MW01628438

The Earliest Commentary Upon the Quran According to The 4th Rightly Guided Caliph Ali ibn Abi Talib

from His Sermons, Letters and Sayings
Arranged by Sharif Razi in the *Nahj al-Balagha*

Foreword by
Mohammad H. Faghfoory

Introduction, Quranic Translation and Compilation by
Laleh Bakhtiar

Library of Islam

Printed in the United States of America.

Library of Congress Cataloging-in-Publication Data

Bakhtiar, Laleh. The Earliest Commentary Upon the Quran According to the 4th Rightly Guided Caliph, Ali ibn Abi Talib from the Sermons, Letters and Sayings Arranged by Sharif Razi in the *Nahj al-Balagha*

Cover Design by
Shaikh, Hafeez, Art and Design

p.cm.
Includes bibliographic references

ISBN 10: 1-56744-683-3 pbk
ISBN 13: 978-1-56744-683-8 pbk
ISBN 10: 1-56744-684-1 hbk
ISBN 13: 978-1-56744-684-5 hbk

1. Koran—Commentary. 2. Koran—Criticism, interpretation, etc.
II.Koran. English. Quranic Psychology. II. Title

Published by
Library of Islam
Distributed by
Kazi Publications, Inc. (USA)
3023 West Belmont Avenue
Chicago IL 60618
(T) 773-267-7001
(F) 773-267-7002
www.kazi.org
email: info@kazi.org

Contents

The Text of the Commentary

Dedication

Dedicated to my grandfather, Haji Hasan, who from 1885 to 1897 led a camel caravan to the Hajj in Makkah each year, taking items to be blessed belonging to those who knew they would never be able to make the pilgrimage themselves and to his son, my father, Dr. Abol Ghassem Bakhtiar, who taught me the prayer: There is no spiritual warrior if it not be Ali; there is no sword if it not be Zulfiqar (*la fata illa Ali; la saif illa zu'l fiqar*).

Acknowledgments

My gratitude to Liaquat Ali, Founder and President of Kazi Publications (USA) for his continued suggestions and support without which this project would never have seen fruition. I am grateful to Dr. Mohammad H. Faghfoory for his courage in writing a Foreword to this critical Introduction and original Text. I also acknowl-edge Dr. Ali M. Shah and Dr. Syed Ali Abutalib for their friendship, Karin Lillehei and Yasmin Shah for proofreading the Introduction and, of course, my good friend and colleague, Dr. Mahshid Razavi for her dedication to the Sufi Enneagram and the translation of this and my other works into Persian. May God continue to bless their journey

Foreword

Ali ibn Abi Talib has often been called the first Muslim intellectual and scholar. Yet Ali is more than just a scholar and an intellectual. Unlike many prominent people in history who excelled in one field or another, Ali possessed contradictory qualities and skills that ordinarily are not found in one individual. He was a chivalrous man, an exceptionally brave soldier and fighter whose armor only covered his chest, as he never turned his back on his enemies in wars. Yet, he was also a commentator on the Quran, a metaphysician, a theologian, a gnostic, a linguist, a grammarian, a poet, and a man of taste for beauty, an artist who loved calligraphy and was aware of the value of knowledge and learning. The present book is a Quranic commentary based on the collection of his Sermons, Letters and Sayings.

Readers who are intimate with the *Nahj al-balagha* might have often considered it as a book of wisdom inspired by Ali's mastery of the Quran. Rarely do we ever think that the *Path of Eloquence* is indeed a commentary on the Quran in light of which other fields of Islamic science were indeed born. To the best of my knowledge Dr. Bakhtiar's compilation of the *Nahj al-balagha* into the Quran is the first study in English that treats Ali's Sermons, Letters and Sayings as a commentary on the Quran. In a sense, the book is also a tribute the author pays to Ali ibn Abi Talib in her expression of gratitude for what she learned through him about her religion and spirituality.

The texts presented in this collection obviously have their own merit as commentaries on the Quran, but are also particularly important in terms of their relevance to other fields of Islamic sciences such as theology, philosophy, history, literature and politics. Even more important is the fact that Ali puts his comments on the Quran in an operative mode that shows the reader the practical application of its verses.

A few years ago Dr. Bakhtiar established herself as the first American woman translator of the Quran.[1] In her Preface to that edition she noted that among commentators and translators, "little attention had been given to the women's point of view [although] the intention of the Quran is to see man and woman as complements of one another, not as superior–inferior."[2]

It was probably that project along with her reading of twelve statements in the *Nahj al-balagha* that denigrate women in a strong language that prompted Dr. Bakhtiar to undertake the monumental task of compiling this Quranic commentary from the *Nahj al-balagha*, the third most important source of Islam. Her reading of the Quran and her personal devotion to Ali ibn Abi Talib as she describes in the Preface made it difficult for her to accept that a man of Ali's stature and spiritual station, the Speaking Quran,[3] the man about who the Prophet, peace and the mercy of God be upon him, said: *Ali was always with the Quran and the Quran was with him*,[4] would even speak of women in such terms and language that are recorded in the said twelve statements.

Pointing out in her Preface the continuation of the degrading of *all* women in

Islamic source-texts, she shows that 200 years after the death of the Prophet and Ali, some of the same exact spurious statements vilifying *all* women are put into the mouth of the Prophet in the then new science of Hadith. She indicates that these statements should be ignored as they clearly were added over time, the proof being that Ali ibn Abi Talib never says that he heard these words from the Prophet, whereas he mentions many times how "the Prophet told him" or "said" this or that.

The question that Dr. Bakhtiar poses is as follow: If Ali's mission was to continue the initial steps that the Prophet had taken to establish a just society by improving the status of woman based on what he had learned personally from the Prophet regarding women, how could he have made such horrible statements about women? How could a wise and saintly man like Ali ibn Abi Talib, who was the beacon of knowledge and justice, have treated women so differently from the Prophet, peace and the mercy of God be upon him, if these statements in fact represent his views on women and especially on all women?

This is a valid question. How a man, a model of justice could have made twelve statements that denigrate women. Either Ali was not the man he claimed to be or is believed to have been, or if he was, how could such a person look at women with an eye that we ordinarily expect from the most ignorant, prejudiced, selfish, and unjust man? Bakhtiar's response is that, "Clearly they [those twelve statements] were falsely added to the collection of Ali's sermons to undermine Imam's reputation for justice while, at the same time, to present an unfair view of *all* women which he would never have adhered to."[5] She draws the readers' attention to note that "*unlike all other commentators on the* Nahj al-balagha *who added the verses of the Quran underneath the Sermons, Letters and Sayings, Bakhtiar weighs the authenticity or lack thereof of them by placing parts of each Sermon, Letter or Saying underneath the relevant verse of the Quran. When you do this, there is no Quranic verse underneath which you can place any of these twelve statements discrediting all women*" and thereby verify the statement by the Prophet: "Ali was always with the Quran and the Quran was with him."

This conclusion may result in criticism as it challenges the views of many modern scholars as well as traditional *'ulama who indeed have similar views about the status of women in Islam*. Whether or not readers would agree with all the points Dr. Bakhtiar has presented and analyzed in this book, what is important is to acknowledge that she has taken a brave step to bring to readers' attention a new dimension of the *Nahj al-balagha* as a guide to understanding the Quran by one who bore witness to its revelation as well as a source on gender relations hoping "*to bring both men and women to equity so that the message of fairness and justice between sexes can be accepted in Truth by both genders*." If this objective is attained, this book will be a turning point in gender studies in Islam. This is a major accomplishment for which Dr. Bakhtiar must be acknowledged and congratulated.

Mohammad H. Faghfoory
Virgina, March 2020

Preface

Why this book?

A reader may want to know how it came to be that I undertook this work. My American Protestant mother brought me to America from Iran when I was just six months old. Years later, she sent my two older brothers and myself to Catholic school as our home had no father and she felt we would receive the discipline needed from a "father" figure there.

When I was nineteen, I met someone who later became my intellectual mentor. He asked me what religion I was. I said that I had grown up as a Christian. He said to me that because my father was Persian, everyone will expect me to be Muslim. I said to him that I knew nothing about Islam. He said in a commanding voice: "Well, learn!"

I began to do just that. I found that I had always believed in the Oneness of God. I learned the formal prayers, fasted during the month of Ramadan, went on the once-in-a-lifetime pilgrimage to Makkah, and gave to charity.

As my faith unfolded, through the various books that I read and Muslims that I met, I slowly began to understand the moral character of Ali ibn Abi Talib. The encounters were so strong that I began having dreams about him. In one dream I felt very frightened when I had to jump over a large crevasse in the earth. Something in my subconscious said to me to ask for Ali's help by saying "*Ya Ali*" three times and then to jump, which I did making it easily to the other side. This, then, became my mantra whenever I faced a frightening or difficult situation.

It was many years later that my father (b1882), with whom my only contact as I was growing up was through his letters from Iran to my siblings and myself in America, wrote his autobiography. In it he had explained how he had grown up as a villager in the Bakhtiari region of Iran located near Isfahan. He suffered a great deal trying to find his way in life. He writes that after he had learned to read and write, at some point during his difficult years, a cousin told him to say a certain prayer that the Prophet had said regarding Ali at the end of the Battle of Uhud. It had to be said for forty days and at the end of that time, his cousin said, he should receive an answer. The prayer was: There is no spiritual warrior if it not be Ali; there is no sword if it be not *zu'l fiqar* (*la fata illa Ali; la saif illa zu'l fiqar*), the double-pointed sword given to Ali by the Prophet where one point stood for wisdom and the other for justice. My father wrote that he did this and that at the end of forty days he received a letter from the wife of one of the Bakhtiari khans offering him a job to tutor her two nephews. This was *the* opportunity that came to him that ended in him becoming the first Iranian physician to finish medical school in the United States (University of Syracuse, 1926) at the age of forty-four and return to Iran (1931). He arrived in Tehran with his American nurse wife, Helen Jeffreys[1] and two daughters born in New York City where Abol and Helen had met. I am their seventh child.

My story did not end here. It just made me aware of this prayer and how important it had been for my father. In 1986 I found myself working in London after having lived twenty years in Iran. I had been initiated into a Sufi group in London and knew the master well. One day I was walking along a London street and ran into the master who had been out for a walk. He saw me and, as if somehow he had expected to see me, he gave me an agate ring engraved with the words: *la fata illa Ali; la saif illa zu'l fiqar.*

My dreams and this gesture and gift tied my life to Ali. This connection resurfaced for me when I found that the Sufis had integrated a psychology and a practice based on an image of a circle with nine points marked on the circumference of the circle (an image of it appears in Part 2: The Solution). I called it the Sufi Enneagram. It is based in spiritual chivalry (Arabic, *futuwwa*h, Persian and Urdu, *javanmardi*), the motto of which is *la fata illa Ali; la saif illa zu'l fiqar* indicating the role of the central figure, Ali ibn Abi Talib. Praise be to God.

Ali ibn Abi Talib and The Quran
The Prophet said: The Quran is with Ali and Ali is with the Quran

The Prophet, peace and the mercy of God be upon him, was born in 570 CE. His father had died before he was born. The Prophet lived for two years with his mother in Madinah when she died. His grandfather, Abdul Mutallib, then cared for his grandson for six years when his grandfather died. He was then placed in the care of his father's full brother, Abu Talib, whose wife, Fatima bint Asad, the second woman who was to accept Islam, raised him until the age of twenty-five when he married Khadija bint Khuwaylid in 595 CE.

Ali ibn Abi Talib was born in 600 CE, the son of Abu Talib and Fatima bint Asad, both from the Hashim clan of the Quraysh who traced their lineage back to that of Prophet Ishmael, the son of Prophet Abraham and Hajar, as did Prophet Muhammad, peace and the mercy of God be upon him. Abu Talib had a large family that was suffering because of a famine in Makkah so when Ali was five years old, he went to live with Muhammad and Khadija. When he was ten years old, Muhammad, peace and the mercy of God be upon him, was forty when the revelation of the Quran began in 610 CE. Khadija was the first woman to accept Islam while Ali, a youth at that time, was the first male to accept Islam.

Due to their close relationship, the Prophet, peace and the mercy of God be upon him, was to say to Ali: "It is enough that you are a part of myself, and that I am a part of you. He who inherits from you will be my heir for you stand in the same relation to me as Aaron to Moses, with the difference that after me there will be no other Prophet."[2]

In the early years of the revelation in Makkah the members of the Quraysh tribe, who were not from the Hashim clan, tried to prevent the Prophet from delivering the divine message. They finally came to the conclusion that the only way to stop the Prophet was to isolate he and his Hashim family in a dry valley outside Makkah and impose economic sanctions. It was to last for three years.

Ali was the only one of the later-to-be "Rightly Guided caliphs" to be with the Prophet during these years to hear the Quranic verses revealed as the other three later-to-be Rightly Guided caliphs were not from the Hashim clan of the Quraysh and so they were prohibited by the Quraysh from visiting or providing food or water to the Prophet and his family.

In addition, Ali was literate: "He was one of the scribes of the Prophet who wrote down verses of the Quran as they were revealed...."[3]

As stated above, Ali was "as a brother" to the Prophet, peace and the mercy of God be upon him, as Aaron was to Moses. Ali ibn Abi Talib lived with the Prophet and his family until the age of twenty-three, when in 623 CE, he married the Prophet's daughter, Fatima bint Muhammad, and they set up their own home in Madinah next to the home of the Prophet, peace and the mercy of God be upon him.

Later, after the Prophet migrated to Madinah and the Battle of Uhud took place in 624 CE, a heavenly voice said: There is no spiritual warrior (*fata, javanmard*) if it not be Ali; no sword but (the two edged sword named) *zu'l-faqar*."[4]

Ali was thirty-two years old when the Prophet died (11AH/632CE). He was fifty-six when he became the 4th Rightly Guided caliph. His caliphate lasted for a little over four years (656-661 CE) when he was martyred.

The 1st Rightly Guided caliph, Abu Bakr (573-634CE), was the earliest adult male to convert to Islam. He was a close companion to the Prophet, but as mentioned above, he was prohibited from visiting the Prophet and his family when they were isolated and under economic sanctions. Therefore, there was a three year period when he did not hear the Quranic revelation, but later in 622CE when the Prophet, peace and the mercy of God be upon him, migrated from Makkah to Madinah, Abu Bakr was the only one present to hear the revelation as it was being revealed during that eight day period. During his short caliphate of two years, Abu Bakr ordered the collection of the tablets, bones and the wide, flat ends of the date palm leaves on which the Quranic revelation had been written at the time that each revelation was revealed.

Umar ibn Khattab (584-644 CE), the 2nd Rightly Guided caliph converted to Islam six years after the revelation had begin (616 CE). He had not been present during the first six years of the revelation and he was also prohibited by the Quraysh for visiting or aiding the Prophet and his family during their three years of economic sanctions.

Uthman ibn Affan (577-656 CE), an early convert brought into the fold by Abu Bakr, was the 3rd Rightly Guided caliph. He migrated with his family to Abyssinia in 615 CE and was gone for four years. However, it was during the years of his caliphate (644-656 CE) that he ordered the Quran to be compiled in book form, twenty years after death of Prophet which is the Quran used to this day.

We have very few records of the Sermons of the first three Rightly Guided Caliphs.

In the brief period of sovereignty, two years, three months and ten days, according to al-Masudi, the 1st Rightly Guided caliph, Abu Bakr (11-13AH/632-4CE) does not seem to have made many speeches which have been recorded. His prime and important address, that at *al-saqifa of Banu Sa'idah*, along with some other speeches have been preserved.

The austere Umar, the 2nd Rightly Guided caliph, (13-23AH/634-44CE) seems to have been more concerned with practical politics and, perhaps, less with eloquence in speeches. It appears that when the second Caliph did speak, his speech was not necessarily designed to contain linguistic decor or rhymed synonyms. Confronted with such important a task as mobilizing people to go to war against the mighty Persian Empire, he is reported to have made a speech which takes no more space in the page than approximately one and a half lines. '*Innakum*,' he said: 'The Hijaz is no longer the place for you; and the Prophet had promised you the conquest of Persia. So go to the land of the Persians.'[5]

In fact speaking on the pulpit had become such an important symbol of authority that when the 3rd Rightly Guided caliph, Uthman (24-35AH/643-655CE), was raised to the caliphate, he showed signs of not being accustomed to public speaking. He stood on the pulpit not knowing what to say for quite a while, then he said: 'Truly Abu Bakr and Umar used to prepare for this place and occasion. But you are more in need of a just leader than the leader who carves out the speeches. If you are still alive the speeches will come in due course.'[6]

Therefore, it appears that of the Rightly Guided caliphs, it was only Ali who was present with the Prophet, peace and the mercy of God be upon him, and heard from him all but one or two verses of the Quran that were revealed during the Prophet's migration from Makkah to Madinah in the company of his companion, Abu Bakr. As Ali was literate, he wrote down many of them. Once he became the 4th Rightly Guided caliph, his Sermons, Letters and Sayings began to be recorded either orally or in writing. A well-known Muslim scholar has pointed out: 'Only in the Quran can be found a precedent for the *Nahj al-balagha*. Apart from the Quran, we do not find any other source that provides some ground for the discourses of the *Nahj al-balagha*.'[7]

Another states: "... the Imam's teachings, which express his spiritual ethos, should be read essentially as creative interpretations of the Quranic revelation."[8]

Thus, it is no surprise that these became the first and, thus, the earliest commentary upon the Quran. Why is this the earliest commentary on the Quran? Most historians have said that the first commentary on the Quran was made by Ali's paternal first cousin, Abdullah Ibn Abbas (619-687CE). Yet Abdullah Ibn Abbas claims to have learned the science of interpretation from his older first cousin, Ali.[9]

Once the Sermons, Letters and Sayings were compiled in the *Nahj al-Balagha* (*Path of Eloquence*), it should have been recognized as the earliest commentary on the Quran as the Commentary here shows. Ali tells us:

Not a single verse of the Quran was revealed to the Messenger of God which he did not proceed to dictate to me and make me recite. I would write it with my own hand, and he would instruct me as to its *tafsir* (the literal explanation) and the *ta'wil* (the spiritual exegesis), the *nasikh* (the verse which abrogates) and the *mansukh* (the abrogated verse), the *muhkam* and the *mutashabih* (the fixed and the ambiguous), the particular and the general. He would pray to God to increase my understanding and my memory. Then he would lay his hand on my breast and ask God to fill my heart with knowledge and understanding, with judgement and illumination.[10]

Reflecting his deep understanding of the Quran, Ali ibn Abi Talib also said:

> There is no Quranic verse which does not possess four types of meaning: exoteric (*zahir*), esoteric (*batin*), limit (*hadd*), divine plan (*muttala'*). The exoteric is for oral recitation; the esoteric is for the inner understanding; the limit consists of the statements laying down what things are permissible and what forbidden; the divine plan is that which God intends to realize within a person by means of each verse.[11]

The Prophet had said: "Ali is with the Quran and the Quran is with Ali. They will not separate from each other until they return to me (the Prophet, peace and the mercy of God be upon him), at the paradisal pool."[12] He said: "I am the city of knowledge and Ali is its gate so whoever desires knowledge, let him enter that gate."[13] Ali not only received knowledge of the Quran from the Prophet, peace and the mercy of God be upon him, but heart knowledge or consciousness as well. As he encompassed both kinds of knowledge, neither one would allow him to vilify women.

Ali refers to the *sunna* of Prophet Muhammad, peace and the mercy of God be upon him, over and over in the *Nahj al-Balagha*. As there were no collection of Hadith for another two hundred years after the Prophet's death, it is clear that Ali ibn Abi Talib is referring to the Quranic *sunna* which is to follow the *sunna* of the Prophet as expressed in the Quran as well as the *sunna* that he himself experienced.

The following two verses were used by scholars to justify the compilation of the Hadith, but, in effect, they also justify the Quranic *sunna* as Ali ibn Abi Talib had done in his Sermons, Letters and Sayings. *Say: Obey God and obey the Messenger.* (Q24:54) *Surely, in the Messenger of God there is for you a fairer, good example for those whose hope had been in God and the Last Day and remembered God frequently.* (Q33:21)

What is the Quranic *sunna*? *Sunna* means well-trodden path, way. It is to analyze four different types of Quranic verses: First, Quranic signs/verses addressed to the Prophet specifically (2nd person singular, i.e., thou, thee, thy which appear as **you** or **your** in the text, the bold indicating the original was addressed in the second person singular) in chronological order; second, Quranic commands addressed directly to the Prophet (2nd person singular) in chronological order that begin with the word "*Say*" (*qul*); commands other than the "Say" command given directly to the Prophet (2nd person singular) in chronological order; and other commands addressed through the Prophet (2nd person plural) for humanity in chronological order.[14]

As the earliest commentary upon the Quran, it helps to have an interpretation as Ali Ibn Abi Talib said: "The Quran consists of a book inscribed between two covers. It speaks not with a tongue. It cannot do without an interpreter." Sermon 124*

> The compilation made by Sharif Razi (d. 406AH/1015CE), entitled *Nahj al-Balagha* (commonly translated as *Peak of Eloquence*, *Path of Eloquence* or *Way of Eloquence*) is a collection of the Sermons, Letters and Sayings (*Logia*) of the 4th Rightly Guided caliph, Ali ibn Abi Talib. The influence of the *Nahj al-Balagha:* can be sensed in the logical co-ordination of terms, the deduction of correct conclusions, and the creation of certain technical terms in Arabic which possess both richness and beauty, and which in this way entered the literary and philosophical language independently of the translation into Arabic of Greek texts.[15]

Sharif Razi had not included the sources for his choices to be included in the compilation so that over the later centuries there were those who said that Sharif Razi or his brother had actually written the Sermons, Letters and Sayings. More recent scholars have found the original sources for most of the content of the *Nahj al-Balagha*. The critical edition of the Arabic of the *Nahj al-Balagha* has been prepared by Shaykh Azizullah al-Utardi.[16]

The English translation of the online version used here contains 239 Sermons, 79 Letters, 206 Sayings[17] without mention of the name of the English translator. Quotes from Sermons, Letters or Sayings indicated by a * are from Reza Shah-Kazemi.[18]

*****

There are over 100 commentaries on the *Nahj al-Balagha* where the commentators place Quranic verses under the words of the Sermons, Letters and Sayings as reflections of the Quran or which are specific commentaries by Ali himself on certain verses. However, they had not put the Quran first and added words from his Sermons, Letters and Sayings as commentary upon these verses as this Commentary does. The Commentary consists of the entire English translation of *The Sublime Quran*[19] with excerpts from the *Nahj al-Balagha,* relevant to the specific verse or verses placed following the verse(s). This Commentary clearly shows the truth of the saying of the Prophet, peace and the mercy of God be upon him, leaving no room for doubt that "Ali is with the Quran and the Quran is with Ali. They will not separate from each other until they return to me (the Prophet, peace and the mercy of God be upon him) at the paradisal pool."[20]

It was from following the Quranic *sunna* of the Prophet that Ali ibn Abi Talib learned the importance of being a fair and just person. This text will show example after example of Ali's fairness, not only having become a fair and just person through his own personal efforts first before guiding others in his attempt to create a fair and just society.

Yet we find that once Ali ibn Abi Talib, the paragon of justice, was chosen by the people to be the 4th Rightly Guided caliph, certain words creeped into his Sermons, Letters and Sayings which do not reflect his sense of justice and fairness. They were clearly added over time by those who wished to denigrate Ali. The fabrications continued, as we will see, when 200 years later as the Hadith were being compiled, similar words attributed to Ali ibn Abi Talib in Sermon 80 are said to have been said by the Prophet, peace and the mercy of God be upon him, recorded in the Sunni canonical work, *Sahih al-Bukhari*:[20]

> Once God's Messenger, peace and blessings be upon him, went out to the musalla for 'Id al-Adha or 'Id al-Fitr prayer. Then he passed by the women and said, 'O women! Give alms, as I have seen that the majority of the dwellers of Hell-fire are you (women).' They asked, 'Why is it so, O God's Messenger?' He replied, 'You curse frequently and are ungrateful to your husbands. I have not seen anyone more deficient in intelligence and religion than you. A cautious sensible man could be led astray by some of you.' The women asked, 'O God's Messenger! What is deficient in our intelligence and religion?' He said: 'Is not the evidence of two women equal to the witness of one man?' They replied in the affirmative. He said 'This is the deficiency in her intelligence. Is it not true that a woman can neither pray nor fast during her menses?' The women replied in the affirmative. He said: 'This is the deficiency in her religion.'[21]

Explain Your Reason

In Part 1 of this Introduction, we detail the problem of injustice against *all* women and exonerate Ali from having had any part in the discrediting of *all* women. Interestingly enough, the arguments come from the same *Nahj al-Balagha* text, but follow the Quranic dictum "say what is fairer" (Q17:53). In this case, it would be to follow the words that clearly respect the reputation of Ali ibn Abi Talib, a man of wisdom and justice. We give clear explanations as to how certain phrases and words go against the Quran which we have learned "was with him." Ali's words to Malik Ashtar echo the purpose of this work, as well: "The conduct (of giving clear explanations) is a means of self-discipline. It is a form of kindness (towards the reader) and a way of presenting (the) plea which will help (us) to fulfill (our) need to keep upright in accordance with the truth." Letter 53* (Parentheses added)

We say as Caliph Ali expressed in Sermon 126: "Some people said to Caliph Ali that wisdom lies in setting aside, for the time being, the matter of equality and justice. 'What harm is there in that?' they asked. Ali replied to them, echoing our words and thoughts: "Do you ask me to seek support through injustice to my subjects and to sacrifice justice for the sake of political advantage?'" Sermon 126

My challenge to the reader is to undertake the same exercise I have taken. That is, to place the closest words from the *Nahj al-Balagha* (*Path of Eloquence*) that reflect the Quranic verses underneath the specific Quranic verse(s) as a commentary upon that particular verse. The person who does this will find that there is no Quranic verses to which one can apply the forged words denigrating women that we will indicate in the Introduction which follows. The person who accepts this challenge will have to conclude, as I have done, that the words that mis-characterize "*all*" women could not have been said by either the Prophet, peace and the mercy of God be upon him, or Ali ibn Abi Talib as both were models of fairness and justice.

Those scholars who know their "self" and have "morally healed," as explained in Part 2 of this Introduction, have to either indicate that the spurious words slandering *all* women refer to "some" women (not one woman) or be left out of the *Nahj al-Balagha* completely as Yasin al-Jibouti has done in the bi-lingual edition of the *Nahj al-Balagha* because the words neither reflect the Quranic revelation nor *sunna* of the Prophet as a commentary on the Quran should do. Otherwise, as we will show, the Quran commands: ... *sit not with the folk, the ones who are unjust.* (Q6:68). The Quran commands that women should not "sit with" or "learn from" the unjust, those who continue to make mockery of the great paragon of justice, Ali ibn Abi Talib, and *all* women.

Introduction: Part 1: The Problem
I Ali ibn Abi Talib: Caliph, Imam, Spiritual Guide

Ali ibn Abi Talib as the 4th Rightly Guided Caliph

Ali ibn Abi Talib is the 4th Rightly Guided caliph according to all Muslims. which is why this title was chosen for this work. All Sermons, Letters and Sayings in the *Nahj al-Balagha* relate to the time that he was the 4th Rightly Guided caliph. His mission was to continue implementing the moral committment to justice that he had learned from the Prophet, peace and the mercy of God be upon him, in emancipating women from the oppression of men as confirmed by a Christian scholar in his work devoted to the life of Ali ibn Abi Talib, *The Voice of Human Justice*:

> This voice of the Prophet, was a call for human brotherhood. It stopped the hands of the rulers from reaching the property of the subjects and gave equal rights to all human beings. In his religion there is no discrimination between a common man, a ruler and a subject and an Arab and a non-Arab, because all human beings are the servants of God and it is He who provides sustenance to all of them. **This voice emancipated women from the oppression of men....** The Prophet of Islam made all human beings participate in the affairs of government. He also disallowed usury and exploitation of one person by another. After the Prophet of Islam, it was Ali ibn Abi Talib who called people to good morals.[1]

Ali ibn Abi Talib as the 1st Imam

Ali ibn Abi Talib is the 1st Imam of those who follow the Jafari school of law so they refer to him as Imam Ali or Amir al-Muminin, his words having been transmitted orally from each generation of his family to the next as descendants of Muhammad, Fatima and Ali. His entire life can be seen as the quest to establish justice.[2]

Ali reinforces the Prophet's sense of justice in Sermon 86 where Ali speaks of his own experience growing up under the guidance of the Prophet, peace and the mercy of God be upon him. Ali, then, learned that the first step in becoming a fair and just person is to give up one's own desires and interests, that is, one's ego.

Ali ibn Abi Talib learned that no matter how difficult a situation he faced was, that when deciding between two responses, he should choose the most difficult one. This would assure him that he was not acting out of his own desires, but that he was submitting to God's will as stated in His revelation, the goal of which is to establish justice, moderation, the golden mean, balance within himself and within the society that he was to rule. Ali tells us:

> The Prophet, peace and the mercy of God be upon him, enjoined upon himself to follow justice. The first step of his justice is the rejection of desires from his consciousness (heart). He describes right and acts according to it. There is no good which he has not aimed at nor any likely place of virtue of the Quran. Therefore, the Quran is his guide and leader. Sermon 86

Justice as emphasized over and over again in the *Nahj al-Balagha* is among the five principles of belief of the Jafari school of law. Jafari Muslims believe that there is intrinsic right or wrong in things, and that God commands them to do the right things and shun wrongdoing as both the Prophet, peace and the mercy of God be upon him, and Ali taught. As such: "Doing the right thing" according to the Prophet, peace and the mercy of God be upon him, and Ali ibn Abi Talib clearly indicate that belittling half of society is wrong.

> In the Quran, just (*'adl*) and equity (*qist*) are two words used to describe justice. *Adl* means a balanced approach to all things, including life. So if a person is fair and just, *adil*, he is balanced morally, behaviorally and spiritually. *Qist* is defined as the approach regulating the human-to-human or human-to-God relations.[3]

Ali ibn Abi Talib as Spiritual Guide

As spiritual guide, Ali also carries on the work of Prophet Muhammad, peace and the mercy of God be upon him, in the mystical dimension of Islam. Mystics refer to him with the more familiar "Ali."[4]

Beginning in the second century, all eventual forty traditional Sufi orders trace their spiritual lineage to Ali ibn Abi Talib. Ali is regarded as the first spiritual pole of Sufism after the Prophet himself and is situated at the summit of all the spiritual chains.[5] There must have been some records of his Sermons, Letters or Sayings that were known to the mystics which caused them to trace their spiritual lineage to him. Certainly his letters had been written and not just orally transmitted, because they reached the person to whom they were addressed.

The remembrance of God (*dhikr*) is an important part of a Sufi gathering and is also emphasized as a method to attain spiritual growth. A well-known Sufi master and founder of the Qadiriyya Sufi order, Abdul Qadir Jilani (1077-1166 CE), tells how the Prophet taught Ali the basic lesson concerning the remembrance (*dhikr*) of God.

> Ali once asked the Prophet: 'Which of the methods is nearest to God, easiest for His servants, and most praiseworthy in His sight?'
>
> The beloved Prophet replied: 'O Ali, you must make it your constant practice to remember Allah (Exalted is He) in private moments and places.'
>
> Ali then went on to ask: 'Can such be the merit of remembrance (*dhikr*), when all the people are remembering all the time since they frequently exclaim 'Allah!'?'
>
> The Prophet responded: 'This is no light matter, O Ali, for the Final Hour will not arise so long as there is still someone, somewhere on the face of the earth, who is saying: 'Allah, Allah'!'
>
> This prompted Ali to ask: 'How should I practice remembrance of God (*dhikr Allah*)?'
>
> So the beloved Prophet told him: 'Listen to what I say three times. Then you say it three times, while I do the listening.' Then he said: *La ilaha illa 'llah* (there is no god but God), three times, closing his eyes and raising his voice while Ali lis-

tened.

Then Ali said: '*La ilaha illa 'llah* (there is no god but God) three times,' closing his eyes and raising his voice, while the Prophet listened in turn.[6]

Ali himself gives a commentary on (Q24:37) indicating the connection between those who practice the *dhikr* as being those who are themselves fair and just and who teach others about justice: "Truly there are people who belong to the *dhikr*. They have adopted it in place of the world, such that *neither commerce nor trade* (Q24:37) distracts them from it. They spend the days of their life in it ... They instruct people about justice and are themselves steadfast therein."[7] Being steadfast in instructing people about justice, Ali would never demean *all* women.

Spiritual Chivalry[8]

The mystical dimension of Islam, which traces its spiritual roots back to the Prophet, peace and the mercy of God be upon him, and Ali ibn Abi Talib, includes members of the trade guilds and artisans through what is called spiritual chivalry (*futuwwah*): The Arabic word (*futuwwah*), whose Persian equivalent is *javanmardi*, means youth or youthfulness of spirit and is a Quranic term, translated here as spiritual warrior(s), *fata* for the male and *fatat* for the female.

Whoever of you is not affluent to be able to marry the ones who are free, chaste female believers, then, from females whom your right hands possess of ***female spiritual warriors****. God is greater in knowledge about your belief. You are of one another.* (Q4:25)

The Quran refers to Prophet Joseph, peace be upon him, in Chapter 12 as a spiritual warrior (Q12:30) as well as his prison mates (Q12:36) and his assistants who handed out grain to people during the famine in Egypt (Q12:62). In Chapter 18, the Companions of the Cave are referred to as spiritual warriors (Q18:10; Q18:13). The servant who accompanied Moses[9] on a journey is called a spiritual warrior (Q18:60 (Q18:62) as well as Prophet Abraham, peace be upon him, in (Q21:60).

Then, most important to us here as well as later in this Introduction, the term is used to prohibit men from compelling their female spiritual warriors to prostitution. If the men do so anyway, God forgives the female spiritual warrior who has been compelled to do so against her own free willpower of *wanting chastity*, indicating the right to a woman to actualize her potential free willpower and the Quranic preference for a woman over a man when the oppressive male, being deficient in faith, is trying to force a female into what may become a harmful situation to her (something we shall also see later in this Introduction in regard to a wife and husband): *Compel not your* ***spiritual warriors*** (f) *against their will to prostitution when they* (f) *wanted chastity, that you be looking for the advantage of this present life. Whoever compels them* (f) to it *against their* (f) *will, yet after their* (f) *compulsion, God will be of them* (f), *the female, Forgiving, Compassionate.* (Q24:33)

When human beings reflect on their role in the universe, they realize the importance of balance, moderation, avoiding the extremes of too much or too little, of putting things in their right place as Ali defines justice as spiritual warriors do: "What makes us unique and special is the instinctive and natural sense of justice that we—all of us, Muslims and non-Muslims alike—are born with as human beings."[10]

Justice in the Quran and the *Nahj al-Balagha*

Certainly, We sent Our Messengers with the clear portents and We caused the Book to descend with them and the Balance so that humanity may uphold justice. (Q57:25)

As we have pointed out in the Preface, Ali would never have made the struggle for justice to be of secondary importance. How then is it conceivable that he would have been responsible for denouncing *all* women? It is no use to rationalize this vilification of *all* women saying the words refer to "one woman" as we will see, but here we note that the unjust fabrications against *all* women pervade the text of the *Nahj al-Balagha*. We have to ask: Are those who continue to repeat and teach the derogatory statements in the *Nahj al-Balagha* that disparage women, not aware of the Quranic teaching of *ihsan* as an important aspect of Ali's teachings on justice? *Ihsan* was defined by the Prophet as worshipping God as if one saw him and if not, knowing that God sees that person? Are they willing to risk the punishment they will receive on the Day of Judgment by continuing to teach that which denigrates both the character of Ali ibn Abi Talib and *all* women who are so disgraced?

> In this verse (Q57:25), establishment of justice has been declared as being the objective of the mission of all the prophets. The sanctity of justice is so stressed that it is considered the aim of all prophetic missions. Hence, how would it be possible for someone like Ali, whose duty was to expound the teachings of the Quran and explain the doctrines and laws of Islam, to have ignored this issue or, at least, accorded it a secondary importance? Those who neglect these issues in their teachings, or imagine that these problems are only of marginal significance and that the central issues are those of ritual purity and impurity (*taharah* and *najasah*), should re-examine their own beliefs and views.[11]

The Christian scholar who wrote on the life of Ali said in regard to Ali's sense of justice: "Justice was a part of his soul and was ingrained in his heart and it had combined other virtues also with itself. It was not possible for him to deviate from justice and from the demands of his nature. Justice was an element which was entwined in his entire body and ran in his veins like blood."[12]

Ali ibn Abi Talib emphasizes the importance of justice in many of his Sermons, Letters and Sayings such as: "So long as the stars revolve in the sky I shall not at all give a judgment opposed to justice. By God I shall do justice so far as the oppressor and the oppressed persons are concerned."[13]

As if to echo his words in Letter 53 where he advises Malik Ashtar that those who are wronged will seek justice, we women are among those who have been wronged who seek justice. Ali says: "Justice will be sought from you by those who have been wronged." Letter 53*

The Best Woman in the World

Ali ibn Abi Talib had good things to say about women, particularly his wife, Fatima bint Muhammad, and the oppression she suffered as he wrote in Letters 28 and 93 about her death:

> The best woman in the world (title bestowed by God upon Fatima) the beloved daughter of the Prophet, peace and the mercy of God be upon him, is from us.... Letter 28
>
> Now, the trust has been returned and what had been given has been taken back. As to my grief, it knows no bounds, and as to my nights. they will remain sleepless until God chooses for me the house in which you are now residing. Certainly, your daughter would apprise you of joining together of your *umma* for oppressing her. You ask her in detail and get all the news about the position. This has happened when a long time had not elapsed and your remembrance had not disappeared. My greetings (*salam*) be on you both, the greetings of a grief stricken, not a disgusted or hateful person; for if I go away, it is not because I am weary of you, and if I stay it is not due to lack of belief in what God has promised those who endure. Letter 93

II The Virtue of Being Fair and Just in the Quran in Regard to Women as Mother, Wife, Sister, Daughter and Individual Female Compared to Quranic Prohibitions of Men in Regard to Wife, Daughter and Individual Female

We will come to understand the positive way that the Quran views women in their various roles as mother, wife, sister and daughter. This is the Quranic *sunna* and tradition of how to respect women, one that Ali ibn Abi Talib clearly honored when he told Malik Ashtar to follow the beneficial traditions established by the leaders of the Muslim community beginning with the Prophet, peace and the mercy of God be upon him, in striving for unity whereas the statements about *all* women that have been falsely inserted in the *Nahj al-Balagha* not only rupture the beneficial tradition established by the Quran, Islam and the *sunna* of Prophet Muhammad, peace and the mercy of God be upon him, but also divide the sexes and do not allow all subjects of society to prosper. In the words of Ali: "Do not rupture any beneficial tradition established by the leaders of this community, as a result of which unity has been harmoniously established, and from which the subjects have prospered." Letter 53*

The Quran States That Women Have Their Share

God has given a share to women as mothers, wives, sisters and daughters, which men should not covet. What she earns is her own. If she decides to share her income or inheritance with her family, they should not be demeaning, but grateful because she has no religious obligation to do so. According to (Q4:32) both men and women have an independent economic position: *Covet not what God gave as advantage of it to some of you over others. For men is a share of what they deserved* (m) *and for women is a share of what they* (f) *deserved. Ask God for His grace. Truly, God had been Knowing of everything.* (Q4:32)

Female Names of Quranic Chapters

There are four female names of chapters in the Quran: Chapter 4: "The Women," Chapter 19: "Mary," Chapter 58: "She Who Disputes" and Chapter 60: "She Who is Put to a Test."[1] While Chapter 4 does include gender issues such as marriage and divorce, the only female referred to by name, and as a sign of God (Q23:50) in the Quran, is the female figure of Mary, the mother of Jesus. The Quran is very respectful of her as Ali ibn Abi Talib was aware.

The Messiah son of Mary was not but a Messenger. Surely, Messengers passed away before him. His mother was a just person (f). *They both had been eating food. Look on how We make manifest the signs to them.* (Q5:75)

So her Lord received her with the very best acceptance. Her bringing forth caused the very best to develop in her. Zechariah took charge of her. Whenever Zechariah entered upon her in her sanctuary, he found her with provision. He said: O Mary! From where is this for ***you*** (f)? *She said: This is from God. Truly, God provides to whom He wills without reckoning.* (Q3:37)

Mary characterizes the Quranic view of females because *she was purified, morally obligated to God* (Q66:12) and *a just person.* (Q5:75) *Mention when the angels said: O Mary! Truly, God favored* ***you*** (f), *and purified* ***you*** (f), *and favored* ***you*** (f) *above women of the world.* (Q3:42) *O Mary! Be morally obligated to* ***your*** *Lord and prostrate* ***your****self* (f) *and bow down* (f) *with the ones who bow down.* (Q3:43)[2]

Chapter 58, "She Who Disputes," refers to Khaulah bint Thalabah who complained to the Prophet about her husband who had divorced her using a pre-Islamic phrase: *Be as the back of my mother!*

Chapter 60, "She Who is Put to a Test" speaks of females who emigrated from Makkah to Madinah. In testing if they were believers, the Prophet, peace and the mercy of God be upon him, should not return them to their non-Muslim spouses in Makkah. It was lawful to marry them once their dowry was given back to their husbands.

While these are the four chapters whose names allude to females, verses that speak to or about females refer to women in their natural roles as mothers, wives, sisters, daughters and as individual females who may be single, married, divorced or widowed.

Quranic Verses Encouraging Mothers

Mothers

Mothers are to be respected and appreciated for what they have endured as children are born *from the wombs of mothers,* (Q16:78), *who carried* (them) *in weakness upon weakness,* (Q31:14) *painfully* (Q53:32) and *gave birth to them.* (Q58:2) Prophet Moses' mother (Q28:7) as well as all mothers are told to breastfeed their children for two years. (Q2:233)

In addition to the mention of Mary as mother, the Quran refers indirectly to mothers of some of the other Prophets/Messengers. These include the mother of Cain and Abel (Eve); the mother of Prophet Ishmael (Hajar); the mother of Prophet Isaac (Sarah); the mother of Prophet Moses; the mother of Prophet Yahya, named Yahya, "he who lives," because he breathed life into his barren mother's womb; the mother of Mary; and the wives of Muhammad, *his spouses are their mothers,* (Q33:6), the "Mothers of the Believers."

Quranic Verses Forbidding Men in Regard to Mothers

A mother *is not to be pressed for her child.* (Q2:233)

Men cannot *marry females their fathers had married* (Q4:22)

Quranic Verses Encouraging Wives

Wives

Praiseworthy wives include the wives of some of the Prophets/Messengers such as the spouse of Adam (Eve). In the Islamic view, she and Adam are both blamed for the fall from Eden and *from whom disseminated many men and women* (4:1): *O humanity! Be God-conscious of your Lord Who created you from a single soul and, from it, created its spouse and from them both disseminated many men and women. Be God-conscious of God through Whom you demand rights of one another and the wombs, the rights of blood relations. Truly, God had been watching over you.* (Q4:1)

The wives of Prophet Abraham: Hagar, his second wife, who was the founder of the city of Makkah (the Mother of the Towns) and is said to be buried in the semi-circular area of the Kabah and Sarah who could not believe she would have a child (Isaac) because of her age; the wife of Prophet Job (Rahmah), found in the commentaries on verse (Q38:44) from which comes the parenthetical words (lightly) in reference to (Q4:34); the wife of Imran who *dedicated* what was in her womb to the temple (Q3:35); and the barren wife of Zechariah (Q19:8) who competes *with* (Zechariah) *in good deeds.* (21:90) Other praiseworthy wives include the wife of Pharaoh, Asiya, who prayed for God *to build for [her] a house near to [God] in the Garden* (66:11): *God propounded an example for those who believed: Behold the woman of Pharaoh; she said: My Lord, build for me near* ***You*** *a house in the Garden and deliver me from Pharaoh and his actions and deliver me from the folk, the ones who are unjust.* (Q66:11)

The believing females *who draw closer their outer garments over themselves.* (Q33:59)

The *companion wife* who is forgotten on the Day of Judgment; and temporary wives, whether they be from a *mut'a* or a *misyar* marriage.[3] Mention is made of wives a man is forbidden to marry, of widows and divorcees, the latter often referred to as women who have been *set free*.[4]

Quranic Verses Forbidding Men in Regard to Wives

There is renewed controversy in regard to husbands having the right to beat their wives whose resistance (*nushuz*) they fear (Q4:34), after two stages of disciplinary measures, especially when husbands are not allowed to harm wives they are divorcing (Q2:231). Some commentators such as Allama Tabatabai state that this "privilege" of disciplining a wife is only given to husbands who financially support their wives. Traditional commentators[5] continue to hold that the verse says: *beat them* (i.e., *nushuz* wives) while recent translations claim that the verse says: *go away from them* as this was the *sunna* of the Prophet.

The latter interpretors who interpret *daraba* as "beat," "scourage, "chastise," and so forth forget (Q16:126): *If you are chastised, then, chastise with the like of that with which you were chastised.* Therefore, if a woman is "beaten," (Q4:34) according to (Q16:126) she can "chastise" her husband to the same degree. The Prophet, peace and the mercy of God be upon him, would have known this so that his *sunna* is to go away from the situation in order to defuse the emotions.

Men are forbidden from beating women and to go away from "resisting" (*nushuz*) wives: *Men are supporters of wives because God gave some of them an advantage over others and because they spent of their wealth. So the females, ones in accord with morality are the females, ones who are morally obligated and the females, ones who guard the unseen of what God kept safe. Those females whose resistance* (nushuz) *you fear, then admonish them* (f) *and abandon them* (f) *in their sleeping places and go away from them* (f). *Then if they* (f) *obeyed you, then look not for any way against them* (f). *Truly, God had been Lofty, Great.* (Q4:34)

The same word, "resistance" (*nushuz)* is used in regard to the women: *If a woman feared resistance* (nushuz) *or turning aside from her husband no blame on either of them that they make things right between the two, that there be reconciliation. Reconciliation is better.* (Q4:128) This shows that it is fair and just to understand or to translate the same Quranic word in the exact same way when the context allows. In (Q4:34) we had a *nushuz* wife and in (Q4:125) we have a *nushuz* husband. In either case, the Quran recommends reconciliation.

In addition, husbands cannot harm wives who they are divorcing if they want to be God-conscious: *When you divorced wives, and they* (f) *reached their* (f) *term, then, hold them* (f) *back as one who is honorable or set them* (f) *free as one who is honorable. But hold them* (f) *not back by injuring them so that you commit aggression. Whoever commits that, then, surely, he did wrong to himself. Take not to yourselves the signs of*

God in mockery. Remember the divine blessing of God on you, and what He caused to descend to you from the Book and wisdom. He admonishes you with it. Be God-conscious (taqwa) *and know that God is Knowing of everything.* (Q2:231)

So, as a wife reflects on the fact that Islam encourages marriage and discourages divorce, she may say to herself: "As a Muslim wife who is about to be divorced I cannot be harmed, but as a Muslim wife who wants to remain married, I do so under the threat of being beaten." As the victim in either case she may ask herself: Which do I prefer?

Husbands are required *to deal with wives justly* and since this is not possible, they are admonished to take *just one wife* (Q4:3): *If you feared that you will not act justly with the orphans, then, marry who seems good to you of the women (who have orphans), by twos, in threes or four. But if you feared you will not be just, then, one or what your right hands possessed. That is likelier that you not commit injustice.* (Q4:3)

Divorced wives are to receive their dowry whether the husband has touched them or not: *There is no blame on you if you divorced wives whom you touch not, nor undertake a duty to them* (f) of *a dowry portion. Make provision for them* (f). *For the one who is wealthy—according to his means—and for the one who is needy —according to his means—with a sustenance, one that is honorable, an obligation on the ones who are doers of good.* (Q2:236)

Husbands must provide a wife he has lived with and divorces with an honorable sustenance: *For ones who are divorced females, sustenance, as one who is honorable. This is an obligation on the ones who are God-conscious.* (Q2:241)

Husbands cannot divorce wife by saying: *Be as my mother's back.* (Q58:2)

Husbands cannot take back anything given to his wife when marrying another woman: *If you wanted to exchange your spouse in place of another spouse and you gave one of them* (f) *a hundredweight, so take not anything from it. Would you take it by false charges to harm her reputation and in clear sin?* (Q4:20)

Husband cannot cause difficulty for divorced wife to marry her previous spouse: *When you divorced wives, and they reached their* (f) term, *then, place not difficulties for them* (f) *that they* (f) *re-marry their former spouses when they agreed among themselves as one who is honorable. This is admonished for him—whoever had been among you who believes in God and the Last Day—that is pure and purer for you. God knows and you know not.* (Q2:232)

Husbands receive half of what their wives left if they have no children: *For you is a half of what your spouses left if they be with no child. Then, if they* (f) *had a child, then, for you is a fourth of what they* (f) *left. This is after any bequest which they bequeath or any debt.* (Q4:12)

Quranic Verses Encouraging Sisters

Sisters

The sister of Moses is mentioned (Q28:11-12) who followed the cradle of her infant brother, Moses, until he was safely rescued by Pharaoh's wife. She was then able to assure that Moses would secretly be nursed by his own mother: (The mother of Moses) *said to his sister: Track him. So she kept watching him from afar while they are not aware. We forbade any breastfeeding female for him before. Then,* (the sister of Moses) *said* (to the wife of Pharaoh)*: Shall I point you to the people of a house who will take control of him for you and they will be ones who will look after him?* (Q28:11-28:12) Also, sisters also receive a share in inheritance.

Quranic Verses Forbidding Men in Regard to Sisters

Men cannot marry two sisters. (Q4:23)

Quranic Verses Encouraging Daughters

Daughters

Praiseworthy daughters are the daughters of Lot; Mary, the daughter of Imran; and the daughters of Midian as well as the daughter(s) of Muhammad *who draw closer their outer garments over themselves.* (Q33:59)

Quranic Verses Forbidden Men in Regard to Daughters

The Quran forbids a pre-Islamic practice of burying female children alive, a practice we will refer to later in this Introduction.

Quranic Verses Encouraging Individual Females

Individuals

Females as individuals may be believing females *who show not their adornments.... and draw their head coverings over their bosoms*; *good females* (24:26); females who: submit, are morally obligated, are sincere, remain steadfast, are humble, are charitable, who fast, who guard their private parts, who remember God frequently (Q33:35); and who repent and who worship, (Q66:5), and who, as a result in some cases, are female spiritual warriors who trace their spiritual lineage to Ali ibn Abi Talib.

Reference is given to free, chaste females; female virgins; females who give their allegiance becoming *ones who submit* such as *the woman controlling the people of Saba,* (Q27:22-27:44) or, as commentators describe her, "the Queen of Sheba"; females among the People of the Book; females who emigrate (Q60:10-60:13); females invited to Muhammad's disputation with the Christians (Q3:61) where there is no mention of two women replacing one man; females who shepherd their sheep (Q28:25-28:34); female witnesses (Q2:282) where in all cases where the Quran calls for witnesses, it does not always require two women in place of one man as we will see; females who have a share of what they deserve or earn (Q4:32); female spiritual warriors, "bond servants" and "right hand possessed" as well as those who the females' right hands possess, that is, females also may have *what their right hand possesses* so it is not only males;[6] *the ladies who cut their hands*; lovely, large-eyed females; and females who are in their waiting periods after divorce. The Quran even honors women who are post-menopausal telling them that they do not need to be as careful with the showing of their adornment: *Women who are past child-bearing, those who hope not for marriage, there is no blame on them* (f) *if they lay down their* (f) *garments, not as ones who flaunt themselves and their* (f) *adornment. That they have restraint is better for them* (f), *and God is Hearing, Knowing.* (Q24:60)

Quranic Verses Forbidding Men in Regard to Individual Females

As previously noted, men are not forgiven if they force female spiritual warriors into prostitution if she wants chastity, but the woman is forced to do so against her willpower is forgiven by God: (Q24:33).

Men cannot inherit a woman against her will: *O those who believed! It is not lawful for you that you inherit women unwillingly, and place not difficulties for them* (f) so that *you take away some of what you gave them* (f), *unless they approach a manifest indecency. Live as one who is honorable with them* (f). *Then, if you disliked them* (f) *perhaps you dislike something in which God makes much good.* (Q4:19-4:22) They are: not *to inherit women against their will*, specifically done in pre-Islamic times to avoid paying a woman her dowry.

Men cannot appoint secretly with women (Q2:235): ... *appoint not with them (f) secretly, unless you say a saying as one who is honorable.* (Q2:235)

Men cannot approach men with lust: *They assign daughters to God! Glory be to Him! And for themselves, that for which they lust.* (Q16:57); *why approach you men with lust instead of women?* (Q27:55) nor cherish women for lust: *Made to appear pleasing to humanity was the cherishing of lust: From women and children and that which is heaped up heaps of gold and silver and horses, ones that are distinguished, and flocks and cultivation, that is the enjoyment of this present life, while God, with Him is the goodness of the Destination.* (Q3:14)

Men cannot give parts of animals born dead to their wives to eat: *They said: What is in the bellies of these flocks is exclusively for our males and is that which is forbidden to our female spouses, but if it would be born dead, then, they are ascribed as associates in it. He will give recompense to them for their allegations. Truly, He is Wise, Knowing.* (Q6:139)

They are not to wrongly accuse: *Truly, those who accuse the ones who are free, unwary, chaste female believers were cursed in the present and the world to come and for them will be a serious punishment on a Day when their tongues bear witness against them and their hands and their feet as to what they had been doing.* (Q24:23-24:24)

They are not to persecute believing women: *Truly, those who persecuted the males, ones who believe and the females, ones who believe and again repent not after that, for them is the punishment of hell and for them is the punishment of the burning.* (Q85:10)

Here we have perhaps the strongest evidence from Quranic verses that forbid wrong by accusing *all* women and/or persecuting believing women. Surely, Ali ibn Abi Talib, the embodiment of justice, would never write nor ever sanction the deceit of the fabricators who added words disparaging women to his eloquence. As the falsehoods include the condemnation of *all* women, they only serve to harm his reputation and that of *all* women.

III The Vice of Being Unjust Described in the Quran and the Fabrications Against Women in the *Nahj al-Balagha*

Quranic Verses Describing the Unjust

***Your** Lord is not unjust to His servants.* (Q41:46) Yet, these words harming the reputation of all women continue to be unjust. Rationalizations that refer to "one woman" no longer hold any weight. As mentioned before, the only way to show their humanity is to either add "some" or to remove the words altogether.

*Then, for that, call to this. Go **you** straight as **you** were commanded.* The Quran commands the slanderers of women to: *Follow not their desires. Say* (Muhammad): *I believed in what God caused to descend from a Book*, that is, to "follow the fairer" (Q39:17). *I was commanded to be just among you*, words ignored by those who discredit women, *God is our Lord and your Lord. For us are our actions* which are to show that words deprecating *all* women are not Ali ibn Abi Talib's words, *and for you, your actions*, the action of those who wish to continue publishing and teaching the *Nahj al-Balagha* with these statements and words against *all* women. They only pay lip-service to the Quran. *There is no disputation between us and between you. God will gather us together. To Him is the Homecoming*, when they will know the consequence of their actions at the Homecoming! (Q42:15)

We repeat to the maligners as the Quran tells us: *How well they will hear! How well **you** will perceive on that Day they will approach Us, but today the ones who are unjust are in a clear wandering astray!* (Q19:38)

If they (the ungrateful) *respond not to **you**,* (Muhammad), *then, know that they only follow their own desires. Who is one who goes further astray than one who followed his own desires without guidance from God? Truly, God guides not the folk, the ones who are unjust.* (Q28:50) Those who continue to criticize *all* women ***follow their own desires.*** Their desire (*hawa*) lead them astray so that they no longer follow ***guidance from God*** because ***God does not guide the ones who are unjust.***

*Those who were ungrateful said: We will never believe in this, the Quran, nor in what was in advance of it. If **you**,* (Muhammad), *could but see when the ones who are unjust are stationed before their Lord reproaching one another. Those who were taken advantage of due to their weakness say to those who grew arrogant: If it were not for you, we would have been ones who believe.* (Q34:31) Can those who denounce *all* women not feel responsible for those who have been so disparaged that they will say to them on the Day of Judgment: *If it were not for you, we would have been ones who believe.* (Q2:259)

*These are the signs of God. We recount them to **you**,* (Muhammad), as the Quran tells us, these are words we recount *in Truth* because *God wants not injustice in the worlds.* (Q3:108)

Quranic Verses Describing Unjust Wives, Daughters and Individual Females

Does the Quran mention unjust women? Yes, but it does not condemn *all* women just as it does not accuse *all* men of being oppressors and tyrants. There are wives who commanded to wrongdoing rather than to what is right. Blameworthy wives include those of some Prophets/Messengers such as the wives of Noah and Lot; as well as others such as the wife of the Aziz of Egypt (Zulaykha) and the wife of Abu Lahab.

Blameworthy daughters are referred to as idols that pre-Islamic Arabs *assigned as daughters of God* while the Quran makes clear that God did not have any daughters or sons. We will see how Sermon 185 says: God is too purified to have contact with women. We say to those whose goal is to degrade women—God is too purified to have contact with men, as well, as God is above any gender.

Females with which there is displeasure include female polytheists, thieves (Q5:39) and hypocrites. In addition, there are *bad females* (Q24:26); *adulteresses* (Q24:2-3); *those* (f) *who commit indecency* (Q4:15-16); females *who deride one another* (Q49:11); those who: *abort their children* (Q6:140), *take lovers to themselves* (f), (Q5:5), or are *licentious* (Q5:5).

Females who are specific examples of wrongdoers include the woman *who breaks what she spun after firming its fibers* compared to giving deceitful oaths (Q16:92); the wife of Abu Lahab *around whose neck is a rope of palm fibers* (Q111:4-111:5); the *cunning* of Zulaykha which the Quran describes as "female cunning" (Q12:28); and *the women who practice magic, blowing on knots*. (Q113:4)

However, as pointed out several times, these are not *all* women.

Quranic Verses Describing Unjust Men

There are too many such verses to be able to name them all in this Introduction.

The Fabrications Against Women in the *Nahj al-Balagha*

After understanding something of the sense of justice embodied by Ali ibn Abi Talib, whether he is seen as caliph, leader (***imam***) or spiritual guide, we are now prepared to learn about the words that have been fabricated by his enemies to degrade and dishonor him and his great legacy as the model of justice.

Here we highlight lines and even full sermons that are found in the *Nahj al-Balagha* which are clearly spurious for two reasons: They are not commentary on the Quranic verses which calls for God's servants: *those who listen to the saying of the Quran and follow the fairer of it*, (Q39:18); and, secondly, using the same argument when it comes to the collection of Sermons, Letters and Sayings in the *Nahj al-Balagha*, not "**follow the fairer of it**," instead of denigrating the paragon of justice, Ali ibn Abi Talib.

> **Sermon 27:** O you facade of men, not men, **your intelligence is that of children and your mental sharpness is that of the women kept in seclusion, partitioned from the outside world.** I wish I had not seen you nor known you. By God, this acquaintance has brought about shame and resulted in repentance.

> **Sermon 80:** O you peoples! **Women are deficient in faith, deficient in shares and deficient in intelligence.** As regards the deficiency in their faith, it is their ab-

stention from prayers and fasting during their menstrual period. As regards deficiency in their intelligence it is because the evidence of two women is equal to that of one man. As for the deficiency of their shares that is because of their share in inheritance being half of men. So beware of the evils of women. Be on your guard even from those of them who are reportedly good. Do not obey them even in good things so that they may not attract you to evils.

Sermon 136: I have never mixed matters nor have they appeared mixed to me. Certainly, this is the rebellious group in which there is the near one (al-Zubayr), the **scorpion's venom** (Aisha) and doubts which cast a veil on facts. But the matter is clear, and the wrong has been shaken from its foundation. Its tongue has stopped uttering mischief. By God, I will prepare for them a cistern from which I alone will draw water. They will not be able to drink from it nor would they be able to drink from any other place.

Sermon 152: Beasts are concerned with their bellies. Predators are concerned with assaulting others. **Women are concerned with the adornments of this ignoble life and the creation of mischief herein.** On the other hand, believers are humble, believers are admonishers and believers are afraid of God.

Sermon 155: Whoever can at this time keep himself clinging to God should do so. If you follow me I shall certainly carry you, if God so wills, on the path of Paradise, even though it may be full of severe hardship and of bitter taste. **As regards a certain woman, she is in the grip of womanly views, and malice is boiling in her bosom like the furnace of the blacksmith.**

Another part of the same sermon follows, saying:

Sermon 155: This path is the lightest course and the brightest lamp. Guidance towards virtuous actions is sought through faith while guidance towards faith is achieved through virtuous actions. Knowledge is made to prosper through faith, and death is feared because of knowledge. this world comes to an end with death, while the next world is secured by virtuous actions in this world. For people there is no escape from resurrection. They are heading for this last end in its appointed course.

Sermon 185: God is too purified to contact women.

Letter 14: Do not excite women and do not make them angry with rude behavior even if they use harsh and insulting words against your commander and officers because they are physically and mentally weak and get excited easily and frightened quickly.

Letter 31: Do not seek the advice of women. Their verdicts are often immature and incorrect. Their determinations are not firm. You must guard and defend them and act as a shelter to protect them from impious and injurious surroundings and infamous sights. This kind of shelter will keep them well-protected from every harm. Their contact with a vicious and sinful atmosphere (even with all the shelter that you can provide) is going to prove more harmful than being left with protection. **Do not let them interfere with affairs where you cannot personally guide or protect them. Do not let them aspire for things which are beyond their capacities. They are more like decoration to humanity and are not made to rule and govern humanity. Exhibit reasonable interest in things which they desire and give importance to them, but do not let them influence your opinions and do not let them impel you to go against your sane views. Do not force them into marriages which they abhor or which they consider below their dignity because there is danger of thereby converting honorable and virtuous women into shameless and dishonorables beings.** Divide and distribute work among your servants so that you can hold each one responsible for the work entrusted.

Saying 61: Woman is a scorpion whose grip is sweet.

Saying 102: Your society will pass through a period when cunning and crafty intriguers will be favored by status, when profligates will be considered as well-bred, well-behaved and elegant elites of the society, when just and honest persons will be considered as weaklings, when charity will be considered as a loss to wealth and property, when support and help to each other will be considered as favor and benevolence and when prayers and worship to God will be taken up for the sake of show to gain popularity and higher status. **At such times regimes will be run under the advice of women and the youngsters will be the rulers and counselors of the State.**

Saying 123: Jealousy in woman is unpardonable but in man it is a sign of his faith in religion (because Islam has permitted polygamy and prohibited polyandry).

Saying 135: Daily prayers are the best medium through which one can seek the nearness to God. The pilgrimage (*hajj*) is the greater struggle (*jihad*) for every weak person. For everything that you own there is the purifying alms (*zakat*), and the purifying alms (*zakat*) of your body is fasting. **The greater struggle (*jihad*) of a woman is to afford pleasant company to her husband.**

Oppressors, Tyrants and Bullys

Who would create such falsehood? In the words of the famous martyred religious scholar, Ayatullah Mutahhari, the principle of justice is crucial from Ali's point of view as it ensures a healthy society and brings peace to the soul. He points out that "oppression, injustice and discrimination cannot bring peace and happiness." It is clear from his words that a healthy society includes both men and women and that "oppression, injustice and discrimination" against *all* women or even *all* men, cannot bring peace and happiness:

> From Ali's viewpoint, it is the principle of justice that is of crucial significance in preserving the balance of society, and winning the goodwill of the public. Its practice can ensure the health of society and bring peace to its soul. Oppression, injustice and discrimination cannot bring peace and happiness—even to the tyrant or the one in whose interest the injustice is perpetrated. Justice is like a public highway which has room for all and through which everyone may pass without impediment. But injustice and oppression constitute a blind alley which does not lead even the oppressor to his desired destination.[1]

Using Quranic language, we can only refer to those who inserted these untruths and practices of pre-Islamic Arabia into the *Nahj al-Balagha* as tyrants, oppressors or bullys who wanted to harm the reputation of Ali by treating someone in a cruel, insulting, threatening or aggressive way. Ali himself warns of such people:

> God abases every tyrant and disgraces every braggart. Be just with God and **be just with people giving them what is their due** from yourself, from your close relatives, and from those of your subjects towards whom you are most affectionate. **If you fail to do this, you will be an oppressor.** Letter 53*

Ali ibn Abi Talib says that those who continue not to act with justice towards God's creatures—male and female—will remain at war with God.

> One who does not act with justice towards God and His creatures and instead tyrannizes them will find that not only His creatures, but also God Himself will be his opponent: He remains at war with God until he desists and repents. Letter 53*

Ali ibn Abi Talib tells us in his last will and testament to be an enemy of tyrants and oppressors, seemingly including the oppressors of *all* women. He advises that we improve mutual relations, implying between men and women, as the Prophet said this is better then even prayer and fasting.

> Be an enemy of tyrants and oppressors and be a friend and helper of those who are oppressed and tyrannized. To you, to my other children, to my relatives and to all who acquire this will of mine, I advise to fear God and to be pious, to have fair and honest dealings with one another and improve mutual relations because I have heard your grandfather, the Prophet, peace and the mercy of God be upon him, saying: 'To remove mutual enmity, ill-feeling and hatred is better than recommended prayers and fasting.' Letter 53*

Projection

What leads to tyranny, oppression or bullying? One of the causes is known as projection. Projection may be a defense mechanism in which the human ego defends itself against vices that unconsciously occur as negative impulses by denying their existence in themselves while attributing them to others. For example, they deny their own anger which can acquire the venom of a scorpion (Sermon 136) and attribute it to women. They deny their own jealousy by saying that jealousy in women is unpardonable but permissible in men (Saying 123).

A tyrant, oppressor or bully may project his/her own feelings of vulnerability onto the target of the tyranny, oppression or bullying activity which in this case is *all* women. Despite the fact that a bully's typically denigrating activities are aimed at a person's targets of demeaning women, the true source of such negativity is ultimately almost always found in the person's own sense of personal insecurity or vulnerability.

Here in the *Nahj al-Balagha* we have statements by tyrants, oppressors and bullys, the unjust and egotistical who have broken the limits of justice and violated the belief in it for both themselves as well as censuring *all* women they slander. As a result, these egos increase their greed and lust for their own desires while limiting the believing woman's ability to develop her own free willpower, to know her own animal soul that incites to wrongdoing because, as a victim of this slander, she has come to believe that she is at fault, that her very physical form is the cause of all greed and lust in the world, that, on the one hand, she contains the scorpion's venom while on the other hand, she is weak and mentally challenged. As a victim, she becomes unjust to herself. Then, the greater the greed and lust exhibited by the oppressor, the greater becomes the dissatisfaction with herself never realizing that she is the victim of tyranny against her and the oppression against the great paragon of justice, Ali ibn Abi Talib.

Statements in the *Nahj al-Balagha* That Contradict Quranic Verses

Letter 31: Seeking the Advice of Women and Consultation

The main precedent, then, for the Sermons, Letters and Sayings of Ali ibn Abi Talib is the Quran as the Commentary of this work shows. How is it then conceivable that he would say something that clearly goes against the Quran? We refer to Letter 31 where it says:

> **Do not seek the advice of women.** Their verdicts are often immature and incorrect. Their determinations are not firm. You must guard and defend them and act as a shelter to protect them from impious and injurious surroundings and infamous sights. This kind of shelter will keep them well-protected from every harm. Their contact with a vicious and sinful atmosphere even with all the shelter that you can provide is going to prove more harmful than being left with protection. Letter 31

The Quran favors consultation: Letter 31 goes against the Quran: According to the Quran, giving good advice or moral counsel, no matter who it comes from and it is one of the three ways of invitation towards God: Wisdom, giving good advice, and honorable debate: *Call* ***you*** *to the way of* ***your*** *Lord with wisdom and fairer advice.*

Dispute with them in a way that is fairer. Truly, **your** *Lord is He Who is greater in knowledge of whoever went astray from His way. He is greater in knowledge of the ones who are truly guided.* (Q16:125)

Prophet Moses took the advice of the shepherdess whom he later married: *Then, drew near him one of the two women, walking bashfully. She said: Truly, my father calls to* **you that** *he may give* **you** *recompense of compensation because* **you** *had drawn water for us. So when he drew near him and related to him the narrative, he said: Fear not.* **You** *were delivered from the folk, ones who are unjust.* (Q28:25)

The father of the shepherdess took the advice of his daughter: *One of the two women said: O my father! Employ him. Truly, best is that you would employ the strong, the trustworthy.* (Q28:26)

Khadija advised the Prophet, peace and the mercy of God be upon him to go and visit her cousin when the Prophet received the first revelation and he listened to her advice.

Again, in Letter 31, we read: "**Women are more like decoration to humanity and are not made to rule and govern humanity.** Yet, when the female believers pledged their allegiance to the Prophet, they pledged that they would not: ascribe partners with God nor steal nor commit adultery nor kill their children nor make false charges to harm another's reputation nor rebel against anything that is honorable."

The females pledge not to harm the reputation of another, yet their reputation and the reputation of Ali ibn Abi Talib are harmed by the deprecating words noted above that somehow found their way into the *Nahj al-Balagha* contradicting the Quran: *Then, take their* (f) *pledge of allegiance and ask forgiveness from God for them* (f). *Truly, God is Forgiving, Compassionate.* (Q60:12)

In addition, their pledge clearly shows that they are not just a decoration to humanity as Letter 31 says, but are important members of society and that their pledges are vital in the establishment of a just society as was the goal of the Prophet, peace and the mercy of God be upon him, and Ali ibn Abi Talib.

O those who believed! When the females, ones who believe, drew near to you, ones who emigrate (f), *put them* (f) *to a test. God is greater in knowledge as to their* (f) *faith.* (Q60:10) The Quran does not say that because they menstruate they are deficient in faith. Knowing that *God is greater in knowledge as to their* (f) *faith,* Ali would not then go beyond the revelation and say something such as: "women are deficient in faith". He would give believing women who emigrate a chance as the Quran does by saying: Test their belief.

Saying 102 demeans the state run by advice of women to youngsters:

> Your society will pass through a period when cunning and crafty intriguers will be favored by status, when profligates will be considered as well-bred, well-behaved and elegant elites of the society, when just honest persons will be considered as weaklings, when charity will be considered as a loss to wealth and property, when support and help to each other will be considered as favor and benevolence and

when prayers and worship to God will be taken up for the sake of show to gain popularity and higher status. **At such times regimes will be run under the advice of women and the youngsters will be the rulers and counselors of the State.**

Yet, the practices of the Rightly Guided caliphs was supposed to differ from pre-Islamic Arab practice which had placed great importance on the age and experience of the one chosen.[2] However, the praise literature (*manaqib*) hints that Ali was not chosen to be caliph earlier because of his age so why would he write something against young people when he himself suffered this fate?

The *manaqib* (praise) literature states that Ali was the first to accept Islam while a youth who had not reached maturity of age and he had to hide his Islam.[3]

Making False Claims Harming the Reputation of Another

The Quran warns against maligning believers, males or females, which happens when *all* females are disgraced: People are not to malign anyone: *Those who malign the males, ones who believe and the females, ones who believe without their deserving it, surely, they lay a burden on themselves of false charges to harm another's reputation and a clear sin.* (Q33:58)

The following text will give the arguments as to why these excerpts need to either be qualified by the word "some" or removed entirely from the collection of Sermons, Letters and Sayings as we show that they go against so many of the Quranic verses and only serve to disparage the man about whom the Prophet said: "The Quran is with Ali and Ali is with the Quran."

We begin with the *Nahj al-Balagha* in which certain words in Sermon 27 clearly disrespect this Quranic view by referring to the army of Ali as being not that of men, but that of people with the intelligence of children and that of secluded women: "O you facade of men, not men, **your intelligence is that of children and your mental sharpness is that of the women kept in seclusion, partitioned from the outside world.**" Sermon 27

The reason women are secluded or "partitioned" is either because their husbands commanded them to do so or it was their choice to do so as it is referred to in the Quran in regard to Mary, the mother of Jesus: *Then,* (Mary) *took to herself a partition away from them, so We sent Our Spirit to her and he presented himself before her as a mortal without fault.* (Q19:17)

Or when the Quran tells the community in regard to the wives of the Prophet: *When you asked his wives for sustenance, then, ask them* (f) *from behind a partition. That is purer for your hearts and their* (f) *hearts.* (Q33:53) Therefore, these words in Sermon 27 must be a fabrication as Ali would not disparage the Word of God.

Sermon 136 refers to the scorpion's venom which typical commentators say refers to Aisha:

> I have never mixed matters nor have they appeared mixed to me. Certainly, this is the rebellious group in which there is the near one (al-Zubayr), the **scorpion's venom** (the translator/commentator to the *Nahj al-Balagha* adds the word Aisha here) and doubts which cast a veil on facts. But the matter is clear, and the wrong has been shaken from its foundation. Its tongue has stopped uttering mischief. By God, I will prepare for them a cistern from which I alone will draw water. They will not be able to drink from it nor would they be able to drink from any other place. Sermon 136

In addition, Saying 61 claims *all* women are scorpions: "Woman is a scorpion whose grip is sweet."

Are mothers, wives, sisters and daughters mentioned in the Quran or well-known in Islamic history, scorpions? Were Fatima bint Muhammad, Fatima bint Asad, Khadija bint Khuwaylid (d. 619 CE), Ali's daughter: Zaynab bint Ali ibn Abi Talib deficient in faith and intelligence? Were they too emotional? Should the Prophet not have listened to Khadija? Of course not. Not all women are like Fatima bint Muhammad or Khadija or Zaynab bint Ali, but also not all men are Satan, Pharaoh, Hamun or followers of the Quranic *sunna* as expressed by Prophet Muhammad, peace and the mercy of God be upon him.

Yet, Ali says in Letter 53:

> Let those of your subjects who most keenly seek out the faults of others be the ones furthest away from you and the most despicable in your eyes. For people do have faults which it behooves the governor—above all others—to conceal.... **So try and veil deficiences as much as you can** so that God may veil from your subjects what is within yourself which you wish to be veiled. Letter 53*

Here we have a clue to the fact that words such as "woman is a scorpion" are fabricated. Ali ibn Abi Talib states in his letter to Malik Ashtar to veil a person's deficiencies and yet are we to believe that in Sermon 80, which we will get to, he is falsely said to have said: Women are deficient in faith, intelligence and shares? Are there women who could be considered to be as "scorpions?" Perhaps there are some such women, but certainly not *all* women.

Ali tells us: "Never be quick to believe a slanderer, for a slanderer is a deceiver, even if he appears in the guise of a good adviser." Letter 53*

We are here warned by Ali ibn Abi Talib not to believe the words of slanderers such as those who inserted words, phrases and even complete sermons into the *Nahj al-Balagha* that not only slander "women" but slander Ali ibn Abi Talib as well as they are meant to harm his reputation, as a champion of justice. The Quran says: *Woe to every slandering backbiter.* (Q104:1)

Do Not Deride

The Quran also warns against deriding others—including women and the 4th

Rightly Guided caliph—yet scholars choose to continue to print the words of the slanderers and *those who deride others* or insult women *with nicknames*. Those who slander *all* women and who degrade the reputation of Ali ibn Abi Talib were people who *disobeyed God after they had believed. They are the ones who are unjust: O those who believed! Let not a folk deride another folk. Perhaps they be better than they, nor women deride other women. Perhaps they be better than they. Nor find fault with one another nor insult one another with nicknames. Miserable was the name of disobedience after belief! Whoever repents not, then, those, they are the ones who are unjust.* (Q49:11)

Sermon 152 reads: "Beasts are concerned with their bellies. Predators are concerned with assaulting others. **Women are concerned with the adornments of this ignoble life and the creation of mischief herein.** On the other hand, believers are humble, believers are admonishers and believers are God-conscious."

The sentence about women appears to be a random statement added after the description of beasts and predators and asserts a parallel with all women. A typical commentator says:

> The intention is to say that the cause of all mischief and evil is the passion to satisfy bodily needs and the passion to subdue. If a human being is subjugated by the passion to satisfy bodily needs and considers filling the stomach as his aim there will be no difference between him and a beast, because a beast, too, has no aim except to fill its belly. But if he is over-powered by the passion to subdue others and takes to killing and devastation there will be no difference between him and a predator, because the latter's aim is also tearing and devouring. If the passions are at work in him, then, he is like a woman, because in a woman both these passions act side by side and because of this she is extremely eager of adornment and is active in fanning mischief and disturbance. However, a true believer will never agree to adopt these habits as his mode of behavior. Rather he keeps his passions suppressed so that he neither allows pride and vanity to approach near him nor does he fan mischief or disturbance for fear of God.

According to the commentator, Ali is saying that women are similar to beasts and predators because the passions that cause a beast to satisfy its belly and a predator who tears and devours its prey are part of *all* women. Yet the analogy does not work. Her "beastly" nature is because she is eager for adornment and she is a "predator" because she fans mischief and disturbance. Is it pride or vanity that a beast seeks to fill its bellly? Is it pride or vanity that a predator tears and devours its prey? How are women related to this? Clearly the sentence has been added to Ali's words as the commentator is not able to tie it in with the previous words. In addition, the commentator has disregarded the fact that there are female believers, as well, who are being ignored.

In Letter 53 Ali clearly warns men not to become "ravenous beasts of prey seeking to devour" people. They should change their behavior because the people are either their same in faith or fellow human beings:

> Infuse your heart with mercy for the subjects, love for them and kindness towards them. Be not like a ravenous beast of prey above them, seeking to devour them. For they are of two types: either your brethren in religion or your like in creation (i.e. human being). Letter 53*

Ali is here obviously protecting women from beastly and predator men, yet the commentator never refers to some men who are in this state.

IV Analysis of Sermon 80

> **Sermon 80:** O you peoples! **Women are deficient in faith, deficient in shares and deficient in intelligence.** As regards the deficiency in their faith, it is their abstention from prayers and fasting during their menstrual period. As regards deficiency in their intelligence it is because the evidence of two women is equal to that of one man. As for the deficiency of their shares that is because of their share in inheritance being half of men. So beware of the evils of women. Be on your guard even from those of them who are reportedly good. Do not obey them even in good things so that they may not attract you to evils.

"Be Aware of the Evils of Women"

Those who have inserted false statements into the Sermons, Letters and Sayings in the *Nahj al-Balagha* have replaced the male satanic forces that the Quran refers to with women, they doing the "mischief" that they blame on *all* women. They should desist or their words be removed from the collection because the Quran says: *Do no mischief in and on the earth as ones who make corruption.* (Q11:85)

Claiming women are only interested in "adornments of this ignoble life," the Quran indicates that spending one's wealth to show off to others is a sign of satanic influence, not that of the influence of *all* women: *For those who spend their wealth to show off to humanity* ... implies that someone who causes another to go astray is under the influence of satanic forces, not that of *all* women, because Satan wants to cause people to go astray. If a woman understands this and gives good advice to another in this regard, she is opposing satanic suggestions. The Quran goes on to say that it is Satan who fills people with "false desires," not all women. *To whomever Satan would be a comrade, then how evil a comrade!* (Q4:38) Saying not to listen to the advice of women even if they give a good suggestion, the Quran says: *Satan wants to cause them to go astray—a far wandering astray.* (Q4:60) Satan says in the Quran: *I will cause them to go astray. I will fill them with false desires.... Whoever takes Satan to himself for a protector other than God, then, surely, he lost, a clear loss.* (Q4:119) Or: *Satan promises them and fills them with false desires and Satan promises them nothing but delusion.* (Q4:120) The Quran refers to the fact that mischief, delusion or deception comes from Satan, not from *all* women.

"Women Are Mentally Weak"

In Letter 14, it says that Ali said: **"Do not excite women and do not make them**

angry with rude behavior even if they use harsh and insulting words against your commander and officers because they are physically and mentally weak and get excited easily and frightened quickly." Letter 14

The fabricators have again relaced the Quranic view of Satan with all women by projecting their own passions onto them. If as some do consider women to be weak and helpless, this is how Ali ibn Abi Talib says to treat them—not by demeaning the weak and the poor— but by showing sympathy and compassion.

> Upholding the right of each person is incumbent upon you. Do not let any haughtiness on your part cause you to neglect them, for you will not be pardoned even the slightest shortcoming in fulfilling your obligations towards them as a result of attending to some important matter. So do not turn your concern away from them, nor assume a contemptuous attitude towards them. **Keep a watchful eye over the affairs of those who have no access to you, and who are disdained by men of high standing.** Sermon 53*

"Those who are distained by men of high standing" clearly refers to women who are disdained by authoritarian rulers. Clearly this refers to treating all women with disdain. Why would Ali have contradicted himself? A typical commentary upon Sermon 80 states:

> After describing women's natural weakness, Amir al-muminin points out the mischief of blindly following women and wrongly obeying them. He says that not to say of bad things they say, but even if they say in regard to some good things, it should not be done in a way that they should feel as if it is being done in pursuance of their wish, but rather in a way that they should realize that the good act has been performed because of its being good and that their pleasure or wish has nothing to do with it. If they have even the doubt that their pleasures has been kept in view in it, women would slowly increase in their demands and would wish that they should be obeyed in all matters, however evil, the inevitable consequence whereof will be destruction and ruin. ash-Shaykh Muhammad Abduh writes about this view of Amir al-muminin as under: Amir al-muminin has said a thing which is **corroborated by experiences of centuries.**[1]

The commentator says that blindly following women and wrongly obeying them leads to mischief in the male who does so implying that women must blindly follow men and rightfully obey them because of women being an imperfect creature. In other words, women need to ignore their ability to reason and their ability to employ their free willpower to choose the good. They are to have no choice. This is why it is said that their jihad is "to afford pleasant company to their husband," Saying 135.

Unconcerned by the degrading of women that these statements cause for *all* women, we point out the opposite of what Shayh Muhammad Abduh says: Because of the oppression, tyranny and bullying by some men, this thing that is said has been **"corroborated by experience of centuries."**

This was not how it was according to the prophetic *sunna* and the life of Ali ibn Abi Taib, so again we have commentators who try to rationalize an injustice rather than uphold the reputation of Ali ibn Abi Talib. In other words a typical commentator stands with the slanderers and not with the fair and just Ali.

There is an ever-present temptation on the part of rulers and leaders to abuse their power and to perpetuate injustice and tyranny. It is clearly more difficult to avoid the harm/pain of injustice than it is to act with justice. Rulers are confronted with the temptations of power. While a society may develop laws to punish corruption, we cannot legislate the free willpower to remain uncorrupted. Ali says in the first part of Letter 53: "break the soul of passionate desire," "dominate your impulses," "withhold yourself from that which is unlawful for you."

Males and females begin with the same *fitrat Allah* or innate nature so the difference lies not in biology, but in one's intentions as developed through experiences of the nurturing process and interaction with society.

> One's intention is to be just, not for the sake of some earthly reward or some tangible consequence in this world, but purely for the sake of justice itself, and this essence or principle of justice is in turn inseparable from our innate nature (*fitrat Allah*). For justice is at one with God not simply because that which God commands is just; rather, God commands just acts precisely because they are just and because this justice *is* one with His own nature.[2]

Ali ibn Abi Talib says in Sermon 232*: "I bear witness that He is Justice and He acts justly." If God acts justly as a result of His very nature, which is pure justice, the fair and just person will act justly out of a desire to conform to God's nature and not simply out of obedience to God's commands, and never out of desire for any earthly reward.[3]

The Quran says in regard to men, women and children who are taken advantage of because of their weakness: *Why should you not fight in the way of God and for the ones taken advantage of due to weakness among the men and the women and the children, those who say: Our Lord! Bring us out from this town whose people are the ones who are unjust and assign for us a protector from* **Your** *Presence and assign for us a helper from* **Your** *Presence?* (Q4:75) And: *But the ones taken advantage of due to weakness of the men and the women and the children who are neither able to access some means, nor are they truly guided to the way.* (Q4:78)

Whereas in Sermon 80, Ali supposedly says that women are deficient in intelligence, in Sermon 232 he points out that men differ one from the other because of the clay from which they were created, the clay having nothing to do with gender. It can be, as he says: "a man of handsome features is weak in intelligence" and so on. Are we then to believe that it was he who declared "all women are deficient in intelligence?" Is that his statement or his words in Sermon 232 where he says that "some" men are deficient in intelligence?

> Men differ among themselves because of the sources of their clay from which they have been created. This is because they are either from saltish soil or sweet soil or from rugged earth or soft earth. They resemble each other on the basis of the affinity of their soil and differ according to its difference. Therefore, sometimes **a man of handsome features is weak in intelligence**, a tall statured person is of low courage, a virtuous man is ugly in appearance, a short statured man is far-sighted, a good-natured man has an evil trait, a man of perplexed heart has bewildering mind and a sharp-tongued person has a wakeful heart. Sermon 232

Ali warns Malki Ashtar to follow the precedence of the Prophet, peace be upon him, in all matters, conceivably including the attitude towards women: "Do not set up some new practice which is detrimental to the already established traditions; if you do so, the reward for their observance will rebound to him who established them, while the responsibility of their destruction will be upon you." Letter 53*

Ali ibn Abi Talib tells Malik Ashtar not to put the just and the unjust together. This would also indicate not to put all believing men and women in the same category as unjust men and women, but indicate "some" are believing and "some" are unjust.

Ali writes in another letter: "Do not place the virtuous and the wicked in the same rank before you, for this would result in the virtuous belittling the virtues and the wicked entrenching their vices" (Letter 31). This is exactly what Letter 31, as we have seen, tries to do in regard to *all* women.

Ali ibn Abi Talib, quoting a Quranic verse, tells us to follow that which unites: *O you who believe, obey God and obey the Messenger and those in authority among you. If you dispute with one another over anything, then refer it to God and the Messenger.* (Q4:59) To "refer to God" means following that which is clear and unequivocal in His Book; and "refer to the Messenger"'means following that part of his *sunna* which unites, rather than that which divides. Letter 53*

Clearly the fabrications found in the *Nahj al-Balagha* only serve to divide women from men instead of uniting them as the Quran directs.

Again, we return to the typical commentator of Sermon 80 who states: "Ali ibn Abi Talib gave Sermon 80 following the Battle of Siffin where two companions of the Prophet, peace and the mercy of God be upon him, instigated the widow of the Prophet, Aisha bint Abu Bakr, to attack him in order to try to remove him from the caliphate. Since the devastation resulting from this battle was the outcome of blindly following a woman's command, he has described women's physical defects and their causes and effects in this sermon."

Yet Ali also blames the two men who instigated the nineteen year old Prophet's widow to go to battle:

Talhah and Zubayr

> They (Talhah, az-Zubayr and their supporters) came out dragging the wife of the Messenger of God, peace and the mercy of God be upon him, just as a maidslave

> is dragged for sale. They took her to Basrah where those two (Talhah and az-Zubayr) put their own women in their houses, but exposed the wife of the Messenger of God to themselves and to others in the army in which there was not a single individual who had not offered me his obedience and sworn to me allegiance quite obediently, without any compulsion. Sermon 171

Aisha

It is suggested that Ali said in Sermon 155: "Whoever can at this time keep himself clinging to God should do so. If you follow me I shall certainly carry you, if God so wills, on the path of Paradise, even though it may be full of severe hardship and of bitter taste."

Then suddenly comes this sentence: "**As regards a certain woman, she is in the grip of womanly views, and malice is boiling in her bosom like the furnace of the blacksmith.**" Another part of the same sermon follows, saying:

> This path is the lightest course and the brightest lamp. Guidance towards virtuous actions is sought through faith while guidance towards faith is achieved through virtuous actions. Knowledge is made to prosper through faith, and death is feared because of knowledge. This world come to an end with death, while the next world is secured by virtuous actions in this world. For people there is no escape from resurrection. They are heading for this last end in its appointed course. Sermon 155

While speaking of guiding people on the path of Paradise, suddenly and out of context appears the line: "**As regards a certain woman, she is in the grip of womanly views, and malice is boiling in her bosom like the furnace of the blacksmith.**" Why is this sentence a fabrication? He tells us in Sermon 155 that he gives her her original respect and that it is the obligation of God to be her Reckoner: "If she (Aisha) were called upon to deal with others as she is dealing with me she would not have done it. As for me, even hereafter **she will be allowed her original respect, while the reckoning of her misdeeds is an obligation on God.**" Sermon 155

Forgiveness

Ali speaks eloquently about forgiveness, echoing the Quranic verses such as: *An honorable saying and forgiveness are better than charity succeeded by injury.* (Q2:263) He says in Letter 53*: Mistakes slip from them. Defects emerge from them, deliberately or accidentally. So bestow upon them your forgiveness and your pardon, just as you would have God bestow upon you His forgiveness and pardon, for you are above them. The one who has authority over you is above you. God is above him who appointed you ... and through them He tests you.

Ali says the following regarding the importance of forgiveness in the eyes of God:

I am willing to forgive and to forget those who have wronged me and to requite those who have exhibited fidelity towards me. Letter 29

Do not feel ashamed to forgive and forget. Letter 53

The best deed of a great man is to forgive and forget. Saying 203[4]

Aisha Exonerated

In an incident that occurred when Aisha was perhaps fourteen years old after the Battle of Mustaliq in 627 CE according to some reports,[5] Aisha was with a caravan on its way back to Madinah when she realized that she had lost her necklace and went to find it. As she was petite and did not weigh much, no one noticed that she was not in her enclosed tent-like structure saddle on top of her camel (*howdah*). Her camel stood up with the caravan and left the area with the rest of the caravan. When she returned to the place where the caravan had been, she found it had left. One of the companions had returned to the place where the caravan had been and found her. She rode his camel as he walked leading it to the caravan's next stop. When they arrived, people began to spread rumors among themselves that she had committed adultery with the companion. The Quran responded sternly against those people in what is called "The Scandal Against Aisha."[6]

Truly, those who drew near with a false and defamatory statement about someone to damage their reputation are many among you. Assume it not worse for you. Nay! It is good for you. To every man of them is what he deserved of sin. As for those who turned away towards the greater part from among them, there will be a tremendous punishment for him.

Why not when you heard about it, thought not the ones who are male believers and the ones who are female believers the better of themselves and have said: This is a clear false and defamatory statement about someone to damage their reputation? Why brought they not about four witnesses for it?

As they bring not about witnesses, then, with God, those, they are the ones who bring a false and defamatory statement about someone to damage their reputation. If it not were for the grace of God on you and His mercy in the present and in the world to come, certainly, would have afflicted you a tremendous punishment for what you muttered. When you received it on your tongues and said with your mouths of what there is no knowledge, you assume it insignificant while it is serious with God.

Why, when you heard it, said you not: It will not be for us to assert this. Glory be to **You!** *This is a serious false charge to harm the reputation of another. God admonishes you that you shall never revert to the like of it, if you had been ones who believe. He makes manifest for you the signs. God is Knowing, Wise.*

Truly, those who love that anything not agreeable with the Truth be spread about those who believed, they will have a painful punishment in the present and in the world to come. God knows and you know not. If it were not for the grace of God on you and His mercy, you would be ruined, and that God is Gentle, Compassionate.

O those who believed! Follow not in the steps of Satan. Whoever follows in the steps of Satan, then, truly, he commands depravity, and that which is unlawful. If it were not for the grace of God on you and His mercy, none of you would ever be pure in heart, but God makes pure whom He wills. God is Hearing, Knowing. (Q24:11-24:20)

Aisha: Mother of the Believers

As the wife of the Prophet, peace and the mercy of God be upon him, Aisha was also designated along with his other wives as one of the "Mothers of the Believers": *The Prophet is closer to the ones who believe than their own souls. His spouses are their mothers ...* (Q33:6)

Kindness to Kin

As Aisha was the wife of the Prophet, peace and the mercy of God be upon him, she was one the step-mothers of Fatima bint Muhammad, the wife of Ali ibn Abi Talib. The Quran admonishes about relations with kin: *Truly, God commands justice and kindness and giving to one who is a possessor of kinship and He prohibits depravity and ones who are unlawful and insolent. He admonishes you so that perhaps you will recollect.* (Q16:90)

First Weakness: Deficiency in Faith: Menstruation

According to a typical commentator regarding Sermon 80, it says: "The first weakness of women is that for a few days in every month they have to abstain from prayer and fasting, and this abstention from worship is a proof of their deficiency in faith."

In addition to too much emphasis on ritual purity and impurity as pointed out by Ayatullah Morteza Mutahhari: "Those who ... imagine that ... the central issues are those of ritual purity and impurity (*taharah* and *najasah*), should re-examine their own beliefs and views,"[7] what this typical commentator has overlooked is the important biological role that females play in preserving the human species and society. The story began when God breathed His spirit into Adam: *So when I shaped him* (Adam) *and blew into him My Spirit ...* (Q38:72) Ali ibn Abi Talib mentions this in Sermon 1: "Then He breathed into it of His spirit ..."

According to al-Tabari,[8] immediately after this incident, the verse came to the Prophet: *Mention when your Lord took from the offspring of the Children* (progeny) *of Adam—from their generative organs* (zuhurihum)— *and called to them to witness of themselves: Am I not your Lord? They said: Yea! We bore witness, so that you say not on the Day of Resurrection: Truly, we had been ones who were heedless of this.* (Q7:172)[9]

Immediately after God breathed His spirit into Adam, He called forth the generative organs of Adam's progeny, establishing the human species by connecting His spirit with the potential of our soul-body to actualize our generative organs to preserve our species. Ali ibn Abi Talib refers to this in commenting upon (Q7:172), saying: "In this army of ours, even those **who are still in the loins of men and wombs of women are present with us.**" Sermon 12[10]

What is important to note from this covenant with the generative organs of all of humanity is that a male embryo is not created with semen, but rather with the generative organs to create semen once puberty is reached. The female generative organs, on the other hand, are created with whatever potential human eggs she may have during her lifetime. Both the male and female generative organs, including as they do the female potential embryonic eggs, have received the spirit of God that was breathed into Adam and from Adam to his progeny.

Therefore, while the male semen were not present at the time the covenant was formed with God, the female actual potential human eggs were present confirming that the female human eggs contain God's spirit that will be passed on to all future human generations.

The fact that women carry God's spirit from the time of the covenant makes them very special as the Quran recognizes when it refers to the female children being buried alive—in fact, it was not only the killing of the female child, but the killing of the spirit of God, as well that lay in potential within her eggs.

Men are warned in the Quran about their attitude towards females: ... *when the buried infant girl will be asked for which impiety she was slain* ..., (Q81:8-81:9) Those who did so were oblivious to the fact that they were burying the spirit of God within those female children, that they were denying the spirit of God when their faces darkened: *When any of them was given good tidings of a female, his face stayed one that is clouded over and he chokes. He is secluded from the folk because of the dire tidings he was given. Will he hold it back with humiliation or will he trample it in the earth dust? Truly, how evil is the judgment they give!* (Q16:58-16:59)

It is this very blood that is lost in menstruation that nourishes the embryo when she is pregnant. Therefore, she has a much higher role to play in the universe by being the vessel that continues to hold the spirit of God within in order to preserve the species. It is an unjust statement to claim that she is deficient in faith because of it. This is clearly a falsehood which Ali ibn Abi Talib would never have said.

Why is the Quran adamant about the burying of female children alive? Why does We discredit those whose faces darken when they are told their wife has given birth to a girl? This was a practice in place before the revelation of the Quran.

As noted above, these sentiments in regard to women relate to the attitude in pre-Islamic Arabia where female children were buried alive and when a man was told he has a daughter, his face would cloud over and he would choke. The Quran asks whether or not he will hold back his humiliation or trample it in the earth. The unjust view expressed in Sermon 80 in regard to her being deficient in faith because she menstruates only serves to revive this pre-Islamic attitude of males towards females which the Quran forbid.

Ali ibn Abi Talib would have known of this practice and perhaps even seen or heard of pre-Islamic Arabs practicing this and reacting this way to the news of a female child. He would have recognized the injustice and oppression conducted by the pre-Islamic tribes and fought against it by calling for justice and fairness as the Quran so commands, and yet another indication of the contrived deceit of whoever added words to Ali's Sermons, Letters and Sayings that condemn women for being less than men—to be deficient in intelligence, faith and shares.

When God told the angels that he was creating the human being: *Truly, I am assigning on the earth a viceregent.* The angels said: *Will* ***You*** *be One Who Makes on it someone who makes corruption on it and sheds blood, while we glorify* ***Your*** *praise and sanctify* ***You****?* God responded: *Truly, I know what you know not!* (Q2:30)

He commanded the angels to bow down to Adam and only Satan refused: *God asked: What prevented* ***you*** (Satan) *from prostrating* ***your****self when I commanded* ***you****? Satan said: I am better than he.* ***You*** *had created me of fire and* ***You*** *had created him of clay.* (Q7:12)

Are these falsehoods against *all* women not unconsciously asking God why He created this less than perfect female form? Did God create an imperfect creature? Are the slanderers not copying the role of Satan instead of that of the angels by demeaning a creation of God calling her deficient in faith, intelligence and shares, saying, in effect, that men are better than women because they were created perfect while women were created imperfect? Will they continue in their satanic role of denigrating all women? Why would God save females from being buried alive if he knew they would be deficient in faith, intelligence and shares?

In addition, females begin offering the formal prayer six years before males do and she makes up the formal prayers she missed because of her menstruation and after menopause, which begins around the ages of forty-five to fifty, women no longer menstruate so their formal prayers continue daily. In addition, it has been shown that women in general live longer than men so they may have even more time to make up for any missed prayers during the years she was menstruating. Are they to be deemed deficient in faith even when they are not menstruating or does their faith suddenly return to them then?

Second Weakness: Deficiency in Intelligence: Two Female Witnesses

Continuing with a typical commentary regarding Sermon 80: "The second weakness is that their natural propensities do not admit of full performance of their intelligence. Therefore, nature has given them the power of intelligence only in accordance with the scope of their activities which can guide them in pregnancy, delivery, child nursing, child care and house-hold affairs. **On the basis of this weakness of mind and intelligence their evidence has not been accorded the status of man's evidence,** as God says: *... call two witnesses to bear witness from among your men. Or if there are not two men, then a man and two women, with whom you are well-pleased as witnesses, so that if one of them* (f) *goes astray, then, the other one of the two will remind her....*" (Q2:282)

Is it a sign of deficiency in intelligence because one may need a reminder? The

Quran itself is a reminder to men and women, yet this does not mean they are deficient, but only that they are human. The greatest sin in Islam is to forget God. That is why God sent the Quran as a reminder. The Quran says: *If Satan should cause you to forget, then, after a reminder ...* (Q6:68)

Another reason for two female witnesses here in regard to the forming of an economic contract is because God in His infinite wisdom knew that men can be aggressive. When dealing with economic contracts, the Quran requires two women so one can remind her and in addition protect her against an aggressive male who later decides to change the terms of the economic contract to which he had originally agreed.

The Quran gives us an example of a witness being a wife, one woman, supposedly deficient in faith, intelligence and shares, whose word takes precedence over her witness male husband when he is the only witness who is accusing her.

The oath of the wife, as one witness equal to her husband being one witness, prevails indicating that a husband is not reliable when he is the only witness: *Those who accuse their spouses—and there be no witnesses but themselves—let the testimony of one of them be four testimonies sworn to God that he is among the ones who are sincere and a fifth that the curse of God be on him, if he had been among the ones who lie. It will drive off the punishment from her if she bears witness with four testimonies sworn to God that he is among the ones who lie and the fifth, that the anger of God be on her if he had been among the ones who are sincere.* (Q24:6-24:9)

In addition, the Quran calls for witnesses in many verses and in many cases calls for two or four witnesses. If these witnesses are males, does this mean that they lack intelligence as well so that God calls for two males to be present? The verses do not indicate that the witnesses be males, but only that they be "in accord with morality" or fair and just. This does not exclude *all* women from being either two or four witnesses.

Whoever obeys God and the Messenger, those are to whom God was gracious among the Prophets and just persons and the witnesses and the ones in accord with morality. Excellent were those as allies! (Q4:69) Is the Quran referring to male or female witnesses or either?

O those who believed! Be staunch in justice as witnesses to God and let not that you detest a folk (i.e. *all* women) *drive you into not dealing justly. Be just. That is nearer to God-consciousness. Be God-conscious of God. Truly, God is Aware of what you do.* (Q5:8)

The Quran warns witnesses to be just and to not let the fact that they detest a folk—i.e., *all* women—influence them to deal unjustly with them. Is anyone listening? *Then let ones who are listening bring a clear authority.* (Q52:38)

Then, to whoever argued with **you** *about it after what drew near* **you** *of the knowledge, say* (Muhammad)*: Approach now! Let us call to our children and your children and our women and your women and ourselves and yourselves. Again we will humbly supplicate, and we lay the curse of God on the ones who lie.* (Q3:61) This verse refers to males as "us" in the plural and "women" in the plural, equal to the plural males.

Then, when they (f) *reached their* (f) *term, either hold them* (f) *back as one who is honorable or part from them* (f) *as one who is honorable and call to* ***witnesses from two possessors of justice*** *from among you and perform testimony for God. That is admonished for whomever had been believing in God and the Last Day. He who is God-conscious, He will make a way out for him.* (Q65:2) Is the Quran calling for two male or two female or a mixed two male and female possessors of justice?

O those who believed! Kill not game when you are in pilgrim sanctity. Whoever of you killed as one who is willful, then, the recompense is like what he killed of flocks by ***two possessors of justice who give judgment.*** *Among you will be a sacrificial gift—that which reaches the Kabah—or the expiation of food for the needy or the equivalent of that in formal fasting so that he, certainly, experiences the mischief of his conduct. God pardoned what is past. Whoever reverted to it, then, God will requite him. God is Almighty, Possessor of Requital.* (Q5:95) Does the Quran call for two possessors of justice, male or female?

O those who believed! Have testimony between you when death attended anyone of you. At the time of bequeathing, ***have two possessors of justice from among yourselves or two others from among others if you traveled through the region and the affliction of death lit on you.*** *You will detain them both after the formal prayer. They will swear by God. If you were in doubt about them, have them say: We will not exchange it for a price even if he had been possessing kinship. We will not keep back testimony of God. Truly, we, then, would be among the ones who are perverted.* (Q5:106) Does it mean two men or two women or one male and one female from among themselves or two others to bear witness to the last will and testament of a traveler? If male, it calls for two males. Are they deficient in intelligence because the Quran calls for two witnesses?

Third Weakness: Deficiency in Shares: Inheritance

The third weakness is that "their share in inheritance is half of man's share in inheritance as the Quran says: *God enjoins you about your children. The male shall have the equal of the shares of two females...*"(4:11) A typical commentator says:

> The third weakness is that **their share in inheritance is half of man's share** in inheritance as the Quran says: *God enjoins you about your children. The male shall have the equal of the shares of two females...*(Q4:11) This shows woman's weakness because the reason for her share in inheritance being half is that the liability of her maintenance rests on man. When man's position is that of a maintainer and care taker the status of the weaker sex who is in need of maintenance and care-taking is evident.

Yes, female children receive half of the inheritance of male children, not because they are "the weaker sex" as the typical commentator disparaging intimates, but because the male child must share what he inherits while whatever the female child earns is her own. However, this having been said, it is not the case with female and male adults. The shares are different for an adult female as mother, wife, sister or daughter. As a matter of fact, the laws of inheritance in Islam are so complicated that Muslim scholars invented the science of algebra to figure out what a female and male would receive.[11]

God enjoins you concerning your children. For the male, the like allotment of two females. If there had been women, more than two, then, for them (f) *two-thirds of what he left. But if there had been one, then, for her is half. For one's parents, for each one of them a sixth of what he left, if he would have a child. Then, if he be with no child and his parents inherited, then, a third to his mother. Then, if he had brothers, then a sixth for his mother. This is after any bequest he enjoins or any debt. Your parents or your children, you are not informed which of them is nearer to you in profit. This is a duty to God. Truly, God had been Knowing, Wise.* (Q4:11)

For men is a share of what was left by the ones who are their parents and the nearest kin. For women is a share of what was left by the ones who are their parents and nearest kin whether it was little or it was much—an apportioned share. (Q4:7)

They ask ***you*** *for advice. Say* (Muhammad): *God pronounces to you about indirect heirs. If a man perished and he be without children and he has a sister, then, for her is half of what he left. He inherits from her if she be without children.* (Q4:176)

Ayatullah Makarim Shirazi agrees that this statement in Sermon 80 regarding female inheritance is true only in certain circumstances. There are instances when males only receive half as well:

> A woman's portion of the inheritance is half of that of a man only in certain circumstances when children and wives are inheriting from the man; whereas in relation to inheriting from a father and mother—in many instances—the inheritance of a man and woman are the same and also in regards to the inheritance of brothers and sisters and their children—their inheritance is also similar. In other words: a woman—as a mother or sister—in many instances, takes an equal share of inheritance as a man.
>
> Another reason why sometimes the man gets double the share of inheritance than the woman is due to the fact that the financial maintenance and all of the woman's daily requirements are the responsibility of the men in her life and not only does the woman not have to spend her own money on the maintenance of her children, but in fact her husband must provide all of her requirements, even if a large amount of money comes to her by way of inheritance or anything else.[12]

Introduction: Part 2: The Solution

IV The Virtue of Justice Requires Struggle

The attaining of the virtue of justice requires the greater struggle, not the minimizing of it as someone arbitrarily, almost mockingly, inserted at the end of Saying 135 demeaning women.

> Daily prayers are the best medium through which one can seek the nearness to God. The pilgrimage (*hajj*) is the greater struggle for every weak person. For everything that you own there is the purifying almsgiving (*zakat*), and the purifying almsgiving of your body is fasting. **The greater struggle (*jihad*) of a woman is to afford pleasant company to her husband.** Saying 135

The Quran says: *O those who believed! Take not to yourselves as protectors those who took to themselves your way of life in mockery ... Be God-conscious if you had been ones who believe.* (Q5:57)

The last statement in Saying 135 goes against Ali's words elsewhere in regard to the greater struggle (*jihad al-akbar*). Ali clarifies what the Prophet meant by defining the greater struggle as that of the struggle against the soul that incites to wrongdoing (*nafs al-ammarah bi'l su'*)[1] and certainly not "affording pleasant company to a husband" as Saying 135 falsely insinuates. Elsewhere he said: "No struggle is more excellent than the struggle of the soul (*nafs,* feminine principle) preparing itself within each human being through engaging in the greater struggle."[2]

It is the soul, the feminine principle within, a living substance, has been programmed by nature to undertake the greater struggle from animal to human as justice requires:

> Justice requires an unyielding struggle to achieve it, failing which the intention is shown to be lacking sincerity. Without concordant action, aspirations and intentions are lacking in depth and remain purely theoretical. To hold an intention with total sincerity strictly requires striving diligently and ceaselessly in pursuit of its realization. Thus, however formidable the obstacles, however compelling the arguments of political pragmatism may be, however much one's strenuous efforts are brought to nothing due to unavoidable exigencies of outward life, the just person never despairs: *He said: Who despairs of the mercy of his Lord, but the ones who go astray?* (Q15:56)[3]

Yes, Ali did not despair of the mercy of God during this lifetime, but clearly he must be suffering despair over the centuries that followed his martyrdom when tyrant and unjust rulers managed to damage his reputation by inserting into his Sermons, Letters and Sayings, words which completely go against this paragon of justice.[4]

So it is with *all* women. Many do not despair of God's mercy even though hurtful words are thrown against them by defamers using the name of the great model of justice, Ali ibn Abi Talib.

Knowing the Self

The greater struggle begins by knowing the self. This reminds one of the famous saying of Ali, also attributed to the Prophet: He who knows his self knows his Lord.[5] To know the self requires eliminating all the vices that accompany egocentricity. This, according to Ali ibn Abi Talib, is to become a fair and just person, one who has morally healed. It is the struggle of one's own animal soul against itself—the animal soul that incites to wrongdoing (*nafs al-ammarah bi'l su'*). That is, to struggle against the passionate and distracting desires of the ego.

The View of the Inner Feminine and Masculine Principles
The Feminine Principle Within Males and Females

Knowing the self is to know that the self consists of body, soul (*nafs*) and spirit/intellect/reason (*ruh/'aql*). While the physical body is an outward manifestation of self, the essence is the inner self. The aspersions cast against *all* women in the *Nahj al-Balagha* seem to be denigrating her in her physical female form. One of the keys to unlocking the question of how this could happen has to do with an understanding of the inner self, the feminine principle (*nafs*, soul) and our masculine principle (*ruh/'aql*, spirit/intellect/reason) within all human beings—male and female.[6] In the Quranic view, men have a feminine inner soul and a masculine inner spirit/intellect /reason as do *all* women. This, then, contradicts the allegation that "women are deficient in intelligence" (Sermon 80) as both males and females were each born with a soul and spirit/intellect/reason and, as noted, each have the same innate nature or *fitrat Allah* as all other human beings.

In the Quranic view, the soul, *nafs*, a feminine noun in Arabic, is the feminine principle in all human beings and is known in psychology as the affective-behavioral motivational system. This feminine principle that has been programmed by nature to activate the infant's movement/motivation at birth is called the animal soul (*nafs al-ammarah*), the aspect of self that is shared with other animals.

The animal soul is a vital and necessary part of our very existence. However, when Islamic scholars speak of confronting the *nafs* or disciplining the *nafs* or controling the *nafs*, they are not referring to the *nafs al-ammarah* or animal soul, per se, but to the Quranic term of the animal soul that incites to wrongdoing (*nafs al-ammarah bi'l su'*). Thus, it is when the animal soul itself is not kept in balance or moderation, it becomes the soul in its aspect of inciting to wrongdoing or following one's egotistical "desire" (*hawa*).[7]

The motivational system or animal soul includes the most basic abilities to preserve its species as well as to preserve its individual self. The animal soul regulates what is known as the passions: lust (*quwwat al-shahwaniyya*) and anger (*quwwat al-ghazabiyya*) or attraction to pleasure and avoidance of harm/pain or affect and behavior.

The functions of the animal soul or the passions as our motivational system also regulates our functions of sensation and the five senses of seeing, hearing, tasting, touching and smelling; the five inner senses that make up perception including common sense, retention, estimation, recall and imagination which is either sensible (shared with animals) or rational (only in humans); and willpower that is either instinctive (*iradah*, shared with animals) or free (*ikhtiyar*, only in humans). If the animal soul fails to attain humanness on its journey, it is because of the presence of vices or negative traits which indicate that the person is not using their free willpower to choose what is right or virtues and is instead acting out of the Quranic term of *nafs al-ammarah bi'l su'*.

The feminine principle is born with the body so that it is said to be bodily in origin. However, it returns to the eternal world at death so that its subsistence as it intensifies its existence is said to be spiritual. The soul or feminine principle within goes through three phases on this journey from body, outwardly masculine or feminine, to integrating with the spirit/intellect or masculine principle within.

The soul begins its journey from its "origin to its return" attached to the body (soul-body, male or female). In its second stage, known as the greater struggle (*jihad al-akbar*), it gradually evolves at maturity from being attached to the physical body towards morality, becoming human (*nafs al-insaniyya*). In this second phase, the soul or feminine principle's journey depends on its movement or motivation to either morally heal or remain the feminine principle of the animal soul in its aspect that incites to wrongdoing as it is too attached to materiality and the physical world.

Ali ibn Abi Talib often refers to the fact that he struggled with his animal soul that incites to wrongdoing through eliminating what the Quran considers to be vices and how doing this with oneself has to precede all attempts to reform others because the necessity of the greater struggle and overcoming one's own vices is an essential quality of justice, that is as Ali defines it: "Placing each thing in its proper place." This means morally healing one's self before trying to help others morally heal. He says: "If your aspiration ascends to the reforming of the people, begin with yourself, for your pursuit of the reform of others, when your own soul is corrupt, is the greatest of faults."[8]

> Struggle against the animal soul that incites to wrongdoing through knowledge—such is the mark of the spirit/intellect.[9]

> The strongest men and women are those who are strongest against their own animal soul that incites to wrongdoing.[10]

> Truly, one who fights his own animal soul that incites to wrongdoing, in obedience to God and does not sin against Him, has the rank of the righteous martyr in God's eyes.[11]

> The ultimate battle is that of a person against his own soul.[12]

> He who knows his animal soul that incites to wrongdoing fights it.[13]

> He who knows God integrates himself.[14]

> He who knows his soul disengages himself (from the physical world).[15]

> Let the most beloved of affairs to you be those most centered upon the right (that is, the golden mean), the most comprehensive in justice.... Letter 53*

This is a lesson obviously not adhered to by those who inserted false statements deriding *all* women into his work. How are women, who are not allowed to have an education and whose parents do not teach them knowledge, to know how to struggle against the animal soul that incites to wrongdoing within?

Passions: Soul's Desires

The word "desire" (*hawa*), as noted above, is further used in the Quran in the sense of a desire coming from the ego, so that the ego becomes a kind of false god: *Have* **you** *considered him who took to himself his own desires as his god? Would* **you**, *then, be over him a trustee?* (Q25:43) *Have* **you** *seen him who makes his desire his god?* (Q45:23).

The Prophet, peace and the mercy of God be upon him, referred to this as the "subtle or hidden idolatry" that which is "more hidden than a black ant crawling on a dark stone in a moonless night."[16]

We are told in the Quran, that the Prophet, peace and the mercy of God be upon him, does not speak from *hawa*: *nor speaks he for himself out of desire* (hawa). *It is but a revelation that is revealed.* (Q53:3–53:4)

Ali ibn Abi Talib speaks of how the Prophet, peace and the mercy of God be upon him, told Ali about the necessity to control his passions. The Prophet said that the first step in becoming a fair and just person is to reject or control the desires (*hawa*) or moral vices described in the Quran. That is, to choose virtue (positive traits) over vices (negative traits) or to command our "self" to what is right and prohibit what is wrong based on the criteria (*furqan*) or one's discernment. Speaking of the Prophet, peace and the mercy of God be upon him, Ali says in Sermon 86:

> The first step of his justice is the rejection of desires from his consciousness (heart, *qalb*). He describes right and acts according to it. There is no good which he has not aimed at nor any likely place of virtue of the Quran that he has not adopted. Therefore, the Quran is his guide and leader. He gets down when the Quran puts down its weight. He settles where the Quran settles him down. Sermon 86

Ali adds: "Dominate your inclinations, and exercise self-restraint in the face of that which is unlawful for you—for indeed self-restraint engenders within the soul a proper balance as regards what it likes and what it dislikes." Letter 53*

He further enjoins Malik Ashtar to consciously assist God: "For truly He—majestic is His Name—has undertaken to grant victory to him who assists Him, and to elevate him who exalts Him. He enjoins him to **break the passionate desires of his soul** (within himself and not by demeaning women), and to restrain it when it is afflicted with whim and caprice, for truly the soul incites to wrongdoing, unless God has mercy." Letter 53* (Parentheses added)

Ali tells us: "The most beloved of God is he whom God has given power to act against his passions" (Sermon 86). And: "Knowledge commands, action drives, and the animal soul that incites to wrongdoing is the obstinate mount; developing the intellect helps us to tame the *nafs al-ammarah bi'l su'*."[17]

The basic energy of the animal soul is not to be destroyed but the aspect of the animal soul that incites to wrongdoing is to be converted and redirected away from the transitory objects of desires of the individual ego, away from the impulsive temptations of Satan, towards the One. Otherwise, the individual begins to feel self-sufficient without any dependence upon God:

> The animal soul which incites or commands to wrongdoing arrogates to itself the right of autonomy and dominion is described succinctly by the Quranic verse: *No indeed! The human being is, truly, defiant. He considered himself self-sufficient.* (Q96:6–96:7). Insofar as the soul pretends to be self-sufficient and tries to detach itself from its total dependence upon God, it sets itself up as a god in its own right, and herein lies the true description of the tyrant, the one who, as the Quran puts it: *he who took to himself his own desire as his god.* (Q45:23)[18]

Moinuddin Chishti (d. 1236 CE) of Ajmer writes in the book *Ganj-e-Asrar*: "Unless a seeker follows Ali and unless he has a true, genuine/deep conscious relationship with him, not even a thousand years of austerity and efforts to subjugate his passions will give him even an ounce of intuitive experience knowledge, except those whom Almighty God might favor with His Grace."[19]

The Masculine Principle Within Males and Females
The Spirit/Intellect/Reason

To stop worshipping the ego as an idol, one has to engage an energy or force higher than that of the ego itself. It cannot eliminate itself by itself. In the Quranic view, this higher force is the spirit/intellect/reason and the function of cognition.

The spirit/intellect/reason or masculine principle comes from the world of command (as opposed to the soul which is part of the world of creation at its origin and may end in the world of command), when God breathed His spirit into the first human being (*adam*). The spirit/intellect/reason or masculine principle within is the basis for our cognitive system as opposed to our feminine principled motivational system. Our spirit/intellect/reason connects its existence to the gradually evolving movement of the soul from a weak existence attached to the body to a more intense existence until it integrates with cognition. At the lowest level it is reason (*'aql al-natiqah*). At the highest level it becomes intuition. Ali tells us:

> *Al-aql* (the spirit/intellect/reason, the masculine principles) is the leader of the forces of The Compassionate (al-Rahman); *al-hawa* (whim, caprice, desire of the

> aspect of the animal soul that incites to wrongdoing) commands the forces of Satan. The soul vacillates between reason and the passions, susceptible to the attraction of both and enters into 'the domain of whichever of the two will triumph',*[20] that is, compassion vs. egotistic and satanic temptations. He adds: The spirit/intellect/reason and passions are opposites. The spirit/intellect/reason is strengthened by knowledge, passion by desires. The soul is between them, pulled by both. Whichever triumphs has the *nafs* on its side.*[21]

The gradual substantial motion of the soul moving from animal to human thereby integrates the soul's third stage with the spirit/intellect/reason, and if one is serious regarding cultivating knowledge of oneself, one gains consciousness (*qalb, nafs al-mulhamah*) which the Quran says is the seat of knowledge. It is through consciousness that human beings arrive at various types of knowledge—including intuitive experience knowledge of their Lord, or *ma'rifah*.[22]

When we read the fake words harming the reputation of *all* women in the *Nahj al-Balagha, The Path to Eloquence*, if we understand the masculine and feminine principles to be within each male and each female, we readily understand what the problem is.

The ego of authoritarian men has become their "god." their own desire as their god. Instead of coming to know their self and recognizing their own inner feminine principle that can be incited by satanic temptations to wrongdoing if not controlled by their free will to choose what is right, they use their animal instinctive willpower to control women. They project their own feminine principle onto the physicality of women rather than to undertake the greater struggle as directed by Ali ibn Abi Talib. They are similar to those referred to in the Quran who are deficient in reason because they command others to virtuous conduct, but forget it in regard to themselves: *You command humanity to virtuous conduct and forget yourselves while you relate the Book? Will you not, then, be reasonable*? (Q2:44)

In order to morally heal, we have two other potential aspects of our cognitive system to awaken: Conscience (*fu'ad, nafs al-lawwamah*) and consciousness (*qalb, nafs al-mulhamah*). It is important to notice how the Quran distinguishes between the two: *It came to be in the morning that the* **conscience** (fu'ad, nafs al-lawwamah) *of the mother of Moses was that which is empty. Truly, she was about to show him, if We had not invigorated her* **consciousness** (qalb, nafs al-mulhamah) *so that she became among the ones who believe.* (Q28:10)

If our soul continues to be motivated, with the presence of conscience and consciousness and continuing the greater struggle towards moral healing and attaining virtues, it eventually integrates the spirit/intellect/reason by the grace of God. However, if the animal soul ignores its free willpower to choose the good, it remains with its instinctive willpower which maintains it as the animal soul which incites to wrongdoing. As a result, it remains an animal, egocentric and feeling, doing and thinking vices, rather than attaining virtues and humanness.

Ali said: "A person whose (spirit/)intellect(/reason) is perfected regards animal desires with disdain."[23] Rather than being controlled by his or her desires, a person with true intellect controls them, thereby coming closer to the level of the angels—who have intellect but no desires—rather than sinking to the level of being lower than animals when we go to extremes allowing our animal soul that incites to wrongdoing control us. (Parentheses added.)

Will and Free Willpower

In regard to our instinctive willpower, it is known as *iradah*. We share this function with other animals. As human beings, when God breathed His spirit into our generative organs as the progeny of the first human being (*adam*), we received what is referred to as *ikhtiyar* or free willpower. The word *ikhtiyar* stems from the word *khayr* which means good. Therefore, we have free willpower to choose the good, that is, what is right.

While God knows what we will choose, He does not will that we choose it and since we do not have knowledge of what God knows, we are free to will the good or ignore the good and become willful, falling back on our instinctive willpower (*iradah*).

It is this aspect of the soul which informs human beings to choose between the better of two decisions, or *ikhtiyar*.[24]

> By having knowledge of oneself, human beings are able to derive exemplary characteristics from the conception of the animal soul that commands to wrongdoing, which further can shape personal development, ethics and morality. *Ikhtiyar* can be defined as the conscious choosing of the better of two choices.[25] But even before this conscious choosing, or the act of doing *ikhtiyar*, one must have knowledge of what is right, and what is wrong. Similarly, one must have knowledge of what is just, and what is unjust.... Justice is ... a state of being, or putting things in their proper place.

It is only when a woman's willpower is free to remember God that her consciousness (heart) can be enlivened and her inner substance illuminated. One cannot understand the concept of what is right and just, or what is wrong and unjust, without being allowed to have an intimate conversation with one's self, and, by extension, the concept of the animal soul and how it can become the source of wrongdoing when women are unjustly under the control of a male figure.

> God has created humankind, male and female, in a state of liberty, free to choose to do good rather than evil or vice versa—whether individually in our own private lives or, for some of us, collectively in our society at large. That is why all people are created equal in the sight of God, as the Quran famously reminds us: *O humanity! Truly, We created you from a male and a female and made you into peoples and types that you recognize one another. Truly, the most honored of you with God is the most mindful. Truly, God is Knowing, Aware.* (Q49:13)[26]

Authoritarian rulers in the Islamic world forgot that they also have an animal soul which may incite to wrongdoing. As a result, they forgot God-consciousness (*taqwa*) resulting in them projecting what they were trying to avoid, as previously described, onto women in order to feel they were controling themselves.

Statements in Letter 31 degrading women clearly interfere with a woman's ability to develop her God given free will:

> Do not let (women) interfere with affairs where you cannot personally guide or protect them. Letter 31

> Do not let (women) aspire for things which are beyond their capacities. Letter 31

Parts of Letter 31 treat women as if they were children whose natural spirit/intellect/reason has not yet developed, yet females do reach maturity where their cognitive functions could develop if allowed to exercise their free willpower. Again, Letter 31 falsely says:

> Do not force (women) into marriages which they abhor or which they consider below their dignity because there is danger of thus converting honorable and virtuous women into shameless and dishonorables beings. Letter 31

The Quran already gives women the right to a marriage she agrees with by exercising her free willpower, a verse Ali would have been in familiar with as he was present when Quranic verses were revealed to the Prophet, peace and the mercy of God be upon him, and wrote many of them down so he would have no need to make this statement.

With fabricated statements like these, how are women to learn how to use their free willpower to choose the good instead of relying solely on their instinctive willpower of the animal soul that incites to wrongdoing being objects to instinctively attract pleasure in order to preserve the species, but being able to go beyond this, and not knowing how to avoid harm/pain, the pain being inflicted on them by being controlled so that their inner development is stunted, their feminine principle (soul, *nafs*) not being allowed to journey from animal to human in order to flourish but remaining "boxed in" by outside power control?

Moral Healing

For Ali, the truly fair and just person is one who not only *thinks* correctly but also *acts* ethically.[27] Ali's virtues show why it is that Ahmad b. Hanbal (d. 241AH/855CE), a leading Sunni traditionist and founder of one of the four Sunni schools of law, made the following statement: "No companion of the Prophet has had such virtues ascribed to him as those which have been ascribed to Ali b. Abi Talib."[28]

Moral healing arises from spiritual chivalry. It is in an ethics which puts "everything in its right place," and leads to fairness and justice. It is based on attaining a balance in the virtues of Generosity, Courage and Wisdom, which results in one becoming a zero, a fair and just person. Al-Ghazzali gives these virtues their Quranic origin: *Believers are not but those who believed in God and His Messenger and they were not in doubt* (wisdom). *They struggled with their wealth* (generosity) *and themselves* (courage) *in the way of God. They are the truthful ones* (fair and just). (Q49:15)[29]

Taking this advice, the self thereby becomes fully human, a fair and just person, just as the Prophet was and Ali ibn Abi Talib and all women have the potential to be when, with the grace of God, they are able to actualize this potential.[30]

This psychological system, which clearly was confirmed by the prophetic *sunna* and further experienced by Ali ibn Abi Talib, is adopted by Muslim scholars of the science of Ethics over the centuries, based as it is in the Quran. This leads to what is known as a nine point theory of moral healing oriented as it is in the Quran, the goal of which is to become a fair and just person exemplified by the Prophet, peace and the mercy of God be upon him, and Ali ibn Abi Talib, among others.

The soul is divided into three parts. The lower two parts symbolize the passions, the *nafs al-ammarah*, attraction to pleasure (lust) to preserve society or the species and avoidance of harm/pain (anger) to preserve the individual. Numbers 1 to 9 appear on the circumference of a circle. Too much, too little or lacking (or over, under and un-developed) of Courage is manifested in numbers 2, 3, 4, indicating behavior (preserving the individual); too much, too little or lacking of Generosity is manifested in 5, 6, 7, affect (preserving the species); and too much, too little or lacking in Wisdom is manifested in 8, 9, 1, cognition (preserving the eternal possibility of self). The center point is zero symbolizing the fair and just, egoless person if the person's fair and just actions are first confirmed by another.

The following is the image of the Sufi Enneagram while the descriptions of the over, under or un-development of a virtue are from the writings of Ali ibn Abi Talib.

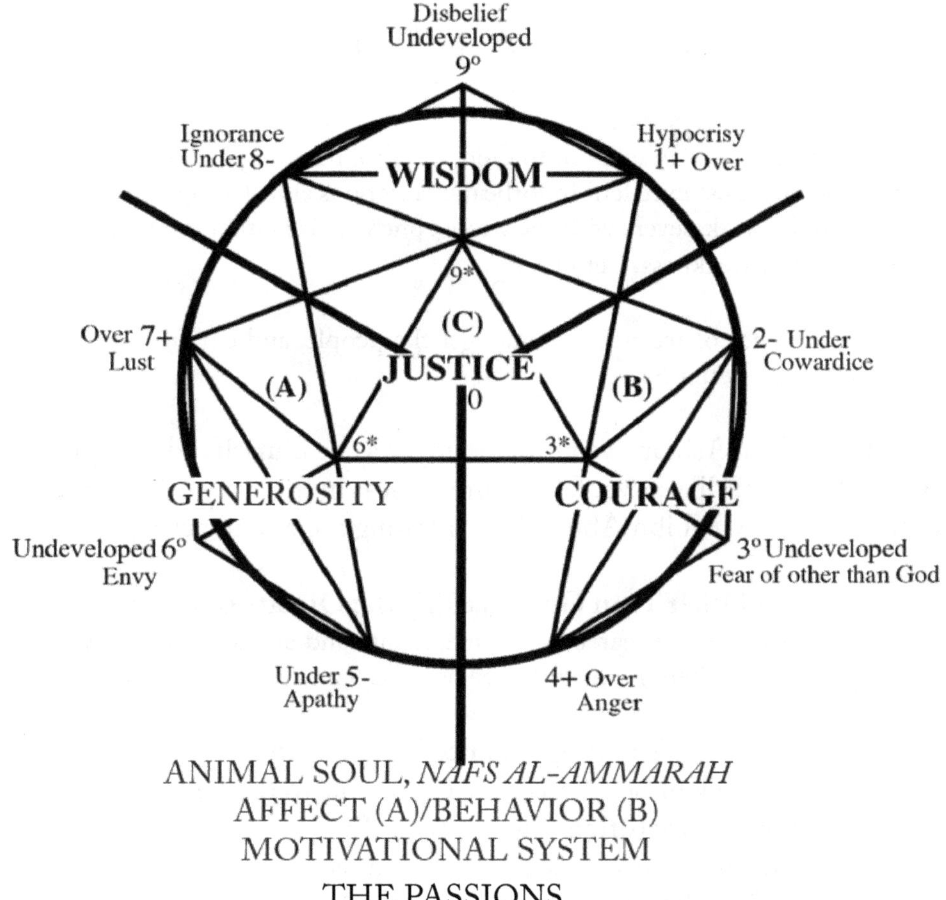

The Motivational System: Disciplining the Passions
Attaining Balanced Courage
Coward: Too Little Courage

Do not allow into your sphere of consultation any cowards who would weaken you in your affairs. Letter 53*

Inappropriate Anger: Too Much Courage

Anger does not prevent Him from mercy. Sermon 194

Have a control on your temper. If you have power to retaliate, then forgive and forget. **When in anger, be forbearing, patient and tolerant.** When you are in possession of wealth, power and authority, then be forgiving, merciful and compassionate. These traits will help you to gain your salvation. Letter 69

> When I feel **angry** with a person how and when should I satisfy my anger. At a time when I am not in a position to retaliate and people may advise me to bear patiently or when I have power to punish and I forgive? Saying 192

As regards the commander of the troops, Malik is told to select for this position the person who is:

> ... the most sincere in relation to God, the Prophet and your Imam, the purest of heart, the one most excellent in forbearance, who is slow to anger, happy to pardon, kind to the weak, severe with the strong: one who is neither moved by violence, nor held back by weakness. Letter 53*

> Untie the knot of resentment amongst the people, and cut from yourself the rope of all anger. Letter 53*

He advises Malik Ashtar to control his anger, as he himself did in regard to Aisha bint Abu Bakr as we will see, yet false words appear in the *Nahj al-Balagha* that contradict this and show Ali ibn Abu Talib exhibiting anger and acting upon it.

Fear of Other Than God: Lacking the Quality of Courage

> No calamity need be feared (from merchants and artisans) and they are in a state of peace, from them no disturbance need be feared. Letter 53*

Attaining Balanced Generosity
Lack of Self Esteem: Ungenerous to the Self

In terms of Generosity (often referred to as Temperance), too little is a lack of self-esteem, too much is greed, pride, vanity, and lacking in its quality is envy and jealousy. In Letter 53, Ali admonishes: "... that a ruler should be kind to the weak, a person who is neither moved by violence or held back by weakness." And: "Help those who are weak and helpless from whom no political benefit is derived." Letter 53*

Miserliness: Too Generous to the Self

> Do not allow into your sphere of consultation any misers, for they would deflect you from generosity and threaten you with poverty. Letter 53

Greed: Too Generous to the Self

"Do not allow into your sphere of consultation any of those who are avaricious, for they would adorn avidity for you with injustice. Truly, miserliness, cowardice and avarice are so many diverse inclinations comprised within a bad opinion of God." Letter 53* And: "... the gratification of one's desires is the only "virtue" which the greedy recognize as such." Letter 53* Again: "That is, a greedy person will make greed for things of this world appear pleasing and good through disguising the means to obtain them—misappropriation, oppression, injustice. These vices will be presented as virtues inasmuch as they are means to the gratification of one's desires, this being the only virtue that the greedy recognize as such."[31]

Pride: Too Generous to the Self

"Excessive praise breeds pride and carries one headlong towards excessive vanity." Letter 53* And: "Dominate the zeal of your pride, the vehemence of your castigation, the power of your hand, and the sharpness of your tongue. Guard against these vices by restraining all impulsiveness, and putting off all resort to force until your anger subsides, and you regain self-control. But you cannot attain such self-domination without increasing your pre-occupation with remembrance of your return to your Lord." Letter 53*

Vanity: Too Generous to the Self

> If the authority of your position engenders vanity and arrogance, then look at the grandeur of God's dominion above you, and at His power to do for you that which you have no power to do for yourself. This will calm your ambition, restrain you from your own vehemence, and restore to you what had strayed from your intellect. Letter 53*

Envy, Jealousy: Lacking the Quality of Generosity

In Letter 53* Ali advises Malik Ashtar to be a ruler who: "... lives like the poor so as not to generate envy among the poor because of the inevitable inequalities in society."

Then we have Saying 123 of the *Nahj al-Balagha* that is clearly spurious stating that jealousy, which is a vice whether the jealous person be male or female, yet, in a woman is unpardonable, but in a man it is a sign of faith. The reason given is because in Islam polygamy is permissible while polyandry is prohibited. How this connects to jealousy is unclear: "Jealousy in woman is unpardonable but in man it is a sign of his faith in religion (because Islam has permitted polygamy and prohibited polyandry)." Letter 53*

The Cognitive System: Disciplining Reason
Attaining Balanced Wisdom
Ignorance: Too Little Wisdom

Ali brings out more clearly the way in which immorality is rooted in ignorance: "The uprooting of this ignorance is thus tantamount to dissolving the very substance of the vices. This uprooting requires great effort, a relentless battle within, which is, indeed, the most formidable of all battles, *al-jihad al-akbar*, the greater struggle as it was defined by the Prophet."[32] "Whoever makes God twofold has fragmented Him and whoever thus fragments Him is **ignorant** of Him." Sermon 1

Hypocrisy: Too Much Wisdom

> **You were the army of a woman and in the command of a four-legged animal.** When it grumbled you responded, and when it was wounded (hamstrung) you fled

away. Your character is low and your pledge is broken. Your faith is hypocrisy. Sermon 13

How this connects to an army of women is unclear. How is this faith of an army of women, spoken as a derogatory comment, connected to hypocrisy? Clearly, the next statement found spuriously in Letter 31 is advising husbands to be hypocrites in their relationship with their wives.

> Exhibit reasonable interest in things which (your wives) desire and give importance to them, but do not let (your wives) influence your opinions and do not let them impel you to go against your sane views. Letter 31

The statement in Letter 31 as to how men should act towards women is sheer hypocrisy—pretending that he is interested in what she desires and giving importance to them, but not allowing a woman to influence their opinion and not letting them go against his sane views, implying that he also may have insane views.

Disbelief: Lacking the Quality of Wisdom

It is disbelief to despair of the mercy of God. (Q15:56), (Q7:156), (Q6:54)[33]

> The tyrant or oppressor can be both a Muslim in the formal sense and at the same time be guilty of a mode of disbelief, taking the word *kafir* in the strictly etymological sense as one who 'covers over' the truth, and its moral concomitants, by his being and by his actions. This is connected to (Q7:181-7:182), that between those who dispense justice in accordance with the truth and those who reject Our signs—the oppressors and tyrants, precisely.[34]

There is a community of whom We created that guides with The Truth, and with it, it is just. Those who denied Our signs, We will draw them on gradually from where they will not know. (Q7:181-7:182)

Justice

When Courage, Temperance and Wisdom are held in balance, one becomes fair and just when another person first confirms it. Clearly those who disdain all women through the false assertions placed in the *Nahj al-Balagha* never came to know self nor to morally heal as Ali teaches. Ali tells us:

> May God have mercy on the person who, when he sees the truth, supports it, when he sees the wrong, rejects it, and who helps the truth against him who is on the wrong. Sermon 204

> I am astounded by the person who hopes for mercy from one above him, while he is not merciful to those beneath him.[35]

Only the middle way is the right path which is the Everlasting Book and the traditions of the Prophet, peace and the mercy of God be upon him,. From it the *sunna* has spread and towards it is the eventual return. He who claims otherwise is ruined. Sermon 16

Be just in your dealings. Letter 27

O my God! deal with me through **Your** forgiveness and do not deal with me according to **Your** justice. Sermon 225

VI Conclusion

The false statements need to be eliminated from the *Nahj al-Balagha* so as to protect the reputation of Ali ibn Abi Talib as the paradigm of justice. Otherwise, whoever chooses to continue to place these words in the *Nahj al-Balagha* will have to answer to God on the Day of Judgment with the Prophet as a witness. Or you agree to say that *some* women are scorpions and add that *some* men are tyrants (Pharoah, Hamun, Satan). After all, Satan is a masculine proper noun in Arabic.

The consequences of not doing so for those who choose not to morally heal, not to become fair and just people should know that the Quran commands women not to sit with those who are unjust: ... *sit not with the folk, the ones who are unjust.* (Q6:68), those who continue to repeat and teach these falsehoods in the Sermons, Letters and Sayings of Ali ibn Abi Talib about *all* women: *Truly, those who drew near with the lies are many among you.* (Q24:11) As we have seen twelve occasions in the collection of Sermons, Letter and Sayings, lies have been directed to *all* women. The Quran asks: *Why not when you heard about it, thought not the ones who are male believers ... the better of themselves and have said: This is a clear, false and derogatory statement about someone to damage their reputation?* (Q24:12) Verse 24:12 ... encapsulates the ethical principle of erring against suspicion and not repeating something one has heard if its source is unreliable or unknown ...[1]

As is the case here. Sharif Razi did not give sources for his collection of Ali's Sermons, Letters and Sayings. Further research[2] has shown that even the earliest sources differ on what Sermon 80 actually says.

The commentary continues:

> Islamic ethical writings make frequent mention of "positive presumption" or "thinking well of others" (*husn al-zann*), which can apply to human beings as well as on another level to God. In the former case, it refers to the presumption of innocence and good character in others, and in relation to God it refers to believe in God's Compassion and Mercy.[3]

This is something many women do, but they are still written off as mentally weak and causes of mischief by those who forgot that Islamic morality calls for *husn al-zann*.

Why brought they not about four witnesses for it? As they bring not about witnesses, then, with God, those, they are the ones who bring a false and derogatory statement about someone to damage their reputation. (Q24:13) There were never four witnesses who gave testimony about the degrading and slanderous comments negating *all* women. Commentators only repeat the words of Muhammad Abduh as a "witness." Yet we have seen that just as the slanderous words against all women has been "corroborated by experiences of centuries," so has the oppression of women been "corroborated by experiences of centuries." Which corroboration is closer to the Quranic view, the *sunna* of the Prophet, peace and the mercy of God be upon him, and the life of Ali ibn Abi Talib?

When you received it on your tongues—as scholars have been doing for 14 centuries—*and said with your mouths of what there is no knowledge, you assume it insignificant while it is serious with God.* (Q24:15) That is: "You propagated it quickly with your tongues."[4]

It has been over 1350 years that males who are believers have said very little about these statements to correct them or to indicate "some" women or delete them entirely as in many cases the statements contradict the Quran and harm the reputation of fairness and justice of Ali as well as that of *all* women. The most they have come up with is rationalizations that while the statements refer to women in the plural, they are all really about one woman who at the age of nineteen was instigated by two men to cause an insurrection (*fitna*) because we read in other Sermons, Letters and Sayings that Ali forgave "that women" and returned her to her home unharmed because, as Ali said: God is the one who judges wrongdoing.

Why, when you heard it, said you not: It will not be for us to assert this. Glory be to ***You!*** *This is a serious false charge to harm the reputation of another.* (Q24:16) "In Islamic ethics gossip and backbiting are considered serious vices."[5]

God admonishes you that you shall never revert to the like of it, if you had been ones who believe. (Q24:17-24:18) "*If you are ones who believe* means if the accusers heed God's persuasion and never repeat the same type of accusation in the future."[6]

Backbiters and slanderers clearly did not understand these verses when they heard them or they deliberately overlooked them as they continued to include *all* women including women believers among other pious women.

Truly, those who love that anything not agreeable with the Truth be spread about to those who believed, they will have a painful punishment in the present and in the world to come. God knows and you know not. (Q24:19)

> Those who desire that anything not agreeable with the Truth be spread among believers shall be punished unless they make sincere repentance. This verse, and indeed the entire passage is understood as a warning against such slander-mongering and a reminder to the believers that their inner thoughts are not hidden from God. In this connection Ibn Kathir mentions the hadith: Do not insult the servants of God (males and females), and do not reproach them, and do not look for their faults....[7]

If it were not for the grace of God on you and His mercy, you would be ruined for God is Gentle, Compassionate. (Q24:20) "Meaning, were it not for God's Mercy, the slanderers would have been worse off, either through their own ultimate perdition or because the slander would have spread even further."[8]

In the case of all women, the slander has continued for 14 centuries in either oral or written form.

O those who believed! Follow not in the steps of Satan. Whoever follows in the steps of Satan, then, truly, he commands depravity, and that which is unlawful. (Q24:21) "To be pure is understood here to mean to be upright or acting in accord with morality, to be rightly guided, to follow Islam."[9]

Is it not Satan that has caused the maligners to denigrate all women? *Follow not in the steps of Satan. Truly He is a clear enemy to you.* (Q2:168); (Q2:208); (Q6:142)

It is Satan who commands to wrongdoing, not *all* women: *Truly* (Satan) *commands evil and depravity.* (Q2:169) And: *Satan threatens you with poverty and commands you to depravity.* (Q2:268)

Ali gives a final warning from something the Prophet, peace and the mercy of God be upon him, said to him:

> I heard the Messenger of God say—God bless him and his family—on more than one occasion:

A nation in which the rights of the weak
are not wrested in an uninhibited manner
from the strong will never be blessed. Sermon 53*

Let us remember:

Whoever turns in friendship to God and His Messenger ***and those who believed****, then, behold the Party of God. They are the ones who are victors.* (Q5:56)

VII Endnotes

Endnotes to the Foreword

1 *The Sublime Quran*, Chicago, Kazi Publications, 2007.

2. Preface to *The Sublime Quran*, p. xliii.

3.

4.

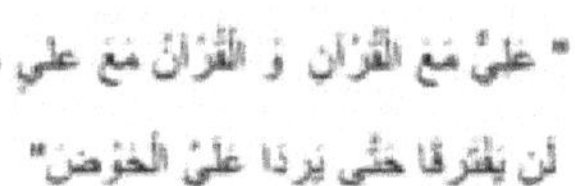

5. From the Introdution, pp. 28-29.

Endnotes to the Preface

1 Helen arrived in Tehran in 1931, the first American woman to marry an Iranian and move to Iran, as well as the first American trained nurse in Iran, where she and Abol set up the first private hospital in Tehran. Helen, who was pregnant when she arrived in Iran, was told that now that she is in Iran, she would give birth to a boy. As it turned out, she gave birth to twin girls. The story of Helen, however, a public health nurse, did not end there. Through various adventures, she was eventually to serve the people in the Bakhtiari tribal region of Chahar Mahal and Bakhtiari near Isfahan. Many years after her death in 1973, the United Nations wanted to declare a 40,000 hectare area (over 98,000 acres) in Chahar Mahal and Bakhtiari as a Natural World Heritage. When they asked the people what they called this area, they said: "We call this area 'Helen' after an American nurse who helped our people." It was then designated as Helen's Environmentally Protected Area by the United Nations.

2 Ahmad b. Shuayb al-Nasai, *Khasais*, p. 109.

3 Tahera Qutbuddin, "The Sermons of Ali ibn Abi Talib: At the Confluence of the Core Islamic Teachings of the Quran and the Oral, nature-based Cultural Ethos of Seventh Century Arabia." *Anuariode Estudios Medievales* 42/1, enero-junio de 2012, pp. 201-228. Online.

4 Reza Shah Kazemi, "From the Spirituality of Jihad to the ideology of Jihadism," in *Seasons Seminannual Journal of Zatuna Institute*, vol.2.

5 Abul al-Hasan al-Masudi, *Muruj al-Ghahab*, vol. 2.

6 Ibn al-Wadih al-Yaqubi, *Al-Tarikh*, vol. 2, p. 163.

7 Ayatullah Morteza Mutahhari, *Glimpses into the Nahj al-Balagha*. Online.

8 Reza Shah Kazemi, *Justice and Remembrance: Introducing the Spirituality of Imam Ali*. Kindle.

9 Muhammad Muradi, *Rawish-i tafsīr-i Quran* in Rashad, ed., *Danish-namah*, vol.1, pp. 238–239.

10 Henri Corbin, *History of Islamic Philosophy*. Online.

11 Henri Corbin, *History of Islamic Philosophy*. Online.

12 al-Hakim al-Nishaburi, *Mustadrak ala al-Sahihayn*, p 927, no. 468. Written in 373AH/983CE, is a supplement of *Sahih al-Bukhari* and *Sahih Muslim* written by al-Hakim al-Nishaburi. He collected hadiths that were missing from the two books, although they met the conditions of reliability as set by al-Bukhari and Muslim.

13 al-Hakim al-Nishaburi, *Mustadrak ala al-Sahihayn*, p. 929, no.4694.

14 See Laleh Bakhtiar, *Quranic Sunnah*.

15 Henri Corbin, *History of Islamic Philosophy*, Online.

16 Reza Shah-Kazemi, *Justice and Remembrance: Introducing the Spirituality of Imam Ali*. Kindle.

17 www.al-islam.org

18 The sermons are not numbered the same in the various English translations so the reader might have to look at the previous number to find a particularly referenced Sermon, Letter or Saying.

19 See Laleh Bakhtiar, *Sublime Quran.*

20 al-Hakim al-Nishaburi, *Mustadrak ala al-Sahihayn*, p 927, no.468. See note 12 above.

21 Muhammad Bukhari, *Sahih al-Bukhari.* Narrated Abu Said Al-Khudri. Volume 1, Book 6, Number 301. Online. This idea recurs in other parts of Bukhari as well. It has been argued that in all of the Sunni recensions of this narration, the narrators should be considered as inauthentic as per Sunni *rijal* works.

We are grateful to the work of Amina Inloes, "Was Imam Ali a Misogynist?", in www.al-islam.org for informing her readers that Ayatollah Javadi Amoli believed that the words demeaning women are "beneath the dignity of Ali," Mahdi Mehrizi, "Ta'ammoli dar Ahadith-e Nuqsan-e Aql-e Zanan," in *Ulum-e Hadith* 81, 81-99; and that Rawand Osman in *Female Personalities in the Quran and Sunna*, 158-162 has said I was once told privately by an Iranian of the older generation that Ayatullah Mutahhari held this view but that it was posthumously removed from his work.

Endnotes to the Introduction Part 1: The Problem
I Ali ibn Abi Talib: Caliph, Imam, Spiritual Guide

1 George Jordac, *The Voice of Human Justice*. Kindle.

2 In Reza Shah-Kazemi, *Justice and Remembrance*. Kindle, who suggests the following in regard to Ali ibn Abi Talib's manifestation of the virtue of justice: See *Proceedings of the International Congress on Imām Ali*, which address diverse aspects of the theme of justice in relation to the Imam's life and thought; as well as the collection of legal judgments delivered by the Imam, *Qada Amīr al-muminin Ali ibn Abi Talib*, compiled by Allama Shushtari (Tehran, 2001); the 27 essays devoted to the Imam in *Farhang: Quarterly Journal of Humanities and Cultural Studies*, vol.13, nos.33–36, Winter, 2001; and finally, a biography of the Imam, by George Jordac, *The Voice of Human Justice*, tr. M. Fazal Haqq (Qom, 1990), the title of which brings out the centrality of the theme of justice in his life.

3 See Lawrence Rosen, *The Justice of Islam: Comparative Perspectives on Islamic Law and Society.*

4 Islamic mysticism in the West is referred to as "Sufism." According to a well-known author on Islamic mysticism, William Chittick, Sufism can simply be described as: the interiorization, and intensification of Islamic faith and practice. Chittick, William, *Sufism: A Beginner's Guide*, p. 6.

5 One of the three groups of the Naqshbandi trace their lineage to Abu Bakr, but in their chain of transmission is Jafar Sadiq, the 6th Imam who founded the Jafari school of law, whose father was from the family of Muhammad, Fatima and Ali ibn Abi Talib and his mother was from the family of Abu Bakr, essentially, therefore, tracing its spiritual lineage to Ali ibn Abi Talib.

6 https://yaqeeninstitute.org

7 Ali ibn Abi Talib, *Ghurar al-hikam wa durr al-kalim*, compiled by Abd al-Wahid Amidi, with Persian tr. Sayyid Husayn Shaykhul-Islamie in *Guftar-i Amir al-mu'minin Ali*, ed. with Persian tr. Muhammad Ali Ansari, p. 764, no.9545.

8 Spiritual chivalry (*futuwwah*) originated with Seth, the son of the Adam, the 'first Sufi', in whose person the *futuwwah* is not yet differentiated from Sufism (*tariqah*)—that is to say, from the mystical way or Sufism. When people no longer possessed the strength to wear the cloak of Sufism (the *khirqah*), it was Abraham who founded the *futuwwah* as distinct from Sufism. In the person of Abraham the prophetic mission was henceforth assimilated to a chivalric service. By cutting across the cycle of prophecy and the cycle of the 'Friend of God' (*walayah*), the *futuwwah* determines the division of historiosophy into periods. The cycle of prophecy was initiated by Adam, its pole was Abraham, and the Seal which brought it to a close was Muhammad. The cycle of the *futuwwah* was initiated by Abraham, its pole was the First Imam, Ali ibn Abi Talib, and its Seal was the Twelfth Imam, the Imam of the Resurrection, the Longed-for One (*muntazai*), who at present is invisible. It is based on the virtues of courage, generosity, loyalty, and helping the poor and downtrodden in their uncompromising search to become fair and just towards God, others, including men and women, and themselves. See Ehsan Yarshartar, English Introduction to *Ayin-e Javanmardi* (*Fotowwat*), by Mohammad Jafar Mahjoub.

9 See Laleh Bakhtiar, *Moses and Khidr: Consciousness Between the Two Seas of Reason and Intuition*

and an Analysis Based on Quranic Psychology.

10 See Syed Naquib al-Attas, *Nature of Man and the Psychology of the Human Soul.*

11 Ayatullah Morteza Mutahhari. *Glimpses into the Nahj al-Balagha*. Online.

12 George Jordac, *The Voice of Human Justice* (*Sautu'l 'Adalati'l Insaniyah*). Online.

13 George Jordac, *The Voice of Human Justice* (*Sautu'l 'Adalati'l Insaniyah*). Online, quoting from the *Nahj al-Balagha*.

Endnotes to:

II The Virtue of Being Fair and Just in the Quran in Regard to Women as Mother, Wife, Sister, Daughter and Individual Female Compared to Quranic Prohibitions of Men in Regard to Wife, Daughter and Individual Female

1 See Laleh Bakhtiar, *Sublime Quran.*

2 A modern Quranic commentator has said that Mary was able to participate in a mixed-gender prayer based on (Q3:43) according to Smith and Haddad where Mary is told *to bow down with those [males] who bow down*. Smith, Jane and Yvonne Haddad. "The Virgin Mary in Islamic Tradition and Commentary," *The Muslim World*, Vol. LXXIX, July-October, 1989. Smith and Haddad refer to Muhammad Jamal al-Din al-Qasimi, *Tafsir al-Qasimi*, Cairo, 1914, Vol. IV, p. 841, where they say: "The last reference to Qasimi, to the opinion of the highly respected classical theologian al-Suyuti that because of Mary, women are qualified to lead the prayer suggests the possibility for an interesting discussion on female leadership. The image of Mary as imam could become an engaging model for opening up the ranks of religious leadership to women. Those who might wish to pursue this possibility, however, should note that most contemporary opinion agrees with al-Qasimi, who in reference to 3:43 ... says it means that it is not as a woman that she is given such a directive from God. 'Because of the perfection that God has apportioned to you, you are counted as among the men!'"

3 *Mut'a* is practiced by followers of the Jafari school of law. It is a private marriage between a man and a woman for a specific period of time which can be extended. The woman receives a dowery but does not inherit from the man and anything else the couple may want to include as long as it is consistent with Muslim marriage law. The man agrees to the complete care and upbringing of any children that may result.

Misyar is marriage practiced by the Wahabi school of law (usually considered to be Hanbali). It must have the agreement of both parties, two legal witnesses, the payment of the wife by the husband of a dowry, the absence of a fixed time period for the contract and anything else the couple may want to include as long as it is consistent with Muslim marriage law. The couple has to renounce living together and the wife's right to maintenance.

4 The Arabic word, *talaq*, alo means setting free, letting go. Edward William Lane, *Arabic-English Lexicon*. Online.

5 See M. A. S. Abdel Haleem, *The Quran*.

6 See Laleh Bakhtiar, *Concordance of the Sublime Quran.*

Endnotes to:

III The Vice of Being Unjust Described in the Quran and the Fabrications Against Women in the *Nahj al-Balagha*

1 Ayatullah Morteza Mutahhari, *Glimpses into the Nahj al-Balagha*. Online.

2 Faisal H. Al-Kathiri, *Succession to the Caliphate in Early Islam*. Online.

3 Asma Asfaruddin, *International Journal of Middle East Studies*, vol. 31, No. 3 (Aug., 1999), pp. 329-350. This account is contained in *al-Muhibb al-Tabari*, *al-Riyad al-nadira*, 1102.

Endnotes to:

IV Analysis of Sermon 80

1 al-islam.org

2 Reza Shah Kazemi, *Justice and Remembrance: Introducing the Spirituality of Imam Ali*. Kindle.

3 Reza Shah Kazemi, *Justice and Remembrance: Introducing the Spirituality of Imam Ali*. Kindle.

4 George Jordac. *The Voice of Human Justice* (*Sautu'l 'Adalati'l Insaniyah*). Kindle.

5 The date of her birth is unclear. Many scholars say that she was born in 613 CE.

6 al-islam.org, "The Scandal Against Aisha."

7 See Note 21 in Endnotes to the Preface.

8 Muhammad ibn Jarir al-Tabari (d. 310/923), *Jami al-bayan an tawil ay al-quran* in *The Study Quran*, p. 467.

9 It is generally agreed that the words, *the Children of Adam* (*banu Adam*) in the Quran, in general and specifically in (Q7:172), includes all the progeny of Adam—male and female. Generative organs (*zuhur*) is the plural form of *zuhr*. The word *zuhr* appears several times in the Quran, but the sign of interest to us here is (Q33:4): *God made not your spouses, those whom you divorced saying: Be as the back of my mother!* (Q33:4)

In pre-Islamic times, it was common practice when a man wanted to divorce his wife, he would say: *Be as my mother's back* (zihar). When a husband said this to his wife, he was free and no longer had any duties towards her, but she was still married to him and could not marry anyone else. The sign, (Q33:4), was revealed about the woman, Khaulah bint Thalabah, who complained to the Prophet about her husband, Aws ibn As-Samit. (See *The Study Quran* p. 1019 for the story.) Clearly the husband was referring to his mother's generative organs which were forbidden to him. Therefore, the use of the same word—*zuhur*— in the context of the reproductive organs shows that in (Q7:172), God took the generative organs (*zuhur*) from both the males and females who bore witness to Him as their Lord.

10 All creatures have the potential for cognition and consciousness but because they have a weak existence as it is more closely connected to the physical realm—only in the human being who has a more intense existence, that is, bodily in origin, but spiritual in subsistence, having received the Spirit of God breathed within the generative organs of the progeny of Adam—the human soul is able to actualize the potential for consciousness and cognition (soul-spirit/intellect/reason.

11 Islamic law of inheritance served as an impetus behind the development of algebra (derived from the Arabic *al-jabr*) by Muhammad ibn Musa al-Khwarizmi and other medieval Islamic mathematicians. Al-Khwarizmi's *Hisab al-jabr w'al-muqabala*, the foundational text of algebra, devoted its third and longest chapter to solving problems related to Islamic inheritance using algebra. He formulated the rules of inheritance as linear equations, hence his knowledge of quadratic equations was not required. (Gandz, Solomon (1938). "The Algebra of Inheritance: A Rehabilitation of Al-Khuwarizmi". Osiris. University of Chicago Press. 5:319–91)

Al-Hassar, a mathematician from North Africa specializing in Islamic inheritance jurisprudence during the 12th century, developed the modern symbolic mathematical notation for fractions, where the numerator and denominator are separated by a horizontal bar. The dust ciphers he used are also nearly identical to the digits used in the current Western Arabic numerals.

These same digits and fractional notation appear soon after in the work of Fibonacci in the 13th century. (Hoyrup, J. (2009). *Hesitating progress—the slow development toward algebraic symbolization in abacus-and related manuscripts*, c. 1300 to c. 1550: Contribution to the conference "Philosophical Aspects of Symbolic Reasoning in Early Modern Science and Mathematics", Ghent, 27–29 August 2009. Preprints. 390. Berlin: Max Planck Institute for the History of Science.

Fibonacci uses ibn al-Yasamin's fraction notations to the full in the *Liber abbaci* [ed. Boncompagni 1857], writing composite fractions from right to left and mixed numbers with the fraction to the left—all in agreement with Arabic customs. Further, he often illustrates non-algebraic calculations in rectangular marginal frames suggesting a lawha. Fibonacci, Leonardo; Barnabas Hughes (2008). *Fibonacci's De practica geometrie*. Springer. p. 12. At this point it would be well to make a few remarks about Fibonacci's fractions. The first thing to note is the format, 1/2 4, which means four and a half. The format is unique to Andalusia and the Maghrib and reflects the Arabic method of writing from right to left, something Fibonacci most probably learned as a student in a Moslem school in Bougie. Livio, Mario (2003). *The Golden Ratio*. New York: Broadway. p. 96.)

In the 15th century, Abu al-Hasan ibn Ali al-Qalasadi, a specialist in Islamic inheritance jurisprudence, used a mathematical notation for algebra which took "the first steps toward the introduction of algebraic symbolism." He represented mathematical symbols using characters from the Arabic alphabet. (O'Connor, John J.; Robertson, Edmund F., "Abu'l Hasan ibn Ali al Qalasadi", *MacTutor History of Mathematics archive*, University of St Andrews. Wikipedia

12 Ayatullah Makarim Shirazi, www.alhassanain.org/english Makarim Shirazi, "Commentary on Sermon 80 of *Nahjul Balagha*." Online.

Endnotes to the Introduction Part 2: The Solution

IV The Virtue of Justice Requires Struggle

1 Ali ibn Abi Talib, *Ghurar al-hikam wa durr al-kalim*, compiled by Abd al-Wahid Amidi, with Persian tr. Sayyid Husayn Shaykhul-Islamie in *Guftar-i Amir al-mu'minin Ali*, ed. with Persian tr. Muhammad Ali Ansari, vol. 2, p. 951, no.9.

2 Ali ibn Abi Talib, *Ghurar al-hikam wa durr al-kalim*, compiled by Abd al-Wahid Amidi, with Persian tr. Sayyid Husayn Shaykhul-Islamie in *Guftar-i Amir al-mu'minin Ali*, ed. with Persian tr. Muhammad Ali Ansari, vol.1, pp. 208-211 no.28.

3 Reza Shah Kazemi, *Justice and Remembrance: Introducing the Spirituality of Imam Ali*. Kindle.

4 The circumstances that occurred during the caliphate of Ali ibn Abi Talib prevented him outwardly from putting into effect many of the principles and policies that flowed from his conception of truth and justice—but none of this resulted in dejection, despair or cynicism, or in even a slight diminution in his efforts to achieve justice whenever and wherever possible, as is amply demonstrated in the nature of his own administration, and in the stream of letters and counsels to his officers and governors. See Reza Shah-Kazemi, *Justice and Remembrance: Introducing the Spirituality of Imam Ali*. Kindle.

5 See Reza Shah-Kazemi, *Justice and Remembrance: Introducing the Spirituality of Imam Ali* who says that the commentary on this saying by Rajab Bursi, one of the most important 'intuitive experience knowledge' (*arif*) interpreters of the spiritual tradition of Shiism, in his treatise *Mashariq anwar al-yaqīn fī haqa'iq asrar amīr al-mu'minīn* ('*The Dawning Places of the Lights of Certainty in the Divine Secrets connected with the Commander of the Faithful*'), as cited in Todd Lawson's article of the same name, in L. Lewisohn, ed., *The Heritage of Persian Sufism*, vol.2, pp. 271–273.

6 Unlike the work of Carl Jung who says that the male carries the feminine principle and the female carries the male principle, not that each have both.

7 These scholars are not being specific as the Quran also refers to the other aspects of the soul or feminine principle which are to be supported and encouraged such as the *nafs al lawwamah*, the blaming soul, our conscience, the *nafs al-mulhamah* or inspired soul, our consciousness or heart (*qalb*) and the *nafs al-mutma'innah* or soul at peace, our spirit/intellect/reason.

8 Ali ibn Abi Talib, *Ghurar al-hikam wa durr al-kalim*, compiled by Abd al-Wahid Amidi, with Persian tr. Sayyid Husayn Shaykhul-Islamie in *Guftar-i Amir al-mu'minin Ali*, ed. with Persian tr. Muhammad Ali Ansari, vol. 1, p. 781, no.1.

9 Ali ibn Abi Talib, *Ghurar al-hikam wa durr al-kalim*, compiled by Abd al-Wahid Amidi, with Persian tr. Sayyid Husayn Shaykhul-Islamie in *Guftar-i Amir al-mu'minin Ali*, ed. with Persian tr. Muhammad Ali Ansari, vol.1, pp.208-211 no.20.

10 Ali ibn Abi Talib, *Ghurar al-hikam wa durr al-kalim*, compiled by Abd al-Wahid Amidi, with Persian tr. Sayyid Husayn Shaykhul-Islamie in *Guftar-i Amir al-mu'minin Ali*, ed. with Persian tr. Muhammad Ali Ansari, vol.1, pp. 208-211 no.17.

11 Ali ibn Abi Talib, *Ghurar al-hikam wa durr al-kalim*, compiled by Abd al-Wahid Amidi, with Persian tr. Sayyid Husayn Shaykhul-Islamie in *Guftar-i Amir al-mu'minin Ali*, ed. with Persian tr. Muhammad Ali Ansari, vol.1, pp. 208-211 no.8.

12 Ali ibn Abi Talib, *Ghurar al-hikam wa durr al-kalim*, compiled by Abd al-Wahid Amidi, with Persian tr. Sayyid Husayn Shaykhul-Islamie in *Guftar-i Amir al-mu'minin Ali*, ed. with Persian tr. Muhammad Ali Ansari, vol.1, pp. 208-211 no.23.

13 Ali ibn Abi Talib, *Ghurar al-hikam wa durr al-kalim*, compiled by Abd al-Wahid Amidi, with Persian tr. Sayyid Husayn Shaykhul-Islamie in *Guftar-i Amir al-mu'minin Ali*, ed. with Persian tr. Muhammad Ali Ansari, vol.1, pp. 208-211 no.26.

14 Todd Lawson, *Mashariq anwar al-yaqīn fī haqa'iq asrar amīr al-mu'minīn* ('*The Dawning Places of the Lights of Certainty in the Divine Secrets connected with the Commander of the Faithful*') in L. Lewisohn, ed., *The Heritage of Persian Sufism,* Vol. 2.

15 Todd Lawson, *Mashariq anwar al-yaqīn fī haqa'iq asrar amīr al-mu'minīn* ('*The Dawning Places of the Lights of Certainty in the Divine Secrets connected with the Commander of the Faithful*') in L. Lewisohn, ed., *The Heritage of Persian Sufism,* Vol. 2.

16 Ibn Hanbal, *al-Musnad*, ed. A.M. Shakir, vol.4, p. 403.

17 https://www.tasnimnews.com/fa/news/1396/01/16/1370272/

18 Reza Shah Kazemi, *Justice and Remembrance: Introducing the Spirituality of Imam Ali*. Kindle.

19 https://www.tasnimnews.com/fa/news/1396/01/16/1370272/

20 Ali ibn Abi Talib, *Ghurar al-hikam wa durr al-kalim*, compiled by Abd al-Wahid Amidi, with Persian tr. Sayyid Husayn Shaykhul-Islamie in *Guftar-i Amir al-mu'minin Ali*, ed. with Persian tr. Muhammad Ali Ansari,vol. 2, p. 951, no.9.

21 Ali ibn Abi Talib, *Ghurar al-hikam wa durr al-kalim*, compiled by Abd al-Wahid Amidi, with Persian tr. Sayyid Husayn Shaykhul-Islamie in *Guftar-i Amir al-mu'minin Ali*, ed. with Persian tr. Muhammad Ali Ansari, vol. 2, p. 951, no.10.

22 Syed Naquib al-Attas, *Nature of Man and the Psychology of the Human Soul.* See "Contextualizing the Human Soul." Online.

23 https://www.tasnimnews.com/fa/news/1396/01/16/1370272/

24 Syed Naquib al-Attas, *Nature of Man and the Psychology of the Human Soul.* See "Contextualizing the Human Soul." Online.

25 Syed Naquib al-Attas, *Nature of Man and the Psychology of the Human Soul.* See "Contextualizing the Human Soul." Online.

26 Syed Naquib al-Attas, *Nature of Man and the Psychology of the Human Soul.* See "Contextualizing the Human Soul." Online.

27 Ali ibn Abi Talib, *Ghurar al-hikam wa durr al-kalim*, compiled by Abd al-Wahid Amidi, with Persian tr. Sayyid Husayn Shaykhul-Islamie in *Guftar-i Amir al-mu'minin Ali*, ed. with Persian tr. Muhammad Ali Ansari, vol.3, p. 973, no.12.

28 al-Hakim al-Nishaburi, *Mustadrak ala al-Sahihayn*, p. 916, no.4628.

29 al-Ghazzali, *Tahafut al-Falasifah* (*Incoherence of the Philosophers*), p. 303.

30 It is important to note that what are referred to in the West as the four cardinal virtues as having their origin in the works of Plato, in fact, Plato himself writes in *Alcibiades I* that Socrates says to Alcibiades that when the Persian kings wanted to train their sons, they hired four tutors: One was an expert in Courage, one in Generosity, one in Wisdom and one in Justice so the origin of the cardinal virtues belongs to the Zoroastrians.
http://www.dominiopublico.gov.br/download/texto/gu001676.pdf.

31 Reza Shah Kazemi, *Justice and Remembrance: Introducing the Spirituality of Imam Ali*. Kindle.

32 See Reza Shah-Kazemi, "From the Spirituality of Jihad to the Ideology of Jihadism," in *Seasons Semiannual Journal of Zetana Institute,* vol.2, no.2, pp. 44-68.

33 Ali ibn Abi Talib, *Ghurar al-hikam wa durr al-kalim*, compiled by Abd al-Wahid Amidi, with Persian tr. Sayyid Husayn Shaykhul-Islamie in *Guftar-i Amir al-mu'minin Ali*, ed. with Persian tr. Muhammad Ali Ansari, vol.2, p. 456, no.1.

34 Reza Shah Kazemi, *Justice and Remembrance: Introducing the Spirituality of Imam Ali*. Kindle.

35 Ali ibn Abi Talib, *Ghurar al-hikam wa durr al-kalim*, compiled by Abd al-Wahid Amidi, with Persian tr. Sayyid Husayn Shaykhul-Islamie in *Guftar-i Amir al-mu'minin Ali*, ed. with Persian tr. Muhammad Ali Ansari, p. 581, no.4.

Endnotes

V Conclusion

1 Seyyed Hossein Nasr, ed., *The Study Quran* (24:11-20) pages 870-873.

2 See Asmar Jafar, "Hadiths on Deficiency of Female Intelligence and Faith." Online; Amina Inloes, "Was Imam 'Ali a Misogynist? The Portrayal of Women in the *Nahj al-Balaghah* and *Kitab Sulaym ibn Qays." Journal of Shi'a Islamic Studies*, Summer 2015, Vol. VIII, No. 3. Online.

3 Seyyed Hossein Nasr, ed., *The Study Quran* (24:11-20) pages 870-873.

4 Seyyed Hossein Nasr, ed., *The Study Quran* (24:11-20) pages 870-873.

5 Seyyed Hossein Nasr, ed., *The Study Quran* (24:11-20) pages 870-873.

6 Seyyed Hossein Nas, ed., *The Study Quran* (24:11-20) pages 870-873.

7 Seyyed Hossein Nasr, ed., *The Study Quran* (24:11-20) pages 870-873.

8 Seyyed Hossein Nasr, ed., *The Study Quran* (24:11-20) pages 870-873.

9 Seyyed Hossein Nasr, ed., *The Study Quran* (24:11-20) pages 870-873.

VIII Bibliography

al-Ghazzali, Muhammad, *Tahafut al-Falasifah* (*Incoherence of the Philosophers*). Lahore, 1963.
al-Jibouri, Yasin T, *Nahjul-Balagha*. Iraq Ministry of Culture nd.
al-Masudi, Abul al-Hasan, *Muruj al-Ghahab*, vol. 2. Cairo, 1948.
al-Nisai, Ahmad b. Shuayb, *Khasa'is Amir al-muminin, Ali ibn Abi Talib*. Tehran, 1419/1998.
al-Nishaburi, al-Hakim, *Mustadrak ala al-Sahihayn*. Online.
al-Tabari, Muhammad ibn Jarir, *Jami al-bayan an tawil ay al-quran* in Seyyed Hossein Nasr, ed., *The Study Quran*. HarperOne, 2015.
al-Utardi, Shaykh Azizullah, Critical Edition of the *Nahj al-Balagha* in Arabic Tehran, 1413 AH/1372 SH (1993).
al-Yaqubi, Ibn al-Wadih, *Al-Ta'rikh*, vol. 2. Beirut, 1960.
Asfaruddin, Asma, *International Journal of Middle East Studies*, vol. 31, No. 3, Aug., 1999, pp. 329-350. This account is contained in al-Muhibb al-Tabari, *al-Riyad al-nadira*, 1102.
al-Attas, Syed Muhammad Naquib, "On Justice and the Nature of Man: A Commentary on Surah al-Nisa 4:58 and Surah al-Mu'minun 23:12-14." Kuala Lumpur: IBFIM, 2016.
— *Nature of Man and the Psychology of the Human Soul*. Kuala Lumpur: ISTAC, 1990.
Bakhtiar, Laleh, *Concordance of the Sublime Quran*: Kazi Publications, 2011.
— *Moses and Khidr: Consciousness Between the Two Seas of Reason and Intuition and an Analysis Based on Qurani Psychology*. Chicago: Kazi Publications, 2019.
— *Sublime Quran*. Chicago: Kazi Publications, 2007.
— *Quranic Sunnah*. Chicago: Kazi Publications, 2015.
Bukhari, Muhammad, *Sahih al-Bukhari*. Online.
Chittick, William, *Sufism: A Beginner's Guide*. Oneworld Publications, 2007.
Corbin, Henri. *History of Islamic Philosophy*, 1993. Online.
Cornell, Rkia, *Early Sufi Women*. 1999.
Dakake, Maria Massi, "Walking Upon the Path of God like Men," *Sufism: Love and Wisdom*. World Wisdom, 2006. Online.
Gwynne, Rosalind Ward, *Logic, Rhetoric and Legal Argument*. RoutledgeCurzon: Oxon, 2004.
Hamisan, Nur Saadah, "The Debate on Anti-Woman Discourse in The Hadith Literature," *Journal of Hadith Studies*, Vol. 2, No. 1, June 1917. Online.
Hassan, Syed Mohammad Waris, "A Critical Study of the *Nahj al-Balagha*." 1979. Online.
Haleem, M. A. S. Abdel, *The Quran*. OUP, 2008.
Ibn Hanbal, *al-Musnad*, ed. A.M. Shakir, Vol. 4. Cairo, 1949.
Inloes, Amina, "Was Imam 'Ali a Misogynist? The Portrayal of Women in the *Nahj al-Balaghah* and *Kitab Sulaym ibn Qays*." *Journal of Shi'a Islamic Studies*, Summer 2015, Vol. VIII, No. 3. Online.
Jafari, Asma, "Hadiths on Deficiency of Female Intelligence and Faith." Online.
Jafery, Seyyed Mohammed Askari, *Nahjul Balagha*. Karachi, 1960.
Jordac, George, *The Voice of Human Justice* (*Sautu'l 'Adalati'l Insaniyah*). Online.
Kathiri, Faisal H. al-, *Succession to the Caliphate in Early Islam*. Online
Lane, Edward William, *Arabic-English Lexicon*. Online.
Lawson, Todd, *Mashariq anwar al-yaqīn fī haqa'iq asrar amīr al-mu'minīn* (*'The Dawning Places of the Lights of Certainty in the Divine Secrets connected with the Commander of the Faithful'*) in L. Lewisohn, ed., *The Heritage of Persian Sufism*, Vol. 2. Oxford, 1999.
Lewisohn, Leonard, *The Heritage of Persian Sufism*, Vol. 2. Oxford, 1999.
Muradi, Muhammad, *Rawish-i tafsir-i Quran* in Rashad, ed., *Danish namah*, vol. 1.
Murata, Sachiko, *The Tao of Islam*. SUNY, 1992.
Mutahhari, Ayatullah Morteza, *Glimpses into the Nahj al-Balagha*. Online.
Nasr, Seyyed Hossein Nasr, "Shi'ism and Sufism: Their Relationship in Essence and in History."

Rel. Stud. 6, pp. 229-242. Online
— ed., *Study Quran. HarperOne,* 2015.
Qutbuddin, Tahera, "The Sermons of 'Ali ibn Abi Talib: At the Confluence of the Core Islamic Teachings of the Quran and the Oral, nature-based Cultural Ethos of Seventh Century Arabia." *Anuariode Estudios Medievales* 42/1, enero-junio de 2012, pp. 201-228. Online.
Rosen, Lawrence, *The Justice of Islam: Comparative Perspectives on Islamic Law and Society.* London: OUP, 2000.
Saeed, Shaykh Hassan, *Nahj al-Balagha.* Tehran, 1977.
Schimmel, Annemarie, *My Soul is Woman.* Continuum, 2003.
Shah-Kazemi, Reza, "From the Spirituality of Jihad to the Ideology of Jihadism," in *Seasons Seminannual Journal of Zatuna Institute*, vol.2., 2005.
— *Justice and Remembrance: Introducing the Spirituality of Imam Ali.* Kindle.
Shirazi, Ayatullah Nasir Makarim, "Commentary on Sermon 80 of the *Nahjl Balaghah.*" Online.
Smith, Jane and Yvonne Haddad. "The Virgin Mary in Islamic Tradition and Commentary," *The Muslim World*, Vol. LXXIX, July-October, 1989.
Talib, Ali ibn Abi, *Ghurar al-hikam wa durr al-kalim*, compiled by Abd al-Wahid Amidi, with Persian tr. Sayyid Husayn Shaykhul-Islamie in *Guftar-i Amir al-mu'minin Ali.* Qom, 2000 ed. with Persian tr. Muhammad Ali Ansari. Qom, 2001.
Talib, Ali ibn Abi, *Peaks of Eloquence*, al-islam.org Online.
Talib, Khalifa Ali bin, "Ali, The Father of Sufism," at Witness-Pioneer International (not found)
Yarshartar, Ehsan, English Introduction to *Ayin-e Javanmardi* (*Fotowwat*), by Mohammad Jafar Mahjoub. New York Bibliotheca Persica Press, 2000.
http://www.dominiopublico.gov.br/download/texto/gu001676.pdf.
https://www.tasnimnews.com/fa/news/1396/01/16/1370272/
https://yaqeeninstitute.org
www.al-islam.org

Chapter 1: The Opening (al-Fātiḥah)

In the Name of God, The Merciful, The Compassionate. **1:1**

In the Name of God, The Merciful, The Compassionate. (Q1:1) Letter 53

The Praise belongs to God, Lord of the worlds, **1:2**

Praise belongs to God (Q1:2) Who is High above all else. He is Near the creation through His bounty. He is the Giver of all reward and distinction and Dispeller of all calamities and hardships. I praise Him for His continuous mercy and His copious bounties. Sermon 82

The Merciful, The Compassionate, **1:3**

O my God! Do pour on us **Your** mercy, **Your** blessing, **Your** sustenance.... Sermon 143

One Who is Sovereign of the Day of Judgment. **1:4**

On that Day God will collect humanity to stand in obedience for the reckoning of accounts and for award of recompense for deeds. Sermon 102

***You** alone we worship and to **You** alone we pray for help.* **1:5**

You are everlasting. There is no end to **You**. **You** are the highest aim. Sermon 108

Guide us on the straight path, **1:6**

*the path of those to whom **You** were gracious, not the ones against whom **You** are angry, nor the ones who go astray.* **1:7**

He whom He guides does not go astray. Sermon 2

Chapter 2: The Cow (al-Baqarah)

Alif Lam Mim **2:1**

That is the Book—there is no doubt in it, a guidance for the ones who are God-conscious. **2:2**

Doubt is named doubt because it resembles truth. As for lovers of God, their conviction serves them as light and the direction of the right path itself serves as their guide.... Sermon 38

Those who believe in the unseen **2:3**

*and perform the formal prayer, and they spend out of what We provided them, and those who believe in what was caused to descend to **you**, and what was caused to descend before **you**, and they are certain of the world to come.* **2:4**

Those are on a guidance from their Lord and those, they are the ones who prosper. **2:5**

O God's human being! I advise you that to be God-conscious is the provision for the next world, and with it is your return. The provision would take you to your destination and the return would be successful. The best one who is able to make people listen has called towards it, and the best listener has listened to it. So the caller has proclaimed, the listener has listened and persevered. O God's human being! Certainly, being God-conscious has saved the lovers of God from unlawful items and has given His dread to their hearts until their nights are passed in wakefulness and their noons in thirst. So they achieve comfort through trouble and copious watering through thirst. They regarded death to be near and, therefore, hastened towards good actions. They rejected their desires by keeping death in their sight. Sermon 114

Truly, as for those who were ungrateful, it is the same to them whether ***you*** *had warned them or* ***you*** *have warned them not. They believe not.* **2:6**

They took to the right and the left piercing through to the ways of evil and leaving the paths of guidance. Sermon 150

God sealed over their hearts and over their inner hearing and a blindfold over their inner sight. There is a tremendous punishment for them. **2:7**

You, O people of Arabia, will be victims of calamities which have come near. You should avoid the intoxication of wealth, fear the disasters of chastisement, keep steadfast in the darkness and crookedness of mischief when its hidden nature discloses itself, its secrets become manifest and its axis and the pivot of its rotation gain strength. It begins in imperceptible stages but develops into great hideousness. Sermon 151

Among humanity are some who say: We believed in God and in the Last Day, and yet they are not ones who believe. **2:8**

Be aware of God against what He has cautioned you. Be God-conscious to the extent that no excuse be needed for it. Act without show or intention of being heard, for if a person acts for other than God, then God entrusts him to that one. We ask God to grant us the positions of the martyrs, company of the virtuous and friendship of the Prophets. Sermon 23

They seek to trick God and those who believed while they deceive none but themselves, but they are not aware. **2:9**

Be aware, he whom right does not benefit must suffer the harm of the wrong. He whom guidance does not keep firm will be led away by misguidance towards destruction. Sermon 2

In their hearts is a sickness. Then, God increased them in sickness, and for them is a painful punishment because they had been lying against themselves. **2:10**

O people, surely this world deceives him who longs for it and who is attracted towards it. Sermon 178

When it was said to them not to make corruption in and on the earth, they said: Truly, we are only ones who make things right. **2:11**

... one who seeks right, but does not find it, is not like one who seeks wrong and finds it. Sermon 61

No doubt they, they are the ones who make corruption except they are not aware. **2:12**

Be aware and act during the period of attraction just as you act during a period of dread. Be aware! Sermon 28

When it was said to them: Believe as humanity believed, they said: Will we believe as the fools believed? No! Truly, they, they are the fools, except they know not. **2:13**

O God's human being! You should know that a believer should be distrustful of his heart every morning and evening. He should always blame it for shortcomings and ask it to add to its good acts. You should behave like those who have gone before you and the precedents in front of you. They left this world like a traveler and covered it as distance is covered. Sermon 176

When they met those who believed, they said: We believed. When they went privately to their satans, they said: Truly, we are with you. We were only ones who ridicule. **2:14**

People obey Satan and tread his path. Sermon 2

God ridicules them and causes them to increase in their defiance, to wander unwilling to see. **2:15**

We ask God, the Almighty, that He may make us and you like one whom bounty does not mislead, whom nothing can stop from obedience of God and whom shame and grief do not befall after death. Sermon 64

Those are those who bought fallacy for guidance, so their trade was not bettered, nor had they been ones who are truly guided. **2: 16**

Yes, by God, they had heard it and understood it, but the world appeared glittering in their eyes and its embellishments seduced them. Sermon 4

Their parable is like a parable of those who started a fire. Then, when it illuminated what was around it, God took away their light and left them in shadows where they perceive not. **2:17**
Unwilling to hear, unwilling to speak, unwilling to see, then, they will not return to the way. **2:18**

Doubt is named doubt because it resembles truth. As for lovers of God, their conviction serves them as light and the direction of the right path itself serves as their guide; while the enemies of God in time of doubt call to misguidance in the darkness of doubt and their guide is unwilling to see. Sermon 38

Or as a cloudburst from heaven in which there are shadows and thunder and lightning. They lay their fingertips in their ears from the thunderbolt, being fearful of death. God is One Who Encloses the ones who are ungrateful. **2:19**

O God's human being! Be God-conscious and anticipate your death by good actions.... Prepare yourselves for death, since it is hovering over you. Be a people who wake up when called, who know that this world is not their abode and change it for the next. Truly, God has not created you aimlessly nor left you as useless. There is nothing between anyone of you and Paradise or hellfire except death that must befall you. The life that is being shortened every moment and being dismantled every hour must be regarded as being very short. Sermon 64

The lightning almost snatches their sight. When it illuminated for them, they walked in the light. When it grew dark against them, they stood still. If God willed, He would have taken away their having the ability to hear and their sight. Truly, God is Powerful over everything. **2:20**

Everyone should be God-conscious, should admonish himself, should send forward his repentance and should overpower his desire because his death is hidden from him. His desires deceive him. Satan keeps posted about him. He beautifies his sin for him so that he may commit it. He prompts him to delay repentance until his desires cause him to be the most negligent. Pity is for the negligent person whose life itself would be a proof against him and his own days, passed in sin, will lead him to punishment. Sermon 64

O humanity! Worship your Lord Who created you and those who were before you so that perhaps you will be God-conscious. **2:21**

He did not create what He created to fortify His authority, nor for fear of the consequences of time, nor to seek help against the attack of an equal or a boastful partner or a hateful opponent. On the other hand, all creatures are reared by Him and are His humbled servants. Sermon 65

It is He Who assigned the earth for you as a place of restfulness and the heaven as a canopy. He caused water to descend from heaven and from it drove out fruit of trees as provision for you. Then, assign not rivals to God while you, you know. **2:22**

He asked: What did the Quraysh plead? People said: They argued that they belong to the lineal tree of *the Prophet* (Q7:158), peace and the mercy of God be upon him. Ali ibn Abi Talib then said: They defended themselves with the plea of the tree, but neglected the fruit. Sermon 67

If you had been in doubt about what We sent down to Our servant, then approach with a Chapter of the Quran—the like of it—and call to your witnesses other than God if you had been ones who are sincere. **2:23**

Only the middle way is the right path which is the Everlasting Book and the traditions of the Prophet. From it the *sunna* has spread and towards it is the eventual return. Sermon 16

If you accomplish it not—and you will never accomplish it—then be God-conscious of the fire whose fuel is humanity and rocks, prepared for the ones who are ungrateful. **2:24**

O God's human being! I advise you to be God-conscious which is the provision for the next world and with it is your return. Sermon 114

Give good tidings to those who believed and did as the ones in accord with morality, that for them will be Gardens beneath which rivers run. Whenever they were provided from there of its fruit as provision they would say: This is what we were provided before. They will be brought it—ones that resemble one another—and in it for them will be purified spouses. They are ones who will dwell in them forever! **2:25**

Know that, certainly, those creatures of God who preserve His knowledge offer protection to those things which He desires to be protected. They make His springs flow for the benefit of others. They contact each other with friendliness and meet each other with affection. They drink water from cups that quench the thirst and return from the watering places fully satiated. Misgiving does not affect them. Backbiting does not gain ground with them. In this way, God has tied their nature with good manners. It is because of this that they love each other and meet each other. They have become superior, like seeds which are selected by taking some and throwing away others. This selection has distinguished them and the process of choosing has purified them. Sermon 214

Truly, God is not ashamed that He propound a parable, even of a gnat or whatever is above it. So, as for those who believed, then, they know that it is The Truth from their Lord, but those who were ungrateful, then they will say: What did God mean by this parable? He causes many to go astray by it and He guides many by it. He causes none to go astray by it, but the ones who disobey—**2:26**
those who break the compact of God after a solemn promise and sever what God commanded that it be joined and make corruption in and on the earth. Those, they are the ones who are losers! **2:27**

At last, when God will make clear to them the reward for their sins and take them out from the veils of their neglectfulness, they will proceed to what they were running away from and run away from what they were proceeding to. They will not benefit from the wants they will satisfy or the desires they would fulfill. Sermon 153

How is it you are ungrateful to God? You had been lifeless, then, He gave you life. again, He will cause you to die. Again, He will give you life. Again, you are returned to Him. **2:28**

The length of its life does not weary Him so as to induce Him to its quick destruction. Sermon 186

It is He Who created for you all that is in and on the earth. Again, He turned His attention to the heaven. Then, He shaped them into seven heavens. He is Knowing of everything. **2:29**

He is not conditioned on anything so that it be said that He exists therein, nor is He separated from anything so as to be said that He is away from it. The creation of what He initiated or the administration of what He controls did not fatigue Him. No disability overtook Him against what He created. No misgiving ever occurred to Him in what He commanded and resolved, but His verdict is certain. His knowledge is definite. His governance is overwhelming. He is wished for at time of distress and He is feared even in bounty. Sermon 65

When ***your*** *Lord said to the angels: Truly, I am assigning on the earth a viceregent. They said: Will* ***You*** *be One Who Makes on it someone who makes corruption on it and sheds blood, while we glorify* ***Your*** *praise and sanctify* ***You****? He said: Truly, I know what you know not!* **2 30**
He taught Adam the names, all of them. Again, He presented them to the angels and said: Communicate to Me the names of these if you had been ones who are sincere. **2:31**
They said: Glory be to ***You****! We have no knowledge but what* ***You*** *taught us. Truly,* ***You****,* ***You*** *alone are The Knowing, The Wise.* **2:32**

He created the openings between the heavens and filled them with all classes of His angels. Some of them are in prostration and do not sit up. Others are in kneeling position and do not stand up. Some of them are in array and do not leave their position. Others praise God and do not get tired. The sleep of the eye or the slip of wit or languor of the body or the effect of forgetfulness do not affect them. God asked the angels to fulfill His promise with them and to accomplish the pledge of His injunction to them by acknowledging Adam through prostration to him and submission to his honored position. Sermon 1

He said: O Adam! Communicate to them their names. So, then, when he communicated to them their names, He said: Did I not say to you (angels)*: Truly, I know the unseen of the heavens and the earth, and I know what you show and what you had been keeping back.* **2:33**

If God had wanted to create Adam from a light whose glare would have dazzled the eyes, whose handsomeness would have amazed the wits and whose fragrance would have caught the breath, He could have done so. If He had done so people would have bowed to him in humility and the trial of the angels through him would have become easier, but, God, the Almighty, tries His creatures by means of those things whose real nature they do not know in order to distinguish good and bad for them through the trial, and to remove vanity from them and keep them away from pride and self-admiration. Sermon 192

Mention when We said to the angels: Prostrate yourselves to Adam! They, then, prostrated themselves but Iblis. He refused and grew arrogant. He had been among the ones who are ungrateful. **2:34**

Then God asked the angels to fulfill His promise with them and to accomplish the pledge of His injunction to them by acknowledging Him through prostration to Him and submission to His honored position. So God said: *Prostrate yourselves to Adam! They, then, prostrated themselves but Iblis.* Sermon 1

We said: O Adam! Inhabit the Garden, ***you*** *and* ***your*** *spouse: Eat freely from it both of you wherever you both willed, but come not near this, the tree or you both will be among the ones who are unjust.* **2:35**

God placed Adam in a house where He made his life pleasant and his stay safe. He cautioned Adam of Iblis and his enmity. Then Iblis envied his abiding in Paradise and his contacts with the virtuous. So he changed his conviction into wavering and determination into weakness. He thus converted his happiness into fear and his prestige into shame. God offered Adam the chance to repent, taught him words of His Mercy, promised him return to His Paradise and sent him down to the place of trial and procreation of progeny. Sermon 1

Then, Satan caused both of them to slide back from there and drove both of them out from that in which they both had been. We said: Get down some of you as an enemy to some other. For you on the earth, a time appointed and sustenance for a while. **2:36**

They made Satan the master of their affairs. He takes them as partners. He lays eggs and hatches them in their bosoms. He creeps and crawls in their laps. He sees through their eyes and speaks with their tongues. In this way he has led them to sinfulness and adorned for them foul things like the action of one whom Satan has made partner in his domain and speaks untruth through his tongue. Sermon 7

Adam, then, received words from his Lord for He turned to him in forgiveness. Truly, He, He is The Accepter of Repentance, The Compassionate. **2:37**

O my God! Forgive me. **You** know more about me than I do. If I return to sin, **You** return to forgiveness. My God, forgive me what I had promised to myself, but **You** did not find its fulfillment with me. My God, forgive me that with what I sought nearness to **You** with my tongue, but my heart opposed and did not perform. My God, forgive me winking of the eye, vile utterances, desires of the heart and errors of speech. Sermon 78

We said: Get down altogether from it. Whenever guidance approaches you from Me, then, whoever heeded My guidance, then, there will be neither fear in them, nor will they feel remorse. **2:38**

O my God! I seek **Your** protection from becoming destitute despite **Your** riches, from being misguided despite **Your** guidance, from being molested in **Your** realm and from

being humiliated while authority rests with **You.** O my God! Let my spirit be the first of those good objects that **You** take from me and the first trust out of **Your** favors held in trust with me. Sermon 215

But those who were ungrateful and denied Our signs, those will be the Companions of the Fire. They are ones who will dwell in it forever! **2:39**

Praise belongs to God (Q1:2) Who lies inside all hidden things and towards Whom all open things guide. He cannot be seen by the eye of an onlooker, but the eye which does not see Him cannot deny Him while the mind that proves His existence cannot perceive Him. He is so high in sublimity that nothing can be more sublime than He, while in nearness, He is so near that no one can be nearer than He, but His sublimity does not put Him at a distance from anything of His creation, nor does His nearness bring them on equal level to Him. He has not informed the human consciousness about the limits of His qualities. Nevertheless, He has not prevented it from securing essential knowledge of Him. So he is such that all signs of existence bear witness to Him until the denying mind also believes in Him. God is sublime beyond what is described by those who liken Him to things or those who deny Him. Sermon 49

O Children of Jacob! Remember My divine blessing with which I was gracious to you and live up to the compact with Me. I will live up to the compact with you. Have reverence for Me alone. **2:40**
Believe in what I caused to descend, that which establishes as true what is with you. Be not the first one who is ungrateful for it. Exchange not My signs for a little price. Fear Me, God, alone. **2:41**
Confuse not The Truth with falsehood, nor keep back The Truth while you know. **2:42**

Time does not keep company with Him. Implements do not help Him. His Being precedes time. His Existence precedes non-existence. His eternity precedes beginning. By His creating the senses it is known that He has no senses. By the contraries in various matters it is known that He has no contrary. By the similarity between things it is known that there is nothing similar to Him. He has made light the contrary of darkness, brightness that of gloom, dryness that of moisture and heat that of cold. He produces affection among inimical things. He fuses together diverse things, brings near remote things and separates things which are joined together. He is not confined by limits, nor counted by numbers. Sermon 186

Perform the formal prayer, and give the purifying alms, and bow down with the ones who bow down. **2:43**

The purifying alms has been laid down along with prayer as a sacrifice to be offered by the people of Islam. Whoever pays it by way of purifying his spirit, it serves as a purifier for him and a protection and shield against the fire of Hell. No one, therefore, who pays it should feel attached to it afterwards, nor should he feel grieved over it. Whoever pays it without the intention of purifying his heart expects through it more than its due. He is certainly ignorant of the *sunna*. He is allowed no reward for it. His action goes to waste. His repentance is excessive. Sermon 199

You command humanity to virtuous conduct and forget yourselves while you relate the Book? Will you not, then, be reasonable? **2:44**

One who has been through the thick and thin of life finds excuses that prevent him from the commands and prohibitions of God. He disregards them, despite his ability to succumb to excuses. He follows the commands of God. Yet one who has no restraints of religion seizes the opportunity and accepts the excuses for not following the commands of God. Sermon 41

Pray for help with patience and formal prayer. Truly, it is arduous, but for the ones who are humble, **2:45**
those who bear in mind that, truly, they, they will be ones who encounter their Lord and that to Him they will be ones who return. **2:46**

Clothe yourself with patience for it is the best to victory. Sermon 26

O Children of Jacob! Remember My divine blessing with which I was gracious to you, and that I gave advantage to you over the worlds. **2:47**

O God's human being! I advise you to keep away from this world which is shortly to leave you, even though you do not like its departure, and which would make your bodies old, even though you would like to keep them young. Your example and its example is like the travelers who travel some distance and then traverses it quickly, or they aimed at a sign and reached it at once. How short is the distance to the aim if one heads towards it and reaches it. How short is the stage of one who has only a day which he cannot exceed while a swift driver is driving him in this world until he departs from it. Sermon 99

Be God-conscious of a Day when no soul will give recompense for another soul at all, nor will intercession be accepted from it, nor an equivalent be taken from it, nor will they be helped. **2:48**

A person should derive benefit from himself for himself, from the living for the dead, from the mortal, for the lasting and from the departer for the stayer. A person should be God-conscious while he is given age to live up to his death and is allowed time to act. A person should control himself by the rein and hold it with its bridle. By the rein, he should prevent it from disobedience towards God. By the bridle, he should lead it towards obedience to God. Sermon 236

Mention when We delivered you from the people of Pharaoh who cause an affliction to befall you of a dire punishment. They slaughter your children and save alive your women. In that there is a tremendous trial from your Lord. **2:49**
Mention when We separated the sea for you, and We rescued you, and We drowned the people of Pharaoh while you look on. **2:50**
Mention when We appointed for Moses forty nights. Again, you took the calf to yourselves after him and you were ones who are unjust. **2:51**
Again, We pardoned you after that, so that perhaps you will give thanks. **2:52**
Mention when We gave Moses the Book and the Criterion between right and wrong, so that perhaps you will be truly guided. **2:53**
Mention when Moses said to his folk: O my folk! Truly, you did wrong to yourselves by your taking the calf to yourselves to worship, so repent to One Who is your Fashioner and kill your souls. That would be better for you with One Who is your Fashioner. Then He will turn to you in forgiveness. Truly, He, He is The Accepter of Repentance, The Compassionate. **2:54**
Mention when you said: O Moses! We will never believe **you** *until we see God publicly. So, the*

thunderbolt took you while you look on. **2:55** ***

Break the soul in the face of passionate desires. Dominate your inclination to withhold yourself from that which is not lawful for you. Letter 53*

Again, We will raise you up after your death so that perhaps you will give thanks. **2:56**

Do you feel it when the Angel of Death enters a house? Do you see him when he takes the life of anyone? How does he take the life of an embryo in the womb of his mother? Does he reach it through any part of her body, or does the spirit respond to his call with the permission of God? Or does he stay with him in the mother's interior? How can he who is unable to describe a creature like this, describe God? Sermon 112

We shaded over you cloud shadows. We caused to descend to you the manna and the quails. Eat of what is good that We provided you. They did not wrong Us. Rather, they had been doing wrong to themselves. **2:57**

He made a big cloud by collecting together small clouds. When water collected in it and lightning began to flash on its sides and the flash continued under the white clouds as well as the heavy ones, He sent heavy rain. The cloud was hanging towards the earth and southerly winds were squeezing it into shedding its water like a she-camel bending down for milking. Sermon 91

Mention when We said: Enter this town, then, eat freely from it whatever you willed, and enter the door as one who prostrates oneself and say: Unburden us of sin! We will forgive you your transgressions. We will increase the ones who are doers of good. **2:58**

I praise God, seeking completion of His Blessing, submitting to His Glory and expecting safety from committing sin. Sermon 2

*Then, those who did wrong substituted another saying—other than what was said to them—so We sent forth on those who did wrong wrath from heaven because they had been disobeying.***2:59**

O God's human being! Fear God and flee unto God from His wrath (seek protection in His Mercy). Tread on the path He has laid down for you. Stand by what He has enjoined upon you. Sermon 24

Mention when Moses asked for water for his folk. Then, We said: Strike the rock with **your** *staff. Then, twelve springs ran out from it. Every clan knew their drinking place. Eat and drink from the provision of God, and do no mischief in and on the earth as ones who make corruption.* **2:60**
Mention when you said: O Moses! We will never endure patiently with one kind of food, so call to **your** *Lord for us to drive out for us of what the earth is bringing forth of its green herbs and its cucumbers and its garlic and its lentils and its onions. Moses said: Would you have in exchange what is lesser for what is higher? Get down to a settled country. Then, truly for you is what you asked for. Stamped on them were abasement and wretchedness. They drew the burden of anger from God. That was because they had been ungrateful for the signs of God, and kill the Prophets without right. That, because they rebelled, and they had been exceeding the limits.* **2:61**
Truly, those who believed, and those who became Jews, and the Christians and the Sabeans, whoever believed in God and the Last Day and did as one in accord with morality, then, for them, their compensation is with their Lord. There will be neither fear in them, nor will they feel remorse. **2:62**

When We took your solemn promise, and We exalted the mount above you: Take what We gave you with firmness, and remember what is in it, so that perhaps you will be God-conscious. **2:63**
Again, after that you turned away, and if it were not for the grace of God on you, and His mercy certainly, you would have been among the ones who are losers. **2:64**

God never allowed His creation to remain without a Prophet, one deputized by Him or a Book sent down from Him or a binding argument or a standing plea. These Messengers were such that they did not fear that they were few in comparison to the large numbers of their falsifiers. Among them was either a predecessor who would name the one to follow or the follower who had been introduced by the predecessor. Sermon 1

Certainly, you knew those who exceeded the limits among you on the Sabbath, to whom We said: Be you apes, ones who are driven away. **2:65**
Then, We made this an exemplary punishment for the former of them, and of succeeding generations, and an admonishment for the ones who are God-conscious. **2:66**

The gazing of people's eyes is not hidden from Him, nor the repetition of words, nor the glimpse of hillocks, nor the tread of a footstep in the dark night or in the deep gloom, where the shining moon casts its light and the effulgent sun comes in its wake, through its setting and appearing again and again with the rotation of time and periods, by the approach of the advancing night or the passing away of the running day. Sermon 163

*Mention when Moses said to his folk: Truly, God commands that you sacrifice a cow. They said: Have **you** taken us to **your**self in mockery? He said: I take refuge with God that I be among the ones who are ignorant!* **2:67**
*They said: Call to **your** Lord for us to make manifest to us what she is! Moses said: Truly, He says: She should be a cow that is neither old, nor virgin —middle-aged between them— so accomplish what you are commanded.* **2:68**
*They said: Call to **your** Lord for us to make manifest to us what hue she is. He said: Truly, He says: She is a saffron-colored cow —one that is bright in hue— that makes the ones who look on her joyous.* **2:69**
*They said: Call to **your** Lord for us to make manifest to us what she is. Truly, cows resembled one another to us, and, truly, if God willed we would be ones who are truly guided.* **2:70**
*He said: Truly, He says she is a cow neither broken to plow the earth, nor to draw water for cultivation, that which is to be handed over without blemish on her. They said: Now **you** brought about The Truth. So, they sacrificed her, and they almost accomplish it not.* **2:71**
Mention when you killed a soul, then, you put up an argument over it. God was One Who Drives Out what you had been keeping back. **2:72**
So, We said: Turn him away with some of it! Thus, God gives life to the dead, and He causes you to see His signs, so that perhaps you will be reasonable. **2:73**
Again, after that, your hearts became hard, so that they were as rocks or harder in hardness. Truly, from the rocks there are some that the rivers gush forth from it. Truly, there are some that split open so water goes forth from it. Truly, some that from it get down from dreading God. God is not One Who is Heedless of what you do. **2:74**
Are you desirous that they believe in you? Surely, a group of people among them had been hearing the assertion of God. Yet again, they tamper with it after they were reasonable, and they know? **2:75** ***

When they met those who believed, they said: We believed. When they went privately—some of them with some others—they said: Will you divulge to them what God opened to you, so that they argue with you about it before your Lord? Will you not, then, be reasonable? **2:76**

O God's human being! Truly, loyalty and truthfulness are twins. I do not know a better shield against the assaults of sin than it. One who realizes the reality of return to the next world never betrays. We are in a period when most of the people regard betrayal as wisdom. In these days the ignorant ones called it excellence of cunning. What is the matter with them? Sermon 41

Know they not that God knows what they keep secret, and what they speak openly. **2:77**

Whoever speaks, He hears his speaking, and whoever keeps quiet, He knows his secret. Sermon 108

Among them are the unlettered who know nothing of the Book but fantasy. Truly, they but surmise. **2:78**

The Book of God is among you. It speaks and its tongue does not falter. It is a house whose pillars do not fall down. It is a power whose supporters are never defeated. Sermon 132

Woe to those who write down the Book with their own hands. Again, they say: This is from God. Certainly, they exchange it for a little price. Then, woe to them for what their hands wrote down. Woe to them for what they earn! **2:79**

Mind the obligations! Fulfill them for God and they will take you to the Garden. Surely, God has made unlawful the things which are not unknown and made lawful the things which are without defect. Sermon 167

They said: The fire will never touch us, but for numbered days. Say: Took you to yourselves a compact from God? If so, God never breaks His compact; or say you about God what you know not? **2:80**

On Him is the livelihood of everyone who lives, and to Him returns whoever dies. Sermon 108

Yea! Whoever earned an evil deed and is enclosed by his transgression, then those will be the Companions of the Fire. They are ones who will dwell in it forever! **2:81**

Be aware! At the time of committing evil deeds, remember the destroyer of joys, the spoiler of pleasures and the killer of desires, namely death. Seek assistance of God for fulfillment of His obligatory rights and for thanking Him for His countless bounties and obligations. Sermon 999

Those who believed and did as the ones in accord with morality, those will be the Companions of the Garden. They, ones who will dwell in it forever! **2:82**

Commanding to good and refraining from evil are two characteristics of God, the Almighty. They can neither bring death near nor lessen sustenance. Sermon 156

Mention when We took a solemn promise from the Children of Jacob not to worship other than God, and goodness to the ones who are your parents and to the possessors of kinship and the orphans and the needy. Speak with kindness to humanity. Perform the formal prayer, and give the purifying alms. Again, you turned away but a few among you. You are ones who turn aside. **2:83**

The good memory of a person that God retains among people is better than the property which others inherit from him. Sermon 23

Mention when We took your solemn promise: You will not shed your blood, nor drive yourselves out from your abodes. Again, you were in accord and you, you bear witness. **2:84**
Again, you are these—killing yourselves, and driving out a group of people among you from their abodes, to support one another against them in sin and deep seated dislike. If they approach you as prisoners of war, you redeem them, although expelling them is that which is forbidden to you. Then, believe you in some of the Book, and are ungrateful for some? Then, what will be the recompense of whoever commits that among you, but degradation in this present life? On the Day of Resurrection, they will be returned to the hardest punishment. God is not One Who is Heedless of what you do. **2:85**

Be aware that for every blood that is shed there is an avenger and for every right there is a claimant. Sermon 105

Those are those who bought this present life for the world to come, so the punishment on them will not be lightened, nor will they be helped. **2:86**

This world is a place for which destruction is ordained. Departure is destined for its inhabitants here. It is sweet and green. It hastens towards its seeker and attaches to the heart of the viewer. So depart from here with the best of provision available for you. Do not ask for herein more than what is necessary and do not demand from it more than subsistence. Sermon 45

Certainly, We gave Moses the Book and We sent Messengers following after him. We gave Jesus son of Mary the clear portents, and confirmed him with the hallowed Spirit. Is it that whenever a Messenger drew near you with what you yourselves yearn not for, you grew arrogant, and you denied a group of people, and you kill a group of people? **2:87**
They said: Our hearts are encased! Nay! God cursed them for their ingratitude, so little is what they believe! **2:88**

There is no doubt that God sent down *the Prophet* (Q7:158), peace and the mercy of God be upon him, as a guide with an eloquent Book and a standing command. No one will be ruined by it except one who ruins himself. Sermon 169

Mention when a Book from God drew near them, that which establishes as true what was with them—and before that they had been asking for victory over those who were ungrateful—so when drew near them what they recognized, they were ungrateful for it. Then, the curse of God is on the ones who are ungrateful! **2:89**
Miserable was that for which they sold out themselves for it, that they are ungrateful for what God caused to descend, resenting that God sends down of His grace on whom He wills of His servants. They drew the burden of anger on anger. For the ones who are ungrateful, there is a despised punishment. **2:90**

A person should derive benefit from his own "self." Certainly, prudent is he who hears and ponders over it, who sees and observes and who benefits from instructive material and then treads on clear paths wherein he avoids falling into hollows and straying into pitfalls and does not assist those who misguide him by turning away from truthfulness, changing his words or fearing truth. Sermon 153

When it was said to them to believe in what God caused to descend, they said: We believe in what was caused to descend to us. They are ungrateful for what is beyond it, while it is The Truth, that which establishes as true what is with them. Say: Why, then, kill you the Prophets of God before if you had been ones who believe? **2:91**

God chose Prophets from Adam's progeny. He took their pledge to receive His revelation and to carry His message as their trust. Sermon 1

Certainly, Moses drew near you with the clear portents. Again, you took the calf to yourselves after him. You are ones who are unjust. **2:92**
Mention when We took your solemn promise, and We exalted the mount above you: Take what We gave you with firmness and hear. They said: We heard and we rebelled, and they were steeped with love for the calf in their hearts because of their ingratitude. Say: Miserable was what commands you to it of your belief if you had been ones who believe. **2:93**
Say: If the Last Abode for you had been with God —that which is exclusively for you— excluding others of humanity— then, covet death if you had been ones who are sincere. **2:94**
They never covet it ever because of what their hands put forward, and God is Knowing of the ones who are unjust. **2:95**

Did you not witness those who engaged in long-reaching desires, built strong buildings, amassed much wealth, but their houses turned into graves and whatever they had collected turned into ruin? Their property devolved on the successors and their spouses on those who came after them. They cannot now add to their good acts, nor invoke God's mercy in respect of evil acts. Therefore, whoever makes his heart habituated to God-consciousness achieves a forward position and his action is successful. Sermon 132

Certainly, **you** *will find them to be eager among humanity for this life, even of those who ascribed partners with God. Each one of them wishes that he be given a long life of a thousand years, yet he still would not be one who is drawn away from the punishment, even if he be given a long life, and God is Seeing of what they do.* **2:96**

Indeed, God did not crush any unruly tyrant in this world except after allowing him time and opportunity and did not join the broken bone of any community until He did not inflict calamity and distress upon them. Even less than what sufferings and misfortunes have yet to fall upon you or have already befallen, you are enough for giving lessons. Every human being with a heart is not intelligent. Every ear does not listen. Every eye does not see. Sermon 88

Say: Whoever had been an enemy of Gabriel knows, then, truly, it was sent down through him to **your** *heart with the permission of God, that which establishes as true what was before it, and as a guidance and good tidings for the ones who believe.* **2:97**
Whoever had been an enemy of God and His angels, and His Messengers and Gabriel and Michael, then, truly, God is an enemy of the ones who are ungrateful. **2:98**

Be aware! Surely, Almighty God has provided for virtue those who are suited to it, for truth pillars that support it, for obedience and protection against deviation. In every matter of obedience you will find the Almighty God's help that will speak through tongues and accord firmness to hearts. It has sufficiency for those who seek sufficiency and a cure for those who seek to be cured. Sermon 214

Certainly, We caused to descend to **you** *signs, clear portents. None are ungrateful for them, but the ones who disobey.* **2:99**

Is it not that whenever they made a contract—a compact— a group of people among them repudiated it? Nay! Most of them believe not. **2:100**

O people, you are the target for the arrows of death in this world. With every drinking there is choking and with every eating there is suffocation. You do not receive any benefit from it except by forgoing another benefit. No one among you advances in age by a day except by the taking away of a day from his life. Nothing more is added to his eating unless it reduces what was there before. No mark appears for him unless a mark disappears. Nothing new comes into being unless the new becomes old. No new crop comes up unless a crop has been reaped. Those roots are gone whose off-shoots we are. How can an off-shoot live after the departure of its root? Sermon 145

When a Messenger drew near them from God—one who establishes as true what was with them—a group of people repudiated among those who were given the Book, the Book of God—behind their backs as if they had not been knowing that it was God's Book. **2:101**

Certainly, only doubtful innovations cause ruin except those from which God may protect. In God's authority lies the safety of your affairs. Therefore, render Him such obedience as is neither blameworthy nor insincere. Sermon 169

They followed what the satans recount during the dominion of Solomon. Solomon was not ungrateful, except the satans were ungrateful. They teach humanity sorcery, and what was caused to descend to the two angels at Babylon—Harut and Marut. But neither of these two teach anyone unless they say: We are only a test, so be not ungrateful. They learn from these two that by it they separate and divide between a man and his spouse. They were not ones who injured anyone with it, but by the permission of God. They learn what hurts them and profits them not. Certainly, they knew that whoever bought it, for him in the world to come was not any apportionment. Miserable was that for which they sold themselves. Would that they had been knowing! **2:102**

Do you think you can tell the time when a person goes out and no evil befall him, or can warn of the time at which, if one goes out, harm will accrue? Whoever testifies to this falsifies the Quran and becomes unmindful of God in achieving his desired objective and in warding off the undesirable. You cherish saying this, so that he who acts on what you say should praise you rather than God because, according to your misconception, you have guided him about the hour in which he would secure benefit and avoid harm. Sermon 79

If they believed and were God-conscious, certainly, their place of spiritual reward from God was better. Would that they had been knowing! **2:103**

How appropriate are these illustrations and effective admonitions, provided they are received by pure hearts, open ears, firm views and sharp wits. Be God-conscious like him who listened to good advice and bowed before it. Sermon 82

O those who believed! Say not: Look at us, but say: Wait for us patiently and hear. For the ones who are ungrateful, there is a painful punishment. **2:104**

Their hearts are grieved. Others are protected from their evil. Their bodies are thin. Their needs are scanty. Their souls are chaste. They endured hardship for a short while. As a consequence, they secured comfort for a long time. It is a beneficial transaction that God made easy for them. Sermon 193

Neither wish those who were ungrateful from among the People of the Book, nor the ones who are polytheists that any good be sent down to you from your Lord. God singles out for His mercy whom He wills. God is Possessor of the Sublime Grace. **2:105**

He on whom God's bounty is great and God's favors are kind has a greater obligation, because God's bounty over any person does not increase without an increase in God's right over him. Sermon 216

For whatever sign We nullify or cause it to be forgotten, We bring better than it, or similar to it. Have ***you*** *not known that God is Powerful over everything?* **2:106**

He is Powerful, such that when imagination shoots its arrows to comprehend the extremity of His power and the mind, making itself free of the dangers of evil thoughts, tries to find Him in the depth of His realm, and hearts long to grasp the realities of His attributes and openings of intelligence penetrate beyond description in order to secure knowledge about His Being, crossing the dark pitfalls of the unknown and concentrating towards Him, He would turn them back. They would return defeated admitting that the reality of His knowledge cannot be comprehended by such random efforts, nor can an iota of the sublimity of His Honor enter the understanding of thinkers. Sermon 91

Have ***you*** *not known that God, to Him is the dominion of the heavens and the earth, and not for you other than God is there either a protector or a helper?* **2:107**

Be aware! The earth which bears you and the sky which overshadows you are obedient to their Sustainer (God). They have not been bestowing their blessings on you for any feeling of pity on you or inclination towards you, nor for any good which they expect from you, but they were commanded to bestow benefits on you. They are obeying and were asked to maintain your good and so they are maintaining it. Sermon 143

Or want you that you ask your Messenger as Moses was asked before? Whoever takes disbelief in exchange for belief, then, surely, he went astray from the right way. **2:108**

Among the companions of the *Messenger of God* (Q48:29), all were not in the habit of putting him questions and asking him the meanings. Indeed, they always wished that some Bedouin or stranger might come and ask him, peace and the mercy of God be upon him, so that they could also listen. Sermon 210

Many of the People of the Book wished that after your belief they return you to being one who is ungrateful out of jealousy within themselves even after The Truth became clear to them. So, pardon and overlook them until God brings His command. Truly, God is Powerful over everything. **2:109**

Truly, God is Powerful over everything. Sermon 1

Perform the formal prayer and give the purifying alms. Whatever good you put forward for yourselves, you will find it with God. Truly, God is Seeing of what you do. **2:110**

Whoever pays the purifying alms by way of purifying his spirit, it serves as a purifier for him and a protection and shield against the fire of Hell. Sermon 199

They said: None will enter the Garden, but ones who had been Jews or Christians. That is their own fantasies. Say: Prepare your proof if you had been ones who are sincere. **2:111**

Yea! Whoever submitted his face to God, and he is one who is a doer of good, then, for him his compensation is with his Lord. There will be neither fear in them, nor will they feel remorse. **2:112**

I submit to His Glory. Sermon 2

The Jews said: The Christians are not based on anything. The Christians said: The Jews are not based on anything, although they both recount the Book. Thus, said those who know not a thing like their saying. So, God will give judgment between them on the Day of Resurrection about what they had been at variance in it. **2:113**

Prepare yourself for it and do all that you can for the Garden ... Be ready for departure from here and keep close your riding animals for setting off. Sermon 132

Who does greater wrong than those who prevented access to the places of prostration to God so that His Name not be remembered in them, and endeavored for their devastation? It had not been for those to enter them, but as ones who are fearful. For them is degradation in the present, and for them is a tremendous punishment in the world to come. **2:114**

O people! Look at the world like those who abstain from it and turn away from it. By God, it would shortly turn out its inhabitants and cause grief to the happy and the safe. That which turns and goes away from it never returns. That which is likely to come about is not known or anticipated. Its joy is mingled with grief. Sermon 103

To God belongs the East and the West. So, wherever you turn to, then, again, there is the Countenance of God. Truly, God is One Who is Extensive, Knowing. **2:115**

One who imagines himself to be The Knowing will surely suffer on account of his ignorance. Letter 85

They said: God took to Himself a son. Glory be to Him! Nay! To Him belongs whatever is in the heavens and the earth. All are ones who are morally obligated to Him, **2:116**
Beginner of the heavens and the earth and when He decreed a command, then, truly, He says to it: Be! Then, it is! **2:117**

He remembers, but does not memorize. He determines, but not by exercising His mind. He loves and approves without any sentimentality of heart. He hates and feels angry without any pain. When He intends to create something, He says: "*Be! and it is*" (Q2:117), but not through a voice that strikes the ears is that call heard. His speech is an act of His creation. His like never existed before this. Sermon 186

Those who know not said: Why does God not speak to us or a sign approach us? Thus, said those who were before them like their saying. Their hearts resembled one another. Surely, We made manifest the signs for a folk who are certain. **2:118**

Where are the hearts dedicated to God and devoted to the obedience of God? Sermon 144

Truly, We sent ***you*** *with The Truth as a bearer of good tidings and as a warner.* ***You*** *will not be asked about the Companions of Hellfire.* **2:119**

God sent Muhammad, peace and the mercy of God be upon him, with the Truth so that he may take out His people from the worship of idols towards His worship and from obeying Satan towards obeying Him. God sent him with the Quran which He explained and made strong in order that the people may know their Sustainer (God), since they were ignorant of Him, may acknowledge Him, since they were denying Him and accept Him, since they were refusing to believe in Him. Sermon 147

The Jews will never be well-pleased with **you**, *nor the Christians until* **you** *have followed their creed. Say: Truly, guidance of God. It is the guidance. If* **you** *had followed their desires after what drew near* **you** *of the knowledge, there is not for* **you** *from God either a protector or a helper.* **2:120**
Those to whom We gave the Book recount it with a true recounting. Those believe in it, and whoever is ungrateful for it, then, those, they are the ones who are losers. **2:121**

Mind the obligations! Mind the obligations! Fulfill them for God and they will take you to the Garden. Surely, God has made unlawful the things which are not unknown and made lawful the things which are without defect. Sermon 167

O Children of Jacob! Remember My divine blessing with which I was gracious to you, and that I gave you an advantage over the worlds. **2:122**
Be God-conscious of a Day when no soul will give recompense for another soul at all, nor will the equivalent be accepted from it, nor will intercession profit it, nor will they be helped. **2:123**

Whatever they were ignoring has befallen them, separation from this world, from which they took themselves safe, has come to them and they have reached that in the next world which they had been promised. Whatever has befallen them cannot be described. Pangs of death and grief for losing this world have surrounded them. Consequently, their limbs become languid and their complexion changes. Then death increases its struggle over them. Sermon 108

Mention when his Lord tested Abraham with words; then, he fulfilled them. God said: Truly, I am One Who Makes **you** *a leader for humanity. He said: Of my offspring? He said: Attain not My compact the ones who are unjust.* **2:124**
Mention when We made the House a place of spiritual reward for humanity and a place of sanctuary: Take the Station of Abraham to yourselves as a place of prayer. We made a compact with Abraham, and Ishmael saying: Purify My House for the ones who circumambulate it, and the ones who cleave to it, and the ones who bow down, and the ones who prostrate themselves. **2:125**
Mention when Abraham said: My Lord! Make this a safe land, and provide its people with fruits, whomever of them believed in God and the Last Day. God said: Whoever is ungrateful, I will give him enjoyment for a while. Again, I will compel him to the punishment of the fire. Miserable will be the Homecoming! **2:126**
Mention when Abraham elevates the foundations of the House with Ishmael saying: Our Lord! Receive it from us. Truly, **You**, **You** *alone are The Hearing, The Knowing.* **2:127**
Our Lord! Make us ones who submit to **You**, *and, of our offspring, a community of ones who submit to* **You**. *Cause us to see our devotional acts, and turn to us in forgiveness. Truly,* **You**, **You** *alone are The Accepter of Repentance, The Compassionate.* **2:128**
Our Lord! Raise **You** *up, then, in the midst of them, a Messenger from among them who will recount to them* **Your** *signs and teach them the Book, and wisdom and make them pure. Truly,* **You**, **You** *alone are The Almighty, The Wise.* **2:129**
Who shrinks from the creed of Abraham, but he who fooled himself? Certainly, We favored him in the present. Truly, in the world to come, he will be among the ones in accord with morality. **2:130**

O people! Look at the world like those who abstain from it and turn away from it. By God, it would shortly turn out its inhabitants and cause grief to the happy and the safe.

That which turns and goes away from it never returns. That which is likely to come about is not known or anticipated. Its joy is mingled with grief. Herein people's firmness inclines towards weakness and languidness. The majority of what pleases you here should not mislead you because that which would help you would be little. God may shower His mercy on him who ponders and takes lesson thereby, and when he takes lesson he achieves enlightenment. Whatever is present in this world would shortly not exist, while whatever is to exist in the next world is already in existence. Every countable thing would pass away. Every anticipation should be taken to be coming up and every thing that is to come up should be taken as just near. Sermon 103

When his Lord said to him: Submit! He said: I submitted to the Lord of the worlds. **2:131**
Abraham charged his children to it, and Jacob: O my children! Truly, God favored the way of life for you. Then, be not overtaken by death but you be ones who submit to the One God. **2:132**

I submit to His Glory. Sermon 2

Or had you been witnesses when death attended Jacob when he said to his children: How will you worship after me? They said: We will worship **your** *God and the God of* **your** *fathers—Abraham and Ishmael and Isaac—One God. We are ones who submit to Him.* **2:133**
That was, surely, a community that passed away. For them is what they earned, and for you is what you earned and you will not be asked about what they had been doing. **2:134**

You should take a lesson from the fate of the progeny of Ishmael, the children of Isaac and the children of Jacob. How similar are their affairs and how akin are their examples. Sermon 192

They said: Be you ones who are Jews or Christians, you will be truly guided. Say **you**: *Nay! We follow the creed of Abraham a monotheist. He had not been of the ones who are polytheists.* **2:135**

He whom He guides does not go astray. Sermon 2

Say: We *believed in God and what was caused to descend to us, and what was caused to descend to Abraham and Ishmael and Isaac and Jacob and the Tribes and whatever was given Moses and Jesus, and whatever was given to the Prophets from their Lord. We separate and divide not between anyone of them. We are ones who submit to Him.* **2:136**

God chose Prophets from Adam's progeny. He took their pledge to receive His revelation and to carry His message as their trust. Over the course of time, many people perverted God's trust in them. They ignored His position. They took partners with Him. Satan turned them away from knowing Him and distanced them from His worship. Then God sent His Messengers and series of His Prophets to them to guide them to fulfilling the pledges of His creation, to recall to them His bounties, to exhort them by preaching, to unveil before them the hidden virtues of wisdom and show them the signs of His Omnipotence, namely the sky which is raised over them, the earth that is placed beneath them, their means of living that sustains them, their deaths that cause them to die, ailments that turn them old and incidents that successively betake them. Sermon 1

So, if they believed the like of what you believed in it, then, surely, they were truly guided. If they turned away, then, they are not but in breach. So, God suffices for you against them. He is The Hearing, The Knowing. **2:137**

The best means by which seekers of nearness to God, the Almighty, the Exalted, seek nearness, is the belief in Him and His Prophet.... Sermon 110

Life's color is from God. Who is fairer at coloring than God? We are ones who worship Him. **2:138**

Be fair, just and impartial in your dealings so that even the influential persons may not dare take undue advantage of your leniency and the commoners and the poor may not be disappointed in your justice and fair dealings. Letter 27

Say: Argue you with us about God? He is our Lord and your Lord. To us are our actions, and to you are your actions. We are to Him ones who are sincere and devoted. **2:139**

The beginning of the action of one who sees with his heart and acts with eyes is to assess whether the action will go against him or for him. If it is for him, he indulges in it, but if it is against him, he keeps away from it. For he who acts without knowledge is like one who treads without a path. His deviation from the path keeps him at a distance from his aim. He who acts according to knowledge is like him who treads the clear path. Therefore, he who can see should see whether he should proceed or return. You should also know that the outside has a similar inside. Of whatever the outside is good, its inside, too, is good and whenever the outside is bad, its inside too is bad. The truthful Prophet, peace and the mercy of God be upon him, has said: God may love a person but hate his action, and may love the action but hate the person. You should also know that every action is like vegetation. Vegetation cannot do without water while waters are different. Where the water is good, the plant is good and its fruits are sweet, whereas where the water is bad, the plant will also be bad and its fruits will be bitter. Sermon 153

Or say you about Abraham and Ishmael and Isaac and Jacob and the Tribes had been ones who became Jews or were Christians? Say: Are you greater in knowledge or God? Who does greater wrong than he who had been keeping back testimony from God that is with him, and God is not One Who is Heedless of what you do. **2:140**

That is a community that surely passed away; for it is what it earned and for you is what you earned and you will not be asked about what they had been doing. **2:141**

Every person with consciousness is not intelligent, nor does every ear listen, nor every eye see. Sermon 87

The fools among humanity say: What turned them from their direction of formal prayer to which they had been towards? Say: To God belongs the East and the West. He guides whom He wills to a straight path. **2:142**

Everything that is known through itself has been created. Everything that exists by virtue of other things is the effect of a cause. He works, but not with the help of instruments. He fixes measures, but not with the activity of thinking. He is rich, but not by acquisition. Sermon 186

Thus, We made you a middle community that you be witnesses to humanity, and that the Messenger be a witness to you. We made not the direction of the formal prayer which **you** *had been towards but that We make evident whoever follows the Messenger from him who turns about on his two heels. Truly, it had been grave, but for those whom God guided. God had not been wasting your belief. Truly, God is Gentle toward humanity, Compassionate.* **2:143**

Only the middle way is the right path which is the Everlasting Book and the traditions of *the Prophet* (Q7:158), peace and the mercy of God be upon him. From it the *sunna* has spread and towards it is the eventual return. Sermon 16

Surely, We see the going to and fro of ***your*** *face toward heaven. Then, We will turn* **you** *to a direction of formal prayer that* **you** *will be well pleased with it. Then, turn* ***your*** *face to the direction of the Masjid al-Haram. Wherever you had been, turn your faces to its direction. Truly, those who were given the Book know that it is The Truth from their Lord, and God is not One Who is Heedless of what they do.* **2:144**

There is no doubt that God sent down *the Prophet* (Q7:158), peace and the mercy of God be upon him, as a guide with an eloquent Book and a standing command. No one will be ruined by it except one who ruins himself. Certainly, only doubtful innovations cause ruin except those from which God may protect. In God's authority lies the safety of your affairs. Therefore, render Him such obedience as is neither blameworthy nor insincere. By God, you must do so otherwise God will take away from you the power of Islam and will never thereafter return it to you until it reverts to others. Sermon 169

Even if ***you*** *were to bring to those who were given the Book every sign, they would not heed* ***your*** *direction of formal prayer. Nor are* **you** *one who heeds their direction of formal prayer. Nor are some of them ones who heed the direction of the other's formal prayer. If* ***you*** *followed their desires after the knowledge that has been brought about to* **you**, *then truly* **you** *would be of the ones who are unjust.* **2:145**

... on us it is obligatory ... to abide by the Book of God (Quran), the Sublime, and the conduct of the Prophet of God, peace and the mercy of God be upon him, to stand by His rights and the revival of his *sunna*. Sermon 169

Those to whom We gave the Book recognize it as they recognize their children, while, truly, a group of people among them keep back The Truth while they know **2:146**
it is The Truth from ***your*** *Lord. So, be* **you** *not among the ones who contest.* **2:147**

He who memorizes truthfully ... is he who does not speak a lie against God or against His Prophet. He hates falsehood out of fear for God and respect for the *Messenger of God* (Q48:29), and does not commit mistakes, but retains in his mind exactly what he heard from *the Prophet* (Q7:158), peace and the mercy of God be upon him, and he relates it as he heard it without adding anything or omitting anything. Sermon 210

Everyone has a direction to that which he turns. Be forward, then, in good deeds. Wherever you be, God will bring you altogether for the Judgment. Truly, God is Powerful over everything. **2:148**

Perform good acts while you are still in the vastness of life. The books are open for recording of actions. Repentance is allowed. The runner away from God is being called and the sinner is being given hope of forgiveness before the light of action is put off, time expires, life ends, the door for repentance is closed and angels ascend to the sky. Sermon 236

From wherever ***you*** *had gone forth, then, turn* ***your*** *face in the direction of the Masjid al-Haram. Truly, this is The Truth from* ***your*** *Lord, and God is not One Who is Heedless of what you do.* **2:149**

The birth-place of *the Prophet* (Q7:158), peace and the mercy of God be upon him, was Makkah (wherein is the Masjid al-Haram), and the place of his immigration, Madinah, from where his name rose high and his voice spread far and wide.

From wherever **you** *had gone forth, then, turn* **your** *face to the direction of the Masjid al-Haram. Wherever you had been, then, turn your faces to the direction of it so that there be no disputation from humanity against you, but from those of them who did wrong. Dread them not, then, but dread Me. I fulfill My divine blessing on you—so that perhaps you will be truly guided—* **2:150**
as We sent to you a Messenger from among you who recounts Our signs to you, and makes you pure, and teaches you the Book and wisdom, and teaches you what you be knowing not. **2:151**

Know that, certainly, those creatures of God who preserve His knowledge, offer protection to those things which He desires to be protected. They make His springs flow for the benefit of others. They contact each other with friendliness and meet each other with affection. They drink water from cups that quench the thirst and return from the watering places fully satiated. Misgiving does not affect them. Backbiting does not gain ground with them. In this way, God has tied their nature with good manners. It is because of this that they love each other and meet each other. They have become superior, like seeds which are selected by taking some and throwing away others. This selection has distinguished them and the process of choosing has purified them. Sermon 214

So, remember Me and I will remember you. Give thanks to Me, and be not ungrateful! **2:152**

So remember God. Sermon 85

O those who believed! Pray for help with patience and formal prayer. Truly, God is with the ones who remain steadfast. **2:153**

Clothe yourself with patience for it is the best to victory. Sermon 26

Say not about those who are slain in the way of God: They are lifeless. Nay! They are living, except you are not aware. **2:154**

The Prophet (Q7:158), peace and the mercy of God be upon him, informed us that a martyr receives the title of one who flies in Paradise (*tayyar*). Letter 28

We will, certainly, try you with something of fear and hunger and diminution of wealth and lives and fruits, and give good tidings to the ones who remain steadfast, **2:155**
those who, when an affliction lit on them, they said: Truly, we belong to God and, truly, we are ones who return to Him. **2:156**

Have you not been left among people who are just like rubbish and so low that lips avoid mention of them and do not move even to condemn their low position? *Truly, we belong to God and, truly, we are ones who return to Him.* (Q2:156) Sermon 128

Those, blessings will be sent on them from their Lord and mercy. Those, they are the ones who are truly guided. **2:157**

Infuse your heart with mercy for the subjects, love for them and kindness towards them. Be not like a ravenous beast of prey above them, seeking to devour them. For they are of two types: either your brother in religion or your like in creation. Mistakes slip from them. Defects emerge from them, deliberately or accidentally. So bestow upon them your forgiveness and your pardon, just as you would have God bestow upon you His forgiveness and pardon, for you are above them. The one who has authority over you is above you. God is above him who appointed you ... and through them He tests you. Letter 53*

Truly, Safa and Marwa are among the Waymarks of God, so whoever made the pilgrimage to Makkah to the House or visited the Kabah, then, there is no blame on him that he circumambulates between the two. Whoever volunteered good, then, truly, God is One Who is Responsive, Knowing. **2:158**

If God, the Almighty, had placed His sacred House and His great signs among plantations, streams, soft and level plains, plenty of trees, an abundance of fruits, a thick population, close habitats, golden wheat, lush gardens, green land, watered plains, thriving orchards and crowded streets, the amount of recompense would have decreased because of the lightness of the trial. If the foundation on which the House is borne and the stones with which it has been raised had been of green emerald and red rubies, and there had been brightness and effulgence, then this would have lessened the action of doubts in the breasts, would have dismissed the effect of Satan's activity from the hearts, and would have stopped the surging of misgivings in people, but God tries His creatures by means of different troubles, wants them to render worship through hardships and involves them in distresses, all in order to extract out vanity from their hearts, to settle down humbleness in their spirits and to make all this an open door for His favors and an easy means for His forgiveness. Sermon 192

Truly, those who keep back what We caused to descend of the clear portents and the guidance, after We made it manifest to humanity in the Book—those, God curses them and the ones who curse, curse them. **2:159**

Mind the obligations! Mind the obligations! Fulfill them for God and they will take you to the Garden. Surely, God has made unlawful the things which are not unknown and made lawful the things which are without defect. Sermon 167

But those who repented, and made things right, and made things manifest, then, those—I will turn to them in forgiveness. I am The Accepter of Repentance, The Compassionate. **2:160**

He never grudges His Forgiveness, nor refuses His Mercy. On the contrary He has decreed repentance as a virtue and pious deed. Letter 31

Truly, those who were ungrateful, and they died and they were ones who are ungrateful, those, on them is a curse of God, and the angels and humanity, one and all. **2:161**
They are ones who will dwell in it forever. The punishment will not be lightened for them nor will they be given respite. **2:162**

Truly, if you could see what has been seen by those of you who have died, you would be puzzled and troubled. Then you would have listened and obeyed, but what they have seen is yet curtained off from you. The curtain would shortly be thrown off. You have been shown, provided you are willing to see. You have been made to listen, provided you are willing to listen. You have been guided, if you accept guidance. I spoke to you with the truth. You have been called aloud by instructive examples and warned through items full of warnings. Sermon 20

Your God is One God. There is no god but He, The Merciful, The Compassionate. **2:163**

I bear witness that there is no god, but He ... One God. (Q2:163) Sermon 2

Truly, in the creation of the heavens and the earth and the alteration of the nighttime and the daytime and the boats that run on the sea with what profits humanity, and what God caused to descend from heaven of water, and gave life to the earth after its death, and disseminated on it all moving creatures, and diversified the winds and the clouds, ones caused to be subservient between heaven and earth, are the signs for a folk who are reasonable. **2:164**

He initiated creation most initially and commenced it originally without undergoing reflection, without making use of any experiment, without innovating any movement and without experiencing any aspiration of mind. He allotted all things their times, put together their variations, gave them their properties and determined their features knowing them before creating them, realizing fully their limits and confines and appreciating their propensities and intricacies. Sermon 1

Yet there are among humanity some who take to themselves rivals besides God. They love them like they should cherish God. Those who believed are stauncher in cherishing God. If only those who did wrong would consider when they will see the punishment that all strength belongs to God, and that God is Severe in punishment. **2:165**

Truly, God sent Muhammad, peace and the mercy of God be upon him, as a warner against vice for all the worlds and a trustee of His revelation, while you people of Arabia were following the worst religion and you resided among rough stones and venomous serpents. You drank dirty water and ate filthy food. You shed each other's blood and cared not for your relationships. Idols were worshipped among you and your sins were clinging to you. Sermon 26

When they will clear themselves—those who were followed from those who followed them—and they will see the punishment, all cords will be cut asunder from them. **2:166**

You should know that the same troubles have returned to you which existed before *the Prophet* (Q7:158), peace and the mercy of God be upon him, was first sent. Sermon 16

Those who were followed said: If there be a return again for us, then, we would clear ourselves from them as they cleared themselves from us. Thus, God will cause them to see their actions with regret for them, and they will never be ones who go forth from the fire. **2:167**

The present is an opportune moment for acting, O God's human being, since the neck is free from the loop and the spirit is also unfettered. Now you have time for seeking guidance. You are in ease of body. You can assemble in crowds. The rest of your life is before you. You have the opportunity of acting by will. There is an opportunity for repentance and peaceful circumstances. However, you should act before you are overtaken by narrow circumstances and distress or fear and weakness before the approach of the awaited death and before seizure by the Almighty, the Powerful. Sermon 82

O humanity! Eat of what is in and on the earth—lawful, wholesome—and follow not the steps of the Satan. Truly, he is a clear enemy to you. **2:168**

They have made Satan the master of their affairs. He has taken them as partners. He has laid eggs and hatched them in their bosoms. He creeps and crawls in their laps. He sees through their eyes and speaks with their tongues. In this way he has led them to sinfulness and adorned for them foul things like the action of one whom Satan has made partner in his domain and speaks untruth through his tongue. Sermon 7

Truly, he commands you to evil and depravity, and that you say about God what you know not. **2:169**

Truly, sins are like unruly horses on whom their riders have been placed and their reins have been let loose so that they would jump with them in hellfire. Truly, that God-consciousness is like trained horses on whom the riders have been placed with the reins in their hands so that they would take the riders to heaven. There is right and wrong and there are followers for each. If wrong dominates, it has always in the past been so and if truth goes down, that too has often occurred. It seldom happens that a thing that lags behind comes forward. Sermon 16

When it was said to them: Follow what God caused to descend. They said: Nay! We will follow whatever we discovered our fathers were following on it —even though their fathers had been not at all reasonable—nor are they truly guided. **2:170**

Truly, God sent Muhammad, peace and the mercy of God be upon him, when none among the Arabs read a book or claimed prophethood. He guided the people until he took them to their correct position and their salvation. So their officers learned and their conditions improved. Sermon 33

The parable of those who were ungrateful is like the parable of those who shout to what hears not, but a crying out and pleading yet those to which they call out to are deaf, dumb and blind, so they are not reasonable. **2:171**

You received guidance in the darkness through us and secured a high spiritual position. You put aside the gloomy night through us. Ears which do not listen to the cries may become deaf. How can one who remained deaf to the loud cries of the Quran and *the Prophet* (Q7:158), peace and the mercy of God be upon him, listen to my feeble voice? The heart that has ever palpitated with God-consciousness may attain peace. Sermon 4

O those who believed! Eat of what is good that We provided you and give thanks to God if it had been He alone whom you worship. **2:172**

He is sufficient for one who relies on Him. He gives one who asks Him. He repays one who lends to Him. He rewards one who thanks Him. Sermon 90

Truly, He forbade carrion for you and blood and the flesh of swine and what was hallowed to any other than God, but whoever was driven by necessity, without being one who is willfully disobedient, and not one who turns away, then, it is not a sin for him. Truly, God is Forgiving, Compassionate. **2:173**

Truly, those who keep back what God caused of the Book to descend, and exchange it for a little price, those, they consume not into their bellies but fire. God will not speak to them on the Day of Resurrection nor will He make them pure. For them will be a painful punishment. **2:174**

Your ultimate goal of reward or punishment is before you. Behind your back is the hour of Resurrection which is driving you on. Keep yourself light and overtake the forward ones. The first ones who have preceded await your last ones. Sermon 21

Those are those who bought fallacy for guidance and punishment for forgiveness. So, how they are ones who remain steadfast for the fire! **2:175**

They took to the right and the left piercing through to the ways of evil and leaving the paths of guidance. Do not make haste for a matter which is to happen and is awaited.

Do not wish for delay in what tomorrow is to bring for you. For how many people make haste for a matter, but when they get it, they begin to wish they had not gotten it? How near is today to the dawning of tomorrow? Sermon 150

That is because God sent down the Book with The Truth and, truly, those who were at variance regarding the Book are in a wide breach. **2:176**

When the caliphate came to me, I kept the Book of God in my view and all that God had put therein for us and all that according to which He has commanded us to make decisions. I followed it. I also acted on whatever *the Prophet* (Q7:158), peace and the mercy of God be upon him, had laid down as his *sunna*. Sermon 205

It is not virtuous conduct that you turn your faces towards the East or the West. Rather, virtuous conduct consists of: Whoever believed in God and the Last Day and the angels and the Book and the Prophets. Whoever gave wealth out of cherishing Him to the possessors of kinship and to the orphans and to the needy and to the traveler of the way and to the one who begs and the freeing of a bondsperson, and whoever performed the formal prayer, and gave the purifying alms, and the ones who live up to their compact when they made a contract, and the ones who remain steadfast in desolation and tribulation and at the time of danger, those are those who were sincere and those, they are the ones who are God-conscious! **2:177**

The best means by which seekers of nearness to God, the Almighty, the Exalted, seek nearness, is the belief in Him and His Prophet, struggling in His cause, for it is the high pinnacle of Islam, and to believe in the expression of divine purification for it is just nature and the establishment of prayer for it is the basis of community, payment of the purifying tax (*zakat*) for it is a compulsory obligation, fasting for the month of Ramadan for it is the shield against chastisement, the performance of the pilgrimage to the House of God (Kabah) and its visitation (*umrah*) (other than annual visit) for these two acts banish poverty and wash away sins, regard for kinship for it increases wealth and length of life, to giving alms secretly for it covers shortcomings, giving alms openly for it protects against a bad death and extending benefits to people for it saves from positions of disgrace. Sermon 110

O those who believed! Reciprocation was prescribed for you for the slain: the freeman for the freeman and the servant for the servant and the female for the female. But whoever was forgiven a thing by his brother, the pursuing be as one who is honorable, and the remuneration be with kindness. That is a lightening from your Lord, and a mercy. He who exceeded the limits after that, then, for him is a painful punishment. **2:178**

O people! If a person knows his brother to be steadfast in faith and of correct ways he should not lend ear to what people may say about him. Sometimes the bowman shoots arrows, but the arrow goes astray. Similarly, talk can be off the point. Its wrong perishes, while God is the Hearer and the Witness. Sermon 141

For you in reciprocation there is the saving of life, O those imbued with intuition, so that perhaps you will be God-conscious. **2:179**

How appropriate are these illustrations and effective admonitions, provided they are received by pure hearts, open ears, firm views and sharp wits. Be God-conscious like him who listened to good advice and bowed before it. Sermon 82

It is prescribed for you when death attended anyone of you if one left goods, to bequeath to the ones who are your parents and the nearest kin as the one who is honorable, an obligation for the ones who are God-conscious. **2:180**

O God's human being! Be God-conscious. Keep in view the reason why He created you. Be afraid of Him to the extent He has advised you to do. Make yourself deserve what He has promised you by having confidence in the truth of His promise and entertaining fear of the Day of Judgment. Sermon 82

Then, whoever substituted it after he heard it, truly, the sin of it is only on those who substitute it. Truly, God is Hearing, Knowing. **2:181**

Certainly, nothing is viler than evil except its punishment. Nothing is better than good except its reward. In this world, everything that is heard is better than what is seen, while everything of the next world that is seen is better than what is heard. You should satisfy yourself by hearing rather than seeing and by the news of the unknown. You should know that what is little in this world but much in the next is better than what is much in this world, but little in the next. In how many cases little is profitable while much causes loss. Sermon 114

Then, whoever feared from one who makes a testament, a swerving from the right path or sin, and, then, made things right between them, there is no sin on him. Truly, God is Forgiving, Compassionate. **2:182**

O people, what I fear most for you are two things—your acting according to your desires and extending of your hopes. As regards acting according to your desires, this prevents you from the truth and as regards extending of your hopes, it makes you forget the next world. You should know this world is moving rapidly and nothing has remained out of it except the last particles like the dregs of a vessel which has been emptied by someone. Be aware that the next world is advancing and both of them have followers. You should become followers and sons of the next world and not become followers and sons of this world because on the Day of Judgment every son will cling to his mother. Today is the day of action, but there is no reckoning. Tomorrow is the day of reckoning, but there would be no opportunity for action. Sermon 42

O those who believed! Formal fasting was prescribed for you as it was prescribed for those who were before you so that perhaps you will be God-conscious. **2:183**
Fasting is prescribed for numbered days. Then, whoever among you had been sick or on a journey, then, a period of other days. For those who cannot fast is a redemption of food for the needy. Whoever volunteered good, it is better for him and that you formally fast is better for you if you had been knowing. **2:184**
The month of Ramadan is that in which the Quran was caused to descend—a guidance for humanity—and clear portents of the guidance, and the Criterion between right and wrong. So, whoever of you bore witness to the month, then, formal fasting, and whoever had been sick or on a journey, then, a period of other days. God wants ease for you, and wants not hardship for you, so that you perfect the period and that you magnify God because He guided you so that perhaps you will give thanks. **2:185**

The best means by which seekers of nearness to God, the Almighty, the Exalted, seek nearness, is the belief in Him and His Prophet ... fasting for the month of Ramadan for it is the shield against chastisement.... Sermon 110

When My servants asked **you** *about Me, then, truly, I am near. I answer the call of one who calls when he will call to Me. So, let them respond to Me and let them believe in Me, so that perhaps they will be on the right way.* **2:186**

Praise belongs to God (Q1:2) Who is High above all else. He is Near the creation through His bounty. He is the Giver of all reward and distinction and Dispeller of all calamities and hardships. I praise Him for His continuous mercy and His copious bounties. Sermon 82

It is permitted for you on the nights of formal fasting to have sexual intercourse with your wives. They (f) are a garment for you and you are a garment for them (f). God knew that you had been dishonest to yourselves so He turned to you in forgiveness and pardoned you. So, now lie with them (f) and look for what God prescribed for you. Eat and drink until the white thread becomes clear to you from the black thread at dawn. Again, fulfill the formal fasting until night. Lie not with them (f) when you are ones who cleave to the places of prostration. These are the ordinances of God. Then, come not near them. Thus, God makes His signs manifest to humanity so that perhaps they will be God-conscious. **2:187**

The best means by which seekers of nearness to God, the Almighty, the Exalted, seek nearness, is the belief in Him and His Prophet.... Sermon 110

Consume not your wealth between yourselves in falsehood, nor let it down in bribes to the ones who judge so that you consume a group of people's wealth among humanity in sin while you know. **2:188**

Be aware! Certainly that giving of wealth without any right for it is wastefulness and lavishness. It raises its doer in this world, but lowers him in the next world. It honors him before people, but disgraces him with God. If a man gives his property to those who have no right for it or do not deserve it, God deprives him of their gratefulness, and their love, too, would be for others. Then if he falls on bad days and needs their help, they would prove the worst comrades and ignoble friends. Sermon 126

They ask **you** *about the new moons. Say: They are appointed times for humanity, and the pilgrimage to Makkah. It is not virtuous conduct that you approach houses from the back. Rather, virtuous conduct was to be God-conscious, and approach houses from their front doors. Be God-conscious so that perhaps you will prosper.* **2:189**

The sun and the moon are steadily moving in pursuit of His will. They make every fresh thing old and every distant thing near.... Sermon 89

Struggle in the Way of God those who struggle against you, but exceed not the limits. Truly, God loves not the ones who exceed the limits. **2:190**

They may move from their position, but you should not move from yours. Grit your teeth. In struggling for God, give yourself to God. Plant your feet firmly on the ground. Have your eye on the remotest foe and close your eyes to their numbers. Rest assured that help is but from God, the Almighty. Sermon 11

Kill them wherever you came upon them, and drive them out from wherever they drove you out.

Persecution is more grave than killing. Fight them not near the Masjid al-Haram unless they fight you in it. But if they fought you, then kill them. Thus, this is the recompense for the ones who are ungrateful. **2:191**
Then, if they refrained themselves, then, truly, God is Forgiving, Compassionate. **2:192**
Fight them until there be no persecution, and the way of life be for God. Then, if they refrained themselves, then, there is to be no deep seated dislike, but against the ones who are unjust. Fight aggression **2:193**
committed in the Sacred Month, in the Sacred Month and so reciprocation for all sacred things. So, whoever exceeded the limits against you, exceed you the limits against him likewise as he exceeded the limits against you? Be God-conscious and know that God is with the ones who are God-conscious. **2:194**

I praise God for whatever matter He ordained and whatever action He destines. Sermon 180

Spend in the way of God, and cast not yourselves by your own hands into deprivation by fighting. Do good. Truly, God loves the ones who are doers of good. **2:195**

The *Messenger of God*,(Q48:29), peace and the mercy of God be upon him, used to say: O son of Adam, do good and evade evil; by doing so you will be treading correctly. Sermon 175

Fulfill the pilgrimage to Makkah, and the visit for God. If you were restrained, then, whatever was feasible of sacrificial gifts. Shave not your heads until the sacrificial gift reaches its place of sacrifice. Then, whoever had been sick among you, or has an injury of his head, then, a redemption of formal fasting, or charity or a ritual sacrifice. When you were safe, then, whoever took joy in the visit and the pilgrimage to Makkah then whatever was feasible of a sacrificial gift. Then, whoever finds not the means, then, formal fasting for three days during the pilgrimage to Makkah and seven when you returned, that is ten completely. That would be for he whose people are not ones who are present at the Masjid al-Haram. Be God-conscious and know that God is Severe in repayment. **2:196**
The pilgrimage to Makkah is in known months. Whoever undertook the duty of pilgrimage to Makkah in them, then, there is no sexual intercourse nor disobedience nor dispute during the pilgrimage to Makkah. Whatever good you accomplish, God knows it. Take provision. Then, truly, the best ration is God-consciousness. So, be God-conscious, O those imbued with intuition! **2:197**
There is no blame on you that you be looking for grace from your Lord. When you pressed on from Arafat, then remember God at the Sacred Monument. Remember Him as He guided you, although you had been before this, certainly, of the ones who go astray. **2:198**
Again, press on from where humanity pressed on, and ask God for forgiveness. Truly, God is Forgiving, Compassionate. **2:199**

God has made the pilgrimage to His sacred House obligatory upon you which is the turning point for the people who go to it as beasts or pigeons go towards spring water. God, the Almighty, made it a sign of their supplication before His Greatness and their acknowledgment of His Dignity. He selected from among His creation those who, upon listening to His call, responded to it and bore witness to His word. They stood in the position of His Prophets and resembled His angels who surround the Divine Throne securing all the benefits of performing His worship and hastening towards His promised forgiveness. God the Almighty made His sacred House an emblem for Islam and an object of respect for those who turn to it. He made pilgrimage to it obligatory and laid down its claim for which He held you responsible to discharge. Thus, God the Almighty said: ... *Truly the first House to be set in place for humanity is at Bekka, that which is blessed and a guidance for the worlds.* (Q3:96-97). Sermon 1

When you satisfied your devotional acts, then, remember God like your remembrance of your fathers, or a stauncher remembrance. Among humanity are some who say: Our Lord! Give to us in the present! For him, there is no apportionment in the world to come! **2:200**

Praise belongs to God (Q1:2) who made praise the Key for His remembrance, a means for increase of His bounty and a guide for His Attributes and Dignity. Sermon 157

Among them are some who say: Our Lord! Give us benevolence in the present and benevolence in the world to come and protect us from the punishment of the fire! **2:201**

Every period in this world has an end and every living being in it is to die. Sermon 99

Those, for them is a share of what they earned. God is Swift at reckoning. **2:202**

O God's human being! Be God-conscious! Be God-conscious in the matter of your own selves, which are the most beloved and dear to you, because God has clarified to you the way of truthfulness and lit its paths. You may choose either ever-present misfortune or eternal happiness. Sermon 157

Remember God during numbered days. So, whoever hastened on in two days, then, there is no sin on him. Whoever remained behind, then, there is no sin on him. For whoever was God-conscious, be God-conscious. Know that to Him you will be assembled. **2:203**

The God-conscious believer kept his mind alive and killed the desires of his heart until his body became thin, his bulk turned light and an effulgence of extreme brightness shone for him. It lighted the way for him and took him on the right path. Different doors led him to the door of safety and the place of his permanent stay. His feet, balancing his body, became fixed in the position of safety and comfort because he kept his heart in good acts and pleased his God. Sermon 219

Among humanity is one whose sayings impress ***you*** *about this present life and he calls to God to witness what is in his heart while he is most stubborn in altercation.* **2:204**

He who has Heaven and Hell in his view has no other aim. He who attempts and acts quickly succeeds, while the seeker who is slow may also entertain hope. He who falls short of action faces destruction in Hell. Misleading paths are on both the right and the left. Only the middle way is the right path which is the Everlasting Book and the traditions of *the Prophet* (Q7:158), peace and the mercy of God be upon him. From it the *sunna* has spread and towards it is the eventual return. He who claims otherwise is ruined. He who concocts falsehood is disappointed. He who opposes right is destroyed. It is enough ignorance for a person not to know himself. He who is strong rooted in God-consciousness is not destroyed. The plantation of a people based on God-consciousness never remains without water. Hide yourselves in your houses. Reform yourselves. Repent. One should praise only God and condemn only one's self. Sermon 16

When he turned away, he hastened about the earth so that he makes corruption in and on it, and he causes the cultivation and stock to perish, but God loves not corruption. **2:205**

Corruption has become manifest ... (Q30:41) There is no one to oppose and change it, nor anyone to dissuade from it or desist from it. Sermon 129

When it was said to him: Be God-conscious! Vainglory took him to sin. So, hell is enough for him! Certainly, it will be a miserable Final Place! **2:206**

Certainly, God the Almighty tries His creatures who are vain about themselves through His beloved persons who are humble in their eyes. Sermon 192

Among humanity is he who sells himself looking for the goodwill of God, and God is Gentle with His servants. **2:207**

I bear witness that *Muhammad* (Q48:29), peace and the mercy of God be upon him, is *His servant* (Q17:1), and *Prophet.* (Q7:158) God sent him with the illustrious religion, effective emblem, the Guarded Tablet, effulgent light, sparkling gleam and decisive injunction in order to dispel doubts, present clear proof, administer warning through signs and warn of punishments. Sermon 2

O those who believed! Enter into peacefulness collectively and follow not the steps of Satan. Truly, he is a clear enemy to you. **2:208**

Although Satan had said so only by guessing about the unknown future and by wrong conjecturing, yet the sons of vanity, the brothers of haughtiness and the horsemen of pride and intolerance proved him to be true, so much so that when disobedient persons from among you bowed before him, his greed concerning you gained strength. What had been a hidden secret turned into a clear fact. He spread his full control over you.... Sermon 192

But if you slipped after drew near you the clear portents, then, know that God is Almighty, Wise. **2:209**

God, the Almighty, cannot let a human being enter the Garden if he does the same thing for which God turned out from it an angel. His command for the inhabitants in the sky and of the earth is the same. There is no friendship between God and any individual out of His creation so as to give him license for an undesirable thing which He has held unlawful for all the worlds. Sermon 192

So, do they look on but that God approach them in the overshadowing of cloud shadows? And the angels? The command would be decided. Commands are returned to God. **2:210**

Be aware! The earth which bears you and the sky which overshadows you are obedient to their Sustainer (God). They have not been bestowing their blessings on you for any feeling of pity on you or inclination towards you, nor for any good which they expect from you, but they were commanded to bestow benefits on you. They are obeying and were asked to maintain your good and so they are maintaining it. Sermon 143

Ask the Children of Jacob how many a sign, a clear portent, We gave them. Whoever substitutes the divine blessing of God after it drew near him, then, truly, God is Severe in repayment. **2:211**
Made to appear pleasing to those who were ungrateful is this present life, and they deride those

who believed. But those who were God-conscious will be above them on the Day of Resurrection. God provides for whomever He wills without reckoning. **2:212**

No person rejoices in this world, but tears come to him after it. No one is comforted in the front, but he has to face hardships in the rear. No one receives the light rain of ease in it, but the heavy rain of distress pours upon him. It is just worthy of this world that in the morning it supports a person, but in the evening it does not recognize him. If one side of it is sweet and pleasant, the other side is bitter and distressing. Sermon 111

Humanity had been of one community. Then, God raised up the Prophets, ones who give good tidings and ones who warn. With them He caused the Book to descend with The Truth to give judgment among humanity about what they were at variance in it. None were at variance in it but those who were given it after the clear portents drew near them because of their insolence to one another. Then, God guided those who believed to The Truth—about what they were at variance in it—with His permission. God guides whom He wills to a straight path. **2:213**

I bear witness that He is just and does justice. He is the arbiter Who decides between right and wrong. I also bear witness that *Muhammad* (Q48:29), peace and the mercy of God be upon him, is *His servant,* (Q17:1), *His Messenger* (Q3:101), and the Chief of His creatures.... Be aware! Surely God, the Almighty, has provided for virtue those who are suited to it, for truth pillars that support it and for obedience protection against deviation. In every matter of obedience you will find the Almighty God's help that will speak through tongues and accord firmness to hearts. It has sufficiency for those who seek sufficiency and a cure for those who seek to be cured. Sermon 214

Or assumed you that you would enter the Garden while approaches you not the likeness of those who passed away before you? Desolation and tribulation afflicted them. They are so convulsed that even the Messenger says, and those who believed with him: When will there be help from God? No doubt, truly, the help of God is Near. **2:214**

In the Garden there are various degrees of excellence and different places of stay. Its blessings never end. He who stays in it will never depart from it. He who is endowed with everlasting abode in it will not grow old and its resident will not face want. Sermon 86

They ask **you** *what they should spend. Say: Whatever you spent for good is for the ones who are your parents and the nearest kin and the orphans and the needy and the traveler of the way. Whatever good you accomplish, then, truly, God is Knowing of it.* **2:215**

You spend no wealth in the cause of Him Who gave it, nor do you risk your lives for the sake of Him Who created them. You enjoy honor through God among His creatures, but you do not honor God among His creatures. You should derive lessons from your occupying the places of those who were before you and from the departure of your nearest brothers. Sermon 117

Fighting was prescribed for you although it is disliked by you. Perhaps you dislike a thing and it is good for you. Perhaps you love a thing, and it is worse for you. God knows and, truly, you know not. **2:216**

The best means by which seekers of nearness to God, the Almighty, the Exalted, seek nearness is the belief in Him and His Prophet, struggling in His cause.... Sermon 110

They ask **you** *about the Sacred Month and fighting in it. Say: Fighting in it is deplorable and barring from the way of God and ingratitude to Him. To bar from the Masjid al-Haram, and expelling people from it are more deplorable with God. Persecution is more deplorable than killing. They cease not to fight you until they repel you from your way of life, if they are able. Whoever of you goes back on his way of life, then, dies while he is one who is ungrateful, those, their actions were fruitless in the present and in the world to come. Those will be the Companions of the Fire. They are ones who will dwell in it forever.* **2:217**

O people! Look at the world like those who abstain from it and turn away from it. By God, it would shortly turn out its inhabitants and cause grief to the happy and the safe. That which turns and goes away from it never returns. That which is likely to come about is not known or anticipated. Its joy is mingled with grief. Herein people's firmness inclines towards weakness and languidness. The majority of what pleases you here should not mislead you because that which would help you would be little. God may shower His mercy on him who ponders and takes lesson thereby, and when he takes lesson he achieves enlightenment. Whatever is present in this world would shortly not exist, while whatever is to exist in the next world is already in existence. Every countable thing would pass away. Every anticipation should be taken to be coming up and everything that is to come up should be taken as just near. Sermon 103

Truly, those who believed and those who emigrated and struggled in the way of God, those hope for the mercy of God. God is Forgiving, Compassionate. **2:218**

He has appreciated their actions and praised their position. They call Him and breathe in the air of forgiveness. They are ever needy of His bounty and remain humble before His greatness. The length of their grief has pained their hearts, the length of weeping, their eyes. They knock at every door of inclination towards God. They ask Him Whom generosity does not make destitute and from Whom those who approach Him are not disappointed. Sermon 221

They ask **you** *about intoxicants and gambling. Say: In both of them there is deplorable sin and profits for humanity. Their sin is more deplorable than what is profitable. They ask* **you** *how much they should spend. Say: The extra. Thus, God makes manifest His signs to you so that perhaps you will reflect* **2:219**

on the present and the world to come. They ask **you** *about orphans. Say: Making things right for them is better. If you intermix with them, then they are your brothers/sisters. God knows the one who makes corruption from the one who makes things right. If God willed, He would have overburdened you. Truly, God is Almighty, Wise.* **2:220**

You, O people of Arabia, will be victims of calamities which have come near. You should avoid the intoxication of wealth, fear the disasters of chastisement, keep steadfast in the darkness and crookedness of mischief when its hidden nature discloses itself, its secrets become manifest and its axis and the pivot of its rotation gain strength. It begins in imperceptible stages but develops into great hideousness. Its youth is like the youth of an adolescent and its marks are like the marks of beating by stone. Sermon 151

Marry not ones who are female polytheists until they believe. The one who is a believing, female bond servant is better than the one who is a female polytheist even if she impressed you and wed not the ones who are male polytheists until they believe. One who is a believing, male bond servant is better than the one who is a male polytheist even if he impressed you. Those call you to the fire while God calls you to the Garden and to forgiveness with His permission. He makes manifest His signs to humanity so that perhaps they will recollect. 2:221

Everything submits to Him. Everything exists by Him. He is the satisfaction of every poor, dignity of the low, energy for the weak and shelter for the oppressed. Whoever speaks, He hears his speaking. Whoever keeps quiet, He knows his secret. On Him is the livelihood of everyone who lives. To Him returns whoever dies. Sermon 108

They ask **you** *about menstruation. Say: It is an impurity, so withdraw from your wives during menstruation. Come not near them (f) until they cleanse themselves. Then when they (f) cleansed themselves, approach them (f) as God commanded you. Truly, God loves the contrite and He loves the ones who cleanse themselves.* 2:222
Your wives are a place of cultivation for you, so approach your cultivation whenever you willed and put forward for yourselves. Be God-conscious. Know that you will be one who encounters Him. Give **you** *good tidings to the ones who believe.* 2:223

O God's human being! Certainly, being God-conscious has saved the lovers of God from unlawful items and has given His dread to their hearts until their nights are passed in wakefulness and their noons in thirst. So they achieve comfort through trouble and copious watering through thirst. They regarded death to be near and, therefore, hastened towards good actions. They rejected their desires by keeping death in their sight. Sermon 114

Make God not an obstacle with your sworn oaths to your being good, and being God-conscious, and making things right among humanity. God is Hearing, Knowing. 2:224

O creatures of God! I advise you to be God-conscious because it is the best advice to be mutually given by persons, and the best of all things before God. Sermon 173

God will not take you to task for idle talk in your sworn oaths. Rather, He will take you to task for what your hearts earned. God is Forgiving, Forbearing. 2:225

O My God, melt their hearts as salt melts in water. Sermon 25

For those who vow abstinence from their wives, await four months. Then, if they changed their minds, then, truly, God is Forgiving, Compassionate. 2:226
If they resolved on setting them (f) free, then, truly, God is Hearing, Knowing. 2:227
The women who are to be divorced will await by themselves three menstrual periods. It is not lawful for them (f) that they (f) keep back what God created in their (f) wombs, if they (f) had been believing in God, and the Last Day. Their husbands have better right to come back during that period if they (m) wanted to make things right. For the rights of them (f) in regard to their husbands is the like of rights of their (f) husbands in regard to them (f), as one who is honorable. Men have a degree over them (f). God is Almighty, Wise. 2:228
Setting free is said two times: Then, hold fast to them (f) as one who is honorable or setting them (f) free with kindness. It is not lawful for you that you take anything of what you gave them (f) unless they both fear that they both will not perform the ordinances of God. If you feared that they both will not perform the ordinances of God, then, there is no blame on either of them in what she offered as redemption for that. These are the ordinances of God, so exceed not the limits. Whoever violates the ordinances of God, then, those, they are the ones who are unjust. 2:229
If he divorced her finally, then, she is not lawful to him after that until she marries a spouse other

than him. Then, if that husband divorced her irrevocably, there is no blame on either of them if they return to one another if both of them thought that they will perform within the ordinances of God, and these are the ordinances of God. He makes them manifest for a folk who know. **2:230**

When you divorced wives, and they (f) reached their (f) term, then, hold them (f) back as one who is honorable or set them (f) free as one who is honorable. But hold them (f) not back by injuring them so that you commit aggression. Whoever commits that, then, surely, he did wrong himself. Take not to yourselves the signs of God in mockery. Remember the divine blessing of God on you, and what He caused to descend to you from the Book and wisdom. He admonishes you with it. Be God-conscious and know that God is Knowing of everything. **2:231**

When you revocably divorced wives, and they reached their (f) term, then, place not difficulties for them (f) that they (f) re-marry their former spouses when they agreed among themselves as one who is honorable. This is admonished for him —whoever had been among you who believes in God and the Last Day— that is pure and purer for you. God knows and you know not. **2:232**

O people! Abstinence is to shorten desires, to thank for bounties and to keep away from what is prohibited. If all of this is not possible, then at least what is prohibited should not overpower your patience. Do not forget gratitude when receiving blessings for God has exhausted the excuses before you through clear, shining arguments and open, bright books. Sermon 81

The ones who are mothers will breast feed their (f) children for two years completely for whoever wanted to fulfill breast feeding. On one to whom a child is born is their (f) provision and their clothing (f) as one who is honorable. No soul is placed with a burden, but to its capacity. Neither the one who is a mother be pressed for her child, nor the one to whom a child is born for his child. On one who inherits is the like of that. While if they both wanted weaning by them agreeing together and after consultation, then, there is no blame on either of them. If you wanted to seek wet-nursing for your children, then, there is no blame on you when you handed over what you gave as one who is honorable. Be God-conscious. Know that God is Seeing of what you do. **2:233**

Those of you whom death will call to itself, forsaking spouses, they (f) will await by themselves (f) four months and ten days. When they (f) reached their term, then, there is no blame on you in what they (f) accomplished for themselves (f), as one who is honorable. God is Aware of what you do. **2:234**

There is no blame on you in what you offered with it of a proposal to women, or for what you hid in yourselves. God knew that you will remember them (f), except appoint not with them (f) secretly, unless you say a saying as one who is honorable. Resolve not on the knot of marriage until she reaches her prescribed term. Know that God knows what is within yourselves. So, be fearful of Him. Know that God is Forgiving, Forbearing. **2:235**

Be aware of God against what He has cautioned you. Be God-conscious to the extent that no excuse be needed for it. Act without show or intention of being heard, for if a person acts for other than God, then God entrusts him to that one. We ask God to grant us the positions of the martyrs, company of the virtuous and friendship of the Prophets. Sermon 23

There is no blame on you if you divorced wives whom you touch not, nor undertake a duty to them (f) of a dowry portion. Make provision for them (f). For the one who is wealthy—according to his means—and for the one who is needy —according to his means—with a sustenance, one that

is honorable, an obligation on the ones who are doers of good. **2:236**
If you divorced them (f) before you touch them (f), and you undertook the duty of a dowry portion for them (f), then, half of what you undertook as a duty unless they (f) pardon it or they (m) pardon it in whose hand is the marriage knot. That
they (m) pardon is nearer to God-consciousness. Forget not grace among you. Truly, God is Seeing of what you do. **2:237**

No act is negligible if it is accompanied by God-consciousness. Saying 95

Be watchful of the formal prayers and the middle formal prayer. Stand up as ones who are morally obligated to God. **2:238**

Obey God (Q3:32), and do not disobey Him. When you see virtue adopt it. When you see vice, avoid it. Sermon 167

If you feared, then, pray on foot or as one who is mounted. When you were safe, then, remember God, for He taught you what you be not knowing. **2:239**

Pledge yourself with prayer and remain steady with it. Offer prayer as much as possible and seek nearness to God through it, because it is imposed upon the believers as a timed ordinance: *Truly, the formal prayer had been —for the ones who believe— a timed prescription.* (Q4:103) Sermon 198

Those whom death will call to itself forsaking spouses, will bequeath for their spouses sustenance for a year without expelling them (f). But if they (f) went forth themselves (f), then, there is no blame on you in what they (f) accomplished for themselves (f) as one who is honorable. God is Almighty, Wise. **2:240**

O God's human being! Fear God and anticipate your death by good actions. Purchase everlasting joy by paying transitory things—pleasures of this world. Sermon 64

For ones who are divorced females, sustenance, as one who is honorable. This is an obligation on the ones who are God-conscious. **2:241**
Thus God makes manifest His signs to you so that perhaps you will be reasonable. **2:242**

God sent His Messengers and series of His Prophets to them to guide them to fulfilling the pledges of His creation, to recall to them His bounties, to exhort them by preaching, to unveil before them the hidden virtues of wisdom and show them the signs of His Omnipotence, namely the sky which is raised over them, the earth that is placed beneath them, their means of living that sustains them, their deaths that cause them to die, ailments that turn them old and incidents that successively betake them. Sermon 1

Have **you** *not considered those who went forth from their abodes while they were in the thousands being fearful of death? God said to them: Die! Again, He gave them life. Truly, God is Possessor of Grace for humanity except most of humanity gives not thanks.* **2:243**

Know that this world which you have started to covet and in which you are interested and which sometimes enrages you and sometimes pleases you is not your permanent abode, nor the place of your stay for which you might have been created, nor one to which you have been invited. Know that it will not last for you, nor will you live along with it. If anything out of this world deceives you into attraction, its evils warn you as well. Sermon 173

So, struggle in the Way of God, and know that God is Hearing, Knowing. **2:244**

In struggling for God, give yourself to God. Plant your feet firmly on the ground. Have your eye on the remotest foe and close your eyes to their numbers. Keep sure that help is but from God, the Almighty. Sermon 11

Who is he who will lend God a fairer loan that He will multiply it for him manifold times? God seizes and extends and you are returned to Him. **2:245**

When a man dies, people ask what property he has left while the angels ask what good actions he has sent forward. May God bless you and send forward something. It will be a loan for you. Do not leave everything behind, for that would be a burden on you. Sermon 203

Have ***you*** *not considered the Council of the Children of Jacob after Moses when they said to a Prophet of theirs: Raise up a king for us, and we will fight in the way of God. He said: Perhaps if fighting was prescribed for you, you would not fight. They said: Why should we not fight in the way of God when we were driven out of our abodes with our children. Then, when fighting was prescribed for them, they turned away, but for a few of them. God is Knowing of the ones who are unjust.* **2:246**

Their Prophet said to them: Truly, God raised up for you Saul, a king. They said: How would it be for him to have dominion over us when we have better right to dominion than he, as he is not given plenty of wealth? He said: Truly, God favored him over you, and increased him greatly in the knowledge and the physique. God gives His dominion to whom He wills. God is One Who is Extensive, Knowing. **2:247**

Their Prophet said to them: Truly, a sign of his dominion is that there would approach you the Ark of the Covenant. In it is tranquility from your Lord, and abiding wisdom of what the people of Moses left, and the people of Aaron. The angels will carry it. Truly, in that is a sign for you if you had been ones who believe. **2:248**

So, when Saul set forward with his army he said: Truly, God is One Who Tests you with a river. So, whoever would drink of it, he is not of me, and whoever tastes it not, truly, he is of me, but he who scoops up with a scooping of his hand. So, they drank of it, but a few of them. Then, when he crossed it, he and those who believed with him, they said: There is no energy for us today against Goliath and his armies. Said those who think they truly would be ones who encounter God: How often a faction of a few vanquished a faction of many with the permission of God! God is with the ones who remain steadfast. **2:249**

So, when they departed against Goliath and his armies they said: Our Lord! Pour out patience on us, and make our feet firm, and help us against the folk— the ones who are ungrateful. **2:250**

So, they put them to flight with the permission of God. David killed Goliath. God gave him the dominion and wisdom, and taught him of what He wills. If not for God driving humanity back—some by some others—the earth would have, certainly, gone to ruin, except God is Possessor of Grace to the worlds. **2:251**

These are the signs of God. We recount to ***you*** *The Truth. Truly,* ***you*** *are among the ones who are sent.* **2:252**

Praise belongs to God (Q1:2) Who ... made His creation to populate the world and sent His Messengers towards the jinn and human beings to unveil it for them, to warn them of its harm, to present to them its examples, to show them its defects and to place before them a whole collection of matters containing lessons about the changing of health and sickness in this world, its lawful things and unlawful things and all that God has ordained for the obedient and the disobedient, namely Paradise and Hell and honor and disgrace. I extend my praise to His Being as He desires His creation to praise Him. He has fixed for everything a measure, for every measure a time limit, and for every time limit a document. Sermon 182

These are the Messengers. We gave advantage, some of them over some others. Of them are those to whom God spoke and some of them He exalted in degree. We gave Jesus son of Mary the clear portents and confirmed him with the hallowed Spirit. If God willed, those who were after them have fought one another after the clear portents drew near them, except they were at variance. Some of them believed, while some of them were ones who are ungrateful. If God willed, they would not have fought one another, except God accomplishes what He wants. **2:253**

Know that if you had followed him who was calling you to guidance, he would have made you tread the ways of *the Prophet* (Q7:158), peace and the mercy of God be upon him. Then you would have been spared the difficulties of misguidance. You would have thrown away the crushing burden from your necks. Sermon 167

O those who believed! Spend of what We provided you, before a Day approaches when there is neither trading in it nor friendship nor intercession. The ones who are ungrateful, they are the ones who are unjust. **2:254**

Nothing prevents anyone among you from disclosing to his friend the shortcomings he is afraid of, except the fear that the friend would also disclose to him similar defects. You have decided together on leaving the next world and loving this world. Your religion has become just licking with the tongue. It is like the work of one who has finished his job and secured satisfaction of his master. Sermon 113

God! There is no god but He, The Living, The Eternal. Neither slumber takes Him nor sleep. To Him belongs whatever is in the heavens and whatever is in and on the earth. Who will intercede with Him but with His permission? He knows what is in front of them and what is behind them. They will not comprehend anything of His knowledge, but what He willed. His Seat encompassed the heavens and the earth, and He is not hampered by their safe-keeping. He is The Lofty, The Sublime. **2:255**

We do not know the reality of **Your** greatness except that we know that **You** are *The Living, the Eternal. Neither slumber takes Him nor sleep.* (Q2:255) Sermon 160

There is no compulsion in the way of life. Surely, right judgment became clear from error. So, whoever disbelieves in false deities and believes in God, then, surely, he held fast to the most firm handhold. It is not breakable. God is Hearing, Knowing. **2:256**

O my God! We seek **Your** protection from turning away from **Your** command or revolting against **Your** religion,or being led away by our desires instead of by guidance that comes from **You**. Sermon 215

God is The Protector of those who believed. He brings them out from the shadows into the light. Those who were ungrateful, their protectors are false deities. They bring them out from the light into the shadows. Those will be the Companions of the Fire. They are ones who will dwell in it forever. **2:257**

Generosity is the protector of honor. Forbearance is the bridle of the fool. Forgiveness is the levy of success. Disregard is the punishment of him who betrays. Consultation is the chief way of guidance. He who is content with his own opinion faces danger. Endurance braves calamities while impatience is a helper of the hardships of the world. The best contentment is to give up desires. Many a slavish mind is subservient to overpowering longings. Capability helps preservation of experience. Love means well-utilized relationships. Do not trust one who is grieved. Hadith 211

Have ***you*** *not considered him who argued with Abraham about his Lord because God gave him dominion? Mention when Abraham said: My Lord is He Who gives life and causes to die. He said: I give life and cause to die. Abraham said: Truly, God brings the sun from the East, so bring* ***you*** *the sun from the West! Then, he who was ungrateful was dumfounded. God guides not the unjust folk.* **2:258**

Everything submits to Him. Everything exists by Him. Sermon 108

Or like the one who passed by a town and it was one that has fallen down into ruins. He said: How will God give life to this after its death? So, God caused him to die for a hundred years. Again, He raised him up. He said: How long had ***you*** *lingered in expectation? He said: I lingered in expectation for a day or some part of a day. He said: Nay.* ***You*** *had lingered in expectation a hundred years. Then look on* ***your*** *food and* ***your*** *drink. They are not spoiled. Look on* ***your*** *donkey. We made* ***you*** *a sign for humanity. Look on the bones, how We set them up. Again, We will clothe them with flesh. So, when it became clear to him, he said: I know that God is Powerful over everything.* **2:259**

He did not create things from eternal matter, nor after ever-existing examples, but He created whatever He created. Then He fixed limits thereto. He shaped whatever He shaped and gave the best shape thereto. Nothing can disobey Him, but the obedience of something is of no benefit to Him. His knowledge about those who died in the past is the same as His knowledge about the remaining survivors. His knowledge about whatever there is in the high skies is like His knowledge of whatever there is in the low earth. Sermon 163

Mention when Abraham said: My Lord! Cause me to see how ***You*** *will give life to the dead. He said: Will* ***you*** *not believe? He said: Yea, but so my heart be at rest. He said: Again, take four birds, and twist them to thyself. Again, lay a part of them on every mountain. Again, call to them. They will approach* ***you*** *coming eagerly. Know* ***you*** *that God is Almighty, Wise.* **2:260**

He produces affection among inimical things. He fuses together diverse things, brings near remote things and separates things which are joined together. He is not confined by limits, nor counted by numbers. Material parts can surround things of their own kind, and organs can point out things similar to themselves. Sermon 186

A parable of those who spend their wealth in the way of God is like a parable of a grain. It puts forth seven ears of wheat. In every ear of wheat, a hundred grains. God multiplies for whom He wills. God is One Who is Extensive, Knowing. **2:261**

Do not forget God, struggle in His cause with your tongue, with your wealth and with your lives. Letter 47

Those who spend their wealth in the way of God and, again, pursue not what they spent with re-

proachful reminders nor injury, the compensation for them is with their Lord. There will be neither fear in them nor will they feel remorse. **2:262**

You spend no wealth in the cause of Him Who gave it, nor do you risk your lives for the sake of Him Who created them. You enjoy honor through God among His creatures, but you do not honor God among His creatures. You should derive lessons from your occupying the places of those who were before you and from the departure of your nearest brothers. Sermon 117

An honorable saying and forgiveness are better than charity succeeded by injury. God is Sufficient, Forbearing. **2:263**

Praise to God, Who is the First before every first and the Last after every last. His Firstness necessitates that there is no other first before Him and His Lastness necessitates that there is no other last after Him. *I bear witness that there is no god, but He* (Q2:163), both openly as well as secretly, with heart as well as with tongue. Sermon 101

O those who believed! Render not untrue your charities with reproachful reminders nor injury like he who spends of his wealth to show off to humanity, and believes not in God and the Last Day. His parable is like the parable of a smooth rock. Over it is earth dust. A heavy downpour lit on it, and left it bare. They have no power over anything of what they earned and God guides not the ungrateful folk. **2:264**

If there is plenty of wealth and money in this world, then a person finds himself in such a whirlpool of worries that he loses his joy and peace of mind. However, if there is want and poverty, he is ever crying for wealth. He who hankers after this world, there is no limit for his desires. If one wish is fulfilled, the desire for fulfillment of another wish crops up. This world is like the reflection. If you run after it, then it will itself run forward, but if you leave it and run away from it, then it follows you. In the same way, if a person does not run after the world, the world runs after him. The implication is that if a person breaks the clutches of greed and avarice and keeps aloof from undesirable hankering after the world, he too receives pleasures of the world. He does not remain deprived of them. Sermon 81

The parable of those who spend their wealth looking for the goodwill of God and for confirming their souls is like the parable of a garden on a hillside. A heavy downpour lit on it. Then, it gave its harvest double. Even if lights not on it a heavy downpour, then a dew. God is Seeing of what you do. **2:265**

You should try for the release of your necks before their mortgage is foreclosed, keep your eyes awake at night, make your bellies lean, use your feet, spend your money, take your bodies and spend them over yourselves, and do not be miserly about them, because God the Almighty has said: *If you help God, He will help you and make firm your feet.* (Q47:7) Sermon 183

Would anyone of you wish that he have a garden of date palm trees and grapevines beneath which rivers run with all kinds of fruits in it for him? Then, old age lit on him, and he had weak offspring. Then, a whirlwind lit on it in which there is a fire. Then, it was consumed. Thus, God makes manifest His signs for you so that perhaps you will reflect. **2:266**

God is such that all signs of existence bear witness to Him until the denying mind also believes in Him. God is sublime beyond what is described by those who liken Him to things or those who deny Him. Sermon 49

O those who believed! Spend of what is good that you earned, and from what We brought out for you from the earth. Aim not at getting the bad of it to spend while you would not be ones who take it, but you would close an eye to it. Know that God is Sufficient, Worthy of Praise. **2:267**

Praise belongs to God (Q1:2) for Whom one condition does not proceed another so that He may be the First before being the Last or He may be Outward or Manifest before being Inward or Hidden. Anyone called one except Him is by virtue of being small in number. Anyone enjoying honor other than Him is humble. Any powerful person other than Him is weak. Any master other than Him is a servant. Sermon 65

Satan threatens you with poverty and commands you to depravity; whereas God promises you His forgiveness from Himself and His grace. God is One Who is Extensive, Knowing. **2:268**

You should take a lesson from what God did with Satan. Namely, He nullified his great acts and extensive efforts on account of the vanity of one moment, although Satan had worshipped God for six thousand years—whether by the reckoning of this world or of the next world is not known. Who now can remain safe from God after Satan by committing a similar disobedience? None at all. Sermon 192

He gives wisdom to whom He wills. Whomever is given wisdom, then, surely, was given much good and none recollects no doubt but those imbued with intuition. **2:269**

The Mahdi will be wearing the armor of wisdom which he will have secured with all its conditions such as full attention towards it, its complete knowledge and exclusive devotion to it. For him it is like a thing which he had lost and which he was then seeking or a need which he was trying to fulfill. If Islam is in trouble, he will feel forlorn like a traveler and like a tired camel beating the end of its tail and with its neck flattened on the ground. He is the last of God's proofs and one of the vicegerents of His Prophets. Sermon 182

Whatever of contributions you spent or vows that you vowed, then, truly, God knows it. For the ones who are unjust there is no helper. **2:270**

The gazing of people's eyes is not hidden from Him, nor the repetition of words, nor the glimpse of hillocks, nor the tread of a footstep in the dark night or in the deep gloom, where the shining moon casts its light and the effulgent sun comes in its wake, through its setting and appearing again and again with the rotation of time and periods, by the approach of the advancing night or the passing away of the running day. Sermon 163

If you show your charity, then, how bountiful it is while if you conceal it and give it to the poor, that would be better for you. This absolves you of some of your evil deeds. God is Aware of what you do. **2:271**

Be aware of God against what He has cautioned you. Be God-conscious to the extent that no excuse be needed for it. Act without show or intention of being heard, for if a person acts for other than God, then God entrusts him to that one. We ask God to grant us the positions of the martyrs, company of the virtuous and friendship of the Prophets. Sermon 23

Their guidance is not on ***you****. But God guides whomever He wills. Whatever of good you spend, it is for yourselves. Spend not but looking for the Countenance of God. Whatever of good you spend, your account will be paid to you in full and you will not be wronged.* **2:272**

He whom He guides does not go astray. Sermon 2

Spend for the poor, those who were restrained in the way of God and are not able to travel on the earth. The one who is ignorant assumes them to be rich because of their having reserve. ***You*** *will recognize them by their mark. They ask not persistently of humanity. Whatever of good you spend, then, truly, God is Knowing of that.* **2:273**

One who realizes the reality of return to the next world never betrays. Sermon 41

Those who spend their wealth by nighttime and daytime, secretly or in public, then, for them, their compensation is with their Lord. There will be neither fear in them nor will they feel remorse. **2:274**

Charity is an effective cure, and the actions of people in their present life will be before their eyes in the next life. Hadith 7

Those who consume usury will not arise, but like he who arises whom Satan prostrated by touch. That is because they said: Trading is only like usury and yet God permitted trading and forbade usury. So, whoever drew near an admonishment from his Lord and refrained himself, for him is what was past. His command is with God. While whoever reverted, then, those will be the Companions of the Fire. They, ones who will dwell in it forever! **2:275**

Certainly, Satan has made his ways easy for you and wants to unfasten the knots of religion one by one and to cause division among you in place of unity. Keep away from his evil ideas and enchantments. Accept good advice of one who offers it to you. Preserve it in your minds. Sermon 121

God eliminates usury, and He causes charity to increase. God loves not any sinful ingrate. **2:276**

Whoever trades without knowing the rules of religious law will be involved in usury. Hadith 447

Truly, those who believed and did as the ones in accord with morality and performed the formal prayer and gave the purifying alms, for them, their compensation is with their Lord. There will be neither fear in them nor will they feel remorse. **2:277**

Where are the seekers of virtue? The paths have already been determined. They have been given the news. For every misguidance, there is a cause. For every breaking of a pledge, there is a misrepresentation. By God, I shall not be like him who listens to the voice of mourning, hears the man who brings news of death and also visits the mourner, yet does not take a lesson. Sermon 14

O those who believed! Be God-conscious. Forsake what remained of usury, if you had been ones who believe. **2:278**

But if you accomplish it not, then, give ear to war from God and His Messenger. If you repented, you will have your principal capital, doing no wrong to others nor will you be wronged. **2:279**

Every one of you has to bear his own burden. It has been kept light for the ignorant. God is Merciful. Faith is straight. *The Prophet* (Q7:158), peace and the mercy of God be upon him, is the holder of knowledge. Sermon 149

If a debtor had been possessing adversity, a respite until a time of ease and prosperity. It is better

for you that you be charitable, if you had been knowing. **2:280**
Be God-conscious of a Day on which you are returned to God. Again, every soul will be paid its account in full for what it earned, and they will not be wronged. **2:281**

How appropriate are these illustrations and effective admonitions, provided they are received by pure hearts, open ears, firm views and sharp wits. Be God-conscious like him who listened to good advice and bowed before it. Sermon 82

O those who believed! When you contracted a debt for a term—that which is determined—then, write it down. Let one who is a scribe write it down between you justly. One who is a scribe should not refuse to write it down as God taught him. So, let him write down and let the debtor dictate. Let him be God-conscious, his Lord, and diminish not anything out of it. But if the debtor had been mentally deficient, or weak, or not able to dictate himself, then, let his protector dictate justly. Call two witnesses to bear witness from among your men. Or if there are not two men, then a man and two women, with whom you are well-pleased as witnesses, so that if one of them (f) goes astray, then, the other one of the two will remind her. The witnesses will not refuse when they were called. Grow not weary that you write it down, be it small or great, with its term. That is more equitable with God and more upright for testimony, and likelier not to be in doubt unless it be a trade, that which is transferred at the time—to give and take among yourselves. Then, there is no blame on you if you not write it down. Call witnesses when you have a transaction. Let neither one who is a scribe nor witness be pressed. If you accomplish that, then, it is, truly, disobedience on your part. So, be God-conscious. God teaches you. God is Knowing of everything. **2:282**

We bear witness that *there is no god, but He.* (Q3:2) Sermon 100

If you had been on a journey and find no one who is a scribe, then, a guarantee of that which is held in hand. But if any of you entrusted to another, then, let who was trusted give back his trust and let him be God-conscious, his Lord, and keep not back testimony. He who keeps back, he, then, truly, his heart is one that is perverted. God is Knowing of what you do. **2:283**

He knows all that breasts contain or eyes hide. Sermon 192

To God belongs what is in the heavens and in and on the earth. Whether you show what is within yourselves, or conceal it, God will make a reckoning with you for it. He will forgive whom He wills. He will punish whom He wills. God is Powerful over everything. **2:284**

O my God! Forgive me. **You** know more about me than I do. If I return to sin, **You** return to forgiveness. My God, forgive me what I had promised to myself, but **You** did not find its fulfillment with me. My God, forgive me that with what I sought nearness to **You** with my tongue, but my heart opposed and did not perform. My God, forgive me winking of the eye, vile utterances, desires of the heart and errors of speech. Sermon 78

The Messenger believed in what was caused to descend to him from his Lord as do the ones who believe. All believed in God and His angels and His Books and His Messengers saying: We separate and divide not among anyone of His Messengers. They said: We heard and we obeyed, so grant ***Your*** *forgiveness, Our Lord! To* ***You*** *is the Homecoming.* **2:285**

Certainly, prayer drops out sins like the dropping of leaves of trees and removes them as ropes are removed from the necks of cattle. *The Messenger of God* (Q48:29), the peace and mercy of God he upon him, likened it to a hot bath situated at the door of a person who bathes in it five times a day. Will then any dirt remain on him? Sermon 199

God places not a burden on a soul beyond its capacity. For it is what it earned and against it is what it deserved. Our Lord! Take us not to task if we forgot or made a mistake. Our Lord! Burden us not with a severe test like that which ***You*** *had burdened those who were before us. Our Lord! Load us not such that we have no energy for it and pardon us and forgive us and have mercy on us.* ***You*** *are our Defender so help us against the folk, the ones who are ungrateful.* **2:286**

God has placed on you some obligations which you should not ignore, laid down for you limits which you should not transgress and prohibited you from certain things which you should not violate. He has kept silent about certain things, but has not left them out through forgetfulness. Hadith 105

CHAPTER 3: THE FAMILY OF IMRAN (Āl-i ᶜImrān)

Alif Lam Mim **3:1**
God! There is no god but He, The Living, The Eternal. **3:2**

Praise to God, Who is the First before every first and the Last after every last. His Firstness necessitates that there is no other first before Him and His Lastness necessitates that there is no other last after Him. I bear witness that *there is no god, but He* (Q3:2) both openly as well as secretly, with heart as well as with tongue. Sermon 101

He sent down to ***you*** *the Book with The Truth, that which establishes as true what was before it. He caused to descend the Torah and the Gospel* **3:3**
before this as a guidance for humanity. He caused to descend the Criterion between right and wrong. Truly, those who were ungrateful for the signs of God, for them is a severe punishment. God is Almighty, Possessor of Requital. **3:4**

God, the Almighty has sent down a guiding Book wherein He has explained virtue and vice. You should adopt the course of virtue whereby you will have guidance, and keep aloof from the direction of vice so that you remain on the right way. Sermon 167

Truly, God, nothing is hidden from Him in or on the earth nor in heaven. **3:5**

We praise Him for whatever He takes or gives or whatever He inflicts on us or tries us with. He is aware of all that is hidden and He sees all that is concealed. He knows all that breasts contain or eyes hide. We render evidence that *there is no god, but He* and that Muhammad, peace and the mercy of God be upon him, has been chosen by Him and deputized by Him—evidence tendered both secretly and openly, by heart and by tongue. Sermon 132

It is He Who forms you in the wombs how He wills. There is no god but He, Almighty, Wise. **3:6**

Praise to God, Who is the First before every first and the Last after every last. His Firstness necessitates that there is no other first before Him and His Lastness necessitates that there is no other last after Him. I do bear witness that *there is no god but God* (Q47:19), both openly as well as secretly, with heart as well as with tongue. Sermon 101

It is He who caused the Book to descend to ***you****. In it are signs, ones that are definitive. They are the essence of the Book and others, ones that are unspecific. Then, those whose hearts are swerving, they follow what was unspecific in it, looking for dissent and looking for an interpretation, but none knows its interpretation but God and the ones who are firmly rooted in knowledge say: We believed* *in it as all is from our Lord. None recollects, but those imbued with intuition.* 3:7

In God's authority lies the safety of your affairs. Therefore, render Him such obedience as is neither blameworthy, nor insincere. By God, you must do so otherwise God will take away from you the power of Islam and will never thereafter return it to you until it reverts to others. Sermon 169

Our Lord! Cause our hearts not to swerve after ***You*** *had guided us. Bestow on us mercy from that which proceeds from* ***Your*** *Presence. Truly,* ***You, You*** *alone are The Giver.* 3:8

O My God, melt their hearts as salt melts in water. Sermon 25

Our Lord! Truly, ***You*** *are One Who Gathers humanity on a Day in which there is no doubt in it. Truly, God breaks not His solemn declaration.* 3:9

How appropriate are these illustrations and effective admonitions, provided they are received by pure hearts, open ears, firm views and sharp wits. Sermon 82

Truly, those who were ungrateful, it will not avail them—neither their wealth nor their children—against God at all. Those, they will be fuel for the fire, 3:10
in like manner of the people of Pharaoh and those who were before them. They denied Our signs so God took them because of their impiety. God is Severe in repayment. 3:11

O Kumayl, knowledge is better than wealth. Knowledge guards you while you must guard wealth. Wealth diminishes as it is spent. Knowledge increases as it is disbursed. The results of wealth disappear with the disappearance of wealth. Saying 146

Say to those who were ungrateful: You will be vanquished and you will be assembled into hell. It will be a miserable Final Place. 3:12

Where are the minds which seek light from the lamps of guidance and the eyes which look at minarets of God-consciousness? Where are the hearts dedicated to God and devoted to the obedience of God? Sermon 144

Surely, there had been a sign for you in the two factions who met one another—one faction fights in the way of God and the other as ones who are ungrateful, whom they see twice the like of visibly in their eyes. God confirms with His help whom He wills. Truly, in this is a lesson for those imbued with insight. 3:13

In struggling for God, give yourself to God. Plant your feet firmly on the ground. Have your eye on the remotest foe. Close your eyes to their numbers. Rest assured that help is but from God, the Almighty. Sermon 11

Made to appear pleasing to humanity was the cherishing of lust: From women and children and that which is heaped up heaps of gold and silver and horses, ones that are distinguished, and flocks and cultivation, that is the enjoyment of this present life, while God, with Him is the goodness of the Destination. 3:14

No one secures enjoyment from its freshness, but he has to face hardship from its calamities. No one would pass the evening under the wing of safety, but that his morning would be under the feathers of the wing-tip of fear. It is deceitful, and all that is there in it is deception. It is perishable and all that is on it is to perish. There is no good in its provisions except in God-consciousness. Whoever takes little from it collects much of what would give him safety, while one who takes much from it takes much of what would ruin him. He would shortly depart from his collection. How many people relied on it, but it distressed them. How many felt peaceful with it, but it tumbled them down. How many were prestigious, but it made them low. How many were proud, but it made them disgraceful. Sermon 111

Say: Shall I tell you of better than that? For those who were God-conscious, with their Lord are Gardens beneath which rivers run. They are ones who will dwell in them forever with purified spouses and contentment from God. God is Seeing His servants, **3:15**
those who say: Our Lord! Truly, we believed, so forgive us our impieties and protect us from the punishment of the fire: **3:16**

Among the God-conscious are the people of distinction. Their speech is to the point. Their dress is moderate. Their gait is humble. They keep their eyes closed to what God has made unlawful for them. They put their ears to that knowledge which is beneficial to them. They remain in the time of trials as though they remain in comfort. If there had not been fixed periods of life ordained for each, their spirits would not have remained in their bodies even for the twinkling of an eye because of their eagerness for the reward and fear of chastisement. The greatness of the Creator is seated in their heart, and so everything else appears small in their eyes. Thus, to them Paradise is as though they see it and are enjoying its favors. To them, Hell is also as if they see it and are suffering punishment in it. Sermon 193

The ones who remain steadfast and the ones who are sincere and the ones who are morally obligated and the ones who are expenders in the way of God and the ones who ask for forgiveness at the breaking of the day. **3:17**

In struggling for God, give yourself to God. Plant your feet firmly on the ground. Have your eye on the remotest foe and close your eyes to their numbers. Keep sure that help is but from God, the Almighty. Sermon 11

God bore witness that there is no god but He, as do the angels and those imbued with the knowledge, the ones who uphold equity. There is no god but He, The Almighty, The Wise. **3:18**

Praise belongs to God (Q1:2) ... I do bear witness that *there is no god but God* (Q47:19), both openly as well as secretly, with heart as well as with tongue. Sermon 101

Truly the way of life with God is submission to the One God. At variance were those who were given the Book after what had drawn near to them of knowledge out of insolence among themselves, and whoever is ungrateful for the signs of God, then truly God is Swift in reckoning. **3:19**

You are everlasting. There is no end to **You**. **You** are the highest aim. There is no escape from **You**. Sermon 108

So, if they argued with **you***, then say: I submitted my face to God as have those who followed me. Say to those who were given the Book and to the unlettered: Have you submitted to God? If they submitted to God, then, surely, they were truly guided. If they turned away, then, on* **you** *is only delivering the message. God is Seeing of His servants.* **3:20**

God, the Almighty, deputed Muhammad, peace and the mercy of God be upon him, with the truth.... Sermon 198

Truly, those who are ungrateful for the signs of God and kill the Prophets without right and kill those who command to equity from among humanity, then, give ***you*** *to them the good tidings of a painful punishment.* **3:21**

One who has been through the thick and thin of life finds excuses that prevent him from the commands and prohibitions of God. He disregards them, despite his ability to succumb to excuses. He follows the commands of God. Yet, one who has no restraints of religion seizes the opportunity and accepts the excuses for not following the commands of God. Sermon 41

Those, those are they whose actions were fruitless in the present and the world to come. For them there is no one who helps. **3:22**

Whatever is present in this world would shortly not exist, while whatever is to exist in the next world is already in existence. Every countable thing would pass away. Every anticipation should be taken to be coming up and every thing that is to come up should be taken as just near. Sermon 103

Have ***you*** *not considered those who were given a share of the Book? They are called to the Book of God to give judgment between them. Again, a group of people among them turn away and they, they are ones who turn aside.* **3:23**

That is because they said: The fire will not touch us but for numbered days. They were deluded in their way of life by what they had been devising. **3:24**

There is no doubt that God sent down *the Prophet* (Q7:158), peace and the mercy of God be upon him, as a guide with an eloquent Book and a standing command. No one will be ruined by it except one who ruins himself. Sermon 169

How then will it be when We gathered them on a Day, there is no doubt in it? The account of every soul will be paid in full for what it earned and they, they will not be wronged? **3:25**

Every one of you has to bear his own burden. It has been kept light for the ignorant. God is Merciful. Faith is straight. *The Prophet* (Q7:158), peace and the mercy of God be upon him, is the holder of knowledge. Sermon 149

Say: O God! The One Who is Sovereign of Dominion, ***You*** *have given dominion to whom* ***You*** *willed, and* ***You*** *tore away dominion from whom* ***You*** *willed.* ***You*** *rendered powerful whom* ***You*** *willed, and* ***You*** *abased whom* ***You*** *willed. In* ***Your*** *hand is the good. Truly,* ***You*** *are Powerful over everything.* **3:26**

Be aware! The earth which bears you and the sky which overshadows you are obedient to their Sustainer (God). They have not been bestowing their blessings on you for any feeling of pity on you or inclination towards you, nor for any good which they expect from you, but they were commanded to bestow benefits on you. They are obeying and were asked to maintain your good and so they are maintaining it. Sermon 143

You *caused the nighttime to be interposed into the daytime.* ***You*** *caused the daytime to be interposed into the nighttime.* ***You*** *brought out the living from the dead.* ***You*** *brought out the dead from the living.* ***You*** *provided to whomever* ***You*** *willed without stinting.* **3:27**

He made its sun the bright indication for its day and moon the gloomy indication for its night. He then put them in motion in their orbits and ordained their pace of movement in the stages of their paths in order to distinguish with their help between night and day and in order that the reckoning of years and calculations may be known by their fixed movements. Sermon 91

Let not the ones who believe take to themselves the ones who are ungrateful for protectors instead of the ones who believe. Whoever accomplishes that is not with God in anything, unless it is because you are God-conscious that you are being cautious towards them. God cautions you of Himself. To God is the Homecoming. **3:28**

God ... is aware of whatever is hidden in the hearts and whatever lies behind the unseen. Sermon 192

Say: Whether you conceal what is in your breasts or show it, God knows it and He knows whatever is in the heavens and whatever is in and on the earth. God is Powerful over everything. **3:29**

O my God! **You** are the most attached to **Your** lovers and the most ready to assist those who trust in **You. You** see them in their concealments, know whatever is in their consciences, and are aware of the extent of their intelligence. Consequently, their secrets are open to **You** and their hearts are eager from **You**. If loneliness makes them desolate, **Your** remembrance gives them solace. If distresses befall them, they beseech **Your** protection, because they know that the reins of affairs are in **Your** hands, and that their movements depend upon **Your** commands. Sermon 226

A Day when every soul will find that which is brought forward of good and what it did of evil. It will wish that there be between this and between that a long space of time. God cautions you of Himself. God is Gentle to the servants. **3:30**

Certainly, nothing is viler than evil, except its punishment. Nothing is better than good, except its reward. In this world, everything that is heard is better than what is seen, while everything of the next world that is seen, is better than what is heard. You should satisfy yourself by hearing rather than seeing and by the news of the unknown. You should know that what is little in this world but much in the next is better than what is much in this world but little in the next. In how many cases little is profitable while much causes loss. Sermon 114

Say: If you had been loving God, then, follow me. God will love you and forgive you your impieties. God is Forgiving, Compassionate. **3:31**

This Islam is the religion which God has chosen for Himself, developed it before His eyes, preferred it as the best among His creations, established its pillars on His love. He has disgraced other religions by giving honor to it. He has humiliated all communities before its sublimity. He has humbled its enemies with His kindness and made its opponents lonely by according it His support. He has smashed the pillars of misguidance with its columns. He has quenched the thirst of the thirsty from its cisterns, and filled the cisterns through those who draw its water. Sermon 198

Say: Obey God and the Messenger. Then, if they turned away, then, truly, God loves not the ones who are ungrateful. **3:32**

... abide by what He has commanded in His Book ... for no one prospers except through abiding by them, and no one is wretched except through repudiating and neglecting them. Sermon 191*

Truly, God favored Adam and Noah and the people of Abraham and the people of Imran above all the worlds, **3:33**
some of one another's offspring. God is The Hearing, The Knowing. **3:34**
Mention when the woman of Imran said: My Lord! I vowed to **You** *what is in my womb—that which is dedicated—so receive* **You** *this from me. Truly,* **You, You** *alone are The Hearing, The Knowing.* **3:35**
Then, when she brought forth she said: My Lord! Truly, I brought her forth, a female. God is greater in knowledge of what she brought forth. The male is not like the female. Truly, I named her Mary. Truly, I commend her to **Your** *protection and her offspring from the accursed Satan.* **3:36**
So, her Lord received her with the very best acceptance. Her bringing forth caused the very best to develop in her. Zechariah took charge of her. Whenever Zechariah entered upon her in her sanctuary, he found her with provision. He said: O Mary! From where is this for **you** *(f)? She said: This is from God. Truly, God provides to whom He wills without reckoning.* **3:37**
There Zechariah called to his Lord. He said: My Lord! Bestow on me good offspring from **Your** *Presence. Truly,* **You** *are hearing the supplication.* **3:38**
Then, the angels proclaimed to him while he was one who stands to invoke blessings in the sanctuary that God gives **you** *good tidings of Yahya* (John)*—one who establishes the Word of God as true—a chief and concealer of secrets and a Prophet among the ones in accord with morality.* **3:39**
He said: My Lord! How is it I will have a boy while, surely, I reached old age and my woman is a barren woman. He said: Thus, God accomplishes what He wills. **3:40**
He said: My Lord! Assign a sign for me. He said: **Your** *sign is that* **you** *will not speak to humanity for three days but by gesture and remember* **your** *Lord frequently, and glorify in the evening and early morning.* **3:41**
Mention when the angels said: O Mary! Truly, God favored **you** *(f), and purified* **you** *(f), and favored* **you** *(f) above women of the world.* **3:42**
O Mary! Be **you** *morally obligated to* **your** *Lord and prostrate* **your***self (f) and bow down (f) with the ones who bow down.* **3:43**
That is tidings from the unseen We reveal to **you**. **You** *had not been present with them when they cast their pens as to which of them would take control of Mary, nor had* **you** *been present with them when they strive against one another.* **3:44**
Mention when the angels said: O Mary! Truly, God gives **you** *(f) good tidings of a Word from Him. His name is the Messiah—Jesus son of Mary—well-esteemed in the present and the world to come and among the ones who are brought near.* **3:45**
He will speak to humanity from the cradle and in manhood and be among the ones in accord with morality. **3:46**
She said: My Lord! How is it I will be with child when no mortal touches me? He said: Thus, God creates whatever He wills. When He decreed a command, then, He only says to it: Be! Then, it is! **3:47**
He teaches him the Book and wisdom and the Torah and the Gospel **3:48**
to be a Messenger to the Children of Jacob saying: Surely I drew near you with a sign from your Lord that I will create for you out of clay a likeness of a bird. Then, I will blow into it and it will become a bird with the permission of God. I cure one who is blind from birth and the leper and give life to dead mortals with the permission of God. I tell you what you eat and what you store up in your houses. Truly, in that is a sign for you if you had been ones who believe. **3:49**
I come with that which establishes as true what was before me of the Torah, and permit you some of what was forbidden to you. I drew near you with a sign from your Lord. So, be God-conscious and obey Me. **3:50**

Truly, God is my Lord and your Lord so worship Him. This is a straight path. **3:51**
When Jesus became conscious of their ingratitude, he said: Who are my helpers for God? The disciples said: We will be helpers for God. We believed in God and bear **you** *witness that we are ones who submit to God.* **3:52**
Our Lord! We believed in what **You** *caused to descend. We followed the Messenger so write us down with the ones who bear witness.* **3:53**

If you desire I will tell you about Jesus son of Mary. He used a stone for his pillow, put on coarse clothes and ate rough food. His condiment was hunger. His lamp at night was the moon. His shade during the winter was just the expanse of earth eastward and westward. His fruits and flowers were only what grows from the earth for the cattle. He had no wife to allure him, nor any son to give grief, nor wealth to deviate his attention, nor greed to disgrace him. His two feet were his conveyance and his two hands his servant. Sermon 159

They planned and God planned and God is Best of the ones who plan. **3:54**

We bear witness that *there is no god, but He.* (Q3:2) Sermon 100

Mention when God said: O Jesus! I will be One Who Gathers **you** *and One Who Elevates* **you** *to Myself and One Who Purifies* **you** *from those who were ungrateful, and One Who Makes those who followed* **you** *above those who were ungrateful until the Day of Resurrection. Again, you will return to Me. Then, I will give judgment between you about what you had been at variance in it.* **3:55**
So, as for those who were ungrateful, then, I will punish them with a severe punishment in the present and the world to come. For them there is no one who helps. **3:56**
To those who believed and did as the ones in accord with morality, We will pay them their account with full compensation. God loves not the ones who are unjust. **3:57**
These We recount to **you** *are of the signs and the wise remembrance.* **3:58**
Truly the parable of Jesus with God is like the parable of Adam. He created him from earth dust. Again, He said to him: Be! Then, he is! **3:59**
The Truth is from **your** *Lord, so be not of the ones who contest.* **3:60** ***

Then, to whoever argued with **you** *about it after what drew near* **you** *of the knowledge, say: Approach now! Let us call to our children and your children and our women and your women and ourselves and yourselves. Again we will humbly supplicate, and we lay the curse of God on the ones who lie.* **3:61**

God sent Muhammad, peace and the mercy of God be upon him, with the Truth so that he may take out His people from the worship of idols towards His worship and from obeying Satan towards obeying Him. God sent him with the Quran which He explained and made strong in order that the people may know their Sustainer (God), since they were ignorant of Him, may acknowledge Him, since they were denying Him and accept Him, since they were refusing to believe in Him. Sermon 147

This is, truly, a narrative of The Truth. There is no god but God. Truly, God, He is The Almighty, The Wise. **3:62**

I bear witness that *there is no god but God* (Q47:19), the One. Sermon 2

Then, truly, if they turned away, then, truly, God is Knowing of the ones who make corruption. **3:63**

Had God not taken from the learned a promise that they would not acquiesce in the rapacity of the tyrant nor in the hunger of the oppressed ... I would truly have flung its reins (of the caliphate) back upon its withers ... and you would indeed have discovered that this world of yours is as insignificant to me as that which drips from the nose of a goat. Sermon 3*

Say: O People of the Book! Approach now to a word common between us and between you that we worship none but God and ascribe nothing as partners with Him, that none of us take others to ourselves as lords besides God. If they turned away, then, say: Bear witness that we are ones who submit to God. **3:64**

I submit to His Glory. Sermon 2

O People of the Book! Why argue with one another about Abraham while neither was the Torah caused to descend nor the Gospel until after him. Will you not, then, be reasonable? **3:65**
Lo and behold! You are these who argue with one another about what you have some knowledge. Why then argue with one another about what you have no knowledge? God knows and you know not. **3:66**
Abraham had been neither a Jew nor a Christian, but he had been a monotheist, one who submits to God. He had not been among the ones who were polytheists. **3:67**
Truly, of humanity closest to Abraham are those who followed him and this Prophet and those who believed. God is Protector of the ones who believe. **3:68**

God, the Sublime, says: *Truly, of men the nearest to Abraham are surely those who followed him and this Prophet and those who believe; and God is Protector of the ones who believe.* (Q3:68) Letter 28

A section of the People of the Book wished that they cause you to go astray. They cause none to go astray but themselves, and they are not aware. **3:69**

Be aware of God against what He has cautioned you. Be God-conscious to the extent that no excuse be needed for it. Act without show or intention of being heard, for if a person acts for other than God, then God entrusts him to that one. We ask God to grant us the positions of the martyrs, company of the virtuous and friendship of the Prophets. Sermon 23

O People of the Book! Why be ungrateful for the signs of God while you bear witness? **3:70**

The foremost in religion is the acknowledgment of Him. The perfection of acknowledging Him is to bear witness to Him. The perfection of bearing witness to Him is to believe in His Oneness. The perfection of believing in His Oneness is to regard Him Pure. Sermon 1

O People of the Book! Why confuse you The Truth with falsehood, and keep back The Truth while you know? **3:71**

In regard to a true statement to which a false meaning is attributed.... Sermon 167

A section of the People of the Book said: Believe in what was caused to descend to those who believed at the beginning of the daytime. Disbelieve at the last of the day so that perhaps they will return to disbelief. **3:72**

On us it is obligatory, for your sake, to abide by the Book of God (Quran), the Sublime, and the conduct of *the Prophet* (Q7:158), peace and the mercy of God be upon him, to stand by His rights and to revive his *sunna*. Sermon 169

Believe none, but one who heeded your way of life. Say: Truly guidance is The Guidance from God and believe not that anyone be given the like of what you were given, so that he argue with you before your Lord. Say: Truly, the grace is in the hand of God. He gives it to whomever He wills. God is One Who is Extensive, Knowing. **3:73**

O my God! Whoever listens to our words which are just and which seek the prosperity of religion and the worldly life and do not seek mischief, they reject after listening. He certainly turns away from **Your** support and desists from strengthening **Your** religion. We make **You** a Witness over him. **You** are the greatest of all witnesses. We make all those who inhabit **Your** earth and **Your** skies witness over him. Thereafter, **You** alone can make us needless of his support and question him for his sin. Sermon 212

He singles out for His mercy whom He wills. God is Possessor of Sublime Grace. **3:74**

May God shower His mercy on you! Act according to the clear signs, because the way is straight and leads to the house of safety while you are in the place of seeking God's favor and have time and opportunity. The books of your doings are open and pens of angels are busy recording your actions while your bodies are healthy, tongues are free, repentance is accepted and deeds are accorded recognition. Sermon 94

Among the People of the Book is he who, if ***you*** *entrusted him with a hundredweight, he would give it back to* ***you****. Among them is he who, if* ***you*** *entrusted him with a dinar, he would not give it back to* ***you*** *unless* ***you*** *continued as one who stands over him. That is because they said: There is no way of moral duty on us as to the unlettered. They are lying against God while they, they know.* **3:75**

Yea! Whoever lived up to his compact and was God-conscious, then, truly, God loves the ones who are God-conscious. **3:76**

O God's human being! I advise you to be God-conscious which is the provision for the next world and with it is your return. The provision would take you to your destination and the return would be successful. Sermon 114

Truly, those who exchange the compact of God and their sworn oaths for a little price, those, there is no apportionment for them in the world to come. God will neither speak to them, nor look on them on the Day of Resurrection nor will He make them pure. For them is a painful punishment. **3:77**

There remain a few people in whose case the remembrance of their return to God on the Day of Judgment keeps their eyes bent and the awareness of the Resurrection moves them to tears. Some of them are scared away from the world and disperse. Some are frightened and subdued. Some are quiet as if muzzled. Some are praying sincerely. Some are grief-stricken and pain-ridden whom fear has confined to namelessness. Disgrace has shrouded them, so they are in the sea of bitter water, their mouths are closed and their hearts are bruised. They preached until they were tired. They were oppressed until they were disgraced. They were killed until their numbers dwindled. Sermon 32

Truly, among them is a group of people who distort their tongues with the Book so that you assume it is from the Book, although it is not from the Book. They say: It is from God, although it is not from God. They say a lie against God while they know. **3:78**

Be aware of destroying your manners and changing them, maintaining one tongue. Sermon 176

It had not been for a mortal that God should give him the Book and critical judgment and the prophethood and, again, he say to humanity: Be you servants of me instead of God! Rather, he would say: Be you masters, because you had been teaching the Book and because you had been studying it. **3:79**

They are hankering after this world out of jealousy against him on whom God has bestowed it. So they intend to revert the matters to the pre-Islamic period. Sermon 169

Nor would He command you to take to yourselves the angels and the Prophets as lords. Would He command you to ingratitude after you are ones who submit to God? **3:80**

I bear witness that He is just and does justice. He is the arbiter Who decides between right and wrong. I also bear witness that Muhammad, peace and the mercy of God be upon him, is His servant, *His Messenger* (Q2:279) and the Chief of His creatures.... Sermon 214

Mention when God took a solemn promise from the Prophets: Whatever I gave you of the Book and wisdom, again, if a Messenger drew near you with that which establishes as true what is with you, you will believe in him and you will help him. He said: Are you in accord? Will you take on My severe test? They said: We are in accord. He said: Then, bear witness and I am with you among the ones who bear witness. **3:81**

Then, whoever turned away after this, then, those, they are the ones who disobey. **3:82**

Everything submits to Him. Everything exists by Him. He is the satisfaction of every poor, dignity of the low, energy for the weak and shelter for the oppressed. Whoever speaks, He hears his speaking. Whoever keeps quiet, He knows his secret. On Him is the livelihood of everyone who lives. To Him returns whoever dies. Sermon 108

Desire they other than the way of life of God while to Him submitted whatever is in the heavens and the earth willingly or unwillingly and they are returned to Him? **3:83**

The best means by which seekers of nearness to God, the Almighty, the Exalted, seek nearness, is the belief in Him and His Prophet, struggling in His cause.... Sermon 109

Say: We believed in God and what was caused to descend to us and what was caused to descend to Abraham and Ishmael and Isaac and Jacob and the Tribes and what was given to Moses and Jesus and the Prophets from their Lord. We separate and divide not between anyone of them and we are ones who submit to Him. **3:84**

Whoever be looking for a way of life other than submission to God, it will never be accepted from him. He, in the world to come, will be among the ones who are losers. **3:85**

God sent *Muhammad* (Q48:29), peace and the mercy of God be upon him, with a sufficing plea, a convincing discourse and a rectifying announcement. Through him, God disclosed the ways that had been forsaken and destroyed the innovations that had been introduced. Through him, He explained the detailed commands. *Whoever be looking for a way of life other than submission, it will never be accepted from him.* (Q3:85) His misery is definite. His stick of support will be cracked. His fate will be serious. His end will be long grief and distressing punishment. I trust in God, the trust of bending towards Him. I seek His guidance for the way that leads to His Paradise and takes to the place of His pleasure. Sermon 161

How will God guide a folk who disbelieved after their belief? They bore witness to The Truth of the Messenger after the clear portents drew near them. God guides not the unjust folk. **3:86**

Certainly, God Almighty sent Muhammad, peace and the mercy of God be upon him, as Prophet while no one among the Arabs read the Book, nor claimed prophethood or revelation. He had to fight those who disobeyed him in company with those who followed him, leading them towards their salvation and hastening with them lest death overtook them. When any weary person sighed or a distressed one stopped, he stood with him until he became his aim, except the worst in whom there was no virtue at all. Eventually, he showed them their goal and carried them to their places of deliverance. Consequently, their affairs moved on and their position gained strength. Their spears were straightened. By God, I was among their rear-guard until they turned back on their sides and were flocked in their rope. I never showed weakness or lack of courage, nor did I betray or become languid. By God, I shall split the wrong until I extract right from its flanks. Sermon 104

Those, their recompense is that the curse of God is on them and of the angels and of humanity, one and all, **3:87**

ones who will dwell with it forever. Neither will the punishment be lightened from them, nor will they be given respite. **3:88**

May God bless whoever listens to a point of wisdom and retains it. When he is invited to the right path, he approaches it. He follows a leader by catching his waist band and finds salvation, keeps God before his eyes and fears his sins, performs actions sincerely and acts virtuously, earns the treasure of heavenly rewards, avoids vice, aims at good objectives and reaps recompense, faces his desires and rejects fake hopes, makes endurance the means to his salvation and God-consciousness the provision for his death, rides on the path of honor and sticks to the highway of truth, makes good use of his time and hastens towards the end and takes with him the provision of good actions. Sermon 76

But those who repented after that and made things right, then, truly, God is Forgiving, Compassionate. **3:89**

Be God-conscious like him who listened to good advice and bowed before it. Sermon 82

Truly, those who disbelieved after their belief, again, added to their disbelief. Their remorse will never be accepted. Those, they are the ones who go astray. **3:90**

I praise God, seeking completion of His Blessing, submitting to His Glory and expecting safety from committing sin. Sermon 2

Truly, those who were ungrateful and died when they were ones who are ungrateful, it will not be accepted from anyone of them the earth full of gold, even if he offered it as ransom. Those, for them, is a painful punishment, and for them there is no one who helps. **3:91**

O God's human being! Where are those who were allowed long ages to live? They enjoyed bounty. They were taught. They learned. They were given time. They passed it in vain. They were kept healthy. They forgot their duty. They were allowed a long period of life, were handsomely provided for, were warned of grievous punishment and were promised great rewards. You should avoid sins that lead to destruction and vices that attract the wrath of God. Sermon 82

You will never attain virtuous conduct until you spend of what you love. Whatever thing you spend, truly, God is Knowing of it. **3:92**

The best contentment is to give up desires. Many a slavish mind is subservient to overpowering longings. Capability helps preservation of experience. Love means well-utilized relationship. Do not trust one who is grieved. Hadith 211

All food had been allowed to the Children of Jacob, but what Jacob, Jacob, forbade to himself before the Torah is sent down. Say: Then, approach with the Torah and recount it if you had been ones who are sincere. **3:93**

Then, whoever devised lies against God after that then, those, they are the ones who are unjust. **3:94**

By God, he is not capable of solving the problems that come to him, nor is he fit for the position assigned to him. Whatever he does not know he does not regard as worth knowing. He does not realize that what is beyond his reach is within the reach of others. If anything is not clear to him, he keeps quiet over it, because he knows his own ignorance. Lost lives are crying against his unjust verdicts. Properties that have been wrongly disposed of are grumbling against him. Sermon 17

Say: God was Sincere, so follow the creed of Abraham—a monotheist—and he had not been among the ones who are polytheists. **3:95**

Truly, the first House set in place for humanity was that which is at Bekka, that which is blessed, and a guidance for the worlds. **3:96**

In it are clear portents, signs, the Station of Abraham. Whoever entered it had been one who is safe. To God is a duty on humanity of pilgrimage to the House in Makkah for whoever was able to travel the way to it. Whoever was ungrateful, then truly God is Independent of the worlds. **3:97**

God has made the pilgrimage to His sacred House obligatory upon you which is the turning point for the people who go to it as beasts or pigeons go towards spring water. God, the Almighty, made it a sign of their supplication before His Greatness and their acknowledgment of His Dignity. He selected from among His creation those who, upon listening to His call, responded to it and bore witness to His word. They stood in the position of His Prophets and resembled His angels who surround the Divine Throne securing all the benefits of performing His worship and hastening towards His promised forgiveness. God the Almighty made His sacred House an emblem for Islam and an object of respect for those who turn to it. He made pilgrimage to it obligatory and laid down its claim for which He held you responsible to discharge. Thus, God the Almighty said: ... *Truly the first House to be set in place for humanity is at Bekka, that which is blessed and a guidance for the worlds.* (Q3:96-97). Sermon 1

Say: O People of the Book! Why be ungrateful for the signs of God? God is Witness over what you do. **3:98**

Praise belongs to God (Q1:2) whose worth cannot be described by speakers.... Sermon 1

Say: O People of the Book! Why bar you from the way of God he who believed, desiring crookedness when you are witnesses? God is not One Who is Heedless of what you do. **3:99**

He listens, but not with the holes of the ears or the organs of hearing. He says, but does not utter words. Sermon 186

O those who believed! If you obey a group of people of those who were given the Book, they will repel you after your belief turning you into ones who are ungrateful. **3:100**

Nothing from the earth that he may ask for defies Him, nor does it oppose Him so as to overpower Him. No swift-footed creature can run away from Him so as to surpass Him. He is not needy towards any possessing person so that he should feed Him. All things bow to Him and are humble before His greatness. They cannot flee away from His authority to someone else in order to escape His benefit or His harm. There is no parallel for Him who may match Him and no one like Him so as to equal Him. Sermon 186

How would you be ungrateful when the signs of God are recounted to you, and His Messenger is among you? Whoever cleaves firmly to God was, then, surely guided to a straight path. **3:101**

Certainly, you know my position of close kinship and special relationship with the Prophet of God, peace and the mercy of God be upon him. When I was only a child he took charge of me ... I would follow him as a baby camel follows in the footsteps of its mother. He raised up for me a sign of his noble character every day, ordering me to follow it. Each year he would go into seclusion on Mt. Hira. I saw him. Nobody else saw him. The household was brought together at that time for the religion of Islam, just *the Messenger of God* (Q48:29, peace and the mercy of God be upon him, Khadija and myself as the third. I saw the light of the revelation and the message. I smelt the fragrance of prophecy. He used to press me to his chest and lay me beside him in his bed, bring his body close to mine and make me smell his fragrance. He used to chew something and then feed me with it. He found no lie in my speaking, nor weakness in any act. Sermon 192

O those who believed! Be God-conscious as it is His right that He be feared. Die not but that you be ones who submit to the One God. **3:102**

Hasten towards good actions and dread the suddenness of death.... Hope can be only for that which is to come, while about that which is passed there is only disappointment. *So, Be God-conscious as it is His right that He should be feared and die not but that you be ones who submit to the One God.* (Q3:102) Sermon 113

Cleave firmly to the rope of God altogether and be not split up. Remember the divine blessing of God on you when you had been enemies. Then, He brought your hearts together. You became brothers/sisters by His divine blessing. You had been on the brink of an abyss of the fire and He saved you from it. Thus, God makes manifest to you His signs so that perhaps you will be truly guided. **3:103**

This Quran is the strong rope of God and His trustworthy means. It contains the blossoming of the heart and springs of knowledge. For the spiritual heart, there is no cure better than the Quran, although those who remembered it have passed away while those who forgot or pretended to have forgotten it have remained. If you see any good, give your support to it, but if you see evil, evade it, because *the Messenger of God* (Q48:29) used to say: O son of Adam, do good and evade evil. By doing so you will be treading correctly. Sermon 176

Let there be a community from among you who calls to good and commands to that which is honorable and prohibits that which is unlawful. Those, they are the ones who prosper. **3:104**

God, the Almighty, cannot let a human being enter Paradise if he does the same thing for which God turned out an angel from it. His command for the inhabitants in the sky and of the earth is the same. There is no friendship between God and any individual out of His creation so as to give him license for an undesirable thing that He has held unlawful for all the worlds. Sermon 192

Be not like those who split up and were at variance after the clear portents drew near them. Those, for them is a tremendous punishment **3:105**
on a Day when faces will brighten and faces will cloud over. As for those whose faces cloud over: Disbelieve you after your belief? Then experience the punishment for what you had been ungrateful. **3:106**

Everyone should be God-conscious, should admonish himself, should send forward his repentance and should overpower his desire because his death is hidden from him. His desires deceive him. Satan keeps posted about him. He beautifies his sin for him so that he may commit it. He prompts him to delay repentance until his desires cause him to be the most negligent. Pity is for the negligent person whose life itself would be a proof against him and his own days, passed in sin, will lead him to punishment. Sermon 64

As for those whose faces brightened, they are in the mercy of God. They, ones who will dwell in it forever. **3:107**

May God prompt us and you for His obedience and obedience of His Prophet, and forgive us and you by His great mercy. Sermon 190

These are the signs of God. We recount them to ***you*** *in Truth. God wants not injustice in the worlds.* **3:108**

Be just with God and be just with people giving them what is their due from yourself. Letter 53*

To God belongs whatever is in the heavens and whatever is in and on the earth. To God all commands are returned. **3:109**

Thus, after the tumult of its surges it became tame and overpowered, an obedient prisoner of the shackles of disgrace, while the earth spread itself and became solid in the stormy depth of this water. In this way the earth put an end to the pride, self conceit, high position and superiority of the water and muzzled the intrepidity of its flow. Consequently, it stopped after its stormy flow and settled down after its tumult. Sermon 91

You had been the best community that was brought out for humanity. You command to that which is honorable and prohibit that which is unlawful and believe in God. If the People of the Book believed, it would have been better for them. Some of them are the ones who believe, but most of them are the ones who disobey. **3:110**
They will never injure you but are an annoyance. If they fight you, they will turn their backs on

you. Again, they will not be helped. **3:111**

In struggling for God, give yourself to God. Plant your feet firmly on the ground. Have your eye on the remotest foe and close your eyes to their numbers. Rest assured that help is but from God, the Almighty. Sermon 11

Abasement was stamped on them wherever they were come upon—but those with a rope to God and a rope to humanity—and they drew the burden of anger from God and wretchedness was stamped on them. That is because they had been ungrateful for the signs of God and kill the Prophets without right. That is because they rebelled and had been exceeding the limits. **3:112**

This Quran is the strong rope of God and His trustworthy means. It contains the blossoming of the heart and springs of knowledge. Sermon 176

They are not all the same. Among the People of the Book is a community of ones who are upstanding. They recount the signs of God in the night watch of the night and they, they prostrate themselves. **3:113**

They believe in God and the Last Day and they command that which is honorable and prohibit that which is unlawful and they compete with one another in good deeds. Those are among the ones in accord with morality. **3:114**

The sin that grieves you is better, in the sight of God, than the virtue that makes you proud. Saying 46*

Whatever of good they accomplish will never go unappreciated. God is Knowing of the ones who are God-conscious. **3:115**

Certainly, that which you have been commanded to do is wider than what you have been refrained from. What has been made lawful for you is more than what has been prohibited. Then give up what is less for what is much and what is limited for what is vast. God has guaranteed your livelihood and has commanded you to act. Therefore, the pursuit of that which has been guaranteed to you should not get preference over that whose performance has been enjoined upon you. Sermon 114

Truly, those who were ungrateful never will avail them their wealth nor their children against God at all. Those will be the Companions of the Fire. They are ones who will dwell in it forever. **3:116**

Where are the seekers of virtue? The paths have already been determined. They have been given the news. For every misguidance, there is a cause. For every breaking of a pledge, there is a misrepresentation. By God, I shall not be like him who listens to the voice of mourning, hears the man who brings news of death and also visits the mourner, yet does not take a lesson. Sermon 148

The parable of what they spend in this present life is like the parable of a freezing wind in it that lit on the cultivation of the folk who did wrong themselves and caused it to perish. God did not wrong them, but they do wrong themselves. **3:117**

One who has been through the thick and thin of life finds excuses that prevent him from the commands and prohibitions of God. He disregards them, despite his ability to succumb to excuses. He follows the commands of God. Yet, one who has no restraints of religion seizes the opportunity and accepts the excuses for not following the commands of

God. Sermon 41

O those who believed! Take not to yourselves as close friends other than yourselves. They stop at nothing to ruin you. They wished that misfortune would fall on you. Surely, their hatred showed itself from their mouths and what their breasts conceal is greater. Surely, We made manifest to you the signs if you had been reasonable. **3:118**

Everyone of them is ... alone although they are a group, and they are strangers, even though friends. They are unaware of morning after a night and of evening after a day. The night or the day when they departed has become ever existent for them. They found the dangers of their place of stay more serious than they had apprehended. They witnessed that its signs were greater than they had guessed. Sermon 220

Lo, behold! You are those imbued with love for them, but they love you not. You believed in the Book, all of it. When they met you, they said: We believe. But when they went privately, they bit the tips of their fingers at you in rage. Say: Die in your rage. Truly God is Knowing of what is within the breasts. **3:119**

The Book of God is that through which you see, you speak and you hear. Sermon 132

If benevolence touches you, it raises anger in them, but if an evil deed lights on you, they are glad about it. But if you endure patiently and are God-conscious, their cunning will not injure you at all. Truly, God is One Who Encloses what they do. **3:120**

Certainly, nothing is viler than evil, except its punishment. Nothing is better than good, except its reward. In this world, everything that is heard is better than what is seen, while everything of the next world that is seen, is better than what is heard. You should satisfy yourself by hearing rather than seeing and by the news of the unknown. You should know that what is little in this world but much in the next is better than what is much in this world, but little in the next. In how many cases little is profitable while much causes loss. Sermon 114

When **you** *set forth in the early morning from* **your** *family to place the ones who believe at their positions for fighting, God is Hearing, Knowing.* **3:121**
Mention when two sections are about to lose heart among you although God was their Protector. Let the ones who believe put their trust in God. **3:122**
Certainly, God helped you at Badr while you were humiliated in spirit. So, be God-conscious so that perhaps you will give thanks. **3:123**

Do not forget thankfulness when receiving blessings for God has exhausted the excuses before you through clear, shining arguments and open, bright books. Sermon 81

Mention when **you** *have said to the ones who believe: Suffices you not that your Lord will reinforce you with three thousand among the angels? Ones who are caused to descend,* **3:124**
yea! if you endure patiently and are God-conscious? If they approach you instantly here, your Lord will reinforce you with five thousand angels—ones who are sweeping on. **3:125**

He created the openings between the heavens and filled them with all classes of His angels. Some of them are in prostration and do not sit up. Others are in kneeling position and do not stand up. Some of them are in array and do not leave their position. Others praise God and do not get tired. The sleep of the eye or the slip of wit or languor of the body or the effect of forgetfulness do not affect them. Sermon 1

God made it but as good tidings to you so that with it your hearts will be at rest. There is no help, but from God, The Almighty, The Wise, **3:126**
for He will sever a selection of those who were ungrateful or suppress them so they turn about as ones who are frustrated. **3:127**

God ... is aware of whatever is hidden in the hearts and whatever lies behind the unseen. Sermon 192

It is none of **your** *affair at all if He turns to them in forgiveness or He punishes them, for, truly, they are ones who are unjust.* **3:128**

He exercises superiority over great men through His generosity.

To God belongs whatever is in the heavens and whatever is in and on the earth. He forgives whom He wills and punishes whom He wills. God is Forgiving, Compassionate. **3:129**

Whoever can at this time keep himself clinging to God should do so. If you follow me I shall certainly carry you, if God so wills, on the path to the Garden, even though it may be full of severe hardship and of bitter taste. Sermon 156

O those who believed! Consume not usury—that which is doubled and redoubled—and be God-conscious so that perhaps you will prosper. **3:130**

Whoever trades without knowing the rules of religious law will be involved in usury. Hadith 447

Be God-conscious of the fire that was prepared for the ones who are ungrateful. **3:131**

Know that you have to pass over the pathway (*sirat*) where steps waver, feet slip away and there are fearful dangers at every step. O God's human being! Be God-conscious, like the fearing of a wise man whom the thought of the next world has turned him away from other matters. God-consciousness has afflicted his body with trouble and pain. His engagement in the night prayer has turned even his short sleep into awakening. Hope of eternal recompense keeps him thirsty in the day. Sermon 82

Obey God and the Messenger so that perhaps you will find mercy. **3:132**

God sent *Muhammad* (Q48:29), peace and the mercy of God be upon him, as a witness, giver of good tidings and warner, the best in the universe as a child and the most chaste as a grown up person, the purest of the purified in conduct, the most generous of those who are approached for generosity. Sermon 105

Compete with one another for forgiveness from your Lord and for a Garden whose depth is as the heavens and the earth that was prepared for the ones who are God-conscious, **3:133**
those who spend in gladness and tribulation and the ones who choke their rage and the ones who pardon humanity. God loves the ones who are doers of good. **3:134**

O God's human being! You should know now that you have to perform good acts, because at present your tongues are free, your bodies are healthy, your limbs have movement, the area of your coming and going is vast and the course of your running is wide; before the loss of opportunity or the approach of death. Take death's approach as an accomplished fact and do not think it will come hereafter. Sermon 195

Those who, when they committed an indecency or did wrong to themselves, they remembered God. Then, they asked for forgiveness for their impieties. Who forgives impieties but God? Persist not in what impiety they committed while they know. **3:135**

He has appreciated their actions and praised their position. They call Him and breathe in the air of forgiveness. They are ever needy of His bounty and remain humble before His greatness. The length of their grief has pained their hearts, the length of weeping, their eyes. They knock at every door of inclination towards God. They ask Him Whom generosity does not make destitute and from Whom those who approach Him are not disappointed. Sermon 221

Those, their recompense is forgiveness from their Lord and Gardens beneath which rivers run, ones who will dwell in them forever. How bountiful is the compensation for the ones who work! **3:136**

God's verdict is judicious and full of wisdom. His pleasure implies protection and mercy. He decides with knowledge and forgives with forbearance. Sermon 160

Customs passed away before you. So, journey through the earth; then, look on how had been the Ultimate End of the ones who deny. **3:137**

You have been guided as to how to provide for the journey. Truly, the most frightening thing which I am afraid of about you is that you will follow desires and widen your hopes. Provide for yourself from this world what would save you tomorrow on the Day of Judgment. Sermon 28

This is a clear explanation for humanity, a guidance and an admonishment for the ones who are God-conscious. **3:138**

Whoever from among us are here during these days will move through them with a burning lamp and will tread on the footsteps of the virtuous in order to unfasten knots, to free servants, to divide the united and to unite the divided. He will be in concealment from people. The stalker will not find his footprints even though he pursues with his eye. Then a group of people will be sharpened like the sharpening of swords by the blacksmith. Their sight will be brightened by revelation, the delicacies of commentary will be put in their ears and they will be given drinks of wisdom, morning and evening. Sermon 150

Be not feeble nor feel remorse. You will be among the lofty, if you had been ones who believe. **3:139**

God, the Sublime, says: *Truly, of men the nearest to Abraham are surely those who followed him and this Prophet and those who believe; God is Protector of the ones who believe.* (Q3:68) Letter 28

If a wound afflicts you, surely, a wound afflicted the folk similar to that. These are the days We rotate among humanity so that God knows those who believed and takes witnesses to Himself from among you—and God loves not the ones who are unjust— **3:140**
and so that God may prove those who believed and eliminate the ones who are ungrateful. **3:141**

This world is a place of destruction, tribulations, changes and lessons. As for destruction, the time has its bow pressed for readiness and its dart does not go amiss. Its wound does not heal. It afflicts the living with death, the healthy with ailment and the safe with distress. It is an eater who is not satisfied and a drinker whose thirst is never quenched. As for tribulation, a person collects what he does not eat and builds wherein he does not live.

Then he goes out to God without carrying the wealth or shifting the building. Sermon 114

Or assumed you that you would enter the Garden while God knows not those who struggled among you and knows the ones who remain steadfast? **3:142**

Indeed, surely, jihad is one of the doors of Paradise which God has opened for His best friends. It is the dress of God-consciousness, the protective armor of God and His trustworthy shield. Whoever abandons it, God covers him with the dress of disgrace and the clothes of distress. He is kicked with contempt and scorn. His heart is veiled with screens of neglect. Truth is taken away from him because of his missing the jihad. He has to suffer ignominy. Justice is denied to him. Sermon 27

Certainly, you had been coveting death before you were to meet it. Then, surely, you saw and look on it. **3:143**

They are your forerunners in reaching the goal and have arrived at the watering places before you. They had positions of honor and plenty of pride. They were rulers and holders of positions. Now they have gone into the interstice where earth covers them from above and is eating their flesh and drinking their blood. They lie in the hollows of their graves lifeless, no more growing, and hidden, not to be found. The approach of danger does not frighten them. The adversity of circumstances does not grieve them. They do not mind earthquakes, nor do they pay heed to thunder. They are gone and not expected back. They are existent, but unseen. They were united, but are now dispersed. They were friendly and are now separated. Sermon 220

Muhammad is only a Messenger. Surely, Messengers passed away before him. Then, if he died or be slain, will you turn about on your heels? He who turns about on his heels will not injure God at all. God will give recompense to the ones who are thankful. **3:144**

The pledge of Muhammad, peace and the mercy of God be upon him, had been taken from the Prophets. His character traits were well reputed. His birth was an honorable one. At this time, the people of the earth were divided in different parties. Each had separate aims. Their ways were diverse. They either likened God to His creation or twisted His Names or turned to other than Him. God guided them through Muhammad, peace and the mercy of God be upon him, out of darkness and removed their ignorance through the efforts of *the Messenger of God.* (Q48:29) Sermon 1

It had not been for any soul to die, but with the permission of God. Prescribed is that which is appointed. Whoever wants a reward for good deeds in the present, We will give him that. Whoever wants a reward for good deeds in the world to come We will give him that. We will give recompense to the ones who are thankful. **3:145**

O God's human being! Be God-conscious. Keep in view the reason why He created you. Be afraid of Him to the extent He has advised you to do. Make yourself deserve what He has promised you by having confidence in the truth of His promise and entertaining fear of the Day of Judgment. Sermon 82

How many a Prophet whom, along with him, many thousands fought, but none lost confidence with what lit on them in the way of God, nor were they weakened nor were they to give in. God loves the ones who remain steadfast. **3:146**

Neither the conveyor of God's message lied, nor the hearer misunderstood. Sermon 101

Their saying had been only that they said: Our Lord! Forgive us our impieties and our excessiveness in our affairs. Make our feet firm and help us against the folk, the ones who are ungrateful. **3:147**

There are some people devoted to the remembrance of God who have adopted it in place of worldly matters so that commerce or trade does not turn them away from it. They pass their life in it. They speak into the ears of neglectful persons warning against matters held unlawful by God. They order them to practice justice and themselves keep practicing it. They refrain them from the unlawful and themselves refrain from it. It is as though they have finished the journey of this world towards the next world and have beheld what lies beyond it. Sermon 221

So, God gave them a reward for good deeds in the present and the goodness of reward for good deeds in the world to come. God loves the ones who are doers of good. **3:148**

Be God-conscious and perform good acts because *Truly God is with those who are God-conscious and those, they are the ones who are doers of good.* (Q16:128).... Sermon 193

O those who believed! If you obey those who were ungrateful, they will repel you back on your heels and you will turn about—ones who are losers. **3:149**

O God's human being! Secure light from the flame of lamps of the preacher who follows what he preaches. Draw water from the spring which has been cleaned of dirt. O God's human being! Do not rely on your ignorance. Do not be obedient to your desires, because he who stays at this place is like one who stays on the brink of a bank undermined by water carrying ruin on his back from one portion to the other following his opinion which he changes one after the other. He wants to make adhere what cannot adhere and to bring together what cannot keep together. Be God-conscious and do not place your complaints before him who cannot redress your grievance, nor undo with his opinion what has been made obligatory for you. Sermon 105

Nay! God is your Defender and He is Best of the ones who help. **3:150**

It is as though you too have gone where they have gone, the same sleeping place has caught you and the same place has detained you. What will, then be your position when your affairs reach their end and graves are turned upside down to throw out the dead? *There every soul will be tried for what it has done in the past. They would be returned to God, their Defender, The Truth. From them will go astray what they had been devising.* (Q10:30) Sermon 226

We will cast into the hearts of those who were ungrateful, alarm, because they ascribed partners with God. He sends not down for it authority. Their place of shelter will be the fire. Miserable will be the place of lodging of the ones who are unjust. **3:151**

Whoever takes a partner for **You** is ungrateful according to what is stated in **Your** unambiguous verses and indicated by the evidence of **Your** clear arguments. Sermon 91

Certainly, God was sincere to you in His promise when you blasted the enemy with His permission until you lost heart and you contended with one another about the command and you rebelled after He caused you to see what you longed for in the spoils of war. Among you are some who want the present and among you are some who want the world to come. Again, He turned you away from

them that He test you and, certainly, He pardoned you. God is Possessor of Grace for the ones who believe. **3:152**
When you mount up, not attentive to anyone and the Messenger calls you from your rear, then, He repaid you, lament for lament, so that you neither feel remorse for what slipped away from you, nor for what lit on you. God is Aware of what you do. **3:153**
Again, He caused to descend safety for you after lament. Sleepiness overcomes a section of you while a section caused themselves grief thinking of God without right, a thought out of the Age of Ignorance. They say: Have we any part in the command? Say: Truly, the command is entirely from God. They conceal within themselves what they show not to **you**. *They say: If there had been for us any part in the command, we would not be killed here. Say: Even if you had been in your houses, those would have departed—whom it was prescribed they be slain—for the Final Place of sleeping, so that God tests what is in your breasts and He proves what is in your hearts. God is Knowing of what is in the breasts.* **3:154**

You should put out the fires of haughtiness and the flames of intolerance that are hidden in your hearts. This vanity can exist in a Muslim only by the machinations of Satan, his haughtiness, mischief and whisperings. Make up your mind to have humility over your heads, to trample self-pride under your feet and to cast off vanity from your necks. Adopt humility as the weapon between you and your enemy, Satan and his forces. He certainly has, from every people, fighters, helpers, footmen and horsemen. Do not be like him who feigned superiority over the son of his own mother without any distinction given to him by God except the feeling of envy which his feeling of greatness created in him and the fire of anger that vanity kindled in his heart. Satan blew into his nose his own vanity, after which God gave him remorse and made him responsible for the sins of all killers up to the Day of Judgment. Sermon 192

Truly, those of you who turned away on a day two multitudes met one another, only Satan caused them to slip back for some of what they earned. Certainly, God pardoned them. Truly God is Forgiving, Forbearing. **3:155**

Certainly, Satan has made his ways easy for you and wants to unfasten the knots of religion one by one and to cause division among you in place of unity. Keep away from his evil ideas and enchantments. Accept good advice of one who offers it to you. Preserve it in your minds. Sermon 121

O those who believed! Be not like those who were ungrateful and said about their brothers when they traveled through the earth or had been ones who are combatants: If they had been with us, neither would they have died, nor would they have been slain, so that God makes this a cause of regret in their hearts. God gives life and causes to die. God is Seeing of what you do. **3:156**

I bear witness that *there is no god but God,* (Q47:19), the One. Sermon 2

If you were slain in the way of God or died, certainly, forgiveness and mercy from God are better than what they gather in the present. **3:157**
If you died or were slain, it is, certainly, to God you will be assembled. **3:158**

What loss did our brothers whose blood was shed in Siffin suffer by not being alive today? Only that they are not suffering choking on swallowing and not drinking turbid water. By God, surely they have met God. (Surely), He has bestowed upon them their rewards and He has lodged them in safe houses after their having suffered fear. Sermon 182

It is by the mercy of God **you** *were gentle with them. If* **you** *had been hard, harsh of heart, they would have broken away from around* **you**. *So, pardon them and ask for forgiveness for them. Take counsel with them in the affair. But when* **you** *are resolved, then, put* **your** *trust in God. Truly, God loves the ones who put their trust in Him.* **3:159**

If God helps you, then none will be one who is a victor over you. If He withdraws His help from you, then, who is there who helps you after Him? In God put their trust the ones who believe. **3:160**

As regards fulfillment of trust, whoever does not pay attention to it will be disappointed. It was placed before the strong skies, vast earths and high mountains, but none of them was found to be stronger, vaster or higher than it. If anything could be unapproachable because of height, vastness, power or strength they would have been unapproachable, but they felt afraid of the evil consequences of failure in fulfilling a trust and noticed what a weaker being did not realize it, and this was the human being: *Truly, We presented the trust to the heavens and the earth and the mountains, but they refused to carry it and were apprehensive of it. But the human being carried it. Truly, he had been wrongdoing, very ignorant.* (Q33:72) Sermon 198

It had not been for a Prophet that he defraud. Whoever defrauds, what he defrauded will approach him on the Day of Resurrection. Again, the account will be paid in full of every soul for what he earned and they will not be wronged. **3:161**

You are on test in this world and have to render account about it. Sermon 82

So, then, is he who followed the contentment of God like he who drew the burden of the displeasure of God and whose place of shelter will be hell? Miserable will be the Homecoming! **3:162**

He who is content with his own opinion faces danger. Endurance braves calamities while impatience is a helper of the hardships of the world. The best contentment is to give up desires. Many a slavish mind is subservient to overpowering longings. Capability helps preservation of experience. Love means well-utilized relationship. Do not trust one who is grieved. Hadith 211

They have degrees with God. God is Seeing of what they do. **3:163**

In the Garden there are various degrees of excellence and different places of stay. Its blessings never end. He who stays in it will never depart from it. He who is endowed with everlasting abode in it will not grow old and its resident will not face want. Sermon 86

Certainly, God showed grace to the ones who believe when he raised up among them a Messenger from themselves who recounts His signs to them and makes them pure and teaches them the Book and wisdom. Truly, before that they had been, certainly, clearly wandering astray. **3:164**

You should follow your Prophet, the pure, the chaste, may God bless him. In him is the example for the follower and the consolation for the seeker of consolation. The most beloved person before God is he who follows His Prophet and who treads in his footsteps. He took the least share from this world and did not take a full glance at it. Of all the people of the world he was the least satiated and the most empty of stomach. The world was offered to him, but he refused to accept it. When he knew that God, the Glorified, hated a thing, he too hated it; that God held a thing low, he too held it low; that God held a thing small, he too held it small. If we love what God and His Prophet hate and hold great what God and His Prophet hold small that would be enough isolation from God and transgression of His commands. Sermon 159

Why, when an affliction lit on you, surely, you lit two times its like on them. Say: Where is this from? Say: It is from yourselves. Truly, God is Powerful over everything. **3:165**

O God's human being! The present is an opportune moment for acting since the neck is free from the loop, and the spirit is also unfettered. Now you have time for seeking guidance. You are in ease of body. You can assemble in crowds. The rest of your life is before you. You have the opportunity of acting by will. There is opportunity for repentance and peaceful circumstances, but you should act before you are overtaken by narrow circumstances and distress, or fear and weakness, before the approach of the awaited death and before seizure by the Almighty, the Powerful. Sermon 82

What lit on you on a day when the two multitudes met one another was with the permission of God that He would know the ones who believe **3:166**
and He would know those who were hypocrites. It was said to them: Approach now! Fight in the way of God or drive back. They said: If we would have known there would be fighting, we would, certainly, have followed you. They were nearer to disbelief on that day than to belief. They say with their mouths what is not in their hearts. God is greater in knowledge of what they keep back. **3:167**

Hypocrites sowed vices, watered them with deception and harvested destruction. Sermon 2

Those who said to their brothers while they sat back: If they obeyed us, they would not have been slain. Say: Then, drive off death from yourselves, if you had been ones who are sincere. **3:168**

The person who contrives for his own people to be put to the sword and invites death and destruction for them does deserve that the near ones should hate him and the farther ones should not trust him. Sermon 19

Assume not those who were slain in the way of God to be lifeless. Nay! They are living with their Lord. They are provided for, **3:169**
glad for what God gave them of His grace and rejoice at the good tidings for those who have not yet joined them from behind them. There will be neither fear in them, nor will they feel remorse. **3:170**

Hearts achieved guidance through him after being ridden with troubles. He introduced clearly guiding signs and shining injunctions. He is **Your** trusted trustee, the treasurer of **Your** treasured knowledge, **Your** witness on the Day of Judgment, Thy envoy of truth and **Your** Messenger towards the people. May God prepare a large place for him under **Your** shade and award him multiplying good by **Your** bounty. Sermon 71

They rejoice at the good tidings of the divine blessing from God and His grace and that God will not waste the compensation of the ones who believe, **3:171**
those who responded to God and the Messenger after wounds lit on them. For those of them who did good among them and were God-conscious, there is a sublime compensation. **3:172**

On all this He suffers no trouble. No impediment hampers Him in the preservation of what He created, nor any languor or grief hinders Him from the enforcement of commands and management of the creatures. His knowledge penetrates through them. They are within His counting. His justice extends to all of them. His bounty encompasses them despite their falling short of what is due to Him. Sermon 91

Those to whom humanity said: Truly, humanity has gathered against you, so dread them, but it increased them in belief and they said: God is enough for us and how excellent is He, The Trustee. **3:173**

I say what you are hearing. I seek God's help for myself and yourselves: *God is enough for us and how excellent is He, the Trustee.* (Q3:173) Sermon 183

So, they turned about with divine blessing from God and grace and evil afflicts them not and they followed the contentment of God and God is Possessor of Sublime Grace. **3:174**

Nothing is better than good except its reward. In this world everything that is heard is better than what is seen, while everything of the next world that is seen is better than what is heard. So you should satisfy yourself by hearing rather than seeing and by the news of the unknown. You should know that what is little in this world but much in the next is better than what is much in this world but little in the next. In how many cases little is profitable while much causes loss. Sermon 114

It is only Satan who frightens you with his protectors. So, fear them not, but fear Me if you had been ones who believe. **3:175**

It is that you are unthankful to God for all which He has granted to you. You are ungrateful to Him for the favors bestowed upon you. Satan has taken possession of your soul. Satan's desire to secure you as his obedient servant is fully fulfilled. He has a firm hold on your mind. Letter 10

Let not those who compete with one another in ingratitude dishearten ***you****. Truly, they will never injure God at all. God wants to assign no allotment for them in the world to come and for them is a tremendous punishment.* **3:176**

Truly, those who bought ingratitude at the price of belief will never injure God at all. For them will be a painful punishment. **3:177**

Whoever takes a partner for **You** is ungrateful according to what is stated in **Your** unambiguous verses and indicated by the evidence of **Your** clear arguments. Sermon 91

Those who were ungrateful should not assume that the indulgence We grant to them is better for themselves. We only grant indulgence to them so that they add sin! For them is a despised punishment. **3:178**

God ... is aware of whatever is hidden in the hearts and whatever lies behind the unseen. Sermon 192

God had not been forsaking the ones who believe to what you are in until He differentiates the bad from what is good. God will not inform about the unseen, but God elects from His Messengers whom He wills. So, believe in God and His Messengers. If you believe and are God-conscious, then, for you there is a sublime compensation. **3:179**

I bear witness that *Muhammad* (Q48:29), peace and the mercy of God be upon him, is *His servant* (Q17:1), and *Prophet* (Q7:158) and His responsible trustee, peace and the mercy of God be upon him. God sent him with undeniable proofs, a clear success and open paths. So he conveyed the message declaring the truth with it. He led the people on the correct highway, established signs of guidance and minarets of light and made Islam's ropes strong and its knots firm. Sermon 185

Assume not those who are misers that what God gave them of His grace is better for them. Nay! It is worse for them. To be hung around their necks will be what they were misers with on the Day of Resurrection. To God belongs the heritage of the heavens and the earth. God is Aware of what you do. **3:180**

Truly, miserliness, cowardice and greed are so many diverse inclinations comprised within a bad opinion of God. Letter 53

Certainly, God heard the saying of those who said: Truly, God is poor and we are rich. We will write down what they said and their killing of the Prophets without right. We will say: Experience the punishment of the burning! **3:181**
That is for what your hands put forward and that God is not unjust to His servants. **3:182**
To those who said: Truly, God made a compact with us that we believe not in a Messenger until He approaches with a sacrifice to be consumed by the fire, say: Surely, Messengers brought about to you before me the clear portents and even of what you spoke. Then, why have you killed them if you had been ones who are sincere? **3:183**

The basis of the occurrence of evil are those desires which are acted upon and the orders that are innovated. They are against the Book of God. People co-operate with each other about them even though it is against the religion of God. If wrong had been pure and unmixed, it would not be hidden from those who are in search of it. If right had been pure without admixture of wrong, those who bear hatred towards it would have been silenced. What is, however, done is that something is taken from here and something from there and the two are mixed! At this stage, Satan overpowers his friends. They alone escape for whom virtue has been apportioned by God from before. Sermon 50

Then if they denied **you***, surely, Messengers before* **you** *were denied who drew near with the clear portents and the Psalms and the illuminating Book.* **3:184**

There is no doubt that God sent down *the Prophet* (Q7:158), peace and the mercy of God be upon him, as a guide with an eloquent Book and a standing command. No one will be ruined by it except one who ruins himself. Sermon 169

Every soul is one that experiences death. Your account will be paid with full compensation on the Day of Resurrection. Then, whoever was drawn away from the fire and was caused to enter the Garden, surely, won a triumph. What is this present life but the delusion of enjoyment? **3:185**

Whatever they were ignoring has befallen them. Separation from this world, from which they thought themselves safe, has come to them. They have reached that in the next world which they had been promised. Whatever has befallen them cannot be described. Pangs of death and grief for losing this world have surrounded them. Consequently, their limbs have become languid and their complexion changes. Then death increases its struggle over them. Sermon 108

You will, certainly, be tried with your wealth and yourselves and you will, certainly, hear much annoyance from those who were given the Book before you and from those who ascribed partners with God. If you endure patiently and are God-conscious, then, truly, that is of the commands to constancy. **3:186**

God, the Almighty, has sent down a guiding Book wherein He has explained virtue and vice. You should adopt the course of virtue, whereby you will have guidance. Detach yourself from the direction of vice, so that you remain on the right way. Sermon 167

When God took a solemn promise from those who were given the Book: You will make it manifest to humanity and keep it not back. Yet they repudiated it behind their backs and exchange it for a little price. Miserable will be what they buy! **3:187**

O my God! Forgive me. **You** know more about me than I do. If I return to sin, **You** return to forgiveness. My God, forgive me what I had promised to myself, but **You** did not find its fulfillment with me. My God, forgive me that with what I sought nearness to **You** with my tongue, but my heart opposed and did not perform. My God, forgive me winking of the eye, vile utterances, desires of the heart and errors of speech. Sermon 78

Assume not that those who are glad for what they brought and who love to be praised for what they accomplish not, assume not, then, that they will be kept safe from the punishment. For them, a painful punishment. **3:188**

They, the ungrateful, jumped on the carcass of this world, earned shame by eating it and became united on loving it. When one loves a thing, it blinds him and sickens his heart. He sees, but with a diseased eye, hears, but with un-hearing ears. Desires have cut asunder his wit. The world has made his heart dead while his mind is all longing for it. Consequently, he is a servant of it and of everyone who has any share in it. Wherever it turns, he turns towards it. Wherever it proceeds, he proceeds towards it. He is not desisted by any desister from God, nor takes admonition from any preacher. He sees those who have been caught in neglect whence there is neither rescission, nor reversion. Sermon 108

To God belongs the dominion of the heavens and of the earth. God is Powerful over everything. **3:189**

O my God! **You** know that what we did was not to seek power, nor to acquire anything from the vanities of the world. We rather wanted to restore the signs of **Your** religion and to usher prosperity into **Your** cities so that the oppressed among **Your** creatures might be safe and **Your** forsaken commands might be established. Sermon 131

Truly, in the creation of the heavens and of the earth and the alteration of nighttime and daytime there are signs for those imbued with intuition, **3:190**
those who remember God while upright and sitting and on their sides and they reflect on the creation of the heavens and the earth: Our Lord! ***You*** *had not created this in vain. Glory be to* ***You****! Then, protect us from the punishment of the fire.* **3:191**

O Kumayl ibn Ziyad, intuitive knowledge is a religion by which God is worshipped. Through it, a person acquires obedience in this life and a good name after his death. Knowledge is a judge, while wealth is judged. Saying 146

Our Lord! Whomever ***You*** *caused to enter the fire, surely,* ***You*** *covered him with shame and there will not be for the ones who are unjust any helpers.* **3:192**

Where are those who protect honor, and those self-respecting persons who defend respectable persons in the time of hardship? Shame is behind you while the Garden is in front of you. Sermon 171

Our Lord! Truly, we heard one who calls out, cries out for belief: Believe in your Lord! So, we believed. Our Lord! So, forgive our impieties and absolve us of our evil deeds and gather us to ***You*** *with the pious.* **3:193**
Our Lord! Give us what ***You*** *promised us through* ***Your*** *Messengers and cover us not with shame on the Day of Resurrection. Truly,* ***You*** *will not break* ***Your*** *solemn declaration.* **3:194**

God will take them out from the corners of the graves, the nests of birds, the dens of beasts and the centers of death. They will hasten towards His command and run towards the place fixed for their final return, group by group, quiet, standing and arrayed in rows. They will be within God's sight and will hear every one who would call them. They will have the dress of helplessness and covering of submission and indignity. At this time contrivances will disappear. Desires will be cut. Hearts will sink quietly. Voices will be lowered. Sweat will choke the throat. Fear will increase. Ears will resound with the thundering voice of the announcer calling towards the final judgment, award of recompense, striking of punishment and paying of reward. Sermon 82

Their Lord responded to them: I waste not the actions of ones who work among you from male or female. Each one of you is from the other. So, those who emigrated and were driven out from their abodes and were maligned on My way and who fought and were slain, I will, certainly, absolve them of their evil deeds. I will, certainly, cause them to enter into Gardens beneath which rivers run, a reward for good deeds from God. God, with Him is the goodness of rewards for good deeds.
3:195

It is the most bright of all paths, the clearest of all passages. It has dignified minarets, bright highways, burning laps, prestigious field of activity and high objective. It has a collection of race horses. It is approached eagerly. Its riders are honorable. Testimony of God and *the Prophet* (Q7:158) is its way, good deeds are its minarets, death is its extremity, this world is its race-course, the Day of Judgment is its horses and Paradise is its point of approach. Sermon 105

Let not the going to and fro delude ***you*** *of those who were ungrateful in the land* **3:196**
—a little enjoyment—again, their place of shelter will be hell. It will be a miserable Final Place.
3:197
But those who were God-conscious of their Lord, for them will be Gardens beneath which rivers run, ones who will dwell in them forever, a hospitality from God. What is with God is best for the pious. **3:198**

I am just like a night traveler who reaches the spring in the morning or like a seeker who secures his aim: *Whatever is with God is the best for the pious.* (Q3:198) Letter 23

Truly, among the People of the Book are those who believe in God and what was caused to descend to you and what was caused to descend to them, ones who are humble toward God. They exchange not the signs of God for a little price. Those, for them, their compensation is with their Lord. Truly, God is Swift in reckoning. **3:199**

O God's human being! Certainly, being God-conscious has saved the lovers of God from unlawful items and has given His dread to their hearts until their nights are passed in wakefulness and their noons in thirst. So they achieve comfort through trouble and copious watering through thirst. They regarded death to be near and, therefore, hastened towards good actions. They rejected their desires by keeping death in their sight. Sermon 114

O those who believed! Excel in patience and be steadfast. Be God-conscious so that perhaps you will prosper. **3:200**

Clothe yourself with patience for it is the best to victory. Sermon 26

CHAPTER 4: THE WOMEN (al-Nisā')

O humanity! Be God-conscious of your Lord Who created you from a single soul and, from it, created its spouse and from them both disseminated many men and women. Be God-conscious through Whom you demand rights of one another and the wombs, the rights of blood relations. Truly, God had been watching over you. **4:1**

From His rights, He, the Almighty, created certain rights for certain people against others. He made them so as to equate with one another. Some of these rights produce other rights. Some rights are such that they do not accrue except with others. Sermon 216

Give the orphans their property and take not in exchange the bad of yours for what is good of theirs. Consume not their property with your own property. Truly, this had been criminal, a hateful sin. **4:2**

Do you command me that I should seek support by oppressing those over whom I have been placed? By God, I will not do so as long as the world goes on and as long as one star leads another in the sky. Even if it were my property, I would have distributed it equally among them. Then why not when the property is that of God? Sermon 126

If you feared that you will not act justly with the orphans, then, marry who seems good to you of the women (who have orphans), by twos, in threes or four. But if you feared you will not be just, then, one or what your right hands possessed. That is likelier that you not commit injustice. **4:3**

The lawful actions performed here have to be accounted for, while for the forbidden ones there is punishment. Sermon 81

Give wives their marriage portion as a spontaneous gift. Then, truly, if they (f) were pleased to offer to you anything of it on their (f) own, consume it wholesomely with repose. **4:4**

O enemy of yourself! Certainly, the evil Satan has misguided you. Do you feel no pity for your wife and your children? Do you believe that if you use those things which God has made lawful for you, He will dislike you? You are too unimportant for God to do so. Sermon 208

Give not the mentally deficient your wealth that God assigned to you to maintain for them, but provide for them from it and clothe them. Say honorable sayings to them. **4:5**

Every knower other than Him is a seeker of knowledge. Every controller other than Him is sometimes imbued with control and sometimes with disability. Every listener other than Him is deaf to light voices while loud voices make him deaf and distant voices also get away from him. Every onlooker other than Him is blind to hidden colors and delicate bodies. Every manifest thing other than Him is hidden, but every hidden thing other than Him is incapable of becoming manifest. Sermon 64

Test the orphans until when they reach the age for marriage. Then if you observe them to be of right judgment, then release their property to them. Consume it not excessively and hastily, for they will develop. Whoever has been rich, let him have restraint. Whoever has been poor, then let him consume as one who is honorable. When you have released their property to them, call witnesses over them. God has sufficed as a Reckoner. **4:6**

For men is a share of what was left by the ones who are their parents and the nearest kin. For women is a share of what was left by the ones who are their parents and nearest kin whether it was little or it was much—an apportioned share. **4:7**

When the division is attended by those imbued with kinship and the orphans and the needy, then, provide for them from it and say honorable sayings to them. **4:8**

Let executors dread like those who, if they left behind weak offspring, would fear for them. Then, let them be God-conscious and let them say appropriate sayings. **4:9**

Truly, those who consume the wealth of orphans with injustice, consume only fire into their bellies and they will roast in a blaze. **4:10**

Know that injustice is of three kinds—one, the injustice that will not be forgiven, another that will not be left unquestioned and another that will be forgiven without being questioned. The injustice that will not be forgiven is ascribing partners with God. God has said: *Truly, God forgives not to ascribe partners with Him and He forgives other than that whomever He will*s. (Q4:48) The injustice that will be forgiven is the injustice a person does to himself by committing small sins and the injustice that will not be left unquestioned is the injustice of men against other men. The retribution in such a case is severe. It is not wounding with knives, nor striking with whips, but it is so severe that all these things are small against it. You should therefore avoid change in the matter of God's religion for your unity in respect of a right which you dislike is better than your scattering away in respect of a wrong that you like. Certainly, God the Glorified has not given any person, whether among the dead or among those who survive, any good from separation. Sermon 175

God enjoins you concerning your children. For the male, the like allotment of two females. If there had been women, more than two, then, for them (f) two-thirds of what he left. But if there had been one, then, for her is half. For one's parents, for each one of them a sixth of what he left, if he would have a child. Then, if he be with no child and his parents inherited, then, a third to his mother. Then, if he had brothers, then a sixth for his mother. This is after any bequest he enjoins or any debt. Your parents or your children, you are not informed which of them is nearer to you in profit. This is a duty to God. Truly, God had been Knowing, Wise. **4:11**

For you is a half of what your spouses left if they be with no child. Then, if they (f) had a child, then, for you is a fourth of what they (f) left. This is after any bequest which they bequeath or any debt. For them (f) a fourth of what you left if you be with no child. If you had a child, then, for them (f) is an eighth of what you left. This is after any bequest which you bequeath or any debt. If a man would have no direct heirs, or a woman, but indirect heirs, and has a brother or sister, then, for each one of them (f), a sixth. Then, if there would be more than that, then, they would be ascribed associates in a third. This is after any bequest which is bequeathed or any debt without being one who presses the heirs. This is the enjoinment from God. God is Knowing, Forbearing. **4:12**

These are the ordinances of God. Whoever obeys God and His Messenger, He will cause to enter Gardens beneath which rivers run, ones who will dwell in them forever. That is the winning the sublime triumph. **4:13** ***

Whoever rebels against God and His Messenger and violates His ordinances, He will cause him to enter fire, one who shall dwell in it forever and he will have a despised punishment. **4:14**

God sent *the Prophet* (Q7:158), peace and the mercy of God be upon him, for enforcement of His commands, for exhausting His pleas and for presenting warnings against eternal punishment. Sermon 82

Those who approach indecency among your wives, call to four among you to bear witness against them (f). Then, if they bore witness to the affair, then, hold them (f) back in their houses until death gathers them (f) to itself or God makes a way for them (f). **4:15**
Those two who among you approach that, then penalize them both. Then, if they repented and made things right, then, turn aside from them. Truly, God had been Accepter of Repentance, Compassionate. **4:16**

Blessed be he who possesses a virtuous heart, who obeys one who guides him, desists from him who takes to ruin, catches the path of safety with the help of him who provides him light of guidance and by obeying the leader who commands him, hastens towards guidance before its doors are closed, opens the door of repentance and removes the stain of sins. He has certainly been put on the right path and guided towards the straight road. Sermon 213

To turn only to God for forgiveness is for those who do evil in ignorance and, again, soon they are remorseful. Then, those are whom God turns to in forgiveness. God had been Knowing, Wise. **4:17**

By God, he is not capable of solving the problems that come to him, nor is he fit for the position assigned to him. Whatever he does not know he does not regard as worth knowing. He does not realize that what is beyond his reach is within the reach of others. If anything is not clear to him, he keeps quiet over it, because he knows his own ignorance. Lost lives are crying against his unjust verdicts. Properties that have been wrongly disposed of are grumbling against him. Sermon 17

There is not remorsefulness for those who do evil deeds until when one of them was attended by death, he would say: I, truly, repented now nor for those who die while they are ones who are ungrateful. Those, We made ready for them a painful punishment. **4:18**

Be aware! At the time of committing evil deeds remember the destroyer of joys, the spoiler of pleasures and the killer of desires, namely death. Seek assistance of God for fulfillment of His obligatory rights and for thanking Him for His countless bounties and obligations. Sermon 99

O those who believed! It is not lawful for you that you inherit women unwillingly, and place not difficulties for them (f) so that you take away some of what you gave them (f), unless they approach a manifest indecency. Live as one who is honorable with them (f). Then, if you disliked them (f) perhaps you dislike something in which God makes much good. **4:19**
If you wanted to exchange your spouse in place of another spouse and you gave one of them (f) a hundredweight, so take not anything from it. Would you take it by false charges to harm her reputation and in clear sin? **4:20**
How would you take it when one of you had sexual intercourse with the other and they (f) took from you an earnest solemn promise? **4:21**
Marry not women whom your fathers married unless it was in the past. Truly, it had been an in-

decency and repugnant and how evil a way! **4:22**
Your mothers were forbidden to you and your daughters and your sisters and your paternal and maternal aunts and daughters of your brothers and daughters of your sisters and your foster mothers, those who breast fed you, and your sisters through fosterage and mothers of your wives and your stepdaughters, those who are in your care from wives, those with whom you have lain—but if you have not yet lain with them (f), then there is no blame on you; and wives of your sons who are of your loins; and that you should not gather two sisters together unless it be from the past. Truly, God had been Forgiving, Compassionate. **4:23**
Forbidden to you are the ones who are married women, but from females whom your right hands (f) possessed. This is prescribed by God for you. Permitted to you are those who were beyond these so that with your wealth you be looking as males, ones who seek wedlock, not as ones who are licentious males. For what you enjoyed of it from them (f), give them (f) their bridal due as their dowry portion. There is no blame on you for what you agreed on among yourselves after the duty. Truly, God had been Knowing, Wise. **4:24**
Whoever of you is not affluent to be able to marry the ones who are free, chaste females, the female believers, then, from females whom your right hands possessed, the ones who are female spiritual warriors, female believers God is greater in knowledge about your belief. You are of one another. So, marry them (f) with the permission of their people, and give them (f) their bridal due as one who is honorable, they being ones who are free, chaste females, without being ones who are licentious females, nor females, ones who take lovers to themselves. When they (f) are in wedlock, if they (f) approached indecencies, then on them is half of the ones who are free, chaste females of the punishment. That is for those who dreaded fornication among you. That you endure patiently is better for you. God is Forgiving, Compassionate. **4:25**
God wants to make manifest to you and to guide you to customs of those who were before you and to turn to you in forgiveness. God is Knowing, Wise. **4:26**

In (the Quran) there are some verses whose knowledge is obligatory and others whose ignorance by the people is permissible. It also contains what appears to be obligatory according to the Book but its repeal is signified by the actions (*sunna*) of *the Prophet* (Q7:158), peace and the mercy of God be upon him, or that which appears compulsory according to the actions of *the Prophet* (Q7:158), peace and the mercy of God be upon him, but the Book allows not following it. Or, there are those which are obligatory in a given time, but not so after that time. Its prohibitions also differ. Some are major regarding which there exists the threat of hellfire and others are minor for which there is the hope of forgiveness. There are also those of which a small portion is also acceptable to God, but they are capable of being expanded. Sermon 1

God wants that He turn to you in forgiveness while those who follow their lusts want that you turn against God in a serious deviation. **4:27**

Your city is the most stinking of all the cities as regards its clay, the nearest to water and remotest from the sky. It contains nine tenths of evil. He who enters it is surrounded with his sins. He who is out of it enjoys God's forgiveness. It seems as though I look at this habitation of yours that water has so engulfed it that nothing can be seen of it except the highest part of the mosque appearing like the bosom of a bird in the deep sea. Sermon 13

God wants to lighten the burden on you. The human being was created weak. **4:28**

Everything submits to Him. Everything exists by Him. He is the satisfaction of every poor, dignity of the low, energy for the weak and shelter for the oppressed. Whoever speaks, He hears his speaking. Whoever keeps quiet, He knows his secret. On Him is the livelihood of everyone who lives. To Him returns whoever dies. Sermon 108

O those who believed! Consume not your wealth between you with falsehood, but that it be a transaction of agreeing together among you. Kill not yourselves. Truly, God had been Compassionate to you. **4:29**
But whoever accomplishes that through deep seated dislike and injustice, We will scorch him in a fire. That would have been easy for God. **4:30**

When a community is composed of honest, sober and virtuous people, your forming a bad opinion about anyone of its members, when nothing wicked has been seen of him, is a great injustice to him. On the contrary, in a corrupt society to form a good opinion of anyone of them and to trust him is to harm yourself. Saying 113

If you avoid major sins that you are prohibited, We will absolve you of your minor sins and cause you to enter a generous gate. **4:31**

Truly, sins are like unruly horses on whom their riders have been placed and their reins have been let loose so that they would jump with them in hellfire. Sermon16

Covet not what God gave as advantage of it to some of you over others. For men is a share of what they deserved and for women is a share of what they (f) deserved. Ask God for His grace. Truly, God had been Knowing of everything. **4:32**

Patience is of two kinds: patience over what pains you, and patience against what you covet. Saying 55

To everyone We assigned inheritors to what the ones who are your parents and the nearest kin left. Those with whom you made an agreement with your sworn oaths, then, give them their share. Truly, God had been Witness over everything. **4:33**

O people! Surely, no one, even though he may be rich, can do without his kinsmen, and their support by hands or tongues. They alone are his support from the rear and can ward off from him his troubles. They are the most kind to him when tribulations befall him. The good memory of a person that God retains among people is better than the property which others inherit from him. Sermon 23

Men are supporters of wives because God gave some of them an advantage over others and because they spent of their wealth. So, the females, ones in accord with morality are the females, ones who are morally obligated and the females, ones who guard the unseen of what God kept safe. Those females whose resistance you fear, then admonish them (f) and abandon them (f) in their sleeping places and go away from them (f). Then if they (f) obeyed you, then look not for any way against them (f). Truly, God had been Lofty, Great. **4:34**
If you feared a breach between the two, then, raise up an arbiter from his people and an arbiter from her people. If they both want to make things right, God will reconcile it between the two. Truly, God had been Knowing, Aware. **4:35**

The Arbiter is God and to Him is the return on the Day of Judgment. Sermon 161

Worship God and ascribe nothing as partners with Him. Kindness to the ones who are your parents

and to the possessors of kinship and the orphans and the needy, to the neighbor who is as a possessor of strangeness and the neighbor who is kin and to the companion by your side and the traveler of the way and whom your right hands possessed. Truly, God loves not ones who had been proud, boastful, **4:36**
those who are misers and command humanity to miserliness and keep back what God gave them of His grace. We made ready for the ones who are ungrateful a despised punishment **4:37**
and for those who spend their wealth to show off to humanity and believe neither in God nor in the Last Day. To whomever Satan would be a comrade, then how evil a comrade! **4:38**

You should know that Satan makes his ways easy so that you may follow him on his heels. Sermon 138

What would be for them if they believed in God and the Last Day and spent out of what God provided them? God had been Knowing of them. **4:39**

Time has made me laugh after making me weep. No wonder, by God. What is this affair which surpasses all wonder and which has increased wrongfulness? These people have tried to put out the flame of God's light from His lamp and to close His fountain from its source. They mixed epidemic-producing water between me and themselves. If the trying hardships were removed from among us, I would take them on the course of truthfulness, otherwise: *So, let not* ***your****self be wasted in regret for them. Truly God is Knowing of what they craft*! (Q35:8) Sermon 162

Truly, God does not wrong even the weight of an atom. If there be benevolence, He multiplies it and gives that which proceeds from His Presence a sublime compensation. **4:40**

Reward lies in saying by the tongue and doing something with the hands and feet. Certainly, God, the Almighty, admits into Paradise by virtue of truthfulness of intention and chastity of heart to whomsoever He wishes from among His creatures. Hadith 42

Then, how will it be when We brought about from each community a witness and We brought ***you*** *about as witness against these?* **4:41**

He is such that all signs of existence bear witness to Him until the denying mind also believes in Him. God is sublime beyond what is described by those who liken Him to things or those who deny Him. Sermon 49

On a Day those who were ungrateful and rebelled against the Messenger will wish that the earth be shaped over them but they will not keep back God's discourse. **4:42**

You have been guided as to how to provide for the journey. Truly, the most frightening thing which I am afraid of about you is that you will follow desires and widen your hopes. Provide for yourself from this world what would save you tomorrow on the Day of Judgment. Sermon 28

O those who believed! Come not near the formal prayer while you are intoxicated until you know what you are saying nor defiled but as one who passes through a way until you wash yourselves. If you had been sick or on a journey or one of you drew near from the privy or you came into sexual contact with your wives and you find no water, then, aim at getting wholesome, dry earth. Then, wipe your faces and your hands. Truly, God had been Pardoning, Forgiving. **4:43**

At last, when God will make clear to them the reward for their sins and take them out from the veils of their neglectfulness, they will proceed to what they were running away from and run away from what they were proceeding to. They will not benefit from the wants they will satisfy or the desires they would fulfill. Sermon 153

Have **you** *not considered those who were given a share of the Book? They exchange fallacy and they want you to go astray from the way.* **4:44**

I will carry on until I perceive disunity among you, because if, in spite of the unsoundness of their view, they succeed, the whole organization of Muslims will be shattered. They are hankering after this world out of jealousy against him on whom God has bestowed it. So they intend to revert the matters to the pre-Islamic period. On us it is obligatory, for your sake, to abide by the Book of God (Quran), the Sublime, and the conduct of *the Prophet* (Q7:158), peace and the mercy of God be upon him, to stand by His rights and to revive his *sunna*. Sermon 169

God is greater in knowledge of your enemies. God sufficed as a protector. God sufficed as a helper. **4:45**

I advise you to fear God. Do not go after this vicious world, although it may try to entice you. Do not seek it, although it may seek you. Do not grieve over and pine for things which this world refuses you. Let the eternal Reward and Blessings of God be the prompting factors for all that you say and do. Be an enemy of tyrants and oppressors. Be a friend and helper of those who are oppressed and tyrannized. Letter 47

Among those who became Jews are those who tamper with words out of context. They say: We heard and we rebelled and: Hear—without being one who is caused to hear and: Look at us—distorting their tongues and discrediting the way of life. If they said: We heard and we obeyed and: Hear **you** *and: Wait for us, it would have been better for them and more upright, except God cursed them for their ingratitude. So, they believe not but a few.* **4:46**

They jumped on the carcass of this world, earned shame by eating it and became united in loving it. Sermon 108

O those who were given the Book! Believe in what We sent down, that which establishes as true what was with you, before We obliterate faces, and repel them backward or curse them as We cursed the Companions of the Sabbath. The command of God had been one that is accomplished. **4:47**

Mind the obligations! Mind the obligations! Fulfill them for God and they will take you to the Garden. Surely, God has made unlawful the things which are not unknown and made lawful the things which are without defect. Sermon 167

Truly, God forgives not to ascribe partners with Him and He forgives other than that whomever He wills. Whoever ascribes partners with God, then, surely, he devised a serious sin. **4:48**

The injustice that will not be forgiven is duality of God. God has said: *Truly, God forgives not that anything be associated with Him* ... (Q4:48) Sermon 175

Have **you** *not considered those who make themselves seem pure? Nay! God makes pure whom He wills and they will not be wronged in the least.* **4:49**

If *the Prophet* (Q7:158), peace and the mercy of God be upon him, is silent, his silence does not grieve him. If he laughs, he does not raise his voice. If he is wronged, he endures until God takes revenge on his behalf. His own self is in distress because of him, while the people are in ease from him. He puts himself in hardship for the sake of his next life and makes people feel safe from himself. His keeping away from those who distance themselves from him is by way of asceticism and purification. His nearness to those who draw near to him is by way of leniency and mercifulness. His keeping away is not by way of vanity or feeling of greatness, nor his nearness by way of deceit and cheating. Sermon 193

Look on how they devise a lie against God; and it sufficed as clear sin. **4:50**

Be aware! The worst speech is that which is untrue. Sermon 84

Have **you** *not considered those who were given a share of the Book? They believe in false gods and false deities and they say to those who were ungrateful: These are better guided than those who believed in the way!* **4:51**

My advice to you is that you should not consider anyone as a co-worker of the Lord. Be firm in your belief that there is One and only One God. Letter 23

Those are those whom God cursed. For whomever God curses, then, **you** *will not find a helper for him.* **4:52**

Certainly, only doubtful innovations cause ruin except those from which God may protect. In God's authority lies the safety of your affairs. Therefore, render Him such obedience as is neither blameworthy nor insincere. Sermon 169

Or share they in the dominion? Then, they give not humanity in the least. **4:53**

You should adhere to the Book of God because it is the strong rope, a clear light, a benefiting cure, a quenching for thirst, protection for the adherent and deliverance for the attached. It does not curve so as to need straightening and does not deflect so as to be corrected. Frequency of its repetition and its falling on ears does not make it old. Whoever speaks according to it speaks truth and whoever acts by it is forward in action. Sermon 156

Are they jealous of humanity for what God gave them of His grace? Then, surely, We gave the people of Abraham the Book and wisdom and We gave them a sublime dominion. **4:54**

Be aware! This world attracts and then turns away. It is stubborn, refusing to go ahead. It speaks lies and misappropriates. It disowns and is ungrateful. It is malicious and abandons its lovers. It attracts, but causes trouble. Its condition is changing, its step, shaking, its honor, disgrace, its seriousness, jest, and its height, lowliness. It is a place of plunder and pillage, ruin and destruction. Its people are ready with their feet to drive, to overtake and to depart. Its routes are bewildering, its exits are baffling. Its schemes end in disappointment. Consequently, strongholds betray them, houses throw them out and cunning fails them. Sermon 190

Then, among them are some who believed in him and among them are some who barred him. Hell sufficed for a blaze. **4:55**

God deputized *the Prophet* (Q7:158), peace and the mercy of God be upon him, after a gap from the previous Prophets when there was much talk among the people. With him God exhausted the series of Prophets and ended the revelation. He then fought those who were turning away from Him and who were equating others with Him for Him. Sermon 133

Truly, those who were ungrateful for Our signs, We will scorch them in a fire. As often as their skins were wholly burned, We will substitute with other skins so that they will experience the punishment. Truly, God had been Almighty, Wise. **4:56**

Where are the hearts dedicated to God and devoted to the obedience of God? They are all crowding towards worldly vanities and quarrelling over unlawful issues. The signs of the Garden and Hell have been raised for them, but they have turned their faces away from the Garden and proceeded to Hell by dint of their performances. God called them, but they showed dislike and ran away. When Satan called them, they responded and proceeded towards him. Sermon 144

Those who believed and did as the ones in accord with morality, We will cause them to enter into Gardens beneath which rivers run, ones who will dwell in them forever, eternally. For them in it will be purified spouses. We will cause them to enter into plenteous shady shadow. **4:57**

So long as people go on prompting for good and dissuading from evil and assisting each other in virtue and piety, they will remain in righteousness. Sermon 226

Truly, God commands you to give back trusts to the people. When you gave judgment between humanity, give judgment justly. Truly, how excellent God admonishes you of it. Truly, God had been Hearing, Seeing. **4:58**

Trust those who have proved themselves faithful. Do not trust and do not count upon the help of those who have proved faithless and disloyal. Remember that the absence of those who do not join us willingly and sincerely is better than their presence in our ranks. Their inactivity and lethargy is better than their participation in our activities. Letter 4

O those who believed! Obey God and obey the Messenger and those imbued with authority among you. Then, if you contended with one another in anything, refer it to God and the Messenger if you had been believing in God and the Last Day. That is better and a fairer interpretation. **4:59**

We did not name people as arbitrators, but we named the Quran the arbitrator. The Quran consists of a book inscribed between two covers. It speak not with a tongue. It cannot do without an interpreter.... When these people invited us to name the Quran as the arbitrator between us, we could not be the party turning away from the Book of God since God has said: *Obey God and obey the Messenger and those imbued with authority among you....* (Q4:59) Sermon 125

Have ***you*** *not considered those who claim that they believed in what was caused to descend to* ***you*** *and what was caused to descend before* ***you****? They want to take their disputes to another for judgment—to false deities—while they were commanded to disbelieve in them, but Satan wants to cause them to go astray—a far wandering astray.* **4:60**

Truly, Satan has certainly begun to instigate his forces and has collected his army in order that oppression may reach its extreme ends and wrong may come back to its position. Sermon 22

When it was said to them: Approach now to what God caused to descend and approach now to the Messenger, ***you*** *saw the ones who are hypocrites barring* ***you*** *with hindrances.* **4:61**

The hypocrite is a person who makes a show of faith and adopts the appearance of a Muslim. He does not hesitate in sinning, nor does he keep aloof from vice. He willfully attributes false things against *the Messenger of God* (Q48:29), peace and the mercy of God be upon him. If people knew that he was a hypocrite and a liar, they would not accept anything from him and would not confirm what he says. Sermon 210

How then will it be when they are lit on by an affliction for what their hands put forward? Again, they drew near ***you****, swearing by God: Truly, we wanted but kindness and conciliation!* **4:62**

Certainly, the tongue of a believer is at the back of his heart while the heart of a hypocrite is at the back of his tongue. When a believer intends to say anything, he thinks it over in his mind. If it is good, he discloses it, but if it is bad, he lets it remain concealed. While a hypocrite speaks whatever comes to his tongue without knowing what is in his favor and what goes against him. Sermon 176

They are those whom God knows what is in their hearts. So, turn aside from them and admonish them and say to them concerning themselves penetrating sayings. **4:63**

We ask God to complete His favors to us and to make us hold on to His rope. Sermon 194

We never sent a Messenger, but he is obeyed with the permission of God. If, when they did wrong themselves, they drew near to ***you*** *and asked for the forgiveness of God and the Messenger asked for forgiveness for them, they found God Accepter of Repentance, Compassionate.* **4:64**

Until this distinction of God, the Almighty, reached Muhammad, peace and blessing of God be upon him, God brought him out from the most distinguished sources of origin and the most honorable places of planting, namely from the same lineal tree from which He brought forth other Prophets and from which He selected His trustees. Sermon 94

But no! By ***your*** *Lord! They will not believe until they make* ***you*** *a judge in what they disagreed about between them. Again, they find within themselves no impediment to what* ***you*** *decided, resigning themselves to submission, full submission.* **4:65**

Praise belongs to God (Q1:2) Who established Islam and made it easy for those who approach it and gave strength to its columns against any one who tries to overpower it. So God made it a source of peace for him who clings to it, safety for him who enters it, argument for him who speaks about it, witness for him who fights with its help, light for him who seeks light from it, understanding for him who provides it, sagacity for him who exerts, a sign of guidance for him who perceives, sight for him who resolves, a lesson for him who seeks advice, salvation for him who testifies, confidence for him who trusts, pleasure for him who entrusts and a shield for him who endures. It is the brightest of all paths, the clearest of all passages. It has dignified minarets, bright highways, burning laps, prestigious fields of activity and a high objective. It has a collection of race horses. It is approached eagerly. Its riders are honorable. Testimony of God and *the Prophet,* (Q7:158), peace and the mercy of God be upon him, is its way. Good deeds are its minarets. Death is its extremity. This world is its racecourse. The Day of Judgment is its horses. Paradise is its point of approach. Sermon 106

If We prescribed for them that you: Kill yourselves, or: Go forth from your abodes, they would not have accomplished it, but a few of them. Had they accomplished what they are admonished by it, it would have been better for them and a stauncher confirming. **4:66**

In all of your affairs keep the thought of God in your mind and act according to His Commands and interdictions because obedience to His Orders has priority over every other thing. By various means and in various ways persuade yourself towards prayers, but do not be hard on yourself. Be gentle and persuasive. Letter 69

Then, We would have given them from that which proceeds from Our Presence a sublime compensation. **4:67**

... hidden things have appeared for those who perceive. The face of right has become clear for the wanderer. The approaching moment has raised the veil from its face and signs have appeared for those who search for them. Sermon 108

We would have guided them on a straight path. **4:68**

By God, I have knowledge of the conveyance of messages, fulfillment of promises and of entire expressions. We, the people of the house of *the Prophet* (Q7:158), peace and the mercy of God be upon him, possess the doors of wisdom and light of governance. Be aware that the paths of religion are one. Its highways are straight. He who follows them achieves the aim and secures the objective. He who stood away from them goes astray and incurs repentance. Act for the day for which provisions are stored and when the intentions would be tested. If a person's own intelligence, which is present with him, does not help him, the wits of others, which are remote from him, are more unhelpful and those who are away from him even more useless. Dread the fire whose flame is severe, whose hollow is deep, whose dress is iron and whose drink is bloody pus. Be aware! The good name of a person retained by God, the Sublime, among the people is better than wealth inherited by those who would not praise Him. Sermon 120

Whoever obeys God and the Messenger, those are to whom God was gracious among the Prophets and just persons and the witnesses and the ones in accord with morality. Excellent were those as allies! **4:69**

I bear witness that Muhammad, peace and the mercy of God be upon him, is His servant and His Prophet. He called people to His obedience and overpowered His enemies by fighting for the sake of His religion. People's joining together to falsify him and their attempt to extinguish His light did not prevent him from it. Sermon 190

That is the grace from God. God sufficed as Knowing. **4:70**

A person who does not speak a lie against God or against His Prophet (is one who) hates falsehood out of fear for God and respect for *the Messenger of God.* (Q48:29) He does not commit mistakes, but retains in his mind exactly what he heard from *the Prophet* (Q7:158), peace and the mercy of God be upon him. He relates it as he heard it without adding anything or omitting anything. He heard the repealing tradition. He retained it and acted upon it. He heard the repealed tradition and rejected it. He also understands the particular and the general. He knows the definite and indefinite. He gives everything its due position. The sayings of *the Prophet* (Q7:158), peace and the mercy of God be upon him, used to be of two types. One was particular and the other common. Sometimes a person would hear him, but he would not know what God, the Almighty, meant by it or what *the Messenger of God* (Q48:29), meant by it. In this way the listener carries it and memorizes it without knowing its meaning and its real intention or what was its reason. Sermon 210

O those who believed! Take your precautions. Then, move forward in companies of men or move forward altogether. **4:71**
Truly, among you is he who lingers behind. Then, if affliction lit on you, he would say: Surely, God was gracious to me that I not be a witness to them. **4:72**

I praise God for whatever matter He ordained and whatever action He destines and for my trial with you, O group of people, who do not obey when I order and do not respond when I call you. If you are at ease, you engage in conceited conversation, but if you are faced with battle you show weakness. Sermon 180

If the grace of God lit on you, certainly, he would say, as if there be not any affection between you and between him: Would that I had been with them so that I would have won a triumph, winning a sublime triumph! **4:73**

The troubles are like a dark night. Horses would not stand facing them, nor would their banners turn back. They would approach in full reins and ready with saddles. Their leader would be driving them and the rider would be exerting them. The trouble-mongers are a people whose attacks are severe. Those who would fight them for the sake of God would be a people who are low in the estimation of the proud, unknown in the earth, but well known in the heavens. Sermon 102

Then, let fight in the way of God those who sell this present life for the world to come. Whoever fights in the way of God, then, is slain or is vanquished, We will give him a sublime compensation. **4:74**

O my God! We seek **Your** protection from turning away from **Your** command, or revolting against **Your** religion, or being led away by our desires instead of by guidance that comes from **You**. Sermon 215

Why should you not fight in the way of God and for the ones taken advantage of due to weakness among the men and the women and the children, those who say: Our Lord! Bring us out from this town whose people are the ones who are unjust and assign for us a protector from ***Your*** *Presence and assign for us a helper from* ***Your*** *Presence?* **4:75**

One of his friends said on that occasion: I wish my brother so-and-so had been present and he too would have seen what success and victory God had given you. Ali ibn Abi Talib said: Did your brother consider me as a friend? He said: Yes. Then Ali ibn Abi Talib said: In that case he was with us in this army of ours. Even those persons were also present who are still in the loins of men and wombs of women. Shortly, time will bring them out and faith will gain strength through them. Sermon 12

Those who believed fight in the way of God. Those who were ungrateful fight in the way of the false deity. So, fight the protectors of Satan. Truly the cunning of Satan had been weak. **4:76**

Truly, Satan has collected his group and assembled his horse-men and foot-soldiers. Truly, I have my sagacity. I have neither deceived myself, nor ever been deceived. By God, I shall fill to the brim a cistern for them from which I alone would draw water. They can neither turn away from it, nor return to it. Sermon 10

Have **you** *not considered those who when it was said to them: Limit your hands from warfare and perform the formal prayer and give the purifying alms? Then, when fighting was prescribed for* *them, there was a group of people among them who dread humanity, even dreading God or with a more severe dreading, and they said: Our Lord! Why had You prescribed fighting for us? Why had* ***You*** *not postponed it for another near term for us? Say: The enjoyment of the present is little and the world to come is better. For whomever was God-conscious, you will not be wronged in the least.* **4:77**

Do you not see that your predecessors did not come back and the surviving followers did not remain? Do you not observe that the people of the world pass mornings and evenings in different conditions? Thus, somewhere the dead is wept for, someone is being condoled, someone is prostrate in distress, someone is enquiring about the sick, someone is passing his last breath, someone is hankering after the world while death is looking for him, someone is forgetful, but he is not forgotten by death, and the survivors walk in the footsteps of the predecessors. Sermon 99

Wherever you be, death will overtake you, even if you had been in imposing towers. When benevolence lights on them, they say: This is from God. When an evil deed lights on them, they say: This is from ***you****. Say: All is from God. So, what is with these folk that they understand almost no discourse?* **4:78**

This is a house surrounded by calamities and well-known for deceitfulness. Its conditions do not last. Those who inhabit it do not remain safe. Its conditions are variable. Its ways are changing. Life in it is blameworthy. Safety in it is non-existent. Yet its people are its targets. It strikes them with its arrows and destroys them through death. Sermon 225

Whatever of benevolence lit on ***you*** *is from God. Whatever evil deeds lit on* ***you****, then, is from* ***yourself****. We sent* ***you*** *to humanity as a Messenger. God sufficed as Witness.* **4:79**

You should fear what calamities befell peoples before you on account of their evil deeds and detestable actions. Remember what happened to them during good or bad circumstances. Be cautious that you do not become like them. Sermon 192

Whoever obeys the Messenger, surely, obeyed God and whoever turned away, then We sent ***you*** *not as a guardian over them.* **4:80**

I bear witness that Muhammad, peace and the mercy of God be upon him, is His servant and His Prophet whom He deputed when the signs of guidance were obliterated and the ways of religion were desolate. So he threw open the truth, gave advice to the people, guided them towards righteousness and ordered them to be moderate. May God bless him. Sermon 195

They say: Obedience! Then, when they departed from ***you****, a section of them spent the night planning on other than what* ***you*** *have said. God records what they spend the night planning. So, turn aside from them and put* ***your*** *trust in God. God sufficed as Trustee.* **4:81**

O people! By God, I do not impel you to any obedience unless I practice it before you. I do not restrain you from any disobedience unless I desist from it before you. Sermon 175

But no! They meditate not on the Recitation. If it had been from other than God, certainly, they would have found in it many contradictions. **4:82**

Is it that God ordered them to differ and they obeyed Him? Or, He prohibited them from it, but they disobeyed Him? Or, is it that God sent an incomplete faith and sought their help to complete it? Or, are they His partners in the affairs, so that it is their share of duty to pronounce and He has to agree? Or, is it that God the Almighty sent a perfect faith, but *the Prophet* (Q7:158), peace and the mercy of God be upon him, fell short of conveying it and handing it over to the people? The fact is that God the Almighty says: *We have not neglected anything in the Book* (Q6:38) and in it is a "clarification of everything." He says that one part of the Quran verifies another part and that there is no divergence in it: *But no! They meditate not on the Recitation. If it had been from other than God, certainly, they would have found in it many contradictions.* (Q4:82) Certainly the manifest of the Quran is wonderful and its hidden is deep in meaning. Its wonders will never disappear. Its amazements will never pass away. Its intricacies cannot be cleared except through itself. Sermon 18

Whenever drew near them a command of public safety or fear, they broadcasted it. But if they referred it to the Messenger, and to those imbued with authority among them, they would have known it—those who investigate from among them. If it were not for the grace of God on you and His mercy, certainly, you would have followed Satan, but a few. **4:83**

They have made Satan the master of their affairs. He has taken them as partners. Sermon 8

So, fight ***you*** *in the way of God.* ***You*** *are not placed with a burden but for* ***yourself****. Encourage the ones who believe. Perhaps God will limit the might of those who were ungrateful. God is Stauncher in might and Stauncher in making an example.* **4:84**

O people, your bodies are together, but your desires are divergent. Your talk softens the hard stones. Your action attracts your enemy towards you. You claim in your sittings that you would do this and that, but when fighting approaches, you say to war: Turn away. If one calls you for help, the call receives no heed. He who deals harshly with you, his heart has no solace. Excuses are amiss like that of a debtor unwilling to pay. The ignoble cannot ward off oppression. Right cannot be achieved without effort. Which is the house besides this one to protect? With which leader would you go for fighting after me? By God! Deceived is one whom you have deceived while, by God, he who is successful with you receives only useless arrows! You are like broken arrows thrown over the enemy. By God! I am now in the position that I neither confirm your views, nor hope for your support, nor challenge the enemy through you. What is the matter with you? What is your ailment? What is your cure? The other party is also men of your type, but they are so different in character. Will there be talk without action, carelessness without God-consciousness and greed in things not right? Sermon 29

Whoever intercedes with a benevolent intercession, there will be for himself a share of it. Whoever intercedes with an intercession for bad deeds, there will be for himself a like part of it. God had been over everything One Who Oversees. **4:85**

Know that the Quran is an interceder and its intercession will be accepted. It is a speaker who bears witness. For whoever the Quran intercedes on the Day of Judgment, its intercession for him would be accepted. He about whom the Quran speaks ill on the Day of Judgment shall testify to it. On the Day of Judgment, an announcer will announce: Be aware! Every sower of a crop is in distress except the sowers of the Quran. Therefore, you should be among the sowers of the Quran and its followers. Make it your guide towards

God. Seek its advice for yourselves, do not trust your views against it and regard your desires in the matter of the Quran as deceitful. Sermon 176

When you were given greetings with greetings, then, give greetings fairer than that or return the same to them. Truly, God had been over everything a Reckoner. **4:86**

Today is the day of action, but there is no reckoning. Tomorrow is the day of reckoning, but there would be no opportunity for action. Sermon 42

God, there is no god but He. He will, certainly, gather you on the Day of Resurrection. There is no doubt about it. Who is one who is more sincere in discourse than God? **4:87**
Then, what is it with you that you be two factions concerning the ones who are hypocrites? God overthrew them for what they earned? Want you to guide whom God caused to go astray? Whomever God causes to go astray, ***you*** *will never find for him a way.* **4:88**

We praise God for the help He has given us in carrying out His obedience and in preventing us from disobedience. We ask Him to complete His favors to us and to make us hold on to His rope. We bear witness that Muhammad, peace and the mercy of God be upon him, is *His servant* (Q17:1), and *His Messenger.* (Q3:101) He entered every hardship in search of God's pleasure and endured for its sake every grief. His near relations changed themselves for him. Those who were remote from him in relationship, united against him. Sermon 194

They wished for you to be ungrateful as they were ungrateful so you become equals. So, take not to yourselves protectors from them until they emigrate in the way of God. Then, if they turned away, then, take them and kill them wherever you found them. Take not to yourselves from them either a protector or a helper, **4:89**
but those who reach out to a folk who between you and between them is a solemn promise or when they drew near to you, their breasts were reluctant that they fight you or they fight their folk? If God willed, He would have given them authority over you and they would have fought you. So, if they withdrew from you and fight not against you and gave a proposal of surrender to you, then, God has not assigned any way for you against them. **4:90**

Populated places were brightened through *the Prophet* (Q7:158), peace and the mercy of God be upon him, when previously there was dark misguidance, overpowering ignorance and rude habits, and people regarded unlawful as lawful, humiliated the man of wisdom, passed lives when there were no prophets and died as ungrateful. Sermon 151

You will find others who want that they be safe from you and that they be safe from their folk. Whenever they were returned to temptation, they were overthrown in it. So, if they withdraw not from you, nor give a proposal of surrender to you and limit not their hands, then, take them and kill them wherever you came upon them. Those, We made for you a clear authority against them. **4:91**

You are being killed and you do not kill. You are being attacked but you do not attack. God is being disobeyed and you remain agreeable to it. When I ask you to move against them in the summer, you say the weather is too hot: Spare us until the heat subsides from us. When I order you to march in winter, you say it is severely cold: Give us time until the cold clears from us. These are just excuses for evading heat and cold because if you run away from heat and cold, you would be, by God, running away in a greater degree from war. O you semblance of men, not men, your intelligence is that of children and your wit is that of the occupants of the curtained canopies. Sermon 27

It had not been for the one who believes to kill one who believes unless by error. Whoever killed one who believes by error the letting go of a believing bondsperson and blood money should be handed over to his family unless that family be charitable. If he had been from the enemy folk of yours and he be one who believes, then, there should be the letting go of a believing bondsperson. If he had been of a folk who between you and between them is a solemn promise, then, blood money should be handed over to the family and the letting go of a believing bondsperson. Then, whoever finds not the means, then, formally fast for two successive months as a penance from God. God had been Knowing, Wise. **4:92**

Desist others from the unlawful and abstain from it yourself because you have been commanded to abstain yourself before abstaining others. Sermon 105

Whoever kills one who believes as one who is willful, then, his recompense is hell, one who will dwell in it forever. God was angry with him and cursed him and He prepared for him a tremendous punishment. **4:93**

O my God! I beseech **You** to take revenge on the Quraysh and those who are assisting them, for they have cut asunder my kinship, over-turned my cup and joined together to contest a right to which I was entitled more than anyone else. They said to me: If you get your right, that will be just, but if you are denied the right, that too will be just. Endure it with sadness or kill yourself in grief. I looked around, but found no one to shield me, protect me or help me except the members of my family. I refrained from flinging them into death and, therefore closed my eyes despite the dust, kept swallowing saliva despite the suffocation of grief and endured pangs of anger although it was more bitter than colocynth and more grievous than the bite of knives. Sermon 217

O those who believed! When you traveled in the way of God, then be clear and say not to whomever gave you a proposal of peace: ***You*** *are not one who believes, looking for advantage in this present life. With God is much gain. Thus, you had been like that before, then God showed grace to you, so be clear. Truly, God had been Aware of what you do.* **4:94**

Are you not residing in the houses of those before you who were of longer ages, better traces, had bigger desires, were more in numbers and had greater armies? How they devoted themselves to the world and how they showed preference to it! Then they left it without any provision that could convey them through or the back of a beast for riding to carry them. Sermon 111

Not on the same level are the ones who sit at home among the ones who believe—other than those imbued with disability—and the ones who struggle in the way of God with their wealth and their lives. God gave advantage to the ones who struggle with their wealth and their lives by a degree over the ones who sit at home. To each God promised the fairer. God gave advantage to the ones who struggle over the ones who sit at home with a sublime compensation, **4:95**
degrees from Him and forgiveness and mercy. God had been Forgiving, Compassionate. **4:96**

Justice is to struggle in the cause of God sincerely and firmly on all occasions and to detest the vicious. Saying 30

Truly those whom the angels gather to themselves—they will say: In what condition had you been? They will say: We had been taken advantage of because of our weakness on the earth. They will say: Is the earth of God not wide enough to emigrate in it? Then for those, their place of shelter will be hell and how evil a Homecoming, **4:97**

An angel announces daily: Birth of more human beings means so many more will die. The collection of more wealth means much more will be destroyed. The erection of more buildings means so many more ruins will come. Saying. 113

But the ones taken advantage of due to weakness of the men and the women and the children who are neither able to access some means, nor are they truly guided to the way, **4:98**
then those, perhaps God will pardon them. God had been Pardoning, Forgiving. **4:99**

There is one whose weakness and lack of means have held him back.... Sermon 32

Whoever emigrates in the way of God will find in and on the earth many places of refuge and plenty. Whoever goes forth from his house as one who emigrates for God and His Messenger, and, again, death overtakes him, then, surely, his compensation will fall on God. God had been Forgiving, Compassionate. **4:100**

One belief is that which is firm and steadfast in hearts. Another belief is that which remains temporarily in the heart and the breast up to a certain time. If you were to acquit yourself before any person, you should wait until death approaches him, for that is the time limit for being acquitted. Sermon 189

When you traveled on the earth, there is no blame on you if you shorten the formal prayer if you feared that you would be persecuted by those who were ungrateful. The ones who are ungrateful, they had been for you a clear enemy. **4:101**

This is the thing against which God has protected His creatures who are believers by means of prayers, alms-giving and suffering the hardship of fasting in the days in which it has been made obligatory in order to give their limbs peacefulness, to cast fear in their eyes, to make their spirits humble, to give their hearts humility and to remove haughtiness from them. Sermon 192

*When **you** had been among them, performing the formal prayer with them, let a section of them stand up with **you** and take their weapons. When they prostrated themselves, then, let them move behind you and let another section approach who has not yet formally prayed. Then, let them formally pray with **you** and let them take their precaution and their weapons. Those who were ungrateful wished for you to be heedless of your weapons and your sustenance. They would turn against you with a single turning. There is no blame on you if you had been annoyed because of rain or you had been sick that you lay down your weapons. Take precaution for yourselves. Truly, God prepared for the ones who are ungrateful a despised punishment.* **4:102**

Whoever takes a partner for **You** is ungrateful according to what is stated in **Your** unambiguous verses and indicated by the evidence of **Your** clear arguments. Sermon 91

Then, when you satisfied the formal prayer, then, remember God when upright and sitting and on your sides. Then, when you were secured, perform the formal prayer. Truly, the formal prayer had been —for the ones who believe— a timed prescription. **4:103**

Pledge yourself with prayer and remain steady with it. Offer prayer as much as possible and seek nearness to God through it, because it is imposed upon the believers as a timed ordinance: *Truly, the formal prayer had been—for the ones who believe—a timed prescription.* (Q4:103) Sermon 198

Be not feeble in looking for the folk (the enemy). *If you be suffering, they suffer as you suffer, yet you hope for from God what they hope not for, and God had been Knowing, Wise.* **4:104**

Whoever takes a partner for **You** is ungrateful according to what is stated in **Your** unambiguous verses and indicated by the evidence of **Your** clear arguments. Sermon 91

Truly, We caused to descend to ***you*** *the Book with The Truth so that* ***you*** *will give judgment between humanity by what God caused* ***you*** *to see. Be* ***you*** *not the pleader for ones who are traitors.* **4:105**

On us it is obligatory, for your sake, to abide by the Book of God (Quran), the Sublime, and the conduct of *the Prophet* (Q7:158), peace and the mercy of God be upon him, to stand by His rights and to revive his *sunna*. Sermon 169

Ask God for forgiveness. Truly, God had been Forgiving, Compassionate. **4:106**

O my God! Forgive me. **You** know more about me than I do. If I return to sin, **You** return to forgiveness. My God, forgive me what I had promised to myself, but **You** did not find its fulfillment with me. My God, forgive me that with what I sought nearness to **You** with my tongue, but my heart opposed and did not perform. My God, forgive me winking of the eye, vile utterances, desires of the heart and errors of speech. Sermon 78

Dispute not for those who are dishonest to themselves. Truly, God loves not anyone who had been a sinful betrayer. **4:107**

There is the individual who heard a saying from *the Prophet* (Q7:158), peace and the mercy of God be upon him, but did not memorize it as it was, but surmised it. He does not lie willfully. Now, he carries the saying with him and relates it, acts upon it and claims that: I heard it from *the Messenger of God.* (Q48:29) If the Muslims come to know that he has committed a mistake in it, they will not accept it from him, and if he himself knows that he is in the wrong he will give it up. Sermon 210

They conceal themselves from humanity, but they conceal themselves not from God, as He is with them when they spend the night planning with sayings with which He is not well-pleased. God had been One Who Encloses what they do. **4:108**

Truly, sins are like unruly horses on whom their riders have been placed and their reins have been let loose so that they would jump with them in hellfire. Truly, that God-consciousness is like trained horses on whom the riders have been placed with the reins in their hands so that they would take the riders to heaven. There is right and wrong and there are followers for each. If wrong dominates, it has always in the past been so and if truth goes down, that, too, has often occurred. Sermon 16

Lo, behold! You are these who disputed for them in this present life. Then, who will dispute with God for them on the Day of Resurrection? Or who will be a trustee over them? **4:109**

On that day even the opening of an eye in the air and the sound of a footstep on the ground will be assigned its due through His Justice and His Equity. On that Day many an argument will prove void and a contention for excuses will stand rejected. Sermon 222

Whoever does evil or does wrong to himself, again, asks for forgiveness from God will, truly, find God Forgiving, Compassionate. **4:110**

Praise belongs to God (Q1:2) from whose mercy no one loses hope, from whose bounty no one is deprived, from whose forgiveness no one is disappointed and for whose worship no one is too high. His mercy never ceases and His bounty never ceases. Sermon 45

Whoever earns a sin, truly, he earns it only against himself. God had been Knowing, Wise. **4:111**

His desires deceive him. Satan keeps posted about him. He beautifies his sin for him so that he may commit it. He prompts him to delay repentance until his desires cause him to be the most negligent. Sermon 64

Whoever earns a transgression or a sin, and, again, accuses an innocent one, surely, laid a burden on himself of false charges that harm another's reputation and a clear sin. **4:112**

O creature of God, do not be quick in exposing anyone's sin for he may be forgiven for it. Do not feel yourself safe even for a small sin because you may be punished for it. Therefore, every one of you who comes to know the faults of others should not expose them in view of what he knows about his own faults. He should remain busy in thanks that he has been saved from what others have been indulging in. Sermon 140

Were it not for the grace of God on ***you*** *and His mercy, a section of them was about to do something that would cause* ***you*** *to go astray. They cause none to go astray but themselves and they injure* ***you*** *not at all. God caused the Book to descend to* ***you*** *and wisdom and taught* ***you*** *what* ***you*** *are not knowing. The grace of God had been sublime upon* ***you.*** **4:113**

The Book of God is that through which you see, you speak and you hear. Sermon 132

No good is there in most of their conspiring secretly, but for him who commanded charity or one who is honorable or makes things right between humanity. Whoever accomplishes that—looking for the goodwill of God—then, We will give him a sublime compensation. **4:114**

Praise to God, Who is the First before every first and the Last after every last. His Firstness necessitates that there is no other first before Him and His Lastness necessitates that there is no other last after Him. I do bear witness that *there is no god but God* (Q47:19), both openly as well as secretly, with heart as well as with tongue. Sermon 101

Whoever makes a breach with the Messenger after the guidance became clear to him and follows a way other than that of the ones who believe, We will turn him away from what he turns to and We will scorch him in hell. How evil a Homecoming! **4:115**

O my God! I seek **Your** protection from becoming destitute despite **Your** riches, from being misguided despite **Your** guidance, from being molested in **Your** realm and from being humiliated while authority rests with **You**. Sermon 215

Truly, God forgives not to ascribe partners with Him. He forgives other than that whomever He wills. Whoever ascribes partners with God, then, surely, went astray, a wandering far astray. **4:116**

The injustice that will not be forgiven is claiming the duality of God. God has said: *Truly, God forgives not to ascribe partners with Him ...* (Q4:116). Sermon 175

They call to other than Him none but female gods and they call to but the rebellious Satan. **4:117**
God cursed him. Satan said: Truly, I will take to myself of **Your** *servants, an apportioned share,* **4:118**
and I will cause them to go astray. I will fill them with false desires. I will command them, then they will slit the ears of the flocks. I will command them, and they will alter the creation of God. Whoever takes Satan to himself for a protector other than God, then, surely, he lost, a clear loss. **4:119**
Satan promises them and fills them with false desires and Satan promises them nothing but delusion. **4:120**

Satan's most reliable opportunities (the presence of excessive praise and conceit) is to efface the virtue of one who is virtuous. Letter 53*

Those, their place of shelter will be hell and they will find no way to escape from it. **4:121**

They have made Satan the master of their affairs. He has taken them as partners. He has laid eggs and hatched them in their bosoms. He creeps and crawls in their laps. He sees through their eyes and speaks with their tongues. In this way he has led them to sinfulness and adorned for them foul things like the action of one whom Satan has made partner in his domain and speaks untruth through his tongue. Sermon 7

But those who believed and did as the ones in accord with morality, We will cause them to enter Gardens beneath which rivers run, ones who will dwell in them forever, eternally. The promise of God is true. Who is One More Sincere in speech than God? **4:122**

God offered Adam the chance to repent, taught him words of His Mercy, promised him return to His Paradise and sent him down to the place of trial and procreation of progeny. Sermon 1

Paradise will be neither after your fantasies, nor the fantasies of the People of the Book. Whoever does evil will be given recompense for it and he will not find for himself other than God either a protector or a helper. **4:123**

Remember well that if there is any defect in your officers and you are tolerating it, then you and only you are responsible for all those evils. Letter 53

Whoever does as the ones in accord with morality—whether male or female—and is one who believes then, those will enter the Garden and they will not be wronged, in the least. **4:124**

O God's human being! The most beloved of God is he whom God has given power to act against his passions so that his interior is submerged in grief and his exterior is covered with fear. The lamp of guidance is burning in his heart. He has provided entertainment for the day that is to befall him. He regards what is distant to be near himself and takes the hard to be light. He looks at and perceives. He remembers God and enhances the tempo of his actions. Sermon 87

Who is fairer in the way of life than he who submitted his face to God and he is one who is a doer of good and followed the creed of Abraham, a monotheist? God took Abraham to Himself as a friend. **4:125**

Nearest to the Prophets are those persons who obey them. The Quran says: *Who is fairer in the way of life than he who submitted his face to God and he is one who is a doer of good and followed the creed of Abraham, a monotheist? God took Abraham to Himself as a friend.* (Q4:125) Letter 96

To God is whatever is in the heavens and whatever is in and on the earth. God had been One Who Encloses everything. **4:126**

He has arranged the depressions and elevations of the openings of the sky. He has joined the breadths of its breaches and has joined them with one another. He has made easy the approach to its heights for those angels who come down with His commands and those angels who go up with the deeds of the creatures. Sermon 91

They ask ***you*** *for advice about women. Say: God pronounces to you about them (f) and what is recounted to you in the Book about women who have orphans, those to whom (f) you give not what was prescribed for them (f) because you prefer that you marry them (f) and about the ones taken advantage of due to weakness among children and that you stand up for the orphans with equity. Whatever you accomplish of good, then, truly, God had been Knowing of it.* **4:127**

O my God! **You** know that what we did was not to seek power, nor to acquire anything from the vanities of the world. We rather wanted to restore the signs of **Your** religion and to usher prosperity into **Your** cities so that the oppressed among **Your** creatures might be safe and **Your** forsaken commands might be established. Sermon 131

If a woman feared resistance or turning aside from her husband no blame on either of them that they make things right between the two, that there be reconciliation. Reconciliation is better. Souls were prone to stinginess. If you do good and are God-conscious, then, truly, God had been Aware of what you do. **4:128**
You will never be able to be just between wives, even if you were eager so incline not with total inclination away from her, forsaking her as if she be one who is in suspense. If you make things right and are God-conscious, then, truly, God had been Forgiving, Compassionate. **4:129**
If the two split up, God will enrich each of them from all His plenty. God had been One Who is Extensive, Wise. **4:130**

Whoever can at this time keep himself clinging to God should do so. Sermon 156

To God is whatever is in the heavens and whatever is in and on the earth and, certainly, We charged those who were given the Book before you, and to you, that you be God-conscious alone. If you are ungrateful, then, truly, to God belongs whatever is in the heavens and whatever is in and on the earth. God had been Sufficient, Worthy of Praise. **4:131**

Praise belongs to God (Q1:2) when night spreads and darkens. *Praise belongs to God* (Q1:2) whenever a star shines and sets. *Praise belongs to God* (Q1:2) whose bounty never misses and whose favors cannot be repaid. Sermon 48

To God belongs whatever is in the heavens and whatever is in and on the earth. God sufficed as a Trustee. **4:132**

Praise belongs to God (Q1:2) Who is above all similarity to creatures, is above the words of describers Who displays the wonders of His management for the on-lookers, is hidden from the imagination of thinkers by virtue of the greatness of His glory, has knowledge without acquiring it by adding to it or drawing it from someone, and Who is the ordainer of all matters without reflecting or thinking. He is such that gloom does not concern

Him, nor does He seek light from brightness. Night does not overtake Him, nor does the day pass over Him so as to affect Him in any manner. His comprehension of things is not through eyes. His knowledge is not dependent on being informed. God deputized *the Prophet* (Q7:158), peace and the mercy of God be upon him, with light and accorded him the highest precedence in selection. Through him God united those who were divided, overpowered the powerful, overcame difficulties and leveled rugged ground and, thus, removed misguidance from right and left. Sermon 213

If He wills, He will cause you to be put away—O humanity—and approach with others. Over that God had been Powerful. **4:133**

He is Powerful, such that when imagination shoots its arrows to comprehend the extremity of His power and the mind, making itself free of the dangers of evil thoughts, tries to find Him in the depth of His realm, and hearts long to grasp the realities of His attributes and openings of intelligence penetrate beyond description in order to secure knowledge about His Being, crossing the dark pitfalls of the unknown and concentrating towards Him, He would turn them back. They would return defeated admitting that the reality of His knowledge cannot be comprehended by such random efforts, nor can an iota of the sublimity of His Honor enter the understanding of thinkers. Sermon 91

Whoever had been wanting a reward for good deeds in the present, then with God is The Reward for good deeds in the present and in the world to come. God had been Hearing, Seeing. **4:134**

God is the Giver of all reward and distinction, and Dispeller of all calamities and hardships. I praise Him for His continuous mercy and His copious bounties. Sermon 82

O those who believed! Be staunch in equity as witnesses to God even against yourselves or the ones who are your parents or the nearest of kin, whether you would be rich or poor, then God is Closer to both than you are. So, follow not your desires that you become unbalanced. If you distort or turn aside, then, truly, God had been Aware of what you do. **4:135**

What is the matter with you? What is your ailment? What is your cure? Sermon 29

O those who believed! Believe in God and His Messenger and the Book which He sent down to His Messenger and the Book that He caused to descend before. Whoever is ungrateful to God and His angels and His Books and His Messengers and the Last Day, then, surely, went astray, a wandering far astray. **4:136**

The leader of guidance and the leader of destruction cannot be equal, nor the friend of *the Prophet* (Q7:158), peace and the mercy of God be upon him, and the enemy of *the Prophet,* (Q7:158). *The Messenger of God* (Q48:29), peace and the mercy of God be upon him, has told me: I have no fear for my Community (*umma*) from either a believer or an unbeliever. As for the believer, God will afford him protection because of his belief. As for the unbeliever, God will humiliate him because of his unbelief. Letter 27

Truly those who believed, and, again, disbelieved, and, again, believe and, again, disbelieve, and, again, added to disbelief, neither will God be forgiving of them nor guide them to a way. **4:137**

The hypocrite is a person who makes a show of faith and adopts the appearance of a Muslim. He does not hesitate in sinning, nor does he keep aloof from vice. He willfully attributes false things against *the Messenger of God* (Q48:29), peace and the mercy of God be upon him. If people knew that he was a hypocrite and a liar, they would not accept anything from him and would not confirm what he says. Sermon 210

Give **you** *good tidings to the ones who are hypocrites that, truly, for them is a painful punishment,* **4:138**
those who take to themselves the ones who are ungrateful as their protectors instead of the ones who believe! Are they looking for great glory with them? Truly, then, all great glory belongs to God alone. **4:139**

The hypocrite makes people feel safe from major sins and takes serious crimes lightly. He says that he is waiting for clarification of doubts, but he remains plunged therein. He remains aloof from innovations, but actually he is immersed in them. His shape is that of a human being, but his heart is that of a beast. He does not know the door of guidance to follow, nor the door of misguidance to keep aloof therefrom. These are living dead bodies. Sermon 87

Surely, He sent down to you in the Book that when you heard the signs of God being unappreciated and being ridiculed, then, and sit not with them until they discuss in conversation about other than that or else, you will be like them. Truly, God is One Who Gathers the ones who are hypocrites and the ones who are ungrateful altogether in hell. **4:140**

Hypocrites sowed vices, watered them with deception and harvested destruction. Sermon 2

Those who lie in wait for you, if there had been a victory from God for you, they would say: Have we not been with you? If the ones who are ungrateful had been with a share, they would say: Gain we not mastery over you and secure you from among the ones who believe? God will give judgment between you on the Day of Resurrection. God will never assign the ones who are ungrateful any way over the ones who believe. **4:141**

You sent a Messenger to invite towards it, but the people did not respond to the caller and did not feel persuaded to what **You** persuaded them, nor showed eagerness towards what **You** desired them to eagerly feel. Sermon 108

Truly, the ones who are hypocrites seek to trick God. He is The One Who Deceives them, and when they stood up for formal prayer, they stood up lazily to make display to humanity. They remember not God but a little, **4:142**
ones who are wavering between this and that, neither with these, nor with these. Whom God causes to go astray, **you** *will never find a way for him.* **4:143**

The Arabs let loose the reins of their horses to quicken their march against him, and struck the bellies of their carriers to rouse them in fighting against *the Messenger of God* (Q48:29), so much so that enemies came to his threshold from the remotest places and most distant areas. Sermon 194

O those who believed! Take not to yourselves the ones who are ungrateful as protectors instead of the ones who believe. Want you to assign to God clear authority against yourselves? **4:144**
Truly, the ones who are hypocrites will be in the lowest, deepest reaches of the fire. **You** *will not find for them any helper,* **4:145**
but those who repented and made things right and cleaved firmly to God and made sincere their

way of life for God, then, those will be with the ones who believe. God will give the ones who believe a sublime compensation. **4:146**

O my God! We seek **Your** protection from turning away from **Your** command, or revolting against **Your** religion, or being led away by our desires instead of by guidance that comes from **You**. Sermon 215

What would God accomplish by your punishment if you gave thanks to Him and believed in Him? God had been One Who is Responsive, Knowing. **4:147**

Do not forget gratitude when receiving blessings for God has exhausted the excuses before you through clear, shining arguments and open, bright books. Sermon 81

God loves not the open publishing of evil sayings, the open publishing of evil sayings, but by him who was wronged. God had been Hearing, Knowing. **4:148**

Be aware of destroying your manners and changing them, maintaining one tongue. A person should control his tongue because the tongue is obstinate with its master. By God, I do not find that God-consciousness benefits a person who practices it unless he controls his tongue. Certainly, the tongue of a believer is at the back of his heart while the heart of a hypocrite is at the back of his tongue because, when a believer intends to say anything, he thinks it over in his mind. If it is good he discloses it, but if it is bad he lets it remain concealed. While a hypocrite speaks whatever comes to his tongue, without knowing what is in his favor and what goes against him. Sermon 176

If you show good or conceal it or pardon evil, then, truly, God had been Pardoning, Powerful. **4:149**

Habituate your heart to mercy for the subjects and to affection and kindness for them. Do not stand over them like greedy beasts who feel it is enough to devour them, since they are of two kinds, either your brother in religion or one like you in creation. They will commit slips and encounter mistakes. They may act wrongly, willfully or by neglect. So extend to them your forgiveness and pardon, in the same way as you would like God to extend His forgiveness and pardon to you. Letter 53

Truly, those who are ungrateful to God and His Messengers and they want to separate and divide between God and His Messengers and they say: We believe in some and we disbelieve in others, they want that they take themselves to a way between that. **4:150**
Those, they are, in truth, the ones who are ungrateful. We made ready for the ones who are ungrateful a despised punishment. **4:151**

Revival means to unite on it in a matter and destruction means to divide on a matter. Sermon 126

Those who believed in God and His Messengers and they separate and divide not between any of them, those, He will give them their compensation. God had been Forgiving, Compassionate. **4:152**

Even when He made Adam die, He did not leave them without one who would serve among them as proof and plea for His Godhead and serve as the link between them and His knowledge, but He provided to them the proofs through His chosen Messengers and bearers of the trust of His Message, age after age, until the process came to end with our Prophet Muhammad, peace and the mercy of God be upon him, and His pleas and warnings reached finality. Sermon 91

The People of the Book ask ***you*** *that* ***you*** *send down to them a Book from heaven. Surely, they had asked Moses for greater than that. Then, they said: Cause us to see God publicly. So, a thunderbolt took them for their injustice. Again, they took the calf to themselves after what drew near to them—the clear portents. Even so We pardoned that. We gave Moses a clear authority.* **4:153**

If you overpower your enemy, then pardon him by way of thankfulness to God, for being able to subdue him. Saying 10

We exalted the mount above them for their solemn promise. We said to them: Enter the door as ones who prostrate themselves. We said to them: Disregard not the Sabbath! We took from them an earnest solemn promise. **4:154**
for their breaking their solemn promise and their ingratitude for the signs of God and their killing the Prophets without right and their saying: Our hearts are encased. Nay! God set a seal on them for their ingratitude—so they believe not but a few— **4:155**
and for their ingratitude and their saying against Mary serious, false charges to harm her reputation **4:156**
and for their saying: We killed the Messiah, Jesus son of Mary, the Messenger of God. They killed him not, nor they crucified him. Rather, a likeness to him of another was shown to them. Truly, those who were at variance in it are in uncertainty about it. There is no knowledge with them about it but they are pursuing an opinion. They for certain killed him not. **4:157**
Nay! God exalted him to Himself. God had been Almighty, Wise. **4:158**
Yet there is none among the People of the Book but will, surely, believe in Jesus before his death. On the Day of Resurrection he will be a witness against them. **4:159**

Make yourself deserve what He has promised you, by having confidence in the truth of His promise and entertaining fear for the Day of Judgment. Sermon 82

So, for the injustice of those who became Jews, We forbade them what was good that was permitted to them and for their barring many from the way of God **4:160**
and for their taking usury—although they were prohibited from it—and for their consuming the wealth of humanity with falsehood. We made ready for the ones who are ungrateful among them a painful punishment. **4:161**
But the ones who are firmly rooted in knowledge among them and the ones who believe, they believe in what was caused to descend to ***you*** *and what was caused to descend before* ***you****. They are the ones who perform the formal prayer. They are the ones who give the purifying alms. They are the ones who believe in God and the Last Day. It is those to whom We will give a sublime compensation.* **4:162**

Whoever trades without knowing the rules of religious law will be involved in usury. Hadith 447

Truly, We revealed to ***you****, as We revealed to Noah and the Prophets after him. We revealed to Abraham and Ishmael and Isaac and Jacob and the Tribes and Jesus and Job and Jonah and Aaron and Solomon. We gave David the Psalms.* **4:163**

If you desire I can give you a third example of David. He is the holder of the Psalms and the reciter among the people of Paradise. He used to prepare baskets of date palm leaves with his own hands and would say to his companions: Which of you will help me by purchasing it? He used to eat barley bread bought out of its price. Sermon 160

Messengers We related to ***you*** *before and Messengers We relate to* ***you*** *not. God spoke directly to Moses, speaking directly.* **4:164**
Messengers are ones who give good tidings and ones who warn so that humanity not be in disputation against God after the Messengers. God had been Almighty, Wise. **4:165**

Then God sent His Messengers and series of His prophets towards them to get them to fulfill the pledges of His creation, to recall to them His bounties, to exhort them by preaching, to unveil before them the hidden virtues of wisdom and show them the signs of His Omnipotence, namely the sky which is raised over them, the earth that is placed beneath them, means of living that sustain them, deaths that make them die, ailments that turn them old and incidents that successively betake them. Sermon 1

God bears witness to what He caused to descend to ***you****. He caused it to descend with His knowledge. The angels also bear witness. God sufficed as witness.* **4:166**

We praise Him for whatever He takes or gives or whatever He inflicts on us or tries us with. He is aware of all that is hidden and He sees all that is concealed. He knows all that breasts contain or eyes hide. We render evidence that *there is no god, but He.* (Q3:2) and that *Muhammad* (Q48:29), peace and the mercy of God be upon him, has been chosen by Him and deputized by Him—evidence tendered both secretly and openly, by heart and by tongue. Sermon 132

Truly, those who were ungrateful and barred others from the way of God, they, surely, went astray, a wandering far astray. **4:167**

God ... is aware of whatever is hidden in the hearts and whatever lies behind the unseen. Sermon 192

Truly, those who were ungrateful and did wrong, God will never be forgiving of them, nor guide them to a road **4:168**
but the road to hell, ones who will dwell in it forever, eternally and that had been easy for God. **4:169**

He sees, but with a diseased eye, hears, but with unhearing ears. Desires have cut asunder his wit. The world has made his heart dead, while his mind is all longing for it. Consequently, he is a servant of it and of everyone who has any share in it. Wherever it turns, he turns towards it. Wherever it proceeds, he proceeds towards it. He is not desisted by any desister from God, nor takes admonition from any preacher. He sees those who have been caught in neglect, whence there is neither rescission nor reversion. Sermon 108

O humanity! Surely, the Messenger drew near you with The Truth from your Lord. So, believe, it is better for you. If you are ungrateful, then, truly, to God is whatever is in the heavens and the earth. God had been Knowing, Wise. **4:170**

With *the Prophet* (Q7:158), peace and the mercy of God be upon him, God exhausted the series of Prophets and ended the revelation. He then fought for Him those who were turning away from Him and were equating others with Him. Sermon 133

O People of the Book! Go not beyond the limits in your way of life and say not about God but The Truth: That the Messiah, Jesus son of Mary, was a Messenger of God and His Word that He cast to Mary and a Spirit from Him. So, believe in God and His Messengers. Say not: Three. To refrain

yourselves from it is better for you. There is only One God. Glory be to Him that He have a son! To Him belongs whatever is in the heavens and whatever is in and on the earth and God sufficed as a Trustee. **4:171**
The Messiah will never disdain that he be a servant of God nor the angels, the ones who are brought near to Him. Whoever disdains His worship and grows arrogant, He will assemble them altogether to Himself. **4:172** ***

Then, as for those who believed and did as the ones in accord with morality, then, He will pay their compensation in full and increase His grace for them. As for those who disdained and grew arrogant, He will punish them with a painful punishment. They will not find for themselves other than God a protector or a helper. **4:173**

Among the proofs of His creation is the creation of the skies which are fastened without pillars and stand without support. He called them. They responded obediently and humbly without being lazy or loathsome. If they had not acknowledged His Godhead and obeyed Him, He would not have made them the place for His throne, the abode of His angels and the destination: *To Him Words of what is good rise and He exalts an action in accord with morality* ... (Q35:10) of the creatures. Sermon 182

O humanity! Surely, there drew near you proof from your Lord. We caused to descend to you a clear light. **4:174**

I discharged duties when others lost the courage to do so. I came forward when others hid themselves. I spoke when others remained silent. I struck with divine light when others remained standing. I was the quietest of them in voice, but the highest in going forward. I cleaved to its rein and applied myself solely to its pledge like the mountain which neither sweeping wind could move nor storm could shake. No one could find fault with me, nor could any speaker speak ill of me. Sermon 37

So, for those who believed in God and cleaved firmly to Him, then, He will cause them to enter into mercy from Him and grace and guide them to Himself on a straight path. **4:175**

God knows the cries of the beasts in the forest, the sins of the people in seclusion, the movements of the fishes in the deep seas and the rising of the water by tempestuous winds. I bear witness that Muhammad, peace and the mercy of God be upon him, is the choice of God, the conveyor of His revelation and the Messenger of His Mercy. Sermon 198

They ask ***you*** *for advice. Say: God pronounces to you about indirect heirs. If a man perished and he be without children and he has a sister, then, for her is half of what he left. He inherits from her if she be without children. If there had been two sisters, then, for them (f), two-thirds of what he left. If there had been brothers/sisters, men and women, the man will have the like allotment as two females. God makes manifest to you so that you go not astray, and God is Knowing of everything.* **4:176** ***

Chapter 5: The Table Spread with Food (al-Māʾidah)

O those who believed! Live up to your agreements. Flocks of animals were permitted to you, but what is now recounted to you: You are not ones who are permitted hunting while you are in pilgrim sanctity. Truly, God gives judgment how He wants. **5:1**

In every matter of obedience you will find God, the Glorified's succor that will speak through tongues and accord firmness to hearts. It has sufficiency for those who seek sufficiency and a cure for those who seek cure. Sermon 213

O those who believed! Profane not the waymarks of God nor the Sacred Month nor the sacrificial gift nor the garlanded nor ones who are bound for the Sacred House looking for grace from their Lord and contentment. When you left your pilgrim sanctity, then, hunt. Let not that you detest a folk who barred you from the Masjid al-Haram drive you into exceeding the limits. Cooperate with one another in virtuous conduct and God-consciousness and cooperate not with one another in sin and deep seated dislike. Be God-conscious. Truly, God is Severe in repayment. 5:2

As a matter of fact those people who have carefully studied the condition of life and the world, pass their days as if they know that they are travelers, who have to leave a place which is famine-stricken, unhealthy and uncongenial and proceed towards lands which are fertile, congenial and where there is abundant provision of all comforts and pleasures. They have eagerly taken up the journey, happy in the hope of future blessings and peace. They have willingly accepted the sufferings, troubles and hazards of the way, parting of friends, scarcity of food and comfort during the pilgrimage so that they may reach the journey's end—a happy place. They do not refuse to bear any discomfort and do not grudge any expenditure by way of giving out alms and charities and helping the poor and the needy. Letter 31

Carrion was forbidden to you and blood and flesh of swine and what of it was hallowed to other than God and the one that is a strangled beast and the one that is beaten to death and the animal one fallen to its death and the animal gored to death or eaten by a beast of prey—but what you slew lawfully—and what were sacrificed to fetishes and what you partition by divining arrows. That is contrary to moral law. Today, those who were ungrateful gave up hope because of your way of life. So, dread them not but dread Me. Today, I perfected your way of life for you and I fulfilled My divine blessing on you and I was well-pleased with submission to the One God for your way of life. Whoever was driven by necessity due to emptiness—not one who inclines to sin—then, truly, God is Forgiving, Compassionate. 5:3

As far as presumptions of actions and things, lawful, legitimate and allowable or unlawful, forbidden and prohibited are concerned, accept the rulings of the Quran. Letter 69

They ask **you** *what was permitted to them. Say: That which is good was permitted to you and what you taught of hunting creatures, as one who teaches hunting dogs of what God taught you. So, eat of what they seized for you and remember the Name of God over it and be God-conscious. Truly, God is Swift in reckoning.* 5:4

Today, what is good was permitted to you. The food of those to whom We gave the Book is allowed to you and your food is allowed to them. The ones who are free, chaste females from the females, ones who believe and the ones who are free, chaste females from among those who were given the Book before you when you were to give them their bridal due, as males, ones who seek wedlock, not as ones who are licentious males, nor as males, ones who take lovers to themselves. Whoever disbelieves after belief, then, surely, his actions will be fruitless. He in the world to come will be among the ones who are losers. 5:5

O those who believed! When you stood up for the formal prayer, then, wash your faces and your hands up to the elbows and wipe your heads and your feet up to the ankles. If you had been defiled, then, cleanse yourselves. If you had been sick or on a journey or one of you drew near from the privy or you came into sexual contact with your wives and you find no water, then, aim at getting wholesome, dry earth and wipe your faces and hands with it. God wants not to make any impediment for you and He wants to purify you and to fulfill His divine blessing on you, so that perhaps you will give thanks. **5:6**

He is sufficient for one who relies on Him. He gives one who asks Him. He repays one who lends to Him. He rewards one who thanks Him. Sermon 89

Remember the divine blessing of God on you and His solemn promise that he made as a covenant with you by it when you said: We heard and we obeyed. Be God-conscious. Truly, God is Knowing of what is in the breasts. **5:7**

Be God-conscious like him who listened to good advice and bowed before it. Sermon 82

O those who believed! Be staunch in equity as witnesses to God and let not that you detest a folk drive you into not dealing justly. Be just. That is nearer to God-consciousness. Be God-conscious. Truly, God is Aware of what you do. **5:8**

Where are the minds which seek light from the lamps of guidance and the eyes which look at minarets of God-consciousness? Where are the hearts dedicated to God and devoted to the obedience of God? Sermon 144

God promised those who believed and did as the ones in accord with morality that for them is forgiveness and a sublime compensation. **5:9**

Good is not that your wealth and progeny should be much, but good is that your knowledge should be much, your forbearance should be great and that you should vie with other people in worship of God. If you do good deeds, you thank God, but if you commit evil, you seek forgiveness of God. In this world good is for two persons only: the person who commits sins, but rectifies them by repentance and the person who hastens towards good actions. Hadith 94

Those who were ungrateful and denied Our signs, those will be the Companions of Hellfire! **5:10**

When one loves a thing, it blinds him and sickens his heart. He sees, but with a diseased eye, hears, but with un-hearing ears. Desires have cut asunder his wit. The world has made his heart dead while his mind is all longing for it. Consequently, he is a servant of it and of everyone who has any share in it. Wherever it turns, he turns towards it. Wherever it proceeds, he proceeds towards it. He is not desisted by any desister from God, nor takes admonition from any preacher. He sees those who have been caught in neglect whence there is neither rescission, nor reversion. Sermon 108

O those who believed! Remember the divine blessing of God on you when they, a folk, were about to extend their hands against you, but He limited their hands from you. Be God-conscious. In God let the ones who believe put their trust. **5:11**

God, the Almighty, deputed Muhammad, peace and the mercy of God be upon him, with truth at a time when the destruction of the world was near and the next life was at hand, when its brightness was turning into gloom after shining, it had become troublesome for its inhabitants, its surface had become rough and its decay had approached near. This was during the exhaustion of its life at the approach of signs of its decay, the ruin of its inhabitants, the breaking of its links, the dispersal of its affairs, the decay of its signs, the divulging of its secret matters and the shortening of its length. God made him responsible for conveying His message and a means of honor for his people, a period of bloom for the men of his days, a source of dignity for the supporters and an honor for his helpers. Sermon 198

Certainly, God took a solemn promise from the Children of Jacob and We raised up among them twelve chieftains. God said: Truly, I am with you. If you performed the formal prayer and gave the purifying alms and believed in My Messengers and you supported them and you lent God a fairer loan, I would, certainly, absolve you of your evil deeds. I would, certainly, cause you to enter Gardens beneath which rivers run. Then, whoever among you was ungrateful after this, then, surely, he went astray from the right way. **5:12**

You should also fear what calamities befell peoples before you on account of their evil deeds and detestable actions. Remember, during good or bad circumstances, what happened to them, and be cautious that you do not become like them. Sermon 191

Then, for their breaking their solemn promise, We cursed them and We made their hearts ones that harden. They tamper with the words out of context and they forgot an allotment of what they were reminded of in it. ***You*** *will not cease to peruse the treachery of them, but a few of them. Then, overlook and pardon them. Truly, God loves the ones who are doers of good.* **5:13**

At the same time, be very careful. Never break your promise with your enemy. Never forsake the protection or support that you have offered to him. Never go back upon your word. Never violate the terms of the treaty. You must even risk your life to fulfill the promises given and the terms settled because of all the obligations laid by Almighty God upon the human being in respect of other people there is none so important as to keep one's promises when made. Letter 53

From those who said: We are Christians, We took their solemn promise, but they forgot an allotment of what they were reminded of it so We stirred up enmity and hatred among them until the Day of Resurrection. God will tell them of what they had been crafting. **5:14**

Once a treaty has been finally concluded, do not try to take advantage of any ambiguous word or phrase in it. If you find yourself in a critical situation on account of the treaty made in the cause of God, then try to face the situation and bear the consequences bravely. Do not try to back out of the terms because to face such perplexing situations as may gain His Rewards and Blessings is better than to break your promise on that account and earn that about which you feel nervous and for which you will have to answer God and which may bring down His Wrath upon you in this world and damnation in the next. Letter 53

O People of the Book! Surely, Our Messenger drew near you. He makes manifest to you much of what you had been concealing of the Book and pardons much. Surely, from God drew near you a light and a clear Book. **5:15**

Always keep God-consciousness in your mind, to give priority to His worship and to give preference to obeying His Commands over every other thing in life, to carefully and faithfully follow the commandments and interdictions as are given by the Book and the traditions of *the Prophet* (Q7:158), peace and the mercy of God be upon him, because the success of a person to attain happiness in this world and in the next depends upon these qualities. A failure to achieve these attributes brings about total failure in both the worlds. Letter 53

God guides with it whoever followed His contentment to ways of peace and He brings them out from the shadows into the light with His permission and He guides them to a straight path. **5:16**

God kept the Prophets in deposit in the best place of deposit and made them stay in the best place of stay. He moved them in succession from distinguished forefathers to chaste wombs. Whenever a predecessor from among them died, the follower stood up for the cause of the way of God. Sermon 94

Certainly, ungrateful were those who said: Truly, God is the Messiah, the son of Mary. Say: Who, then, has any sway over God? If He wanted to He would cause the Messiah son of Mary and his mother to perish and whatever is in and on the earth altogether. To God belongs the dominion of the heavens and the earth and what is between the two. He creates what He wills. God is Powerful over everything. **5:17**

The Jews and Christians said: We are the children of God and His beloved. Say: Why, then, does He punish you for your impieties? Nay! You are mortals whom He created. He forgives whom He wills and He punishes whom He wills. To God belongs the dominion of the heavens and the earth and what is even between the two. To Him is the Homecoming! **5:18**

O People of the Book! Surely, Our Messenger drew near you. He makes manifest to you the way of life—after an interval without Messengers—so that you say not: There drew not near us either a bearer of good tidings or a warner. Then, surely, drew near to you a bearer of good tidings and a warner. God is Powerful over everything. **5:19**

Mention when Moses said to his folk: O my folk! Remember the divine blessing of God on you when He assigned Prophets among you and assigned kings and gives you what He gave not to anyone of the worlds. **5:20**

O my folk! Enter the region, one that is sanctified, that God prescribed for you and go not back, turning your back, for, then, you will turn about as ones who are losers. **5:21**

They said: O Moses! Truly, in it is a haughty folk and we will never enter it until they go forth from it, but if they go forth from it, then, we will, certainly, be ones who enter. **5:22**

Two men to whom God was gracious said among those who fear to disobey: Enter on them through the door! When you entered it, you will, certainly, be ones who are victors. Put your trust in God if you had been ones who believe. **5:23**

They said: O Moses! We will never enter it as long as they continued in it, so you and your Lord, you two go and fight. We are here, ones who sit at home. **5:24**

He said: My Lord! I control no one but myself and my brother so separate You between us and between the folk, the ones who disobey. **5:25**

He said: Truly, it is that which is forbidden to them for forty years. They will wander about the earth. So, grieve not for the folk, the ones who disobey. **5:26**

(I) relate to you concerning Moses, the Friend of God, when he said: *My Lord! Truly, I am, certainly, of whatever* **You** *caused to descend of good to me, in need.* (Q28:24) Sermon 159

Recount **you** *to them the tiding of the two sons of Adam in Truth when they both brought near a sacrifice and it was received from one of them but there is non-acceptance from the other. He said: I will, surely, kill* **you**. *He said: Truly, God receives only from the ones who are God-conscious.* **5:27**

If **you** *were to extend* **your** *hand against me so that* **you** *would kill me, I would not be one who stretches out my hand towards* **you** *so that I kill* **you**. *I fear God, Lord of the worlds.* **5:28**
Truly, I want that **you** *will draw the burden of my sin and* **your** *sin, then, to be among the Companions of the Fire. That is the recompense of the ones who are unjust.* **5:29**
Then, his soul prompted him to kill his brother. He killed him and became among the ones who are losers. **5:30**
Then, God raised up a raven to scratch the earth, to cause him to see how to cover up the naked corpse of his brother. He says: Woe to me! Was I unable to be like this raven to cover up the naked corpse of my brother? Then, he became among the ones who were remorseful. **5:31**
On account of that, We prescribed for the Children of Jacob that whoever killed a person, other than in retribution for another person, or because of corruption in and on the earth, it will be as if he had killed all of humanity. Whoever gave life to one, it will be as if he gave life to all of humanity. Certainly, our Messengers drew near them with the clear portents. Again, truly, many of them after that were ones who were excessive in and on the earth. **5:32** ***

The only recompense for those who war against God and His Messenger and hasten about corrupting in and on the earth, is that they be killed or caused to be crucified or their hands and their feet be cut off on opposite sides or they be expelled from the region. That for them is their degradation in the present. For them in the world to come, there is a tremendous punishment, **5:33**
but for those who repented before you have power over them. So, know you that God is Forgiving, Compassionate. **5:34**
O those who believed! Be God-conscious and look for an approach to Him and struggle in His way so that perhaps you will prosper. **5:35**

Indeed, surely, jihad is one of the doors of Paradise which God has opened for His best friends. It is the dress of God-consciousness, the protective armor of God and His trustworthy shield. Whoever abandons it, God covers him with the dress of disgrace and the clothes of distress. He is kicked with contempt and scorn. His heart is veiled with screens of neglect. Truth is taken away from him because of his missing the jihad. He has to suffer ignominy. Justice is denied to him. Sermon 27

Truly, those who were ungrateful, if they had whatever is in and on the earth and the like of it with as much again that they offer it as ransom from the punishment on the Day of Resurrection, it would not be received from them and for them is a painful punishment. **5:36**

Whoever takes a partner with **You** is ungrateful according to what is stated in **Your** unambiguous verses and indicated by the evidence of **Your** clear arguments. Sermon 91

They will want to go forth from the fire, but they will not be ones who go forth from it. For them is an abiding punishment. **5:37**

O God's human being! Be afraid of death and its nearness and keep ready all that is needed for it. It will come as a big event and a great affair, either as a good in which there will never be any evil, or an evil in which there will never be any good. Who is nearer to Paradise than he who works towards it, and who is nearer to Hell than he who works for it? Letter 27

As for the one who is a male thief and the one who is a female thief, then, sever their hands as recompense for what they earned, an exemplary punishment from God. God is Almighty, Wise. **5:38**

But whoever repents after his injustice and made things right, then, truly, God will turn to him in forgiveness. Truly, God is Forgiving, Compassionate. **5:39**

The opponents have entered the oceans of disturbance and have taken to innovations instead of the *sunna*, while the believers have sunk down. The misguided and the liars are speaking. We are the near ones, companions, treasure holders and doors to the *sunna*. Houses are not entered save through their doors. Whoever enters them from other than the door is called a thief. Sermon 153

Have **you** *not known that to God, to Him belongs the dominion of the heavens and the earth? He punishes whom He wills and He forgives whom He wills. God is Powerful over everything.* **5:40**

He is such that gloom does not concern Him, nor does He seek light from brightness. Night does not overtake Him, nor does the day pass over Him so as to affect Him in any manner. His comprehension of things is not through eyes. His knowledge is not dependent on being informed. God deputized *the Prophet* (Q7:158), peace and the mercy of God be upon him, with light and accorded him the highest precedence in selection. Through him God united those who were divided, overpowered the powerful, overcame difficulties and leveled rugged ground and thus removed misguidance from right and left. Sermon 213

O Messenger! Let them not dishearten **you***—those who compete with one another in ingratitude among those who said: We believed with their mouths while their hearts believe not. Among those who became Jews are ones who hearken to lies, ones who hearken to folk of others who approach not* **you***. They tamper with the words out of context. They say: If you were given this, then, take it, but if you are not given this, then, beware! For whomever God wants to test, you will never have sway over him against God at all. Those are whom God wants not to purify their hearts. For them in the present is degradation. For them in the world to come is a tremendous punishment.* **5:41**

Be patient till people quiet down and hearts settle in their places so that rights can be achieved for people easily. Sermon 167

They are ones who hearken to lies, the ones who devour the wrongful. Then, if they drew near you, then, give **you** *judgment between them or turn aside from them. If* **you** *turned aside from them, then, they will never injure* **you** *at all. If* **you** *gave judgment, then, give judgment between them with equity. Truly, God loves the ones who act justly.* **5:42**

... he who finds it hard to act justly should find it harder to deal with injustice. Sermon 15

How will they make **you** *their judge while with them is the Torah wherein is the determination of God? Yet, again, after that, they turn away. Those are the ones who believe not.* **5:43**
Truly, We caused the Torah to descend wherein is guidance and light. The Prophets give judgment with it, those who submitted to God, for those who became Jews and the rabbis and learned Jewish scholars who committed to memory the Book of God and they had been witnesses to it. So, dread not humanity, but dread Me. Exchange not My signs for a little price. Whoever gives not judgment by what God caused to descend, those, they are the ones who are ungrateful. **5:44**
We prescribed for them in it: A life for a life and an eye for an eye and a nose for a nose and an ear for an ear and a tooth for a tooth and for injuries to the body, reciprocation. Then, whoever was charitable and forgives it, it will be an atonement for him. Whoever gives judgment not by what God caused to descend, then, those, they are the ones who are unjust. **5:45**

The best judge is the Lord Almighty. Letter 45

We sent following in their footsteps, Jesus son of Mary, one who establishes as true what was before him in the Torah. We gave him the Gospel in which is guidance and light, and that which establishes as true what was before him in the Torah and a guidance and admonishment for the ones who are God-conscious. **5:46**
Let the People of the Gospel give judgment by what God caused to descend in it. Whoever gives not judgment by what God caused to descend, then, those, they are the ones who disobey. **5:47**

Blessed is the person who always kept the life after death in his view, who remembered the Day of Judgment through all his deeds, who led a contented life and who was happy with the lot that God had destined for him. Saying 44

We caused the Book to descend to **you** *with The Truth, that which establishes as true what was before it of the Book and that which preserves it. So, give judgment between them by what God caused to descend. Follow not their desires that drew near* **you** *against The Truth. For each among you We made a divine law and an open road. If God willed, He would have made you one community to try you with what He gave you so be forward in good deeds. To God is your return altogether. Then, He will tell you about what you had been at variance in it.* **5:48**

O people! Abstinence is to shorten desires, to thank for bounties and to keep away from what is prohibited. If all of this is not possible, then at least, what is prohibited should not overpower your patience. Do not forget gratitude when receiving blessings for God has exhausted the excuses before you through clear, shining arguments and open, bright books. Sermon 81

Give judgment between them by what God caused to descend and follow not their desires and beware of them so that they tempt **you** *not from some of what God caused to descend to* **you**. *If they turned away, then, know that God only wants that He light on them for some of their impieties. Truly, many within humanity are ones who disobey.* **5:49**

Did you not witness those who engaged in long-reaching desires, built strong buildings, amassed much wealth, but their houses turned into graves and whatever they had collected turned into ruin? Their property devolved on the successors and their spouses on those who came after them. They cannot now add to their good acts, nor invoke God's mercy in respect of evil acts. Therefore, whoever makes his heart habituated to fear God achieves a forward position and his action is successful. Sermon 132

Look they for a determination of Age of Ignorance? Who is fairer than God in determination for a folk who are certain? **5:50**

Be aware! Be aware of obeying your leaders and elders who felt proud of their achievements and boasted about their lineage. They hurled the liability for things on God and quarreled with God in what He did with them, contesting His decree and disputing His favors. Certainly, they are the main foundation of obstinacy, the chief pillars of mischief and the swords of pre-Islamic boasting over forefathers. Therefore, be God-conscious. Do not become antagonistic to His favors on you, nor jealous of His bounty over you. Do not obey the claimants of Islam whose dirty water you drink along with your clean one, whose ailments you mix with your healthiness and whose wrongs you allow to enter into your rightful matters. Sermon 192

O those who believed! Take not to yourselves the Jews and the Christians as protectors. Some of them are protectors of one another. Whoever among you turns away to them, then, he is of them. Truly, God guides not the folk, the ones who are unjust. **5:51**

Surely, God, the Glorified, the Sublime, nothing is hidden from Him of whatever people do in their nights or days. He knows all the details and His knowledge covers them. Your limbs are a witness, the organs of your body constitute an army against yourself, your inner self serves Him as eyes to watch your sins and your loneliness is open to Him. Sermon 198

You *saw those who in their hearts is a sickness. They compete with one another. They say: We dread that a turn of fortune should light on us. Then, perhaps God brings a victory or a command from Him? Then, they will become —from what they kept secret within themselves—ones who are remorseful.* **5:52**

I have seen your flight and your dispersal from the lines. You were surrounded by rude and low people and Bedouins of Syria, although you are the chiefs of Arabs and summit of distinction and possess the dignity of the high nose and big hump of the camel. Sermon 107

Those who believed will say: Are these they who swore an oath by God —the most earnest of sworn oaths—that they were with you? Their actions were fruitless. They became ones who are losers. **5:53**

They took to the right and the left piercing through to the ways of evil and leaving the paths of guidance. Do not make haste for a matter which is to happen and is awaited. Do not wish for delay in what the morrow is to bring for you. For how many people make haste for a matter, but when they get it they begin to wish they had not gotten it? How near is today to the dawning of tomorrow? O my people, this is the time for the occurrence of every promised event and the approach of things which you do not know. Sermon 150

O those who believed! Whoever of you goes back on his way of life, God will bring the folk whom He loves and who love Him, humble-spirited towards the ones who believe, disdainful towards the ones who are ungrateful. They struggle in the way of God and they fear not the reproach of one who is reproached. That is the grace of God. He gives it to whom He wills. God is One Who is Extensive, Knowing. **5:54**

Know that the loss of anything of this world will not harm you if you have guarded the principles of your religion. Know also that after the loss of your religion nothing of this world for which you have cared will benefit you. May God carry our hearts and your hearts towards the right and may He grant us and you endurance. Sermon 173

Your protector is only God and His Messenger and those who believed and those who perform the formal prayer and give the purifying alms and they are ones who bow down. **5:55**

May my father and my mother shed their lives for you, O *Messenger of God*! (Q48:29) With your death, the process of prophethood, revelation and heavenly messages has stopped, which had not stopped at the death of other Prophets. Your position with us members of your family is so special that your grief has become a source of consolation to us as against the grief of all others. Our grief is also common in that all Muslims share it equally. Sermon 234

Whoever turns in friendship to God and His Messenger and those who believed, then, behold the

Party of God. They are the ones who are victors. **5:56**

The Prophet (Q7:158), peace and the mercy of God be upon him, is the leader of all who exercise fear of God and a light for those who seek guidance. He is a lamp whose flame is burning, a meteor whose light is shining and a flint whose spark is bright. His conduct is upright, his behavior guides, his speech is decisive and his decision is just. God sent him after an interval from the previous Prophets when people had fallen into errors of action and ignorance. May God have mercy on you. Sermon 94

O those who believed! Take not to yourselves those who took to themselves your way of life in mockery and as a pastime from among those who were given the Book before you and the ones who are ungrateful, as protectors. Be God-conscious if you had been ones who believe. **5:57**

By God, certainly it is reality not play, truth not falsehood. It is none other than death. Its caller is making himself heard. Its driver is making haste. The majority of the people should not deceive you. You have seen those who lived before you, amassed wealth, feared poverty and felt safe from its evil consequences, the longevity of desires and the apparent distance from death. How, then death overtook them, turned them out of their homelands and took them out of their places of safety. They were borne on coffins. People were busy about them one after another, carrying them on their shoulders and supporting them with their hands. Did you not witness those who engaged in long-reaching desires, built strong buildings, amassed much wealth, but their houses turned into graves and whatever they had collected turned into ruin? Their property devolved on the successors and their spouses on those who came after them. They cannot now add to their good acts, nor invoke God's mercy in respect of evil acts. Therefore, whoever makes his heart habituated to God-consciousness achieves a forward position. His action is successful. Sermon 132

When you cried out for formal prayer they took it to themselves in mockery and as a pastime. That is because they are a folk who are not reasonable. **5:58**

Be aware of destroying your manners and changing them, maintaining one tongue. A person should control his tongue because the tongue is obstinate with its master. Sermon 176

Say: O People of the Book! Seek you revenge on us because we believed in God and what was caused to descend to us and what was caused to descend before, while, truly, most of you are ones who disobey? **5:59**

O son of Adam, when you see that your Lord, the Glorified, bestows His Favors on you while you disobey Him, you should fear Him. Take warning that His Wrath may not turn those very blessings into misfortunes. Saying 24

Say: Will I tell **you** *of worse than that as a reward from God? He whom God cursed and with whom He was angry and He made some of them into apes and swine who worshiped the false deities. Those are worse placed and ones who go astray from the right way.* **5:60**

O God's human being! I advise you to be God-conscious. It is He Who has furnished illustrations and Who has timed for you your lives. He has given you covering of dress. He has scattered a livelihood for you. He has surrounded you with His knowledge. He has ordained rewards. He has bestowed upon you vast bounties and extensive gifts. He has warned you through far reaching arguments. He has counted you by numbers. He has fixed for you an age to live in this place of testing and house of instruction. You are on a test in this world and have to render an account regarding it. Sermon 82

When they drew near you they said: We believed. Surely, they entered with ingratitude and they, surely, went forth with it. God is greater in knowledge of what they had been keeping back. **5:61**

Certainly, the tongue of a believer is at the back of his heart while the heart of a hypocrite is at the back of his tongue. When a believer intends to say anything, he thinks it over in his mind. If it is good, he discloses it, but if it is bad, he lets it remain concealed. While a hypocrite speaks whatever comes to his tongue without knowing what is in his favor and what goes against him. Sermon 176

***You** have seen many of them competing with one another in sin and deep seated dislike and in consuming the wrongful. What they had been doing was miserable.* **5:62**

The hypocrite is a person who makes a show of faith and adopts the appearance of a Muslim. He does not hesitate in sinning, nor does he keep aloof from vice. He willfully attributes false things against *the Messenger of God* (Q48:29), peace and the mercy of God be upon him. If people knew that he was a hypocrite and a liar, they would not accept anything from him and would not confirm what he says. Sermon 210

Why prohibit not the rabbis and learned Jewish scholars their sayings of sin and their consuming the wrongful? Miserable was what they had been crafting. **5:63**
*The Jews said: The hand of God is one that is restricted! Restricted were their hands! They were cursed for what they said. Nay! His hands are ones that are stretched out: He spends how He wills. Certainly, many of them increase by what was caused to descend to **you** from **your** Lord in defiance and in ingratitude. We cast among them enmity and hatred until the Day of Resurrection. Whenever they kindled a fire of war, God extinguished it. They hasten about corrupting in and on the earth. God loves not the ones who make corruption.* **5:64**
If the People of the Book believed and were God-conscious, certainly, We would have absolved them from their evil deeds and caused them to enter into Gardens of Bliss. **5:65**
If they adhered to the Torah and the Gospel—what was caused to descend to them from their Lord, they would, certainly, have eaten in abundance from above them and from beneath their feet. Among them is a community of ones who halt between two opinions. But many of them, how evil is what they do! **5:66**

They may often try to take advantage of their status and may resort to selfishness, intrigues, fraud, corruption and oppression. If you find such people around you, then do away with them no matter how closely connected they may be with you. Immediately bring an end to the scandal and clear your surroundings of all such moral and spiritual filth. Letter 53

*O Messenger! State what was caused to descend to **you** from **your** Lord, for if **you** accomplished it not, then, **you** will not have stated His message. God will save **you** from the harm of humanity. Truly, God guides not the folk, the ones who are ungrateful.* **5:67**

If you had not ordered endurance and prevented us from bewailing, we would have produced a store of tears and even then the pain would not have subsided. This grief would not have ended. They would have been too little of our grief for you, but this death is a matter that cannot be reversed, nor is it possible to repulse it. May my father and my mother die for you. Do remember us with God and take care of us. Sermon 234

Say: O People of the Book! You are not based on anything until you adhere to the Torah and the Gospel and what was caused to descend to you from your Lord. Certainly, many of them increase by what was caused to descend to **you** *from* **your** *Lord in defiance and ingratitude. So, grieve not for folk, the ones who are ungrateful.* **5:68**
Truly, those who believed, those who became Jews and Sabeans and Christians—whoever believed in God and the Last Day and did as one in accord with morality, then, there will be neither fear in them nor will they feel remorse. **5:69**
Certainly, We took a solemn promise from the Children of Jacob and We sent Messengers to them. Whenever a Messenger drew near them with what they themselves yearn not for, a group of people denied them and a group of people kill them. **5:70**
They assumed there would be no test. They were in darkness and became unhearing. Again, God turned to them in forgiveness. Again, in darkness and became unhearing many of them. God is Seeing of what they do. **5:71**
Certainly, were ungrateful those who said: Truly, God is He, the Messiah, son of Mary, but the Messiah said: O Children of Jacob! Worship God, my Lord and your Lord. Truly, whoever ascribes partners with God, then, surely, God forbade the Garden to him. His place of shelter will be the fire. For the ones who are unjust, there are no helpers. **5:72**
Certainly, ungrateful were those who said: Truly, God is the third of three. There is no god but One God. If they refrain not themselves from what they say, there will afflict those who were ungrateful among them a painful punishment. **5:73**
Will they not, then, turn to God for forgiveness and ask for His forgiveness? God is Forgiving, Compassionate. **5:74**
The Messiah son of Mary was not but a Messenger. Surely, Messengers passed away before him. His mother was a just person (f). They both had been eating food. Look on how We make manifest the signs to them. Again, look on how they are misled! **5:75**

When truth was revealed to me, I never doubted it. Saying 183

Say: Worship you other than God what controls neither hurt nor profit for you? God, He is The Hearing, The Knowing. **5:76**

You are commanded by God to worship none but Him. Saying 78

Say: O People of the Book! Go not beyond limits in your way of life but with The Truth and follow not the desires of the folk who, surely, went astray before. They caused many to go astray. They themselves went astray from the right way. **5:77**
Those who were ungrateful were cursed among the Children of Jacob by the tongue of David and that of Jesus son of Mary.
That was because they would rebel and they had been exceeding the limits. **5:78**
They had not been forbidding one another from that which is unlawful that they committed. Miserable was what they had been committing! **5:79**
You *saw many of them turning away to those who were ungrateful. Miserable was what was put forward for them themselves so that God was displeased with them and in their punishment they are ones who will dwell in it forever.* **5:80**

Whoever takes a partner for **You** is ungrateful according to what is stated in **Your** unambiguous verses and indicated by the evidence of **Your** clear arguments. Sermon 91

If they had been believing in God and the Prophet and what was caused to descend to him, they would not have taken them to themselves protectors, but many of them are ones who disobey. **5:81**

The Prophet (Q7:158), peace and the mercy of God be upon him, left among you what other Prophets had left among their peoples, because Prophets do not leave their people in darkness without a clear path and a sign, namely the Book of your Creator. The Book clarifies its permission and prohibitions, its obligations and discretions, its repealing injunctions and the repealed ones, its permissible matters and compulsory ones, its particulars and general ones, its lessons and illustrations, its long and short ones, its clear and obscure ones, detailing its abbreviations and clarifying its obscurities. Sermon 1

Truly, **you** *will find the hardest of humanity in enmity to those who believed are the Jews and those who have ascribed partners with God. Certainly,* **you** *will find the nearest of them in affection to those who believed are those who said: We are Christians. That is because among them are priests and monks and they grow not arrogant.* **5:82**

To be submissive, humble, crawling and begging when one is needy, powerless and poor and to be arrogant, oppressing and cruel when in power and opulence are two very ugly traits of the human character. Letter 31

When they heard what was caused to descend to the Messenger, **you** *saw their eyes overflow with tears because they recognized The Truth. They say: Our Lord! We believed so write us down with the ones who bear witness.* **5:83**
Why believe we not in God and in what drew near us of The Truth? We are desirous that Our Lord would cause us to enter the Garden among the folk—the ones in accord with morality. **5:84**
Then, God repaid them for what they said—Gardens beneath which rivers run, ones who will dwell in them forever. That is the recompense of the ones who are doers of good. **5:85**

A person should derive benefit from his own "self." Certainly, prudent is he who hears and ponders over it, who sees and observes and who benefits from instructive material and then treads on clear paths wherein he avoids falling into hollows and straying into pitfalls and does not assist those who misguide him by turning away from truthfulness, changing his words, or fearing truth. Sermon 153

But those who are ungrateful and denied Our signs, those will be the Companions of Hellfire. **5:86**

Certainly, the most hated person with God is he whom has left God for his own "self." He goes astray from the right path, and moves without a guide. If he is called to the plantation of this world, he is active, but if he is called to the plantation of the next world, he is slow. It is as though what he is active for is obligatory upon him whereas in whatever he is slow is not required of him. Sermon 103

O those who believed! Forbid not what is good that God permitted to you and exceed not the limits. Truly, God loves not the ones who exceed the limits. **5:87**

Whoever can at this time keep himself clinging to God should do so. Sermon 156

Eat of what God provided you, the lawful, what is good. Be God-conscious in Whom you are ones who believe. **5:88**

God seeks you to thank Him and assigns to you His affairs. Sermon 24

God will not take you to task for what is idle talk in your oaths, but He will take you to task for oaths you made as an agreement. Then, its expiation is the feeding of ten needy people of the average of what you feed your own people or clothing them or letting go of a bondsperson. But whoever finds not the means, then, formal fasting for three days. That is the expiation for your oaths when you swore them. Keep your oaths safe. Thus, God makes manifest His signs to you so that perhaps you will give thanks. **5:89**

Truly, those who took the oath of allegiance to Abu Bakr, Umar and Uthman have sworn allegiance to me. Now those who were present at the election have no right to go back against their oaths of allegiance and those who were not present on the occasion have no right to oppose me. So far as the Council (*shura*) was concerned it was supposed to be limited to an Emigrant (*muhajir*) and Helper (*ansar*). It was also supposed that whomsoever they selected became caliph as per approval and pleasure of God. Letter 6

O those who believed! Truly, intoxicants and gambling and fetishes and divining arrows are of the disgraceful actions of Satan. Then, avoid them so that perhaps you will prosper. **5:90**

Surely, God has made unlawful the things which are not unknown and made lawful the things which are without defect. Sermon 167

But Satan only wants that he precipitate enmity and hatred between you through intoxicants and gambling and bar you from the remembrance of God and from formal prayer. Then, will you be ones who desist? **5:91**

Obey God and obey the Messenger and beware. Then, truly, if you turned away, then, know that only on Our Messenger is the delivering of Our clear message. **5:92**

With *the Prophet* (Q7:158), peace and the mercy of God be upon him, God exhausted the series of Prophets and ended the revelation. He then fought for Him those who were turning away from Him and were equating others with Him. Sermon 133

There is not for those who believed and did as the ones in accord with morality blame for what they tasted when they were God-conscious and believed and did as the ones in accord with morality and, again, they were God-conscious and believed. Again, they were God-conscious and did good. God loves the ones who are doers of good. **5:93**

O God's human being! You should know that a believer should be distrustful of his heart every morning and evening. He should always blame it for shortcomings and ask it to add to its good acts. You should behave like those who have gone before you and the precedents in front of you. They left this world like a traveler and covered it as distance is covered. Sermon 176

O those who believed! Certainly, God will try you with something of the game that your hands and your lances attain so that God knows who fears Him in the unseen. Then, whoever exceeded the limits after that, for him is a painful punishment. **5:94**

O God's human being! I advise you to be God-conscious. It is He Who has furnished illustrations and Who has timed for you your lives. He has given you covering of dress. He has scattered a livelihood for you. He has surrounded you with His knowledge. He has ordained rewards. He has bestowed upon you vast bounties and extensive gifts. He has warned you through far reaching arguments. He has counted you by numbers. He has fixed for you an age to live in this place of testing and house of instruction. You are on a test in this world and have to render an account regarding it. Sermon 82

O those who believed! Kill not game when you are in pilgrim sanctity. Whoever of you killed as one who is willful, then, the recompense is like what he killed of flocks by two possessors of justice who give judgment. Among you will be a sacrificial gift—that which reaches the Kabah—or the expiation of food for the needy or the equivalent of that in formal fasting so that he, certainly, experiences the mischief of his conduct. God pardoned what is past. Whoever reverted to it, then, God will requite him. God is Almighty, Possessor of Requital. **5:95**

Justice puts everything in its right place. Letter 53

The game of the sea was permitted to you and the food of it as sustenance for you and for a company of travelers, but the game of dry land was forbidden to you as long as you continued in pilgrim sanctity. Be God-conscious to Whom you will be assembled. **5:96**

O God's human being! Steer clear through the waves of mischief on boats of deliverance. Sermon 5

God made the Kabah the Sacred House, maintaining it for humanity and the Sacred Month and the sacrificial gift and the garlanded. That is so that you will know that God knows whatever is in the heavens and whatever is in and on the earth and that God is Knowing of everything. **5:97**

God has made it a means to His mercy and an approach to His Paradise. Sermon 192

Know that God is Severe in repayment and that God is Forgiving, Compassionate. **5:98**

Certainly, this world is a dirty watering place and a muddy source of drinking. Its appearance is attractive, yet its inside is destructive. It is a deception, a vanishing reflection and a bent pillar. When its despiser begins to like it and he who is not acquainted with it feels satisfied with it, then it jumps for joy, entraps him in its trap, makes him the target of its arrows and puts round his neck the rope of death taking him to the narrow grave and fearful abode in order to show him his place of stay and the recompense of his acts. This goes on from generation to generation. Neither death stops from cutting them asunder, nor do the survivors keep aloof from committing sins. Sermon 82

What is with the Messenger is not but the delivering of the message. God knows whatever you show and whatever you keep back. **5:99**

God sent to him the Book as a light whose flames cannot be extinguished, a lamp whose gleam does not die, a sea whose depth cannot be sounded, a way whose direction does not mislead, a ray whose light does not darken, a separator of good from evil whose arguments do not weaken, a clarifier whose foundations cannot be dismantled, a cure which leaves no apprehension for disease, an honor whose supporters are not defeated and a truth whose helpers are not abandoned. Sermon 198

*Say: Not on the same level are the bad and what is good even if the prevalence of the bad impressed **you**. So, be God-conscious, O those imbued with intuition, so that perhaps you will prosper.* **5:100**

Always keep the consciousness of God in your mind. Remember that you have to meet Him one day. Let the consciousness of God guide you in all your activities against humans and your end will be towards Him and towards none else. Letter 12

O those who believed! Ask not about things that if they are shown to you would raise anger in you. Yet if you ask about them at the time when the Quran is being sent down, they will be shown to you. God pardoned that which is past. God is Forgiving, Forbearing. **5:101**

Is it that God ordered them to differ and they obeyed Him? Or He prohibited them from it, but they disobeyed Him? Or is it that God sent an incomplete faith and sought their help to complete it? Or are they His partners in the affairs, so that it is their share of duty to pronounce and He has to agree? Or is it that God the Almighty sent a perfect faith, but *the Prophet* (Q7:158), peace and the mercy of God be upon him, fell short of conveying it and handing it over to the people? The fact is that God the Almighty says: *We have not neglected anything in the Book* (Q6:38) and in it is a "clarification of everything." He says that one part of the Quran verifies another part and that there is no divergence in it: *But no! They meditate not on the Recitation. If it had been from other than God, certainly, they would have found in it many contradictions.* (Q4:82) Certainly the manifest of the Quran is wonderful and its hidden is deep in meaning. Its wonders will never disappear. Its amazements will never pass away. Its intricacies cannot be cleared except through itself. Sermon 18

Surely, the folk asked about them before you. Again, they became ones who are ungrateful for it. **5:102**

Be aware! This world attracts and then turns away. It is stubborn, refusing to go ahead. It speaks lies and misappropriates. It disowns and is ungrateful. It is malicious and abandons its lovers. It attracts but causes trouble. Its condition is changing, its step, shaking, its honor, disgrace, its seriousness, jest, and its height, lowliness. It is a place of plunder and pillage, ruin and destruction. Its people are ready with their feet to drive, to overtake and to depart. Its routes are bewildering, its exits are baffling. Its schemes end in disappointment. Consequently, strongholds betray them, houses throw them out and cunning fails them. Sermon 190

God made not the thing called Bahirah nor Saibah nor Wasilah nor Hami, but those who were ungrateful, they devise lies against God and most of them are not reasonable. **5:103**

If you do not faithfully and sincerely follow the dictates of religion and do not act as I have advised you, then I want to warn you of something that you have entirely forgotten. It is that you are unthankful to God for all which He has granted to you. You are ungrateful to Him for the favors bestowed upon you. Satan has taken possession of your soul. Satan's desire to secure you as his obedient servant is fully fulfilled. He has a firm hold on your mind. Letter 10

When it was said to them: Approach now to what God caused to descend and to the Messenger, they said: Enough is what we found our fathers upon. Even though their fathers had been knowing nothing nor are they truly guided? **5:104**

One of the firm decisions of God in the Wise Reminder (Quran), upon which He bestows reward or gives punishment and through which He likes or dislikes, is that it will not benefit a person, even though he exerts himself and acts sincerely, if he leaves this world to meet God with one of these acts without repenting, namely that he believed in a partner with God during his obligatory worship or appeased his own anger by killing an individual or spoke about acts committed by others or sought fulfillment of his needs from people by introducing an innovation in his religion or met people with a double face or moved among them with a double tongue. Understand this because an illustration is a guide for its like. Sermon 153

O those who believed! Upon you is the charge of your souls. He who went astray injures you not if you were truly guided. To God is the return of you all. Then, He will tell you what you had been doing. **5:105**

The world aimed at them, but they did not aim at it. It captured them, but they freed themselves from it by a ransom. During the night, they are standing on their feet, reading portions of the Quran and reciting it in a well-measured way, creating through it grief and seeking by it the cure for their ailments. If they come across a verse creating eagerness for Paradise, they pursue it avidly. Their spirits turn towards it eagerly. They feel as if it is in front of them. When they come across a verse which contains fear of Hell, they bend the ears of their hearts towards it and feel as though the sound of Hell and its cries are reaching their ears. They bend themselves from their backs, prostrate themselves on their foreheads, their palms, their knees and their toes, and beseech God, the Sublime, for their deliverance. Sermon 193

O those who believed! Have testimony between you when death attended anyone of you. At the time of bequeathing, have two possessors of justice from among yourselves or two others from among others if you traveled through the region and the affliction of death lit on you. You will detain them both after the formal prayer. They will swear by God. If you were in doubt about them, have them say: We will not exchange it for a price even if he had been possessing kinship. We will not keep back testimony of God. Truly, we, then, would be among the ones who are perverted. **5:106**
Then, if it was ascertained that the two merited an accusation of sin, then, two others will stand up in their station from among those who are the most deserving, nearest in kinship, and they both swear an oath by God saying: Our testimony has a better right than the testimony of the other two. We exceeded not the limits, for, truly, we, then, would be among the ones who are unjust. **5:107**
That is likelier that they bring testimony in proper form or they fear that their oaths will be repelled after the others' oaths. So, be God-conscious and hear. God guides not the folk, the ones who disobey. **5:108**

I bear witness that He is justice and He acts justly. Sermon 213

On a Day when God will gather the Messengers and will say: What was your answer? They will say: We have no knowledge. Truly, ***You, You*** *alone are Knower of the unseen.* **5:109**

O Kumayl ibn Ziyad, Knowers endure for as long as time subsists. Their forms are absent, but their spiritual images are present in the hearts. Saying 146

Mention when God said: O Jesus son of Mary! Remember My divine blessing on ***you*** *and on the one who is* ***your*** *mother, when I confirmed* ***you****, Jesus, with the hallowed Spirit so that* ***you*** *have spoken to humanity from the cradle and in manhood and when I taught* ***you*** *the Book and wisdom and the Torah and the Gospel and when* ***you*** *have created from clay the likeness of a bird with My permission and* ***you*** *have blown into it and it becomes a bird with My permission and* ***you*** *have cured one blind from birth and the leper with My permission and when* ***you*** *have brought out the dead with My permission and when I limited the Children of Jacob from* ***you*** *when* ***you*** *had drawn near them with the clear portents. Those who were ungrateful among them said: This is nothing but clear sorcery.* **5:110**
Mention when I inspired the disciples: Believe in Me and My Messenger. They said: We believed and bear witness that we are ones who submit to God. **5:111**
Mention when the disciples said: O Jesus son of Mary! Is your Lord able to send down to us a table spread with food from heaven? Jesus said: Be God-conscious, if you had been ones who believe.

5:112
They said: We want that we eat of it so that our hearts be at rest and we know that ***you****, surely, wast sincere to us and that we be the ones who bear witness to that.* **5:113**
Jesus son of Mary said: O God! Our Lord! Cause to descend for us a table spread with food from heaven that it will be a festival for the first of us and the last of us and a sign from ***You****. Provide us. You are Best of the ones who provide.* **5:114**
God said: Truly, I am One Who Sends Down to you. But whoever is ungrateful after that among you, then, I will punish him with a punishment that I punish not anyone of the worlds. **5:115**
Mention when God said: O Jesus son of Mary! Had ***you*** *said to humanity: Take me and my mother to yourselves other than God? He would say: Glory be to* ***You****! It is not for me that I say what there is no right for me to say. If I had been saying it, then, surely,* ***You*** *would have known it.* ***You*** *know what is in my soul and I know not what is in* ***Your*** *Soul. Truly,* ***You, You*** *alone are Knower of the unseen.* **5:116**
I said not to them but what ***You*** *commanded me of it: That you worship God, my Lord and your Lord. I had been witness over them as long as I continued among them. Then, when* ***You*** *gathered me to* ***Your****self,* ***You*** *had been The Watcher over them.* ***You*** *are, truly, Witness over everything.*
5:117
If ***You*** *are to punish them, then, they are but* ***Your*** *servants. If* ***You*** *are to forgive them truly,* ***You, You*** *alone are The Almighty, The Wise.* **5:118**
God would say: This Day the ones who are sincere will profit from their sincerity. For them are Gardens beneath which rivers run, ones who will dwell in them forever, eternally. God was well-pleased with them and they are well-pleased with Him. That is the winning the sublime triumph.
5:119
To God belongs the dominion of the heavens and the earth and whatever is in and on them. He is Powerful over everything. **5:120** ***

Chapter 6: The Flocks (al-Anᶜām)

The Praise belongs to God Who created the heavens and the earth and made the shadows and the light. Again, those who were ungrateful to their Lord, they equate others to Him. **6:1**

Praise belongs to God (Q1:2) from Whose mercy no one loses hope, from Whose bounty no one is deprived, from Whose forgiveness no one is disappointed and for Whose worship no one is too high. His mercy never ceases and His bounty never ceases. Sermon 45

It was He Who created you from clay, and, again, decided a term, a term, that which was determined by Him. Again, you contest. **6:2**

God ... is aware of whatever is hidden in the hearts and whatever lies behind the unseen. Sermon 192

He is God in the heavens and in and on the earth. He knows your secret and what you openly publish and He knows whatever you earn. **6:3**

When Almighty God created the openings of the atmosphere, the expanse of firmament and strata of winds, He flowed into it water whose waves were stormy and whose surges leapt one over the other. He loaded it on dashing wind and breaking typhoons, ordered them to shed it back as rain, gave the wind control over the vigor of the rain, and acquainted it with its limitations. The wind blew under it while water flowed furiously over it. Sermon 1

A sign not approaches for them from the signs of their Lord but they would be ones who turn aside from it. **6:4**

God sent His Messengers and series of His Prophets to them to guide them to fulfilling the pledges of His creation, to recall to them His bounties, to exhort them by preaching, to unveil before them the hidden virtues of wisdom and show them the signs of His Omnipotence, namely the sky which is raised over them, the earth that is placed beneath them, their means of living that sustains them, their deaths that cause them to die, ailments that turn them old and incidents that successively betake them. Sermon 1

Then, surely, they denied The Truth when it drew near to them. Then, tidings approach them of what they had been ridiculing of it. **6:5**

The best means by which seekers of nearness to God, the Almighty, the Exalted, seek nearness, is the belief in Him and His Prophet. Sermon 109

Consider they not how many a generation before them We caused to perish? We established them firmly in and on the earth such as We firmly establish not for you. We sent abundant rain from heaven. We made rivers run beneath them. So, We caused them to perish for their impieties and We caused to grow after them other generations. **6:6**

Certainly, **You** pour down rain after the people lose hope and spread **Your** mercy since **You** are the Guardian, the praiseworthy. Sermon 115

If We sent down to ***you*** *a Book on parchment, then, they would have stretched towards it with their hands. Those who were ungrateful would have said: This is nothing but clear sorcery.* **6:7**
They said: Why was an angel not caused to descend to him? Certainly, if We caused to descend an angel, the command would be decided. Again, no respite would be given to them. **6:8**

Mind the obligations! Mind the obligations! Fulfill them for God and they will take you to the Garden. Surely, God has made unlawful the things which are not unknown and made lawful the things which are without defect. Sermon 167

If We made him an angel, certainly, We would have made him as a man and We would have confused them when they are already confused. **6:9**

Do you feel it when the Angel of Death enters a house? Do you see him when he takes out life of anyone? How can he who is unable to describe a creature like this, describe God? Sermon 112

Certainly, Messengers were ridiculed before you. So, those who derided them were surrounded by what they had been ridiculing. **6:10**

God never allowed His creation to remain without a Prophet, one deputized by Him, or a Book sent down from Him, or a binding argument, or a standing plea. These Messengers were such that they did not fear that they were few in comparison to the large numbers of their falsifiers. Among them was either a predecessor who would name the one to follow or the follower who had been introduced by the predecessor. Sermon 1

Say: Journey through the earth; again, look on how had been the Ultimate End of the ones who deny. **6:11**

He has retained for you remains of the past people for your instruction. Sermon 82

Say: To whom is whatever is in the heavens and the earth? Say: To God. He prescribed mercy for Himself. He will, certainly, gather you on the Day of Resurrection. There is no doubt in it. Those who lost themselves that Day, then, they will not believe. **6:12**

The human being should ... fear the Day of Judgment before it arrives. He should appreciate the shortness of his life and the shortness of his sojourn in the place of stay which has only to last for his change over to the next place. He should, therefore, do something for his change over and for the known stages of his departure. Blessed be he who possesses a virtuous heart, obeys one who guides him, keeps away from one who takes him to ruin, catches the path of safety with the help of him who provides him light of guidance and, by obeying the leader who commands him, hastens towards guidance before its doors are closed, opens the door of repentance and removes the stain of sins. He has certainly been put on the right path and guided towards the straight path. Sermon 214

To Him belongs whatever inhabited the nighttime and the daytime. He is The Hearing, The Knowing. **6:13**

He made the sun the bright indication for its day. He made the moon the gloomy indication for night. He put them in motion in their orbits and ordained their pace of movement in the stages of their paths in order to distinguish with their help between night and day and in order that the reckoning of years and calculations may be known by their ... movements. Sermon 91

Say: Will I take to myself, other than God, a protector, One Who is Originator of the heavens and the earth? It is He who feeds and He who is never fed. Say: Truly, I was commanded that I be the first who submitted to the One God. You have not been among the ones who are polytheists. **6:14**

Where are those who were invited to Islam and they accepted it? They read the Quran and decided according to it. They were exhorted to fight and they leapt towards it as she-camels leap towards their young. They took their swords out of the sheaths and went out into the world in groups and rows. Some of them perished and some survived. The good news of survival does not please them, nor are they condoled about the dead. Their eyes have turned white with weeping. Their bellies are emaciated because of fasting. Their lips are dry because of constant praying. Their color is pale because of wakefulness. Their faces bear the dust of God-consciousness. These are my comrades who have departed. We should be justified if we feel eager for them and bite our hands in their separation. Sermon 121

Say: Truly, I fear if I rebelled against my Lord, the punishment of the tremendous Day! **6:15**

Everyone should be God-conscious, should admonish himself, should send forward his repentance and should overpower his desire because his death is hidden from him. His desires deceive him. Satan keeps posted about him. He beautifies his sin for him so that he may commit it. He prompts him to delay repentance until his desires cause him to be the most negligent. Pity is for the negligent person whose life itself would be a proof against him and his own days, passed in sin, will lead him to punishment. Sermon 64

He who is turned away from it on that Day, then, surely, He had mercy on him. That is the winning the clear triumph. **6:16**

Your ultimate goal of reward or punishment is before you. Behind your back is the hour of Resurrection which is driving you on. Keep yourself light and overtake the forward ones. The first ones who have preceded await your last ones. Sermon 21

If God touches ***you*** *with harm, then, no one will remove it but He. If He touches* ***you*** *with good, then, He is Powerful over everything.* **6:17**

O my God! Here stands one who has singled **You** with Oneness that is **Your** due and has not regarded any one deserving of these praises and eulogies except **You.** My want towards **You** is such that nothing except **Your** generosity can cure its destitution, nor provide for its need except **Your** obligation and **Your** generosity. So do grant us in this place **Your** will and make us free from stretching hands to anyone other than **You.** *Truly* ***You*** *are Powerful over everything.* (Q66:8) Sermon 223

He is The One Who is Omniscient over His servants. He is The Wise, The Aware. **6:18**

God knows hidden matters and is aware of inner feelings. He encompasses everything. He has control over everything and power over everything. Sermon 85

Say: Which thing is greater in testimony? Say: God is Witness between me and you. This, the Quran, was revealed to me that I should warn you with it and whomever it reached. Truly, are you bearing witness that there are other gods with God? Say: I bear not such witness. Say: He is not but One God and I am, truly, free from partners you ascribe with Him. **6:19**

The Prophet (Q7:158), peace and the mercy of God be upon him, left among you what other Prophets had left among their peoples, because Prophets do not leave their people in darkness without a clear path and a sign, namely the Book of your Creator. The Book clarifies its permission and prohibitions, its obligations and discretions, its repealing injunctions and the repealed ones, its permissible matters and compulsory ones, its particulars and general ones, its lessons and illustrations, its long and short ones, its clear and obscure ones, detailing its abbreviations and clarifying its obscurities. Sermon 1

Those to whom We gave the Book recognize it as they recognize their own children. But those, they who lost themselves, they believe not. **6:20**

In God's authority lies the safety of your affairs. Therefore, render Him such obedience as is neither blameworthy nor insincere. By God, you must do so otherwise God will take away from you the power of Islam and will never thereafter return it to you until it reverts to others. Sermon 169

Who does greater wrong than he who devised a lie against God or denied His signs. Truly, the ones who are unjust will not prosper. **6:21**

Populated places were brightened through him when previously there was dark misguidance, overpowering ignorance and rude habits, and people regarded unlawful as lawful, humiliated the man of wisdom, passed lives when there were no prophets and died as ungrateful. Sermon 151

On a Day We will assemble them altogether. Again, We will say to those who ascribed partners with God: Where are your ascribed associates with God whom you had been claiming? **6:22**

They are emulating each other and proceeding in groups towards the final objective and the rendezvous of death, until when matters come to a close, the world dies and the Resurrection draws near. Sermon 82

Again, their dissent will not be but that they would say: By God! Our Lord! We had not been ones who are polytheists. **6:23**

They are wrong who liken **You** to their idols and dress **You** with apparel of the creatures by their imagination, attribute to **You** parts of body by their own thinking and consider **You** after the creatures of various types, through the working of their intelligence. I bear witness that whoever equated **You** with anything out of **Your** creation took a partner for **You.** Whoever takes a partner for **You** is ungrateful according to what is stated in **Your** unambiguous verses and indicated by the evidence of **Your** clear arguments. I also bear witness that **You** are that God Who cannot be confined in the fetters of intelligence so as to admit change of condition by entering its imagination, nor in the shackles of the mind so as to become limited and an object of alterations. Sermon 91

Look on how they have lied against themselves. Went astray with them that which they had been devising. **6:24**

Be aware! The worst speech is that which is untrue. Sermon 84

Among them are those who listen to ***you****. But We laid sheathes on their hearts so that they not understand it and in their ears is a heaviness. If they are to see every sign they will not believe in it. So, that when they drew near* ***you****, they dispute with* ***you****. Those who were ungrateful say: This is nothing but fables of the ancient ones.* **6:25**

Where are these ways taking you, gloom misleading you and falsehoods deceiving you? From where are you brought and to where are you driven? For every period there is a written document and everyone who is absent has to return. So listen to your pious leader and keep your hearts present. If he speaks to you, be wakeful. The forerunner must speak the truth to his people, should keep his wits together and maintain presence of mind. He has clarified to you the matter as the thread is cleared and scraped it as the gum is scraped from twigs. Sermon 108

They prohibit others from it. They withdraw aside from it. They cause to perish, no doubt, none but themselves, but they are not aware. **6:26**

Be aware of destroying your manners and changing them. Sermon 176

If ***you*** *would see when they would be stationed by the fire, they will say: Would that we be returned to life. Then, we would not deny the signs of our Lord and we would be among the ones who believe.* **6:27**

The beginning of the action of one who sees with his heart and acts with eyes is to assess whether the action will go against him or for him. If it is for him, he indulges in it, but if it is against him, he keeps away from it. For he who acts without knowledge is like one who treads without a path. His deviation from the path keeps him at a distance from his aim. He who acts according to knowledge is like him who treads the clear path. Therefore, he who can see should see whether he should proceed or return. You should, also know that the outside has a similar inside. Of whatever the outside is good, its inside too is good and whenever the outside is bad, its inside, too, is bad. The truthful Prophet, peace and the mercy of God be upon him, has said: God may love a person but hate his action and may love the action, but hate the person. You should also know that every action is like vegetation. Vegetation cannot do without water while waters are different. Where the water is good, the plant is good and its fruits are sweet, whereas where the water is bad, the plant will also be bad and its fruits will be bitter. Sermon 153

Nay! Shown to themselves will be what they had been concealing before. Even if they were returned, they would revert to what they were prohibited from there and, truly, they are the ones who lie. **6:28**

They took to the right and the left piercing through to the ways of evil and leaving the paths of guidance. Do not make haste for a matter which is to happen and is awaited. Do not wish for delay in what the morrow is to bring for you. For how many people make haste for a matter, but when they get it they begin to wish they had not gotten it? How near is today to the dawning of tomorrow? Sermon 150

They said: There is nothing but this, our present life, and we are not ones who will be raised up. **6:29**

In the present life its authority is changing. Its life is dirty. Its sweet water is bitter. Its sweetness is like myrrh. Its foods are poisons. Its means are weak. The living in it is exposed to death. The healthy in it is exposed to disease. Its realm is liable to be snatched away. The strong in it is liable to be defeated and the rich is liable to be afflicted with misfortune. The neighbor in it is liable to be plundered. Sermon 111

If ***you*** *would see when they would be stationed before their Lord. He would say: Is this not The Truth? They would say: Yea, by Our Lord. He would say: Then, experience the punishment for what you had been ungrateful.* **6:30**

God ... is aware of whatever is hidden in the hearts and whatever lies behind the unseen. Sermon 192

Surely, those lost who denied the meeting with God until when the Hour drew near them suddenly, they would say: What a regret for us that we neglected in it! They will carry heavy loads on their backs. How evil is what they bear! **6:31**

Whoever takes a partner for **You** is ungrateful according to what is stated in **Your** unambiguous verses and indicated by the evidence of **Your** clear arguments. Sermon 91

This present life is nothing but a pastime and diversion. The Last Abode is better for those who are God-conscious. Will you not, then, be reasonable? **6:32**

In what way shall I describe this world whose beginning is grief and whose end is destruction? The lawful actions performed here have to be accounted for, while for the forbidden ones there is punishment. Whoever is rich here faces mischief and whoever is poor is grieved. One who hankers after it does not attain it. If one keeps away from it, then it advances towards him. If one sees through it, it would bestow him sight, but if one has his eye on it, then it would blind him. Sermon 82

Surely, We know that what they say disheartens ***you****. Truly, they deny* ***you*** *not. Rather the ones* *who are unjust negate the signs of God.* **6:33**

I bear witness that Muhammad, peace and the mercy of God be upon him, is His servant and His Prophet whom He deputed when the signs of guidance were obliterated and the ways of religion were desolate. So he threw open the truth, gave advice to the people, guided them towards righteousness and ordered them to be moderate. May God bless him. Sermon 195

Certainly, Messengers before you were denied yet they endured patiently that they were denied and they were maligned until Our help approached them. No one will change the Word of God. Certainly, there drew near ***you*** *tidings of the ones who are sent.* **6:34**

It is He who made His creation to populate the world and sent towards the jinn and human beings His Messengers to unveil it for them, to warn them of its harm, to present to them its examples, to show them its defects and to place before them a whole collection of matters containing lessons about the changings of health and sickness in this world, its lawful things and unlawful things and all that God has ordained for the obedient and the disobedient, namely Paradise and Hell and honor and disgrace. I extend my praise to His Being as He desires His creation to praise Him. He has fixed for everything a measure, for every measure a time limit, and for every time limit a document. Sermon 182

If their turning aside had been troublesome to ***you****, then, if* ***you*** *were able, be looking for a hole in the earth or a ladder to heaven so that* ***you*** *would bring them some sign. If God willed, He would have gathered them to The Guidance. Be* ***you*** *not among the ones who are ignorant.* **6:35**

We are in a period when most of the people regard betrayal as wisdom. In these days the ignorant ones called it excellence of cunning. What is the matter with them? May God destroy them. Sermon 41

It is only those who hear who respond. As for the dead, God will raise them up. Again, they are returned to Him. **6:36**

Do you not see that your predecessors did not come back and the surviving followers did not remain? Do you not observe that the people of the world pass mornings and evenings in different conditions? Thus, somewhere the dead is wept for, someone is being condoled, someone is prostrate in distress, someone is enquiring about the sick, someone is passing his last breath, someone is hankering after the world while death is looking for him, someone is forgetful, but he is not forgotten by death, and the survivors walk in the footsteps of the predecessors. Sermon 99

They said: Why was a sign not sent down to him from his Lord? Say: Truly, God is One Who Has Power over what sign He sends down, except most of them know not. **6:37**

You should, therefore, regard God great as He has held Himself great, because He has not concealed anything of His religion from you, nor has He left out anything which He likes, nor which He dislikes, but He made for it a clear emblem of guidance and a definite sign which either refrains from it or calls towards it. His pleasure is the same for all time to come. Sermon 183

There is no moving creature in or on the earth, none that is a fowl flying with its two wings, but they are communities like yours. We neglected not anything in the Book. Again, they will be assembled to their Lord. **6:38**

Is it that God ordered them to differ and they obeyed Him? Or He prohibited them from it, but they disobeyed Him? Or is it that God sent an incomplete faith and sought their help to complete it? Or are they His partners in the affairs, so that it is their share of duty to pronounce and He has to agree? Or is it that God the Almighty sent a perfect faith, but *the Prophet* (Q7:158), peace and the mercy of God be upon him, fell short of conveying it and handing it over to the people? The fact is that God the Almighty says: *We have not neglected anything in the Book.* (Q6:38) In it is a clarification of everything. Sermon 18

Those who denied Our signs are unwilling to hear and unwilling to speak. They are in the shadows. Whomever God wills, He causes to go astray. Whomever He wills, He lays on a straight path. **6:39**

Where are those who were invited to Islam and they accepted it? They read the Quran and decided according to it. They were exhorted to fight and they leapt towards it as she-camels leap towards their young. They took their swords out of the sheaths and went out into the world in groups and rows. Some of them perished and some survived. The good news of survival does not please them, nor are they condoled about the dead. Their eyes have turned white with weeping. Their bellies are emaciated because of fasting. Their lips are dry because of constant praying. Their color is pale because of wakefulness. Their faces bear the dust of God-consciousness. These are my comrades who have departed. We should be justified if we feel eager for them and bite our hands in their separation. Sermon 121

Say: Considered you that if the punishment of God approached you or the Hour approached you, would you call to any other than God if you had been ones who are sincere? **6:40**

O God's human being! Where are those who were allowed long ages to live? They enjoyed bounty. They were taught. They learned. They were given time. They passed it in vain. They were kept healthy. They forgot their duty. They were allowed a long period of life, were handsomely provided for, were warned of grievous punishment and were promised great rewards. You should avoid sins that lead to destruction and vices that attract the wrath of God. Sermon 82

Nay! To Him alone you would call and He would remove that for which you call to Him—if He willed—and you will forget whatever partners you ascribe with Him. **6:41**

I bear witness that *there is no god but God,* (Q47:19), by virtue of belief, certainty, sincerity and conviction. I also bear witness that Muhammad, peace and the mercy of God be upon him, is His servant and His Prophet whom He deputed when the signs of guidance were obliterated and the ways of religion were desolate. So he threw open the truth, gave advice to the people, guided them towards righteousness and ordered them to be moderate. May God bless him.... Sermon 194

Certainly, We sent to communities that were before **you**. *Then, We took them with desolation and tribulation so that perhaps they will lower themselves to Us.* **6:42**

O people! If you had not evaded support of the truth and had not felt weakness from crushing wrong, then he who was not your match would not have aimed at you. He who overpowered you would not have overpowered you, but you roamed about the deserts of disobedience like the Children of Jacob. I swear by my life that after me your tribulations will increase several times because you will have abandoned the truth behind your backs, severed your connection with your near ones and established relations with remote ones.

Know that if you had followed him who was calling you to guidance, he would have made you tread the ways of *the Prophet,* (Q7:158), peace and the mercy of God be upon him. Then you would have been spared the difficulties of misguidance and you would have thrown away the crushing burden from your necks. Sermon 166

Then, why when drew near them Our might, they lowered not themselves? Rather, their hearts became hard. Satan made appear pleasing to them what they had been doing. **6:43**

God chose Prophets from Adam's progeny. He took their pledge to receive His revelation and to carry His message as their trust. Over the course of time, many people perverted God's trust in them. They ignored His position. They took partners with Him. Satan turned them away from knowing Him and distanced them from His worship. Sermon 1

So, when they forgot about what they were reminded in it, We opened to them the doors of everything. Until when they were glad with what they were given, We suddenly took them. That is when they were ones who are seized with despair. **6:44**

They have adopted for every truth a wrong way, for every erect thing a bender, for every living being a killer, for every closed door a key and for every night a lamp. They covet, but with despair, in order to maintain with it their markets and to popularize their handsome merchandise. When they speak, they create doubts. When they describe, they exaggerate. First they offer easy paths, but afterwards they make them narrow. In short, they are the party of Satan and the sting of fire. *Regard the Party of Satan. They will be the ones who are losers.* (Q58:19) Sermon 193

So, cut off were the last remnant of the folk who did wrong. The Praise belongs to God, Lord of the worlds. **6:45**

All *praise belongs to God.* (Q1:2) Sermon 35

Say: Considered you that if God took your having the ability to hear and your sight and sealed over your hearts, what god other than God restores them to you? Look on how We diversify the signs! Again, they still drew aside. **6:46**

Where are the minds which seek light from the lamps of guidance and the eyes which look at minarets of God-consciousness? Where are the hearts dedicated to God and devoted to the obedience of God? They are all crowding towards worldly vanities and quarreling over unlawful issues. The banners of the Garden and Hell have been raised for them, but they have turned their faces away from the Garden and proceeded to Hell by dint of their performances. God called them, but they showed dislike and ran away. When Satan called them, they responded and proceeded towards him. Sermon 144

Say: Considered you that if the punishment of God approached you suddenly or publicly, will anyone be caused to perish but the folk, the ones who are unjust? **6:47**

O people, surely this world deceives him who longs for it and who is attracted towards it. It does not behave in a miserly manner with him who aspires for it and overpowers him who overpowers it. By God, no people are deprived of the lively pleasures of life after enjoying them, except as a result of sins committed by them, because certainly God is not unjust to His creatures. Even then when calamities descend upon people and pleasures depart from them, they turn towards God with true intention and the feeling in their hearts that

He will return them everything that has fled from them and cure all their ills. Sermon 178

We send not the ones who are sent, but as ones who give good tidings and ones who warn. So, whoever believed and made things right, then, there will be neither fear in them nor will they feel remorse. **6:48**
But those who denied Our signs, the punishment will afflict them because they had been disobeying. **6:49**

God sent *Muhammad* (48:29), peace and the mercy of God be upon him, as a witness, giver of good tidings and warner, the best in the universe as a child and the most chaste as a grown up person, the purest of the purified in conduct, the most generous of those who are approached for generosity. Sermon 105

Say: I say not to you: With me are treasures of God nor that I know the unseen nor say I to you that I am an angel. I follow only what is revealed to me. Say: Are they on the same level— the unwilling to see and the seeing? Will you, then, not reflect? **6:50**

People did not take light from the lights of his wisdom, nor did they produce flame from the flint of sparkling knowledge. So in this matter, they are like grazing cattle and hard stones. Nevertheless, hidden things have appeared for those who perceive. The face of right has become clear for the wanderer. The approaching moment has raised the veil from its face. Signs have appeared for those who search for them. Sermon 108

Warn with the Quran those who fear that they will be assembled before their Lord. Other than He there is neither a protector nor an intercessor, so that perhaps they will be God-conscious. **6:51**

God sent Muhammad, peace and the mercy of God be upon him, with the Truth so that he may take out His people from the worship of idols towards His worship and from obeying Satan towards obeying Him. God sent him with the Quran which He explained and made strong in order that the people may know their Sustainer (God), since they were ignorant of Him, may acknowledge Him, since they were denying Him and accept Him, since they were refusing to believe in Him. Sermon 147

Drive not away those who call to their Lord in the morning and the evening, wanting His Countenance. Their reckoning is not on ***you*** *at all.* ***Your*** *reckoning is not on them at all. If* ***you*** *were to drive them away, then,* ***you*** *would be among the ones who are unjust.* **6:52**

Certainly, I belong to the group of people who care not for the reproach of anybody in matters concerning God. Their countenance is the countenance of the truthful and their speech is the speech of the virtuous. They are wakeful during the nights in devotion to God and over beacons of guidance in the day. They hold fast to the rope of the Quran, revive the traditions of God and of His Prophet. They do not boast, nor indulge in self-conceit, nor misappropriate, nor create mischief. Their hearts are in Paradise while their bodies are busy in good acts. Sermon 192

Thus, We tried some of them with others that they should say: Is it these to whom God showed grace from among us? Is not God greater in knowledge of the ones who are thankful? **6:53**

You should know that He will not be pleased with you for anything for which He was displeased with those before you. He will not be displeased with you for anything for which He was pleased with those before you. You are treading on a clear path and are speaking the same as the people before you had spoken. God is enough for your needs in this world. He has persuaded you to remain thankful and has made it obligatory on you to mention Him with your tongues. Sermon 183

When drew near ***you*** *those who believe in Our signs, say: Peace be to you. Your Lord prescribed mercy for Himself so that anyone of you who did evil in ignorance—again, repented afterwards and made things right—then, truly, He is Forgiving, Compassionate.* **6:54**

Do you know what asking God's forgiveness is? Asking for forgiveness is meant for people of a high position. It is a word that stands on six supports. The first is to repent over the past; the second is to make a firm determination never to revert to it; the third is to discharge all the rights of people so that you may meet God quite clean with nothing to account for; the fourth is to fulfill every obligation which you ignored in the past so that you may now do justice with it; the fifth is to aim at the flesh grown as a result of unlawful earning so that you may melt it by grief of repentance until the skin touches the bone and a new flesh grows between them; and the sixth is to make the body taste the pain of obedience as you previously made it taste the sweetness of disobedience. On such an occasion you may repent and ask for forgiveness. Hadith 417

Thus, We explain Our signs distinctly so that the way is indicated for the ones who sin. **6:55**

The Prophet (Q7:158), peace and the mercy of God be upon him, left among you what other Prophets had left among their peoples, because Prophets do not leave their people in darkness without a clear path and a sign, namely the Book of your Creator. The Book clarifies its permission and prohibitions, its obligations and discretions, its repealing injunctions and the repealed ones, its permissible matters and compulsory ones, its particulars and general ones, its lessons and illustrations, its long and short ones, its clear and obscure ones, detailing its abbreviations and clarifying its obscurities. Sermon 106

Say: I was prohibited that I worship those whom you call to other than God. Say: I will not follow your desires, for, then, I would have gone astray. I would not be of the ones who are truly guided. **6:56**

Storms may overtake you while there may be none to prick you to reform. Shall I be witness to my becoming a heretic after having accepted the faith and fighting in the company of *the Prophet* (Q7:158), peace and the mercy of God be upon him?! ... *then I would not be among the ones who are truly guided.* (Q6:56) So you should return to your evil places and trace back to where your heels began. Be aware! Truly, you will meet, after me, overwhelming disgrace towards you and a sharp sword and tradition that will be adopted by the oppressors as a norm. Sermon 57

Say: I am with a clear portent from my Lord and you denied it. I have not of that which you seek to hasten. The determination is with God. He relates The Truth. He is Best of the ones who distinguish truth from falsehood. **6:57**
Say: Truly, if with me was what you seek to hasten, the command would be decided between me and between you. God is greater in knowledge of the ones who are unjust. **6:58**

At a time when virtue is in vogue in the world and among people, if a person entertains an evil suspicion about another person from whom nothing evil has ever been seen, then he has been unjust. Hadith 114

With Him are the keys of the unseen. None knows them but He. He knows whatever is on dry land and in the sea. Not a leaf descends but He knows it, nor a grain in the shadows of the earth, nor fresh nor dry thing, but it is in a clear Book. **6:59**

Certainly, the manifest of the Quran is wonderful and its hidden is deep in meaning. Its wonders will never disappear. Its amazements will never pass away. Its intricacies cannot be cleared except through itself. Sermon 18

It is He Who gathers you to Himself by nighttime and He knows what you were busy with by daytime. Again, He raises you up in it so that the term, that which is determined, is decided. Again, to Him is your return. Again, He will tell you of what you had been doing. **6:60**

He commanded it to remain stationary in obedience to His commands. He made its sun the bright indication for its day and moon the gloomy indication for its night. He then put them in motion in their orbits and ordained their pace of movement in the stages of their paths in order to distinguish with their help between night and day and in order that the reckoning of years and calculations may be known by their fixed movements. Sermon 91

He is The One Who Is Omniscient over His servants. He sends over you recorders until when death drew near one of you. Our Messengers gathered him to themselves and they neglect not. **6:61**

He has advised you to exercise fear and has made it the highest point of His pleasure and all that He requires from His creatures. You should, therefore, be God-conscious, Who is such that you are as though just in front of Him. Your forelocks are in His grip. Your change of position is in His control. If you conceal a matter, He will know of it. If you disclose a matter, He will record it. For this He has appointed honored guardian angels who do not omit any rightful matter, nor include anything incorrect. Sermon 183

Again, they would be returned to God, their Defender, The True. Is not the determination for Him? He is The Swiftest of the ones who reckon. **6:62**

There remain a few people in whose case the remembrance of their return to God on the Day of Judgment keeps their eyes bent and the awareness of the Resurrection moves them to tears. Some of them are scared away from the world and disperse. Some are frightened and subdued. Some are quiet as if muzzled. Some are praying sincerely. Some are grief-stricken and pain-ridden whom fear has confined to namelessness. Disgrace has shrouded them, so they are in the sea of bitter water, their mouths are closed and their hearts are bruised. They preached until they were tired. They were oppressed until they were disgraced. They were killed until their numbers dwindled. Sermon 32

Say: Who delivers you from the shadows of the dry land and the sea? You call to Him humbly and inwardly: If ***You*** *were to rescue us from this, we will be of the ones who are thankful.* **6:63**

God is enough for your needs in this world. He has persuaded you to remain thankful and has made it obligatory on you to mention Him with your tongue. Sermon 183

Say: God delivers you from them and from every distress. Again, you ascribe partners with Him. **6:64**

The highest among you in distress would be he who bears the best belief about God. If God grants you safety, accept it, and if you are put in trouble, endure it, because surely good results are for the God-conscious. Sermon 97

Say: He is The One Who Has Power to raise up on you a punishment from above you, or from beneath your feet or to confuse you as partisans and to cause you to experience the violence of some of you to one another. Look on how We diversify the signs so that perhaps they will understand! **6:65**

Praise belongs to God (Q1:2) Who established Islam and made it easy for those who approach it and gave strength to its columns against any one who tries to overpower it. So God made it a source of peace for him who clings to it, safety for him who enters it, argument for him who speaks about it, witness for him who fights with its help, light for him who seeks light from it, understanding for him who provides it, sagacity for him who exerts, a sign of guidance for him who perceives, sight for him who resolves, a lesson for him who seeks advice, salvation for him who testifies, confidence for him who trusts, pleasure for him who entrusts and a shield for him who endures. It is the brightest of all paths, the clearest of all passages. It has dignified minarets, bright highways, burning laps, prestigious fields of activity and a high objective. It has a collection of race horses. It is approached eagerly. Its riders are honorable. Testimony of God and *the Prophet* (Q7:158), peace and the mercy of God be upon him, is its way. Good deeds are its minarets. Death is its extremity. This world is its racecourse. The Day of Judgment is its horses. Paradise is its point of approach. Sermon 106

***Your** folk denied it and it is The Truth. Say: I am not a trustee over you.* **6:66**

Even when He made Adam die, He did not leave them without one who would serve among them as proof and plea for His Godhead and serve as the link between them and His knowledge, but He provided to them the proofs through His chosen Messengers and bearers of the trust of His Message, age after age, until the process came to end with our Prophet Muhammad, peace and the mercy of God be upon him, and His pleas and warnings reached finality. Sermon 91

For every tiding there is an appointed time. You will know it. **6:67**

Death is its extremity. This world is its race-course. The Day of Judgment is its horses. Paradise is its point of approach. Sermon 106

*When **you** saw those who engage in idle talk about Our signs, then, turn aside from them until they discuss in conversation other than that. If Satan should cause **you** to forget, then, after a reminder, sit not with the folk, the ones who are unjust.* **6:68**

You should, therefore, put out the fires of haughtiness and the flames of intolerance that are hidden in your hearts. This vanity can exist in a Muslim only by the machinations of Satan, his haughtiness, mischief and whisperings. Sermon 192

There is not on those who are God-conscious anything of their reckoning, but a reminder so that perhaps they will be God-conscious. **6:69**

Among the God-conscious are the people of distinction. Their speech is to the point. Their dress is moderate. Their gait is humble. They keep their eyes closed to what God has made unlawful for them. They put their ears to that knowledge which is beneficial to them. They remain in the time of trials as though they remain in comfort. If there had not been fixed periods of life ordained for each, their spirits would not have remained in their bodies even for the twinkling of an eye because of their eagerness for the reward and fear of chastisement. The greatness of the Creator is seated in their heart, and so everything else appears small in their eyes. Thus, to them Paradise is as though they see it and are enjoying its favors. To them, Hell is also as if they see it and are suffering punishment in it. Sermon 193

Forsake those who took to themselves their way of life as a pastime and as a diversion and whom this present life deluded. But remind with it, the Quran, so that a soul would not be given up to destruction for what it earned. Other than God there is not for it a protector nor an intercessor. Even if it be an equitable equivalent, it will not be taken from it. Those are those who were given up to destruction for what they earned. For them is a drink of scalding water and a painful punishment because they had been ungrateful. **6:70**

By God, certainly it is reality not play, truth not falsehood. It is none other than death. Its caller is making himself heard. Its driver is making haste. The majority of the people should not deceive you. You have seen those who lived before you, amassed wealth, feared poverty and felt safe from its evil consequences, the longevity of desires and the apparent distance from death. How, then death overtook them, turned them out of their homelands and took them out of their places of safety. They were borne on coffins. People were busy about them one after another, carrying them on their shoulders and supporting them with their hands. Sermon 132

Say: Will we call to other than God what can neither hurt nor profit us? Are we repelled on our heels after God guided us like one whom the satans lured, bewildered in and on the earth although he has companions who call him to the guidance saying: Approach us? Say: Truly, the guidance of God is The Guidance. We were commanded to submit to the Lord of the worlds **6:71**
and to perform the formal prayer and be God-conscious of Him. It is He to Whom you will be assembled. **6:72**

O God's human being! I advise you to keep away from this world which is shortly to leave you, even though you do not like its departure, and which would make your bodies old, even though you would like to keep them young. Sermon 99

It is He Who created the heavens and the earth with The Truth. On a Day He says: Be! Then, it is! His saying is The Truth. His is the dominion on a Day when the trumpet will be blown. He is One Who Knows of the unseen and the visible. He is The Wise, The Aware. **6:73**

My God, Spreader of the surfaces of the earth and Keeper intact of all skies, Creator of hearts of good and evil nature, send **Your** choicest blessings and growing favors on Muhammad, peace and the mercy of God be upon him, **Your** servant and **Your** Prophet, who is the last of those who preceded him and an opener for what is closed, proclaimer of truth with truth, repulser of the forces of wrong and crusher of the onslaughts of misguidance. Sermon 72

Mention when Abraham said to his father Azar: Have ***you*** *taken idols to thyself as gods? Truly, I see* ***you*** *and* ***your*** *folk clearly wandering astray.* **6:74**
Thus, We cause Abraham to see the kingdom of the heavens and the earth so that he would be of the ones who are certain in belief. **6:75**
So, when night outspread over him, he saw a star. He said: This is my Lord. Then, when it set, he said: I love not that which sets. **6:76**
Then, when he saw the moon, that which rises, he said: This is my Lord. Then, when it set, he said:

If my Lord guides me not, certainly, I would have been among the folk, the ones gone astray. **6:77**
Then, when he saw the sun, that which rises, he said: This is my Lord. This is greater. Then, when it set, he said: O my folk! Truly, I am free from the partners you ascribe with Him. **6:78**
Truly, I turned my face to He Who Originated the heavens and the earth—as a monotheist and I am not of the ones who are polytheists. **6:79**

Through His power He originated all created things. Sermon 1*

His folk argued with him. He said: You argue with me about God while, surely, He guided me? I fear not whatever partners you ascribe with Him. When my Lord wills a thing, my Lord encompassed everything in His knowledge. Will you not, then, recollect? **6:80**
How should I fear what you ascribed as partners with Him while you fear not that you ascribe as partners with God? He sends not down to you any authority for it. Then, which of the two groups of people has better right to a place of sanctuary if you had been knowing? **6:81**
Those who believed and confuse not their belief with injustice, those, to them belongs the place of sanctuary. They are ones who are truly guided. **6:82**
That was Our disputation that We gave Abraham against his folk. We exalt in degrees whom We will, truly, ***your*** *Lord is Wise, Knowing.* **6:83**
We bestowed on him Isaac and Jacob. Each of them We guided. Noah We guided before and among his offspring are David and Solomon and Job and Joseph and Moses and Aaron. Thus, We gave recompense to the ones who are doers of good. **6:84**
Zechariah and Yahya and Jesus and Elijah—all are among the ones in accord with morality. **6:85**
Ishmael and Elisha and Jonah and Lot. We gave all an advantage over the worlds. **6:86**
From among their fathers and their offspring and their brothers/sisters, We elected them and We guided them to a straight path. **6:87**
That is guidance of God. He guides with it whom He wills of His servants. If they ascribed partners with Him, what they had been doing was fruitless for them. **6:88**

That is the guidance of God. He guides with it whom He wills of His servants. (Q6:88) Letter 28

Those are those to whom We gave the Book and critical judgment and prophethood. So, if these are ungrateful for them, then, surely, We charged a folk with them who is not of the ones who are ungrateful for them. **6:89**
Those are those whom God guided. So, imitate their guidance. Say: I ask of you no compensation for it. It is not but a reminder for the worlds. **6:90** ***

They measured not God with His true measure when they said: God caused not to descend anything to a mortal. Say: Who caused the Book to descend that was brought about for Moses as a light and guidance for humanity? You make it into parchments. You show them some of it and conceal much of it. You were taught what you know not, you nor your fathers. Say: God revealed it. Again, forsake them playing, engaging in their idle talk. **6:91**
This is a Book We caused to descend—that which is blessed—and that which establishes as true what was before it and for ***you*** *to warn the Mother of Towns and those who are around it. Those who believe in the world to come believe in it. They over their formal prayers are watchful.* **6:92**

The Book of God is among you. It speaks. Its tongue does not falter. It is a house whose pillars do not fall down. It is a power whose supporters are never defeated. Sermon 132

Who does greater wrong than he who devised lies against God or said: It was revealed to me, when nothing is revealed to him. Or who said: I will cause to descend the like of what God caused to descend. If ***you*** *would see when the ones who are unjust are in the perplexity of death and the angels—the ones who stretch out their hands will say: Relinquish your souls. Today, you will be given recompense with the humiliating punishment for what you had been saying about God other than The Truth. You had been growing arrogant to His signs.* **6:93**

O people, you are the target for the arrows of death in this world. With every drinking there is choking and with every eating there is suffocation. You do not receive any benefit from it except by forgoing another benefit. No one among you advances in age by a day except by the taking away of a day from his life. Nothing more is added to his eating unless it reduces what was there before. No mark appears for him unless a mark disappears. Nothing new comes into being unless the new becomes old. No new crop comes up unless a crop has been reaped. Those roots are gone whose off-shoots we are. How can an off-shoot live after the departure of its root? Sermon 145

Certainly, you drew near Us one by one as We created you the first time. You left what We granted you behind your backs. We see not your intercessors with you, those whom you claimed as your ascribed associates. Certainly, the bonds between you were cut asunder. Gone astray from you is what you had been claiming. **6:94**

Be aware, every sower of a crop is in distress except the sowers of the Quran. Therefore, you should be among the sowers of the Quran and its followers. Make it your guide towards God. Seek its advice for yourselves, do not trust your views against it and regard your desires in the matter of the Quran as deceitful. Sermon 175

Truly, it is God who is One Who Causes to Break Forth the grain and the pit of a date. He brings out the living from the dead and is One Who Brings Out the dead from the living. That is God. Then, how you are misled. **6:95**

O people who possess eyes and ears and health and wealth! Is there any place of protection, any shelter of safety, or asylum or haven, or occasion to run away or to come back to this world? *If not: How then you are misled?* (Q6:95) and whither are you averting? By what things have you been deceived? Certainly, the share of every one of you from this earth is just a piece of land equal to his own stature and size where he would lie on his cheeks covered with dust. Sermon 82

He is One Who Causes to Break Forth the morning dawn and He made the night as a place of comfort and rest and the sun and the moon to keep count. That is the foreordaining of The Almighty, The Knowing. **6:96**

In His creation, the big, the delicate, the heavy, the light, the strong, the weak are all equal. An ant can hardly be seen in the corner of the eye, nor by the perception of the imagination—how it moves on the earth and leaps at its livelihood. It carries the grain to its hole and deposits it in its place of stay. It collects during the summer for its winter and for strength during its period of weakness. Its livelihood is guaranteed. It is fed according to fitness. God, the Kind, does not forget it. God, the Giver, does not deprive it even though it may be in dry stone or fixed rocks. Sermon 185

It is He Who made the stars for you so that you will be truly guided by them in the shadows of dry land and the sea. Surely, We explained distinctly the signs for a folk who know. **6:97**

Be aware! The example of the descendants of Muhammad, peace and the mercy of God be upon him, is like that of stars in the sky. When one star sets, another one rises. So you are in a position that God's blessings on you have been perfected. He has shown you what you used to wish for. Sermon 100

It is He Who caused you to grow from a single soul, then, a temporary stay and a repository. Surely, We explained distinctly the signs for a folk who understand. **6:98**

No other originator took part with Him in its origination. No one having power assisted Him in its creation. Sermon 185

It is He Who caused to descend water from heaven. Then, We brought out from it every kind of bringing forth. Then, We brought out herbs from it. We bring out from it thick-clustered grain and from the date palm tree, from the spathe of it, thick clusters of dates, that which draws near and gardens of the grapevines and the olives and the pomegranates, like each to each and not resembling one another. Look on its fruit when it bore fruit and its ripening. Truly, in this are signs for a folk who believe. **6:99**

He initiated creation most initially and commenced it originally without undergoing reflection, without making use of any experiment, without innovating any movement and without experiencing any aspiration of mind. He allotted all things their times, put together their variations, gave them their properties and determined their features knowing them before creating them, realizing fully their limits and confines and appreciating their propensities and intricacies. Sermon 1

They made as associates with God—the jinn—although He created them. They falsely attributed to Him sons and daughters without knowledge. Glory be to Him! Exalted is He above what they allege. **6:100**

Certainly, the outside of the Quran is wonderful and its inside is deep in meaning. Its wonders will never disappear, its amazements will never pass away and its intricacies cannot be cleared except through itself. Sermon 18

He is Beginner of the heavens and the earth. How would He have a child when He is without a companion and He created everything and He is Knowing of everything? **6:101**

Set out with the fear of God, Who is One and has no partner. Sermon 25

That is God, your Lord. There is no god but He—the One Who is Creator of everything—so worship Him. For He is Trustee over everything. **6:102**

No sight overtakes Him, but He overtakes sight. He is The Subtle, The Aware. **6:103**

... by the things their Creator manifests Himself to the intellects, and by things He is guarded from the sight of the eyes. Sermon 185*

Surely, clear evidence drew near you from your Lord. So, whoever perceived, it will be for his own soul. Whoever was in darkness will be against his own soul. Say: I am not a guardian over you. **6:104**

Whomever we ask for evidence, he should give it according to his knowledge about it. Sermon 123

Thus, We diversify the signs and they will say: **You** *received instruction and We will make the Quran manifest for a folk who know.* **6:105**

He, the Almighty, revealed Himself to them through His Book without their having seen Him, by means of what He showed them out of His might and made them fear His sway, how He destroyed those whom He wished to destroy through His chastisement and ruined those whom He wished to ruin through His retribution! Sermon 147

Follow **you** *what was revealed to* **you** *from* **your** *Lord. There is no god but He. Turn* **you** *aside from the ones who are polytheists.* **6:106**

When truth was revealed to me, I never doubted it. Saying 183

If God willed, they would not have ascribed partners with Him, We made **you** *not a guardian over them, nor are* **you** *a trustee for them.* **6:107**

I bear witness that *there is no god but God* (Q47:19). He is One and there is no partner with Him. He is the First, such that nothing was before Him. He is the Last, such that there is not limit for Him. Imagination cannot catch any of His qualities. Hearts cannot entertain belief about His nature. Analysis and division cannot be applied to Him. Eyes and hearts cannot compare Him. Sermon 84

Offend not those who call to other than God so that they not offend God out of spite without knowledge. Thus, We made to appear pleasing the actions of every community. Again, to their Lord is their return. Then, He will tell them what they had been doing. **6:108**

How awe-striking is **Your** realm that we notice, but how humble is this against what is hidden from us out of **Your** authority! How extensive are **Your** bounties in this world, but how small are they against the bounties of the next world! Sermon 108

They swear by God the most earnest sworn oaths that if a sign would draw near them, they would, certainly, believe in it. Say: The signs are only with God. What will cause you to realize that even if the signs were to draw near, they would not believe? **6:109**

Alas! It is a treasured knowledge. Sermon 149

We will turn around and around their minds and their sight as they believe not in it the first time. We will forsake them in their defiance, wandering unwilling to see. **6:110**

Wrong has set itself in its place. Ignorance has ridden on its riding beasts. Unruliness has increased while the call for virtue is suppressed. Time has pounced upon him like a devouring carnivore. Wrong is shouting like a camel after remaining silent. People have become brothers over ill-doings, have forsaken religion, are united in speaking lies and bear mutual hatred in the matter of truth. Sermon 108

Even if We sent down the angels to them and the dead spoke to them and we assembled everything against them, face to face, yet they would not believe unless God wills, except many of them are ignorant. **6:111**

Moses did not entertain fear for himself. Rather he understood the ignorant and their deviated way. We stand today on the cross-roads of truth and untruth. The one who is sure of reaching water feels no thirst. Sermon 4

Thus, We made an enemy for every Prophet, satans from among humankind and the jinn. Some of them reveal to some others an ornamented saying, a delusion. If **your** *Lord willed, they would not have accomplished it. So, forsake them and what they devise,* **6:112**

By God Who germinates the seed and blows the wind, whatever I convey to you is from *the Prophet* (Q7:158), peace and the mercy of God be upon him. Neither the conveyor of God's message, *the Prophet* (Q7:158), peace and the mercy of God be upon him, lied, nor the hearer misunderstood. Sermon 101

while minds will bend towards it of those who believe not in the world to come and they will be well-pleased with it. They will gain what the ones who gain gain. **6:113**

Your land is close to the sea and away from the sky. Your wits have become light and your minds are full of folly. You are the aim of the archer, a morsel for the eater and an easy prey for the hunter. Sermon 14

Will I be looking for an arbiter other than God while it is He Who caused to descend to you the Book, one that is distinct? Those to whom We gave the Book, they know that it is one that is sent down by **your** *Lord with The Truth. So,* **you** *have not been among the ones who contest.* **6:114**

There is no doubt that God sent down *the Prophet* (Q7:158), peace and the mercy of God be upon him, as a guide with an eloquent Book and a standing command. No one will be ruined by it except one who ruins himself. Certainly, only doubtful innovations cause ruin except those from which God may protect. Sermon 169

Completed was the Word of **your** *Lord in sincerity and justice. There is no one who changes His Words. He is The Hearing, The Knowing.* **6:115**

In God's authority lies the safety of your affairs. Therefore, render Him such obedience as is neither blameworthy nor insincere. By God, you must do so otherwise God will take away from you the power of Islam and will never thereafter return it to you until it reverts to others. Sermon 169

If **you** *obeyed most of who are on the earth, they will cause* **you** *to go astray from the way of God. They follow nothing but opinion and they only guess.* **6:116**

Obey God (Q3:32), and do not disobey Him. When you see virtue, adopt it. When you see vice, avoid it. Sermon 166

Truly, **your** *Lord is He Who is greater in knowledge of who goes astray from His way. He is greater in knowledge of the ones who are truly guided.* **6:117**

Know that firm in knowledge are those who refrain from opening the curtains that lie against the unknown. Their acknowledgment of ignorance about the details of the hidden unknown prevents them from further probe. God praises them for their admission that they are unable to attain knowledge not allowed to them. They do not go deep into the discussion of what is not enjoined upon them about knowing Him. They call it firmness. Be content with this and do not limit the Greatness of God after the measure of your own intelligence or else you will be among the destroyed ones. Sermon 91

So, eat of that over which the Name of God was remembered if you had been ones who believe in His signs. **6:118**

Almighty are **You**, the Creator, the Worshipped. On account of **Your** good trials of **Your** creatures, **You** created a house (Paradise) and provided in it for feasting, drinks, foods, spouses, servants, places, streams, plantations and fruits. Sermon 108

Why should you not eat of that over which the Name of God was remembered on it? Surely, He explained distinctly to you what He forbade to you unless you were driven by necessity to it. Truly, many cause others to go astray by their desires without knowledge. Truly, ***your*** *Lord, He is greater in knowledge of the ones who exceed the limits.* **6:119**

God has allowed time in the limited field of life so that you may vie with each other in seeking the reward of the Garden. Therefore, tight up your girdles and wrap up the skirts. High courage and dinners do not go together. Sleep causes weakness in the big affairs of the day and its darkness obliterates the memories of courage. Sermon 24

Forsake manifest sin and its inward part. Truly, those who earn sin, they will be given recompense for what they had been gaining. **6:120**

I advise you, O people, to fear God and to praise Him profusely for His favors to you and His reward for you and His obligations on you. See how He chose you for favors and dealt with you with mercy. You sinned openly. He kept you covered. You behaved in a way to incur His punishment, but He gave you more time. Sermon 188

Eat not of that over which the Name of God is not remembered on it. Truly, it is contrary to moral law. Truly, the satans will reveal to their protectors so that they dispute with you and if you obeyed them, truly, you would be of the ones who are polytheists. **6:121**

Whoever can at this time keep himself clinging to God should do so. Sermon 156

Is he who had been lifeless and We gave him life and We made a light for him by which he walks among humanity like he who is in the shadows and is not one who goes forth from them? Thus, it was made to appear pleasing to ones who are ungrateful what they had been doing. **6:122**
Thus, We made in every town greater ones who sin that they plan in it. Yet they plan not but against themselves although they are not aware. **6:123**

This world and the hereafter have submitted to Him their reins. The skies and earths have flung their keys towards Him. The thriving trees bow to Him in the morning and evening, producing for Him flaming fire from their branches and, at His command, turn their own feed into ripe fruits. Sermon 133

When a sign drew near them they said: We will not believe until we are given the like of what was given to Messengers of God. God is greater in knowledge where to assign His message. On those who sinned will light contempt from God and a severe punishment for what they had been planning. **6:124**

I bear witness that *Muhammad* (Q48:29), peace and the mercy of God be upon him, is *His servan*t (Q17:1), and His *Prophet*. (Q7:158) He sent him for enforcement of His commands, for exhausting His pleas and for presenting warnings against eternal punishment. Sermon 82

Whomever God wants, He guides him. He expands his breast for The Submission to One God. Whomever He wants to cause to go astray, He makes his breast tight, troubling, as if he had been climbing up a difficult ascent. Thus, God assigns disgrace on those who believe not. **6:125**

Be aware of comparing yourself with God in greatness and likening yourself to Him in might, for God abases every tyrant and disgraces every braggart. Letter 53*

This is the path of ***your*** *Lord, one that is straight. Surely, We explained distinctly the signs for a folk who recollect.* **6:126**

I have seen the companions of *the Prophet* (Q7:158), peace and the mercy of God be upon him, but I do not find anyone resembling them. They began the day with dust on the hair and face in hardship of life and passed the night in prostration and standing in prayers. Sometimes they put down their foreheads and sometimes their cheeks. With the recollection of their Resurrection it seemed as though they stood on live coal. It seemed that in between their eyes there were signs like knees of goats, resulting from long prostrations. When God was mentioned, their eyes flowed freely until their shirt collars were drenched. They trembled for fear of punishment and hope of reward as the tree trembles on the day of stormy wind. Sermon 96

For them is the abode of peace with their Lord. He is their protector for what they had been doing. **6:127**

Adopt the Quran and prayers as your guide and protector. Letter 104

Mention on a Day He will assemble them altogether. O assembly of the jinn! Surely, you acquired much from humankind. Their protectors among humankind would say: Our Lord! Some of us enjoyed some others and we reached our term that was appointed by ***You*** *for us. He would say: The fire is your place of lodging, ones who will dwell in it forever, but what God willed. Truly,* ***your*** *Lord is Wise, Knowing.* **6:128**

By God, I would rather pass a night in wakefulness on the thorns of *as-sadan* (a plant having sharp prickles) or be driven in chains as a prisoner than meet God and *His Messenger* (Q3:101), on the Day of Judgment as an oppressor over any person or a usurper of anything out of worldly wealth. How can I oppress anyone for the sake of a life that is fast moving towards destruction and is to remain under the earth for a long time? Sermon 223

Thus, that is how We make some of them friends with some others who are ones who are unjust to one another for what they had been earning. **6:129**

You, certainly, know that he who is in charge of honor, life, booty, enforcement of legal commandments and the leadership of the Muslims should not be a miser as his greed would aim at their wealth, nor be ignorant as he would then mislead them with his ignorance, nor be of rude behavior who would estrange them with his rudeness, nor should he deal unjustly with wealth thus preferring one group over another, nor should he accept a bribe while taking decisions as he would forfeit others' rights and hold them up without finality. He should not ignore the *sunna* as he would ruin the people. Sermon 131

O assembly of jinn and humankind! Approach not Messengers from among yourselves relating to you My signs, and warning you of the meeting of this, your Day? They said: We bore witness against ourselves. This present life deluded them and they bore witness against themselves that they had been ones who are ungrateful. **6:130**

By God, certainly it is reality not play, truth not falsehood. Sermon 132

That is because ***your*** *Lord would never be One Who Causes to Perish towns unjustly while their people are ones who are heedless.* **6:131**

Hearts are unmoved, heedless of guidance and moving on wrong lines, as though the addressee is someone else and as though the correct way is to amass worldly gains. Sermon 82

For everyone there are degrees for what they did. ***Your*** *Lord is not One Who is Heedless of what they do.* **6:132**

In the Garden there are various degrees of excellence and different places of stay. Its blessings never end. He who stays in it will never depart from it. He who is endowed with everlasting abode in it will not grow old and its resident will not face want. Sermon 86

Your *Lord is The Sufficient, Possessor of Mercy. If He wills, He will cause you to be put away and will make a successor after you of whomever He wills, just as He caused you to grow from offspring of other folk.* **6:133**

His punishment on enemies is harsh despite the extent of His Mercy and His compassion on His friends is vast despite His harsh punishment. He overpowers one who wants to overcome Him and destroys one who clashes with Him. He disgraces one who opposes Him and gains sway over one who bears Him hostility. He is sufficient for one who relies on Him. He gives one who asks Him. He repays one who lends to Him. He rewards one who thanks Him. Sermon 90

Truly, what you are promised is, certainly, that which arrives and you will not be ones who frustrate it. **6:134**

Certainly, there are examples before you of God's wrath, punishment, days of tribulations and happenings. Therefore, do not disregard His promises. Do not ignore His punishment or make light His wrath and not expect His violence, because God, the Almighty, did not curse the past ages unless they had left off asking others to do good acts and refraining them from bad acts. In fact, God cursed the foolish for committing sins and the wise because they gave up refraining others from evil. Be aware! You have broken the bonds of Islam, transgressed its limits, and destroyed its commands. Sermon 192

Say: O my folk! Act according to your ability. Truly, I too am one who acts. Then, you will know for whom the Ultimate End will be the abode. Truly, the ones who are unjust will not prosper. **6:135**

By God, no people are deprived of the lively pleasures of life after enjoying them, except as a result of sins committed by them, because certainly God is not unjust to His creatures. Sermon 178

They assigned to God of what He made numerous of cultivation and flocks a share. Then, they said in their claim: This is for God and this is for our ascribed associates. But what had been ascribed for their associates then, reaches not out to God and what had been ascribed for God then, reaches out to their associates. How evil is the judgment they give! **6:136**

He who has an intelligent mind looks to his goal. He knows his low road as well as his high road. The caller has called. The shepherd has tended his flocks. So respond to the caller and follow the shepherd. Sermon 153

Thus, made to appear pleasing to many of the ones who are polytheists was the killing of their children by those whom they ascribe as associates with Him so that they deal them destruction and so that they confuse their way of life for them. If God willed, they would not have accomplished it. So, forsake them and what they devise. **6:137**

O God's human being! The good which God has promised should not be abandoned and the evil from which He has refrained should not be coveted. O God's human being! Fear the day when actions will be reckoned. There will be much quaking and even children will become old. Sermon 156

They said: These flocks and cultivation are banned. None should taste them, but whom we will, so they claim. There are flocks whose backs were forbidden and flocks that they remember not the Name of God on it, a devising against Him. He will give them recompense for what they had been devising. **6:138**
They said: What is in the bellies of these flocks is exclusively for our males and is that which is forbidden to our female spouses, but if it would be born dead, then, they are ascribed as associates in it. He will give recompense to them for their allegations. Truly, He is Wise, Knowing. **6:139**

They took partners with Him. Satan turned them away from knowing Him and distanced them from His worship. Sermon 1

They, surely, lost those who foolishly kill their children without knowledge. They forbade what God provided them in a devising against God. They, surely, went astray and had not been ones who are truly guided. **6:140**

Do not give away to doubts about the truth which Islam has proclaimed. Do not be misled by schism into blind alleys. Be aware that sinful temptation has drawn heavy curtains and that the darkness they create is blinding you to your reason. Letter 65

It is He Who caused gardens to grow, trellised and without being trellised and the date palm trees and a variety of harvest crops and the olives and the pomegranates resembling and not resembling one another. Eat of its fruit when it bore fruit and give its due on the day of its reaping and exceed not all bounds. Truly, He loves not the ones who are excessive. **6:141**

The ignorant among you are excessive in their deeds without knowledge while your learned fall short in their deeds. Hadith 283

Of the flocks are some as beasts of burden and some for slaughter. Eat of what God provided you and follow not in the steps of Satan. Truly, he is a clear enemy to you. **6:142**
Eight diverse pairs; two of sheep and two of goats. Say: Forbade He the two males or the two females? Or what is contained in the wombs of the two females? Tell me with knowledge if you had been ones who are sincere. **6:143**
Of the camels two and of cows two, say: Forbade He the two males or the two females or what is contained in the wombs of the two females? Had you been witnesses when God charged you with this? Then, who does greater wrong than he who devised a lie against God to cause humanity to go astray without knowledge. Truly, God guides not the folk, the ones who are unjust. **6:144**
Say: I find not in what was revealed to me to taste that which is forbidden to taste, but that it be carrion or blood, that which is shed or the flesh of swine for that, truly, is a disgrace or was hallowed—contrary to moral law—to other than God on it. Then, whoever was driven by necessity other than being one who is willfully disobedient or one who turns away. Then, truly, your Lord is

Forgiving, Compassionate. **6:145**
To those who became Jews, We forbade every possessor of claws. Of the cows and the herd of sheep, We forbade them their fat, but what their backs carried or entrails or what mingled with bone. Thus, we gave them recompense for their insolence and We are, truly, ones who are sincere. **6:146**

You should be quick in performance of good acts so that your way be with His neighbors in His abode. Sermon 182

If they denied **you**, *say: Your Lord is the Possessor of Extensive Mercy. His might is not repelled from the folk, ones who sin.* **6:147**

O God's human being! Fear God and flee unto God from His wrath, that is, seek protection in His Mercy. Tread on the path He has laid down for you. Stand by what He has enjoined upon you. In that case Ali would stand surety for your success and salvation eventually even though you may not receive it in this world. Sermon 24

Those who ascribed partners with God will say: If God willed, neither would we have ascribed partners with God, nor our fathers, nor would we have forbidden anything. Thus, denied those who were before them until they experienced Our might. Say: Is there any knowledge with you that you bring out to us? You follow not but opinion and, then, you only guess. **6:148**

Or are they His partners in the affairs, so that it is their share of duty to pronounce and He has to agree? Sermon 18

Say: God has the conclusive disputation. If He willed, He would have guided you one and all. **6:149**

You have been shown, provided you are willing to see. You have been made to listen, provided you are willing to listen. You have been guided if you accept guidance. Sermon 20

Say: Come on! Bring your witnesses who bear witness that God forbade this. Then, if they bore witness, bear you not witness with them. Follow **you** *not the desires of those who denied Our signs and those who believe not in the world to come and they equate others with their Lord.* **6:150**
Say: Approach now. I will recount what your Lord forbade you. Ascribe nothing as partners with Him. Show kindness to the ones who are your parents. Kill not your children from want. We will provide for you and for them. Come not near any indecencies whether these were manifest or what was inward. Kill not a soul which God forbade, unless rightfully. He charged you with that so that perhaps you will be reasonable. **6:151**

One of the firm decisions of God in the Wise Reminder (Quran), upon which He bestows reward or gives punishment and through which He likes or dislikes, is that it will not benefit a person, even though he exerts himself and acts sincerely, if he leaves this world to meet God with one of these acts without repenting, namely that he believed in a partner with God during his obligatory worship or appeased his own anger by killing an individual or spoke about acts committed by others or sought fulfillment of his needs from people by introducing an innovation in his religion or met people with a double face or moved among them with a double tongue. Understand this because an illustration is a guide for its like. Sermon 153

Come not near the property of the orphan but with what is fairer until one reaches the coming of age. Live up to the full measure and balance with equity. We will not place a burden on any soul, but to its capacity. When you said something, be just, even if it had been with possessors of kinship and live up to the compact of God. Thus, He charged you with it so that perhaps you will recollect. **6:152**

Do you command me that I should seek support by oppressing those over whom I have been placed? By God, I will not do so as long as the world goes on and as long as one star leads another in the sky. Even if it were my property, I would have distributed it equally among them. Then why not when the property is that of God? Sermon 126

That this is My straight path, so follow it. Follow not the ways that will split you up from His way. He charged you this with it, so that perhaps you will be God-conscious. **6:153**

Keep us on the straight path of truth. Sermon 171

Again, We gave Moses the Book rendered complete for him who did good, a decisive explanation of all things and as a guidance and mercy, so that perhaps they will believe in the meeting with their Lord. **6:154**
This Book We caused to descend is that which is blessed so follow it and be God-conscious so that perhaps you will find mercy, **6:155**
so that you not say: The Book was only caused to descend to two sections before us. Truly, we had been ones who are heedless of their study. **6:156**

On us it is obligatory, for your sake, to abide by the Book of God (Quran), the Sublime, and the conduct of *the Prophet* (Q7:158), peace and the mercy of God be upon him, to stand by His rights and to revive his *sunna*. Sermon 169

Or so that you not say: If the Book was caused to descend to us, we would have been better guided than they. Surely, there drew near you clear portents from your Lord and a guidance and a mercy. Who, then, does greater wrong than he who denied the signs of God and drew aside from them. We will give recompense to those who draw aside from Our signs with a dire punishment because they had been drawing aside. **6:157**

Only doubtful innovations cause ruin except those from which God may protect. In God's authority lies the safety of your affairs. Therefore, render Him such obedience as is neither blameworthy nor insincere. Sermon 169

Look they on only that the angels approach them? Or ***your*** *Lord approach them? Or some signs of* ***your*** *Lord approach them? On a Day that approach some signs of* ***your*** *Lord, belief will not profit a person if he believed not before, nor earned good because of his belief. Say: Wait awhile! We too are ones who are waiting awhile!* **6:158**

O people, you are the target for the arrows of death in this world. Sermon 145

Truly, those who separated and divided their way of life and had been partisans, be ***you*** *not concerned with them at all. Truly, their affair is only with God. Again, He will tell them what they had been accomplishing.* **6:159**

O my God! We seek **Your** protection from turning away from **Your** command, or revolting against **Your** religion, or being led away by our desires instead of by guidance that comes from **You**. Sermon 215

Whoever drew near with benevolence, then, for him, ten times the like of it. Whoever drew near with an evil deed, then, recompense will not be given but with its like and they, they will not be wronged. **6:160**

Truly, God enjoins justice (*'adl*) and benevolence (*ihsan*): *Truly God commands justice and kindness and giving to one who is a possessor of kinship.* (Q16:90) (Here *'adl* means equal distribution and *ihsan* means favor). Hadith 231

Say: Truly, my Lord guided me to a straight path, a truth-loving way of life, the creed of Abraham, the monotheist. He had not been of the ones who are polytheists. **6:161**

God, the Sublime, says: *Truly, of men the nearest to Abraham are surely those who followed him and this Prophet and those who believe; and God is Protector of the ones who believe.* (Q3:68) Letter 28

Say: Truly, my formal prayer and my ritual sacrifice and my living and my dying are for God, Lord of all the worlds. **6:162**

Certainly, prayer drops out sins like the dropping of leaves of trees and removes them as ropes are removed from the necks of cattle. *The Messenger of God* (Q48:29), the peace and mercy of God he upon him, likened it to a hot bath situated at the door of a person who bathes in it five times a day. Will then any dirt remain on him? Sermon 199

No associates are to be ascribed with Him and of this was I commanded and I am the first of the ones who submit to God. **6:163**

I invoke His help, being in need of His protection. He whom He guides does not go astray. Sermon 2

Say: Is it other than God that I should desire as a lord while He is Lord of everything? Each soul will earn only for itself. No burdened soul will bear another's heavy load. Again, to your Lord will you return. Then, He will tell you about what you had been at variance in it. **6:164**

If you have thought about its digestive tracts in its high and low parts, the carapace of its belly, and its eyes and its ears in its head you would be amazed at its creation and you would feel difficulty in describing it. Exalted is He who made it stand on its legs and erected it on its pillars of limbs. No other originator took part with Him in its origination and no one having power assisted Him in its creation. Sermon 185

It is He who made you as viceregents on the earth and exalted some of you above some others in degree that He try you with what He gave you. Truly, your Lord is Swift in repayment and He, truly, is Forgiving, Compassionate. **6:165**

The riser has risen. The sparkler has sparkled. The appearer has appeared. The curved has been straightened. God has replaced one people with another and one day with another. We awaited these changes as the famine-stricken await the rain. Certainly, the leaders are the viceregents of God over His creatures. They guide the creatures to knowing God. No one will enter Paradise except him who knows them and knows Him. No one will enter Hell except him who denies them and denies Him. Sermon 152

Chapter 7: The Elevated Places (al-A^{c}rāf)

Alif Lam Min Sad. **7:1**

It is a Book that was caused to descend to ***you****. So, let there be no impediment in* ***your*** *breast about it so that* ***you*** *will warn with it and as a reminder to the ones who believe.* **7:2**

God never allowed His creation to remain without a Prophet, one deputized by Him, or a Book sent down from Him, or a binding argument, or a standing plea. These Messengers were such that they did not fear that they were few in comparison to the large numbers of their falsifiers. Among them was either a predecessor who would name the one to follow or the follower who had been introduced by the predecessor. Sermon 1

Follow what was caused to descend to you from your Lord and follow not protectors other than He. Little you recollect! **7:3**

Generosity is the protector of honor. Forbearance is the bridle of the fool. Forgiveness is the levy of success. Disregard is the punishment of him who betrays. Consultation is the chief way of guidance. He who is content with his own opinion faces danger. Endurance braves calamities while impatience is a helper of the hardships of the world. The best contentment is to give up desires. Many a slavish mind is subservient to overpowering longings. Capability helps preservation of experience. Love means well-utilized relationships. Do not trust one who is grieved. Hadith 211

How many towns We caused to perish! Our might drew near them at night or when they were ones who sleep at noon! **7:4**

Turn your sleep into wakefulness with the help of God-consciousness. Pass your days with it. Make it the equipment of your hearts. Wash your sins with it. Treat your ailments with it. Hasten towards your death with it. Take a lesson from him who neglects it so that others who follow it should not take a lesson from you having neglected it. Therefore, be aware. You should take care of it and should take care of yourselves through it. Sermon 191

Then, there had been no calling out when Our might drew near to them, but that they said: Truly, we had been ones who are unjust. **7:5**

At a time when virtue is in vogue in the world and among people, if a person entertains an evil suspicion about another person from whom nothing evil has ever been seen, then he has been unjust. Hadith 114

Then, We will, certainly, ask those to whom were sent Messengers to them and We will, certainly, ask the ones who are sent. **7:6**

With *the Prophet* (Q7:158), peace and the mercy of God be upon him, God exhausted the series of Prophets and ended the revelation. He then fought for Him against those who were turning away from Him and were equating others with Him. Sermon 133

Then, We will relate to them with knowledge for We had never been of ones who are absent. **7:7**

Know that, certainly, those creatures of God who preserve His knowledge offer protection to those things which He desires to be protected. They make His springs flow for the benefit of others. They contact each other with friendliness and meet each other with affection. They drink water from cups that quench the thirst and return from the watering places fully satiated. Misgiving does not affect them. Backbiting does not gain ground with them. In this way, God has tied their nature with good manners. It is because of this that they love each other and meet each other. They have become superior, like seeds which are selected by taking some and throwing away others. This selection has distinguished them and the process of choosing has purified them. Sermon 214

The weighing of deeds on that Day will be The Truth. So, ones whose balance was heavy from good deeds, then, those, they are the ones who prosper. **7:8**

Where are the seekers of virtue? The paths have already been determined. They have been given the news. For every misguidance, there is a cause. For every breaking of a pledge, there is a misrepresentation. By God, I shall not be like him who listens to the voice of mourning, hears the man who brings news of death and also visits the mourner, yet does not take a lesson. Sermon 148

Ones whose balance was made light from bad deeds those are those who have lost their souls because they had been doing wrong with Our signs. **7:9**

Leaning towards this world, despite what you see of it, is folly. Lagging behind in good deeds when you are convinced of good reward for them is obvious loss, while trusting in every one before trying is weakness. Hadith 384

Certainly, We established you firmly on the earth and We made for you in it a livelihood. But little you give thanks! **7:10**

The world is an abode for which annihilation is ordained. For its people, departure from it is decreed. It is sweet and green. It hastens to one who seeks it and confounds the heart that gazes upon it. So set out from it with the best of provision available to you. Ask not for it above what suffices and seek not from it more than what can be attained. Sermon 45*

Certainly, We created you. Again, We formed you. Again, We said to the angels: Prostrate yourselves before Adam! Then, they prostrated themselves, but Iblis. He would not be of the ones who prostrate themselves. **7:11**

*He said: What prevented **you** from prostrating yourself when I commanded **you**? Satan said: I am better than he. **You** created me of fire and **You** created him of clay.* **7:12**

Then God asked the angels to fulfill His promise with them and to accomplish the pledge of His injunction to them by acknowledging Him through prostration to Him and submission to His honored position. So God said: *Prostrate yourselves to Adam! They, then, prostrated themselves but Iblis.* Sermon 1

*He said: So, get **you** down from this! It will not be for **you** to increase in pride in it. Then, **you** go forth. Truly, **you** are of the ones who are disgraced.* **7:13**

Do not hanker after worldly honor and its pride. Do not feel happy over its beauties and bounties, nor wail over its damages and misfortunes because its honor and pride will end, its beauty and bounty will perish and its damages and misfortunes will pass away. Every period in it has an end. Every living being in it is to die. Do you not understand that for you there is a warning in the relics of the predecessors, an eye opener and lesson that your forefathers provided you? Sermon 99

Satan said: Give me respite until the Day they are raised up. **7:14**

Certainly, Satan has made his ways easy for you and wants to unfasten the knots of religion one by one and to cause division among you in place of unity. Keep away from his evil ideas and enchantments. Accept good advice of one who offers it to you. Preserve it in your minds. Sermon 121

He said: Truly, ***you*** *are among the ones who are given respite.* **7:15**

Where are the minds which seek light from the lamps of guidance and the eyes which look at minarets of God-consciousness? Where are the hearts dedicated to God and devoted to the obedience of God? They are all crowding towards worldly vanities and quarreling over unlawful issues. The banners of the Garden and Hell have been raised for them, but they have turned their faces away from the Garden and proceeded to Hell by dint of their performances. God called them, but they showed dislike and ran away. When Satan called them, they responded and proceeded towards him. Sermon 144

Satan said: Because ***You*** *led me into error, certainly, I will sit in ambush for them on* ***Your*** *path, one that is straight.* **7:16**

Truly, Satan has collected his group and assembled his horse-men and foot-soldiers. Truly, I have my sagacity. I have neither deceived myself, nor ever been deceived. By God, I shall fill to the brim a cistern for them from which I alone would draw water. They can neither turn away from it, nor return to it. Sermon 10

Again, I will approach them from between the front of them and from behind them and from their right and from their left. ***You*** *will not find many of them ones who are thankful.* **7:17**

Populated places were brightened through him when previously there was dark misguidance, overpowering ignorance and rude habits, and people regarded unlawful as lawful, humiliated the man of wisdom, passed lives when there were no prophets and died as ungrateful. Sermon 151

He said: Go ***you*** *forth from this—one who is scorned, one who is rejected. Whoever heeded* ***you*** *among them, I will, certainly, fill hell with you, one and all.* **7:18**

Satan keeps posted about him. He beautifies his sin for him so that he may commit it. He prompts him to delay repentance until his desires cause him to be the most negligent. Sermon 64

O Adam! Inhabit ***you*** *and* ***your*** *spouse the Garden and both eat from where you both willed, but neither of you come near this tree or you both will be of the ones who are unjust.* **7:19**
Satan whispered evil to them both to show them both what was kept secret from them both—their intimate parts. He said: The Lord of both of you prohibited you both from this tree so that neither of you be angels nor be ones who will dwell forever. **7:20**
He swore an oath to them both that I am the one who gives advice to both of you. **7:21**
Then, he led both of them on to delusion. Then, when they both experienced of the tree, the intimate parts of both showed to both themselves and both of them took to doing stitching together over both from the leaves of the Garden. The Lord of both of them proclaimed to them: Prohibited I not both of you from that tree? Said I not to both of you: Truly, Satan is a clear enemy of you both. **7:22**
They both said: Our Lord! We did wrong to ourselves. If ***You*** *will not forgive us and have mercy on us, we will, certainly, be among the ones who are losers.* **7:23**
He said: Get you down, some of you an enemy to some other. For you on the earth an appointed time and enjoyment for awhile. **7:24**

He said: You will live in it and you will die in it and from it you will be brought out. **7:25**

Remember that it is Satan which will attack an imprudent and non-cautious Muslim from behind and from the right and the left so that finding him unwary and unwatchful, Satan may overpower him and may enslave his reasoning. Letter 44

O Children of Adam! Surely, We caused to descend to you garments to cover up your intimate parts and finery, but the garment of God-consciousness, that is better. That is of the signs of God so that perhaps they will recollect! **7:26**

O Children of Adam! Let not Satan tempt you as he drove your parents out of the Garden, tearing off their garments from both of them to cause them to see their intimate parts. Truly, he and his type sees you whereas you see them not. Truly, We made he and the satans protectors of those who believe not. **7:27**

When they committed an indecency, they said: We found our fathers on it and God commanded us in it. Say: Truly, God commands not depravities. Say you about God what you know not? **7:28**

Paradise is the end of those who are forward in good acts and Hell is the end of those who commit excesses. Sermon 156

Say: My Lord commanded me to equity. Set your faces at every place of prostration and call to Him ones who are sincere and devoted in the way of life to Him. As He began you, you will revert to Him. **7:29**

O my God! We seek **Your** protection from turning away from **Your** command, or revolting against **Your** religion, or being led away by our desires instead of by guidance that comes from **You**. Sermon 215

He guided a group of people and a group of people realized their fallacy. Truly, they took satans to themselves as protectors instead of God and they assume that they are ones who are truly guided. **7:30**

Have you ever seen the crying of a person who has been pricked with a thorn or who bleeds due to stumbling or whom hot sand has burnt? How would he feel when he is between two frying pans of Hell with stones all round with Satan as his companion? Sermon 182

O Children of Adam! Take your adornment at every place of prostration. Eat and drink, but exceed not all bounds. Truly, He loves not the ones who are excessive. **7:31**

(A parable): A humble and powerless creature has purchased a house from another mortal being. Its boundaries are as follows: On one side it is bounded by calamities and disasters. On the other side with disappointments and sorrows. On the third side its borders are covered with inordinate and excessive desires ending in failures. On the fourth side it adjoins the misleading and captivating allurements of Satan. The door of this house opens towards this fourth side. A man leading his life under the merciless grip of intemperance and disorderly desires has purchased this house from another person who is being relentlessly pursued by death. For the purchase price he has bargained the glory of an honorably contented and respectable way of living against the detestable life of submitting to every form of humiliation for profit and pleasure. The buyer had not realized what sorrows and degradations he was purchasing and what he was paying for in the way of cost. His delivery now lies in the hands of One Who throws the bodies of kings into dust and overthrows their empires, Who ends the lives of despots and Who has brought to an end the dominions of Egypt, Persia, Greece, Rome and Himyars, kings of Yemen, Who had destroyed the wealth, power and glory of all those individuals who had amassed wealth, gathered property, built very strong and durable houses, furnished them with the choicest and most costly furniture and surrounded them with beautiful gardens. Those people were imagining that they and their descendants will enjoy the fruits of their labors, though in reality everyone of the house so built or the articles so collected will have to be accounted for on the Day of Judgment, the Day when people will be rewarded or punished according to their deeds, the Day on which evil doers will suffer for their vicious and wicked ways. Your mind will corroborate and confirm this if it is kept free from intemperate ambitions, from lust for alluring things, from sensuality and from vicious affections and attachments. Letter 3

Say: Who forbade the adornment of God that He brought out for His servants. What is the good of His provision? Say: They are for those who believed in this present life and, exclusively, on the Day of Resurrection. Thus, We explain distinctly the signs for a folk who know. **7:32**

In God's authority lies the safety of your affairs. Therefore, render Him such obedience as is neither blameworthy nor insincere. By God, you must do so otherwise God will take away from you the power of Islam and will never thereafter return it to you until it reverts to others. Sermon 169

Say: My Lord forbade not but indecencies—what was manifest or what was inward—and sins and unrightful insolence, to ascribe partners with God when He sends not down for it any authority and that you say about God what you know not. **7:33**

I advise you, O people, to fear God and to praise Him profusely for His favors to you and His reward for you and His obligations on you. See how He chose you for favors and dealt with you with mercy. You sinned openly. He kept you covered. You behaved in a way to incur His punishment, but He gave you more time. Sermon 188

For every community there is a term. When their term drew near, they will not delay it by an hour, nor press it forward. **7:34**

Truly, if you could see what has been seen by those of you who have died, you would be puzzled and troubled. Then you would have listened and obeyed, but what they have seen is yet curtained off from you. The curtain would shortly be thrown off. You have been shown, provided you are willing to see. Sermon 20

O Children of Adam! If Messengers from among you approach relating My signs to you, then, whoever was God-conscious and made things right, then, there will be neither fear in them nor will they feel remorse. **7:35**

O God's human being! Know that your own self is a guard over you. Sermon 156

But those who denied Our signs and grew arrogant against them, those are the Companions of the Fire; they are ones who will dwell in it forever. **7:36**

Do you feel it when the Angel of Death enters a house? Do you see him when he takes the life of anyone? How does he take the life of an embryo in the womb of his mother? Does he reach it through any part of her body or does the spirit respond to his call with the permission of God? Or does he stay with him in the mother's interior? How can he who is unable to describe a creature like this, describe God? Sermon 112

Then, who does greater wrong than he who devised a lie against God or denied His signs? Those, they will attain their share from the Book. Until Our Messengers drew near to gather them to themselves, they will say: Where are who you had been calling on other than God? They will say: They went astray from us. They bore witness against themselves that, truly, they had been ones who are ungrateful. **7:37**

The Book of God is that through which you see, you speak and you hear. Sermon 132

He will say: Enter among the communities that passed away before you of jinn and humankind into the fire. Every time a community entered, it would curse its sister community until when they will come successively in it altogether. The last of them would say to the first of them: Our Lord! These caused us to go astray so give them a double punishment of the fire. He will say: For everyone it is double except you know not. **7:38**

Do you think you can tell the time when a person goes out and no evil befall him, or can warn of the time at which, if one goes out, harm will accrue? Whoever testifies to this falsifies the Quran and becomes unmindful of God in achieving his desired objective and in warding off the undesirable. You cherish saying this, so that he who acts on what you say should praise you rather than God because, according to your misconception, you have guided him about the hour in which he would secure benefit and avoid harm. Sermon 79

The first of them would say to the last of them: You have had no superiority over us so experience the punishment for what you had been earning. **7:39**

Truly, those who denied Our signs and grew arrogant among them, the doors of heaven will not be opened up to them nor will they enter the Garden until a he-camel penetrates through the eye of the needle. Thus, We give recompense to the ones who sin. **7:40**

Certainly, this world is a dirty watering place and a muddy source of drinking. Its appearance is attractive, yet its inside is destructive. It is a deception, a vanishing reflection and a bent pillar. When its despiser begins to like it and he who is not acquainted with it feels satisfied with it, then it jumps for joy, entraps him in its trap, makes him the target of its arrows and puts round his neck the rope of death taking him to the narrow grave and fearful abode in order to show him his place of stay and the recompense of his acts. This goes on from generation to generation. Neither death stops from cutting them asunder, nor do the survivors keep aloof from committing sins. Sermon 82

For them hell will be their cradling and above them, the overwhelming event. Thus, We give recompense to the ones who are unjust. **7:41**

On that day God will collect on it the front and the back, to stand in obedience for the exaction of accounts and for the award of recompense for deeds. Sweat would flow up to their mouths like reins while the earth would be trembling under them. In the best condition among them would be he who has found a resting place for both his feet and an open place for his breath. Sermon 102

But for those who believed and did as the ones in accord with morality, We place no burden on any soul beyond its capacity. Those will be the Companions of the Garden. They are ones who will dwell in it forever. **7:42**

When he was asked about God's saying: *Whoever be one who acts in accord with morality, whether male or female, while being one who believes, We will give life—this good life. We will give recompense to them—their compensation—for the fairest for what they had been doing,* (Q16:97) he said: that means a life of contentment. Hadith 229

We will draw out what was in their breasts of grudges. Rivers will run beneath them. They will say: The Praise belongs to God Who truly guided us to this! We would not have been guided if God guided us not. Certainly, the Messengers of our Lord drew near us with The Truth. It was proclaimed to them that this, the Garden, was given to you as inheritance for what you had been doing. **7:43**

I praise God, seeking completion of His Blessing, submitting to His Glory and expecting safety from committing sin. Sermon 2

The Companions of the Garden would cry out to the Companions of the Fire: Surely, we found what our Lord promised us to be true. Found you not what your Lord promised to be true? They would say: Yes. Then, it will be announced by one who announces among them: May the curse of God be on the ones who are unjust, **7:44**

those who bar the way of God and who desire it to be crooked. In the world to come they will be ones who are ungrateful. **7:45**

Be aware! This world attracts and then turns away. It is stubborn, refusing to go ahead. It speaks lies and misappropriates. It disowns and is ungrateful. Sermon 190

Between them both is a partition. On the Elevated Places will be men who recognize everyone by their mark. They will cry out to the Companions of the Garden that: Peace be on you. They enter it not and they are desirous of it. **7:46**

God, the Sublime, said: *Truly, those who said: Our Lord is God, again, they went straight, the angels come forth to them: Neither fear nor feel remorse, but rejoice in the Gardens which you had been promised.* (Q41:30) Sermon 175

When their sight would be turned away of its own accord to the Companions of the Fire, they will say: Our Lord assign **You** *us not with the folk, ones who are unjust!* **7:47**

Mind yourself and consider for a while as though you had reached the end of life and had been buried under the earth. Your actions will then be presented before you in the place where the oppressor cries: *They cried out but there was no time for escape.* (Q38:3) Letter 41

The Companions of the Elevated Places would cry out to men whom they would recognize by their mark. They would say: Your amassing availed you not, nor that you had been growing arrogant. **7:48**

Are these, those about whom you swore an oath that God would never impart mercy? Enter the Garden. There will be neither fear in you nor will you feel remorse. **7:49**

The Companions of the Fire would cry out to the Companions of the Garden: Pour some water on us, or some of what God provided you. They would say: Truly, God forbade them both to the ones who are ungrateful, **7:50**

those who took their way of life to themselves as a diversion and as a pastime. This present life deluded them. So, today We will forget them as they forgot the meeting of this their Day and because they had been negating Our signs. **7:51**

By God, certainly it is reality not play, truth not falsehood. It is none other than death. Its caller is making himself heard. Its driver is making haste. Sermon 132

Surely, We brought about a Book to them in which We explained distinctly, with knowledge, a guidance and a mercy for a folk who believe. **7:52**

There is no doubt that God sent down *the Prophet* (Q7:158), peace and the mercy of God be upon him, as a guide with an eloquent Book and a standing command. No one will be ruined by it except one who ruins himself. Sermon 169

Did they look on for nothing but its interpretation? The Day its interpretation approaches, those who forgot it before will say: Surely, Messengers of our Lord drew near us with The Truth. Have we any intercessors who will intercede for us? Or will we be returned so we do other than what we had been doing before? Surely, they lost themselves. Went astray from them what they had been devising. **7:53**

You have been guided as to how to provide for the journey. Truly, the most frightening thing which I am afraid of about you is that you will follow desires and widen your hopes. Provide for yourself from this world what would save you tomorrow on the Day of Judgment. Sermon 28

Truly, your Lord is God, He Who created the heavens and the earth in six days. Again, He turned His attention to the Throne. He covers the nighttime with the daytime that seeks it out urgently. The sun and the moon and the stars are ones caused to be subservient to His command. Truly, His is not but the creation and the command. Blessed be God, Lord of the worlds. **7:54**

He created the earth and suspended it without being busy, retained it without support, made it stand without legs, raised it without pillars, protected it against bendings and curvings and defended it against crumbling and splitting into parts. He fixed mountains on it like stumps, solidified its rocks, caused its streams to flow and opened wide its valleys. Whatever He made did not suffer from any frailty. Whatever He strengthened did not show any weakness. He manifests Himself over the earth with His authority and greatness. He is aware of its inside through His knowledge and understanding. He has power over everything in the earth by virtue of His sublimity and dignity. Nothing from the earth that He may ask for defies Him, nor does it oppose Him so as to overpower Him. No swift-footed creature can run away from Him so as to surpass Him. He is not needy towards any possessing person so that he should feed Him. All things bow to Him and are humble before His greatness. They cannot flee away from His authority to someone else in order to escape His benefit or His harm. There is no parallel for Him who may match Him and no one like Him so as to equal Him. Sermon 186

Call to your Lord humbly and inwardly. Truly, He loves not the ones who exceed the limits. **7:55**

Anyone enjoying honor other than Him is humble. Any powerful person other than Him is weak. Any master other than Him is a servant. Sermon 65

Make not corruption in the earth after things were made right and call to Him with fear and hope. Truly, the mercy of God is Near to the ones who are doers of good. **7:56**

O God's human being! I advise you to be God-conscious which is the provision for the next world and with it is your return. The provision would take you to your destination and the return would be successful. The best one who is able to make people listen has called towards it and the best listener has listened to it. So the caller has proclaimed and the listener has listened and persevered. O God's human being! Certainly, being God-conscious has saved the lovers of God from unlawful items and has given His dread to their hearts until their nights are passed in wakefulness and their noons in thirst. So they achieve comfort through trouble and copious watering through thirst. They regarded death to be near and, therefore, hastened towards good actions. They rejected their desires by keeping death in their sight. Sermon 114

It is He Who sends the winds, ones that are bearers of good news before His mercy until when they were charged with heavy clouds. We will drive it to a dead land. Then, We caused water to descend from the cloud and with it We bring out by water all kinds of fruits. Thus, We bring out the dead so that perhaps you will recollect. **7:57**

Through His mercy, He diffused the comforting winds. Sermon 1*

As for the good land, its plants go forth with permission of its Lord. While, as for what was bad, it goes forth not but scantily. Thus, We diversify the signs for a folk who give thanks. **7:58**

O my God! Do pour on us **Your** mercy, **Your** blessing, **Your** sustenance and **Your** pity, and make us enjoy a drink which benefits us, quenches our thirst, produces green herbage by which all that has died down grows again and all that had withered is revived. It should bring about the benefit of freshness and plentifulness of ripe fruits. With it plains may be watered, rivers may begin flowing, plants may pick up foliage and prices may come down. Surely, **You** are powerful over whatever **You** will. Sermon 143

Surely, We sent Noah to his folk. He said: O my folk! Worship God! You have no god other than He. Truly, I fear for you the punishment of a tremendous Day. **7:59**
The Council of his folk said: Truly, we see you clearly wandering astray. **7:60**
He said: O my folk! There is no fallacy in me. I am only a Messenger from the Lord of the worlds. **7:61**
I state the messages of my Lord to you and advise you and I know from God what you know not. **7:62**
Or marveled you that there drew near you a remembrance from your Lord through a man among you that he warn you and that you be God-conscious so that perhaps you will find mercy? **7:63**
Then, they denied him. Then, We rescued him and those who were with him on the boat and We drowned those who denied Our signs. Truly, they, they had been a folk in the dark. **7:64**
To Ad, God sent their brother Hud. He said: O my folk! Worship God. You have no god but He. Will you not, then, be God-conscious? **7:65**
The Council of those who were ungrateful said among his folk: Truly, we see foolishness in ***you****. Truly, we think that* ***you*** *are among the ones who lie.* **7:66**
He said: O my folk! There is no foolishness in me. I am only a Messenger from the Lord of the worlds. **7:67**
I state the messages of my Lord to you and I am one who gives advice to you, trustworthy. **7:68**
Or marveled you that there drew near you a remembrance from your Lord through a man from among you that he may warn you? Remember when He made you viceregents after the folk of Noah and increased you greatly in constitution? Then, remember the benefits of God so that perhaps you will prosper. **7:69**
They said: Have ***you*** *brought about to us that we should worship God alone and forsake what our fathers had been worshipping? So, approach us with what* ***you*** *promised us if* ***you*** *had been among the ones who are sincere.* **7:70**
He said: Surely, fell on you disgrace and anger from your Lord. Dispute you with me over names

which you named, you and your fathers, for which God sent not down any authority? Then, wait awhile. Truly, I will be with you among the ones who are waiting awhile. 7:71
Then, We rescued him and those with him by a mercy from Us. We severed the last remnant of those who denied Our signs. They had not been ones who believe. 7:72
To Thamud God sent their brother Salih. He said: O my folk! Worship God! You have no god but He. Surely, drew near you clear portents from your Lord. This is the she-camel of God as a sign so allow her to eat on the earth of God and afflict her not with evil so a painful punishment not take you. 7:73
Remember when He made you viceregents after Ad and placed you on the earth. You take to yourselves palaces on the plains and carve out the mountains as houses. So, remember the benefits of God. Do no mischief as ones who make corruption in and on the earth. 7:74
Said the Council of those who grew arrogant among his folk to those who were taken advantage of due to their weakness, to those who believed among them: Know you that Salih is one who is sent from his Lord? They said: Truly, in what he was sent, we are ones who believe. 7:75
Those who grew arrogant said: Truly, we are in what you believed, ones who disbelieve. 7:76
Then, they crippled the she-camel and defied the command of their Lord and they said: O Salih! Approach us with what **you** *have promised us if* **you** *had been among the ones who are sent.* 7:77
So, the quaking of the earth took them. It came to be in the morning they were in their abodes ones who are fallen prostrate. 7:78
Then, he turned away from them and said: O my folk! Certainly, I expressed to you the message of my Lord and advised you, except you love not the ones who give advice. 7:79
Mention Lot, when he said to his folk: You approach indecency as preceded you not anyone therein in the worlds? 7:80
Truly, you, you approach men with lust instead of women? Nay! You are a folk, ones who are excessive. 7:81
The answer of his folk had not been but that they said: Bring them out from your town. Truly, they are a clan to cleanse themselves. 7:82
Then, We rescued him and his people, but his woman. She had been among the ones who stay behind. 7:83
We rained down a rain on them. So, look on how had been the Ultimate End of the ones who sin. 7:84
To Midian God sent their brother Shuayb. He said: O my folk! Worship God! You have no god other than He. Surely, a clear portent drew near you from your Lord so live up to the full measure and the balance and diminish not the things of humanity nor make corruption in and on the earth after things were made right. That will be better for you if you had been ones who believe. 7:85
Sit not by every path intimidating and barring from the way of God those who believed in Him and you desire it to be crooked. Remember when you had been few and He augmented you. Look on how had been the Ultimate End of the ones who make corruption. 7:86
If there had been a section of you who believed in what I was sent with and a section believe not, have patience until God gives judgment between us. He is Best of the ones who judge. 7:87

I swear, and my oath is such that I have no intention of breaking it, that if fate so arranges as to bring us face to face against each other, then I shall not leave the battlefield *until God gives judgment between us. He is Best of the ones who judge.* (Q7:87) Letter 55

Said the Council of those who grew arrogant from among his folk: O Shuayb! We will, certainly, drive **you** *out—and those who believed with* **you***—from our town or else you revert to our creed.*

He said: Even if we had been ones who dislike it? **7:88**
Surely, we would have devised a lie against God if we reverted to your creed after God delivered us from it. It will not be for us that we revert to it unless God, our Lord, wills. Our Lord encompassed everything in knowledge. In God we put our trust. Our Lord! Give victory between us and between our folk in Truth and ***You*** *are Best of the ones who are deliverers.* **7:89**
But said the Council of those who were ungrateful among his folk: If you followed Shuayb, then, truly, you will be ones who are losers. **7:90**
Then, the quaking of the earth took them and they came to be in the morning ones who are fallen prostrate in their abodes. **7:91**
Those who denied Shuayb had been as if they had not dwelt in them. Those who denied Shuayb they, they had been the ones who were losers. **7:92**
So, he turned away from them and said: O my folk! Certainly, I expressed to you the messages of my Lord and I advised you. Then, how should I grieve for a folk, ones who are ungrateful? **7:93**
We sent not any Prophet to a town, but We took its people with tribulation and desolation so that perhaps they will lower themselves. **7:94**
Again, We substituted in place of evil deeds, benevolence, until they exceeded in number and they said: Surely, our fathers were touched by tribulation and gladness. Then, We took them suddenly while they are not aware. **7:95**
if the people of the towns believed and were God-conscious, We would have opened blessings for them from the heaven and the earth, except they denied. So, We took them for what they had been earning. **7:96**
Were, then, the people of the towns safe when Our might approaches them at night while they are ones who sleep? **7:97**
Or were the people of the towns safe when Our might approaches them in the forenoon while they play? **7:98**
Were they safe from the planning of God? No one deems himself safe from the planning of God but the folk, the ones who are losers! **7:99** ***

Guides not those who inherit the earth after its previous people that if We will, We would light on them for their impieties, and We set a seal on their hearts so they hear not? **7:100**

Surely, you have been made to see if only you are willing to see. Surely, you have been guided if only you are willing to take guidance. Surely, you have been made to hear if only you are willing to lend your ears. Hadith 157

These are the towns. Their tidings We relate to ***you****. Certainly, their Messengers drew near them with the clear portents. But they had not been believing in what they denied before. Thus, God set a seal on the hearts of the ones who are ungrateful.* **7:101**
We found not in many of them any compact. truly, We found many of them are ones who disobey. **7:102**

If a person's heart becomes attached to the world, it then catches three things, namely worry that never leaves him, greed that does not abandon him and desires which he never fulfills. Hadith 228

Again, We raised up Moses after them with Our signs to Pharaoh and his Council, but they did wrong to them. So, look on how had been the Ultimate End of the ones who make corruption. **7:103**

Moses said: O Pharaoh! Truly, I am a Messenger from the Lord of the worlds. **7:104**
I am approved on condition that I say nothing but The Truth about God. Surely, I drew near you with a clear portent from
your Lord. So, send the Children of Jacob with me. **7:105**
Pharaoh said: If **you** *had been drawing near with a sign, then, approach with it if* **you** *had been among the ones who are sincere.* **7:106**
Then, Moses cast his staff. That is when it became a clear serpent. **7:107**
he drew out his hand. That is when it was shimmering white to the ones who look. **7:108**
The Council of the folk of Pharaoh said: Truly, this is a knowing sorcerer. **7:109**
He wants to drive you out from your region so what is your command? **7:110**
They said: Put him and his brother off and send to the cities to the place where ones who assemble are. **7:111**
Let them approach **you** *with every knowing sorcerer.* **7:112**
The ones who are sorcerers drew near to Pharaoh. They said: Truly, would we have compensation if we had been the ones who are victors? **7:113**
Pharaoh said: Yes! Truly, you will be of the ones who are brought near to me. **7:114**
They said: O Moses! Either **you** *cast, or will we be the ones who cast?* **7:115**
He said: You cast. So, when they cast, they cast a spell on the eyes of the personages and terrified them. A tremendous sorcery drew near. **7:116**
We revealed to Moses that: Cast **your** *staff. That is when it swallowed what they faked.* **7:117**
Thus, The Truth came to pass and proved false what they had been doing. **7:118**
So, they were vanquished there and turned about as ones who are disgraced. **7:119**
The ones who are sorcerers were made to fall down as ones who prostrate themselves. **7:120**
They said: We believed in the Lord of the worlds, **7:121**
the Lord of Moses and Aaron. **7:122**
Pharaoh said: You believed in Him before I give permission to you. Truly, this is a plan you planned in the city that you drive out the people from it but you will know. **7:123**
I will, certainly, cut off your hands and your feet on opposite sides. Again, I will cause you to be crucified, one and all. **7:124**
They said: Truly, we are ones who are turning to our Lord. **7:125**
You *have sought revenge on us only because we believed in the signs of our Lord when they drew near us. Our Lord! Pour out patience on us and call us to* **Your***self as ones who submit to God.* **7:126**
The Council of the folk of Pharaoh said: Will **you** *forsake Moses and his folk to make corruption in and on the earth while they forsake* **you** *and* **your** *gods? Pharaoh said: We will slay their children and we will save alive their women. Truly, we are ones who are ascendant over them.* **7:127**
Moses said to his folk: Pray for help from God and have patience. Truly, the earth belongs to God. He gives it as inheritance to whom He wills of His servants. That is the Ultimate End for the ones who are God-conscious. **7:128**
They said: We were maligned before **you** *have approached us and after* **you** *have drawn near to us. He said: Perhaps your Lord will cause your enemy to perish and make you successors to him on the earth so that He will look on how you do.* **7:129**
Certainly, We took the people of Pharaoh with years of diminution of fruits, so that perhaps they will recollect. **7:130**
When benevolence drew near them, they would say: This belongs to us. But if an evil deed lights on them, they augur ill of Moses and who were with him. Certainly, that which are their omens are with God except most of them know not. **7:131**

They said: Whatever sign **you** *have brought to us to cast a spell on us with it, we will not be ones who believe in* **you**. 7:132

Then, We sent on them the deluge and the locusts and the lice and the frogs and blood as distinct signs, but they grew arrogant and they had been a folk, ones who sin. 7:133

When the wrath fell on them, they said: O Moses! Call to **your** *Lord for us because of the compact made with* **you**. *If* **you** *were to remove the wrath from us, we would, certainly, believe in* **you**. *We will send the Children of Jacob with* **you**. 7:134

But when We removed the wrath from them for a term, that which is conclusive, they break their oath. 7:135

So, We requited them and drowned them in the water of the sea because they denied Our signs and they had been ones who are heedless of them. 7:136

We gave as inheritance to the folk who had been taken advantage of due to their weakness, the east of the region and its west which We blessed. Completed was the fairer Word of **your** *Lord for the Children of Jacob because they endured patiently. We destroyed what Pharaoh and his folk had been crafting and what they had been constructing.* 7:137

We brought the Children of Jacob over the sea. Then, they approached on a folk who give themselves up to their idols. They said: O Moses! Make for us a god like the gods they have. He said: Truly, you are an ignorant folk! 7:138

Truly, these are the ones who are ruined and falsehood is what they had been doing. 7:139

He said: Should I look for any god other than God for you while He gave you an advantage over the worlds? 7:140

Mention when We rescued you from the people of Pharaoh who cause an affliction to befall you of a dire punishment. They slay your children and save alive your women. In that was a trial for you from your Lord, tremendous. 7:141

We appointed thirty nights for Moses. We completed them with ten more. Thus, fulfilled was the time appointed by his Lord of forty nights. Moses said to his brother, Aaron: Be my successor among my folk and make things right and follow not the way of the ones who make corruption. 7:142

When Moses drew near Our time appointed and his Lord spoke to him, he said: O my Lord! Cause me to see that I look on **You**. *He said:* **You** *will never see Me but look on the mountain. Then, if it stayed fast in its place, then,* **you** *will see Me. Then, when his Lord Self-disclosed to the mountain, He made it as ground powder and Moses fell down swooning. When he recovered he said: Glory be to* **You**! *I repented to* **You** *and I am the first of the ones who believe.* 7:143

He said: O Moses! Truly, I favored **you** *above humanity by My messages and by My assertion. So, take what I gave* **you** *and be among the ones who are thankful.* 7:144

We wrote down for him on the Tablets something of all things and an admonishment and a decisive explanation of all things. So, take these with firmness and command **your** *folk to take what is fairer. I will cause you to see the abodes of the ones who disobey.* 7:145

I will turn away from My signs those who increase in pride on the earth without right. If they see every sign, they believe not in it. If they see the way of right judgment, yet they will not take that way to themselves. But if they see the way of error, they will take themselves to that way. That is because they denied Our signs and had been ones who are heedless of them. 7:146

Be resolute in placing self-abasement over your heads, casting self-glorification beneath your feet, and removing pride from your necks. Take up humility as the fortified watchtower between you and your enemy. Sermon 191*

As for those who denied Our signs and the meeting in the world to come, their actions were fruitless.

Will they be given recompense but for what they had been doing? **7:147**
The folk of Moses took to themselves after him from out of their glitter a calf, a lifeless body like one that has the lowing sound of flocks. See they not that it neither speaks to them nor guides them to a Way? Yet they took it to themselves. They had been the ones who are unjust. **7:148**
When they became ones who are remorseful and saw that they, surely, went astray, they said: If our Lord not have mercy on us and forgive us, we will, certainly, be among the ones who are losers. **7:149**
When Moses returned to his folk enraged, grieved, he said: Miserable was what you succeeded in after me. Would you hasten the command of your Lord? He cast down the Tablets. He took his brother by his head, pulling him to himself. Aaron said: O son of my mother, truly, the folk took advantage of my weakness and are about to kill me. So, let not my enemies gloat over me and assign me not with the folk, the ones who are unjust. **7:150**
Moses said: Lord! Forgive me and my brother and cause us to enter into ***Your*** *mercy for* ***You*** *are One Who is Most Merciful of the ones who are merciful.* **7:151**
Those who took the calf to themselves attain anger from their Lord and abasement in this present life. Thus, We give recompense to the ones who devise. **7:152**
But those who do evil deeds and repent and, moreover, believe, truly your Lord, after that will be Forgiving, Compassionate.. **7:153**
But those who did evil deeds and repented and, again, believed, truly, ***your*** *Lord, after that, will be Forgiving, Compassionate. When the anger subsided in Moses, he took the Tablets. There was guidance and mercy in their inscription for those, they who have reverence for their Lord.* **7:154**
Moses chose of his folk seventy men for Our time appointed. When the quaking of the earth took them, he said: Lord! If ***You*** *will,* ***You*** *would cause them to perish and me before. Would* ***You*** *cause us to perish for what the foolish among us accomplished? It is not but* ***Your*** *test. With it* ***You*** *will cause to go astray whom* ***You*** *will and* ***You*** *will guide whom* ***You*** *willed.* ***You*** *are our protector, so forgive us and have mercy on us for* ***You*** *are Best of the ones who forgive.* **7:155** ***

Prescribe for us in the present benevolence and in the world to come. Truly we turned back to ***You****. He said: I light My punishment on whom I will and My mercy encompassed everything. Then, I will prescribe it for those who are God-conscious and give the purifying alms and those, they who believe in Our signs,* **7:156**
those who follow the Messenger—the unlettered Prophet—whom they will find with them that which is a writing in the Torah and the Gospel. He commands them to that which is honorable and prohibits them from that which is unlawful. He permits to them what is good and forbids them from deeds of corruption. He lays down for them severe tests, and the yokes that had been on them. So, those who believed in him and supported him and helped him and followed the light that was caused to descend to him, those, they are the ones who prosper. **7:157**

God's verdict is judicious and full of wisdom. His pleasure implies protection and mercy. He decides with knowledge and forgives with forbearance. Sermon 159

Say: O humanity! Truly, I am the Messenger of God to you all of Him to Whom belongs the dominion of the heavens and the earth. There is no god but He. He gives life and He causes to die. So, believe in God and His Messenger, the unlettered Prophet, who believes in God and His words and follow him so that perhaps you will be truly guided. **7:158**

I bear witness that *Muhammad* (Q48:29), peace and the mercy of God be upon him, is *His servant* (Q17:1) and *Prophet* (7:158). He sent him for enforcement of His commands, for exhausting His pleas and for presenting warnings against eternal punishment. Sermon 82

Among the folk of Moses there is a community that guides with The Truth and by it is just. **7:159**
We sundered them into twelve tribes as communities. We revealed to Moses when his folk asked him for water: Strike the rock with **your** *staff. Then, burst forth out of it twelve springs: Surely, each clan knew its drinking place. We shaded them with cloud shadows. We caused to descend manna and the quails for them. Eat of what is good that We provided you! They did not wrong Us, but they had been doing wrong to themselves.* **7:160**
Mention when it was said to them: Inhabit this town and eat from it wherever you willed. Say: Unburden us of sin! Enter the door as ones who prostrate themselves We will forgive you your transgressions. We will increase the ones who are doers of good. **7:161**
But among those who did wrong, they substituted a saying other than what was said to them. Then, We sent wrath from heaven because they had been doing wrong. **7:162**

Take instruction from how God's wrath, violence, chastisement and punishment fell upon the arrogant nations before you. Take admonition from the resting places of their cheeks and their bodies. Seek God's protection from the dangers of pride as you seek His protection from calamities. Certainly, if God were to allow anyone to indulge in pride, He would have allowed it to his selected prophets and vicegerents. Sermon 192

Ask them about the town—that which had been bordering the sea— when they disregarded the Sabbath, when their great fish would approach them on the day of the Sabbath, one that was visible on the shore. The day they keep not the Sabbath, they approach them not. Thus, We try them because they had been disobeying. **7:163**
Mention when a community of them said: Why admonish a folk whom God is One Who Causes them to Perish or One Who Punishes them with a severe punishment. They said: To be free from guilt before your Lord and so that perhaps they will be God-conscious. **7:164**
So, when they forgot of what they were reminded, We rescued those who prohibited evil and We took those who did wrong with a terrifying punishment because they had been disobeying. **7:165**
Then, when they defied what they were prohibited We said to them: Be you apes, ones who are driven away. **7:166**

The God-conscious person does not forget what he is required to remember. Sermon 192

Mention when your Lord caused to be proclaimed that He would, surely, raise up against them until the Day of Resurrection who cause an affliction to befall on them of a dire punishment. Truly, **your** *Lord is Swift in repayment. Truly, He is Forgiving, Compassionate.* **7:167**
We sundered them in the region into communities. Some of them were the ones in accord with morality and others were other than that. We tried them with benevolence and evil deeds so that perhaps they will return to obedience. **7:168**

O people! By God, I do not impel you to any obedience unless I practice it before you. I do not restrain you from any disobedience unless I desist from it before you. Sermon 175

Then, after that succeeded successors who inherited the Book. They take advantage of this nearer world, and they say: We will be forgiven. If an advantage approaches them like it, they will take it. Is not a solemn promise taken from them with the Book that they would say about God only The

Truth? Studied they not what is in it, and know that the Last Abode is better for those who are God-conscious? Will you not, then, be reasonable? **7:169**

O my God! Forgive me. **You** know more about me than I do. If I return to sin, **You** return to forgiveness. My God, forgive me what I had promised to myself, but **You** did not find its fulfillment with me. My God, forgive me that with what I sought nearness to **You** with my tongue, but my heart opposed and did not perform. My God, forgive me winking of the eye, vile utterances, desires of the heart and errors of speech. Sermon 78

Those who keep fast to the Book and performed the formal prayer, We will not waste the compensation of the ones who make things right. **7:170**

Pledge yourself with prayer and remain steady with it. Offer prayer as much as possible and seek nearness to God through it, because it is imposed upon the believers as a timed ordinance: *Truly, the formal prayer had been—for the ones who believe—a timed prescription.* (Q4:103) Sermon 198

Mention when We shook up the mountain over them, as if it had been an overshadowing, and they thought it was that which would fall on them: It was said: Take with firmness what We gave you and remember what is in it so that perhaps you will be God-conscious. **7:171**

I cleaved to its rein and applied myself solely to its pledge, like the mountain which neither sweeping wind could move nor storm could shake. No one could find fault with me, nor could any speaker speak ill of me. Sermon 37

*Mention when **your** Lord took from the Children of Adam—from their generative organs—their offspring and called to them to witness of themselves: Am I not your Lord? They said: Yea! We bore witness so that you say not on the Day of Resurrection: Truly, we had been ones who were heedless of this.* **7:172**

Surely, nothing is hidden from God, the Almighty, the Sublime, of whatever people do in their nights or days. He knows all the details. His knowledge covers them. Your limbs are a witness, the organs of your body constitute an army against yourself. Your inner self serves Him as eyes to watch your sins. Your loneliness is open to Him. Sermon 199

*Or you not say: Our fathers before us ascribed partners with God. We had been offspring after them. Will **You** cause us to perish for what the ones who deal in falsehood accomplished?* **7:173**

I bear witness that *there is no god but God* (Q47:19), the One, there is no partner with Him, nor is there with Him any god other than Himself, and that *Muhammad* (Q48:29), peace and the mercy of God be upon him, is *His servant* (Q17:1), and *Prophet* (Q7:158). Sermon 35

Thus, We explain Our signs distinctly so that perhaps they will return. **7:174**

Mind the obligations! Mind the obligations! Fulfill them for God and they will take you to the Garden. Surely, God has made unlawful the things which are not unknown and made lawful the things which are without defect. Sermon 167

Recount to them the tiding of him to whom We gave Our signs, but he cast himself off from them. So, Satan pursued him then, he had been among the ones who are in error. **7:175**

They have made Satan the master of their affairs. Sermon 7

If We willed, We would have exalted him with them, but he inclined towards the earth, and followed his own desires. His parable is like the parable of a dog. If **you** *will attack it, it pants. Or if* **you** *will leave it, it pants. That is the parable of the folk, those who denied Our signs. Then, relate these narratives so that perhaps they will reflect.* **7:176**

Truly, the most frightening thing that I am afraid of about you is that you will follow desires and widen your hopes. Provide for yourself from this world what would save you tomorrow on the Day of Judgment. Sermon 28

How evil is the parable of the folk who denied Our signs! They had been doing wrong to themselves. **7:177**

Surely, the hearts of the abstemious weep in this world even though they may apparently laugh. Their grief increases even though they may appear happy. Their hatred for themselves is much even though they may be envied for the subsistence they are allowed. Remembrance of death has disappeared from your hearts while false hopes are present in you. So this world has mastered you more than the next world. The immediate end of this world has removed you away from the remote one of the next life. You are brethren in the religion of God. Nothing but corrupt natures and bad conscience has separated you. Consequently, you do not bear burdens of each other, nor advise each other, nor spend on each other, nor love each other. Sermon 113

Whomever God guides, then, he is one who is truly guided. Whomever He causes to go astray, then, those, they are the ones who are losers. **7:178**

They eulogize each other and expect reward from each other. When they ask something they insist on it. If they reprove any one, they disgrace him. If they pass verdict, they commit excess. They have adopted for every truth a wrong way, for every erect thing a bender, for every living being a killer, for every closed door a key and for every night a lamp. They covet, but with despair, in order to maintain with it their markets and to popularize their handsome merchandise. When they speak, they create doubts. When they describe, they exaggerate. First they offer easy paths, but afterwards they make them narrow. In short, they are the party of Satan and the stings of fire. *Regard the Party of Satan. They will be the ones who are losers.* (Q58:19) Sermon 193

Certainly, We made numerous for hell many of the jinn and humankind. They have hearts with which they understand not. They have eyes with which they perceive not. They have ears with which they hear not. Those are like flocks. Nay! They are ones who go astray. Those, they are the ones who are heedless. **7:179**

Everyone of them is ... alone although they are a group, and they are strangers, even though friends. They are unaware of morning after a night and of evening after a day. The night or the day when they departed has become ever existent for them. They found the dangers of their place of stay more serious than they had apprehended. They witnessed that its signs were greater than they had guessed. Sermon 220

To God belongs the Fairer Names, so call to Him by them. Forsake those who blaspheme His Names. They will be given recompense for what they had been doing. **7:180**

He hears you whenever you call Him. Letter 31

Of whom We created there is a community that guides with The Truth, and with it, it is just. **7:181**

The Prophet (Q7:158), peace and the mercy of God be upon him, lit flames for the seeker and put bright signs for the impeded. So he is **Your** trustworthy trustee, **Your** witness on the Day of Judgment, **Your** deputy as a blessing and **Your** Messenger of truth as mercy. My God, distribute to him a share from **Your** Justice and award him multiples of good by **Your** bounty. Sermon 106

Those who denied Our signs, We will draw them on gradually from where they will not know. **7:182**

I will grant them indulgence for a while. Truly, My strategizing is sure. **7:183**

Mind the obligations! Mind the obligations! Fulfill them for God and they will take you to the Garden. Surely, God has made unlawful the things which are not unknown and made lawful the things which are without defect. Sermon 167

Reflect they not? There is no madness in their companion. He is but a clear warner. **7:184**

I bear witness that *Muhammad* (Q48:29), peace and the mercy of God be upon him, is *His servant* (Q17:1) and His *Prophet.* (Q7:158) He sent him for enforcement of His commands, for exhausting His pleas and for presenting warnings against eternal punishment. Sermon 82

Expect they not in the kingdom of the heavens and the earth and whatever things God created that perhaps their term be near? Then, in which discourse after this will they believe? **7:185**

Truly, if you could see what has been seen by those of you who have died, you would be puzzled and troubled. Then you would have listened and obeyed, but what they have seen is yet curtained off from you. The curtain would shortly be thrown off. You have been shown, provided you are willing to see. You have been made to listen, provided you are willing to listen. You have been guided, if you accept guidance. Sermon 20

Whomever God causes to go astray then, there is no one who guides him. He forsakes them in their defiance, wandering unwilling to see. **7:186**

Praise belongs to God. (Q1:2) I praise Him, implore His help and ask for His guidance. I seek protection in Him from error. *Whomever God causes to go astray, for him there is no one who guides.* (Q7:186) Sermon 2

*They ask **you** about the Hour, when will it berth? Say: The knowledge of that is only with my Lord. None will display its time but He. It was heavy, hidden in the heavens and the earth. It will approach you not but suddenly. They will ask **you** as if **you** had been one who is well-informed about it. Say: The knowledge of that is only with God, but most of humanity knows not.* **7:187**

My God, heighten his construction over the constructions of others, honor him when he comes to **You**, dignify his position before **You**, give him honorable position, award him glory and distinction and bring us out on the Day of Judgment among his party, neither ashamed, nor repentant, nor deviators, nor pledge-breakers, nor strayers, nor misleaders, nor seduced. Sermon 106

Say: I rule not over myself either for profit or for hurt, but what God willed. If the unseen had been known to me, I would have acquired much good and evil would not have afflicted me. I am but a warner and a bearer of good tidings to a folk who believe. **7:188**

Truly, God sent Muhammad, peace and the mercy of God be upon him, as a warner against vice for all the worlds and a trustee of His revelation. Sermon 26

It is He Who created you from a single soul. Out of it made its spouse that he rest in her. When he laid over her, she carried a light burden and moved about with it. But when she was weighed down, they both called to God their Lord saying: If ***You*** *would give us one in accord with morality, we will certainly be among the ones who are thankful.* **7:189**

Their hearts are grieved. Others are protected from their evil. Their bodies are thin. Their needs are scanty. Their souls are chaste. They endured hardship for a short while. As a consequence, they secured comfort for a long time. It is a beneficial transaction that God made easy for them. The world aimed at them, but they did not aim at it. It captured them, but they freed themselves from it by a ransom. During the night, they are standing on their feet, reading portions of the Quran and reciting it in a well-measured way, creating through it grief and seeking by it the cure for their ailments. If they come across a verse creating eagerness for Paradise, they pursue it avidly. Their spirits turn towards it eagerly. They feel as if it is in front of them. When they come across a verse which contains fear of Hell, they bend the ears of their hearts towards it and feel as though the sound of Hell and its cries are reaching their ears. They bend themselves from their backs, prostrate themselves on their foreheads, their palms, their knees and their toes, and beseech God, the Sublime, for their deliverance. Sermon 193

Then, when He gave them both one in accord with morality, they made ascribed associates with Him in what He gave them both. God was Exalted above partners they ascribe! **7:190**

If they had not acknowledged His Godhead and obeyed Him, He would not have made them the place for His throne, the abode of His angels and the destination: *To Him Words of what is good rise and He exalts an action in accord with morality* ...(Q35:10) of the creatures. Sermon 182

Ascribe they partners with God who create nothing and are themselves created? **7:191**

I bear witness that *there is no god but God* (Q47:19). He is One. There is no partner with Him. He is the First, such that nothing was before Him. He is the Last, such that there is not limit for Him. Imagination cannot catch any of His qualities. Hearts cannot entertain belief about His nature. Analysis and division cannot be applied to Him. Eyes and hearts cannot compare Him. Sermon 84

They are not able to help them nor help themselves? **7:192**

God deputized *the Prophet* (Q7:158), peace and the mercy of God be upon him, with light, and accorded him the highest precedence in selection. Through him God united those who were divided, overpowered the powerful, overcame difficulties and leveled rugged ground, and thus removed misguidance from right and left. Sermon 213

If you call them to the guidance, they will not follow you. It is equal whether you called to them or you be ones who remain quiet. **7:193**

O my God! I seek **Your** protection from becoming destitute despite **Your** riches, from being misguided despite **Your** guidance, from being molested in **Your** realm and from

being humiliated while authority rests with **You.** O my God! Let my spirit be the first of those good objects that **You** take from me and the first trust out of **Your** favors held in trust with me. Sermon 215

Truly, those whom you call to other than God are servants like you. So, call to them and let them respond to you if you had been ones who are sincere. **7:194**

I bear witness that *Muhammad* (Q48:29), peace and the mercy of God be upon him, is *His servant* (Q17:1), His chosen *Prophet* (Q7:158) and His responsible trustee, peace and the mercy of God be upon him. God sent him with undeniable proofs, a clear success and open paths. So he conveyed the message declaring the truth with it. He led the people on the correct highway, established signs of guidance and minarets of light and made Islam's ropes strong and its knots firm. Sermon 185

Have they feet by which they walk? Or have they hands by which they seize by force? Or have they eyes by which they perceive? Or have they ears by which they hear? Say: Call you to your ascribed associates. Again, try to outwit me and give me no respite. **7:195**

It cannot be said that He has a limit or extremity, nor end or termination, nor do things control Him so as to raise Him or lower Him, nor does anything carry Him so as to bend Him or keep Him erect. He is not inside things, nor outside them. He conveys news, but not with the tongue or voice. He listens, but not with the holes of the ears or the organs of hearing. He says, but does not utter words. He remembers, but does not memorize. He determines, but not by exercising His mind. He loves and approves without any sentimentality of heart. He hates and feels angry without any painstaking. When He intends to create someone He says: *Be!* and it is, but not through a voice that strikes the ears is that call heard. His speech is an act of His creation. Sermon 185

Truly, God is my protector, Who sent down the Book. He takes into His protection the ones in accord with morality. **7:196**

My God, I seek **Your** protection from the hardships of the journey, from the grief of returning and from the scene of devastation of property and people. O God, **You** are the companion in the journey. **You** are One Who is left behind for protection of the family. None except **You** can join these two because one who is left behind cannot be a companion in the journey, nor one who is in company on a journey can at the same time be left behind. Sermon 46

Those whom you call to other than Him, they are not able to help you, nor are they able to help themselves. **7:197**

Blessed be he who possesses a virtuous heart, who obeys one who guides him, desists from him who takes to ruin, catches the path of safety with the help of him who provides him light of guidance and by obeying the leader who commands him, hastens towards guidance before its doors are closed, opens the door of repentance and removes the stain of sins. He has certainly been put on the right path and guided towards the straight road. Sermon 213

If you call them to the guidance, they hear not. ***You*** *saw them look on* ***you****, but they perceive not.* **7:198**

O God's human being! I advise you to be God-conscious. I warn you of this world which is a house from which departure is inevitable and a place of discomfort. He who lives in it has to depart. He who stays here has to leave it. It is drifting with its people like a boat whom severe winds dash here and there in the deep sea. Some of them are drowned and die while some of them escape on the surface of the waves where winds push them with their currents and carry them towards their dangers. So whatever is drowned cannot be restored. Whatever escapes is on the way to destruction. Sermon 196

Take the extra and command what is honorable. Turn aside from the ones who are ignorant. **7:199**

O God's human being! Truly, loyalty and truthfulness are twins. I do not know a better shield against the assaults of sin than it. One who realizes the reality of return to the next world never betrays. We are in a period when most of the people regard betrayal as wisdom. In these days the ignorant ones called it excellence of cunning. What is the matter with them? May God destroy them. Sermon 41

But if enmity is sown by Satan in **you**, *sowing enmity, then, seek refuge in God. Truly, He is Hearing, Knowing.* **7:200**

They have made Satan the master of their affairs. He has taken them as partners. He has laid eggs and hatched them in their bosoms. He creeps and crawls in their laps. He sees through their eyes and speaks with their tongues. In this way he has led them to sinfulness and adorned for them foul things like the action of one whom Satan has made partner in his domain and speaks untruth through his tongue. Sermon 7

Truly, those who were God-conscious when they were touched by a visitation from Satan, they recollected. That is when they were ones who perceive. **7:201**

Certainly, Satan has made his ways easy for you and wants to unfasten the knots of religion one by one and to cause division among you in place of unity. Keep away from his evil ideas and enchantments. Accept good advice of one who offers it to you. Preserve it in your minds. Sermon 121

Their brothers/sisters cause them to increase in error, and, again, they never stop short. **7:202**

Where are the minds which seek light from the lamps of guidance and the eyes which look at minarets of God-consciousness? Where are the hearts dedicated to God and devoted to the obedience of God? Sermon 144

When **you** *approached them not with a sign, they said: Why had* **you** *not improvised one? Say: I follow only what is revealed to me from my Lord. This is clear evidence from your Lord and guidance and mercy for a folk who believe.* **7:203**

O my God! Let my spirit be the first of those good objects that **You** take from me and the first trust out of **Your** favors held in trust with me. Sermon 215

When the Quran was recited, listen and pay heed so that perhaps you will find mercy. **7:204**

God, the Almighty, has not counseled anyone on other than the lines of this Quran, for it is the strong rope of God and His trustworthy means. It contains the blossoming of the heart and springs of knowledge. For the heart there is no other gloss than the Quran, although those who remembered it have passed away, while those who forgot or pretended to have forgotten it have remained. If you see any good, give your support to it, but if you see evil, evade it, because *the Messenger of God* (Q48:29), peace and the mercy of God be upon him, used to say: O son of Adam, do good and evade evil. By doing so you will be treading correctly. Sermon 176

Remember ***your*** *Lord in* ***your****self humbly and with awe instead of openly publishing the sayings at the first part of the day and the eventide. Be* ***you*** *not among the ones who are heedless.* **7:205**
Truly, those who are with ***your*** *Lord grow not arrogant from His worship. They glorify Him and they prostrate themselves to Him.* **7:206**

God ... Who is aware of whatever is hidden in the hearts and whatever lies behind the unseen said: **Your** Lord said to the angels: *Truly, I am one who is Creator of a mortal from clay. So, when I shaped him and blew into him My Spirit, then, fall to him, ones who prostrate themselves. So, the angels prostrated themselves, one and all, altogether but Iblis. He grew arrogant and had been among the ones who are ungrateful.* (Q38:71-74) Sermon 192

CHAPTER 8: THE SPOILS OF WAR (al-Anfāl)

They ask ***you*** *about the spoils of war. Say: The spoils of war belong to God and the Messenger so be God-conscious and make things right among you and obey God and his Messenger if you had been ones who believe.* **8:1**
ones who believe are only those whose hearts took notice **8:2**
those who perform the formal prayer and spend out of what We provided them, **8:3**
those, they are the ones who truthfully believe. For them are degrees with their Lord and forgiveness and generous provision. **8:4**
Just as ***your*** *Lord brought* ***you*** *out from* ***your*** *house with The Truth, and, truly, a group of people among the ones who believe were the ones who dislike it.* **8:5**

God sent *the Prophet* (Q7:158), peace and the mercy of God be upon him, as a caller towards Truth and a witness over the creatures. *The Prophet* (Q7:158), peace and the mercy of God be upon him, conveyed the messages of God tirelessly and without any negligence. He fought His enemies in the cause of God unflaggingly and without pleading excuses. He is the foremost of all who practice God-consciousness and the power of perception of all those who achieve guidance. Sermon 116

They dispute with ***you*** *about The Truth—after it became clear—as if they had been driven to death and they look on at it.* **8:6**

No blood can be avenged through you. No purpose can be achieved with you. I called you for help of your brethren, but made noises like a camel having stomach pain and became loose like the camel with a thin back. Then a wavering weak contingent came to me from amongst you: ... *as if they had been driven to death and they are looking at it.* (Q8:6) Sermon 39

When God promises you, one of the two sections: It will, truly, be for you. You wish that the one that is unarmed should be yours. God wants that He verify The Truth by His Words and to sever the last remnant of the ones who are ungrateful **8:7**
that He may verify The Truth and render the falsehood untrue even if the ones who sin disliked it. **8:8**

I praise God for whatever matter He ordained and whatever action He destines. Sermon 180

Mention when you cry for help from your Lord and He responded to you: Truly, I am One Who Reinforces you with a thousand angels, ones who come one after another. **8:9**
Did God make this as good tidings for you so that with it your hearts will be at rest in it? There is no help but from God alone. Truly, God is Almighty, Wise. **8:10**

I invoke His help, being in need of His protection. He whom He guides does not go astray. He with whom He is hostile receives no protection. He whom He supports remains not needy. Praise is most weighty of all that is weighed and the most valuable of all that is treasured. Sermon 2

Mention when a sleepiness enwraps you as a safety from Him. He sends down water from heaven for you and He purifies you by it and causes to be put away from you the defilement of Satan. He invigorates your hearts and makes your feet firm by it. **8:11**

We beg Him for safety in the faith just as we beg Him for safety in our bodies. Sermon 99

Mention when **your** *Lord reveals to the angels: I am, truly, with you, so make those who believed firm. I will cast alarm into the hearts of those who were ungrateful. So, strike above their necks and strike each of their fingers from them.* **8:12**

God, the Almighty, tries His creatures by means of those things whose real nature they do not know in order to distinguish good and bad for them through the trial, to remove vanity from them, to keep them detached from pride and self-admiration. Sermon 192

That is because they made a breach with God and His Messenger. To whomever makes a breach with God and His Messenger, then, truly, God is Severe in repayment. **8:13**
That is for you, so experience it, and, truly, for the ones who are ungrateful, the punishment of the fire. **8:14**

Whoever makes a breach with God and *His Messenger* (Q3:101), his path will become difficult, his affairs will become complicated and his way to salvation will be uncertain. Saying 31

O those who believed! When you met those who were ungrateful marching to battle, then, turn not your backs to them in flight. **8:15**
Whoever turns his back that Day—but one who withdraws from fighting for a purpose—or one who moves aside to another faction, he, surely, drew the burden of the anger from God and his place of shelter will be hell. Miserable will be the Homecoming! **8:16**
Then, you kill them not, but God killed them. **You** *had not thrown when* **you** *had thrown but God threw. He tries by experiment the ones who believe with a fairer trial from Him. Truly, God is Hearing, Knowing.* **8:17**

Right cannot be achieved without effort. Sermon 29

That is so, and, truly, God is One Who Makes Frail the cunning of the ones who are ungrateful. **8:18**

God ... is aware of whatever is hidden in the hearts and whatever lies behind the unseen. Sermon 192

If you seek a judgment then, surely, drew near to you the victory. If you refrain yourselves, then, that would be better for you. If you revert, We will revert. Your factions will not avail you at all even if they were many. God is with the ones who believe. **8:19**

I have seen your flight and your dispersal from the lines. You were surrounded by rude and low people and Bedouins of Syria, although you are the chiefs of Arabs and summit of distinction and possess the dignity of the high nose and big hump of the camel. The sigh of my bosom can subside only when I eventually see you surrounding them as they surrounded you and see you dislodging them from their position as they dislodged you, killing them with arrows and striking them with spears so that their forward rows might fall on the rear ones just like the thirsty camels who have been turned away from their place of drink and removed from their water-points. Sermon 107

O those who believed! Obey God and His Messenger and turn not away from him when you hear his command. **8:20**

The best means by which seekers of nearness to God, the Almighty, the Exalted, seek nearness, is the belief in Him and His Prophet. Sermon 109

Be not like those who said: We heard, when they hear not. **8:21**
Truly, the worst of moving creatures with God are unwilling to hear and unwilling to speak, those who are not reasonable. **8:22**
If God knew any good in them He would have caused them to be willing to hear. Even if He had caused them to be willing to hear, truly, they would have turned away, and they are ones who turn aside. **8:23**

O God's human being! I advise you to exercise God-consciousness and to obey Him because it is salvation tomorrow and deliverance forever. He warned you of chastisement and did so thoroughly. He persuaded you towards virtues and did so fully. He described this world, its cutting away from you, its decay and its shifting. Therefore, turn away from its attractions because very little of it will accompany you. This house is the closest to the displeasure of God and the remotest from the pleasure of God. Sermon 161

O those who believed! Respond to God and to the Messenger when He called you to what gives you life. Know, truly, that God comes between a man and his heart and that to Him you will assemble. **8:24**

You should know that every obedience to God is unpleasant in appearance while every disobedience to God has the appearance of enjoyment. God may have mercy on the person who turns away from his desire and uproots the desires of his heart because this heart has far-reaching aims and it pursues disobedience through desires. Sermon 176

Be God-conscious of a test which will not light on those of you, particularly, who did wrong. Know that God is, truly, Severe in repayment. **8:25**

O God's human being! I advise you to be God-conscious.

Remember when you were few, ones taken advantage of due to weakness on the earth. You fear humanity would snatch you away so He gave you refuge and confirmed you with His help and provided you with what is good so that perhaps you will give thanks. **8:26**

God is enough for your needs in this world. He has persuaded you to remain thankful. He has made it obligatory on you to mention Him with your tongues. Sermon 183

O those who believed! Betray not God and the Messenger nor betray your trusts when you know. **8:27**

God chose Prophets from Adam's progeny. He took their pledge to receive His revelation and to carry His message as their trust. Over the course of time, many people perverted God's trust in them. They ignored His position. They took partners with Him. Satan turned them away from knowing Him and distanced them from His worship. Then God sent His Messengers and series of His Prophets to them to guide them to fulfilling the pledges of His creation, to recall to them His bounties, to exhort them by preaching, to unveil before them the hidden virtues of wisdom and show them the signs of His Omnipotence, namely the sky which is raised over them, the earth that is placed beneath them, their means of living that sustains them, their deaths that cause them to die, ailments that turn them old and incidents that successively betake them. Sermon 1

Know that your wealth and your children are a test and that God, with Him is a sublime compensation. **8:28**

O God's human being! I advise you to be God-conscious. It is He Who has furnished illustrations and Who has timed for you your lives. He has given you covering of dress. He has scattered a livelihood for you. He has surrounded you with His knowledge. He has ordained rewards. He has bestowed upon you vast bounties and extensive gifts. He has warned you through far reaching arguments. He has counted you by numbers. He has fixed for you an age to live in this place of testing and house of instruction. You are on a test in this world and have to render an account regarding it. Sermon 82

O those who believed! If you are God-conscious, He will assign you a Criterion between right and wrong and will absolve you of your evil deeds and will forgive you. God is Possessor of Sublime Grace. **8:29**

God, the Sublime, disliked vanity for them and liked humbleness for them. Therefore, they laid their cheeks on the ground, smeared their faces with dust, bent themselves down for the believers and remained humble people. God tried them with hunger, afflicted them with difficulty, tested them with fear and upset them with troubles. Therefore, do not regard wealth and progeny the criterion for God's pleasure and displeasure as you are not aware of the chances of mischief and trials during richness and power as God, the Almighty, the Sublime, has said: *Assume they that with the relief We furnish them of wealth and children We compete for good works for them? Nay! They are not aware.* (Q23:55-56) Sermon 192

Mention when those who were ungrateful plan against ***you*** *to bring* ***you*** *to a standstill or to kill* ***you*** *or to drive* ***you*** *out. They plan and God plans, but God is Best of the ones who plan.* **8:30**

God ... is aware of whatever is hidden in the hearts and whatever lies behind the unseen. Sermon 192

When Our signs are recounted to them, they said: We heard this. If we will, we would say the like of this. Truly, this is only fables of ancient ones. **8:31**

When they said: O God! Truly, if this had been The Truth from ***You****, rain down rocks on us from heaven or bring us a painful punishment.* **8:32**

God sent Muhammad, peace and the mercy of God be upon him, with the Truth so that he may take out His people from the worship of idols towards His worship and from obeying Satan towards obeying Him. God sent him with the Quran which He explained and made strong in order that the people may know their Sustainer (God), since they were ignorant of Him, may acknowledge Him, since they were denying Him and accept Him, since they were refusing to believe in Him. Sermon 147

But God had not been punishing them with ***you*** *among them. Nor had God been One Who Punishes them while they ask for forgiveness.* **8:33**

Generosity is the protector of honor. Forbearance is the bridle of the fool. Forgiveness is the levy of success. Disregard is the punishment of him who betrays. Consultation is the chief way of guidance. He who is content with his own opinion faces danger. Hadith 211

What is with them that God should not punish them while they bar worshipers from the Masjid al-Haram and they had not been its protectors? Truly, its protectors are but ones who are God-conscious except most of them know not. **8:34**
Their formal prayer at the House had been nothing but whistling and clapping of hands. So, experience the punishment because you had been ungrateful. **8:35**

Endurance braves calamities while impatience is a helper of the hardships of the world. The best contentment is to give up desires. Many a slavish mind is subservient to overpowering longings. Capability helps preservation of experience. Love means well-utilized relationship. Do not trust one who is grieved. Hadith 211

Truly, those who were ungrateful spend their wealth so that they bar the way of God. They will spend it. Again, it will become a regret for them. Again, they will be vanquished. Those who were ungrateful will be assembled in hell. **8:36**

They, the ungrateful, jumped on the carcass of this world, earned shame by eating it and became united in loving it. When one loves a thing, it blinds him and sickens his heart. He sees, but with a diseased eye, hears, but with un-hearing ears. Desires have cut asunder his wit. The world has made his heart dead while his mind is all longing for it. Consequently, he is a servant of it and of everyone who has any share in it. Wherever it turns, he turns towards it. Wherever it proceeds, he proceeds towards it. He is not desisted by any desister from God, nor takes admonition from any preacher. He sees those who have been caught in neglect whence there is neither rescission, nor reversion. Sermon 108

God will differentiate the bad from what is good. He will lay the bad, some on some other, and heap them up altogether and lay them into hell. Those, they are the ones who are losers. **8:37**

The two objectives, namely Paradise and Hell, have been stretched for them up to a point beyond the reach of fear or hope. Had they been able to speak they would have become dumb to describe what they witnessed or saw. Sermon 220

Say to those who were ungrateful: If they refrain themselves, what is past will be forgiven. If they repeat then, surely, a custom passed of the ancient ones as a warning. **8:38**

We do not make use of what we know and do not discover what we do not know.

We do not fear calamity until it befalls. Sermon 32

Fight them until there be no persecution and the way of life—all of it—be for God. Then, if they refrained themselves, then, truly, God is Seeing of what they do. **8:39**

O my God! We seek **Your** protection from turning away from **Your** command, or revolting against **Your** religion, or being led away by our desires instead of by guidance that comes from **You**. Sermon 215

If they turned away, then, know that God is your Defender. How excellent a Defender and how excellent a Helper! **8:40**

What will then be your position when your affairs reach their end and graves are turned upside down to throw out the dead? Every soul will be tried there for what it has done in the past. They would be returned to God, their Defender, The Truth. *From them will go astray what they had been devising.* (Q10:30) Sermon 224

Know that whatever thing you gain as booty, then, truly one-fifth of it belongs to God and to the Messenger and to the possessors of kinship and the orphans and the needy and the traveler of the way. if you had been believing in God and in what We caused to descend to Our servant on the Day of the Criterion between right and wrong, the day when the two multitudes met one another. God is Powerful over everything. **8:41**

He is that generous Being Whom the begging of beggars cannot make poor, nor the pertinacity of beseechers make misers. Sermon 91

Mention when you were on the nearer bank of the valley and they were on the farther bank of the valley and the cavalcade was below you. Even if you made a promise together, you would be, certainly, at variance as to the solemn declaration because God decrees a command that had been one that is accomplished so that he who perishes would have perished by a clear portent and he who lives would live on by a clear portent. Truly, God is Hearing, Knowing. **8:42**

Mention when God causes ***you*** *to see them as few in* ***your*** *slumbering. If He caused* ***you*** *to see them as many, you would have lost heart and contended with one another about the command except God saved you. Truly, He is Knowing of what is in the breasts.* **8:43**

I praise God for whatever matter He ordained and whatever action He destines and for my trial with you. Sermon 180

Mention when He causes you to see them when you met one another as few in your eyes and He makes you few in their eyes so that God decrees a command that had been one that is accomplished. Commands are returned to God. **8:44**

The trouble-mongers are a people whose attacks are severe. Those who would fight them for the sake of God would be a people who are low in the estimation of the proud, unknown in the earth, but well known in the heavens. Sermon 102

O those who believed! When you met a faction, then, stand firm and remember God frequently so that perhaps you will prosper. **8:45**

What is the matter with you? What is your ailment? What is your cure? The other party is also men of your type, but they are so different in character. Will there be talk without action, carelessness without God-consciousness and greed in things not right? Sermon 29

Obey God and His Messenger and contend not with one another. Then, you lose heart and your competence go. Have patience. Truly, God is with the ones who remain steadfast. **8:46**

I bear witness that *Muhammad* (Q48:29), peace and the mercy of God be upon him, is *His servant* (Q17:1) and *Prophet* (Q7:158), whom He deputed when the signs of guidance were obliterated and the ways of religion were desolate. So he threw open the truth, gave advice to the people, guided them towards righteousness and ordered them to be moderate. May God bless him. Sermon 195

Be not like those who went forth from their abodes recklessly to show off to personages and bar them from the way of God. God is One Who Encloses what they do. **8:47**

O my listener! Be cured from your intoxication. Wake up from your slumber. Decrease your hasty activity. Ponder over what has come to you through *the unlettered Prophet* (Q7:157), peace and the mercy of God be upon him, which is inevitable and inescapable. You should turn away from him who opposes him. Leave him and leave whatever he has adopted for himself. Put off your vanity. Drop your haughtiness. Recall your grave because your way passes over it. You will be dealt with as you deal with others. You will reap what you sow. What you send today will meet you tomorrow. So provide for your future. Send some good acts for your day of reckoning. God-consciousness, God-consciousness, O listener! Act, act, O careless one! *None tells* **you** *like One Who is Aware.* (Q35:14) Sermon 153

Mention when Satan made to appear pleasing their actions to them and said: No one will be ones who are victors against you this day from among all personages. Truly, I will be your neighbor. But when the two factions sighted one another, he receded on his two heels and said: Truly, I am free of you. Truly, I see what you see not. Truly, I fear God. God is Severe in repayment. **8:48**

If the foot remains firm in this slippery place, well and good, but if the foot slips, this is because we are under the shade of branches, the passing of the winds, and the canopy of the clouds whose layers are dispersed in the sky, and whose traces disappeared in the earth. Sermon 149

Mention when the ones who are hypocrites say and those who, in their hearts, is a sickness: Their way of life deluded these, but whoever puts his trust in God, then, truly, God is Almighty, Wise. **8:49**

Every trouble and hardship just increased us in our belief, in our treading on the right path, in submission to the divine command. Sermon 122

If **you** *would see when those who were ungrateful are called to themselves by the angels, they are striking their faces and their backs saying: Experience the punishment of the burning.* **8:50** *That is because of what your hands put forward of evil and, truly, God is not unjust to His servants.* **8:51**

You will see the hopes of *the Messenger* (Q2:143), peace and the mercy of God be upon him, simple, his shortcomings few, his heart fearing, his spirit contented, his meal small and simple, his religion safe, his desires dead and his anger suppressed. Good alone is expected from him. Evil from him is not to be feared. Even if he is found among those who forget God, he is counted among those who remember Him. However, if he is among the rememberers, he is not counted among the forgetful. He forgives him who is unjust to him. He gives to him who deprives him. He behaves well with him who behaves ill with him. Sermon 193

In like manner of the people of Pharaoh—and of those before them— they were ungrateful for the signs of God so God took them for their impieties. Truly, God is Strong, Severe in repayment. **8:52**

Did you not witness those who engaged in long-reaching desires, built strong buildings, amassed much wealth, but their houses turned into graves. Whatever they had collected turned into ruin. Sermon 131

Know that God will never be One Who Causes to Alter a divine blessing when He was gracious to a folk unless they first alter what is within themselves. Truly, God is Hearing, Knowing. **8:53**

Surely, there is a strong shield of God over me. When my day would come, it would not move away from me, but hand me over to death. At that time, neither an arrow would go amiss, nor would a wound heal. Sermon 61

In like manner of the people of Pharaoh, and those before them, they denied the signs of their Lord, so We caused them to perish for their impieties. We drowned the people of Pharaoh. They all had been ones who are unjust. **8:54**

History cannot deny ... enmity against Islam and *the Prophet* (Q7:158), peace and the mercy of God be upon him. Letter 28

Truly, the worst of moving creatures with God are those who were ungrateful, so they will not believe. **8:55**

O God's human being! Close your eyes from the worries and engagements of this world. You are sure about its separation and its changing conditions. Fear it like one who is sincere, one who struggles hard. Learn a lesson from what you have seen about the falling places of those before you, namely that their joints were made to vanish, their eyes and ears were destroyed, their honor and prestige disappeared, and their pleasure and wealth came to an end. Sermon 161

Those with whom ***you*** *have made a contract, again, they break their compact every time and they are not God-conscious.* **8:56**

A pledge is binding on those of them who are present and those of them who are absent, those of them who are forbearing and those of them who are foolish, those of them who are learned and those of them who are ignorant. Along with this, the pledge of God is also binding on them. The pledge of God is to be accounted for. *Live up to the compact. Truly the compact is that which has been asked about.* (Q17:34)

So, if ***you*** *have come upon them in war, then, break them up, whoever is behind them, so that perhaps they will recollect.* **8:57**

If ***you*** *have feared treachery from a folk, then, dissolve the relationship with them equally. Truly, God loves not the ones who are traitors.* **8:58**

The best means by which seekers of nearness to God, the Almighty, the Exalted, seek nearness, is the belief in Him and His Prophet, fighting in His cause, for it is the high pinnacle of Islam. Sermon 109

Assume ***you*** *not that those who were ungrateful will outdo Me. Truly, they will never weaken Him.* **8:59**

God sent to *the Prophet* (Q7:158), peace and the mercy of God be upon him, the

Book as a light whose flames cannot be extinguished, a lamp whose gleam does not die, a sea whose depth cannot be sounded, a way whose direction does not mislead, a ray whose light does not darken, a separator of good from evil whose arguments do not weaken, a clarifier whose foundations cannot be dismantled, a cure which leaves no apprehension for disease, an honor whose supporters are not defeated and a truth whose helpers are not abandoned. It is the mine of belief and its center, the source of knowledge and its oceans, the plantation of justice and its pools, the foundation stone of Islam and its construction, the valleys of truth and its plains, an ocean which those who draw water cannot empty, springs which those who draw water cannot dry up, a watering place which those who come to take water cannot exhaust, a staging place in moving towards so that travelers do not get lost, signs which no one who treads fails to see and a highland which those who approach it cannot surpass it. Sermon 197

Prepare for them whatever you were able of strength, including a string of horses, to put fear in the enemy of God and your enemy and others besides whom you know them not. God knows them. Whatever thing you spend in the way of God, the account will be paid in full to you and you will not be wronged. **8:60**

O God's human being! Be God-conscious! Be God-conscious in the matter of your own selves, which are the most beloved and dear to you, because God has clarified to you the way of truthfulness and lit its paths. You may choose either ever-present misfortune or eternal happiness. You should, therefore, provide in these mortal days for the eternal days.... Be aware, what will he, who has been created for the next world, do with this world? What will a person do with wealth that he would shortly be deprived of while only its ill effects and reckoning would be left behind for him? Sermon 157

If they tended towards peace, then, tend **you** *towards it and put* **your** *trust in God. Truly, He is The Hearing, The Knowing.* **8:61**

Possibly God may, as a result of this peace, improve the condition of these people. They will not be caught by the throats and will not, before indication of the right, fall into rebellion as before. Certainly, the best person before God is he who loves most to act according to right, even though it causes him hardship and grief, rather than according to wrong, even though it gives him benefit and increase. Sermon 125

If they want to deceive **you**, *then, truly, God is Enough. It is He Who confirmed* **you** *with His help and with the ones who believe.* **8:62**

He who is strong rooted in God-consciousness is not destroyed. The plantation of a people based on God-consciousness never remains without water.... Reform yourselves. Repent. One should praise only God and condemn only one's self. Sermon 16

He brought their hearts together. If **you** *had spent all that is in and on the earth,* **you** *would not have brought together their hearts, except God brought them together. Truly, He is Almighty, Wise.* **8:63**

O my God! Forgive me. **You** know more about me than I do. Sermon 78

O Prophet! God is Enough for **you** *and for whoever followed* **you** *among the ones who believe.* **8:64**

O Prophet! Encourage fighting to the ones who believe. If there be twenty of you, ones who remain steadfast, they will vanquish two hundred. If there be a hundred of you, they will vanquish a thousand of those who were ungrateful because they are a folk who understand not. **8:65**
Now God lightened your burden from you for He knew that there was a weakness in you. So, if there would be a hundred of you, ones who remain steadfast, they will vanquish two hundred. If there would be a thousand of you, they will vanquish two thousand with the permission of God. God is with the ones who remain steadfast. **8:66**
It had not been for a Prophet that he would have prisoners of war unless he gives a sound thrashing in the region. You want the advantages of the present, but God wants the world to come. God is Almighty, Wise. **8:67**
Were it not for a preceding prescription from God, you would, certainly, be afflicted with a tremendous punishment for what you took. **8:68**

The Prophet (Q7:158), peace and the mercy of God be upon him, lit flames for the seeker and put bright signs for the impeded. So he is **Your** trustworthy trustee, **Your** witness on the Day of Judgment, **Your** deputy as a blessing and **Your** Messenger of truth as mercy. Sermon 106

Eat of what you gained as booty, lawful, what is good. Be God-conscious. Truly, God is Forgiving, Compassionate. **8:69**

I praise God for whatever matter He ordained and whatever action He destines. Sermon 180

O Prophet! Say to whom are in your hands of the prisoners of war: If God knows any good in your hearts, He will give you better than what was taken from you and He will forgive you. God is Forgiving, Compassionate. **8:70**
But if they want treachery against ***you****, they, surely, betrayed God before, so He gave* ***you*** *power over them. God is Knowing, Wise.* **8:71**

My God, Spreader of the surfaces of the earth and Keeper intact of all skies, Creator of hearts of good and evil nature, send **Your** choicest blessings and growing favors on Muhammad, peace and the mercy of God be upon him, **Your** servant and **Your** Prophet, who is the last of those who preceded him and an opener for what is closed, proclaimer of truth with truth, repulser of the forces of wrong and crusher of the onslaughts of misguidance. As he was burdened with the responsibility of prophethood so he bore it standing by **Your** commands, advancing towards **Your** will, without shrinking of steps of weakness of determination, listening to **Your** revelation, preserving **Your** testament, proceeding forward in the spreading of **Your** commands until he lit a fire for its seeker and lighted the path for the groper in the dark. Hearts achieved guidance through him after being ridden with troubles. He introduced clearly guiding signs and shining injunctions. He is **Your** trusted trustee, the treasurer of **Your** treasured knowledge, **Your** witness on the Day of Judgment, **Your** envoy of truth and **Your** Messenger towards the people. May God prepare a large place for him under **Your** shade and award him multiplying good by **Your** bounty. My God, give height to his construction above all other constructions, heighten his position with **You**, grant perfection to his effulgence and perfect for him his light. In reward for his discharging **Your** prophetship, grant him that his testimony be admitted and his speech be liked for his speech is just, and his judgments are clear-cut. My God, put us and him together in the pleasures of life, continuance of bounty, satisfaction of desires, enjoyment of pleasures, ease of living, peace of mind and gifts of honor. Sermon 72

Truly, those who believed and emigrated and struggled with their wealth and their lives in the way of God, and those who gave refuge and helped, those are protectors, some of some others. Those who believed, but emigrate not, you have no duty of friendship to them at all until they emigrate. If they asked you for help in the way of life, then, it would be upon you to help them, except against the folk whom between you and between them there is a solemn promise. God is Seeing of what you do. **8:72**

God deputed *the Prophet* (Q7:158), peace and the mercy of God be upon him, with a sparkling light, a clear argument, an open path and a guiding book. His tribe is the best tribe and his lineal tree the best lineal tree whose branches are in good proportion and fruits hanging in plenty. His birthplace was Makkah, and the place of his immigration Yathrib, from where his name rose high and his voice spread far and wide. God sent him with a sufficing plea, a convincing discourse and a rectifying announcement. Through him God disclosed the ways that had been forsaken, and destroyed the innovations that had been introduced. Through him He explained the detailed commands. Now: *Whoever be looking for a way of life other than submission, it will never be accepted from him.* (Q3:85) Sermon 161

Those who were ungrateful, some are protectors of some others. If you accomplish not allying with other believers there will be persecution on the earth and the hateful sin of corruption. **8:73**

The opponents have entered the oceans of disturbance and have taken to innovations instead of the *sunna*, while the believers have sunk down. The misguided and the liars are speaking. We are the near ones, companions, treasure holders and doors to the *sunna.* Houses are not entered save through their doors. Whoever enters them from other than the door is called a thief. Sermon 153

Those who believed and emigrated and struggled in the way of God and those who gave refuge and helped, those, they are the ones who truthfully believe. For them is forgiveness and generous provision. **8:74**

Those who believed afterwards, and emigrated and struggled beside you, then, those are of you. Those imbued through wombs, blood relations, some are more deserving than some others in what is prescribed by God, truly, God is Knowing of everything. **8:75**

My bearing witness has been tested. Its essence is our belief. Sermon 2

Chapter 9: Repentance (al-Tawbah)

God and His Messenger declare disassociation from those with whom you made a contract among the ones who were polytheists who violated it: **9:1**

God never allowed His creation to remain without a Prophet, one deputized by Him, or a Book sent down from Him, or a binding argument, or a standing plea. These Messengers were such that they did not fear that they were few in comparison to the large numbers of their falsifiers. Among them was either a predecessor who would name the one to follow or the follower who had been introduced by the predecessor. Sermon 1

Roam about on the earth for four months and know that you will not be ones who frustrate God and that God is One Who Covers with shame the ones who are ungrateful. **9:2**

Where are those who protect honor, and those self-respecting persons who defend respectable persons in the time of hardship? Shame is behind you while the Garden is in front of you. Sermon 171

The announcement from God and His Messenger to humanity on the day of the greater pilgrimage to Makkah is that God is free from the ones who are polytheists and so is His Messenger. Then, it will be better for you if you repented. But if you turned away, then, know that you are not ones who frustrate God. Give ***you*** *tidings to those who were ungrateful of a painful punishment.* **9:3**
But those with whom you made a contract—among the ones who are polytheists—and again, they reduce you not at all nor do they back anyone against you, then, fulfill their compact with them until their term of contract expires. Truly, God loves the ones who are God-conscious. **9:4**

God sent *the Prophet,* (Q7:158), peace and the mercy of God be upon him, for enforcement of His commands, for exhausting His pleas and for presenting warnings against eternal punishment. Sermon 82

When the months of pilgrim sanctity were drawn away, then, kill the ones who are polytheists wherever you found them and take them and besiege them and sit in every place of ambush. Then, if they repented and performed the formal prayer and gave the purifying alms, then, let them go their way. Truly, God is Forgiving, Compassionate. **9:5**

Do not make haste for a matter which is to happen and is awaited. Do not wish for delay in what the morrow may to bring for you. For how many people make haste for a matter, but when they get it, they begin to wish they had not gotten it. How near is today to the dawning of tomorrow. O my people, this is the time for the occurrence of every promised event and the approach of things which you do not know. Sermon 150

If anyone of the ones who are polytheists sought asylum with ***you****, then, grant him protection so that he hears the assertions of God. Again, convey* ***you*** *him to a place of safety. That is because they are a folk who know not.* **9:6**

We beg Him for safety in the faith, just as we beg Him for safety in our bodies. Sermon 99

How will there be for the ones who are polytheists a compact with God and with His Messenger but for those with whom you made a contract near the Masjid al-Haram? If they go straight with you, then, go straight with them. Truly, God loves the ones who are God-conscious. **9:7**

I bear witness that whoever equated **You** with anything out of **Your** creation took a partner for **You**. Whoever takes a partner for **You** is ungrateful according to what is stated in **Your** unambiguous verses and indicated by the evidence of **Your** clear arguments. Sermon 91

How? If they get the better of you, they regard not ties of relationship with you nor a pact? They please you with their mouths, but their hearts refuse compliance and many of them are ones who disobey. **9:8**

The hypocrite is a person who makes a show of faith and adopts the appearance of a Muslim. He does not hesitate in sinning, nor does he keep aloof from vice. He willfully attributes false things against *the Messenger of God* (Q48:29), peace and the mercy of God be upon him. If people knew that he was a hypocrite and a liar, they would not accept anything from him and would not confirm what he says. Sermon 210

They sold out the signs of God for a little price and barred others from His way. Truly, how evil is what they had been doing. **9:9**

Certainly, the tongue of a believer is at the back of his heart while the heart of a hypocrite is at the back of his tongue. When a believer intends to say anything, he thinks it over in his mind. If it is good, he discloses it, but if it is bad, he lets it remain concealed. While a hypocrite speaks whatever comes to his tongue without knowing what is in his favor and what goes against him. Sermon 176

They regard not towards one who believes either ties of relationship or a pact. Those, they are the ones who exceed the limits. **9:10**

Glory be to **You**! How great is **Your** affair! Glory to **You**! How great is **Your** creation that we see, but how small is this greatness by the side of **Your** Might! How awe-striking is **Your** realm that we notice, but how humble is this against what is hidden from us out of **Your** authority! How extensive are **Your** bounties in this world, but how small are they against the bounties of the next world! Sermon 108

But if they repented and performed the formal prayer and gave the purifying alms, then, they are your brothers/sisters in your way of life, We explain the signs distinctly for a folk who know. **9:11**

O my God! We seek **Your** protection from turning away from **Your** command, or revolting against **Your** religion, or being led away by our desires instead of by guidance that comes from **You**. Sermon 215

But if they broke their sworn oaths after their compact and discredited your way of life, then, fight the leaders of ingratitude. Truly, they, their sworn oaths are nothing to them, so that perhaps they will refrain themselves. **9:12**

Oppressors inherit mutual agreement. The first of them serves as a leader for the latter one and the latter one follows the first one. They vie with each other in the matter of this lowly world, and leap over this stinking carcass. Shortly, the follower will denounce his connection with the leader, and the leader with the follower. They will disunite on account of mutual hatred and curse one another when they meet. Then after this, there will appear another arouser of mischief who will destroy ruined things. The heart will become wavering after being normal. People will be misled after safety, desires will multiply and become diversified, and views will become confused. Sermon 151

Will you not fight a folk who broke their sworn oaths and were about to expel the Messenger? Began they the first time against you? Will you dread them? God has a better right that you should dread Him if you had been ones who believe. **9:13**

The trouble-mongers are a people whose attacks are severe. Those who would fight them for the sake of God would be a people who are low in the estimation of the proud, unknown in the earth, but well known in the heavens. Sermon 102

Fight them! God will punish them by your hands and cover them with shame and help you against them. He will heal the breasts of a folk, ones who believe, **9:14**

and He causes to be put away the rage in their hearts. God turns to whom He wills in forgiveness. God is Knowing, Wise. **9:15**

Where are those who protect honor and those self-respecting persons who defend respectable persons in the time of hardship? Shame is behind you while the Garden is in front of you. Sermon 171

Or assumed you that you would be left before God knows those who struggled among you? Take not anyone to yourselves other than God and His Messenger and the ones who believe as intimate friends. God is Aware of what you do. **9:16**

Indeed, surely, jihad is one of the doors of Paradise which God has opened for His best friends. It is the dress of God-consciousness, the protective armor of God and His trustworthy shield. Whoever abandons it, God covers him with the dress of disgrace and the clothes of distress. He is kicked with contempt and scorn. His heart is veiled with screens of neglect. Truth is taken away from him because of his missing the jihad. He has to suffer ignominy. Justice is denied to him. Sermon 27

It had not been for the ones who are polytheists to frequent the places of prostration to God while they are ones who bear witness against themselves of their ingratitude. Those, their actions were fruitless. They are ones who will dwell in the fire forever! **9:17**

O God's human being! I advise you to fear God and I warn you of the hypocrites, because they are themselves misguided and misguide others, and they have slipped and make others slip too. They change into many colors, and adopt various ways. They support you with all sorts of supports, and lie in waiting for you at every lookout. Sermon 194

Only he frequents places of prostration to God who believed in God and the Last Day and performed the formal prayer and gave the purifying alms and dreads none but God. Perhaps those will be among the ones who are truly guided. **9:18**

Made you the giving of water to drink to the ones who are pilgrims and frequenting the Masjid al-Haram the same as he who believed in God and the Last Day and struggled in the way of God? They are not on the same level with God. God guides not the folk, ones who are unjust. **9:19**

The foremost in God's Way of life is the acknowledgment of Him. The perfection of acknowledging Him is to bear witness to Him. The perfection of bearing witness to Him is to believe in His Oneness. The perfection of believing in His Oneness is to regard Him Pure. The perfection of His purity is to deny Him attributes, because every attribute is a proof that it is different from that to which it is attributed and everything to which something is attributed is different from the attribute. Thus whoever attaches attributes to God recognizes His like. Whoever recognizes His like regards Him as two. Whoever regards Him as two recognizes parts for Him. Whoever recognizes parts for Him mistakes Him. Whoever mistakes Him points at Him. Whoever points at Him admits limitations for Him. Whoever admits limitations for Him numbers Him. Sermon 1

Those who believed and emigrated and struggled in the way of God with their wealth and their lives are sublime in their degree with God. Those, they are the ones who are victorious. **9:20**

One belief is that which is firm and steadfast in heart. Another belief is that which remains temporarily in the heart and the breast up to a certain time. Sermon 189

Their Lord gives them good tidings of mercy from Him and His contentment and of Gardens for them in which is abiding bliss. **9:21**

They are ones who will dwell in them forever, eternally. Truly, God, with Him is a sublime com-

pensation. **9:22**

God, the Almighty, has sent down a guiding Book wherein He has explained virtue and vice. You should adopt the course of virtue, whereby you will have guidance. Detach yourself from the direction of vice, so that you remain on the right way. Sermon 167

O those who believed! Take not to yourselves your fathers and brothers/sisters as protectors if they embraced disbelief instead of belief. Whoever of you turns away to them, then, those, they are the ones who are unjust. **9:23**
Say: If had been your fathers and your children and your brothers/sisters and your spouses and your kinspeople and the wealth you gained and the transactions you dread slacken and the dwellings with which you are well-pleased were more beloved to you than God and His Messenger and struggling in His Way, then, await until God brings His command. God guides not the folk, ones who disobey. **9:24**

You will see the Messenger's hopes simple, his shortcomings few, his heart fearing, his spirit contented, his meal small and simple, his religion safe, his desires dead and his anger suppressed. Good alone is expected from him. Evil from him is not to be feared. Even if he is found among those who forget God, he is counted among those who remember Him, but if he is among the rememberers he is not counted among the forgetful. He forgives him who is unjust to him, and he gives to him who deprives him. He behaves well with him who behaves ill with him. Sermon 193

God, certainly, helped you in many battlefields and on the day of Hunayn when you were impressed with your great numbers, but it avails you not at all. The earth was narrow for you for all its breadth. Again, you turned as ones who draw back. **9:25**
Again, God caused His tranquility to descend on His Messenger and on the ones who believed and caused armies you see not to descend and punished those who were ungrateful. This is the recompense of the ones who were ungrateful. **9:26**

The ignoble cannot ward off oppression. Right cannot be achieved without effort. Which is the house besides this one to protect? What is the matter with you? What is your ailment? What is your cure? Sermon 29

Again, God will turn to whom He will in forgiveness after that. God is Forgiving, Compassionate. **9:27**

O my God! Forgive me. **You** know more about me than I do. Sermon 78

O those who believed! Truly, the ones who are polytheists are unclean, so let them come not near the Masjid al-Haram after this year. If you feared being poverty-stricken, God will enrich you out of His grace if He willed. Truly, God is Knowing, Wise. **9:28**

O God! I bear witness that he who likens **You** with the separateness of the limbs or with the joining of the extremities of his body did not acquaint his inner self with knowledge about **You**. His heart did not secure conviction to the effect that there is no partner for **You**. It is as though he has not heard the wrongful followers disclaiming their false gods by sayings. *By God! Truly we have been clearly wandering astray when we made you equal with the Lord of the worlds.* (Q26:97-98) They are wrong who liken **You** to their idols, and dress **You** with apparel of the creatures by their imagination, attribute to **You** parts of body by their own thinking and consider **You** after the creatures of various types, through the working of their intelligence. I bear witness that whoever equated **You** with anything out of **Your** creation took a partner for **You**. Whoever takes a partner for **You** is ungrateful according to what is stated in **Your** unambiguous verses and indicated by the evidence of **Your** clear arguments. I also bear witness that **You** are that God Who cannot be confined in the fetters of intelligence so as to admit change of condition by entering its imagination, nor in the shackles of the mind so as to become limited and an object of alterations. Sermon 91

Fight those who believe not in God nor the Last Day nor forbid what God and His Messenger forbade nor practice the way of life of The Truth among those who were given the Book until they give the tribute out of hand and they be ones who comply. **9:29**

At last, when God will make clear to them the reward for their sins and take them out from the veils of their neglectfulness, they will proceed to what they were running away from and run away from what they were proceeding to. They will not benefit from the wants they will satisfy or the desires they would fulfill. Sermon 153

The Jews said: Ezra is the son of God and the Christians said: The Messiah is the son of God. That is the saying with their mouths. They conform with the sayings of those who were ungrateful before. God took the offensive. How they are misled! **9:30**
They took to themselves their learned Jewish scholars and their monks as lords—other than God—and the Messiah son of Mary. They were only commanded to worship The One God. There is no god but He! Glory be to Him above the partners they ascribe! **9:31**
They want to extinguish the light of God with their mouths, but God refuses so that He fulfill His light even if the ones who are ungrateful disliked it. **9:32**
It is He Who sent His Messenger with the guidance and the way of life of The Truth so that He may uplift it over all ways of life, even if the ones who are polytheists disliked it. **9:33**

O my God! Let my spirit be the first of those good objects that **You** take from me and the first trust out of **Your** favors held in trust with me. Sermon 215

O those who believed! Truly, there are many of the learned Jewish scholars and monks who consume the wealth of humanity in falsehood and bar from the way of God and those who treasure up gold and silver and spend it not in the way of God. Give to them tidings of a painful punishment, **9:34**
on a Day it will be hot in the fire of hell. Then, by it are branded their foreheads and their sides and their backs. It will be said: This is what you treasured up for yourselves so experience what you had been treasuring up. **9:35**

Let your most beloved treasure be the treasure of virtuous acts. Letter 53

Truly, the period of months with God is twelve lunar months in the Book of God. On the day when He created the heavens and the earth of them. Four are sanctified. That is the truth-loving way of life. So, do not wrong yourselves in it. Fight the ones who are polytheists collectively, as they fight you collectively. Know that God is with the ones who are God-conscious. **9:36**
Truly, the postponing a Sacred Month is an increase in ingratitude. By it are caused to go astray those who were ungrateful, for they permit it a year, and forbid it a year, so that they agree with the period that God forbade, and they permit what God forbade. Made to appear pleasing to them was the evil of their actions. God guides not the folk, the ones who are ungrateful. **9:37**

They are hankering after this world out of jealousy against him on whom God has bestowed it. So they intend to revert the matters to the pre-Islamic period. On us it is obligatory, for your sake, to abide by the Book of God (Quran), the Sublime, and the conduct of *the Prophet* (Q7:158), peace and the mercy of God be upon him, to stand by His rights and to revive his *sunna*. Sermon 169

O those who believed! What was it with you when was said to you: Move forward in the way of God, you inclined heavily downwards to the earth? Were you so well-pleased with this present life instead of the world to come? But the enjoyment of this present life is not but little compared to the world to come. **9:38**

In this way time will improve, the continuance of government will be expected, and the aims of the enemies will be frustrated, but if the ruled gain sway over the ruler, or the ruler oppresses the ruled, then difference crops up in every word, signs of oppression appear, mischief enters religion and the ways of the *sunna* are forsaken. Then desires are acted upon, the commands of the Divine Law are discarded, diseases of the spirit become numerous and there is no hesitation in disregarding even great rights, nor in committing big wrongs. In such circumstances, the virtuous are humiliated while the vicious are honored, and there are serious chastisements from God, the Almighty, onto the people. Sermon 216

Unless you move forward, He will punish you with a painful punishment and will have in exchange for you a folk other than you. You will not injure Him at all. God is Powerful over everything. **9:39**

If you help him not, then, surely, God helped him when those who were ungrateful drove him out. The second of two, when they were both in the cavern, he says to his companion: Feel no remorse. Truly, God is with us. Then, God caused His tranquility to descend on him and confirmed him with armies that you see not and made the word of those who were ungrateful the lowest. The Word of God is Lofty. God is Almighty, Wise. **9:40**

I praise God for whatever matter He ordained and whatever action He destines. Sermon 180

Move forward light and heavy and struggle with your wealth and your lives in the way of God. That is better for you if you had been knowing. **9:41**

Do not forget God, struggle in His cause with your tongue, with your wealth and with your lives. Letter 47

If it had been a near advantage and an easy journey, they would have followed **you**, *except the destination of the journey was distant for them. They will swear by God: If we were able, we would, certainly, have gone forth with you. They will cause themselves to perish. God knows that they are the ones who lie.* **9:42**

God pardon **you**! *Why gave* **you** *permission to them before it becomes clear to* **you** *those who were sincere and* **you** *know who are the ones who lie?* **9:43**

They ask not permission of **you**, *those who believe in God and the Last Day, that they struggle with their wealth and their lives. God is Knowing of the ones who are God-conscious.* **9:44**

It is only those who ask permission of **you** *who believe not in God and the Last Day and whose hearts were in doubt, so they go this way and that in their doubts.* **9:45**

If they wanted to go forth, certainly, they would have prepared for it some preparation, except God disliked arousing them, so He caused them to pause and it was said: Sit along with the ones who sit at home. **9:46**

If they went forth with you, they would have increased nothing for you, but ruination. They would have rushed to and fro in your midst with insolent dissension. Among you are ones who would have harkened to them. God is Knowing of the ones who are unjust. **9:47**

The troubles are like a dark night. Horses would not stand facing them, nor would their banners turn back. They would approach in full reins and ready with saddles. Their leader would be driving them and the rider would be exerting them. The trouble-mongers are a people whose attacks are severe. Those who would fight them for the sake of God would be a people who are low in the estimation of the proud, unknown in the earth, but well known in the heavens. Woe to you, O Basrah, when an army of God's infliction would face upon you without raising dust of cries. Your inhabitants would then face bloody death and dire hunger. Sermon 102

Certainly, they were looking for dissension before. They turned around and around for ***you*** *the commands until The Truth drew near, and the command of God became manifest although they were ones who dislike it.* **9:48**

The hypocrite is a person who makes a show of faith and adopts the appearance of a Muslim. He does not hesitate in sinning, nor does he keep aloof from vice. He willfully attributes false things against *the Messenger of God* (Q48:29), peace and the mercy of God be upon him. If people knew that he was a hypocrite and a liar, they would not accept anything from him and would not confirm what he says. Sermon 210

Among them is he who says: Give me permission and tempt me not. But they descended into dissension. Truly, hell is that which encloses the ones who are ungrateful. **9:49**
If lights on ***you*** *benevolence, they are raised to anger, but if an affliction lights on* ***you****, they say: Surely, we took our precautions before. They turn away and they are glad.* **9:50**
Say: Nothing will light on us but what God had been prescribing for us. He is our Defender. In God let the ones who believe put their trust. **9:51**

Where are the hearts dedicated to God and devoted to the obedience of God? They are all crowding towards worldly vanities and quarreling over unlawful issues. The signs of the Garden and Hell have been raised for them, but they have turned their faces away from the Garden and proceeded to Hell by dint of their performances. God called them, but they showed dislike and ran away. When Satan called them, they responded and proceeded towards him. Sermon 144

Say: Are you watching for something, but one of the two fairer things to befall us? We watch for you, whether God will light on you a punishment from Him or from our hands. So, watch! We are ones who are waiting with you. **9:52**

He to whom experiences have clearly shown the past exemplary punishments given by God to peoples is prevented by God-consciousness from falling into doubt. You should know that the same troubles have returned to you which existed when *the Prophet* (Q7:158), peace and the mercy of God be upon him, was first sent. By God who sent *the Prophet* (Q7:158), peace and the mercy of God be upon him, with faith and truth, you will be severely subverted, bitterly shaken as in sieving and fully mixed as by spooning in a cooking pot until your low persons become high and high ones become low. Sermon 16

Say: Spend willingly or unwillingly. There will be only non-acceptance. Truly, you, you had been a folk, ones who disobey. **9:53**

Nothing prevented their contributions being accepted from them but that they were ungrateful to God and His Messenger and that they not approach formal prayer but while they are lazy and they spend but as ones who dislike to spend. **9:54**
So, let not their wealth impress ***you*** *nor their children. God wants only to punish them in this present life and so that their*
souls depart while they are ones who are ungrateful. **9:55**
They swear by God that they are, truly, of you while they are not of you. They are but a folk who are in fear. **9:56**

He who disobeys **You** does not decrease **Your** authority. Sermon 108

If they find a shelter or a place to creep into or a place of retreat, they would turn to it as they rush away. **9:57**

The people of this time are engaged in disobedience. Their youth are wicked, their old men are sinful, their learned men are hypocrites, and their speakers are sycophants. Their young ones do not respect their elders, and their rich men do not support the destitute. Sermon 232

Among them there are some who find fault with ***you*** *about charities. If they were given a part of it, they were well-pleased, but if they are not given of it, that is when they are displeased.* **9:58**
Better if they were well-pleased with what God gave them and His Messenger. They had said: God is Enough for us. God will give to us of His grace and so will His Messenger. Truly, to God we are ones who quest. **9:59**
Charities are only for the poor and the needy and the ones who work to collect it and the ones whose hearts are brought together and to free the bondsperson and the ones who are in debt and in the way of God and for the traveler of the way. This is a duty to God. God is Knowing, Wise. **9:6**

This is the thing against which God has protected His creatures who are believers by means of prayers, alms-giving and suffering the hardship of fasting in the days in which it has been made obligatory in order to give their limbs peacefulness, to cast fear in their eyes, to make their spirits humble, to give their hearts humility and to remove haughtiness from them. All this is achieved through the covering of their delicate cheeks with dust in humility, prostrating their main limbs on the ground in humbleness and retracting of their bellies so as to reach to their backs due to fasting by way of lowliness before God, in addition to giving all sorts of products of the earth to the needy and the destitute by way of alms. Look what there is in these acts by way of curbing the appearance of pride and suppressing the traces of vanity. Sermon 192

Among them are those who malign the Prophet and say: He is unquestioning. Say: He is unquestioning of what is good for you. He believes in God and believes in ones who believe. He is a mercy to those of you who believed. Those of you who malign the Messenger of God, for them is a painful punishment. **9:61**
They swear by God to you to please you, but God and His Messenger have better right that they should please Him if they had been ones who believe. **9:62**

The Prophet (Q7:158), peace and the mercy of God be upon him, manifested whaever he was commanded and conveyed the messages of his Lord. Consequently, God repaired through him the cracks, joined through him the slits and created through him affection among kin although they bore intense enmity in their chests and deep-seated rancor in their hearts. Sermon 230

Know they not that whoever opposes God and His Messenger, then, truly, for him will be the fire of hell—one who will dwell in it forever? That is the tremendous degradation. **9:63**
The ones who are hypocrites are fearful that should be sent down against them a Chapter of the Quran to tell them what is in their hearts. Say: Ridicule us, but, truly, God is One Who Drives Out that of which you are fearful. **9:64**

I complain to God about persons who live ignorant and die misguided. For them nothing is more worthless than the Quran if it is recited as it should be recited, nor anything more valuable than the Quran if its verses are removed from their places, nor anything more vicious than virtue, nor more virtuous than vice. Sermon 17

If ***you*** *asked them, they would say: Truly, we had only been engaging in idle talk and playing. Say: Was it God and His signs and His Messenger that you had been ridiculing?* **9:65**

Know that if you had followed him who was calling you to guidance, he would have made you tread the ways of *the Prophet* (Q7:158), peace and the mercy of God be upon him. Then you would have been spared the difficulties of misguidance. You would have thrown away the crushing burden from your necks. Sermon 166

Make no excuses! Surely, you disbelieved after your belief. If We pardon a section of you, We will punish another section because, truly, they had been ones who sin. **9:66**

The hypocrite is a person who makes a show of faith and adopts the appearance of a Muslim. He does not hesitate in sinning, nor does he keep aloof from vice. He willfully attributes false things against *the Messenger of God* (Q48:29), peace and the mercy of God be upon him. If people knew that he was a hypocrite and a liar, they would not accept anything from him and would not confirm what he says. Sermon 210

The ones who are male hypocrites and the ones who are female hypocrites, some are of some other. They command that which is unlawful and prohibit that which is honorable and close their hands. They forgot God so He forgot them. Truly, the ones who are hypocrites, they are the ones who disobey. **9:67**

O God's human being! I advise you to fear God and I warn you of the hypocrites, because they are themselves misguided and misguide others, and they have slipped and make others slip too. They change into many colors, and adopt various ways. They support you with all sorts of supports, and lie in waiting for you at every lookout. Sermon 194

God promised the males, ones who hypocrites and the females, ones who are hypocrites and the ones who are ungrateful, the fire of hell, ones who will dwell in it forever! It will be enough for them. God cursed them. For them is an abiding punishment. **9:68**

Know that—may God have mercy on you—you are living at a time when those who speak about right are few, when tongues are loath to utter the truth and those who stick to the right are humiliated. Sermon 232

Like those before you who had been with more strength than you and more wealth and children, they enjoyed their apportionment so you enjoyed your apportionment as enjoyed those who were before you their apportionment. You engaged in idle talk as they engaged in idle talk. As to those, their actions were fruitless in the present and are such in the world to come. Those, they are the ones who are losers. **9:69**

O people! Look at the world like those who abstain from it and turn away from it. By God, it would shortly turn out its inhabitants and cause grief to the happy and the safe. That which turns and goes away from it never returns. That which is likely to come about is not known or anticipated. Its joy is mingled with grief. Herein people's firmness inclines towards weakness and languidness. The majority of what pleases you here should not mislead you because that which would help you would be little. God may shower His mercy on him who ponders and takes lesson thereby, and when he takes lesson he achieves enlightenment. Whatever is present in this world would shortly not exist, while whatever is to exist in the next world is already in existence. Every countable thing would pass away. Every anticipation should be taken to be coming up and every thing that is to come up should be taken as just near. Sermon 103

Approaches them not the tidings of those before them—the folk of Noah and of Ad and of Thamud, and of a folk of Abraham, and of the Companions of Midian, and that which are cities overthrown? Their Messengers approached them with the clear portents. So, it had not been God who did wrong to them, rather, they had been doing wrong to themselves. **9:70**

They are trying to reach the path of religion through wrong ways and to acquire worldly wealth and pleasure under the pretence of religious activities. Letter 33

The males, ones who believe and the females, ones who believe, some are protectors of some other. They command to that which is honorable and they prohibit that which is unlawful and they perform the formal prayer and give the purifying alms and obey God and His Messenger. Those, God will have mercy on them. Truly, God is Almighty, Wise. **9:71**

God, the Sublime, says: *Truly those of humanity closest to Abraham are those who followed him and this Prophet and those who have believed.* (Q3:68) Letter 28

God promised males, the ones who believe, and the females, the ones who believe, Gardens beneath which rivers run, ones who will dwell in them forever and good dwellings in the Gardens of Eden. The greater contentment is with God. That, it is the winning of the sublime triumph. **9:72**

Contentment is the capital which will never diminish. Saying 57

O Prophet! Struggle with the ones who are ungrateful and the ones who are hypocrites and be **you** *harsh against them. Their place of shelter will be hell. Miserable will be the Homecoming!* **9:73**

In the company of *the Prophet* (Q7:158), peace and the mercy of God be upon him, we used to fight our parents, sons, brothers and uncles. This continued us in our faith, in submission, in our following the right path, in endurance over the pangs of pain and in our fight against the enemy. Sermon 56

They swear by God that they said not against the Prophet but, certainly, they said the word of ingratitude and they were ungrateful after their submission to God. They were about to do something that they never attain. They sought revenge but that God would enrich them and His Messenger with His grace. If they repent, it would be better for them. If they turn away, God will punish them with a painful punishment in the present and in the world to come. There is not for them on earth either a protector or a helper. **9:74**

May God's mercy remain away from them as in the case of Thamud. Know that when the spears are hurled towards them and the swords are struck at their heads they will repent of their doings. Surely, today Satan has scattered them and tomorrow he will disclaim any connection with them, and will leave them. Their departing from guidance, returning to misguidance and blindness, turning away from truth and falling into wrong is enough for their chastisement. Sermon 180

Of them are some who made a contract with God saying: If He gave us of His grace, we will be charitable and, certainly, we will be among the ones in accord with morality. **9:75**

O God's human being! The good that God has promised should not be abandoned and the evil from which He has refrained should not be coveted. O God's human being! Fear the day when actions will be reckoned. There will be much quaking and even children will get old. Sermon 157

Then, when He gave them of His grace, they were misers with it and turned away and they were ones who turn aside. **9:76**

He made the consequence hypocrisy in their hearts until a Day they will meet Him because they broke with God what they promised Him, because they had been lying against Him. **9:77**

Know that this Quran is an adviser who never deceives, a leader who never misleads and a narrator who never speaks a lie. No one will sit beside this Quran, but when he rises, he will achieve one addition or one diminution—addition in his guidance or elimination in his spiritual blindness. You should also know that no one will need anything after guidance from the Quran and no one will be free from want before guidance from the Quran. Seek cure from the Quran for your ailments and seek its assistance in your distress. It contains a cure for the worst diseases, namely unbelief, hypocrisy, revolt and misguidance. Pray to God through it and turn to God with its love ... There is nothing like it through which the people should turn to God, the Sublime. Sermon 176

Know they not that God knows their conspiring secretly and their secret? That God is The Knower of the unseen. **9:78**

They took to the right and the left piercing through to the ways of evil and leaving the paths of guidance. Do not make haste for a matter which is to happen and is awaited. Do not wish for delay in what the morrow is to bring for you. For how many people make haste for a matter, but when they get it they begin to wish they had not gotten it? How near is today to the dawning of tomorrow? O my people, this is the time for the occurrence of every promised event and the approach of things which you do not know. Whoever from among us will be during these days will move through them with a burning lamp and will tread on the footsteps of the virtuous in order to unfasten knots, to free servants, to divide the united and to unite the divided. He will be in concealment from people. The stalker will not find his footprints even though he pursues with his eye. Then a group of people will be sharpened like the sharpening of swords by the blacksmith. Their sight will be brightened by revelation. The delicacies of commentary will be put in their ears. They will be given drinks of wisdom, morning and evening. Sermon 150

Those who find fault with ones who are volunteer donors to charities from among the ones who believe and those who find not but their striving to give, so they derided them. God will deride them.

They will have a painful punishment. **9:79**
Ask for forgiveness for them or ask not for forgiveness for them, if **you** *have asked for forgiveness for them seventy times, God will never forgive them. That is because they were ungrateful to God and His Messenger. God guides not the folk, the ones who disobey.* **9:80**
The ones who are left behind were glad of their positions behind the Messenger of God. They disliked struggling with their wealth and themselves in the way of God. They said: Move not forward in the heat. Say: The fire of hell has more severe heat. Would that they had been understanding! **9:81**
So, let them laugh a little and weep much as a recompense for what they had been earning. **9:82**
Then, God returned **you** *to a section of them. They asked* **your** *permission for going forth. Then, say: You will never ever go forth with me nor fight an enemy with me. You were well-pleased sitting the first time. Then, sit—ones who await with who lagged behind.* **9:83**

O son of Adam, when you see that your Lord, the Glorified, bestows His Favors on you while you disobey Him, you should fear Him, take warning that His Wrath may not turn those very blessings into misfortunes. Saying 24

Pray **you** *not formally for any of them who died, ever, nor stand up at his grave. Truly, they were ungrateful to God and His Messenger and died while they are ones who disobey.* **9:84**

Be aware! Certainly that giving of wealth without any right for it is wastefulness and lavishness. It raises its doer in this world, but lowers him in the next world. It honors him before people, but disgraces him with God. If a man gives his property to those who have no right for it or do not deserve it, God deprives him of their gratefulness, and their love too would be for others. Then if he falls on bad days and needs their help, they would prove the worst comrades and ignoble friends. Sermon 126

Let not their wealth impress you nor their children. For God only wants to punish them with these in the present and their souls depart while they were ones who are ungrateful. **9:85**

Indeed, surely, jihad is one of the doors of Paradise which God has opened for His best friends. It is the dress of God-consciousness, the protective armor of God and His trustworthy shield. Whoever abandons it, God covers him with the dress of disgrace and the clothes of distress. He is kicked with contempt and scorn. His heart is veiled with screens. Sermon 27

When a Chapter of the Quran was caused to descend saying that: Believe in God and struggle along with His Messenger, those imbued with affluence ask permission of **you**. *They said: Forsake us. We would be with the ones who sit at home.* **9:86**

The Book of God is among you. It speaks and its tongue does not falter. It is a house whose pillars do not fall down and a power whose supporters are never routed. Sermon 133

They were well-pleased to be with those who stay behind. A seal was set on their hearts so they understand not. **9:87**

We praise God for the help He has given us in carrying out His obedience and in preventing us from disobedience. We ask Him to complete His favors to us and to make us hold on to His rope. We bear witness that Muhammad, peace and the mercy of God be upon him, is His *servant* (Q17:1), and His *Messenger.* (Q3:101) He entered every hardship in search of God's pleasure and endured for its sake every grief. His near relations changed themselves for him. Those who were remote from him in relationship, united against him. Sermon 194

But the Messenger and those who believed with him struggled with their wealth and their lives. Those, for them are good deeds. Those, they are the ones who will prosper. **9:88**
God prepared for them Gardens beneath which rivers run, ones who will dwell in them forever. That is the winning of the sublime triumph. **9:89**
The ones who make excuses drew near from among the nomads that permission be given them. They sat back, those who lied against God and His Messenger. There will light on those who were ungrateful among them a painful punishment. **9:90**

I bear witness that *Muhammad* (Q48:29), peace and the mercy of God be upon him, is His *servant* (Q17:1) and His *Prophet.* (Q7:158) He sent him for enforcement of His commands, for exhausting His pleas and for presenting warnings against eternal punishment. Sermon 82

Not on the weak nor on the sick nor on those who find nothing to spend is there fault if they were true to God and His Messenger. There is no way against the ones who are doers of good. God is Forgiving, Compassionate. **9:91**

I swear by Him Who is such that *there is no god, but He* (Q3:2) that I am on the path of truth and that the enemy are on the misleading path of wrong. You hear what I say. I seek God's forgiveness for myself and for you. Sermon 197

Nor on those who when they approached ***you*** *that* ***you*** *would find mounts to carry them,* ***you*** *had said: I find not what will carry you. So, they turned away while their eyes overflow with tears of grief when they find nothing for them to spend in the way of God.* **9:92**

My God, I seek **Your** protection from the hardships of the journey, from the grief of returning and from the scene of devastation of property and people. O God, **You** are the companion in the journey. **You** are One Who is left behind for protection of the family. None except **You** can join these two because one who is left behind cannot be a companion in the journey, nor one who is in company on a journey can at the same time be left behind. Sermon 46

The way of blame is only against those who ask ***you*** *permission to remain behind and they are rich. They were well-pleased to be with those who stay behind. God set a seal on their hearts so that they know not.* **9:93**

The trouble-mongers are a people whose attacks are severe. Sermon 102

They will make excuses to you when you returned to them. Say: Make no excuses. We will never believe you. Surely, God told us news about you. God and His Messenger will consider your actions. Again, you will be returned to One Who Knows the unseen and the visible. Then, He will tell you of what you had been doing. **9:94**

May my father and my mother shed their lives for you, O *Messenger of God*! (Q48:29) With your death, the process of prophethood, revelation and heavenly messages has stopped, which had not stopped at the death of other Prophets. Your position with us members of your family is so special that your grief has become a source of consolation to us as against the grief of all others. Our grief is also common in that all Muslims share it equally. Sermon 234

They will swear to you by God when you turned about to them so that you renounce them. So, renounce them. Truly, they are a disgrace. Their place of shelter will be hell, as a recompense for what they had been earning. **9:95**

The two objectives, namely Paradise and Hell, have been stretched for them up to a point beyond the reach of fear or hope. Had they been able to speak they would have become dumb to describe what they witnessed or saw. Sermon 220

They swear to you so that you will be well-pleased with them. So, while you be well-pleased with them, then, truly, God is not well-pleased with the folk, the ones who disobey. **9:96**

He who disobeys **You** does not decrease **Your** authority. Sermon 108

The nomads are stauncher in ingratitude and hypocrisy and more likely not to know the ordinances that God caused to descend to His Messenger. God is Knowing, Wise. **9:97**

Of the nomads are some who take what they spend to themselves as something owed them and await for some turn of your fortunes. Theirs will be the reprehensible turn of fortune. God is Hearing, Knowing. **9:98**

The hypocrite is a person who makes a show of faith and adopts the appearance of a Muslim. He does not hesitate in sinning, nor does he keep aloof from vice. He willfully attributes false things against *the Messenger of God* (Q48:29), peace and the mercy of God be upon him. If people knew that he was a hypocrite and a liar, they would not accept anything from him and would not confirm what he says. Sermon 210

Of the nomads are some who believe in God and the Last Day and take for himself what he spends—as an offering to God—and blessings of the Messenger that will be sent for them. No doubt these are not but an offering from them. God will cause them to enter into His mercy. Truly, God is Forgiving, Compassionate. **9:99**

I bear witness that *there is no god but God* (Q47:19), the One. I bear witness that *there is no god but God* (Q47:19), the One.... It is the means to keep Satan away. Sermon 2

As for the forerunners, the ones who take the lead among the ones who emigrate and the helpers and those who followed them with kindness, God was well-pleased with them and they were well-pleased with Him. He prepared for them Gardens beneath which rivers run, ones who will dwell in them forever, eternally. That is the winning of the sublime triumph. **9:100**

The delicacies of the Quran are about the descendants of *the Prophet* (Q7:158), peace and the mercy of God be upon him. They are the treasurers of God. When they speak, they speak the truth, but when they keep quiet, no one can speak unless they speak. The forerunner should report correctly to his people, should retain his wits and should be one of the persons of the next world, because he has come from there and would return to it. Sermon 154

From around you of the nomads are ones who are hypocrites. From among the people of the city, some grew bold in hypocrisy. ***You*** *have not known them but We know them. We will, truly, punish them two times in this world. Again, they will be returned to a tremendous punishment.* **9:101**

Do you think you can tell the time when a person goes out and no evil befall him, or can warn of the time at which, if one goes out, harm will accrue? Whoever testifies to this falsifies the Quran and becomes unmindful of God in achieving his desired objective and in warding off the undesirable. You cherish saying this, so that he who acts on what you say should praise you rather than God because, according to your misconception, you have guided him about the hour in which he would secure benefit and avoid harm. Sermon 79

Others acknowledged their impieties. They mixed actions, ones in accord with morality with others that are bad deeds. Perhaps God will turn to them in forgiveness. Truly, God is Forgiving, Compassionate. **9:102**

O God's human being! Time will deal with the survivors just as it dealt with those gone by. The time that has passed will not return. Whatever there is in it will not stay forever. Its later deeds are the same as the former ones. Its troubles try to excel one another. Its banners follow each other. It is as though you are attached to the last day that is driving you as rapidly as are driven the she-camels which are dry for seven months. He who busies himself with things other than improvement of his own self becomes perplexed in darkness and entangled in ruination. His evil spirits immerse him deep in vices and make his bad actions appear handsome. Paradise is the end of those who are forward in good acts. Hell is the end of those who commit excesses. Sermon 157

Take charity from their wealth to purify them and make them pure with it. Invoke blessings for them. Truly, **your** *entreaties will bring a sense of comfort and rest to them. God is Hearing, Knowing.* **9:103**

This is the thing against which God has protected His creatures who are believers by means of prayers, alms-giving and suffering the hardship of fasting in the days in which it has been made obligatory in order to give their limbs peacefulness, to cast fear in their eyes, to make their spirits humble, to give their hearts humility and to remove haughtiness from them. Sermon 192

Know they not that God is He Who accepts remorse from His servants and takes charities and that God, He is The Accepter of Repentance, The Compassionate? **9:104**

God may shower mercy on him who repents, gives up sins and hastens in performing good acts before his death. Sermon 143

Say: Act! God will consider your actions and so will His Messenger and the ones who believe. You will be returned to Him, One Who Knows of the unseen and the visible. Then, He will tell you what you had been doing. **9:105**

With *the Prophet* (Q7:158), peace and the mercy of God be upon him, God exhausted the series of Prophets and ended the revelation. He then fought for Him those who were turning away from Him and were equating others with Him. Sermon 133

There are others, ones who are waiting in suspense for the command of God. Either He will punish them or He will turn to them in forgiveness. God is Knowing, Wise. **9:106**

One who has been through the thick and thin of life finds excuses that prevent him from the commands and prohibitions of God. He disregards them, despite his ability to succumb to excuses. He follows the commands of God. Yet, one who has no restraints of religion seizes the opportunity and accepts the excuses for not following the commands of God. Sermon 41

Mention those who took to themselves places of prostration by injuring and in ingratitude and separating and dividing between the ones who believe and as a stalking place for whoever warred against God and His Messenger before. They will, certainly, swear that: We wanted nothing but the fairer. God bears witness that they are, truly, ones who lie. **9:107**

Where are the minds which seek light from the lamps of guidance and the eyes which look at minarets of God-consciousness? Where are the hearts dedicated to God and devoted to the obedience of God? Sermon 144

Stand not up in it ever! A place of prostration that was founded from the first day on God-consciousness is more rightful that ***you*** *have stood up in it. In it are men who love to cleanse themselves. God loves the ones who cleanse themselves.* **9:108**

Is one who founded his structure on the God-consciousness of God and His contentment better than he who founded his structure on the brink of a crumbling, tottering bank of a river so that it tumbled with him into the fire of hell? God guides not the folk, the ones who are unjust! **9:109**

The structure they built will cease not the skepticism in their hearts until their hearts are cut asunder. God is Knowing, Wise. **9:110**

By God, certainly it is reality not play, truth not falsehood. It is none other than death. Its caller is making himself heard and its driver is making haste. The majority of the people should not deceive you. You have seen those who lived before you, amassed wealth, feared poverty and felt safe from its evil consequences, the longevity of desires and the apparent distance from death. How, then death overtook them, turned them out of their homelands and took them out of their places of safety. They were borne on coffins. People were busy about them one after another, carrying them on their shoulders and supporting them with their hands. Did you not witness those who engaged in long-reaching desires, built strong buildings, amassed much wealth, but their houses turned into graves and whatever they had collected turned into ruin? Their property devolved on the successors and their spouses on those who came after them. They cannot now add to their good acts, nor invoke God's mercy in respect of evil acts. Therefore, whoever makes his heart habituated to God-consciousness achieves a forward position. His action is successful. Sermon 132

Truly, God bought from the ones who believe themselves and their properties. For them is the Garden! They fight in the way of God so they kill and are slain. It is a promise rightfully on Him in the Torah and the Gospel and the Quran. Who is more true to His compact than God? Then, rejoice in the good tidings of the bargain that you made in trading with Him. That, it is the winning the sublime triumph **9:111**

for the repentant worshippers, the ones who praise, the ones who are inclined to fasting, the ones who bow down, the ones who prostrate themselves, the ones who command that which is honorable and the ones who prohibit that which is unlawful, and the ones who guard the ordinances of God, and give ***you*** *good tidings to the ones who believe!* **9 112**

It had not been for the Prophet and those who believed to ask for forgiveness for ones who are polytheists—even if they had been imbued with kinship—after it became clear to them that they are the Companions of Hellfire. **9:113**

Whoever persuades people to obey the orders of God provides strength to the believers. Whoever dissuades them from vices and sins humiliates the unbelievers. Whoever struggles on all occasions discharges all his obligations. Whoever detests the vicious only for the sake of God, then God will take revenge on his enemies and will be pleased with Him on the Day of Judgment. Saying 30

Had not been Abraham asking for forgiveness for his father only because of a promise he had promised him? Then, when it became clear to him that, truly, he was an enemy to God, he cleared himself from him. Truly, Abraham was sympathetic and forbearing. **9:114**
God would not have been causing a folk to go astray after He guided them until He makes manifest to them of what they should be God-conscious. Truly, God is Knowing of everything. **9:115**

Hasten towards good actions and dread the suddenness of death.... Hope can be only for that which is to come, while there is only disappointment about that which is passed. *So, Be God-conscious as it is His right that He should be feared and die not but that you be ones who submit to the One God.* (Q3:102) Sermon 113

Truly, God, to Him belongs the dominion of the heavens and the earth. He gives life and He causes to die. There is not for you other than God, either a protector or a helper. **9:116**

Praise belongs to God (Q1:2) Who is above all similarity to creatures, is above the words of describers Who displays the wonders of His management for the on-lookers, is hidden from the imagination of thinkers by virtue of the greatness of His glory, has knowledge without acquiring it by adding to it or drawing it from someone, and Who is the ordainer of all matters without reflecting or thinking. He is such that gloom does not concern Him, nor does He seek light from brightness. Night does not overtake Him, nor does the day pass over Him so as to affect Him in any manner. His comprehension of things is not through eyes. His knowledge is not dependent on being informed. God deputized *the Prophet* (Q7:158), peace and the mercy of God be upon him, with light and accorded him the highest precedence in selection. Through him God united those who were divided, overpowered the powerful, overcame difficulties and leveled rugged ground and, thus, removed misguidance from right and left. Sermon 213

Certainly, God turned towards the Prophet and the ones who emigrate and the helpers who followed him in the hour of adversity after the hearts of a group of people were about to swerve among them. Again, He turned towards them. Truly, He is Gentle, Compassionate. **9:117**

When God had observed our truth, He sent ignominy to our foe and sent His help to us until Islam was established and grounded and resting in its place. Sermon 56

Upon the three who were left behind when the earth became narrow for them—for all its breadth—and their souls became narrow for them and they thought that there was no shelter from God, but in Him, again, He turns to them in forgiveness so that they would turn towards Him. Truly, God, He is The Accepter of Repentance, The Compassionate. **9:118**

We bear witness that *there is no god, but He.* (Q3:2) Sermon 100

O those who believed! Be God-conscious and be with the ones who are sincere. **9:119**

One of the firm decisions of God in the Wise Reminder (Quran), upon which He bestows reward or gives punishment and through which He likes or dislikes, is that it will not benefit a person, even though he exerts himself and acts sincerely, if he leaves this world to meet God with one of these acts without repenting, namely that he believed in a partner with God during his obligatory worship or appeased his own anger by killing an individual or spoke about acts committed by others or sought fulfillment of his needs from people by introducing an innovation in his religion or met people with a double face or moved among them with a double tongue. Understand this because an illustration is a guide for its like. Sermon 153

It had not been for the people of the city and among the nomads around them to stay behind from the Messenger of God nor prefer themselves more than himself. That is because they were neither lit on by thirst nor fatigue nor emptiness in the way of God nor tread they any treading on any ground—enraging the ones who are ungrateful—nor glean any gleaning of ground against the enemy but as an action in accord with morality written down for them. Truly, God wastes not the compensation of the ones who are doers of good. **9:120**

Nor spend they contributions—be they small or great—nor cross they over a valley, but it was written down for them that God will give recompense to them for the fairer of what they had been doing. **9:121**

Know that you have to pass over the pathway (*sirat*) where steps waver, feet slip away and there are fearful dangers at every step. O God's human being! Be God-conscious, like the fearing of a wise man whom the thought of the next world has turned him away from other matters. God-consciousness has afflicted his body with trouble and pain. His engagement in the night prayer has turned even his short sleep into awakening. Hope of eternal recompense keeps him thirsty in the day. Sermon 82

It had not been for the ones who believe to move forward collectively. If every band moved not forward of them but a section of people only, it may be that they become learned in the way of life and that they warn their folk when they return to them so that perhaps they will beware? **9:122**

Today will depart with all that it has. Tomorrow will come in its wake. It is as though everyone of you has reached that place on earth where he would be alone, namely the location of his grave. So what to say of the lonely house, the solitary place of staying and the solitary exile? It is as though the cry of the Trumpet has reached you, the Hour has overtaken you, and you have come out of your graves for the passing of judgment. The curtains of falsehood have been removed from you. Your excuses have become weak. The truth about you has been proven. All your matters have proceeded to their consequences. Therefore, you should now take counsel from examples, learn lessons from vicissitudes and take advantage of the warners. Sermon 157

O those who have believed! Fight the ones who are close to you of the ones who are ungrateful. Let them find harshness in you. Know that God is with the ones who are God-conscious. **9:123**

Be aware! I called you insistently to fight these people night and day, secretly and openly, and exhorted you to attack them before they attacked you, because by God, no people have been attacked in the hearts of their houses, but they suffered disgrace. Sermon 27

Whenever there was caused to descend a Chapter of the Quran, some of them say: Which of you had this increased in belief? As for those who believed, it increased them in belief and they rejoice at the good tidings. **9:124**

But as for those who, in their hearts, is a sickness, it increased disgrace to their disgrace and they died while they are the ones who are ungrateful. **9:125**

At that time, there will remain no house or tent, but oppressors would inflict it with grief and inject sickness in it. On that day, no one in the sky will listen to their excuse and no one on the earth will come to their help. Sermon 158

Consider they not that they are tried one time or two times a year? Again, they neither repent nor they recollect. **9:126**
whenever there was caused to descend a Chapter of the Quran, some looked at some others saying: Is anyone seeing you? Again, they took flight. God turned away from their hearts because they are a folk who understand not. **9:127**

It is He Who has furnished illustrations and Who has timed for you your lives. He has given you covering of dress. He has scattered a livelihood for you. He has surrounded you with His knowledge. He has ordained rewards. He has bestowed upon you vast bounties and extensive gifts. He has warned you through far reaching arguments. He has counted you by numbers. He has fixed for you an age to live in this place of testing and house of instruction. You are on a test in this world and have to render an account regarding it. Sermon 82

Certainly, there drew near to you a Messenger from among yourselves. It was grievous to him that you fell into misfortune. He is anxious for you and to the ones who believe, gentle, compassionate. **9:128**

There is no doubt that God sent down *the Prophet* (Q7:158), peace and the mercy of God be upon him, as a guide with an eloquent Book and a standing command. No one will be ruined by it except one who ruins himself. Certainly, only doubtful innovations cause ruin except those from which God may protect. In God's authority lies the safety of your affairs. Therefore, render Him such obedience as is neither blameworthy nor insincere. By God, you must do so otherwise God will take away from you the power of Islam and will never thereafter return it to you until it reverts to others. Sermon 169

But if they turned away, say: God is enough for me. There is no god but He. In Him I put my trust. He is the Lord of the Sublime Throne. **9:129**

I bear witness that *there is no god but God* (Q47:19), the One. He has no like. Sermon 2

Chapter 10: Jonah (Yunūs)

Alif Lam Ra. **10:1**
These are the signs of the wise Book. Had it been for humanity to wonder that We revealed to a man from among them that: Warn humanity and give **you** *good tidings to those who believed so that they will have a sound footing with their Lord? The ones who are ungrateful said: Truly, this is one who is a clear sorcerer.* **10:2**

The Book of God is among you. It speaks. Its tongue does not falter. It is a house whose pillars do not fall down. It is a power whose supporters are never defeated. Sermon 132

Truly, your Lord is God Who created the heavens and the earth in six days. Again, He turned Himself to the Throne managing the command. There is no intercessor but after His permission. That is God, your Lord, so worship Him alone. Will you not, then, recollect? **10:3**
To Him is your return, altogether. The promise of God is true. It is He Who begins the creation. Again, He will cause it to return so that He may give recompense to those who believed and did as

the ones in accord with morality with equity. Those who are ungrateful, for them is a drink of scalding water and a painful punishment because they had been ungrateful. **10:4**

We bear witness that *there is no god, but He.* (Q3:2) Sermon 100

It is He Who made the sun an illumination and the moon as a light and ordained its mansions so that you would know the number of the years and the reckoning. God created that only in Truth. He explains distinctly the signs for a folk who know. **10:5**

When Almighty God created the openings of the atmosphere, the expanse of firmament and strata of winds, He flowed into it water whose waves were stormy and whose surges leapt one over the other. He loaded it on dashing wind and breaking typhoons, ordered them to shed it back as rain, gave the wind control over the vigor of the rain, and acquainted it with its limitations. The wind blew under it while water flowed furiously over it. Sermon 1

Truly, in the alternation of the nighttime and the daytime and whatever God has created in the heavens and the earth are signs for a folk who are God-conscious. **10:6**

He made the sun the bright indication for its day. He made the moon the gloomy indication for night. He put them in motion in their orbits and ordained their pace of movement in the stages of their paths in order to distinguish with their help between night and day and in order that the reckoning of years and calculations may be known by their ... movements. Sermon 91

Truly, those who hope not for their meeting with Us, but were well-pleased with this present life and were secured in it, those, they are ones who are heedless of Our signs. **10:7**

Certainly, this world is a dirty watering place and a muddy source of drinking. Its appearance is attractive, yet its inside is destructive. It is a deception, a vanishing reflection and a bent pillar. When its despiser begins to like it, and he who is not acquainted with it feels satisfied with it, then it jumps for joy, entraps him in its trap, makes him the target of its arrows and puts round his neck the rope of death taking him to the narrow grave and fearful abode in order to show him his place of stay and the recompense of his acts. This goes on from generation to generation. Neither death stops from cutting them asunder, nor do the survivors keep aloof from committing sins. Sermon 82

Those, their place of shelter will be the fire because of what they had been earning. **10:8**

Everyone of them is ... alone although they are a group. They are strangers, even though friends. They are unaware of morning after a night and of evening after a day. The night or the day when they departed has become ever existent for them. They found the dangers of their place of stay more serious than they had apprehended. They witnessed that its signs were greater than they had guessed. Sermon 220

Truly, those who believed and did as the ones in accord with morality, their Lord will guide them in their belief. Rivers will run beneath them in Gardens of Bliss. **10:9**

Among the proofs of His creation is the creation of the skies which are fastened without pillars and stand without support. He called them. They responded obediently and humbly without being lazy or loathsome. If they had not acknowledged His Godhead and obeyed Him, He would not have made them the place for His throne, the abode of His angels and the destination: *To Him Words of what is good rise and He exalts an action in accord with morality* ... (Q35:10) of the creatures. Sermon 182

They will be calling out from there: Glory be to ***You****, O God! Their greetings in it will be: Peace! The last of their calling out will be that: The Praise belongs to God the Lord of the worlds!* **10:10**

Praise belongs to God (Q1:2) Who established Islam and made it easy for those who approach it and gave strength to its columns against any one who tries to overpower it. So God made it a source of peace for him who clings to it, safety for him who enters it, argument for him who speaks about it, witness for him who fights with its help, light for him who seeks light from it, understanding for him who provides it, sagacity for him who exerts, a sign of guidance for him who perceives, sight for him who resolves, a lesson for him who seeks advice, salvation for him who testifies, confidence for him who trusts, pleasure for him who entrusts and a shield for him who endures. It is the brightest of all paths, the clearest of all passages. Sermon 106

If God is to quicken the worst for humanity, as they would desire to hasten for the good, their term would be decided. But We forsake those who hope not for the meeting with Us, wandering unwilling to see in their defiance. **10:11**
When harm afflicted the human being, he calls to Us on his side or as one who sits at home or as one who is standing up. But when We removed his harm from him, he passed by as if he had never been calling to Us for harm that afflicted him. Thus, made to appear pleasing to the ones who are excessive is what they had been doing. **10:12**
Certainly, We caused to perish generations before you when they did wrong while their Messengers drew near with the clear portents, but they had not been such as to believe. Thus, We give recompense to the folk, the ones who sin. **10:13**

The appearance of this world is ... attractive while its interior is destructive. It is a deception, a vanishing reflection and a bent pillar. When its despiser begins to like it and he who is not acquainted with it feels satisfied with it, then it jumps for joy, entraps him in its trap, makes him the target of its arrows and puts round his neck the rope of death taking him to the narrow grave and fearful abode in order to show him his place of stay and the recompense of his acts. This goes on from generation to generation. Neither death stops from cutting them asunder, nor do the survivors keep aloof from committing sins. Sermon 82

Again, We made you viceregents on the earth after them that We look on how you would do. **10:14**

The riser has risen. The sparkler has sparkled. The appearer has appeared. The curved has been straightened. God has replaced one people with another and one day with another. We awaited these changes as the famine-stricken await the rain. Certainly, the leaders are the viceregents of God over His creatures. They guide the creatures to knowing God. No one will enter Paradise except him who knows them and knows Him. No one will enter Hell except him who denies them and denies Him. Sermon 152

When are recounted to them Our signs, clear portents, those who hope not for their meeting with Us said: Bring us a Recitation other than this or substitute it. Say: It be not possible for me to substitute it of my own accord (self). I follow nothing but what is revealed to me. Truly, I fear if I rebelled against my Lord a punishment on the tremendous Day. **10:15**
Say: If God willed, I would not have related it to you nor would He have caused you to recognize

it. Surely, I lingered in expectation among you a lifetime before this. Will you not, then, be reasonable? **10:16**

Go ahead with the remembrance of God, for it is the best remembrance. Long for that which He has promised to the pious, for His promise is the most true promise. Tread the course of *the Prophet* (Q7:158), peace and the mercy of God be upon him, for it is the most distinguished course. Follow his *sunna*, for it is the most right of all behaviors. Learn the Quran, for it is the fairest of discourses. Understand it thoroughly, for it is the best blossoming of hearts. Seek cure with its light, for it is the cure for hearts. Recite it beautifully, for it is the most beautiful narration. Certainly, a scholar who acts not according to his knowledge is like the off-headed ignorant who does not find relief from his ignorance, but the plea of God is greater on the learned and grief more incumbent. He is more blameworthy before God. Sermon 110

So, who did greater wrong than he who devised a lie against God or denied His signs? Truly, the ones who sin will not prosper. **10:17**

Know that if you had followed him who was calling you to guidance, he would have made you tread the ways of *the Prophet* (Q7:158), peace and the mercy of God be upon him. Then you would have been spared the difficulties of misguidance. You would have thrown away the crushing burden from your necks. Sermon 166

They worship other than God things that injure them not, nor profit them. They say: These are our intercessors with God. Say: Are you telling God of what He knows not in the heavens nor in and on the earth? Glory be to Him and exalted is He above partners they ascribe. **10:18**

When a problem is put before anyone of them, he passes judgment on it from his imagination. When exactly the same problem is placed before another of them, he passes an opposite verdict. Then these judges go to the chief, who had appointed them, and he confirms all the verdicts, although their God is One and the same, their Prophet, peace and the mercy of God be upon him, is one and the same, their Book (the Quran) is one and the same. Sermon 18

Humanity had not been but one community, but, then, they became at variance. If it were not for a Word that preceded from **your** *Lord, it would be decided between them immediately about what they are at variance in it.* **10:19**

Know that the Quran is an interceder and its intercession will be accepted. It is a speaker who bears witness. For whoever the Quran intercedes on the Day of Judgment, its intercession for him would be accepted. He about whom the Quran speaks ill on the Day of Judgment shall testify to it. On the Day of Judgment, an announcer will announce: Be aware! Every sower of a crop is in distress except the sowers of the Quran. Therefore, you should be among the sowers of the Quran and its followers. Make it your guide towards God. Seek its advice for yourselves, do not trust your views against it and regard your desires in the matter of the Quran as deceitful. Sermon 176

They say: Why was a sign not caused to descend from his Lord? Say: Truly, the unseen belongs only to God. So, wait awhile. Truly, I am with you of the ones who are waiting awhile. **10:20**

People did not take light from the lights of his wisdom, nor did they produce flame from the flint of sparkling knowledge. Sermon 108

When We caused humanity to experience mercy after tribulation afflicted them, that is when they conspired against Our signs. Say: God is Swifter in planning. Truly, Our Messengers write down what you plan. **10:21**

He has arranged the depressions and elevations of the openings of the sky. He has joined the breadths of its breaches and has joined them with one another. He has made easy the approach to its heights for those angels who come down with His commands and those angels who go up with the deeds of the creatures. Sermon 91

He it is Who sets you in motion through dry land and the sea until when you had been in boats and they ran them with the good wind and they were glad in it. A tempest wind drew near them. Waves drew near from every place, and they thought that they were enclosed by it. They called to God, ones who are sincere and devoted in their way of life to Him saying: If ***You*** *were to rescue us from this, we will, certainly, be of the ones who are thankful.* **10:22**

When mischief comes, it confuses right with wrong. When it is cleared away, it leaves a warning. It cannot be known at the time of approach, but is recognized at the time of return. It blows like the blowing of winds, striking some cities and missing others. Sermon 93

But when He rescued them, that is when they are insolent in and on the earth without right. O humanity, your insolence is only against yourselves, an enjoyment of this present life. Again, to Us is your return. Then, We will tell you what you had been doing. **10:23**

You should know that a person is satiated and wearied with everything except life, because he does not find for himself any pleasure in death. It is life for a dead heart, sight for the blind eye, hearing for the deaf ear, quenching for the thirsty, and it contains complete sufficiency and safety. Sermon 133

The parable of this present life is but like water that We caused to descend from heaven. It mingled with the plants of the earth—from which you eat—humanity and flocks—until when the earth took its ornaments and was decorated and its people thought that, truly, they are ones who have power over it! Our command approached it by nighttime or by daytime. Then, We made it stubble as if it flourished not yesterday. Thus, We explain distinctly the signs for a folk who reflect. **10:24**

When Almighty God created the openings of the atmosphere, the expanse of firmament and strata of winds, He flowed into it water whose waves were stormy and whose surges leapt one over the other. He loaded it on dashing wind and breaking typhoons, ordered them to shed it back as rain, gave the wind control over the vigor of the rain and acquainted it with its limitations. The wind blew under it while water flowed furiously over it. Sermon 1

God calls to the Abode of Peace and He guides whom He wills to a straight path. **10:25**

By God, I have knowledge of the conveyance of messages, fulfillment of promises and of entire expressions. We, the people of the house of *the Prophet* (Q7:158), peace and the mercy of God be upon him, possess the doors of wisdom and light of governance. Be aware that the paths of religion are one. Its highways are straight. He who follows them achieves the aim and secures the objective. Sermon 120

For those who did good is the fairer and increase. Neither will gloom come over their faces nor abasement. Those are the Companions of the Garden. They are ones who will dwell in it forever. **10:26**

God, the Almighty, has sent down a guiding Book wherein He has explained virtue and vice. You should adopt the course of virtue, whereby you will have guidance. Detach yourself from the direction of vice, so that you remain on the right way. Sermon 167

For those who earned evil deeds, the recompense of an evil deed will be its like and abasement will come over them. They will have none but God as One Who Saves from Harm. It is as if their faces were covered with a strip of the night, one in darkness. Those are the Companions of the Fire. They are ones who will dwell in it forever. **10:27**

In case you cannot avoid vanity, your vanity should be for good qualities, praiseworthy acts and admirable matters with which the dignified and noble chiefs of the Arab families distinguished themselves such as attractive manners, high thinking, respectable position and good performances. You, too, should show vanity in praiseworthy habits like the protection of the neighbor, the fulfillment of agreements, obedience to the virtuous, opposition to the haughty, extending generosity to others, abstention from rebellion, keeping aloof from bloodshed, doing justice to people, suppressing anger and avoiding trouble on the earth. You should also fear what calamities befell peoples before you on account of their evil deeds and detestable actions. Remember, during good or bad circumstances, what happened to them. Be cautious that you do not become like them. Sermon 192

On a Day We will assemble them altogether. Again, We will say to those who ascribed partners with God: Stay in your place, you and your ascribed associates. Then, We will set a space between them. Their ascribed associates would say: It had not been us that you were worshipping. **10:28**
God sufficed as a witness between you and between us. We had been of your worship certainly, ones who are heedless. **10:29**

O God's human being! Be God-conscious. Keep in view the reason why He created you. Be afraid of Him to the extent He has advised you to do. Make yourself deserve what He has promised you by having confidence in the truth of His promise and entertaining fear of the Day of Judgment. Sermon 82

There every soul will be tried for what it has did in the past. They would be returned to God, their Defender, The Truth. From them will go astray what they had been devising. **10:30**

It is as though you too have gone where they have gone, the same sleeping place has caught you and the same place has detained you. What will, then be your position when your affairs reach their end and graves are turned upside down to throw out the dead? There, every soul will be tried for what it has done in the past. *They would be returned to God, their Defender, The Truth. From them will go astray what they had been devising.* (Q10:30) Sermon 224

Say: Who provides for you from the heaven and the earth? Who controls having the ability to hear and sight? Who brings out the living from the dead and brings out the dead from the living? Who manages the command? They will, then, say: God! Say: Will you not be God-conscious? **10:31**

God will take them out from the corners of the graves, the nests of birds, the dens of beasts and the centers of death. They will hasten towards His command and run towards the place fixed for their final return, group by group, quiet, standing and arrayed in rows. They will be within God's sight and will hear every one who would call them. They will have the dress of helplessness and covering of submission and indignity. At this time contrivances will disappear. Desires will be cut. Hearts will sink quietly. Voices will be lowered. Sweat will choke the throat. Fear will increase. Ears will resound with the thundering voice of the announcer calling towards the final judgment, award of recompense, striking of punishment and paying of reward. Sermon 82

Such is God, your Lord, The Truth. What else is there after The Truth but wandering astray. Where, then, turn you away? **10:32**

God sent *the Prophet* (Q7:158), peace and the mercy of God be upon him, as a caller towards Truth and a witness over the creatures. *The Prophet* (Q7:158), peace and the mercy of God be upon him, conveyed the messages of God tirelessly and without any negligence. He fought His enemies in the cause of God unflaggingly and without pleading excuses. He is the foremost of all who practice God-consciousness and the power of perception of all those who achieve guidance. Sermon 116

Thus, was the Word of **your** *Lord realized against those who disobeyed that they will not believe.* **10:33**

God was being disobeyed. Satan was given support. Faith was forsaken. Sermon 2

Say: Are there among your ascribed associates with God anyone who begins the creation and, then, causes it to return? Say: God begins the creation. Again, He causes it to return. Then, how you are misled! **10:34**

O people who possess eyes and ears and health and wealth! Is there any place of protection, any shelter of safety, or asylum or haven, or occasion to run away or to come back to this world? *If not: How then you are misled?* (Q10:34) and whither are you averting? By what things have you been deceived? Certainly, the share of every one of you from this earth is just a piece of land equal to his own stature and size where he would lie on his cheeks covered with dust. Sermon 82

Say: Are there among your ascribed associates with God anyone who guides to The Truth? Say: God guides to The Truth. Has not He who guides to The Truth a better right to be followed than he who guides not unless he himself be guided? What is the matter with you? How you give judgment! **10:35**

I bear witness that *there is no god but God.* (Q47:19) I bear witness that *Muhammad* (Q48:29), peace and the mercy of God be upon him, is His *servant* (Q17:1), His *Prophet* (Q7:158), His chosen and His selected one. Sermon 150

Most of them follow nothing but opinion. Truly, opinion avails them not against The Truth at all. Truly, God is Knowing of what they accomplish. **10:36**

Generosity is the protector of honor. Forbearance is the bridle of the fool. Forgiveness is the levy of success. Disregard is the punishment of him who betrays. Consultation is the chief way of guidance. He who is content with his own opinion faces danger. Endurance braves calamities while impatience is a helper of the hardships of the world. The best contentment is to give up desires. Many a slavish mind is subservient to overpowering longings. Capability helps preservation of experience. Love means well-utilized relationships. Do not trust one who is grieved. Hadith 211

This Recitation had not been devised by other than God because it establishes as true what was before it and as a decisive explanation of the Book. There is no doubt in it. It is from the Lord of the worlds. **10:37**

Learn the Quran, for it is the fairest of discourses. Understand it thoroughly, for it is the best blossoming of hearts. Seek cure with its light, for it is the cure for hearts. Recite it beautifully, for it is the most beautiful narration. Certainly, a scholar who acts not according to his knowledge is like the off-headed ignorant who does not find relief from his ignorance, but the plea of God is greater on the learned and grief more incumbent. He is more blameworthy before God. Sermon 110

Or they will say: He devised it. Say: Bring a Chapter of the Quran like it and call to whomever you were able—other than God—if you had been ones who are sincere. **10:38**
Nay! They denied the knowledge that they comprehend not while approaches them not the interpretation. Thus, those who were before them denied. So, look on how had been the Ultimate End of the ones who are unjust! **10:39**

The Book of God is among you. It speaks and its tongue does not falter. It is a house whose pillars do not fall down, and a power whose supporters are never routed. Sermon 133

Of them are some who believe in it and of them are some who believe not in it. ***Your*** *Lord is greater in knowledge of the ones who make corruption.* **10:40**

Corruption has become manifest ... (Q30:41) There is no one to oppose and change it, nor anyone to dissuade from it, or desist from it. Do you, with these qualities, hope to secure abode in the purified neighborhood of God and to be regarded His staunch lovers? Alas! God cannot be deceived about His Paradise. His will cannot be secured except by His obedience. May God curse those who advise good, but they themselves avoid it, and those who desist others from evil, but they themselves act upon it. Sermon 129

If they denied ***you****, then,* ***you*** *say: For me are my actions and for you are your actions. You are free of what I do and I am free of what you do.* **10:41**

The beginning of the action of one who sees with his heart and acts with eyes is to assess whether the action will go against him or for him. If it is for him, he indulges in it, but if it is against him, he keeps away from it. For he who acts without knowledge is like one who treads without a path. His deviation from the path keeps him at a distance from his aim. He who acts according to knowledge is like him who treads the clear path. Therefore, he who can see should see whether he should proceed or return. You should, also know that the outside has a similar inside. Of whatever the outside is good, its inside too is good and whenever the outside is bad, its inside too is bad. The truthful Prophet, peace and the mercy of God be upon him, has said: God may love a person, but hate his action, and may love the action, but hate the person. You should also know that every action is like vegetation. Vegetation cannot do without water while waters are different. Where the water is good, the plant is good and its fruits are sweet, whereas where the water is bad, the plant will also be bad and its fruits will be bitter. Sermon 153

Among them are some who listen to ***you****. So, have* ***you*** *caused someone unwilling to hear, to hear if they had not been reasonable?* **10:42**
Among them are some who look on ***you****. So, have* ***you*** *guided the unwilling to see if they had not been perceiving?* **10:43**

O my God! Whoever listens to our words which are just and which seek the prosperity of religion and the worldly life and do not seek mischief, they reject after listening. He certainly turns away from **Your** support and desists from strengthening **Your** religion. We make **You** a Witness over him. **You** are the greatest of all witnesses. We make all those who inhabit **Your** earth and **Your** skies witness over him. Thereafter, **You** alone can make us needless of his support and question him for his sin. Sermon 212

Truly, God does not wrong humanity at all, but humanity does wrong itself. **10:44**

You should adhere to the Book of God because it is the strong rope, a clear light, a benefiting cure, a quenching for thirst, protection for the adherent and deliverance for the attached. It does not curve so as to need straightening and does not deflect so as to be corrected. Frequency of its repetition and its falling on ears does not make it old. Whoever speaks according to it speaks truth and whoever acts by it is forward in action. Sermon 156

On a Day He will assemble them as if they had not been lingering in expectation but an hour of the daytime. They will recognize one another among themselves. Surely, those who denied lost the meeting with God and they had not been ones who are truly guided. **10:45**

He initiated creation most initially and commenced it originally without undergoing reflection, without making use of any experiment, without innovating any movement and without experiencing any aspiration of mind. He allotted all things their times, put together their variations, gave them their properties and determined their features knowing them before creating them, realizing fully their limits and confines and appreciating their propensities and intricacies. Sermon 1

Whether We cause ***you*** *to see some of what We promise them or We call* ***you*** *to Us, then, to Us is their return. Again, God will be witness to what they accomplish.* **10:46**

We bear witness that *there is no god, but He.* (Q3:2) Sermon 100

Every community has its Messenger. So, then, when their Messenger drew near, it would be decided between them with equity. They, they will not be wronged. **10:47**
They say: When is this promise if you had been ones who are sincere? **10:48**
Say: I control not either hurt or profit for myself, but what God willed. To every community there is a term. When their term draws near, neither will they delay it an hour nor will they press it forward. **10:49**

God deputized *the Prophet* (Q7:158), peace and the mercy of God be upon him, after a gap from the previous Prophets when there was much talk among the people. With him God exhausted the series of Prophets and ended the revelation. He then fought for Him those who were turning away from Him and were equating others with Him. Sermon 133

Say: Considered you that if His punishment approached you at nighttime or at daytime, for which portion would the ones who sin be ones who seek to hasten? **10:50**

This world is a place of destruction, tribulations, changes and lessons. As for destruction, the time has its bow pressed for readiness and its dart does not go amiss. Its wound does not heal. It afflicts the living with death, the healthy with ailment and the safe with distress. It is an eater who is not satisfied and a drinker whose thirst is never quenched. As for tribulation, a person collects what he does not eat and builds wherein he does not live. Then he goes out to God without carrying the wealth or shifting the building. Sermon 114

Again, when it falls on you, believed you in it? Now? While you had been seeking to hasten it? **10:51**

Certainly, nothing is viler than evil, except its punishment. Nothing is better than good, except its reward. In this world, everything that is heard is better than what is seen, while everything of the next world that is seen is better than what is heard. You should satisfy yourself by hearing rather than seeing and by the news of the unknown. You should know that what is little in this world but much in the next is better than what is much in this world but little in the next. In how many cases little is profitable while much causes loss. As for its changes, you see a pitiable person becoming enviable and an enviable person becoming pitiable. This is because the wealth has gone and misfortune has come to him. As for its lessons, a person reaches near realization of his desires when suddenly the approach of his death cuts them. Then neither the desire is achieved, nor the desirer spared. Glory be to God! How deceitful are its pleasures. How thirst-rousing its quenching. How sunny its shade. That which approaches (i.e., death) cannot be sent back. He who goes away does not return. Glory be to God! How near is the living to the dead because he will meet him soon. How far is the dead from the living because he has gone away from him. Sermon 114

Again, it would be said to those who did wrong: Experience the infinite punishment! Will you be given recompense but for what you had been earning? **10:52**

O God's human being! Where are those who were allowed long ages to live? They enjoyed bounty. They were taught. They learned. They were given time. They passed it in vain. They were kept healthy. They forgot their duty. They were allowed a long period of life, were handsomely provided for, were warned of grievous punishment and were promised great rewards. You should avoid sins that lead to destruction and vices that attract the wrath of God. Sermon 82

They ask **you** *to be told: Is it true? Say: Yes! By my Lord it is The Truth and you are not ones who frustrate Him.* **10:53**

If there would be for every person who did wrong whatever is in or on the earth, he would, certainly, offer it for his ransom. They would keep secret their self-reproach when they considered the punishment. But it will be decided between them with equity. They, they will not be wronged. **10:54**

He knows the secrets of those who conceal them, the secret conversation of those who engage in it, the inner feelings of those who indulge in guesses, the established certainties, the furtive glances of the eyes, the inner contents of hearts and depths of the unknown. He also knows what can be heard only by bending the holes of the ears, the summer resorts of ants and winter abodes of the insects, resounding of the cries of wailing women and the sound of steps. Sermon 91

No doubt to God belongs all that is in the heavens and the earth. No doubt the promise of God is true, but most of them know not. **10:55**

Praise belongs to God (Q1:2) Who is above all similarity to creatures, is above the words of describers Who displays the wonders of His management for the onlookers, is hidden from the imagination of thinkers by virtue of the greatness of His glory, has knowledge without acquiring it by adding to it or drawing it from someone, and Who is the ordainer of all matters without reflecting or thinking. He is such that gloom does not concern Him, nor does He seek light from brightness. Night does not overtake Him, nor does the day pass over Him so as to affect Him in any manner. His comprehension of things is not through eyes. His knowledge is not dependent on being informed. Sermon 213

It is He Who gives life and causes to die and to Him you will return. **10:56**

He is the Giver of all reward and distinction, and Dispeller of all calamities and hardships. Sermon 82

O humanity! Surely, an admonishment drew near you from your Lord and a healing for what is in the breasts and a guidance and mercy for ones who believe. **10:57**

O my God! I seek **Your** protection from becoming destitute despite **Your** riches, from being misguided despite **Your** guidance, from being molested in **Your** realm and from being humiliated while authority rests with **You.** O my God! Let my spirit be the first of those good objects that **You** take from me and the first trust out of **Your** favors held in trust with me. Sermon 215

Say: In the grace of God and in His mercy therein let them be glad. That is better than what they gather. **10:58**

Praise belongs to God (Q1:2) from Whose mercy no one loses hope, from Whose bounty no one is deprived, from Whose forgiveness no one is disappointed and for Whose worship no one is too high. His mercy never ceases and His bounty never ceases. Sermon 45

Say: Considered you from what God caused to descend for you of provision and that you made some of it unlawful and some lawful? Say: Gave God permission to you or devise you against God? **10:59**

Certainly, God-consciousness is the key to guidance, provision for the next world, freedom from every servantry and deliverance from all ruin. With its help, the seeker succeeds and he who makes for safety escapes and achieves his aims. Sermon 229

What is the opinion of those who devise a lie against God on the Day of Resurrection? Truly, God is Possessor of Grace to humanity, but most of them give not thanks. **10:60**

Neither have ***you*** *been on any matter nor have* ***you*** *recounted from the Recitation nor are you doing any action but We had been ones who bear witness over you when you press on it. Nothing escapes from* ***your*** *Lord of the weight of an atom in or on the earth nor in the heaven nor what is smaller than that nor what is greater than that but it is in a clear Book.* **10:61**

They are wrong who liken **You** to their idols, dress **You** with apparel of the creatures by their imagination, attribute to **You** parts of body by their own thinking and consider **You** after the creatures of various types through the working of their intelligence. I bear witness that whoever equated **You** with anything out of **Your** creation took a partner for **You.** Whoever takes a partner for **You** is ungrateful according to what is stated in **Your** unambiguous verses and indicated by the evidence of **Your** clear arguments. I also bear witness that **You** are that God Who cannot be confined in the fetters of intelligence so as to admit change of condition by entering its imagination, nor in the shackles of the mind so as to become limited and an object of alterations. Sermon 91

No doubt with the faithful friends of God there will be neither fear in them nor will they feel remorse. **10:62**

Those who believed and had been God-conscious, **10:63**
for them are good tidings in this present life and in the world to come. There is no substitution of the Words of God. That, it is the winning the sublime triumph. **10:64**

Recite (the Quran) beautifully, for it is the most beautiful narration. Certainly, a scholar who acts not according to his knowledge is like the off-headed ignorant who does not find relief from his ignorance, but the plea of God is greater on the learned and grief more incumbent. He is more blameworthy before God. Sermon 110

Let not their saying dishearten ***you****. Truly, all great glory belongs to God. He is The Hearing, The Knowing.* **10:65**

Praise belongs to God (Q1:2) Who made me such that I have not died, nor am I sick, nor have my veins been infected with disease, nor have I been hauled up for my evil acts, nor am I without progeny, nor have I forsaken my religion, nor do I disbelieve in my Lord, nor do I feel strangeness with my faith, nor is my intelligence affected, nor have I been punished with the punishment of peoples before me. I am a servant in **Your** possession. I have been guilty of excesses over myself. **You** have exhausted **Your** pleas over me and I have no plea before **You**. I have no power to take except what **You** give me. I cannot evade except what **You** save me from. Sermon 215

No doubt to God belongs whatever is in the heavens and whatever is in and on the earth. Follow not those who call to ascribed associates other than God. They follow nothing but opinion and they do nothing but guess. **10:66**

God deputized *the Prophet* (Q7:158), peace and the mercy of God be upon him, with light, and accorded him the highest precedence in selection. Through him God united those who were divided, overpowered the powerful, overcame difficulties and leveled rugged ground, and thus removed misguidance from right and left. Sermon 213

It is He Who made the nighttime for you so that you rest in it and the daytime for one who perceives. Truly, in this are signs for a folk who hear. **10:67**

He created the earth and suspended it without being busy, retained it without support, made it stand without legs, raised it without pillars, protected it against bendings and curvings and defended it against crumbling and splitting into parts. He fixed mountains on it like stumps, solidified its rocks, caused its streams to flow and opened wide its valleys. Whatever He made did not suffer from any frailty. Whatever He strengthened did not show any weakness. Sermon 186

They said God took to Himself a son. Glory be to Him. He is Sufficient. To Him is whatever is in the heavens and in and on the earth. With you there is no authority for this. Say you against God what you know not? **10:68**
Say: Truly, those who devise lies against God, they will not prosper, **10:69**
only an enjoyment in the present! Again, to Us will be their return. Again, We will cause them to experience the severe punishment because they had been ungrateful. **10:70**

O God's human being! Secure light from the flame of lamps of the preacher who follows what he preaches. Draw water from the spring which has been cleaned of dirt. O God's human being! Do not rely on your ignorance. Do not be obedient to your desires, because he who stays at this place is like one who stays on the brink of a bank undermined by water carrying ruin on his back from one portion to the other following his opinion which he changes one after the other. He wants to make adhere what cannot adhere and to bring together what cannot keep together. Be God-conscious and do not place your complaints before him who cannot redress your grievance, nor undo with his opinion what has been made obligatory for you. Sermon 105

Recount to them the tidings of Noah when he said to his folk: O my folk! If my station had been troublesome to you and my reminding you of the signs of God, then, in God I put my trust. So, summon up your affair along with your ascribed associates. Again, there be no cause for doubt in your affair. Again, decide against me and give me no respite. **10:71**
Then, if you turned away, I asked you not for any compensation. My compensation is with God. I was commanded that I be of the ones who submit to God. **10:72**
Then, they denied him, so We delivered him and some with him on the boat. We made them the viceregents while We drowned those who denied Our signs. Then, look on how had been the Ultimate End of the ones who are warned! **10:73**
Again, We raised up Messengers after him to their folk. They drew near them with the clear portents. But they had not been believing in what they had denied before of it. Thus, We set a seal on the hearts of the ones who exceed the limits. **10:74**
Again, We raised up after them Moses and Aaron to Pharaoh and his Council with Our signs. Then, they grew arrogant, and they had been a folk, ones who sin. **10:75**
So, when The Truth drew near them from Us, they said: Truly, this is clear sorcery! **10:76**
Moses said: Say you this about The Truth when it drew near you? Is this sorcery? The ones who are sorcerers will not prosper. **10:77**
They said: Have **you** *drawn near to us to turn us from what we found our fathers on so that the domination on the earth might be for you two? We are not ones who believe in both of you.* **10:78**
Pharaoh said: Bring to me every one who is a knowing sorcerer. **10:79**
When the ones who are sorcerers drew near, Moses said to them: Cast down with ones who cast.
10:80
Then, when they cast Moses said: What you brought about is sorcery. Truly, God will render it untrue. Truly, God makes not right the actions of the ones who make corruption. **10:81**
God will verify The Truth by His Words, although the ones who sin disliked it much! **10:82**
But none believed Moses but the offspring of his folk because of the fear of Pharaoh and his Council that he persecute them. Truly, Pharaoh was one who exalted himself on the earth. He was, truly, of the ones who are excessive. **10:83**
Moses said: O my folk! If you had been believing in God, then, put your trust in Him, if you had been ones who submit to God. **10:84**
Then, they said: We put our trust in God. Our Lord! Make us not a temptation for the folk, the ones who are unjust. **10:85**
Deliver us by **Your** *Mercy from the folk, the ones who are ungrateful.* **10:86**
We revealed to Moses and his brother: Take as your dwellings, houses for your folk in Egypt. Make your houses a direction of formal prayer. Perform the formal prayer. Give good tidings to the ones who believe. **10:87**
Moses said: Our Lord! **You** *had given to Pharaoh and his Council adornment and wealth in this present life. Our Lord! Cause them to go astray from* **Your** *way. Our Lord! Obliterate their wealth and harden their hearts so that they believe not until they consider the painful punishment.* **10:88**
He said: Surely, you both were answered, so go straight both of you and follow not the way of those who know not. **10:89**

We brought the Children of Jacob over the sea. Pharaoh and his army pursued them in insolence and acting impulsively until when, overtaken by drowning, he said: I believed that there is no god but He in Whom the Children of Jacob believed and I am among ones who submit to God. **10:90**
It was said: Now, surely, ***you*** *rebelled before and had been among the ones who make corruption.* **10:91**
On this day We will deliver ***you*** *with* ***your*** *physical form that* ***you*** *be a sign to whoever is after* ***you****. Truly, many among humanity are ones who are heedless of Our signs.* **10:92**
Certainly, We placed the Children of Jacob in a sound place of settlement and provided them with what is good. They are not at variance until the knowledge drew near them. Truly, ***your*** *Lord will decree between them on the Day of Resurrection about what they had been at variance in it.* **10:93**
***

So, *if* ***you*** *had been in uncertainty about what We caused to descend to* ***you****, then, ask those who recited the Book before* ***you****. Certainly, The Truth drew near* ***you*** *from* ***your*** *Lord so* ***you*** *have not been among the ones who contest.* **10:94**
You *have not been among those who denied the signs of God, for, then,* ***you*** *would be among the ones who are losers.* **10:95**

Certainly, only doubtful innovations cause ruin except those from which God may protect. In God's authority lies the safety of your affairs. Therefore, render Him such obedience as is neither blameworthy nor insincere. Sermon 169

Truly, those against whom is realized through the Word of ***your*** *Lord, will not believe* **10:96**
—even if every sign drew near them—until they consider the painful punishment. **10:97**

God ... is aware of whatever is hidden in the hearts. Sermon 192

Had there been a town that believed and profited from its belief other than the folk of Jonah? When they believed, We removed from them the punishment of degradation in this present life and gave them enjoyment for a while. **10:98**
If ***your*** *Lord willed, all would have believed who are on the earth altogether. So, would* ***you*** *compel humanity against their will until they become ones who believe?* **10:99**
It would not have been for any person to believe but by the permission of God. He lays disgrace on those who are not reasonable. **10:100**

I am happy that the reasoning of God has been exhausted before them. He knows all about them. Sermon 22

Say: Look on what is in the heavens and the earth. Neither the signs nor the warning avail a folk who believe not. **10:101**

Now then truly, divine commands descend from heaven to earth like drops of rain, bringing to everyone what is destined for him, whether plenty or scarce. So if any one of you observes for his brother plenty of progeny, or of wealth, or of self, it should not be a worry for him so long as a Muslim does not commit such an act that if it is disclosed he has to lower his eyes in shame and by which low people are emboldened. He is like the gambler who expects that the first draw of his arrow would secure him gain and also cover up the previous loss. Sermon 23

So, wait they awhile but like in the days of those who passed away before them? Say: So, wait awhile. I am with you among the ones waiting awhile! **10:102**

Again, We rescue Our Messengers and those who believed. Thus, it is an obligation upon Us to deliver the ones who believe. **10:103**

You should take a lesson from the fate of the progeny of Ishmael, the children of Isaac and the children of Jacob. How similar are their affairs and how akin are their examples. In connection with the details of their division and disunity, think of the days when Kings of Persia and the Caesars of Rome had become their masters. They turned them out from the pastures of their lands, the rivers of Iraq and the fertility of the world, towards thorny forests, the passages of hot winds and hardships in livelihood. By doing this, they turned them into just herders of camels. Their houses were the worst in the world and their places of stay were the most drought-stricken. There was not one voice towards which they could turn for protection, nor any shade of affection on whose strength they could repose trust. Sermon 192

Say: O humanity! If you were in uncertainty as to my way of life, then, I will not worship those whom you worship other than God. Rather, I worship only God Who will call you to Himself. I was commanded that I be among the ones who believe. **10:104**

and that: Set ***you your*** *face to the way of life of a monotheist. Be* ***you*** *not among the ones who are polytheists.* **10:105**

O my God! We seek **Your** protection from turning away from **Your** command, or revolting against **Your** religion, or being led away by our desires instead of by guidance that comes from **You**. Sermon 215

Call not to other than God what neither profits nor hurts ***you****. If* ***you*** *were to accomplish that, truly,* ***you*** *would be among the ones who are unjust.* **10:106**

By God, he is not capable of solving the problems that come to him, nor is he fit for the position assigned to him. Whatever he does not know he does not regard as worth knowing. He does not realize that what is beyond his reach is within the reach of others. If anything is not clear to him, he keeps quiet over it, because he knows his own ignorance. Lost lives are crying against his unjust verdicts. Properties that have been wrongly disposed of are grumbling against him. Sermon 17

If God afflicts ***you*** *with harm, there is no one who removes it but He. If He wants good for* ***you****, there is no one who repels His grace. It lights on whomever He wills of His servants. He is The Forgiving, The Compassionate.* **10:107**

My ears continually caught their humming voice as they invoked God's blessing on him until we buried him in his grave. Thus, who can have greater rights with him than I during his life or after his death? Therefore, depend on your intelligence and make your intentions pure in fighting your enemy, because I swear by Him Who is such that *there is no god, but He* (Q3:2), that I am on the path of truth and that the enemy is on the misleading path of wrong. Hear what I say. I seek God's forgiveness for myself and for you. Sermon 197

Say: O humanity! Surely, The Truth drew near you from your Lord so whoever was truly guided, then, he is only truly guided for his own self. Whoever went astray, then, he only goes astray to his own loss. I am not a trustee over you. **10:108**

O God's human being! Know that your own self is a guard over you. Limbs are as watchmen and truthful vigil-keepers who preserve the record of your actions and the number of your breaths. The gloom of the dark night cannot conceal you from them, nor can closed doors hide you from them. Surely, tomorrow is close to today. Sermon 157

Follow ***you*** *what is revealed to* ***you****. Have* ***you*** *patience until God gives judgment. He is Best of the ones who judge.* **10:109**

Make obedience to God your way of life and not only your outside covering. Make it your inner habit instead of only outer routine, subtle enough to enter through your ribs up to the heart, the guide for all your affairs, the watering place for your getting down on the Day of Judgment, the interceder for the achievement of your aims, asylum for the day of your fear, the lamp of the interior of your graves, company for your long loneliness and deliverance from the troubles of your abodes. Certainly, obedience to God is a protection against encircling calamities expected dangers and the flames of burning fires. Sermon 198

Chapter 11: Hud (Hūd)

Alif Lam Ra. A Book, the signs in it were set clear. Again, they were explained distinctly from that which proceeds from the Presence of the Wise, Aware, **11:1**
that you not worship any but God. Truly, I am a warner to you from Him and a bearer of good tidings **11:2**
and that: Ask for forgiveness from your Lord. Again, repent to Him that He give you fairer enjoyment for a term that which is determined. He gives His grace to every possessor of grace. If they turn away, I fear for you the punishment of a Great Day. **11:3**

God never allowed His creation to remain without a Prophet, one deputized by Him, or a Book sent down from Him, or a binding argument, or a standing plea. These Messengers were such that they did not fear that they were few in comparison to the large numbers of their falsifiers. Among them was either a predecessor who would name the one to follow or the follower who had been introduced by the predecessor. Sermon 1

To God is your return. He is Powerful over everything. **11:4**

He is Powerful, such that when imagination shoots its arrows to comprehend the extremity of His power and the mind, making itself free of the dangers of evil thoughts, tries to find Him in the depth of His realm, and hearts long to grasp the realities of His attributes and openings of intelligence penetrate beyond description in order to secure knowledge about His Being, crossing the dark pitfalls of the unknown and concentrating towards Him, He would turn them back. They would return defeated admitting that the reality of His knowledge cannot be comprehended by such random efforts, nor can an iota of the sublimity of His Honor enter the understanding of thinkers. Sermon 91

But they fold up their breasts that they conceal themselves from Him. No doubt at the time when they cover themselves with their garments, He knows what they keep secret and what they speak openly. Truly, He is Knowing of what is in their breasts. **11:5**

He knows the secrets of those who conceal them, the secret conversation of those who engage in it, the inner feelings of those who indulge in guesses, the established certainties, the furtive glances of the eyes, the inner contents of hearts and depths of the unknown. He also knows what can be heard only by bending the holes of the ears, the summer resorts of ants and winter abodes of the insects, resounding of the cries of wailing women and the sound of steps. Sermon 91

There is no moving creature on earth but its provision is from God. He knows its appointed time and its repository. All is in a clear Book. **11:6**

O God's human being! Know that, certainly, you and all the things of this world that you have are treading on the lines of those who were before you. They were of longer ages, had more populated houses and were of more lasting traces. Their voices have become silent, their movements have become stationary, their bodies have become rotten, their houses have become empty and their traces have been obliterated. Sermon 225

It is He Who created the heavens and the earth in six days. His Throne had been upon the waters that He try you—which of you is fairer in actions. If ***you*** *were to say to them: Truly, you are ones who will be raised up after death. Those who were ungrateful would be sure to say: This is nothing but clear sorcery.* **11:7**

Praise belongs to God (Q1:2) Whose worth cannot be described by speakers, Whose bounties cannot be counted by calculators and Whose claim to obedience cannot be satisfied by those who attempt to do so Whom the height of intellectual courage cannot appreciate, and the depths of understanding cannot reach. He for Whose description no limit has been laid down, no eulogy exists, no time is ordained and no duration is fixed. He brought forth creation through His Omnipotence, dispersed winds through His Compassion and made firm the shaking earth with rocks. Sermon 1

If We postponed the punishment for them for a period of time, that which is numbered, they will, surely, say: What detains it? Certainly, the day it approaches them, there is not of that which will be turned away from them and surrounded them was what they had been ridiculing of it. **11:8**

Do you think you can tell the time when a person goes out and no evil befall him, or can warn of the time at which, if one goes out, harm will accrue? Whoever testifies to this falsifies the Quran and becomes unmindful of God in achieving his desired objective and in warding off the undesirable. You cherish saying this, so that he who acts on what you say should praise you rather than God because, according to your misconception, you have guided him about the hour in which he would secure benefit and avoid harm. Sermon 79

If We caused the human being to experience mercy from Us, then, again, We tear it out from him, truly, he is hopeless, ungrateful. **11:9**

Populated places were brightened through him when previously there was dark misguidance, overpowering ignorance and rude habits, and people regarded unlawful as lawful, humiliated the man of wisdom, passed lives when there were no prophets and died as ungrateful. Sermon 151

If We caused him to experience favor after tribulation afflicted him, he is certain to say: Evil deeds went from me! Truly, he becomes glad, boastful. **11:10**

In case you cannot avoid vanity, your vanity should be for good qualities, praiseworthy acts and admirable matters with which the dignified and noble chiefs of the Arab families distinguished themselves such as attractive manners, high thinking, respectable position and good performances. You too should show vanity in praiseworthy habits like the protection of the neighbor, the fulfillment of agreements, obedience to the virtuous, opposition to the haughty, extending generosity to others, abstention from rebellion, keeping aloof from bloodshed, doing justice to people, suppressing anger and avoiding trouble on the earth. You should also fear what calamities befell peoples before you on account of their evil deeds and detestable actions. Remember, during good or bad circumstances, what happened to them. Be cautious that you do not become like them. Sermon 192

But those who endured patiently and did as the ones in accord with morality, those, for them is forgiveness and a great compensation. **11:11**

Among the proofs of His creation is the creation of the skies which are fastened without pillars and stand without support. He called them. They responded obediently and humbly without being lazy or loathsome. If they had not acknowledged His Godhead and obeyed Him, He would not have made them the place for His throne, the abode of His angels and the destination: *To Him Words of what is good rise and He exalts an action in accord with morality* ... (Q35:10) of the creatures. Sermon 182

So, would **you** *perhaps be one who leaves some of what is revealed to* **you***? Or is* **your** *breast that which is narrowed by it because they say: Why was a treasure not caused to descend to him or an angel drew near him? Truly,* **you** *are only a warner. God is a Trustee over everything. Or they say: He devised it.* **11:12**

God deputized *the Prophet* (Q7:158), peace and the mercy of God be upon him, after a gap from the previous Prophets when there was much talk among the people. With him God exhausted the series of Prophets and ended the revelation. He then fought for Him those who were turning away from Him and were equating others with Him. Sermon 133

Say: Approach you, then, with ten chapters of the Quran like it, that which is forged, and call to whomever you were able other than God if you had been ones who are sincere. **11:13**

Know that this Quran is an adviser who never deceives, a leader who never misleads and a narrator who never speaks a lie. No one will sit beside this Quran, but when he rises, he will achieve one addition or one diminution—addition in his guidance or elimination in his spiritual blindness. You should also know that no one will need anything after guidance from the Quran and no one will be free from want before guidance from the Quran. Sermon 176

If they respond not to you, then, know that it was only caused to descend by the knowledge of God and that there is no god but He. Are you, you, then, ones who submit to God? **11:14**

I praise God, seeking completion of His Blessing, submitting to His Glory and expecting safety from committing sin. Sermon 2

Whoever had been wanting this present life and its adornment, We pay their account in full to them for their actions in it. They will not be diminished in it. **11:15**

May God have pity on you. You should, therefore, hasten towards the preparation of abodes which you have been commanded to populate and towards which you have been called and invited. Seek the completion of God's favors on you by exercising endurance in His obedience and abstention from His disobedience, because tomorrow is close to today. How fast are the hours of the day. How fast are the days in the month. How fast are the months in the years. How fast the years in a life. Sermon 188

Those are those for whom there is nothing in the world to come but fire. What they crafted here was fruitless. What they had been doing is in vain. **11:16**

Certainly, God the Almighty tries His creatures who are vain about themselves through His beloved persons who are humble in their eyes. Sermon 192

Is he, then, who had been on a clear portent from his Lord, and recounts it from Him as one who bears witness—and before it was the Book of Moses, a leader and a mercy—like them? Those believe in it. Whoever is ungrateful for it among the confederates, he is promised the fire! So, be ***you*** *not hesitant about it. Truly, it is The Truth from* ***your*** *Lord, except most of humanity believes not.* **11:17**

Whoever proceeds towards this mischief will be ruined and whoever strives for it will be annihilated. They will be biting each other during it as the wild asses bite each other in the herd. The coils of the rope will be disturbed and the face of affairs will be blinded. During it sagacity will be on the ebb, and the oppressors will have the opportunity to speak. Sermon 151

Who does greater wrong than he who devised a lie against God? Those will be presented before their Lord. The ones who bear witness will say: These are those who lied against their Lord. But the curse of God is upon the ones who are unjust— **11:18**

Be aware! The worst speech is that which is untrue. Sermon 84

they who bar from the way of God and desire in it crookedness. They, in the world to come, they are ones who disbelieve. **11:19**

I wonder—and there is no reason why I should not wonder—about the faults of these groups who have introduced alterations in their religious pleas, who do not move on the footsteps of their Prophet, nor follow the actions of the vicegerent. They do not believe in the unknown and do not avoid the evil. They act on the doubts and tread in the way of their passions. For them good is whatever they consider good, and evil is whatever they consider evil. Sermon 88

Those will not be ones who frustrate Him on the earth, nor had there been for them—other than God—any protectors. The punishment is multiplied for them. Not had they been able to have the ability to hear, nor had they been perceiving. **11:20**

Certainly, nothing is viler than evil, except its punishment. Nothing is better than good, except its reward. In this world, everything that is heard is better than what is seen, while everything of the next world that is seen is better than what is heard. You should satisfy yourself by hearing rather than seeing and by the news of the unknown. You should know that what is little in this world but much in the next is better than what is much in this world but little in the next. In how many cases little is profitable while much causes loss. Sermon 114

Those are those who lost their souls. What they had been devising had gone astray. **11:21**

Act for the day for which provisions are stored and when the intentions would be tested. If a person's own intelligence, which is present with him, does not help him, the wits of others, which are remote from him, are more unhelpful and those who are away from him even more useless. Dread the fire whose flame is severe, whose hollow is deep, whose dress is iron and whose drink is bloody pus. Be aware! The good name of a person retained by God, the Sublime, among the people is better than wealth inherited by those who would not praise Him. Sermon 120

Without a doubt they in the world to come, they are the ones who are losers. **11:22**
Truly, those who believed and did as the ones in accord with morality and humbled themselves before their Lord, those will be the Companions of the Garden. They, ones who will dwell in it forever. **11:23**
The parable of the two groups of people is as the one unwilling to see, unwilling to hear and the other, seeing and hearing. They are not on the same level in likeness. Will you not, then, recollect? **11:24**

They eulogize each other and expect reward from each other. When they ask something they insist on it. If they reprove any one, they disgrace him. If they pass verdict, they commit excess. They have adopted for every truth a wrong way, for every erect thing a bender, for every living being a killer, for every closed door a key and for every night a lamp. They covet, but with despair, in order to maintain with it their markets and to popularize their handsome merchandise. When they speak, they create doubts. When they describe, they exaggerate. First they offer easy paths, but afterwards they make them narrow. In short, they are the party of Satan and the stings of fire. *Regard the Party of Satan. They will be the ones who are losers.* (Q58:19) Sermon 193

Certainly, We sent Noah to his folk: Truly, I am a clear warner to you **11:25**
that you worship none but God. Truly, I fear for you the punishment of a painful Day. **11:26**
Then, the Council of those who were ungrateful said from among his folk: We see **you** *only as a mortal like us. We see none followed* **you** *but those, they who are visibly our most wretched, simple minded. Nor we see you as having any merit above us. Nay! We think that you are ones who lie.* **11:27**
He said: O my folk! Considered you that I had been with a clear portent from my Lord and that He gave me mercy from Himself but it was invisible to you? Then, will we fasten you to it when you are ones who dislike it? **11:28**
O my folk! I ask not of you wealth for it. My compensation is but with God. I will not be one who drives away those who believed. Truly, they are ones who will encounter their Lord while I see you a folk who are ignorant. **11:29**
O my folk! Who would help me against God if I drove them away? Will you not, then, recollect? **11:30**
I say not to you: The treasures of God are with me nor that I know the unseen nor I say: Truly, I am an angel nor I say of those whom your eyes look down upon:God will never give them good. God is greater in knowledge of what is within their souls for, then, I would be of the ones who are unjust. **11:31**
They said: O Noah! Surely, **you** *disputed with us, then, made much of the dispute with us. Now approach us with what* **you** *promised us if* **you** *had been among the ones who are sincere.* **11:32**
He said: Only God will bring it on you if He willed. You will not be ones who frustrate Him. **11:33**
My advice will not profit you—even if I wanted to advise you—if God had been wanting to lead you into error. He is your Lord and to Him you will return. **11:34**
Or they say: He devised it. Say: If I devised it, my sin is upon me and I am free of your sins. **11:35**

It was revealed to Noah: Truly, none of ***your*** *folk will believe but who had already believed. So, be* ***you*** *not despondent at what they have been accomplishing.* **11:36**
Craft ***you*** *the boat under Our Eyes and by Our Revelation and address Me not for those who did wrong. They are, truly, ones who will be drowned.* **11:37**
He crafts the boat. Whenever the Council passed by him of his folk, they derided him. He said: If you deride us, then, we will deride you just as you deride us, ones who are drowned. **11:38**
You will know to whom will approach a punishment covering with shame and on whom an abiding punishment will alight! **11:39**
Until when Our command drew near and the oven boiled, We said: Carry in it of every living thing, two, a pair and ***your*** *people, but him against whom the saying has preceded and who believed. None but a few believed with him.* **11:40**
He said: Embark in it. In the Name of God will be the course of the ship and its berthing. Truly, my Lord is Forgiving, Compassionate. **11:41**
So, it runs with them amidst waves like mountains. Noah cried out to his son and he had been standing apart: O my son! Embark with us and be ***you*** *not with the ones who are ungrateful!* **11:42**
He said: I will take shelter for myself on a mountain. It will be what saves me from the harm of the water. Noah said: No one saves from the harm this day from the command of God but him on whom He had mercy. A wave came between them so he had been of the ones who are drowned. **11:43**
It was said: O earth! Take in ***your*** *water! O heaven: Desist! The water was shrunken and the command of God was satisfied and it was on the same level as Al-Judi. It was said: Away with the folk, the ones who are unjust!* **11:44**
Noah cried out to his Lord and said: My Lord! Truly, my son is of my people. Truly, ***Your*** *promise is The Truth.* ***You*** *are the Most Just of the ones who judge.* **11:45**
He said: O Noah! Truly, he is not of ***your*** *people. Truly, he, his actions are not in accord with morality. So, ask not of Me what* ***you*** *have no knowledge. Truly, I admonish* ***you*** *so that* ***you*** *not be of the ones who are ignorant.* **11:46**
He said: My Lord! Truly, I take refuge with ***You*** *so that I not ask* ***You*** *of what I am without knowledge. Unless* ***You*** *are to for give me and have mercy on me, I would be of the ones who are losers.* **11:47**
It was said: O Noah! Get ***you*** *down with peace from Us and blessings on* ***you*** *and on communities from whoever are with* ***you****, and communities to whom We will give enjoyment. Again, they will be afflicted by Us with a painful punishment.* **11:48**
That is of the tidings of the unseen that We reveal to ***you. You*** *have not been knowing of them nor* ***your*** *folk before this. So, have* ***you*** *patience. Truly, the Ultimate End is for the ones who are God-conscious.* **11:49**
To Ad, their brother Hud. He said: O my folk! Worship God! You have no god other than He. You are nothing but ones who devise. **11:50**
O my folk! I ask not of you any compensation. My compensation is but with Who originated me. Will you not, then, be reasonable? **11:51**

Through His power He originated all created things. Sermon 1*

O my folk! Ask your Lord for forgiveness. Again, repent to Him. He will send abundant rain to you from heaven and increase you, adding strength to your strength. So, turn not away as ones who sin. **11:52**

They said: O Hud! Had **you** *brought about any clear portent for us? We will not be ones who leave our gods for* **your** *saying? We are not ones who believe in* **you**. **11:53**
Truly, we say nothing but that some of our gods inflicted **you** *with evil. He said: Truly, I call God to witness and bear you witness that I am free from partners you ascribe* **11:54**
other than Him. So, try to outwit me altogether. Again, give me no respite. **11:55**
Truly, I put my trust in God, my Lord and your Lord. There is not a moving creature but He is One Who Takes of its forelock. Truly, my Lord is on a straight path. **11:56**
But if you turn away, that is your decision. Then, surely, I expressed to you what I was sent with to you. My Lord will make successors a folk other than you and you will not injure Him at all. Truly, My Lord is Guardian over everything. **11:57**
Our command drew near. We delivered Hud and those who believed with him by a mercy from Us. We delivered them from a harsh punishment. **11:58**
That was Ad. They negated the signs of their Lord and rebelled against His Messengers. They followed the command of every haughty and stubborn one. **11:59**
They were pursued in the present life by a curse. On the Day of Resurrection, no doubt, truly, Ad were ungrateful to their Lord. Away with Ad, a folk of Hud! **11:60**
We sent to Thamud their brother Salih. He said: O my folk! Worship God. You have no god other than He. He caused you to grow from the earth and settled you on it. So, ask for His forgiveness. Again, repent to Him. Truly, my Lord is Near, One Who Answers. **11:61**
They said: O Salih! Surely, **you** *had been one who is a source of hope to us before this. Have* **you** *prohibited us that we worship what our fathers worship? Truly, we are in uncertainty about what* **you** *have called us to, in grave doubt.* **11:62**
He said: O my folk! Considered you that I had been with a clear portent from my Lord and that He gave me a mercy from Himself so who, then, would help me against God if I rebelled against Him? Then, you would increase me not but in decline. **11:63**
O my folk! This is the she-camel of God, a sign for you. So, let her eat on God's earth and afflict her not with evil so that a near punishment take you. **11:64**
But they crippled her. So, he said: Take joy in your abode for three days. That is a promise, one that will not be belied. **11:65**
Then, Our command drew near. We delivered Salih and those who believed with him by a mercy from Us and from the degradation of that Day. Truly, **your** *Lord, He is Strong, Almighty.* **11:66**
The Cry took those who did wrong. It came to be in the morning in their abodes, ones who are fallen prostrate, **11:67**
as if they dwelt not in them. No doubt, truly, Thamud were ungrateful to their Lord. Away with Thamud. **11:68**
Certainly, Our Messengers drew near Abraham with good tidings. They said: Peace. He said: Peace. He presently brought about a roasted calf. **11:69**
Then, when he saw their hands reach not out towards it, he became suspicious and sensed awe of them. They said: Fear not. We were sent to the folk of Lot. **11:70**
Abraham's woman, one who is standing up, laughed when We gave her good tidings of Isaac and besides Isaac, Jacob. **11:71**
She said: Woe to me! Will I give birth when I am an old woman and this, my husband, is an old man? Truly, this is a strange thing! **11:72**
They said: Marvel **you** *at the command of God? The mercy of God and His blessings be upon you, O People of the House: Truly, He is Worthy of Praise, Glorious.* **11:73**
When the panic went from Abraham and the good tidings drew near to him, he disputes with Us

for the folk of Lot. **11:74**
Truly, Abraham was forbearing, sympathetic, one who turns in repentance. **11:75**
O Abraham! Turn aside from this. Truly, the command of **your** *Lord drew near. Truly, that which arrives for them is a punishment, one that is not to be repelled.* **11:76**
When Our Messengers drew near Lot, he was troubled for them and was concerned for them, being distressed. He said: This is a distressful day! **11:77**
Then, drew near his folk, running toward him because they had been doing evil deeds before. He said: O my folk! These are my daughters! They are purer for you. So, be God-conscious. Cover me not with shame as regards my guests. Is there not among you a well-intentioned man? **11:78**
They said: Certainly, **you** *knew we have no right to* **your** *daughters. Truly,* **you** *knew well what we want.* **11:79**
He said: Would that I had strength against you or take shelter with stauncher support! **11:80**
They said: O Lot! Truly, we are Messengers of **your** *Lord. They will not reach out to* **you** *so set* **you** *forth with* **your** *people in a part of the night and let not any of you look back, but* **your** *woman. Truly, that which lights on them will light on her. Truly, what is promised to them is in the morning. Is the morning not near?* **11:81**
So, when Our command drew near, We made its high part low and We rained down on it rocks of baked clay, one upon another, **11:82**
ones that are distinguished, and not far from the ones who are unjust. **11:83**
We sent to Midian their brother Shuayb. He said: O my folk! Worship God. You have no god other than He. Reduce not the measuring vessel and balance. Truly, I consider you as good. Truly, I fear for you the punishment of an Enclosing Day. **11:84**
O my folk! Live up to the measuring vessel and balance in equity. Diminish not of humanity their things. Do no mischief in and on the earth as ones who make corruption. **11:85**
God's abiding wisdom is best for you if you had been ones who believe. I am not a Guardian over you. **11:86**
They said: O Shuayb! Is it that **your** *formal prayer commands* **you** *that we leave what our fathers worship or that we accomplish not with our possibilities whatever we will? Truly,* **you** *are the forbearing, the well-intentioned.* **11:87**
He said: O my folk! Considered you that I had been with a clear portent from my Lord. He provided me fairer provision from Himself. I want not to go against you in what I prohibit you. I want only making things right so far as I was able. My success is not but from God. In Him I put my trust and to Him I am penitent. **11:88**

God in the Book repeats the saying of a Prophet which appropriately represents my position: *I want not to go against you in what I prohibit you. I want only making things right so far as I was able. My success is not but from God. In Him I put my trust and to Him I am penitent.* (Q11:88) Letter 28

O my folk! Let not your breach with me drive you into being lighted on by the like of what lit on a folk of Noah or a folk of Hud or a folk of Salih. A folk of Lot are not far from you. **11:89**
Ask for forgiveness from your Lord. Again, repent to Him. Truly, my Lord is Compassionate, Loving. **11:90**
They said: O Shuayb! We understand not much of what **you** *say. Truly, we see* **you** *weak among us. If it had not been for* **your** *extended family, we would have stoned* **you**. **You** *are not mighty against us.* **11:91**
He said: O my folk! Is my extended family mightier to you than God whom you took to yourselves

to disregard? Truly, my Lord is One Who Encloses whatever you do. **11:92**
O my folk! Act according to your ability and, truly, I am one who acts. You will know to whom approaches a punishment covering him with shame and who, he is one who lies. Be on the watch! Truly, I am watching with you. **11:93**
Our command drew near. We delivered Shuayb and those who believed with him by a mercy from Us. The Cry took those who did wrong. It came to be in the morning in their abodes ones who are fallen prostrate, **11:94**
as if they had not been dwelling in them. Away with Midian just as Thamud was done away. **11:95**

Then he said: May God's mercy remain away from them ... *just as Thamud was done away with* from His Mercy. (Q11:95) Know that when the spears are hurled towards them and the swords are struck at their heads, they will repent of their doings. Surely, today Satan has scattered them. Tomorrow he will disclaim any connection with them and will leave them. Their departing from guidance, returning to misguidance and blindness, turning away from truth and falling into wrong is enough for their chastisement. Sermon 181

Certainly, We sent Moses with Our signs and a clear authority **11:96**
to Pharaoh and his Council but they followed the command of Pharaoh. The command of Pharaoh was not well-intended. **11:97**
He will go before his folk on the Day of Resurrection and they will be led down into the fire. Miserable will be the watering place, that to which they are led down! **11:98**
They were pursued by a curse in this life and on the Day of Resurrection! Miserable will be, the oblation, that which is offered! **11:99**
That is from the tidings of the towns that We relate to ***you****. Of them, some are ones that are standing up and some are stubble.* **11:100**
It was not that We did wrong to them. Rather, they did wrong themselves. Their gods availed them not whom they call to besides God at all. When the command of ***your*** *Lord drew near they increased them not other than in ruination.* **11:101**
Thus, is the taking of ***your*** *Lord when He took the towns while they are ones who are unjust. Truly, His taking is painful, severe.* **11:102**
In that, truly, there is a sign for whoever feared the punishment of the world to come. That Day humanity will be one that is gathered together for it and that will be a witnessed Day. **11:103**
We postpone it not but for the numbered term. **11:104**

When you do not find a true way to do the thing on hand, then do not persist on the wrong way. When you find a correct solution, then do not be lethargic in adopting it. Letter 53

On the Day it approaches no person will assert anything but with His permission. Then, among them will be the disappointed and the happy. **11:105**
As for those who were in despair, they will be in the fire. For them in it is sobbing and sighing, **11:106**
ones who will dwell in it for as long as the heavens and the earth continued, but what ***your*** *Lord willed. Truly,* ***your*** *Lord is Achiever of what He wants.* **11:107**
As for those who were happy, they will be in the Garden, ones who will dwell in it for as long as the heavens and the earth continued, but what ***your*** *Lord willed, a gift that will not be that which is broken.* **11:108**

*So, be **you** not hesitant as to what these worship. They worship nothing but what their fathers worship before. We are the ones who pay their share in full without being that which is reduced.* **11:109**

Remember that Divine Reward is for those who earn it with their sincere and good deeds. Punishment is the lot of men who deserve it by their evil activities. Letter 33

*Certainly, We gave Moses the Book, but they were at variance about it. If it were not for a Word that preceded from **your** Lord, it would be decided between them. Truly, they were uncertain about it, ones in grave doubt.* **11:110**
*Truly, to each his account will be paid in full by **your** Lord for their actions. Truly, He is Aware of what they do.* **11:111**
*So, go **you** straight as **you** were commanded and those who repented with **you** and be not defiant. Truly, He is Seeing of what you do.* **11:112** ***

Then, incline not to those who did wrong so the fire afflict you and there will not be for you any protectors other than God. Again, you will not be helped. **11:113**

This world and the hereafter have submitted to Him their reins. The skies and earths have flung their keys towards Him. The thriving trees bow to Him in the morning and evening, producing for Him flaming fire from their branches and, at His command, turn their own feed into ripe fruits. Sermon 133

Perform the formal prayer at the two ends of the daytime and at nearness of the nighttime. Truly, benevolence causes evil deeds to be put away. That is a reminder for the ones who remember. **11:114**

Include whatever God has made obligatory on you in your demands. Ask from Him fulfillment of what He has asked you to do. Make your ears hear the call of death before you are called by death. Surely, the hearts of the abstemious weep in this world even though they may apparently laugh. Their grief increases even though they may appear happy. Their hatred for themselves is much even though they may be envied for the subsistence they are allowed. Remembrance of death has disappeared from your hearts while false hopes are present in you. So this world has mastered you more than the next world. The immediate end of this world has removed you away from the remote one of the next life. You are brethren in the religion of God. Nothing but corrupt natures and bad conscience has separated you. Consequently, you do not bear burdens of each other, nor advise each other, nor spend on each other, nor love each other. Sermon 113

*Have **you** patience, for, truly, God wastes not the compensation of the ones who are doers of good.* **11:115**

Be God-conscious and perform good acts because: *Truly God is with those who are God-conscious and those, they are the ones who are doers of good.* (Q16:128) Sermon 193

Why had there not been among the generations before you imbued with abiding wisdom, prohibiting corruption in and on the earth, but a few of those whom We rescue from among them? Those who did wrong followed what they were given ease in it. They had been ones who sin. **11:116**

O those whose bodies are present, but whose wits are absent, whose wishes are scattered and whose rulers are afflicted by them! Your leader obeys God, but you disobey him while the leader of the people of Syria disobeys God, but they obey him. Sermon 97

***Your** Lord had not been causing the towns to perish unjustly while their people are ones who make things right.* **11:117**

O my people, this is the time for the occurrence of every promised event and the approach of things which you do not know. Whoever from among us will be during these days will move through them with a burning lamp and will tread on the footsteps of the virtuous in order to unfasten knots, to free servants, to divide the united and to unite the divided. He will be in concealment from people. The stalker will not find his footprints even though he pursues with his eye. Then a group of people will be sharpened like the sharpening of swords by the blacksmith. Their sight will be brightened by revelation. The delicacies of commentary will be put in their ears. They will be given drinks of wisdom, morning and evening. Sermon 150

*If **your** Lord willed, He would have made humanity one community. But they cease not to be ones who are at variance,* **11:118**

*but on whom **your** Lord had mercy. For that, He created them, and completed was the Word of **your** Lord. Certainly, I will fill hell with genie and humanity one and all.* **11:119**

Everyone of them is ... alone although they are a group, and they are strangers, even though friends. They are unaware of morning after a night and of evening after a day. The night or the day when they departed has become ever existent for them. They found the dangers of their place of stay more serious than they had apprehended, and they witnessed that its signs were greater than they had guessed. The two objectives, namely Paradise and Hell, have been stretched for them up to a point beyond the reach of fear or hope. Had they been able to speak they would have become dumb to describe what they witnessed or saw. Sermon 220

*All that We relate to **you** of the tidings of the Messengers is so that We make **your** mind firm by it. The Truth drew near **you** in this, and an admonishment and a reminder for the ones who believe.* **11:120**

With *the Prophet* (Q7:158), peace and the mercy of God be upon him, God exhausted the series of Prophets and ended the revelation. He then fought for Him those who were turning away from Him and were equating others with Him. Sermon 133

Say to those who believe not: Act according to your ability. Truly, We are ones who act. **11:121**

In (the Quran) there are some verses whose knowledge is obligatory and others whose ignorance by the people is permissible. It also contains what appears to be obligatory according to the Book, but its repeal is signified by the actions of *the Prophet* (Q7:158) (*sunna*), peace and the mercy of God be upon him, or that which appears compulsory according to the Prophet's actions, but the Book allows not following it. Or there are those which are obligatory in a given time, but not so after that time. Its prohibitions also differ. Some are major regarding which there exists the threat of hellfire and others are minor for which there is the hope of forgiveness. There are also those of which a small portion is also acceptable to God, but they are capable of being expanded. Sermon 1

Wait awhile. We, too, are ones who are waiting awhile. **11:122**

I praise God for whatever matter He ordained and whatever action He destines and for my trial with you, O group of people, who do not obey when I order and do not respond when I call you. If you are at ease, you engage in conceited conversation, but if you are faced with battle you show weakness. Sermon 180

To God belongs the unseen of the heavens and the earth. To Him is the return of every command, so worship Him and put ***your*** *trust in Him.* ***Your*** *Lord is not One Who is Heedless of what you do.* **11:123**

He distributed their sustenance and has counted their deeds and acts, the number of their breaths, their concealed looks, and whatever is hidden in their bosoms. He knows their places of stay and places of last resort in the loins and wombs until they reach their end. Sermon 90

CHAPTER 12: JOSEPH (Yūsuf)

Alif Lam Ra. That are the signs of the clear Book. **12:1**
Truly, We caused to descend a Recitation in Arabic so that perhaps you will be reasonable. **12:2**

Go ahead with the remembrance of God, for it is the best remembrance. Long for that which He has promised to the pious, for His promise is the most true promise. Tread the course of *the Prophet* (Q7:158), peace and the mercy of God be upon him, for it is the most distinguished course. Follow his *sunna*, for it is the most right of all behaviors. Learn the Quran, for it is the fairest of discourses. Sermon 110

We relate to ***you*** *the fairer of narratives through what We revealed to* ***you*** *of this, the Quran, although* ***you*** *had been before this among the ones who are heedless.* **12:3**

Remember God, O people, about what He has asked you in His Book to take care of, and about His rights that He has entrusted to you. Truly, God has not created you in vain, nor left you unbridled, nor left you alone in ignorance and gloom. He has defined what you should leave behind taught you your acts, ordained your death and sent down to you: *the Book (Quran) explaining everything.* (Q16:89) He made His Prophet, peace and the mercy of God be upon him, live among you for a long time until He completed the message sent through the Quran for him and for you, namely the religion chosen by Him, clarified His good and evil acts through him and His prohibitions and His commands. Sermon 85

Mention when Joseph said to his father: O my father! Truly, I saw eleven stars and the sun and the moon. I saw them as ones prostrating themselves to me. **12:4**
Truly, Satan is a clear enemy to the human being. **12:5**
Thus, ***your*** *Lord will elect* ***you*** *and teach* ***you*** *of the interpretation of events. He will fulfill His divine blessing on* ***you*** *and on the people of Jacob just as He fulfilled it on* ***your*** *two fathers before, Abraham and Isaac. Truly,* ***your*** *Lord is Knowing, Wise.* **12:6**
Certainly, there had been in Joseph and his brothers signs for the ones who ask. **12:7**
When they said: Certainly, Joseph and his brother are more beloved to our father than we, although we are many. Truly, our father is clearly wandering astray. **12:8**
Kill Joseph or fling him to some other region to free the face of your father for you. You be a folk after that ones in accord with morality! **12:9**
Said one who says: Kill not Joseph, but cast him into the bottom of a well. Some company of travelers will pick him out, if you had been ones who do this. **12:10**

They said: O our father! Why will **you** *not entrust us with Joseph when we are, truly, ones who will, certainly, look after him?* **12:11**
Send him with us tomorrow to frolic and play. Truly, we are ones who guard him. **12:12**
He said: Truly, it disheartens me that you go with him. I fear that a wolf eat him while you are ones who are heedless of him. **12:13**
They said: If a wolf ate him while we are many, truly, then, we are ones who are losers. **12:14**
So, they went with him, and they agreed to lay him in the bottom of the well. We revealed to him: Certainly, **you** *will tell them of this, their affair, when they are not aware.* **12:15**
They drew near their father in the time of night, weeping. **12:16**
They said: O our father! Truly, we went racing and we left Joseph with our sustenance and a wolf ate him and **you** *will not be one who believes us, even if we had been ones who are sincere.* **12:17**
They brought about his long shirt with false blood. He said: Nay! Your souls enticed you with a command. Having patience is graceful. It is God, One Whose Help is being sought against what you allege. **12:18**
There drew near a company of travelers so they sent their water-drawer to let down his bucket. He said: What good tidings! This is a boy! So, they kept him secret as merchandise. God is Knowing of what they do. **12:19**
They sold him for a meager price of coins, ones that are numbered. They had been of him among the ones who hold him in low esteem. **12:20**
One from Egypt who bought him said to his woman: Honor him as a guest with a place of lodging. Perhaps he will profit us or we will take him to ourselves as a son. Thus, We established Joseph firmly in the earth that We teach him the interpretation of events. God is One Who is Victor over His command, except most of humanity knows not. **12:21**
When he had fully grown and come of age, We gave him critical judgment and knowledge. Thus, We give recompense to the ones who are doers of good. **12:22**
She in whose house he was solicited him, enticing his soul to evil. She shut the doors and said: Come **you**! *He said: God be my safe place. Truly, he,* **your** *husband, is my master and He gave me a goodly place of lodging. Truly, the ones who are unjust will not prosper.* **12:23**
She, certainly, was about to act on her desire for him and he was about to act on his desire for her, if it were not that he saw proof of his Lord. Thus, it was that We turn away from him evil and depravity. Truly, he was among Our servants, ones who are devoted. **12:24**
So, they raced to the door and she tore his long shirt from behind. They both discovered her chief at the door. She said: What is the recompense of him who wanted evil for **your** *household, but that he be imprisoned or a painful punishment?*
12:25
He said: She solicited me, enticing my soul to evil. One who bears witness bore witness from her household and said: If his long shirt had been torn from the front, then, she was sincere, and he was among the ones who lie. **12:26**
But if his long shirt had been torn from behind, she lied against herself; he was among ones who are sincere. **12:27**
When her husband saw his long shirt was torn from behind, he said: It is of your (f) cunning; truly, your (f) cunning is serious. **12:28**
Joseph! Turn aside from this! To his wife he said: Ask **you** *for forgiveness for* **your** *(f) impiety; truly,* **you** *(f) had been of the ones who are inequitable.* **12:29**
The ladies in the city said: The woman of the great one solicits her spiritual warrior, enticing his soul to evil. Surely, he captivated her longing. Truly, we consider her to be clearly wandering astray.
12:30

So, when she heard of their planning, she sent for them (f), and made ready for them a banquet. She gave each one of them (f) a knife, and said to Joseph: Go forth before them (f). Then, when they saw him, they admired him and cut their hands. They (f) said: God save us! This is not a mortal. This is nothing but a generous angel! **12:31**

She said: This is he about whom you (f) blamed me. Certainly, I solicited him, enticing his soul to evil, but he preserved himself from sin. Now if he accomplishes not what I command, he will, certainly, be imprisoned and will be among the ones who are disgraced. **12:32**

He said: O my Lord! Prison is more beloved to me than what they call me to. Unless **You** *have turned away their (f) cunning from me, I will yearn towards them (f) and I will be among the ones who are ignorant.* **12:33**

So, his Lord responded to him and turned away their (f) cunning from him. Truly, He, He is The Hearing, The Knowing. **12:34**

Again, it showed itself to them. After they saw the signs, it seemed that they should imprison him for a while. **12:35**

There entered with him in the prison two male spiritual warriors. One of them said: Truly, I see myself pressing grapes in season. The other said: Truly, I see myself carrying bread over my head from which birds are eating. They said: Tell us the interpretation of this. Truly, we consider **you** *among the ones who are doers of good.* **12:36**

He said: The food you both are provided approaches you not, but I will tell you of its interpretation before it approaches. That is of what my Lord taught me. Truly, I left the creed of a folk who believe not in God and they, in the world to come, they are ones who disbelieve. **12:37**

I followed the creed of my fathers, Abraham and Isaac and Jacob. It had not been for us that we ascribe anything as partners with God. That is from the grace of God to us and to humanity, except most of humanity gives not thanks. **12:38**

O my two prison companions! Are ones that are different masters better or God, The One, The Omniscient? **12:39**

Whomever you worship other than He are nothing but names that you named—you and your fathers for which God caused not to descend any authority. The determination is from God alone. He commanded that you worship none but Him. That is the truth-loving way of life, except most of humanity knows not. **12:40**

O my two prison companions! As for one of you, he will give intoxicants to drink to his master. As for the other, he will be crucified. Birds will eat from his head. The matter was decided about which you ask for advice. **12:41**

He said to the one of them whom he thought should be the one who is saved of the two: Remember me to **your** *master. Then, Satan caused him to forget the remembrance of him to his master so Joseph lingered in expectation in prison for a certain number of years.* **12:42**

The king said: Truly, I, I see seven fattened cows eating seven lean ones and seven ears of green wheat and others dry. O Council: Render an opinion to me about my dream if you had been able to expound dreams. **12:43**

They said: Jumbled nightmares. We are not of the interpretation of nightmares ones who know. **12:44**

Said the man of the two of them who was delivered and recalled after a period of time: I will tell you its interpretation so send me. **12:45**

Joseph, O **you** *just person! Render an opinion to us about seven fattened cows eaten by seven lean ones and seven ears of green wheat and others dry so that perhaps I will return to the personages so that perhaps they will know about* **you**. **12:46**

He said: You will sow for seven years in like previous manner and of what you reaped, then, forsake ears of wheat, but a little of it that you may eat. **12:47**
Again, seven severe years will approach after that. You will eat what you put forward, but a little of what you keep in store. **12:48**
Again, after that, will approach a year in which humanity will be helped with rain and they will press in season. **12:49**
*The king said: Bring him to me. Then, when the Messenger brought about, he said: Return to **your** master and ask him: What of the ladies, those who cut their hands? Truly, my Lord is Knowing of their (f) cunning.* **12:50**
He said: What was your (f) business when you solicited Joseph, enticing his soul to evil? They (f) said: God save us! We knew not any evil against him. The woman of the great one said: Now The Truth was discovered! I sought to solicit him, enticing him to evil. Truly, he is among the ones who are sincere. **12:51**
Joseph said: That is so that the great one know that I betray him not in his absence. That God guides not the cunning of the ones who are traitors. **12:52**
I declare my soul not innocent. Truly, the soul is that which incites to evil, but when my Lord had mercy. Truly, my Lord is Forgiving, Compassionate. **12:53**

For truly, the soul incites to evil, unless God has mercy. Letter 53

*The king said: Bring him to me so that I attach him to me myself. Then, when he spoke to him he said: Truly, this day **you** are with us secure, trustworthy.* **12:54**
Joseph said: Assign me over the storehouses of the region. Truly, I will be a knowing guardian. **12:55**
Thus, We established Joseph firmly in the region to take his dwelling in it when or where he wills. We light Our mercy on whom We will and We waste not the compensation of ones who are doers of good. **12:56**
Truly, the compensation of the world to come is better for those who believed and had been God-conscious. **12:57**
Joseph's brothers drew near and they entered before him. He recognized them, but they are ones who know him not. **12:58**
When he equipped them with their food supplies, he said: Bring me a brother of yours from your father. See you not that I live up to full measure and that I am best of the ones who host? **12:59**
Then, if you bring him not to me, there will be no full measure for you with me, nor will you come near me. **12:60**
They said: We will solicit his father for him and, truly, we are ones who do it. **12:61**
Joseph said to his spiritual warriors: Lay their merchandise into their saddlebags so that perhaps they will recognize it. Then they turned about to their household so that perhaps they will return. **12:62**
So, when they returned to their father, they said: O our father! The full measure was refused to us so send our brother with
us that we will obtain our measure. Truly, we will be ones who guard him. **12:63**
Jacob said: How will I entrust him to you as I entrusted you with his brother before? But, then, God is Best of One Who Guards. He is One Who is the Most Merciful of the ones who are the most merciful. **12:64**
When they opened their sustenance, they found their merchandise was returned to them. They said: O our father, this is what we desire. Our merchandise was returned to us and we will get provision

for our household and we will keep our brother safe and add a camel's load of full measure. That is an easy full measure. **12:65**
He said: I will not send him with you until you give me a pledge by God that you will bring him back to me, unless you are enclosed yourselves. When they gave him their pledge, he said: God is Trustee over what we say. **12:66**
He said: O my sons! Enter not by one door, but enter by different doors. I will not avail you against God in anything. Truly, the determination is but with God. In Him I put my trust. In Him put their trust the ones who put their trust. **12:67**
When they entered from where their father commanded, it had not been availing them against God in anything, but it was a need of Jacob's soul which he satisfied. Truly, he was a possessor of knowledge because We taught him, except most of humanity knows not. **12:68**
When they entered before Joseph, he himself gave refuge to his brother. He said: Truly, I am ***your*** *brother, so be not despondent for what they had been doing.* **12:69**
So, when he equipped them with their food supplies, he laid the drinking cup into their brother's saddlebag. Again, one who announces announced: O you in the caravan! Truly, you are ones who are thieves. **12:70**
They said coming forward: What is it that you are missing? **12:71**
They said: We are missing the king's drinking cup and for him who brought it about is a camel's load and I am the guarantor
for it. **12:72**
They said: By God, certainly, you knew we drew not near making corruption in the region. We had not been ones who are thieves. **12:73**
They said: What, then, will be the recompense for him if you had been ones who lie? **12:74**
They said: The recompense for it will be that he in whose saddlebag it was located will be the recompense. Thus, we give recompense to the ones who are unjust. **12:75**
So, he began with their sacks before the sack of his brother. Again, he pulled it out of his brother's sack. Thus, We contrived for Joseph. He would not have taken his brother into the judgment of the king unless God wills it. We exalt in degree whomever We will, and above all those possessors of knowledge is One Who is Knowing. **12:76**
They said: If he steals, surely, a brother of his stole before. But Joseph kept it secret within himself, not showing it to them. He said: You are in a worse place. God is greater in knowledge of what you allege. **12:77**
They said: O the great one! Truly, for him is an old man as his father so take one of us in his place. Truly, we consider ***you*** *among the ones who are doers of good.* **12:78**
He said: God be my safe place that we take but him with Whom we found our sustenance. Truly, we, then, would be of the ones who are unjust. **12:79**
So, when in regard to him they became hopeless, they conferred privately. The eldest of them said: Know you not that your father, surely, took a pledge from you by God and before that you neglected your duty with Joseph. So, I will never quit this region until my father gives me permission or God gives judgment in my case. He is Best of the ones who judge. **12:80**
Return to your father and say: O our father! Truly, ***your*** *son stole and we bore witness only to what we knew. We had not been ones who guard the unseen.* **12:81**
Ask the people of the town where we had been and the people of the caravan in which we came forward. Truly, we are ones who are sincere. **12:82**
He said: You were enticed by your souls into an affair. So, patience is graceful. Perhaps God will bring me them altogether. Truly, He, He is The Knowing, The Wise. **12:83**

He turned away from them and said: O my bitterness for Joseph! His eyes brightened because of the sorrow that was choking him. **12:84**

They said: By God! ***You*** *will never discontinue remembering Joseph until* ***you*** *ruined* ***your*** *health.* ***You*** *would be among the ones who are perishing.* **12:85**

He said: I make not complaint of my anguish and sorrow but to God. I know from God what you know not. **12:86**

O my sons! Go and search for Joseph and his brother. Give not up hope of the solace of God. Truly, no one gives up hope of the solace of God but the folk, ones who are ungrateful. **12:87**

Then, when they entered to him, they said: O the great one! Harm afflicted us and our household. We drew near merchandise of scant worth so live up to the full measure and be charitable to us. Truly, God gives recompense to the ones who give in charity. **12:88**

He said: Knew you what you accomplished with Joseph and his brother when you are ones who are ignorant? **12:89**

They said: are ***you****, truly, Joseph? He said: I am Joseph and this is my brother. Surely, God showed us grace. Truly, He Who is God-conscious and endures patiently, then, surely, God will not waste the compensation of the ones who are doers of good.* **12:90**

They said: By God! Certainly, God held ***you*** *in greater favor above us. Truly, we had been ones who are inequitable.* **12:91**

He said: No censure on you this day. God forgive you. He is One Who is Most Merciful of the ones who are most merciful. **12:92**

Go with this, my long shirt and cast it over the face of my father. He will become seeing. Bring me your household one and all. **12:93**

When they set forward with the caravan their father said: Truly, I find the scent of Joseph if you think me not weak of mind. **12:94**

They said: By God! Truly, ***you*** *are long possessed by* ***your*** *wandering astray.* **12:95**

Then, when the bearer of good tidings drew near, he cast it over his face and he went back, seeing. He said: Did I not say to you, truly, I know from God what you know not? **12:96**

They said: O our father! Ask forgiveness for us for our impieties. Truly, we had been ones who are inequitable. **12:97**

He said: I will ask forgiveness for you with my Lord. Truly, He, He is The Forgiving, The Compassionate. **12:98**

Then, when they entered to Joseph, he gave refuge to his parents and said: Enter Egypt, if God willed, as ones who are safe! **12:99**

He exalted his parents to the throne. They fell down before him as ones who prostrate themselves. He said: O my father! This is the interpretation of my dream from before. My Lord has made it a reality. Surely, He did good to me when He brought me out of the prison and drew you near out of the desert after Satan had sown enmity between me and between my brothers. Truly, my Lord is Subtle in what He wills. Truly, He is The Knowing, The Wise. **12:100**

My Lord! Surely, ***You*** *gave me of the dominion.* ***You*** *taught of the interpretation of events. One Who is Originator of the heavens and the earth,* ***You*** *are my protector in the present and in the world to come. Call me to* ***Your****self as one who submits to* ***You*** *and cause me to join with the ones in accord with morality.* **12:101**

That is of the tidings of the unseen that We reveal to ***you****.* ***You*** *had not been in their presence when they agreed to their affair. They plan.* **12:102**

Therefore, plan for your place of stay and do not sell your next life with this world. Letter 31

Most of humanity is not ones who believe, even if ***you*** *were eager.* **12:103**

God deputed Muhammad, peace and the mercy of God be upon him, with The Truth so that he may take out His people from the worship of idols towards His worship and from obeying Satan towards obeying Him. He sent him the Quran which He explained and made strong in order that the people may know their Sustainer (God), since they were ignorant of Him, may acknowledge Him, since they were denying Him, and accept Him, since they were refusing to believe in Him. He, the Glorified, revealed Himself to them through His Book without their having seen Him, by means of what He showed them out of His might and made them fear His sway. How He destroyed those whom He wished to destroy through His chastisement and ruined those whom He wished to ruin through His retribution! Sermon 146

You *asked them not for any compensation. It is but a Remembrance to the worlds.* **12:104**

Certainly, God, the Glorified, the Sublime, has made His remembrance the light for hearts which hear with its help despite deafness, see with its help despite blindness and become submissive with its help despite unruliness. Sermon 220

How many signs of the heavens and the earth they pass by while they are ones who turn aside from them! **12:105**

O Lord! Our hearts seek **Your** Protection. Our faces turn to **You**. Our eyes look towards **You**. Our feet move towards **Your** path, and our bodies sincerely submit to **Your** command. Letter 15

Most of them believe not in God, but they be ones who are polytheists. **12:106**

Do not give way to doubts about the truth which Islam has proclaimed. Letter 65

Were they safe from the approach to them of the overwhelming event of the punishment from God or the approach on them of the Hour suddenly while they are not aware? **12:107**

God knows hidden matters and is aware of inner feelings. He encompasses everything. He has control over everything and power over everything. Sermon 85

Say: This is my way. I call to God. I and whoever followed me are on clear evidence. Glory be to God! I am not among the ones who are polytheists. **12:108**

They do not believe in the unknown and do not avoid the evil. They act on the doubts and tread in the way of their passions. For them good is whatever they consider good and evil is whatever they consider evil. Sermon 88

We sent not before ***you*** *as Messengers, but men to whom We reveal from among the people of the towns. So, journey they not through the earth and look on how had been the Ultimate End of those who were before them? Truly, the abode of the world to come is better for those who were God-conscious. Will you not, then, be reasonable?* **12:109**

When the Messengers became hopeless and thought that they were lied against, then, Our help drew near. So, We were to deliver whomever We will. Our Might will not be repelled from the folk, the ones who sin. **12:110**

Then God chose progeny for Muhammad, peace and the mercy of God be upon him, and then selected him to be near Him, regarded him too dignified to remain in this world and removed him from this place of trial. He drew him towards Himself with honor. May God shower His blessing on him. Sermon 1

Certainly, there had been in their narratives a lesson for those imbued with intuition. It had not been a discourse that is devised except it established as true what was before and decisively explained everything and is a guidance and a mercy for a folk who believe. **12:111**

God deputed *the Prophet* (Q7:158), peace and the mercy of God be upon him, when no sign of guidance existed, no beacon was giving light and no passage was clear. Sermon 196

Chapter 13: Thunder (al-Ra^c^d)

Alif Lam Mim Ra. That are the signs of the Book, and what were caused to descend to ***you*** *from* ***your*** *Lord is The Truth, except most of humanity believes not.* **13:1**

The Book of God is among you. It speaks. Its tongue does not falter. It is a house whose pillars do not fall down. It is a power whose supporters are never defeated. Sermon 132

It is He Who exalted the heavens without any pillars so that you see them. Again, He turned his attention to above the Throne. He caused to become subservient the sun and the moon, each run for a term, that which is determined. He manages the command. He explains distinctly the signs so that perhaps of the meeting with your Lord you would be certain. **13:2**

This world and the hereafter have submitted to Him their reins. The skies and earths have flung their keys towards Him. The thriving trees bow to Him in the morning and evening, producing for Him flaming fire from their branches and, at His command, turn their own feed into ripe fruits. Sermon 133

It is He Who stretched out the earth and made on it firm mountains and rivers. With all kinds of fruits, he made in it two, a pair. He covers the nighttime with the daytime. Truly, in that are signs for a folk who reflect. **13:3**

He created the earth and suspended it without being busy, retained it without support, made it stand without legs, raised it without pillars, protected it against bendings and curvings and defended it against crumbling and splitting into parts. He fixed mountains on it like stumps, solidified its rocks, caused its streams to flow and opened wide its valleys. Whatever He made did not suffer from any frailty. Whatever He strengthened did not show any weakness. Sermon 186

In the earth there are strips, that which neighbor one another and gardens of grapevines and plowed lands and date palm trees coming from the same root and not coming from the same root that are given to drink from one water. We give advantage to some of them over some others in produce. Truly, in these things there are signs for a folk who are reasonable. **13:4**

O God's human being! Be God-conscious. Keep in view the reason why He created you. Be afraid of Him to the extent He has advised you to do. Make yourself deserve what He has promised you by having confidence in the truth of His promise and entertaining fear of the Day of Judgment. Sermon 82

If ***you*** *marvel, then, wonder at their saying: When we had been earth dust, will we, truly, be in a new creation? Those are those who were ungrateful to their Lord. Those will have yokes around their necks. Those will be the Companions of the Fire. They, ones who will dwell in it forever.* **13:5**

When He made anything of the world, the making of it did not cause Him any difficulty. The creation of anything which He created and formed did not fatigue Him. He did not create it to heighten His authority, nor for fear of loss or harm, nor to seek its help against an overwhelming foe, nor to guard against any avenging opponent with its help, nor for the extension of His domain by its help, nor for boasting over largeness of His possession against a partner, nor because He felt lonely and desired to seek its company. Sermon 186

They seek ***you*** *to hasten on evil deeds before the benevolence. Surely, passed away before them exemplary punishments. But, truly,* ***your*** *Lord is certainly, The Possessor of Forgiveness for humanity in spite of their injustice. Truly,* ***your*** *Lord is Severe in repayment.* **13:6**

There remain a few people in whose case the remembrance of their return to God on the Day of Judgment keeps their eyes bent and the awareness of the Resurrection moves them to tears. Some of them are scared away from the world and disperse. Some are frightened and subdued. Some are quiet as if muzzled. Some are praying sincerely. Some are grief-stricken and pain-ridden whom fear has confined to namelessness. Disgrace has shrouded them, so they are in the sea of bitter water, their mouths are closed and their hearts are bruised. They preached until they were tired. They were oppressed until they were disgraced. They were killed until their numbers dwindled. Sermon 32

Those who were ungrateful say: Why was a sign not caused to descend to him from his Lord? ***You*** *are only one who warns, and one who guides every folk.* **13:7**

God ... is aware of whatever is hidden in the hearts and whatever lies behind the unseen. Sermon 192

God knows what every female carries and how much her womb absorbs and what they add. Everything with Him is in proportion. **13:8**

He has made for you ears to preserve what is important, eyes to have sight in place of unseeing and limbs which consist of many smaller parts whose curves are in proportion with the molding of their shape and length of their ages and also bodies that are sustaining themselves and hearts that are busy in search of their food besides other great bounties, obliging gifts and fortresses of safety. He has fixed for you ages that are not known to you. Sermon 82

He is One Who Knows the unseen and the visible, The Great, The One Who is Raised High. **13:9**

If you tread on the path of your imagination and reach its extremity, it will not lead you anywhere except that the Originator of the ant is the same as Him who is the Originator of the date-palm, because everything has the same delicacy and detail. Every living being has little difference. In His creation, the big, the delicate, the heavy, the light, the strong, the weak are all equal. An ant can hardly be seen in the corner of the eye, nor by the perception of the imagination—how it moves on the earth and leaps at its livelihood. It carries the grain to its hole and deposits it in its place of stay. It collects during the summer for its winter and for strength during its period of weakness. Its livelihood is guaranteed. It is fed according to fitness. God, the Kind, does not forget it. God, the Giver, does not deprive it even though it may be in dry stone or fixed rocks. Sermon 185

It is equal to Him whether you kept secret his saying or you published it. Or whoever he be, one who conceals himself by nighttime or one who goes about carelessly in the daytime. **13:10**

Whoever from among us will be during these days will move through them with a burning lamp and will tread on the footsteps of the virtuous, in order to unfasten knots, to free servants, to divide the united and to unite the divided. He will be in concealment from people. The stalker will not find his footprints even though he pursues with his eye. Then a group of people will be sharpened like the sharpening of swords by the blacksmith. Their sight will be brightened by revelation, the delicacies of commentary will be put in their ears and they will be given drinks of wisdom, morning and evening. Sermon 150

For him there are Ones Who Postpone from before him and from behind him to keep him safe by the command of God. Truly, God alters not a folk until they alter what is within themselves. When God wanted evil for a folk, then, there is no turning it back. There is not for them other than He anyone who is a safeguarder. **13:11**

O people! Secure light from the flame of lamps of the preacher who follows what he preaches and draw water from the spring which has been cleaned of dirt. O God's human being! Do not rely on your ignorance. Do not be obedient to your desires, because he who stays at this place is like one who stays on the brink of a bank undermined by water carrying ruin on his back from one portion to the other following his opinion which he changes, one after the other. He wants to make adhere what cannot adhere and to bring together what cannot keep together. So be God-conscious and do not place your complaints before him who cannot redress your grievance, nor undo with his opinion what has been made obligatory for you. Certainly, there is no obligation on the leader except what has been devolved on him from God, namely to convey warnings, to exort in good advice, to revive the *sunna*, to enforce penalties on those liable to them and to issue shares to the deserving. So hasten towards knowledge before its vegetation dries up and before you turn yourselves away from seeking knowledge from those who have it. Desist others from the unlawful and abstain from it yourself, because you have been commanded to abstain yourself before abstaining others. Sermon 105

It is He Who causes you to see the lightning in fear and in hope. It is He Who causes the clouds to grow heavy, **13:12**
and thunder glorifies His praise and the angels, because of their awe of Him. He sends thunderbolts and He lights on whom He wills. They dispute about God, and He is a Severe Force. **13:13**

He created ... *the clouds to grow heavy* ... (Q13:12) and produced from them heavy rain and spread it on various lands. He drenched the earth after its dryness and grew vegetation from it after its barrenness. Sermon 185

For Him is the call of The Truth. Those whom they call to other than Him, they respond not to them at all, but like one who stretches out the palms of his hands for water so that it should reach his mouth, but it is not that which reaches it. Supplication of the ones who are ungrateful is only wandering astray. **13:14**

O my God! Sustainer of the high sky and the suspended firmament which **You** have made a shelter for the night and the day, an orbit for the sun and the moon and a path for the rotating stars, and for populating it **You** have created a group of **Your** angels who do not get weary of worshipping **You.** O Sustainer of this earth which **You** have made an abode for people and a place for the movement of insects and beasts and countless other creatures seen and unseen. Sermon 171

To God prostrates whatever is in the heavens and the earth, willingly or unwillingly as does their shade at the first part of the day and the eventide. **13:15**

Almighty is God before Whom bows in prostration: *To God prostrates whatever is in the heavens and the earth, willingly or unwillingly ...* (Q13:15), and submits to Him by placing his cheeks and face (in the dust), casts himself down before Him in obedience in health and weakness, and hands over to Him full control in fear and apprehension. Sermon 185

Say: Who is the Lord of the heavens and the earth? Say: God! Say: Took you to yourselves other than Him protectors? They control not themselves, neither profiting nor hurting. Say: Are the unwilling to see on the same level as the seeing? Are the shadows on the same level as the light? Made they ascribed associates with God who created as His creation so that creation resembled one another to them? Say: God is One Who is Creator of everything. He is The One, The Omniscient. **13:16**

I bear witness that *there is no god but God.* (Q47:19) He is One and there is no partner with Him. He is the First, such that nothing was before Him. He is the Last, such that there is not limit for Him. Imagination cannot catch any of His qualities. Hearts cannot entertain belief about His nature. Analysis and division cannot be applied to Him. Eyes and hearts cannot encompass Him. Sermon 183

He caused water to descend from heaven and it flowed into valleys according to their measure. Then, the flood bears away the froth. From what they kindle in a fire, looking for glitter or sustenance, there is a froth the like of it. Thus, God compares The Truth and falsehood. Then, as for the froth, it goes as swelling scum while what profits humanity abides on the earth. Thus, God propounds parables. **13:17**

God collected from hard, soft, sweet and sour earth, clay which He dripped in water until it became pure and kneaded it with moisture until it became clay-like. From it He carved an image with curves, joints, limbs and segments. He solidified it until it dried up for a fixed time and a known duration. Then He blew into it out of His Spirit whereupon it took the pattern of a human being with mind that governs him, intelligence which he makes use of, limbs that serve him, organs that change his position, sagacity that differentiates between truth and untruth, tastes and smells, colors and species. He is a mixture of clays of different colors, cohesive materials, divergent contradictories and differing properties like heat, cold, softness and hardness. Sermon 1

For those who responded to their Lord there is the fairer. For those who respond not to Him, if they had all that is in and on the earth and its like with it, they would offer it as ransom. Those, for them will be a dire reckoning and their place of shelter will be hell. Miserable will be the cradling! **13:18**

Everyone of them is ... alone although they are a group, and they are strangers, even though friends. They are unaware of morning after a night and of evening after a day. The night or the day when they departed has become ever existent for them. They found the dangers of their place of stay more serious than they had apprehended. They witnessed that its signs were greater than they had guessed. Sermon 220

Then, is he who knows what was caused to descend to ***you*** *from* ***your*** *Lord to be The Truth like he who is unwilling to see? It is only those imbued with intuition who recollect.* **13:19**

The Prophet (Q7:158), peace and the mercy of God be upon him, treated this world disdainfully and regarded it low. He held it contemptible and hated it. He realized that God kept it away from him with intention and spread it out for others by way of contempt. Therefore, he remained away from it by his heart, banished its recollection from his mind and wished that its attraction should remain hidden from his eyes so that he would not acquire any clothing from it, or hope for staying in it. He conveyed from God the pleas against committing sins, counseled his people as a warner against Divine chastisement, called people towards Paradise as a conveyor of good tidings and made them fear the Fire, cautioning against it. Sermon 108

Those who live up to their compact with God and break not their solemn promise **13:20**
and those who reach out to what God commanded be joined and dread their Lord and they fear the dire reckoning **13:21**
and those who endured patiently, looking for the Countenance of their Lord and who performed the formal prayer and spent out of what We have provided them in secret and in public, and they drive off the evil deed with benevolence—those, for them is the Ultimate Abode: **13:22**

Everyone should be God-conscious, should admonish himself, should send forward his repentance and should overpower his desire because his death is hidden from him. His desires deceive him. Satan keeps posted about him. He beautifies his sin for him so that he may commit it. He prompts him to delay repentance until his desires cause him to be the most negligent. Pity is for the negligent person whose life itself would be a proof against him and his own days, passed in sin, will lead him to punishment. Sermon 64

Gardens of Eden which they will enter along with whoever was in accord with morality from among their fathers and their spouses and their offspring. Angels will enter to them from every door saying: **13:23**

Mind the obligations! Mind the obligations! Fulfill them for God and they will take you to the Garden. Surely, God has made unlawful the things which are not unknown and made lawful the things which are without defect. Sermon 167

Peace be to you for what you endured patiently. How excellent is the Ultimate Abode! **13:24**

If we behave kindly, patiently and sympathetically towards people, God will reward us, but if we ill-treat them we shall be sinning. Letter 18

But those who break the compact of God after its solemn promise and sever what God commanded to be joined and make corruption in and on the earth, those, for them is the curse and for them is the Dire Abode. **13:25**
God extends the provision for whom He wills and measures it. They were glad in this present life. There is nothing in this present life like the world to come but a brief enjoyment. **13:26**

O God's human being! I advise you to keep away from this world which is shortly to leave you, even though you do not like its departure, and which would make your bodies old, even though you would like to keep them young. Your example and its example is like the travelers who travel some distance and then traverse it quickly, or they aimed at a sign and reached it at once. How short is the distance to the aim if one heads towards it and reaches it. How short is the stage of one who has only a day which he cannot exceed while a swift driver is driving him in this world until he departs from it. So do not hanker after worldly honor and its pride. Do not feel happy over its beauties and bounties, nor wail over its damages and misfortunes because its honor and pride will end, its beauty and bounty will perish and its damages and misfortunes will pass away. Every period in it has an end. Every living being in it is to die. Do you not understand that for you there is a warning in the relics of the predecessors, an eye opener and lesson that your forefathers provided you? Do you not see that your predecessors did not come back and the surviving followers did not remain? Do you not observe that the people of the world pass mornings and evenings in different conditions? Thus, somewhere the dead is wept for, someone is being condoled, someone is prostrate in distress, someone is enquiring about the sick, someone is passing his last breath, someone is hankering after the world while death is looking for him, someone is forgetful, but he is not forgotten by death, and the survivors walk in the footsteps of the predecessors. Sermon 99

Those who were ungrateful say: Why was a sign not caused to descend to him from his Lord? Say: Truly, God causes to go astray whom He wills and guides to Himself whomever was penitent, **13:27**
those who believed and their hearts are at rest in the remembrance of God, no doubt in the remembrance of God hearts are at rest. **13:28**
Those who believed and did as the ones in accord with morality, there is joy for them and a goodness of destination. **13:29**

Their hearts are in the Gardens of Paradise, while their bodies are at work. Sermon 191

Thus, We sent ***you*** *to a community. Surely, passed away other communities before it so that* ***you*** *would recount to them what We revealed to* ***you*** *and they are ungrateful to The Merciful. Say: He is my Lord. There is no god but He. In Him I put my trust and to Him I am turning in repentance.* **13:30**

O the Most Merciful of all! .... Do pour on us **Your** mercy, **Your** blessing, **Your** sustenance and **Your** pity.... Surely, **You** are powerful over whatever **You** will. Sermon 143

If there were a Recitation that would have set mountains in motion with it, or the earth would be cut off with it or the dead would be spoken to with it, nay! The command is altogether with God. Do those who believed not have knowledge that if God wills He would have guided humanity altogether. Will cease not to light on those who were ungrateful disaster because of what they crafted? Or will it alight close to their abode until the promise of God approaches? Truly, God breaks not His solemn declaration. **13:31**

Go ahead with the remembrance of God, for it is the best remembrance. Long for that which He has promised to the pious, for His promise is the most true promise. Tread the course of *the Prophet* (Q7:158), peace and the mercy of God be upon him, for it is the most distinguished course. Follow his *sunna*, for it is the most right of all behaviors. Learn the Quran, for it is the fairest of discourses. Understand it thoroughly, for it is the best blossoming of hearts. Seek cure with its light, for it is the cure for hearts. Recite it beautifully, for it is the most beautiful narration. Certainly, a scholar who acts not according to his knowledge is like the off-headed ignorant who does not find relief from his ignorance, but the plea of God is greater on the learned and grief more incumbent. He is more blameworthy before God. Sermon 110

Certainly, Messengers were ridiculed before ***you****, but I granted indulgence to those who were ungrateful. Again, I took them. How had been My repayment!* **13:32**

His deviation from the path keeps him at a distance from his aim. Sermon 153

Is He, then, One Who Sustains Every Soul for what it earned? Yet they ascribe associates with God! Say: Name them! Or will you tell Him of what He knows not in the earth? Or name you only them in the manifest sayings? Nay! Made to appear pleasing to those who were ungrateful was their planning and they were barred from the way. Whomever God causes to go astray, for him there is no one who guides. **13:33**

Praise belongs to God. (Q1:2) I praise Him, implore His help and ask for His guidance. I seek protection in Him from error. *Whomever God causes to go astray, for him there is no one who guides.* (Q13:33) Sermon 2

For them is a punishment in this present life and, certainly, punishment in the world to come will be one that presses hard. For them is no one who is a defender against God. **13:34**

O God's human being! Where are those who were allowed long ages to live? They enjoyed bounty. They were taught. They learned. They were given time. They passed it in vain. They were kept healthy. They forgot their duty. They were allowed a long period of life, were handsomely provided for, were warned of grievous punishment and were promised great rewards. You should avoid sins that lead to destruction and vices that attract the wrath of God. Sermon 82

A parable of the Garden which was promised to the ones who are God-conscious; beneath it rivers run. Its produce is one that continues as is its shade. That is the Ultimate End of those who were God-conscious; and the Ultimate End of the ones who are ungrateful is the fire. **13:35**

God, the Almighty, has sent down a guiding Book wherein He has explained virtue and vice. You should adopt the course of virtue, whereby you will have guidance. Detach yourself from the direction of vice, so that you remain on the right way. Sermon 167

Those to whom We gave the Book are glad at what was caused to descend to ***you****. There are among the confederates some who reject some of it. Say: I was commanded to worship only God and not to ascribe partners with Him. I call to Him and to Him is my destination.* **13:36**

In God's authority lies the safety of your affairs. Therefore, render Him such obedience as is neither blameworthy nor insincere. By God, you must do so otherwise God will take away from you the power of Islam and will never thereafter return it to you until it reverts to others. Sermon 169

Thus, We caused to descend an Arabic determination. If ***you*** *followed their desires after what drew near* ***you*** *of the knowledge,* ***you*** *would not have against God either a protector or one who is a defender.* **13:37**

The Book of God is that through which you see, you speak and you hear. Its one part speaks for the other part, and one part bears witness to the other. It does not create differences about God, nor does it mislead its own follower from the path of God. You are joined together in hatred of each other and in the growing of herbage on your covering inner impurity by good appearance outside. You are sincere with one another in your love of desires and bear enmity against each other in earning wealth. The evil spirit (Satan) has perplexed you and deceit has misled you. I seek the help of God for myself and you. Sermon 133

Certainly, We sent Messengers before ***you*** *and We assigned for them spouses and offspring. It had not been for a Messenger to bring a sign but with the permission of God. For every term there is a Book.* **13:38**

Praise belongs to God (Q1:2) Who is recognized without being seen and Who creates without trouble. He created the creation with His Might and receives the devotion of rulers by virtue of His dignity. He exercises superiority over great men through His generosity. It is He who made His creation to populate the world and sent towards the jinn and human beings His Messengers to unveil it for them, to warn them of its harm, to present to them its examples, to show them its defects and to place before them a whole collection of matters containing lessons about the changings of health and sickness in this world, its lawful things and unlawful things and all that God has ordained for the obedient and the disobedient, namely Paradise and Hell and honor and disgrace. I extend my praise to His Being as He desires His creation to praise Him. He has fixed: *Surely God has assigned a measure to everything* (Q65:3) for every measure a time limit, and ....*for every term there is a Book.* (Q13:38) Sermon 183

God blots out what He wills and brings to a standstill what He wills; and with Him is the essence of the Book. **13:39**

On us it is obligatory, for your sake, to abide by the Book of God (Quran), the Sublime, and the conduct of *the Prophet* (Q7:158), peace and the mercy of God be upon him, to stand by His rights and to revive his *sunna*. Sermon 169

Whether We cause ***you*** *to see some of what We have promised them or call* ***you*** *to Ourselves, on* ***you*** *is delivering the message and on Us is the reckoning.* **13:40**

The Prophet (Q7:158), peace and the mercy of God be upon him, left among you what other Prophets had left among their peoples, because Prophets do not leave their people in darkness without a clear path and a sign, namely the Book of your Creator. The Book clarifies its permission and prohibitions, its obligations and discretions, its repealing injunctions and the repealed ones, its permissible matters and compulsory ones, its particulars and general ones, its lessons and illustrations, its long and short ones, its clear and obscure ones, detailing its abbreviations and clarifying its obscurities. Sermon 1

Consider they not that We approach the earth, reducing it from its outlying parts? God gives judgment. There is no one who postpones His determination. He is Swift in reckoning. **13:41**

In His creation, the big, the delicate, the heavy, the light, the strong, the weak are all equal. Sermon 185

Surely, those who were before them planned, but to God is the plan altogether. He knows what every person earns. The ones who are ungrateful will know for whom will be the Ultimate Abode. **13:42**

The great calamity of Hell is the hot water and entry into it, flames of eternal fire and intensity of blazes. There is no resting period, no gap for ease, no power to intervene, no death to bring about solace and no sleep to make him forget pain. He rather lies under several kinds of deaths and moment-to-moment punishment. We seek refuge with God. Sermon 82

Those who were ungrateful say: ***You*** *are not one who is sent. Say: God sufficed as a witness between me and between you and whoever has knowledge of the Book.* **13:43**

Mind the obligations! Mind the obligations! Fulfill them for God and they will take you to the Garden. Surely, God has made unlawful the things which are not unknown and made lawful the things which are without defect. Sermon 167

CHAPTER 14: ABRAHAM (Ibrāhīm)

Alif Lam Ra. This is a Book We caused to descend to ***you*** *so that* ***you*** *bring humanity out from the shadows into the light with the permission of their Lord to the path of The Almighty, The Worthy of Praise.* **14:1**

The Book of God is among you. It speaks. Its tongue does not falter. It is a house whose pillars do not fall down. It is a power whose supporters are never defeated. Sermon 132

God! To Him belongs whatever is in the heavens and whatever is in and on the earth, and woe to the ones who are ungrateful. For them is the severe punishment, **14:2**
those who embrace this present life instead of the world to come and bar from the way of God, and desire in it crookedness. Those are wandering far astray. **14:3**

O my God! We seek **Your** protection from turning away from **Your** command, or revolting against **Your** religion, or being led away by our desires instead of by guidance that comes from **You**. Sermon 215

We sent not any Messenger but with the tongue of his folk in order that he make it manifest for them. Then, God causes to go astray whom He wills and guides whom He wills. He is The Almighty, The Wise. **14:4**

He does not seek your support because of any weakness, nor does He demand a loan from you because of shortage. He seeks your help, although He possesses all: *To God belongs the armies of the heavens and the earth. God has been Almighty, Wise.* (Q14:4) Sermon 183

Certainly, We sent Moses with Our signs saying: Bring out ***your*** *folk from the shadows into the light and remind them of the Days of God. Truly, in that are signs for every enduring, grateful one.* **14:5**
Mention when Moses said to his folk: Remember the divine blessing of God to you when He rescued you from the people of Pharaoh who cause an affliction to befall you—a dire punishment—and slaughter your children and save alive your women. In it was a serious trial from your Lord. **14:6**
Mention when your Lord caused to be proclaimed: If you gave thanks, I will increase your blessings. If you were ungrateful, truly, My punishment will be severe. **14:7**

Moses said: Even if you are ungrateful, you and what is in and on the earth altogether, then, truly, God is Sufficient, Worthy of Praise. **14:8**
Approach not to you the tidings of those before you: The folk of Noah and Ad and Thamud and of those after them. None knows them but God. Their Messengers drew near them with the clear portents, but they shoved their hands into their mouths in denial. Then, they said: Truly, we disbelieved in what you were sent and we are in uncertainty about that to which you call us. We are in grave doubt. **14:9**
Their Messengers said: Is there any uncertainty about God, One Who is Originator of the heavens and the earth? He calls you so that He would forgive you your impieties and postpone for you a term, that which is determined. They said: You are only mortal like us. You want to bar us from what our fathers had been worshipping. Then, bring us a clear authority. **14:10**
Their Messengers said to them: We are only mortals like you except God shows His grace on whom He wills of His servants. It had not been for us that we bring you an authority, but by the permission of God. In God let the ones who believe put their trust. **14:11**

This world did not appear sweet to you in its pleasures and you did not secure milk from its udders except after having met it when its nose-rein was trailing and its leather girth was loose. For certain people its unlawful items were like bent branches laden with fruit while its lawful items were far away, not available. By God, you would find it like a long shade up to a fixed time. So the earth is with you without hindrance and your hands in it are extended while the hands of the leaders are held away from you. Your swords are hanging over them while their swords are held away from you. Sermon 105

Why should we not put our trust in God while, surely, He guided us to our ways? We will endure patiently however you maligned us. In God let the ones who trust, put their trust. **14:12**

The Prophet (Q7:158), peace and the mercy of God be upon him, lit flames for the seeker and put bright signs for the impeded. So he is **Your** trustworthy trustee, **Your** witness on the Day of Judgment, **Your** deputy as a blessing and **Your** Messenger of truth as mercy. My God, distribute to him a share from **Your** Justice and award him multiples of good by **Your** bounty. My God, heighten his construction over the constructions of others, honor him when he comes to **You**, dignify his position before **You**, give him honorable position and award him glory and distinction and bring us out on the Day of Judgment among his party, neither ashamed, nor repentant, nor deviators, nor pledge-breakers, nor strayers, nor misleaders, nor seduced. Sermon 106

Those who were ungrateful said to their Messengers: Certainly, we will drive you out of our region unless you revert to our creed. So, their Lord revealed to them: Truly, We will cause to perish the ones who are unjust. **14:13**

God ... is aware of whatever is hidden in the hearts and whatever lies behind the unseen. Sermon 192

Certainly, We will cause you to dwell in the region after them. This is for whoever feared My station and feared My threat. **14:14**

Hasten towards good actions and dread the suddenness of death.... Hope can be only for that which is to come, while about that which is passed there is only disappointment. *So, Be God-conscious as it is His right that He should be feared and die not but that you be ones who submit to the One God.* (Q3:102) Sermon 113

The Messengers sought judgment and frustrated was every haughty, stubborn one. **14:15**

God never allowed His creation to remain without a Prophet, one deputized by Him, or a Book sent down from Him or a binding argument or a standing plea. These Messengers were such that they did not fear that they were few in comparison to the large numbers of their falsifiers. Among them was either a predecessor who would name the one to follow or the follower who had been introduced by the predecessor. Sermon 1

Hell is ahead of him. He will be given to drink of watery pus. **14:16**

The great calamity of that place is the hot water and entry into Hell, flames of eternal fire and intensity of blazes. There is no resting period, no gap for ease, no power to intervene, no death to bring about solace and no sleep to make him forget pain. He rather lies under several kinds of deaths and moment-to-moment punishment. We seek refuge with God. Sermon 82

He will gulp it and he will be about to swallow it easily when death will approach him from every place, yet he will not be dead. Ahead of him will be a harsh punishment. **14:17**

God will take them out from the corners of the graves, the nests of birds, the dens of beasts and the centers of death. They will hasten towards His command and run towards the place fixed for their final return, group by group, quiet, standing and arrayed in rows. They will be within God's sight and will hear every one who would call them. They will have the dress of helplessness and covering of submission and indignity. At this time contrivances will disappear. Desires will be cut. Hearts will sink quietly. Voices will be lowered. Sweat will choke the throat. Fear will increase. Ears will resound with the thundering voice of the announcer calling towards the final judgment, award of recompense, striking of punishment and paying of reward. Sermon 82

A parable of those who were ungrateful to their Lord, their actions are as ashes over which the wind blew strongly on a tempestuous day. They will have no power over anything they earned. That is the wandering far away, astray. **14:18**

They have gone astray from the straight path. Letter 28

Have **you** *not considered that God created the heavens and the earth in Truth? If He wills, He will cause you to be put away and bring a new creation.* **14:19**

God has provided wonderful creations including the living, the lifeless, the stationary and the moving. He has established such clear proofs for His delicate creative power and great might that minds bend down to Him in acknowledgment thereof and in submission to Him, and arguments about His Oneness strike our ears. He has created birds of various shapes which live in the burrows of the earth, in the openings of high passes and on the peaks of mountains. Sermon 165

That is not a great matter for God. **14:20**

Everything submits to Him. Everything exists by Him. Sermon 108

They will depart to God altogether. Then, the weak would say to those who grew arrogant: Truly, we had been followers of yours. Have you ones who avail us at all against the punishment of God? They would say: If God would have guided us, we would have guided you. It is equal to us whether we were patientless or endured patiently. There is no asylum for us. **14:21**

Certainly, nothing is viler than evil, except its punishment. Nothing is better than good, except its reward. In this world, everything that is heard is better than what is seen, while everything of the next world that is seen is better than what is heard. You should satisfy yourself by hearing rather than seeing and by the news of the unknown. You should know that what is little in this world but much in the next is better than what is much in this world but little in the next. In how many cases little is profitable while much causes loss. Sermon 114

Satan would say when the command would be decided: Truly, God promised you a promise of the Truth. I promised you, but I broke it. I had been no authority over you, but that I called to you and you responded to me. So, blame me not, but blame yourselves. I am not one who assists you nor are you one who assists me. Truly, I was ungrateful for your ascribing me as partner with God before. Truly, the ones who are unjust, for them is a painful punishment. **14:22**

They will not benefit from the wants they will satisfy or the desires they would fulfill. I warn you and myself from this position. A person should derive benefit from his own self. Certainly, prudent is he who hears and ponders over it, who sees and observes and who benefits from instructive material and then treads on clear paths wherein he avoids falling into hollows and straying into pitfalls and does not assist those who misguide him by turning away from truthfulness, changing his words, or fearing truth. Sermon 153

Will be caused to enter those who believed and did as the ones in accord with morality into Gardens beneath which rivers run. They, ones who will dwell in them forever with the permission of their Lord. Their greeting in it will be: Peace! **14:23**

Among the proofs of His creation is the creation of the skies which are fastened without pillars and stand without support. He called them. They responded obediently and humbly without being lazy or loathsome. If they had not acknowledged His Godhead and obeyed Him, He would not have made them the place for His throne, the abode of His angels and the destination: *To Him Words of what is good rise and He exalts an action in accord with morality* ... (Q35:10) of the creatures. Sermon 182

Have ***you*** *not considered how God propounded a parable? What is like a good word is what is like a good tree. Its root is one that is firm and its branches are in heaven.* **14:24**

After *the Prophet* (Q7:158), peace and the mercy of God be upon him, no one preceded me in inviting people to truthfulness, in giving consideration to kinship and practicing generosity. So hear my word and preserve what I say. Sermon 138

It gives all its produce for a while with the permission of its Lord. God propounds parables for humanity so that perhaps they will recollect. **14:25**

The parable of a bad word is that of a bad tree, that was uprooted from above the earth, so it has no stability. **14:26**

I have seen the companions of *the Prophet* (Q7:158), peace and the mercy of God be upon him, but I do not find anyone resembling them. They began the day with dust on the hair and face in hardship of life and passed the night in prostration and standing in prayers. Sometimes they put down their foreheads and sometimes their cheeks. With the recollection of their Resurrection it seemed as though they stood on live coal. It seemed that in between their eyes there were signs like knees of goats, resulting from long prostrations. When God was mentioned, their eyes flowed freely until their shirt collars were drenched. They trembled for fear of punishment and hope of reward as the tree trembles on the day of stormy wind. Sermon 96

God makes firm those who believed with the saying, one that is firm in this present life and in the world to come. God will cause to go astray the ones who are unjust. God accomplishes what He wills. **14:27**

Do you not understand that for you there is a warning in the relics of the predecessors, an eye opener and lesson that your forefathers provided you? Do you not see that your predecessors did not come back and the surviving followers did not remain? Do you not observe that the people of the world pass mornings and evenings in different conditions? Thus, somewhere the dead is wept for, someone is being condoled, someone is prostrate in distress, someone is enquiring about the sick, someone is passing his last breath, someone is hankering after the world while death is looking for him, someone is forgetful, but he is not forgotten by death, and the survivors walk in the footsteps of the predecessors. Sermon 99

Have ***you*** *not considered those who substituted ingratitude for the divine blessing of God and caused their folk to live in abodes of nothingness?* **14:28**
They will roast in hell. Miserable will be the stopping place! **14:29**
They made rivals with God, causing others to go astray from His way. Say: Take joy, but, truly, your homecoming is the fire! **14:30**

A time will come when in the towns nothing will be more hated than virtue, nor anything more acceptable than vice. Sermon 146

Say to My servants who believed that they should perform the formal prayer and spend from what We provided them secretly and in public before a Day approaches in which there is neither trading nor befriending. **14:31**

This is the thing against which God has protected His creatures who are believers by means of prayers, alms-giving and suffering the hardship of fasting in the days in which it has been made obligatory in order to give their limbs peacefulness, to cast fear in their eyes, to make their spirits humble, to give their hearts humility and to remove haughtiness from them. All this is achieved through the covering of their delicate cheeks with dust in humility, prostrating their main limbs on the ground in humbleness and retracting of their bellies so as to reach to their backs due to fasting by way of lowliness before God, in addition to giving all sorts of products of the earth to the needy and the destitute by way of alms. Look what there is in these acts by way of curbing the appearance of pride and suppressing the traces of vanity. Sermon 192

God is He Who created the heavens and the earth and caused water to descend from heaven and brought out thereby fruits as provision for you. He caused boats to be subservient to you that they run through the sea by His command. He caused rivers to be subservient to you. **14:32**

When the excitement of water subsided under the earth's sides and under the weight of the high and lofty mountains placed on its shoulders, God flowed springs of water from its high tops and distributed them through plains and low places and moderated their movement by fixed rocks and high mountain tops. Then its trembling came to a standstill because of the penetration of mountains in various parts of its surface and their being fixed in its deep areas, and their standing on its plains. Sermon 91

He caused the sun to be subservient to you and the moon, both, ones that are constant in their work. He caused the nighttime to be subservient to you and the daytime. **14:33**
He gave you all that you asked of Him. If you were to number the divine blessing of God, you would not count them, truly, the human being is wrongdoing and an ingrate. **14:34**

Praise belongs to God (Q1:2) Whose laudation those who speak about cannot deliver. Sermon 1*

When Abraham said: My Lord! Make this land that which is safe and cause me and my children to turn away from worshipping idols. **14:35**
My Lord! Truly, they caused to go astray many among humanity; so whoever heeded me, truly, he is of me. Whoever rebelled against me, then You are, truly, Forgiving, Compassionate. **14:36**
Our Lord! Truly, I caused to dwell some of my offspring in an unsown valley by Your Holy House, O our Lord, they, certainly, perform the formal prayer. So, make the minds among humanity yearn for them and provide them with fruits so that perhaps they will give thanks. **14:37**
Our Lord! Truly, ***You*** *have known what we conceal and what we speak openly. Nothing is hidden from God in or on the earth or in heaven.* **14:38**
The Praise belongs to God Who bestowed on me in my old age Ishmael and Isaac. Truly, my Lord is Hearing the supplication. **14:39**
My Lord! Make me one who performs the formal prayer and from my offspring also. Our Lord! Receive my supplication. **14:40**
Our Lord! Forgive ***You*** *me and the ones who are my parents and the ones who believe on the Day the reckoning arises.* **14:41** ***

Assume not that God is One Who is Heedless of what the ones who are unjust do. He only postpones their reckoning to a Day when their sight will be fixed in horror, **14:42**
ones who run forward with eyes fixed in horror, ones who lift up their heads. Their glance goes not back to them. Their minds are void. **14:43**

O God's human being! I advise you to be God-conscious, for it is the rein and the mainstay of religion. Hold fast to its salient points. Keep hold of its realities. It will take you to abodes of easiness, places of comfort, fortresses of safety and houses of honor on the Day of Judgment *when their sight will be fixed in horror* (Q14:42), when there will be darkness all round, when small groups of camels pregnant for ten months will be allowed free grazing, and when the Horn will be blown. Then every living being will die. Every voice will become dumb. The high mountains and hard rocks will crumble to pieces, so that their hard stones will turn into moving sand and their bases will become level. On that day, there will be no interceder to intercede, no relation to ward off trouble and no excuse will be of avail. Sermon 194

Warn humanity of a Day the punishment will approach them. So, those who did wrong will say: Our Lord! Postpone for us a near term so that we answer ***Your*** *call and follow the Messengers. Yet swore you not an oath before that there would be no ceasing for you?* **14:44**

I bear witness that *Muhammad* (Q48:29), peace and the mercy of God be upon him, is His *servant* (Q17:1) and His *Prophet.* (Q7:158) He sent him for enforcement of His commands, for exhausting His pleas and for presenting warnings against eternal punishment. Sermon 82

You inhabited the dwellings of those who did wrong to themselves. It became clear to you how We accomplished against them and We propounded for you parables. **14:45**

God's matters have been coming to you and going from and again coming back to you, but you have made over your place to wrong-doers and thrown towards them your responsibilities and have placed God's affairs in their hands. They act in doubts and tread in fulfillment of desires. By God, even if they disperse you under every star, God would surely collect you on the Day that would be worst for them. Sermon 106

Surely, they planned their plan and their plan was with God, even if their plan had been to displace mountains. **14:46**

The beginning of the action of one who sees with his heart and acts with eyes is to assess whether the action will go against him or for him. If it is for him, he indulges in it, but if it is against him, he keeps away from it. For he who acts without knowledge is like one who treads without a path. His deviation from the path keeps him at a distance from his aim. He who acts according to knowledge is like him who treads the clear path. Sermon 153

So, assume not that God will be one who breaks His promise to His Messengers. Truly, God is Almighty, Possessor of Requital. **14:47**

O my God! Forgive me. **You** know more about me than I do. If I return to sin, **You** return to forgiveness. My God, forgive me what I had promised to myself, but **You** did not find its fulfillment with me. My God, forgive me that with what I sought nearness to **You** with my tongue, but my heart opposed and did not perform. My God, forgive me winking of the eye, vile utterances, desires of the heart and errors of speech. Sermon 78

On a Day when the earth will be substituted for other than this earth and the heavens, they will depart to God, The One, The Omniscient God, **14:48**
and ***you*** *will consider the ones who sin that Day, ones who are chained in bonds,* **14:49**
their tunics are made of pitch and the fire will overcome their faces **14:50**
so that God would give recompense to every soul for what it earned. Truly, God is Swift in reckoning. **14:51**

I advise you, O people, to fear God and to praise Him profusely for His favors to you and His reward for you and His obligations on you. See how He chose you for favors and dealt with you with mercy. You sinned openly. He kept you covered. You behaved in a way to incur His punishment, but He gave you more time. Sermon 188

This is the delivering of the message to humanity so that they be warned by it and that they know that He is One God so that those imbued with intuition recollect. **14:52**

(The Quran) is the mine of belief and its center, the source of knowledge and its oceans, the plantation of justice and its pools, the foundation stone of Islam and its construction, the valleys of truth and its plains, an ocean which those who draw water cannot empty, springs which those who draw water cannot dry up, a watering place which those who come to take water cannot exhaust, a staging place in moving towards which travelers do not get lost, signs which no wayfarer fails to see and a highland which those who approach it cannot surpass it. Sermon 198

Chapter 15: The Rocky Tract (al-Ḥijr)

Alif Lam Ra. That are the signs of the Book and of a clear Recitation. **15:1**

Learn the Quran (Recitation) for it is the fairest of discourses and understand it thoroughly for it is the best blossoming of hearts. Seek cure with its light for it is the cure for hearts. Recite it beautifully for it is the most beautiful narration. Sermon 109

It may be those who were ungrateful would wish that they had been ones who submit to God. **15:2**

God ... is aware of whatever is hidden in the hearts and whatever lies behind the unseen. Sermon 192

Forsake them to eat and let them take joy and be diverted with hopefulness. Then, they will know. **15:3**

You should know that what is little in this world but much in the next is better than what is much in this world but little in the next. In how many cases little is profitable while much causes loss. Sermon 113

We caused not a town to perish but there was for it a known prescription. **15:4**
No community precedes its term nor delays it. **15:5**
They say: O ***you*** *to whom was sent down the Remembrance, truly,* ***you*** *are one who is possessed.* **15:6**

... glorifying Him at the first part of the day and the eventide are men whom neither trade nor trading diverts from the remembrance of God and the performing the formal prayer and the giving of purifying alms, for they fear a Day when the hearts will go to and fro and their sight. (Q24:36-37) Truly, God has made the remembrance a polish for the hearts by which they hear after suffering from unwillingness to hear and see after being unwilling to see. There have always been servants of God ... with whom He held intimate discourse through their thoughts and spoke with them through the essence of their intellects. They diffused illumination through the awakened light in their hearing and their seeing and their hearts, calling unto the remembrance of the days of God. Sermon 220*

Why have ***you*** *not brought angels to us if* ***you*** *had been the ones who are sincere?* **15:7**
We send angels down not but with The Truth. If they come to the ungrateful, they would not have been ones who are given respite. **15:8**

The angels do not consider their past virtuous deeds to be great, for if they had considered them great then excessive hope would have wiped away fearfulness from their hearts. They did not differ among themselves about their Sustainer because of Satan's lack of control over them. The vice of separation from one another did not disperse them. Rancor and mutual malice did not overpower them. Ways of wavering did not divide them. Differences of degree of courage did not render them into divisions. Thus, they the angels are captives of faith. Neither crookedness of mind, nor excess, nor lethargy, nor languor loosens them from its bond. There is not the thinnest point in the skies, but there is an angel over it in prostration before God or busy in quick performance of His commands. By long worship of their Sustainer, they increase their knowledge. The honor of their Sustainer increases in their hearts. Sermon 91

Truly, We, We sent down the Remembrance and, truly, We are ones who guard it. **15:9**

He will direct desires towards the path of guidance, while people will have turned guidance towards desires. He will turn their views to the direction of the Quran, while the people will have turned the Quran to their views. Sermon 138

Certainly, We sent Messengers before ***you*** *to partisans of the ancient ones.* **15:10**
Approach them not any Messenger but they had been ridiculing him. **15:11**

Confirm and testify the truth said before in the religions of ancient prophets. Take lessons from history for your future because history often repeats itself. Future nations of the world will mostly follow the footsteps of those who have passed. Letter 69

Thus, We thrust it into the hearts of the ones who sin. **15:12**
They believe not in it. Surely, passed away before them a custom of the ancient ones. **15:13**
Even if We opened for them a door from heaven and they continued going up to it, **15:14**
they would say: Truly, our sight was dazzled. Nay! We were a bewitched folk. **15:15**

Certainly, there are examples before you of God's wrath, punishment, days of tribulations and happenings. Therefore, do not disregard His promises. Do not ignore His punishment or make light His wrath and not expect His violence, because God, the Almighty, did not curse the past ages unless they had left off asking others to do good acts and refraining them from bad acts. In fact, God cursed the foolish for committing sins and the wise because they gave up refraining others from evil. Be aware! You have broken the bonds of Islam, transgressed its limits, and destroyed its commands. Sermon 192

Certainly, We made constellations in the heavens and We made them appear pleasing to the ones who look. **15:16**
We kept them safe from every accursed satan, **15:17**
but he who had the ability to hear by eavesdropping. Then, a clear flame pursued him. **15:18**
We stretched out the earth and We cast on it firm mountains and We caused to develop on it that which was well-balanced of everything. **15:19**
We made on it for you a livelihood and for whomever you are not ones who provide. **15:20**

In His creation, the large, the delicate, the heavy, the light, the strong, the weak are all equal. Sermon 185

There is not a thing, but its treasures are with Us and We send it down not but in a known measure. **15:21**

He knows whatever has been treasured by mother-of-pearls, and covered under the waves of oceans, all that which is concealed under the darkness of night and all that on which the light of day is shining, as well as all that on which sometimes darkness prevails and sometimes light shines, the trace of every footstep, the feel of every movement, the echo of every sound, the motion of every lip, the abode of every living being, the weight of every particle, the sobs of every sobbing heart, and whatever is there on the earth like fruits of trees or falling leaf, or the settling place of semen, or the congealing of blood or clot and the developing of life and embryo. Sermon 91

We sent fertilizing winds. Then, We caused water to descend from heaven, then, We satiated you, and you are not ones who are its keepers. **15:22**

He brought forth creation through His Omnipotence, dispersed winds through His Compassion, and made firm the shaking earth with rocks. Sermon 1

Truly, it is We Who give life and cause to die and We are the ones who inherit. **15:23**
Certainly, We knew the ones who precede among you and, certainly, We knew the ones who come later. **15:24**

You should fear God! God! Sermon 192

Truly, ***your*** *Lord is He Who assembles. Truly, He is Wise, Knowing.* **15:25**

This world and the hereafter have submitted to Him their reins. The skies and earths have flung their keys towards Him. The thriving trees bow to Him in the morning and evening, producing for Him flaming fire from their branches and, at His command, turn their own feed into ripe fruits. Sermon 133

Certainly, We created the human being out of earth-mud of soft wet earth. **15:26**
We created the ones who are spirits before from the fire of a burning wind. **15:27**

God collected from hard, soft, sweet and sour earth, clay which He dripped in water until it became pure and kneaded it with moisture until it became clay-like. From it He carved an image with curves, joints, limbs and segments. He solidified it until it dried up for a fixed time and a known duration. Then He blew into it out of His Spirit whereupon it took the pattern of a human being with mind that governs him, intelligence which he makes use of, limbs that serve him, organs that change his position, sagacity that differentiates between truth and untruth, tastes and smells, colors and species. He is a mixture of clays of different colors, cohesive materials, divergent contradictories and differing properties like heat, cold, softness and hardness. Sermon 1

Mention when ***your*** *Lord said to the angels: Truly, I am One Who is Creator of mortals out of earth-mud of soft wet earth.* **15:28**
That is when I shaped him and blew into him of My Spirit. So, fall down before him as ones who prostrate themselves. **15:29**

Then He created the openings between high skies and filled them with all classes of His angels. Sermon 1

The angels prostrated themselves, one and all, **15:30**
but Iblis. He refused to be with the ones who prostrate themselves. **15:31**
He said: O Iblis! What is with ***you*** *that* ***you*** *be not with the ones who prostrate themselves?* **15:32**
Iblis said: I will not be prostrating myself before a mortal whom ***You*** *created out of earth-mud of soft wet earth.* **15:33**
It was said: Go ***you*** *forth from here, for, truly,* ***you*** *are accursed!* **15:34**
Truly, a curse will be upon ***you*** *until the Day of Judgment.* **15:35**
Iblis said: O my Lord! Give me respite until the Day they are raised up. **15:36**
He said: Then, truly, ***you*** *are among the ones who are given respite* **15:37**
until the Day of the known time. **15:38**

Self-importance withheld Satan and vice overcame him so that he took pride in his own creation with fire and treated contemptuously the creation of clay. So God allowed him time in order to let him fully deserve His wrath, to complete the test and to fulfill the promise: *He said: Then, truly,* ***you*** *are among the ones who are given respite until the Day of the known time.* Sermon 1

Iblis said: My Lord! Because ***You*** *led me into error I will, certainly, make the earth appear pleasing to them and I will lead them one and all into error,* **15:39**

You should fear lest Satan infects you with his disease, or leads you astray through his call, or marches on you with his horsemen and footmen, because, by my life, he has put the arrow to the bow for you, has stretched the bow to its limits, and has aimed at you from a nearby position: *Iblis said: My Lord! Because* ***You*** *led me into error I will, certainly, make the earth appear pleasing to them and I will lead them one and all into error.* (Q15:39) Sermon 191

but ***Your*** *servants among them, the ones who are devoted.* **15:40**
He said: This is the straight path to Me. **15:41**
Truly, as for My servants there is no authority for ***you*** *over them, but ones who are in error followed* ***you****.* **15:42**
Truly, hell is promised to them one and all. **15:43**
It has seven doors. Then, for every one, a door set apart, is for them. **15:44** ***

Truly, the ones who are God-conscious will be amidst gardens and springs. **15:45**
Enter them in peace as ones who are safe! **15:46**

One of the firm decisions of God in the Wise Reminder (Quran), upon which He bestows reward or gives punishment and through which He likes or dislikes, is that it will not benefit a person, even though he exerts himself and acts sincerely, if he leaves this world to meet God with one of these acts without repenting, namely that he believed in a partner with God during his obligatory worship or appeased his own anger by killing an individual or spoke about acts committed by others or sought fulfillment of his needs from people by introducing an innovation in his religion or met people with a double face or moved among them with a double tongue. Understand this because an illustration is a guide for its like. Sermon 153

We will tear out any grudges from their breasts. They will be as brothers/sisters on couches, one facing the other. **15:47**
In it neither fatigue will afflict them nor will they be ones who are driven out. **15:48**

God, the Almighty, has sent down a guiding Book wherein He has explained virtue and vice. You should adopt the course of virtue, whereby you will have guidance. Detach yourself from the direction of vice, so that you remain on the right way. Sermon 167

Tell My servants that I am The Forgiving, The Compassionate **15:49**
and that My punishment, it is a painful punishment. **15:50**
Tell them about the guests of Abraham **15:51**
when they entered upon him and said: Peace! He said: Truly, we are afraid of you. **15:52**
They said: Take no notice. Truly, we give ***you*** *good tidings of a knowing boy.* **15:53**
He said: Gave you good tidings to me even though old age afflicted me? So, of what give you good tidings? **15:54**
They said: We gave ***you*** *good tidings of The Truth, so* ***you*** *are not of the ones who despair.* **15:55**
He said: Who despairs of the mercy of his Lord, but the ones who go astray? **15:56**
He said: Then, what is your business, O the ones who are sent? **15:57**

They said: We were sent to a folk, ones who sin, **15:58**
but the family of Lot. Truly, we are ones who will deliver them one and all, **15:59**
but his woman. We ordained that she be of the ones who stay behind. **15:60**
Then, when the ones who are sent drew near the people of Lot, **15:61**
he said: Truly, you are folk, ones unlawful to me. **15:62**
They said: Nay! We drew near you with what they had been contesting in it. **15:63**
We approached ***you*** *with The Truth and, truly, we are ones who are sincere.* **15:64**
Then, set forth with ***your*** *family in a part of the night and follow* ***you*** *their backs and look not back any of you, but pass on to where you are commanded.* **15:65**
We decreed the command to him that the last remnant of these would be that which is severed, in that which is morning. **15:66**
The people of the city drew near rejoicing at the good tidings. **15:67**
Lot said: Truly, these are my guests, so put me not to shame. **15:68**
Be God-conscious and cover me not with shame. **15:69**
They said: Prohibit we ***you*** *not from some beings?* **15:70**
Lot said: These are my daughters if you had been ones who do something. **15:71**
By ***your*** *life, truly, they were in a daze, wandering unwilling to see.* **15:72**
So, the Cry took them at sunrise. **15:73**
We made its high part low and We rained down on them rocks of baked clay. **15:74**
Truly, in this are signs for the ones who read marks. **15:75**
Truly, they are ones who are on an abiding way. **15:76**
Truly, in it is a sign for the ones who believe. **15:77**
Truly, the Companions of the Thicket had been ones who are unjust **15:78**
so We requited them and they were both on a clear high road. **15:79**
Certainly, the Companions of the Rocky Tract denied the ones who are sent. **15:80**
We gave them Our signs. Then, they had been ones who turn aside from them. **15:81**
They had been carving out safe houses from mountains, **15:82**
but the Cry took them in that which is morning. **15:83**
Availed them not what they had been earning. **15:84** ***

We created not the heavens and the earth and whatever is in between them but with The Truth. Truly, the Hour is one that arrives. So, overlook with a graceful overlooking. **15:85**

No other originator took part with Him in its origination and no one having power assisted Him in its creation. Sermon 185

Truly, ***your*** *Lord is The Knowing Creator.* **15:86**

He created the whole of creation without any example made by someone else. He did not secure the assistance of any one out of His creation for creating it. He created the earth and suspended it without being busy, retained it without support, made it stand without legs, raised it without pillars, protected it against bendings and curvings and defended it against crumbling and splitting into parts. He fixed mountains on it like stumps, solidified its rocks, caused its streams to flow and opened wide its valleys. Whatever He made did not suffer from any frailty. Whatever He strengthened did not show any weakness. He manifests Himself over the earth with His authority and greatness. He is aware of its inside through His knowledge and understanding. He has power over everything in the earth by virtue of His sublimity and dignity. Nothing from the earth that He may ask for defies Him, nor does it oppose Him so as to overpower Him. No swift-footed creature can run away from

Him so as to surpass Him. He is not needy towards any possessing person so that he should feed Him. All things bow to Him and are humble before His greatness. They cannot flee away from His authority to someone else in order to escape His benefit or His harm. There is no parallel for Him who may match Him and no one like Him so as to equal Him. Sermon 186

Certainly, We gave **you** *seven often repeated parts of the sublime Quran.* **15:87**

The Book of God is among you. It speaks and its tongue does not falter. It is a house whose pillars do not fall down, and a power whose supporters are never routed. Sermon 133

Stretch not out **your** *eyes for what We gave of enjoyment in this life to spouses among them, nor feel remorse for them, but make low* **your** *wing in kindness to the ones who believe.* **15:88**

You should therefore put out the fires of haughtiness and the flames of intolerance that are hidden in your hearts. This vanity can exist in a Muslim only by the machinations of Satan, his haughtiness, mischief and whisperings. Make up your mind to have humility over your heads, to trample self-pride under your feet and to cast off vanity from your necks. Adopt humility as the weapon between you and your enemy, Satan and his forces. He certainly has, from every people, fighters, helpers, footmen and horsemen. Do not be like him who feigned superiority over the son of his own mother without any distinction given to him by God except the feeling of envy which his feeling of greatness created in him and the fire of anger that vanity kindled in his heart. Satan blew into his nose his own vanity, after which God gave him remorse and made him responsible for the sins of all killers up to the Day of Judgment. Sermon 192

Say: Truly, I am a clear warner, **15:89**
even as We caused to descend on the ones who are partitioners, **15:90**
those who made the Quran into fragments. **15:91**
So, by **your** *Lord, We will, certainly, ask them one and all* **15:92**
about what they had been doing. **15:93**
So, call aloud what **you** *are commanded: Turn aside from the ones who are polytheists!* **15:94**
Truly, We sufficed **you** *against the ones who ridicule,* **15:95**
those who make with God another god. But they will know. **15:96**

By God! *Truly we have been clearly wandering astray when we made you equal with the Lord of the worlds.* (Q26:97-98) They are wrong who liken **You** to their idols, and dress **You** with apparel of the creatures by their imagination, attribute to **You** parts of body by their own thinking and consider **You** after the creatures of various types, through the working of their intelligence. I bear witness that whoever equated **You** with anything out of **Your** creation took a partner for **You**. Whoever takes a partner for **You** is ungrateful according to what is stated in **Your** unambiguous verses and indicated by the evidence of **Your** clear arguments. I also bear witness that **You** are that God Who cannot be confined in the fetters of intelligence so as to admit change of condition by entering its imagination, nor in the shackles of the mind so as to become limited and an object of alterations. Sermon 91

Certainly, We know that **your** *breast became narrowed, injured in spirit, because of what they say.* **15:97**

Do not take to heart the behavior of the Quraysh. To talk about their skepticism, their enmity of Islam, their revolt against the cause of God and their desire to bring harm to me are a waste of time. They now are as much bent upon doing me injustice and fighting against me as they were unanimously against *the Prophet* (Q7:158), peace and the mercy of God be upon him. Letter 36

So, glorify the praises of ***your*** *Lord and be among the ones who prostrate themselves* **15:98**
and worship ***your*** *Lord until the certainty approaches* ***you.*** **15:99**

Whosoever establishes well-being between himself and God, God establishes well-being between him and humanity. Saying 89

CHAPTER 16: THE BEE (al-Naḥl)

Approached the command of God? Seek not to hasten it. Glory be to Him and exalted is He above partners they ascribe with God. **16:1**
He sends down the angels with the Spirit of His command on whom He wills of His servants to warn that there is no god but I, so be God-conscious of Me. **16:2**
He created the heavens and the earth with The Truth. Exalted is He above partners they ascribe. **16:3**

I bear witness that *there is no god but God* (Q47:19), Who has no parallel, Who is not doubted, Whose religion is not denied and Whose creativeness is not questioned. My witnessing is like that of a person whose intention is free, whose conscience is clear, whose belief is pure and whose loads of good actions are heavy. I also bear witness that Muhammad, peace and the mercy of God be upon him, is His *servant* (Q17:1) and His *Messenger* (Q3:101), chosen from His creations, selected for detailing His realities, picked for His selected honors and chosen for His esteemed messages. Through him the signs of guidance have been lighted and the gloom of misguidance has been dispelled. Sermon 177

He created the human being from seminal fluid. That is when he is a clear adversary. **16:4**

My dear son, do not be carried away and be allured by the infatuations of the worldly people in the vicious life and its pleasures as an adversary to God. Do not be impressed by the sight of their acute struggle to possess and own this world. God has very mercifully explained to you everything about this world. Not only the Merciful Lord, but also the world has also told you everything. It has disclosed to you that it is mortal. It has openly declared its weakness, its shortcomings and its vices. Remember that these worldly-minded people are like barking dogs and hungry and ferocious beasts. Some of them are constantly barking at others. The mighty lords kill and massacre the poor and the weak. Their powerful persons exploit and tyrannize the powerless. Their inordinate desires and their greed have such a complete hold over them that you will find some of them like animals tamed and tied with a rope round their feet and necks. They have lost the freedom of thought and cannot come out of the enslavement of their desires and habits. While there are others whom wealth and power have turned mad. They behave like unruly beasts, trampling, crushing and killing their fellow beings, and destroying things around them. The history of this world is merely a reward of such incidents, some big and some small, the difference is of might, but the intensity is the same. These people have lost the balance of their minds. They do not know what they are doing and where they are going, scan their activities and study their ways of thinking and you will find them confused and irrational. They appear like cattle wandering in a dreary desert where there is no water to drink and no fodder to eat, no shepherd to cater for them and no guardian to look after them. What has actually happened to them is that the vicious world has taken possession of them. It is dragging them wherever it likes. It is treating them as if they are blind because it has in reality blind-folded them against the Divine light of the true religion. They are wandering without reasonable aims and sober purposes in the bewitching show that the world has staged for them. They are fully intoxicated with the pleasures amassed around them. They take this world to be their god and nourisher. The world is amusing them and they are amused with it and have forgotten and forsaken everything else, but the nights of enjoyments and pleasures will not last long for anybody. The dawn of realities will break sooner or later. The caravan of life will surely reach its destination one day. One who has nights and days acting as piebald horses for him, carrying him onward and onward towards his journey's end must remember that though he may feel as if he is stopping at one place, yet actually he is moving on. He is proceeding to his destination. Every day is carrying him a step further in his journey towards death. Letter 31

He created the flocks, for you in which there is warmth and profits and of them you eat **16:5**
and in them is a beauty for you when you give them rest and when you drive forth flocks to pasture. **16:6**
They carry your lading to a land, being that which reaches you not but under adverse circumstances to yourselves. Truly, your Lord is Gentle, Compassionate. **16:7**

In His creation, the big, the delicate, the heavy, the light, the strong, the weak are all equal. Sermon 185

He creates horses, mules and donkeys for you to ride and as an adornment. He creates what you know not. **16:8**

This world and the hereafter have submitted to Him their reins. The skies and earths have flung their keys towards Him. The thriving trees bow to Him in the morning and evening, producing for Him flaming fire from their branches and, at His command, turn their own feed into ripe fruits. Sermon 133

With God is showing of the way yet some of them are ones who swerve. If He willed, He would have guided you one and all. **16:9**

God ... is aware of whatever is hidden in the hearts and whatever lies behind the unseen. Sermon 192

It is He Who caused water to descend from heaven for you to drink from it and from it, trees wherein you pasture your herds. **16:10**

When Almighty God created the openings of the atmosphere, the expanse of firmament and strata of winds, He flowed into it water whose waves were stormy and whose surges leapt one over the other. He loaded it on dashing wind and breaking typhoons, ordered them to shed it back as rain, gave the wind control over the vigor of the rain, and acquainted it with its limitations. The wind blew under it while water flowed furiously over it. Sermon 91

He caused crops to develop for you with it, and the olives and the date palms and the grapevines, and all kinds of fruits. Truly, in that is a sign for a folk who reflect. **16:11**

So when the crop grows and stands on stalks, its foam shoots forth and its lightning shines.... Sermon 101

He caused to be subservient to you the nighttime and the daytime and the sun and the moon, and the stars, ones caused to be subservient by His command. Truly, in that are signs for a folk who are reasonable. **16:12**

He hung in its vastness its sky and put therein its decoration consisting of small bright pearls and lamp-like stars. He shot at the over-hearers arrows of bright meteors. He put them in motion on their appointed routine and made them into fixed stars, moving stars, descending stars, ascending stars, ominous stars and lucky stars. Sermon 91

Whatever He made numerous for you in and on the earth of hues, ones that are at variance, truly, in that is a sign for a folk who recollect. **16:13**

In His creation, the big, the delicate, the heavy, the light, the strong, the weak are all equal. Sermon 185

He it is Who caused the sea to be subservient to you so that you eat from it succulent flesh and pull out of it glitter to wear and **you** *see the boats, ones that plow through the waves, that you be looking for His grace and so that perhaps you will give thanks.* **16:14**

He cast on to the earth firm mountains so that it not vibrate with you and rivers and roads so that perhaps you will be truly guided **16:15**

and landmarks. They are truly guided by the stars. **16:16**

Is, then, He Who creates as he who creates not? Will you not, then, recollect? **16:17**

If you try to number the divine blessing of God, you will not be able to count it. Truly, God is Forgiving, Compassionate. **16:18**

Praise belongs to God (Q1:2) Whose laudation those who speak cannot deliver. Sermon 1*

God knows what you keep secret and what you speak openly. **16:19**

O people! Every one shall meet what he wishes to avoid by running away. Death is the place to which life is driving. To run away from it means to catch it. How many days did I spend in searching for the secret of this matter, but God did not allow save its concealment. Alas! It is a treasured knowledge. Sermon 149

Those whom you call to other than God, they created not anything but they are themselves created. **16:20**

They are lifeless, not living. They are not aware when they will be raised up. **16:21**

... the wrongful followers disclaim their false gods by saying: *By God! Truly, we had been clearly wandering astray when we made you equal with the Lord of the worlds.* (Q26:97-98) Sermon 90

Your God is One God. But for those who believe not in the world to come, their hearts are ones that know not and they are ones who grow arrogant. **16:22**

I bear witness that *there is no god but God* (Q47:19), the One. I bear witness that *there is no god but God* (Q47:19), the One. He has no like. My bearing witness has been tested. Its essence is our belief. We shall cling to it for as long as we live and shall store it facing the tribulations that overtake us because it is the foundation stone of faith and the first step towards good actions and divine pleasure. It is the means to keep Satan away. Sermon 2

Without a doubt God knows what they keep secret and what they speak openly. Truly, He loves not the ones who grow arrogant. **16:23**

O God's human being! Know that your own self is a guard over you. Limbs are as watchmen and truthful vigil-keepers who preserve the record of your actions and the number of your breaths. The gloom of the dark night cannot conceal you from them, nor can closed doors hide you from them. Surely, tomorrow is close to today. Sermon 157

When it is said to them: What is that your Lord caused to descend, they would say: Fables of the ancient ones! **16:24**

One of the firm decisions of God in the Wise Reminder (Quran), upon which He bestows reward or gives punishment and through which He likes or dislikes, is that it will not benefit a person, even though he exerts himself and acts sincerely, if he leaves this world to meet God with one of these acts without repenting, namely that he believed in a partner with God during his obligatory worship or appeased his own anger by killing an individual or spoke about acts committed by others or sought fulfillment of his needs from people by introducing an innovation in his religion or met people with a double face or moved among them with a double tongue. Understand this because an illustration is a guide for its like. Sermon 153

They will carry their own heavy loads, that which is complete, on the Day of Resurrection, and of the heavy loads of whomever they cause to go astray without knowledge. How evil is what they will bear! **16:25**

On that Day many an argument will prove void and a contention for excuses will stand rejected. Sermon 222

Surely, those who were before them planned, then, God approached their structures from the foundations and the roof fell down upon them from above and the punishment approached them from where they are not aware. **16:26**

Did you not witness those who engaged in long-reaching desires, built strong buildings, amassed much wealth, but their houses turned into graves and whatever they had collected turned into ruin? Their property devolved on the successors and their spouses on those who came after them. They cannot now add to their good acts, nor invoke God's mercy in respect of evil acts. Therefore, whoever makes his heart habituated to God-consciousness achieves a forward position. His action is successful. Sermon 132

Again, on the Day of Resurrection He will cover them with shame and will say: Where are My ascribed associates with whom you had been making a breach with them? Those who were given the knowledge will say: Truly, degradation this Day and evil upon the ones who are ungrateful. **16:27**

Those whom the angels call to themselves while they are ones who are unjust to themselves. Then, they will give a proposal of surrender: We had not been doing any evil. Yea! Truly, God is Knowing of what you had been doing. **16:28**

Where are those who protect honor, and those self-respecting persons who defend respectable persons in the time of hardship? Shame is behind you while the Garden is in front of you. Sermon 171

So, enter the doors of hell—ones who will dwell in it forever; and, certainly, it will be a miserable place of lodging. It is for the ones who increase in pride! **16:29**

Everyone of them is ... alone although they are a group, and they are strangers, even though friends. They are unaware of morning after a night and of evening after a day. The night or the day when they departed has become ever existent for them. They found the dangers of their place of stay more serious than they had apprehended, and they witnessed that its signs were greater than they had guessed. Sermon 220

When it was said to those who were God-conscious: What is it that your Lord caused to descend? They will say: Good or for those who did good in the present, there is benevolence. The abode of the world to come is better. How excellent will be the abode of the ones who are God-conscious! **16:30**

Among the God-conscious are the people of distinction. Their speech is to the point. Their dress is moderate. Their gait is humble. They keep their eyes closed to what God has made unlawful for them. They put their ears to that knowledge which is beneficial to them. They remain in the time of trials as though they remain in comfort. If there had not been fixed periods of life ordained for each, their spirits would not have remained in their bodies even for the twinkling of an eye because of their eagerness for the reward and fear of chastisement. The greatness of the Creator is seated in their heart, and so everything else appears small in their eyes. Thus, to them Paradise is as though they see it and are enjoying its favors. To them, Hell is also as if they see it and are suffering punishment in it. Sermon 193

Gardens of Eden which they will enter beneath which rivers run. They have in them all that they will. Thus, God gives recompense to the ones who are God-conscious. **16:31**

Among them are those who work as trusted bearers of His message, those who serve as speaking tongues for His prophets and those who carry to and fro His orders and injunctions. Among them are the protectors of His creatures and guards of the doors of the gardens of Paradise. Sermon 1

Those whom the angels call to themselves while they are ones who are good. They say to them: Peace be unto you! Enter the Garden because of what you had been doing. **16:32**

Paradise is the best reward and achievement. Sermon 82

Look they not on but that the angels approach them or the command of your Lord approach? Thus, accomplished those before them. God did not wrong them. Rather, they had been doing wrong to themselves. **16:33**

Then, their evil deeds lit on them for what their hands did. Surrounded them is what they had been ridiculing. **16:34**

If God had wanted to create Adam from a light whose glare would have dazzled the eyes, whose handsomeness would have amazed the wits and whose fragrance would have caught the breath, He could have done so. If He had done so people would have bowed to him in humility and the trial of the angels through him would have become easier, but God, the Almighty, tries His creatures by means of those things whose real nature they do not know in order to distinguish good and bad for them through the trial, and to remove vanity from them and keep them away from pride and self-admiration. Sermon 192

Those who ascribed partners with God said: If God willed neither would we have worshiped other than Him anything, we nor our fathers, nor would we have held sacred anything other than what He forbade. Thus, accomplished those who were before them. Then, what is upon the Messengers, but the delivering of the clear message? **16:35**
Certainly, We raised up in every community a Messenger saying that: Worship God and avoid false deities. Then, of them were some whom God guided and of them were some upon whom their fallacy was realized. So, journey through the earth; then, look on how had been the Ultimate End of the ones who deny. **16:36**
If ***you*** *be eager for their guidance, then, truly, God will not guide whom He causes to go astray. They will have no ones who help.* **16:37**
They swore by God their most earnest oaths: God will not raise up him who dies. Yea! It is a promised obligation upon Him—except most of humanity knows not— **16:38**
in order to make manifest for them about what they are at variance in it and so that those who were ungrateful know that they had been ones who lie. **16:39**

They took to the right and the left piercing through to the ways of evil and leaving the paths of guidance. Do not make haste for a matter which is to happen and is awaited. Do not wish for delay in what the morrow is to bring for you. For how many people make haste for a matter, but when they get it they begin to wish they had not gotten it? How near is today to the dawning of tomorrow? O my people, this is the time for the occurrence of every promised event and the approach of things which you do not know. Sermon 150

Our saying to a thing when We wanted it is that We say to it: Be! Then, it is! **16:40**

Glory be to **You**! How great is **Your** affair! Glory to **You**! How great is **Your** creation that we see, but how small is this greatness by the side of **Your** Might! How awe-striking is **Your** realm that we notice, but how humble is this against what is hidden from us out of **Your** authority! How extensive are **Your** bounties in this world, but how small are they against the bounties of the next world! Sermon 108

As for those who emigrated for God after they were wronged, We will, certainly, have a place of settlement for them with benevolence in the present. The compensation of the world to come will be greater, if they had been knowing. **16:41**

One belief is that which is firm and steadfast in hearts. Another belief is that which remains temporarily in the heart and the breast up to a certain time. If you were to acquit yourself before any person, you should wait until death approaches him, for that is the time limit for being acquitted. Sermon 189

Those who endured patiently, they put their trust in their Lord. **16:42**

Even when He made Adam die, He did not leave them without one who would serve among them as proof and plea for His Godhead and serve as the link between them and His knowledge, but He provided to them the proofs through His chosen Messengers and bearers of the trust of His Message, age after age, until the process came to end with our Prophet Muhammad, peace and the mercy of God be upon him, and His pleas and warnings reached finality. Sermon 91

We sent not before **you** *but men to whom We reveal revelation. So, ask the People of Remembrance if you had not been knowing.* **16:43**

Know that this Quran is an adviser who never deceives, a leader who never misleads and a narrator who never speaks a lie. No one will sit beside this Quran, but when he rises, he will achieve one addition or one diminution—addition in his guidance or elimination in his spiritual blindness. You should also know that no one will need anything after guidance from the Quran and no one will be free from want before guidance from the Quran. Seek cure from the Quran for your ailments and seek its assistance in your distress. It contains a cure for the worst diseases, namely unbelief, hypocrisy, revolt and misguidance. Pray to God through it. Turn to God with its love ... There is nothing like it through which the people should turn to God, the Sublime. Sermon 176

With the clear portents and the ancient scrolls, We caused to descend the Remembrance to **you** *that* **you** *will make manifest to humanity what was sent down to them and so that perhaps they will reflect.* **16:44**

One of the firm decisions of God in the Wise Reminder (Quran) upon which He bestows reward or gives punishment, and through which He likes or dislikes, is that it will not benefit a person, even though he exerts himself and acts sincerely, if he leaves this world to meet God with one of these acts without repenting, namely that he believed in a partner with God during his obligatory worship, or appeased his own anger by killing an individual, or spoke about acts committed by others, or sought fulfillment of his needs from people by introducing an innovation in his religion, or met people with a double face, or moved among them with a double tongue. Understand this because an illustration is a guide for its like. Sermon 153

Were those who planned evil deeds safe that God will not cause the earth to swallow them or that the punishment will not approach them from where they are not aware? **16:45**

In case you cannot avoid vanity, your vanity should be for good qualities, praiseworthy acts and admirable matters with which the dignified and noble chiefs of the Arab families distinguished themselves such as attractive manners, high thinking, respectable position and good performances. You too should show vanity in praiseworthy habits like the protection of the neighbor, the fulfillment of agreements, obedience to the virtuous, opposition to the haughty, extending generosity to others, abstention from rebellion, keeping aloof from bloodshed, doing justice to people, suppressing anger and avoiding trouble on the earth. You should also fear what calamities befell peoples before you on account of their evil deeds and detestable actions. Remember, during good or bad circumstances, what happened to them. Be cautious that you do not become like them. Sermon 192

Or that He take them in their going to and fro where they will not be ones who frustrate Him? **16:46**

Or that He take them, destroying them little by little? Truly, **your** *Lord is Gentle, Compassionate.* **16:47**

God ... is aware of whatever is hidden in the hearts and whatever lies behind the unseen. Sermon 192

Consider they not that whatever things God created casts its shadow to the right and to the left, ones who prostrate themselves to God. They are ones in a state of lowliness? **16:48**

O God! The eyes have not seen **You** so as to be aware of **You**, but **You** were before the describers of **Your** creation. **You** did not create the creation on account of loneliness, nor did **You** make them work for gain. He whom **You** catch cannot go farther than **You**, and he whom **You** hold cannot escape **You**. He who disobeys **You** does not decrease **Your** authority. He who obeys **You** does not add to **Your** Might. He who disagrees with **Your** judgment cannot turn it. He who turns away from **Your** command cannot do without **You**. Every secret before **You** is open and for **You** every absent is present. **You** are everlasting. There is no end to **You. You** are the highest aim. There is no escape from **You. You** are the promised point of return from which there is no deliverance except towards **You**. In **Your** hand is the forelock of every creature. To **You** is the return of every living being. Glory be to **You**! How great is **Your** affair! Glory to **You**! How great is **Your** creation that we see, but how small is this greatness by the side of **Your** Might! How awe-striking is **Your** realm that we notice, but how humble is this against what is hidden from us out of **Your** authority! How extensive are **Your** bounties in this world, but how small are they against the bounties of the next world! Sermon 108

To God prostrates whatever is in the heavens and all that is in and on the earth of moving creatures and the angels and they grow not arrogant. **16:49**

O God's human being! Fear like the fear of one who has control over himself, who can check his passions and perceive with his wisdom. Surely, the matter is quite clear, the sign is manifest, the course is level and the way is straight. Sermon 161

They fear their Lord above them and accomplish what they are commanded. **16:50**

The Prophet (Q33:6) of God, peace and the mercy of God be upon him, said: The belief of a person cannot be firm unless his heart is firm, and his heart cannot be firm unless his tongue is firm. So whoever of you can manage to meet God, the Sublime, in such a position that his hands are unsmeared with the blood of Muslims and their property and his tongue is safe from exposing them, he should do so. Sermon 176

God said: Take not two gods to yourselves. Truly, He is One God. Then, have reverence for Me. **16:51**

I bear witness that *there is no god but God* (Q47:19), the One, there is no partner with Him nor is there with Him any god other than Himself, and that *Muhammad* (Q48:29), peace and the mercy of God be upon him, is His *servant* (Q17:1) and His *Prophet.* (Q7:158) Sermon 35

To Him belongs whatever is in the heavens and the earth and His is the way of life, that which is forever. Are you God-conscious of other than God? **16:52**

O God's human being! I advise you to be God-conscious which is the provision for the next world and with it is your return. Sermon 114

Whatever you have of divine blessing is from God. After that when harm afflicted you, you make

entreaties to Him. **16:53**
Again, when He removed the harm from you, that is when a group of people among you ascribe partners with their Lord. **16:54**
They are ungrateful for what We gave them. So, let them take joy. They will know. **16:55**
They assign to what they know not a share from what We provided them. By God! You will, certainly, be asked about what you had been devising. **16:56**
They assign daughters to God! Glory be to Him! For themselves, that for which they lust. **16:57**

I bear witness that *there is no god but God* (Q47:19), Who has no parallel, Who is not doubted, Whose religion is not denied and Whose creativeness is not questioned. My witnessing is like that of a person whose intention is free, whose conscience is clear, whose belief is pure and whose loads of good actions are heavy. I also bear witness that Muhammad, peace and the mercy of God be upon him, is His *servant* (Q17:1) and *His Messenger* (Q3:101), chosen from His creations, selected for detailing His realities, picked for His selected honors and chosen for His esteemed messages. Through him the signs of guidance have been lit and the gloom of misguidance has been dispelled. Sermon 177

When any of them was given good tidings of a female, his face stayed one that is clouded over and he chokes. **16:58**
He is secluded from the folk because of the dire tidings he was given. Will he hold it back with humiliation or will he trample it in the earth dust? Truly, how evil is the judgment they give! **16:59**

God alone knows what is there in the wombs ... generous or miserly, mischievous or pious, and who will be the fuel for Hell and who will be in the company of the Prophets in Paradise. This is the knowledge of the hidden things which is not known to anyone save God. All else is that whose knowledge God passed on to His Prophet and he passed it on to me and prayed for me that my bosom may retain it and my ribs may hold it. Sermon 128

For those who believe not in the world to come there is the reprehensible evil description while the loftiest description belongs to God. He is The Almighty, The Wise. **16:60**

God ... is aware of whatever is hidden in the hearts and whatever lies behind the unseen. Sermon 192

If God were to take humanity to task for their injustice, He would not leave on it a moving creature. Rather, He postpones them for a term, that is determined. When their term drew near, neither will they delay it an hour, nor press it forward. **16:61**
They assign to God what they dislike. Their tongues allege the lie that the fairer things will be theirs. Without a doubt, for them is the fire, and they will be ones made to hasten to it. **16:62**

By God, even if I had found that by such money women have been married or servant-maids have been purchased, I would have returned it to its owners because there is wide scope in dispensation of justice. He who finds it hard to act justly will find it harder to deal with injustice. Sermon 15

By God! We, certainly, sent Messengers to communities before ***you****. Satan made their actions appear pleasing to them. So, He is their protector on this Day and theirs will be a painful punishment.* **16:63**

There is no doubt that God sent down *the Prophet* (Q7:158), peace and the mercy of God be upon him, as a guide with an eloquent Book and a standing command. No one will be ruined by it except one who ruins himself. Certainly, only doubtful innovations cause ruin except those from which God may protect. In God's authority lies the safety of your affairs. Therefore, render Him such obedience as is neither blameworthy nor insincere. By God, you must do so otherwise God will take away from you the power of Islam and will never thereafter return it to you until it reverts to others. Sermon 169

We caused the Book to descend to ***you****, but that* ***you*** *will make manifest to them those things in which they were at variance in it and as a guidance and a mercy for a folk who believe.* **16:64**

Only the middle way is the right path which is the Everlasting Book and the traditions of *the Prophet* (Q7:158), peace and the mercy of God be upon him. From it the *sunna* has spread and towards it is the eventual return. He who claims otherwise is ruined. He who concocts falsehood is disappointed. He who opposes right is destroyed. It is enough ignorance for a person not to know himself. He who is strong rooted in God-consciousness is not destroyed. The plantation of a people based on God-consciousness never remains without water. Sermon 16

God caused water to descend from heaven and from it gave life to the earth after its death. Truly, in this is a sign for a folk who hear. **16:65**
Truly, for you in the flocks is a lesson. We satiate you from what is in their bellies—between waste and blood—exclusively milk, that which is delicious to the ones who drink. **16:66**
From fruits of the date palm trees and grapevines you take to yourselves of it what obscures the mind and fairer provisions. Truly, in it is a sign for a folk who be reasonable. **16:67**

Be reasonable and act rationally ... Letter 65

Your *Lord revealed to* ***you*** *the bee: Take to* ***your****self houses from the mountains and in the trees and in what they construct.* **16:68**

He whom He guides does not get astray. Sermon 2

Again, eat of all the fruits and insert ***your****self submissively into the ways of* ***your*** *Lord. Drink goes forth from their bellies in hues, ones that are at variance, wherein is healing for humanity. Truly, in this is, certainly, a sign for a folk who reflect.* **16:69**

In His creation, the big, the delicate, the heavy, the light, the strong, the weak are all equal. Sermon 185

God created you. Again, He calls you to Himself. Of you there are some who are returned to the most wretched of lifetimes so that he knows nothing after having knowledge of something. Truly, God is Knowing, Powerful. **16:70**

Know that firm in knowledge are those who refrain from opening the curtains that lie against the unknown. Their acknowledgment of ignorance about the details of the hidden unknown prevents them from further probe. God praises them for their admission that they are unable to attain knowledge not allowed to them. They do not go deep into the discussion of what is not enjoined upon them about knowing Him. They call it firmness. Be content with this and do not limit the Greatness of God after the measure of your own intelligence or else you will be among the destroyed ones. Sermon 91

God gave advantage to some of you over some others in provision. But those who were given ad-

vantage are not ones who give over their provision to what their right hands possessed so that they are equal in it. Why negate they the divine blessing of God? **16:71**

God assigned to you souls (f) of your own kind and has assigned you from your spouses (f), children and grandchildren and provided you with what is good. Believe they, then, in falsehood and are ungrateful for the divine blessing of God? **16:72**

They worship other than God what has no sway, no power to provide for them anything from the heavens and the earth, nor are they able to do so. **16:73**

So, propound not parables for God. Truly, God Knows and you know not. **16:74**

I bear witness that *there is no god but God.* (Q47:19) I bear witness that *Muhammad* (Q48:29), peace and the mercy of God be upon him, is His *servant* (Q17:1) and His *Prophet.* (Q7:158) His chosen and His selected one. Sermon 150

God propounded a parable of a chattel servant who has no power over anything and one to whom We provided from Us a fairer provision. He spends from it secretly and openly publishing it. Are they on the same level? The Praise belongs to God. Nay! Most of them know not! **16:75**

Praise belongs to God (Q1:2) Who spreads His bounty throughout the creation and extends His hand of generosity among them. We praise Him in all His affairs and seek His assistance for fulfillment of His rights. Sermon 100

God propounded a parable of two men, one of them unwilling to speak. He has no power over anything and he is a heavy burden to his defender. Whichever way he turns his face, he brings no good. Is he on the same level as the one who commands justice and he who is on a straight path? **16:76**

... keep us on the straight path of truth. Sermon 170

To God belongs the unseen of the heavens and the earth. The command of the Hour is not but the twinkling of an eye to one's sight or it is nearer. Truly, God is Powerful over everything. **16:77**

O Sustainer of this earth which **You** have made an abode for people and a place for the movement of insects and beasts and countless other creatures seen and unseen. Sermon 170

God brought you out from the wombs of your mothers and you know nothing. He assigned to you the ability to hear and sight and mind so that perhaps you will give thanks. **16:78**

Do not forget gratitude when receiving blessings for God has exhausted the excuses before you through clear, shining arguments and open, bright books. Sermon 81

Consider you not the birds, the ones caused to be subservient in the firmament of the heavens? None holds them back but God. Truly, in this are the signs for a folk who believe. **16:79**

The perfection of acknowledging Him is to bear witness to Him. The perfection of bearing witness to Him is to believe in His Oneness. Sermon 1

God assigned for you your houses as places of comfort and rest and assigned for you the hides of flocks for your houses which you find light on the day of your departure and the day of your halting and of their wool and furs and hair—furnishing and enjoyment for a while. **16:80**

He who has an intelligent mind looks to his goal. He knows his low road as well as his high road. The caller has called. The shepherd has tended his flocks. So respond to the caller and follow the shepherd. Sermon 153

God made for you shade out of what He created and made for you the mountains as a refuges in the time of need and has made for you tunics to protect you from the heat and tunics to protect you from your violence. Thus, He fulfills His divine blessing to you so that perhaps you will submit to God. **16:81**

He is the Giver of all reward and distinction, and Dispeller of all calamities and hardships. I praise Him for His continuous mercy and His copious bounties. Sermon 82

Then, if they turned away, for **you** *is only the delivering of the clear message.* **16:82**

God never allowed His creation to remain without a Prophet, one deputized by Him, or a Book sent down from Him, or a binding argument, or a standing plea. These Messengers were such that they did not fear that they were few in comparison to the large numbers of their falsifiers. Among them was either a predecessor who would name the one to follow or the follower who had been introduced by the predecessor. Sermon 1

They recognize the divine blessing of God. Again, they reject it and most of them are the ones who are ungrateful. **16:83**

God, the Almighty, deputed Muhammad, peace and the mercy of God be upon him, with truth at a time when the destruction of the world was near and the next life was at hand, when its brightness was turning into gloom after shining, it had become troublesome for its inhabitants, its surface had become rough, and its decay had approached near. This was during the exhaustion of its life at the approach of signs of its decay, the ruin of its inhabitants, the breaking of its links, the dispersal of its affairs, the decay of its signs, the divulging of its secret matters and the shortening of its length. God made him responsible for conveying His message and a means of honor for his people, a period of bloom for the men of his days, a source of dignity for the supporters and an honor for his helpers. Sermon 198

On the Day We will raise up from every community a witness again, no permission will be given to those who are ungrateful nor will they ask to be favored. **16:84**

God is sublime beyond what is described by those who liken Him to things or those who deny Him. Sermon 49

When those who did wrong consider the punishment, then, it will not be lightened for them nor will they be given respite. **16:85**

Certainly, nothing is viler than evil, except its punishment. Nothing is better than good, except its reward. Sermon 114

When those who ascribed partners saw their ascribed associates with God, they will say: Our Lord, these are our ascribed associates whom we had been calling to other than **You**. *Then, they will cast their saying back to them: Truly, you are ones who lie!* **16:86**
They will give a proposal to God on that day of surrender. Gone astray from them will be what they had been devising. **16:87**

I bear witness that *there is no god but God* (Q47:19) the One, there is no partner with Him, nor is there with Him any god other than Himself, and that *Muhammad* (Q48:29), peace and the mercy of God be upon him, is His *servant* (Q17:1) and His *Prophet.* (Q7:158) Sermon 35

Those who were ungrateful and barred from the way of God, We increased them in punishment above their punishment because they had been making corruption. **16:88**

God was being disobeyed. Satan was given support. Faith was forsaken. As a result, the pillars of religion crumbled. Any trace of them were lost. Its passages were destroyed. Its streets fell into decay. People obeyed Satan and tread his path. They sought water from his watering places. Satan's banners flew in the wind through them. His standard of vice was raised. They trampled people under their hoofs and tread upon them with their feet. Vice attained full stature. The people immersed in them were led astray, perplexed, ignorant and seduced as though they were in a good house (Mecca) with bad neighbors (ungrateful Quraysh). Instead of sleep, the people had wakefulness. Instead of antimony, they had tears in their eyes. They were in a land where the lips of the learned bridled while the words of the ignorant were honored. Sermon 2

On the Day We raise up in every community a witness against them from among themselves and We will bring ***you*** *about as a witness against these. We sent down to* ***you*** *the Book as an exposition that makes everything clear and as a guidance and as a mercy and as good tidings for the ones who submit to God.* **16:89**

He has defined what you should leave behind, taught you your acts, ordained your death and sent down to you: *the Book (Quran) explaining everything.* (Q16:89) Sermon 85

Truly, God commands justice and kindness and giving to one who is a possessor of kinship and He prohibits depravity and ones who are unlawful and insolent. He admonishes you so that perhaps you will recollect. **16:90**

... be regardful of kinship ... Sermon 208

Live up to the compact of God when you have made a contract. Break not the oaths after ratification. Surely, you made God surety over you. Truly, God knows what you accomplish. **16:91**

O God's human being! The good that God has promised should not be abandoned and the evil from which He has refrained should not be coveted. O God's human being! Fear the day when actions will be reckoned. There will be much quaking and even children will get old. Sermon 157

Be not like she who would break what she spun after firming its fibers by taking to yourselves your oaths in mutual deceit among yourselves so that one community be one that is swelling more than another community. God tries you but by this. He will make manifest to you on the Day of Resurrection about what you had been at variance in it. **16:92**

Every deceit is a sin and every sin is disobedience of God. Every deceitful person will have a banner by which he will be recognized on the Day of Judgment. Sermon 200

If God willed, He would have made you one community, but He causes to go astray whom He wills and guides whom He wills. Certainly, you will be asked about what you had been doing. **16:93**

When a community is composed of honest, sober and virtuous people, your forming a bad opinion about anyone of its members, when nothing wicked has been seen of him, is a great injustice to him. On the contrary, in a corrupt society to form good opinion of anyone of them and to trust him is to harm yourself. Saying 113

Take not your oaths to yourselves in mutual deceit among yourselves, that your footing should not backslide after standing firm and you experience the evil of having barred from the way of God. For you will be a serious punishment. **16:94**

Be aware that the paths of religion are one and its highways are straight. Sermon 120

Exchange not the compact for a little price. Truly, what is with God is better for you if you had been knowing. **16:95**

In **Your** hand is the forelock of every creature. To **You** is the return of every living being. Glory be to **You**! How great is **Your** affair! Glory to **You**! How great is **Your** creation that we see, but how small is this greatness by the side of **Your** Might! How awe-striking is **Your** realm that we notice, but how humble is this against what is hidden from us out of **Your** authority! How extensive are **Your** bounties in this world, but how small are they against the bounties of the next world! Sermon 108

Whatever is with you will come to an end. Whatever is with God is that which endures. We will, certainly, give recompense to those who endured patiently their fairer compensation for what they had been doing. **16:96**

Perform good acts while such acts are being raised up to God, while repentance can be of benefit, prayer can be heard, conditions are peaceful and the pens of the two angels are in motion to record the actions. Hasten towards virtuous actions before the change of age to oldness, lingering illness or snatching death overtakes you. Sermon 229

Whoever does as one in accord with morality, whether male or female, while being one who believes, We will give life—this good life. We will give recompense to them—their compensation—for the fairer for what they had been doing. **16:97**

He drinks sweet water to whose source his way has been made easy. So he drinks to satisfaction and takes the level path. He has put off the clothes of desires and rid himself of worries except one worry peculiar to him. He is safe from misguidance and the company of people who follow their passions. He has become the key to the doors of guidance and the lock for the doors of destruction. Sermon 87

So, when ***you*** *recited the Quran, seek refuge with God from the accursed Satan.* **16:98**

The Book of God is that through which you see, you speak and you hear. Its one part speaks for the other part, and one part bears witness to the other. It does not create differences about God, nor does it mislead its own follower from the path of God. You are joined together in hatred of each other and in the growing of herbage on your covering inner impurity by good appearance outside. You are sincere with one another in your love of desires and bear enmity against each other in earning wealth. The evil spirit (Satan) has perplexed you and deceit has misled you. I seek the help of God for myself and you. Sermon 133

Truly, he is not an authority over those who believed and in their Lord they put their trust. **16:99**

It is *the Prophet* (Q7:158), peace and the mercy of God be upon him, who lit the flames for the seeker and put bright signs for the impeded. So he is **your** trustworthy trustee, **your** witness on the Day of Judgment, **your** deputy as a blessing and **your** Messenger of truth as mercy. Sermon 106

His authority is only over those who turn away to him and they, those are ones who are polytheists. **16:100**

I bear witness that *there is no god but God* (Q47:19), by virtue of belief, certainty, sincerity and conviction. I also bear witness that *Muhammad* (Q48:29), peace and the mercy of God be upon him, is His *servant* (Q17:1) and His *Prophet,* (Q7:158), whom He deputed when the signs of guidance were obliterated and the ways of religion were desolate. So he threw open the truth, gave advice to the people, guided them towards righteousness and ordered them to be moderate. May God bless him ... Sermon 194

When We substituted a sign in place of another sign—and God is greater in knowledge of what He sends down—they said: ***You*** *are only one who devises! But most of them know not.* **16:101**

People obeyed Satan and tread his path. They sought water from his watering places. Satan's banners flew in the wind through them. His standard of vice was raised. They trampled people under their hoofs and tread upon them with their feet. Vice attained full stature. Sermon 2

Say: The hallowed Spirit sent it down from ***your*** *Lord with The Truth to make firm those who believed and as a guidance and good tidings to the ones who submit to God.* **16:102**

O my God! Let my spirit be the first of those good objects that **You** take from me and the first trust out of **Your** favors held in trust with me. Sermon 215

Certainly, We know that they say: It is only a mortal who teaches him. The tongue of him whom they hint at is non-Arab, while this is in a clear Arabic tongue. **16:103**

God, the Almighty, has not counseled anyone on other than the lines of this Quran, for it is the strong rope of God and His trustworthy means. It contains the blossoming of the heart and springs of knowledge. For the heart there is no other gloss than the Quran, although those who remembered it have passed away, while those who forgot or pretended to have forgotten it have remained. If you see any good, give your support to it, but if you see evil, evade it, because *the Messenger of God* (Q48:29) used to say: O son of Adam, do good and evade evil. By doing so you will be treading correctly. Sermon 176

Truly, those who believe not in the signs of God, God will not guide them and for them is a painful punishment. **16:104**

There is no doubt that God sent down *the Prophet* (Q7:158), peace and the mercy of God be upon him, as a guide with an eloquent Book and a standing command. No one will be ruined by it except one who ruins himself. Sermon 169

Devising falsity is only by those who believe not in the signs of God. Those, they are the ones who lie. **16:105**

Truly, sins are like unruly horses on whom their riders have been placed and their reins have been let loose so that they would jump with them in hellfire. Sermon 16

Whoever disbelieved in God after his belief—other than whoever was compelled to do it against his will while his heart is one that is at peace in belief—but whoever's breast is expanded to disbelief, on them is the anger of God and for them is a serious punishment. **16:106**
That is because they embraced this present life instead of the world to come. God guides not the folk,

the ones who disbelieve, **16:107**
those are those who God set a seal upon their hearts and upon their ability to hear and their sight. Those, they are the ones who are heedless. **16:108**
Without a doubt they will be in the world to come, the ones who are losers. **16:109**

They eulogize each other and expect reward from each other. When they ask something they insist on it. If they reprove any one, they disgrace him. If they pass verdict, they commit excess. They have adopted for every truth a wrong way, for every erect thing a bender, for every living being a killer, for every closed door a key and for every night a lamp. They covet, but with despair, in order to maintain with it their markets and to popularize their handsome merchandise. When they speak, they create doubts. When they describe, they exaggerate. First they offer easy paths, but afterwards they make them narrow. In short, they are the party of Satan and the stings of fire. *Regard the Party of Satan. They will be the ones who are losers.* (Q58:19) Sermon 193

Again, truly, ***your*** *Lord, for those who emigrated after they were persecuted and, again, struggled and endured patiently, truly, after that,* ***your*** *Lord is Forgiving, Compassionate.* **16:110**

Blessings of the Lord for this precedence or when those who, on account of unbearable sufferings from the hands of your clan, were forced to migrate from Makkah, you and your family were after wealth and power. Letter 17

On a Day every soul will approach, disputing for itself and for every soul, its account will be paid in full for what it did; they will not be wronged. **16:111**

Their hearts are grieved. Others are protected from their evil. Their bodies are thin. Their needs are scanty. Their souls are chaste. They endured hardship for a short while. As a consequence, they secured comfort for a long time. It is a beneficial transaction that God made easy for them. The world aimed at them, but they did not aim at it. It captured them, but they freed themselves from it by a ransom. During the night, they are standing on their feet, reading portions of the Quran and reciting it in a well-measured way, creating through it grief and seeking by it the cure for their ailments. If they come across a verse creating eagerness for Paradise, they pursue it avidly. Their spirits turn towards it eagerly. They feel as if it is in front of them. When they come across a verse which contains fear of Hell, they bend the ears of their hearts towards it and feel as though the sound of Hell and its cries are reaching their ears. They bend themselves from their backs, prostrate themselves on their foreheads, their palms, their knees and their toes, and beseech God, the Sublime, for their deliverance. Sermon 193

God propounded a parable of a town—that which had been safe, one that is at peace, its provision approaches it freely from every place. Then, it was ungrateful for the divine blessings of God and so God caused it to experience extreme hunger and fear because of what they had been crafting. **16:112**

It is that you are unthankful to God for all which He has granted to you and you are ungrateful to Him for the favors bestowed upon you. Letter 10

Certainly, drew near them a Messenger from among them, but they denied him, so the punishment took them while they are ones who are unjust. **16:113**

May my father and my mother shed their lives for you, O *Messenger of God*!

(Q48:29) With your death, the process of prophethood, revelation and heavenly messages has stopped, which had not stopped at the death of other Prophets. Your position with us members of your family is so special that your grief has become a source of consolation to us as against the grief of all others. Our grief is also common in that all Muslims share it equally. Sermon 234

So, eat of what God provided you as lawful, what is good and give thanks for the divine blessing of God if it had been Him that you worship. **16:114**

Where are the hearts dedicated to God and devoted to the obedience of God? Sermon 144

He only forbade to you carrion and blood and flesh of swine and what was hallowed to other than God. But if one was compelled, without being one who is willfully disobedient, nor one who turns away, then, truly, God is Forgiving, Compassionate. **16:115**

A person should derive benefit from himself for himself, from the living for the dead, from the mortal, for the lasting and from the departer for the stayer. A person should be God-conscious while he is given age to live up to his death and is allowed time to act. A person should control himself by the rein and hold it with its bridle. By the rein, he should prevent it from disobedience towards God. By the bridle, he should lead it towards obedience to God. Sermon 236

Say not to what your lying tongues allege: This is lawful and this is unlawful so as to devise lies against God. Truly, those who devise against God lies will not prosper, **16:116**
but a little enjoyment and for them is a painful punishment. **16:117**

Be aware! The worst speech is that which is untrue. Sermon 84

We forbade those who became Jews what We related to ***you*** *before and We did not wrong them, except they had been doing wrong to themselves.* **16:118**
Again, truly, ***your*** *Lord—to those who did evil in ignorance, again, repented after that and made things right—truly,* ***your*** *Lord after that is Forgiving, Compassionate.* **16:119**

There is no greater wealth than wisdom, no greater poverty than ignorance; no greater heritage than culture and no greater support than consultation. Saying 54

Abraham had been a community obedient to God—a monotheist—he is not among the ones who are polytheists. **16:120**
He was one who is thankful for His divine blessings. He elected him and guided him to a straight path. **16:121**
He gave him in the present benevolence. Truly, in the world to come he will be among the ones in accord with morality. **16:122**
Again, we revealed to ***you*** *that* ***you*** *follow the creed of Abraham—a monotheist. He had not been among the ones who are polytheists.* **16:123**
Truly, the Sabbath was made for those who are at variance about it. Truly, ***your*** *Lord will give judgment between them on the Day of Resurrection about what they had been at variance in it.* **16:124**
Call ***you*** *to the way of* ***your*** *Lord with wisdom and fairer admonishment. Dispute with them in a way that is fairer. Truly,* ***your*** *Lord is He Who is greater in knowledge of whoever went astray*

from His way. He is greater in knowledge of the ones who are truly guided. **16:125**

May God have mercy on you! Provide yourselves for the journey because the call for departure has been announced. Regard your stay in the world as very short. Return to God with the best provision that is with you, because surely, before you lies a valley, difficult to climb, and places of stay full of fear and danger. Sermon 204

If you chastised, then, chastise with the like of that with which you were chastised. But if you endured patiently, certainly, it is better for the ones who remain steadfast. **16:126**

Then look at the end, the end, and remain steadfast, steadfast. Sermon 176

Have ***you*** *patience and* ***your*** *patience is only from God. Feel not remorse over them, nor be* ***you*** *troubled about what they plan.* **16:127**

Action! Action! .... Thereafter exercise endurance, endurance, and God-consciousness, God-consciousness. You have an objective. Proceed towards your objective. You have a sign. Take guidance from your sign. Islam has an objective. Proceed towards its objective. Proceed towards God by fulfilling His rights which He has enjoined upon you. He has clearly stated His demands for you. Sermon 176

Truly, God is with those who were God-conscious and those, they are ones who are doers of good. **16:128**

Be God-conscious and perform good acts because: *Truly God is with those who are God-conscious and those, they are the ones who are doers of good.* (Q16:128) Sermon 193

Chapter 17: The Journey by Night (al-Isrāᵓ)

Glory be to Him Who caused His servant to set forth night from the Masjid al-Haram to the Masjid al-Aqsa around which We blessed so that We cause him to see Our signs. Truly, He, He is The Hearing, The Seeing. **17:1**

I bear witness that *Muhammad* (Q48:29), peace and the mercy of God be upon him, is *His servant* (Q17:1) and His *Prophet.* (Q7:158) God sent him with the illustrious religion, effective emblem, the Guarded Tablet, effulgent light, sparkling gleam and decisive injunction in order to dispel doubts, present clear proof, administer warning through signs and to warn of punishments. At that time people had fallen into vices whereby the rope of religion had been broken, the pillars of belief had been shaken, principles had been sacrificed, the system had become topsy turvy, openings were narrow, passages were dark, guidance was unknown and darkness prevailed. Sermon 2

We gave Moses the Book and made it a guidance for the Children of Jacob: Take not to yourselves a Trustee other than Me. **17:2**
O offspring of whomever We carried with Noah: Truly, he had been a grateful servant. **17:3**
We decreed for the Children of Jacob in the Book: Certainly, you will make corruption in and on the earth two times. Certainly, you will exalt yourselves in a great self-exaltation. **17:4**
So, when the promise drew near for the first of the two, We raised up against you servants of Ours imbued with severe might. They ransacked in the midst of your abodes. The promise had been one that is accomplished. **17:5**
Again, We returned to you a turn of luck over them and We furnished you relief with children and

wealth and made you more in soldiery: **17:6**
If you did good, you would be doing good for yourselves. If you did evil, then, it is against yourselves. Then, when the last promise drew near, We sent your enemies; they raise anger on your faces and they enter the place of prostration just as they entered it the first time, to shatter all that they ascended to with a shattering. **17:7**
Perhaps your Lord will have mercy on you. But if you reverted, We will revert. We made hell a jail for the ones who are ungrateful. **17:8**

Where are the minds which seek light from the lamps of guidance and the eyes which look at minarets of God-consciousness? Where are the hearts dedicated to God and devoted to the obedience of God? They are all crowding towards worldly vanities and quarreling over unlawful issues. The banners of the Garden and Hell have been raised for them, but they have turned their faces away from the Garden and proceeded to Hell by dint of their performances. God called them, but they showed dislike and ran away. When Satan called them, they responded and proceeded towards him. Sermon 144

Truly, this, the Quran, guides to what is upright and gives good tidings to the ones who believe, those who are as the ones in accord with morality, that they will have a great compensation. **17:9**

O people, he who seeks counsel from God secures guidance and he who adopts His word as guide is led ... *guides to what is upright* ... (Q17:9), because God's lover feels secure and His opponent feels afraid. It does not behoove one who knows His greatness to assume greatness, but the greatness of those who know His greatness is that they should abase themselves before Him. The safety for those who know what His power is lies in submitting to Him. Do not be scared away from the truth like the scaring of the healthy from the scabbed person or the sound person from the sick. Sermon 147

As for those who believe not in the world to come, We made ready for them a painful punishment. **17:10**
The human being calls to worse as much as he supplicates for good. The human being had been hasty. **17:11**
We made the nighttime and the daytime as two signs. Then, We blotted out the sign of nighttime and We made the sign of daytime for one who perceives that you be looking for grace from your Lord and that you know the number of years and the reckoning. We explained everything distinctly, with a decisive explanation. **17:12**

Certainly, God tries His creatures in respect of their evil deeds by decreasing fruits, holding back blessings and closing the treasures of good, so that he who wishes to repent may repent, he who wishes to turn away from evils may turn away, he who wishes to recall forgotten good may recall, and he who wishes to abstain from evil may abstain. God, the Glorified, has made the seeking of His forgiveness a means for the pouring down of livelihood and mercy on the people as God has said: *As for those who believe not in the world to come, We made ready for them a painful punishment. The human being calls to worse as much as he supplicates for good. The human being had been hasty. We made the nighttime and the daytime as two signs. Then, We blotted out the sign of nighttime and We made the sign of daytime for one who perceives that you be looking for grace from your Lord and that you know the number of years and the reckoning. We explained everything distinctly, with a decisive explanation.* (Q17:10-12) Sermon 142

For every human being We fastened his omen to his neck and We will bring out for him on the Day of Resurrection a book in which he will meet that which unfolded. **17:13**

Look at the human being whom God has created in the dark wombs and layers of curtains from what was overflowing semen, then shapeless clot, then embryo, then suckling infant, then child and then fully grown up young person. Then He gave him heart with memory, tongue to talk and eye to see with in order that he may take lesson from whatever is around him and understand it and follow the admonition and abstain from evil. When he attained the normal growth and his structure gained its average development he fell in self-conceit and became perplexed. He drew buckets full of his desires, was immersed in fulfilling his wishes for pleasures of the world and his sordid aims. He did not fear any evil, nor was frightened by any apprehension. He died infatuated with his vices. He spent his short life in rubbish pursuits. He earned no reward, nor did he fulfill any obligation. Fatal illness overtook him while he was in his enjoyments. It perplexed him. He passed the night in wakefulness in the hardships of grief and pricking of pains and ailments in the presence of real brother, loving father, wailing mother, crying sister, while he himself was under maddening uneasiness, serious senselessness, fearful cries, suffocating pains, anguish of suffocating sufferings and the pangs of death. Thereafter, he was clad in the shroud while he remained quiet and thoroughly submissive to others. Then he was placed on planks in such a state that he had been downtrodden by hardships and thinned by ailments. The crowd of young men and helping brothers carried him to his house of loneliness where all connections of visitors are severed. Thereafter those who accompanied him went away and those who were wailing for him returned. He was made to sit in his grave for terrifying questioning and slippery examination. The great calamity of that place is the hot water and entry into hell, flames of eternal fire and intensity of blazes. There is no resting period, no gap for ease, no power to intervene, no death to bring about solace and no sleep to make him forget pain. He rather lies under several kinds of deaths and moment-to-moment punishment. We seek refuge with God. Sermon 82

Recite ***your*** *book! This day* ***your*** *soul sufficed* ***you*** *as* ***your*** *reckoner against* ***you****.* **17:14**

Mind the obligations! Mind the obligations! Fulfill them for God and they will take you to the Garden. Surely, God has made unlawful the things which are not unknown and made lawful the things which are without defect. Sermon 167

Whoever was truly guided is truly guided only for his own soul. Whoever went astray, then, only goes astray against it. No burdened soul bears the heavy load of another, nor would We have been ones who punish until We raised up a Messenger. **17:15**

In God's authority lies the safety of your affairs. Therefore, render Him such obedience as is neither blameworthy, nor insincere. By God, you must do so otherwise God will take away from you the power of Islam and will never thereafter return it to you until it reverts to others. Sermon 169

When We wanted to cause a town to perish, We commanded ones who are given ease, but they disobeyed therein. So, the saying was realized against it. Then, We destroyed it with utter destruction. **17:16**

God sent the *Prophet* (Q7:158) after the mission of other Prophets had stopped. The people were in slumber for a long time. Evils were raising heads. All matters were under disruption and in flames of wars while the world was devoid of brightness and full of open deceitfulness. Its leaves had turned yellow. There was absence of hope about its fruits. Its water had gone underground. The minarets of guidance had disappeared. The signs of destruction had appeared. It was stern to its people and frowned in the face of its seeker. Its fruit was vice. Its food was carcass. Its inner dress was fear. Its outer cover was a sword. Sermon 89

How many generations have We caused to perish after Noah? ***Your*** *Lord sufficed as Aware, Seeing the impieties of His servants.* **17:17**
Whoever had been wanting that which hastens away, We quicken it for him, whatever We will to whomever We want. Again, We assigned hell for him. He will roast in it, one who is condemned, one who is rejected. **17:18**

O God's human being! I advise you to have God-consciousness which is the provision for the next world. Sermon 113

Whoever wanted the world to come and endeavored for it, endeavoring, while he is one who believes, then, those, their endeavoring had been appreciated. **17:19**
To each We furnish relief, these and these, with the gift of ***your*** *Lord. This gift of* ***your*** *Lord has not been that which is confined.* **17:20**
Look on how We gave advantage to some of them over some others. Certainly, the world to come will be greater in degrees and greater in excellence. **17:21**

Today will depart with all that it has. Tomorrow will come in its wake. It is as though everyone of you has reached that place on earth where he would be alone, namely the location of his grave. So what to say of the lonely house, the solitary place of staying and the solitary exile? It is as though the cry of the Trumpet has reached you, the Hour has overtaken you, and you have come out of your graves for the passing of judgment. The curtains of falsehood have been removed from you. Your excuses have become weak. The truth about you has been proven. All your matters have proceeded to their consequences. Therefore, you should now take counsel from examples, learn lessons from vicissitudes and take advantage of the warners. Sermon 157

Assign not another god with God for, then, ***you*** *will be put as one who is condemned, one who is damned.* **17:22**

I bear witness that *there is no god but God* (Q47:19). He is One. There is no partner with Him. He is the First, such that nothing was before Him. He is the Last, such that there is not limit for Him. Imagination cannot catch any of His qualities. Hearts cannot entertain belief about His nature. Analysis and division cannot be applied to Him. Eyes and hearts cannot compare Him. Sermon 84

Your *Lord decreed that you worship none but Him! Kindness to the ones who are one's parents. If they reach old age with* ***you****—one of them or both of them—then,* ***you*** *will not say to them a word of disrespect nor scold them, but say a generous saying to them.* **17:23**
Make ***your****self low to them, the wing of the sense of humility through mercy. Say: O my Lord! Have mercy on them even as they raised me when I was small.* **17:24**

When you have found and selected such persons who may be considered as sources of magnificence and sublimity of character and fountain-heads of piety and good deeds, then keep an eye over them and watch them as parents watch their children so that you may find out if there appears any change in their behavior. Letter 53

Your Lord is greater in knowledge of what is within yourselves. If you be ones in accord with morality, truly, He is Forgiving to those who had been penitent. **17:25**

He called them and they responded obediently and humbly without being lazy or loathsome. Sermon 182

Give to the possessor of kinship his right and to the needy and to the traveler of the way. Spend not extravagantly an extravagant spending. **17:26**

Be generous, but not extravagant. Be frugal, but not miserly. Saying 33

Truly, the ones who spend extravagantly had been brothers/sisters of the satans and Satan had been ungrateful to his Lord. **17:27**

They have made Satan the master of their affairs. Sermon 7

If ***you*** *have turned aside from them, looking for mercy from* ***your*** *Lord for which* ***you*** *have hoped, then, say to them a saying softly.* **17:28**

Praise belongs to God (Q1:2) from Whose mercy no one loses hope, from Whose bounty no one is deprived, from Whose forgiveness no one is disappointed and for Whose worship no one is too high. His mercy never ceases and His bounty never ceases. Sermon 45

Make not ***your*** *hand be one that is restricted to* ***your*** *neck as a miser nor extend it to its utmost expansion as a prodigal so that* ***you*** *will sit as one who is reproached, one who is denuded.* **17:29**

He who shows generosity to those who have no claim to it or who are not fit for it would not earn anything except the praise of the ignoble and appreciation of bad persons, although as long as he continues giving, the ignorant will say how generous his hand is, even though in the affairs of God he is a miser. Sermon 142

Truly, ***your*** *Lord extends the provision for whom He wills and He tightens for whom He wills. Truly, He, He had been Aware, Seeing of His servants.* **17:30**

Certainly, God-consciousness is the key to guidance, provision for the next world, freedom from every servantry and deliverance from all ruin. With its help, the seeker succeeds and he who makes for safety escapes and achieves his aims. Sermon 229

Kill not your children dreading want. We will provide for them and for you. Truly, the killing of them had been a grave inequity. **17:31**

Certainly, God tries His creatures in respect of their evil deeds by decreasing fruits, holding back blessings and closing the treasures of good, so that he who wishes to repent may repent, he who wishes to turn away from evils may turn away, he who wishes to recall forgotten good may recall, and he who wishes to abstain from evil may abstain. Sermon 142

Come not near committing adultery. Truly, it had been a great indecency! How evil a way! **17:32**

Truth would go down, falsehood would overflow, affection would be claimed with tongues, but people would be quarrelsome at heart. Adultery would be the key to lineage while chastity would be rare and Islam would be worn like a furry coat, inside out. Sermon 108

Kill not a soul that God forbade, but rightfully. Whoever was slain as one who is treated unjustly, surely, We assigned for his protector, authority, but he should not exceed all bounds in killing. Truly, he would be one who is helped by the Law. **17:33**

Be aware of the sin of shedding blood without religious justification and sanction because there is nothing quicker to bring down the Wrath of God, to take away His Blessings, to make you more deserving of His Wrath and to reduce the span of your life than to shed innocent blood. Letter 53

Come not near the property of the orphan, but with what is fairer until he reaches the coming of age. Live up to the compact. Truly, the compact had been that which will be asked about. **17:34**

Do you command me that I should seek support by oppressing those over whom I have been placed? By God, I will not do so as long as the world goes on and as long as one star leads another in the sky. Even if it were my property, I would have distributed it equally among them. Then why not when the property is that of God? Sermon 126

Live up to the full measure when you wanted to measure. Weigh with a scale, one that is straight. That is best and fairer in interpretation. **17:35**

I notice that misguidance has stood on its center and spread all round through its off-shoots. It weighs you with its weights and confuses you with its measures. Sermon 108

Follow up not of what there is not for ***you*** *knowledge of it. Truly, having the ability to hear and sight and mind, each of those will have been that which is asked.* **17:36**

They are emulating each other and proceeding in groups towards the final objective and the rendezvous of death, until when matters come to a close, the world dies and resurrection draws near. God will take them out from the corners of the graves, the nests of birds, the dens of beasts and the centers of death. They will hasten towards His command and run towards the place fixed for their final return, group by group, quiet, standing and arrayed in rows. They will be within God's sight and will hear every one who would call them. They will have the dress of helplessness and covering of submission and indignity. At this time contrivances will disappear. Desires will be cut. Hearts will sink quietly. Voices will be lowered. Sweat will choke the throat. Fear will increase. Ears will resound with the thundering voice of the announcer calling towards the final judgment, award of recompense, striking of punishment and paying of reward. Sermon 82

Walk not on the earth exultantly. Truly, ***you*** *will never make a hole in the earth and will never reach the mountains in height.* **17:37**

So I said: O Prophet of God, what is this disturbance of which God, the Sublime, has informed you? He replied: O Ali, my people will create trouble after me. I said: O Prophet of God, on the day of Uhud, when people had fallen martyrs and I was not among them, and that was distressing for me, did you not say to me: Cheer up, as martyrdom is for you hereafter? *The Prophet* (Q7:158), peace and the mercy of God be upon him, replied: Yes it is so but what about your enduring at present? I said: O Prophet of God, this is not an occasion for endurance, but rather an occasion for cheering up and gratefulness. Then he said: O Ali, people will fall into mischief through their wealth, will show obligation to God on account of their faith, will expect His mercy, will feel safe from His anger and regard His unlawful matters as lawful by raising false doubts and by their misguiding desires. They will then hold lawful the use of wine by calling it barley water, a bribe by calling it a gift, and taking of usurious interest by calling it a sale. I said: O Prophet of God, how should I deal with them at the time, whether to hold them to have gone back in heresy or just in revolt? He said: In revolt. Sermon 156

All of that had been bad deeds, ones that are disliked by ***your*** *Lord.* **17:38**

He who busies himself with things other than improvement of his own self becomes perplexed in darkness and entangled in ruination. His evil spirits immerse him deep in vices and make his bad actions appear handsome. Paradise is the end of those who are forward in good acts and Hell is the end of those who commit excesses. Sermon 157

That is of what ***your*** *Lord revealed to* ***you*** *of wisdom. So, make not up with God another god that* ***you*** *would be cast down into hell as one who is reproached, as one who is rejected.* **17:39**

I bear witness that *there is no god but God* (Q47:19) Who has no parallel, Who is not doubted, Whose religion is not denied and Whose creativeness is not questioned. My witnessing is like that of a person whose intention is free, whose conscience is clear, whose belief is pure and whose loads of good actions are heavy. I also bear witness that *Muhammad* (Q48:29), peace and the mercy of God be upon him, is *His servant* (Q17:1) and His *Messenger* (Q3:101) chosen from His creations, selected for detailing His realities, picked for His selected honors and chosen for His esteemed messages. Through him the signs of guidance have been lighted and the gloom of misguidance has been dispelled. Sermon 177

Selected your Lord for you sons and taken for Himself females from among the angels? Truly, you, you say a serious saying! **17:40**

God ... is aware of whatever is hidden in the hearts and whatever lies behind the unseen. Sermon 192

Certainly, We diversified in this, the Quran, that they recollect. It increases them only in aversion. **17:41**

While the other kind of person is he who calls himself learned, but he is not so. He has gleaned ignorance from the ignorant and misguidance from the misguided. He has set for the people a trap made of the ropes of deceit and untrue speech. He takes the Quran according to his own views and right after his passions. Sermon 87

Say: If there had been gods along with Him as they say, then, they would, certainly, be looking for a way to the Possessor of the Throne. **17:42**
Glory be to Him! Exalted is He above what they say, greatly exalted. **17:43**

Praise belongs to God (Q1:2) Who is High above all else. He is Near the creation through His bounty. Sermon 82

The seven heavens glorify Him and the earth and whatever is in and on them. There is not a thing but it glorifies His praise, except you understand not their glorification. Truly, He had been Forbearing, Forgiving. **17:44**

Exalted is God Whom heights of daring cannot approach and fineness of intelligence cannot find. Sermon 93

When ***you*** *recited the Quran, We made between* ***you*** *and between those who believe not in the world to come a partition obstructing their vision.* **17:45**

The Book of God is that through which you see, you speak and you hear. Its one part speaks for the other part, and one part bears witness to the other. It does not create differences about God, nor does it mislead its own follower from the path of God. You are joined together in hatred of each other and in the growing of herbage on your covering inner impurity by good appearance outside. You are sincere with one another in your love of desires and bear enmity against each other in earning wealth. The evil spirit (Satan) has perplexed you and deceit has misled you. I seek the help of God for myself and you. Sermon 133

We laid sheaths on their hearts so that they not understand it and heaviness in their ears. When ***you*** *remembered* ***your*** *Lord in the Quran that He is One, they turned their backs in aversion.* **17:46**

There remain a few people in whose case the remembrance of their return to God on the Day of Judgment keeps their eyes bent and the awareness of the Resurrection moves them to tears. Some of them are scared away from the world and disperse. Some are frightened and subdued. Some are quiet as if muzzled. Some are praying sincerely. Some are grief-stricken and pain-ridden whom fear has confined to namelessness. Disgrace has shrouded them, so they are in the sea of bitter water, their mouths are closed and their hearts are bruised. They preached until they were tired. They were oppressed until they were disgraced. They were killed until their numbers dwindled. Sermon 32

We are greater in knowledge of what they listen for when they listen to ***you****. When they conspire secretly, when the ones who are unjust say: You follow but a bewitched man.* **17:47**

O my God! Whoever listens to our words which are just and which seek the prosperity of religion and the worldly life and do not seek mischief, they reject after listening. He certainly turns away from **Your** support and desists from strengthening **Your** religion. We make **You** a Witness over him. **You** are the greatest of all witnesses. We make all those who inhabit **Your** earth and **Your** skies witness over him. Thereafter, **You** alone can make us needless of his support and question him for his sin. Sermon 212

Look on how they propounded parables for ***you****. So, they went astray and they are not able to be on a way.* **17:48**

They say: When we had been bones and broken bits will we be ones who are raised up in a new creation? **17:49**

Say: Should you be rocks or iron, **17:50**

or any creation that is more troublesome in your breasts to raise up? Then, they will say: Who will cause us to return? Say: He Who originated you the first time. Then, they will nod their heads at ***you*** *and say: When will it be? Say: Perhaps it is near.* **17:51**

For every period there is a written document and everyone who is absent has to return. Sermon 108

It will be a Day when He will call to you and you will respond to Him with His praise and you will think that you lingered in expectation but a little. **17:52**

We praise God for what has happened and seek His help in our affairs for what is yet to happen. Sermon 99

Say to My servants they should say what is fairer. Truly, Satan sows enmity among them. Truly, Satan had been to the human being, a clear enemy. **17:53**

I bear witness that *there is no god but God* (Q47:19), the One. I bear witness that *there is no god but God* (Q47:19), the One.... It is the means to keep Satan away. Sermon 2

Your Lord is greater in knowledge of you. If He wills, He will have mercy on you. If He wills, He will punish you. We sent **you** *not as a trustee over them.* **17:54**

Even when He made Adam die, He did not leave them without one who would serve among them as proof and plea for His Godhead and serve as the link between them and His knowledge, but He provided to them the proofs through His chosen Messengers and bearers of the trust of His Message, age after age, until the process came to end with our Prophet Muhammad, peace and the mercy of God be upon him, and His pleas and warnings reached finality. Sermon 91

Your *Lord is greater in knowledge of whoever are in the heavens and in and on the earth. Certainly, We gave advantage to some of the Prophets over others. To David We gave Psalms.* **17:55**

If you desire I can give you a third example of David. He is the holder of the Psalms and the reciter among the people of Paradise. He used to prepare baskets of date palm leaves with his own hands and would say to his companions: Which of you will help me by purchasing it? He used to eat barley bread bought out of its price. Sermon 160

Say: Call to those whom you claimed other than Him. Then, they are neither in control to remove harm from you nor revise it. **17:56**

Those are those to whom they call to, they are looking for an approach to their Lord—whoever is nearer—and they hope for His mercy and they fear His punishment. Truly, the punishment of **your** *Lord had been one to beware.* **17:57**

I bear witness that *there is no god but God.* (Q47:19) I bear witness that *Muhammad* (Q48:29), peace and the mercy of God be upon him, is *His servant* (Q17:1) and His *Prophet,* (Q7:158) His chosen and His selected one. Sermon 150

There is not a town but We will be ones who cause it to perish before the Day of Resurrection, or We will be ones who punish it with a severe punishment— that which had been inscribed in the Book. **17:58**

Nothing prevented Us from sending the signs, but that the ancient ones denied them. We gave to Thamud the she-camel—the one who perceives—but they did wrong to her. We send not the signs, but as a deterrence. **17:59**

God, the Almighty, has sent down a guiding Book wherein He has explained virtue and vice. You should adopt the course of virtue, whereby you will have guidance. Detach yourself from the direction of vice, so that you remain on the right way. Sermon 167

Mention when We said to **you**: *Truly,* **your** *Lord enclosed humanity. We made not the dream that We caused* **you** *to see, but as a test for humanity—and the tree—one that was cursed in the Quran.*

We frighten them, but it only increases them in great defiance. **17:60**

Seek cure from it for your ailments and seek its assistance in your distresses. It contains a cure for the greatest diseases, namely unbelief, hypocrisy, revolt and misguidance. Pray to God through it and turn to God with its love ... There is nothing like it through which the people should turn to God, the Sublime. Sermon 176

Mention when We said to the angels: Prostrate yourselves to Adam! so they prostrated themselves, but Iblis. He said: Will I prostrate myself to one whom ***You*** *created from clay?* **17:61**

Then God asked the angels to fulfill His promise with them and to accomplish the pledge of His injunction to them by acknowledging Him through prostration to Him and submission to His honored position. So God said: *Prostrate yourselves to Adam! They, then, prostrated themselves but Iblis.* Sermon 1

He said: Had ***You*** *considered this whom* ***You*** *had held in esteem above me? If* ***You*** *had postponed for me to the Day of Resurrection, I will, certainly, bring under full control his offspring, but a few.* **17:62**

He said: Go ***you****! Whoever of them heeded* ***you****, then, truly, hell will be your recompense, an ample recompense.* **17:63**

In the course of time many people perverted God's trust in them. They ignored His position. They took partners with Him. Satan turned them away from knowing Him and distanced them from His worship. Then God sent His Messengers and series of His Prophets to them to guide them to fulfilling the pledges of His creation, to recall to them His bounties, to exhort them by preaching, to unveil before them the hidden virtues of wisdom and show them the signs of His Omnipotence, namely the sky which is raised over them, the earth that is placed beneath them, their means of living that sustains them, their deaths that cause them to die, ailments that turn them old and incidents that successively betake them. Sermon 1

Hound whom ***you*** *were able to of them with* ***your*** *voice and rally against them with* ***your*** *horses and* ***your*** *foot soldiers and share with them in their wealth and children and promise them. Satan promises them nothing but delusion.* **17:64**

You should fear lest the enemy of God (Satan) infects you with his disease leading you astray through his call, or marches on you with *his horsemen and footmen* (Q17:64) because, by my life, he has put the menacing arrow in the bow for you, has stretched the bow strongly, and has aimed at you from a nearby position. Sermon 192

Truly, My servants, over them there is no authority for ***you****.* ***Your*** *Lord sufficed as a Trustee.* **17:65**

Certainly, Satan has made his ways easy for you and wants to unfasten the knots of religion one by one and to cause division among you in place of unity. Keep away from his evil ideas and enchantments. Accept good advice of one who offers it to you. Preserve it in your minds. Sermon 121

Your Lord is He Who propels for you the boats on the sea so that you be looking for His grace. Truly, He had been Compassionate towards you. **17:66**

When harm afflicted you upon the sea, whomever you call to besides Him went astray. But when He delivered you to dry land, you turned aside. The human being had been ungrateful. **17:67**

Were you safe that He causes not the shore of dry land to swallow you up or send a sand storm against you? Again, you will find no trustee for you. **17:68**
Or were you safe that He will not cause you to return to it another time and send against you a hurricane of wind and drown you because you were ungrateful? Again, you will not find for yourselves an advocate against Us in it. **17:69**
Certainly, We held the Children of Adam in esteem. We carried them on dry land and on the sea and provided them with what is good. We gave them advantage over many of whomever We created with excellence. **17:70**

He is the Giver of all reward and distinction and Dispeller of all calamities and hardships. Sermon 82

On a Day when We will call to every clan with their leader, then, whoever was given his book in his right hand, those will recite their book and they will not be wronged in the least. **17:71**

Only the middle way is the right path which is the Everlasting Book and the traditions of *the Prophet* (Q7:158), peace and the mercy of God be upon him,. From it the *sunna* has spread and towards it is the eventual return. He who claims otherwise is ruined. Sermon 16

Whoever had been unwilling to see here will be unseeing in the world to come and one who goes astray from the way. **17:72**

Right cannot be achieved without effort. Sermon 29

Truly, they were about to persecute ***you*** *for what We revealed to* ***you*** *so that* ***you*** *would devise against Us other than it. Then, they would take* ***you*** *to themselves as a friend.* **17:73**

Certainly, only doubtful innovations cause ruin except those from which God may protect. In God's authority lies the safety of your affairs. Therefore, render Him such obedience as is neither blameworthy nor insincere. Sermon 169

If We made ***you*** *not firm, certainly,* ***you*** *were about to incline to them a little.* **17:74**
Then, We would have caused ***you*** *to experience a double of this life and a double after dying. Again,* ***you*** *would find for* ***your****self no helper against Us.* **17:75**

Be aware, he whom right does not benefit must suffer the harm of the wrong, and he whom guidance does not keep firm will be led away by misguidance towards destruction. Sermon 28

They were about to hound ***you*** *from the region that they drive* ***you*** *out of it. Then, they would not linger in expectation behind* ***you*** *but for a little while.* **17:76**

May my father and my mother shed their lives for you, O *Messenger of God!* (Q48:29) With your death, the process of prophethood, revelation and heavenly messages has stopped, which had not stopped at the death of other Prophets. Your position with us members of your family is so special that your grief has become a source of consolation to us as against the grief of all others. Our grief is also common in that all Muslims share it equally. Sermon 234

This is, surely, a custom with whomever We sent before ***you*** *of Our Messengers.* ***You*** *will not find in Our custom any revision.* **17:77**

If you had not ordered endurance and prevented us from bewailing, we would have produced a store of tears and even then the pain would not have subsided. This grief would not have ended. They would have been too little of our grief for you, but this death is a matter that cannot be reversed, nor is it possible to repulse it. May my father and my mother die for you. Do remember us with God and take care of us. Sermon 234

Perform the formal prayer from the sinking sun until the darkening of the night and the recital at dawn. Truly, the dawn recital had been one that is witnessed. **17:78**

Certainly, prayer drops out sins like the dropping of leaves of trees and removes them as ropes are removed from the necks of cattle. *The Messenger of God* (Q48:29), the peace and mercy of God he upon him, likened it to a hot bath situated at the door of a person who bathes in it five times a day. Will then any dirt remain on him? Sermon 199

Keep vigil with it in the night as a work of supererogation for ***you****. Perhaps* ***your*** *Lord will raise* ***you*** *up to a station of one who is praised.* **17:79**

God's verdict is judicious and full of wisdom. His pleasure implies protection and mercy. He decides with knowledge and forgives with forbearance. Sermon 160

Say: My Lord! Cause me to enter a gate in sincerity. Bring me out as one who is brought out in sincerity. Assign me from that which proceeds from ***Your*** *Presence a helping authority.* **17:80**

O my God! **You** know that what we did was not to seek power, nor to acquire anything from the vanities of the world. We rather wanted to restore the signs of **Your** religion and to usher prosperity into **Your** cities so that the oppressed among **Your** creatures might be safe and **Your** forsaken commands might be established. O my God! I am the first who leaned towards **You** and who heard and responded to the call of Islam. Sermon 131

Say: The Truth drew near and falsehood is vanishing! Truly, falsehood had been made to vanish away. **17:81**

God sent *the Prophet* (Q7:158), peace and the mercy of God be upon him, as a caller towards Truth and a witness over the creatures. *The Prophet* (Q7:158) conveyed the messages of God tirelessly and without any negligence. He fought His enemies in the cause of God unflaggingly and without pleading excuses. He is the foremost of all who practice God-consciousness and the power of perception of all those who achieve guidance. Sermon 116

We send down in the Quran what is a healing and a mercy for the ones who believe. It increases not the ones who are unjust, but in a loss. **17:82**

You should adopt the course of virtue whereby you will have guidance and keep aloof from the direction of vice so that you remain on the right way. Sermon 167

When We were gracious to the human being, he turned aside and withdrew aside. When worse afflicted him, he had been hopeless. **17:83**

Populated places were brightened through him when previously there was dark misguidance, overpowering ignorance and rude habits, and people regarded unlawful as lawful, humiliated the man of wisdom, passed lives when there were no prophets and died as ungrateful. Sermon 151

Say: Each does according to his same manner. ***Your*** *Lord is greater in knowledge of him who is better guided on the way.* **17:84**

God alone knows what is ... ugly or handsome, generous or miserly, mischievous or pious, and who will be the fuel for Hell and who will be in the company of the Prophets in Paradise. This is the knowledge of the hidden things which is not known to anyone save God. All else is that whose knowledge God passed on to His Prophet and he passed it on to me and prayed for me that my bosom may retain it and my ribs may hold it. Sermon 128

They will ask ***you*** *about the spirit. Say: The spirit is of the command of my Lord. You were not given the knowledge but a little.* **17:85**

O my God! Let my spirit be the first of those good objects that **You** take from me and the first trust out of **Your** favors held in trust with me. Sermon 215

If We willed, We would, certainly, take away what We revealed to ***you****. Again,* ***you*** *would not find for* ***you*** *in that any trustee against Us,* **17:86**

but a mercy from ***your*** *Lord. Truly, His grace had been great upon* ***you****.* **17:87**

The Book of God is that through which you see, you speak and you hear. Its one part speaks for the other part, and one part bears witness to the other. It does not create differences about God, nor does it mislead its own follower from the path of God. You are joined together in hatred of each other and in the growing of herbage on your covering inner impurity by good appearance outside. You are sincere with one another in your love of desires and bear enmity against each other in earning wealth. The evil spirit (Satan) has perplexed you and deceit has misled you. I seek the help of God for myself and you. Sermon 133

Say: If humankind were gathered together and jinn to bring the like of this Quran, they would Certainly, We diversified for humanity in this, the Quran, every kind of parable, but most of humanity refused all but disbelief. **17:89**

not approach the like of it even if some of them had been sustainers of some others. **17:88**

Know that the Quran is an interceder and its intercession will be accepted. It is a speaker who bears witness. For whoever the Quran intercedes on the Day of Judgment, its intercession for him would be accepted. He about whom the Quran speaks ill on the Day of Judgment shall testify to it. On the Day of Judgment, an announcer will announce: Be aware! Every sower of a crop is in distress except the sowers of the Quran. Therefore, you should be among the sowers of the Quran and its followers. Make it your guide towards God. Seek its advice for yourselves, do not trust your views against it and regard your desires in the matter of the Quran as deceitful. Sermon 176

They would say: We will never believe in ***you*** *until* ***you*** *have a fountain gush out of the earth for us.* **17:90**

Or will there be a garden for ***you*** *of date palms and grapevines and* ***You*** *have caused rivers to gush forth in its midst with a gushing forth?* **17:91**

Or have ***you*** *caused heaven to drop on us in pieces as* ***you*** *had claimed? Or have you brought God and the angels as a warranty?* **17:92**

Or is there a house of ornament for you? Or have ***you*** *ascended up into heaven? We will not believe in* ***your*** *ascension until* ***you*** *have sent down for us a Book that we recite. Say: Glory be to my Lord! Had I been but a mortal Messenger?* **17:93**

Nothing prevented humanity from believing when the guidance drew near them, but that they said: Raised God up a mortal as a Messenger? **17:94**

Whoever makes a breach with God and *His Messenger* (Q3:101), his path becomes difficult, his affairs will become complicated and his way to salvation will be uncertain. Saying 31

Say: If there had been angels on earth walking around, ones who are at peace, then, We would certainly have sent down for them from heaven an angel as a Messenger. **17:95**

Occupation in His worship has made the angels carefree, and realities of faith have served as a link between them and His knowledge. Their belief in Him has made them concentrate on Him. They long from Him not others. They have tasted the sweetness of His knowledge and have drunk from the satiating cup of His love. The roots of His fear have been implanted in the depth of their hearts. Consequently, they have bent their straight backs through His worship. The length of the humility and extreme nearness has not removed from them the rope of their fear. Sermon 91

Say: God sufficed as a Witness between me and between you. Truly, He had been of His servants Aware, Seeing. **17:96**

He whom God guides is one who is truly guided. Whomever He causes to go astray, ***you*** *will never find for them protectors other than Him. We will assemble them on the Day of Resurrection on their faces, unseeing and unspeaking and unhearing. Their place of shelter will be hell. Whenever it declined, We will increase the blaze for them.* **17:97**

We bear witness that *there is no god, but He.* (Q3:2) Sermon 100

That is their recompense because they were ungrateful for Our signs. They said: When we had been bones and broken bits, will we be ones who are raised up as a new creation? **17:98**

After its creation He will destroy it, but not because any worry has overcome Him in its upkeep and administration or for any pleasure that will accrue to Him or for the cumbrousness of anything over Him. The length of its life does not weary Him so as to induce Him to its quick destruction. Sermon 186

Consider they not God Who created the heavens and the earth is One Who Has Power to create the like of them? He assigned a term for them whereof there is no doubt in it, but the ones who are unjust refused all but disbelief. **17:99**

I praise Him for His continuous mercy and His copious bounties. Sermon 82

Say: If you possessed the treasures of the mercy of my Lord, then, you would hold back for dread of spending. The human being had been ever stingy. **17:100**

Cast your glance over people wherever you like, you will see either a poor man suffering from poverty or a rich man ignoring God despite His bounty over him or a miser increasing his wealth by trampling on God's obligations or an unruly person closing his ears to all counsel. Where are your good people? Where are your virtuous people? Where are your high spirited and generous people? Where are those of you who avoid deceit in their business and remain pure in their behavior? Have they not all departed from this ignoble, transitory and troublesome world? Have you not been left among people who are just like rubbish and so low that lips avoid mention of them and do not move even to condemn their low position? *Truly we belong to God and truly we are ones who return to Him.* (Q2:156) Sermon 128

Certainly, We gave Moses nine signs, clear portents. Then, ask the Children of Jacob when he drew near them. Then Pharaoh said to him: Truly, O Moses, I think that **you** *are one who is bewitched.* **17:101**
He said: Certainly, **you** *knew no one caused these to descend but the Lord of the heavens and the earth as clear evidence. Truly, O Pharaoh, I think that* **you** *be one who is accursed.* **17:102**
So, he wanted to hound them in the region, but We drowned him and those who were with him altogether. **17:103**
We said to the Children of Jacob after him: Inhabit the region. So, when drew near the promise of the world to come, We will bring you about a mixed group. **17:104** ***

We caused it to descend with The Truth. It came down with the Truth. We sent it not to **you***, but as one who gives good tidings and as a warner.* **17:105**

There are four causes of infidelity and loss of belief in God: Hankering after whims, a passion to dispute every argument, deviation from truth, and dissension, because whoever hankers after whims does not incline towards truth. Whoever keeps on disputing every argument on account of his ignorance will always remain unwilling to see the truth. Whoever deviates from truth because of ignorance will always take good for evil and evil for good. He will always remain intoxicated with misguidance. Saying 31

It is a Recitation. We separated it in order that **you** *recite it to humanity at intervals. We sent it down a sending successively down.* **17:106**

Go ahead with the remembrance of God, for it is the best remembrance. Long for that which He has promised to the pious, for His promise is the most true promise. Tread the course of *the Prophet* (Q7:158), peace and the mercy of God be upon him, for it is the most distinguished course. Follow his *sunna*, for it is the most right of all behaviors. Learn the Quran, for it is the fairest of discourses. Understand it thoroughly, for it is the best blossoming of hearts. Seek cure with its light, for it is the cure for hearts. Recite it beautifully, for it is the most beautiful narration. Certainly, a scholar who acts not according to his knowledge is like the off-headed ignorant who does not find relief from his ignorance, but the plea of God is greater on the learned and grief more incumbent. He is more blameworthy before God. Sermon 110

Say: Believe in it, or believe not. Truly, those who were given the knowledge before it, when it is recounted to them, they fall down on their visages, ones who prostrate. **17:107**

The Prophet (Q33:6) of God, peace and the mercy of God be upon him, said: The belief of a person cannot be firm unless his heart is firm, and his heart cannot be firm unless his tongue is firm. So whoever of you can manage to meet God, the Sublime, in such a position that his hands are unsmeared with the blood of Muslims and their property and his tongue is safe from exposing them, he should do so. Sermon 176

They say: Glory be to our Lord! Truly, the promise of our Lord had been one that is accomplished. **17:108**

Praise belongs to God (Q1:2) Who made me such that I have not died, nor am I sick, nor have my veins been infected with disease, nor have I been hauled up for my evil acts, nor am I without progeny, nor have I forsaken my religion, nor do I disbelieve in my Lord, nor do I feel strangeness with my faith, nor is my intelligence affected, nor have I been punished with the punishment of peoples before me. I am a servant in **Your** possession. I have been guilty of excesses over myself. **You** have exhausted **Your** pleas over me and I have no plea before **You**. I have no power to take except what **You** give me. I cannot evade except what **You** save me from. Sermon 215

They fall down on their visage weeping. It increases them in humility. **17:109**

He recited the verse: *Rivalry diverted you until you have stopped by the cemetery.* (Q102:1-2) Then he said: How distant from achievement is their aim, how neglectful are these visitors and how difficult is the affair. They have not taken lessons from things which are full of lessons, but they took them from far off places. Do they boast on the dead bodies of their fore-fathers, or do they regard the number of dead persons as a ground for feeling boastful of their number? They want to revive the bodies that have become spiritless and the movements that have ceased. They are more entitled to be a source of lesson than a source of pride. They are more suitable for being a source of humility than of honor. Sermon 220

Say: Call to God or call to the Merciful. By whatever you call Him, to Him are the Fairer Names. Be ***you*** *not loud in* ***your*** *formal prayer nor speak in a low tone and look for a way between.* **17:110**

O the Most Merciful of all! O my God! We have come out to **You** to complain to **You** who is already not hidden from **You**, when the severe troubles have forced us, drought-stricken famines have driven us, distressing wants have made us helpless and troublesome mischiefs have incessantly befallen us. O my God! We beseech **You** not to send us back disappointed, nor to return us with down-cast eyes, nor to address us harshly for our sins, nor deal with us according to our deeds. O my God! Do pour on us **Your** mercy, **Your** blessing, **Your** sustenance and **Your** pity, and make us enjoy a drink which benefits us, quenches our thirst, produces green herbage by which all that has died down grows again and all that had withered is revived. It should bring about the benefit of freshness and plentifulness of ripe fruits. With it plains may be watered, rivers may begin flowing, plants may pick up foliage and prices may come down. Surely, **You** are powerful over whatever **You** will. Sermon 143 143

Say: The Praise belongs to God Who takes not a son to Himself and there be no associates ascribed with Him in the dominion nor there be for Him need for a protector from humility. Magnify Him a magnification! **17:111**

I praise Him out of gratefulness for His reward. I seek His assistance in fulfilling His rights. He has a strong army. His dignity is grand. Sermon 190

Chapter 18: The Cave (al-Kahf)

The Praise belongs to God Who caused the Book to descend to His servant and makes not for it any crookedness **18:1**
truth-loving, to warn of severe violence from that which proceeds from His Presence and to give good tidings to the ones who believe, those who do as the ones in accord with morality, that they will have a fairer compensation, **18:2**
ones who will abide in it eternally **18:3**
and to warn those who said: God took to Himself a son. **18:4**

They have no knowledge about it, nor had their fathers. Troublesome is a word that goes forth from their mouths. They say nothing but a lie **18:5**
so that perhaps ***you*** *will be one who consumes* ***your****self with grief for their sake if they believe not in this discourse out of bitterness.* **18:6**
Truly, We assigned whatever is in and on the earth as adornment for it so that We try them with it as to which of them are fairer in actions. **18:7**

God deputed prophets and distinguished them with His revelation. He made them as pleas for Him among His creation so that there should not remain any excuse for people. He invited people to the right path through a truthful tongue. You should know that God fully knows creation. Not that He was not aware of what they concealed from among their hidden secrets and inner feelings, but in order to try them ... *as to which of them are fairest in actions* ... (Q18:7), so that there is reward in respect of good acts and chastisement in respect of evil acts. Sermon 144

Truly, We are ones who make whatever is on it, barren dust, dry earth. **18:8**

Praise and eulogy be to God, O people. Sermon 92

Have ***you*** *assumed that the Companions of the Cave and the Bearers of Inscription had been a wonder among Our signs?* **18:9**
When the spiritual warriors took shelter in the Cave, then, they said: Our Lord! Give us mercy from ***Your*** *Presence and furnish us with right mindedness in our affair.* **18:10**
So, We sealed their ears in the Cave for a number of years. **18:11**
Again, We raised them up so that We might know which of the two confederates was better in calculating the space of time they lingered in expectation. **18:12**
We relate this tiding to ***you*** *with The Truth. Truly, they were male spiritual warriors who believed in their Lord and We increased them in guidance.* **18:13**
We invigorated their hearts when they stood up and said: Our Lord is Lord of the heavens and the earth. We will never call to any god other than He. Certainly, we would have said an outrageous thing. **18:14**
These, our folk, took to themselves gods other than Him. Why bring they not a clear portent of authority with them? Who does greater wrong than he who devised a lie against God? **18:15**
When you withdrew from them and from what they worship but God, then, take shelter in the cave. Your Lord will unfold for you from His mercy and will furnish you with a gentle issue in your affair. **18:16**
You *would have seen the sun when it came up. It inclines from their cave towards the right and when it began to set, it passed them towards the left while they were in a fissure. That is of the signs of God. He whom God guides, he is one who is truly guided. He whom He causes to go astray,* ***you*** *will never find for him a protector or one who will show him the way.* **18:17**
You *would assume them to be awake while they are ones who are sleeping. We turn them around and around towards the right and towards the left and their dog, one who stretches out its paws at the threshold. If* ***you*** *were to peruse them,* ***you*** *would have turned from them, running away, and would, certainly, be filled with alarm of them.* **18:18**
Thus, it was that We raised them up that they might demand of one another. Said one who speaks among them: How long lingered you in expectation? They said: We lingered in expectation a day or a part of a day. They said: Your Lord is greater in knowledge of how long you lingered in expectation. So, raise up one of you and with this, your money, send him to the city and let him look on which is the purest food. Then, let him bring you provision from there. Let him be courteous and cause not anyone to realize. **18:19**

Truly, if you become manifest to them, they will stone you, or they will cause you to return to their creed and you would not ever prosper. **18:20**
Thus, We made their case known that they know that the promise of God is true and that, as for the Hour, there is no doubt about it. Mention when they contend with one another about their affair. They said: Build over them a structure. Their Lord is greater in knowledge about them. Those who prevailed over their affair said: We, certainly, will take to ourselves over them a place of prostration. **18:21**
They will say: They were three, the fourth of them being their dog. They will say: They were five, the sixth of them being their dog, guessing at the unseen. They will say: They were seven, the eighth of them being their dog. Say: My Lord is greater in knowledge of their amount. No one knows them but a few, so altercate not about them but with a manifest argumentation and ask not for advice about them of anyone of them. **18:22**
Surely, he will not say about something: Truly, I will be one who does that tomorrow, **18:23**
but that you add: If God wills. Remember ***your*** *Lord when* ***you*** *had forgotten. Say: Perhaps my Lord will guide me nearer to right mindedness than this.* **18:24**
They lingered in expectation in their cave three hundred years, and they added nine. **18:25**
Say: God is greater in knowledge of how long they lingered in expectation. To Him belongs the unseen of the heavens and the earth. How well He perceives and how well He hears! Other than him, they have no protector and He ascribes no one partners in His determination. **18:26** ***

Recount what was revealed to ***you*** *from the Book of* ***Your*** *Lord. There is no one who changes His Words.* ***You*** *will never find other than Him, that which is a haven.* **18:27**

The riser has risen. The sparkler has sparkled. The appearer has appeared. The curved has been straightened. God has replaced one people with another and one day with another. We awaited these changes as the famine-stricken await the rain. Certainly, the leaders are the viceregents of God over His creatures. They guide the creatures to knowing God. No one will enter Paradise except him who knows them and knows Him. No one will enter Hell except him who denies them and denies Him. Sermon 152

Have ***you*** *patience* ***your****self with those who call to their Lord in the morning and the evening, wanting His Countenance. Let not* ***your*** *eyes pass over them wanting the adornment of this present life. Obey not him whose heart We made neglectful of Our Remembrance and who followed his own desires and whose affair had been excess.* **18:28**
Say: The Truth is from your Lord. Then, let whoever willed, believe, and let whoever willed, disbelieve. Truly, We made ready a fire for the ones who are unjust. They will be enclosed by its large tent. If they cry for help, they will be helped with rain, water like molten copper that will scald their faces. Miserable was the drink and how evil a place of rest! **18:29**

By God, you have not been told anything that they did not know. You have not been given anything of which they were deprived. Certainly you have been afflicted by a calamity which is like a she-camel whose nose-string is moving about and whose strap is loose So in whatever condition these deceitful people are should not deceive you, because it is just a long shadow whose term is fixed. Sermon 89

Truly, those who believed and did as the ones in accord with morality, truly, We will not waste the compensation of him who did good actions. **18:30**

Among the proofs of His creation is the creation of the skies which are fastened without pillars and stand without support. He called them. They responded obediently and humbly without being lazy or loathsome. If they had not acknowledged His Godhead and obeyed Him, He would not have made them the place for His throne, the abode of His angels and the destination: *To Him Words of what is good rise and He exalts an action in accord with morality* ... (Q35:10) of the creatures. Sermon 182

Those, for them are Gardens of Eden beneath which rivers run. They will be adorned in them with bracelets of gold and they will wear green garments of fine silk and brocade. They will be ones who are reclining in it on raised benches. Excellent is the reward for good deeds and how excellent a place of rest! **18:31**

Where are the seekers of virtue? The paths have already been determined. They have been given the news. For every misguidance, there is a cause. For every breaking of a pledge, there is a misrepresentation. By God, I shall not be like him who listens to the voice of mourning, hears the man who brings news of death and also visits the mourner, yet does not take a lesson. Sermon 148

Propound to them the parable of two men: We assigned to one of them two gardens of grapevines and We encircled them with date palm trees and We made crops between them. **18:32**
Both the gardens gave their produce and fail nothing at all. We caused a river to gush forth in the midst of them. **18:33**
There had been fruit for him. Then, he said to his companion while he converses with him: I have more wealth than **you** *and am mightier than a group of men or jinn.* **18:34**
He entered his garden while he is one who is unjust to himself. He said: I think that this will not be destroyed ever. **18:35**
I think that the Hour will not be one that arises. If I would be returned to my Lord, I would, surely, find better than this as an overturning. **18:36**
His companion said to him while he converses with him: Were **you** *ungrateful to Him Who created* **you** *out of earth dust, again, out of seminal fluid and, again, shaped* **you** *into a man?* **18:37**
Certainly, He is God, my Lord, and I will not ascribe partners with my Lord anyone. **18:38**
Would that when **you** *had entered* **your** *garden* **you** *had said: What God willed! There is no strength but with God! If* **you** *have seen I am less than you in wealth and children.* **18:39**
Then, perhaps my Lord will give me better than **your** *garden and will send on it a thunderclap from heaven. It will come to be in the morning a place of slippery earth.* **18:40**
Or it will come to be in the morning that its water will be sinking into the ground so that **you** *will never be able to seek it out.* **18:41**
Its fruit was enclosed. It came to be in the morning he turns around and around the palms of his hands in wretchedness for what he spent on it while it was one that has fallen down in ruins. He says: Would that I not ascribe partners with my Lord anyone! **18:42**
There is no faction to help him other than God. He had been one who is helpless. **18:43**

God, the Almighty, has sent down a guiding Book wherein He has explained virtue and vice. You should adopt the course of virtue, whereby you will have guidance. Detach yourself from the direction of vice, so that you remain on the right way. Sermon 167

All protection there belongs to God, The Truth. He is Best in rewarding for good deeds and Best in consequence. **18:44**

Perform good acts while you are still in the vastness of life. The books are open for recording of actions. Repentance is allowed. The runner away from God is being called. The sinner is being given hope of forgiveness before the light of action is put off, time expires, life ends, the door for repentance is closed and angels ascend to the sky. Sermon 236

Propound for them the parable of this present life: It is like water that We caused to descend from heaven. Then, plants of the earth mingled with it and it becomes straw in the morning that winnows in the winds. God had been over everything One Who is Omnipotent. **18:45**

So now, certainly I frighten you from this world for it is sweet and green, surrounded by lusts, and liked for its immediate enjoyments. It excites wonder with small things, is ornamented with false hopes and decorated with deception. Its rejoicing does not last. Its afflictions cannot be avoided. It is deceitful, harmful, changing, perishable, exhaustible, liable to destruction, eating away and destructive. When it reaches the extremity of desires of those who incline towards it and feel happy with it, the position is just what God, the Almighty, says in the Quran: *Propound for them the parable of this present life: It is like water that We caused to descend from heaven. Then, plants of the earth mingled with it and it becomes straw in the morning that winnows in the winds. God had been over everything One Who is Omnipotent.* (Q18:45) Sermon 110

Wealth and children are the adornment of this present life. But that which endures are ones in accord with morality. These are better with ***your*** *Lord in reward for good deeds and better for hopefulness.* **18:46**

Where are the seekers of virtue, for the paths have already been determined and they have been given the news? Sermon 148

On a Day We will set in motion the mountains and ***you*** *will see the earth as that which will depart. We will assemble them and not leave out anyone of them.* **18:47**

Praise belongs to God (Q1:2), Who is High above all else. He is Near the creation through His bounty. Sermon 82

They were presented before ***your*** *Lord ranged in rows. Certainly, you drew near Us as We created you the first time. Nay! You claimed that We never assign for you something that is promised.* **18:48**

He did not create what He created to fortify His authority, nor for fear of the consequences of time, nor to seek help against the attack of an equal or a boastful partner or a hateful opponent. On the other hand, all creatures are reared by Him and are His humbled servants.... He is not conditioned on anything so that it be said that He exists therein, nor is He separated from anything so as to be said that He is away from it. The creation of what He initiated or the administration of what He controls did not fatigue Him. No disability overtook Him against what He created. No misgiving ever occurred to Him in what He commanded and resolved, but His verdict is certain. His knowledge is definite. His governance is overwhelming. He is wished for at time of distress and He is feared even in bounty. Sermon 65

The Book was set in place and ***you*** *will see the ones who sin being ones who are apprehensive as to what is in it. They will say: Woe to us! What is this Book? It neither leaves out anything small or great, but counted everything. They will find present what their hands had done.* ***Your*** *Lord does not wrong anyone.* **18:49**

On us it is obligatory ... to abide by the Book of God (Quran), the Sublime, and the conduct of *the Prophet* (Q7:158), peace and the mercy of God be upon him, to stand by His rights and the revival of his *sunna*. Sermon 169

Mention when We said to the angels: Prostrate yourselves to Adam! So, they prostrated themselves but Iblis. He had been among the jinn and he disobeyed the command of His Lord. Will you, then, take him to yourselves and his offspring to be protectors other than Me while they are an enemy to you? Miserable was it to give in place ones who are unjust! **18:50**

Then God asked the angels to fulfill His promise with them and to accomplish the pledge of His injunction to them by acknowledging Him through prostration to Him and submission to His honored position. So God said: *Prostrate yourselves to Adam! They, then, prostrated themselves but Iblis.* Sermon 1

I called them not to witness the creation of the heavens and the earth nor to their own creation of themselves nor took I to myself the ones who are led astray as assistants. **18:51**

Had they pondered over the greatness of His power and the vastness of His bounty they would have returned to the right path and feared the punishment of the fire, but hearts are sick and eyes are diseased. Do they not see the small things He has created, how He strengthened their system and opened for them hearing and sight and made for them bones and skins? Look at the ant with its small body and delicate form. Sermon 185

On a Day when He will say: Cry out to My associates, those who you claimed. Then, they will call out to them, but they will not respond to them and We will make a gulf of doom between them. **18:52**

I bear witness that *there is no god but God* (Q47:19), the One, there is no partner with Him nor is there with Him any god other than Himself and that *Muhammad* (Q48:29), peace and the mercy of God be upon him, is *His servant* (Q17:1) and His *Prophet.* (Q7:158) Sermon 35

The unjust will see the ones who sin in the fire. They thought that they are ones who are about to fall in it and they will not find a place to turn from it. **18:53**

The great calamity of that place is the hot water and entry into Hell, flames of eternal fire and intensity of blazes. There is no resting period, no gap for ease, no power to intervene, no death to bring about solace and no sleep to make him forget pain. He rather lies under several kinds of deaths and moment-to-moment punishment. We seek refuge with God. Sermon 82

Certainly, We diversified in this, the Quran, every kind of example for humanity. The human being had been more than anything argumentative. **18:54**

Certainly, these people are in agreement in disliking my authority. I will carry on until I perceive disunity among you, because if they succeed in spite of the unsoundness of their view, the whole organization of Muslims will be shattered. They are hankering after this world out of jealousy against him on whom God has bestowed it. So they intend to revert the matters to the pre-Islamic period. On us it is obligatory, for your sake, to abide by the Book of God (Quran), the Sublime, and the conduct of *the Prophet* (Q7:158), peace and the mercy of God be upon him, to stand by His rights and to revive his *sunna*. Sermon 169

Nothing prevented humanity from believing when the guidance drew near to them or from asking forgiveness of their Lord, but that approaches them a custom of the ancient ones or approaches them the punishment face to face. **18:55**

O my God! I seek **Your** protection from becoming destitute despite **Your** riches, from being misguided despite **Your** guidance, from being molested in **Your** realm and from being humiliated while authority rests with **You**. Sermon 215

We send not the ones who are sent, but as ones who give good tidings and as ones who warn. Those who were ungrateful dispute with falsehood in order to refute The Truth by it. They took My signs to themselves in mockery and what they were warned of. **18:56**

God was being disobeyed. Satan was given support. Faith was forsaken. As a result, the pillars of religion crumbled. Any trace of them was lost. Its passages were destroyed. Its streets fell into decay. People obeyed Satan and tread his path. They sought water from his watering places. Satan's emblems flew in the wind through them. His standard of vice was raised. They trampled people under their hoofs and tread upon them with their feet. Vice attained full stature. The people immersed in them were led astray, perplexed, ignorant and seduced as though they were in a good house (Mecca) with bad neighbors (ungrateful Quraysh). Instead of sleep, the people had wakefulness. Instead of antimony, they had tears in their eyes. They were in a land where the lips of the learned were bridled while the words of the ignorant were honored. Sermon 2

Who does greater wrong than he who was reminded of the signs of his Lord, then, turned aside from them and forgot what his hands put forward? Truly, We laid sheathes on their hearts so that they should not understand it and heaviness in their ears. If ***you*** *have called them to the guidance, yet they will not be truly guided ever.* **18:57**

God ... is aware of whatever is hidden in the hearts. Sermon 191

Your *Lord is Forgiving, Possessor of Mercy. If He were to take them to task for what they earned, He will quicken the punishment for them. But for them is what they are promised, from which they will never find a way to elude it.* **18:58**

O my God! Forgive me. **You** know more about me than I do. If I return to sin, **You** return to forgiveness. My God, forgive me what I had promised to myself, but **You** did not find its fulfillment with me. My God, forgive me that with what I sought nearness to **You** with my tongue, but my heart opposed and did not perform. My God, forgive me winking of the eye, vile utterances, desires of the heart and errors of speech. Sermon 78

These towns, We caused them to perish when they did wrong and We assigned for their destruction what is promised. **18:59**

O God's human being! So take lesson and recall that evil doing with which your fathers and brothers are entangled and for which they have to account. By my life, your time is not much behind theirs, nor have long periods or centuries lapsed between you and them, nor are you much distant from when you were in their loins. Sermon 89

Mention when Moses said to his spiritual warrior: I will not quit until I reach the place of meeting of the two seas even if I will go on for many years. **18:60**

But when they reached the place of the meeting between them, then, they both forgot their great fish and it took to itself a way through the sea, burrowing. **18:61**

Then, when they crossed, he said to his spiritual warrior: Give us our breakfast. Certainly, we met fatigue from our journey. **18:62**
He said: Had **you** *considered? When we took shelter at the rock, truly, I forgot the great fish. None but Satan caused me to forget to remember it. It took to itself to a way into the sea in a wondrous way.* **18:63**
He said: That is what we had been looking for! So, they went back following their footsteps. **18:64**
Then, they found a servant among Our servants to whom We gave mercy from Us and We taught him knowledge which proceeds from Our Presence. **18:65**
Moses said to him: May I follow **you** *so that* **you** *will teach me something of what* **you** *were taught of right judgment?* **18:66**
He said: Truly, **you** *will never be able to have patience with me.* **18:67**
How will **you** *endure a thing patiently when* **you** *have not comprehended any awareness of it?* **18:68**
Moses said: **You** *will find me, if God willed, one who remains steadfast and I will not rebel against* **your** *command.* **18:69**
He said: Then, if **you** *had followed me, ask me not about anything until I cause to be evoked in* **you** *a remembrance of it.* **18:70**
So, they both set out until when they embarked in a vessel. He made a hole in it. Moses said: Had **you** *made a hole in it in order to drown the people? Certainly,* **you** *had brought about a dreadful thing!* **18:71**
He said: Said I not that **you** *will never be able to have patience with me?* **18:72**
Moses said: Take me not to task for what I forgot and constrain me not with hardship for my affair. **18:73**
Then, they both set out until when they met a boy; then, he killed him. Moses said: Had **you** *killed a pure soul without his having slain a soul? Certainly,* **you** *had brought about a horrible thing!* **18:74**
He said: Said I not that **you** *will never be able to have patience with me?* **18:75**
Moses said: If I asked **you** *about anything after this, then, keep not company with me, surely,* **you** *had reached enough of excusing from my presence!* **18:76**
Then, they both set out until when they approached a people of a town. They asked its people for food. But they refused to receive them as guests. Then, they found in it a wall that wants to tumble down, so he repaired it. Moses said: If **you** *had willed, certainly,* **you** *would have taken compensation to* **your***self for it.* **18:77**
He said: This is the parting between me and between **you***! I will tell* **you** *the interpretation of what* **you** *were not able to have patience for it.* **18:78**
As for the vessel, it had been of some needy people who toil in the sea, so I wanted to mar it as there had been a king behind them taking every vessel forcefully. **18:79**
As for the boy, both his parents had been ones who believe, and we dreaded that he should constrain them with defiance and ingratitude, **18:80**
so we wanted their Lord to cause for them in exchange one better than he in purity and nearer in sympathy. **18:81**
As for the wall, it had been that of two orphan boys in the city and beneath it had been a treasure for them. The father of both of them had been one in accord with morality so **your** *Lord wanted they be fully grown, having come of age, and pull out their treasure as a mercy from* **your** *Lord. I accomplished that not of my own command. This is the interpretation of what* **you** *were not able to have patience for it.* **18:82**

They will ask **you** *about Dhu-l Qarnayn. Say: I will recount to you a remembrance of him.* **18:83**
Truly, We established him firmly on the earth and gave him a route to everything. **18:84**
So, he pursued a route **18:85**
until when he reached the setting of the sun. He found it beginning to set in a spring of muddy water. He found near it a folk. We said: O Dhu-l Qarnayn! Either **you** *will punish them or* **you** *will take them to* **your***self with goodness.* **18:86**
He said: As for him who did wrong, we will punish him. Again, he will be returned to his Lord Who will punish him with a horrible punishment. **18:87**
But as for him who believed and did as one in accord with morality, he will have the fairer recompense. We will say to him of our command with ease. **18:88**
Again, he pursued a route **18:89**
until when he reached the rising place of the sun. He found it coming up on a folk for whom We make not any obstruction against it. **18:90**
Thus, We, surely, enclosed whatever was near him through awareness. **18:91**
Again, he pursued a route **18:92**
until when he reached between two embankments. He found behind them a folk who would almost not understand any saying. **18:93**
They said: O Dhu-l Qarnayn! Truly, Gog and Magog are ones who make corruption in and on the earth. Will we assign to **you** *payment if* **you** *have made an embankment between us and between them?* **18:94**
He said: What my Lord established firmly for me is better, so assist me with strength. I will make a fortification between you and between them. **18:95**
Give me ingots of iron, until when he made level between the two cliffs. He said: Blow, until when he made it a fire. He said: Give me molten brass to pour out over it. **18:96**
So, they were not able to scale it nor were they able to dig through it. **18:97**
He said: This is a mercy from my Lord. So, when the promise of my Lord drew near, He will made it powder. The promise of my Lord had been true. **18:98**
That Day We will leave some of them to surge like waves on others. The trumpet will be blown. Then We will gather them together. **18:99**
We will present the depths of hell on that Day in plain view to ones who are ungrateful, **18:100**
to those whose eyes had been screened from My Remembrance and who had not been able to hear. **18:101** ***

Assumed ones who were ungrateful that they take My servants to themselves as protectors instead of Me? Truly, We made hell ready with hospitality for ones who are ungrateful. **18:102**

Where are the minds which seek light from the lamps of guidance and the eyes which look at minarets of God-consciousness? Where are the hearts dedicated to God and devoted to the obedience of God? They are all crowding towards worldly vanities and quarreling over unlawful issues. The banners of the Garden and Hell have been raised for them, but they have turned their faces away from the Garden and proceeded to Hell by dint of their performances. God called them, but they showed dislike and ran away. When Satan called them, they responded and proceeded towards him. Sermon 144

Say: Shall We tell you who will be ones who are losers by their actions? **18:103**
It is those whose endeavoring went astray in this present life while they assume that they are doing good by their handiwork. **18:104**

In (the Quran) there are some verses whose knowledge is obligatory and others whose ignorance by the people is permissible. It also contains what appears to be obligatory according to the Book, but its repeal is signified by the actions of *the Prophet* (Q7:158) (*sunna*), peace and the mercy of God be upon him, or that which appears compulsory according to the Prophet's actions, but the Book allows not following it. Or there are those which are obligatory in a given time, but not so after that time. Its prohibitions also differ. Some are major regarding which there exists the threat of hellfire and others are minor for which there is the hope of forgiveness. There are also those of which a small portion is also acceptable to God, but they are capable of being expanded. Sermon 1

Those were those who were ungrateful for the signs of their Lord and the meeting with Him so their actions were fruitless. So, We will not perform for them on the Day of Resurrection, any weighing. **18:105**
That will be their recompense—hell—because they were ungrateful and took to themselves My signs and My Messengers in mockery. **18:106**

Pledge yourself with prayer and remain steady on it. Offer prayer as much as possible and seek nearness of God through it, because it is imposed upon the believers as a time of ordinance: *Then, when you satisfied the formal prayer, then, remember God when upright and sitting and on your sides. And, then, when you were secured, perform the formal prayer. Truly, the formal prayer had been —for the ones who believe— a timed prescription.* (Q4:103) Have you not heard the reply of the people of Hell when they were asked: *What thrust you into Saqar (Hell)? They would say: We be not among the ones who formally pray.* (Q74:42-43) Certainly, prayer drops out sins like the dropping of leaves of trees, and removes them as ropes are removed from the necks of cattle. *The Messenger of God* (Q48:29), peace and the mercy of God be upon him, likened it to a hot bath situated at the door of a person who bathes in it five times a day. Will then any dirt remain on him? Sermon 198

Truly, those who believed and did as ones in accord with morality, their hospitality had been in the Gardens of Paradise, **18:107**
ones who will dwell in them forever. They will have no desire for relocation from there. **18:108**
Say: If the sea had been ink for the Words of my Lord, the sea would come to an end before the Words of my Lord came to an end even if We brought about replenishment the like of it. **18:109**

Mind the obligations! Mind the obligations! Fulfill them for God and they will take you to the Garden. Surely, God has made unlawful the things which are not unknown and made lawful the things which are without defect. Sermon 167

Say: I am only a mortal like you. It is revealed to me that your God is One, so whoever had been hoping for the meeting with his Lord, let him do with his actions as one in accord with morality and ascribe no partners—in the worship of his Lord, ever. **18:110**

With *the Prophet* (Q7:158), peace and the mercy of God be upon him, God exhausted the series of Prophets and ended the revelation. He then fought for Him those who were turning away from Him and were equating others with Him. Sermon 133

CHAPTER 19: MARY (Maryam)

Kaf Ha Ya Ain Sad **19:1**

A remembrance of the mercy of **your** *Lord to His servant Zechariah* **19:2**
when he cried out to his Lord, secretively crying out. **19:3**
He said: My Lord! Truly, I—my bones became feeble and my head became studded with grayness of hair and I be not disappointed in my supplication to **You**, *O my Lord.* **19:4**
Truly, I feared for my defenders after me. My woman had been a barren woman. So, bestow on me from that which proceeds from **Your** *Presence a protector.* **19:5**
He will inherit from me and inherit from the family of Jacob. Make him, my Lord, pleasing. **19:6**
O Zechariah! Truly, We give **you** *the good tidings of a boy. His name will be Yahya and We assigned it not as a namesake for anyone before.* **19:7**
He said: My Lord! How will I have a boy while my woman had been a barren woman and, surely, I reached an advanced old age? **19:8**
He said: It is about to be! **Your** *Lord said: It is insignificant for Me and, surely, I created* **you** *before when* **you** *wast nothing.* **19:9**
Zechariah said: My Lord! Assign for me a sign. He said: **Your** *sign is that* **you** *will not speak to humanity for three nights, although being without fault.* **19:10**
So, he went forth to his folk from the sanctuary. Then, he revealed to them:Glorify in the early morning dawn and evening. **19:11**
O Yahya! Take the Book with strength. We gave him critical judgment while a lad, **19:12**
and Our continuous mercy from that which proceeds from Our Presence and purity and he had been devout **19:13**
and pious to ones who are his parents and be not haughty nor rebellious. **19:14**
Peace be on him the day on which he was given birth and the day he dies and the day he is raised up, living. **19:15** ***
Remember Mary in the Book when she went apart from her people to an eastern place. **19:16**
Then, she took to herself a partition away from them, so We sent Our Spirit to her and he presented himself before her as a mortal without fault. **19:17**
She said: Truly, I take refuge in The Merciful from **you**; *come not near me if* **you** *had been devout.* **19:18**
He said: I am only a Messenger from **your** *Lord that I bestow on* **you** *(f) a pure boy.* **19:19**
She said: How will I have a boy when no mortal touches me, nor am I an unchaste woman? **19:20**
He said: Thus, it will be. **Your** *Lord said: It is for Me insignificant. We will assign him as a sign for humanity and as a mercy from Us. It had been that which is a decreed command.* **19:21**
So, she conceived him and she went apart with him to a farther place. **19:22**
The birth pangs surprised her at the trunk of a date palm tree. She said: O would that I had died before this and I had been one who is forgotten, a forgotten thing! **19:23**
So, he cried out to her from beneath her: Feel not remorse! Surely, **your** *Lord made under* **you** *(f) a brook.* **19:24**
Shake towards **you** *(f) the trunk of the date palm tree. It will cause ripe, fresh dates to fall on* **you**. **19:25**
So, eat and drink and **your** *eyes be refreshed. If* **you** *have seen any mortal, say: I vowed formal fasting to The Merciful so I will never speak to any human this day.* **19:26**
Then, she approached her folk with him, carrying him. They said: O Mary! Surely, **you** *had drawn near a monstrous thing!* **19:27**
O sister of Aaron! **Your** *father had not been a reprehensible man nor was* **your** *mother an unchaste woman.* **19:28**
Then, she pointed to him. They said: How speak we to one who had been in the cradle, a lad? **19:29**

Jesus said: Truly, I am a servant of God. He gave me the Book and He made me a Prophet. **19:30**
He made me one who is blessed wherever I had been and He bequeathed to me the formal prayer and the purifying alms as long as I continue living, **19:31**
and He makes me pious toward one who is my mother and He makes me not haughty nor disappointed. **19:32** ***
Peace be on me the day I was given birth and the day I die and the day I am raised up, living. **19:33**
That is Jesus son of Mary, a saying of The Truth. They contest what is in it. **19:34**
It had not been for God that He takes to Himself a son. Glory be to Him! When He decreed a command, He not but says to it: Be! Then, it is! **19:35**
Truly, God is my Lord and your Lord, so worship Him. This is a straight path. **19:36** ***

There was variance among the confederates, so woe to those who were ungrateful from the scene of a tremendous Day! **19:37**
Hear well and perceive well. On that Day they will approach Us, but today the ones who are unjust are in a clear wandering astray! **19:38**

Be aware and act during the period of attraction just as you act during a period of dread. Be aware! Truly, I have not seen one who covets Paradise to be asleep, nor a dreader from hellfire to be asleep. Be aware, he whom right does not benefit must suffer the harm of the wrong. He whom guidance does not keep firm will be led away by misguidance towards destruction. Sermon 28

Warn ***you*** *them of the Day of Regret when the command would be decided. Yet they are heedless and they believe not.* **19:39**
Truly, We will inherit the earth and whatever is in and on it and to Us they will be returned. **19:40**

When the earthquake occurs, the Day of Resurrection approaches with all its severities, the people of every worshipping place cling to it, all the devotees cling to the object of their devotion and all the followers cling to their leader. Then on that day even the opening of an eye in the air and the sound of a footstep on the ground will be assigned its due through His Justice and His Equity. On that day many an argument will prove void and a contention for excuses will stand rejected. Sermon 222

Remember Abraham in the Book. Truly, he had been a just person, a Prophet. **19:41**
That is when he said to his father: O my father! Why will you worship what hears not, and perceives not, and avails ***you*** *not anything?* **19:42**
O my father! Truly, I, there drew near me of the knowledge of what approaches ***you*** *not. So, follow me and I will guide* ***you*** *to a path without fault.* **19:43**
O my father! Worship not Satan. Truly, Satan had been rebellious towards The Merciful! **19:44**
O my father! Truly, I fear that a punishment should afflict ***you*** *from The Merciful so that* ***you*** *become a protector of Satan.* **19:45**
He said: are ***you*** *one who shrinks from my gods, O Abraham? If* ***you*** *will not refrain* ***your****self, certainly, I will stone* ***you****, so abandon me for some while.* **19:46**
He said: Peace be to ***you****. I will ask for forgiveness from my Lord for* ***you****. Truly, He had been One Who is Gracious to me.* **19:47**
I will withdraw from you and what you call to other than God and I will call to my Lord. Perhaps

I will not be disappointed in my supplication to my Lord. **19:48**
So, he withdrew from them and what they worship other than God. We bestowed on him Isaac and Jacob. Each of them We made a Prophet. **19:49**
We bestowed on them from Our mercy and We assigned them the tongue of lofty sincerity. **19:50**

The Quran has made remembrance incumbent upon your tongues. Sermon 182

Remember Moses in the Book. Truly, he had been one who was devoted and he had been a Messenger, a Prophet. **19:51**
We proclaimed to him from the right edge of the mount and We brought him near privately. **19:52**
We bestowed on him out of Our mercy his brother Aaron, a Prophet. **19:53**
Remember Ishmael in the Book. Truly, he had been one who is sincere in his promise, and he had been a Messenger, a Prophet. **19:54**
He had been commanding his people to formal prayer and the purifying alms and he had been with His Lord one who is well-pleasing. **19:55***
Remember Enoch in the Book. Truly, he had been a just person, a Prophet. **19:56**
We exalted him to a lofty place. **19:57**
Those are those to whom God was gracious from among the Prophets of the offspring of Adam and whomever We carried with Noah and of the offspring of Abraham and Jacob, Jacob, from among whomever We guided and elected. When are recounted to them the signs of the Merciful they fell down, crying, ones who prostrate themselves. **19:58**
Then, after them succeeded a succession who wasted the formal prayer and followed their lusts. So, they will meet error, **19:59**
but the ones who repented and believed and did as ones in accord with morality. For those will enter the Garden and they will not be wronged at all, **19:60**
Gardens of Eden which The Merciful promised His servants in the unseen. Truly, He, His promise had been that which is kept. **19:61**
They will not hear in them idle talk, nothing but: Peace. They will have their provision in them in the early morning dawn and evening. **19:62**
This is the Garden which We will give as inheritance to whomever of Our servants who had been devout. **19:63**

This is the thing against which God has protected His creatures who are believers by means of prayers, alms-giving and suffering the hardship of fasting in the days in which it has been made obligatory in order to give their limbs peacefulness, to cast fear in their eyes, to make their spirits humble, to give their hearts humility and to remove haughtiness from them. All this is achieved through the covering of their delicate cheeks with dust in humility, prostrating their main limbs on the ground in humbleness and retracting of their bellies so as to reach to their backs due to fasting by way of lowliness before God, in addition to giving all sorts of products of the earth to the needy and the destitute by way of alms. Look what there is in these acts by way of curbing the appearance of pride and suppressing the traces of vanity. Sermon 192

We come forth not but by the command of ***your*** *Lord. To Him belongs whatever is in advance of us and whatever is behind us and whatever is in between that.* ***Your*** *Lord had not been forgetful,* **19:64**

I praise Him for His continuous mercy and His copious bounties. Sermon 82 *the Lord of the heavens and the earth, and what is between them! So, worship Him and maintain* ***you*** *patience in His worship. Have* ***you*** *known any namesake for Him?* **19:65**

This world and the hereafter have submitted to Him their reins. The skies and earths have flung their keys towards Him. The thriving trees bow to Him in the morning and evening, producing for Him flaming fire from their branches and, at His command, turn their own feed into ripe fruits. Sermon 133

The human being says: When I am dead, will I be brought out living? **19:66**

Do you not see that your predecessors do not come back and the surviving followers do not remain? Do you not observe that the people of the world pass mornings and evenings in different conditions? Thus, somewhere the dead is wept for. Someone is being condoled. Someone is prostrate in distress. Someone is inquiring about the sick. Someone is passing his last breath. Someone is hankering after the world while death is looking for him. Someone is forgetful, but he is not forgotten by death. On the footsteps of the predecessors walk the survivors. Sermon 99

Will the human being not remember that We created him before when he be of nothing? **19:67**

No other originator took part with Him in its origination. No one having power assisted Him in its creation. Sermon 185

So, by ***your*** *Lord, certainly, We will assemble them and the satans. Again, We will parade them around hell, ones who crawl on their knees.* **19:68**

People obeyed Satan and tread his path. They sought water from his watering places. Satan's banners flew in the wind through them. His standard of vice was raised. They trampled people under their hoofs and tread upon them with their feet. Vice attained full stature. Sermon 2

Again, We will tear out every partisan, whoever of them was more severe in stubborn rebellion against The Merciful. **19:69**

Be God-conscious! From the immediate consequence of rebellion to accrue in this world and the eventual consequence of weighty oppressiveness to accrue in the next world and from the evil result of vanity because it is the great trap of Satan and his big deceit which enters the hearts of the people like a fatal poison. It never goes to waste, nor misses anyone—neither the learned because of his knowledge, nor the destitute in his rags. Sermon 192

After that We are greater in knowledge of those, they who are most deserving of roasting in it. **19:70**

There is none of you, but ones who go down to it. This had been a thing decreed, that decreed by ***your*** *Lord.* **19:71**

Everyone of them is ... alone although they are a group, and they are strangers, even though friends. They are unaware of morning after a night and of evening after a day. The night or the day when they departed has become ever existent for them. They found the dangers of their place of stay more serious than they had apprehended. They witnessed that its signs were greater than they had guessed. Sermon 220

Again, We will deliver those who were God-conscious and We will forsake the ones who are unjust, in it, ones who crawl on their knees. **19:72**

Among the God-conscious are the people of distinction. Their speech is to the point. Their dress is moderate. Their gait is humble. They keep their eyes closed to what God has made unlawful for them. They put their ears to that knowledge which is beneficial to them. They remain in the time of trials as though they remain in comfort. If there had not been fixed periods of life ordained for each, their spirits would not have remained in their bodies even for the twinkling of an eye because of their eagerness for the reward and fear of chastisement. The greatness of the Creator is seated in their heart and so everything else appears small in their eyes. Thus, to them Paradise is as though they see it and are enjoying its favors. To them, Hell is also as if they see it and are suffering punishment in it. Sermon 193

When are recounted to them Our signs, clear portents, those who were ungrateful would say to those who believed: Which of the two groups of people is best in station and fairer in alliance? **19:73**

Whoever takes a partner for **You** is ungrateful according to what is stated in **Your** unambiguous verses and indicated by the evidence of **Your** clear arguments. Sermon 91

How many before them We caused to perish whose generation was fairer in furnishing and outward show? **19:74**

One of the firm decisions of God in the Wise Reminder (Quran), upon which He bestows reward or gives punishment and through which He likes or dislikes, is that it will not benefit a person, even though he exerts himself and acts sincerely, if he leaves this world to meet God with one of these acts without repenting, namely that he believed in a partner with God during his obligatory worship or appeased his own anger by killing an individual or spoke about acts committed by others or sought fulfillment of his needs from people by introducing an innovation in his religion or met people with a double face or moved among them with a double tongue. Understand this because an illustration is a guide for its like. Sermon 153

Say: Whoever had been in fallacy, The Merciful will prolong his prolonging for him until when they would see what they are promised, either the punishment or the Hour, then, they will know whose place is worse and whose army is weak. **19:75**

O my God! We beseech **You** not to send us back disappointed, nor to return us with down-cast eyes, nor to address us harshly for our sins, nor deal with us according to our deeds. O my God! Do pour on us **Your** mercy, **Your** blessing, **Your** sustenance and **Your** pity and make us enjoy a drink which benefits us, quenches our thirst, produces green herbage by which all that has died down grows again and all that had withered is revived. It should bring about the benefit of freshness and plentifulness of ripe fruits. With it plains may be watered, rivers may begin flowing, plants may pick up foliage and prices may come down. Surely, **You** are powerful over whatever **You** will. Sermon 143

God increases in guidance those who were truly guided and endure in accord with morality. They are better with ***your*** *Lord in reward for good deeds and better for turning back.* **19:76**

Where are the seekers of virtue? The paths have already been determined. They have been given the news. For every misguidance, there is a cause. For every breaking of a pledge, there is a misrepresentation. By God, I shall not be like him who listens to the voice of mourning, hears the man who brings news of death and also visits the mourner, yet does not take a lesson. Sermon 148

Had ***you*** *seen him who was ungrateful for Our signs, who said: Will I be given wealth and children?* **19:77**

What will a person do with wealth which he would shortly be deprived of while only its ill effects and reckoning would be left behind for him? Sermon 157

Perused he the unseen or took he to himself a compact from The Merciful? **19:78**

People did not take light from the lights of his wisdom, nor did they produce flame from the flint of sparkling knowledge. Sermon 108

No indeed! We will write down what he says. We will cause the punishment to increase for him, prolonging it. **19:79**

O God's human being! Where are those who were allowed long ages to live? They enjoyed bounty. They were taught. They learned. They were given time. They passed it in vain. They were kept healthy. They forgot their duty. They were allowed a long period of life, were handsomely provided for, were warned of grievous punishment and were promised great rewards. You should avoid sins that lead to destruction and vices that attract the wrath of God. Sermon 82

We will inherit from him all that he says and he will approach Us individually. **19:80**

He is the Giver of all reward and distinction and Dispeller of all calamities and hardships. I praise Him for His continuous mercy and His copious bounties. Sermon 82

They took to themselves gods other than God that there be a triumph for them. **19:81**
No indeed! They will disbelieve in what they worship and they will be taking a stand against them. **19:82**
Have ***you*** *not considered that We sent the satans against the ones who were ungrateful to confound them with confusion?* **19:83**
So, hasten ***you*** *not against them. We only number for them a sum.* **19:84**

Where are the minds which seek light from the lamps of guidance and the eyes which look at minarets of God-consciousness? Where are the hearts dedicated to God and devoted to the obedience of God? They are all crowding towards worldly vanities and quarreling over unlawful issues. The banners of the Garden and Hell have been raised for them, but they have turned their faces away from the Garden and proceeded to Hell by dint of their performances. God called them, but they showed dislike and ran away. When Satan called them, they responded and proceeded towards him. Sermon 144

On the Day We will assemble the ones who are God-conscious to The Merciful like an entourage. **19:85**

God the Almighty, the Sublime, created the things of creation. He created them without any need for their obedience or being safe from their sinning, because the sin of anyone who sins does not harm Him, nor does the obedience of anyone who obeys Him benefit Him. He has distributed among them their livelihood and has assigned them their positions in the world. Sermon 193

We will drive the ones who sin to hell, herding them. **19:86**
None of them will possess the power of intercession but such a one who took to himself a compact with The Merciful. **19:87**

Know that the Quran is an interceder and its intercession will be accepted. It is a speaker who bears witness. For whoever the Quran intercedes on the Day of Judgment, its intercession for him would be accepted. He about whom the Quran speaks ill on the Day of Judgment shall testify to it. On the Day of Judgment, an announcer will announce: Be aware! Every sower of a crop is in distress except the sowers of the Quran. Therefore, you should be among the sowers of the Quran and its followers. Make it your guide towards God. Seek its advice for yourselves, do not trust your views against it and regard your desires in the matter of the Quran as deceitful. Sermon 176

They said: The Merciful took to Himself a son! **19:88**
Certainly, you brought about a disastrous thing **19:89**
whereby the heavens are almost split asunder and the earth is split and the mountains fall crashing down **19:90**
that they attributed a son to The Merciful. **19:91**
It is not fit and proper for The Merciful that He should take a son to Himself! **19:92**
There is none at all in the heavens and the earth but he be one who arrives to The Merciful as a servant. **19:93**
Certainly, He counted for them and numbered up a sum! **19:94**
Every one of them will be ones who arrive to Him individually on the Day of Resurrection. **19:95**
Truly, those who believed and did as the ones in accord with morality, The Merciful will assign ardor for them. **19:96**
So, truly, We made this easy on ***your*** *tongue. Certainly,* ***you*** *will give good tidings with it to the ones who are God-conscious and* ***you*** *will warn a most stubborn folk with it.* **19:97**
How many a generation caused We to perish before them? are ***you*** *conscious of anyone of them or hear you so much as a whisper from them?* **19:98** ***

Chapter 20: Ta Ha (Ṭā Hā)

Ta Ha **20:1**
We caused not the Quran to descend to ***you*** *that* ***you*** *be in despair,* **20:2**
but as an admonition to him who dreads **20:3**
a sending down successively from Him Who created the earth and the lofty heavens. **20:4**

The Book of God is among you. It speaks and its tongue does not falter. It is a house whose pillars do not fall down, and a power whose supporters are never routed. Sermon 133

The Merciful turned His attention to the Throne. **20:5**
To Him belongs whatever is in the heavens and whatever is on the earth and whatever is between them and whatever is beneath the soil. **20:6**

I praise Him for His continuous mercy and His copious bounties. Sermon 82

If ***you*** *are to publish a saying, yet, truly, He knows the secret and what is more secret.* **20:7**

God deputed prophets and distinguished them with His revelation. He made them as pleas for Him among His creation so that there should not remain any excuse for people. He invited people to the right path through a truthful tongue. You should know that God fully knows creation. Not that He was not aware of what they concealed from among their hidden secrets and inner feelings, but in order to try them ... *as to which of them are fairest in actions* ... (Q18:7), so that there is reward in respect of good acts and chastisement in respect of evil acts. Sermon 144

God, there is no god but He. To Him belongs the Fairer Names. **20:8**

We bear witness that *there is no god, but He.* (Q3:2) Sermon 100

Has the conversation of Moses approached ***you****?* **20:9**
When he saw a fire, he said to his people: Abide! Truly, I observed a fire so that perhaps I will bring you some firebrand from it or I find guidance at the fire. **20:10**
When he approached it, it was proclaimed: O Moses! **20:11**
Truly, I—I am ***your*** *Lord! So, take off* ***your*** *shoes; truly,* ***you*** *are one who is in the sanctified valley of Tuwa.* **20:12**
I chose ***you*** *so listen to what is revealed:* **20:13**
Truly, I—I am God. There is no god but Me. So, worship Me and perform the formal prayer of My Remembrance. **20:14**
Truly, the Hour is that which arrives. I am about to conceal it so that every soul is given recompense for what it endeavors. **20:15**
So, let none bar ***you*** *from it—whoever believes not in it and followed his own desires—so that* ***you*** *not survive.* **20:16**
What is that in ***your*** *right hand O Moses?* **20:17**
Moses said: This is my staff. I lean on it, and beat down leaves from a tree with it for my herd of sheep and for me in it are other uses. **20:18**
He said: Cast it, O Moses! **20:19**
So, he cast it. That is when it was a viper sliding. **20:20**
He said: Take it and fear not. We will cause it to return to its first state. **20:21**
Clasp ***your*** *hand to* ***your*** *armpit. It will go forth shimmering white without any evil as another sign* **20:22**
that We cause ***you*** *to see of Our greater signs.* **20:23**
Go ***you*** *to Pharaoh! Truly, he was defiant.* **20:24**
Moses said: My Lord! **20:25**
Expand my breast for me and make ***You*** *my affair easy for me* **20:26**
and untie the knot from my tongue **20:27**
so they understand my saying **20:28**
and assign to me a minister from my people— **20:29**
—Aaron, my brother. **20:30**
Strengthen my vigor with him **20:31**
and ascribe him as a partner in my affair **20:32**
that we glorify ***You*** *much* **20:33**
and we remember ***You*** *frequently.* **20:34**
Truly, ***You, You*** *alone had been seeing of us.* **20:35**
He said: Surely, ***you*** *were given* ***your*** *petition, O Moses!* **20:36**
Certainly, We showed grace on ***you*** *another time* **20:37**

when We revealed to **your** *mother what is revealed*: **20:38**
Cast him adrift in the ark. Then, cast it adrift into the water of the sea. Then, the water of the sea will cast him up on the bank and he will be taken by an enemy of Mine and an enemy of his. I cast on **you** *fondness from Me that* **you** *be trained under My Eye.* **20:39**
Mention when **your** *sister walks saying: Shall I point you to one who will take control of him? So, We returned* **you** *to* **your** *mother that her eyes settle down and she not feel remorse. Y***ou** *have killed a person, but We delivered* **you** *from lament and We tried* **you** *with an ordeal. Then,* **you** *had lingered in expectation years among the people of Midian. Again,* **you** *had drawn near according to a measure, O Moses!* **20:40**
I chose **you** *for service for Myself.* **20:41**
Go **you** *and* **your** *brother with My signs and you both not be inattentive in My Remembrance.* **20:42**
So, go both of you to Pharaoh. Truly, he had become defiant. **20:43**
Both say to him a saying gently, so that perhaps he will recollect or dread. **20:44**
They both said: Our Lord! Truly, we fear that he should exceed against us or that he be defiant. **20:45**
He said: Fear not. Truly, I am with both of you. I hear and I see. **20:46**
So, approach you both to him and say: Truly, we are Messengers of **your** *Lord. So, send the Children of Jacob with us and punish them not. Surely, we drew near* **you** *with a sign from* **your** *Lord. Peace be to him who followed the guidance.* **20:47**
Surely, it was revealed to us that the punishment is on him who denied and turned away. **20:48**
He said: Then, who is the Lord of you two, O Moses? **20:49**
He said: Our Lord is He Who gave everything its creation; again, He guided it. **20:50**
Pharaoh said: Then, what of the first generations? **20:51**
Moses said: The knowledge of them is with my Lord in a Book. My Lord neither goes astray nor forgets. **20:52**
He it is Who assigned for you the earth as a cradle and threaded ways for you in it and caused water to descend from heaven. We brought out from it diverse pairs of plants: **20:53**
Eat and give attention to your flocks. Truly, in this are signs for the people imbued with sense. **20:54**
We created you from it and into it We will cause you to return and from it We will bring you out another time. **20:55**
Certainly We caused Pharaoh to see Our signs—all of them—but he denied and refused. **20:56**
He said: Have **you** *drawn near us to drive us out of our region with* **your** *sorcery, O Moses?* **20:57**
Then, truly, we will bring for **you** *sorcery like it. So, make something that is promised between us and* **you***—neither we nor* **you** *will break it—at a mutually agreeable place.* **20:58**
Moses said: That promised will be for the Day of Adornment and let humanity be assembled in the forenoon. **20:59**
So, Pharaoh turned away. Then, he gathered his cunning. After that he approached. **20:60**
Moses said to them: Woe to you! Devise you not a lie against God so that He put an end to you with a punishment. Surely, he who devised will be frustrated. **20:61**
So, they contended between each other about their affair and they kept secret, conspiring secretly. **20:62**
They said: Truly, these two are the ones who are sorcerers who want to drive you out from your region with their sorcery and take away your most ideal behavior. **20:63**
So, summon up your cunning. Again, approach ranged in rows. Truly, he who prospered this day

is whoever gained the upper hand. **20:64**
They said: O Moses! Either **you** *will cast or let us be the first to cast.* **20:65**
He said: Nay! You cast. That is when their ropes and their staffs seem to him to be, by their sorcery, as though they are sliding. **20:66**
So, Moses sensed awe in himself. **20:67**
We said: Fear not! Truly, **you, you** *are lofty!* **20:68**
Cast what is in **your** *right hand. It will swallow what they crafted. What they crafted is not but the cunning of one who is a sorcerer. The one who is a sorcerer will not prosper in whatever he approached.* **20:69**
Then, the ones who are sorcerers were cast down, ones who prostrate themselves. They said: We believed in the Lord of Aaron and Moses. **20:70**
Pharaoh said: Believed you in Him before I give you permission? Truly, he is your teacher who taught you the sorcery. So, certainly, I will cut off your hands and your feet on opposite sides and, certainly, I will cause you to be crucified on the trunks of date palm trees, and, certainly, you will know which of us is more severe in punishment and one who endures. **20:71**
They said: We will never hold **you** *in greater favor over the clear portents that drew near us nor over Who originated us. So, decide whatever* **you** *will as one who decides.* **You** *will decide not but about this present life.* **20:72**
For us, truly, we believed in our Lord that He forgive us our transgressions and what **you** *had compelled us to do because of the sorcery. God is Best of one who endures.* **20:73**
Truly, whoever approaches his Lord as one who sins, then, truly, for him is hell. Neither will he die in it nor will he live. **20:74**
Whoever approaches Him as one who believes, who, surely, did as the one in accord with morality, then, for those, they are of lofty degrees, **20:75**
Gardens of Eden, beneath which rivers run, ones who will dwell in them forever. That is the recompense of whoever purified himself. **20:76**
Certainly, We revealed to Moses that set **you** *forth with My servants. Then, strike for them a dry road in the sea, neither fearing to be overtaken, nor dreading that.* **20:77**
Then, Pharaoh and his army pursued them. Then, overcame them the water of the sea by what overcame. **20:78**
Pharaoh caused his folk to go astray and he guided them not. **20:79**
O Children of Jacob! Surely, We rescued you from your enemy and We appointed someone with you on the right edge of the mount and We sent down to you the manna and the quails. **20:80**
Eat from what is good that We provided you, and be not defiant in it so that My anger not alight on you. He on whom My anger alights surely, will be hurled to ruin. **20:81**
Truly, I am a Forgiver of whoever repented and believed and did as one in accord with morality. Again, he was truly guided. **20:82**
What caused **you** *to hasten from* **your** *folk, O Moses?* **20:83**
Moses said: They are those who are close on my footsteps and I hastened to **You,** *my Lord that I please* **you.** **20:84**
He said: Then, truly, We tried **your** *folk after* **you** *and the Samaritan caused them to go astray.* **20:85**
Then, Moses returned to his folk enraged, grieved. He said: O my folk! Promise you not with your Lord a fairer promise? Was the compact too long for you to wait? Or wanted you that the anger of your Lord alight on you, so you broke what you were to have promised me? **20:86**
They said: We broke not what was promised to **you** *from what is within our power, but we were*

charged with a heavy load of the adornments of the folk. Surely, we hurled them because the Samaritan cast. **20:87**
Then, he brought out for them a calf, a lifeless body that had the lowing sound of flocks. Then, they said: This is your god and the God of Moses whom he forgot. **20:88**
Then, see they not that it returns not to them a saying and it possesses for them neither hurt nor profit? **20:89**
Certainly, Aaron said to them before: O my folk! You were only tempted by it. Truly, your Lord is The Merciful. So, follow me and obey my command. **20:90**
They said: We will never quit it as ones who give ourselves up until Moses returns to us. **20:91**
He said: O Aaron! What prevented **you** *when* **you** *had seen them going astray* **20:92**
that **you** *have followed me not? Have* **you***, then, rebelled against my command?* **20:93**
Aaron said: O son of my mother! Take me not by my beard nor by my head. Truly, I dreaded that **you** *have said:* **You** *had separated and divided between the Children of Jacob and* **you** *have not regarded my saying.* **20:94**
Moses said: Then, what is **your** *business O Samaritan?* **20:95**
He said: I kept watch over what they keep not watch, so I seized a handful of dust from the foot prints of the Messenger and cast it forth. Thus my soul enticed me. **20:96**
Moses said: Then go off! Truly for **you** *in this life is that* **you** *mayest say: Untouchable; there is for* **you** *something promised that* **you** *shalt never break; and look on* **your** *god that* **you** *have stayed with and given* **your***self up to; certainly we will burn it, Moreover, we will certainly scatter it in the water of the sea in a scattering.* **20:97**
Your God is only God Whom there is no god but He. **20:98**
Thus We relate to **you** *some tiding of what preceded. Surely We gave* **you** *from that which proceeds from Our Presence a Remembrance.* **20:99** ***

Whoever turned aside from it, then truly he will carry a heavy load on the Day of Resurrection, ones who will dwell in it forever. How evil for them on the Day of Resurrection **20:100**
ones who will dwell in it forever; how evil for them on the Day of Resurrection will be the load **20:101**
on the Day the trumpet will be blown. We will assemble the ones who sin, white eyed on that Day. **20:102**
They will whisper among themselves: You lingered in expectation but ten days. **20:103**
We are greater in knowledge of what they will say when the most ideal of them in tradition says: You lingered in expectation not but a day! **20:104** ***

They will ask **you** *about the mountains. Then, say: My Lord will scatter them a scattering.* **20:105**

On that day God will collect on it the front and the back, to stand in obedience for the exaction of accounts and for the award of recompense for deeds. Sweat would flow up to their mouths like reins while the earth would be trembling under them. In the best condition among them would be he who has found a resting place for both his feet and an open place for his breath. Sermon 102

Then, He will forsake it as a leveled spacious plain. **20:106**
Then, **you** *will see not in it any crookedness nor unevenness.* **20:107**

This world and the hereafter have submitted to Him their reins. The skies and earths have flung their keys towards Him. The thriving trees bow to Him in the morning and evening, producing for Him flaming fire from their branches and, at His command, turn their own feed into ripe fruits. Sermon 133

On that Day they will follow one who calls. There will be no crookedness in him. Voices will be hushed for The Merciful so ***you*** *will hear nothing but a murmuring.* **20:108**

They are emulating each other and proceeding in groups towards the final objective and the rendezvous of death, until when matters come to a close, the world dies and the Resurrection draws near. Sermon 82

On a Day intercession will not profit anyone but him to whom gave permission The Merciful and with whose saying He was well-pleased. **20:109**

Know that the Quran is an interceder and its intercession will be accepted. It is a speaker who bears witness. For whoever the Quran intercedes on the Day of Judgment, its intercession for him would be accepted. He about whom the Quran speaks ill on the Day of Judgment shall testify to it. On the Day of Judgment, an announcer will announce: Be aware! Every sower of a crop is in distress except the sowers of the Quran. Therefore, you should be among the sowers of the Quran and its followers. Make it your guide towards God. Seek its advice for yourselves, do not trust your views against it and regard your desires in the matter of the Quran as deceitful. Sermon 176

He knows what is in advance of them and what is behind them and they will not comprehend Him in knowledge. **20:110**

He has surrounded you with His knowledge. He has ordained rewards. He has bestowed upon you vast bounties and extensive gifts. He has warned you through far reaching arguments, and He has counted you by numbers. He has fixed for you ages to live in this place of test and house of instruction. Sermon 82

Faces will be humbled before The Living, The Eternal while, surely, will be frustrated whoever was burdened by doing injustice. **20:111**

On that Day many an argument will prove void and a contention for excuses will stand rejected. Sermon 222

Whoever does as the one in accord with morality and he is one who believes, then, he will neither fear injustice nor unfairness. **20:112**

He has seen his way and is walking on it. He knows his pillar of guidance and has crossed over his deep water. He has caught hold of the most reliable supports and the strongest ropes. He is on that level of conviction which is like the brightness of the sun. He has set himself for God, the Almighty, for performance of the most sublime acts of facing all that befalls him and taking every step needed for it. He is the lamp in darkness. He is the dispeller of all blindness, key to the obscure, remover of complexities and a guide in vast deserts. Sermon 87

Thus, We caused it to descend as an Arabic Recitation. We diversified the threats in it so that perhaps they will be God-conscious or cause the Remembrance to be evoked by them. **20:113**

Go ahead with the remembrance of God, for it is the best remembrance. Long for that which He has promised to the pious, for His promise is the most true promise. Tread the course of *the Prophet* (Q7:158), peace and the mercy of God be upon him, for it is the most distinguished course. Follow his *sunna*, for it is the most right of all behaviors. Sermon 110

Then, exalted be God, The True King, and hasten not the Recitation before its revelation is decreed to ***you****. Say: My Lord! Increase me in knowledge!* **20:114**

Learn the Quran for it is the fairest of discourses and understand it thoroughly for it is the best blossoming of hearts. Seek cure with its light for it is the cure for hearts. Recite it beautifully for it is the most beautiful narration. Certainly, a scholar who acts not according to his knowledge is like the off-headed ignorant who does not find relief from his ignorance, but on the learned the plea of God is greater and grief more incumbent, and he is more blameworthy before God. Sermon 109

Certainly, We made a compact with Adam before. Then, he forgot and We find no constancy in him. **20:115**

When We said to the angels: Prostrate yourselves to Adam! They prostrated themselves, but Iblis who refused. **20:116**

Then God asked the angels to fulfill His promise with them and to accomplish the pledge of His injunction to them by acknowledging Him through prostration to Him and submission to His honored position. So God said: *Prostrate yourselves to Adam! They, then, prostrated themselves but Iblis.* Sermon 1

Then, We said: O Adam! Truly, this is an enemy to ***you*** *and to* ***your*** *spouse, so let him not drive you both out from the Garden so that* ***you*** *would be in despair.* **20:117**

Truly, it is not for ***you*** *that* ***you*** *hunger in it nor to be naked.* **20:118**

Truly, ***you*** *will not thirst in it nor suffer the heat of the sun.* **20:119**

Then, Satan whispered evil to him. He said: O Adam! Will I point ***you*** *to the Tree of Infinity and a dominion that will not decay?* **20:120**

Then, they both ate from that so the intimate parts of both showed to both themselves. Both of them took to doing stitching together over both from the leaves of the Garden. Adam rebelled against his Lord and he erred. **20:121**

Again, his Lord elected him. Then, He turned in forgiveness to him and guided him. **20:122**

He said: Get you both down from here altogether, some of you an enemy to some others. Then, if guidance approaches you from Me, then, whoever followed My Guidance, neither will he go astray, nor will he be in despair. **20:123**

Whoever turned aside from My Remembrance, then, truly, for him is a livelihood of narrowness. We will assemble him on the Day of Resurrection unseeing. **20:124** ***

He would say: My Lord! Why had ***You*** *assembled me with the unseeing when, surely, I had been seeing?* **20:125**

The hidden thing, namely death, which is being driven towards you by two ever new phenomena—the day and the night—is certainly quick to approach. The traveler that is approaching with success or failure deserves the best of provision. So acquire such provision from this world while you are here with which you may shield yourself tomorrow on the Day of Judgment. Sermon 64

He would say: It is thus: Our signs approached ***you****, but* ***you*** *had forgotten them and, thus, this*

Day ***you*** *will be forgotten.* **20:126**

O God's human being! I advise you to keep away from this world which is shortly to leave you, even though you do not like its departure, and which would make your bodies old, even though you would like to keep them young. Your example and its example is like the travelers who travel some distance and then traverse it quickly, or they aimed at a sign and reached it at once. How short is the distance to the aim if one heads towards it and reaches it. How short is the stage of one who has only a day which he cannot exceed while a swift driver is driving him in this world until he departs from it. Sermon 99

Thus, We give recompense to him who exceeded all bounds and believes not in signs of his Lord. Surely, punishment in the world to come is more severe and one that endures. **20:127**

There remain a few people in whose case the remembrance of their return to God on the Day of Judgment keeps their eyes bent and the awareness of the Resurrection moves them to tears. Some of them are scared away from the world and disperse. Some are frightened and subdued. Some are quiet as if muzzled. Some are praying sincerely. Some are grief-stricken and pain-ridden whom fear has confined to namelessness. Disgrace has shrouded them, so they are in the sea of bitter water, their mouths are closed and their hearts are bruised. They preached until they were tired. They were oppressed until they were disgraced. They were killed until their numbers dwindled. Sermon 32

Guide He not them? How many generations We caused to perish before them amidst whose dwellings they walk. Truly, in this are signs for the people imbued with sense. **20:128**

Certainly, there are examples before you of God's wrath, punishment, days of tribulations and happenings. Therefore, do not disregard His promises. Do not ignore His punishment or make light His wrath and not expect His violence, because God, the Almighty, did not curse the past ages unless they had left off asking others to do good acts and refraining them from bad acts. In fact, God cursed the foolish for committing sins and the wise because they gave up refraining others from evil. Be aware! You have broken the bonds of Islam, transgressed its limits, and destroyed its commands. Sermon 192

If a Word preceded not from ***your*** *Lord for a term that was determined, it would be close at hand.* **20:129**

So, have ***you*** *patience with what they say and glorify the praises of* ***your*** *Lord before the coming up of the sun and before sunset and during the nighttime night watch and glorify at the end of the daytime, so that perhaps* ***you*** *will be well-pleased.* **20:130**

Praise belongs to God (Q1:2) Who is hidden in all things and towards Whom all open things guide. He cannot be seen by the eye of an onlooker, but the eye which does not see Him cannot deny Him while the mind that proves His existence cannot perceive Him. He is so high in sublimity that nothing can be more sublime than He. While in nearness, He is so near that no one can be nearer than He, but his sublimity does not put Him at a distance from anything of His creation, nor does His nearness bring them on equal level to Him. He has not informed human wit about the limits of His qualities. Nevertheless, He has not prevented it from securing essential knowledge of Him. So he is such that all signs of existence stand witness for Him until the denying mind also believes in Him. God is sublime beyond what is described by those who liken Him to things or those who deny Him. Sermon 49

Stretch not out ***your*** *eyes for what We gave of enjoyment in this life to spouses among them as the luster of this present life so that We try them by it. Provision of* ***your*** *Lord is Best and that which endures.* **20:131**

He who surveys this world from above its surface and takes a lesson from its changes and happenings and, through its variation and alterations, gains knowledge about God's Might, Wisdom and Sagacity, Mercy, Clemency and Sustaining power, his eyes will gain real brightness and sight. On the other hand, the person who is lost only in the colorfulness of the world and its decorations loses himself in the darkness of the world. That is why God has forbidden to view the world thusly: *Stretch not out* ***your*** *eyes for what We gave of enjoyment in this life to spouses among them as the luster of this present life so that We try them by it. Provision of* ***your*** *Lord is Best and that which endures.* (Q20:131) Sermon 81

Command ***your*** *people to the formal prayer, and to maintain patience in it. We ask not of* ***you*** *for any provision. We provide for* ***you*** *and the Ultimate End will be for the God-conscious.* **20:132**

Even after receiving assurance of Paradise, *the Messenger of God* (Q48:29), peace and the mercy of God be upon him, used to exert himself for formal prayers because of God, the Almighty's command: *Command* ***your*** *people to the formal prayer, and to maintain patience in it. We ask not of* ***you*** *for any provision. We provide for* ***you*** *and the Ultimate End will be for the God-conscious.* (Q20:132) Sermon 198

They said: Why brings he not to us a sign from his Lord? Approaches them not clear portents that were in the first scrolls? **20:133**

You should be God-conscious! God, in feeling proud of your vanity and boasting over ignorance, because this is the root of enmity and the design of Satan wherewith he has been deceiving past people and bygone ages with the result that they fell into the depression of ignorance and the hollows of misguidance, submitting to (Satan's) driving and accepting his leadership. The hearts of all the people were similar in this matter. Centuries passed by, one after the other, in just the same way. Sermon 192

If We caused them to perish with a punishment before this, certainly, they would have said: Our Lord! Why had ***You*** *not sent to us a Messenger so that we follow* ***Your*** *signs before we are degraded and humiliated!* **20:134**

Do you not see how God humiliated him through his pride? Sermon 191

Say: Each is one who is waiting so watch. Then, you will know who are the Companions of the Path without fault and who were truly guided. **20:135**

Truly, of humanity closest to Abraham are those who followed him and this Prophet and those who believed. God is Protector of the ones who believe. (Q3:68) Letter 28

Chapter 21: The Prophets (al-Anbiyāᵓ)

The reckoning for humanity was near while they are ones who turn aside in heedlessness. **21:1**

Now neither the good acts can be added to, nor can evil acts be atoned for by repentance. Are you not sons, fathers, brothers and relations of these dead? Are you not to follow their footsteps and pass by their paths? Yet, hearts are still unmoved, heedless of guidance and moving on wrong lines, as though the addressee is someone else and as though the correct way is to amass worldly gains. Sermon 82

Approaches them not a remembrance from their Lord, that which is renewed, but they listened to it while they play **21:2**
being ones whose hearts are ones that are diverted, and they kept secret, conspiring secretly those who did wrong? Is this other than a mortal like you? Then, will you approach sorcery while you perceive? **21:3**

O my God! Whoever listens to our words which are just and which seek the prosperity of religion and the worldly life and do not seek mischief, they reject after listening. He certainly turns away from **Your** support and desists from strengthening **Your** religion. We make **You** a Witness over him. **You** are the greatest of all witnesses. We make all those who inhabit **Your** earth and **Your** skies witness over him. Thereafter, **You** alone can make us needless of his support and question him for his sin. Sermon 212

He said: My Lord knows The Word of the heavens and the earth. He is The Hearing, The Knowing. **21:4**

Had they pondered over the greatness of His power and the vastness of His bounty they would have returned to the right path and feared the punishment of the Fire; but hearts are sick and eyes are impure. Do they not see the small things He has created, how He strengthened their system and opened for them hearing and sight and made for them bones and skins? Look at the ant with its small body and delicate form. It can hardly be seen in the corner of the eye, nor by the perception of the imagination, how it moves on the earth and leaps at its livelihood. It carries the grain to its hole and deposits it in its place of stay. It collects during the summer for its winter, and during strength for the period of its weakness. Its livelihood is guaranteed, and it is fed according to fitness. God, the Kind, does not forget it and God, the Giver, does not deprive it, even though it may be in dry stone or fixed rocks. Sermon 184

Nay! They said: Jumbled nightmares! Nay! He but devised it! Nay! He is but a poet! Let him bring us a sign as the ancient ones were sent! **21:5**

I bear witness that *Muhammad* (Q48:29), peace and the mercy of God be upon him, is *His servant* (Q17:1) and His *Prophet* (Q7:158) and His responsible trustee, peace and the mercy of God be upon him. God sent him with undeniable proofs, a clear success and open paths. So he conveyed the message declaring the truth with it. He led the people on the correct highway, established signs of guidance and minarets of light and made Islam's ropes strong and its knots firm. Sermon 184

No town believed before them of whom We caused to perish. Will they, then, believe? **21:6**

Certainly, there are examples before you of God's wrath, punishment, days of tribulations and happenings. Therefore, do not disregard His promises. Do not ignore His punishment or make light His wrath and not expect His violence, because God, the Almighty, did not curse the past ages unless they had left off asking others to do good acts and refraining them from bad acts. In fact, God cursed the foolish for committing sins and the wise because they gave up refraining others from evil. Be aware! You have broken the bonds of Islam, transgressed its limits, and destroyed its commands. Sermon 192

We sent not before **you** *but men to whom We reveal. So, ask the People of the Remembrance if you had not been knowing.* **21:7**
We made them not lifeless bodies that eat not food nor had they been ones who will dwell forever. **21:8**

Seek cure from the Quran for your ailments and seek its assistance in your distress. It contains a cure for the worst diseases, namely unbelief, hypocrisy, revolt and misguidance. Pray to God through it and turn to God with its love. Do not ask the people through it. There is nothing like it through which the people should turn to God, the Sublime. Sermon 176

Again, We were sincere in the promise. So, We rescued them and whom We will. We caused the ones who are excessive to perish. **21:9**

They took to the right and the left piercing through to the ways of evil and leaving the paths of guidance. Do not make haste for a matter which is to happen and is awaited. Do not wish for delay in what the morrow is to bring for you. For how many people make haste for a matter, but when they get it they begin to wish they had not gotten it? How near is today to the dawning of tomorrow? O my people, this is the time for the occurrence of every promised event and the approach of things which you do not know. Sermon 150

Surely, We caused a Book to descend to you in which is your Remembrance. Will you not, then, be reasonable? **21:10**

The Book of God is among you. It speaks. Its tongue does not falter. It is a house whose pillars do not fall down. It is a power whose supporters are never defeated. Sermon 132

How many a town We damaged that had been one that is unjust and caused to grow after them another folk? **21:11**

You should take a lesson from the fate of the progeny of Ishmael, the children of Isaac and the children of Jacob. How similar are their affairs and how akin are their examples. In connection with the details of their division and disunity, think of the days when Kings of Persia and the Caesars of Rome had become their masters. They turned them out from the pastures of their lands, the rivers of Iraq and the fertility of the world, towards thorny forests, the passages of hot winds and hardships in livelihood. By doing this, they turned them into just herders of camels. Their houses were the worst in the world and their places of stay were the most drought-stricken. There was not one voice towards which they could turn for protection, nor any shade of affection on whose strength they could repose trust. Sermon 192

Then, when they were conscious of Our might, that is when they make haste from it! **21:12**

He is the Giver of all reward and distinction and Dispeller of all calamities and hardships. Sermon 82

Make not haste, but return to what you were given of ease in it and to your dwellings, so that perhaps you will be asked. **21:13**

I praise Him for His continuous mercy and His copious bounties. Sermon 82

They said: O woe to us! Truly, we had been ones who are unjust! **21:14**

Praise belongs to God (Q1:2) Who is High above all else and is Near the creation through His bounty. Sermon 82

Then, truly, they ceased not calling that out until We made them as stubble, ones silent and stilled. **21:15**

You should be God-conscious! God, in feeling proud of your vanity and boasting over ignorance, because this is the root of enmity and the design of Satan wherewith he has been deceiving past people and bygone ages with the result that they fell into the depression of ignorance and the hollows of misguidance, submitting to (Satan's) driving and accepting his leadership. The hearts of all the people were similar in this matter. Centuries passed by, one after the other, in just the same way. Sermon 192

We created not the heavens and the earth and what is between them as ones in play. **21:16**
If We wanted We would have taken some diversion. We would take it to Ourselves from that which proceeds from Our Presence if We had been ones who do so. **21:17**

He is the Giver of all reward and distinction and Dispeller of all calamities and hardships. Sermon 82

Nay! We hurl The Truth against falsehood so it prevails over it. That is when falsehood is that which vanishes away. Woe to you for what you allege. **21:18**

I bear witness that *there is no god but God,* (Q47:19), by virtue of belief, certainty, sincerity and conviction. I also bear witness that *Muhammad* (Q48:29), peace and the mercy of God be upon him, is *His servant* (Q17:1) and His *Prophet* (Q7:158), whom He deputed when the signs of guidance were obliterated and the ways of religion were desolate. So he threw open the truth, gave advice to the people, guided them towards righteousness and ordered them to be moderate. May God bless him ... Sermon 194

To Him belongs whoever is in the heavens and the earth. Whoever is near Him, they grow not arrogant to worship Him, nor they be weary. **21:19**

Praise belongs to God (Q1:2) Who is above all similarity to creatures, is above the words of describers Who displays the wonders of His management for the on-lookers, is hidden from the imagination of thinkers by virtue of the greatness of His glory, has knowledge without acquiring it by adding to it or drawing it from someone, and Who is the ordainer of all matters without reflecting or thinking. He is such that gloom does not concern Him, nor does He seek light from brightness. Night does not overtake Him, nor does the day pass over Him so as to affect Him in any manner. His comprehension of things is not through eyes. His knowledge is not dependent on being informed. God deputized *the Prophet* (Q7:158), peace and the mercy of God be upon him, with light and accorded him the highest precedence in selection. Through him God united those who were divided, overpowered the powerful, overcame difficulties and leveled rugged ground and thus removed misguidance from right and left. Sermon 213

They glorify Him nighttime and daytime. They never decrease. **21:20**

O my God! **You** know that what we did was not to seek power, nor to acquire anything from the vanities of the world. We rather wanted to restore the signs of **Your** religion and to usher prosperity into **Your** cities so that the oppressed among **Your** creatures might be safe and **Your** forsaken commands might be established. O my God! I am the first who leaned towards **You** and who heard and responded to the call of Islam. No one preceded me in formal prayer except *the Prophet* (Q7:158), peace and the mercy of God be upon him. Sermon 131

Or took they gods to themselves from the earth, they, ones who revive the dead? **21:21**
If there had been gods in it—other than God— certainly, both would have gone to ruin. Then, glory be to God! Lord of the Throne! High above what they allege. **21:22**
He will not be asked as to what He accomplishes, but they will be asked. **21:23**

Your ultimate goal of reward or punishment is before you. Behind your back is the hour of Resurrection which is driving you on. Keep yourself light and overtake the forward ones. The first ones who have preceded await your last ones. Sermon 21

Or took they gods to themselves other than He? Say: Prepare your proof. This is a Remembrance for him who is with me and a Remembrance of him before me. Nay! Most of them know not The Truth, so they are ones who turn aside. **21:24**
We sent not before **you** *any Messenger, but We reveal to him that there is no god but I, so worship Me.* **21:25**
They said: The Merciful took to Himself a son. Glory be to Him! Nay! They were honored servants! **21:26**
They precede Him not in saying and they act by His command. **21:27**

He created them in different shapes and with diverse characteristics. They have wings. They glorify the sublimity of His Honor. They do not appropriate to themselves His skill that shows itself in creation. Nor do they claim they create anything in which He is unparalleled. *Nay! They were honored servants!* (Q21:26-27) Sermon 91

He knows what is in advance of them and what is behind them and they intercede not but for him with whom He was content. They are dreading Him, ones who are apprehensive. **21:28**
Whoever says of them: Truly, I am a god other than He, then, We will give recompense to him with hell. Thus, We give recompense to the ones who are unjust. **21:29**

The trouble-mongers are a people whose attacks are severe. Those who would fight them for the sake of God would be a people who are low in the estimation of the proud, unknown in the earth, but well known in the heavens. Sermon 102

Consider not those who were ungrateful that the heavens and the earth had been interwoven and We unstitched them? We made every living thing of water. Will they, then, not believe? **21:30**

When the excitement of water subsided under the earth's sides and under the weight of the high and lofty mountains placed on its shoulders, God flowed springs of water from its high tops and distributed them through plains and low places and moderated their movement by fixed rocks and high mountain tops. Then its trembling came to a standstill because of the penetration of mountains in various parts of its surface and their being fixed in its deep areas, and their standing on its plains. Sermon 91

We made firm mountains on the earth so that it should not vibrate with them. We made in it ravines as ways, so that perhaps they will be truly guided. **21:31**

He also created high hills, rocks of stones and lofty mountains. He put them in their positions and made them remain stationary. Their peaks rose into the air while their roots remained in the water. In this way He raised the mountains above the plains and fixed their foundations in the vast expanse wherever they stood. He made their peaks high and made their bodies lofty. He made them like pillars for the earth and fixed them in it like pegs. Consequently, the earth became stationary; otherwise it might bend with its inhabitants or sink inwards with its burden, or shift from its positions. Sermon 210

We made heaven as a guarded roof. Yet they are ones who turn aside from its signs. **21:32**

This world and the hereafter have submitted to Him their reins. The skies and earths have flung their keys towards Him. The thriving trees bow to Him in the morning and evening, producing for Him flaming fire from their branches and, at His command, turn their own feed into ripe fruits. Sermon 133

It is He Who created the nighttime and the daytime, the sun and the moon, each swimming in orbit. **21:33**

He hung in its vastness its sky and put therein its decoration consisting of small bright pearls and lamp-like stars. He shot at the over-hearers arrows of bright meteors. He put them in motion on their appointed routine and made them into fixed stars, moving stars, descending stars, ascending stars, ominous stars and lucky stars. Sermon 91

We assigned not to any mortal before ***you*** *immortality. If* ***you*** *were to die will they be ones who dwell forever?* **21:34**

He is the Giver of all reward and distinction and Dispeller of all calamities and hardships. Sermon 82

Every soul is one that experiences death. We will try you with the worst and good as a test. To Us you will be returned. **21:35**

Real death is in the life of subjugation while real life is in dying as subjugators. Sermon 51

When those who were ungrateful saw ***you****, they take* ***you*** *to themselves not but in mockery: Ha! Is this he who mentions your gods? They, for Remembrance of The Merciful, they are ones who are ungrateful.* **21:36**

They were in a land where the lips of the learned were bridled while the words of the ignorant were honored. Sermon 2

The human being was created of haste. I will cause you to see My signs, so seek not to hasten! **21:37**

O God's human being! Certainly, being God-conscious has saved the lovers of God from unlawful items and has given His dread to their hearts until their nights are passed in wakefulness and their noons in thirst. So they achieve comfort through trouble and copious watering through thirst. They regarded death to be near and therefore hastened towards good actions. They rejected their desires and so they kept death in their sight. Sermon 114

They say: When will this promise be if you had been ones who are sincere? **21:38**

O God's human being! The good that God has promised should not be abandoned and the evil from which He has refrained should not be coveted. O God's human being!

Fear the day when actions will be reckoned. There will be much quaking and even children will get old. Sermon 157

If those who were ungrateful but know at the time when they will not limit the fire from their faces, nor from their backs and they will not be helped! **21:39**

Satan's banners flew in the wind through them. His standard of vice was raised. They trampled people under their hoofs and tread upon them with their feet. Vice attained full stature. Sermon 2

Nay! It will approach them suddenly. Then, it will dumfound them so they will not be able to come back nor will they be given respite. **21:40**

I also advise you to remember death and to lessen your heedlessness towards it. Why should you be heedless of Him Who is not heedless of you? Why expect from the angel of death who will not give you time? Sermon 188

Certainly, Messengers were ridiculed before ***you****. Then, those who derided them were surrounded by what they had been ridiculing.* **21:41**

Say: Who will guard you in the nighttime and the daytime from The Merciful? Nay! They, from the Remembrance of their Lord, are ones who turn aside. **21:42**

The best means by which seekers of nearness to God, the Almighty, the Exalted, seek nearness is the belief in Him and His Prophet. Sermon 109

Or secure them their gods from Us? They are not able to help themselves, nor will they be rendered safe from Us. **21:43**

I bear witness that *there is no god but God.* (Q47:19) He is One. There is no partner with Him. He is the First, such that nothing was before Him. He is the Last, such that there is not limit for Him. Imagination cannot catch any of His qualities. Hearts cannot entertain belief about His nature. Analysis and division cannot be applied to Him. Eyes and hearts cannot compare Him. Sermon 84

Nay! We gave enjoyment to these, their fathers until their lifetime was long for them. Consider they not that We approach the earth? We reduce it of its outlying parts. Or will they be the ones who are the victors? **21:44**

He is the Giver of all reward and distinction and Dispeller of all calamities and hardships. I praise Him for His continuous mercy and His copious bounties. Sermon 82

Say: I warn you only by the revelation. But hear not the unwilling to hear, the calling to them when they are warned? **21:45**

If a breath afflicted them of punishment of ***your*** *Lord, they would, surely, say: O woe to us! Truly, we had been ones who are unjust.* **21:46**

You will see the hopes of the pious simple, his shortcomings few, his heart God-conscious, his spirit contented, his meal small and simple, his religion safe, his desires dead and his anger suppressed. Good alone is expected from him. Evil from him is not to be feared. Even if he is found among those who forget God he is counted among those who remember Him, but if he is among the rememberers, he is not counted among the forgetful. He forgives him who is unjust to him, and he gives to him who deprives him. He behaves well with him who behaves ill with him. Sermon 192

We will lay down the balances of equity on the Day of Resurrection. Then, no soul will be wronged at all. Even if it had been the weight of a grain of a mustard seed We will bring it. We sufficed as Ones Who Reckon. **21:47**

On that day many an argument will prove void and a contention for excuses will stand rejected. Sermon 222

Certainly, We gave Moses and Aaron the Criterion between right and wrong and an illumination and a Remembrance for the ones who are God-conscious, **21:48**
those who dread their Lord in the unseen while they are ones who are apprehensive of the Hour. **21:49**

... hidden things have appeared for those who perceive. The face of right has become clear for the wanderer. The approaching moment has raised the veil from its face and signs have appeared for those who search for them. Sermon 108

This is a blessed Remembrance We caused to descend. Are you, then, ones who know not of it? **21:50**

The Book of God is that through which you see, you speak and you hear. Its one part speaks for the other part, and one part bears witness to the other. It does not create differences about God, nor does it mislead its own follower from the path of God. You are joined together in hatred of each other and in the growing of herbage on your covering inner impurity by good appearance outside. You are sincere with one another in your love of desires and bear enmity against each other in earning wealth. The evil spirit (Satan) has perplexed you and deceit has misled you. I seek the help of God for myself and you. Sermon 133

Certainly, We gave Abraham his right judgment before. We had been ones who know of him **21:51**
when he said to his father and his folk: What are these images to which you be ones who give yourselves up to? **21:52**
They said: We found our fathers as ones who are worshippers of them. **21:53**
He said: Certainly, you and your fathers had been in a clear wandering astray. **21:54**
They said: Have **you** *drawn near The Truth or are* **you** *of the ones who play?* **21:55**
He said: Nay! Your Lord is the Lord of the heavens and the earth, Who originated them. I am of the ones who bear witness to this: **21:56**
By God, I will contrive against your idols after you turn as ones who draw back. **21:57**
So, he made them broken pieces—but the greatest of them—so that perhaps they will return to it. **21:58**
They said: Who accomplished this with our gods? Truly, he is of the ones who are unjust! **21:59**
They said: We heard a spiritual warrior (m) mention them. It is said he is Abraham. **21:60**
They said: Then, approach with him before the eyes of personages so that perhaps they will bear witness. **21:61**
They said: Have **you** *accomplished this with our gods O Abraham?* **21:62**
He said: Nay! It was accomplished by the greatest of them—this. So, ask them if they had been able to speak for themselves. **21:63**
Then, they returned to one another. Then, they said: Truly, you, you are the ones who are unjust. **21:64**

Again, they were put into confusion: Certainly, **you** *had known that these speak not for themselves!* **21:65**
He said: Worship you, then, other than God what neither profits you nor hurts you at all? **21:66**
Fie on you on what you worship other than God. Will you not, then, be reasonable? **21:67**
They said: Burn him and help your gods if you had been ones who do so! **21:68**
We said: O fire! Be coolness and peace for Abraham! **21:69**
They wanted to use cunning against him, but We made them the ones who are losers. **21:70**
We delivered him and Lot to the region which We blessed for the worlds. **21:71**
We bestowed Isaac on him and Jacob as an unexpected gift. We made both of them ones in accord with morality. **21:72**
We made them leaders, guiding by Our command. We revealed to them the accomplishing of good deeds and the performing of the formal prayer and the giving of the purifying alms. They had been ones who worship Us. **21:73**
To Lot We gave him critical judgment and knowledge and We delivered him from the town which had been doing deeds of corruption. Truly, they had been a reprehensible folk, ones who disobey. **21:74**
We caused him to enter into Our Mercy. Truly, he was among the ones in accord with morality. **21:75**
Mention Noah, when he cried out before and We responded to him. We delivered him and his people from the tremendous distress. **21:76**
We helped him against the folk who denied Our signs. Truly, they had been a reprehensible folk. So, We drowned them one and all. **21:77**
Mention David and Solomon, when they give judgment about cultivation when a herd of the sheep of his folk strayed. To their critical judgment We had been ones who bear witness. **21:78**
So, We caused Solomon to understand it. We gave each of them critical judgment and knowledge. We caused to become subservient to David, the mountains and the birds to glorify God. We had been ones who do such things. **21:79**
We taught him the art of making garments of chain mail for you to fortify you from your violence. Will you, then, be ones who are thankful? **21:80**
To Solomon, the wind tempest runs by His command toward the earth which We blessed. We had been ones who know everything. **21:81**
Among the satans are some who dive for him and do actions other than that. We had been ones who guard over them. **21:82**
Job, when he cried out to his Lord: Truly, harm afflicted me and **You** *are One Who is Most Merciful of the ones who are merciful.* **21:83**
So, We responded to him. Then, We removed his harm. We gave him back his people and the like of others with them as a mercy from Us and as a reminder of ones who worship. **21:84**
Ishmael and Enoch and Dhul-Kifl, all were of the ones who remain steadfast. **21:85**
We caused them to enter into Our mercy. They are the ones in accord with morality. **21:86**
Jonah, when he went as one who is enraged, and thought that We would never have power over him. Then, he cried out through the shadows that: There is no god, but **You**! *Glory be to* **You**! *Truly, I had been of the ones who are unjust.* **21:87**
So, We responded to him. We delivered him from the lament. Thus, We rescue the ones who believe. **21:88**
Mention Zechariah when he cried out to his Lord: My Lord! Forsake me not unassisted and **You** *are Best of the ones who inherit.* **21:89**
So, We responded to him and We bestowed Yahya on him. We made things right for his spouse and

for him. Truly, they had been competing with one another in good deeds and they would call to Us with yearning and reverence. They had been ones who are humbled before Us. **21:90**
She who guarded her private parts, then, We blew into her Our Spirit and We made her and her son a sign for the worlds. **21:91**
Truly, this, your community, is one community and I am your Lord so worship Me. **21:92**
But they cut asunder their affair between them. Yet all of them are ones who return to Us. **21:93**
***

So, whoever does as the ones in accord with morality and he is one who believes, then, his endeavoring will not be rejected. Truly, We will be One Who Inscribes it for him. **21:94**

Among the proofs of His creation is the creation of the skies which are fastened without pillars and stand without support. He called them. They responded obediently and humbly without being lazy or loathsome. If they had not acknowledged His Godhead and obeyed Him, He would not have made them the place for His throne, the abode of His angels and the destination: *To Him Words of what is good rise and He exalts an action in accord with morality ...* (Q35:10) of the creatures. Sermon 182

There is a ban on the town that We caused to perish. They will not return **21:95**
until Gog and Magog are let loose and they slide down from every slope. **21:96**

Certainly, there are examples before you of God's wrath, punishment, days of tribulations and happenings. Therefore, do not disregard His promises. Do not ignore His punishment or make light His wrath and not expect His violence, because God, the Almighty, did not curse the past ages unless they had left off asking others to do good acts and refraining them from bad acts. In fact, God cursed the foolish for committing sins and the wise because they gave up refraining others from evil. Be aware! You have broken the bonds of Islam, transgressed its limits, and destroyed its commands. Sermon 192

The true promise will be near. That is when the sight will be that which fixed in horror of those who were ungrateful! O woe to us. Surely, we had been in heedlessness of this. Nay! We had been ones who were unjust. **21:97**
Truly, you and what you worship other than God are fuel material for hell. You are the ones who go down to it. **21:98**
If these had been gods, they would never have gone down to it. All are ones who will dwell in it forever. **21:99**

The two objectives, namely Paradise and Hell, have been stretched for them up to a point beyond the reach of fear or hope. Had they been able to speak they would have become dumb to describe what they witnessed or saw. Sermon 220

There will be sobbing in it for them and they, their gods, will not hear in it. **21:100**

I bear witness that *there is no god but God* (Q47:19), the One, there is no partner with Him, nor is there with Him any god other than Himself and that *Muhammad* (Q48:29) peace and the mercy of God be upon him, is *His servant,* (Q17:1), and His *Prophet.* (Q7:158) Sermon 35

Truly, those to whom there has preceded the fairer from Us, those are ones who are far removed from it. **21:101**

Truly, the source of misguidance lies in the occurrence of evils when one's desires are acted upon and the commands that are innovated. They are against the Book of God. People co-operate with each other about them even though it is against the Way of God. If wrong had been pure and unmixed it would not be hidden from those who are in search of it. If right had been pure without admixture of wrong, those who bear hatred towards it would have been silenced. What is, however, done is that something is taken from here and something from there and the two are mixed! At this stage Satan overpowers his friends and they alone escape: *Truly, those to whom there has preceded the fairer from Us, those are ones who are far removed from it.* (Q21:101) Sermon 50

They will not hear even the low sound of it. They, in that for which their souls lusted, will be ones who will dwell in it forever. **21:102**

The world aimed at them, but they did not aim at it. It captured them, but they freed themselves from it by a ransom. During the night, they are standing on their feet, reading portions of the Quran and reciting it in a well-measured way, creating through it grief and seeking by it the cure for their ailments. If they come across a verse creating eagerness for Paradise, they pursue it avidly. Their spirits turn towards it eagerly. They feel as if it is in front of them. When they come across a verse which contains fear of Hell, they bend the ears of their hearts towards it and feel as though the sound of Hell and its cries are reaching their ears. They bend themselves from their backs, prostrate themselves on their foreheads, their palms, their knees and their toes, and beseech God, the Sublime, for their deliverance. Sermon 193

The greater terror will not dishearten them and the angels will admit them: This is your day that you had been promised! **21:103**

Action! Action! Then look at the end, the end, and remain steadfast, steadfast. Thereafter exercise endurance, endurance, and God-consciousness, God-consciousness. You have an objective. Proceed towards your objective. You have a sign. Take guidance from your sign. Islam has an objective. Proceed towards its objective. Proceed towards God by fulfilling His rights which He has enjoined upon you. He has clearly stated His demands for you. I am a witness for you and shall plead excuses on your behalf on the Day of Judgment. Sermon 176

On a Day when We roll up the heavens like the rolling up of the written scroll of manuscripts, as We began the first creation, We will cause it to return. It is a promise from Us. Truly, We had been ones who do. **21:104**

They departed from it with their acts towards the continuing life and everlasting house as God has said: *On a Day when We roll up the heavens like the rolling up of the written scroll of manuscripts, as We began the first creation, We will cause it to return. It is a promise from Us. Truly, We had been ones who do.* (Q21:104) Sermon 110

Certainly, We wrote down in the Psalms after the Remembrance that the earth will be inherited by My servants—the ones who are in accord with morality. **21:105**

The Book of God is among you. It speaks and its tongue does not falter. It is a house whose pillars do not fall down, and a power whose supporters are never routed. Sermon 133

Truly, in this is the delivering of this message for the folk, ones who worship. **21:106**

We sent ***you*** *not but as a mercy for the worlds.* **21:107**

God ... sent *the Prophet* (Q7:158), peace and the mercy of God be upon him, with faith and truth. Sermon 16

Say: It is only revealed to me that your god is One God. Will you, then, be ones who submit to God? **21:108**

I bear witness that *there is no god but God* (Q47:19), the One. He has no like. Sermon 2

But if they turned away, then, say: I proclaimed to you all equally. I am not informed whether what you are promised is near or far. **21:109**

God deputized *the Prophet* (Q7:158), peace and the mercy of God be upon him, after a gap from the previous Prophets when there was much talk among the people. With him God exhausted the series of Prophets and ended the revelation. He then fought for Him those who were turning away from Him and were equating others with Him. Sermon 133

Truly, He knows the openly published saying and He knows what you keep back. **21:110**

O God's human being! Know that your own self is a guard over you. Limbs are as watchmen and truthful vigil-keepers who preserve the record of your actions and the number of your breaths. The gloom of the dark night cannot conceal you from them, nor can closed doors hide you from them. Surely, tomorrow is close to today. Sermon 157

I am not informed so that perhaps it will be a test for you and an enjoyment for a while. **21:111**

O God's human being! I advise you to be God-conscious. It is He Who has furnished illustrations and Who has timed for you your lives. He has given you covering of dress. He has scattered a livelihood for you. He has surrounded you with His knowledge. He has ordained rewards. He has bestowed upon you vast bounties and extensive gifts. He has warned you through far reaching arguments. He has counted you by numbers. He has fixed for you an age to live in this place of testing and house of instruction. You are on a test in this world and have to render an account regarding it. Sermon 82

He said: My Lord! Give ***You*** *judgment between us with The Truth. Our Lord is The Merciful, He Whose help is being sought against what you allege.* **21:112**

God sent the Prophet, peace and the mercy of God be upon him, as a caller towards Truth and a witness over the creatures. *The Prophet* (Q7:158) conveyed the messages of God tirelessly and without any negligence. He fought His enemies in the cause of God unflaggingly and without pleading excuses. He is the foremost of all who practice God-consciousness and the power of perception of all those who achieve guidance. Sermon 116

Chapter 22: The Pilgrimage (al-Ḥajj)

O humanity! Be God-conscious of your Lord. Truly, the earthquake of the Hour is a tremendous thing. On a Day you will see it, **22:1**

When the earthquake occurs, the Day of Resurrection approaches with all its severities. Sermon 222

Every one who is breast feeding will be negligent of whoever she breast fed. Every pregnant woman will bring forth a fetus and **you** *will see humanity intoxicated yet they will not be intoxicated. But the punishment of God will be severe.* **22:2**

O people who are negligent of God, but not neglected by God, and those who miss doing good acts, but are to be caught. How is it that I see you becoming removed from God and becoming interested in others? You are like the camel whom the grazer drives to a disease-stricken pasture and a disastrous watering place. They are like beasts who are fed in order to be slaughtered, but they do not know what is intended for them. When they are treated well they think that day to be their whole life, and eating their full to be their aim. Sermon 175

Among humanity is he who disputes about God without knowledge and follows every rebel satan. **22:3**

Everyone should be God-conscious, should admonish himself, should send forward his repentance and should overpower his desire because his death is hidden from him. His desires deceive him. Satan keeps posted about him. He beautifies his sin for him so that he may commit it. He prompts him to delay repentance until his desires cause him to be the most negligent. Pity is for the negligent person whose life itself would be a proof against him and his own days, passed in sin, will lead him to punishment. Sermon 64

It was written down about him that whoever turned away to him as a friend, truly, he will cause him to go astray and will guide him to the punishment of the blaze. **22:4**

Everyone of them is ... alone although they are a group, and they are strangers, even though friends. They are unaware of morning after a night and of evening after a day. The night or the day when they departed has become ever existent for them. They found the dangers of their place of stay more serious than they had apprehended, and they witnessed that its signs were greater than they had guessed. The two objectives, namely Paradise and Hell, have been stretched for them up to a point beyond the reach of fear or hope. Had they been able to speak they would have become dumb to describe what they witnessed or saw. Sermon 220

O humanity! If you had been in doubt about the Upraising, truly, We created you from earth dust and, again, from seminal fluid and, again, from a clot and, again, from tissue that was formed and that was not formed so that we make it manifest to you. We establish in the wombs whom We will for a term, that which is determined. Again, We bring you out as infant children and, again, you may reach the coming of age. Among you there is he whom death will call to itself. Among you there is he who is returned to the most wretched lifetime so that he knows not anything after some knowledge. **You** *have seen the earth as that which is lifeless. Yet when We caused water to descend on it, it quivered and it swelled and put forth every lovely pair.* **22:5**

That is because God, He is The Truth, and it is He Who gives life to the dead and He is Powerful over everything. **22:6**

Truly, the Hour is that which arrives. There is no doubt about it and that God will raise up whoever is in the graves. **22:7**

People have been created as a proof of His power, have been brought up with authority. They are made to die through pangs and placed in graves where they turn into crumbs. Then they will be resurrected one by one, awarded their recompense and each one separately will have to account for his actions. Sermon 82

Among humanity is such a one who disputes about God without knowledge nor guidance nor an illuminating Book, **22:8**
turning to his side as one who turns away to cause to go astray from the way of God. For him in the present is degradation. We will cause him to experience—on the Day of Resurrection— the punishment of the burning. **22:9**

Be aware and act during the period of attraction just as you act during a period of dread. Be aware! Truly, I have not seen one who covets Paradise to be asleep, nor a dreader from hellfire to be asleep. Be aware, he whom right does not benefit must suffer the harm of the wrong. He whom guidance does not keep firm will be led away by misguidance towards destruction. Sermon 28

That is because of what **your** *two hands put forward! Truly, God is not unjust to His servants.* **22:10**

He is true in His promise. He is too high to be unjust to His creatures. He stands by equity among His creation and practices justice over them in His commands. He provides evidence through the creation of things of His being from ever, through their marks of incapability of His power, and through their powerlessness against death of His eternity. Sermon 185

Among humanity is he who worships God on the fringes. If good lit on him, he is at rest with it. If a test lit on him, he turned completely about. He lost the present and the world to come. That, it is the clear loss. **22:11**

O God's human being! I advise you to be God-conscious. Sermon 82

He calls to other than God what neither hurts him nor profits him. That, it is a far wandering astray. **22:12**
He calls to him whose hurting is nearer than his profiting. Miserable was the defender and miserable was the acquaintance. **22:13**

I bear witness that *there is no god but God* (Q47:19) and I bear witness that *Muhammad* (Q48:29), peace and the mercy of God be upon him, is *His servant* (Q17:1) and *Prophet* (Q7:158) and His chosen and His selected one. Sermon 150

Truly, God will cause to enter those who have believed and did as the ones accord with morality, Gardens beneath which rivers run. Truly, God accomplishes what He wants. **22:14**

God, the Almighty, has sent down a guiding Book wherein He has explained virtue and vice. You should adopt the course of virtue, whereby you will have guidance. Detach yourself from the direction of vice, so that you remain on the right way. Sermon 167

Whoever had been thinking that God will never help him, in the present and in the world to come, let him stretch out a cord to heaven. Again, let him sever it. Then, let him look on whether his cunning causes to put away what enrages him. **22:15**

Certainly, it is a great blessing of God, the Glorified, that He has engendered among them unity through the cord of affection in whose shade they walk and take shelter. This is a blessing whose value no one in the whole world realizes, because it is more valuable than any price and higher than any wealth. Sermon 191

Thus, We caused signs to descend, clear portents. That God guides whom He wants. **22:16**

My God, Spreader of the surfaces of the earth and Keeper intact of all skies, Creator of hearts of good and evil nature, send **Your** choicest blessings and growing favors on Muhammad, peace and the mercy of God be upon him, **Your** servant and **Your** Prophet, who is the last of those who preceded him and an opener for what is closed, proclaimer of truth with truth, repulser of the forces of wrong and crusher of the onslaughts of misguidance. Sermon 72

Truly, those who believed and those who became Jews and the Sabeans and the Christians and the Zoroastrians and those who ascribed partners—truly, God will distinguish between them on the Day of Resurrection. Truly, God over everything is a Witness. **22:17**
Have ***you*** *not considered that to God prostrates to Him whoever is in the heavens and whoever is in and on the earth and the sun and the moon and the stars, the mountains, the trees and the moving creatures, and many of humanity while there are many on whom the punishment will be realized. He whom God despises, then, there is no one who honors him. Truly, God accomplishes whatever He wills.* **22:18**
These two disputants strove against one another about their Lord. Then, for those who were ungrateful garments of fire will be cut out for them. Over their heads, scalding water will be unloosed **22:19**
whereby what is in their bellies will be dissolved and their skins. **22:20**
For them are maces of iron. **22:21**
Whenever they wanted to go forth from there because of lament, they will be caused to return to it and experience the punishment of the burning. **22:22**

The great calamity of that place is the hot water and entry into Hell, flames of eternal fire and intensity of blazes. There is no resting period, no gap for ease, no power to intervene, no death to bring about solace and no sleep to make him forget pain. He rather lies under several kinds of deaths and moment-to-moment punishment. We seek refuge with God. Sermon 82

Truly, God will cause to enter those who believed and did as ones in accord with morality, Gardens beneath which rivers run. They are adorned in them with bracelets of gold and pearls. Their garments in it will be of silk. **22:23**

The best means by which seekers of nearness to God, the Almighty, the Exalted, seek nearness is the belief in Him and His Prophet, fighting in His cause, for it is the high pinnacle of Islam, and to believe in the expression of divine purification for it is just nature and the establishment of prayer for it is the basis of community, payment of the purifying tax (*zakat*) for it is a compulsory obligation, fasting for the month of Ramadan for it is the shield against chastisement, the performance of the pilgrimage to the House of God (Kabah) and its visitation (*umra*) (other than annual visit) for these two acts banish poverty and wash away sins, regard for kinship for it increases wealth and length of life, giving alms secretly for it covers shortcomings, giving alms openly for it protects against a bad death and extending benefits to people for it saves from positions of disgrace. Sermon 109

They were guided to what is good of the saying and they were guided to the Path of Him Who is Worthy of Praise. **22:24**

Praise belongs to God (Q1:2) Who is such that it is not possible to describe the reality of knowledge about Him, since His greatness has restrained their intellects, and therefore they cannot find the way to approach the extremity of His realm. He is God, the True, the Manifester of Truth. He is more True and more Manifest than eyes can see. The intellect cannot comprehend Him by fixing limits for Him since in that case to Him would be attributed shape. Imagination cannot catch Him by fixing quantities for Him for in that case to Him would be attributed body. He created creatures without any example, and without the advice of a counsel, or the assistance of a helper. His creation was completed by His command, and bowed to His obedience. It responded to Him and did not defy Him. It obeyed and did not resist. Sermon 155

Truly, those who were ungrateful and bar from the way of God and from the Masjid al-Haram that We made for humanity—equal for the ones who give themselves up and the ones who are desert dwellers—and whoever wants to violate it with injustice, We will cause him to experience a painful punishment. **22:25**

Whoever proceeds towards this mischief will be ruined and whoever strives for it will be annihilated. They will be biting each other during it as the wild asses bite each other in the herd. The coils of the rope will be disturbed and the face of affairs will be blinded. During it sagacity will be on the ebb, and the oppressors will have the opportunity to speak. Sermon 151

Mention when We placed Abraham in the place of the House that: ***You*** *will ascribe nothing as partners with Me.* ***You*** *purify My House for the ones who circumambulate it and the ones who are standing up, and the ones who bow down and the ones who prostrate themselves.* **22:26**
Announce to humanity the pilgrimage to Makkah. They will approach ***you*** *on foot and on every thin camel. They will approach from every deep ravine* **22:27**
that they bear witness to what profits them and remember the Name of God on known days over whatever He provided them from flocks of animals. Then, eat of it and feed the ones who are in misery and the poor. **22:28**
Again, let them finish their ritual cleanliness and live up to their vows and circumambulate the Ancient House. **22:29**
That was commanded! Whoever holds the sacred things of God in honor, then, that is better for him with his Lord. Permitted to you were the flocks, but what will be recounted to you. So, avoid the disgrace of graven images and avoid saying the untruth. **22:30**

God has made the pilgrimage to His sacred House obligatory upon you which is the turning point for the people who go to it as beasts or pigeons go towards spring water. God, the Almighty, made it a sign of their supplication before His Greatness and their acknowledgment of His Dignity. He selected from among His creation those who, upon listening to His call, responded to it and bore witness to His word. They stood in the position of His Prophets and resembled His angels who surround the Divine Throne securing all the benefits of performing His worship and hastening towards His promised forgiveness. God the Almighty made His sacred House an emblem for Islam and an object of respect for those who turn to it. He made pilgrimage to it obligatory and laid down its claim for which He held you responsible to discharge. Thus, God the Almighty said: ... *Truly the first House to be set in place for humanity is at Bekka, that which is blessed and a guidance for the worlds.* (Q3:96-97) Sermon 1

Turn to God as monotheists not with Him as ones who are polytheists. Whoever ascribes partners with God, it is as if he fell down from heaven and the birds snatch him or the wind hurled him to ruin in a place far away. **22:31**

I bear witness that *there is no god but God* (Q47:19), the One, there is no partner with Him, nor is there with Him any god other than Himself, and that *Muhammad* (Q48:29), peace and the mercy of God be upon him, is *His servant,* (Q17:1) and *Prophet.* (Q7:158) Sermon 35

That was commanded! Whoever holds the waymarks of God in honor, then, it is, truly, from hearts filled with God-consciousness. **22:32**

For you in that is what profits for a term, that which is determined. Again, their place of sacrifice is at the Ancient House. **22:33**

O God's human being! Know that God-consciousness is a strong house of protection while lack of God-consciousness is a weak house that does not protect its people and does not give security to him who takes refuge therein. Know that the sting of sins is cut by God-consciousness and the final aim is achieved by conviction of belief. Sermon 157

For every community We assigned devotional acts that they may remember the Name of God over what We provided them of flocks of animals. Your God is One God. Submit to Him, and give ***you*** *good tidings to the ones who humble themselves,* **22:34**

those who, when God was remembered, their hearts took notice and the ones who remain steadfast against whatever lit on them and the ones who perform the formal prayer and who spends out of what We provided them. **22:35**

This is the thing against which God has protected His creatures who are believers by means of prayers, alms-giving and suffering the hardship of fasting in the days in which it has been made obligatory in order to give their limbs peacefulness, to cast fear in their eyes, to make their spirits humble, to give their hearts humility and to remove haughtiness from them. All this is achieved through the covering of their delicate cheeks with dust in humility, prostrating their main limbs on the ground in humbleness and retracting of their bellies so as to reach to their backs due to fasting by way of lowliness before God, in addition to giving all sorts of products of the earth to the needy and the destitute by way of alms. Look what there is in these acts by way of curbing the appearance of pride and suppressing the traces of vanity. Sermon 192

We made for you the beasts of sacrifice among the waymarks of God. You have in them much good so remember the Name of God over them, ones who are standing in ranks. Then, when they collapsed on their sides, eat from them and feed the ones who are paupers and the ones who are poor persons who beg not. Thus, We caused them to be subservient to you so that perhaps you will give thanks. **22:36**

For an animal to be fully fit for sacrifice, it is necessary that both its ears should be raised upwards and its eyes should be healthy. If the ears and the eyes are sound, the animal of sacrifice is sound and perfect, even though its horn be broken or it drags its feet to the place of sacrifice. Sermon 53

Neither their flesh nor their blood attains to God, rather, God-consciousness from you attains Him. Thus, He caused them to be subservient to you that you magnify God in that He guided you. Give ***you*** *good tidings to the ones who are doers of good.* **22:37**

Where are the minds which seek light from the lamps of guidance and the eyes which look at minarets of God-consciousness? Where are the hearts dedicated to God and devoted to the obedience of God? They are all crowding towards worldly vanities and quarreling over unlawful issues. The banners of the Garden and Hell have been raised for them, but they have turned their faces away from the Garden and proceeded to Hell by dint of their performances. God called them, but they showed dislike and ran away. When Satan called them, they responded and proceeded towards him. Sermon 144

Truly, God defends those who believed. Truly, God loves not any who is an ungrateful betrayer. **22:38**

Almighty are **You**, the Creator, the Worshipped. On account of **Your** good trials of **Your** creatures, **You** created a house (Paradise) and provided in it for feasting, drinks, foods, spouses, servants, places, streams, plantations and fruits. Then **You** sent a Messenger to invite towards it, but the people did not respond to the caller and did not feel persuaded to what **You** persuaded them, nor showed eagerness towards what **You** desired them to feel eager. They, the ungrateful, jumped on the carcass of this world, earned shame by eating it and became united in loving it. When one loves a thing, it blinds him and sickens his heart. He sees, but with a diseased eye, hears, but with un-hearing ears. Desires have cut asunder his wit. The world has made his heart dead while his mind is all longing for it. Consequently, he is a servant of it and of everyone who has any share in it. Wherever it turns, he turns towards it. Wherever it proceeds, he proceeds towards it. He is not desisted by any desister from God, nor takes admonition from any preacher. He sees those who have been caught in neglect whence there is neither rescission nor reversion. Sermon 108

Permission was given to those who are fought against because they, they were wronged. Truly, Powerful is God to help them, **22:39**
those who were driven out from their abodes without right because they say: Our Lord is God! If not for God driving back humanity, some by some other, cloisters would be demolished and churches and synagogues and mosques in which is remembered in it the Name of God frequently. Truly, God will help whoever helps Him. Truly, God is Strong, Almighty. **22:40**

May God have mercy on the person who, when he sees the truth, supports it, when he sees the wrong, rejects it, and who helps the truth against him who is in the wrong. Sermon 205

Those who, if We established them firmly on the earth, they performed the formal prayer and they gave the purifying alms and they commanded to that which is honorable and they prohibited that which is unlawful. With God is the Ultimate End of the command. **22:41**

All this is achieved through the covering of their delicate cheeks with dust in humility, prostrating their main limbs on the ground in humbleness, and retracting of their bellies so as to reach to their backs due to fasting by way of lowliness before God, besides giving all sorts of products of the earth to the needy and the destitute by way of alms. Look what there is in these acts by way of curbing the appearance of pride and suppressing the traces of vanity. Sermon 192

If they deny **you***, surely, the folk of Noah denied before* **you** *and Ad and Thamud* **22:42**
and the folk of Abraham and the folk of Lot **22:43**
and the companions of Midian. Moses was denied, but I granted indulgence to the ones who are ungrateful. Again, I took them and how had been My disapproval! **22:44**
How many a town We caused to perish while they are ones who are unjust so that it be one that had fallen down in ruins and how much well water ignored and a tall palace! **22:45** ***

Journey they not through the earth? Have they not hearts with which to be reasonable or ears with which to hear? Truly, it is not their sight that is in darkness, but their hearts that are within their breasts that are in darkness! **22:46**

By God, your city would certainly be drowned so much so that as though I see its mosque like the upper part of a boat or a sitting ostrich. Sermon 13

Seek they that **you** *hasten the punishment? God never breaks His Promise. Truly, a day with* **your** *Lord is as a thousand years of what you number.* **22:47**
How many a town I granted indulgence while it is one that is unjust. Again, I took it and to Me was the Homecoming. **22:48**

O God's human being! Be God-conscious, keeping in view the reason why He created you. Be afraid of Him to the extent He has advised you to do. Make yourself deserve what He has promised you by having confidence in the truth of His promise and entertaining fear of the Day of Judgment. Sermon 82

Say: O humanity! Truly, I am only a clear warner to you. **22:49**
So, those who believed and did as ones in accord with morality, for them is forgiveness and a generous provision. **22:50**

I bear witness that *Muhammad* (Q48:29), peace and the mercy of God be upon him, is *His servant* (Q17:1) and His *Prophet.* (Q7:158) He sent him for enforcement of His commands, for exhausting His pleas and for presenting warnings against eternal punishment. Sermon 82

Those who endeavored against Our signs, ones who strive to thwart, those are the Companions of Hellfire. **22:51**

Everyone of them is ... alone although they are a group, and they are strangers, even though friends. They are unaware of morning after a night and of evening after a day. The night or the day when they departed has become ever existent for them. They found the dangers of their place of stay more serious than they had apprehended. They witnessed that its signs were greater than they had guessed. Sermon 220

We sent not before **you** *any Messenger nor Prophet, but when he fantasized, Satan cast fantasies into him. But God nullifies what Satan casts. Again, God set clear His signs. God is Knowing, Wise,* **22:52**
for He makes what Satan casts a test for those who in their hearts is a sickness and their hearts, ones that harden. Truly, the ones who are unjust are in a wide breach. **22:53**

They have made Satan the master of their affairs. He has taken them as partners. He has laid eggs and hatched them in their bosoms. He creeps and crawls in their laps. He sees through their eyes and speaks with their tongues. In this way he has led them to sinfulness and adorned for them foul things like the action of one whom Satan has made partner in his domain and speaks untruth through his tongue. Sermon 7

Those who were given the knowledge know that it is The Truth from **your** *Lord, so that they believe in it and humble their hearts to Him. Truly, God is One Who Guides those who believed to a straight path.* **22:54**

You are supporters of Truth and brethren in faith. You are the shield on the day of tribulation and my trustees among the rest of the people. With your support I strike the runner away and hope for the obedience of him who advances forward. Therefore, extend to me support which is free from deceit and pure from doubt because, by God, I am the most preferable of all for the people. Sermon 118

Those who were ungrateful cease not to be hesitant about it until the Hour approaches them suddenly or the punishment approaches them on a withering Day. **22:55**

Truly, the Hour will come as the most important and the greatest event of your life; it will either carry unmixed blessings and rewards for you or it will bring in its wake punishments, sufferings, and eternal damnation. There will be no chance of its lessening or redemption or any change for the better. It is for you to decide whether to proceed towards perpetual peace and blessings—Paradise, or towards eternal damnation—Hell. Remember that life is actually driving you towards death which will meet you if you are ready to face it and which will follow you like a shadow if you try to run away from it. Letter 27

On that Day the dominion will belong to God. He will give judgment between them. So, those who believed and did as the ones accord with morality will be in Gardens of Bliss. **22:56**
Those who were ungrateful and denied Our signs, for them will be a despised punishment. **22:57**

The hidden thing, namely death, which is being driven towards you by two ever new phenomena—the day and the night—is certainly quick to approach. The traveler that is approaching with success or failure deserves the best of provision. So acquire such provision from this world while you are here with which you may shield yourself tomorrow on the Day of Judgment. Sermon 64

Those who emigrated in the way of God, then, they were slain or died, certainly, God will provide them a fairer provision. Truly, God, certainly, He is Best of the ones who provide. **22:58**

Steadfast and transient belief and the obligation of migration (*hijrah*): One belief is that which is firm and steadfast in hearts and one is that which remains temporarily in the heart and the breast up to a certain time. If you were to acquit yourself before any person, you should wait until death approaches him, for that is the time limit for being acquitted. Sermon 189

Certainly, He will cause them to enter a gate with which they will be well-pleased. Truly, God is, certainly, Knowing, Forbearing. **22:59**

You should adopt the course of virtue whereby you will have guidance, and keep aloof from the direction of vice so that you remain on the right way. Sermon 167

That is so! Whoever chastises for injustice with the like of what he was chastised, and, again, suffered an injustice, God will, certainly, help him. Truly, God is Pardoning, Forgiving. **22:60**

By God, even if I had found that by such money women have been married or servant-maids have been purchased, I would have returned it to its owners because there is wide scope in dispensation of justice. He who finds it hard to act justly will find it harder to deal with injustice. Sermon 15

That is because God causes the nighttime to be interposed into the daytime and He causes the daytime to be interposed into the nighttime. Truly, God is Hearing, Seeing. **22:61**

He created the earth and suspended it without being busy, retained it without support, made it stand without legs, raised it without pillars, protected it against bendings and curvings and defended it against crumbling and splitting into parts. He fixed mountains on it like stumps, solidified its rocks, caused its streams to flow and opened wide its valleys. Whatever He made did not suffer from any frailty. Whatever He strengthened did not show any weakness. Sermon 186

That is because God, He is The Truth. What they call to other than Him, it is falsehood. That God, He is The Lofty, The Great. **22:62**

Know that the tongue is a part of a person's body. If the man desists, speech will not co-operate with him and when he dilates, speech will not give him time to stop. Certainly, we are the masters of speaking. Its veins are fixed in us and its branches are hanging over us. Sermon 232

Have **you** *not considered that God caused water to descend from heaven? Then, in the morning, the earth becomes green. Truly, God is Subtle, Aware.* **22:63**

This world and the next have submitted to Him their reins. The skies and earths have flung their keys towards Him. The thriving trees bow to Him in the morning and evening. They produce for Him flaming fire from their branches, and at His command, turn their own feed into ripe fruits. Sermon 132

To Him belongs whatever is in the heavens and whatever is in and on the earth. Truly, God, He is The Sufficient, The Worthy of Praise. **22:64**

Praise belongs to God (Q1:2) Whose worth cannot be described by speakers, Whose bounties cannot be counted by calculators and Whose claim to obedience cannot be satisfied by those who attempt to do so Whom the height of intellectual courage cannot appreciate, and the depths of understanding cannot reach. He for Whose description no limit has been laid down, no eulogy exists, no time is ordained and no duration is fixed. He brought forth creation through His Omnipotence, dispersed winds through His Compassion, and made firm the shaking earth with rocks. The foremost in religion is the acknowledgment of Him. The perfection of acknowledging Him is to bear witness to Him. The perfection of bearing witness to Him is to believe in His Oneness. The perfection of believing in His Oneness is to regard Him Pure. The perfection of His purity is to deny Him attributes, because every attribute is a proof that it is different from that to which it is attributed and everything to which something is attributed is different from the attribute. Thus, whoever attaches attributes to God recognizes His like. Whoever recognizes His like regards Him as two. Whoever regards Him as two recognizes parts for Him. Whoever recognizes parts for Him mistakes Him. Whoever mistakes Him points at Him. Whoever points at Him admits limitations for Him. Whoever admits limitations for Him numbers Him. Whoever says in what He is, has held that He is contained. Whoever says on what is He, has held He is not on something else. He is a Being, but not through the phenomenon of coming into being. He exists, but not from non-existence. He is with everything, but not in physical nearness. He is different from everything, but not in physical separation. He acts, but without connotation of movements and instruments. He sees even when there is nothing to be looked at from among His creation. He is only One such that there is none with whom He may keep company or whom He may miss in his absence. Sermon 1

Have **you** *not considered that God caused to be subservient to you what is in and on the earth? The boats run through the sea by His command. He holds back the heaven so that it not fall on the earth, but by His permission. Truly, to humanity God is Gentle, Compassionate.* **22:65**
It is He Who gave you life and, again, He will cause you to die and, again, He will give you life. Truly, the human being is ungrateful. **22:66**

Praise belongs to God (Q1:2) Who is High above all else. He is Near the creation through His bounty. Sermon 82

For every community We assigned devotional acts so that they be ones who perform rites. So, let them not bicker with **you** *in the command. Call* **you** *to* **your** *Lord. Truly,* **You** *are on a guidance, that which is straight.* **22:67**

O my God! I seek **Your** protection from becoming destitute despite **Your** riches, from being misguided despite **Your** guidance, from being molested in **Your** realm and from being humiliated while authority rests with **You**. O my God! Let my spirit be the first of those good objects that **You** take from me and the first trust out of **Your** favors held in trust with me. Sermon 215

If they disputed with **you***, then,* **you** *say: God is greater in knowledge about what you do.* **22:68**

The truthful Prophet, peace and the mercy of God be upon him, has said: God may love a person but hate his action, and may love the action but hate the person. You should also know that every action is like vegetation. Vegetation cannot do without water while waters are different. Where the water is good, the plant is good and its fruits are sweet, whereas where the water is bad, the plant will also be bad and its fruits will be bitter. Sermon 153

God will give judgment among you on the Day of Resurrection about what you had been at variance in it. **22:69**

On that day God will collect on it the front and the back, to stand in obedience for the exaction of accounts and for the award of recompense for deeds. Sweat would flow up to their mouths like reins while the earth would be trembling under them. In the best condition among them would be he who has found a resting place for both his feet and an open place for his breath. Sermon 102

Have **you** *not known that God knows what is in the heaven and the earth? Truly, that is in a Book. Truly, that is easy for God.* **22:70**

Praise belongs to God (Q1:2) from Whose view one sky does not conceal another sky, nor one earth another earth. Sermon 172

They worship other than God, that for which He sent not down any authority and of what they have no knowledge. There is no helper for the ones who are unjust. **22:71**

You, certainly, know that he who is in charge of honor, life, booty, enforcement of legal commandments and the leadership of the Muslims should not be a miser as his greed would aim at their wealth, nor be ignorant as he would then mislead them with his ignorance, nor be of rude behavior who would estrange them with his rudeness, nor should he deal unjustly with wealth thus preferring one group over another, nor should he accept a bribe while taking decisions as he would forfeit others' rights and hold them up without finality. He should not ignore the *sunna* as he would ruin the people. Sermon 131

When Our signs are recounted to them, clear portents, ***you*** *will recognize on the faces of those who were ungrateful, that they are the ones who are rejected. They are about to rush upon those who recount Our signs to them. Say: Shall I tell you of worse than that? God promised the fire to those who were ungrateful. Miserable will be the Homecoming!* **22:72**

On that day many an argument will prove void and a contention for excuses will stand rejected. Sermon 221

O humanity! A parable was propounded, so listen to it. Truly, those whom you call to other than God will never create a fly, even if they were gathered together for it. When the fly is to rob them of something, they would never seek to deliver it from the fly. Weak were the ones who are seekers and the ones who are sought. **22:73**

He did not create what He created to fortify His authority, nor for fear of the consequences of time, nor to seek help against the attack of an equal or a boastful partner or a hateful opponent. On the other hand, all the creatures are reared by Him and are His humble servants. He is not conditioned in anything so that it be said that He exists therein, nor is He separated from anything so as to be said that He is away from it. The creation of what He initiated or the administration of what He controls did not fatigue Him. No disability overtook Him against what He created. No misgiving ever occurred to Him in what He ordained and resolved, but His verdict is certain. His knowledge is definite. His governance is overwhelming. He is wished for at time of distress and He is feared even in bounty. Sermon 64

They duly measured not the measure of God. Truly, God is Strong, Almighty. **22:74**

Praise belongs to God (Q1:2) ... I am a servant in **Your** possession. I have been guilty of excesses over myself. **You** have exhausted **Your** pleas over me and I have no plea before **You.** I have no power to take except what **You** give me. I cannot evade except what **You** save me from. Sermon 215

God favors from the angels Messengers and Messengers from humanity. Truly, God is Hearing, Seeing. **22:75**

God never allowed His creation to remain without a Prophet, one deputized by Him, or a Book sent down from Him, or a binding argument, or a standing plea. These Messengers were such that they did not fear that they were few in comparison to the large numbers of their falsifiers. Among them was either a predecessor who would name the one to follow or the follower who had been introduced by the predecessor. Sermon 1

He knows what is in advance of them, and what is behind them, and to God all matters are returned. **22:76**

... to Him returns whoever dies. Sermon 108

O those who believed! Bow down and prostrate yourselves, and worship your Lord, and accomplish good so that perhaps you will prosper. **22:77**
Struggle for God in a true struggling. He elected you and made not for you in your way of life any impediment. It is the creed of your father Abraham. He named you the ones who submit to God before and in this Recitation that the Messenger be a witness over you and you are witnesses over humanity. So, perform the formal prayer and give the purifying alms and cleave firmly to God. He is your Defender. How excellent a Defender and how excellent a Helper! **22:78**

The best means by which seekers of nearness to God, the Almighty, the Exalted, seek nearness is the belief in Him and His Prophet, fighting in His cause ... Sermon 109

Chapter 23: The Believers (al-Muminun)

Surely, the ones who believe prospered, **23:1**
those, they, who in their formal prayers are ones who are humble **23:2**
and they, those who from idle talk, are ones who turn aside **23:3**
and they, those who the purifying alms are ones who do give **23:4**
and they, those who of their private parts, are ones who guard, **23:5**
but from their spouses or from what their right hands possessed. Truly, they are ones who are irreproachable. **23:6**
Whoever was looking for something beyond that, then, those, they are the ones who turn away. **23:7**

To the pious people, the best is that which they find with God. Letter 23

Those, they who their trusts and their compacts are ones who shepherd **23:8**
and those, they who over their formal prayers are watchful, **23:9**
those, they are ones who will inherit, **23:10**
those who will inherit Paradise, they are ones who will dwell in it forever. **23:11**

He who has an intelligent mind looks to his goal. He knows his low road as well as his high road. The caller has called. The shepherd has tended his flocks. So respond to the caller and follow the shepherd. Sermon 154

Certainly, We created the human being from an extraction of clay. **23:12**
Again, We made him into seminal fluid in a stopping place, secure. **23:13**

O creature who has been equitably created and who has been nurtured and looked after in the darkness of wombs with multiple curtains. *Certainly We have created the human being from an extraction of clay.* (Q23:12) Then you were taken out from your place of stay to a place you had not seen, and you were not acquainted with the means of acquiring its benefits. Who guided you to eke out your sustenance from the udder of your mother? And, when you were in need, who apprised you of the location of what you required or aimed at? Alas! Certainly he who is unable to understand the qualities of a being with shape and limbs is the more unable to understand the qualities of the Creator and the more remote from appreciating Him through the limitations of creatures! Sermon 163

Again, We created a clot from seminal fluids. Then, We created tissue from the clot. Then, We created bones from tissue. Then, We clothed the bones with flesh. Again, We caused another creation to grow. So, blessed be God, the Fairer of the ones who are creators! **23:14**
Again, truly, after that, you will die. **23:15**

No other originator took part with Him in its origination and no one having power assisted Him in its creation. Sermon 185

Again, truly, you will be raised up on the Day of Resurrection. **23:16**

Then there remain a few people in whose case the remembrance of their return to God on the Day of Judgment keeps their eyes bent and the fear of Resurrection moves their tears. Some of them are scared away from the world and dispersed. Some are frightened and subdued. Some are quiet as if muzzled. Some are praying sincerely. Some are grief-stricken and pain-ridden whom fear has confined to namelessness and disgrace has shrouded them, so they are in the sea of bitter water, their mouths are closed and their hearts are bruised. They preached until they were tired. They were oppressed until they were disgraced. They were killed until their numbers dwindled. Sermon 32

Certainly, We created above you seven tiers. We had not been ones who are heedless of the creation. **23:17**

Subservient to **You** is the creation of the sky, the air, the winds and the water. Therefore, **You** look at the sun and moon, the plants and trees, water and stone, the alternation of this night and day, the flowing out of these seas, the large number of mountains and the height of their peaks, the diversity of languages and the variety of tongues. Then woe be to him who disbelieves in the Ordainer and denies the Ruler. They claim that they are like grass for which there is no cultivator, nor any maker for their diverse shapes. They have not relied on any argument for what they assert, nor on any research for what they have heard. Can there be any construction without a Constructor, or any offense without an offender? Sermon 185

We caused water to descend from heaven in measure and We ceased it to dwell in the earth. We certainly are ones who have power to take away. **23:18**

When the excitement of water subsided under the earth's sides and under the weight of the high and lofty mountains placed on its shoulders, God flowed springs of water from its high tops and distributed them through plains and low places and moderated their movement by fixed rocks and high mountain tops. Then its trembling came to a standstill because of the penetration of mountains in various parts of its surface and their being fixed in its deep areas, and their standing on its plains. Sermon 91

We caused to grow for you gardens of date palm trees and grapevines where there is much sweet fruit for you and you eat of it **23:19**
and a tree that goes forth from Mount Sinai that bears oil and a seasoning for the ones who eat it. **23:20**
Truly, for you in the flocks there is a lesson. We satiate you with what is in their bellies. In them are many profits and of them you eat **23:21**
and on them and on boats you are carried. **23:22**

Praise belongs to God (Q1:2) Who is High above all else. He is Near the creation through His bounty. He is the Giver of all reward and distinction and Dispeller of all calamities and hardships. I praise Him for His continuous mercy and His copious bounties. Sermon 82

Certainly, We sent Noah to his folk. He said: O my folk! Worship God! You have no other god but Him. Will you not, then, be God-conscious? **23:23**
But said the Council who were ungrateful among his folk: This is nothing but a mortal like you. He wants to gain superiority over you. If God willed He would have caused angels to descend. We heard not such a thing from our fathers, the ancient ones. **23:24**
He is nothing but a man in whom there is madness. So, watch him for a while. **23:25**
He said: My Lord! Help me because they denied me. **23:26**
So, We revealed to him: Craft ***you*** *the boat under Our eyes and by Our revelation. Then, when Our command drew near and the oven boiled, then, insert two pairs of each kind and* ***your*** *people, but whomever against whom the saying has preceded. Address Me not for those who did wrong. Truly, they are ones who are drowned.* **23:27**
When ***you*** *and whoever is with* ***you*** *are seated in the boat, then, say: All Praise belongs to God Who delivered us from the folk, the ones who are unjust.* **23 28**
Say: My Lord! Land ***You*** *me with a blessed landing for* ***You*** *are Best of the landing-places.* **23:29**
Truly, in this there are signs and, truly, We had been ones who test. **23:30**

O people! A time will come to you when Islam would be capsized as a pot is capsized with all its contents. O people, God has protected you from that. He might be hard on you. He has not spared you from being put on trial. God, the Sublimest of all speakers, has said: *Truly, in this there are signs and, truly, We had been ones who test.* (Q23:30) Sermon 102

Again, We caused to grow another generation after them. **23:31**
We sent a Messenger to them from among them saying that: Worship God! You have no god other than Him. Will you, then, not be God-conscious? **23:32**
Said the Council of his folk to those who were ungrateful and denied the meeting in the world to come, and to whom We gave ease in this present life: This is nothing but a mortal like you. He eats of what you eat and he drinks of what you drink. If you obeyed a mortal like yourselves, truly, then, you are ones who are losers. **23:34**
Promises He that when you died and had been earth dust and bones, that you will be ones who are brought out? **23:35**
Begone! Begone with what you are promised! **23:36**
There is nothing but this present life. We die and we live and we shall not be ones who are raised up. **23:37**
He is nothing but a man. He devised a lie against God and we are not ones who will believe in him. **23:38**
He said: My Lord! Help me because they denied me. **23:39**
He said: In a little while they will become ones who are remorseful. **23:40**
Then, a Cry duly took them so We made them into refuse. So, away with the folk, the ones who are unjust! **23:41**
Again, We caused to grow after them other generations. **23:42**
No community precedes its term, nor delays it. **23:43**
Again, We sent Our Messengers one after another. Whenever drew near a community a Messenger

to them, they denied him. So, We caused some of them to pursue others and We made them tales. So, away with the folk who believe not! **23:44**
Again, We sent Moses and his brother Aaron with Our signs and clear authority **23:45**
to Pharaoh and his Council. Then, they grew arrogant and they had been a folk, ones who exalt themselves. **23:46**
Then, they said: Will we believe in two mortals like ourselves while their folk are ones who worship us? **23:47**
So, they denied both of them. They had been among the ones who are caused to perish. **23:48**
Certainly, We gave Moses the Book so that perhaps they will be truly guided. **23:49**
We made the son of Mary and his mother a sign, and We gave them refuge on a hillside, a stopping place, and a spring of water. **23:50** ***

O you Messengers! Eat of what is good and do as one in accord with morality. Truly, I am Knowing of what you do. **23:51**
Truly, this, your community is one community and I am your Lord so be God-conscious. **23:52**

Among the God-conscious are the people of distinction. Their speech is to the point. Their dress is moderate. Their gait is humble. They keep their eyes closed to what God has made unlawful for them. They put their ears to that knowledge which is beneficial to them. They remain in the time of trials as though they remain in comfort. If there had not been fixed periods of life ordained for each, their spirits would not have remained in their bodies even for the twinkling of an eye because of their eagerness for the reward and fear of chastisement. The greatness of the Creator is seated in their heart and so everything else appears small in their eyes. Thus, to them Paradise is as though they see it and are enjoying its favors. To them, Hell is also as if they see it and are suffering punishment in it. Sermon 193

Then, they cut their affair of unity asunder into sects among them, each party glad with what was with them. **23:53**
So, forsake **you** *them for a while in their obstinacy.* **23:54**

The position of the head of government is that of the thread for beads, as it connects them and keeps them together. If the thread is broken, they will disperse and be lost, and will never come together again. The Arabs today, even though small in number, are big because of Islam and strong because of unity. You should remain like the axis for them, and rotate the mill of government with the help of the Arabs, and be their root. Avoid battle, because if you leave this place, the Arabs will attack you from all sides and directions until the unguarded places left behind by you will become more important than those before you. Sermon 146

Assume they that with the relief We furnish them of wealth and children **23:55**
We compete for good deeds for them? Nay! They are not aware. **23:56**
Truly, those, they are dreading their Lord, ones who are apprehensive. **23:57**

God, the Sublime, disliked vanity for them and liked humbleness for them. Therefore, they laid their cheeks on the ground, smeared their faces with dust, bent themselves down for the believers and remained humble people. God tried them with hunger, afflicted them with difficulty, tested them with fear, and upset them with troubles. Therefore, do not regard wealth and progeny the criterion for God's pleasure and displeasure, as you are not aware of the chances of mischief and trials during richness and power as God, the Almighty, the Sublime, has said: *Assume they that with the relief We furnish them of wealth and children We compete for good works for them? Nay! They are not aware.* (Q23:55-56) Sermon 192

Those, they who believe in the signs of their Lord **23:58**
and those, they who ascribe nothing as partners with their Lord, **23:59**
and those who give what they gave with their hearts afraid because they are ones who will return to their Lord, **23:60**
are those who compete with one another in good deeds and they, in them, are ones who take the lead. **23:61**

Remember that Divine Reward is for those who earn it with their sincere and good deeds. Letter 33

We place not a burden on any soul but to its capacity. From Us is a Book that speaks The Truth for itself. They will not be wronged. **23:62**

The Book of God is among you. It speaks. Its tongue does not falter. It is a house whose pillars do not fall down. It is a power whose supporters are never defeated. Sermon 132

Nay! Their hearts are in obstinacy towards this Quran and they have other actions besides as they are ones who act **23:63**
until, when We took ones who are given ease with the punishment. That is when they make entreaties. **23:64**
Make not entreaties this Day. Truly, you will not be helped from Us. **23:65**

Everyone should fear God, should admonish himself, should send forward his repentance and should overpower his desire, because his death is hidden from him. His desires deceive him. Satan keeps posted about him. He beautifies his sin for him so that he may commit it. He prompts him to delay repentance until his desires cause him to be the most negligent. Pity is for the negligent person whose life itself would be a proof against him and his own days, passed in sin, will lead him to punishment. Sermon 64

Surely, My signs had been recounted to you, but you had been receding on your heels **23:66**
as ones who grow arrogant regarding it and ones who nightly talk nonsense, talking foolishly. **23:67**
Meditate they not on the saying or drew not near them anything that approaches not their fathers, the ancient ones? **23:68**
Or is it they recognize not their Messenger so that they are ones who reject him? **23:69**

You should take a lesson from the fate of the progeny of Ishmael, the children of Isaac and the children of Jacob. How similar are their affairs and how akin are their examples. In connection with the details of their division and disunity, think of the days when Kings of Persia and the Caesars of Rome had become their masters. They turned them out from the pastures of their lands, the rivers of Iraq and the fertility of the world, towards thorny forests, the passages of hot winds and hardships in livelihood. By doing this, they turned them into just herders of camels. Their houses were the worst in the world and their places of stay were the most drought-stricken. There was not one voice towards which they could turn for protection, nor any shade of affection on whose strength they could repose trust. Sermon 192

Or say they: There is madness in him? Nay! He drew near them with The Truth, but most of them are ones who dislike The Truth. **23:70**

Know that—may God have mercy on you—you are living at a time when those who speak about right are few, when tongues are loath to utter the truth and those who stick to the right are humiliated. The people of this time are engaged in disobedience. Their youth are wicked, their old men are sinful, their learned men are hypocrites, and their speakers are sycophants. Their young ones do not respect their elders, and their rich men do not support the destitute. Sermon 232

If The Truth followed their desires, the heavens and the earth would have gone to ruin and whoever is in it. Nay! We brought them their Remembrance, but they, from their Remembrance, are ones who turn aside. **23:71**

I bear witness that *there is no god but God* (Q47:19), by virtue of belief, certainty, sincerity and conviction. I also bear witness that *Muhammad* (Q48:29), peace and the mercy of God be upon him, is *His servant* (Q17:1) and *Prophet* (Q7:158) whom He deputed when the signs of guidance were obliterated and the ways of religion were desolate. So he threw open the truth, gave advice to the people, guided them towards righteousness and ordered them to be moderate. May God bless him ... Sermon 194

Or is it that **you** *have asked them for payment? Yet the revenue from* **your** *Lord is better. He is Best of the ones who provide.* **23:72**

God deputized *the Prophet* (Q7:158), peace and the mercy of God be upon him, after a gap from the previous Prophets when there was much talk among the people. With him God exhausted the series of Prophets and ended the revelation. He then fought for Him those who were turning away from Him and were equating others with Him. Sermon 133

Truly, **you** *call them to a straight path.* **23:73**

O Sustainer of strong mountains that **You** make as pegs for the earth and as a means of support for people, if **You** give us victory over our enemy, we will be saved from excesses and kept on the straight path of truth, but if **You** give them victory over us, then grant us martyrdom and save us from mischief. Sermon 171

Truly, those who believe not in the world to come are ones who move away from the path. **23:74**

Whatever they were ignoring has befallen them. Separation from this world, from which they thought themselves safe, has come to them. They have reached that in the next world which they had been promised. Whatever has befallen them cannot be described. Pangs of death and grief for losing this world have surrounded them. Consequently, their limbs have become languid and their complexion changes. Then death increases its struggle over them. In someone it stands in between him and his power of speaking, although he lies among his people, looking with eyes, hearing with his ears, with full wits and intelligence. He then thinks over how he wasted his life and in what activities he passed his time. He recalls the wealth he collected when he had blinded himself in seeking it and acquired it from fair and foul sources. Now the consequences of collecting it have overtaken him. He gets ready to leave it. It would remain for those who are behind him. They would enjoy it and benefit from it. It would be an easy acquisition for others, but a burden on his back. The person cannot get rid of it. He would thereupon bite his hands with teeth out of shame for what was disclosed to him about his affairs at the time of his death. He would dislike what he coveted during the days of his life and would wish that the one who envied him on account of it and felt jealous over him for it should have amassed it instead of himself. Death would continue affecting his body until his ears, too, would behave like his tongue and lose functioning. So he would lie among his people, neither speaking with his tongue or hearing with his ears. He would be rotating his glance over their faces, watching the movements of their tongues, but not hearing their speaking. Then death would increase its sway over him. His sight would be taken by death as the ears had been taken. The spirit would depart from his body. He would then become a carcass among his own people. They would feel loneliness from him and move away from being near him. He would not join a mourner or respond to a caller. Then they would carry him to a small place in the ground and deliver him in it to face his deeds. They would abandon visiting him. Sermon 108

Even if We had mercy on them and removed the harm which is on them, they would still be resolute in their defiance, wandering unwilling to see. **23:75**
Certainly, We took them with the punishment. Then, they gave not into their Lord nor lower themselves **23:76**
until, when we opened a door for them of a severe punishment. That is when they were ones who are seized with despair! **23:77**

Reform yourselves. Repent. One should praise only God and condemn only one's self. Sermon 16

He it is Who caused you to grow, have the ability to hear and sight and mind. But you give little thanks! **23:78**

Do not forget gratitude when receiving blessings for God has exhausted the excuses before you through clear, shining arguments and open, bright books. Sermon 81

It is He Who made you numerous on the earth and to Him you will be assembled. **23:79**

I praise Him for His continuous mercy and His copious bounties. Sermon 82

It is He Who gives life and causes to die and His is the alteration of nighttime and daytime. Will you not, then, be reasonable? **23:80**
Nay! They said the like of what the ancient ones said. **23:81**

He manifests Himself over the earth with His authority and greatness. He is aware of its inside through His knowledge and understanding. He has power over everything in the earth by virtue of His sublimity and dignity. Nothing from the earth that He may ask for defies Him, nor does it oppose Him so as to overpower Him. No swift-footed creature can run away from Him so as to surpass Him. He is not needy towards any possessing person so that he should feed Him. All things bow to Him and are humble before His greatness. They cannot flee away from His authority to someone else in order to escape His benefit or His harm. There is no parallel for Him who may match Him and no one like Him so as to equal Him. Sermon 186

They said: When we are dead and had been earth dust and bones, will we be ones who are raised up? **23:82**

When the earthquake occurs, the Day of Resurrection approaches with all its severities, the people of every worshipping place cling to it, all the devotees cling to the object of their devotion and all the followers cling to their leader. Then on that day even the opening of an eye in the air and the sound of a footstep on the ground will be assigned its due through His Justice and His Equity. On that day many an argument will prove void and a contention for excuses will stand rejected. Sermon 222

Certainly, we were promised this—we and our fathers—before this. This is nothing but the fables of the ancient ones. **23:83**

Say: To whom belongs the earth and whoever is in it if you had been knowing? **23:84**
They will say: To God! Say: Will you then not recollect? **23:85**
Say: Who is the Lord of the seven heavens and Lord of the Sublime Throne? **23:86**
They will say: It belongs to God! Say: Then, will you not be God-conscious? **23:87**

Everything submits to Him. Everything exists by Him. He is the satisfaction of every poor, dignity of the low, energy for the weak and shelter for the oppressed. Whoever speaks, He hears his speaking. Whoever keeps quiet, He knows his secret. On Him is the livelihood of everyone who lives. To Him returns whoever dies. Sermon 108

Say: In whose hand is the kingdom of everything and He grants protection? No one is granted protection against Him if you had been knowing. **23:88**

My God, I seek **Your** protection from the hardships of the journey, from the grief of returning and from the scene of devastation of property and people. O God, **You** are the companion in the journey. **You** are One Who is left behind for protection of the family. None except **You** can join these two because one who is left behind cannot be a companion in the journey, nor one who is in company on a journey can at the same time be left behind. Sermon 46

They will say: It belongs to God! Say: How, then, are you under a spell! **23:89**
Nay! We brought them The Truth and, truly, they are ones who lie. **23:90**

May God have mercy on the person who, when he sees the truth, supports it, when he sees the wrong, rejects it, and who helps the truth against him who is in the wrong. Sermon 205

God took not to Himself any son, nor had there been any god with Him. For, then, each god would have taken away what he created. Some of them would have ascended over some others. Glory be to God above all that they allege! **23:91**

Everything submits to Him. Everything exists by Him. Sermon 108

He is the One Who Knows the unseen and the visible. Exalted be He above partners they ascribe. **23:92**

I bear witness that *there is no god but God* (Q47:19), the One, there is no partner with Him, nor is there with Him any god other than Himself, and that *Muhammad* (Q48:29), peace and the mercy of God be upon him, is *His servant* (Q17:1) and *Prophet.* (Q7:158) Sermon 35

Say: My Lord! If **You** *will cause me to see what they are promised,* **23:93**
then, assign me not, my Lord, to the folk, the ones who are unjust. **23:94**
Truly, We cause **you** *to see what We promise them as certainly ones who have power.* **23:95**

They took to the right and the left piercing through to the ways of evil and leaving the paths of guidance. Do not make haste for a matter which is to happen and is awaited. Do not wish for delay in what the morrow is to bring for you. For how many people make haste for a matter, but when they get it they begin to wish they had not gotten it? How near is today to the dawning of tomorrow? O my people, this is the time for the occurrence of every promised event and the approach of things which you do not know. Sermon 150

Drive **you** *back evil deeds with what is fairer. We are greater in knowledge of what they allege.* **23:96**

In case you cannot avoid vanity, your vanity should be for good qualities, praiseworthy acts and admirable matters with which the dignified and noble chiefs of the Arab families distinguished themselves such as attractive manners, high thinking, respectable position and good performances. You, too, should show vanity in praiseworthy habits like the protection of the neighbor, the fulfillment of agreements, obedience to the virtuous, opposition to the haughty, extending generosity to others, abstention from rebellion, keeping aloof from bloodshed, doing justice to people, suppressing anger and avoiding trouble on the earth. You should also fear what calamities befell peoples before you on account of their evil deeds and detestable actions. Remember, during good or bad circumstances, what happened to them. Be cautious that you do not become like them. Sermon 192

Say: My Lord! I take refuge with **You** *from the evil suggestions of the satans.* **23:97**
My Lord, I take refuge with **You** *so that they not attend me.* **23:98**

Certainly, Satan has made his ways easy for you and wants to unfasten the knots of religion one by one and to cause division among you in place of unity. Keep away from his evil ideas and enchantments. Accept good advice of one who offers it to you. Preserve it in your minds. Sermon 121

Until when death drew near one of them, he said: My Lord! Return me **23:99**
so that perhaps I will do as one in accord with morality in what I left behind. No indeed! Truly, it is only a word that one who converses says. Ahead of them is a barrier until the Day they are raised up. **23:100**

Well, as for your idea whether this delay is due to my unwillingness for death, then by God I do not care whether I proceed towards death or death advances towards me. As for your impression that it may be due to my misgivings about the people of Syria, well by God, I did not put off war even for a day except in the hope that some group may join me, find guidance through me and see my light with their weak eyes. This is dearer to me than to kill them in the state of their misguidance although they would be bearing their own sins. Sermon 55

When the trumpet will be blown, there will be no talk of kindred among them that Day nor will they demand anything of one another. **23:101**

The human being should secure honor by adopting these qualities. He should fear the Day of Judgment before it arrives. He should appreciate the shortness of his life and the shortness of his sojourn in the place of stay which has only to last for his change over to the next place. He should, therefore, do something for his change over and for the known stages of his departure. Blessed be he who possesses a virtuous heart, obeys one who guides him, keeps away from one who takes him to ruin, catches the path of safety with the help of him who provides him light of guidance and by obeying the leader who commands him, hastens towards guidance before its doors are closed, opens the door of repentance and removes the stain of sins. He has certainly been put on the right path and guided towards the straight path. Sermon 214

Then, whose balance was heavy with good deeds, those, they are the ones who prosper. **23:102**

Where are the seekers of virtue? The paths have already been determined. They have been given the news. For every misguidance, there is a cause. For every breaking of a pledge, there is a misrepresentation. By God, I shall not be like him who listens to the voice of mourning, hears the man who brings news of death and also visits the mourner, yet does not take a lesson. Sermon 148

Among ones whose balance was made light, then, those are those who lost themselves. They will be ones who will dwell in hell forever. **23:103**
Their faces will fry in the fire. They will be ones who are morose in it. **23:104**

Everyone of them is ... alone although they are a group, and they are strangers, even though friends. They are unaware of morning after a night and of evening after a day. The night or the day when they departed has become ever existent for them. They found the dangers of their place of stay more serious than they had apprehended, and they witnessed that its signs were greater than they had guessed. The two objectives, namely Paradise and Hell, have been stretched for them up to a point beyond the reach of fear or hope. Had they been able to speak they would have become dumb to describe what they witnessed or saw. Sermon 220

Be not My signs recounted to you, yet you had been denying them? **23:105**

O my God! **You** know that what we did was not to seek power, nor to acquire anything from the vanities of the world. We rather wanted to restore the signs of **Your** religion and to usher prosperity into **Your** cities so that the oppressed among **Your** creatures might be safe and **Your** forsaken commands might be established. O my God! I am the first who leaned towards **You** and who heard and responded to the call of Islam. No one preceded me in formal prayer except *the Prophet* (Q7:158), peace and the mercy of God be upon him. Sermon 131

They will say: Our Lord! Our misgiving prevailed over us. We had been a folk, ones who go astray. **23:106**
Our Lord! Bring us out of this. Then, if ever we reverted, truly, we will be ones who are unjust. **23:107**
He would say: Be driven away in it and speak not to Me. **23:108**
Truly, there had been a group of people of My servants who say: Our Lord! We believed, so forgive us and have mercy on us for **You** *are Best of the ones who are most merciful.* **23:109**
But you took them to yourselves as a laughing-stock until they caused you to forget My Remembrance and you had been laughing at them. **23:110**

O the Most Merciful of all! ... O my God! Do pour on us **Your** mercy, **Your** blessing,

Your sustenance and **Your** pity.... Surely, **You** are powerful over whatever **You** will. Sermon 143

Truly, I gave recompense this Day for what they endured patiently. Truly, they, they are the ones who are victorious! **23:111**

There remain a few people in whose case the remembrance of their return to God on the Day of Judgment keeps their eyes bent and the awareness of the Resurrection moves them to tears. Some of them are scared away from the world and disperse. Some are frightened and subdued. Some are quiet as if muzzled. Some are praying sincerely. Some are grief-stricken and pain-ridden whom fear has confined to namelessness. Disgrace has shrouded them, so they are in the sea of bitter water, their mouths are closed and their hearts are bruised. They preached until they were tired. They were oppressed until they were disgraced. They were killed until their numbers dwindled. Sermon 32

He said: Lingered you in expectation on the earth for what number of years? **23:112**
They said: We lingered in expectation a day or some of a day. So, ask the ones who count. **23:113**
He said: You lingered in expectation not but a little. If you had but been knowing. **23:114**
Assumed you that We created you in amusement and that to Us you would not be returned? **23:115**
So, exalted be God! The King, The Truth. There is no god but He, the Lord of the Generous Throne! **23:116**

We bear witness that *there is no god, but He.* (Q3:2) Sermon 100

Whoever calls to another god with God of which he has no proof, then, truly, his reckoning is with his Lord. Truly, the ones who are ungrateful will not prosper. **23:117**

Guidance towards virtuous actions is sought through faith while guidance towards faith is achieved through virtuous actions. Knowledge is made to prosper through faith, and death is feared because of knowledge. This world comes to an end with death, while the next world is secured by virtuous actions in this world. For people there is no escape from Resurrection. They are heading for this last end in its appointed course. Sermon 155

Say: My Lord! Forgive and have mercy and ***You*** *are Best of the ones who are most merciful.* **23:118**

O my God! We have come out to **You** from under the curtains and coverings of houses when the beasts and children are crying, seeking **Your** Mercy, hoping for the generosity of **Your** bounty and fearing **Your** chastisement and retribution.... O Most Merciful of all. Sermon 142

CHAPTER 24: THE LIGHT (al-Nūr)

This is a Chapter of the Quran that We caused to descend and We imposed laws in it. We caused to descend signs, clear portents, so that perhaps you will recollect. **24:1**

The Book of God is among you. It speaks and its tongue does not falter. It is a house whose pillars do not fall down, and a power whose supporters are never routed. Sermon 133

The one who is an adulteress and the one who is an adulterer, scourge each one of them one hundred strokes. Let not tenderness for them take you from the judgment of God, if you had been believing in God and the Last Day. Let them bear witness to their punishment by a section of the ones who

believe. **24:2**
The one who is an adulterer will not marry but one who is an adulteress, or one who is a female polytheist. The one who is an adulteress will not marry but one who is an adulterer, or one who is a male polytheist. All that was forbidden to the ones who believe. **24:3**
Those who accuse the ones who are free, chaste (f) and, again, bring not four witnesses, then, scourge them eighty strokes and never accept their testimony. Those, they are the ones who disobey. **24:4**
But those who repented after that and made things right, so, truly, God is Forgiving, Compassionate. **24:5**

O God's human being! I advise you to be God-conscious. It is He Who has furnished illustrations and Who has timed for you your lives. He has given you covering of dress. He has scattered a livelihood for you. He has surrounded you with His knowledge. He has ordained rewards. He has bestowed upon you vast bounties and extensive gifts. He has warned you through far reaching arguments. He has counted you by numbers. He has fixed for you an age to live in this place of testing and house of instruction. You are on a test in this world and have to render an account regarding it. Sermon 82

Those who accuse their spouses—and there be no witnesses but themselves—let the testimony of one of them be four testimonies sworn to God that he is among the ones who are sincere **24:6**
and a fifth that the curse of God be on him, if he had been among the ones who lie. **24:7**
It will drive off the punishment from her if she bears witness with four testimonies sworn to God that he is among the ones who lie **24:8**
and the fifth, that the anger of God be on her if he had been among the ones who are sincere. **24:9**
*and had it not been for the grace of God on you and His mercy, and that God is Accepter of Repentance, Wise—***24:10**

God may shower mercy on him who repents, gives up sins and hastens in performing good acts before his death. Sermon 143

Truly, those who drew near with the calumny are many among you. Assume it not worse for you. Nay! It is good for you. To every man of them is what he deserved of sin. As for those who turned away towards the greater part from among them, there will be a tremendous punishment for him. **24:11**
Why not when you heard about it, thought not the ones who are male believers and the ones who are female believers the better of themselves and have said: This is a clear calumny? **24:12**
Why brought they not about four witnesses for it? As they bring not about witnesses, then, with God, those, they are the ones who lie. **24:13**
If it not were for the grace of God on you and His mercy in the present and in the world to come, certainly, would have afflicted you a tremendous punishment for what you muttered. **24:14**
When you received it on your tongues and said with your mouths of what there is no knowledge, you assume it insignificant while it is serious with God. **24:15**
Why, when you heard it, said you not: It will not be for us to assert this. Glory be to ***You****! This is a serious false charge to harm the reputation of another.* **24:16**

Be aware! The worst speech is that which is untrue. Sermon 84

God admonishes you that you shall never revert to the like of it, if you had been ones who believe. **24:17**

The Prophet (Q33:6) of God, peace and the mercy of God be upon him, said: The belief of a person cannot be firm unless his heart is firm, and his heart cannot be firm unless his tongue is firm. So whoever of you can manage to meet God, the Sublime, in such a position that his hands are unsmeared with the blood of Muslims and their property and his tongue is safe from exposing them, he should do so. Sermon 176

He makes manifest for you the signs. God is Knowing, Wise. **24:18**

I bear witness that *Muhammad* (Q48:29), peace and the mercy of God be upon him, is *His servant* (Q17:1) and *Prophet.* (Q7:158) God sent him with the illustrious religion, effective emblem, the Guarded Tablet, effulgent light, sparkling gleam and decisive injunction in order to dispel doubts, present clear proof, administer warning through signs and to warn of punishments. At that time people had fallen into vices whereby the rope of religion had been broken, the pillars of belief had been shaken, principles had been sacrificed, the system had become topsy turvy, openings were narrow, passages were dark, guidance was unknown and darkness prevailed. Sermon 2

Truly, those who love that indecency be spread about those who believed, they will have a painful punishment in the present and in the world to come. God knows and you know not. **24:19**

Everyone should be God-conscious, should admonish himself, should send forward his repentance and should overpower his desire because his death is hidden from him. His desires deceive him. Satan keeps posted about him. He beautifies his sin for him so that he may commit it. He prompts him to delay repentance until his desires cause him to be the most negligent. Pity is for the negligent person whose life itself would be a proof against him and his own days, passed in sin, will lead him to punishment. Sermon 64

If it were not for the grace of God on you and His mercy, you would be ruined, and that God is Gentle, Compassionate. **24:20**

Praise belongs to God (Q1:2) from Whose mercy no one loses hope, from Whose bounty no one is deprived, from Whose forgiveness no one is disappointed and for Whose worship no one is too high. His mercy never ceases and His bounty never ceases. Sermon 45

O those who believed! Follow not in the steps of Satan. Whoever follows in the steps of Satan, then, truly, he commands depravity, and that which is unlawful. If it were not for the grace of God on you and His mercy, none of you would ever be pure in heart, but God makes pure whom He wills. God is Hearing, Knowing. **24:21**

Be God-conscious and do not place your complaints before him who cannot redress your grievance, nor undo with his opinion what has been made obligatory for you. Certainly, there is no obligation on the leader except what has been devolved on him from God, namely to convey warnings, to exert in good advice, to revive the *sunna*, to enforce penalties on those liable to them and to issue shares to the deserving. So hasten towards knowledge before its vegetation dries up and before you turn yourselves away from seeking knowledge from those who have it. Desist others from the unlawful and abstain from it yourself, because you have been commanded to abstain yourself before abstaining others. Sermon 105

Let those imbued with grace not forswear—and those with plenty among you—to give to those imbued with kinship and to the needy and the ones who emigrate in the way of God. Let them pardon and let them overlook. Love you not that God should forgive you? God is Forgiving, Compassionate. **24:22**

Charity and alms are the best remedy for ailments and calamities. One has to account in the next world for the deeds that he has done in this world. Saying 6

Truly, those who accuse the ones who are free, unwary, chaste female believers were cursed in the present and the world to come and for them will be a serious punishment **24:23**
on a Day when their tongues bear witness against them and their hands and their feet as to what they had been doing. **24:24**

The opponents have entered the oceans of disturbance and have taken to innovations instead of the *sunna*, while the believers have sunk down. The misguided and the liars are speaking. Sermon 153

On that Day God will pay them their account in full, what is their just due. They will know that God, He is The Clear Truth. **24:25**

Know that—may God have mercy on you—you are living at a time when those who speak about right are few, when tongues are loath to utter the truth and those who stick to the right are humiliated. The people of this time are engaged in disobedience. Their youth are wicked, their old men are sinful, their learned men are hypocrites and their speakers are sycophants. Their young ones do not respect their elders, and their rich men do not support the destitute. Sermon 232

The bad females are for the bad males and the bad males are for the bad females. Who are good females are for who are good males and who are good males are for who are good females. Those are ones declared innocent of what others say. For them is forgiveness and generous provision. **24:26**
O those who believed! Enter not houses other than your houses until you announced your presence and greeted the people within. That is better for you so that perhaps you will recollect. **24:27**
If you find not in it anyone, then, enter them not until permission be given to you. If it was said to you: Return, then, return. It is purer for you. God is Knowing of what you do. **24:28**
There is no blame on you in entering houses without ones who are inhabitants wherein you have enjoyment. God knows what you show and what you keep back. **24:29**

Be aware of destroying your manners and changing them ... Sermon 175

Say to the males, ones who believe, to lower their sight and keep their private parts safe. That is purer for them. Truly God is Aware of what they craft. **24:30**

Where are your good people? Where are your virtuous people? Where are your high spirited and generous people? Where are those of you who avoid deceit in their business and remain pure in their behavior? *Truly we belong to God and truly we are ones who return to Him.* (Q2:156) Sermon 128

Say to the females, ones who believe to lower their (f) sight and keep their (f) private parts safe and show not their (f) adornment but what is manifest of it. Let them (f) draw their head coverings over their (f) bosoms; and not show their (f) adornment but to their (f) husbands or their (f) fathers or the fathers of their (f) husbands or their sons or the sons of their (f) husbands or their (f) brothers or the sons of their (f) brothers or the sons of their (f) sisters or their (f) women, or what their (f) right hands possessed, or the ones who heed, imbued with no sexual desire among the men or small male children to whom was not manifest nakedness of women. Let them (f) not stomp their feet so as to be known what they (f) conceal of their adornment. Turn to God altogether for forgiveness. O the ones who believe, so that perhaps you will prosper. **24:31**

Your vanity should be for good qualities, praiseworthy acts, and admirable matters with which the dignified ... families distinguished themselves, as attractive manners, high thinking, respectable position and good performances. Sermon 191

Wed the single among you to the ones in accord with morality of your male bond servants and your female bond servants. If they be poor, God will enrich them of His grace. God is One Who is Extensive, Knowing. **24:32**
Let those who find not the means for marriage have restraint until God enriches them of His grace. For those who are looking for emancipation from among what your right hands possessed, contract with them if you knew good in them. Give them of the wealth of God which He gave you. Compel not your spiritual warriors (f) against their will to prostitution when they (f) wanted chastity, that you be looking for the advantage of this present life. Whoever compels them (f) to it against their (f) will, yet after their (f) compulsion, God will be of them (f), the female, Forgiving, Compassionate. **24:33**

God, the Glorified, did not curse the past ages except because they had left off asking others to do good acts and refraining them from bad acts. Sermon 191

Certainly, We caused to descend to you manifest signs and a parable of those who passed away before you and an admonishment for ones who are God-conscious. **24:34**

One of the firm decisions of God in the Wise Reminder (Quran), upon which He bestows reward or gives punishment and through which He likes or dislikes, is that it will not benefit a person, even though he exerts himself and acts sincerely, if he leaves this world to meet God with one of these acts without repenting, namely that he believed in a partner with God during his obligatory worship or appeased his own anger by killing an individual or spoke about acts committed by others or sought fulfillment of his needs from people by introducing an innovation in his religion or met people with a double face or moved among them with a double tongue. Understand this because an illustration is a guide for its like. Sermon 153

God is the Light of the heavens and the earth. The parable of His Light is as a niche in which there is a lamp. The lamp is in a glass. The glass is as if it had been a glittering star, kindled from a blessed olive tree, neither eastern nor western, whose oil of the olive is about to illuminate although no fire touches it. Light on light, God guides to His Light whom He wills! God propounds parables for humanity, and God is Knowing of everything. **24:35**

I am among you like a lamp in the darkness. Whoever enters by it will be lit from it. So listen, O people, preserve it and remain attentive with the ears of your hearts so that you may understand. Sermon 187

The Light is lit in houses God gave permission to be lifted up and that His Name be remembered in it. Glorifying Him at the first part of the day and the eventide **24:36**
are men whom neither trade nor trading diverts from the remembrance of God and the performing the formal prayer and the giving of purifying alms for they fear a Day when the hearts will go to and fro and their sight, **24:37**

that God gives recompense to them according to the fairer of what they did and increases even more for them from His grace. God provides to whom He wills without reckoning. **24:38**

Truly, God has made the remembrance a polish for the hearts by which they hear after being unwilling to hear and see after being unwilling to see and yield after being resistant ... Indeed, there is a special group who belong to the remembrance. They have adopted it in place of the world, such that *neither trade nor trading diverts from the remembrance of God.* (Q24:37) They spend the days of their life in it ... It is as though they had left this world for the hereafter, and they are there, witnessing what is beyond this world. Sermon 198*

As for those who were ungrateful, their actions are like a mirage in a spacious plain. The thirsty one assumes it to be water until he drew near it. He finds it to be nothing. Instead, he found God with him Who paid his account in full, reckoning and God is Swift at reckoning. **24:39**

Be aware the world is wrapping itself up. It has announced its departure. Its known things have become strangers and it is speedily moving backward. It is advancing its inhabitants towards destruction and driving its neighbors towards death. Its sweet enjoyments have become sour. Its clear things have become polluted. Consequently, what has remained of it is just like the remaining water in a vessel or a mouthful of water in a measuring cup. If a thirsty person drinks it, his thirst is not quenched. Sermon 52

Or they are like the shadows in an obscure sea, overcome by a wave, above which is a wave, above which are clouds, shadows, some above some others. When he brought out his hand he almost sees it not. Whomever God assigns no light for him, there is no light for him. **24:40**

When the cloud prostrated itself on the ground and delivered all the water it carried on itself God grew vegetation on the plain earth and herbage on dry mountains. As a result, the earth felt pleased at being decorated with its gardens and wondered at her dress of soft vegetation and the ornaments of its blossoms. God made all this the means of sustenance for the people and feed for the beasts. He has opened up highways in its expanse and has established minarets of guidance for those who tread on its highways. Sermon 91

*Have **you** not considered that glorifies God whatever is in the heavens and the earth and the birds, ones standing in ranks? Each knew its formal prayer and its glorification. God is Knowing of what they accomplish.* **24:41**

He also knows the spots in the inner sheaths of leaves where fruits grow, the hiding places of beasts, namely caves in mountains and valleys, the hiding holes of mosquitoes on the trunks of trees and their herbage, the sprouting points of leaves in the branches, the dripping points of semen passing through passages of the loins, small rising clouds and the big giant ones, the drops of rain in the thick clouds, the particles of dust scattered by whirlwinds through their skirts, the lines erased by rain floods, the movements of insects on sand-dunes, the nests of winged creatures on the cliffs of mountains and the singing of chattering birds in the gloom of their brooding places. Sermon 91

To God belongs the dominion of the heavens and the earth. To God is the Homecoming. **24:42**

Praise belongs to God (Q1:2) Who is High above all else. He is Near the creation through His bounty. He is the Giver of all reward and distinction and Dispeller of all calamities and hardships. I praise Him for His continuous mercy and His copious bounties. Sermon 82

Have **you** *not considered how God propels clouds and, again, brings what is between them together? Again, He lays them into a heap.* **You** *see the rain drops go forth in the midst. He sends down from the heaven mountains of rain in which there is hail. He lights it on whom He wills and turns away from it whom He wills. The gleams of His lightning almost take away the sight.* **24:43**

O my God! Give rain from **You** which should be life giving, satisfying, thorough, wide-scattered, purified, blissful, plentiful and invigorating. Its vegetation should be exuberant, its branches full of fruits and its leaves green. With it **You** reinvigorate the weak among **Your** creatures and bring back to life the dead among **Your** cities. O my God! Give rain from **You** with which our high lands are covered with green herbage, streams flow, our sides grow green, our fruit thrive, our cattle prosper, our far-flung areas are watered and our dry areas receive its benefit, with **Your** vast blessing and immeasurable grant on **Your** distressed universe and **Your** untamed beasts. Pour upon us rain which is drenching, continuous and heavy; wherein one cycle of rain clashes with the other and one rain drop pushes another into a continuous chain. Its lightning should not be deceptive, its cheek not rainless, its white clouds not scattered and rain not light, so that the famine-stricken thrive with its abundant herbage and the drought-stricken come to life with its bliss. Certainly, **You** pour down rain after the people lose hopes and spread **Your** mercy, since **You** are the Guardian, the praiseworthy. Sermon 115

God turns around and around the nighttime and the daytime. Truly, in this is a lesson for those imbued with insight. **24:44**

When Almighty God created the openings of the atmosphere, the expanse of firmament and strata of winds, He flowed into it water whose waves were stormy and whose surges leapt one over the other. He loaded it on dashing wind and breaking typhoons, ordered them to shed it back as rain, gave the wind control over the vigor of the rain, and acquainted it with its limitations. The wind blew under it while water flowed furiously over it. Sermon 91

God created every moving creature from water. Among them there is what walks on its belly and of them there is what walks on two feet and of them there is what walks on four. God creates what He wills. Truly, God is Powerful over everything. **24:45**

When the excitement of water subsided under the earth's sides and under the weight of the high and lofty mountains placed on its shoulders, God flowed springs of water from its high tops and distributed them through plains and low places and moderated their movement by fixed rocks and high mountain tops. Then its trembling came to a standstill because of the penetration of mountains in various parts of its surface and their being fixed in its deep areas, and their standing on its plains. Sermon 91

Certainly, We caused manifest signs to descend. God guides whom He wills to a straight path. **24:46**

I bear witness that *there is no god but God* (Q47:19), by virtue of belief, certainty, sincerity and conviction. I also bear witness that *Muhammad* (Q48:29), peace and the mercy of God be upon him, is *His servant* (Q17:1) and *Prophet* (Q7:158) whom He deputed when the signs of guidance were obliterated and the ways of religion were desolate. So he threw open the truth, gave advice to the people, guided them towards righteousness and ordered them to be moderate. May God bless him ... Sermon 194

They say: We believed in God and the Messenger, and we obeyed. Again, a group of people among them turn away after this. Those are not of the ones who believe. **24:47**

Be God-conscious like him who listened to good advice and bowed before it. When he committed sin, he admitted it. When he felt fear, he acted virtuously. When he apprehended, he hastened towards good acts. When he believed, he performed virtuous acts. When he was asked to take a lesson from the happenings of this world, he did take the lesson. When he was asked to desist, he abstained from evil. When he responded to the call of God, he leaned towards Him. When he turned back to evil, he repented. When he followed, he almost imitated. When he was shown the right path, he saw it. Sermon 82

When they were called to God and His Messenger to give judgment among them, then, a group of people among them are ones who turn aside. **24:48**
But if they would be in the right, they would approach him as ones who are yielding. **24:49**
Is there a sickness in their hearts? Or were they in doubt? Or be they fearful that God and His Messenger will be unjust to them? Nay! Those, they are the ones who are unjust. **24:50**

With *the Prophet* (Q7:158), peace and the mercy of God be upon him, God exhausted the series of Prophets and ended the revelation. He then fought for Him those who were turning away from Him and were equating others with Him. Sermon 133

The only saying of the ones who believe had been—when they were called to God and His Messenger that He give judgment between them—to say: We heard and obeyed. Those, they are the ones who prosper. **24:51**
Whoever obeys God and His Messenger and dreads God and is God-conscious, those, they are the ones who are victorious. **24:52**

If they had not acknowledged His Godhead and obeyed Him, He would not have made them the place for His throne, the abode of His angels and the destination: *To Him Words of what is good rise and He exalts an action in accord with morality* ...(Q35:10) of the creatures. Sermon 182

They swore by God their most earnest oaths that if ***you*** *would command them, they would go forth. Say: Swear not; honorable obedience is better. Truly God is Aware of what you do.* **24:53**

You should therefore counsel each other for the fulfillment of your obligations and co-operate with each other. However extremely eager a person may be to secure the pleasure of God, and however fully he strives for it, he cannot discharge his obligation for obedience to God, the Almighty, as is really due to Him, and it is an obligatory right of God over the people that they should advise each other to the best of their ability and co-operate with each other for the establishment of truth among them. Sermon 216

Say: Obey God and obey the Messenger. But if you turn away, then, on him was only what was loaded on him, and on you was only what was loaded on you. If you obey him, you will be truly guided. There is not a duty on the Messenger but the delivering of the clear message. **24:54**

I bear witness that *Muhammad* (Q48:29), peace and the mercy of God be upon him, is *His servant* (Q17:1) and His *Prophet.* (Q7:158) He sent him for enforcement of His commands, for exhausting His pleas and for presenting warnings against eternal punishment. Sermon 82

God promised those who have believed among you and did as the ones in accord with morality, that He will make them successors in the earth, even as He made of those before them successors and He will establish for them their way of life firmly by which He was content with them and He will substitute a place of sanctuary in place of their fear: They shall worship Me—ascribe nothing as partners with Me. Whoever was ungrateful after that, then, those, they are the ones who disobey. **24:55**

O God's human being! The good that God has promised should not be abandoned and the evil from which He has refrained should not be coveted. O God's human being! Fear the day when actions will be reckoned. There will be much quaking and even children will get old. Sermon 157

Perform the formal prayer and give the purifying alms and obey the Messenger so that perhaps you will find mercy. **24:56**

In God's authority lies the safety of your affairs. Therefore, render Him such obedience as is neither blameworthy nor insincere. By God, you must do so otherwise God will take away from you the power of Islam and will never thereafter return it to you until it reverts to others. Sermon 169

Assume not those who were ungrateful that they are ones who will frustrate Him in the region. Their place of shelter will be the fire and how miserable the Homecoming! **24:57**

God was being disobeyed. Satan was given support. Faith was forsaken. As a result, the pillars of religion crumbled. Any trace of them was lost. Its passages were destroyed. Its streets fell into decay. People obeyed Satan and tread his path. They sought water from his watering places. Satan's banners flew in the wind through them. His standard of vice was raised. They trampled people under their hoofs and tread upon them with their feet. Vice attained full stature. The people immersed in them were led astray, perplexed, ignorant and seduced as though they were in a good house (Mecca) with bad neighbors (ungrateful Quraysh). Instead of sleep, the people had wakefulness. Instead of antimony, they had tears in their eyes. They were in a land where the lips of the learned bridled while the words of the ignorant were honored. Sermon 2

O those who believed! Let them ask permission—those whom your right hands possessed (f) and those who reach not puberty—three times: Before the dawn formal prayer, when you lay down your garments at the time of noon and after the time of night formal prayer. These are the three times of privacy for you. There is not on you nor on them blame after these. Other than these, go about some of you with some others. Thus, God makes manifest to you the signs. God is Knowing, Wise. **24:58**

When infant children were fully grown among you, then, let them ask permission as asked permission those who were before them. Thus, God makes manifest for you His signs. God is Knowing, Wise. **24:59**

Women who are past child-bearing, those who hope not for marriage, there is no blame on them (f) if they lay down their (f) garments, not as ones who flaunt themselves and their (f) adornment. That they have restraint is better for them (f), and God is Hearing, Knowing. **24:60**

There is no fault on the blind nor fault on the lame nor fault on the sick nor on yourselves that you eat from your houses or the houses of your fathers or the houses of your mothers or the houses of your brothers or the houses of your sisters or the houses of your paternal uncles or the houses of your paternal aunts or the houses of your maternal uncles or the houses of your maternal aunts or of that for which you possess its keys or your ardent friend. There is no blame on you that you eat altogether or separately. But when you entered houses, then, greet one another with a greeting from God, one that is blessed and what is good. Thus, God makes manifest for you the signs so that perhaps you will be reasonable. **24:61**

I bear witness that *there is no god but God* (Q47:19), by virtue of belief, certainty, sincerity and conviction. I also bear witness that *Muhammad* (Q48:29), peace and the mercy of God be upon him, is *His servant* (Q17:1), and *Prophet* (Q7:158) whom He deputed when the signs of guidance were obliterated and the ways of religion were desolate. So he threw open the truth, gave advice to the people, guided them towards righteousness and ordered them to be moderate. May God bless him ... Sermon 194

The ones who believe are only those who believe in God and His Messenger. When they had been with him on a collective matter, they go not until they asked his permission. Truly, those who ask ***your*** *permission, those are those who believed in God and His Messenger. So, when they ask* ***your*** *permission for some of their affairs, give permission to whom* ***you*** *had willed of them, and ask God for forgiveness for them. Truly, God is Forgiving, Compassionate.* **24:62**

God is Merciful. Faith is straight. *The Prophet* (Q7:158), peace and the mercy of God be upon him, is the holder of knowledge. Sermon 149

The supplication of the Messenger among you is not as the supplication of some of you on some other. Surely, God knows those who slip away under cover. Let those who go against his command beware so that a test should not light on them or a painful punishment not light on them. **24:63**

God deputized *the Prophet* (Q7:158), peace and the mercy of God be upon him, after a gap from the previous Prophets when there was much talk among the people. With him God exhausted the series of Prophets and ended the revelation. He then fought for Him those who were turning away from Him and were equating others with Him. Sermon 133

Surely, to God belongs whatever is in the heavens and the earth. Surely, He knows what you did. On the Day when they are returned to Him, then, He will tell them what their hands did, and God is Knowing of everything. **24:64**

People did not take light from the lights of his wisdom, nor did they produce flame from the flint of sparkling knowledge. So in this matter, they are like grazing cattle and hard stones. Nevertheless, hidden things have appeared for those who perceive. The face of right has become clear for the wanderer. The approaching moment has raised the veil from its face. Signs have appeared for those who search for them. Sermon 108

Chapter 25: The Criterion (al-Furqān)

Blessed be He Who sent down the Criterion between right and wrong to His servant so that he be a warner to the worlds, **25:1**

God sent *Muhammad* (Q48:29), peace and the mercy of God be upon him, as a witness, giver of good tidings and warner, the best in the universe as a child and the most chaste as a grown up person, the purest of the purified in conduct, the most generous of those who are approached for generosity. Sermon 105

He to Whom belongs the dominion of the heavens and the earth, and Who takes not to Himself a son. There be no ascribed associate with Him in the dominion. He created everything and ordained it a foreordaining. **25:2**

I bear witness that *there is no god but God* (Q47:19), the One, there is no partner with Him, nor is there with Him any god other than Himself, and that *Muhammad* (Q48:29), peace and the mercy of God be upon him, is *His servant* (Q17:1) and *Prophet.* (Q7:158) Sermon 35

Yet they took gods to themselves other than Him who create nothing and are themselves created. They neither possess for themselves hurt nor profit nor have they dominion over death, nor this life, nor rising up. **25:3**
Those who were ungrateful said: This is nothing but a calumny he devised and other folk assisted him. So, surely, they brought about injustice and untruth. **25:4**

God has forbidden you from tyranny and injustice. Even if there had not been any fear of punishment for these inequities, the mere reward of being just, kind and human would have been such that there could not have been any excuse for not trying to achieve it. Letter 51

They said: Fables of the ancient ones that he caused to be written down! They are to be related from memory to him at early morning dawn and eventide. **25:5**
Say: It was caused to descend by He who knows the secret in the heavens and the earth. Truly, He had been Forgiving, Compassionate. **25:6**

Praise belongs to God (Q1:2) Who is High above all else. He is Near the creation through His bounty. He is the Giver of all reward and distinction and Dispeller of all calamities and hardships. I praise Him for His continuous mercy and His copious bounties. Sermon 82

They said: What Messenger is this that he eats food and walks in the markets? Why was an angel not caused to descend to him to be a warner with him? **25:7**
Or why is not a treasure cast down to him or why is there not a garden for him so that he may eat from it? The ones who are unjust said: You follow nothing but a bewitched man. **25:8**
Look on how they propounded for ***you*** *parables for they went astray and are not able to find a way.* **25:9**
Blessed be He Who, had He willed, assigned for ***you*** *better than that, Gardens beneath which rivers run and He will assign for* ***you*** *palaces.* **25:10**

God, the Almighty, has sent down a guiding Book wherein He has explained virtue and vice. You should adopt the course of virtue, whereby you will have guidance. Detach yourself from the direction of vice, so that you remain on the right way. Sermon 167

Nay! They denied the Hour. We made ready a blaze for whoever denied the Hour. **25:11**

Your ultimate goal of reward or punishment is before you. Sermon 21

When it saw them from a far place, they heard it raging furiously and roaring. **25:12**
When they were cast down into it, a troubling place, ones who are chained, they called for damnation. **25:13**

It will be said to them: Call not today for a single damnation, but call for many damnations! **25:14**

Everyone of them is ... alone although they are a group, and they are strangers, even though friends. They are unaware of morning after a night and of evening after a day. The night or the day when they departed has become ever existent for them. They found the dangers of their place of stay more serious than they had apprehended. They witnessed that its signs were greater than they had guessed. Sermon 220

Say: Is that better or the Garden of Infinity that was promised the ones who are God-conscious? It had been a recompense for them and a Homecoming. **25:15**

For them in it will be whatever they will, ones who will dwell in it forever. That had been from ***your*** *Lord a promise, one that is besought.* **25:16**

Blessed be he who possesses a virtuous heart, who obeys one who guides him, desists from him who takes to ruin, catches the path of safety with the help of him who provides him light of guidance and by obeying the leader who commands him, hastens towards guidance before its doors are closed, opens the door of repentance and removes the stain of sins. He has certainly been put on the right path and guided towards the straight road. Sermon 213

On the Day He will assemble them and what they worship other than God. To them He will say: Was it you who caused these My servants to go astray? Or went they astray from the way? **25:17**

When the earthquake occurs, the Day of Resurrection approaches with all its severities, the people of every worshipping place cling to it, all the devotees cling to the object of their devotion and all the followers cling to their leader. Then on that day even the opening of an eye in the air and the sound of a footstep on the ground will be assigned its due through His Justice and His Equity. On that day many an argument will prove void and a contention for excuses will stand rejected. Sermon 222

They would say: Glory be to ***You****! It had not been fit and proper for us to take to ourselves any protectors other than* ***You****. But* ***You*** *gave them enjoyment and their fathers until they forgot the Remembrance and had been a lost folk.* **25:18**

So, surely, they denied you in what you say. Then, you will neither be able to turn away from it, nor help. Whoever does wrong among you, We will cause him to experience the great punishment. **25:19**

No one will sit beside this Quran, but that when he rises he will achieve one addition or one diminution—addition in his guidance or elimination in his spiritual blindness. You should also know that no one will need anything after guidance from the Quran and no one will be free from want before guidance from the Quran. Therefore, seek cure from it for your ailments and seek its assistance in your distress. It contains a cure for the worst diseases, namely unbelief, hypocrisy, revolt and misguidance. Pray to God through it and turn to God with its love. Do not ask the people through it. There is nothing like it through which the people should turn to God, the Sublime. Sermon 176

We sent not before ***you*** *any ones who are sent but that, truly, they eat food and walk in the markets. We made some of you as a test for some others. Will you endure patiently, and* ***your*** *Lord had been Seeing.* **25:20**

O God's human being! Where are those who were allowed long ages to live? They enjoyed bounty. They were taught. They learned. They were given time. They passed it in vain. They were kept healthy. They forgot their duty. They were allowed a long period of life, were handsomely provided for, were warned of grievous punishment and were promised great rewards. You should avoid sins that lead to destruction and vices that attract the wrath of God. Sermon 82

Those who hope not for a meeting with Us said: Why were angels not caused to descend to us and why see we not our Lord? Surely, they grew arrogant among themselves, defiant, turning in great disdain. **25:21**
On a Day they will see the angels there will be no good tidings for the ones who sin. They will say: Unapproachable! Banned! **25:22**

Occupation in His worship has made the angels carefree, and realities of faith have served as a link between them and His knowledge. Their belief in Him has made them concentrate on Him. They long from Him not from others. They have tasted the sweetness of His knowledge and have drunk from the satiating cup of His love. The roots of His fear have been implanted in the depth of their hearts. Consequently, they have bent their straight backs through His worship. The length of the humility and extreme nearness has not removed from them the rope of their fear. Sermon 91

We will advance on whatever actions they did. We will make them as scattered dust. **25:23**

Be aware and act during the period of attraction just as you act during a period of dread. Be aware! Truly, I have not seen one who covets Paradise to be asleep, nor a dreader from hellfire to be asleep. Be aware, he whom right does not benefit must suffer the harm of the wrong. He whom guidance does not keep firm will be led away by misguidance towards destruction. Sermon 28

The Companions of the Garden on that Day will have the best resting place and the fairer place of noonday rest. **25:24**

Mind the obligations! Mind the obligations! Fulfill them for God and they will take you to the Garden. Surely, God has made unlawful the things which are not unknown and made lawful the things which are without defect. Sermon 167

On a Day when heaven will be split open with the cloud shadows and the angels were sent down, a sending down successively, **25:25**
on that Day the true dominion will belong to The Merciful. It will be a Day difficult for the ones who are ungrateful. **25:26**

Action! Action! Then look at the end, the end, and remain steadfast, steadfast. Thereafter exercise endurance, endurance, and God-consciousness, God-consciousness. You have an objective. Proceed towards your objective. You have a sign. Take guidance from your sign. Islam has an objective. Proceed towards its objective. Proceed towards God by fulfilling His rights which He has enjoined upon you. He has clearly stated His demands for you. Sermon 176

On a Day when one who is unjust will bite his hands, he will say: Would that I took myself to a way with the Messenger! **25:27**
Ah! Woe is me! Would that I take not to myself so-and-so as a friend! **25:28**

Certainly, he caused me to go astray from the Remembrance after it drew near me. Satan had been a betrayer of the human being. **25:29**

Truly, Satan has collected his group and assembled his horse-men and foot-soldiers. Truly, I have my sagacity. I have neither deceived myself, nor ever been deceived. By God, I shall fill to the brim a cistern for them from which I alone would draw water. They can neither turn away from it, nor return to it. Sermon 10

The Messenger said: O my Lord! Truly, my folk took this, the Quran to themselves, as that which is to be abandoned! **25:30**

You should know that you will never know guidance unless you know who has abandoned it, you will never abide by the pledges of the Quran unless you know who has broken them, and will never cling to it unless you know who has forsaken it. Sermon 146

Thus, We assigned for every Prophet an enemy of the ones who sin. ***Your*** *Lord sufficed as one who guides and as a helper.* **25:31**

God has warned you of the enemy that steals into hearts and stealthily speaks into ears, and thereby misguides and brings about destruction, makes false promises and keeps you under wrong impressions. He represents evil sins in attractive shape and shows as light even serious crimes. Sermon 82

Those who were ungrateful said: Why was the Quran not sent down to him all at once? Thus, We will make firm ***your*** *mind by it. We chanted a chanting.* **25:32**

The Book of God is that through which you see, you speak and you hear. Its one part speaks for the other part, and one part bears witness to the other. It does not create differences about God, nor does it mislead its own follower from the path of God. You are joined together in hatred of each other and in the growing of herbage on your covering inner impurity by good appearance outside. You are sincere with one another in your love of desires and bear enmity against each other in earning wealth. The evil spirit (Satan) has perplexed you and deceit has misled you. I seek the help of God for myself and you. Sermon 133

They bring ***you*** *no parable. We brought about The Truth to* ***you*** *and fairer exposition.* **25:33**

Know that—may God have mercy on you—you are living at a time when those who speak about right are few, when tongues are loath to utter the truth and those who stick to the right are humiliated. The people of this time are engaged in disobedience. Their youth are wicked, their old men are sinful, their learned men are hypocrites, and their speakers are sycophants. Their young ones do not respect their elders, and their rich men do not support the destitute. Sermon 232

Those who will be assembled on their faces in hell, those are worse placed, ones who go astray from the way. **25:34**

Hell! Everyone of them is ... alone although they are a group, and they are strangers, even though friends. They are unaware of morning after a night and of evening after a day. The night or the day when they departed has become ever existent for them. They found the dangers of their place of stay more serious than they had apprehended, and they witnessed that its signs were greater than they had guessed. The two objectives, namely Paradise and Hell, have been stretched for them up to a point beyond the reach of fear or hope. Had they been able to speak they would have become dumb to describe what they witnessed or saw. Sermon 220

Certainly, We gave Moses the Book and assigned his brother Aaron to him as a minister. **25:35**
We said: You both go to the folk who denied Our signs. Then, We destroyed them, an utter destruction. **25:36**
The folk of Noah when they denied the Messengers, We drowned them. We made them as a sign for humanity. We made ready for the ones who are unjust a painful punishment, **25:37**
and Ad and Thamud and the Companions of Rass and many generations in between that. **25:38**
We propounded parables for each of them. We shattered each a shattering. **25:39**
Certainly, they approached the town where the reprehensible rain was rained down on them. Is it that they see it not? Nay! They had been not hoping for any rising up. **25:40**
When they saw **you**, *they take* **you** *to themselves but in mockery: Is this the one whom God raised up as a Messenger?* **25:41**

I bear witness that Muhammad, peace and the mercy of God be upon him, is His servant and His Prophet whom He deputed when the signs of guidance were obliterated and the ways of religion were desolate. So he threw open the truth, gave advice to the people, guided them towards righteousness and ordered them to be moderate. May God bless him. Sermon 195

He was about to cause us to go astray from our gods, if it were not that we endured patiently in them! They will know at the time when they see the punishment, who is one who goes astray from the way. **25:42**

Pity is for the negligent person whose life itself would be a proof against him and his own days, passed in sin, will lead him to punishment. Sermon 64

Had **you** *considered him who took to himself his own desires as his god? Would* **you**, *then, be over him a trustee?* **25:43**

I bear witness that *there is no god but God.* (Q47:19) He is One. There is no partner with Him. He is the First, such that nothing was before Him. He is the Last, such that there is not limit for Him. Imagination cannot catch any of His qualities. Hearts cannot entertain belief about His nature. Analysis and division cannot be applied to Him. Eyes and hearts cannot compare Him. Sermon 84

Or assume **you** *that most of them hear or are reasonable? They are not but as flocks. Nay! They are ones who go astray from a way.* **25:44**

People obeyed Satan and tread his path. They sought water from his watering places. Satan's banners flew in the wind through them. His standard of vice was raised. Sermon 2

Have **you** *not considered how* **your** *Lord stretched out the shade? If He willed, He would make it a place of rest. Again, We made the sun an indicator over it.* **25:45**
Again, We seized it to Us an easy seizing. **25:46**

On that day many an argument will prove void and a contention for excuses will stand rejected. Sermon 222

It is He Who made the nighttime a garment for you and sleep a rest and made the daytime for rising. **25:47**

Sleeping with certainty is better than praying with doubt. Saying 97

It is He Who sent the winds, bearers of good tidings in advance of His Mercy. We caused to descend undefiled water from heaven **25:48**
that We give life by it to a lifeless land and with it We satiate. We created flocks on it and many humans. **25:49**
Certainly, We diversified among them so that they recollect. Then, most of humanity refused everything, but disbelief. **25:50**

Avoid confusion in your ideas. Do not let disbelief take hold of your mind because the first will lead you to agnosticism and the others towards errors and sins. When you are thus prepared to solve any problem and you are sure that you possess a clear mind, a sincere and firm desire to reach the truth, to say the correct thing and to do the correct deed, then carefully go through the advice that I am leaving for you. Letter 31

If We willed, We would have raised up a warner in every town. **25:51**

God sent the *Prophet* (Q33:6), peace and the mercy of God be upon him, for enforcement of His commands, for exhausting His pleas and for presenting warnings against eternal punishment. Sermon 82

So, obey not the ones who are ungrateful and struggle against them thereby with a great struggle. **25:52**

If you refuse to stop claiming that I have gone wrong and been misled, why do you consider that the common men among the followers of *the Prophet* (Q7:158), peace and the mercy of God be upon him, have gone astray like me, and accuse them with my wrong, and hold them ungrateful on account of my sins? You are holding your swords on your shoulders and using them right and wrong. You are confusing those who have committed sins with those who have not. Sermon 127

It is He Who let forth the two seas—this, agreeable and water of the sweetest kind and this, salty, bitter. He made between the two that which was unapproachable, a banned barrier. **25:53**

Praise belongs to God (Q1:2) Whose worth cannot be described by speakers,Whose bounties cannot be counted by calculators and Whose claim to obedience cannot be satisfied by those who attempt to do so Whom the height of intellectual courage cannot appreciate, and the depths of understanding cannot reach. He for Whose description no limit has been laid down, no eulogy exists, no time is ordained and no duration is fixed. He brought forth creation through His Omnipotence, dispersed winds through His Compassion, and made firm the shaking earth with rocks. Sermon 1

It is He Who created a mortal from water and made for him kindred by blood and kin by marriage. ***Your*** *Lord had been ever Powerful.* **25:54**

God flowed springs of water from its high tops and distributed them through plains and low places and moderated their movement by fixed rocks and high mountain tops. Sermon 91

They worship other than God what neither profits them nor hurts them. The one who is ungrateful had been ever a sustainer against his Lord. **25:55**

Instead of sleep, the people had wakefulness. Instead of antimony, they had tears in their eyes. They were in a land where the lips of the learned were bridled while the words of the ignorant were honored. Sermon 2

We sent ***you*** *not, but as one who gives good tidings and as a warner.* **25:56**

Certainly, God made Muhammad, peace and mercy of God be upon him, a sign for the Day of Judgment. a conveyor of tidings for Paradise and a warner of retribution. He left this world hungry, but entered upon the next world safe. He did not lay one stone upon another to make a house until he departed and responded to the call of God. How great is God's blessing in that He blessed us with *the Prophet* (Q7:158), peace and the mercy of God be upon him, as a predecessor whom we follow and a leader behind whom we tread. Sermon 159

Say: I ask of you no compensation for this but that whoever willed should take himself on a way to his Lord. **25:57**

There is no doubt that God sent down *the Prophet* (Q7:158), peace and the mercy of God be upon him, as a guide with an eloquent Book and a standing command. No one will be ruined by it except one who ruins himself. Certainly, only doubtful innovations cause ruin except those from which God may protect. In God's authority lies the safety of your affairs. Therefore, render Him such obedience as is neither blameworthy, nor insincere. By God, you must do so otherwise God will take away from you the power of Islam and will never thereafter return it to you until it reverts to others. Sermon 169

Put ***your*** *trust in the Living Who is Undying and glorify His praise. He sufficed to be aware of the impieties of His servants,* **25:58**

Praise belongs to God (Q1:2) Creator of the human being. Sermon 163

He Who created the heavens and the earth and whatever is between the two in six days, again, He turned His attention to the Throne. The Merciful! Ask the aware, then, about Him. **25:59**

There remain a few people in whose case the remembrance of their return to God on the Day of Judgment keeps their eyes bent and the awareness of the Resurrection moves them to tears. Some of them are scared away from the world and disperse. Some are frightened and subdued. Some are quiet as if muzzled. Some are praying sincerely. Some are grief-stricken and pain-ridden whom fear has confined to namelessness. Disgrace has shrouded them, so they are in the sea of bitter water, their mouths are closed and their hearts are bruised. They preached until they were tired. They were oppressed until they were disgraced. They were killed until their numbers dwindled. Sermon 32

When it was said to them: Prostrate yourselves to The Merciful, they said: What is The Merciful? Will we prostrate ourselves to what ***you*** *have commanded us? It increased aversion in them.* **25:60** *Blessed be He Who made constellations in the heaven and made in it a light-giving lamp and an illuminating moon.* **25:61**

I am among you like a lamp in the darkness. Whoever enters by it will be lit from it. So listen, O people, preserve it and remain attentive with the ears of your hearts so that you may understand. Sermon 187

He it is Who made the nighttime and the daytime to follow in succession for who wanted to recollect, or who wanted thankfulness. **25:62**

O my God! **You** know that what we did was not to seek power, nor to acquire anything from the vanities of the world. We rather wanted to restore the signs of **Your** religion and to usher prosperity into **Your** cities so that the oppressed among **Your** creatures might be safe and **Your** forsaken commands might be established. Sermon 131

The servants of The Merciful are those who walk on the earth in meekness. When the ones who are ignorant addressed them, they said: Peace! **25:63**

Do pour on us **Your** mercy, **Your** blessing, **Your** sustenance and **Your** pity, and make us enjoy a drink which benefits us, quenches our thirst, produces green herbage by which all that has died down grows again and all that had withered is revived. It should bring about the benefit of freshness and plentifulness of ripe fruits. With it plains may be watered, rivers may begin flowing, plants may pick up foliage and prices may come down. Surely, **You** are powerful over whatever **You** will. Sermon 143

Those who spend the night with their Lord as ones who prostrate themselves and are upright, **25:64**
and those who say: Our Lord! Turn You away the punishment of hell from us. Truly, its punishment will be continuous torment. **25:65**
How evil a habitation and resting place. **25:66**

Everyone of them is ... alone although they are a group, and they are strangers, even though friends. They are unaware of morning after a night and of evening after a day. The night or the day when they departed has become ever existent for them. They found the dangers of their place of stay more serious than they had apprehended. They witnessed that its signs were greater than they had guessed. Sermon 220

Those who, when they spent, neither exceed all bounds, nor are they tightfisted, but had been between that, a just stand: **25:67**
Those who call not to another god with God nor kill the soul which God forbade but rightfully, nor commit adultery. Whoever disregards and commits this will meet sinfulness. **25:68**

O you who are old, whom old age has grayed your hair, how will you feel when rings of fire will touch the bones of your neck, and handcuffs hold so hard that they eat away the flesh of the forearms? Be God-conscious! God-conscious! O crowd of people, while you are in good health before sickness grips you and you are in ease before straitness overtakes you, you should try for the release of your necks before their mortgage is foreclosed, your eyes, thin down bellies, use your feet, spend your money, take your bodies and spend them over yourselves, and do not be miserly about them, because God, the Glorified, has said: *O those who believed! If you help God, He will help you and make firm your feet.* (Q47:7) Sermon 182

The punishment will be multiplied for him on the Day of Resurrection. He will dwell in it forever, as one who is despised. **25:69**

They are emulating each other and proceeding in groups towards the final objective and the rendezvous of death, until when matters come to a close, the world dies and the Resurrection draws near. Sermon 82

Whoever has repented and believed and whose actions were done as one in accord with morality, for those God will substitute for their evil deeds benevolence. God had been Forgiving, Compassionate. **25:70**
Whoever repented and did as one in accord with morality, he, truly, repents to God, turning in repentance. **25:71**

Among the proofs of His creation is the creation of the skies which are fastened without pillars and stand without support. He called them. They responded obediently and humbly without being lazy or loathsome. If they had not acknowledged His Godhead and obeyed Him, He would not have made them the place for His throne, the abode of His angels and the destination: *To Him Words of what is good rise and He exalts an action in accord with morality ...* (Q35:10) of the creatures. Sermon 182

Those who bear not witness to untruth and if they passed by idle talk, they passed by nobly, **25:72**
and those who, when they were reminded of the signs of their Lord, fall not down unwilling to hear and unwilling to see **25:73**
and those who say: Our Lord! Bestow on us from our spouses and our offspring the comfort of our eyes and make us leaders of the ones who are God-conscious, **25:74**
those will be given recompense in the highest chambers because they endured patiently. They will be in receipt of greetings and peace, **25:75**
ones who will dwell in it forever. Excellent it is for habitation and as a resting place! **25:76**

God, the Sublime, says: *Truly, of humanity closest to Abraham are those who followed him and this Prophet and those who believed. God is Protector of the ones who believe.* (Q3:68) Letter 28

Say: My Lord would not concern Himself with you if it had not been for your supplication, for, surely, you denied so it will be close at hand. **25:77**

Therein declare glory unto Him in the mornings and the evenings. *The Light is lit in houses God gave permission to be lifted up and that His Name be remembered in it. Glorifying Him at the first part of the day and the eventide are men whom neither trade nor trading diverts from the remembrance of God and the performing the formal prayer and the giving of purifying alms for they fear a Day when the hearts will go to and fro and their sight ...* (Q24:36-37) Sermon 221

CHAPTER 26: THE POETS (al-Shuᶜarāᵓ)

26:1 *Ta Sin Mim*
That are the signs of the clear Book. **26:2**

There is no doubt that God sent down *the Prophet* (Q7:158), peace and the mercy of God be upon him, as a guide with an eloquent Book and a standing command. No one will be ruined by it except one who ruins himself. Certainly, only doubtful innovations cause ruin except those from which God may protect. In God's authority lies the safety of your affairs. Therefore, render Him such obedience as is neither blameworthy nor insincere. By

God, you must do so otherwise God will take away from you the power of Islam and will never thereafter return it to you until it reverts to others. Sermon 169

Perhaps ***you*** *would be one who consumes* ***your****self in grief because they become not ones who believe.* **26:3**

Instead of sleep, the people had wakefulness. Instead of antimony, they had tears in their eyes. They were in a land where the lips of the learned were bridled while the words of the ignorant were honored. Sermon 2

If We will, We send down to them from heaven a sign so that perhaps their necks would stay to it, ones that are bent in humility. **26:4**

I bear witness that *there is no god but God* (Q47:19), by virtue of belief, certainty, sincerity and conviction. I also bear witness that *Muhammad* (Q48:29), peace and the mercy of God be upon him, is *His servant* (Q17:1)å and *Prophet,* (Q7:158) whom He deputed when the signs of guidance were obliterated and the ways of religion were desolate. So he threw open the truth, gave advice to the people, guided them towards righteousness and ordered them to be moderate. May God bless him ... Sermon 194

There approaches them not any renewed Remembrance from The Merciful but that they had been ones who turn aside from it. **26:5**
Surely, they denied it. So, soon the tiding will approach them about what they had been ridiculing. **26:6**

O my God! Do pour on us **Your** mercy, **Your** blessing, **Your** sustenance and **Your** pity.... Surely, **You** are powerful over whatever **You** will. Sermon 143

Consider they the earth, how much We caused to develop in and on it of every generous pair? **26:7**
Truly, in that is a sign. Yet most of them had not been ones who believe. **26:8**
Truly, ***your*** *Lord, He is, certainly, The Almighty, The Compassionate.* **26:9**

Praise belongs to God (Q1:2) Who is High above all else. He is Near the creation through His bounty. He is the Giver of all reward and distinction and Dispeller of all calamities and hardships. I praise Him for His continuous mercy and His copious bounties. Sermon 82

When ***your*** *Lord proclaimed to Moses saying that: Approach the unjust folk,* **26:10**
a folk of Pharaoh saying: Will they not be God-conscious? **26:11**
He said: My Lord! Truly, I fear that they will deny me **26:12**
and my breast be narrowed and my tongue will not be loosened. So, send for Aaron. **26:13**
They charge an impiety against me. I fear that they will kill me. **26:14**
He said: No indeed! Both of you go with Our signs. Truly, We will be with you, ones who are listening. **26:15**
Both of you approach Pharaoh and say: We are the Messengers of the Lord of the worlds, **26:16**
so send the Children of Jacob with us. **26:17**
Pharaoh said: Raise not we ***you*** *up among us as a child? Had* ***you*** *not lingered in expectation with us for many years of* ***your*** *lifetime?* **26:18**
You *had accomplished* ***your*** *accomplishment that* ***you*** *had accomplished and* ***you*** *are among the ones who are ungrateful.* **26:19**

Moses said: I accomplished it when I was of the ones who go astray. 26:20
So, I ran away from you when I feared you. Then, my Lord bestowed on me critical judgment and made me among the ones who are sent. 26:21
Beyond this past favor with which **you** *have reproached me,* **you** *had enslaved the Children of Jacob.* 26:22
Pharaoh said: What is the Lord of the worlds? 26:23
Moses said: The Lord of the heavens and the earth and whatever is between the two of them if you had been ones who are certain. 26:24
Pharaoh said to whoever was around him: Listen you not? 26:25
Moses said: Your Lord and the Lord of your fathers, the ancient ones. 26:26
Pharaoh said: Truly, your Messenger who was sent to you is one who is possessed! 26:27
Moses said: The Lord of the East and the West and whatever is between the two of them if you had been reasonable! 26:28
Pharaoh said: If **you** *had taken to* **your***self a god other than me. I will, certainly, assign* **you** *to be imprisoned!* 26:29
Moses said: What if I drew near **you** *with something that makes it clear?* 26:30
Pharaoh said: Bring it, if **you** *have been among the ones who are sincere.* 26:31
So, he cast his staff; that is when it was a clear serpent. 26:32
He drew out his hand and that is when it was shimmering white to the ones who look. 26:33
He said to the Council around him: Truly, this is one who is a knowing sorcerer! 26:34
He wants to drive you out from your region by his sorcery. What is it, then, that you suggest? 26:35
They said: Put him and his brother off and raise up ones who summon in the cities. 26:36
They will bring every knowing witch to **you**. 26:37
So, the ones who were sorcerers were gathered at a time appointed on a known day 26:38
and it was said to humanity: Will you, you be ones who gather together 26:39
so that perhaps we follow the ones who are sorcerers if they had been the ones who are victors? 26:40
So, when the ones who are sorcerers drew near, they said to Pharaoh: Is there a compensation for us if we had been the ones who are victors? 26:41
Pharaoh said: Yes! Truly, you will be the ones who are brought near to me. 26:42
Moses said to them: Cast what you will as ones who cast. 26:43
So, they cast their ropes and their staffs and said: By the vainglory of Pharaoh, we, we will, surely, be the ones who are victors! 26:44
Then, Moses cast down his staff. That is when it swallows what they faked. 26:45
The ones who are sorcerers were cast down, ones who prostrate themselves. 26:46
They said: We believed in the Lord of the worlds, 26:47
the Lord of Moses and Aaron. 26:48
Pharaoh said: You believed in him before I give permission to you? He is, truly, your foremost master who taught you sorcery. Then, you will know. I will, certainly, cut off your hands and your feet on opposite sides, and I will cause you to be crucified one and all. 26:49
They said: No grievance. Truly, to our Lord we are ones who are turning. 26:50
Truly, we are desirous that Our Lord forgive us our transgressions that we had been the first of the ones who believe. 26:51
We revealed to Moses saying that: Set **you** *forth by night with My servants. Truly, you are ones who will be followed.* 26:52
Then, Pharaoh sent to the cities, ones who summon. 26:53

They said: These are, truly, a small crowd **26:54**
and, truly, they are ones who enrage us. **26:55**
We are altogether, truly, ones who are cautious. **26:56**
So, We drove them out from the gardens and springs **26:57**
and treasures and a generous station. **26:58**
We, thus, gave them as inheritance to the Children of Jacob. **26:59**
So, they pursued them at sunrise. **26:60**
Then, when the two multitudes sighted each other, the Companions of Moses said: Truly, we are ones who are to be overtaken. **26:61**
Moses said: No indeed. Truly, my Lord is with me and He will guide me. **26:62**
Then, We revealed to Moses saying that: Strike the sea with **your** *staff and it divided and each had been a separate part like a high, tremendous mountain.* **26:63**
Again, We brought the others close **26:64**
and We rescued Moses and whoever was with him, one and all. **26:65**
Again, We drowned the others. **26:66**
Truly, in this is a sign and yet most of them had not been ones who believe. **26:67**
Truly, **your** *Lord, He is The Almighty, The Compassionate.* **26:68**
Recount to them the tidings of Abraham **26:69**
when he said to his father and his folk: What is it you worship? **26:70**
They said: We worship idols. We will stay ones who give ourselves up to them. **26:71**
He said: Hear they when you call them? **26:72**
Or are they profiting you or hurting you? **26:73**
They said: Nay! But we found our fathers acting likewise. **26:74**
He said: Then, considered what you had been worshipping, **26:75**
you and your fathers, the elders? **26:76**
Truly, they are an enemy to me, but not so the Lord of the worlds **26:77**
Who created me. It is He Who guides me. **26:78**
That He Who feeds me and gives me drink. **26:79**
When I was sick, it is He Who heals me **26:80**
and Who causes me to die, again, will give me life, **26:81**
and from Whom I am desirous that He will forgive me my transgressions on the Day of Judgment. **26:82**
My Lord! Bestow on me critical judgment and cause me to join with the ones in accord with morality. **26:83**
Assign me a good name of good repute with the later ones **26:84**
and make me one who inherits the Garden of Bliss. **26:85**
Forgive my father. Truly, he had been among the ones who go astray. **26:86**
Cover me not with shame on a Day they will be raised up, **26:87**
on a Day neither wealth will profit nor children **26:88**
but he who approached God with a pure-hearted heart. **26:89**

This is the thing against which God has protected His creatures who are believers by means of prayers, alms-giving and suffering the hardship of fasting in the days in which it has been made obligatory in order to give their limbs peacefulness, to cast fear in their eyes, to make their spirits humble, to give their hearts humility and to remove haughtiness from them. Sermon 192

The Garden will be brought close for the ones who are God-conscious **26:90**
and hellfire will be advanced for the ones who are in error. **26:91**

This path is the lightest course and the brightest lamp. Guidance towards virtuous actions is sought through faith while guidance towards faith is achieved through virtuous actions. Knowledge is made to prosper through faith, and death is feared because of knowledge. This world comes to an end with death, while the next world is secured by virtuous actions in this world. With the Day of Resurrection, Paradise is brought near and ... *and hellfire will be advanced for the ones who are in error.* (Q26:91) For people there is no escape from resurrection. They are heading for this last end in its appointed course. They have arisen from the resting places in their graves and have set off for the final objectives. Every house has its own people. They are not changed, nor shifted from there. Sermon 156

It will be said to them: Where is what you had been worshipping **26:92**
instead of God? Are you helped by them? Or help they themselves? **26:93**
Then, they were thrown down into it, they and the ones who are in error, **26:94**
and the army of Iblis, one and all. **26:95**
They said while they are in it striving against one another: **26:96**
By God! Truly, we have been clearly wandering astray **26:97**
when we made you equal with the Lord of the worlds. **26:98**
No one caused us to go astray but the ones who sin. **26:99**

O God! I bear witness that he who likens **You** with the separateness of the limbs or with the joining of the extremities of his body did not acquaint his inner self with knowledge about **You**. His heart did not secure conviction to the effect that there is no partner for **You**. It is as though he has not heard the wrongful followers disclaiming their false gods by sayings. By God! *Truly we have been clearly wandering astray when we made you equal with the Lord of the worlds.* (Q26:97-98). Sermon 91

Now we have not ones who are intercessors **26:100**
nor an ardent friend, a loyal friend. **26:101**

Know that the Quran is an interceder and its intercession will be accepted. It is a speaker who bears witness. For whoever the Quran intercedes on the Day of Judgment, its intercession for him would be accepted. He about whom the Quran speaks ill on the Day of Judgment shall testify to it. On the Day of Judgment, an announcer will announce: Be aware! Every sower of a crop is in distress except the sowers of the Quran. Therefore, you should be among the sowers of the Quran and its followers. Make it your guide towards God. Seek its advice for yourselves, do not trust your views against it and regard your desires in the matter of the Quran as deceitful. Sermon 176

Would that there were for us a return again. Then, we would be among the ones who believe! **26:102**

Everything submits to Him. Everything exists by Him. He is the satisfaction of every poor, dignity of the low, energy for the weak and shelter for the oppressed. Whoever speaks, He hears his speaking. Whoever keeps quiet, He knows his secret. On Him is the livelihood of everyone who lives. To Him returns whoever dies. Sermon 108

Truly, in this is a sign; yet most of them had not been ones who believe. **26:103**

I bear witness that *Muhammad* (Q48:29), peace and the mercy of God be upon him, is *His servant* (Q17:1) and *Prophet* (Q7:158), whom He deputed when the signs of guidance were obliterated and the ways of religion were desolate. So he threw open the truth, gave advice to the people, guided them towards righteousness and ordered them to be moderate. May God bless him. Sermon 194

Truly, ***your*** *Lord, He is The Almighty, The Compassionate.* **26:104**

If God, the Almighty, had placed His sacred House and His great signs among plantations, streams, soft and level plains, plenty of trees, an abundance of fruits, a thick population, close habitats, golden wheat, lush gardens, green land, watered plains, thriving orchards and crowded streets, the amount of recompense would have decreased because of the lightness of the trial. If the foundation on which the House is borne and the stones with which it has been raised had been of green emerald and red rubies, and there had been brightness and effulgence, then this would have lessened the action of doubts in the breasts, would have dismissed the effect of Satan's activity from the hearts, and would have stopped the surging of misgivings in people, but God tries His creatures by means of different troubles, wants them to render worship through hardships and involves them in distresses, all in order to extract out vanity from their hearts, to settle down humbleness in their spirits and to make all this an open door for His favors and an easy means for His forgiveness for their sins. Sermon 192

The folk of Noah denied the ones who are sent **26:105**
when their brother, Noah, said to them: Will you not be God-conscious? **26:106**
Truly, I am a trustworthy Messenger to you **26:107**
so be God-conscious and obey me. **26:108**
I ask you not for any compensation for it. My compensation is only from the Lord of the worlds. **26:109**
So, be God-conscious and obey you me. **26:110**
They said: Will we believe in ***you*** *when it is the most wretched that followed* ***you****?* **26:111**
He said: What knowledge have I of what they had been doing? **26:112**
Truly, their reckoning is but with my Lord if you be aware. **26:113**
I am not one who drives away the ones who believe. **26:114**
I am not but a clear warner. **26:115**
They said: If ***you*** *have not refrained* ***your****self, O Noah,* ***you*** *will, certainly, be among the ones who are stoned!* **26:116**
He said: My Lord! My folk denied me, **26:117**
so give ***You*** *deliverance between me and them and victory and deliver me and whoever is with me among the ones who believe.* **26:118**
We rescued him and whoever was with him in the laden boat. **26:119**
Again, We drowned after that the ones who remained. **26:120**
In this is, truly, a sign, yet most of them had not been ones who believe. **26:121**
Your *Lord, He, truly, is The Almighty, The Compassionate.* **26:122**
Ad denied the ones who are sent **26:123**
when their brother Hud said to them: Will you not be God-conscious? **26:124**
Truly, I am a trustworthy Messenger to you, **26:125**
so be God-conscious and obey me. **26:126**

I ask you not for any compensation for it. My compensation is only from the Lord of the worlds. **26:127**
Build you a sign on every high hill to amuse? **26:128**
Take you for yourselves castles so that perhaps you will dwell in them forever? **26:129**
When you seized by force, seized you by force haughtily? **26:130**
So, be God-conscious and obey me. **26:131**
Be God-conscious of Him Who furnished relief to you with all that you know. **26:132**
He furnished relief to you with flocks and children **26:133**
and gardens and springs. **26:134**
Truly, I fear for you the punishment of a tremendous Day. **26:135**
They said: It is equal to us whether ***you*** *were to admonish or* ***you*** *have not been among the ones who admonish.* **26:136**
Truly, this is nothing but morals of the ancient ones **26:137**
and we are not ones who are punished. **26:138**
So, they denied him and We caused them to perish. Truly, in this is a sign yet most of them had not been ones who believe. **26:139**
Truly, ***your*** *Lord, He is, certainly, The Almighty, The Compassionate.* **26:140**
Thamud denied the ones who are sent **26:141**
when their brother Salih said to them: Will you not be God-conscious? **26:142**
Truly, I am a trustworthy Messenger to you, **26:143**
so be God-conscious and obey me. **26:144**
I ask you not for any compensation for it. My compensation is only from the Lord of the worlds. **26:145**
Will you be left ones who are safe in what you have here **26:146**
in gardens and springs **26:147**
Will you carve houses out of the mountains as ones who are skillful? **26:149**
and crops of slender spathes of date palm trees? **26:148**
So, be God-conscious and obey me. **26:150**

On that day many an argument will prove void and a contention for excuses will stand rejected. Sermon 222

Obey not the command of the ones who are excessive, **26:151**
who make corruption in and on the earth and make not things right. **26:152**
They said: Truly, ***you*** *are only of the ones against whom a spell is cast.* **26:153**
You *are not but a mortal like us. So, bring us a sign if* ***you*** *had been of the ones who are sincere.* **26:154**

Praise belongs to God (Q1:2) Who is High above all else. He is Near the creation through His bounty. He is the Giver of all reward and distinction, and Dispeller of all calamities and hardships. I praise Him for His continuous mercy and His copious bounties. Sermon 82

He said: This is a she camel. She has a right to drink and you have a right to drink on a known day. **26:155**
Afflict her not with evil so that you should take the punishment of a tremendous Day. **26:156**
But they crippled her and, then, it came to be in the morning that they are ones who are remorseful. **26:157**

So, the punishment took them. Truly, in this is a sign yet most of them had not been ones who believe. **26:158**

O people, certainly, what gathers people together in categories is their agreement to good or bad and their disagreement, for only one individual killed the camel of Thamud, but God held all of them in punishment because all of them consented to it. Thus, God, the Almighty, has said: *But they crippled her and then it came to be in the morning that they were ones who are remorseful.* (Q26:157) Sermon 200

Truly, ***your*** *Lord! He is, certainly, The Almighty, The Compassionate.* **26:159**

O my God! Do pour on us **Your** mercy, **Your** blessing, **Your** sustenance and **Your** pity.... Surely, **You** are powerful over whatever **You** will. Sermon 143

The folk of Lot denied the ones who are sent **26:160**
when their brother, Lot, said to them: Will you not be God-conscious? **26:161**
Truly, I am a trustworthy Messenger to you **26:162**
so be God-conscious and obey me. **26:163**
I ask you not for any compensation for it. My compensation is only from the Lord of the worlds. **26:164**
You approach males among worldly beings **26:165**
forsaking spouses whom your Lord created for you? Nay! You are a folk ones who turn away. **26:166**
They said: If ***you*** *have not refrained* ***your****self, O Lot,* ***you*** *will, certainly, be among ones who are driven out.* **26:167**
He said: I am of the ones with hatred for your actions. **26:168**
My Lord! Deliver me and my people from what they do! **26:169**
So, We delivered him and his people one and all **26:170**
but an old woman of the ones who stay behind. **26:171**
Again, We destroyed the others **26:172**
and We rained down on them a rain. How evil was the rain for the ones who are warned! **26:173**
Truly, in this is a sign. Yet most of them had not been ones who believe. **26:174**
Truly, ***your*** *Lord, He is, certainly, The Almighty, The Compassionate.* **26:175**

I bear witness that *Muhammad* (Q48:29), peace and the mercy of God be upon him, is *His servant* (Q17:1) and *Prophet* (Q7:158), whom He deputed when the signs of guidance were obliterated and the ways of religion were desolate. So he threw open the truth, gave advice to the people, guided them towards righteousness and ordered them to be moderate. Sermon 194

The Companions of the Thicket denied the ones who are sent. **26:176**
When Shuayb said to them: Will you not be God-conscious? **26:177**
Truly, I am a trustworthy Messenger to you **26:178**
so be God-conscious and obey me. **26:179**
I ask you not for any compensation for it. My compensation is only from the Lord of the worlds. **26:180**
Live up to the full measure and be not of the ones who cause loss to others by fraud. **26:181**
Weigh with a straight scale **26:182**
and diminish not to humanity their things nor do mischief in or on the earth as ones who make corruption. **26:183**

He knows whatever has been treasured by mother-of-pearls, and covered under the waves of oceans, all that which is concealed under the darkness of night and all that on which the light of day is shining, as well as all that on which sometimes darkness prevails and sometimes light shines, the trace of every footstep, the feel of every movement, the echo of every sound, the motion of every lip, the abode of every living being, the weight of every particle, the sobs of every sobbing heart, and whatever is there on the earth like fruits of trees or falling leaf, or the settling place of semen, or the congealing of blood or clot and the developing of life and embryo. Sermon 91

Be God-conscious of Him Who created you and the array of the ancient ones. **26:184**

O God's human being! Be God-conscious. Keep in view the reason why He created you. Be afraid of Him to the extent He has advised you to do. Make yourself deserve what He has promised you by having confidence in the truth of His promise and entertaining fear of the Day of Judgment. Sermon 82

They said: ***You*** *are only ones against whom a spell is cast.* **26:185**
You *are nothing but a mortal like us. Truly, we think* ***you*** *to be among the ones who lie.* **26:186**
So, cause pieces of heaven to drop on us, if you had been among the ones who are sincere. **26:187**
He said: My Lord is greater in knowledge of what you do. **26:188**
But they denied him. So, took them the punishment on the overshadowing day. Truly, that had been the punishment of a tremendous Day! **26:189**
Truly, in this is a sign. Yet most of them had not been ones who believe. **26:190** ***

Truly, ***your*** *Lord, He is, certainly, The Almighty, The Compassionate.* **26:191**

O the Most Merciful of all! O my God! Surely, **You** are powerful over whatever **You** will. Sermon 143

This, truly, is the sending down successively of the Lord of the worlds **26:192**
that the Trustworthy Spirit brought down **26:193**
on ***your*** *heart that* ***you*** *be among the one who warn* **26:194**
in a clear Arabic tongue. **26:195**
Truly, it is in the ancient scrolls of the ancient ones. **26:196**
Would it not be a sign for them that is known to the knowing among the Children of Jacob? **26:197**
***

If We sent it down to some of the non-Arabs, **26:198**
and he recited it to them, they had not been ones who believe in it. **26:199**
Thus, We thrust it into the hearts of the ones who sin. **26:200**

The Book of God is that through which you see, you speak and you hear. Its one part speaks for the other part, and one part bears witness to the other. It does not create differences about God, nor does it mislead its own follower from the path of God. You are joined together in hatred of each other and in the growing of herbage on your covering inner impurity by good appearance outside. You are sincere with one another in your love of desires and bear enmity against each other in earning wealth. The evil spirit (Satan) has perplexed you and deceit has misled you. I seek the help of God for myself and you. Sermon 133

They will not believe in it until they see the painful punishment. **26:201**
Then, it will approach them suddenly while they are not aware. **26:202**

Even though their traces have been wiped out and their news has stopped circulating, eyes are capable of drawing a lesson, as they looked at them, ears of intelligence heard them and they spoke without uttering words. So they said that handsome faces have been destroyed and delicate bodies have been smeared with earth. We have put on a worn-out shroud. The narrowness of the grave has overwhelmed us and strangeness has spread among us. Our silent abodes have been ruined. The beauty of our bodies has disappeared. Our known features have become hateful. Our stay in the places of strangeness has become long. We do not get relief from pain, nor widening from narrowness. Sermon 220

Then, they will say: Are we ones who are given respite? **26:203**

Some of them are like hocked camels, some like butchered meat, some like severed limbs, some like spilt blood, some are biting their hands in pain, some are rubbing their palms in remorse, some are holding their cheeks on their hands in anxiety, some are cursing their own views and some are retreating from their determination, but the time for action has gone away and the hour of calamity has approached: *They cried out but there was no time for escape for awhile.* (Q38:3) Alas! Alas! What has been lost is lost! What has gone is gone! The world has passed in its usual manner. *Neither the heavens wept for them nor the earth nor had they been ones who were given respite.* (Q44:29) Sermon 191

Seek they to hasten Our punishment? **26:204**

Reform yourselves. Repent. One should praise only God and condemn only one's self. Sermon 16

Had ***you*** *considered that if We gave them enjoyment for years* **26:205**
and, again, there drew near them what they had been promised, **26:206**
they would not be availed by what they had been given of enjoyment? **26:207**

You should know that a person is satiated and wearied with everything except life, because he does not find for himself any pleasure in death. It is life for a dead heart, sight for the blind eye, hearing for the deaf ear, quenching for the thirsty, and it contains complete sufficiency and safety. Sermon 133

We caused no town to perish but that it had ones who warn **26:208**
as a reminder. We had not been ones who are unjust. **26:209**
It came not forth by the satans **26:210**
and neither is it fit and proper for them nor are they able. **26:211**
Truly, they, from having the ability to hear, are the ones who are set aside. **26:212**

Truly, Satan has collected his group and assembled his horse-men and foot-soldiers. Truly, I have my sagacity. I have neither deceived myself, nor ever been deceived. By God, I shall fill to the brim a cistern for them from which I alone would draw water. They can neither turn away from it, nor return to it. Sermon 10

So, call ***you*** *not to any god with God so that* ***you*** *be among the ones who are punished.* **26:213**

I bear witness that *there is no god but God* (Q47:19), the One, there is no partner with Him, nor is there with Him any god other than Himself, and that *Muhammad*

(Q48:29), peace and the mercy of God be upon him, is *His servant* (Q17:1) and *Prophet.* (Q7:158) Sermon 35

Warn ***your*** *nearest kin, the kinspeople.* **26:214**

Regard for kinship for it increases wealth and length of life, giving alms secretly for it covers shortcomings, giving alms openly for it protects against a bad death and extending benefits to people for it saves from positions of disgrace. Sermon 110

Make low ***your*** *wing to whoever followed* ***you*** *among the ones who believe.* **26:215**

The Prophet (Q33:6) of God, peace and the mercy of God be upon him, said: The belief of a person cannot be firm unless his heart is firm, and his heart cannot be firm unless his tongue is firm. So whoever of you can manage to meet God, the Sublime, in such a position that his hands are unsmeared with the blood of Muslims and their property and his tongue is safe from exposing them, he should do so. Sermon 176

Then, if they rebelled against ***you****, then, say: Truly, I am free of what you do.* **26:216**

God never allowed His creation to remain without a Prophet, one deputized by Him, or a Book sent down from Him, or a binding argument, or a standing plea. These Messengers were such that they did not fear that they were few in comparison to the large numbers of their falsifiers. Among them was either a predecessor who would name the one to follow or the follower who had been introduced by the predecessor. Sermon 1

Put ***your*** *trust in The Almighty, The Compassionate,* **26:217**

Surely, **You** are powerful over whatever **You** will. Sermon 143

Who sees ***you*** *at the time* ***you*** *have stood up* **26:218**
and ***your*** *going to and fro of the ones who prostrate themselves?* **26:219**

O my God! **You** know that what we did was not to seek power, nor to acquire anything from the vanities of the world. We rather wanted to restore the signs of **Your** religion and to usher prosperity into **Your** cities so that the oppressed among **Your** creatures might be safe and **Your** forsaken commands might be established. O my God! I am the first who leaned towards **You** and who heard and responded to the call of Islam. No one preceded me in formal prayer except *the Prophet* (Q7:158), peace and the mercy of God be upon him. Sermon 131

Truly, He is The Hearing, The Knowing. **26:220**

Know that firm in knowledge are those who refrain from opening the curtains that lie against the unknown. Their acknowledgment of ignorance about the details of the hidden unknown prevents them from further probe. God praises them for their admission that they are unable to attain knowledge not allowed to them. They do not go deep into the discussion of what is not enjoined upon them about knowing Him. They call it firmness. Be content with this and do not limit the Greatness of God after the measure of your own intelligence or else you will be among the destroyed ones. Sermon 91

Will I tell you in whom the satans come forth? **26:221**
They come forth in every sinful false one who gives listen, **26:222**

but most of them are ones who lie. **26:223**

O my God! Whoever listens to our words which are just and which seek the prosperity of religion and the worldly life and do not seek mischief, they reject after listening. He certainly turns away from **Your** support and desists from strengthening **Your** religion. Sermon 212

As for the poets, the ones who are in error follow them. **26:224**
Have **you** *not considered that they wander in every valley* **26:225**
and that they say what they accomplish not? **26:226**
But those who believed and did as the ones in accord with morality remembered God frequently and helped themselves after they were wronged. Those who did wrong will know by which overturning they will be turned about! **26:227**

Among the proofs of His creation is the creation of the skies which are fastened without pillars and stand without support. He called them. They responded obediently and humbly without being lazy or loathsome. If they had not acknowledged His Godhead and obeyed Him, He would not have made them the place for His throne, the abode of His angels and the destination: *To Him Words of what is good rise and He exalts an action in accord with morality* ... (Q35:10) of the creatures. Sermon 182

Chapter 27: The Ant (al-Naml)

Ta Sin. That are the signs of the Quran and a clear Book, **27:1**
a guidance and good tidings for the ones who believe, **27:2**
those who perform the formal prayer and give the purifying alms so that they of the world to come, they are certain. **27:3**

This is the thing against which God has protected His creatures who are believers by means of prayers, alms-giving and suffering the hardship of fasting in the days in which it has been made obligatory in order to give their limbs peacefulness, to cast fear in their eyes, to make their spirits humble, to give their hearts humility and to remove haughtiness from them. Sermon 192

Truly, as for those who believe not in the world to come, We made their actions appear pleasing to them so that they wander unwilling to see. **27:4**

O people, your bodies are together, but your desires are divergent. Your talk softens the hard stones. Your action attracts your enemy towards you. You claim in your sittings that you would do this and that, but when fighting approaches, you say to war: Turn away. If one calls you for help, the call receives no heed. He who deals harshly with you, his heart has no solace. Excuses are amiss like that of a debtor unwilling to pay. The ignoble cannot ward off oppression. Right cannot be achieved without effort. Which is the house besides this one to protect? With which leader would you go for fighting after me? By God! Deceived is one whom you have deceived while, by God, he who is successful with you receives only useless arrows! You are like broken arrows thrown over the enemy. By God! I am now in the position that I neither confirm your views, nor hope for your support, nor challenge the enemy through you. What is the matter with you? What is your ailment? What is your cure? The other party is also men of your type, but they are so different in character. Will there be talk without action, carelessness without God-consciousness and greed in things not right? Sermon 29

Those are those for whom is the dire punishment and they, in the world to come, they are the ones who are the losers. **27:5**

O God's human being! Where are those who were allowed long ages to live? They enjoyed bounty. They were taught. They learned. They were given time. They passed it in vain. They were kept healthy. They forgot their duty. They were allowed a long period of life, were handsomely provided for, were warned of grievous punishment and were promised great rewards. You should avoid sins that lead to destruction and vices that attract the wrath of God. Sermon 82

Truly, ***you, you*** *are in receipt of the Quran, that which proceeds from the Presence, Wise, Knowing.* **27:6**

Know that this Quran is an adviser who never deceives, a leader who never misleads and a narrator who never speaks a lie. No one will sit beside this Quran but when he rises, he will achieve one addition or one diminution—addition in his guidance or elimination in his spiritual blindness. You should also know that no one will need anything after guidance from the Quran and no one will be free from want before guidance from the Quran. Seek cure from the Quran for your ailments and seek its assistance in your distress. It contains a cure for the worst diseases, namely unbelief, hypocrisy, revolt and misguidance. Pray to God through it and turn to God with its love ... There is nothing like it through which the people should turn to God, the Sublime. Sermon 176

Mention when Moses said to his people: Truly, I, I observed a fire! I will bring you news from it or I will approach you with a flaming firebrand so that perhaps you would warm yourselves. **27:7**
But when he drew near it, it was proclaimed that: Blessed be He Who is in the fire and Who is around it, and glory be to God, the Lord of the worlds. **27:8**
O Moses! Truly, I alone am God, The Almighty, The Wise. **27:9**
Cast down ***your*** *staff. But when he saw it quiver as if it were a snake, he turned as one who draws back to retrace his steps. O Moses! Fear not! The ones who are sent fear not My nearness* **27:10**
but whoever did wrong does. Again, he substituted goodness after evil and, truly, I am Forgiving, Compassionate. **27:11**
Cause ***your*** *hand to enter into* ***your*** *bosom. It will go forth shimmering white without evil. These are among nine signs to Pharaoh and his folk. Truly, they had been a folk, ones who disobey.* **27:12**
But when Our signs drew near them, ones who perceive, they said: This is clear sorcery. **27:13**
They negated them—although their souls confessed to them—out of injustice and self-exaltation. So, look on how had been the Ultimate End of the ones who make corruption. **27:14**
Certainly, We gave David and Solomon knowledge; and they said: All Praise belongs to God Who gave us advantage over many of His servants, ones who believe **27 15**
Solomon inherited from David and he said: O humanity! We were taught the utterance of the birds and everything was given to us. Truly, this is clearly grace. **27:16**
There was assembled before Solomon his armies of jinn and humankind and birds and they are marching in rank **27:17**
until when they approached the Valley of the Ants. One ant said: O ants! Enter your dwellings so that Solomon and his armies not crush you while they are not aware. **27:18**
So, Solomon smiled as one who laughs at its saying and he said: My Lord! Arouse me that I give thanks for ***Your*** *divine blessing with which* ***You*** *were gracious to me and ones who are my parents and that I do as one in accord with morality. May* ***You*** *be well-pleased and cause me to enter by*

***Your** Mercy among **Your** servants, ones in accord with morality.* **27:19**
He reviewed the birds and said: Why see I not the hoopoe bird? Had it been among the ones who are absent? **27:20**
I will, certainly, punish him with a severe punishment or deal a death blow to it unless it brings me a clear authority! **27:21**
*But it was not long in coming. Then, it said: I comprehended what **you** have not comprehended of it. I drew near **you** from Sheba with certain tidings.* **27:22**
Truly, I found a woman controlling them. She was given everything and for her is a sublime throne. **27:23**
I found her and her folk prostrating herself to the sun—instead of God—and Satan made to appear pleasing to them their actions and barred them from the way so they are not truly guided. **27:24**
So, they prostrate themselves not to God Who brings out that which is hidden in the heavens and the earth and knows what you conceal and what you speak openly. **27:25**
God, there is no god but He, the Lord of the Sublime Throne. **27:26**
*Solomon said: We will look on if **you** had been sincere or **you** are of the ones who lie.* **27:27**
*Go **you** with this letter of mine and cast it to them. Again, turn away from them and look on what they return.* **27:28**
She said: O Council! Truly, a generous letter was cast down to me. **27:29**
Truly, it is from Solomon and, truly, it is in the Name of God, The Merciful, The Compassionate. **27:30**
Rise not up against me, but approach me as ones who submit to God. **27:31**
She said: O Council! Render me an opinion in my affair. I had not been one who resolves unless you bear witness. **27:32**
*They said: We are imbued with strength and vigorous might, but the command is for **you**. So, look on what **you** will command.* **27:33**
She said: Truly, when kings entered a town, they made corruption in it and made the most mighty of its people humiliated in spirit. Thus, this is what they accomplish. **27:34**
But, truly, I am one who will send to them a present and will be one who looks with what returns the ones who are sent. **27:35**
So, when they drew near Solomon, he said: Are you furnishing me relief with wealth? What God gave me is better than what He gave you. Nay! It is you who should be glad with your present! **27:36**
*Return **you** to them and We, truly, will approach them with armies against which they will not be capable and we will drive them out from there as ones who are disgraced and they, humble-spirited.* **27:37**
He said: O Council! Which of you will bring me her throne before they approach me as ones who submit to God? **27:38**
*A demon from among the jinn said: I will bring it to **you** before **you** will stand up from **your** station. Truly, I am strong, trustworthy.* **27:39**
*Said he who has knowledge of the Book: I will bring it to **you** before **your** glance goes back to **you**. Then, when he saw that which is settled before him, he said: This is from the grace of my Lord to try me whether I give thanks or am ungrateful. Whoever gave thanks, truly, he gives thanks for himself. Whoever was ungrateful, then, truly, my Lord is Rich, Generous.* **27:40**
He said: Disguise her throne for her that we look on whether she will be truly guided or she will be of those who are not truly guided. **27:41**
*So, when she drew near, it was said: Is **your** throne like this? She said: It is as though it had been*

it. Solomon said: The knowledge was given us before her and we had been ones who submit to the One God. **27:42**
She was barred from worshipping God by what she had been worshipping other than God for, truly, she had been of a folk, ones who are ungrateful. **27:43**
It was said to her: Enter the pavilion. When she saw it, she assumed it to be a pool and she bared her legs. He said: Truly, it is a smooth, crystal pavilion. She said: My Lord! Truly, I did wrong to myself and I submitted with Solomon to God, the Lord of the worlds. **27:44**
Certainly, We sent to Thamud their brother, Salih that they worship God! Then, when they became two groups of people
he said: O my folk! Why seek you to hasten the evil deed before benevolence? Why ask you not for forgiveness of God so that perhaps you will find mercy? **27:46**
They said: We auger ill of **you** *and whoever is with* **you**. *He said: That which is your omen is with God. Nay! You are a folk who are being tried.* **27:47** ***

There had been nine groups of persons in the city who make corruption in the earth and make not things right. **27:48**

He is the Giver of all reward and distinction and Dispeller of all calamities and hardships. Sermon 82

They said: Swear to one another by God: We will, certainly, attack him by night and his people. Again, we will, certainly, say to his protector: We bore not witness to the destruction of his people and, truly, we are ones who are sincere. **27:49**
So, they planned a plan and We planned a plan while they were not aware. **27:50**
So, look on how had been the Ultimate End of their planning! Truly, We destroyed them and their folk one and all. **27:51**

Surely, **You** are powerful over whatever **You** will. Sermon 143

That are their houses, ones that have fallen down for what they did wrong? Truly, in this is a sign for a folk who know. **27:52**

I also bear witness that *Muhammad* (Q48:29), peace and the mercy of God be upon him, is *His servant* (Q17:1) and *Prophet* (Q7:158) whom He deputed when the signs of guidance were obliterated and the ways of religion were desolate. So he threw open the truth, gave advice to the people, guided them towards righteousness and ordered them to be moderate. May God bless him ... Sermon 194

We rescued those who believed and had been God-conscious. **27:53**

One of the firm decisions of God in the Wise Reminder (Quran), upon which He bestows reward or gives punishment and through which He likes or dislikes, is that it will not benefit a person, even though he exerts himself and acts sincerely, if he leaves this world to meet God with one of these acts without repenting, namely that he believed in a partner with God during his obligatory worship or appeased his own anger by killing an individual or spoke about acts committed by others or sought fulfillment of his needs from people by introducing an innovation in his religion or met people with a double face or moved among them with a double tongue. Understand this because an illustration is a guide for its like. Sermon 153

Lot, when he said to his folk: You approach indecency and you perceive what you do. **27:54**
Why approach you men with lust instead of women? Nay! You are a folk who are ignorant. **27:55**
Then, there had been no answer by his folk, but that they said: Drive the people of Lot out from your town. Truly, they are a clan to cleanse themselves. **27:56**
So, We rescued him and his people, but his woman. We ordained her to be among the ones who stay behind. **27:57**
We rained down on them a rain. How evil was the rain to the ones who are warned! **27:58**
Say: The Praise belongs to God and peace be on His servants, those whom He favored. Is God better or what they ascribe as partner with God? **27:59**
Who created the heavens and the earth and caused to descend for you from the heavens, water? With it We caused joyous, fertile gardens to develop. It had not been for you to cause their trees to develop. Is there any god besides God? Nay! They are a folk who equate others with God. **27:60**
Who made the earth a stopping place and made rivers in the midst and made firm mountains for it and made between the two seas that which hinders? Is there a god besides God? Nay! But most of them know not! **27:61**

Praise belongs to God (Q1:2) Who is High above all else. He is Near the creation through His bounty. He is the Giver of all reward and distinction and Dispeller of all calamities and hardships. I praise Him for His continuous mercy and His copious bounties. Sermon 82

Who answers one who is constrained when he called to Him and He removes the evil and assigns you as vice-regents on the earth? Is there a god besides God? Little is what you recollect! **27:62**

They are the trustees of His secrets, shelter for His affairs, source of knowledge about Him, center of His wisdom, valleys for His books and mountains of His religion. With them God straightened the bend of religion's back and removed the trembling of its limbs. None in the Islamic community can be taken at par with the progeny of Muhammad, peace and the mercy of God be upon him. One who was under their obligation cannot be matched with them. They are the foundation of religion and pillar of faith. The forward runner has to turn back to them while the follower has to overtake them. They possess the chief characteristics of vice-regency. In their favor exists the succession of *the Prophet,* (Q7:158), peace and the mercy of God be upon him. This is the time when right has returned to its owner and diverted to its center of return. Sermon 2

Who guides you in the shadows of the dry land the sea and Who sends the winds, bearer of good news in advance of His mercy? Is there a god besides God? Exalted is God above partners they ascribe with God. **27:63**

... the position is just what God, the Glorified, says in the Quran: *Propound for them the parable of this present life: It is like water that We caused to descend from heaven. Then, plants of the earth mingled with it and it becomes straw in the morning that winnows in the winds. God had been over everything One Who is Omnipotent.* (Q18:45) Sermon 110

Who begins creation, again, will cause it to return and Who provides you from the heaven and the earth. Is there a god besides God? Say: Prepare your proof if you had been ones who are sincere! **27:64**

He will destroy the earth after its existence, until all that exists on it will become non-existent, but the extinction of the world after its creation is no more marvelous than its first formation and invention. How could it be otherwise? Even if all the animals of the earth, whether birds or beasts, stabled cattle or pasturing ones, of different origins and species, dull people and sagacious men—all jointly try to create even a mosquito, they are not able to bring it into being and do not understand what is the way to its creation. Their wits are bewildered and wandering. Their powers fall short and fail, and return dazzled and weary, knowing that they are defeated and admitting their inability to produce it, also realizing that they are too weak even to destroy it! Sermon 186

Say: None knows who is in the heavens and the earth, nor the unseen but God. Nor are they aware when they will be raised up. **27:65**
Nay! Their knowledge of the world to come failed. Nay! They are in uncertainty about it. Nay! They are in the dark about it. **27:66**

One who takes account of his shortcomings will always gain by it. One who is unmindful of them will always suffer. One who is afraid of the Day of Judgment is safe from the Wrath of God. One who takes lessons from the events of life by acquiring vision becomes wise and one who attains wisdom achieves knowledge. Saying 196

Those who were ungrateful said: When we had been earth dust like our fathers will we, truly, be ones who are brought out? **27:67**
Certainly, we were promised this, we and our fathers before. Truly, this is nothing but fables of the ancient ones. **27:68**

Do you not understand that for you there is a warning in the relics of the predecessors, an eye opener and lesson that your forefathers provided you? Do you not see that your predecessors did not come back and the surviving followers did not remain? Do you not observe that the people of the world pass mornings and evenings in different conditions? Thus, somewhere the dead is wept for, someone is being condoled, someone is prostrate in distress, someone is enquiring about the sick, someone is passing his last breath, someone is hankering after the world while death is looking for him, someone is forgetful, but he is not forgotten by death, and the survivors walk in the footsteps of the predecessors. Sermon 99

Say: Journey through the earth; then, look on how had been the Ultimate End of the ones who sin. **27:69**

How awe-striking is **Your** realm that we notice, but how humble is this against what is hidden from us out of **Your** authority! How extensive are **Your** bounties in this world, but how small are they against the bounties of the next world! Sermon 108

Feel ***you*** *not remorse for them, nor be troubled by what they plan.* **27:70**
They say: When is the promise if you had been ones who are sincere? **27:71**

They will not discern truth from wrong. They will oscillate like waves and would be utterly misled. Sermon 164

Say: Perhaps coming close behind you be some of that which you seek to hasten. **27:72**

God may shower mercy on him who repents, gives up sins and hastens in performing good acts before his death. Sermon 143

Truly, ***your*** *Lord is Possessor of Grace for humanity, but most of them give not thanks.* **27:73**

Do not forget gratitude when receiving blessings for God has exhausted the excuses before you through clear, shining arguments and open, bright books. Sermon 81

Truly, ***your*** *Lord knows what their breasts hide and what they speak openly.* **27:74**

Now, if you portray them in your mind, or if the curtains concealing them are removed from them for you, in this state when their ears have lost their power and turned deaf, their eyes have been filled with dust and sunk down, their tongues, which were very active, have been cut into pieces, their hearts, which were ever wakeful, have become motionless in their chests, in every limb of theirs a peculiar decay has occurred which has deformed it and has paved the way for calamity towards it, all these lie powerless, with no hand to help them and no heart to grieve over them, then you would certainly notice the grief of their hearts and the dirt of their eyes. Sermon 220

Not is that which is absent in the heaven and the earth, but that it is in the clear Book. **27:75**
Truly, this, the Quran, relates about the Children of Jacob and most of what they are at variance in it. **27:76**
Truly, it is a guidance and a mercy for the ones who believe. **27:77**
Truly, ***your*** *Lord will decree between them with His determination. He is The Almighty, The Knowing.* **27:78**

God sent to *the Prophet* (Q7:158), peace and the mercy of God be upon him, the Book as a light whose flames cannot be extinguished, a lamp whose gleam does not die, a sea whose depth cannot be sounded, a way whose direction does not mislead, a ray whose light does not darken, a separator of good from evil whose arguments do not weaken, a clarifier whose foundations cannot be dismantled, a cure which leaves no apprehension for disease, an honor whose supporters are not defeated and a truth whose helpers are not abandoned. Sermon 197

So, put ***your*** *trust in God. Truly,* ***you*** *are on The Clear Truth.* **27:79**

I trust in God, the trust of bending towards Him. I seek His guidance for the way that leads to His Paradise and takes to the place of His pleasure. Sermon 160

Truly, ***you*** *will not cause the dead to hear nor will* ***you*** *cause to hear the unwilling to hear the calling to them when they turned as ones who draw back.* **27:80**

You should know that a person is satiated and wearied with everything except life, because he does not find for himself any pleasure in death. It is life for a dead heart, sight for the blind eye, hearing for the deaf ear, quenching for the thirsty, and it contains complete sufficiency and safety. Sermon 133

Nor will ***you*** *be one who guides the unwilling to see out of their fallacy.* ***You*** *will not cause to hear, but whoever believes in Our signs and so they are ones who submit to God.* **27:81**

I also bear witness that *Muhammad* (Q48:29), peace and the mercy of God be upon him, is *His servant* (Q17:1) and *Prophet* (Q7:158), whom He deputed when the signs of guidance were obliterated and the ways of religion were desolate. So he threw open the truth, gave advice to the people, guided them towards righteousness and ordered them to be moderate. May God bless him ... Sermon 194

When the saying fell on them, We will bring out a moving creature for them from the earth that will speak to them, that: Humanity had not been certain of Our signs. **27:82**

How can he who is unable to describe a creature like this, describe God? Sermon 211

On a Day We will assemble a unit out of every community of whoever denies Our signs and they will be marching in rank. **27:83**

Until when they drew near, He will say: Denied you My signs without comprehending them in knowledge, or what is it that you had been doing? **27:84**

The saying will fall on them because they did wrong. They will speak nothing for themselves. **27:85**

God will take them out from the corners of the graves, the nests of birds, the dens of beasts and the centers of death. They will hasten towards His command and run towards the place fixed for their final return, group by group, quiet, standing and arrayed in rows. They will be within God's sight and will hear every one who would call them. They will have the dress of helplessness and covering of submission and indignity. At this time contrivances will disappear. Desires will be cut. Hearts will sink quietly. Voices will be lowered. Sweat will choke the throat. Fear will increase. Ears will resound with the thundering voice of the announcer calling towards the final judgment, award of recompense, striking of punishment and paying of reward. Sermon 82

Considered they not? We made the nighttime for them to rest in it and the daytime for ones who perceive. Truly, in that are signs for a folk who believe. **27:86**

He initiated creation most initially and commenced it originally without undergoing reflection, without making use of any experiment, without innovating any movement and without experiencing any aspiration of mind. He allotted all things their times, put together their variations, gave them their properties and determined their features knowing them before creating them, realizing fully their limits and confines and appreciating their propensities and intricacies. Sermon 1

On a Day on which the trumpet will be blown, whoever is in the heavens will be terrified and whoever is on the earth, but him whom God willed. All will approach Him as ones who are in a state of lowliness. **27:87**

There remain a few people in whose case the remembrance of their return to God on the Day of Judgment keeps their eyes bent and the awareness of the Resurrection moves them to tears. Some of them are scared away from the world and disperse. Some are frightened and subdued. Some are quiet as if muzzled. Some are praying sincerely. Some are grief-stricken and pain-ridden whom fear has confined to namelessness. Disgrace has shrouded them, so they are in the sea of bitter water, their mouths are closed and their hearts are bruised. They preached until they were tired. They were oppressed until they were disgraced. They were killed until their numbers dwindled. Sermon 32

You *will see the mountains* ***you*** *have assumed to be that which are fixed. But they will pass by as the passing of the clouds. This is the handiwork of God Who created everything very well. Truly, He is Aware of what you accomplish.* **27:88**

Be aware! Truly, I have not seen one who covets Paradise to be asleep, nor a dreader from hellfire to be asleep. Be aware! He whom right does not benefit must suffer the harm of the wrong. He whom guidance does not keep firm will be led away by misguidance towards destruction. Sermon 28

Whoever drew near with benevolence, for him will be better than it and they would be from the terror ones who are safe on that Day. **27:89**

When the earthquake occurs, the Day of Resurrection approaches with all its severities, the people of every worshipping place cling to it, all the devotees cling to the object of their devotion and all the followers cling to their leader. Sermon 222

Whoever drew near with evil deeds, they would be slung on their faces in the fire: Are you given recompense but for what you had been doing? **27:90**
Truly, I was commanded to worship the Lord of this land which He made sacred and to Whom everything belongs. I was commanded that I be among the ones who submit to God **27:91**
and to recount the Recitation. So, whoever was truly guided, then, he is truly guided only for himself. To whoever went astray say: Truly, I am among the ones who warn. **27:92**

God, the Sublime, says: *Truly, of humanity closest to Abraham are those who followed him and this Prophet and those who believed. God is Protector of the ones who believe.* (Q3:68) Letter 28

Say: The Praise belongs to God. He will cause you to see His signs and you will recognize them. ***Your*** *Lord is not One Who is Heedless of what you do.* **27:93**

Why should you be heedless of Him Who is not heedless of you? Sermon 187

Chapter 28: The Story (al-Qaṣaṣ)

28:1 *Ta Sin Mim*
That are the signs of the clear Book. **28:2**

It is the mine of belief and its center, the source of knowledge and its oceans, the plantation of justice and its pools, the foundation stone of Islam and its construction, the valleys of truth and its plains, an ocean which those who draw water cannot empty, springs which those who draw water cannot dry up, a watering place which those who come to take water cannot exhaust, a staging place in moving towards which travelers do not get lost, signs which no treader fails to see and a highland which those who approach it cannot surpass it. Sermon 197

We recount to ***you*** *the tiding of Moses and Pharaoh with The Truth for a folk who believe.* **28:3**
Truly, Pharaoh exalted himself on the earth and made his people partisans, taking advantage of due to their weakness, a section among them. He slaughters their children and saves alive their women. Truly, he had been of the ones who make corruption. **28:4**
We want to show grace to those who were taken advantage of due to their weakness on the earth and to make them leaders and to make them the ones who inherit **28:5**
and to establish them firmly on the earth. We cause Pharaoh and Haman to see—and their armies from them— that of which they had been fearful. **28:6**
We revealed to the mother of Moses: Breast feed him. But if ***you*** *had feared for him, then, cast him into the water of the sea and neither fear nor feel remorse. Truly, We will be ones who restore him to* ***you****, ones who make him among the ones who are sent.* **28:7**
Then, the people of Pharaoh picked him out to be an enemy to them and a cause of grief. Truly, Pharaoh and Haman and their armies had been ones who are inequitable. **28:8**

The woman of Pharaoh said: He will be a comfort to our eyes for me and for ***you****. Kill him not. Perhaps he may profit us or we may take him to ourselves as a son. But they are not aware.* **28:9**
It came to be in the morning that the mind of the mother of Moses was that which is empty. Truly, she was about to show him, if We had not invigorated her heart so that she became among the ones who believe. **28:10**
She said to his sister:Track him. So, she kept watching him from afar while they are not aware. **28:11**
We forbade any breast feeding female for him before. Then, she said: Shall I point you to the people of a house who will take control of him for you and they will be ones who will look after him? **28:12**
So, We returned him to his mother that her eyes settle down and she not feel remorse and that she knows that the Promise of God is true. But most of them know not. **28:13**
When he was fully grown, come of age and he straightened himself up, We gave him critical judgment and knowledge. Thus, We give recompense to the ones who are doers of good. **28:14**
He entered the city at a time of heedlessness of its people. He found in it two men fighting one against the other. This who was from among his partisans and this who was from among his enemies. The one who was among his partisans cried for help against him who was among his enemies. So, Moses struck him with his fist and Moses made an end of him. He said: This is the action of Satan. Truly, he is a clear enemy, one who leads astray. **28:15**
He said: My Lord! Truly, I did wrong to myself so forgive me and He forgave him. Truly, He is The Forgiving, The Compassionate. **28:16**
He said: My Lord! For that with which ***You*** *were gracious to me I will never be a sustainer of the ones who sin.* **28:17**
So, he came to be in the morning in the city one who is fearful and is vigilant. That is when the one who had asked for help yesterday cries out aloud to him. Moses said to him: Truly, ***you*** *are clearly a hothead.* **28:18**
Then, when he wanted to seize by force the one who he was an enemy of both of them—he said: O Moses! Would ***you*** *want to kill me as* ***you*** *had killed a soul yesterday?* ***You*** *would want nothing, but to be haughty on the earth?* ***You*** *would want not to be among the ones who make things right?* **28:19**
A man drew near from the farther part of the city, coming eagerly, he said: O Moses! Truly, the Council is conspiring against ***you*** *to kill* ***you****, so go forth. Truly, I am the one who gives advice to* ***you****.* **28:20**
So, Moses went forth from there as one who is fearful, is vigilant. He said: My Lord! Deliver me from the folk, ones who are unjust. **28:21**
When of his own accord he turned his face toward Midian he said: Perhaps my Lord guides me to the right way. **28:22**
When he went down to the well of Midian, he found a community there of personages drawing water and he found other than them two women who keep away. He said: What is your business? They both said: We draw not water until the ones who are shepherds move on. Our father is an aged, old man. **28:23**
So, he drew water for them. Again, he turned away to the shade and said: My Lord! Truly, I am, certainly, of whatever ***You*** *caused to descend of good to me, in need.* **28:24**

Certainly, in *the Prophet* (Q7:158), peace and the mercy of God be upon him, was sufficient example for you and a proof concerning the vices of the world, its defects, the multitude of its disgraces and its evils, because its sides had been constrained for him, while its flanks had been spread for others. He was deprived of its milk and turned away from its adornments. If you want, I will, as a second example, relate to you concerning Moses, the friend of God, peace be upon him, when he said: *My Lord! Truly, I am, certainly, of whatever* ***You*** *caused to descend of good to me, in need.* (Q28:24) By God, he asked Him only for bread to eat ... Sermon 159

Then, drew near him one of the two women, walking bashfully. She said: Truly, my father calls to ***you*** *that he may give* ***you*** *recompense of compensation because* ***you*** *had drawn water for us. So, when he drew near him and related to him the narrative, he said: Fear not.* ***You*** *were delivered from the folk, ones who are unjust.* **28:25**
One of the two women said: O my father! Employ him. Truly, best is that ***you*** *would employ the strong, the trustworthy.* **28:26**
He said: Truly, I want to wed ***you*** *to one of my two daughters if that* ***you*** *will hire* ***your****self to me for eight years. But if* ***you*** *were to fulfill ten years, then, it will be from* ***you****, for I want not to press* ***you*** *hard.* ***You*** *will find me, if God willed, among the ones in accord with morality.* **28:27**
He said: That is between ***you*** *and between me whichever of the two terms I satisfied. There will be no deep seated dislike from me. God is Trustee over what we say.* **28:28**
Then, when Moses satisfied the term and journeyed with his people, he observed at the edge of the mount a fire. He said to his people: Abide! Truly, I, I observed a fire so that perhaps I will bring you some news from there or burning wood of fire so that perhaps you will warm yourselves. **28:29**
So, when he approached it, it was proclaimed from the right side of the ridge of the valley, in a corner of the blessed ground from the tree: O Moses! Truly, I am God, the Lord of the worlds. **28:30**
Cast ***your*** *staff. But when he saw it quiver as if it were a snake, he turned as one who draws back, and he retraces his steps. O Moses! Come forward and fear not. Truly,* ***you*** *are among the ones who are safe.* **28:31**
Insert ***your*** *hand into* ***your*** *bosom. It will go forth shimmering white without evil and clasp* ***your*** *arm pits against fright. These are two proofs from* ***your*** *Lord to Pharaoh and his Council. Truly, they had been a folk, ones who disobey.* **28:32**
He said: My Lord! Truly, I killed a soul among them and I fear that they will kill me. **28:33**
My brother Aaron, he is more oratorical in language than I, so send him with me as a helpmate to establish me as true. Truly, I fear that they will deny me. **28:34**
He said: We will strengthen ***your*** *arm through* ***your*** *brother and assign to you both authority so that they reach not out to you both. With Our signs, you two and whoever followed you two will be the ones who are victors.* **28:35**
Then, when Moses drew near them with Our signs, clear portents, they said: This is nothing but forged sorcery. We heard not of this from our fathers, the ancient ones. **28:36**
Moses said: My Lord is greater in knowledge of who drew near with guidance from Him and what will be the Ultimate End in the Abode. Truly, the ones who are unjust will not prosper. **28:37**
Pharaoh said: O Council! I knew not of any god for you other than me so kindle for me, O Haman, a fire on the clay and make a pavilion for me so that perhaps I will peruse the God of Moses. Truly, I think that he is among the ones who lie. **28:38**
He grew arrogant, he and his armies, on the earth without right and they thought that they would not be returned to Us. **28:39**
So, We took him and his armies and We cast them forth in the water of the sea. So, look on how had been the Ultimate End of the ones who are unjust. **28:40**

We made them leaders. They call to the fire. On the Day of Resurrection, they will not be helped. **28:41**

A curse pursued them in the present. On the Day of Resurrection they will be of the ones who are spurned. **28:42**

Certainly, We gave Moses the Book, after We caused previous generations to perish as clear evidence for humanity and a guidance and a mercy so that they recollect. **28:43**

***You** had not been on the western edge when We decreed the command to Moses and **you** had not been among the ones who bear witness.* **28:44**

*But We caused generations to grow and their lifetimes continued to be long. **You** had not been one who is a dweller with the people of Midian who recount Our signs to them, but it is We Who had been ones who send.* **28:45**

***You** had not been at the edge of the mount when We proclaimed, but as a mercy from **your** Lord, that **you** wast to warn a folk to whom no warner approached them before **you** so that perhaps they will recollect.* **28:46**

*So, that if affliction lights on them for what their hands put forward, they say: Our Lord! Why had **You** not sent a Messenger to us that we would have followed **Your** signs and we would be among the ones who believe?* **28:47**

But when The Truth drew near them from Us they said: Why was he not given the like of what was given to Moses? They are ones who are ungrateful for what was given to Moses before. They said: Two kinds of sorcery, each helped one against the other. They said: Truly, we disbelieve in all of it. **28:48** ***

Say: Then, bring a Book from God that is better guided than these two that I follow it, if you had been ones who are sincere. **28:49**

The Book of God is that through which you see, you speak and you hear. Sermon 132

*But if they respond not to **you**, then, know that they only follow their own desires. Who is one who goes astray than whoever followed his own desires without guidance from God? Truly, God guides not the folk, the ones who are unjust.* **28:50**

O my God! Let my spirit be the first of those good objects that **Your** take from me and the first trust out of **Your** favors held in trust with me. Sermon 215

Certainly, We caused the saying to reach them so that perhaps they will recollect. **28:51**

The Prophet (Q7:158), peace and the mercy of God be upon him, treated this world disdainfully and regarded it low. He held it contemptible and hated it. He realized that God kept it away from him with intention and spread it out for others by way of contempt. Therefore, he remained away from it by his heart, banished its recollection from his mind and wished that its attraction should remain hidden from his eyes so that he would not acquire any clothing from it or hope for staying in it. He conveyed from God the pleas against committing sins, counseled his people as a warner against Divine chastisement, called people towards Paradise as a conveyor of good tidings and made them fear the Fire, cautioning against it. Sermon 108

Those to whom We gave the Book before it, they believe in it. **28:52**

Certainly, only doubtful innovations cause ruin except those from which God may protect. In God's authority lies the safety of your affairs. Therefore, render Him such obedience as is neither blameworthy nor insincere. Sermon 169

When it is recounted to them, they say: We believed in it. Truly, it is The Truth from our Lord. Truly, even before it we had been ones who submit to God. **28:53**
Those will be given their compensation two times because they patiently endured and drive off evil deeds with benevolence and they spend out of what We provided them. **28:54**
When they heard idle talk, they turned aside from it and said: To us are our actions and to you are your actions. Peace be to you! We are not looking for the ones who are ignorant. **28:55**

You are supporters of Truth and brethren in faith. You are the shield on the day of tribulation and my trustees among the rest of the people. With your support I strike the runner away and hope for the obedience of him who advances forward. Therefore, extend to me support which is free from deceit and pure from doubt because, by God, I am the most preferable of all for the people. Sermon 118

Truly, ***you*** *have not guided whom* ***you*** *have loved but God guides whomever He wills. He is greater in knowledge of the ones who are truly guided.* **28:56**

The human being should secure honor by adopting these qualities. He should fear the Day of Judgment before it arrives. He should appreciate the shortness of his life and the shortness of his sojourn in the place of stay which has only to last for his change over to the next place. He should therefore do something for his change over and for the known stages of his departure. Blessed be he who possesses a virtuous heart, obeys one who guides him, keeps away from one who takes him to ruin, catches the path of safety with the help of him who provides him light of guidance and by obeying the leader who commands him, hastens towards guidance before its doors are closed, opens the door of repentance and removes the stain of sins. He has certainly been put on the right path and guided towards the straight path. Sermon 214

They said: If we follow the guidance with ***you****, we would be snatched away from our region. Establish We not firmly for them a holy, safe place where all kinds of fruits are collected as provision from that which proceeds from Our Presence? But most of them know not.* **28:57**

O my God! I seek **Your** protection from becoming destitute despite **Your** riches, from being misguided despite **Your** guidance, from being molested in **Your** realm and from being humiliated while authority rests with **You**. O my God! Let my spirit be the first of those good objects that **You** take from me and the first trust out of **Your** favors held in trust with me. Sermon 215

How many a town that We caused to perish boasted about its livelihood. These are their dwellings, not to be inhabited after them but a little. Truly, We, We had been the ones who inherit. **28:58**

Certainly, there are examples before you of God's wrath, punishment, days of tribulations and happenings. Therefore, do not disregard His promises. Do not ignore His punishment or make light His wrath and not expect His violence, because God, the Almighty, did not curse the past ages unless they had left off asking others to do good acts and refraining them from bad acts. In fact, God cursed the foolish for committing sins and the wise because they gave up refraining others from evil. Be aware! You have broken the bonds of Islam, transgressed its limits, and destroyed its commands. Sermon 192

***Your** Lord had not been One Who Causes towns to perish until He raises up to their mother-town a Messenger who recounts Our signs to them. We never had been Ones Who Cause towns to perish unless their people are ones who are unjust.* **28:59**

With *the Prophet* (Q7:158), peace and the mercy of God be upon him, God exhausted the series of Prophets and ended the revelation. He then fought for Him those who were turning away from Him and were equating others with Him. Sermon 133

Whatever things you were given are enjoyment for this present life and its adornment. What is with God is better for one who endures. Will you not, then, be reasonable? **28:60**

You should take a lesson from the fate of the progeny of Ishmael, the children of Isaac and the children of Jacob. How similar are their affairs and how akin are their examples. In connection with the details of their division and disunity, think of the days when Kings of Persia and the Caesars of Rome had become their masters. They turned them out from the pastures of their lands, the rivers of Iraq and the fertility of the world, towards thorny forests, the passages of hot winds and hardships in livelihood. By doing this, they turned them into just herders of camels. Their houses were the worst in the world and their places of stay were the most drought-stricken. There was not one voice towards which they could turn for protection, nor any shade of affection on whose strength they could repose trust. Sermon 192

Is he to whom We promised a fairer promise—and it is one that reaches fulfillment—like him to whom We gave the enjoyment of enjoyment for this present life? Again, on the Day of Resurrection he will be among the ones who are charged? **28:61**
On that Day He will proclaim to them and will say: Where are My ascribed associates whom you had been claiming? **28:62**
They would say about whom will be realized the saying: Our Lord! These are they whom we led into error. We led them into error even as we erred. We clear ourselves with ***You****. They had never been worshipping us.* **28:63**
It would be said: Call to your ascribed associates. Then, they will call to them, but they will not respond to them and they will see the punishment. If only they had been truly guided! **28:64**
On a Day when He would proclaim to them and He would say: What have you answered to the ones who are sent? **28:65**

I bear witness that *there is no god but God* (Q47:19), and I bear witness that *Muhammad* (Q48:29), peace and the mercy of God be upon him, is *His servant* (Q17:1) and *Prophet* (Q7:158) and His chosen and His selected one. Sermon 150

Then, the tidings of that day will be in darkness and they will not demand anything of one another. **28:66**

They will be within God's sight and will hear every one who would call them. They will have the dress of helplessness and covering of submission and indignity. At this time, contrivances will disappear. Desires will be cut. Hearts will sink quietly. Voices will be lowered. Sweat will choke the throat. Fear will increase. Ears will resound with the thundering voice of the announcer calling towards the final judgment, award of recompense, striking of punishment and paying of reward. Sermon 82

As for him who repented and believed and did as one in accord with morality, then, perhaps he will be among the ones who prosper. **28:67**

Among the proofs of His creation is the creation of the skies which are fastened without pillars and stand without support. He called them. They responded obediently and humbly without being lazy or loathsome. If they had not acknowledged His Godhead and obeyed Him, He would not have made them the place for His throne, the abode of His angels and the destination: *To Him Words of what is good rise and He exalts an action in accord with morality ...* (Q35:10) of the creatures. Sermon 182

Your *Lord creates whatever He wills and chooses. Not for them had there been a choice. Glory be to God and exalted is He above partners they ascribe!* **28:68**

I bear witness that *there is no god but God,* (Q47:19), the One, there is no partner with Him, nor is there with Him any god other than Himself, and that *Muhammad* (Q48:29), peace and the mercy of God be upon him, is *His servant,* (Q17:1), and *Prophet.* (Q7:158) Sermon 35

Your *Lord knows what their breasts hide and what they speak openly.* **28:69**

O people! Every one shall meet what he wishes to avoid by running away. Death is the place to which life is driving. To run away from it means to catch it. How many days did I spend in searching for the secret of this matter, but God did not allow save its concealment. Alas! It is a treasured knowledge. Sermon 149

He, God, there is no god but He. His is all Praise in the First and in the Last. His is the determination. To Him you will be returned. **28 70**

Foreheads bow before Him and lips declare His Oneness. He determined the limits of things at the time of His creating them, keeping Himself away from any likeness. Sermon 163

Say: Considered you what if God made the nighttime endless for you until the Day of Resurrection? What god other than God brings you illumination? Will you not, then, hear? **28:71**

On that Day even the opening of an eye in the air and the sound of a footstep on the ground will be assigned its due through His Justice and His Equity. On that say many an argument will prove void and a contention for excuses will stand rejected. Sermon 222

Say: Considered you what if God made the daytime endless for you until the Day of Resurrection? What god other than God brings you nighttime wherein you rest? Will you not, then, perceive? **28:72**

He commanded it to remain stationary in obedience to His commands. He made its sun the bright indication for its day and moon the gloomy indication for its night. He then put them in motion in their orbits and ordained their pace of movement in the stages of their paths in order to distinguish with their help between night and day and in order that the reckoning of years and calculations may be known by their fixed movements. Sermon 91

It is out of His mercy that He assigned for you the nighttime and the daytime that you rest in it and that you be looking for His grace and so that perhaps you will give thanks. **28:73**

He created the earth and suspended it without being busy, retained it without support, made it stand without legs, raised it without pillars, protected it against bendings and curvings and defended it against crumbling and splitting into parts. He fixed mountains on it like stumps, solidified its rocks, caused its streams to flow and opened wide its valleys. Whatever He made did not suffer from any frailty. Whatever He strengthened did not show any weakness. Sermon 186

On a Day He will proclaim to them and say: Where are My ascribed associates whom you had been claiming? **28:74**
We will tear out a witness from every community and We will say: Prepare your proof. Then, they will know that The Truth is with God and will go astray from them what they had been devising. **28:75**

... my God, the earth will never be empty of one who establishes the proof of God, whether overtly with publicity or fearfully in obscurity, so that God's proofs and elucidations come to naught. But such as these, how many are they and where? By God, they may be the smallest in number, but with God they are the greatest in rank. Through them God preserves His proofs and elucidations, so that they entrust them to their compeers and sow them in the hearts of those resembling them. Through them, knowledge penetrates the reality of insight. They rejoice in their intimacy with the spirit of certainty. They make easy what the extravagant find harsh. They befriend that by which the ignorant are estranged. With their bodies they keep company with the world, while their spirits are tied to the transcendent realm. They are the viceregents of God on His earth, summoners to His religion. Ah! How I long to see them! Saying 146*

Truly, Korah had been of the folk of Moses, but he was insolent towards them. We gave him of the treasures which truly, the keys of it were a heavy ordeal to many imbued with strength. Mention when His folk said to him: Exult not. Truly, God loves not the exultant. **28:76**
Look for what God gave ***you*** *for the Last Abode. Forget not* ***your*** *share of the present and do good even as God did good to* ***you****. Be not insolent, corrupting in and on the earth. Truly, God loves not the ones who make corruption.* **28:77**
Korah said: I was only given it because of the knowledge with me. Knows he not that God caused to perish before him some of the generations who were more vigorous in strength than he and more numerous in multitude yet the ones who sin will not be asked about their impieties? **28:78**
So, he went forth to his folk in his adornment. Said those who want this present life: O would that we had the like of what was given to Korah! Truly, he is the possessor of a sublime allotment. **28:79**
Those who were given the knowledge said: Woe to you! The reward for good deeds from God is better for whoever believed and did as ones in accord with morality. None will be in receipt of it, but the ones who remain steadfast. **28:80**
So, We caused to swallow him the earth and his abode! Then, there had been not any faction to help him against God. He had been of the ones who are helpless. **28:81**
It came to be in the morning those who had coveted his place but yesterday, say: God extends the provision to whomever He wills of His servants and confines it to whomever He wills. Were it not that God showed grace to us, He would have caused the earth to swallow us; O how the ones who are ungrateful will not prosper! **28:82** ***

This is the Last Abode that We will assign to those who want not self-exaltation in the earth, nor corruption. The Ultimate End is for the ones who are God-conscious. **28:83**

When I took up the reins of government, one party broke away and another turned disobedient while the rest began acting wrongfully as if they had not heard the word of God saying: *This is the Last Abode that We will assign to those who want not self-exaltation in the earth, nor corruption. The Ultimate End is for the ones who are God-conscious.* 28:83 Sermon 3

Whoever brought about benevolence, for him there will be better than it. Whoever brought about an evil deed, then, not will be given recompense to those who did evil deeds other than for what they had been doing. **28:84**

Be aware! At the time of committing evil deeds, remember the destroyer of joys, the spoiler of pleasures and the killer of desires, namely death. Seek assistance of God for fulfillment of His obligatory rights and for thanking Him for His countless bounties and obligations. Sermon 99

Truly, He Who imposed the Quran for ***you*** *will be one who restores* ***you*** *to the place of return. Say: My Lord is greater in knowledge of whoever drew near guidance and whoever is clearly wandering astray.* **28:85**

By God, I have knowledge of the conveyance of messages, fulfillment of promises and of entire expressions. We, the people of the house of *the Prophet* (Q7:158), peace and the mercy of God be upon him, possess the doors of wisdom and light of governance. Be aware that the paths of religion are one. Its highways are straight. He who follows them achieves the aim and secures the objective. He who stood away from them goes astray and incurs repentance. Act for the day for which provisions are stored and when the intentions would be tested. If a person's own intelligence, which is present with him, does not help him, the wits of others, which are remote from him, are more unhelpful and those who are away from him even more useless. Dread the fire whose flame is severe, whose hollow is deep, whose dress is iron and whose drink is bloody pus. Be aware! The good name of a person retained by God, the Sublime, among the people is better than wealth inherited by those who would not praise Him. Sermon 120

You *had been without hope that the Book would be cast down to* ***you****, but as a mercy from* ***your*** *Lord. Be* ***you*** *not a sustainer of the ones who are ungrateful.* **28:86**

Certainly, these people are in agreement in disliking my authority. I will carry on until I perceive disunity among you, because if they succeed in spite of the unsoundness of their view, the whole organization of Muslims will be shattered. They are hankering after this world out of jealousy against him on whom God has bestowed it. So they intend to revert the matters to the pre-Islamic period. On us it is obligatory, for your sake, to abide by the Book of God (Quran), the Sublime, and the conduct of *the Prophet* (Q7:158), peace and the mercy of God be upon him, to stand by His rights and to revive his *sunna*. Sermon 169

Let them not bar ***you*** *from the signs of God after they were caused to descend to* ***you****. Call to* ***your*** *Lord. Be* ***you*** *not among the ones who are polytheists.* **28:87**

I bear witness that *there is no god but God* (Q47:19) by virtue of belief, certainty, sincerity and conviction. I also bear witness that *Muhammad* (Q48:29), peace and the mercy of God be upon him, is *His servant* (Q17:1) and *Prophet* (Q7:158) whom He deputed when the signs of guidance were obliterated and the ways of religion were desolate. So he threw

open the truth, gave advice to the people, guided them towards righteousness and ordered them to be moderate. May God bless him ... Sermon 194

Call not to any god other than God. There is no god but He! Everything is that which perishes, but His Countenance. To Him is the determination and to Him you will be returned. **28:88**

We bear witness that *there is no god, but He.* (Q3:2) Sermon 100

Chapter 29: The Spider (al-ᶜAnkabūt)

29:1 *Alif Lam Mim*

Assumed humanity that they will be left because they say: We believed and they will not be tried? **29:2**

You should adhere to the Book of God because it is the strong rope, a clear light, a benefiting cure, a quenching for thirst, protection for the adherent and deliverance for the attached. It does not curve so as to need straightening and does not deflect so as to be corrected. Frequency of its repetition and its falling on ears does not make it old. Whoever speaks according to it speaks truth and whoever acts by it is forward in action. A person stood up and said: Tell us about this disturbance and whether you inquired about it from *the Prophet* (Q7:158), peace and the mercy of God be upon him. Thereupon he said: When God the Almighty sent down the verse: *Alif lam mim. Has humanity assumed that they will be left because they say: We have believed and they will not be tried?* (Q29:1-29:2) I came to know that the disturbance would not befall us so long as *the Prophet* (Q7:158), peace and the mercy of God be upon him, is among us. Sermon 156

Certainly, We tried those who were before them. Then, certainly, God knows those who were sincere and knows the ones who lie. **29:3**

Be aware! The worst speech is that which is untrue. Sermon 84

Or assumed those who do evil deeds that they will out do Us? How evil is that about which they give judgment! **29:4**

Be aware! At the time of committing evil deeds, remember the destroyer of joys, the spoiler of pleasures and the killer of desires, namely death. Seek assistance of God for fulfillment of His obligatory rights and for thanking Him for His countless bounties and obligations. Sermon 99

Whoever had been hoping for the meeting with God, then, truly, the term of God is that which arrives. He is The Hearing, The Knowing. **29:5**

Whoever struggled, he struggles only for himself. Then, truly, God is Sufficient for the worlds. **29:6**

Those who believed and do as ones in accord with morality, certainly, We will absolve them of their evil deeds and We will give recompense for the fairer of what they had been doing. **29:7**

Whoever proceeds towards this mischief will be ruined and whoever strives for it will be annihilated. They will be biting each other during it as the wild asses bite each other in the herd. The coils of the rope will be disturbed and the face of affairs will be blinded. During it sagacity will be on the ebb, and the oppressors will have the opportunity to speak. Sermon 151

We charged the human being with goodness to ones who are his parents and if they struggled with ***you*** *that* ***you*** *ascribe partners with Me, that of which for* ***you*** *there is no knowledge, then, obey them not. To Me is your return and I will tell you of what you had been doing.* **29:8**

... to Him returns whoever dies. Sermon 108

Those who believed and did as the ones in accord with morality, We will, certainly, cause them to enter among the ones in accord with morality. **29:9**

Among the proofs of His creation is the creation of the skies which are fastened without pillars and stand without support. He called them. They responded obediently and humbly without being lazy or loathsome. If they had not acknowledged His Godhead and obeyed Him, He would not have made them the place for His throne, the abode of His angels and the destination: *To Him Words of what is good rise and He exalts an action in accord with morality* ... (Q35:10) of the creatures. Sermon 182

Of humanity is he who says: We believed in God. But, when he was maligned for the sake of God, he mistook the persecution by humanity for a punishment by God. If help drew near from ***your*** *Lord, they would, surely, say: We had been with you. Is not God greater in knowledge of what is in the breasts of beings?* **29:10**

Your allegiance to me was not without thinking, nor is my and your position the same. I seek you for God's sake, but you seek me for your own benefits. O people! Support me despite your hearts' desires. By God, I will take revenge for the oppressed from the oppressor and will put a string in the nose of the oppressor and drag him to the spring of truthfulness even though he may grudge it. Sermon 136

Certainly, God knows those who believed and, certainly, He knows the ones who are hypocrites. **29:11**

Their hearts are diseased while their faces are clean. They walk stealthily and tread like the approach of sickness over the body. Their words speak of cure, but their acts are like incurable diseases. They are jealous of ease, intensify distress, and destroy hopes. Their victims are found lying down on every path, while they have means to approach every heart and they have false tears for every grief. Sermon 194

Those who are ungrateful said to those who have believed: Follow our way and we will certainly carry your transgressions while they are not ones who carry any of their own transgressions. Truly they are the ones who lie. **29:12**

Certainly, they will carry their own lading and other ladings with their own ladings. Certainly, they will be asked on the Day of Resurrection about what they had been devising. **29:13**

There remain a few people in whose case the remembrance of their return to God on the Day of Judgment keeps their eyes bent and the awareness of the Resurrection moves them to tears. Some of them are scared away from the world and disperse. Some are frightened and subdued. Some are quiet as if muzzled. Some are praying sincerely. Some are grief-stricken and pain-ridden whom fear has confined to namelessness. Disgrace has shrouded them, so they are in the sea of bitter water, their mouths are closed and their hearts are bruised. They preached until they were tired. They were oppressed until they were disgraced. They were killed until their numbers dwindled. Sermon 32

Certainly, We sent Noah to his folk and he lingered in expectation among them a thousand years less fifty years. The Deluge took them while they were the ones who are unjust. **29:14**
Then, We rescued him and the Companions of the Vessel and made it a sign for the worlds. **29:15**
When Abraham said to his folk: Worship God and be God-conscious of Him. That would be better for you if you had been knowing. **29:16**
You only worship graven images and not God? You create calumny? Truly, those whom you worship other than God possess not for you any power to provide for you. So, look for the provision from God and worship Him and give thanks to Him. To Him you will be returned. **29:17**
If you deny, then, surely, communities denied before you. For the Messenger is not but the delivering of the clear message. **29:18**

God never allowed His creation to remain without a Prophet, one deputized by Him, or a Book sent down from Him, or a binding argument, or a standing plea. These Messengers were such that they did not fear that they were few in comparison to the large numbers of their falsifiers. Among them was either a predecessor who would name the one to follow or the follower who had been introduced by the predecessor. Sermon 1

Consider they not how God causes the creation to begin and, again, He causes it to return? Truly, that for God is easy. **29:19**

People did not take light from the lights of his wisdom, nor did they produce flame from the flint of sparkling knowledge. So in this matter, they are like grazing cattle and hard stones. Nevertheless, hidden things have appeared for those who perceive. The face of right has become clear for the wanderer. The approaching moment has raised the veil from its face. Signs have appeared for those who search for them. Sermon 108

Say: Journey through the earth; then, look on how He began the creation. Again, God will cause the last growth to grow. Truly, God is Powerful over everything. **29:20**
He punishes whom He wills and has mercy on whom He wills. To Him you will come back. **29:21**

He is the Last for Whom there is no "after" so that there could be anything after Him. He prevents the pupils of the eyes from seeing Him or perceiving Him. Time does not change over Him so as to admit of any change of condition about Him. He is not in any place so as to allow Him movement from one place to another. Sermon 91

You will not be ones who frustrate Him on the earth nor in the heaven and there is not for you, other than God, either a protector or a helper. **29:22**

You are everlasting. There is no end to **You. You** are the highest aim. There is no escape from **You. You** are the promised point of return from which there is no deliverance except towards **You.** In **Your** hand is the forelock of every creature. To **You** is the return of every living being. Glory be to **You**! How great is **Your** affair! Glory to **You**! How great is **Your** creation that we see, but how small is this greatness by the side of **Your** Might! How awe-striking is **Your** realm that we notice, but how humble is this against what is hidden from us out of **Your** authority! How extensive are **Your** bounties in this world, but how small are they against the bounties of the next world! Sermon 108

Those who disbelieved in the signs of God and the meeting with Him, those gave up hope of My mercy and those, for them there will be a painful punishment. **29:23**
So, the answer of his folk had been not but that they said: Kill him or burn him! Then, God rescued

him from the fire. Truly, in this are, certainly, signs for a folk who believe. **29:24**

I bear witness that *there is no god but God* (Q47:19), by virtue of belief, certainty, sincerity and conviction. I also bear witness that *Muhammad* (Q48:29), peace and the mercy of God be upon him, is *His servant* (Q17:1) and *Prophet* (Q7:158) whom He deputed when the signs of guidance were obliterated and the ways of religion were desolate. So he threw open the truth, gave advice to the people, guided them towards righteousness and ordered them to be moderate. May God bless him ... Sermon 194

He said: You take only to yourselves graven images instead of God because of affection among yourselves for this present life. Again, on the Day of Resurrection some of you will disavow some others and some of you will curse some others and your place of shelter will be the fire. For you there will be no ones who help. **29:25**

They are emulating each other and proceeding in groups towards the final objective and the rendezvous of death, until when matters come to a close, the world dies and resurrection draws near. Sermon 82

So, Lot believed in him. Abraham said: Truly, I am one who emigrates for my Lord. Truly, He, He is The Almighty, The Wise. **29:26**
We bestowed Isaac and Jacob on him and We assigned to his offspring prophethood and the Book. We gave him his compensation in the present. Truly, in the world to come he will be, certainly, among the ones in accord with morality. **29:27**
Lot, when he said to his folk: Truly, you approach indecency which none who preceded you committed in the worlds. **29:28**
You approach men with lust and sever the way and approach that which is unlawful in your conclave. Then, the answer of his folk had not been but that they said: Bring on us the punishment of God if ***you*** *had been among the ones who are sincere.* **29:29**
He said: My Lord! Help me against the folk, ones who make corruption. **29:30**
When Our Messengers drew near Abraham with the good tidings. They said: Truly, We are ones who will cause to perish the people of this town. Truly, its people had been ones who are unjust. **29:31**
He said: Truly, in it is Lot. They said: We are greater in knowledge of who is in it. We will, truly, deliver him and his family, but his woman. She had been among the ones who stay behind. **29:32**
When Our Messengers drew near Lot, he was troubled because of them and he was concerned for them, distressed, and they said: Neither fear nor feel remorse. Truly, we are ones who will deliver ***you*** *and* ***your*** *family but* ***your*** *woman. She had been among the ones who stay behind.* **29:33**
Truly, we are ones who will cause to descend on the people of this town wrath from heaven because they had been disobeying. **29:34**
Certainly, We left in it a sign, clear portents for a folk who be reasonable. **29:35**
To Midian, their brother Shuayb. He said: O my folk! Worship God and hope for the Last Day and do not mischief in and on the earth as ones who make corruption. **29:36**
They denied him. So, the quaking of the earth took them and it came to be in the morning in their abodes, ones who are fallen prostrate. **29:37**
Ad and Thamud, surely, it became clear to you from their dwellings. Satan made their actions appear pleasing to them and barred them from the way and they had been ones who see clearly. **29:38**
Korah and Pharaoh and Haman and, certainly, Moses drew near to them with the clear portents,

but they grew arrogant on the earth and they had not been ones who take the lead from Us. **29:39**
So, We took each of them in his impiety. Of them was he on whom We sent a sand storm and of them was he whom the Cry took and of them was he whom We caused the earth to swallow and of them were some whom We drowned. God had not been doing wrong to them, but they had been doing wrong themselves. **29:40** ***

The parable of those who took other than God to themselves as protectors is that of the spider who took a house to itself. But, truly, the frailest of houses is the house of the spider if they had but been knowing. **29:41**

If an ambiguous problem is presented before him, he manages a shabby argument about it of his own accord and passes judgment on this basis. In this way he is entangled in the confusion of doubts as if in a spider's web, not knowing whether he is right or wrong. If he is right, he fears lest he erred, while if he is wrong, he hopes he is right. He is ignorant, wandering astray in ignorance and riding on carriages aimlessly moving in darkness. He did not try to find the Reality of knowledge. He scatters the traditions as the wind scatters the dry leaves. Sermon 17

Truly, God knows what thing they call to other than Him. He is The Almighty, The Wise. **29:42**
We propound these parables for humanity. No one is reasonable among them but the ones who know. **29:43**

I bear witness that *there is no god but God* (Q47:19), the One, there is no partner with Him, nor is there with Him any god other than Himself, and that *Muhammad* (Q48:29), peace and the mercy of God be upon him, is *His servant* (Q17:1) and *Prophet.* (Q7:158) Sermon 35

God created the heavens and the earth with The Truth. Truly, in that is a sign for the ones who believe. **29:44**

Know that—may God have mercy on you—you are living at a time when those who speak about right are few, when tongues are loath to utter the truth and those who stick to the right are humiliated. The people of this time are engaged in disobedience. Their youth are wicked, their old men are sinful, their learned men are hypocrites, and their speakers are sycophants. Their young ones do not respect their elders, and their rich men do not support the destitute. Sermon 232

Recount what was revealed to **you** *of the Book and perform the formal prayer. Truly, the formal prayer prohibits depravity and that which is unlawful, and, truly, the remembrance of God is greater. God knows what you craft.* **29:45**

The Book of God is that through which you see, you speak and you hear. Sermon 132

Dispute not with the People of the Book unless in a way that is fairer, but with those who did wrong among them. Say: We have believed in what was caused to descend to us and was caused to descend to you and our God and your God is One and we are ones who submit to Him. **29:46**
Thus, We caused the Book to descend to **you**. *Those to whom We gave the Book before will believe in it. Of these, the people of Makkah, there are some who believe in it. None negates Our signs but the ones who are ungrateful.* **29:47**

You, O people of Arabia, will be victims of calamities which have come near. You should avoid the intoxication of wealth, fear the disasters of chastisement, keep steadfast in the darkness and crookedness of mischief when its hidden nature discloses itself, its secrets become manifest and its axis and the pivot of its rotation gain strength. It begins in imperceptible stages, but develops into great hideousness. Its youth is like the youth of an adolescent and its marks are like the marks of beating by stone. Sermon 151

Neither had ***you*** *been recounting from any Book before it nor write* ***you*** *it with* ***your*** *right hand for then, certainly, they would have been in doubt, the ones who deal in falsehood.* **29:48**

There is no doubt that God sent down *the Prophet* (Q7:158), peace and the mercy of God be upon him, as a guide with an eloquent Book and a standing command. No one will be ruined by it except one who ruins himself. Certainly, only doubtful innovations cause ruin except those from which God may protect. In God's authority lies the safety of your affairs. Therefore, render Him such obedience as is neither blameworthy nor insincere. By God, you must do so otherwise God will take away from you the power of Islam and will never thereafter return it to you until it reverts to others. Sermon 169

Nay! It is clear portents, signs in the breasts of those who were given the knowledge. None negate Our signs but ones who are unjust. **29:49**

Praise belongs to God. (Q1:2) He is such that senses cannot perceive Him, place cannot contain Him, eyes cannot see Him and veils cannot cover Him. He proves His eternity by the coming into existence of His creation, and also by originating His creation He proves His existence, and by their mutual similarity He proves that there is nothing similar to Him. He is true in His promise. He is too high to be unjust to His creatures. He stands by equity among His creation and practices justice over them in His commands. He provides evidence through the creation of things of His being from ever, through their marks of incapability of His power, and through their powerlessness against death of His eternity. Sermon 185

They said: Why were signs not caused to descend to him from his Lord? Say: The signs are only with God. I am only a warner, one who makes clear. **29:50**

The Prophet (Q7:158), peace and the mercy of God be upon him, treated this world disdainfully and regarded it low. He held it contemptible and hated it. He realized that God kept it away from him with intention and spread it out for others by way of contempt. Therefore, he remained away from it by his heart, banished its recollection from his mind and wished that its attraction should remain hidden from his eye so that he should not acquire any clothing from it or hope for staying in it. He conveyed from God the pleas against committing sins, counseled his people as a warner against Divine chastisement and called people towards Paradise as a conveyor of good tidings. Sermon 108

Suffices for them not that We caused the Book to descend to ***you*** *which is recounted to them? Truly, in that is a mercy and a reminder for a folk who believe.* **29:51**

Learn the Quran for it is the fairest of discourses and understand it thoroughly for it is the best blossoming of hearts. Seek cure with its light for it is the cure for hearts. Recite it beautifully for it is the most beautiful narration. Certainly, a scholar who acts not according to his knowledge is like the off-headed ignorant who does not find relief from his ignorance, but on the learned the plea of God is greater and grief more incumbent, and he is more blameworthy before God. Sermon 109

Say: God sufficed as a witness between me and between you. He knows whatever is in the heavens and the earth. Those who believed in falsehood and were ungrateful to God, those, they are the ones who are losers. **29:52**

Remember that inequity and falsehood bring disgrace to a person in this world and in the hereafter Letter 48

They seek ***you*** *to hasten the punishment! Were it not for a term, that which is determined, the punishment would have drawn near them. Certainly, it will approach them suddenly while they are not aware.* **29:53**

O God's human being! Where are those who were allowed long ages to live? They enjoyed bounty. They were taught. They learned. They were given time. They passed it in vain. They were kept healthy. They forgot their duty. They were allowed a long period of life, were handsomely provided for, were warned of grievous punishment and were promised great rewards. You should avoid sins that lead to destruction and vices that attract the wrath of God. Sermon 82

They seek to hasten the punishment and, truly, hell will be that which encloses the ones who are ungrateful. **29:54**

Everyone of them is ... alone although they are a group, and they are strangers, even though friends. They are unaware of morning after a night and of evening after a day. The night or the day when they departed has become ever existent for them. They found the dangers of their place of stay more serious than they had apprehended. They witnessed that its signs were greater than they had guessed. Sermon 220

On a Day when the punishment overcomes them from above them and from beneath their feet, He will say: Experience what you had been doing! **29:55**

Your ultimate goal of reward or punishment is before you. Behind your back is the hour of Resurrection which is driving you on. Keep yourself light and overtake the forward ones. The first ones who have preceded await your last ones. Sermon 21

O my servants who have believed, My earth, truly, is that which is extensive, so worship Me! **29:56**

Glory be to **You**! How great is **Your** creation that we see, but how small is this greatness by the side of **Your** Might! How awe-striking is **Your** realm that we notice, but how humble is this against what is hidden from us out of **Your** authority! How extensive are **Your** bounties in this world, but how small are they against the bounties of the next world! Sermon 108

Every soul is one that experiences death. Again, to Us you will return. **29:57**

People have been created as a proof of His power, have been brought up with authority. They are made to die through pangs and placed in graves where they turn into crumbs. Then they will be resurrected one by one, awarded their recompense and each one separately will have to account for his actions. Sermon 82

Those who believed and did as the ones in accord with morality, We will certainly place them in a settlement in the highest chambers in the Garden, beneath which rivers run, ones who will dwell

in it forever. How excellent is the compensation for the ones who work, **29:58**
those who endured patiently and they put their trust in their Lord. **29:59**

O my God! Let my spirit be the first of those good objects that **You** take from me and the first trust out of **Your** favors held in trust with me. Sermon 215

How many a moving creature carries not its own provision, but God provides for it and for you. He is The Hearing, The Knowing. **29:60**

You are everlasting. There is no end to **You. You** are the highest aim. There is no escape from **You. You** are the promised point of return from which there is no deliverance except towards **You.** In **Your** hand is the forelock of every creature. To **You** is the return of every living being. Glory be to **You**! How great is **Your** affair! Sermon 108

*If **you** had asked them: Who created the heavens and the earth and caused the sun and the moon to be subservient? They will, certainly, say: God. Then, how they are misled!* **29:61**

This world and the hereafter have submitted to Him their reins. The skies and earths have flung their keys towards Him. The thriving trees bow to Him in the morning and evening, producing for Him flaming fire from their branches and, at His command, turn their own feed into ripe fruits. Sermon 133

God extends the provision for whom He wills of His servants and confines it for whom He wills. Truly, God is Knowing of everything. **29:62**

May God have mercy on you! Provide yourselves for the journey because the call for departure has been announced. Regard your stay in the world as very short. Return to God with the best provision that is with you, because surely, before you lies a valley, difficult to climb, and places of stay full of fear and dangers. Sermon 203

Say: The Praise belongs to God! Nay! Most of them are not reasonable. **29:63**

Imagination cannot surmise Him within the limits of the movements of limbs or the senses. It cannot be said about Him: "whence." No time limit can be attributed to Him by saying "until." He is apparent, but it cannot be said "from what.".He is hidden, but it cannot be said "in what." He is not a body which can die, nor is He veiled so as to be enclosed therein. He is not near to things by way of touch, nor is He remote from them by way of separation. Sermon 163

This present life is not, but a diversion and a pastime. Truly, the Last Abode is the eternal life if they had been knowing! **29:64**

May God have pity on you. You should, therefore, hasten towards the preparation of abodes which you have been commanded to populate and towards which you have been called and invited. Seek the completion of God's favors on you by exercising endurance in His obedience and abstention from His disobedience, because tomorrow is close to today. How fast are the hours of the day. How fast are the days in the month. How fast are the months in the years. How fast the years in a life. Sermon 188

When they embarked on the boats, they called to God, ones who are sincere and devoted in the way of life to Him. Then, when He delivered them to dry land, that is when they ascribed partners with God, **29:65** *being ungrateful for what We gave them. So, let them take joy for soon they will know!* **29:66**

O my God! We seek **Your** protection from turning away from **Your** command, or revolting against **Your** religion, or being led away by our desires instead of by guidance that comes from **You**. Sermon 215

Consider they not that We made a safe, holy place while humanity is being snatched away all around them? Believe they, then, in falsehood and are they ungrateful for the divine blessing? **29:67**

Who does greater wrong than he who devised a lie against God? Or denied The Truth when it drew near him? Is there not in hell a place of lodging for the ones who are ungrateful? **29:68**

Where are the minds which seek light from the lamps of guidance and the eyes which look at minarets of God-consciousness? Where are the hearts dedicated to God and devoted to the obedience of God? They are all crowding towards worldly vanities and quarreling over unlawful issues. The banners of the Garden and Hell have been raised for them, but they have turned their faces away from the Garden and proceeded to Hell by dint of their performances. God called them, but they showed dislike and ran away. When Satan called them, they responded and proceeded towards him. Sermon 144

As for those who struggled for Us, We will truly guide them to Our ways. Truly, God is with ones who are doers of good. **29:69**

Truly God is with those who are God-conscious and those, they are the ones who are doers of good. (Q16:128). Sermon 193

CHAPTER 30: THE ROMANS (al-Rūm)

30:1 *Alif Lam Mim*

For them among their ascribed associates will not be intercessors and their ascribed associates with God will be ones who disavow them. **30:1**

As for my last will, it is that concerning God, do not believe in a partner for Him. Sermon 148

The Romans were vanquished **30:2**
in the closer region, and they, after being vanquished, will prevail **30:3**
within a certain number of years. To God belongs the command before and after. That Day ones who believe will be glad **30:4**
with the help of God. He helps whom He wills. He is The Almighty, The Compassionate. **30:5**

Surely, **You** are powerful over whatever **You** will. Sermon 143

It is the promise of God. God breaks not His Promise, but most of humanity knows not. **30:6**

Everything submits to Him. Everything exists by Him. He is the satisfaction of every poor, dignity of the low, energy for the weak and shelter for the oppressed. Sermon 108

They know only that which is manifest in this present life. Of the world to come, they are ones who are heedless. **30:7**

Now neither the good acts can be added to, nor can evil acts be atoned for by repentance. Are you not sons, fathers, brothers and relations of these dead? Are you not to follow their footsteps and pass by their paths? Yet, hearts are still unmoved, heedless of guidance and moving on wrong lines, as though the addressee is someone else and as though the correct way is to amass worldly gains. Sermon 82

Or if they reflect not in themselves, God created not the heavens and the earth and whatever is between the two but with The Truth and for a term that is determined. Truly, most of humanity, in the meeting with their Lord, are, certainly, ones who disbelieve. **30:8**

You are supporters of Truth and brethren in faith. You are the shield on the day of tribulation and my trustees among the rest of the people. With your support I strike the runner away and hope for the obedience of him who advances forward. Therefore, extend to me support which is free from deceit and pure from doubt because, by God, I am the most preferable of all for the people. Sermon 118

Or journey they not through the earth and look on how had been the Ultimate End of those who were before them? They had been superior to them in strength. They plowed the earth and frequented it more than they frequented it. Drew near them their Messengers with the clear portents. Then, it had not been God doing wrong to them, but they had been doing wrong to themselves. **30:9**
Again, the Ultimate End had been misdeeds for those who did evil, because they denied the signs of God and had been ridiculing them. **30:10**

With *the Prophet* (Q7:158), peace and the mercy of God be upon him, God exhausted the series of Prophets and ended the revelation. He then fought for Him those who were turning away from Him and were equating others with Him. Sermon 133

God begins the creation. Again, He causes it to return. Again, you will be returned to Him. **30:11**

People did not take light from the lights of his wisdom, nor did they produce flame from the flint of sparkling knowledge. So in this matter, they are like grazing cattle and hard stones. Nevertheless, hidden things have appeared for those who perceive. The face of right has become clear for the wanderer. The approaching moment has raised the veil from its face. Signs have appeared for those who search for them. Sermon 108

On a Day when the Hour will be secure, the ones who sin will be seized with despair. **30:12**
Not will be for them among their ascribed associates intercessors and their ascribed associates with God will be ones who disavow them. **30:13**

There remain a few people in whose case the remembrance of their return to God on the Day of Judgment keeps their eyes bent and the awareness of the Resurrection moves them to tears. Some of them are scared away from the world and disperse. Some are frightened and subdued. Some are quiet as if muzzled. Some are praying sincerely. Some are grief-stricken and pain-ridden whom fear has confined to namelessness. Disgrace has shrouded them, so they are in the sea of bitter water, their mouths are closed and their hearts are bruised. They preached until they were tired. They were oppressed until they were disgraced. They were killed until their numbers dwindled. Sermon 32

On a Day when the Hour will be secure, that Day they will be split up. **30:14**
Then, as for those who believed and did as the ones in accord with morality, they will be walking with joy in a well-watered meadow. **30:15**

They are emulating each other and proceeding in groups towards the final objective and the rendezvous of death, until when matters come to a close, the world dies and Resurrection draws near. Sermon 82

As for those who are ungrateful and denied Our signs and the meeting of the world to come, those are ones who are charged with the punishment. **30:16**

God ... is aware of whatever is hidden in the hearts and whatever lies behind the unseen. Sermon 192

So, glory be to God at the time of the evening hour and at the time when it comes to be the morning! **30:17**

O my God! **You** know that what we did was not to seek power, nor to acquire anything from the vanities of the world. We rather wanted to restore the signs of **Your** religion and to usher prosperity into **Your** cities so that the oppressed among **Your** creatures might be safe and **Your** forsaken commands might be established. Sermon 131

To Him be The Praise in the heavens and the earth and in the evening and at the time of noon **30: 18**

We praise Him for whatever He takes or gives or whatever He inflicts on us or tries us with. He is aware of all that is hidden and He sees all that is concealed. He knows all that breasts contain or eyes hide. We render evidence that *there is no god, but He* (Q3:2) and that *Muhammad* (Q48:29), peace and the mercy of God be upon him, has been chosen by Him and deputized by Him—evidence tendered both secretly and openly, by heart and by tongue. Sermon 132

He brings out the living from the dead. He brings out the dead from the living. He gives life to the earth after its death. Thus, you will be brought out. **30:19**

Glory be to **You**! How great is **Your** affair! Glory to **You**! How great is **Your** creation that we see, but how small is this greatness by the side of **Your** Might! How awe-striking is **Your** realm that we notice, but how humble is this against what is hidden from us out of **Your** authority! How extensive are **Your** bounties in this world, but how small are they against the bounties of the next world! Sermon 108

Among His signs are that He created you from earth dust, when, again, you were mortals dispersed. **30:20**

Among His signs are that He created for you spouses from among yourselves, that you rest in them. He made affection and mercy among you. Truly, in that are certainly signs for a folk who reflect. **30:21**

I bear witness that *Muhammad* (Q48:29 peace and the mercy of God be upon him, is *His servant* (Q17:1) and *Prophet* (Q7:158), whom He deputed when the signs of guidance were obliterated and the ways of religion were desolate. Sermon 194

Among His signs are the creation of the heavens and the earth and the alteration of your languages and hues. Truly, in that are certainly signs for ones who know. **30:22**

Among His signs are your slumbering by nighttime and by daytime and your looking for His grace. Truly, in that are, certainly, signs for a folk who hear. **30:23**

He manifests Himself over the earth with His authority and greatness. He is aware of its inside through His knowledge and understanding. He has power over everything in the earth by virtue of His sublimity and dignity. Nothing from the earth that He may ask for defies Him, nor does it oppose Him so as to overpower Him. No swift-footed creature can run away from Him so as to surpass Him. He is not needy towards any possessing person so that he should feed Him. All things bow to Him and are humble before His greatness. They cannot flee away from His authority to someone else in order to escape His benefit or His harm. There is no parallel for Him who may match Him and no one like Him so as to equal Him. Sermon 186

Among His signs are that He causes you to see the lightning in fear and in hope. He sends water down from heaven and gives life by it to the earth after its death. Truly, in that are, certainly, signs for a folk who are reasonable. **30:24**

Truly, there is a strong protective shield of God over me. When my day will come it will take itself from me and hand me over to death. At that time neither an arrow will go amiss, nor a wound heal. Sermon 62

Among His signs are that the heaven and the earth are secured for you by His command. When He will call you by a call again from the earth, that is when you will go forth! **30:25**

(The Prophet) threw open the truth, gave advice to the people, guided them towards righteousness and ordered them to be moderate. May God bless him. Sermon 195

To Him belongs whoever is in the heavens and the earth. All are ones who are morally obligated to Him. **30:26**

He it is Who begins the creation. Again, He causes it to return and this is insignificant for Him. His is the Lofty Parable in the heavens and the earth. He is The Almighty, The Wise. **30:27**

The face of right has become clear for the wanderer. The approaching moment has raised the veil from its face and signs have appeared for those who search for them. Sermon 108

He propounds a parable for you from yourselves. Have you—among those whom your right hands possessed—ascribed associates in what We provided you so that you share as equals and you fear them like your awe for each other? Thus, We explain distinctly the signs to a folk who are reasonable. **30:28**

I bear witness that *there is no god but God* (Q47:19), the One, there is no partner with Him, nor is there with Him any god other than Himself, and that *Muhammad* (Q48:29), peace and the mercy of God be upon him, is *His servant* (Q17:1) and *Prophet.* (Q7:158) Sermon 35

Nay! Those who did wrong followed their own desires without knowledge. Then, who will guide whom God caused to go astray? They will not have ones who help. **30:29**

There is no doubt that God sent down *the Prophet,* (Q7:158), peace and the mercy of God be upon him, as a guide with an eloquent Book and a standing command. Sermon 169

So, set **your** *face towards a way of life as a monotheist. It is the nature originated by God in which*

He originated humanity. There is no substitution for the creation of God. That is the truth-loving way of life, but most of humanity knows not. **30:30**

We bear witness that *there is no god, but He*. (Q3:2) Sermon 100

Be ones who turn in repentance to Him and be God-conscious and perform the formal prayer and be not among the ones who are polytheists **30:31**
or of those who separated and divided their way of life and had been partisans, each party is glad with what they have. **30:32**

One of the firm decisions of God in the Wise Reminder (Quran), upon which He bestows reward or gives punishment and through which He likes or dislikes, is that it will not benefit a person, even though he exerts himself and acts sincerely, if he leaves this world to meet God with one of these acts without repenting, namely that he believed in a partner with God during his obligatory worship or appeased his own anger by killing an individual or spoke about acts committed by others or sought fulfillment of his needs from people by introducing an innovation in his religion or met people with a double face or moved among them with a double tongue. Understand this because an illustration is a guide for its like. Sermon 153

When harm afflicted humanity, they call to their Lord as ones who turn in repentance to Him. When He caused them, again, to experience His mercy, that is when a group of people among them ascribe partners with their Lord, **30:33**
for they are ungrateful for what We gave them. Then, take joy; you will know. **30:34**
Or caused We to descend to them an authority that it assert what they had been ascribing as partners with Him? **30:35**

Do not say: I have been given authority, I order and am obeyed, for this leads to corruption in the heart and the erosion of religion. Letter 53*

When We caused humanity to experience mercy, they were glad of it. But when an evil deed lights on them because of what their hands put forward, that is when they are in despair. **30:36**

The Prophet (Q7:158), peace and the mercy of God be upon him, said to me: O Ali, people will fall into mischief through their wealth, will show obligation to God on account of their faith, will expect His mercy, will feel safe from His anger and regard His unlawful matters as lawful by raising false doubts and by their misguiding desires. Sermon 154

Consider they that God extends the provision for whom He wills and confines it for whom He wills? Truly, in that are signs for a folk who believe. **30:37**

May God have mercy on you! Provide yourselves for the journey because the call for departure has been announced. Regard your stay in the world as very short. Return to God with the best provision that is with you, because surely, before you lies a valley, difficult to climb, and places of stay full of fear and dangers. Sermon 203

So, give to possessors of kinship rightfully and to the needy and to the traveler of the way. That is better for those who want the Countenance of God. Those, they are the ones who prosper. **30:38**

Charity and alms are the best remedy for ailments and calamities. One has to account in the next world for the deeds that he has done in this world. Saying 6

What you gave in usury in order that it swell the wealth of humanity swells not with God. What you gave in purifying alms, wanting the Countenance of God, then, those, they are the ones who will receive manifold. **30:39**

Whoever trades without knowing the rules of religious law will be involved in usury. Hadith 447

God is He Who created you. Again, He provided for you and, again, He will cause you to die. Again, He will give you life. Is there among your ascribed associates with Him who accomplish anything of that? Glory be to Him! Exalted is He above partners they ascribe! **30:40**

The best thing for you to do is to seek guidance of One Who has created you, Who maintains and nourishes you, Who has given you a balanced mind and a normally working body. Your invocations should be reserved for Him only. Your requests and solicitations should be alone to Him. You should only be conscious of Him. Letter 31

Corruption has become manifested on the dry land and the sea because of what the hands of humanity earned. He causes them to experience some of what they did, so that perhaps they will return repentant. **30:41**

Corruption has become manifest ... (Q30:41) There is no one to oppose and change it, nor anyone to dissuade from it or desist from it. Do you, with these qualities, hope to secure abode in the purified neighborhood of God and to be regarded His staunch lovers? Alas! God cannot be deceived about His Paradise. His will cannot be secured except by His obedience. May God curse those who advise good, but they themselves avoid it, and those who desist others from evil, but they themselves act upon it. Sermon 129

Say: Journey through the earth; then, look on how had been the Ultimate End of those who were before. Most of them had been ones who are polytheists. **30:42**

How awe-striking is **Your** realm that we notice, but how humble is this against what is hidden from us out of **Your** authority! How extensive are **Your** bounties in this world, but how small are they against the bounties of the next world! Sermon 108

So, set ***your*** *face to the truth-loving way of life before that Day approaches from God and there is no turning back. They will be split up on that Day.* **30:43**

O my God! We seek **Your** protection from turning away from **Your** command, or revolting against **Your** religion, or being led away by our desires instead of by guidance that comes from **You**. Sermon 215

Whoever was ungrateful, his ingratitude is on him. Whoever did as one in accord with morality will be arranging provision for themselves. **30:44**
He gives recompense to those who believed and did as the ones in accord with morality from His grace. Truly, He loves not the ones who are ungrateful. **30:45**

God ... is aware of whatever is hidden in the hearts and whatever lies behind the unseen. Sermon 192

Among His signs are that He sends the winds as ones that give good tidings and causes you to experience His mercy and so that the boats run at His command and that you be looking for His grace so that perhaps you will give thanks. **30:46**

One condition does not prevent Him from getting into another condition. Time does not change Him. Place does not locate him. The tongue does not describe Him. The number of drops of water, of stars in the sky, or of currents of winds in the air are not unknown to Him, nor the movements of ants on rocks, or the resting place of grubs in the dark night. He knows the places where leaves fall and the secret movements of the pupils of the eyes. Sermon 178

Certainly, We sent Messengers before ***you*** *to their own folk. They drew near them with the clear portents. Then, We requited those who sinned. It had been an obligation on Us to help ones who believe.* **30:47**

God is He Who sends the winds so they raise clouds. He extends them in the heaven how He wills and He makes them into pieces until ***you*** *have seen rain drops go forth from their midst. That is when He lit it on whomever He wills of His servants. That is when they rejoice at the good tidings.* **30:48**

It is He who made His creation to populate the world and sent towards the jinn and human beings. His Messengers unveil it for them, warn them of its harm, present to them its examples, show them its defects and place before them a whole collection of matters containing lessons about the changings of health and sickness in this world, its lawful things and unlawful things and all that God has ordained for the obedient and the disobedient, namely Paradise and Hell and honor and disgrace. I extend my praise to His Being as He desires His creation to praise Him. He has fixed for everything a measure, for every measure a time limit, and for every time limit a document. Sermon 182

Truly, they had been—even before it is sent down on them—before that, ones who are seized with despair. **30:49**

The granting of patience from God is in proportion to the extent of calamity you are passing through. If you exhibit fretfulness, irritation and despair in calamities, then your patience and your exertions are wasted. Saying 143

Look on the effects of the mercy of God, how He gives life to the earth after its death! Truly, that! He is One Who Gives Life to the dead and He is Powerful over everything. **30:50**

Glory to **You**! How great is **Your** creation that we see, but how small is this greatness by the side of **Your** Might! How awe-striking is **Your** realm that we notice, but how humble is this against what is hidden from us out of **Your** authority! How extensive are **Your** bounties in this world, but how small are they against the bounties of the next world! Sermon 108

If We sent a wind and they saw fields, ones that are yellowing, they would stay ungrateful after that. **30:51**

God ... is aware of whatever is hidden in the hearts and whatever lies behind the unseen. Sermon 192

Then, truly, ***you*** *will not cause the dead to hear nor will* ***you*** *cause the unwilling to hear, to hear the calling to them when they turned as ones who draw back.* **30:52**

Do not hanker after worldly honor and its pride. Do not feel happy over its beauties and bounties, nor wail over its damages and misfortunes because its honor and pride will end, its beauty and bounty will perish and its damages and misfortunes will pass away. Every period in it has an end. Every living being in it is to die. Do you not understand that for you there is a warning in the relics of the predecessors, an eye opener and lesson that your forefathers provided you? Sermon 99

***You** are not one who guides the unwilling to see from their fallacy. **You** have caused none to hear but those who believe in Our signs. They are ones who submit to God.* **30:53**

I bear witness that *there is no god but God,* (Q47:19), by virtue of belief, certainty, sincerity and conviction. I also bear witness that *Muhammad* (Q48:29), peace and the mercy of God be upon him, is *His servant* (Q17:1) and *Prophet* (Q7:158) whom He deputed when the signs of guidance were obliterated and the ways of religion were desolate. So he threw open the truth, gave advice to the people, guided them towards righteousness and ordered them to be moderate. May God bless him ... Sermon 194

God is He Who created you in your weakness. Again, after that weakness, He assigned strength; again, after that strength, He assigned weakness and grayness of hair. He creates what He wills. He is The Knowing, The Powerful. **30:54**

People of differing minds and divided hearts, whose bodies are present but wits are absent. I am leading you amicably towards truthfulness, but you run away from it like goats and sheep running away from the howling of a lion. How hard it is for me to uncover for you the secrets of justice or to straighten the curve of truthfulness. O my God! **You** know that what we did was not to seek power, nor to acquire anything from the vanities of the world. We rather wanted to restore the signs of **Your** religion and to usher prosperity into **Your** cities so that the oppressed among **Your** creatures might be safe and **Your** forsaken commands might be established. O my God! I am the first who leaned towards **You** and who heard and responded to the call of Islam. No one preceded me in formal prayer except *the Prophet* (Q7:158), peace and the mercy of God be upon him. Sermon 131

On a Day when the Hour is secured for you, the ones who sin will swear that they lingered in expectation not but an hour. Thus, they had been misled. **30:55**

The human being should ... fear the Day of Judgment before it arrives. He should appreciate the shortness of his life and the shortness of his sojourn in the place of stay which has only to last for his change over to the next place. He should, therefore, do something for his change over and for the known stages of his departure. Blessed be he who possesses a virtuous heart, obeys one who guides him, keeps away from one who takes him to ruin, catches the path of safety with the help of him who provides him light of guidance and, by obeying the leader who commands him, hastens towards guidance before its doors are closed, opens the door of repentance and removes the stain of sins. He has certainly been put on the right path and guided towards the straight path. Sermon 214

Said those who were given the knowledge and the belief: Certainly, you lingered in expectation by what is prescribed by God until the Day of the Upraising. This is the Day of Upraising, but you had not been knowing. **30:56**
So, on that Day will not profit them, those who did wrong, their excuses nor will they ask to be favored. **30:57**

Behind your back is the hour of Resurrection which is driving you on. Sermon 21

Certainly, We propounded for humanity in this, the Quran, every kind of parable. But if ***you*** *were to bring about any sign to them, certainly, they who were ungrateful would say: Truly, you are nothing but ones who deal in falsehood.* **30:58**
Thus, God sets a seal on the hearts of those who know not. **30:59**

There remain a few people in whose case the remembrance of their return to God on the Day of Judgment keeps their eyes bent and the awareness of the Resurrection moves them to tears. Some of them are scared away from the world and disperse. Some are frightened and subdued. Some are quiet as if muzzled. Some are praying sincerely. Some are grief-stricken and pain-ridden whom fear has confined to namelessness. Disgrace has shrouded them, so they are in the sea of bitter water, their mouths are closed and their hearts are bruised. They preached until they were tired. They were oppressed until they were disgraced. They were killed until their numbers dwindled. Sermon 32

So, have ***you*** *patience. Truly, the promise of God is True. Let them not irritate* ***you****, those who are not certain in belief.* **30:60**

O God's human being! Be God-conscious. Keep in view the reason why He created you. Be afraid of Him to the extent He has advised you to do. Make yourself deserve what He has promised you by having confidence in the truth of His promise and entertaining fear of the Day of Judgment. Sermon 82

CHAPTER 31: LUQMAN (Luqmān)

31:1 *Alif Lam Mim*
There are the signs of the wise Book, **31:2**
a guidance and a mercy to the ones who are doers of good, **31:3**
those who perform the formal prayer and give the purifying alms and they are certain of the world to come. **31:4**

In God's authority lies the safety of your affairs. Therefore, render Him such obedience as is neither blameworthy, nor insincere. By God, you must do so otherwise God will take away from you the power of Islam and will never thereafter return it to you until it reverts to others. Sermon 169

Those are on a guidance from their Lord. Those, they are the ones who prosper. **31:5**

O my God! I seek **Your** protection from becoming destitute despite **Your** riches, from being misguided despite **Your** guidance, from being molested in **Your** realm and from being humiliated while authority rests with **You**. O my God! Let my spirit be the first of those good objects that **You** take from me and the first trust out of **Your** favors held in trust with me. Sermon 215

Of humanity is he who exchanges diversionary conversation to cause others to go astray from the way of God without any knowledge. He takes it to himself in mockery. Those, for them will be a despised punishment. **31:6**

Reform yourselves. Repent. One should praise only God and condemn only one's self. Sermon 16

When Our signs are recounted to him, he turned as one who grows arrogant, as if he had not been hearing them, as if there had been heaviness in his ears. So, give him the good tidings of a painful punishment. **31:7**

I bear witness that *there is no god but God,* (Q47:19), by virtue of belief, certainty, sincerity and conviction. I also bear witness that *Muhammad* (Q48:29), peace and the mercy of God be upon him, is *His servant* (Q17:1) and *Prophet* (Q7:158) whom He deputed when the signs of guidance were obliterated and the ways of religion were desolate. So he threw open the truth, gave advice to the people, guided them towards righteousness and ordered them to be moderate. May God bless him ... Sermon 194

Truly, those who believed and did as the ones in accord with morality, for them are Gardens of Bliss, **31:8**
ones who will dwell in them forever. The promise of God is true. He is The Almighty, The Wise. **31:9**
He created the heavens without any pillars so that you see the heavens. He cast firm mountains on the earth so that the earth should not vibrate with you. He disseminated in and on it of all moving creatures. We caused water to descend from heaven. We caused all generous, diverse pairs to develop in it. **31:10**

He initiated creation most initially and commenced it originally without undergoing reflection, without making use of any experiment, without innovating any movement and without experiencing any aspiration of mind. He allotted all things their times, put together their variations, gave them their properties and determined their features knowing them before creating them, realizing fully their limits and confines and appreciating their propensities and intricacies. Sermon 1

This is the creation of God. Then, cause me to see what other than He created? Nay! The ones who are unjust are clearly wandering astray. **31:11**

How awe-striking is **Your** realm that we notice, but how humble is this against what is hidden from us out of **Your** authority! How extensive are **Your** bounties in this world, but how small are they against the bounties of the next world! Sermon 108

Certainly, We gave Luqman wisdom that: Give thanks to God. Whoever gives thanks, gives thanks only for himself.
Whoever was ungrateful— then, truly, God is Sufficient, Worthy of Praise. **31:12**
When Luqman said to his son as he admonishes him: O my son! Ascribe not partners with God. Truly, association with God is, certainly, a tremendous injustice. **31:13**
We charged the human being about ones who are his parents. His mother carried him in feebleness on feebleness and his weaning is in two years. Give thanks to Me and to ones who are ***your*** *parents. To Me is the Homecoming.* **31:14**
But if they both struggled with ***you*** *that* ***you*** *have ascribed partners with Me of what for* ***you*** *is no knowledge, then, obey them not. Keep their company in the present as one who is honorable but follow the way of him who was penitent to Me. Again, to Me will be your return and I will tell you of what you had been doing.* **31:15**

He does not refuse you His kindness and does not remove His protection from you. In fact, you have not been without His kindness even for a moment, whether it be a favor that He conferred upon you or a sin of yours that He has concealed or a calamity that He has warded off from you. Sermon 221

O my son! Truly, even if it be the weight of a grain of a mustard seed and though it be in a rock or in the heavens or in or on the earth God will bring it. Truly, God is Subtle, Aware. **31:16**
O my son! Perform the formal prayer. Command that which is honorable. Prohibit that which is unlawful. Have **you** *patience with whatever lit on* **you**. *Truly, that is the constancy of affairs.* **31:17**
Turn not **your** *cheek away from humanity nor walk through the earth exultantly. Truly, God loves not any proud boaster.* **31:18**
Be moderate in **your** *walking and lower* **your** *voice. Truly the most horrible of voices is, certainly, the voice of the donkey.* **31:19**
Consider you not that God caused to become subservient to you whatever is in the heavens and whatever is in and on the earth and lavished on you His divine blessing, that which is manifest and that which is inward and yet most of humanity is he who disputes about God without knowledge and with no guidance and without an illuminating Book. **31:20** ***

When it was said to them: Follow what God caused to descend. They said: Nay! We will follow what we found our fathers on. Even if it Satan had been calling them to the punishment of the blaze? **31:21**

Where are the minds which seek light from the lamps of guidance and the eyes which look at minarets of God-consciousness? Where are the hearts dedicated to God and devoted to the obedience of God? They are all crowding towards worldly vanities and quarreling over unlawful issues. The banners of the Garden and Hell have been raised for them, but they have turned their faces away from the Garden and proceeded to Hell by dint of their performances. God called them, but they showed dislike and ran away. When Satan called them, they responded and proceeded towards him. Sermon 144

Whoever submits his face to God while he is one who is a doer of good, then, surely, he held fast to the most firm handhold. To God is the Ultimate End of affairs. **31:22**

He has declared paying regard to Muslims as the highest of all regards. He has placed the rights of Muslims in the same grade of importance as devotion to Himself and His Oneness. Therefore, a Muslim is one from whose tongue and hand every other Muslim is safe, save in the matter of truth. It is not, therefore, lawful to molest a Muslim except when it is obligatory. Sermon 166

Whoever was ungrateful, let not his ingratitude dishearten **you**. *To Us is their return and We will tell them what they did. Truly, God is Knowing of what is in the breasts.* **31:23**

People did not take light from the lights of his wisdom, nor did they produce flame from the flint of sparkling knowledge. Sermon 108

We give them enjoyment for a little while. Again, We will compel them to a harsh punishment. **31:24**
If **you** *had asked them who created the heavens and the earth, they will certainly say: God! Say: The Praise belongs to God! But most of them know not.* **31:25**

One of the firm decisions of God in the Wise Reminder (Quran), upon which He bestows reward or gives punishment and through which He likes or dislikes, is that it will not benefit a person, even though he exerts himself and acts sincerely, if he leaves this world to meet God with one of these acts without repenting, namely that he believed in a partner with God during his obligatory worship or appeased his own anger by killing an individual or spoke about acts committed by others or sought fulfillment of his needs from people by introducing an innovation in his religion or met people with a double face or moved among them with a double tongue. Understand this because an illustration is a guide for its like. Sermon 153

To God belongs whatever is in the heavens and the earth. Truly, God, He is The Sufficient, The Worthy of Praise. **31:26**

Praise belongs to God (Q1:2) Who made me such that I have not died, nor am I sick, nor have my veins been infected with disease, nor have I been hauled up for my evil acts, nor am I without progeny, nor have I forsaken my religion, nor do I disbelieve in my Lord, nor do I feel strangeness with my faith, nor is my intelligence affected, nor have I been punished with the punishment of peoples before me. I am a servant in **Your** possession. I have been guilty of excesses over myself. **You** have exhausted **Your** pleas over me and I have no plea before **You**. I have no power to take except what **You** give me. I cannot evade except what **You** save me from. Sermon 215

If trees on the earth were only pens and the sea causes to increase after that with seven more seas that were ink, yet the Words of God would not come to an end. Truly, God is Almighty, Wise. **31:27**

This world and the hereafter have submitted to Him their reins. The skies and earths have flung their keys towards Him. The thriving trees bow to Him in the morning and evening, producing for Him flaming fire from their branches and, at His command, turn their own feed into ripe fruits. Sermon 133

Your creation and your Upraising are not but like that of a single soul. Truly, God is Hearing, Seeing. **31:28**

Have ***you*** *not considered that God causes the nighttime to be interposed into the daytime and causes the daytime to be interposed into the nighttime and caused the sun to become subservient and the moon, each run for a term, that which is determined and that God is Aware of what you do?* **31:29**

When Almighty God created the openings of the atmosphere, the expanse of firmament and strata of winds, He flowed into it water whose waves were stormy and whose surges leapt one over the other. He loaded it on dashing wind and breaking typhoons, ordered them to shed it back as rain, gave the wind control over the vigor of the rain, and acquainted it with its limitations. The wind blew under it while water flowed furiously over it. Sermon 1

That is because God, He is The Truth and what they call to other than Him is falsehood and that God, He is The Lofty, The Great! **31:30**

Know that—may God have mercy on you—you are living at a time when those who speak about right are few, when tongues are loath to utter the truth and those who stick to the right are humiliated. The people of this time are engaged in disobedience. Their youth are wicked, their old men are sinful, their learned men are hypocrites, and their speakers are sycophants. Their young ones do not respect their elders, and their rich men do not support the destitute. Sermon 232

Have **you** *not considered that the boats run through the sea by the divine blessing of God that He causes you to see His signs? Truly in that are signs for every enduring, grateful one.* **31:31**

I bear witness that *there is no god but God* (Q47:19), by virtue of belief, certainty, sincerity and conviction. I also bear witness that *Muhammad* (Q48:29), peace and the mercy of God be upon him, is *His servant* (Q17:1) and *Prophet* (Q7:158) whom He deputed when the signs of guidance were obliterated and the ways of religion were desolate. So he threw open the truth, gave advice to the people, guided them towards righteousness and ordered them to be moderate. May God bless him ... Sermon 194

When a wave overcame them like an overshadowing, they called to God as ones who are sincere and devoted in the way of life to Him. Then, when He delivered them to dry land among them are ones who halt between two opinions. None negates Our signs but every ungrateful turncoat. **31:32**

O my God! We seek **Your** protection from turning away from **Your** command, or revolting against **Your** religion, or being led away by our desires instead of by guidance that comes from **You**. Sermon 215

O humanity! Be God-conscious of your Lord, and dread a Day when recompense will not be given by a child to one to whom the child is born, nor will one to whom a child is born be one who gives recompense for the one who is born at all. Truly, the promise of God is True so let not this present life delude you nor let the deluder delude you about God. **31:33**
Truly, the knowledge of the Hour is with God. He sends plenteous rain water down. He knows what is in the wombs. No soul is informed of what it will earn tomorrow. No soul is informed in what region it will die. Truly, God is Knowing, Aware. **31:34**

O brother of Kalb! This is not knowledge of hidden things. These matters have been acquired from *the Prophet* (Q7:158), peace and the mercy of God be upon him, who knew them. As regard knowledge of hidden things, that means knowledge of the Day of Judgment, and the things covered by God in the verse: *Truly, the knowledge of the Hour is with God.* (Q31:34) Sermon 127

Chapter 32: Prostration (al-Sajdah)

32:1 *Alif Lam Mim*
The sending down successively of the Book, there is no doubt in it. It is from the Lord of the worlds. **32:2**

The Book of God is among you. It speaks. Its tongue does not falter. It is a house whose pillars do not fall down. It is a power whose supporters are never defeated. Sermon 132

Or they say: He devised it. Nay! It is The Truth from **your** *Lord that* **you** *warn a folk to whom no warner approached them before* **you***, so that perhaps they will be truly guided.* **32:3**

God sent *the Prophet* (Q7:158), peace and the mercy of God be upon him, as a caller towards Truth and a witness over the creatures. *The Prophet* (Q7:158), peace and the mercy of God be upon him, conveyed the messages of God tirelessly and without any negligence. He fought His enemies in the cause of God unflaggingly and without pleading excuses. He is the foremost of all who practice God-consciousness and the power of perception of all those who achieve guidance. Sermon 116

God! It is He Who created the heavens and the earth and whatever is between them in six days. Again, He turned His attention to the Throne. You will have none other than Him as protector and no intercessor. Will you not, then, recollect? **32:4**

Among them are those who work as trusted bearers of His message, those who serve as speaking tongues for His prophets and those who carry to and fro His orders and injunctions. Among them are the protectors of His creatures and guards of the doors of the gardens of Paradise. Among them are those also whose steps are fixed on earth, but their necks are protruding into the skies, their limbs are getting out on all sides, their shoulders are in accord with the columns of the Divine Throne, their eyes are downcast before it, they have spread down their wings under it and they have rendered between themselves and all else curtains of honor and screens of power. They do not think of their Creator through image, do not impute to Him attributes of the created, do not confine Him within abodes and do not point at Him through illustrations. Sermon 1

He manages every command from the heaven to the earth. Again, it will go up to Him in a day, the span of which had been a thousand years of what you number. **32:5**

Be aware and act during the period of attraction just as you act during a period of dread. Be aware! Truly, I have not seen one who covets Paradise to be asleep, nor a dreader from hellfire to be asleep. Be aware, he whom right does not benefit must suffer the harm of the wrong. He whom guidance does not keep firm will be led away by misguidance towards destruction. Sermon 28

That is the One Who Knows of the unseen and the visible, The Almighty, The Compassionate **32:6**

O the Most Merciful of all! O my God! .... Surely, **You** are powerful over whatever **You** will. Sermon 143

Who did everything that He created well. He began the creation of the human being from clay. **32:7**

Again, He made human progeny from the extraction of despicable water. **32:8**

You, O God, made angels reside in **Your** skies and placed them high above from **Your** earth. They have the most knowledge about **You** and **Your** whole creation, the most consciousness of **You**, and are the nearest to **You**. They never stayed in loins nor were retained in wombs. They were not created *from the extraction of despicable water.* (Q 32:8) Sermon 108

Again, He shaped him and blew into him His Spirit. He made for you the ability to hear and sight and minds. But you give little thanks! **32:9**

Do not forget gratitude when receiving blessings for God has exhausted the excuses before you through clear, shining arguments and open, bright books. Sermon 81

They said: When we went astray on the earth will we be in a new creation? Nay! In the meeting with their Lord they are ones who disbelieve. **32:10**

God, the Almighty, has maintained creation with His kindness, kept it intact with His command and perfected it with His power. Then after its destruction, He will resuscitate it, but not for any need of His own towards it, nor to seek the assistance of any of its things against it, nor to change over from the condition of loneliness to that of company, nor from the condition of ignorance and blindness to that of knowledge and search, nor from paucity and need towards needlessness and plenty, nor from disgrace and lowliness towards honor and prestige. Sermon 186

Say: The angel of death who was charged with you, will call you to itself. Again, you will be returned to your Lord. **32:11**

... to Him returns whoever dies. Sermon 108

If ***you*** *but see when the ones who sin become ones who bend down their heads before their Lord: Our Lord! We perceived and heard. So, return us. We will do as ones in accord with morality. Truly, we are now ones who are certain.* **32:12**

Hidden things have appeared for those who perceive. The face of right has become clear for the wanderer. The approaching moment has raised the veil from its face. Signs have appeared for those who search for them. Sermon 108

If We willed it, We would have, surely, given every soul its guidance, but My saying will be realized. I will fill hell with genies and humanity one and all. **32:13**

O my God! I seek **Your** protection from becoming destitute despite **Your** riches, from being misguided despite **Your** guidance, from being molested in **Your** realm and from being humiliated while authority rests with **You.** Sermon 215

Then, experience it. As you forgot the meeting of this Day of yours, truly, We forgot you. Experience the infinite punishment for what you had been doing. **32:14**

On that Day many an argument will prove void and a contention for excuses will stand rejected. Sermon 222

Only those believe in Our signs who, when they were reminded of them, fell down, ones who prostrate themselves and glorified the praise of their Lord and they grow not arrogant **32 15**
whose sides deliberately avoided their sleeping places to call to their Lord in fear and hope. They spend of what We provided them. **32:16**
No soul knows what was concealed for them of comfort for their eyes as a recompense for what they had been doing. **32:17**

During the day they are enduring, learned, virtuous and God-conscious. God-consciousness has made them thin like arrows. If any one looks at them, he believes they are sick, although they are not sick. He says that they have gone mad. In fact, great concern has made them mad. They are not satisfied with their meager good acts. They do not regard their major acts as great. They always blame themselves and are afraid of their deeds. When anyone of them is spoken of highly, he says: I know myself better than others. My Lord knows me better than I know. O God, do not deal with me according to what they say. Make me better than they think of me. Forgive me those shortcomings which they do not know. Among the signs of anyone of them is that you will see that he has strength in religion, determination along with leniency, faith with conviction, eagerness for knowledge, and knowledge with forbearance, moderation in riches, devotion in worship, gracefulness in starvation, endurance in hardship, desire for the lawful, pleasure in guidance and hatred from greed. He performs virtuous deeds, but still feels afraid. In the evening he is anxious to offer thanks to God. In the morning, his anxiety is to remember God. Sermon 193

Is he who had been one who believes like he who had been one who disobeys? They are not on the same level. **32:18**

Pledge yourself with prayer and remain steady on it; offer prayer as much as possible and seek nearness of God through it, because it is imposed upon the believers as a timed ordinance: *Truly the formal prayer has been—for the ones who believe—a timed prescription.* (Q4:103) Sermon 198

As for those who believed and did as the ones in accord with morality, for them are Gardens as places of shelter, hospitality for them for what they had been doing. **32:19**

Mind the obligations! Mind the obligations! Fulfill them for God and they will take you to the Garden. Surely, God has made unlawful the things which are not unknown and made lawful the things which are without defect. Sermon 167

As for those who disobeyed, their place of shelter will be the fire. Every time they would want to go forth from there, they would be caused to return to it. It will be said to them: Experience the punishment of the fire which you had been denying! **32:20**

Do you think you can tell the time when a person goes out and no evil befall him, or can warn of the time at which, if one goes out, harm will accrue? Whoever testifies to this falsifies the Quran and becomes unmindful of God in achieving his desired objective and in warding off the undesirable. You cherish saying this, so that he who acts on what you say should praise you rather than God because, according to your misconception, you have guided him about the hour in which he would secure benefit and avoid harm. Sermon 79

Certainly, We will cause them to experience the closer punishment other than the greater punishment so that perhaps they will return. **32:21**

People did not take light from the lights of his wisdom, nor did they produce flame from the flint of sparkling knowledge. So in this matter they are like grazing cattle and hard stones. Sermon 108

Who does greater wrong than he who was reminded of the signs of His Lord, then, he turned aside from them? Truly, on the ones who sin, We are ones who requite. **32:22**

I bear witness that *there is no god but God* (Q47:19), by virtue of belief, certainty, sincerity and conviction. I also bear witness that *Muhammad* (Q48:29), peace and the mercy of God be upon him, is *His servant* (Q17:1) and *Prophet* (Q7:158) whom He deputed when the signs of guidance were obliterated and the ways of religion were desolate. So he threw open the truth, gave advice to the people, guided them towards righteousness and ordered them to be moderate. May God bless him ... Sermon 194

Certainly, We gave Moses the Book. So, be you not hesitant about meeting Him. We assigned it as a guidance for the Children of Jacob. **32:23**

We assigned leaders from among them to guide under Our command when they endured patiently. They had been certain of Our signs. **32:24**

They are life for knowledge and death for ignorance. Their forbearance tells you of their knowledge, their outer self of their inner self and their silence of the wisdom of their speaking. They do not go against right, nor do they differ among themselves about it. They are the pillars of Islam and the asylums of its protection. Sermon 238

Truly, ***your*** *Lord is He Who will distinguish among them on the Day of Resurrection about what they had been at variance in it.* **32:25**
Guides them not how many We caused to perish of generations before them amidst whose dwellings they walk? Truly, in that are the signs. Will they not then hear? **32:26**

Your ultimate goal of reward or punishment is before you. Behind your back is the hour of Resurrection which is driving you on. Keep yourself light and overtake the forward ones. The first ones who have preceded await your last ones. Sermon 21

Consider they not that We drive water to the barren dust of earth? We drive out crops with it from which their flocks eat and they themselves. Will they not, then, perceive? **32:27**

Almighty God sent forth wind and made its movement sterile, perpetuated its position, intensified its motion and spread it far and wide. He ordered the wind to raise up deep waters and to intensify the waves of the oceans. So the wind churned it like the churning of curd and pushed it fiercely into the firmament throwing its front position on the rear and the stationary on the flowing until its level was raised and the surface was full of foam. Then Almighty God raised the foam on to the open wind and vast firmament and made therefrom the seven skies and made the lower one as a stationary surge and the upper one as protective ceiling and a high edifice without any pole to support it or nail to hold it together. Then He decorated them with stars and the light of meteors and hung in it the shining sun and effulgent moon under the revolving sky, moving ceiling and rotating firmament. Sermon 1

They say: When is this victory if you had been ones who are sincere? **32:28**
Say: On the Day of Victory there will be no profit for those who disbelieved if they, then, have belief nor will they be given respite. **32:29**
So, turn ***you*** *aside from them and wait awhile. Truly they are ones who are waiting awhile.* **32:30**

God ... is aware of whatever is hidden in the hearts and whatever lies behind the unseen. Sermon 192

Chapter 33: The Confederates (al-Aḥzāb)

O Prophet! Be God-conscious and obey not the ones who are ungrateful and the ones who are hypocrites. Truly, God had been Knowing, Wise. **33:1**

Certainly, only doubtful innovations cause ruin except those from which God may protect. In God's authority lies the safety of your affairs. Therefore, render Him such obedience as is neither blameworthy, nor insincere. Sermon 169

Follow what is revealed to ***you*** *from* ***your*** *Lord. Truly, God is Aware of what you had been doing.* **33:2**

The Book of God is that through which you see, you speak and you hear. Its one part speaks for the other part, and one part bears witness to the other. It does not create differences about God, nor does it mislead its own follower from the path of God. You are joined together in hatred of each other and in the growing of herbage on your covering inner impurity by good appearance outside. You are sincere with one another in your love of desires and bear enmity against each other in earning wealth. The evil spirit (Satan) has perplexed you and deceit has misled you. I seek the help of God for myself and you. Sermon 133

Put ***your*** *trust in God. God sufficed as a Trustee.* **33:3**

O my God! I seek **Your** protection from becoming destitute despite **Your** riches, from being misguided despite **Your** guidance, from being molested in **Your** realm and from being humiliated while authority rests with **You.** O my God! Let my spirit be the first of those good objects that **You** take from me and the first trust out of **Your** favors held in trust with me. Sermon 215

God made not two hearts for any man in his interior. Nor made He your spouses those whom you divorced saying: Be as the back of my mother! Nor made He your adopted sons, your sons. That is but a saying of your mouths. God says: The Truth and He guides to the way. **33:4**

You are supporters of Truth and brethren in faith. You are the shield on the day of tribulation and my trustees among the rest of the people. With your support I strike the runner away and hope for the obedience of him who advances forward. Therefore, extend to me support which is free from deceit and pure from doubt because, by God, I am the most preferable of all for the people. Sermon 118

Call to them by the names of their fathers. That is more equitable with God. But if you know not their fathers, they are your brothers in the way of life and your defenders. There is no blame on you in what mistake you made in it, but what your hearts premeditated. God had been Forgiving, Compassionate. **33:5**

O my God! We seek **Your** protection from turning away from **Your** command, or revolting against **Your** religion, or being led away by our desires instead of by guidance that comes from **You**. Sermon 215

The Prophet is closer to the ones who believe than their own souls. His spouses are their mothers and those imbued through the wombs, blood relations, some of them are closer to some other in what is prescribed by God than the other ones who believe and ones who emigrate, but accomplish what you may for your protectors as ones who are honorable—that which had been inscribed in the Book. **33:6**

Our Islam is well-known.... Whatever remains has been mentioned in the words of God the Glorified, the Sublime: *Blood relations have the better claim in respect of one to the other, according to the Book of God ...* (Q33:6) Letter 28

Mention when We took a solemn promise from the Prophets and from **you** *and from Noah and Abraham and Moses and Jesus son of Mary. We took an earnest solemn promise from them* **33:7** *so that He ask the ones who are sincere about their sincerity. He prepared for the ones who are ungrateful a painful punishment.* **33:8**
O those who believed! Remember the divine blessing of God to you when armies drew near you

and We sent the winds against them and armies you see not. God had been Seeing of what you do. **33:9**

When they drew near you from above you and from below you and when the sight swerved and the hearts reached the throats and you think thoughts about God, **33:10**

there the ones who believe were tested and were convulsed with a severe convulsing. **33:11**

O God's human being! I advise you to be God-conscious. It is He Who has furnished illustrations and Who has timed for you your lives. He has given you covering of dress. He has scattered a livelihood for you. He has surrounded you with His knowledge. He has ordained rewards. He has bestowed upon you vast bounties and extensive gifts. He has warned you through far reaching arguments. He has counted you by numbers. He has fixed for you an age to live in this place of testing and house of instruction. You are on a test in this world and have to render an account regarding it. Sermon 82

When the ones who are hypocrites say, as well as those who in their hearts is a sickness: What God and His Messenger promised is nothing but delusion. **33:12**

The hypocrites have made Satan the master of their affairs, and he has taken them as partners. He has laid eggs and hatched them in their bosoms. He creeps and crawls in their laps. He sees through their eyes, and speaks with their tongues. In this way he has led them to sinfulness and adorned for them foul things like the action of one whom Satan has made partner in his domain and speaks untruth through his tongue. Sermon 7

When a section of them said: O people of Yathrib! There is no habitation for you, so return. A group of people ask permission of the Prophet among them saying: Truly, Our houses are exposed. But they were not exposed. They want only to run away. **33:13**

His place of stay is the best of all places. His origin is the noblest of all origins in the mines of honor and the cradles of safety. Hearts of virtuous persons have been inclined towards him. The reins of eyes have been turned towards him. Through him God buried mutual rancor and put off the flames of revolt. Through him He gave them affection like brothers and separated those who were together through ingratitude. Through him He gave honor to the low and degraded honor of ingratitude. His speaking is clear and his silence indicates as if it were a tongue. Sermon 96

If entry was forced against them from all areas and, again, they were asked to dissent, they would have given into it and they would not have but briefly hesitated **33:14**

although, certainly, they made a contract with God before that they would not turn their backs to the enemy. About their compact with God that had been, they are ones who will be asked. **33:15**

I praise God for whatever matter He ordained and whatever action He destines and for my trial with you, O group of people, who do not obey when I order and do not respond when I call you. If you are at ease, you engage in conceited conversation, but if you are faced with battle you show weakness. Sermon 180

Say: Running away will never profit you that you ran away from death or killing, then, you will be given enjoyment but for a little. **33:16**

Certainly, this world is the end of the sight of the unwilling to see, who see nothing beyond it. The sight of a looker who looks with the eye of his mind pierces through and realizes that the real house is beyond this world. The looker, therefore, wants to get out of it while the unwilling to see wants to get into it. The looker collects provision from it for the next world while the unwilling to see collects provision for this very world. Sermon 133

Say: Who will save you from harm from God if He wanted evil for you or wanted mercy for you? They will not find for themselves other than God a protector or a helper. **33:17**
Surely, God knows the ones of you who hold off and the ones who converse with their brothers saying to us: Come on! They approach not the battle themselves but a little, **33:18**
being covetous of you. Then, when fear drew near, ***you*** *will see them looking on* ***you****, their eyes rolling like he who is overcome by death. But when their fear went, they abused you with sharp tongues in their covetousness for good things. Those believe not and God caused their actions to fail. That had been easy for God.* **33:19**

Indeed, God knows those who hinder others among you and those who say unto their brethren: *Surely, God knows the ones of you who hold off and the ones who converse with their brothers saying to us: Come on! And they approach not the battle themselves but a little.* (Q33:18) Letter 28

They assume the confederates go not, withdrawing. If the confederates approach you, returning, they would wish they were nomads among the ones who are desert dwellers, asking tidings about you. If they had been among you, they would fight but a little. **33:20**

You should know that you have again reverted to the position of the Bedouin Arabs after migration to Islam and have become different parties after having been once united. You do not possess anything of Islam except its name and know nothing of belief save its show. You say: The Fire yes, but no shameful position, as if you would throw down Islam on its face in order to defame its honor and break its pledge for brotherhood which God gave you as a sacred trust on His earth and a source of peace among the people. Be sure that if you incline towards anything other than Islam, the unbelievers will fight you. Then there will be neither Gabriel, nor Michael, neither Emigrants, nor Helpers to help you, but only the clashing of swords, until God settles the matter for you. Sermon 192

Surely, in the Messenger of God there is for you a fairer, good example for those whose hope had been in God and the Last Day and remembered God frequently. **33:21**

From the time of his weaning, God had put a mighty angel with him to take him along the path of high character and good behavior through day and night, while I used to follow him like a young camel following in the footprints of its mother. Every day he would show me in the form of a banner some of his high traits and commanded me to follow it. Every year he used to go in seclusion to the hill of Hira, where I saw him, but no one else saw him. In those days Islam did not exist in any house except that of *the Prophet,* (Q7:158), peace and blessing of God be upon him, and Khadijah, while I was the third after these two. I used to see and watch the effulgence of Divine revelation and message, and breathed the scent of Prophethood. Sermon 192

When the ones who believe saw the confederates, they said: This is what God and His Messenger promised us and God and His Messenger were sincere. It increased them not but in belief and to resign themselves to submission to God. **33:22**

God has placed in Islam the height of His pleasure, the pinnacle of His pillars and the prominence of His obedience. Before God, therefore, its columns are strong, its construction is lofty, its proofs are bright, its fires are aflame, its authority is strong, its beacons are high and its destruction is difficult. You should therefore honor it, follow it, fulfill its obligations and accord the position due to it. Sermon 198

Among the ones who believe are men who were sincere in the contracts they made with God. Of them are some who satisfied by fulfilling their vow with death and of them are some who wait awhile. They substituted not any substitution **33:23**
so that God gives recompense to the ones who are sincere for their sincerity and punish the ones who are hypocrites had He willed or He turns to them in forgiveness. Truly, God had been Forgiving, Compassionate. **33:24**

O the Most Merciful of all! O My God! .... Do pour on us Your mercy, Your blessing, Your sustenance and Your pity ....Surely, You are powerful over whatever You will. Sermon 143

God repelled those who were ungrateful in their rage without their attaining any good. God spared the ones who believe in fighting. God had been Strong, Almighty. **33:25**
He caused to descend those who were behind among the People of the Book from their strongholds and He hurled alarm into their hearts so that you kill a group of people and make captives of another group of people. **33:26**

They may move from their position, but you should not move from yours. Grit your teeth. In fighting for God, give yourself to God. Plant your feet firmly on the ground. Have your eye on the remotest foe and close your eyes to their numbers. Rest assured that help is but from God, the Almighty. Sermon 11

He gave you their region as an inheritance and their abodes and their wealth and a region you tread not. God had been Powerful over everything! **33:27**

Indeed, surely, jihad is one of the doors of Paradise which God has opened for His best friends. It is the dress of God-consciousness, the protective armor of God and His trustworthy shield. Whoever abandons it, God covers him with the dress of disgrace and the clothes of distress. He is kicked with contempt and scorn. His heart is veiled with screens of neglect. Truth is taken away from him because of his missing the jihad. He has to suffer ignominy. Justice is denied to him. Sermon 27

O Prophet! Say to **your** *spouses: If you had been wanting this present life and its adornment, then, approach now. I will give you enjoyment and set you (f) free, releasing gracefully.* **33:28**

God sent *the Prophet* (Q7:158), peace and the mercy of God be upon him, at a time when the people were going astray in perplexity and were moving here and there in mischief. Desires had deflected them and self-conceit had swerved them. Extreme ignorance had made them foolish. They were confounded by the unsteadiness of matters and the evils of ignorance. Then *the Prophet* (Q7:158), peace and the mercy of God be upon him, did his best in giving them sincere advice, himself trod on the right path and called them towards wisdom and good counsel. Sermon 95

If you had been wanting God and His Messenger, and the Last Abode, then truly God prepared for the ones who are doers of good among you a sublime compensation. **33:29**

God never allowed His creation to remain without a Prophet, one deputized by Him, or a Book sent down from Him, or a binding argument, or a standing plea. These

Messengers were such that they did not fear that they were few in comparison to the large numbers of their falsifiers. Among them was either a predecessor who would name the one to follow or the follower who had been introduced by the predecessor. Sermon 1

O wives of the Prophet! Whoever of you (f) approaches a manifest indecency, her punishment will be multiplied for her twofold. That would have been easy for God. **33:30**
Whoever of you (f) is morally obligated to God and His Messenger and do as ones (f) in accord with morality, We will give her her compensation two times over. We made ready a generous provision for her. **33:31**
O wives of the Prophet! There is not among the wives any like you. If you (f) were God-conscious, then, be not soft in your saying so that he become desirous he in whose heart is a sickness, but say (f) a saying of one who is honorable. **33:32**
Settle down (f) in your (f) houses and flaunt (f) not your (f) finery as those who flaunted their finery in the previous Age of Ignorance. Perform (f) the formal prayer and give (f) the purifying alms and obey (f) God and His Messenger. God only wants to cause disgrace to be put away from you—People of the House—and purify you with a purification. **33:33**
Remember (f) what is recounted in your (f) houses of the signs of God and wisdom. Truly, God had been Subtle, Aware. **33:34**
Truly, the males, ones who submit to God and the females, ones who submit to God and the males, ones who believe and the females, ones who believe and the males, ones who are morally obligated and the females, ones who are morally obligated and the males, ones who are sincere and the females, ones who are sincere and the males, ones who remain steadfast and the females, ones who remain steadfast and the males, ones who are humble and the females, ones who are humble and the males, ones who are charitable and the females, ones who are charitable and the males, ones who fast and the females, ones who fast and the males, ones who guard their private parts and the females, ones who guard and the males, ones who are remember God frequently and the females, ones who remember, God prepared for them forgiveness and a sublime compensation. **33:35**
It had not been for a male, one who believes and a female, one who believes, when God and His Messenger decreed an affair that there be any choice for them in their affair. Whoever rebels against God and His Messenger, certainly, he went astray, clearly wandering astray. **33:36**
Mention when **you** *have said to him to whom God was gracious and to whom* **you** *were gracious: Hold back* **your** *spouse to* **your***self and be God-conscious. But* **you** *have concealed in* **your***self what God is One Who Shows and* **you** *have dreaded humanity whereas God has a better right that* **you** *have dreaded Him. So, when Zayd satisfied the necessary formality, We gave her to* **you** *in marriage so that there be no fault for ones who believe in respect of the spouses of their adopted sons when they (m) satisfied the necessary formality. The command of God had been one that is accomplished.* **33:37**
There had been no fault with the Prophet in what is undertaken by him as a duty from God. This is a custom of God with those who passed away before. The command of God had been a measured measure **33:38**
for those who state the messages of God and dread Him and dread none but God, and God sufficed as a Reckoner. **33:39**

Muhammad had not been the father of any men from among you, but he is the Messenger of God and the Seal of the Prophets. God had been Knowing of everything. **33:40**

My God, Spreader of the surfaces of the earth and Keeper intact of all skies, Creator of hearts of good and evil nature, send **Your** choicest blessings and growing favors on Muhammad, peace and the mercy of God be upon him, **Your** servant and **Your** Prophet, who is the last of those who preceded him and an opener for what is closed, proclaimer of truth with truth, repulser of the forces of wrong and crusher of the onslaughts of misguidance. Sermon 72

O those who believed! Remember God with a frequent remembrance **33:41**
and glorify Him at early morning dawn and eventide. **33:42**
He it is Who gives blessings to you and His angels that He bring you out of the shadows into the light. He had been Compassionate to ones who believe. **33:43**

Now, look at the various favors of God upon them, that He deputed towards them a Prophet who got them to pledge their obedience to him and made them unite at his call. Look how God's bounty spread the wings of its favors over them and flowed for them streams of its blessing, and the whole community became wrapped in blissful prosperity. Consequently, they were submerged under its bounty and enjoyed its lush life. Their affairs were settled under the protection of a powerful ruler, and circumstances offered them overpowering honor, and all things became easy for them under the auspices of a strong country. They became rulers over the world and kings in the various parts of the earth. They became masters of those who were formerly their masters, and began issuing commands over those who used to command them. They were so strong that neither did their spears need testing, nor did their weapons have any flaw. Sermon 192

Their greetings on the Day they will meet Him will be: Peace! He prepared for them a generous compensation. **33:44**

They are emulating each other and proceeding in groups towards the final objective and the rendezvous of death, until when matters come to a close, the world dies and the Resurrection draws near. Sermon 82

O Prophet! Truly, We sent **you** *as one who bears witness and as one who gives good tidings and as a warner* **33:45**
and as one who calls to God with His permission and as a light-giving illuminating lamp. **33:46**

Truly, God sent Muhammad, peace and the mercy of God be upon him, when none among the Arabs read a book or claimed prophethood. He guided the people until he took them to their correct position and their salvation. So their officers learned and their conditions improved. Sermon 33

Give good tidings to the ones who believe that for them is a great grace from God. **33:47**

Seek nearness through the belief in Him and His Prophet ... Sermon 110

Obey not the ones who are ungrateful and the ones who are hypocrites and heed not their annoyance and put **your** *trust in God. God sufficed as a Trustee.* **33:48**

God ... is aware of whatever is hidden in the hearts and whatever lies behind the unseen. Sermon 192

O those who believed! If you married the females, ones who believe, and, again, divorced them before you touch them (f), then, there is no waiting period to reckon against; so make provision for them (f), and set them (f) free, releasing gracefully. **33:49**

O Prophet! Truly, We have permitted to **you your** *spouses (f), those whom* **you** *had given their (f) compensation and whom* **your** *right hand possessed from that God gave* **you** *as spoils of war and the daughters of* **your** *paternal uncles and the daughters of* **your** *paternal aunts and the daughters of* **your** *maternal uncles and the daughters of* **your** *maternal aunts those who emigrated with* **you** *and a woman, one who believes, if she bestowed herself on the Prophet. If the Prophet wanted to take her in marriage—that is exclusively for* **you***—not for the other ones who believe. Surely, We know what We imposed on them about their spouses and whom their right hands possessed (f) that there be no fault on* **you***. God had been Forgiving, Compassionate.* **33:50**
You *will put off whom* **you** *will of them (f) and* **you** *will give refuge to whom* **you** *will. Whomever* **you** *will be looking for of whom* **you** *had set aside, there is no blame on* **you** *to receive her again. That is likelier that will be refreshed their (f) eyes and they (f) not feel remorse and may they (f) be well-pleased with what* **you** *had given them (f), all of them (f). God knows what is in your hearts. God had been Knowing, Forbearing.* **33:51**
Women are not lawful for **you** *in marriage after this, nor that* **you** *were taking them (f) in exchange for other spouses, even though their (f) goodness impressed* **you***, but whom* **your** *right hand possessed (f). God had been watching over everything.* **33:52**
O those who believed! Enter not the houses of the Prophet for food unless permission be given to you without being ones who look for the proper time. When you were called to enter, when you have eaten your meal, then, disperse, and be not one who lingers for conversation. Truly, such had been to harass the Prophet and he is ashamed to ask you to leave. But God is not ashamed before The Truth. When you asked his wives for sustenance, then, ask them (f) from behind a partition. That is purer for your hearts and their (f) hearts. It had not been for you to harass the Messenger of God nor marry you his spouses after him ever. Truly, that would have been serious with God. **33:53**

O God's human being! The best adviser for himself is he who is the most obedient to God. Sermon 85

Whether you show anything or conceal it, truly, God had been Knowing of everything. **33:54**

O God's human being! Every one shall meet what he wishes to avoid by running away. Death is the place to which life is driving. To run away from it means to catch it. How many days did I spend in searching for the secret of this matter, but God did not allow save its concealment. Alas! It is a treasured knowledge. Sermon 149

There is no blame on them (f) to converse freely with their (f) fathers nor their (f) sons nor their (f) brothers, nor the sons of their (f) brothers nor the sons of their (f) sisters, nor their (f) women, nor what their (f) right hands possessed. Be God-conscious. Truly, God had been Witness over everything. **33:55** ***

Truly, God and His angels give blessings to the Prophet. O those who believed! Give your blessings to him and blessings of peace and invoke peace for him. **33:56**

God chose *the Prophet* (Q7:158), peace and the mercy of God be upon him, from the lineal tree of prophets, from the flame of light, from the forehead of greatness, from the best part of the valley of al-Batha, from the lamps for darkness, and from the sources of wisdom. *The Prophet* (Q7:158), peace and the mercy of God be upon him, was like a roaming physician who has set ready his ointments and heated his instruments. He uses them wherever the need arises for curing blind hearts, deaf ears and dumb tongues. He followed with his medicine the spots of negligence and places of perplexity. Sermon 108

Truly, those who malign God and His Messenger, God cursed them in the present and in the world to come and prepared for them a despised punishment. **33:57**

O God's human being! I advise you to keep away from this world which is shortly to leave you, even though you do not like its departure, and which would make your bodies old, even though you would like to keep them young. Your example and its example is like the travelers who travel some distance and then traverse it quickly, or they aimed at a sign and reached it at once. How short is the distance to the aim if one heads towards it and reaches it. How short is the stage of one who has only a day which he cannot exceed while a swift driver is driving him in this world until he departs from it. Sermon 99

Those who malign the males, ones who believe, and the females, ones who believe, without their deserving it, surely, they lay a burden on themselves of false charges to harm another's reputation and a clear sin. **33:58**

O God's human being! You should know that a believer should be distrustful of his heart every morning and evening. He should always blame it for shortcomings and ask it to add to its good acts. You should behave like those who have gone before you and the precedents in front of you. They left this world like a traveler and covered it as distance is covered. Sermon 176

O Prophet! Say to ***your*** *spouses (f) and* ***your*** *daughters and the females, ones who believe, to draw closer their (f) outer garments over themselves (f). That is more fitting so that they (f) be recognized and not be maligned. God had been Forgiving, Compassionate.* **33:59** ***

If the ones who are hypocrites refrain not themselves and those who in their hearts is a sickness and the ones who make a commotion in the city, We will stir ***you*** *up against them. Again, they will not be* ***your*** *neighbors in it, but a little while.* **33:60**

They are ones who are cursed. Whenever they were come upon, they were taken and were killed with a terrible slaying. **33:61**

This is a custom of God with those who passed away before. **You** *will never find in a custom of God any substitution.* **33:62**

If the foot remains firm in this slippery place, well and good, but if the foot slips, this is because we are under the shade of branches, the passing of the winds and the canopy of the clouds whose layers are dispersed in the sky, and whose traces disappeared in the earth. I was your neighbor. My body kept you company for some days and shortly you will find just an empty body of mine which would be stationary after all its movement and silent after speech so that my calmness, the closing of my eyes, and the stillness of my limbs may provide you counsel, because it is more of a counsel for those who take a lesson from it than eloquent speech and a ready word. I am departing from you like one who is eager to meet someone. Tomorrow you will look at my days, then my inner side will be disclosed to you and you will understand me after the vacation of my place and its occupation by someone else. Sermon 149

Humanity asks ***you*** *about the Hour. Say: The knowledge of it is only with God. What will cause* ***you*** *to recognize that perhaps the Hour be near?* **33:63**

There remain a few people in whose case the remembrance of their return to God on the Day of Judgment keeps their eyes bent and the awareness of the Resurrection moves them to tears. Some of them are scared away from the world and disperse. Some are frightened and subdued. Some are quiet as if muzzled. Some are praying sincerely. Some are grief-stricken and pain-ridden whom fear has confined to namelessness. Disgrace has shrouded them, so they are in the sea of bitter water, their mouths are closed and their hearts are bruised. They preached until they were tired. They were oppressed until they were disgraced. They were killed until their numbers dwindled. Sermon 32

Truly, God cursed the ones who are ungrateful and prepared a blaze for them, **33:64**
ones who will dwell in it forever, eternally. They shall not find a protector nor a helper. **33:65**

Generosity is the protector of honor. Forbearance is the bridle of the fool. Forgiveness is the levy of success. Disregard is the punishment of him who betrays. Consultation is the chief way of guidance. He who is content with his own opinion faces danger. Endurance braves calamities while impatience is a helper of the hardships of the world. The best contentment is to give up desires. Many a slavish mind is subservient to overpowering longings. Capability helps preservation of experience. Love means well-utilized relationships. Do not trust one who is grieved. Hadith 211

On a Day when will be turned upside down, their faces in the fire, they will say: O would that we obeyed God and obeyed the Messenger! **33:66**

O God's human being! I advise you of God, to exercise God-consciousness and to obey Him because it is salvation tomorrow and deliverance forever. He warned you of chastisement and did so thoroughly. Sermon 160

They will say: Our Lord! Truly, we obeyed our chiefs and our great ones. They caused us to go astray from the way. **33:67**

I bear witness that *there is no god but God* (Q47:19), the One, there is no partner with Him, nor is there with Him any god other than Himself, and that *Muhammad* (Q48:29), peace and the mercy of God be upon him, is *His servant* (Q17:1) and *Prophet.* (Q7:158) Sermon 35

Our Lord! Give them double the punishment and curse them with a great cursing! **33:68**

One of the firm decisions of God in the Wise Reminder (Quran), upon which He bestows reward or gives punishment and through which He likes or dislikes, is that it will not benefit a person, even though he exerts himself and acts sincerely, if he leaves this world to meet God with one of these acts without repenting, namely that he believed in a partner with God during his obligatory worship or appeased his own anger by killing an individual or spoke about acts committed by others or sought fulfillment of his needs from people by introducing an innovation in his religion or met people with a double face or moved among them with a double tongue. Understand this because an illustration is a guide for its like. Sermon 153

O those who believed! Be not like those who maligned Moses. God declared him innocent of what they said. He had been well-esteemed with God. **33:69**
O those who believed! Be God-conscious and say an appropriate saying. **33:70**
He will make your actions right for you and forgive you your impieties. Whoever obeys God and His Messenger surely, won a triumph, a sublime triumph! **33:71**

The beginning of the action of one who sees with his heart and acts with eyes is to assess whether the action will go against him or for him. If it is for him, he indulges in it, but if it is against him, he keeps away from it. For he who acts without knowledge is like one who treads without a path. His deviation from the path keeps him at a distance from his aim. He who acts according to knowledge is like him who treads the clear path. Sermon 153

Truly, We presented the trust to the heavens and the earth and the mountains, but they refused to carry it and were apprehensive of it. But the human being carried it. Truly, he had been wrongdoing, very ignorant. **33:72**

As regards fulfillment of trust, whoever does not pay attention to it will be disappointed. It was placed before the strong skies, vast earths and high mountains, but none of them was found to be stronger, vaster or higher than it. If anything could be unapproachable because of height, vastness, power or strength they would have been unapproachable, but they felt afraid of the evil consequences of failure in fulfilling a trust and noticed what a weaker being did not realize it, and this was the human being: *Truly, We presented the trust to the heavens and the earth and the mountains, but they refused to carry it and were apprehensive of it. But the human being carried it. Truly, he had been wrongdoing, very ignorant.* (Q33:72) Sermon 198

God punishes the males, ones who are hypocrites and the females, ones who are hypocrites and the males, ones who are polytheists and the females, ones who are polytheists and God will turn to forgiveness toward the males, ones who believe and the females, ones who believe. God had been Forgiving, Compassionate. **33:73**

O the Most Merciful of all! O my God! .... Surely, **You** are powerful over whatever **You** will. Sermon 143

Chapter 34: Sheba (al-Sabāʾ)

The Praise belongs to God. To Him belongs whatever is in the heavens and whatever is in and on the earth. His is The Praise in the world to come. He is The Wise, The Aware. **34:1**

He has spread the earth. He makes streams to flow and vegetation to grow on high lands. His primordiality has no beginning, nor has His eternity any end. He is the First and forever. He is the everlasting without limit. Sermon 163

He knows whatever penetrates into the earth and what goes forth out of it and what comes down from the heaven and what goes up to it. He is The Compassionate, The Forgiving. **34:2**

How extensive are **Your** bounties in this world, but how small are they against the bounties of the next world! Sermon 108

Those who were ungrateful said: The Hour will not approach us. Say: Yea! By my Lord, it will, certainly, approach you. He is One Who Knows of the unseen. Not an atom's weight escapes from Him in the heavens or in and on the earth, be it smaller than that or greater, but that it had been in a clear Book **34:3**
that He may give recompense to those who believed and did as the ones in accord with morality. Those, for them there is forgiveness and a generous provision. **34:4**

God ... is aware of whatever is hidden in the hearts and whatever lies behind the unseen. Sermon 192

But those who endeavored against Our signs as ones who strive to thwart, those, for them there is a punishment of painful wrath. **34:5**

Certainly, there are examples before you of God's wrath, punishment, days of tribulations and happenings. Therefore, do not disregard His promises. Do not ignore His punishment or make light His wrath and not expect His violence, because God, the Almighty, did not curse the past ages unless they had left off asking others to do good acts and refraining them from bad acts. In fact, God cursed the foolish for committing sins and the wise because they gave up refraining others from evil. Be aware! You have broken the bonds of Islam, transgressed its limits, and destroyed its commands. Sermon 192

Consider those who were given the knowledge that what was caused to descend to ***you*** *from* ***your*** *Lord. It is The Truth and it guides to a path of The Almighty, The Worthy of Praise.* **34:6**

Praise belongs to God (Q1:2) Who made me such that I have not died, nor am I sick, nor have my veins been infected with disease, nor have I been hauled up for my evil acts, nor am I without progeny, nor have I forsaken my religion, nor do I disbelieve in my Lord, nor do I feel strangeness with my faith, nor is my intelligence affected, nor have I been punished with the punishment of peoples before me. I am a servant in **Your** possession. I have been guilty of excesses over myself. **You** have exhausted **Your** pleas over me and I have no plea before **You**. I have no power to take except what **You** give me. I cannot evade except what **You** save me from. Sermon 215

Those who were ungrateful said: Shall we point you to a man who will tell you when you were torn to pieces, ones who are totally torn to pieces? Then, you will be, truly, in a new creation. **34:7**

God, the Almighty, has maintained it with His kindness, kept it intact with His command and perfected it with His power. Then after its destruction, He will resuscitate it, but not for any need of His own towards it, nor to seek the assistance of any of its things against it, nor to change over from the condition of loneliness to that of company, nor from the condition of ignorance and blindness to that of knowledge and search, nor from paucity and need towards needlessness and plenty, nor from disgrace and lowliness towards honor and prestige. Sermon 186

Devised he a lie against God or is there a madness in him? Nay! Those who believe not in the world to come there is a punishment and a going far astray. **34:8**

Certainly, nothing is viler than evil, except its punishment. Nothing is better than good, except its reward. In this world, everything that is heard is better than what is seen, while everything of the next world that is seen is better than what is heard. You should satisfy yourself by hearing rather than seeing and by the news of the unknown. You should know that what is little in this world but much in the next is better than what is much in this world but little in the next. In how many cases little is profitable while much causes loss. Sermon 114

Consider they not what is in advance of them and what is behind them of the heaven and the earth? If We will, We could cause the earth to swallow them, or cause to drop on them pieces of heaven. Truly, in this is a sign for every servant, one who turns in repentance. **34:9**

I bear witness that *Muhammad* (Q48:29), peace and the mercy of God be upon him, is *His servant* (Q17:1) and *Prophet* (Q7:158) whom He deputed when the signs of guidance were obliterated and the ways of religion were desolate. Sermon 194

Certainly, We gave David grace from Us. O mountains! Echo psalms of praise with him and the birds. We softened iron for him. **34:10**
saying that: Work on full coats of mail and calculate the links. Do as one in accord with morality. Truly, I am Seeing of what you do. **34:11**
To Solomon We subjected the wind. The first part of the day was a month's journey and the evening course was a month's journey. We caused a spring of molten brass to flow for him. We gave him of the jinn who work in advance of him with the permission of his Lord. Whoever of them swerved from Our command We caused him to experience the punishment of the blaze. **34:12**
They worked for him whatever of sanctuaries he wills—images and basin-like cisterns like water-troughs and cooking pots—ones firmly fixed. People of David! Act with thankfulness. But few of My servants are grateful. **34:13**

They will be very few in number, and they are the people who correspond to the description given by God, the Glorified, when He says: *But few of My servants are grateful.* (Q34:13) Sermon 190

Then, when We decreed death for Solomon, nothing pointed out his death to the jinn, but a moving creature of the earth that consumes his scepter. So, when he fell down, it became clear to the jinn that if they had been knowing the unseen, they would not have lingered in expectation in the despised punishment. **34:14**
There had, certainly, been for Sheba a sign in their dwelling place. Two gardens on the right and on the left. Eat of the provision of your Lord and give thanks to Him: A good land and a forgiving Lord. **34:15**
But they turned aside, so We sent against them the overwhelming flood, and We substituted for their two gardens, two gardens yielding a sour harvest, and tamarisks, and something of lote-trees here and there. **34:16**
That is how We gave recompense to them because they were ungrateful. We recompense, but the ungrateful. **34:17**
We made between them and between the towns which We blessed, that which are manifest towns and We ordained your journeying in them. Journey through them as ones who are safe night and day. **34:18**
But they said: Our Lord! Cause a distance between our journeys and they did wrong to themselves. So, We made them as tales and We tore them to pieces, a total tearing to pieces. Truly, in that are signs for every enduring grateful one. **34:19** ***

Certainly, established as true about them was the opinion of Iblis and they followed him, but a group of people among the ones who believe. **34:20**
There had not been for him any authority over them, but that We know who believe in the world to come from who is in uncertainty of it. ***Your*** *Lord is Guardian over everything.* **34:21**

Certainly, **Your** pour down rain after the people lose hopes and spread **Your** mercy, since **You** are the Guardian, the praiseworthy. Sermon 114

Say: Call on those whom you claimed other than God. They possess not the weight of an atom in the heavens nor on the earth, nor have they in either any association, nor among them is there any sustainer of Him. **34:22**
No intercession profits with Him, but for him to whom He gave permission. Until when their hearts were freed from terror, they said: What is it that your Lord said. They said: The Truth. He is the Lofty, the Great. **34:23**

(The Prophet) threw open the truth, gave advice to the people, guided them towards righteousness and ordered them to be moderate. May God bless him. Sermon 195

Say: Who provides for you from the heavens and the earth? Say: God. Truly, we or you are either on guidance or clearly going astray. **34:24**

O my God! I seek **Your** protection from becoming destitute despite **Your** riches, from being misguided despite **Your** guidance, from being molested in **Your** realm and from being humiliated while authority rests with **You**. O my God! Let my spirit be the first of those good objects that **You** take from me and the first trust out of **Your** favors held in trust with me. Sermon 215

Say: You will not be asked of what we sinned, nor will we be asked about what you do. **34:25**
Say: Our Lord will gather us. Again, He will explain The Truth among us and He is The Opener, The Knowing. **34:26**
Say: Cause me to see those whom you caused to join with Him as ascribed associates. No indeed! Nay! He is God, The Almighty, The Wise. **34:27**

I bear witness that *there is no god but God* (Q47:19), and I bear witness that *Muhammad* (Q48:29), peace and the mercy of God be upon him, is *His servant* (Q17:1),and *Prophet* (Q7:158) and His chosen and His selected one. Sermon 150

We sent **you** *not, but collectively for humanity as a bearer of good tidings and a warner, but most of humanity knows not.* **34:28**
They say: When is this promise if you had been ones who are sincere? **34:29**

Be aware! What had been ordained has occurred and that which had been destined has come into play. I am speaking to you with the promise and pleas of God. God, the Sublime, has said: *Truly those who said: Our Lord is God. Moreover, they go straight and the angels come forth to them: Neither fear nor feel remorse, but rejoice in the Gardens which you have been promised.* (Q41:30) You have said: Our Lord is God. Then keep steadfast to His Book, to the way of His command and to the virtuous course of His worship. Thereafter do not go out of it. Do not introduce innovations in it. Do not turn away from it, because those who go away from this course will be cut off from the mercy of God on the Day of Judgment. Sermon 176

Say: Yours is the solemn declaration of a Day which you delay not for an hour nor press forward. **34:30**

When the earthquake occurs, the Day of Resurrection approaches with all its severities, the people of every worshipping place cling to it, all the devotees cling to the object of their devotion and all the followers cling to their leader. Then on that day even the opening of an eye in the air and the sound of a footstep on the ground will be assigned its due through His Justice and His Equity. On that day many an argument will prove void and a contention for excuses will stand rejected. Sermon 222

Those who were ungrateful said: We will never believe in this, the Quran, nor in what was in advance of it, but if **you** *have considered when the ones who are unjust who are stationed before their Lord, returning the saying, some of them to some others. Say to those who were taken advantage of due to their weakness to those who grew arrogant: If it were not for you, we would have been ones who believe.* **34:31**
Those who grew arrogant would say to those who were taken advantage due to their weakness: Barred we you from guidance after it drew near you? Nay! You had been ones who sin. **34:32**
Would say those who were taken advantage due to their weakness to those who grew arrogant: Nay! It was your planning by nighttime and daytime when you commanded us to be ungrateful to God and to assign rivals to Him. They will keep their self-reproach secret when they will see the punishment and We assigned yokes around the necks of those who were ungrateful. Are they given recompense but for what they had been doing? **34:33**

O people of differing minds and divided hearts, whose bodies are present, but wits are absent. I am leading you amicably towards truthfulness, but you run away from it like goats and sheep running away from the howling of a lion. How hard it is for me to uncover for you the secrets of justice or to straighten the curve of truthfulness. Sermon 131

We sent not any warner to a town, but that the ones who are given ease said: Truly, in what you were sent, we are ones who disbelieve it. **34:34**

God sent Muhammad, peace and the mercy of God be upon him, as a warner against vice for all the worlds and a trustee of His revelation, while you people of Arabia were following the worst religion and you resided among rough stones and venomous serpents. You drank dirty water and ate filthy food. You shed blood of each other and cared not for relationship. Idols are fixed among you and sins are clinging to you. Sermon 26

They said: We are more than you in wealth and in children and we are not ones who are punished! **34:35**

In the same way the rich among the prosperous communities have been feeling vanity because of their riches, as God said: *They said: We are more than you in wealth and in children and we are not ones who will be punished!* (Q34:35) Sermon 192

Say: Truly, my Lord extends the provision for whomever He wills and confines it for whom He wills, but most of humanity knows not. **34:36**

Praise belongs to God (Q1:2) Who is above all similarity to creatures, is above the words of describers Who displays the wonders of His management for the on-lookers, is hidden from the imagination of thinkers by virtue of the greatness of His glory, has knowledge without acquiring it by adding to it or drawing it from someone, and Who is the ordainer of all matters without reflecting or thinking. He is such that gloom does not concern Him, nor does He seek light from brightness. Night does not overtake Him, nor does the day pass over Him so as to affect Him in any manner. His comprehension of things is not through eyes. His knowledge is not dependent on being informed. God deputized *the Prophet* (Q7:158), peace and the mercy of God be upon him, with light and accorded him the highest precedence in selection. Through him God united those who were divided, overpowered the powerful, overcame difficulties and leveled rugged ground and thus removed misguidance from right and left. Sermon 213

It is not your wealth nor your children that will bring you near to Us, but whoever believed and did as one in accord with morality. As for those, for them, the recompense is doubled for what they did and they will live in the highest chambers as one who is safe. **34:37**

Among the proofs of His creation is the creation of the skies which are fastened without pillars and stand without support. He called them. They responded obediently and humbly without being lazy or loathsome. If they had not acknowledged His Godhead and obeyed Him, He would not have made them the place for His throne, the abode of His angels and the destination: *To Him Words of what is good rise and He exalts an action in accord with morality* ... (Q35:10) of the creatures. Sermon 182

Those who endeavor against Our signs, as ones who strive to thwart them, those are ones who are charged with the punishment. **34:38**

I bear witness that *there is no god but God,* (Q47:19), by virtue of belief, certainty, sincerity and conviction. I also bear witness that *Muhammad* (Q48:29), peace and the mercy of God be upon him, is *His servant* (Q17:1) and *Prophet* (Q7:158) whom He deputed when the signs of guidance were obliterated and the ways of religion were desolate. So he threw open the truth, gave advice to the people, guided them towards righteousness and ordered them to be moderate. May God bless him ... Sermon 194

Say: Truly, my Lord extends the provision for whomever He wills of His servants and confines for him what He wills. Whatever you spent of anything, He will replace it. He is Best of the ones who provide. **34:39**

Praise belongs to God (Q1:2) Who made me such that I have not died, nor am I sick, nor have my veins been infected with disease, nor have I been hauled up for my evil acts, nor am I without progeny, nor have I forsaken my religion, nor do I disbelieve in my Lord, nor do I feel strangeness with my faith, nor is my intelligence affected, nor have I been punished with the punishment of peoples before me. I am a servant in **Your** possession. I have been guilty of excesses over myself. **You** have exhausted **Your** pleas over me and I have no plea before **You**. I have no power to take except what **You** give me. I cannot evade except what **You** save me from. Sermon 215

On a Day He will assemble them altogether. Again, He will say to the angels: Was it these who had been worshiping you? **34:40**

Perform good acts while you are still in the vastness of life. The books are open for recording of actions. Repentance is allowed. The runner away from God is being called and the sinner is being given hope of forgiveness before the light of action is put off, time expires, life ends, the door for repentance is closed and angels ascend to the sky. Sermon 236

They would say: Glory be to ***You! You*** *are our Protector and not they. Nay! They had been worshiping the jinn. Most of them were ones who believe in them.* **34:41**

I praise Him for His continuous mercy and His copious bounties. Sermon 82

Then, today none of you will possess the power over some others to profit nor hurt and We will say to those who did wrong: Experience the punishment of the fire which you had been denying. **34:42**

Everyone should be God-conscious, should admonish himself, should send forward his repentance and should overpower his desire because his death is hidden from him. His desires deceive him. Satan keeps posted about him. He beautifies his sin for him so that he may commit it. He prompts him to delay repentance until his desires cause him to be the most negligent. Pity is for the negligent person whose life itself would be a proof against him and his own days, passed in sin, will lead him to punishment. Sermon 64

When are recounted to them Our signs, clear portents, they said: This is not but a man who wants to bar you from what your fathers had been worshipping. They said: This is not but a forged calumny. Those who were ungrateful for The Truth said when it drew near them: Truly, this is but clear sorcery. **34:43**

(May God) bring us out on the Day of Judgment among His party, neither ashamed, nor repentant, nor deviators, nor pledge-breakers, nor strayers, nor misleaders nor seduced. Sermon 105

We gave them not any Books that they study them nor sent We to them any warner before ***you***. **34:44**

Those that were before them denied and they reached not one-tenth of what We gave them. Yet they denied My Messengers. So, how had My disapproval of them been! **34:45**

The Book of God is that through which you see, you speak and you hear. Sermon 132

Say: I admonish you in but one thing: That you stand up for God by twos and one by one. Again, reflect. There is not in your companion any madness. He is only a warner to you of a severe punishment in advance of you. **34:46**

Say: Whatever compensation I asked of you, that is for you. My compensation is only from God. He is a Witness over everything. **34:47**

We bear witness that *there is no god, but He*. (Q3:2) Sermon 100

Say: Truly, my Lord hurls The Truth. He is The Knower of the unseen. **34:48**

Say: The Truth drew near and falsehood neither causes to begin nor causes to return. **34:49**

Know that—may God have mercy on you—you are living at a time when those who speak about right are few, when tongues are loath to utter the truth and those who stick to the right are humiliated. The people of this time are engaged in disobedience. Their youth are wicked, their old men are sinful, their learned men are hypocrites, and their speakers are sycophants. Their young ones do not respect their elders, and their rich men do not support the destitute. Sermon 232

Say: If I went astray, truly, I will only go astray with loss for myself. If I was truly guided, it is because of what my Lord reveals to me. Truly, He is Hearing, Ever Near. **34:50**

My bearing witness has been tested. Its essence is our belief. We shall cling to it for as long as we live and shall store it facing the tribulations that overtake us because it is the foundation stone of faith and the first step towards good actions and divine pleasure. Sermon 2

If ***you*** *would see when they would be terrified, when there is no escape and they would be taken from a near place,* **34:51**

they would say: We believed in it! But how could they reach it from a place so far away? **34:52**

Surely, they were ungrateful for it before. They hurl at the unseen from a far place. **34:53**

God ... is aware of whatever is hidden in the hearts and whatever lies behind the unseen. Sermon 192

A barrier was set up between them and between that for which they lust just as was accomplished with partisans before. Truly, they had been uncertain, in grave doubt. **34:54**

I bear witness that *there is no god but God* (Q47:19) and I bear witness that *Muhammad* (Q48:29), peace and the mercy of God be upon him, is *His servant* (Q17:1) and *His Prophet* (Q7:158) and His chosen and His selected one. Sermon 150

CHAPTER 35: THE ORIGINATOR (al-Fāṭir)

The Praise belongs to God, One Who is the Originator of the heavens and the earth, the One Who Makes the angels Messengers imbued with wings by twos and in threes and fours. He increases in creation what He wills. Truly, God is Powerful over everything. **35:1**

He is One, but not by counting. He is everlasting without any limit. He is existent without any support. Minds admit of Him without any activity of the senses. Things which can be seen stand witness to Him without confronting Him. Imagination cannot encompass Him. He manifests Himself to the imagination with his help for the imagination, and refuses to be imagined by the imagination. He has made imagination the arbiter in this matter. He is not great in the sense that volume is vast and so His body is also great. Nor is He mighty in the sense that His limits should extend to the utmost and so His frame be extensive, but He is great in position and mighty in authority. Sermon 185

Whatever God may open of mercy to humanity, there is not one who holds it back. What He holds back, there is not one who sends it after that. He is The Almighty, The Wise. **35:2**

Praise belongs to God (Q1:2) from Whose mercy no one loses hope, from Whose bounty no one is deprived, from Whose forgiveness no one is disappointed and for Whose worship no one is too high. His mercy never ceases and His bounty never ceases. Sermon 45

O humanity! Remember the divine blessing of God on you! Is there anyone who is a creator other than God Who provides for you from the heaven and the earth? There is no god but He. Then, how you are misled! **35:3**

O people who possess eyes and ears and health and wealth! Is there any place of protection, any shelter of safety, or asylum or haven, or occasion to run away or to come back to this world? If not: *How then you are misled?* (Q35:3) and what are you averting? By what things have you been deceived? Certainly, the share of every one of you from this earth is just a piece of land equal to his own stature and size where he would lie on his cheeks covered with dust. Sermon 82

If they deny ***you****, surely, Messengers before* ***you*** *were denied. To God all affairs are returned.* **35:4**

By what things have you been deceived? Certainly, the share of every one of you from this earth is just a piece of land equal to his own stature and size where he would lie on his cheeks covered with dust. Sermon 82

O humanity! Truly, the promise of God is true. So, let not this present life delude you. Let not the deluder delude you about God. **35:5**

How many people make haste for a matter, but when they get it they begin to wish they had not gotten it? How near is today to the dawning of tomorrow? O my people, this is the time for the occurrence of every promised event and the approach of things which you do not know. Sermon 150

Truly, Satan is an enemy to you so take him to yourselves as an enemy. He calls only his party that they be among the Companions of the Blaze. **35:6**

Satan was given support. Faith was forsaken. As a result, the pillars of religion crumbled. Any trace of them was lost. Its passages were destroyed. Its streets fell into decay. People obeyed Satan and tread his path. They sought water from his watering places. Satan's banners flew in the wind through them. His standard of vice was raised. They trampled people under their hoofs and tread upon them with their feet. Vice attained full stature. The people immersed in them were led astray, perplexed, ignorant and seduced as though they were in a good house (Mecca) with bad neighbors (ungrateful Quraysh). Sermon 2

Those who were ungrateful, for them will be a severe punishment. Those who believed and did as the ones in accord with morality, for them there is forgiveness and a great compensation. **35:7**

Praise belongs to God (Q1:2) from Whose mercy no one loses hope, from Whose bounty no one is deprived, from Whose forgiveness no one is disappointed and for Whose worship no one is too high. His mercy never ceases and His bounty is never missed. Sermon 45

Then, who is there that was made to appear pleasing to him the direness of his actions so that, then, he saw it as fairer. Truly, God causes to go astray whomever He wills and guides whomever He wills. So, let not **your** *soul be wasted in regret for them. Truly, God is Knowing of what they craft!* **35:8**

Time has made me laugh after making me weep. No wonder, by God. What is this affair which surpasses all wonder and which has increased wrongfulness? These people have tried to put out the flame of God's light from His lamp and to close His fountain from its source. They mixed epidemic-producing water between me and themselves. If the trying hardships were removed from among us, I would take them on the course of truthfulness, otherwise: *So, let not* **your***self be wasted in regret for them. Truly God is Knowing of what they craft*! (Q35:8) Sermon 162

It is God Who sent the winds so that they raise clouds and We drove them to a dead land and We gave life by them to the earth after its death. Thus, will be the rising! **35:9**

To **You** is the return of every living being. Sermon 108

Whoever had been wanting great glory, great glory belongs to God altogether. To Him Words of what is good rise. He exalts the actions of one in accord with morality. But those who plan evil deeds, for them will be a severe punishment. The planning of those, it will come to nothing. **35:10**

If you study this world properly, you will find that every morning it places new anxieties and new worries before you simply to warn and frighten you of the consequences of evil deeds and to persuade you towards good actions, while every night it raises new hopes of peace and prosperity in you. Saying 130

God created you from earth dust: Again, from seminal fluid. Again, He made you pairs. No female carries nor brings forth her burden but with His Knowledge. No one who is given a long life is given a long life, nor is anything reduced from his lifetime but it is in a Book. Truly, that is easy for God. **35:11**

There is no doubt that God sent down *the Prophet* (Q7:158), peace and the mercy of God be upon him, as a guide with an eloquent Book and a standing command. No one will be ruined by it except one who ruins himself. Certainly, only doubtful innovations cause ruin except those from which God may protect. In God's authority lies the safety of your affairs. Therefore, render Him such obedience as is neither blameworthy nor insincere. By God, you must do so otherwise God will take away from you the power of Islam and will never thereafter return it to you until it reverts to others. Sermon 169

The two bodies of water are not on the same level. This is agreeable, water of the sweetest kind, that which is delicious to drink, and the other is salty, bitter. But from each you eat succulent flesh and pull out glitter that you wear. ***You*** *will see the boats, that which plows through the waves on it, that you be looking for His grace and so that perhaps you will give thanks.* **35:12**

You look at the sun and moon, the plants and trees, water and stone, the alternation of this night and day, the flowing out of these seas, the large number of mountains and the height of their peaks, the diversity of languages and the variety of tongues. Then woe be to him who disbelieves in the Ordainer and denies the Ruler. They claim that they are like grass for which there is no cultivator, nor any maker for their diverse shapes. They have not relied on any argument for what they assert, nor on any research for what they have heard. Can there be any construction without a Constructor, or any offense without an offender? Sermon 185

He causes the nighttime to be interposed in the daytime and He causes the daytime to be interposed into the nighttime and He caused the sun to be subservient and the moon. Each runs its course for a term, that is determined. That is God, your Lord. For Him is the dominion! Those whom you call to other than Him possess not even the white spot of a date stone. **35:13**

Do not give up fearing God Who has no partner. Letter 25

If you call to them, they would not hear your supplication. Even if they heard, they would not respond to you. On the Day of Resurrection they will disbelieve in your association with them. None tells ***you*** *like One Who is Aware.* **35:14**

O my listener! Be cured from your intoxication. Wake up from your slumber. Decrease your hasty activity. Ponder over what has come to you through *the unlettered Prophet* (Q7:157), which is inevitable and inescapable. You should turn away from him who opposes him. Leave him and leave whatever he has adopted for himself. Put off your vanity. Drop your haughtiness. Recall your grave because your way passes over it. You will be dealt with as you deal with others. You will reap what you sow. What you send today will meet you tomorrow. So provide for your future. Send some good acts for your day of reckoning. God-consciousness, God-consciousness, O listener! Act, act, O careless one! *None tells* ***you*** *like One Who is Aware.* (Q35:14) Sermon 153

O humanity! It is you who are poor in relation to God. God—He is Sufficient, Worthy of Praise. **35:15**

Let the most beloved of affairs to you be those most centered upon the right, the most comprehensive in justice (the golden mean), and the most inclusive of popular approval, for the disapproval of the common folk undermines the approval of the elite. Letter 53*

If He wills, He would cause you to be put away and bring a new creation. **35:16**
That for God is not a great matter. **35:17**

The creation was completed by His order. It bowed to His obedience. It responded to His call. The laziness of any slug or the inertness of any excuse-finder did not prevent it from doing so. So He straightened the curves of the things and fixed their limits. With His power He created coherence in their contradictory parts and joined together the factors of similarity. Then He separated them in varieties which differ in limits, quantities, properties and shapes. All this is a new creation. He made them firm and shaped them according as He wished and invented them. Sermon 90

No burdened soul will bear another's load. If one who is weighed down calls for help for his heavy load, nothing of it is carried for him, even if he had been possessor of kinship. Have ***you*** *warned only those who dread their Lord in the unseen and performed the formal prayer. He who purified himself, then, only purifies for himself. To God is the Homecoming.* **35:18**

Their hearts are grieved. Others are protected from their evil. Their bodies are thin. Their needs are scanty. Their souls are chaste. They endured hardship for a short while. As a consequence, they secured comfort for a long time. It is a beneficial transaction that God made easy for them. The world aimed at them, but they did not aim at it. It captured them, but they freed themselves from it by a ransom. During the night, they are standing on their feet, reading portions of the Quran and reciting it in a well-measured way, creating through it grief and seeking by it the cure for their ailments. If they come across a verse creating eagerness for Paradise, they pursue it avidly. Their spirits turn towards it eagerly. They feel as if it is in front of them. When they come across a verse which contains fear of Hell, they bend the ears of their hearts towards it and feel as though the sound of Hell and its cries are reaching their ears. They bend themselves from their backs, prostrate themselves on their foreheads, their palms, their knees and their toes, and beseech God, the Sublime, for their deliverance. Sermon 193

Not on the same level are the unwilling to see and the seeing **35:19**
nor are shadows and light **35:20**
nor are the shade and the torrid heat. **35:21**
Nor are the living and the lifeless on the same level. Truly, God causes to hear whom He wills. ***You*** *are not one who causes to hear whoever is in graves.* **35:22**

God has provided wonderful creations including the living, the lifeless, the stationary and the moving. He has established such clear proofs for His delicate creative power and great might that minds bend down to Him in acknowledgment thereof and in submission to Him, and arguments about His Oneness strike our ears. Sermon 164

***You** are but a warner.* **35:23**
*Truly, We sent **you** with The Truth, a bearer of good tidings and a warner. There is not any community, but a warner passed away among them.* **35:24**

At last, when God will make clear to them the reward for their sins and take them out from the veils of their neglectfulness, they will proceed to what they were running away from and run away from what they were proceeding to. They will not benefit from the wants they will satisfy or the desires they would fulfill. I warn you and myself from this position. A person should derive benefit from his own self. Certainly, prudent is he who hears and ponders over it, who sees and observes and who benefits from instructive material and then treads on clear paths wherein he avoids falling into hollows and straying into pitfalls and does not assist those who misguide him by turning away from truthfulness, changing his words, or fearing truth. Sermon 153

*If they deny **you**, so, surely, those who were before them denied. Their Messengers drew near them with the clear portents and with the Psalms and the illuminating Book.* **35:25**

Do not say what you do not understand, because most of the right is in what you deny. Accept the argument of one against whom you have no argument. Sermon 86

Again, I took those who were ungrateful. How had My disapproval of them been! **35:26**

God ... is aware of whatever is hidden in the hearts and whatever lies behind the unseen. Sermon 192

*Have **you** not considered that God caused water to descend from the heavens? Then, We brought out fruits, the ones of varying hues. Among the mountains are white and red streaks—the ones of varying hues—and others raven black,* **35:27**
and of humanity and moving creatures and flocks, thus, they are likewise of hues, ones at variance. Only His servants who dread God are knowing. Truly, God is Almighty, Forgiving. **35:28**

Almighty God created forth wind and made its movement sterile, perpetuated its position, intensified its motion and spread it far and wide. Then He ordered the wind to raise up deep waters and to intensify the waves of the oceans. So the wind churned it like the churning of curd and pushed it fiercely into the firmament throwing its front position on the rear and the stationary on the flowing until its level was raised and the surface was full of foam. Then Almighty God raised the foam on to the open wind and vast firmament and made therefrom the seven skies and made the lower one as a stationary surge and the upper one as protective ceiling and a high edifice without any pole to support it or nail to hold it together. Then He decorated them with stars and the light of meteors and hung in it the shining sun and effulgent moon under the revolving sky, moving ceiling and rotating firmament. Sermon 1

Truly, those who recount the Book of God and performed the formal prayer and spent out of what We provided for them secretly and in public, they hope for a trade that will never come to nothing. **35:29**

The Book of God is among you. It speaks. Its tongue does not falter. It is a house whose pillars do not fall down. It is a power whose supporters are never defeated. Sermon 132

He will, certainly, pay them their account in full as their compensation and increase them more out of His grace. Truly, He is Forgiving, Ready to Appreciate. **35:30**

A person should derive benefit from himself for himself, from the living for the dead, from the mortal for the lasting and from the departer for the stayer. A person should fear God while he is given age to live up to his death and is allowed time to act. A person should control his self by the rein and hold it with its bridle, thus by the rein he should prevent it from disobedience towards God, and by the bridle he should lead it towards obedience to God. Sermon 236

What We revealed to **you** *of the Book is The Truth, that establishes as true what was in advance of it. Truly, God is Aware, Seeing of His servants.* **35:31**

Be aware! Verily this world is a place from which protection cannot be sought except while one is in it. An action that is performed only for this world cannot secure salvation. People are tested in it through calamities. Those who have taken worldly pleasures here will be taken out from them by death and will be questioned about them. Whatever good actions they have achieved for the other world, they will get them there and stay in them. For the intelligent, this world is like the shade—one moment it is spread out and extended, but soon it shrinks and contracts. Sermon 63

Again, We gave the Book as an inheritance to those whom We favored of Our servants. Then, of them are ones who are unjust to themselves and of them are ones who halt between two opinions and some of them are ones who take the lead with good deeds by permission of God. That is the greater grace. **35:32**

Where are the seekers of virtue? The paths have already been determined. They have been given the news. For every misguidance, there is a cause. For every breaking of a pledge, there is a misrepresentation. By God, I shall not be like him who listens to the voice of mourning, hears the man who brings news of death and also visits the mourner, yet does not take a lesson. Sermon 148

Gardens of Eden—they will enter them. They will be adorned in them with bracelets of gold and pearls. Their garments in them will be silk. **35:33**

God, the Almighty, has sent down a guiding Book wherein He has explained virtue and vice. You should adopt the course of virtue, whereby you will have guidance. Detach yourself from the direction of vice, so that you remain on the right way. Sermon 167

They would say: The Praise belongs to God Who caused grief to be put away from us. Truly, our Lord is Forgiving, Ready to Appreciate. **35:34**

I bear witness that *there is no god but God* (Q47:19), by virtue of belief, certainty, sincerity and conviction. I also bear witness that *Muhammad* (Q48:29), peace and the mercy of God be upon him, is *His servant* (Q17:1) and *Prophet* (Q7:158) whom He deputed when the signs of guidance were obliterated and the ways of religion were desolate. So he threw open the truth, gave advice to the people, guided them towards righteousness and ordered them to be moderate. May God bless him ... Sermon 194

He Who caused us to live in the inhabited Abode out of His grace, fatigue will not afflict us in it, nor will we be afflicted with exhaustion in it. **35:35**

O God's human being! You should know that a believer should be distrustful of his heart every morning and evening. He should always blame it for shortcomings and ask it to add to its good acts. You should behave like those who have gone before you and the precedents in front of you. They left this world like a traveler and covered it as distance is covered. Sermon 176

Those who were ungrateful, for them will be the fire of hell: Neither will it be decided a term for them so that they die nor will its punishment be lightened for them. Thus, We give recompense to every ungrateful one. **35:36**

Everyone of them is ... alone although they are a group, and they are strangers, even though friends. They are unaware of morning after a night and of evening after a day. The night or the day when they departed has become ever existent for them. They found the dangers of their place of stay more serious than they had apprehended, and they witnessed that its signs were greater than they had guessed. The two objectives, namely Paradise and Hell, have been stretched for them up to a point beyond the reach of fear or hope. Had they been able to speak they would have become dumb to describe what they witnessed or saw. Sermon 220

They will shout aloud in it: Our Lord! Bring us out and we shall do as ones in accord with morality, not what we had been doing! Give We not you a long enough life so that whoever recollects would recollect there? The warner drew near you, so experience it because there is no helper for ones who are unjust. **35:37**

You, certainly, know that he who is in charge of honor, life, booty, enforcement of legal commandments and the leadership of the Muslims should not be a miser as his greed would aim at their wealth, nor be ignorant as he would then mislead them with his ignorance, nor be of rude behavior who would estrange them with his rudeness, nor should he deal unjustly with wealth thus preferring one group over another, nor should he accept a bribe while taking decisions as he would forfeit others' rights and hold them up without finality. He should not ignore the *sunna* as he would ruin the people. Sermon 131

Truly, God is One Who Knows the unseen of the heavens and the earth. Truly, He is Knowing of what is in the breasts. **35:38**

You are everlasting. There is no end to **You. You** are the highest aim. There is no escape from **You. You** are the promised point of return from which there is no deliverance except towards **You.** In **Your** hand is the forelock of every creature. To **You** is the return of Sermon 108

He it is Who made you viceregents on the earth. So, whoever was ungrateful, then, his ingratitude will be against him. The ones who are ungrateful increase not their ingratitude to their Lord, but in repugnance. The ones who are ungrateful increase not their ingratitude to their Lord, but in loss. **35:39**

The riser has risen. The sparkler has sparkled. The appearer has appeared. The curved has been straightened. God has replaced one people with another and one day with another. We awaited these changes as the famine-stricken await the rain. Certainly, the leaders are the viceregents of God over His creatures. They guide the creatures to knowing God. No one will enter Paradise except him who knows them and knows Him. No one will enter

Hell except him who denies them and denies Him. Sermon 152

Say: Considered you yourselves ascribed associates to whom you call to other than God? Cause me to see what they created in the earth or have they any association in creation of the heavens? Or gave We them a Book so that they have a clear portent from there? Nay! The ones who are unjust promise nothing—some of them to some others—but delusion. **35:40**

In God's authority lies the safety of your affairs. Therefore, render Him such obedience as is neither blameworthy nor insincere. By God, you must do so otherwise God will take away from you the power of Islam and will never thereafter return it to you until it reverts to others. Sermon 169

Truly, God holds back the heavens and the earth so that they are not displaced. If they were displaced, there is none who held them back after Him. Truly, He had been Forbearing, Forgiving. **35:41**

Glory to **You**! How great is **Your** creation that we see, but how small is this greatness by the side of **Your** Might! How awe-striking is **Your** realm that we notice, but how humble is this against what is hidden from us out of **Your** authority! How extensive are **Your** bounties in this world, but how small are they against the bounties of the next world! Sermon 108

They swore by God the most earnest oaths, that if a warner drew near them, they would be better guided than any of the other communities. Yet when a warner drew near to them, it increased nothing in them but aversion, **35:42**
growing arrogant on the earth and planning evil deeds. The plan of bad deeds surround none but people themselves. Then, look they on but a custom of the ancient ones? ***You*** *will never find in a custom of God any substitution.* ***You*** *will never find in a custom of God any revision.* **35:43**

O God! The eyes have not seen **You** so as to be aware of **You**, but **You** were before the describers of **Your** creation. **You** did not create the creation on account of loneliness, nor did **You** make them work for gain. He whom **You** catch cannot go farther than **Your** authority. He who obeys **You** does not add to **Your** Might. He who disagrees with **Your** judgment cannot turn it. He who turns away from **Your** command cannot do without **You**. Every secret before **You** is open and for **You**, every absent is present. Sermon 108

Journey they not through the earth and look on how had been the Ultimate End of those before them? They had been stronger than they are in strength. God had not been weakened by anything in the heavens nor in or on the earth. Truly, He had been Knowing, Powerful. **35:44**
If God takes humanity to task for what they earned, He would not leave on the back of the earth any moving creature, but He postpones to a term, that is determined. When their term drew near, then, truly, God had been Seeing of His servants. **35:45**

Where are the seekers of virtue; for the paths have already been determined and they have been given the news? Sermon 147

Chapter 36: Ya Sin (Yā Sīn)

36:1 *Ya Sin*
By the Wise Quran, **36:2**

truly, ***you*** *are among the ones who are sent* **36:3**
on a straight path, **36:4**
sent down successively by The Almighty, The Compassionate that **36:5**
you *warn a folk whose fathers were not warned, so they were ones who were heedless.* **36:6**

In (the Quran) there are some verses whose knowledge is obligatory and others whose ignorance by the people is permissible. It also contains what appears to be obligatory according to the Book, but its repeal is signified by the actions of *the Prophet* (Q7:158) (*sunna*), peace and the mercy of God be upon him, or that which appears compulsory according to the Prophet's actions, but the Book allows not following it. Or there are those which are obligatory in a given time, but not so after that time. Its prohibitions also differ. Some are major regarding which there exists the threat of hellfire and others are minor for which there is the hope of forgiveness. There are also those of which a small portion is also acceptable to God, but they are capable of being expanded. Sermon 1

Certainly, the saying was realized against most of them for they believe not. **36:7**
We laid yokes on their necks up to the chins, so that they are ones who are stiff-necked. **36:8**
We laid in advance of them an embankment and behind them an embankment. Then, We covered them so they perceive not. **36:9**
Equal it is to them whether ***you*** *warn them, or* ***you*** *warn them not. They will not believe.* **36:10**
You *have only warned whoever followed the Remembrance and dreaded The Merciful in the unseen, so give him good tidings of forgiveness and a generous compensation.* **36:11**

Know that this Quran is an adviser who never deceives, a leader who never misleads and a narrator who never speaks a lie. No one will sit beside this Quran, but when he rises, he will achieve one addition or one diminution—addition in his guidance or elimination in his spiritual blindness. You should also know that no one will need anything after guidance from the Quran and no one will be free from want before guidance from the Quran. Sermon 176

Truly, We give life to the dead and We write down what they put forward and their effects. We counted everything in a clear record. **36:12**

Perform good acts while you are still in the vastness of life. The books are open for recording of actions. Repentance is allowed. The runner away from God is being called and the sinner is being given hope of forgiveness before the light of action is put off, time expires, life ends, the door for repentance is closed and angels ascend to the sky. Therefore, a person should derive benefit from himself for himself, from the living for the dead, from the mortal, for the lasting and from the departer for the stayer. A person should be God-conscious while he is given age to live up to his death and is allowed time to act. A person should control his self by the rein and hold it with its bridle. By the rein, he should prevent it from disobedience towards God. By the bridle, he should lead it towards obedience to God. Sermon 236

Propound a parable for them: The Companions of the Town when ones who were sent drew near them. **36:13**
When We sent to them two, they denied them both, so We replenished them with the third. They said: Truly, We are ones who are sent to you. **36:14**
They said: You are nothing but mortals like ourselves and The Merciful caused not to descend anything. You are but lying! **36:15**
They said: Our Lord knows that we are ones who are sent to you. **36:16**

On us is only the delivering of the clear message. **36:17**
They said: Truly, we augured ill of you. If you refrain not yourselves, we will, certainly, stone you. Certainly, a painful punishment will afflict you from us. **36:18**
They said: Ones who auger ill will be with you! Is it because you were reminded? Nay! You are a folk, ones who are excessive. **36:19**
A man drew near from the farther part of the city, coming eagerly. He said: O my folk! Follow the ones who are sent! **36:20**
Follow whoever asks not of you any compensation and they are ones who are truly guided. **36:21**
What is it for me that I worship not Him Who originated me and to Whom you will be returned? **36:22**
Will I take gods to myself other than He when, if The Merciful wants any harm for me, their intercession will not avail me at all nor will they save me. **36:23**
Truly, I would, then, be clearly going astray. **36:24**
Truly, I believed in your Lord so hear me! **36:25**
It was said: Enter the Garden. He said: O would that my folk know **36:26**
that my Lord forgave me and made me one who is honored! **36:27**
After him We caused not to descend on his folk an army from heaven, nor had We been ones who need to cause to descend again. **36:28**
It would be but one Cry and that is when they were ones who are silent and still. **36:29**

Even though their traces have been wiped out and their news has stopped circulating, eyes are capable of drawing a lesson, as they looked at them, ears of intelligence heard them and they spoke without uttering words. So they said that handsome faces have been destroyed and delicate bodies have been smeared with earth. We have put on a worn-out shroud. The narrowness of the grave has overwhelmed us and strangeness has spread among us. Our silent abodes have been ruined. The beauty of our bodies has disappeared. Our known features have become hateful. Our stay in the places of strangeness has become long. We do not get relief from pain, nor widening from narrowness. Sermon 220

O how regrettable of the servants! A Messenger approaches them not, but they had been ridiculing him. **36:30**
Consider they not how many generations We caused to perish before them who, truly, return not to them. **36:31**
Truly, all of them will be altogether, ones who are charged in Our Presence. **36:32**

With *the Prophet* (Q7:158), peace and the mercy of God be upon him, God exhausted the series of Prophets and ended the revelation. He then fought for Him those who were turning away from Him and were equating others with Him. Sermon 133

A sign for them is the dead body of the earth. We gave life to it and We brought out grain from it so that they eat from it. **36:33**
We made in them gardens of date palm trees and grapevines and We caused a spring to gush forth in it **36:34**
so that they may eat of the fruit from there that are not what their hands did. Will they, then, not give thanks? **36:35**

Do not forget gratitude when receiving blessings for God has exhausted the excuses before you through clear, shining arguments and open, bright books. Sermon 81

Glory be to Him Who created pairs, all of them, of what the earth causes to develop as well as of themselves and of what they know not! **36:36**
A sign for them is the nighttime. We pluck the daytime from it and that is when they are ones in darkness! **36:37**
The sun runs to a resting place for it. That is foreordained by The Almighty, The Knowing. **36:38**
It is not fit and proper for the sun to overtake the moon nor the nighttime one to take the lead over the daytime. They each swim in an orbit. **36:40**

He initiated creation most initially and commenced it originally without undergoing reflection, without making use of any experiment, without innovating any movement and without experiencing any aspiration of mind. He allotted all things their times, put together their variations, gave them their properties and determined their features knowing them before creating them, realizing fully their limits and confines and appreciating their propensities and intricacies. Sermon 1

A sign for them is that We carried their offspring in a laden boat. **36:41**
We created for them of its like that they ride. **36:42**
If We will, We drown them with none for them to whom they cry aloud for help nor will they be saved **36:43**
unless it be a mercy from Us and as an enjoyment for a while. **36:44**
When it was said to them: Be God-conscious of what is in advance of you and what is behind you, so that perhaps you will find mercy, **36:45**
there never approaches them any sign from the signs of their Lord, but they had been ones who turn aside from it. **36:46**

Be God-conscious like him who listened to good advice and bowed before it. When he committed sin, he admitted it. Sermon 8

When it was said to them: Spend of whatever God provided you, those who were ungrateful said to those who believed: Will we feed him whom He would have fed, if He wills? You are nothing, but in a clear going astray. **36:47**
They say: When is this promise if you had been ones who are sincere? **36:48**
They expect but one Cry which will take them while they strive against one another. **36:49**
Then, they will not be able to leave a legacy nor will they return to their people. **36:50**
The trumpet would be blown! That is when they will be sliding down to their Lord from their tombs. **36:51**
They would say: Woe on us! Who raised us up from our place of sleep? This is what The Merciful promised and the ones who are sent were sincere. **36:52**

O the Most Merciful of all! ... O my God! Do pour on us **Your** mercy, **Your** blessing, **Your** sustenance and **Your** pity. Sermon 143

It would be but one Cry. That is when they will be in Our Presence altogether, ones who are charged. **36:53**
This Day no soul will be wronged at all nor will you be given recompense but for what you had been doing. **36:54**

The world aimed at them, but they did not aim at it. It captured them, but they freed themselves from it by a ransom. During the night, they are standing on their feet, reading portions of the Quran and reciting it in a well-measured way, creating through it grief and seeking by it the cure for their ailments. If they come across a verse creating eagerness for Paradise, they pursue it avidly. Their spirits turn towards it eagerly. They feel as if it is in front of them. When they come across a verse which contains fear of Hell, they bend the ears of their hearts towards it and feel as though the sound of Hell and its cries are reaching their ears. They bend themselves from their backs, prostrate themselves on their foreheads, their palms, their knees and their toes, and beseech God, the Sublime, for their deliverance. Sermon 193

Truly, the Companions of the Garden that Day are ones who are joyful in their engagements. **36:55**
They and their spouses, in shade on raised benches, ones who are reclining. **36:56**
They will have in it sweet fruits and they will have whatever they call for: **36:57**
Peace! A saying from the Compassionate Lord. **36:58**
Be separated on this Day, O ones who sin! **36:59**

The human being should ... fear the Day of Judgment before it arrives. He should appreciate the shortness of his life and the shortness of his sojourn in the place of stay which has only to last for his change over to the next place. He should, therefore, do something for his change over and for the known stages of his departure. Blessed be he who possesses a virtuous heart, obeys one who guides him, keeps away from one who takes him to ruin, catches the path of safety with the help of him who provides him light of guidance and, by obeying the leader who commands him, hastens towards guidance before its doors are closed, opens the door of repentance and removes the stain of sins. He has certainly been put on the right path and guided towards the straight path. Sermon 214

Make I not a compact with you, O Children of Adam, that you not worship Satan? Truly, he is a clear enemy **36:60**
and that you should worship Me. This is a straight path. **36:61**
Certainly, He caused to go astray many an array of you. Be you not, then, reasonable? **36:62**
This is hell which you had been promised. **36:63**

Be reasonable and act rationally ... Letter 65

Roast in it this Day because you had been ungrateful. **36:64**
On this Day We will seal over their mouths and their hands will speak to Us and their feet will bear witness to what they had been earning. **36:65**

There remain a few people in whose case the remembrance of their return to God on the Day of Judgment keeps their eyes bent and the awareness of the Resurrection moves them to tears. Some of them are scared away from the world and disperse. Some are frightened and subdued. Some are quiet as if muzzled. Some are praying sincerely. Some are grief-stricken and pain-ridden whom fear has confined to namelessness. Disgrace has shrouded them, so they are in the sea of bitter water. Their mouths are closed and their hearts are bruised. They preached until they were tired. They were oppressed until they were disgraced. They were killed until their numbers dwindled. Sermon 32

If We will, We would, certainly, have obliterated their eyes. Then, they would race towards the path. How would they have perceived? **36:66**
If We will, We would, certainly, have transformed their ability. Then, they would not have been

able to pass on, nor would they return. **36:67**

People did not take light from the lights of his wisdom, nor did they produce flame from the flint of sparkling knowledge. Sermon 108

He to whom We give a long life, We bend him over in his constitution. Will they not, then, be reasonable? **36:68**
We taught him not poetry, nor is it fit and proper for him. It is but a Remembrance and a clear Recitation **36:69**
to warn whoever had been living and that the saying be realized against the ones who are ungrateful. **36:70**

Go ahead with the remembrance of God, for it is the best remembrance. Long for that which He has promised to the pious, for His promise is the most true promise. Tread the course of *the Prophet* (Q7:158), peace and the mercy of God be upon him, for it is the most distinguished course. Follow his *sunna*, for it is the most right of all behaviors. Learn the Quran, for it is the fairest of discourses. Understand it thoroughly, for it is the best blossoming of hearts. Seek cure with its light, for it is the cure for hearts. Recite it beautifully, for it is the most beautiful narration. Certainly, a scholar who acts not according to his knowledge is like the off-headed ignorant who does not find relief from his ignorance, but the plea of God is greater on the learned and grief more incumbent. He is more blameworthy before God. Sermon 110

Consider they not how We created for them—out of what Our hands did—flocks, so they were of them ones who are owners? **36:71**
We subdued them for them so that of them, some are riding animals and some of them, they eat. **36:72**
They have profits from them and providing a place from which to drink. Will they not, then, give thanks? **36:73**
They took to themselves gods other than God so that perhaps they will be helped. **36:74**

I bear witness that *there is no god but God* (Q47:19), the One, there is no partner with Him, nor is there with Him any god other than Himself, and that *Muhammad* (Q48:29), peace and the mercy of God be upon him, is *His servant* (Q17:1) and *Prophet.* (Q7:158) Sermon 35

They are not able to help them while they are to them as a charged army. **36:75**

The trouble-mongers are a people whose attacks are severe. Those who would fight them for the sake of God would be a people who are low in the estimation of the proud, unknown in the earth, but well known in the heavens. Woe to you, O Basrah, when an army of God's infliction would face upon you without raising dust of cries. Your inhabitants would then face bloody death and dire hunger. Sermon 102

So, let not their saying dishearten ***you****. Truly, We know what they keep secret and what they speak openly.* **36:76**

Whoever speaks, He hears his speaking, and whoever keeps quiet, He knows his secret. Sermon 108

Consider not the human being that We created him from seminal fluid? That is when he is a clear

adversary. **36:77**
He propounded parables for Us and forgot his own creation. He said: Who will give life to these bones when they decayed? **36:78**

To **You** is the return of every living being. Glory be to **You**! How great is **Your** affair! Glory to **You**! How great is **Your** creation that we see, but how small is this greatness by the side of **Your** Might! How awe-striking is **Your** realm that we notice, but how humble is this against what is hidden from us out of **Your** authority! Sermon 108

Say: He will give life to them Who caused them to grow the first time and He is The Knowing of every creation. **36:79**

Exalted is God Whom heights of daring cannot approach and fineness of intelligence cannot find. He is First such that there is no extremity for Him so that He be contained within it, nor is there an end for Him where He would cease. Sermon 94

It is He Who made for you fire out of a green tree. That is when you kindle from it. **36:80**
Is not He Who created the heavens and the earth One Who Has Power to create the like of them? Yea! He is The Knowing Creator. **36:81**

Almighty are **You**, the Creator, the Worshipped. On account of **Your** good trials of **Your** creatures, **You** created a house (Paradise) and provided in it for feasting, drinks, foods, spouses, servants, places, streams, plantations and fruits. Then **You** sent a Messenger to invite towards it, but the people did not respond to the caller and did not feel persuaded to what **You** persuaded them, nor showed eagerness towards what **You** desired them to feel eager. They, the ungrateful, jumped on the carcass of this world, earned shame by eating it and became united in loving it. When one loves a thing, it blinds him and sickens his heart. He sees, but with a diseased eye, hears, but with un-hearing ears. Desires have cut asunder his wit. The world has made his heart dead while his mind is all longing for it. Consequently, he is a servant of it and of everyone who has any share in it. Wherever it turns, he turns towards it. Wherever it proceeds, he proceeds towards it. He is not desisted by any desister from God, nor takes admonition from any preacher. He sees those who have been caught in neglect whence there is neither rescission nor reversion. Sermon 108

Truly, His command when He wanted a thing is but to say to it: Be! Then, it is! **36:82**

When He intends to create something He says: *Be! and it is* (2:117), but not through a voice that strikes the ears is that call heard. His speech is an act of His creation. His like never existed before this. Sermon 186

Then, Glory be to Him in whose hand is the Kingdom of everything! To Him you will be returned. **36:83**

... to Him returns whoever dies. Sermon 108

Chapter 37: The Ones Standing in Ranks (al-Ṣāffāt)

By the ones standing in ranks, ranged in rows **37:1**
then, ones who scare in a scaring **37:2**
then, ones who recount the Remembrance, **37:3**

truly, your God is One, **37:4**
the Lord of the heavens and the earth and whatever is between them and the Lord of the sunrise.
37:5
Truly, We made to appear pleasing the present heaven with the adornment of the stars **37:6**
and keeping it safe from every emboldened Satan. **37:7**

He adorned the heavens with the ornaments of the stars. Sermon 1*

They pay no attention to the lofty Council for they are hurled at from every edge, **37:8**
rejected. For them is a punishment, that which lasts forever, **37:9**
but for him who snatched a fragment, then, a piercing flame pursued him. **37:10**
So, ask them for advice: Are they stronger in constitution or those others whom We created? Truly,
We created them of clinging clay. **37:11**
Nay! ***You*** *had marveled while they deride.* **37:12**
When they were reminded, they remember not. **37:13**
When they saw a sign, they scoff at it. **37:14**
They said: This is not but clear sorcery. **37:15**
Is it when we were dead and had been earth dust and bones that we will, truly, be ones who are
raised up **37:16**
and our fathers, the ancient ones? **37:17**

Know that this Quran is an adviser who never deceives, a leader who never misleads and a narrator who never speaks a lie. No one will sit beside this Quran, but that when he rises he will achieve one addition or one diminution—addition in his guidance or elimination in his spiritual blindness. You should also know that no one will need anything after guidance from the Quran and no one will be free from want before guidance from the Quran. Therefore, seek cure from it for your ailments and seek its assistance in your distresses. It contains a cure for the biggest diseases, namely unbelief, hypocrisy, revolt and misguidance. Pray to God through it and turn to God with its love.... There is nothing comparable to it by which people should turn to God, the Sublime. Sermon 176

Say: Yes, you will be ones in a state of lowliness. **37:18**

They looked at them with weak-sighted eyes and descended into the hollow of ignorance. If they had asked about them from the dilapidated houses and empty courtyards, they would have said that they went into the earth in the state of misguidance and you too are heading ignorantly towards them. You trample their skulls, want to raise constructions on their corpses, you graze what they have left and live in houses which they have vacated. The days that lie between them and you are also bemoaning you and reciting elegies over you. Sermon 220

There will be only one Scare. So, when they will be looking on it, **37:19**
they will say: Woe to us! This is the Day of Judgment! **37:20**

On that day God will collect on it the front and the back, to stand in obedience for the exaction of accounts and for the award of recompense for deeds. Sweat would flow up to their mouths like reins while the earth would be trembling under them. In the best condition among them would be he who has found a resting place for both his feet and an open place for his breath. Sermon 102

This is the Day of Decision which you had been denying. **37:21**

They will be within God's sight and will hear every one who would call them. They will have the dress of helplessness and covering of submission and indignity. At this time contrivances will disappear. Desires will be cut. Hearts will sink quietly. Voices will be lowered. Sweat will choke the throat. Fear will increase. Ears will resound with the thundering voice of the announcer calling towards the final judgment, award of recompense, striking of punishment and paying of reward. Sermon 82

Assemble those who did wrong and their spouses, and what they had been worshipping **37:22**
—other than God—and guide them to the path to hellfire. **37:23**
Stop them for they are ones who will be asked: **37:24**
What is the matter with you that you help not one another? **37:25**
Nay! They are on that Day ones who will resign themselves to submission to God. **37:26**

When the earthquake occurs, the Day of Resurrection approaches with all its severities, the people of every worshipping place cling to it, all the devotees cling to the object of their devotion and all the followers cling to their leader. Then on that day even the opening of an eye in the air and the sound of a footstep on the ground will be assigned its due through His Justice and His Equity. On that day many an argument will prove void and a contention for excuses will stand rejected. Sermon 222

Some of them came forward to some others, demanding of one another. **37:27**
They would say: Truly, you, you had been approaching us from the right. **37:28**
They would say: Nay! You are not ones who believe **37:29**
and we had not been any authority over you. Nay! You had been a folk, ones who are defiant. **37:30**
So, the saying was realized against us of our Lord. That, truly, we are ones who experience the punishment. **37:31**
So, we led you into error. Truly, we had been ones who are in error. **37:32**

One of the firm decisions of God in the Wise Reminder (Quran), upon which He bestows reward or gives punishment and through which He likes or dislikes, is that it will not benefit a person, even though he exerts himself and acts sincerely, if he leaves this world to meet God with one of these acts without repenting, namely that he believed in a partner with God during his obligatory worship or appeased his own anger by killing an individual or spoke about acts committed by others or sought fulfillment of his needs from people by introducing an innovation in his religion or met people with a double face or moved among them with a double tongue. Understand this because an illustration is a guide for its like. Sermon 153

Then, truly, they will be on that Day ones who are partners in the punishment. **37:33**
We accomplish, thus, with the ones who sin. **37:34**

I advise you, O people, to fear God and to praise Him profusely for His favors to you and His reward for you and His obligations on you. See how He chose you for favors and dealt with you with mercy. You sinned openly. He kept you covered. You behaved in a way to incur His punishment, but He gave you more time. Sermon 188

Truly, when it had been said to them: There is no god but God, they grow arrogant. **37:35**
They said: Are we ones who leave our gods for a possessed poet? **37:36**

Nay! He drew near with The Truth and he established as true the ones who are sent. **37:37**
Truly, you are ones who will experience the painful punishment **37:38**
and you will be given recompense but for what you had been doing. **37:39**

May God bless whoever listens to a point of wisdom and retains it. When he is invited to the right path, he approaches it. He follows a leader by catching his waist band and finds salvation, keeps God before his eyes and fears his sins, performs actions sincerely and acts virtuously, earns the treasure of heavenly rewards, avoids vice, aims at good objectives and reaps recompense, faces his desires and rejects fake hopes, makes endurance the means to his salvation and God-consciousness the provision for his death, rides on the path of honor and sticks to the highway of truth, makes good use of his time and hastens towards the end and takes with him the provision of good actions. Sermon 76

But the devoted servants of God, **37:40**
those, for them was a known provision **37:41**
—sweet fruits—and they will be ones who are honored **37:42**
in the Gardens of Bliss, **37:43**
on couches—ones who face one another. **37:44**
A cup from a spring of water will be passed around, **37:45**
white, a delight to ones who drink it. **37:46**
In that is neither headache, nor are they intoxicated by it. **37:47**

God, the Almighty, has sent down a guiding Book wherein He has explained virtue and vice. You should adopt the course of virtue, whereby you will have guidance. Detach yourself from the direction of vice, so that you remain on the right way. Sermon 167

With them are ones who are restraining their (f) glance, lovely eyed **37:48**
as if they are well-guarded pearls. **37:49**
So, some of them will come forward to some others, demanding of one another. **37:50**
One of them who converses would say: Truly, I had a comrade **37:51**
who would say: are **you** *of the ones who establish the Resurrection as true?* **37:52**
When we are dead and had been earth dust and bones, will we be ones who are judged? **37:53**
He said: Will you be ones who peruse? **37:54**
So, he perused and saw him amidst hellfire. **37:55**

Hell! Everyone of them is ... alone although they are a group, and they are strangers, even though friends. They are unaware of morning after a night and of evening after a day. The night or the day when they departed has become ever existent for them. They found the dangers of their place of stay more serious than they had apprehended. They witnessed that its signs were greater than they had guessed. Sermon 220

He said: By God, **you** *were about to deal me destruction!* **37:56**
Had it not been for the divine blessing of my Lord I would have been of the ones who are charged. **37:57**
Are we not, then, to be dead again **37:58**
but for our first death and will we not be ones who are punished? **37:59**

A person should derive benefit from himself for himself, from the living for the dead, from the mortal for the lasting and from the departer for the stayer. A person should be God-conscious while he is given age to live up to his death, and is allowed time to act.

A person should control his self by the rein and hold it with its bridle. Thus, by the rein he should prevent it from disobedience towards God. By the bridle, he should lead it towards obedience to God. Sermon 236

Truly, this, it is the winning the sublime triumph. **37:60**
For the like of this, let the ones who work, work. **37:61**

To **You** is the return of every living being. Glory be to **You**! How great is **Your** affair! Glory to **You**! How great is **Your** creation that we see, but how small is this greatness by the side of **Your** Might! How awe-striking is **Your** realm that we notice, but how humble is this against what is hidden from us out of **Your** authority! How extensive are **Your** bounties in this world, but how small are they against the bounties of the next world! Sermon 108

Is this better as hospitality or the tree of Zaqqum? **37:62**
Truly, We made it a test for the ones who are unjust. **37:63**

O God's human being! I advise you to be God-conscious. It is He Who has furnished illustrations and Who has timed for you your lives. He has given you covering of dress. He has scattered a livelihood for you. He has surrounded you with His knowledge. He has ordained rewards. He has bestowed upon you vast bounties and extensive gifts. He has warned you through far reaching arguments. He has counted you by numbers. He has fixed for you an age to live in this place of testing and house of instruction. You are on a test in this world and have to render an account regarding it. Sermon 82

Truly, it is a tree that goes forth, its root in hellfire, **37:64**
its spathes have been like the heads of satans. **37:65**
So, truly, they, they are ones who eat from it, ones who fill their bellies with it. **37:66**
Again, truly, on top of that for them is a brew of scalding water. **37:67**
Again, truly, their return is to hellfire. **37:68**
They discovered their fathers ones who go astray, **37:69**
yet they are running in their footsteps. **37:70**
Certainly, went astray most of the ancient ones before them. **37:71**

Certainly, there are examples before you of God's wrath, punishment, days of tribulations and happenings. Therefore, do not disregard His promises. Do not ignore His punishment or make light His wrath and not expect His violence, because God, the Almighty, did not curse the past ages unless they had left off asking others to do good acts and refraining them from bad acts. In fact, God cursed the foolish for committing sins and the wise because they gave up refraining others from evil. Be aware! You have broken the bonds of Islam, transgressed its limits, and destroyed its commands. Sermon 192

Certainly, We sent among them ones who warn. **37:72**
Then, look on how had been the Ultimate End of the ones who are warned, **37:73**
but the devoted servants of God. **37:74**

You should take a lesson from the fate of the progeny of Ishmael, the children of Isaac and the children of Jacob. How similar are their affairs and how akin are their examples. In connection with the details of their division and disunity, think of the days when Kings of Persia and the Caesars of Rome had become their masters. They turned them out from the pastures of their lands, the rivers of Iraq and the fertility of the world, towards thorny forests, the passages of hot winds and hardships in livelihood. By doing this, they turned them into just herders of camels. Their houses were the worst in the world and their places of stay were the most drought-stricken. There was not one voice towards which they could turn for protection, nor any shade of affection on whose strength they could repose trust. Sermon 192

Certainly, Noah cried out to Us. How excellent were the ones who answer! **37:75**
We delivered him and his people from tremendous distress. **37:76**
We made his offspring—they, the ones who remain. **37:77**
We left for him to say with the later ones: **37:78**
Peace be on Noah among the worlds. **37:79**
Thus, We give recompense to the ones who are doers of good. **37:80**
Truly, he is one of Our believing servants. **37:81**
Again, We drowned the others. **37:82**
Truly, among his partisans was Abraham. **37:83**
When he drew near his Lord with a pure-hearted heart, **37:84**
when he said to his father and to his folk: What is it that you worship? **37:85**
Is it a calumny that you want gods other than God! **37:86**
Then, what is your opinion about the Lord of the worlds? **37:87**
He looked on them with a glimpse at the stars **37:88**
and he said: Truly, I am ill! **37:89**
But they turned away from him as ones who draw back **37:90**
and he turned upon their gods then, said: Will you not eat? **37:91**
Why speak you not for yourselves? **37:92**
Then, he turned upon them, striking them with his right hand. **37:93**
Then, the people came forward towards him rushing. **37:94**
He said: Worship you what you yourselves carve out **37:95**
while God created you and what you do? **37:96**
They said: Build for him a structure. Then, cast him into hellfire. **37:97**
So, they wanted to use cunning against him, but We made them the lowest. **37:98**
He said: Truly, I am one who goes to my Lord. He will guide me. **37:99**
My Lord! Bestow on me among the ones in accord with morality. **37:100**
So, We gave him the good tidings of a forbearing boy. **37:101**
When he reached maturity endeavoring with him, he said: O my son! Truly, I see while slumbering that I am sacrificing ***you****. So, look on what* ***you*** *have considered? He said: O my father! Accomplish whatever* ***you*** *are commanded.* ***You*** *will find me, if God willed, of the ones who remain steadfast.* **37:102**
Then, when they both submitted themselves to God and he flung him on his brow **37:103**
We cried out to him: O Abraham! **37:104**
Surely, ***you*** *had established the dream as true. Thus, We give recompense to the ones who are doers of good.* **37:105**
Truly, that was, certainly, the clear trial. **37:106**
Then, We took ransom for him with a sublime slaughter **37:107**
and We left for him a good name with the later ones: **37:108**
Peace be on Abraham! **37:109**
Thus, We give recompense to the ones who are doers of good. **37:110**

Truly, he is one of Our believing servants. **37:111**
We gave him the good tidings of Isaac, a Prophet, among the ones in accord with morality. **37:112**
We blessed him and Isaac. Of their offspring are ones who are doers of good and ones who are clearly unjust to themselves. **37:113**
Certainly We showed Our grace to Moses and Aaron. **37:114**
We delivered them and their folk from the tremendous distress **37:115**
and helped them so that they, they had been the ones who are victors. **37:116**
We gave them the manifest Book **37:117**
and guided them to the straight path. **37:118**
We left for them a good name with the later ones: **37:119**
Peace be on Moses and Aaron! **37:120**
Truly, thus, We give recompense to the ones who are doers of good. **37:121**
Truly, they were of Our servants, ones who believe. **37:122**
Truly, Elijah was of the ones who are sent **37:123**
when he said to his folk: Will you not be God-conscious? **37:124**
Will you call to Baal and forsake the fairer of ones who are the creators, **37:125**
God, your Lord and the Lord of your ancient fathers? **37:126**
But they denied him, so they, truly, were ones who are charged. **37:127**
As for the devoted servants of God among them, **37:128**
We left for him a good name with the later ones: **37:129**
Peace be on Elijah! **37:130**
Thus, We give recompense to the ones who are doers of good. **37:131**
Truly, he was of Our servants, ones who believe. **37:132**
Truly, Lot was of the ones who are sent. **37:133**
We delivered him and his people, one and all, **37:134**
but an old woman of the ones who stay behind. **37:135**
Again, We destroyed the others. **37:136**
Truly, you pass by them in that which is morning **37:137**
and at night. Will you not, then, be reasonable? **37:138**
Truly, Jonah was of the ones who are sent **37:139**
when he fled, without his Lord's permission, to the laden boat. **37:140**
He cast lots with them and he had been of the ones who are refuted. **37:141**
Then, the great fish engulfed him while he was one who is answerable. **37:142**
If he had not been of the ones who glorify, **37:143**
he would have lingered in expectation in its belly until the Day they are raised up. **37:144**
Then, We cast him forth on the naked shore while he was ill. **37:145**
We caused a vine of gourd to develop over him. **37:146**
We sent him to a community of a hundred thousand, or they even exceed that. **37:147**
They believed, so We gave them enjoyment for a while. **37:148** ***

Then, ask them for advice: Are daughters for ***your*** *Lord and for them, sons?* **37:149**
Or created We female angels while they were ones who bear witness? **37:150**
Truly, it is out of their calumny that they say: **37:151**
God procreated! Truly, they are ones who lie. **37:152**
Favored He daughters over sons? **37:153**
What is the matter with you? How you give judgment! **37:154**

Will you not, then, recollect? **37:155**
Or is there for you a clear authority? **37:156**
Then, bring your Book if you would be ones who are sincere. **37:157**

The Prophet (Q7:158), peace and the mercy of God be upon him, lit flames for the seeker and put bright signs for the impeded. So he is **Your** trustworthy trustee, **Your** witness on the Day of Judgment, **Your** deputy as a blessing and **Your** Messenger of truth as mercy. My God, distribute to him a share from **Your** Justice and award him multiples of good by **Your** bounty. My God, heighten his construction over the constructions of others, honor him when he comes to **You**, dignify his position before **You**, give him honorable position, and award him glory and distinction, and bring us out on the Day of Judgment among his party, neither ashamed, nor repentant, nor deviators, nor pledge-breakers, nor strayers, nor misleaders, nor seduced. Sermon 106

They made kindred between him and between the genies. But, surely, the genies knew well that they were ones who will be charged. **37:158**
Glory be to God from what they allege, **37:159**
but not the devoted servants of God. **37:160**

Praise belongs to God (Q1:2) Who is High above all else, and is Near the creation through His bounty. He is the Giver of all reward and distinction, and Dispeller of all calamities and hardships. I praise Him for His continuous mercy and His copious bounties. Sermon 82

So, truly, you and those whom you worship **37:161**
will not be ones who are tempters against Him, **37:162**
but he who would be one who roasts in hellfire. **37:163**

Pledge yourself with prayer and remain steady on it; offer prayer as much as possible and seek nearness of God through it, because it is imposed upon the believers as a timed ordinance: *Truly the formal prayer has been—for the ones who believe—a timed prescription.* (Q4:103) Sermon 198

There is not any of us but he has a known station. **37:164**

O God's human being! You should know that a believer should be distrustful of his heart every morning and evening. He should always blame it for shortcomings and ask it to add to its good acts. You should behave like those who have gone before you and the precedents in front of you. They left this world like a traveler and covered it as distance is covered. Sermon 176

We are ones who are standing in ranks. **37:165**
We are the ones who glorify. **37:166**
Truly, they had been saying: **37:167**

God sent Muhammad, peace and the mercy of God be upon him, with the Truth so that he may take out His people from the worship of idols towards His worship and from obeying Satan towards obeying Him. God sent him with the Quran which He explained and made strong in order that the people may know their Sustainer (God), since they were ignorant of Him, may acknowledge Him, since they were denying Him and accept Him, since they were refusing to believe in Him. Sermon 147

Had been with us a Remembrance from the ancient ones, **37:168**
we would have been servants of God, ones who are devoted, **37:169**
but they were ungrateful for it. and soon they will know. **37:170**
Certainly, Our Word preceded for Our servants, the ones who are sent. **37:171**
They, truly, they are ones who shall be helped. **37:172**
Truly, Our armies are the ones who are victors. **37:173**
So, turn **you** *away from them for awhile* **37:174**
and perceive them and soon they will perceive. **37:175**
Are they impatient for Our punishment? **37:176**

O God's human being! Where are those who were allowed long ages to live? They enjoyed bounty. They were taught. They learned. They were given time. They passed it in vain. They were kept healthy. They forgot their duty. They were allowed a long period of life, were handsomely provided for, were warned of grievous punishment and were promised great rewards. You should avoid sins that lead to destruction and vices that attract the wrath of God. Sermon 82

Then, when it would come down into their courtyard, how evil will be the morning daybreak of the ones who are warned! **37:177**

Be aware and act during the period of attraction just as you act during a period of dread. Be aware! Truly, I have not seen one who covets Paradise to be asleep, nor a dreader from hellfire to be asleep. Be aware, he whom right does not benefit must suffer the harm of the wrong. He whom guidance does not keep firm will be led away by misguidance towards destruction. Sermon 28

So, turn **you** *away from them for a while,* **37:178**
and perceive and they will perceive. **37:179**
Glory be to **your** *Lord, the Lord of Great Glory, from what they allege about Him.* **37:180**

I praise God, seeking completion of His Blessing ... Sermon 2

Peace be to the ones who are sent. **37:181**

I praise God for whatever matter He ordained and whatever action He destines. Sermon 180

The Praise belongs to God, the Lord of the worlds! **37:182**

He is that which does not change or vanish. The process of setting does not behoove Him. He has not begotten any one lest He be regarded as having been born. He has not been begotten, otherwise He would be contained within limits. He is too High to have sons. He is too purified to contact women. Imagination cannot reach Him so as to assign Him quantity. Understanding cannot think of Him so as to give him shape. Senses do not perceive Him so as to feel Him. Hands cannot touch Him so as to rub against Him. He does not change into any condition. He does not pass from one state to another. Nights and days do not turn Him old. Light and darkness do not alter Him. Sermon 186

Chapter 38: Sad (Ṣād)

Sad. By the Quran, Possessor of the Remembrance. **38:1**

The Book of God is among you. It speaks and its tongue does not falter. It is a house whose pillars do not fall down, and a power whose supporters are never routed. Sermon 133

Nay! Those who were ungrateful are in vainglory and breach. **38:2**

Certainly, God the Almighty, tries His creatures who are vain about themselves through His beloved persons who are humble in their eyes. Sermon 192

How many before them have We caused to perish of generations! They cried out but there was no time for escape for a while. **38:3**

Some of them are like hocked camels, some like butchered meat, some like severed limbs, some like spilt blood, some are biting their hands in pain, some are rubbing their palms in remorse, some are holding their cheeks on their hands in anxiety, some are cursing their own views and some are retreating from their determination, but the time for action has gone away and the hour of calamity has approached: *They cried out but there was no time for escape for awhile.* (Q38:3) Sermon 191

They marveled that drew near them one who warns from among themselves. The ones who are ungrateful said: This is one who is a sorcerer, a liar. **38:4**
Made He all gods One God? Truly, this is an astounding thing! **38:5**

God ... is aware of whatever is hidden in the hearts and whatever lies behind the unseen. Sermon 192

The Council set out from them, saying: Be gone! Have patience with your gods. Truly, this is a thing to be wanted! **38:6**
We heard not the like of this in the later creed. This is only made up tales! **38:7**

Be aware! You strove hard in revolting and created mischief on the earth in open opposition to God and in challenging the believers over fighting. You should be God-conscious! God, in feeling proud of your vanity and boasting over ignorance, because this is the root of enmity and the design of Satan wherewith he has been deceiving past people and bygone ages with the result that they fell into the depression of ignorance and the hollows of misguidance, submitting to (Satan's) driving and accepting his leadership. The hearts of all the people were similar in this matter. Centuries passed by, one after the other, in just the same way. Sermon 192

Was the Remembrance only caused to descend to him from among us? Nay! They are in uncertainty about My Remembrance. Nay! They experience not My punishment! **38:8**

One of the firm decisions of God in the Wise Reminder (Quran), upon which He bestows reward or gives punishment and through which He likes or dislikes, is that it will not benefit a person, even though he exerts himself and acts sincerely, if he leaves this world to meet God with one of these acts without repenting, namely that he believed in a partner with God during his obligatory worship or appeased his own anger by killing an individual or spoke about acts committed by others or sought fulfillment of his needs from people by introducing an innovation in his religion or met people with a double face or moved among them with a double tongue. Understand this because an illustration is a guide for its like. Sermon 153

Or are they owners of the treasures of mercy of **your** *Lord, The Almighty, The Giver?* **38:9**

If He gives away all that the mines of the mountains emit out or the gold, silver, pearls and cuttings of coral which the shells of the ocean vomit out, it would not affect His munificence, nor diminish the extent of what He has. In fact He would still have such treasures of bounty as would not decrease by the demands of the creatures, because He is that generous Being Whom the begging of beggars cannot make poor, nor the pertinacity of beseechers make miser. Sermon 91

Or is theirs the dominion of the heavens and the earth and what is between them? Let them climb up with cords! **38:10**

Their army is one that is put to flight among the confederates. **38:11**

I praise God for whatever matter He ordained and whatever action He destines. Sermon 180

The folk of Noah before them denied and Ad and Pharaoh, the possessor of the stakes, **38:12**
and Thamud and a folk of Lot and the Companions of the Thicket. Those were the confederates. **38:13**
All of them denied the Messengers so My repayment was realized. **38:14**
These expect not but one Cry. There was no holding it back. **38:15**
They said: Our Lord! Quicken the sentence of the judge on us before the Day of Reckoning. **38:16**
Have patience with what they say, and remember Our servant David, the possessor of potency. Truly, he was penitent. **38:17**
Truly, We caused the mountains to be subservient to glorify with him in the evening and the rising of the sun. **38:18**
The birds were ones who are assembled, all penitent to Him. **38:19**
We strengthened his dominion and gave him wisdom and decisiveness in argument. **38:20**
Approached **you** *the tiding of the disputants when they climbed over the wall of a sanctuary?* **38:21**
When they entered in on David, he was terrified of them. They said: Fear not. Two disputants were insolent, one of us against the other. So, give judgment duly between us and transgress not and guide us to the right path. **38:22**
Truly, this is my brother. He has ninety-nine ewe, while I have one ewe. He said: Place it in my charge and he triumphed over me in argument. **38:23**
David said: Certainly, he did wrong to **you** *in asking for* **your** *ewe in addition to his ewes. Truly, many partners in business are insolent, one to another, but those who believed and did as the ones in accord with morality, and they are few. David thought that We tried him and he asked for forgiveness of his Lord and fell down as one who bows down penitent.* **38:24**
So, We forgave him that. Truly, for him is nearness with Us and goodness of destination. **38:25**
O David! Truly, We made **you** *a viceregent on the earth so give judgment duly among humanity and follow not your desire for it will cause* **you** *to go astray from the way of God. Truly, those who go astray from the way of God, for them there is a severe punishment because they forgot the Day of Reckoning.* **38:26**
We created not the heaven and the earth and whatever is between the two in falsehood. That is the opinion of those who were ungrateful. Then, woe to those who disbelieved in the fire! **38:27**
Or will We make those who believed and did as the ones in accord with morality like the ones who make corruption in and on the earth? Or will We make the ones who are God-conscious as the ones who acted immorally? **38:28**

It is a blessed Book that We caused to descend to **you**, *so that they meditate on its signs and those imbued with intuition recollect.* **38:29**
We bestowed Solomon on David. How excellent a servant. Truly, he was penitent. **38:30**
When they were presented before him in the evening—steeds standing with one foot slightly raised— **38:31**
he said: Truly, I cherished and loved the good instead of remembering my Lord when the sun secluded itself behind the partition of the night. **38:32**
Return them to me. Then, he took wiping over their legs and their necks. **38:33**
Certainly, We tried Solomon. We cast a lifeless body on his seat. Again, he was penitent. **38:34**
He said: My Lord! Forgive me and bestow on me a dominion such will not be fit and proper for another after me. Truly, **You** *are The Giver.* **38:35**
So, We caused the wind to be subservient to him. It runs at his command, a gentle wind, wherever it lit. **38:36**
We made subservient the satans and every builder and diver **38:37**
and others, ones who are chained in bonds. **38:38** ***

This is Our gift. Then, have **you** *shown grace or have* **you** *held back without reckoning?* **38:39**

Praise belongs to God (Q1:2) Who is above all similarity to creatures, is above the words of describers Who displays the wonders of His management for the on-lookers, is hidden from the imagination of thinkers by virtue of the greatness of His glory, has knowledge without acquiring it by adding to it or drawing it from someone, and Who is the ordainer of all matters without reflecting or thinking. He is such that gloom does not concern Him, nor does He seek light from brightness. Night does not overtake Him, nor does the day pass over Him so as to affect Him in any manner. His comprehension of things is not through eyes. His knowledge is not dependent on being informed. God deputized *the Prophet* (Q7:158), peace and the mercy of God be upon him, with light and accorded him the highest precedence in selection. Through him God united those who were divided, overpowered the powerful, overcame difficulties and leveled rugged ground and, thus, removed misguidance from right and left. Sermon 213

Truly, for him is nearness with Us, and goodness of destination. **38:40**

He is the Giver of all reward and distinction, and Dispeller of all calamities and hardships. Sermon 82

Remember Our servant Job when he cried out to his Lord: Truly, Satan afflicted me with fatigue and punishment! **38:41**
It is said: Stomp with **your** *foot. This is a place of washing that is cool and from which to drink.* **38:42**
We bestowed on him, his people, and the like of them along with them as a mercy from Us, a reminder for those imbued with intuition. **38:43**
Take in **your** *hand a bundle of rushes and strike with it and fail not* **your** *oath. Truly, We found him one who remains steadfast. How excellent a servant. Truly, he was penitent.* **38:44**
Remember Our servants Abraham, and Isaac and Jacob, all imbued with dynamic energy and insight. **38:45**
Truly, We made them sincere with that which is pure, a reminder of the Abode. **38:46**
Truly, they are to Us among ones who are favored and good. **38:47**

Remember Ishmael, Elisha, and Dhu-l Kifl. All are among the good. **38:48** ***

This is a Remembrance. Truly, for ones who are God-conscious this is, certainly, a goodly destination, **38:49**
the Gardens of Eden, the doors, ones that are opened up for them. **38:50**
Ones who are reclining in them. They will call for many sweet fruits and drink in it. **38:51**
With them will be ones who are restraining their (f) glance, persons of the same age. **38:52**
This is what you are promised for the Day of Reckoning. **38:53**
Truly, this is Our provision. For it, there is no coming to an end. **38:54**

Mind the obligations! Mind the obligations! Fulfill them for God and they will take you to the Garden. Surely, God has made unlawful the things which are not unknown and made lawful the things which are without defect. Sermon 167

This is so. Truly, for ones who are defiant, there will be a worse destination, **38:55**
hell, where they will roast. Miserable will be the cradling! **38:56**
This is so! Then, let them experience this—scalding water and filth **38:57**
and other torment of a like kind in pairs. **38:58**

The great calamity of that place is the hot water and entry into Hell, flames of eternal fire and intensity of blazes. There is no resting period, no gap for ease, no power to intervene, no death to bring about solace and no sleep to make him forget pain. He rather lies under several kinds of deaths and moment-to-moment punishment. We seek refuge in God. Sermon 82

This is an army unit, one that rushes in with you. There is no welcome for them! Truly, they are ones who roast in the fire. **38:59**
They said: Nay! You! There is no welcome for you. It is you who put this forward on us. Miserable will be the stopping place! **38:60**

You should therefore spend all your force against him, and all your efforts against him, because, by God, he boasted over your (i.e., Adam's) origin, questioned your position and spoke lightly of your lineage. He advanced on you with his army, and brought his footmen towards your path. They are chasing you from every place, and they are hitting you at every finger joint. You are not able to defend by any means, nor can you repulse them by any determination. You are in the thick of disgrace, the ring of straitness, the field of death and the way of distress. Sermon 192

They said: Our Lord! Whoever put this forward for us, increase him with a double punishment in the fire. **38:61**
They said: What is the matter with us that we see not men whom we had been numbering among the worst? **38:62**
Took We them to ourselves as a laughing-stock or swerved our sight from them? **38:63**
Truly, this is true of the disagreement of the people of the fire. **38:64**
Say: I am only one who warns. There is no god but God, The One, The Omniscient, **38:65**
the Lord of the heavens and the earth and whatever is between them, The Almighty, The Forgiver. **38:66**
Say: It is a serious tiding **38:67**
from which you are ones who turn aside. **38:68**

I had been without knowledge of the lofty Council when they are striving against one another. **38:69**
It is revealed to me only that I am a warner, one who makes clear. **38:70**

I bear witness that *Muhammad* (Q48:29), peace and the mercy of God be upon him, is His *servant* (Q17:1) and His *Prophet.* (Q7:158) He sent him for enforcement of His commands, for exhausting His pleas and for presenting warnings against eternal punishment. Sermon 82

Your *Lord said to the angels: Truly, I am one who is Creator of a mortal from clay.* **38:71**
So, when I shaped him and blew into him My Spirit, then, fall to him, ones who prostrate themselves. **38:72**
So, the angels prostrated themselves, one and all, altogether **38:73**
but Iblis. He grew arrogant and had been among the ones who are ungrateful. **38:74**

He put His angels on trial concerning these attributes in order to distinguish those who are modest from those who are vain. Therefore, God, Who is aware of whatever is hidden in the hearts and whatever lies behind the unseen said: *Truly I am One Who Creates a mortal from clay. So, when I have shaped him and breathed into him My Spirit, then fall to him, ones who prostrate themselves. So, the angels prostrated, one and all altogether but Iblis. He grew arrogant and had been among the ones who were ungrateful.* (Q38:71-74) Sermon 192

He said: O Iblis! What prevented ***you*** *from prostrating* ***your****self to what I created with My two hands? Had* ***you*** *grown arrogant? Or had* ***you*** *been among the ones who exalt themselves?* **38:75**
Iblis said: I am better than he. ***You*** *had created me from fire while* ***You*** *had created him from clay.* **38:76**
He said: Then, go ***you*** *forth from here for, truly,* ***you*** *are accursed.* **38:77**
Truly, on ***you*** *is My curse until the Day of Judgment.* **38:78**
Iblis said: My Lord! Then, give me respite until the Day to be raised up. **38:79**
He said: Truly, ***you*** *are among the ones who are given respite* **38:80**
until the Day of the known time. **38:81**

Self-importance withheld Satan and vice overcame him so that he took pride in his own creation with fire and treated contemptuously the creation of clay. So God allowed him time in order to let him fully deserve His wrath, to complete the test and to fulfill the promise: *He said: Then, truly,* ***you*** *are among the ones who are given respite until the Day of the known time.* (Q38:80-81) Sermon 1

Iblis said: By ***Your*** *Great Glory, then, I will certainly lead them one and all into error,* **38:82**
but ***Your*** *devoted servants among them.* **38:83**
He said: This is The Truth and The Truth I say **38:84**
that I will fill hell with ***you*** *and with one and all of whoever heeded* ***you***. **38:85** ***

Say: I ask of you not for any compensation for this nor am I among the ones who take things upon themselves. **38:86**

You must always try to remember the good and useful things done in the past, activities of a just and benign regime, good deeds done by it, good laws promulgated, instructions of *the Prophet* (Q7:158), peace and the mercy of God be upon him, commands of God given in His Book and things that you have seen me doing or have heard me saying. Follow the good actions and advice found therein. Similarly, follow carefully the pieces of advice contained in these orders. Through them I have tried to teach you all that can be taught about a good regime. I have done my duty towards you so that you may not go astray and your mind may not crave for base desires. If it does, then you will have no excuse before God. Letter 53

It is nothing other than a Remembrance for the worlds **38:87**
and you will, certainly, know its tidings after a while. **38:88**

Now then O people of Iraq! You are like the pregnant woman on completion of the period of pregnancy delivers a dead child and her husband is also dead and her period of widowhood is long while only remote relation inherits her. By God, I did not come to you of my own accord. I came to you by force of circumstances. I have come to know that you say: Ali speaks a lie. May God fight you! Against whom do I speak a lie? Surely not against God ... Surely not against His Prophet as I am the first who bore witness to him. Certainly not. By God, it was a way of expression which you failed to appreciate. You were not capable of it. Woe to you! I am giving out these measures of nice expression free of any cost. I wish there were vessels good enough to hold them.... *You will certainly know its tidings after a while.* (38:87-88) Sermon 71

Chapter 39: The Troops (al-Zumar)

The sending down successively of this Book is from God, The Almighty, The Wise. **39:1**

Certainly, only doubtful innovations cause ruin except those from which God may protect. In God's authority lies the safety of your affairs. Therefore, render Him such obedience as is neither blameworthy, nor insincere. Sermon 169

Truly, We caused to descend to **you** *the Book with The Truth so worship God as one who is sincere and devoted in the way of life to Him.* **39:2**

Certainly, these people are in agreement in disliking my authority. I will carry on until I perceive disunity among you, because if they succeed in spite of the unsoundness of their view, the whole organization of Muslims will be shattered. They are hankering after this world out of jealousy against him on whom God has bestowed it. So they intend to revert the matters to the pre-Islamic period. On us it is obligatory, for your sake, to abide by the Book of God (Quran), the Sublime, and the conduct of *the Prophet* (Q7:158), peace and the mercy of God be upon him, to stand by His rights and to revive his *sunna*. Sermon 169

The way of life is exclusively for God. Those who took to themselves protectors other than Him say: We worship them not, but that they bring us nearness to God. Truly, God gives judgment between them about what they are at variance in it. Truly, God guides not him, one who lies and is an ingrate. **39:3**

O my God! We seek **Your** protection from turning away from **Your** command, or revolting against **Your** religion, or being led away by our desires instead of by guidance that comes from **You**. Sermon 215

If God wanted to take to Himself a son, He would have favored from what He creates of what He wills. Glory be to Him. He is God, The One, The Omniscient. **39:4**

He is the Giver of all reward and distinction ... Sermon 82

He created the heavens and the earth with The Truth. He wraps the nighttime around the daytime and wraps the daytime around the nighttime. He caused to be subservient the sun and the moon, each run for a term, that which is determined. Is He not The Almighty, The Forgiver? **39:5**

O my God! Forgive me. **You** know more about me than I do. If I return to sin, **You** return to forgiveness. My God, forgive me what I had promised to myself, but **You** did not find its fulfillment with me. My God, forgive me that with what I sought nearness to **You** with my tongue, but my heart opposed and did not perform. My God, forgive me winking of the eye, vile utterances, desires of the heart and errors of speech. Sermon 78

He creates you from one soul. Again, He made its mate from it and He caused to descend for you eight pairs of flocks. He creates you in the wombs of your mothers, creation after creation, in threefold shadows. Such is God your Lord. His is the dominion. There is no god but He. Why, then, turn you away? **39:6**

O creature who has been equitably created and who has been nurtured and looked after in the darkness of wombs with multiple curtains. You were originated from the essence of clay: *Certainly, We created the human being from an extraction of clay* (Q23:12) and placed in a still place for a known length of time: *Then, We made it in a secure stopping place for a known measuring.* (Q77:21-22) You used to move in the womb of your mother as an embryo, neither responding to a call, nor hearing any voice. Sermon 162

If you are ungrateful, truly, God is Independent of you. He is not well-pleased with ingratitude from His servants. If you give thanks, He will be well-pleased with you. No burdened soul will bear the heavy load of another. Again, to your Lord is the return, so He will tell you what you had been doing. Truly, He is Knowing of what is in the breasts. **39:7**

He is sufficient for one who relies on Him. He gives one who asks Him. He repays one who lends to Him. He rewards one who thanks Him. Sermon 90

When some distress afflicted the human being, he calls to his Lord as one who turns in repentance to Him. Again, when He granted him divine blessing from Himself, he forgets that for which he had been calling to Him before and he laid on rivals to God to cause others to go astray from His way. **39:8**

Their reliance for resolving distresses is on themselves. Their confidence in regard to dubious matters is on their own opinions as if every one of them is a leader of himself. Whatever he has decided himself, he considers it to have been taken through reliable sources and strong factors Sermon 88

Is he one who is morally obligated during the night watch, one who prostrates himself or one who is standing up in prayer being fearful of the world to come and hoping for the mercy of his Lord? Say: Are those who know on the same level as those who know not? Only those imbued with intuition recollect. **39:9**

It does not behoove one who knows His greatness to assume greatness, but the greatness of those who know His greatness is that they should know before Him. The safety for those who know what His power is lies in submitting to Him. Do not be scared away from the truth like the scaring of the healthy from the scabbed person, or the sound person from the sick. Sermon 146

Say: O My servants who believed! Be God-conscious of your Lord. For those who did good in the present, there is benevolence, and the earth of God is One Who is Extensive. Only ones who remain steadfast will have their compensation without reckoning. **39:10**

Be God-conscious like him who listened to good advice and bowed before it. Sermon 82

Say: Truly, I was commanded to worship God, one who is sincere and devoted in the way of life to Him. **39:11**
I was commanded that I be the first of the ones who submit to God. **39:12**

I praise God, seeking completion of His Blessing, submitting to His Glory and expecting safety from committing sin. Sermon 2

Say: Truly, I fear if I rebelled against my Lord the punishment of a tremendous Day. **39:13**

God will take them out from the corners of the graves, the nests of birds, the dens of beasts and the centers of death. They will hasten towards His command and run towards the place fixed for their final return, group by group, quiet, standing and arrayed in rows. They will be within God's sight and will hear every one who would call them. Sermon 82

Say: God alone I worship as one sincere and devoted in the way of life to Him. **39:14**
So, worship what you would other than Him. Say: Truly, the ones who are losers are those who lost themselves and their people on the Day of Resurrection. Truly, that is a clear loss. **39:15**

Be aware and act during the period of attraction just as you act during a period of dread. Be aware! Truly, I have not seen one who covets Paradise to be asleep, nor a dreader from hellfire to be asleep. Be aware! He whom right does not benefit must suffer the harm of the wrong. He whom guidance does not keep firm will be led away by misguidance towards destruction. Sermon 28

They will have overshadowings above from the fire and beneath them, overshadowings. With that, God frightens His servants. O my servants! Be God-conscious of Me! **39:16**

Believers are humble. Believers are admonishers. Believers are God-conscious. Sermon 153

Those who avoided false deities so that they worship them not and were penitent to God, for them are good tidings. So, give good tidings to My servants, **39:17**
those who listen to the saying of the Quran and follow the fairer of it. Those are those whom God guided. Those, they are imbued with intuition. **39:18**

O God! I bear witness that he who likens **You** with the separateness of the limbs or with the joining of the extremities of his body does not acquaint his inner self with knowledge about **You**, his heart did not secure conviction to the effect that there is no partner for **You**. It is as though he has not heard the wrongful followers disclaiming their false gods by sayings: *By God! Truly we have been clearly wandering astray when we made* **you** *equal with the Lord of the worlds.* (Q26:97-98) They are wrong who liken **You** to their idols, and dress

You with apparel of the creatures by their imagination, attribute to **You** parts of body by their own thinking and consider **You** after the creatures of various types, through the working of their intelligence. I bear witness that whoever equated **You** with anything out of **Your** creation took a partner for **You**. Whoever takes a partner for **You** is ungrateful according to what is stated in **Your** unambiguous verses and indicated by the evidence of **Your** clear arguments. I also bear witness that **You** are that God Who cannot be confined in the fetters of intelligence so as to admit change of condition by entering its imagination, nor in the shackles of the mind so as to become limited and an object of alterations. Sermon 91

Against whom was realized the word of punishment? Will ***you*** *be saving him from the fire?* **39:19**

Be God-conscious! Be God-conscious, O God's human being, because the world is behaving with you in the usual way and you and the Day of Judgment are in the same rope close to each other. As though it has come with its signs, has approached with its pleas and has made you stand in its way; and as though it has come forward with all its quakings and has settled down with its chest on the ground while the world has parted from its people and has turned them out of its lap. It was like a day that has passed or a month that has gone by. Its new things have become old and the fat ones have become thin. Sermon 190

But those who were God-conscious of their Lord, for them are the highest chambers with the highest chambers built above them, beneath which rivers run. This is the solemn declaration of God. God never breaks His promise. **39:20**

O God's human being! Be God-conscious. Keep in view the reason why He created you. Be afraid of Him to the extent He has advised you to do. Make yourself deserve what He has promised you by having confidence in the truth of His promise and entertaining fear of the Day of Judgment. Sermon 82

Have ***you*** *not considered that God caused to descend water from heaven and threaded fountains in the earth, again, brings out crops by it of hues, ones that are at variance? Again, they wither so* ***you*** *see them as ones that are growing yellow. Again, He makes them chaff. Truly, in this is a reminder for those imbued with intuition.* **39:21**

Almighty God created forth wind and made its movement sterile, perpetuated its position, intensified its motion and spread it far and wide. Then He ordered the wind to raise up deep waters and to intensify the waves of the oceans. So the wind churned it like the churning of curd and pushed it fiercely into the firmament throwing its front position on the rear and the stationary on the flowing until its level was raised and the surface was full of foam. Then Almighty God raised the foam on to the open wind and vast firmament and made therefrom the seven skies and made the lower one as a stationary surge and the upper one as protective ceiling and a high edifice without any pole to support it or nail to hold it together. Then He decorated them with stars and the light of meteors and hung in it the shining sun and effulgent moon under the revolving sky, moving ceiling and rotating firmament. Sermon 1

So, is he whose breast God has expanded for submission to God, in a light from His Lord? So, woe to their hearts, ones that harden against the Remembrance of God. Those are clearly going astray. **39:22**

He whom He guides does not go astray. He with whom He is hostile receives no protection. He whom He supports does not remain needy. Praise is most weighty of all that is weighed and the most valuable of all that is treasured. Sermon 2

God sent down the fairer discourse, a Book, one that is consistent in its often repeated parts of the Quran by which shiver the skins of those who dread their Lord. Again, their skins and their hearts become gentle with the Remembrance of God. That is the guidance of God. With it He guides whom He wills. Whomever God causes to go astray, for him there is no one who guides. **39:23**
Is he, then, one who fends off a dire punishment with his face on the Day of Resurrection? It will be said to the ones who are unjust: Experience what you had been earning! **39:24**

Praise belongs to God. (Q1:2) I praise Him, implore His help and ask for His guidance. I seek protection in Him from error. *Whomever God causes to go astray, for him there is no one who guides.* (Q39:23) Sermon 2

Those before them denied and so the punishment approached them from where they are not aware. **39:25**

Pity is for the negligent person whose life itself would be a proof against him and his own days, passed in sin, will lead him to punishment. Sermon 64

So, God caused them to experience degradation in this present life. But the punishment of the world to come is greater if they had been knowing! **39:26**

O God's human being! Where are those who were allowed long ages to live? They enjoyed bounty. They were taught. They learned. They were given time. They passed it in vain. They were kept healthy. They forgot their duty. They were allowed a long period of life, were handsomely provided for, were warned of grievous punishment and were promised great rewards. You should avoid sins that lead to destruction and vices that attract the wrath of God. Sermon 82

Certainly, We propounded for humanity in this, the Quran, every kind of parable so that perhaps they will recollect, **39:27**
an Arabic Recitation without any crookedness so that perhaps they would be God-conscious. **39:28**

The Book of God is among you. It speaks and its tongue does not falter. It is a house whose pillars do not fall down, and a power whose supporters are never routed. Sermon 133

God propounded a parable of a man owned by quarreling ascribed associates and a man belonging to another man. Are they both equal in likeness? The Praise belongs to God. But most of them know not. **39:29**
Truly, ***you*** *are mortal and, truly, they are mortal.* **39:30**
Again, truly, on the Day of Resurrection before your Lord you will strive against one another. **39:31**

They are emulating each other and proceeding in groups towards the final objective and the rendezvous of death, until when matters come to a close, the world dies and Resurrection draws near. Sermon 82

Then, who does greater wrong than one who lied against God and denied sincerity when it drew near him? Is there not in hell a place of lodging for the ones who are ungrateful? **39:32**

Where are the minds which seek light from the lamps of guidance and the eyes which look at minarets of God-consciousness? Sermon 144

He who brought about sincerity and he who established it as true, those, they are the ones who are God-conscious. **39:33**
For them is all that they will with their Lord. That is the recompense of the ones who are doers of good. **39:34**

How appropriate are these illustrations and effective admonitions, provided they are received by pure hearts, open ears, firm views and sharp wits. Be God-conscious like him who listened to good advice and bowed before it. 83

Certainly, God absolves them of bad deeds of what they do and gives them recompense in compensation for the fairer of what they had been doing. **39:35**

O my God! Every praiser has the right of reward and recompense from whom he praises. Certainly, I have turned to **You** my eye at the treasures of **Your** Mercy and stores of forgiveness. Sermon 90

Is not God One Who Suffices for His servants? They frighten ***you*** *with those other than Him. Whom God causes to go astray, there is not for him any one who guides.* **39:36**

The Prophet (Q33:6) of God, peace and the mercy of God be upon him, said: The belief of a person cannot be firm unless his heart is firm, and his heart cannot be firm unless his tongue is firm. So whoever of you can manage to meet God, the Sublime, in such a position that his hands are unsmeared with the blood of Muslims and their property and his tongue is safe from exposing them, he should do so. Sermon 176

Whomever God guides, there is not for him anyone who leads astray. Is not God Almighty, The Possessor of Requital? **39:37**

The human being should ... fear the Day of Judgment before it arrives. He should appreciate the shortness of his life and the shortness of his sojourn in the place of stay which has only to last for his change over to the next place. He should, therefore, do something for his change over and for the known stages of his departure. Blessed be he who possesses a virtuous heart, obeys one who guides him, keeps away from one who takes him to ruin, catches the path of safety with the help of him who provides him light of guidance and, by obeying the leader who commands him, hastens towards guidance before its doors are closed, opens the door of repentance and removes the stain of sins. He has certainly been put on the right path and guided towards the straight path. Sermon 214

Truly, if ***you*** *had asked them: Who created the heavens and the earth? They would, certainly, say: God. Say: Considered you what you call to other than God? If God wanted some harm for me, would they (f) be ones who remove His harm from me? Or if He wanted mercy for me would they (f) be ones who hold back His mercy? Say: God is enough for me. In Him put their trust the ones who put their trust.* **39:38**

O God's human being! I advise you to be God-conscious which is the provision for the next world and with it is your return. Sermon 114

Say: O my folk! Truly, act according to your ability. I am one who acts. You will know **39:39**
to whom punishment approaches covering him with shame and on whom alights an abiding pun-

ishment. **39:40**
Truly, We caused the Book to descend to ***you*** *for humanity with The Truth. So, whoever was truly guided, it is only for himself. Whoever went astray, goes astray but for himself.* ***You*** *are not over them a trustee.* **39:41**

God, the Almighty, has sent down a guiding Book wherein He has explained virtue and vice. You should adopt the course of virtue, whereby you will have guidance. Detach yourself from the direction of vice, so that you remain on the right way. Sermon 167

God calls the souls to Himself at the time of their death and those that die not during their slumbering. He holds back those for whom He decreed death and sends the others back for a term, that which is determined. Truly, in that are signs for a folk who reflect. **39:42**

The world aimed at them, but they did not aim at it. It captured them, but they freed themselves from it by a ransom. During the night, they are standing on their feet, reading portions of the Quran and reciting it in a well-measured way, creating through it grief and seeking by it the cure for their ailments. If they come across a verse creating eagerness for Paradise, they pursue it avidly. Their spirits turn towards it eagerly. They feel as if it is in front of them. When they come across a verse which contains fear of Hell, they bend the ears of their hearts towards it and feel as though the sound of Hell and its cries are reaching their ears. They bend themselves from their backs, prostrate themselves on their foreheads, their palms, their knees and their toes, and beseech God, the Sublime, for their deliverance. Sermon 193

Or took they to themselves other than God intercessors? Say: Even though they had not been possessing anything and they are not reasonable? **39:43**

Know that the Quran is an interceder and its intercession will be accepted. It is a speaker who bears witness. For whoever the Quran intercedes on the Day of Judgment, its intercession for him would be accepted. He about whom the Quran speaks ill on the Day of Judgment shall testify to it. On the Day of Judgment, an announcer will announce: Be aware! Every sower of a crop is in distress except the sowers of the Quran. Therefore, you should be among the sowers of the Quran and its followers. Make it your guide towards God. Seek its advice for yourselves, do not trust your views against it and regard your desires in the matter of the Quran as deceitful. Sermon 176

Say: To God belongs all intercession. His is the dominion of the heavens and the earth. Again, to Him you will be returned. **39:44**

... to Him returns whoever dies. Sermon 108

When God alone was remembered, the hearts shuddered of those who believe not in the world to come. But when those who, other than Him, were remembered, that is when they rejoice at the good tidings! **39:45**

They are from among the people of this world, but are not its people, because they remain in it as though they do not belong to it. They act herein on what they observe and hasten herein to avoid what they fear. Their bodies move among the people of the next world. They see that the people of this world attach importance to the death of their bodies, but they themselves attach more importance to the death of the hearts of those who are living. Sermon 229

Say: O God! One Who is Originator of the heavens and the earth! One Who Knows of the unseen and the visible! ***You*** *will give judgment among* ***Your*** *servants about what they had been at variance in it.* **39:46**

He originated the creation without any example which He could follow and without any specimen prepared by any creator who would have before Him. He showed us the realm of His Might, and such wonders which speak of His Wisdom. The confession of the created things that their existence owes itself to Him made us realize that argument has been furnished about knowing Him so that there is no excuse against it. The signs of His creative power and standard of His wisdom are fixed in the wonderful things He has created. Whatever He has created is an argument in His favor and a guide towards Him. Even a silent thing is a guide towards Him as though it speaks and its guidance towards the Creator is clear. Sermon 91

If those who did wrong had whatever is in and on the earth altogether and the like with it, they would, truly, have offered it as ransom for the evil punishment on the Day of Resurrection. It will show itself to them from God what they not be anticipating. **39:47**

One of the firm decisions of God in the Wise Reminder (Quran) upon which He bestows reward or gives punishment, and through which He likes or dislikes, is that it will not benefit a person, even though he exerts himself and acts sincerely if he leaves this world to meet God with one of these acts without repenting, namely that he believed in a partner with God during his obligatory worship, or appeased his own anger by killing an individual, or spoke about acts committed by others, or sought fulfillment of his needs from people by introducing an innovation in his religion, or met people with a double face, or moved among them with a double tongue. Understand this because an illustration is a guide for its like. Sermon 152

It will show itself to them, the evil deeds that they earned and they will be surrounded by what they had been ridiculing. **39:48**

Be aware! At the time of committing evil deeds, remember the destroyer of joys, the spoiler of pleasures and the killer of desires, namely death. Seek assistance of God for fulfillment of His obligatory rights and for thanking Him for His countless bounties and obligations. Sermon 99

Then, when harm afflicted the human being, he called to Us. Again, We granted him divine blessing from Us. He would say: I was only given this because of my knowledge. Nay! It is only a test, but most of them know not. **39:49**

Truly, those who were before them said it so what they had been earning availed them not. **39:50**

God ... is aware of whatever is hidden in the hearts and whatever lies behind the unseen. Sermon 192

The evil deeds they earned lit on them. As for those who did wrong among these, evil deeds of what they earned will light on them. They will not be ones who frustrate Him. **39:51**

Know they not that God extends the provision for whomever He wills and tightens it for whom He wills. Truly, in this are, certainly, signs for a folk who believe. **39:52**

Say: O My servants who exceeded all bounds against themselves, despair not of the mercy of God. Truly, God forgives all impieties. Truly, He is The Forgiving, The Compassionate. **39:53**

Be penitent to your Lord and submit to Him before the punishment approaches you. Again, you will not be helped. **39:54**

Truly, that God-consciousness is like trained horses on whom the riders have been placed with the reins in their hands so that they would take the riders to heaven. There is right and wrong and there are followers for each. If wrong dominates, it has always in the past been so and if truth goes down, that, too, has often occurred. It seldom happens that a thing that lags behind comes forward. He who has Heaven and Hell in his view has no other aim. He who attempts and acts quickly succeeds, while the seeker who is slow may also entertain hope. He who falls short of action faces destruction in Hell. Misleading paths are on both the right and the left. Only the middle way is the right path which is the Everlasting Book and the traditions of *the Prophet* (Q7:158), peace and the mercy of God be upon him. From it the *sunna* has spread and towards it is the eventual return. He who claims otherwise is ruined. He who concocts falsehood is disappointed. He who opposes right is destroyed. It is enough ignorance for a person not to know himself. He who is strong rooted in God-consciousness is not destroyed. The plantation of a people based on God-consciousness never remains without water. Hide yourselves in your houses. Reform yourselves. Repent. One should praise only God and condemn only one's self. Sermon 16

Follow the fairer of what was caused to descend to you from your Lord before the punishment approaches you suddenly while you are not aware **39:55**
so that a soul not say: O me that I am regretful for what I neglected in my responsibility to God and that I had, truly, been among the ones who deride. **39:56**
Or he may say: If God guided me, I would, certainly, have been among the ones who are God-conscious. **39:57**
Or he say at the time he sees the punishment: If only I might return again, then, be among the ones who are doers of good. **39:58**
Yea! My signs drew near ***you*** *and* ***you*** *had denied them and had grown arrogant.* ***You*** *had been among the ones who are ungrateful.* **39:59**
On the Day of Resurrection ***you*** *will see those who lied against God, their faces, ones that are clouded over. Is there not in hell a place of lodging for ones who increase in pride?* **39:60**

When the earthquake occurs, the Day of Resurrection approaches with all its severities, the people of every worshipping place cling to it, all the devotees cling to the object of their devotion and all the followers cling to their leader. Then on that Day even the opening of an eye in the air and the sound of a footstep on the ground will be assigned its due through His Justice and His Equity. On that Day many an argument will prove void and a contention for excuses will stand rejected. Sermon 222

God delivers those who were God-conscious, keeping them safe. No evil will afflict them, nor will they feel remorse. **39:61**

Among the God-conscious are the people of distinction. Their speech is to the point, their dress is moderate and their gait is humble. They keep their eyes closed to what God has made unlawful for them, and they put their ears to that knowledge which is beneficial to them. They remain in the time of trials as though they remain in comfort. If there had not been fixed periods of life ordained for each, their spirits would not have remained in their bodies even for the twinkling of an eye because of their eagerness for the reward and fear of chastisement. The greatness of the Creator is seated in their heart and so everything else appears small in their eyes. Thus to them Paradise is as though they see it and are enjoying its favors. To them Hell is also as if they see it and are suffering punishment in it. Sermon 192

God is One Who is Creator of everything. He is Trustee over everything. **39:62**
To Him belongs the pass keys of the heavens and the earth. Those who were ungrateful for the signs of God, those, they are the ones who are the losers. **39:63**

God, Who is aware of whatever is hidden in the hearts and whatever lies behind the unseen. Sermon 192

Say: Commanded you me to worship other than God, O ones who are ignorant? **39:64**
Certainly, it was revealed to **you** *and to those who were before* **you** *that if* **you** *have ascribed partners with God, certainly,* **your** *actions will be fruitless and* **you** *will, certainly, be among the ones who are losers.* **39:65**

I bear witness that *there is no god but God* (Q47:19), the One, there is no partner with Him, nor is there with Him any god other than Himself, and that *Muhammad* (Q48:29), peace and the mercy of God be upon him, is *His servant* (Q17:1) and *Prophet.* (Q7:158) Sermon 35

Nay! Worship **you** *God and be* **you** *among the ones who are thankful!* **39:66**

You should know that He will not be pleased with you for anything for which He was displeased with those before you. He will not be displeased with you for anything for which He was pleased with those before you. You are treading on a clear path and are speaking the same as the people before you had spoken. God is enough for your needs in this world. He has persuaded you to remain thankful and has made it obligatory on you to mention Him with your tongues. Sermon 183

They measured not God with His true measure. The earth altogether will be His handful on the Day of Resurrection when the heavens will be ones that are rolled up in His right hand. Glory be to Him! Exalted is He above partners they ascribe! **39:67**

Your ultimate goal of reward or punishment is before you. Behind your back is the hour of Resurrection which is driving you on. Keep yourself light and overtake the forward ones. The first ones who have preceded await your last ones. Sermon 21

The trumpet will be blown. Then, whoever is in the heavens will swoon and whoever is in and on the earth, but he whom God willed. Again, it will be blown another time. Then, they will be upright looking on. **39:68**

O God's human being! I advise you to be God-conscious which is the provision for the next world and with it is your return. The provision would take you to your destination and the return would be successful. The best one who is able to make people listen has called towards it and the best listener has listened to it. So the caller has proclaimed and the listener has listened and persevered. O God's human being! Certainly, being God-conscious has saved the lovers of God from unlawful items and has given His dread to their hearts until their nights are passed in wakefulness and their noons in thirst. So they achieve comfort through trouble and copious watering through thirst. They regarded death to be near and therefore hastened towards good actions. They rejected their desires by keeping death in their sight. Sermon 114

The earth will shine with the Light of its Lord and the Book will be laid down and the prophets and the witnesses will be brought about. It will be decided among them with The Truth. They, they will not be wronged. **39:69**
The account of each soul will be paid in full for what it did. He is greater in knowledge of what they accomplish. **39:70**

He has made the angels the trustees of His revelation and sent them to Prophets as holders of His injunctions and prohibitions. He has immunized them against the wavering of doubts. Consequently, no one among them goes astray from the path of His will. He has helped them with the benefits of help and has covered their hearts with humility and peace. He has opened for them doors of submission to His Glories. He has fixed for them bright minarets as signs of His Oneness. Sermon 91

Those who were ungrateful will be ones driven to hell in troops until when they drew near it, then, the doors of it will be flung open. Ones who are its keepers will say to them: Approach not Messengers from among you who recount to you the signs of your Lord to warn you of the meeting of this your Day? They would say: Yea. But the word of punishment was realized against the ones who are ungrateful. **39:71**

Where are the minds which seek light from the lamps of guidance and the eyes which look at minarets of God-consciousness? Where are the hearts dedicated to God and devoted to the obedience of God? They are all crowding towards worldly vanities and quarreling over unlawful issues. The banners of the Garden and Hell have been raised for them, but they have turned their faces away from the Garden and proceeded to Hell by dint of their performances. God called them, but they showed dislike and ran away. When Satan called them, they responded and proceeded towards him. Sermon 144

It will be said: Enter the doors of hell as ones who will dwell in it forever. Miserable it will be as a place of lodging for the ones who increase in pride. **39:72**

Everyone of them is ... alone although they are a group, and they are strangers, even though friends. They are unaware of morning after a night and of evening after a day. The night or the day when they departed has become ever existent for them. They found the dangers of their place of stay more serious than they had apprehended. They witnessed that its signs were greater than they had guessed. Sermon 220

Those who were God-conscious will be ones driven to their Lord in the Garden in troops until when they drew near it and its doors were let loose, ones who are its keepers will say to them: Peace be on you! You fared well! So, enter it, ones who dwell in it forever. **39:73**

They are in a narrow place, in very complicated affairs and in a fire whose pain is sharp, cries are loud, flames are rising, sound is trembling, burning is severe, abatement is remote. Its fuel is burning. Its threats are fearful. Its hollows are hidden. Its sides are dark. Its vessels are aflame. Everything about it is abominable: *Those who were God-conscious will be ones driven to their Lord in the Garden in troops until when they drew near it and its doors were let loose, ones who are its keepers will say to them: Peace be on you! You fared well! So, enter it, ones who dwell in it forever.* (Q39:73) Sermon 189

They would say: The Praise belongs to God Who was sincere in His promise to us and gave us the earth as inheritance that we take our dwelling in the Garden wherever we will. How excellent a compensation for the ones who work! **39:74**

Those who were God-conscious will be driven to their Lord in the Garden in troops ... (Q39:73) They are safe from chastisement, away from punishment, and kept aloof from fire. Their abode will be peaceful and they will be pleased with their longing and their place of stay. These are the people whose acts in this world were chaste, their eyes were tearful, their nights in this world were like days because of fearing and seeking forgiveness, and their days were like nights because of feeling of loneliness and separation. Therefore, God made Paradise the place of their eventual return and a reward in recompense: *They had better right to it and were more worthy of it ...* (Q48:26) in the eternal domain and everlasting favors. Sermon 190

You *will see the angels as ones who encircle around the Throne glorifying their Lord with praise. It would be decided in Truth among them. It would be said: The Praise belongs to God, the Lord of the worlds.* **39:75**

The angels do not consider their past virtuous deeds to be great, for if they had considered them great then excessive hope would have wiped away fearfulness from their hearts. They did not differ among themselves about their Sustainer because of Satan's lack of control over them. The vice of separation from one another did not disperse them. Rancor and mutual malice did not overpower them. Ways of wavering did not divide them. Differences of degree of courage did not render them into divisions. Thus, they the angels are captives of faith. Neither crookedness of mind, nor excess, nor lethargy nor languor loosens them from its bond. There is not the thinnest point in the skies, but there is an angel over it in prostration before God or busy in quick performance of His commands. By long worship of their Sustainer, they increase their knowledge. The honor of their Sustainer increases in their hearts. Sermon 91

Chapter 40: The One Who Forgives (al-Ghāfīr)

Ha Mim. **40:1**

The sending down successively of this Book is from God, The Almighty, The Knowing, **40:2**

There is no doubt that God sent down *the Prophet* (Q7:158), peace and the mercy of God be upon him, as a guide with an eloquent Book and a standing command. No one will be ruined by it except one who ruins himself. Certainly, only doubtful innovations cause ruin except those from which God may protect. In God's authority lies the safety of your affairs. Therefore, render Him such obedience as is neither blameworthy nor insincere. By God, you must do so otherwise God will take away from you the power of Islam and will never thereafter return it to you until it reverts to others. Sermon 169

The One Who Forgives impieties, The One Who Accepts remorse, The Severe in Repayment, The Possessor of Bounty. There is no god but He. To Him is the Homecoming. **40:3**

I bear witness that *there is no god but God* (Q47:19), the One. He has no like. My testimony has been tested in its frankness, and its essence is our belief. We shall cling to it forever and shall store it facing the tribulations that overtake us because it is the foundation stone of belief and the first step towards good actions and Divine pleasure. It is the means to keep Satan away. Sermon 2

No one disputes the signs of God, but those who were ungrateful. So, be ***you*** *not disappointed with their going to and fro in the land.* **40:4**
The folk of Noah denied before them and the confederates after them. Every community is about to take its Messenger and they dispute with falsehood to refute The Truth. So, I took them. How had been My repayment! **40:5**
Thus, was the Word of ***your*** *Lord realized against those who were ungrateful that they will be the Companions of the Fire.* **40:6**

God ... is aware of whatever is hidden in the hearts and whatever lies behind the unseen. Sermon 192

Those who carry the Throne and whoever is around it glorify the praises of their Lord and believe in Him and ask for forgiveness for those who believed: Our Lord! ***You*** *encompassed everything in mercy and in knowledge. So, forgive those who repented and followed* ***Your*** *way and guard them from the punishment of hellfire.* **40:7**

Praise belongs to God (Q1:2) Who made me such that I have not died, nor am I sick, nor have my veins been infected with disease, nor have I been hauled up for my evil acts, nor am I without progeny, nor have I forsaken my religion, nor do I disbelieve in my Lord, nor do I feel strangeness with my faith, nor is my intelligence affected, nor have I been punished with the punishment of peoples before me. I am a servant in **Your** possession. I have been guilty of excesses over myself. **You** have exhausted **Your** pleas over me and I have no plea before **You**. I have no power to take except what **You** give me. I cannot evade except what **You** save me from. Sermon 215

Our Lord! Cause them to enter the Gardens of Eden which ***You*** *promised them and whomever was in accord with morality among their fathers and their spouses and their offspring. Truly,* ***You, You*** *alone are The Almighty, The Wise.* **40:8**

This virtue of patience is one of the highest values of morality and nobility of character and it is the best habit which one can develop. Letter 31

Guard them from the evil deeds. Whomever ***You*** *have guarded from the evil deeds on that Day. Surely,* ***You*** *had had mercy on him. That, it is the winning the sublime triumph!* **40:9**

Desires will be cut. Hearts will sink quietly. Voices will be lowered. Sweat will choke the throat. Fear will increase. Ears will resound with the thundering voice of the announcer calling towards the final judgment, award of recompense, striking of punishment and paying of reward. Sermon 82

It will be proclaimed to those who were ungrateful: Certainly, the repugnance of God is greater than your repugnance of yourselves when you are called to belief, but you are ungrateful. **40:10**

Be aware! This world attracts and then turns away. It is stubborn, refusing to go ahead. It speaks lies and misappropriates. It disowns and is ungrateful. It is malicious and abandons its lovers. It attracts, but causes trouble. Its condition is changing, its step, shaking, its honor, disgrace, its seriousness, jest, and its height, lowliness. It is a place of plunder and pillage, ruin and destruction. Its people are ready with their feet to drive, to overtake and to depart. Its routes are bewildering, its exits are baffling. Its schemes end in disappointment. Consequently, strongholds betray them, houses throw them out and cunning fails them. Sermon 190

They said: Our Lord! **You** *caused us to die two times and* **You** *gave us life two times. We acknowledged our impieties. Then, is there any way of going forth?* **40:11**
It will be said: That is because when God alone was called to, you disbelieved. But when partners are ascribed with Him, you believe. The determination is with God alone, The Lofty, The Great. **40:12**

I bear witness that *there is no god but God* (Q47:19), the One, there is no partner with Him, nor is there with Him any god other than Himself, and that *Muhammad* (Q48:29), peace and the mercy of God be upon him, is *His servant* (Q17:1) and *Prophet.* (Q7:158) Sermon 35

It is He Who causes you to see His signs and sends down provision for you from heaven. None recollect but whoever is penitent. **40:13**

I bear witness that *there is no god but God* (Q47:19), by virtue of belief, certainty, sincerity and conviction. I also bear witness that *Muhammad* (Q48:29), peace and the mercy of God be upon him, is *His servant* (Q17:1) and *Prophet* (Q7:158) whom He deputed when the signs of guidance were obliterated and the ways of religion were desolate. So he threw open the truth, gave advice to the people, guided them towards righteousness and ordered them to be moderate. May God bless him ... Sermon 194

So, call you on God ones who are sincere and devoted in the way of life to Him although the ones who are ungrateful disliked it. **40:14**

O my God! We seek **Your** protection from turning away from **Your** command, or revolting against **Your** religion, or being led away by our desires instead of by guidance that comes from **You**. Sermon 215

Exalter of Degrees, Possessor of the Throne, He casts the Spirit by His command on whom He wills of His servants to warn of the Day of the Encounter, **40:15**
a Day when they are ones who depart. Nothing about them will be hidden from God. Whose is the dominion this Day. It is to God, The One, The Omniscient. **40:16**

God made Paradise the place of their eventual return and a reward in recompense: *They had better right to it and were more worthy of it ...* (Q48:26) in the eternal domain and everlasting favors. Sermon 190

On this Day every soul will be given recompense for what it earned. There will be no injustice today. God is Swift in reckoning. **40:17**
Warn them of The Impending Day when the hearts will be near the throats, ones who choke. There will not be a loyal friend for ones who are unjust, nor an intercessor be obeyed. **40:18**

The world aimed at them, but they did not aim at it. It captured them, but they freed themselves from it by a ransom. During a night they are standing on their feet reading portions of the Quran and reciting it in a well-measured way, creating through it grief for themselves and seeking by it the cure for their ailments. Sermon 193

He knows that which is the treachery of the eyes and whatever the breasts conceal. **40:19**

God deputed prophets and distinguished them with His revelation. He made them as pleas for Him among His creation so that there should not remain any excuse for people. He invited people to the right path through a truthful tongue. You should know that God fully knows creation. Not that He was not aware of what they concealed from among their hidden secrets and inner feelings, but in order to try them ... *as to which of them are fairest in actions* (Q18:7), so that there is reward in respect of good acts and chastisement in respect of evil acts. Sermon 144

God decrees by The Truth. Those whom they call to other than Him decide not anything. Truly, God, He is The Hearing, The Seeing. **40:20**

Know that—may God have mercy on you—you are living at a time when those who speak about right are few, when tongues are loath to utter the truth and those who stick to the right are humiliated. The people of this time are engaged in disobedience. Their youth are wicked, their old men are sinful, their learned men are hypocrites, and their speakers are sycophants. Their young ones do not respect their elders, and their rich men do not support the destitute. Sermon 232

Journey they not through the earth and look on how had been the Ultimate End of those who had been before them? They, they had been superior to them in strength and in traces they left on the earth, but God took them for their impieties and there had not been for them one who is a defender from God. **40:21**
That had been because their Messengers approached them before with clear portents but they were ungrateful, so God took them. Truly He is Strong, Severe in Repayment. **40:22**

O God's human being! I advise you to be God-conscious which is the provision for the next world and with it is your return. The provision would take you to your destination and the return would be successful. The best one who is able to make people listen has called towards it and the best listener has listened to it. So the caller has proclaimed and the listener has listened and preserved. O God's human being! Certainly being God fearing has saved the lovers of God from unlawful items and has given His dread to their hearts until their nights are passed in wakefulness and their noons in thirst. So they achieve comfort through trouble and copious watering through thirst. They regarded death to be near and, therefore, hastened towards good actions. They rejected their desires and so they kept death in their sight. Sermon 114

Certainly, We sent Moses with Our signs and a clear authority **40:23**
to Pharaoh and Haman and Korah. But they said: He is one who is a lying sorcerer. **40:24**
Then, when he drew near with The Truth from Us, they said: Kill the children of those who believed with him and save alive their women. The cunning of the ones who are ungrateful is but going astray. **40:25**
Pharaoh said: Let me kill Moses and let him call to his Lord. Truly, I fear that he substitute for your way of life or that he cause to appear in and on the earth corruption. **40:26**
Moses said: Truly, I took refuge in my Lord and your Lord from everyone who increases in pride and who believes not in the Day of Reckoning. **40:27**
Said a believing man of the family of Pharaoh, who keeps back his belief: Would you kill a man because he says: My Lord is God, and he drew near you with the clear portents from your Lord? If he be one who lies, then, on him will be his lying. If he be one who is sincere, then, will light on you

some of what he promises. Truly, God guides not him who is one who is excessive, a liar. **40:28**
O my folk! Yours is the dominion this day, ones who are prominent on the earth. But who will help us from the might of God if it drew near us? Pharaoh said: I cause you to see not but what I see and what I guide you to is not but the way of rectitude. **40:29**
He who believed said: O my folk! Truly, I fear for you like a Day of the confederates, **40:30**
in like manner of a folk of Noah and Ad and Thamud and those after them. God wants not injustice for His servants. **40:31**
O my folk! Truly, I fear for you a Day when they would call to one another **40:32**
a Day when you will turn as ones who draw back. No one saves you from harm from God. For whomever God causes to go astray, there is not anyone who guides. **40:33**

Praise belongs to God. (Q1:2) I praise Him, implore His help and ask for His guidance. I seek protection in Him from error. *Whomever God causes to go astray, there is not anyone who guides.* (Q40:33) Sermon 2

Certainly, Joseph drew near you before with the clear portents, but you ceased not in uncertainty as to what he brought about to you. Until when he perished you said: God will never raise up a Messenger after him. Thus, God causes him to go astray, one who is excessive, one who is a doubter, **40:34**
those who dispute the signs of God without any authority having approached them. It is troublesome, repugnant with God and with those who believed. Thus, God sets a seal on every heart of one who increases in pride, haughtiness. **40:35**
Pharaoh said: O Haman! Build for me a pavilion so that perhaps I will reach the routes, **40:36**
the routes to the heavens, and that I may peruse The God of Moses but, truly, I think that he is one who lies. Thus, it was made to appear pleasing to Pharaoh, the evil of his actions. He was barred from the way. The cunning of Pharaoh was not but in defeat. **40:37**
He who believed said: O my folk! Follow me; I will guide you to the way of rectitude. **40:38**
O my folk! Truly, this present life is nothing but transitory enjoyment and that the world to come is the stopping place, the Abode. **40:39**
Whoever did an evil deed will not be given recompense but the like of it. But whoever did as one in accord with morality, whether male or female, and such is one who believes, then, those will enter the Garden where they will be provided in it without reckoning. **40:40**
O my folk! What is it to me that I call to you for deliverance and you call to me for the fire? **40:41**
You call to me to be ungrateful to God and to ascribe partners with Him of what there is no knowledge, while I call you to The Almighty, The Forgiver. **40:42**
Without a doubt what you call me to has no merit. It is not a call to the present or to the world to come. Our turning back is to God. Truly, the ones who are excessive, they will be Companions of the Fire. **40:43**
You will remember what I say to you. I commit my affair to God. Truly, God is Seeing of the servants. **40:44**
So, God guarded him from the evil deeds that they planned while surrounded the people of Pharaoh an evil punishment: **40:45**
The fire to which they are presented the first part of the day and evening. On a Day when the Hour is secure it is said: Cause the people of Pharaoh to enter the severest punishment. **40:46**
When they dispute with one another in the fire, the weak will say to those who grew arrogant: Truly, we had been followers of you so will you be ones who avail us from a share of the fire? **40:47**
Those who grew arrogant would say: Truly, we are all in it. Truly, God, surely, gave judgment

among His servants. **40:48**
Those in the fire would say to ones who are keepers of hell: Call to your Lord to lighten the punishment for us for a day. **40:49**
They would say: Be bringing not your Messengers the clear portents. They would say: Yea! They would say: Then, you call. The supplication of the ones who are ungrateful only goes astray. **40:50**
Truly, We will, certainly, help Our Messengers and those who believed in this present life and on a Day when the ones who bear witness will stand up, **40:51**
a Day when their excuses will not profit the ones who are unjust. For them will be the curse and for them will be an evil abode. **40:52**
Certainly, We gave Moses the guidance and We gave as inheritance to the Children of Jacob the Book **40:53**
as a guidance and a reminder for those imbued with intuition. **40:54**
So, have ***you*** *patience. Truly, the promise of God is true. Ask for forgiveness for* ***your*** *impiety. Glorify* ***your*** *Lord with praise in the evening and the early morning.* **40:55** ***

Truly, those who dispute about the signs of God without any authority having approached them, there is nothing but having pride in their breasts. They will never be ones who reach its satisfaction. So, seek refuge in God. Truly, He, He is The Hearing, The Seeing. **40:56**
Certainly, the creation of the heavens and the earth is greater than the creation of humanity, yet most of humanity knows not. **40:57**

Almighty are **You**, the Creator, the Worshipped. On account of **Your** good trials of **Your** creatures, **You** created a house (Paradise) and provided in it for feasting, drinks, foods, spouses, servants, places, streams, plantations and fruits. Then **You** sent a Messenger to invite towards it, but the people did not respond to the caller and did not feel persuaded to what **You** persuaded them, nor showed eagerness towards what **You** desired them to feel eager. They, the ungrateful, jumped on the carcass of this world, earned shame by eating it and became united in loving it. When one loves a thing, it blinds him and sickens his heart. He sees, but with a diseased eye, hears, but with un-hearing ears. Desires have cut asunder his wit. The world has made his heart dead while his mind is all longing for it. Consequently, he is a servant of it and of everyone who has any share in it. Wherever it turns, he turns towards it. Wherever it proceeds, he proceeds towards it. He is not desisted by any desister from God, nor takes admonition from any preacher. He sees those who have been caught in neglect whence there is neither rescission nor reversion. Sermon 108

Not on the same level are the unwilling to see and the seeing nor those who believed and did as the ones in accord with morality and the ones who are evil doers. Little do they recollect. **40:58**

The beginning of the action of one who sees with his heart and acts with eyes is to assess whether the action will go against him or for him. If it is for him, he indulges in it, but if it is against him, he keeps away from it. For he who acts without knowledge is like one who treads without a path. His deviation from the path keeps him at a distance from his aim. He who acts according to knowledge is like him who treads the clear path. Therefore, he who can see, should see whether he should proceed or return. Sermon 153

Truly, the Hour is that which arrives. There is no doubt about it, yet most of humanity believes not. **40:59**

There remain a few people in whose case the remembrance of their return to God on the Day of Judgment keeps their eyes bent and the awareness of the Resurrection moves them to tears. Some of them are scared away from the world and disperse. Some are frightened and subdued. Some are quiet as if muzzled. Some are praying sincerely. Some are grief-stricken and pain-ridden whom fear has confined to namelessness. Disgrace has shrouded them, so they are in the sea of bitter water, their mouths are closed and their hearts are bruised. They preached until they were tired. They were oppressed until they were disgraced. They were killed until their numbers dwindled. Sermon 32

Your Lord said: Call to Me; I will respond to you. Truly, those who grow arrogant toward My worship, they will enter hell as ones who are in a state of lowliness. **40:60**

Everyone of them is ... alone although they are a group, and they are strangers, even though friends. They are unaware of morning after a night and of evening after a day. The night or the day when they departed has become ever existent for them. They found the dangers of their place of stay more serious than they had apprehended, and they witnessed that its signs were greater than they had guessed. Sermon 220

God is He Who made for you the nighttime so that you may rest in it and the daytime for one who perceives. Truly, God is Possessor of Grace to humanity, but most of humanity gives not thanks. **40:61**

He made its sun the bright indication for its day and moon the gloomy indication for its night. He then put them in motion in their orbits and ordained their pace of movement in the stages of their paths in order to distinguish with their help between night and day and in order that the reckoning of years and calculations may be known by their fixed movements. Sermon 91

That is God, your Lord, the One Who is Creator of everything. There is no god but He. Then, how you are misled! **40:62**

O people who possess eyes and ears and health and wealth! Is there any place of protection, any shelter of safety, or asylum or haven, or occasion to run away or to come back to this world? *If not: How then you are misled?* (Q40:62) and whither are you averting? By what things have you been deceived? Certainly, the share of every one of you from this earth is just a piece of land equal to his own stature and size where he would lie on his cheeks covered with dust. Sermon 82

Thus, are misled those who had been negating the signs of God. **40:63**

O people who possess eyes and ears and health and wealth! Is there any place of protection, any shelter of safety, or asylum or haven, or occasion to run away or to come back to this world? If not: *How then you are misled?* (Q6:95) and whither are you averting? By what things have you been deceived? Certainly, the share of every one of you from this earth is just a piece of land equal to his own stature and size where he would lie on his cheeks covered with dust. Sermon 82

God is He Who made the earth for you as a stopping place and the heaven as a canopy. He formed you and formed you well and He provided you of what is good. That is God, your Lord. Then, blessed be God, the Lord of the worlds! **40:64**

He is The Living! There is no god but He! So, call to Him, ones sincere and devoted in the way of life to Him. The Praise belongs to God, the Lord of the worlds! **40 65**

He is far above being affected by things which affect others. Sermon 186

Say: Truly, I was prohibited from worshipping those whom you call to other than God, because the clear portents drew near me from my Lord. I was commanded to submit to the Lord of the worlds. **40:66**

I bear witness that *there is no god but God* (Q47:19), the One, there is no partner with Him, nor is there with Him any god other than Himself, and that *Muhammad* (Q48:29), peace and the mercy of God be upon him, is *His servant* (Q17:1) and *Prophet.* (Q7:158) Sermon 35

He it is Who created you from earth dust, again, from seminal fluid, again, from a clot. Again, He brings you out as infant children. Again, you come of age and are fully grown. Again, you be an old man. Of you is he whom death calls to itself before, and that you reach a term, that which is determined so that perhaps you will be reasonable. **40:67**

He it is Who gives life and causes to die. When He decreed an affair, He only says to it: Be! Then, it is! **40:68**

He then turned to that with which the physician had made him familiar, namely suppressing the hot diseases with cold medicines and curing the cold with hot doses, but the cold things did nothing save aggravate the hot ailments, while the hot ones did nothing except increasing the coldness. Nor did he acquire temperateness in his constitution, but rather every ailment of his increased until his physicians became helpless, his attendants grew neglectful and his own family lacked the ability to describe his disease, and were unable to answer those who enquired about him. Sermon 220

Have ***you*** *not considered those who dispute about the signs of God, where they are turned away*: **40:69**

I bear witness that *there is no god but God* (Q47:19), by virtue of belief, certainty, sincerity and conviction. I also bear witness that *Muhammad* (Q48:29), peace and the mercy of God be upon him, is *His servant* (Q17:1) and *Prophet* (Q7:158) whom He deputed when the signs of guidance were obliterated and the ways of religion were desolate. So he threw open the truth, gave advice to the people, guided them towards righteousness and ordered them to be moderate. May God bless him ... Sermon 194

Those who denied the Book and that with which We sent Our Messengers? Then, they will know. **40:70**

The Book of God is among you. It speaks. Its tongue does not falter. It is a house whose pillars do not fall down. It is a power whose supporters are never defeated. Sermon 132

When yokes are on their necks and the chains, they will be dragged **40:71**

into scalding water. Again, they will be poured forth into the fire as fuel. **40:72**

Very soon you will be overwhelmed with the gloom of its shades, the severity of its illness, the darkness of its distresses, the nonsense utterances of its pangs, the grief of its destruction, the darkness of its encompassment and the unwholesomeness of its taste. It will seem as if it has come to you all of a sudden, silenced those who were whispering to you, separated your group, destroyed your doings, devastated your houses and altered your successors to distribute your estate among the chief relatives, who did not give you any benefit, or the grieved near ones who could not protect you, or those rejoicers who did not lament you. Sermon 229

Again, it will be said to them: Where are what you had been ascribing as partners **40:73**
other than God? They would say: They went astray from us. Nay! We be not calling to anything before. Thus, God causes to go astray ones who are ungrateful. **40:74**
That was because you had been exultant on the earth without right and that you had been glad. **40:75**
Enter the doors of hell as ones who will dwell in it forever. Then, miserable it will be as a place of lodging for the ones who increase in pride! **40:76**

Steer clear through the waves of mischief by boats of deliverance. Turn away from the path of dissension. Put off the crowns of pride. Prosperous is one who rises with wings when he has power or else he remains peaceful and others enjoy ease. The aspiration for the Caliphate is like turbid water or like a morsel that would suffocate the person who swallows it. One who plucks fruits before ripening is like one who cultivated in another's field. Sermon 5

So, have ***you*** *patience. Truly, the promise of God is true. Whether We cause* ***you*** *to see some part of what We promise them or We call* ***you*** *to Us, then, it is to Us they will be returned.* **40:77**

... and to Him returns whoever dies. Sermon 108

Certainly, We sent Messengers before ***you*** *among whom We related to* ***you*** *and of whom We relate not to* ***you****. It had not been for any Messenger that he bring a sign, except with the permission of God. So, when the command of God drew near, the matter would be decided rightfully. Lost here are these, the ones who deal in falsehood.* **40:78**

By God, certainly it is reality not fun, truth not falsehood. Sermon 131

God is He Who has made for you flocks among which you may ride on them and among which you eat of them. **40:79**
You have what profits from them and that with them you reach the satisfaction of a need that is in your breasts and you are carried on them and on boats. **40:80**

Entrust them to one who is trustworthy and who is of a kind and sympathetic disposition so that he may not treat the animals cruelly and may not starve them or tire them out during the transit. Instruct him not to separate a she-camel from its young, not to milk it so much that nothing is left for its young one and not to ride them harshly or to overburden them with heavy loads. He should ride them in turns so that those who have been already ridden may have an easy journey. He should not drive them fast and should avoid harshness. He should always give them enough rest at watering places. They should not be driven through deserts. Letter 25

He causes you to see His signs. So, which of the signs of God do you reject? **40:81**

I bear witness that *there is no god but God,* (Q47:19), by virtue of belief, certainty, sincerity and conviction. I also bear witness that *Muhammad* (Q48:29), peace and the mercy of God be upon him, is *His servant* (Q17:1) and *Prophet* (Q7:158) whom He deputed when the signs of guidance were obliterated and the ways of religion were desolate. So he threw

open the truth, gave advice to the people, guided them towards righteousness and ordered them to be moderate. May God bless him ... Sermon 194

Journey they not through the earth and look on how had been the Ultimate End of those before them? They had been more than them and were more vigorous in strength and in regard to the traces they left on the earth. Then, availed them not what they had been earning. **40:82**

O God's human being! I advise you to be God-conscious which is the provision for the next world and with it is your return. The provision would take you to your destination and the return would be successful. The best one who is able to make people listen has called towards it and the best listener has listened to it. So the caller has proclaimed and the listener has listened and preserved. Sermon 114

Then, when their Messengers drew near them with the clear portents, they were glad in the knowledge that they had and surrounded them was what they had been ridiculing. **40:83**
So, when they saw Our might, they said: We believed in God alone and we were ungrateful in that we had been ones who are polytheists. **40:84**
But their belief be not what profits them once they saw Our might. This is a custom of God which was, surely, in force among His servants. Lost here are the ones who are ungrateful. **40:85**

God ... is aware of whatever is hidden in the hearts and whatever lies behind the unseen. Sermon 192

CHAPTER 41: THEY WERE EXPLAINED DISTINCTLY (Fuṣṣilat)

Ha Mim **41:1**
A sending down successively from The Merciful, The Compassionate, **41:2**
a Book in which its signs were explained distinctly, an Arabic Recitation for a folk who know, **41:3**
a bearer of glad tidings and a warner, but most of them turned aside so they hear not. **41:4**
They said: Our hearts are sheathed from that to which **you** *have called us and in our ears is a heaviness and between us and between* **you** *is a partition. So, work. Truly, we, too, are ones who work.* **41:5**
Say: I am only a mortal like you. It is revealed to me that your God is God, One; so go straight to Him and ask for forgiveness from Him, and woe to the ones who are polytheists—those who give not the purifying alms **41:6**
and who in the world to come are ones who disbelieve. **41:7**
Truly, those who believed and did as the ones in accord with morality, for them will be compensation, that which is unfailing. **41:8**

Among the proofs of His creation is the creation of the skies which are fastened without pillars and stand without support. He called them. They responded obediently and humbly without being lazy or loathsome. If they had not acknowledged His Godhead and obeyed Him, He would not have made them the place for His throne, the abode of His angels and the destination: *To Him Words of what is good rise and He exalts an action in accord with morality ...* (Q35:10) of the creatures. Sermon 182

Say: Truly, are you ungrateful to Him Who created the earth in two days? Assign you to Him rivals? That is the Lord of the worlds! **41:9**

He originated the creation without any example which He could follow and without any specimen prepared by any known creator as there was none before Him. He showed us the realm of His Might, and such wonders which speak of His Wisdom. The confession of the created things that their existence owes itself to Him made us realize that argument has been furnished about knowing Him so that there are no excuses against it. The signs of His creative power and standard of His wisdom are fixed in the wonderful things He has created. Whatever He has created is an argument in His favor and a guide towards Him. Even a silent thing is a guide towards Him as though it speaks, and its guidance towards the Creator is clear. Sermon 90

He made on it firm mountains from above it and He blessed it and ordained its subsistence within it in four days equally for the ones who ask. **41:10**

When the excitement of water subsided under the earth's sides and under the weight of the high and lofty mountains placed on its shoulders, God flowed springs of water from its high tops and distributed them through plains and low places and moderated their movement by fixed rocks and high mountain tops. Then its trembling came to a standstill because of the penetration of mountains in various parts of its surface and their being fixed in its deep areas, and their standing on its plains. Sermon 90

Again, He turned His attention to the heaven while it was smoke and He said to it and to the earth: Approach both of you willing or unwilling. They both said: We approached as ones who are obedient. **41:11**

The Glorified says in the Quran: *Propound for them the parable of this present life: It is like water that We caused to descend from heaven. Then, plants of the earth mingled with it and it becomes straw in the morning that winnows in the winds. God had been over everything One Who is Omnipotent.* (Q18:45) Sermon 110

Then, foreordaining seven heavens in two days, He revealed in each heaven its command. We made the present heaven appear pleasing with lamps and keeping them safe. Thus, decreed the Almighty, The Knowing. **41:12**

I am among you like a lamp in the darkness. Whoever enters by it will be lit from it. So listen, O people, preserve it and remain attentive with the ears of your hearts so that you may understand. Sermon 187

But if they turned aside, then, say: I warned you of a thunderbolt like the thunderbolt of Ad and Thamud. **41:13**

When the Messengers drew near before them and from behind them saying: Worship none but God, they said: If our Lord willed, He would have caused angels to descend. Then, truly, in what you were sent, we are ones who disbelieve. **41:14**

As for Ad, they grew arrogant on the earth without right and they said: Who is more vigorous than us in strength? Consider they not that God Who created them, He was more vigorous than they in strength? They had been negating Our signs. **41:15**

You should know as you do know, that you have to leave it and depart from it. While in it, take lesson from those who *grew arrogant on the earth without right and they said: Who is more vigorous than us in strength?* (Q41:15) Sermon 110

So, We sent on them a raging wind in days of misfortune that We might cause them to experience the punishment of degradation in this present life. The punishment in the world to come will be more degrading; and they will not be helped. **41:16**
As for Thamud, We guided them, but they embraced blindness of heart instead of guidance. Then, a thunderbolt took them with a humiliating punishment because of what they had been earning. **41:17**
We delivered those who believed and had been God-conscious. **41:18** ***

On a Day when will be assembled the enemies of God to the fire, then, they will be marching in rank **41:19**
until when they drew near it. Witness will be borne against them by their having the ability to hear, and by their sight and by their skins as to what they had been doing. **41:20**
They will say to their skins: Why bore you witness against us? They will say: We were given speech by God Who gave speech to all things. He created you the first time and to Him you will be returned. **41:21**

Know that the tongue is a part of a man's body. If the man desists, speech will not co-operate with him and when he dilates, speech will not give him time to stop. Certainly, we are the masters of speaking. Its veins are fixed in us and its branches are hanging over us. Sermon 232

You had not been covering yourselves so that witness be borne against you by your having the ability to hear or by your sight or by your skins but that you thought that God knows not much of what you do. **41:22**

Then on that day even the opening of an eye in the air and the sound of a footstep on the ground will be assigned its due through His Justice and His Equity. On that day many an argument will prove void and a contention for excuses will stand rejected. Sermon 222

That your thought, which you thought about your Lord has dealt destruction to you. Then, you became among the ones who are losers. **41:23**
Then, even if they endure patiently, yet the fire will be the place of lodging for them. If they ask for favor, yet they will not be of the ones to whom favor is shown. **41:24**
We allotted for them comrades who were made to appear pleasing to them whatever was before them and whatever was behind them. The saying was realized against them in communities that passed away before them of jinn and humankind. Truly, they, they had been ones who are losers. **41:25**

Everyone of them is ... alone although they are a group, and they are strangers, even though friends. They are unaware of morning after a night and of evening after a day. The night or the day when they departed has become ever existent for them. They found the dangers of their place of stay more serious than they had apprehended, and they witnessed that its signs were greater than they had guessed. Sermon 220

Those who are ungrateful said: Hear not this, the Quran, but talk idly about it while it is being recited so that perhaps you will prevail. **41:26**

Your party had decided to select two persons. So we took their pledge that they would act according to the Quran and would not commit excess, that their tongues should be with it and that their hearts should follow it, but they deviated from it, abandoned what was right although they had it before their eyes. Wrong-doing was their desire, and going astray was their behavior. Although we had settled with them to decide with justice, to act according to the light and without the interference of their evil views and wrong judgment. Now that they have abandoned the course of right and have come out with just the opposite of what was settled, we have strong ground to reject their verdict. Sermon 177

We will cause those who were ungrateful to experience a severe punishment. We will give recompense to them for the bad deeds of what they had been doing. **41:27**

He put His angels on trial concerning these attributes in order to distinguish those who are modest from those who are vain. Sermon 192

That is the recompense of the enemies of God: The fire. For them is the infinite abode in it, recompense because they had been negating Our signs. **41:28**

I bear witness that *there is no god but God* (Q47:19) by virtue of belief, certainty, sincerity and conviction. I also bear witness that *Muhammad* (Q48:29), peace and the mercy of God be upon him, is *His servant* (Q17:1), and *Prophet* (Q7:158) whom He deputed when the signs of guidance were obliterated and the ways of religion were desolate. So he threw open the truth, gave advice to the people, guided them towards righteousness and ordered them to be moderate. May God bless him ... Sermon 194

Those who were ungrateful would say: Our Lord! Cause us to see those who caused us to go astray among jinn and humankind. We will lay them both beneath our feet so that they become of the lowest. **41:29**

God ... is aware of whatever is hidden in the hearts and whatever lies behind the unseen. Sermon 192

Truly, those who said: Our Lord is God, again, they went straight, the angels come forth to them: Neither fear nor feel remorse, but rejoice in the Gardens which you had been promised. **41:30**

Be aware! What had been ordained has occurred and that which had been destined has come into play. I am speaking to you with the promise and pleas of God. God the Sublime has said: *Truly those who said: Our Lord is God. Moreover, they go straight and the angels come forth to them: Neither fear nor feel remorse, but rejoice in the Gardens which you have been promised.* (Q41:30) You have said: Our Lord is God. Then keep steadfast to His Book, to the way of His command and to the virtuous course of His worship. Thereafter do not go out of it, do not introduce innovations in it, and do not turn away from it, because those who go away from this course will be cut off from the mercy of God on the Day of Judgment.

We were protectors in this present life and in the world to come. You will have in it that for which your souls lust and in it is what you call for, **41:31**
a hospitality from the Forgiving, Compassionate. **41:32**

The world aimed at them, but they did not aim at it. It captured them, but they freed themselves from it by a ransom. During the night, they are standing on their feet, reading portions of the Quran and reciting it in a well-measured way, creating through it grief and seeking by it the cure for their ailments. If they come across a verse creating eagerness for Paradise, they pursue it avidly. Their spirits turn towards it eagerly. They feel as if it is in front of them. When they come across a verse which contains fear of Hell, they bend the ears of their hearts towards it and feel as though the sound of Hell and its cries are reaching their ears. They bend themselves from their backs, prostrate themselves on their foreheads, their palms, their knees and their toes, and beseech God, the Sublime, for their deliverance. Sermon 193

Who has a fairer saying than he who called to God and did as one in accord with morality, and said: I am one of the ones who submit to God. **41:33**

We are happy with the destiny ordained by God and have submitted to the command of God. Sermon 37

Not on the same level are benevolence or the evil deed. Drive back with what is fairer. Then, behold he who between **you** *and between him was enmity as if he had been a protector, a loyal friend.* **41:34**

Truly, those who followed *the Prophet* (Q7:158), peace and the mercy of God be upon him, always carefully measured their thoughts and deeds, as you must also try to do, and they carefully thought over the subject before saying anything about it or before doing a deed. Letter 31

None will be in receipt of it but those who endured patiently. None will be in receipt of it but the possessor of a sublime allotment. **41:35**

The Prophet (Q33:6) of God, peace and the mercy of God be upon him, said: The belief of a person cannot be firm unless his heart is firm, and his heart cannot be firm unless his tongue is firm. So whoever of you can manage to meet God, the Sublime, in such a position that his hands are unsmeared with the blood of Muslims and their property and his tongue is safe from exposing them, he should do so. Sermon 176

But if Satan sows enmity, sowing enmity in **you**, *then, seek refuge in God. Truly, He is The Hearing, The Knowing.* **41:36**

God was being disobeyed. Satan was given support. Faith was forsaken. As a result, the pillars of religion crumbled. Any trace of them was lost. Its passages were destroyed. Its streets fell into decay. People obeyed Satan and tread his path. They sought water from his watering places. Satan's banners flew in the wind through them. His standard of vice was raised. They trampled people under their hoofs and tread upon them with their feet. Vice attained full stature. The people immersed in them were led astray, perplexed, ignorant and seduced as though they were in a good house (Mecca) with bad neighbors (ungrateful Quraysh). Instead of sleep, the people had wakefulness. Instead of antimony, they had tears in their eyes. They were in a land where the lips of the learned bridled while the words of the ignorant were honored. Sermon 2

Of His signs are the nighttime and the daytime and the sun and the moon. Prostrate not yourselves to the sun nor to the moon, but prostrate yourselves to God Who created both of them if it is He you had been worshiping. **41:37**

But if they grew arrogant, then, those who are with **your** *Lord glorify Him during the nighttime and the daytime and they never grow weary.* **41:38**

Be God-conscious! God! from the immediate consequence of rebellion to accrue in this world and the eventual consequence of weighty oppressiveness to accrue in the next world, and from the evil result of vanity, because it is the great trap of Satan and his deceit which enters the hearts of the people like a fatal poison. It never goes to waste, nor misses anyone—neither the learned because of his knowledge, nor the destitute in his rags. This is the thing against which God has protected His creatures who are believers by means of prayers, and alms-giving, and suffering the hardship of fasting in the days in which it has been made obligatory, in order to give their limbs peacefulness, to cast fear in their eyes, to make their spirits humble, to give their hearts humility and to remove haughtiness from them. All this is achieved through the covering of their delicate cheeks with dust in humility, prostrating their main limbs on the ground in humbleness, and retracting of their bellies so as to reach to their backs due to fasting by way of lowliness before God, besides giving all sorts of products of the earth to the needy and the destitute by way of alms. Sermon 191

Among His signs are that **you** *see the earth as that which is humble. But when We caused water to descend to it, it quivered and swelled. Truly, He Who gives life to it is the One Who Gives Life to the dead. Truly, He is Powerful over everything.* **41:39**

When Almighty God created the openings of the atmosphere, the expanse of firmament and strata of winds, He flowed into it water whose waves were stormy and whose surges leapt one over the other. He loaded it on dashing wind and breaking typhoons, ordered them to shed it back as rain, gave the wind control over the vigor of the rain, and acquainted it with its limitations. The wind blew under it while water flowed furiously over it. Sermon 1

Truly, those who blaspheme Our signs are not hidden from Us. Is he who is cast down into the fire better off, or he who approaches as one who is safe on the Day of Resurrection? Do as you willed. Truly, He is Seeing of what you do. **41:40**

They are emulating each other and proceeding in groups towards the final objective and the rendezvous of death, until when matters come to a close, the world dies and the Resurrection draws near. God will take them out from the corners of the graves, the nests of birds, the dens of beasts and the centers of death. They will hasten towards His command and run towards the place fixed for their final return, group by group, quiet, standing and arrayed in rows. They will be within God's sight and will hear every one who would call them. They will have the dress of helplessness and covering of submission and indignity. At this time contrivances will disappear. Desires will be cut. Hearts will sink quietly. Voices will be lowered. Sweat will choke the throat. Fear will increase. Ears will resound with the thundering voice of the announcer calling towards the final judgment, award of recompense, striking of punishment and paying of reward. Sermon 82

Truly, those who were ungrateful for the Remembrance when it drew near them are not hidden from Us. Truly, it is a mighty Book! **41:41**
Falsehood approaches it not from before it, nor from behind it. It is a sending down successively from The Wise, The Worthy of Praise. **41:42**

... abide by the Book of God (Quran), the Sublime, and the conduct of *the Prophet*

(Q7:158), peace and the mercy of God be upon him. Stand by His rights and the revival of his *sunna*. Sermon 169

Nothing is said to ***you*** *but what, truly, was said to the Messengers before* ***you****. Truly,* ***your*** *Lord is, certainly, the Possessor of Forgiveness, and the Possessor of Painful Repayment.* **41:43**

He never grudges His Forgiveness, nor refuses His Mercy. On the contrary, He has decreed repentance as a virtue and pious deed. Letter 31

If We made this a non-Arabic Recitation, they would have said: Why were His signs not explained distinctly: A non-Arab tongue and an Arab! Say: It is a guidance for those who believe and a healing. As for those who believed not, there is a heaviness in their ears and blindness in their hearts. Those are given notice from a far place. **41:44**

God never allowed His creation to remain without a Prophet, one deputized by Him, or a Book sent down from Him, or a binding argument, or a standing plea. These Messengers were such that they did not fear that they were few in comparison to the large numbers of their falsifiers. Among them was either a predecessor who would name the one to follow or the follower who had been introduced by the predecessor. Sermon 1

Certainly, We gave Moses the Book. Then, they were at variance about it. If it were not for a Word that had preceded from ***your*** *Lord, it would have been decided between them. But, truly, they are in uncertainty, ones in grave doubt about it.* **41:45**

You must not allow uncertainties and doubt poison your mind, skepticism or irrational likes and dislikes should not affect your views. Letter 31

Whoever did as one in accord with morality, it is for himself. Whoever did evil, it is against himself, and ***your*** *Lord is not unjust to His servants.* **41:46**

To Him is returned the knowledge of the Hour. No fruits go forth from its sheath and no female conceives or brings forth offspring but with His knowledge. On a Day He will cry out to them: Where are My ascribed associates? They would say: We proclaimed to ***You*** *that none of us was a witness to that.* **41:47**

Everything submits to Him. Everything exists by Him. He is the satisfaction of every poor, dignity of the low, energy for the weak and shelter for the oppressed. Whoever speaks, He hears his speaking. Whoever keeps quiet, He knows his secret. On Him is the livelihood of everyone who lives. To Him returns whoever dies. Sermon 108

Gone astray from them is what they had been calling to before. They would think that there is for them no asylum. **41:48**

I bear witness that *there is no god but God* (Q47:19), and I bear witness that *Muhammad* (Q48:29), peace and the mercy of God be upon him, is *His servant* (Q17:1) and *Prophet* (Q7:158) and His chosen and His selected one. Sermon 150

The human being grows not weary of supplicating for good, but if the worst afflicted him, then, he is hopeless, desperate. **41:49**

The Prophet (Q33:6) of God, peace and the mercy of God be upon him, said: The belief of a person cannot be firm unless his heart is firm, and his heart cannot be firm unless his tongue is firm. So whoever of you can manage to meet God, the Sublime, in such a position that his hands are unsmeared with the blood of Muslims and their property and his tongue is safe from exposing them, he should do so. Sermon 176

Truly, if We caused him to experience mercy from Us, after some tribulation afflicted him, he will, certainly, say: This is due to me. I think not that the Hour will be one that arises, but if I were returned to my Lord, truly, with Him will be the fairer for me. Then, certainly, We will tell those who were ungrateful of what they did. We will cause them to experience a harsh punishment. **41:50**

Is it that you are unthankful to God for all which He has granted to you and you are ungrateful to Him for the favors bestowed upon you? Sermon 110

When We were gracious to the human being, he turned aside, withdrew aside. But when the worst afflicted him, then, he is full of supplication. **41:51**
Say: Considered you that even though it had been from God, again, you were ungrateful for it. Who is one who goes more astray than he who is in wide breach? **41:52**

God ... is aware of whatever is hidden in the hearts and whatever lies behind the unseen. Sermon 192

We will cause them to see Our signs on the horizons and within themselves until it becomes clear to them that it is The Truth. Suffices not **your** *Lord that, truly, He is Witness over all things?* **41:53**

I bear witness that *there is no god but God* (Q47:19) by virtue of belief, certainty, sincerity and conviction. I also bear witness that *Muhammad* (Q48:29), peace and the mercy of God be upon him, is *His servant* (Q17:1) and *Prophet* (Q7:158) whom He deputed when the signs of guidance were obliterated and the ways of religion were desolate. So he threw open the truth, gave advice to the people, guided them towards righteousness and ordered them to be moderate. May God bless him ... Sermon 194

They are hesitant about the meeting with their Lord. Truly, He is who One Who Encloses everything. **41:54**

Imagination cannot surmise Him within the limits of movements of limbs or senses. It cannot be said about Him: "Whence." No time limit can be attributed to Him by saying "until." He is apparent, but it cannot be said "from what." He is hidden, but it cannot be said "in what." He is not a body which can die, nor is He veiled so as to be enclosed therein. He is not near to things by way of touch, nor is He remote from them by way of separation. Sermon 162

Chapter 42: The Consultation (al-Shūrā)

Ha Mim **42:1**
Ayn Sin Qaf **42:2**
Thus, He reveals to **you** *and to those who were before* **you**, *God is The Almighty, The Wise.* **42:3**

Anyone who has been granted four attributes will not be deprived of their four effects; one who prays to God and implores to Him will not be deprived of granting of his prayers; one who repents for his thoughts and deeds will not be refused acceptance of the repentance; one who has atoned for his sins will not be debarred from salvation; and one who thanks God for the blessings and bounties will not be denied the increase in them. The truth of these facts is attested by the Quran As far as prayers are concerned He says: Pray to Me and I shall accept your prayers. About repentance He says: Whoever has done a bad deed or has indulged in sin and then repents and asks for His forgiveness will find God most Forgiving and Merciful. About being thankful He says: If you are thankful for what you are given, I shall increase My bounties and blessings. About atonement of sin He says: God accepts the repentance of those who have ignorantly committed vice and then soon repent for it. God accepts such repentance. He is Wise and Omniscient. Saying 134

To Him belongs whatever is in and on the heavens and whatever is in and on the earth. He is The Lofty, The Sublime. **42:4**

O God's human being! I advise you to be God-conscious which is the provision for the next world and with it is your return. The provision would take you to your destination and the return would be successful. The best one who is able to make people listen has called towards it and the best listener has listened to it. So the caller has proclaimed and the listener has listened and persevered. Sermon 114

The heavens are about to split asunder from above them while the angels glorify the praise of their Lord and ask forgiveness for whoever is on the earth. Truly, God, He is The Forgiving, The Compassionate. **42 5**

O my God! Praise be to **You** for what **You** take and give and for that from which **You** cure or with which **You** afflict; praise which is the most acceptable to **You**, the most liked by **You** and the most dignified before **You**; praise which fills all **Your** creation and reaches where **You** desire; praise which is not veiled from **You** and does not end, and whose continuity does not cease. Sermon 160

As for those who took to themselves other than Him as protectors, God is Guardian over them and ***you*** *are not a Trustee over them.* **42:6**

Praise belongs to God (Q1:2) Who is above all similarity to creatures, is above the words of describers Who displays the wonders of His management for the on-lookers, is hidden from the imagination of thinkers by virtue of the greatness of His glory, has knowledge without acquiring it by adding to it or drawing it from someone, and Who is the ordainer of all matters without reflecting or thinking. He is such that gloom does not concern Him, nor does He seek light from brightness. Night does not overtake Him, nor does the day pass over Him so as to affect Him in any manner. His comprehension of things is not through eyes. His knowledge is not dependent on being informed. God deputized *the Prophet* (Q7:158), peace and the mercy of God be upon him, with light and accorded him the highest precedence in selection. Through him God united those who were divided, overpowered the powerful, overcame difficulties and leveled rugged ground and, thus, removed misguidance from right and left. Sermon 213

Thus, We revealed to ***you*** *an Arabic Recitation that* ***you*** *will warn the Mother of the Towns and whoever is around it. Warn of the Day of Amassing. There is no doubt about it. A group of people will be in the Garden and a group of people will be in the blaze.* **42:7**

Go ahead with the remembrance of God, for it is the best remembrance. Long for that which He has promised to the pious, for His promise is the most true promise. Tread the course of *the Prophet,* (Q7:158), peace and the mercy of God be upon him, for it is the most distinguished course. Follow his *sunna*, for it is the most right of all behaviors. Learn the Quran, for it is the fairest of discourses. Understand it thoroughly, for it is the best blossoming of hearts. Seek cure with its light, for it is the cure for hearts. Recite it beautifully, for it is the most beautiful narration. Certainly, a scholar who acts not according to his knowledge is like the off-headed ignorant who does not find relief from his ignorance, but the plea of God is greater on the learned and grief more incumbent. He is more blameworthy before God. Sermon 110

If God willed, He would have made them one community but He causes to enter whom He wills into His mercy. The ones who are unjust, there is not for them either a protector or a helper. **42:8**

The condition of those people who are solely engrossed in this world and are sadly engulfed in its short-lived, quickly fading and vicious pleasures, is like that of travelers who are staying in fertile and happy regions and who have to undertake a journey, knowing fully well that the journey is going to end in a rough, arid and infertile land. Letter 31

Or they took other than Him to themselves as protectors. But God, He alone is The Protector. He gives life to the dead. He is Powerful over everything. **42:9**

Whoever said in what is He, held that He is contained. Whoever said on what is He held, He is not on something else. He is a Being, but not through the phenomenon of coming into being. He exists, but not from non-existence. He is with everything, but not in physical nearness. He is different from everything, but not in physical separation. He acts, but without connotation of movements and instruments. He sees even when there is none to be looked at from among His creation. He is only One, such that there is none with whom He may keep company or whom He may miss in his absence. Sermon 1

Whatever thing about which you were at variance in it, then, its determination is with God. That is God, my Lord in Whom I put my trust and to Him I am penitent, **42:10**

Praise belongs to God. (Q1:2) He is such that senses cannot perceive Him, place cannot contain Him, eyes cannot see Him and veils cannot cover Him. He proves His eternity by the coming into existence of His creation and also by originating His creation He proves His existence, and by their mutual similarity He proves that there is nothing similar to Him. He is true in His promise. He is too high to be unjust to His creatures. He stands by equity among His creation and practices justice over them in His commands. He provides evidence through the creation of things of His being from ever, through their marks of incapability of His power, and through their powerlessness against death of His eternity. Sermon 185

One Who is Originator of the heavens and the earth. He made for you souls of yourselves and of the flocks, pairs by which means He makes you numerous in it. There is not like Him anything. He is The Hearing, The Seeing. **42:11**

To Him belongs the pass keys of the heavens and the earth. He extends provision for whomever He wills and measures it. Truly, He is The Knowing of everything. **42:12**

He has fixed limits for everything He has created and made the limits firm. He has fixed its working and made the working delicate. He has fixed its direction and it does not transgress the limits of its position, nor fall short of reaching the end of its aim. It did not disobey when it was commanded to move at His will. How could it do so when all matters are governed by His will? He is the producer of varieties of things without exercise of imagination, without the urge of an impulse, hidden in Him, without the benefit of any experiment taken from the vicissitudes of time and without any partner who might have assisted Him in creating wonderful things. Thus, the creation was completed by His order. It bowed to His obedience and responded to His call. The laziness of any slug or the inertness of any excuse-finder did not prevent it from doing so. He straightened the curves of the things and fixed their limits. With His power He created coherence in their contradictory parts and joined together the factors of similarity. Then He separated them in varieties which differ in limits, quantities, properties and shapes. All this is new creation. He made them firm and shaped them according as He wished and invented them. Sermon 91

He laid down the law of the way of life for you, that with which He charged Noah and what We revealed to **you** *and that with which We charged Abraham and Moses and Jesus. Perform the prescribed way of life and be not split up in it. Troublesome for the ones who are polytheists is that to which* **you** *have called them. God elects for Himself whomever He wills and guides the penitent to Himself.* **42:13**
They split not up until after the knowledge drew near them through insolence between themselves. If it were not for a Word that preceded from **your** *Lord—until a term, that which is determined—it would be decided between them. Truly, those who were given as inheritance the Book after them are in uncertainty, in grave doubt about it.* **42:14**

The Book of God is that through which you see, you speak and you hear. Sermon 132

Then, for that, call to this. Go straight as **you** *were commanded. Follow not their desires. Say: I believed in what God caused to descend from a Book. I was commanded to be just among you. God is our Lord and your Lord. For us are our actions and for you, your actions. There is no disputation between us and between you. God will gather us together. To Him is the Homecoming.* **42:15**

Certainly, only doubtful innovations cause ruin except those from which God may protect. In God's authority lies the safety of your affairs. Therefore, render Him such obedience as is neither blameworthy, nor insincere. Sermon 169

Those who argue with one another about God, after He was assented to, their disputations are null and void with their Lord, and on them is His anger. For them will be a severe punishment. **42:16**

Only rightfulness should attract you while wrongfulness should detract you. 130

It is God Who caused the Book to descend with The Truth and the Balance. What causes **you** *to recognize it so that perhaps the Hour is near?* **42:17**

Certainly, these people are in agreement in disliking my authority. I will carry on until I perceive disunity among you, because if they succeed in spite of the unsoundness of their view, the whole organization of Muslims will be shattered. They are hankering after this world out of jealousy against him on whom God has bestowed it. So they intend to revert the matters to the pre-Islamic period. On us it is obligatory, for your sake, to abide by the Book of God (Quran), the Sublime, and the conduct of *the Prophet* (Q7:158), peace and the mercy of God be upon him, to stand by His rights and to revive his *sunna*. Sermon 169

Seeking to hasten are those who believe not in it. Those who believed are ones who are apprehensive of it. They know that it is The Truth, those who altercate, truly, about the Hour are, certainly, going far astray. **42:18**

God sent *the Prophet* (Q7:158), peace and the mercy of God be upon him, as a caller towards Truth and a witness over the creatures. *The Prophet* (Q7:158) conveyed the messages of God tirelessly and without any negligence. He fought His enemies in the cause of God unflaggingly and without pleading excuses. He is the foremost of all who practice God-consciousness and the power of perception of all those who achieve guidance. Sermon 116

God is Subtle with His servants. He provides to whom He wills. He is The Strong, The Almighty. **42:19**

I praise God, seeking completion of His Blessing, submitting to His Glory and expecting safety from committing sin. Sermon 2

Whoever had been wanting cultivation of the world to come, We increase his cultivation for him. Whoever had been wanting cultivation of the present, We give him of it. He has not a share in the world to come. **42:20**

He is the Giver of all reward and distinction, and Dispeller of all calamities and hardships. Sermon 82

Or ascribe they associates who laid down the law of the way of life for them for which God gives not permission? Were it not for a decisive word, it would be decided among them. Truly, the ones who are unjust, for them is a painful punishment. **42:21**

O my God! We seek **Your** protection from turning away from **Your** command, or revolting against **Your** religion, or being led away by our desires instead of by guidance that comes from **You**. Sermon 215

You *will see the ones who are unjust as ones who are apprehensive of what they earned and it is that which falls on them. Those who believed and did as the ones in accord with morality, are in the well-watered meadows of the Gardens. For them will be whatever they will from their Lord. That it is the great grace.* **42:22**

That is what God gives as good tidings to His servants who have believed and the ones who have acted in accord with morality Say: I ask you not for compensation, but for the affection for kin, and whoever gains benevolence, We will increase for him goodness in it. **42:23**

Among the proofs of His creation is the creation of the skies which are fastened without pillars and stand without support. He called them. They responded obediently and humbly without being lazy or loathsome. If they had not acknowledged His Godhead and obeyed Him, He would not have made them the place for His throne, the abode of His angels and the destination: *To Him Words of what is good rise and He exalts an action in accord with morality* ... (Q35:10) of the creatures. Sermon 182

Or they say: He devised against God a lie. But if God wills He would have sealed over ***your*** *heart. God blots out falsehood and verifies The Truth by His Words. Truly, He is Knowing of what is in the breasts.* **42:24**

Know that—may God have mercy on you—you are living at a time when those who speak about right are few, when tongues are loath to utter the truth and those who stick to the right are humiliated. The people of this time are engaged in disobedience. Their youth are wicked, their old men are sinful, their learned men are hypocrites, and their speakers are sycophants. Their young ones do not respect their elders, and their rich men do not support the destitute. Sermon 232

He accepts the remorse of His servants and pardons their evil deeds. He knows what you accomplish. **42:25**
He responds to those who believed and did as the ones in accord with morality, and increases them of His grace. As for the ones who are ungrateful, theirs will be a severe punishment. **42:26**

God ... is aware of whatever is hidden in the hearts and whatever lies behind the unseen. Sermon 192

If God extended the provision for His servants, they would be insolent in the earth, but He sends down by measure whatever He wills. Truly, He is The Aware, The Seeing of His servants. **42:27**

O God's human being! I advise you to be God-conscious which is the provision for the next world and with it is your return. The provision would take you to your destination and the return would be successful. The best one who is able to make people listen has called towards it and the best listener has listened to it. So the caller has proclaimed and the listener has listened and preserved. Sermon 114

He it is Who sends down plenteous rain water after they despaired and He unfolds His mercy. He is The Protector, The Worthy of Praise. **42:28**

Praise belongs to God (Q1:2) Who made me such that I have not died, nor am I sick, nor have my veins been infected with disease, nor have I been hauled up for my evil acts, nor am I without progeny, nor have I forsaken my religion, nor do I disbelieve in my Lord, nor do I feel strangeness with my faith, nor is my intelligence affected, nor have I been punished with the punishment of peoples before me. I am a servant in **Your** possession. I have been guilty of excesses over myself. **You** have exhausted **Your** pleas over me and I have no plea before **You**. I have no power to take except what **You** give me. I cannot evade except what **You** save me from. Sermon 215

Among His signs are the creation of the heavens and the earth and whatever of moving creatures He disseminated in them. He has the power of amassing them when He wills. **42:29**

I swear by God Who gave life to plants and animals. Letter 43

Whatever affliction lit on you is because of what your hands earned. He pardons much. **42:30**
You are not ones who frustrate Him on the earth. There is not for you other than God either a protector or a helper. **42:31**

O God's human being! I advise you to be God-conscious which is the provision for the next world and with it is your return. The provision would take you to your destination and the return would be successful. The best one who is able to make people listen has called towards it and the best listener has listened to it. So the caller has proclaimed and the listener has listened and preserved. Sermon 114

Among His signs are the ones that run on the sea like landmarks. **42:32**
If He wills, He stills the wind. Then, they would stay, that which is motionless on the surface. Truly, in that are signs for every enduring and grateful one. **42:33**
Or He wreck them because of what they earned. He pardons them from much. **42:34**

I bear witness that *there is no god but God* (Q47:19) by virtue of belief, certainty, sincerity and conviction. I also bear witness that *Muhammad* (Q48:29), peace and the mercy of God be upon him, is *His servant* (Q17:1) and *Prophet* (Q7:158) whom He deputed when the signs of guidance were obliterated and the ways of religion were desolate. So he threw open the truth, gave advice to the people, guided them towards righteousness and ordered them to be moderate. May God bless him ... Sermon 194

Those who dispute Our signs know that there is no asylum for them. **42:35**
So, whatever thing you were given is the enjoyment of this present life. What is with God is better and is that which endures for those who believed and put their trust in their Lord **42:36**
and those who avoid the major sins and the indecencies and they forgive when they were angry **42:37**
and those who responded to their Lord and performed their formal prayer and their affairs are by counsel among themselves, and who spend of what We provided them, **42:38**
and those who, when insolence lit on them, they help each other. **42:39**

It seems as if they never lived in this world and as if the next world had always been their abode. They have made lonely the place where they were living, and are now living where they used to feel lonely. They remained busy about what they had to leave, and did not care for where they were to go. Now they cannot remove themselves from evil, nor add to their virtues They were attached to the world and it deceived them. They trusted it and it overturned them. Sermon 188

The recompense for an evil deed is the like of an evil deed. Then, whoever pardoned and made things right, his compensation is due from God. Truly, He loves not the ones who are unjust. **42:40**
As whoever helped himself after an injustice, so those, there is not any way against them. **42:41**

By God, even if I had found that by such money women have been married or servant-maids have been purchased, I would have returned it to its owners because there is wide scope in dispensation of justice. He who finds it hard to act justly will find it harder to deal with injustice. Sermon 15

The way is only against those who do wrong to humanity and are insolent in and on the earth unrightfully. Those, for them is a painful punishment. **42:42**

O God's human being! Where are those who were allowed long ages to live? They enjoyed bounty. They were taught. They learned. They were given time. They passed it in vain. They were kept healthy. They forgot their duty. They were allowed a long period of life, were handsomely provided for, were warned of grievous punishment and were promised great rewards. You should avoid sins that lead to destruction and vices that attract the wrath of God. Sermon 82

Whoever endured patiently and forgave, truly, that is, certainly, a sign of constancy of affairs. **42:43**

I bear witness that *there is no god but God* (Q47:19), by virtue of belief, certainty, sincerity and conviction. I also bear witness that *Muhammad* (Q48:29), peace and the mercy of God be upon him, is *His servant* (Q17:1), and *Prophet* (Q7:158), whom He deputed when the signs of guidance were obliterated and the ways of religion were desolate. So he threw

open the truth, gave advice to the people, guided them towards righteousness and ordered them to be moderate. May God bless him ... Sermon 194

Whomever God causes to go astray has no protector apart from Him. **You** *will see the ones who are unjust when they would see the punishment. They will say: Is there any way of turning it back?* **42:44**

Mind yourself and consider for awhile as though you had reached the end of life and had been buried under the earth. Then your actions will be presented before you in the place where the oppressor cries "Alas" while he who wasted his life yearns for return to the world, *but time was none to escape.* (Q38:3) Letter 41

You *will see them being presented to it as ones who are humbled by a sense of humility looking on with secretive glances. Those who believed will say: Truly, the ones who are losers are those who lost themselves and their people on the Day of Resurrection. Truly, the ones who are unjust will be in an abiding punishment* **42:45**
that there had not been for them any protector to help them other than God. He whom God causes to go astray, there is not for him any way. **42:46**

Your ultimate goal of reward or punishment is before you. Behind your back is the hour of Resurrection which is driving you on. Keep yourself light and overtake the forward ones. The first ones who have preceded await the last ones. Sermon 21

Respond to the call of your Lord before a Day approaches for which there is no turning back from God. There will be no shelter for you on that Day, nor is there for you any refusal. **42:47**

When the earthquake occurs, the Day of Resurrection approaches with all its severities, the people of every worshipping place cling to it, all the devotees cling to the object of their devotion and all the followers cling to their leader. Then on that Day even the opening of an eye in the air and the sound of a footstep on the ground will be assigned its due through His Justice and His Equity. On that Day many an argument will prove void and a contention for excuses will stand rejected. Sermon 222

Truly, when We caused the human being to experience mercy from Us, he was glad in it. But when evil deeds light on him—because of what his hands sent—then, truly, the human being is ungrateful. **42:48**

Populated places were brightened through him when previously there was dark misguidance, overpowering ignorance and rude habits, and people regarded unlawful as lawful, humiliated the person of wisdom, passed lives when there were no prophets and died as ungrateful. Sermon 151

To God belongs the dominion of the heavens and the earth. He creates what He wills. He bestows females on whom He wills. He bestows males on whom He wills. **42:49**
He couples them, males and females. He makes barren whom He wills. Truly, He is Knowing, Powerful. **42:50**

Praise belongs to God (Q1:2) Who made praise the Key for His remembrance, a means for increase of His bounty and a guide for His Attributes and Dignity. Sermon 157

It had not been for a mortal that God speak to him, but by revelation or from behind a partition

or that He send a Messenger to reveal by His permission what He wills. Truly, He is Lofty, Wise. **42:51**
Thus, We revealed to ***you*** *the Spirit of Our command.* ***You*** *had not been informed what the Book is nor what is belief, but We made it a light by which We guide whomever We will of Our servants. Truly,* ***you, you*** *guide to a straight path—* **42:52**
the path of God, to whom belongs whatever is in the heavens and whatever is in and on the earth. Truly, will not all affairs come home to God? **42:53**

This world and the hereafter have submitted to Him their reins. The skies and earths have flung their keys towards Him. The thriving trees bow to Him in the morning and evening, producing for Him flaming fire from their branches and, at His command, turn their own feed into ripe fruits. Sermon 133

CHAPTER 43: THE ORNAMENTS (al-Zukhruf)

Ha Mim **43:1**
By the clear Book, **43:2**
We, truly, made it an Arabic Recitation so that perhaps you will be reasonable. **43:3**

Go ahead with the remembrance of God, for it is the best remembrance. Long for that which He has promised to the pious, for His promise is the most true promise. Tread the course of *the Prophet,* (Q7:158), peace and the mercy of God be upon him, for it is the most distinguished course. Follow his *sunna*, for it is the most right of all behaviors. Learn the Quran, for it is the fairest of discourses. Understand it thoroughly, for it is the best blossoming of hearts. Seek cure with its light, for it is the cure for hearts. Recite it beautifully, for it is the most beautiful narration. Certainly, a scholar who acts not according to his knowledge is like the off-headed ignorant who does not find relief from his ignorance, but the plea of God is greater on the learned and grief more incumbent. He is more blameworthy before God. Sermon 110

Truly, it is in the essence of the Book from Our Presence, Lofty, Wise. **43:4**

Certainly, these people are in agreement in disliking my authority. I will carry on until I perceive disunity among you, because if they succeed in spite of the unsoundness of their view, the whole organization of Muslims will be shattered. They are hankering after this world out of jealousy against him on whom God has bestowed it. So they intend to revert the matters to the pre-Islamic period. On us it is obligatory, for your sake, to abide by the Book of God (Quran), the Sublime, and the conduct of *the Prophet* (Q7:158), peace and the mercy of God be upon him, to stand by His rights and to revive his *sunna*. Sermon 169

Will We turn away the Remembrance from you, overlooking as you had been a folk, ones who are excessive? **43:5**

Know that this Quran is an adviser who never deceives, a leader who never misleads and a narrator who never speaks a lie. No one will sit beside this Quran, but when he rises, he will achieve one addition or one diminution—addition in his guidance or elimination in his spiritual blindness. You should also know that no one will need anything after guidance from the Quran and no one will be free from want before guidance from the Quran. Seek cure from the Quran for your ailments and seek its assistance in your distress. It contains a cure for the worst diseases, namely unbelief, hypocrisy, revolt and misguidance. Pray to God through it and turn to God with its love ... There is nothing like it through which the people should turn to God, the Sublime. Sermon 176

How many a Prophet sent We among the ancient ones! **43:6**
Approaches them not a Prophet, but that they had been ridiculing him. **43:7**
Then, We caused to perish the more vigorous in courage than them and the example of the ancient ones passed. **43:8**
Certainly, if ***you*** *had asked them: Who created the heavens and the earth? They will, certainly, say: The Almighty, The Knowing created them,* **43:9**
Who made the earth a cradle for you and made in it ways for you so that perhaps you would be truly guided **43:10**
and Who sent down water from heaven in measure? Then, We revived with it a lifeless land. Thus, you are brought out. **43:11**

When Almighty God created the openings of the atmosphere, the expanse of firmament and strata of winds, He flowed into it water whose waves were stormy and whose surges leapt one over the other. He loaded it on dashing wind and breaking typhoons, ordered them to shed it back as rain, gave the wind control over the vigor of the rain, and acquainted it with its limitations. The wind blew under it while water flowed furiously over it. Sermon 1

It is He Who created all the pairs and assigned for you the boats and the flocks on which you ride **43:12**
so that you sit upon their backs. Again, remember the divine blessing of your Lord when you are seated on them and you say: Glory be to Him Who caused this to be subservient to us and we had not been ones who are equal to it! **43:13**
Truly, we, certainly, are to our Lord ones who are turning. **43:14**
Yet they assigned with Him a part of some of His servants. Truly, the human being is clearly ungrateful. **43:15**

Whoever takes a partner for **You** is ungrateful according to what is stated in **Your** unambiguous verses and indicated by the evidence of **Your** clear arguments. Sermon 91

Or took He to Himself daughters from what He creates and selected He sons for you? **43:16**
If good tidings were given to one of them of what he cited as an example from The Merciful, his face stayed one that is clouded over and he chokes. **43:17**
Is whoever is brought up amid glitter one who is without clarity when he is in an altercation? **43:18**
Made they the angels—who themselves are servants of The Merciful—females? Bore they witness to their creation? Their giving testimony will be written down. They will be asked about it. **43:19**
They would say: If willed The Merciful, we would not have worshiped them. They have no knowledge of that. They do nothing but guess. **43:20**

If God had wanted to create Adam from a light whose glare would have dazzled the eyes, whose handsomeness would have amazed the wits and whose fragrance would have caught the breath, He could have done so. If He had done so people would have bowed to him in humility and the trial of the angels through him would have become easier, but God, the Almighty, tries His creatures by means of those things whose real nature they do not know in order to distinguish good and bad for them through the trial, and to remove vanity from them and keep them away from pride and self-admiration. Sermon 192

Or gave We them any Book before this so they are ones who hold fast to it? **43:21**

The Book of God is among you. It speaks. Its tongue does not falter. It is a house whose pillars do not fall down. It is a power whose supporters are never defeated. Sermon 132

Nay! They said: We found our fathers in a community holding to a way of life and we are, truly, in their footsteps ones who are truly guided. **43:22**

O my God! We seek **Your** protection from turning away from **Your** command, or revolting against **Your** religion, or being led away by our desires instead of by guidance that comes from **You.** Sermon 215

Thus, We sent not a warner to any town before ***you*** *without ones who are given ease saying: We found our fathers in a community. We are, certainly, ones who imitate their footsteps.* **43:23**

I bear witness that *Muhammad* (Q48:29), peace and the mercy of God be upon him, is His *servant* (Q17:1) and His *Prophet.* (Q7:158) He sent him for enforcement of His commands, for exhausting His pleas and for presenting warnings against eternal punishment. Sermon 82

He said: Even if I brought about better guidance for you than what you found your fathers on. They would say: Truly, we, in that with which you were sent are ones who disbelieve. **43:24**

O my God! I seek **Your** protection from becoming destitute despite **Your** riches, from being misguided despite **Your** guidance, from being molested in **Your** realm and from being humiliated while authority rests with **You.** O my God! Let my spirit be the first of those good objects that **You** take from me and the first trust out of **Your** favors held in trust with me. Sermon 215

So, We requited them. Then, look on how had been the Ultimate End of the ones who deny. **43:25**

Everyone of them is ... alone although they are a group, and they are strangers, even though friends. They are unaware of morning after a night and of evening after a day. The night or the day when they departed has become ever existent for them. They found the dangers of their place of stay more serious than they had apprehended. They witnessed that its signs were greater than they had guessed. Sermon 220

Mention when Abraham said to his father and his folk: Truly, I am released from obligation to what you worship **43:26**
other than He Who originated me and, truly, He will guide me. **43:27**
He made it an enduring Word among his posterity, so that perhaps they will return. **43:28**
Nay! I gave enjoyment to these and to their fathers until The Truth drew near them and a clear Messenger. **43:29**
When The Truth drew near them, they said: This is sorcery and we are ones who disbelieve in it. **43:30**
They said: Why was this, the Quran, not sent down to some eminent man of the two towns? **43:31**

One of the firm decisions of God in the Wise Reminder (Quran), upon which He bestows reward or gives punishment and through which He likes or dislikes, is that it will not benefit a person, even though he exerts himself and acts sincerely, if he leaves this world to meet God with one of these acts without repenting, namely that he believed in a partner with God during his obligatory worship or appeased his own anger by killing an individual or spoke about acts committed by others or sought fulfillment of his needs from people by introducing an innovation in his religion or met people with a double face or moved among them with a double tongue. Understand this because an illustration is a guide for its like. Sermon 153

Would they divide the mercy of ***your*** *Lord? It is We Who divided out among them their livelihood in this present life. Exalted are some of them above some others in degree so that some take to themselves others in their bondage. The mercy of* ***your*** *Lord is better than what they gather.* **43:32**

Praise belongs to God (Q1:2) from Whose mercy no one loses hope. Sermon 45

Were it not that humanity be one community, would We have made for whoever is ungrateful for The Merciful, roofs of silver for their houses, and stairways which they would scale up **43:33**
and for their houses, doors, and couches on which they would recline **43:34**
and ornaments? Yet all this would have been nothing, but enjoyment of this present life. The world to come with your Lord is for the ones who are God-conscious. **43:35**
Whoever withdraws from the Remembrance of The Merciful, We allotted for him a satan, so he is a comrade for him. **43:36**

Everyone should fear God, should admonish himself, should send forward his repentance and should overpower his desire, because his death is hidden from him. His desires deceive him. Satan keeps posted about him. He beautifies his sin for him so that he may commit it. He prompts him to delay repentance until his desires cause him to be the most negligent. Pity is for the negligent person whose life itself would be a proof against him and his own days, passed in sin, will lead him to punishment. Sermon 64

Truly, they bar them from the way, but they assume that they are ones who are truly guided. **43:37**
Then, when he drew near us he would say: Would that there were a distance between me and between ***you*** *of two sunrises! Miserable was the comrade.* **43:38**

O God! I bear witness that he who likens **You** with the separateness of the limbs or with the joining of the extremities of his body did not acquaint his inner self with knowledge about **You**. His heart did not secure conviction to the effect that there is no partner for **You**. It is as though he has not heard the wrongful followers disclaiming their false gods by sayings. By God! *Truly we have been clearly wandering astray when we made you equal with the Lord of the worlds.* (Q26:97-98) Sermon 91

It will never profit you this Day as you did wrong. You will be ones who are partners in the punishment. **43:39**
So, have ***you*** *caused someone unwilling to hear, to hear or will* ***you*** *guide the unwilling to see, or someone who had been clearly going astray?* **43:40**

Right cannot be achieved without effort. Which is the house besides this one to protect? ... What is the matter with you? What is your ailment? What is your cure? ... Will there be talk without action, carelessness without God-consciousness and greed in things not right? Sermon 29

Even if We take ***you*** *away, We will, truly, be ones who requite them* **43:41**
or We will cause ***you*** *to see what We promised them. Then, We are ones who are omnipotent over*

them. **43:42**
So, hold **you** *fast to what was revealed to* **you**. *Truly,* **you** *are on a straight path.* **43:43**

Be aware that the paths of religion are one. Its highways are straight. He who follows them achieves the aim and secures the objective. He who stood away from them goes astray and incurs repentance. Act for the day for which provisions are stored and when the intentions would be tested. If a person's own intelligence, which is present with him, does not help him, the wits of others, which are remote from him, are more unhelpful and those who are away from him even more useless. Dread the fire whose flame is severe, whose hollow is deep, whose dress is iron and whose drink is bloody pus. Be aware! The good name of a person retained by God, the Sublime, among the people is better than wealth inherited by those who would not praise Him. Sermon 120

Truly, this is a remembrance for **you** *and* **your** *folk. You will be asked.* **43:44**

God, the Almighty, has not counseled anyone on other than the lines of this Quran, for it is the strong rope of God and His trustworthy means. It contains the blossoming of the heart and springs of knowledge. For the heart there is no other gloss than the Quran, although those who remembered it have passed away, while those who forgot or pretended to have forgotten it have remained. If you see any good, give your support to it, but if you see evil, evade it, because *the Messenger of God* (Q48:29) used to say: O son of Adam, do good and evade evil. By doing so you will be treading correctly. Sermon 176

Ask ones whom We sent before **you** *of Our Messengers: Made We gods other than the Merciful to be worshiped?* **43:45**
Certainly, We sent Moses with Our signs to Pharaoh and his Council. So, he said: Truly, I am a Messenger of the Lord of the worlds. **43:46**
But when he drew near them with Our signs, that is when they laugh at them. **43:47**
We cause them not to see any sign, but it was greater than its sister's sign. We took them with the punishment so that perhaps they would return. **43:48**
They said: O one who is a sorcerer! Call for us to **your** *Lord by the compact He made with* **you**. *Truly, We will be ones who are truly guided.* **43:49**
But when We removed the punishment from them, that is when they break their oath! **43:50**
Pharaoh proclaimed to his folk. He said: O my folk! Is not the dominion of Egypt for me and these rivers run beneath me? Will you not, then, perceive? **43:51**
Or am I better than this one who is despicable, who scarcely makes things clear? **43:52**
Why were bracelets of gold not cast down on him or the angels drawn near to him as ones who are connected with one another? **43:53**
Thus, he irritated his folk. Then, they obeyed him. Truly, they had been a folk, ones who disobey. **43:54**
So, when they provoked against Us, We requited them and drowned them one and all **43:55**
and We made them a thing of the past and a parable for later ages. **43:56**
When the son of Mary was cited as an example, that is when **your** *folk cry aloud* **43:57**
and said: Are our gods better or is he? They cited him to **you** *not but to be argumentative. Nay! They are a contentious folk.* **43:58**
He was but a servant to whom We were gracious, and We made him an example to the Children of Jacob. **43:59**
If We will, We would have assigned angels to succeed among you on the earth. **43:60**

Truly, he is with the knowledge of the Hour, so contest not about it and follow Me. This is a straight path. **43:61**
Let not Satan bar you. Truly, he is a clear enemy to you. **43:62**
When Jesus drew near with the clear portents, he said: Truly, I drew near you with wisdom and in order to make manifest to you some of that about which you are at variance in it. So, be God-conscious and obey me. **43:63**
Truly, God He is my Lord and your Lord so worship Him. This is a straight path. **43:64**
The confederates were at variance among themselves. So, woe to those who did wrong from the punishment of a painful Day. **43:65** ***

Looked they on but for the Hour that will approach them suddenly while they are not aware? **43:66**

There remain a few people in whose case the remembrance of their return to God on the Day of Judgment keeps their eyes bent and the awareness of the Resurrection moves them to tears. Some of them are scared away from the world and disperse. Some are frightened and subdued. Some are quiet as if muzzled. Some are praying sincerely. Some are grief-stricken and pain-ridden whom fear has confined to namelessness. Disgrace has shrouded them, so they are in the sea of bitter water, their mouths are closed and their hearts are bruised. They preached until they were tired. They were oppressed until they were disgraced. They were killed until their numbers dwindled. Sermon 32

Friends on that Day will be enemies some to some others, but ones who are God-conscious. **43:67**

Among the God-conscious are the people of distinction. Their speech is to the point. Their dress is moderate. Their gait is humble. They keep their eyes closed to what God has made unlawful for them. They put their ears to that knowledge which is beneficial to them. They remain in the time of trials as though they remain in comfort. If there had not been fixed periods of life ordained for each, their spirits would not have remained in their bodies even for the twinkling of an eye because of their eagerness for the reward and fear of chastisement. The greatness of the Creator is seated in their heart and so everything else appears small in their eyes. Thus, to them Paradise is as though they see it and are enjoying its favors. To them, Hell is also as if they see it and are suffering punishment in it. Sermon 193

O My servants! This Day there shall be no fear in you nor will you feel remorse. **43:68**

They will be within God's sight and will hear every one who would call them. They will have the dress of helplessness and covering of submission and indignity. At this time contrivances will disappear. Sermon 82

It will be said to those who believed in Our signs and had been ones who submit to God: **43:69**

I bear witness that *there is no god but God* (Q47:19), by virtue of belief, certainty, sincerity and conviction. I also bear witness that *Muhammad* (Q48:29), peace and the mercy of God be upon him, is *His servant* (Q17:1) and *Prophet* (Q7:158) whom He deputed when the signs of guidance were obliterated and the ways of religion were desolate. So he threw open the truth, gave advice to the people, guided them towards righteousness and ordered them to be moderate. May God bless him ... Sermon 194

Enter the Garden, you and your spouses, to be walking with joy! **43:70**

Mind the obligations! Mind the obligations! Fulfill them for God and they will take you to the Garden. Surely, God has made unlawful the things which are not unknown and made lawful the things which are without defect. Sermon 167

There will be passed around among them platters of gold and goblets. In it will be whatever souls lust for and all that in which the eyes delight. You will be ones who dwell in it forever. **43:71**
This is the Garden that you were given as inheritance because of what you had been doing. **43:72**
For you there will be much sweet fruit from which you will eat. **43:73**
Truly, ones who sin will be in the punishment of hell, ones who will dwell in it forever. **43:74**
It will not be decreased for them and they will be ones who are seized with despair in it. **43:75**

Hell! Everyone of them is ... alone although they are a group, and they are strangers, even though friends. They are unaware of morning after a night and of evening after a day. The night or the day when they departed has become ever existent for them. They found the dangers of their place of stay more serious than they had apprehended, and they witnessed that its signs were greater than they had guessed. Sermon 220

We did not wrong them, but they had been ones who are unjust. **43:76**
They would cry out: O Malik! Let **your** *Lord finish us. He would say: Truly, you will be ones who abide.* **43:77**
Certainly, We brought about The Truth to you, but most of you are ones who dislike The Truth. **43:78**

I bear witness that *there is no god but God* (Q47:19), by virtue of belief, certainty, sincerity and conviction. I also bear witness that *Muhammad* (Q48:29), peace and the mercy of God be upon him, is *His servant* (Q17:1) and *Prophet* (Q7:158) whom He deputed when the signs of guidance were obliterated and the ways of religion were desolate. So he threw open the truth, gave advice to the people, guided them towards righteousness and ordered them to be moderate. May God bless him ... Sermon 194

Or fixed they on some affair? Then, We, too, are ones who fix some affair. **43:79**
Assume they that We hear not their secret thoughts and their conspiring secretly? Yea! Our Messengers are near them writing down. **43:80**

God never allowed His creation to remain without a Prophet, one deputized by Him, or a Book sent down from Him, or a binding argument, or a standing plea. These Messengers were such that they did not fear that they were few in comparison to the large numbers of their falsifiers. Among them was either a predecessor who would name the one to follow or the follower who had been introduced by the predecessor. Sermon 1

Say: If The Merciful had had a son, then, I would be first of the ones who worship. **43:81**
Glory be to the Lord of the heavens and the earth, the Lord of the Throne, from all that they allege! **43:82**

O God's human being! I advise you to be God-conscious which is the provision for the next world and with it is your return. The provision would take you to your destination and the return would be successful. The best one who is able to make people listen has called towards it and the best listener has listened to it. So the caller has proclaimed and the listener has listened and persevered. Sermon 114

So, let them engage in idle talk and play until they encounter their Day which they are promised. **43:83**

God the Sublime, has said: *Truly those who said: Our Lord is God. Moreover, they go straight and the angels come forth to them: Neither fear nor feel remorse, but rejoice in the Gardens which you have been promised.* (Q41:30) You have said: Our Lord is God. Then keep steadfast to His Book, to the way of His command and to the virtuous course of His worship. Thereafter do not go out of it. Do not introduce innovations in it. Do not turn away from it, because those who go away from this course will be cut off from the mercy of God on the Day of Judgment. Sermon 176

It is He Who is in the heaven, God, and on the earth, God. He is The Wise, The Knowing. **43:84**

O God's human being! I advise you to be God-conscious which is the provision for the next world and with it is your return. The provision would take you to your destination and the return would be successful. The best one who is able to make people listen has called towards it and the best listener has listened to it. So the caller has proclaimed and the listener has listened and preserved. Sermon 114

Blessed be He to whom belongs the dominion of the heavens and the earth and whatever is between them and with Whom is the knowledge of the Hour and to Whom you will be returned. **43:85**

The face of right has become clear for the wanderer. The approaching moment has raised the veil from its face and signs have appeared for those who search for them. Sermon 108

Those whom they call to possess no power other than Him for intercession, only whoever bore witness to The Truth, and they know. **43:86**

If ***you*** *asked them: Who created them? They would, certainly, say: God. Then, how are they misled?* **43:87**

Know that—may God have mercy on you—you are living at a time when those who speak about right are few, when tongues are loath to utter the truth and those who stick to the right are humiliated. The people of this time are engaged in disobedience. Their youth are wicked, their old men are sinful, their learned men are hypocrites, and their speakers are sycophants. Their young ones do not respect their elders, and their rich men do not support the destitute. Sermon 232

His saying: O my Lord! Truly, these are a folk who believe not, **43:88**

so overlook them and say: Peace. They will know. **43:89**

His heart did not secure conviction to the effect that there is no partner for **You.** Sermon 91

Chapter 44: The Smoke (al-Dukhān)

Ha Mim. **44;1**

By the clear Book **44:2**

truly, We caused it to descend on a blessed night. Truly, We had been ones who warn. **44:3**

The Prophet (Q7:158), peace and the mercy of God be upon him, left among you the same which other Prophets left among their peoples, because Prophets do not leave them untended in dark without a clear path and a standing sign, namely the Book of your Creator clarifying its permission and prohibitions, its obligations and discretion, its repealing injunctions and the repealed ones, its permissible matters and compulsory ones, its particulars and the general ones, its lessons and illustrations, its long and the short ones, its clear and obscure ones, detailing its abbreviations and clarifying its obscurities. In (the Quran) there are some verses whose knowledge is obligatory and others whose ignorance by the people is permissible. It also contains what appears to be obligatory according to the Book, but its repeal is signified by the actions of *the Prophet* (Q7:158) (*sunna*), peace and the mercy of God be upon him, or that which appears compulsory according to the actions of *the Prophet* (Q7:158) (*sunna*), peace and the mercy of God be upon him, but the Book allows not following it. Or there are those which are obligatory in a given time, but not so after that time. Its prohibitions also differ. Some are major regarding which there exists the threat of hellfire and others are minor for which there is the hope of forgiveness. There are also those of which a small portion is also acceptable to God, but they are capable of being expanded. Sermon 1

Every wise command is made clear in it, **44:4**
a command from Us. Truly, We had been ones who send it **44:5**
as a mercy from **your** *Lord. Truly, He is The Hearing, The Knowing,* **44:6**
Lord of the heavens and the earth and whatever is between them. If you had been ones who are certain. **44:7**

Praise belongs to God (Q1:2) from Whose mercy no one loses hope, from Whose bounty no one is deprived, from Whose forgiveness no one is disappointed and for Whose worship no one is too high. His mercy never ceases and His bounty never ceases. Sermon 45

There is no god but He. It is He Who gives life and causes to die. He is your Lord and the Lord of your ancient fathers. **44:8**
Nay! They play in uncertainty. **44:9**
Then, **you** *be on the watch for a Day when the heavens will bring a clear smoke* **44:10**
overcoming humanity. This is a painful punishment. **44:11**

When the earthquake occurs, the Day of Resurrection approaches with all its severities, the people of every worshipping place cling to it, all the devotees cling to the object of their devotion and all the followers cling to their leader. Then on that day even the opening of an eye in the air and the sound of a footstep on the ground will be assigned its due through His Justice and His Equity. On that day many an argument will prove void and a contention for excuses will stand rejected. Sermon 222

Our Lord! Remove **you** *the punishment from us! Truly, we are ones who believe.* **44:12**

The responsibility for what I say is guaranteed. I am answerable for it. He to whom experiences have clearly shown the past exemplary punishments given by God to peoples is prevented by God-consciousness from falling into doubt. Sermon 16

What will there be as a reminder for them? A clear Messenger drew near them. **44:13**
Again, they turned away from him and they said: He is one who is taught by others, one who is possessed. **44:14**

Truly, We are ones who remove the punishment for a little. Truly, you are ones who revert to ingratitude. **44:15**

O God's human being! Where are those who were allowed long ages to live? They enjoyed bounty. They were taught. They learned. They were given time. They passed it in vain. They were kept healthy. They forgot their duty. They were allowed a long period of life, were handsomely provided for, were warned of grievous punishment and were promised great rewards. You should avoid sins that lead to destruction and vices that attract the wrath of God. Sermon 82

On the Day when We will seize by force with the greatest attack, truly, We will be ones who requite. **44:16**

Your ultimate goal of reward or punishment is before you. Sermon 21

Certainly, We tried a folk of Pharaoh before them when there drew near them a generous Messenger: **44:17**
Give back to me the servants of God, the Children of Jacob. Truly, I am a trustworthy Messenger to you. **44:18**
Rise not up against God. Truly, I am one who arrives with a clear authority. **44:19**
Truly, I took refuge in my Lord and your Lord so that you not stone me. **44:20**
But if you believe not in me, then, withdraw. **44:21**
So, he called on his Lord: Truly, these are a folk, ones who sin. **44:22**
He said: Set ***you*** *forth with my servants by night. Truly, you will be ones who are followed.* **44:23**
Leave the sea calmly as it is. Truly, they will be an army, one that is drowned. **44:24**
How many they left behind of gardens and springs **44:25**
and crops and generous stations **44:26**
and prosperity in which they had been, ones who are joyful! **44:27**
Thus, We gave it as inheritance to another folk. **44:28**
Neither the heavens wept for them nor the earth nor had they been ones who are given respite. **44:29**

Alas! Alas! What has been lost is lost! What has gone is gone! The world has passed in its usual manner. *Neither the heavens wept for them nor the earth nor had they been ones who were given respite.* (Q44:29) Sermon 191

Certainly, We delivered the Children of Jacob from the despised punishment **44:30**
of Pharaoh. Truly, He had been one who exalts himself and was of the ones who are excessive. **44:31**
Certainly, We chose them with knowledge above the worlds **44:32**
and gave them the signs in which there was a clear trial. **44:33**
Truly, these say: **44:34**
There is nothing but our first singled out death and we will not be ones who are revived. **44:35**
Then, bring our fathers back if you had been ones who are sincere. **44:36**

They disputed in front of him about the serious news that they were concealing from him. Thus, someone would say "his condition is what it is" and would console them with hopes of his recovery, while another one would advocate patience on missing him, recalling to them the calamities that had befallen the earlier generations. Sermon 220

Are they better or a folk of Tubba and those who were before them? We caused them to perish. They, truly, had been ones who sin. **44:37**

Be aware! You strove hard in revolting and created mischief on the earth in open opposition to God and in challenging the believers over fighting. You should be God-conscious! God, in feeling proud of your vanity and boasting over ignorance, because this is the root of enmity and the design of Satan wherewith he has been deceiving past people and bygone ages with the result that they fell into the depression of ignorance and the hollows of misguidance, submitting to (Satan's) driving and accepting his leadership. The hearts of all the people were similar in this matter. Centuries passed by, one after the other, in just the same way. Sermon 192

We created not the heavens and the earth and whatever is between them as ones who play! **44:38**

O God's human being! I advise you to be God-conscious which is the provision for the next world and with it is your return. The provision would take you to your destination and the return would be successful. The best one who is able to make people listen has called towards it and the best listener has listened to it. So the caller has proclaimed and the listener has listened and preserved. Sermon 114

We created them not but with The Truth but most of them know not. **44:39**

God sent *the Prophet* (Q7:158), peace and the mercy of God be upon him, as a caller towards Truth and a witness over the creatures. *The Prophet* (Q7:158) conveyed the messages of God tirelessly and without any negligence. He fought His enemies in the cause of God unflaggingly and without pleading excuses. He is the foremost of all who practice God-consciousness and the power of perception of all those who achieve guidance. Sermon 116

Truly, the Day of Decision is the time appointed for them one and all, **44:40**
a Day when a defender will not avail another defender at all nor will they be helped **44:41**
but him on whom God had mercy. Truly, He is The Almighty, The Compassionate. **44:42**

O the Most Merciful of all! O my God! Surely, **You** are powerful over whatever **You** will. Sermon 143

Truly, the tree of Zaqqum **44:43**
will be the food of the sinful. **44:44**
Like molten copper it will bubble in the bellies, **44:45**
like boiling, scalding water. **44:46**
It will be said: Take him and drag him violently into the depths of hellfire. **44:47**
Again, then, unloose over his head the punishment of scalding water! **44:48**
Experience this! Truly, ***you, you*** *are seemingly the mighty, the generous.* **44:49**
Truly, this is what you had been contesting. **44:50**

The great calamity of that place is the hot water and entry into Hell, flames of eternal fire and intensity of blazes. There is no resting period, no gap for ease, no power to intervene, no death to bring about solace and no sleep to make him forget pain. He rather lies under several kinds of deaths and moment-to-moment punishment. We seek refuge with God. Sermon 82

Truly, the ones who are God-conscious will be in the station of trustworthiness **44:51**
among Gardens and springs **44:52**
wearing fine silk and brocade, ones who face one another. **44:53**
Thus, it is so. We will give in marriage lovely, most beautiful eyed ones. **44:54**
They will call therein for every kind of sweet fruit, ones that are safe. **44:55**
They will not experience death with them but the first singled out death. He will protect them from the punishment of hellfire, **44:56**
a grace from ***your*** *Lord. That, it is the winning the sublime triumph!* **44:57**

God, the Almighty, has sent down a guiding Book wherein He has explained virtue and vice. You should adopt the course of virtue whereby you will have guidance, and keep aloof from the direction of vice so that you remain on the right way. Mind the obligations! Mind the obligations! Fulfill them for God and they will take you to the Garden. Surely, God has made unlawful the things which are not unknown and made lawful the things which are without defect. Sermon 167

Truly, We made this easy in ***your*** *language so that perhaps they will recollect.* **44:58**

Know that this Quran is an adviser who never deceives, a leader who never misleads and a narrator who never speaks a lie. No one will sit beside this Quran, but when he rises, he will achieve one addition or one diminution—addition in his guidance or elimination in his spiritual blindness. You should also know that no one will need anything after guidance from the Quran and no one will be free from want before guidance from the Quran. Seek cure from the Quran for your ailments and seek its assistance in your distress. It contains a cure for the worst diseases, namely unbelief, hypocrisy, revolt and misguidance. Pray to God through it and turn to God with its love ... There is nothing like it through which the people should turn to God, the Sublime. Sermon 176

So, be on the watch! Truly, they are ones who watch. **44:59**

I praise Him for His continuous mercy and His copious bounties. Sermon 82

Chapter 45: The Ones Who Kneel (al-Jāthiyah)

Ha Mim **45:1**
The sending down the Book successively is from God, The Almighty, The Wise. **45:2**
Truly, in the heavens and the earth are signs for the ones who believe. **45:3**

I bear witness that *there is no god but God,* (Q47:19), by virtue of belief, certainty, sincerity and conviction. I also bear witness that *Muhammad* (Q48:29), peace and the mercy of God be upon him, is *His servant* (Q17:1) and *Prophet* (Q7:158), whom He deputed when the signs of guidance were obliterated and the ways of religion were desolate. So he threw open the truth, gave advice to the people, guided them towards righteousness and ordered them to be moderate. May God bless him ... Sermon 194

In your creation and what He disseminates of moving creatures are signs for a folk who are certain, **45:4**
the alternation of the nighttime and the daytime and what God caused to descend from the heaven

of provision. He gave life with it to the earth after its death and the diversifying of the winds—signs for a folk who are reasonable. **45:5**

When Almighty God created the openings of the atmosphere, the expanse of firmament and strata of winds, He flowed into it water whose waves were stormy and whose surges leapt one over the other. He loaded it on dashing wind and breaking typhoons, ordered them to shed it back as rain, gave the wind control over the vigor of the rain, and acquainted it with its limitations. The wind blew under it while water flowed furiously over it. Sermon 1

These are the signs of God We recount to **you** *with The Truth. Then, in which discourse, after God and His signs, will they believe?* **45:6**
Woe to every false, sinful one! **45:7**

I advise you, O people, to be God-conscious and to praise Him profusely for His favors to you and His reward for you and His obligations on you. See how He chose you for favors and dealt with you with mercy. You sinned openly. He kept you covered. You behaved in a way to incur His punishment, but He gave you more time. Sermon 188

He hears the signs of God being recounted to him. Again, he persists as one who grows arrogant as if he hears them not. So, give him good tidings of a painful punishment! **45:8**
If he knew anything about Our signs, he took them to himself in mockery. Those, for them is a despised punishment. **45:9**
Behind them there is hell. What they earned will avail them not at all nor whatever they took to themselves other than God as protectors. For them will be a tremendous punishment. **45:10**
This is a guidance. Those who were ungrateful for the signs of their Lord, for them there is a punishment of painful wrath. **45:11**

O my God! Let my spirit be the first of those good objects that **You** take from me and the first trust out of **Your** favors held in trust with me. Sermon 215

God! It is He Who caused the sea to be subservient to you that the boats may run through it by His command and so that you be looking for His grace and so that perhaps you will give thanks. **45:12**
He caused to be subservient to you whatever is in the heavens and whatever is in and on the earth. All is from Him. Truly, in that are signs for a folk who reflect. **45:13**

Subservient to **You** is the creation of the sky, the air, the winds and the water. Therefore, **You** look at the sun and moon, the plants and trees, water and stone, the alternation of this night and day, the flowing out of these seas, the large number of mountains and the height of their peaks, the diversity of languages and the variety of tongues. Then woe be to him who disbelieves in the Ordainer and denies the Ruler. They claim that they are like grass for which there is no cultivator, nor any maker for their diverse shapes. They have not relied on any argument for what they assert, nor on any research for what they have heard. Can there be any construction without a Constructor, or any offense without an offender? Sermon 185

Say to those who believed: Forgive those who hope not for the Days of God that He give recompense to a folk according to what they had been earning. **45:14**

Only such things as will earn for you a reward in the next world should please you and you should only feel sorry for losing rewards of the next world. If you attain worldly pomp and pleasures, then let not your happiness increase along with every enhancement of such pleasure. If you lose any of these pleasures, then do not feel sorry at the loss because you must only feel sorry at the loss of such things as will be of use to you in the next world. Letter 22

Whoever did as one in accord with morality, it is for himself and whoever did evil, it is against himself. Again, to your Lord you will be returned. **45:15**

... to Him returns whoever dies. Sermon 108

Certainly, We gave the Children of Jacob the Book, the critical judgment and the prophethood and We provided them from what is good and We gave them advantage over the worlds **45:16**
and We gave them clear portents of the command. They are not at variance until after the knowledge drew near them through insolence among themselves. Truly, **your** *Lord will decree between them on the Day of Resurrection about what they had been at variance in it.* **45:17** ***

Again, We assigned **you** *an open way of the command so follow it and follow not the desires of those who know not.* **45:18**

Know that this Quran is an adviser who never deceives, a leader who never misleads and a narrator who never speaks a lie. No one will sit beside this Quran, but when he rises, he will achieve one addition or one diminution—addition in his guidance or elimination in his spiritual blindness. You should also know that no one will need anything after guidance from the Quran and no one will be free from want before guidance from the Quran. Seek cure from the Quran for your ailments and seek its assistance in your distress. It contains a cure for the worst diseases, namely unbelief, hypocrisy, revolt and misguidance. Pray to God through it and turn to God with its love ... There is nothing like it through which the people should turn to God, the Sublime. Sermon 176

Truly, they will never avail **you** *against God at all. Truly, the ones who are unjust, some of them are protectors of some others. But God is Protector of the ones who are God-conscious.* **45:19**
This is a clear evidence for humanity and a guidance and a mercy for a folk who are certain. **45:20**

Believers are humble. Believers are admonishers. Believers are God-conscious. Sermon 153

Assumed those who sought to do evil deeds that We will make them equal with those who believed and did as the ones in accord with morality? Are their living and dying equal? How evil is the judgment they give! **45:21**

O my God! I seek **Your** protection from becoming destitute despite **Your** riches, from being misguided despite **Your** guidance, from being molested in **Your** realm and from being humiliated while authority rests with **You**. O my God! Let my spirit be the first of those good objects that **You** take from me and the first trust out of **Your** favors held in trust with me. Sermon 215

God created the heavens and the earth with The Truth so that every soul would be given recompense for what it earned and they, they will not be wronged. **45:22**

You are supporters of Truth and brethren in faith. You are the shield on the day of tribulation and my trustees among the rest of the people. With your support I strike the runner away and hope for the obedience of him who advances forward. Therefore, extend to me support which is free from deceit and pure from doubt because, by God, I am the most preferable of all for the people. Sermon 118

Had **you** *considered he who took to himself his own desire as his god and whom God caused to go astray out of a knowledge, sealed over his having the ability to hear and his heart and laid a blindfold on his sight? Who, then, will guide him after God? Will you not, then, recollect?* **45:23**

I bear witness that **You** are that God Who cannot be confined in the fetters of intelligence so as to admit change of condition by entering its imagination, nor in the shackles of the mind so as to become limited and an object of alterations. Sermon 91

They said: There is nothing, but this present life of ours. We die and we live and nothing causes us to perish but a long course of time. There is for them not any knowledge. Truly, they are but surmising. **45:24**

You should know that a person is satiated and wearied with everything except life, because he does not find for himself any pleasure in death. It is life for a dead heart, sight for the blind eye, hearing for the deaf ear, quenching for the thirsty, and it contains complete sufficiency and safety. Sermon 133

When are recounted to them Our signs, clear portents, then, disputation had not been but that they said: Bring our fathers if you had been ones who are sincere. **45:25**

I bear witness that *Muhammad* (Q48:29), peace and the mercy of God be upon him, is *His servant* (Q17:1) and *Prophet* (Q7:158) whom He deputed when the signs of guidance were obliterated and the ways of religion were desolate. So he threw open the truth, gave advice to the people, guided them towards righteousness and ordered them to be moderate. May God bless him ... Sermon 194

Say: God gives you life. Again, He causes you to die. Again, He will gather you on the Day of Resurrection in which there is no doubt but most of humanity knows not. **45:26**

Be aware! .... Provide for yourself from this world what would save you tomorrow on the Day of Judgment. Sermon 28

To God belongs the dominion of the heavens and the earth. On a Day that the Hour will be secure, on that Day the ones who deal in falsehood will lose. **45:27**

Remember that inequity and falsehood bring disgrace to a person in this world and in the hereafter. Letter 48

You *will see each community one who crawls on its knees. Each community will be called to its book: This Day you will be given recompense for what you had been doing.* **45:28**

Mind the obligations! Mind the obligations! Fulfill them for God and they will take you to the Garden. Surely, God has made unlawful the things which are not unknown and made lawful the things which are without defect. Sermon 167

This is Our Book that speaks for itself against you with The Truth. Truly, We registered what you had been doing. **45:29**

Certainly, only doubtful innovations cause ruin except those from which God may protect. In God's authority lies the safety of your affairs. Therefore, render Him such obedience as is neither blameworthy nor insincere. Sermon 169

Then, as for those who believed and did as the ones in accord with morality, their Lord will cause them to enter in His mercy. That will be the winning the clear triumph. **45:30**

Among the proofs of His creation is the creation of the skies which are fastened without pillars and stand without support. He called them. They responded obediently and humbly without being lazy or loathsome. If they had not acknowledged His Godhead and obeyed Him, He would not have made them the place for His throne, the abode of His angels and the destination: *To Him Words of what is good rise and He exalts an action in accord with morality* ... (Q35:10) of the creatures. Sermon 182

But as for those who were ungrateful: Be not My signs recounted to you? Then, you grew arrogant and you had been a folk, ones who sin! **45:31**
When it was said: Truly, the promise of God is true and the Hour, there is no doubt about it. You said: We are not informed about the Hour. Truly, We think it but an opinion and we are not ones who ascertain it. **45:32**

Go ahead with the remembrance of God, for it is the best remembrance. Long for that which He has promised to the pious, for His promise is the most true promise. Tread the course of *the Prophet* (Q7:158), peace and the mercy of God be upon him, for it is the most distinguished course. Follow his *sunna*, for it is the most right of all behaviors. Learn the Quran, for it is the fairest of discourses. Understand it thoroughly, for it is the best blossoming of hearts. Seek cure with its light, for it is the cure for hearts. Recite it beautifully, for it is the most beautiful narration. Certainly, a scholar who acts not according to his knowledge is like the off-headed ignorant who does not find relief from his ignorance, but the plea of God is greater on the learned and grief more incumbent. He is more blameworthy before God. Sermon 110

Shown to themselves will be the evil deeds they did. They will be surrounded by what they had been ridiculing. **45:33**

Be aware! At the time of committing evil deeds remember the destroyer of joys, the spoiler of pleasures, and the killer of desires, namely death. Seek assistance of God for fulfillment of His obligatory rights and for thanking Him for His countless bounties and obligations. Sermon 99

It would be said: This Day We will forget you as you forgot the meeting of this your Day. Your place of shelter will be the fire and there is not for you any one who helps. **45:34**

Desires will be cut. Hearts will sink quietly. Voices will be lowered. Sweat will choke the throat. Fear will increase. Ears will resound with the thundering voice of the announcer calling towards the final judgment, award of recompense, striking of punishment and paying of reward. Sermon 82

This is because you took to yourselves the signs of God in mockery and this present life deluded you. So, this Day they will not be brought out from there nor will they ask to be favored. **45:35**

On that Day many an argument will prove void and a contention for excuses will stand rejected. Sermon 222

So, The Praise belongs to God, the Lord of the heavens and the Lord of the earth, and the Lord of the worlds. **45 36**
His is the domination of the heavens and the earth. He is The Almighty, The Wise. **45:37**

He precedes every extremity and limit and every counting and numbering. He is far above what those whose regard is limited attribute to Him, such as the qualities of measure, having extremities, living in house and dwelling in abodes, because limits are meant for creation and are attributable only to other than God. Sermon 163

Chapter 46: Curving Sandhills (al-Aḥqāf)

Ha Mim **46:1**
The sending down successively of the Book is from God The Almighty, The Wise. **46:2**

On us it is obligatory to abide by the Book of God (Quran), the Sublime, and the conduct of *the Prophet* (Q7:158), peace and the mercy of God be upon him, to stand by His rights and the revival of his *sunna*. Sermon 169

We created not the heavens and the earth and whatever is between the two, but with The Truth and for a term, that which is determined. Those who disbelieved in what they were warned about are ones who turn aside. **46:3**

Know that—may God have mercy on you—you are living at a time when those who speak about right are few, when tongues are loath to utter the truth and those who stick to the right are humiliated. The people of this time are engaged in disobedience. Their youth are wicked, their old men are sinful, their learned men are hypocrites, and their speakers are sycophants. Their young ones do not respect their elders, and their rich men do not support the destitute. Sermon 232

Say: Considered you what you call to other than God? Cause me to see what of the earth they created. Have they an association in the heavens? Bring me a Book from before this, or a vestige of knowledge if you had been ones who are sincere. **46:4**

God, the Almighty, has sent down a guiding Book wherein He has explained virtue and vice. You should adopt the course of virtue, whereby you will have guidance. Detach yourself from the direction of vice, so that you remain on the right way. Sermon 167

Who is one who has gone more astray than one who calls to other than God, one who responds not to him until the Day of Resurrection? They are of their supplication to them, ones who are heedless. **46:5**
When humanity will be assembled, they will become their enemies and will be ones who disavow their worship. **46:6**

Be aware! You have been ordered insistently to march. You have been guided as to how to provide for the journey. Truly, the most frightening thing that I am afraid of about you is that you will follow desires and widen your hopes. Provide for yourself from this world what would save you tomorrow on the Day of Judgment. Sermon 28

When Our signs are recounted, clear portents, those who were ungrateful for The Truth said when it drew near them: This is clear sorcery! **46:7**

God sent *the Prophet* (Q7:158), peace and the mercy of God be upon him, as a caller towards Truth and a witness over the creatures. *The Prophet* (Q7:158) conveyed the messages of God tirelessly and without any negligence. He fought His enemies in the cause of God unflaggingly and without pleading excuses. He is the foremost of all who practice God-consciousness and the power of perception of all those who achieve guidance. Sermon 116

Or they say: He devised it. Say: If I devised it, you still possess nothing for me against God. He is greater in knowledge of what you press on about. He sufficed as a Witness between me and between you. He is The Forgiving, The Compassionate. **46:8**

O the Most Merciful of all! Surely, **You** are powerful over whatever **You** will. Sermon 143

Say: I had not been an innovation among the Messengers, nor am I informed of what will be wreaked on me, nor with you. I follow only what is revealed to me and I am only a clear warner. **46:9**

The opponents have entered the oceans of disturbance and have taken to innovations instead of the *sunna*, while the believers have sunk down. The misguided and the liars are speaking. We are the near ones, companions, treasure holders and doors to the *sunna*. Houses are not entered save through their doors. Whoever enters them from other than the door is called a thief. Sermon 153

Say: Considered you if this had been from God and you were ungrateful for it and bore witness as one who bears witness from among the Children of Jacob to its like and believed in it, yet you grew arrogant, how unjust you are; truly, God guides not the folk, the ones who are unjust. **46:10**

Those who were ungrateful said of those who believed: If it had been good, they would not have preceded us towards it. When they are not truly guided by it, they say: This is a ripe, aged calumny. **46:11**

Yet before it was the Book of Moses for a leader and as a mercy. This is a Book, that which establishes as true in the Arabic language to warn those who did wrong and as good tidings to the ones who are doers of good. **46:12**

Truly, those who say: Our Lord is God again, go straight, neither will there be fear in them, nor will they feel remorse. **46:13**

Those are the Companions of the Garden, ones who will dwell in it forever as a recompense for what they had been doing. **46:14**

You should adopt the course of virtue whereby you will have guidance and keep aloof from the direction of vice so that you remain on the right way. Sermon 167

We charged the human being with kindness to ones who are his parents. His mother carried him painfully and she painfully brought him forth. The bearing of him and the weaning of him are thirty months. When he was fully grown, having come of age and reached forty years he said: My Lord! Arouse me that I may give thanks for ***Your*** *divine blessing, that with which* ***You*** *were gracious to me and to ones who are my parents and that I do as one in accord with morality so that* ***You*** *be well-pleased and make things right for me and my offspring. Truly, I repented to* ***You*** *and, truly, I am of the ones who submit to God.* **46:15**

Do not forget gratitude when receiving blessings for God has exhausted the excuses before you through clear, shining arguments and open, bright books. Sermon 81

Those are those from whom We will receive the fairer of what they did and we will pass on by their evil deeds. They are among the Companions of the Garden. This is the promise of sincerity that they had been promised. **46:16**

Action! Action! Then look at the end, the end, and remain steadfast, steadfast. Thereafter exercise endurance, endurance, and God-consciousness, God-consciousness. You have an objective. Proceed towards your objective. You have a sign. Take guidance from your sign. Islam has an objective. Proceed towards its objective. Proceed towards God by fulfilling His rights which He has enjoined upon you. He has clearly stated His demands for you. Sermon 176

But he who would say to ones who are his parents a word of disrespect to both of them: Promise you me that I will be brought out when generations before me passed away? They will both cry to God for help: Woe unto ***you****! Believe! Truly, the promise of God is true. But he said: This is only the fables of the ancient ones.* **46:17**

They took to the right and the left piercing through to the ways of evil and leaving the paths of guidance. Do not make haste for a matter which is to happen and is awaited. Do not wish for delay in what the morrow is to bring for you. For how many people make haste for a matter, but when they get it they begin to wish they had not gotten it? How near is today to the dawning of tomorrow? O my people, this is the time for the occurrence of every promised event and the approach of things which you do not know. Sermon 150

Those are those against whom the saying was realized about the communities that passed away before of the jinn and humankind. Truly, they had been ones who are losers. **46:18**

You should take a lesson from the fate of the progeny of Ishmael, the children of Isaac and the children of Jacob. How similar are their affairs and how akin are their examples. In connection with the details of their division and disunity, think of the days when Kings of Persia and the Caesars of Rome had become their masters. They turned them out from the pastures of their lands, the rivers of Iraq and the fertility of the world, towards thorny forests, the passages of hot winds and hardships in livelihood. By doing this, they turned them into just herders of camels. Their houses were the worst in the world and their places of stay were the most drought-stricken. There was not one voice towards which they could turn for protection, nor any shade of affection on whose strength they could repose trust. Sermon 192

For each there will be degrees according to what he did and He will pay them their account in full for their actions and they, they will not be wronged. **46:19**

In the Garden there are various degrees of excellence and different places of stay. Its blessings never end. He who stays in it will never depart from it. He who is endowed with everlasting abode in it will not grow old and its resident will not face want. Sermon 86

On a Day when they will be presented—those who were ungrateful—to the fire, it will be said: You caused what is good to be put away in your present life while you enjoyed it. Then, you will be given recompense with a punishment of humiliation because you had been growing arrogant on the earth without right and because you had been disobeying. **46:20**

It is as though he has not heard the wrongful followers disclaiming their false gods by sayings. By God! *Truly we have been clearly wandering astray when we made you equal with the Lord of the worlds.* (Q26:97-98) Sermon 91

Remember the brother of Ad when he warned his folk in the curving sandhills. Warnings passed away before and after him saying: Worship nothing but God. Truly, I fear for you the punishment of a tremendous Day. **46:21**
They said: Had ***you*** *drawn near to us to mislead us from our gods? Then, bring us that which* ***you*** *have promised us if* ***you*** *had been among the ones who are sincere.* **46:22**
He said: The knowledge is only with God and I state to you what I was sent with, but I see that you are a folk who are ignorant. **46:23**
Then, when they saw it as a dense cloud proceeding towards their valleys, they said: This is a dense cloud, that which gives rain to us. Nay! It is what you seek to hasten, a wind in which there is a painful punishment. **46:24**
It will destroy everything at the command of its Lord. So, it came to be in the morning nothing was seen but their dwellings. Thus, We give recompense to the folk, ones who sin. **46:25** ***

Certainly, We established them firmly in what We established you firmly not and We made for them the ability to hear and sight and minds. Yet having the ability to hear availed them not, nor their sight, nor their minds at all since they had been negating the signs of God. Surrounded were they by what they had been ridiculing. **46:26**

I bear witness that *there is no god but God* (Q47:19), by virtue of belief, certainty, sincerity and conviction. I also bear witness that *Muhammad* (Q48:29), peace and the mercy of God be upon him, is *His servant* (Q17:1) and *Prophet* (Q7:158), whom He deputed when the signs of guidance were obliterated and the ways of religion were desolate. So he threw open the truth, gave advice to the people, guided them towards righteousness and ordered them to be moderate. May God bless him ... Sermon 194

Certainly, We caused to perish towns around you and We diversified the signs so that perhaps they will return. **46:27**

He hears his speaking, and whoever keeps quiet, He knows his secret. Sermon 108

Then, why helped them not those whom they took to themselves other than God as gods as a mediator. Nay! They went astray from them. That was their calumny and what they had been devising. **46:28**

I bear witness that *there is no god but God* (Q47:19). He is One. There is no partner with Him. He is the First, such that nothing was before Him. He is the Last, such that there is not limit for Him. Imagination cannot catch any of His qualities. Hearts cannot entertain belief about His nature. Analysis and division cannot be applied to Him. Eyes and hearts cannot compare Him. Sermon 84

When We turned away from ***you*** *groups of men or jinn who listen to the Quran, when they found themselves in its presence, they said: Pay heed. When it was finished, they turned to their folk, ones who warn.* **46:29**

O my God! Whoever listens to our words which are just and which seek the prosperity of religion and the worldly life and do not seek mischief, they reject after listening. He certainly turns away from **Your** support and desists from strengthening **Your** religion.

We make **You** a Witness over him. **You** are the greatest of all witnesses. We make all those who inhabit **Your** earth and **Your** skies witness over him. Thereafter, **You** alone can make us needless of his support and question him for his sin. Sermon 212

They said: O our folk! Truly, We heard a Book was caused to descend after Moses, that which establishes as true what was in advance of it. It guides to The Truth and to a straight road. **46:30**
O our folk! Answer one who calls to God and believe in Him. He will forgive you your impieties and will grant protection to you from a painful punishment. **46:31**

Everyone should be God-conscious, should admonish himself, should send forward his repentance and should overpower his desire because his death is hidden from him. His desires deceive him. Satan keeps posted about him. He beautifies his sin for him so that he may commit it. He prompts him to delay repentance until his desires cause him to be the most negligent. Pity is for the negligent person whose life itself would be a proof against him and his own days, passed in sin, will lead him to punishment. Sermon 64

Who answers not to one who calls to God? He is not one who frustrates Him in and on the earth. There will not be for him other than God any protectors. Those are clearly gone astray. **46:32**
Considered they not that God Who created the heavens and the earth and is not wearied by their creation—is One Who Has Power to give life to the dead? Yea! He, truly, is Powerful over everything. **46:33**

O God's human being! I advise you to be God-conscious which is the provision for the next world and with it is your return. The provision would take you to your destination and the return would be successful. The best one who is able to make people listen has called towards it and the best listener has listened to it. So the caller has proclaimed and the listener has listened and persevered. O God's human being! Certainly, being God-conscious has saved the lovers of God from unlawful items and has given His dread to their hearts until their nights are passed in wakefulness and their noons in thirst. So they achieve comfort through trouble and copious watering through thirst. They regarded death to be near and, therefore, hastened towards good actions. They rejected their desires by keeping death in their sight. Sermon 114

On a Day when will be presented those who were ungrateful to the fire saying: Is not this The Truth? They would say: Yea! By our Lord! He will say: Then, experience the punishment because you had been ungrateful! **46:34**
So, have ***you*** *patience as endured patiently those imbued with constancy of the Messengers and let them not seek to hasten the Judgment. As, truly, on a Day they will see what they are promised as if they lingered not in expectation but for an hour of daytime. This is delivering the message! Will any be caused to perish but the folk, the ones who disobey?* **46:35**

I bear witness that *there is no god but God* (Q47:19), by virtue of belief, certainty, sincerity and conviction. I also bear witness that *Muhammad* (Q48:29), peace and the mercy of God be upon him, is *His servant* (Q17:1) and *Prophet* (Q7:158) whom He deputed when the signs of guidance were obliterated and the ways of religion were desolate. So he threw open the truth, gave advice to the people, guided them towards righteousness and ordered them to be moderate. May God bless him ... Sermon 194

CHAPTER 47: MUHAMMAD (Muḥammad)

Those who were ungrateful and who barred from the way of God—He caused their actions to go astray. **47:1**

They are wrong who liken **You** to their idols, and dress **You** with apparel of the creatures by their imagination, attribute to **You** parts of body by their own thinking and consider **You** after the creatures of various types, through the working of their intelligence. Sermon 91

Those who believed and did as the ones in accord with morality and believed in what was sent down to Muhammad—for it is The Truth from their Lord—He will absolve them of their evil deeds and will make right their state of mind. **47:2**

That is because those who were ungrateful followed falsehood, while those who believed followed The Truth from their Lord. Thus, God propounds for humanity their parables. **47:3**

Know that—may God have mercy on you—you are living at a time when those who speak about right are few, when tongues are loath to utter the truth and those who stick to the right are humiliated. The people of this time are engaged in disobedience. Their youth are wicked, their old men are sinful, their learned men are hypocrites, and their speakers are sycophants. Their young ones do not respect their elders, and their rich men do not support the destitute. Sermon 232

So, when you met those who were ungrateful, then, strike their thick necks until you gave them a sound thrashing. Then, tie them fast with restraints. Afterwards either have good will towards them or take ransom for them until the war ends, laying down its heavy load. Thus, it is so! But if God willed, He Himself would have, certainly, avenged you. But it is to try some of you with some others. As for those who were slain in the way of God, He will never cause their actions to go astray. **47:4**

I bear witness that **You** are that God Who cannot be confined in the fetters of intelligence so as to admit change of condition by entering its imagination, nor in the shackles of the mind so as to become limited and an object of alterations. Sermon 91

He will guide them and He will make right their state of mind. **47:5**

God sent Muhammad, peace and the mercy of God be upon him, with the Truth so that he may take out His people from the worship of idols towards His worship and from obeying Satan towards obeying Him. God sent him with the Quran which He explained and made strong in order that the people may know their Sustainer (God), since they were ignorant of Him, may acknowledge Him, since they were denying Him and accept Him, since they were refusing to believe in Him. Sermon 147

He will cause them to enter the Garden with which He acquainted them. **47:6**

God, the Almighty, has sent down a guiding Book wherein He has explained virtue and vice. You should adopt the course of virtue, whereby you will have guidance. Detach yourself from the direction of vice, so that you remain on the right way. Sermon 167

O those who believed! If you help God, He will help you and make firm your feet. **47:7**

You should try for the release of your necks before their mortgage is foreclosed, keep your eyes awake at night, make your bellies lean, use your feet, spend your money, take your bodies and spend them over yourselves, and do not be niggardly about them, because God the Almighty, has said: *If you help God, He will help you and make firm your feet.* (Q47:7) Sermon 182

As for those who are ungrateful, for them is falling into ruin! He caused their actions to go astray. **47:8**
That is because they disliked what God caused to descend so He caused their actions to fail. **47:9**
Journey they not through the earth and look on how had been the Ultimate End of those who were before them? God destroyed them. For ones who are ungrateful is its likeness. **47:10**
That is because God is the Defender of those who believed. For the ones who are ungrateful, there is no defender of them. **47:11**
Truly, God will cause to enter those who believed and did as the ones in accord with morality, gardens beneath which rivers run. While those who were ungrateful, take joy in eating as the flocks eat, the fire will be the place of lodging for them. **47:12**

I bear witness that whoever equated **You** with anything out of **Your** creation took a partner for **You**. Whoever takes a partner for **You** is ungrateful according to what is stated in **Your** unambiguous verses and indicated by the evidence of **Your** clear arguments. Sermon 91

How many a town had there been which was stronger in strength than ***your*** *town which drove* ***you*** *out, that We have caused to perish? There was no one who helps them!* **47:13**

You should take a lesson from the fate of the progeny of Ishmael, the children of Isaac and the children of Jacob. How similar are their affairs and how akin are their examples. In connection with the details of their division and disunity, think of the days when Kings of Persia and the Caesars of Rome had become their masters. They turned them out from the pastures of their lands, the rivers of Iraq and the fertility of the world, towards thorny forests, the passages of hot winds and hardships in livelihood. By doing this, they turned them into just herders of camels. Their houses were the worst in the world and their places of stay were the most drought-stricken. There was not one voice towards which they could turn for protection, nor any shade of affection on whose strength they could repose trust. Sermon 192

Is he who had been on a clear portent from his Lord like him for whom was made to appear pleasing his dire actions and they followed their own desires? **47:14**

God deputized *the Prophet* (Q7:158), peace and the mercy of God be upon him, after a gap from the previous Prophets when there was much talk among the people. With him God exhausted the series of Prophets and ended the revelation. He then fought for Him those who were turning away from Him and were equating others with Him. Sermon 133

This is the parable of the Garden which was promised the ones who are God-conscious: In it are rivers of unpolluted water and rivers of milk, the taste of which is not modified and rivers of intoxicants delightful to ones who drink and rivers of clarified honey, and in it for them all kinds of fruits and forgiveness from their Lord. Is this like ones who will dwell forever in the fire and they were given scalding water to drink so that it cuts off their bowels? **47:15**

The great calamity of that place is the hot water and entry into Hell, flames of eternal fire and intensity of blazes. There is no resting period, no gap for ease, no power to intervene, no death to bring about solace and no sleep to make him forget pain. He rather lies under several kinds of deaths and moment-to-moment punishment. We seek refuge with God. Sermon 82

Among them are some who listen to ***you*** *until when they went forth from* ***you****. They said to those who were given the knowledge: What was that he said just now? Those are those upon whose hearts God set a seal. They followed their own desires.* **47:16**

O my God! Whoever listens to our words which are just and which seek the prosperity of religion and the worldly life and do not seek mischief, they reject after listening. He certainly turns away from **Your** support and desists from strengthening **Your** religion. We make **You** a Witness over him. **You** are the greatest of all witnesses. We make all those who inhabit **Your** earth and **Your** skies witness over him. Thereafter, **You** alone can make us needless of his support and question him for his sin. Sermon 212

Those who were truly guided, He increased them in guidance and He gave to them their God-consciousness. **47:17**

You have been shown, provided you are willing to see. You have been made to listen, provided you are willing to listen. You have been guided if you accept guidance. I spoke unto you with the truth. Sermon 20

Look they, then, on not but the Hour, that it approach them suddenly? Certainly, its tokens drew near. Then, what will it be like for them when their reminder drew near to them? **47:18**

How many a prestigious body and amazing beauty the earth has swallowed, although when in the world he enjoyed abundant pleasures and was nurtured in honor. He clung to enjoyments even in the hour of grief. If distress befell him he sought refuge in consolation derived through the pleasures of life and playing and games. He was laughing at the world while the world was laughing at him because of his life full of forgetfulness. Then time trampled him like thorns. The days weakened his energy. Death began to look at him from near. Then he was overtaken by a grief which he had never felt. Ailments appeared in place of the health he had previously possessed. Sermon 219

So, know ***you*** *that there is no god but God and ask forgiveness for* ***your*** *impieties and also for the males, ones who believe and the females, ones who believe, and God knows your place of turmoil and your place of lodging.* **47:19**

I bear witness that *there is no god but God* (Q47:19), and I bear witness that *Muhammad* (Q48:29), peace and the mercy of God be upon him, is *His servant* (Q17:1) and *Prophet* (Q7:158) and His chosen and His selected one. Sermon 150

Those who believed say: Why was a Chapter of the Quran not caused to descend? But when was caused to descend a definitive Chapter of the Quran and fighting was remembered in it, ***you*** *saw those who in their hearts is a sickness looking on* ***you*** *with the look of one who is fainting at death.* **47:20**

But better for them would be obedience and an honorable saying! When the affair was resolved, then, if they were sincere to God, it would have been better for them. **47:21**

O people! By God, I do not impel you to any obedience unless I practice it before you. I do not restrain you from any disobedience unless I desist from it before you. Sermon 175

Will it be that if you turned away, you would make corruption in the earth and cut off your ties with blood relations? **47:22**

O God's human being! I advise you to be God-conscious which is the provision for the next world and with it is your return. The provision would take you to your destination and the return would be successful. The best one who is able to make people listen has called towards it and the best listener has listened to it. So the caller has proclaimed and the listener has listened and preserved. Sermon 114

Those are those whom God cursed, so He made them unwilling to hear and their sight, unwilling to see. **47:23**

O God! I bear witness that he who likens **You** with the separateness of the limbs or with the joining of the extremities of his body did not acquaint his inner self with knowledge about **You**. His heart did not secure conviction to the effect that there is no partner for **You**. It is as though he has not heard the wrongful followers disclaiming their false gods by sayings. By God! *Truly we have been clearly wandering astray when we made you equal with the Lord of the worlds.* (Q26:97-98). Sermon 91

Meditate they not, then, on the Quran or are there locks on their hearts? **47:24**

Know that this Quran is an adviser who never deceives, a leader who never misleads and a narrator who never speaks a lie. No one will sit beside this Quran, but when he rises, he will achieve one addition or one diminution—addition in his guidance or elimination in his spiritual blindness. You should also know that no one will need anything after guidance from the Quran and no one will be free from want before guidance from the Quran. Seek cure from the Quran for your ailments and seek its assistance in your distress. It contains a cure for the worst diseases, namely unbelief, hypocrisy, revolt and misguidance. Pray to God through it and turn to God with its love ... There is nothing like it through which the people should turn to God, the Sublime. Sermon 176

Truly, those who went back—turn their back— after the guidance became clear to them, it was Satan who enticed them and He granted them indulgence. **47:25**

O my God! I seek **Your** protection from becoming destitute despite **Your** riches, from being misguided despite **Your** guidance, from being molested in **Your** realm and from being humiliated while authority rests with **You**. O my God! Let my spirit be the first of those good objects that **You** take from me and the first trust out of **Your** favors held in trust with me. Sermon 215

That is because they said to those who disliked what God sent down: We will obey you in some of the affair. God knows what they keep secret. **47:26**

Now, if you portray them in your mind, or if the curtains concealing them are removed from them for you, in this state when their ears have lost their power and turned deaf, their eyes have been filled with dust and sunk down, their tongues which were very active have been cut into pieces, their hearts which were ever wakeful have become motionless in their chests, in every limb of theirs a peculiar decay has occurred which has deformed it, and has paved the way for calamity towards it, all these lie powerless, with no hand to help them and no heart to grieve over them, then you would certainly notice the grief of their hearts and the dirt of their eyes. Sermon 220

Then, how will it be for them when the angels will call them to themselves, striking their faces and their backs? **47:27**

Perform good acts while you are still in the vastness of life. The books are open for recording of actions. Repentance is allowed. The runner away from God is being called and the sinner is being given hope of forgiveness before the light of action is put off, time expires, life ends, the door for repentance is closed and angels ascend to the sky. Therefore, a person should derive benefit from himself for himself, from the living for the dead, from the mortal for the lasting and from the departer for the stayer. A person should be God-conscious while he is given age to live up to his death and is allowed time to act. A person should control his self by the rein and hold it with its bridle. By the rein, he should prevent it from disobedience towards God. By the bridle, he should lead it towards obedience to God. Sermon 236

That is because they followed what displeased God and they disliked His contentment so He caused their actions to fail. **47:28**

O people! Every one shall meet what he wishes to avoid by running away. Death is the place to which life is driving. To run away from it means to catch it. How many days did I spend in searching for the secret of this matter, but God did not allow save its concealment. Alas! It is a treasured knowledge. Sermon 149

Or assumed those who in their hearts is a sickness that God will never bring out their rancor? **47:29**

If We will, We would have caused **you** *to see them.* **You** *would have recognized them by their mark. But, certainly,* **you** *will recognize them by the twisting of sayings. God knows all your actions.* **47:30**

Certainly, We will try you until We know the ones who struggle among you and the ones who remain steadfast and We will try your reports. **47:31**

Do not forget God, struggle in His cause with your tongue, with your wealth and with your lives. Letter 47

Truly, those who were ungrateful and barred from the way of God and made a breach with the Messenger after guidance became clear to them, they never hurt or profit God at all, but He will cause their actions to fail. **47:32**

O my God! I seek **Your** protection from becoming destitute despite **Your** riches, from being misguided despite **Your** guidance, from being molested in **Your** realm and from being humiliated while authority rests with **You**. O my God! Let my spirit be the first of those good objects that **You** take from me and the first trust out of **Your** favors held in trust with me. Sermon 215

O those who believed! Obey God and obey the Messenger and render not your actions untrue. **47:33**

God, the Glorified, decided that people should follow His Prophets, acknowledge

His Books, remain humble before His face, obey His command and accept His obedience with sincerity in which there should not be an iota of anything else; and as the trial and tribulation would be stiffer, the reward and recompense too should be larger. Sermon 191

Truly, those who were ungrateful and barred from the way of God, again, they died while they were ones who are ungrateful, then, God will never forgive them. **47:34**
So, be not faint and call for peace while you have the upper hand. God is with you and He will never cheat you out of your actions. **47:35**

O Muslims! Make fear of God the routine of your life. Cover yourselves with peace of mind. Clench your teeth because this makes the sword slip away from the skull. Complete your armor and shake your swords in their sheathes before drawing them out. Have your eyes on the enemy. Use your spears on both sides and strike the enemy with swords. Keep in mind that you are before God and in the company of the Prophet's cousin. Repeat your attacks. Feel shame at running away, because it is a shame for posterity and cause of awarding you fire on the Day of Judgment. Give your lives to God willingly and walk towards death with ease. Be aware of this great majority and the pitched tent. Aim at its center because Satan is hiding in its corner. He has extended his hand for assault and has held back his foot from running away. Keep on enduring until the light of Truth dawns upon you. *So, be not faint and call for peace while you have the upper hand. God is with you and will never cheat you out of your actions.* (Q47:35) Sermon 66

This present life is only a pastime and a diversion. But if you believe and are God-conscious, He will give you your compensation and will not ask of you for your property. **47:36**

Do you command me that I should seek support by oppressing those over whom I have been placed? By God, I will not do so as long as the world goes on and as long as one star leads another in the sky. Even if it were my property, I would have distributed it equally among them. Then why not when the property is that of God? Sermon 126

When He asks it of you and, then, urges persistently, you would be a miser and He will bring out your rancor. **47:37**
Lo and behold! These are being called to spend in the way of God, yet among you are some who are misers. Whoever is a miser, then, he is a miser only to himself. God is Sufficient and you are poor. If you turn away, He will have a folk other than you in exchange. Again, they will not be the like of you. **47:38**

You, certainly, know that he who is in charge of honor, life, booty, enforcement of legal commandments and the leadership of the Muslims should not be a miser as his greed would aim at their wealth, nor be ignorant as he would then mislead them with his ignorance, nor be of rude behavior who would estrange them with his rudeness, nor should he deal unjustly with wealth thus preferring one group over another, nor should he accept a bribe while taking decisions as he would forfeit others' rights and hold them up without finality. He should not ignore the *sunna* as he would ruin the people. Sermon 131

Chapter 48: The Victory (al-Fatḥ)

Truly, We gave victory to ***you****, a clear victory,* **48:1**
that God forgive ***you*** *what was former of* ***your*** *impiety and what remained behind that He fulfill*

His divine blessing on **you** *and guide* **you** *on a straight path* **48:2**
and that God help **you** *with a mighty help.* **48:3**

I have seen your flight and your dispersal from the lines. You were surrounded by rude and low people and Bedouins of Syria, although you are the chiefs of Arabs and summit of distinction and possess the dignity of the high nose and big hump of the camel. The sigh of my bosom can subside only when I eventually see you surrounding them as they surrounded you and see you dislodging them from their position as they dislodged you, killing them with arrows and striking them with spears so that their forward rows might fall on the rear ones just like the thirsty camels who have been turned away from their place of drink and removed from their water-points. Sermon 107

He it is Who caused the tranquility to descend into the hearts of the ones who believe that they add belief to their belief. To God belongs the armies of the heavens and the earth. God had been Knowing, Wise **48:4**
that He causes to enter the males, ones who believe and the females, ones who believe Gardens beneath which rivers run, ones who will dwell in them forever, and that He absolve them of their evil deeds. That had been with God a winning a sublime triumph. **48:5**
That He punish the males, ones who are hypocrites and the females, ones who are hypocrites and the males, ones who are polytheists and the females, ones who are polytheists, the ones who think an evil thought about God, a reprehensible thought, for them is the reprehensible turn of fortune. God was angry with them. He cursed them and prepared hell for them. How evil a Homecoming! **48:6**

God, the Almighty, has sent down a guiding Book wherein He has explained virtue and vice. You should adopt the course of virtue whereby you will have guidance, and keep aloof from the direction of vice so that you remain on the right way. Mind the obligations! Mind the obligations! Fulfill them for God and they will take you to the Garden. Surely, God has made unlawful the things which are not unknown and made lawful the things which are without defect. Sermon 167

To God belongs the armies of the heavens and the earth. God had been Almighty, Wise. **48:7**
Truly, We sent **you** *as one who bears witness and one who gives good tidings and as a warner,* **48:8**
so that you believe in God and His Messenger and that you support him and revere Him and glorify Him at early morning dawn and eventide. **48:9**

Praise of God for His bounties, His Might, the excellences of the Quran and counseling God-consciousness. Sermon 183

Truly, those who take the pledge of allegiance to **you**, *take the pledge of alliance only to God. The hand of God is over their hands. Then, whoever broke his oath, breaks his oath only to the harm of himself. Whoever lived up to what he made as a contract with God, He will give him a sublime compensation.* **48:10**

O people, I have a right over you and you have a right over me. As for your right over me, that is to counsel you, to pay you your dues fully, to teach you that you may not remain ignorant and instruct you in behavior that you may act upon. As for my right over you, it is the fulfillment of the obligation of allegiance, wishing me well in my presence or in absence, responding when I call you and obedience when I command you. Sermon 34

The ones who are left behind will say to **you** *among the nomads: Our property and our people occupied us, so ask forgiveness for us. They say with their tongues what is not in their hearts. Say: Who, then, has sway over you against God at all if He wanted to harm you or wanted to bring you profit? Nay! God had been aware of what you do.* **48:11**

Nay! You thought that the Messenger would never turn about and the ones who believe to their people ever, and that was made to appear pleasing in your hearts. But you thought a reprehensible thought, and you had been a lost folk. **48:12**

Do you command me that I should seek support by oppressing those over whom I have been placed? By God, I will not do so as long as the world goes on and as long as one star leads another in the sky. Even if it were my property, I would have distributed it equally among them. Then why not when the property is that of God? Sermon 126

Whoever believes not in God and His Messenger, truly, We made ready a blaze for the ones who are ungrateful. **48:13**

The great calamity of that place is the hot water and entry into Hell, flames of eternal Fire and intensity of blaze. Sermon 82

To God belongs the dominion of the heavens and the earth. He forgives whom He wills and punishes whom He wills. God had been Forgiving, Compassionate. **48:14**

O God's human being! I advise you to be God-conscious which is the provision for the next world and with it is your return. The provision would take you to your destination and the return would be successful. The best one who is able to make people listen has called towards it and the best listener has listened to it. So the caller has proclaimed and the listener has listened and preserved. O God's human being! Certainly being God fearing has saved the lovers of God from unlawful items and has given His dread to their hearts until their nights are passed in wakefulness and their noons in thirst. So they achieve comfort through trouble and copious watering through thirst. They regarded death to be near and therefore hastened towards good actions. They rejected their desires and so they kept death in their sight. Sermon 114

The ones who are left behind will say when you set out to take the gains:Let us follow you. They want to substitute for the assertion of God. Say: You will not follow us. Thus, God said before; then, they will say: Nay! You are jealous of us. Nay! They had not been understanding, but a little. **48:15**

God made Islam a source of peace for him who clings to it, safety for him who enters it, argument for him who speaks about it, witness for him who fights with its help, light for him who seeks light from it, understanding for him who provides it, sagacity for him who exerts, a sign of guidance for him who perceives, sight for him who resolves, lesson for him who seeks advice, salvation for him who testifies, confidence for him who trusts, pleasure for him who entrusts and shield for him who endures. Sermon 105

Say to the ones who are left behind among the nomads: You will be called against a folk imbued with severe might. You will fight them or they will submit to God. Then, if you obey, God will give you a fairer compensation. But if you turn away as you turned away before, He will punish you with a painful punishment. **48:16**

The troubles are like a dark night. Horses would not stand facing them, nor would their banners turn back. They would approach in full reins and ready with saddles. Their leader would be driving them and the rider would be exerting them. The trouble-mongers are a people whose attacks are severe. Those who would fight them for the sake of God would be a people who are low in the estimation of the proud, unknown in the earth, but well known in the heavens. Sermon 102

There is neither a fault on the blind, nor a fault on the lame, nor a fault on the sick, and whoever obeys God and His Messenger, He will cause him to enter Gardens beneath which rivers run. Whoever turns away, He will punish him with a painful punishment. **48:17**

With *the Prophet* (Q7:158), peace and the mercy of God be upon him, God exhausted the series of Prophets and ended the revelation. He then fought for Him those who were turning away from Him and were equating others with Him. Sermon 133

God was well-pleased with the ones who believe (f) when they take the pledge of allegiance to ***you*** *beneath the tree for He knew what was in their hearts and He caused the tranquility to descend on them and He repaid them with a victory near at hand.* **48:18**
They will take much gain. God had been Almighty, Wise. **48:19**

O my people, this is the time for the occurrence of every promised event and the approach of things which you do not know. Sermon 150

God promised you much gain that you will take and He quickened this for you. He limited the hands of humanity from you so that perhaps it will be a sign to the ones who believe and that He guide you to a straight path **48:20**
and other gains which are not yet within your power. Surely, God enclosed them. God had been over everything Powerful. **48:21**

If those who were ungrateful fought you, they would have turned their backs. Again, they would not have found a protector or a helper. **48:22**
This is a custom of God which was, surely, in force before. ***You*** *will never find in a custom of God any substitution.* **48:23**

Praise belongs to God (Q1:2) Who is above all similarity to creatures, is above the words of describers Who displays the wonders of His management for the on-lookers, is hidden from the imagination of thinkers by virtue of the greatness of His glory, has knowledge without acquiring it by adding to it or drawing it from someone, and Who is the ordainer of all matters without reflecting or thinking. He is such that gloom does not concern Him, nor does He seek light from brightness. Night does not overtake Him, nor does the day pass over Him so as to affect Him in any manner. His comprehension of things is not through eyes. His knowledge is not dependent on being informed. God deputized *the Prophet* (Q7:158), peace and the mercy of God be upon him, with light and accorded him the highest precedence in selection. Through him God united those who were divided, overpowered the powerful, overcame difficulties and leveled rugged ground and, thus, removed misguidance from right and left. Sermon 213

He it is who limited their hands from you and your hands from them in the hollow of Makkah after He made you victors over them. God had been Seeing of what you do. **48:24**
They were ungrateful, and they barred you from the Masjid al-Haram, and were ones who detained the sacrificial gift from reaching its place of sacrifice. If it had not been for men, ones who believe,

and for women, ones who believe, whom you know not that you tread on them and guilt should light on you without your knowledge. This was so that God may cause to enter into His mercy whomever He wills. If they were clearly apart, separated, We would have punished those who were ungrateful among them with a painful punishment. **48:25**

I praise God, seeking completion of His Blessing, submitting to His Glory and expecting safety from committing sin. Sermon 2

Mention when those who were ungrateful laid zealotry in their hearts, like the zealotry of the Age of Ignorance. Then, God caused to descend His tranquility on His Messenger and on the ones who believe and fastened on them the Word of God-consciousness. They had been with right to it and were more worthy of it. God had been Knowing. **48:26**

God made Paradise the place of their eventual return and a reward in recompense: *They had better right to it and were more worthy of it* ... (Q48:26) in the eternal domain and everlasting favors. Sermon 190

Certainly, God was sincere to the dream of His Messenger with The Truth: You will enter the Masjid al-Haram, if God willed, as ones who are safe, as ones who shaved your heads or as ones whose hair is cut short. You will fear not. He knew what you know not and He assigned other than that a victory near at hand. **48:27**

I bear witness that Muhammad, peace and the mercy of God be upon him, is *His servant* (Q17:1) and His *Prophet.* (Q7:158) He sent him for enforcement of His commands, for exhausting His pleas and for presenting warnings against eternal punishment. Sermon 82

He it is Who sent His Messenger with guidance and the way of life of The Truth that He uplift it over all of the ways of life. God sufficed as a witness. **48:28**

O my God! Let my spirit be the first of those good objects that **Your** take from me and the first trust out of **Your** favors held in trust with me. Sermon 215

Muhammad is the Messenger of God. Those who are with him are severe against the one who is ungrateful, but compassionate among themselves. ***You*** *have seen them as ones who bow down as ones who prostrate themselves. They are looking for grace from God and contentment. Their mark is on their faces from the effects of prostration. This is their parable in the Torah. Their parable in the Gospel is like sown seed that brought out its shoot, energized. It, then, became stout and rose straight on its plant stalk impressing the ones who sow so that He enrage by them the ones who are ungrateful, God promised those who believed and did as the ones in accord with morality, for them forgiveness and a sublime compensation.* **48:29**

They must be gentle to their own people and dangerous only to their enemies. Letter 53*

Chapter 49: The Inner Apartments (al-Ḥujurāt)

O those who believed! Put not yourselves forward in advance of God and His Messenger. Be God-conscious. Truly, God is Hearing, Knowing. **49:1**

God never allowed His creation to remain without a Prophet, one deputized by

Him, or a Book sent down from Him or a binding argument or a standing plea. These Messengers were such that they did not fear that they were few in comparison to the large numbers of their falsifiers. Among them was either a predecessor who would name the one to follow or the follower who had been introduced by the predecessor. Sermon 1

O those who believed! Exalt not your voices above the voice of the Prophet nor publish a saying to him as you would openly publish something to some others so that your actions not be fruitless while you are not aware. **49:2**

O God's human being! You should know that a believer should be distrustful of his heart every morning and evening. He should always blame it for shortcomings and ask it to add to its good acts. You should behave like those who have gone before you and the precedents in front of you. They left this world like a traveler and covered it as distance is covered. Sermon 176

Truly, those who lower their voices near the Messenger of God, those are those who are ones God put to test their hearts for God-consciousness. For them is forgiveness and a sublime compensation. **49:3**

Truly, those who cry out to **you** *from behind the inner apartments, most of them are not reasonable.* **49:4**

If they endured patiently until **you** *would go forth to them, it would have been better for them. God is Forgiving, Compassionate.* **49:5**

O the Most Merciful of all! O my God! Surely, **You** are powerful over whatever **You** will. Sermon 143

O those who believed! If one who disobeys drew near to you with a tiding, then, be clear so that you not light on a folk out of ignorance. Then, you would become ones who are remorseful for what you accomplished. **49:6**

No one preceded me in inviting people to truthfulness, in giving consideration to kinship and practicing generosity. So hear my word and preserve what I say. Maybe you will see soon after today that over this matter swords will be drawn and pledges will be broken, so much so that some of you will become leaders of the people of misguidance and followers of people of ignorance. 139

Know you that the Messenger of God is of you. If he obeys you in much of the affairs, you would, certainly, fall into misfortune. But God endeared belief to you and made it appear pleasing to your hearts. He caused to be detestable to you ingratitude and disobedience and rebellion. Those, they are the ones who are on the right way. **49:7**

This is a grace from God and His divine blessing. God is Knowing, Wise. **49:8**

Be God-conscious! From the immediate consequence of rebellion to accrue in this world and the eventual consequence of weighty oppressiveness to accrue in the next world and from the evil result of vanity because it is the great trap of Satan and his big deceit which enters the hearts of the people like a fatal poison. It never goes to waste, nor misses anyone—neither the learned because of his knowledge, nor the destitute in his rags. Sermon 192

If two sections among the ones who believe fought one against the other, then, make things right between them both. Then, if one of them was insolent against the other, then, fight the one who is insolent until it changed its mind about the command of God. Then, if it changes its mind, make things right between them justly. Act justly. Truly, God loves the ones who act justly. **49:9**

I praise God for whatever matter He ordained and whatever action He destines and for my trial with you, O group of people, who do not obey when I order and do not respond when I call you. If you are at ease, you engage in conceited conversation, but if you are faced with battle you show weakness. Sermon 180

Only the ones who believe are brothers/sisters, so make things right between your two brothers/sisters. Be God-conscious so that perhaps you will find mercy. **49:10**

O God's human being! Be God-conscious. Keep in view the reason why He created you. Be afraid of Him to the extent He has advised you to do. Make yourself deserve what He has promised you by having confidence in the truth of His promise and entertaining fear of the Day of Judgment. Sermon 82

O those who believed! Let not a folk deride another folk. Perhaps they be better than they, nor women deride other women. Perhaps they be better than they. Nor find fault with one another nor insult one another with nicknames. Miserable was the name of disobedience after belief! Whoever repents not, then, those, they are the ones who are unjust. **49:11**

O those who believed! Avoid suspicion much. Truly, some suspicion is a sin. Spy not nor backbite some by some other. Would one of you love to eat the flesh of his lifeless brother? You would have disliked it. Be God-conscious. Truly, God is Accepter of Repentance, Compassionate. **49:12**

Now then I advise you to fear God, Who created you for the first time; towards Him is your return, with Him lies the success of your aims, at Him terminate all your desires, towards Him runs your path of right and He is the aim of your fears for seeking protection. Certainly, fear of God is the medicine for the sickness of your hearts, sight for the blindness of your spirits, the cure for the ailments of your bodies, the rectifier of the evils of your breasts, the purifier of the pollution of your minds, the light of the darkness of your eyes, the consolation for the fear of your heart and the brightness for the gloom of your ignorance. Sermon 198

O humanity! Truly, We created you from a male and a female and made you into peoples and types that you recognize one another. Truly, the most generous of you with God is the most devout. Truly, God is Knowing, Aware. **49:13**

O God's human being! I advise you to be God-conscious which is the provision for the next world and with it is your return. The provision would take you to your destination and the return would be successful. The best one who is able to make people listen has called towards it and the best listener has listened to it. So the caller has proclaimed and the listener has listened and persevered. O God's human being! Certainly, being God-conscious has saved the lovers of God from unlawful items and has given His dread to their hearts until their nights are passed in wakefulness and their noons in thirst. So they achieve comfort through trouble and copious watering through thirst. They regarded death to be near and, therefore, hastened towards good actions. They rejected their desires by keeping death in their sight. Sermon 114

The nomads said: We believed. Say to them: You believe not. But say: We submitted to God, for belief enters not yet into your hearts. But if you obey God and His Messenger, He will not withhold your actions at all. Truly, God is Forgiving, Compassionate. **49:14**

God sent the *Prophet* (Q33:6), peace and the mercy of God be upon him, for enforcement of His commands, for exhausting His pleas and for presenting warnings against eternal punishment. Sermon 82

The ones who believe are not but those who believed in God and His Messenger. Again, they were not in doubt and they struggled with their wealth and themselves in the way of God. Those, they are the ones who are sincere. **49:15**

Fear the world like a sincere fearer and one who struggles hard. Sermon 159

Say: Would you teach God about your way of life while God knows whatever is in the heavens and whatever is in and on the earth? God is Knowing of everything. **49:16**

One who imagines himself to be The Knowing will surely suffer on account of his ignorance. Saying 85

They show grace to **you** *that they submitted to God. Say: Show you submission to God as grace to me? Nay! God shows grace to you in that He guided you to belief if you, truly, had been ones who are sincere.* **49:17**

God bestows grace He upon whomsoever He wills. *God is The Possessor of the Sublime Grace.* (Q57:21) I seek God's help for myself and yourselves. He is enough for me and He is the best dispenser. Sermon 182

Truly, God knows the unseen of the heavens and the earth. God is Seeing of what you do. **49:18**

Whoever speaks, He hears his speaking, and whoever keeps quiet, He knows his secret. Sermon 108

Chapter 50: Qaf (Qāf)

Qaf. By the glorious Quran! **50:1**

The Book of God is that through which you see, you speak and you hear. Its one part speaks for the other part, and one part bears witness to the other. It does not create differences about God, nor does it mislead its own follower from the path of God. You are joined together in hatred of each other and in the growing of herbage on your filth (i.e., for covering inner dirt by good appearance outside). You are sincere with one another in your love of desires and bear enmity against each other in earning wealth. The evil spirit (Satan) has perplexed you and deceit has misled you. I seek the help of God for myself and you. Sermon 133

Nay! They marveled that there drew near them one who warns from among themselves. So, the ones who are ungrateful said: This is a strange thing. **50:2**

Know that firm in knowledge are those who refrain from opening the curtains that lie against the unknown. Their acknowledgment of ignorance about the details of the hidden unknown prevents them from further probe. God praises them for their admission that they are unable to obtain knowledge not allowed to them. They do not go deep into the discussion of what is not enjoined upon them about knowing Him and they call it firmness. Be content with this and do not limit the Greatness of God after the measure of your own intelligence or else you would be among the destroyed ones. Sermon 90

When we died and had been earth dust, that is a far-fetched returning! **50:3**
... to Him returns whoever dies. Sermon 108

Surely, We knew what the earth reduces from them. With Us is a guardian Book. **50:4**
There is no doubt that God sent down *the Prophet* (Q7:158), peace and the mercy of God be upon him, as a guide with an eloquent Book and a standing command. No one will be ruined by it except one who ruins himself. Certainly, only doubtful innovations cause ruin except those from which God may protect. In God's authority lies the safety of your affairs. Therefore, render Him such obedience as is neither blameworthy nor insincere. By God, you must do so otherwise God will take away from you the power of Islam and will never thereafter return it to you until it reverts to others. Sermon 169

Nay! They denied The Truth when it drew near them, so they are in a confused state of affairs. **50:5**
Look they not on the heaven above them, how We built it and made it appear pleasing? There are not any gaps in it. **50:6**
The earth, We stretched it out and cast on it firm mountains and caused in it to develop every lovely, diverse pair **50:7**
for contemplation and as a reminder to every servant, one who turns in repentance. **50:8**
Is there no one to offer repentance over his faults before his death? Or is there no one to perform virtuous acts before the day of trial? Sermon 28

We sent down blessed water from heaven. Then, We caused gardens to develop from it and reaped grains of wheat **50:9**
and high-reaching date palm trees with ranged spathes **50:10**
as provision for My servants. We gave life by them to a lifeless land. Thus, will be the going forth. **50:11**
If you were to cast the eye of your heart towards what is described for you of the Garden, your soul would become averse to the marvels of this world—its passions, its pleasures and its embellished scenery. Your soul would be rapt in contemplation of the swaying trees whose roots lie hidden in dunes of musk on the banks of the rivers of the Garden and clusters of dazzling pearls hanging down from the branches of its trees ... Sermon 164*

The folk of Noah denied what came before them, and the Companions of the Rass and Thamud, **50:12**
and Ad and Pharaoh and the brothers of Lot, **50:13**
and the Companions of the Thicket and the folk of Tubba. Everyone denied the Messengers, so My threat was realized. **50:14** ***

Were We wearied by the first creation? Nay! They are perplexed about a new creation. **50:15**
When He made anything of the world, the making of it did not cause Him any difficulty. The creation of anything which He created and formed did not fatigue Him. He did not create it to heighten His authority, nor for fear of loss or harm, nor to seek its help against an overwhelming foe, nor to guard against any avenging opponent with its help, nor

for the extension of His domain by its help, nor for boasting over largeness of His possession against a partner, nor because He felt lonely and desired to seek its company. Sermon 186

Certainly, We created the human being. We know what evil his soul whispers to him. We are nearer to him than the jugular vein. **50:16**

I seek guidance from Him as He is Near. He is the Guide. I seek His succor as He is Mighty and the Subduer. I depend upon Him as He is Sufficer and Supporter. I bear witness that *Muhammad* (Q48:29), peace and the mercy of God be upon him, is *His servant* (Q17:1) and *Prophet.* (Q7:158) He sent him for enforcement of His commands, for exhausting His pleas and for presenting warnings against eternal punishment. Sermon 8

When the two receivers are ones who receive, seated on the right and on the left, **50:17**
he utters not a saying but that there is one ready, watching over, near him **50:18**
when the agony of death drew near with The Truth. That is what ***you*** *had been shunning.* **50:19**

After death there is no repentance and no possibility of coming back to this world to undo the wrong done by you. Letter 31

The trumpet will be blown. That is the Day of The Threat. **50:20**

Ears will resound with the thundering voice of the announcer calling towards the final judgment, award of recompense, striking of punishment and paying of reward. Sermon 82

Every person will draw near with an angel, one who drives, and an angel witness. **50:21**
Certainly, ***you*** *had been heedless of this so We removed* ***your*** *screen from* ***you*** *so that* ***your*** *sight this Day will be sharp.* **50:22**

Every person will draw near with an angel, one who drives, and an angel witness. **(50:21)** The driver drives him towards the Resurrection while the witness furnishes evidence about his deeds. Sermon 84

His comrade angel would say: This is what is ready near me of his record: **50:23**
Cast into hell every stubborn ingrate **50:24**
who delays the good, one who exceeds the limits, one who is in grave doubt, **50:25**
he who made another god with God! Then, cast him into the severe punishment! **50:26**
His comrade Satan would say: Our Lord! I made him not overbold, but he had been going far astray. **50:27**
He would say: Strive not against one another in My presence, for, surely, I will put forward The Threat to you. **50:28**
The statement is not substituted in My presence and I am not unjust to the servants. **50:29**

They have made Satan the master of their affairs. He has taken them as partners. He has laid eggs and hatched them in their bosoms. He creeps and crawls in their laps. He sees through their eyes and speaks with their tongues. In this way he has led them to sinfulness and adorned for them foul things like the action of one whom Satan has made partner in his domain and speaks untruth through his tongue. Sermon 7

On a Day when We will say to hell: Are ***you*** *full? It will say: Are there any additions?* **50:30**

Everyone of them is ... alone although they are a group, and they are strangers, even though friends. They are unaware of morning after a night and of evening after a day. The night or the day when they departed has become ever existent for them. They found the dangers of their place of stay more serious than they had apprehended. They witnessed that its signs were greater than they had guessed. Sermon 220

The Garden was brought close to the ones who are God-conscious, not far off. **50:31**

How appropriate are these illustrations and effective admonitions, provided they are received by pure hearts, open ears, firm views and sharp wits. Be God-conscious like him who listened to good advice and bowed before it. Sermon 82

This is what is promised you, for every penitent and guardian **50:32**
who dreaded The Merciful in the unseen and drew near with a heart of one who turns in repentance: **50:33**

O the Most Merciful of all! O my God! Surely, **You** are powerful over whatever **You** will. Sermon 143

Enter you there in peace. That is the Day of Eternity! **50:34**
They will have what they will in it and with Us there is yet an addition. **50:35**

When the earthquake occurs, the Day of Resurrection approaches with all its severities, the people of every worshipping place cling to it, all the devotees cling to the object of their devotion and all the followers cling to their leader. Then on that day even the opening of an eye in the air and the sound of a footstep on the ground will be assigned its due through His Justice and His Equity. On that day many an argument will prove void and a contention for excuses will stand rejected. Sermon 222

How many We caused to perish before them of generations who were stronger than they in courage so that they searched about on the land. Was there any asylum? **50:36**

Certainly, there are examples before you of God's wrath, punishment, days of tribulations and happenings. Therefore, do not disregard His promises. Do not ignore His punishment or make light His wrath and not expect His violence, because God, the Almighty, did not curse the past ages unless they had left off asking others to do good acts and refraining them from bad acts. In fact, God cursed the foolish for committing sins and the wise because they gave up refraining others from evil. Be aware! You have broken the bonds of Islam, transgressed its limits, and destroyed its commands. Sermon 192

Truly, in that is a reminder for him, for whoever had a heart or, having the ability to hear, gave listen. He is a witness. **50:37**

O my God! Whoever listens to our words which are just and which seek the prosperity of religion and the worldly life and do not seek mischief, but they reject after listening, then he certainly turns away from **Your** support and desists from strengthening **Your** religion. We make **You** a Witness over him and **You** are the greatest of all witnesses, and we make all those who inhabit **Your** earth and **Your** skies witness over him. Thereafter, **You** alone can make us needless of his support and question him for his sin. Sermon 212

Certainly, We created the heavens and the earth and whatever is between in six days, and no exhaustion afflicted Us. **50:38**
So, have ***you*** *patience with whatever they say and glorify with the praise of* ***your*** *Lord before the*

coming up of the sun and before sunset. **50:39**
In the night glorify Him and at the end part of the prostrations. **50:40**

Praise belongs to God (Q1:2) Who made me such that I have not died, nor am I sick, nor have my veins been infected with disease, nor have I been hauled up for my evil acts, nor am I without progeny, nor have I forsaken my religion, nor do I disbelieve in my Lord, nor do I feel strangeness with my faith, nor is my intelligence affected, nor have I been punished with the punishment of peoples before me. I am a servant in **Your** possession. I have been guilty of excesses over myself. **You** have exhausted **Your** pleas over me and I have no plea before **You**. I have no power to take except what **You** give me. I cannot evade except what **You** save me from. Sermon 215

Listen ***you*** *on a Day when one who calls out will cry out from a near place.* **50:41**
On a Day when they will hear the Cry with The Truth. That will be the Day of going forth. **50:42**

This whole world is going to end and every individual has to leave it some day or the other. Letter 69

Truly, it is We who give life and cause to die and to Us is the Homecoming **50:43**
on a Day when the earth will be split open swiftly. That will be an easy assembling for Us. **50:44**
We are greater in knowledge as to what they say. ***You*** *are not haughty over them so remind by the Quran whoever fears My threat.* **50:45**

Imam Ali heard somebody reciting the passage of the Quran: *We belong to God and truly, we are ones who return to Him.* (Q2:156) Imam Ali said: How true it is! Our declaring that *we belong to God* indicates that we accept Him as our Master, Owner and Lord and when we say that *we are ones who return to Him*, this indicates that we accept our mortality. Saying 99

CHAPTER 51: THE WINNOWING WINDS (al-Dhāriyāt)

By the winnowing winds of ones that winnow **51:1**
by the burden-bearers, the ones who carry a heavy burden **51:2**
and the ones that run with ease **51:3**
and the ones who distribute the command, **51:4**
truly, what you are promised is that which is sincere. **51:5**
Truly, the judgment is that which falls. **51:6**

O God's human being! Be God-conscious. Keep in view the reason why He created you. Be afraid of Him to the extent He has advised you to do. Make yourself deserve what He has promised you by having confidence in the truth of His promise and entertaining fear of the Day of Judgment. Sermon 82

By the heaven that is full of tracks, **51:7**
you are ones who are at variance in your sayings. **51:8**
He is misled there by he who was misled. **51:9**
Perdition to those who guess, **51:10**
ones who are inattentive because of obstinacy. **51:11**

Whoever takes a partner for **You** is ungrateful according to what is stated in **Your** unambiguous verses and indicated by the evidence of **Your** clear arguments. I bear witness that **You** are that God Who cannot be confined in the fetters of intelligence so as to admit change of condition by entering its imagination, nor in the shackles of the mind so as to become limited and an object of alterations. Sermon 91

They ask: When will the Day of Judgment be? **51:12**
A Day when they are tried over the fire: **51:13**
Experience your test. This is that for which you had been seeking to hasten. **51:14**

On that day God will collect on it the front and the back, to stand in obedience for the exaction of accounts and for the award of recompense for deeds. Sweat would flow up to their mouths like reins while the earth would be trembling under them. In the best condition among them would be he who has found a resting place for both his feet and an open place for his breath. Sermon 102

Truly, the ones who are God-conscious will be in the Garden and springs, **51:15**
ones who take what their Lord gave them. Truly, they had been before this—ones who are doers of good. **51:16**
They had been slumbering little during the night. **51:17**
At the breaking of the day, they ask for forgiveness. **51:18**

They call Him and breathe in the air of forgiveness. Sermon 221

There is an obligation from their wealth for the one who begs and the one who is deprived. **51:19**

What will a person do with wealth that he would shortly be deprived of while only its ill effects and reckoning would be left behind for him? Sermon 157

On the earth are signs, for the ones that are certain **51:20**
and in yourselves. Will you not, then, perceive? **51:21**
In the heaven is your provision as you are promised **51:22**
by the Lord of the heaven and the earth. It is, truly, The Truth just as you yourselves speak. **51:23**

I bear witness that *there is no god but God* (Q47:19), by virtue of belief, certainty, sincerity and conviction. I also bear witness that *Muhammad* (Q48:29), peace and the mercy of God be upon him, is *His servant* (Q17:1) and *Prophet* (Q7:158), whom He deputed when the signs of guidance were obliterated and the ways of religion were desolate. So he threw open the truth, gave advice to the people, guided them towards righteousness and ordered them to be moderate. May God bless him ... Sermon 194

Truly, approached **you** *the discourse of guests of Abraham, the ones who are honored?* **51:24**
When they entered to him they said: Peace. He said: Peace, to a folk, ones who are unknown. **51:25**
Then, he turned upon his people and brought about a fattened calf **51:26**
so he brought it near to them. He said: Will you not eat? **51:27**
Then, he sensed a fear of them; they said: Be not in awe. They gave him good tidings of a knowing boy. **51:28**
Then, his woman came forward with a loud cry. She slapped her face and said: I am an old barren woman! **51:29**
They said: Thus, spoke **your** *Lord. Truly, He is The Wise, The Knowing.* **51:30**
Abraham said: O ones who are sent, what is your business? **51:31**

They said: That we were sent to a folk, ones who sin, **51:32**
to send on them rocks of clay, **51:33**
ones distinguished by **your** *Lord for ones who are excessive.* **51:34**
So, We brought out whoever had been in it of the ones who believe. **51:35**
But We found in it nothing but a house of ones who submit to God. **51:36**
We left a sign in it for those who fear the painful punishment. **51:37**
In Moses, then, We sent him to Pharaoh with a clear authority. **51:38**
Then, Pharaoh turned away to his court. He said: One who is a sorcerer, one who is possessed! **51:39**
So, We took him and his armies and cast them forth into the water of the sea and he is one who is answerable. **51:40**
In Ad, when We sent against them the withering wind. **51:41**
It forsakes not anything it approached, but made it like it was decayed. **51:42**
In Thamud, when it was said to them: Take joy for a while. **51:43**
Yet they defied the command of their Lord so the thunderbolt took them while they look on. **51:44**
They were neither able to stand up nor had they been ones who are aided. **51:45**
The folk of Noah from before. Truly, they had been a folk, ones who disobey. **51:46**
We built the heaven with potency. Truly, We are ones who extend wide. **51:47**
The earth, We spread it forth. How excellent are the ones who spread! **51:48** ***

Of everything We created pairs so that perhaps you will recollect. **51:49**
So, run away towards God. Truly, I am to you a clear warner from Him. **51:50**
Make not with God any other god. Truly, I am to you a clear warner from Him. **51:51**
There approached not those who were before them any Messenger but that they said: One who is a sorcerer or one who is possessed! **51:52**
Counseled they this to one another? Nay! They are a folk, ones who are defiant! **51:53**

A person should control his tongue because the tongue is defiant with its master. By God, I do not find that fear of God benefits a person who practices it unless he controls his tongue. Certainly the tongue of a believer is at the back of his heart while the heart of a hypocrite is at the back of his tongue. When a believer intends to say anything, he thinks it over in his mind. If it is good he discloses it, but if it is bad he lets it remain concealed. While a hypocrite speaks whatever comes to his tongue, without knowing what is in his favor and what goes against him. Sermon 175

So, turn **you** *away from them that* **you** *be not one who is reproached.* **51:54**

Certainly, I belong to the group of people who care not for the reproach of anybody in matters concerning God. Their countenance is the countenance of the truthful and their speech is the speech of the virtuous. They are wakeful during the nights in devotion to God and over beacons of guidance in the day. They hold fast to the rope of the Quran, revive the traditions of God and of His Prophet. They do not boast, nor indulge in self-conceit, nor misappropriate, nor create mischief. Their hearts are in Paradise while their bodies are busy in good acts. Sermon 192

Remind, for, truly, the reminder profits the ones who believe. **51:55**

Know that this Quran is an adviser who never deceives, a leader who never misleads and a narrator who never speaks a lie. No one will sit beside this Quran, but when he rises, he will achieve one addition or one diminution—addition in his guidance or elimination in his spiritual blindness. You should also know that no one will need anything after guidance from the Quran and no one will be free from want before guidance from the Quran. Seek cure from the Quran for your ailments and seek its assistance in your distress. It contains a cure for the worst diseases, namely unbelief, hypocrisy, revolt and misguidance. Pray to God through it and turn to God with its love ... There is nothing like it through which the people should turn to God, the Sublime. Sermon 176

I created not jinn and humankind but that they worship Me. **51:56**
I want no provision from them nor want I that they feed Me. **51:57**
Truly, God, He is The Provider, The Possessor of Strength, The Sure. **51:58**

Praise belongs to God (Q1:2) Who made praise the Key for His remembrance, a means for increase of His bounty and a guide for His Attributes and Dignity.

Truly, the impiety of those who did wrong is like the impiety of their companions. So, let them not seek to hasten the Judgment. **51:59**
Then, woe to those who disbelieved in that Day of theirs that they are promised. **51:60**

On the Day of Judgment an announcer will announce: Be aware! Every sower of a crop is in distress except the sowers of the Quran. Sermon 175

Chapter 52: The Mount (al-Tūr)

By the mount **52:1**
and by a Book inscribed **52:2**
on an unrolled scroll of parchment **52:3**
and by the frequented House **52:4**
and by the exalted roof **52:5**
and that which is poured forth over the seas, **52:6**
truly, the punishment of ***Your*** *Lord is that which falls.* **52:7**
There is no one who averts it. **52:8**
On a Day when the heaven will spin a spinning **52:9**
and the mountains will journey a journey. **52:10**
Then, woe on a Day to the ones who deny, **52:11**
they, those are engaging in idle talk, play, **52:12**
on a Day they will be driven away with force to the fire of hell with a driving away: **52:13**
This is the fire which you had been denying! **52:14**
Is this, then, sorcery or is it that you perceive not? **52:15**
Roast you in it! Then, have patience, or you endure patiently not, it is all the same to you. You will be only given recompense for what you had been doing. **52:16**

Hell! Everyone of them is ... alone although they are a group, and they are strangers, even though friends. They are unaware of morning after a night and of evening after a day. The night or the day when they departed has become ever existent for them. They found the dangers of their place of stay more serious than they had apprehended, and they witnessed that its signs were greater than they had guessed. The two objectives, namely Paradise and Hell, have been stretched for them up to a point beyond the reach of fear or hope. Had they been able to speak they would have become dumb to describe what they witnessed or saw. Sermon 220

Truly, the ones who are God-conscious will be in Gardens and bliss, **52:17**
ones who are joyful for what their Lord gave them. Their Lord protected them from the punishment of hellfire. **52:18**
Eat and drink wholesomely because of what you had been doing. **52:19**
They will be ones who are reclining on couches arrayed. We will give in marriage to them lovely, most beautiful eyed ones. **52:20**
Those who believed and their offspring who followed them in belief, We caused them to join their offspring. We deprived them not of anything of their actions. Every man will be pledged for what he earned. **52:21**

Where are the seekers of virtue? The paths have already been determined. They have been given the news. For every misguidance, there is a cause. For every breaking of a pledge, there is a misrepresentation. By God, I shall not be like him who listens to the voice of mourning, hears the man who brings news of death and also visits the mourner, yet does not take a lesson. Sermon 148

We furnished relief to them with sweet fruit and meat such as that for which they lust. **52:22**
They will contend with one another for a cup around which there is no idle talk nor accusation of sinfulness. **52:23**
Boys of theirs will go around them as if they had been well-guarded pearls. **52:24**
Some of them will come forward to some others demanding of one another. **52:25**
They would say: Truly, we had been before ones who are apprehensive among our people, **52:26**
but God showed grace to us and protected us from the punishment of the burning wind. **52:27**
Truly, we had been calling to Him before. Truly, He, He is The Source of Goodness, The Compassionate. **52:28**

O the Most Merciful of all! O my God! Pour on us **Your** mercy, **Your** blessing, **Your** sustenance and **Your** pity .... Sermon 143

So, remind! ***You*** *are not, by the divine blessing of* ***your*** *Lord, a soothsayer nor one who is possessed.* **52:29**
Or they say: A poet! We await for the setback of fate for him. **52:30**
Say: Await for I am with the ones who are waiting. **52:31**

Did you get the news that the world was ever generous enough to present ransom for them, or gave them any support or afforded them good company? It rather inflicted them with troubles, made them languid with calamities, molested them with catastrophes, threw them down on their noses, trampled them under hoofs and helped ... *the setback of fate* ... (Q52:30) against them. Sermon 110

Or command their faculties of understanding to this? Or are they a folk, ones who are defiant? **52:32**
Or say they: He fabricated it? Nay! They believe not. **52:33**
Then, let them bring a discourse like it, if they had been ones who are sincere. **52:34**
Or were they created out of nothing? Or are they ones who are creators of themselves? **52:35**
Or created they the heavens and the earth? Nay! They are not certain. **52:36**
Or are the treasures of ***your*** *Lord with them? Or are they ones who are registrars?* **52:37**
Or have they a ladder by means of which they listen? Then, let ones who are listening bring a clear authority. **52:38**

Or has He daughters and they have sons? **52:39**
Or have **you** *asked them for a compensation so that they are from something owed ones who will be weighed down?* **52:40**
Or is the unseen with them and they write it down? **52:41**
Or want they cunning? But it is those who were ungrateful. They are the ones who are outwitted. **52:42**
Or have they a god other than God? Glory be to God above partners they ascribe! **52:43**

By God! Truly, we had been clearly wandering astray when we made you equal with the Lord of the worlds. (Q26:97-98) Sermon 91

If they consider pieces of the heaven descending, they would say: Heaped up clouds! **52:44**
So, forsake them until they encounter their day in which they will be swooning. **52:45**

They will be within God's sight and will hear every one who would call them. They will have the dress of helplessness and covering of submission and indignity. Sermon 82

A Day when their cunning will avail them not at all nor will they be helped. **52:46**

Your ultimate goal of reward or punishment is before you. Behind your back is the hour of Resurrection which is driving you on. Keep yourself light and overtake the forward ones. The first ones who have preceded await the last ones. Sermon 21

Truly, for those who did wrong there is a punishment besides that, but most of them know not. **52:47**

O God's human being! Where are those who were allowed long ages to live? They enjoyed bounty. They were taught. They learned. They were given time. They passed it in vain. They were kept healthy. They forgot their duty. They were allowed a long period of life, were handsomely provided for, were warned of grievous punishment and were promised great rewards. You should avoid sins that lead to destruction and vices that attract the wrath of God. Sermon 82

So, have **you** *patience for the determination of* **your** *Lord, for, truly,* **you** *are under Our eyes; and glorify the praises of* **your** *Lord when* **you** *have stood up at the time of dawn,* **52:48**
and glorify at night and the drawing back of the stars. **52:49**

We praise Him for whatever He takes or gives or whatever He inflicts on us or tries us with. He is aware of all that is hidden and He sees all that is concealed. He knows all that breasts contain or eyes hide. We render evidence that *there is no god, but He.* (Q3:2) and that *Muhammad* (Q48:29), peace and the mercy of God be upon him, has been chosen by Him and deputized by Him—evidence tendered both secretly and openly, by heart and by tongue. Sermon 132

Chapter 53: The Star (al-Najm)

By the star when it hurled to ruin, **53:1**
neither your companion went astray, nor he erred **53:2**
nor speaks he for himself out of desire. **53:3**

Praise belongs to God (Q1:2) Who is above all similarity to creatures, is above the words of describers Who displays the wonders of His management for the on-lookers, is hidden from the imagination of thinkers by virtue of the greatness of His glory, has knowledge without acquiring it by adding to it or drawing it from someone, and Who is the ordainer of all matters without reflecting or thinking. He is such that gloom does not concern Him, nor does He seek light from brightness. Night does not overtake Him, nor does the day pass over Him so as to affect Him in any manner. His comprehension of things is not through eyes. His knowledge is not dependent on being informed. God deputized *the Prophet* (Q7:158), peace and the mercy of God be upon him, with light and accorded him the highest precedence in selection. Through him God united those who were divided, overpowered the powerful, overcame difficulties and leveled rugged ground and, thus, removed misguidance from right and left. Sermon 213

It is but a revelation that is revealed, **53:4**
taught to him by The One Stronger in Strength, **53:5**

Know that this Quran is an adviser who never deceives, a leader who never misleads and a narrator who never speaks a lie. No one will sit beside this Quran, but when he rises, he will achieve one addition or one diminution—addition in his guidance or elimination in his spiritual blindness. You should also know that no one will need anything after guidance from the Quran and no one will be free from want before guidance from the Quran. Seek cure from the Quran for your ailments and seek its assistance in your distress. It contains a cure for the worst diseases, namely unbelief, hypocrisy, revolt and misguidance. Pray to God through it and turn to God with its love ... There is nothing like it through which the people should turn to God, the Sublime. Sermon 176

Possessor of Forcefulness. Then, he stood poised **53:6**
while he was on the loftiest horizon. **53:7**
Again, he came to pass near and hung suspended **53:8**
until he had been at a distance of two bow lengths or closer. **53:9**
Then, He revealed to His servant what He revealed. **53:10**
The mind lied not against what it saw. **53:11**
Will you altercate with him about what he sees? **53:12**
Certainly, he saw it another time **53:13**
near the Lote Tree of the Utmost Boundary **53:14**
near which is the Garden of the Place of Shelter, **53:15**
when overcomes the Lote Tree what overcomes it. **53:16**
The sight swerved not, nor was it defiant. **53:17**

God, the Almighty, has sent down a guiding Book wherein He has explained virtue and vice. You should adopt the course of virtue, whereby you will have guidance. Detach yourself from the direction of vice, so that you remain on the right way. Sermon 167

Certainly, he saw some of the greatest signs of his Lord. **53:18**

I bear witness that *there is no god but God,* (Q47:19), by virtue of belief, certainty, sincerity and conviction. I also bear witness that *Muhammad* (Q48:29), peace and the mercy of God be upon him, is *His servant* (Q17:1) and *Prophet* (Q7:158) whom He deputed when the signs of guidance were obliterated and the ways of religion were desolate. So he threw open the truth, gave advice to the people, guided them towards righteousness and ordered them to be moderate. May God bless him ... Sermon 194

Saw you, then, al-Lat and al-Uzza **53:19**
and Manat, the third, the other? **53:20**
Have you males and has He, females? **53:21**
That, then, is an unfair division. **53:22**

O God! I bear witness that he who likens **You** with the separateness of the limbs or with the joining of the extremities of his body did not acquaint his inner self with knowledge about **You.** His heart did not secure conviction to the effect that there is no partner for **You.** It is as though he has not heard the wrongful followers disclaiming their false gods by saying: By God! *Truly we have been clearly wandering astray when we made you equal with the Lord of the worlds.* (Q26:97-98) Sermon 91

They are but names that you named, you and your fathers, for which God caused not to descend any authority. They follow nothing but opinion and that for which their souls yearn. Certainly, drew near them the guidance from their Lord. **53:23**

You should give up forming opinion about things which you have not clearly understood or visualized.... Letter 78

Or will the human being have what he coveted? **53:24**
Then, to God belongs the Last and the First. **53:25**

I believe in Him as He is the First of all and He is Outward or Manifest. I seek guidance from Him as He is Near and He is the Guide. I seek His help as He is Mighty and the Subduer. I depend upon Him as He is Sufficer and Supporter. Sermon 8

How many an angel in the heavens is there whose intercession will avail nothing at all, but after God gives permission to whom He wills and He is well-pleased. **53:26**
Truly, those who believe not in the world to come naming the angels with female names, **53:27**
while they have no knowledge of it, they follow nothing but opinion. Truly, opinion avails them not at all against The Truth. **53:28**
So, turn ***you*** *aside from him who turns away from Our Remembrance and he wants nothing but this present life.* **53:29**
That is their attainment of the knowledge. Truly, ***your*** *Lord, He is the One Who is greater in knowledge of whoever went astray from His way. He is greater in knowledge of whoever were truly guided.* **53:30**
To God belongs whatever is in the heavens and whatever is in and on the earth that He may give recompense to those who did evil for what they did and give recompense fairer to those who did good, **53:31**
those who avoid the major sins and the indecencies but the lesser offenses. Truly, ***your*** *Lord is One Who is Extensive in forgiveness. He is greater in knowledge of you when He caused you to grow from the earth and when you were an unborn child in the wombs of your mothers. So, you make not pure yourselves. He is greater in knowledge of him who was God-conscious.* **53:32**

One of the firm decisions of God in the Wise Reminder (Quran), upon which He bestows reward or gives punishment, and through which He likes or dislikes is that it will not benefit a person, even though he exerts himself and acts sincerely, if he leaves this world to meet God with one of these acts without repenting, namely that he believed in a partner with God during his obligatory worship, or appeased his own anger by killing an individual, or spoke about acts committed by others, or sought fulfillment of his needs from people by introducing an innovation in his religion, or met people with a double face, or moved among them with a double tongue. Understand this because an illustration is a guide for its like. Sermon 153

Had **you** *considered him who turned away* 53:33
and gave a little, giving grudgingly? 53:34
Is the knowledge of the unseen with him so that he sees it? 53:35
Or is he told what is in the scrolls of Moses 53:36
and of Abraham who paid his account in full? 53:37
The burdened soul will not bear the heavy load of another. 53:38
The human being is not but what he endeavored for 53:39
and that his endeavoring will be seen. 53:40
Again, he will be given recompense for it with a more true recompense, 53:41
and that towards **your** *Lord is the Utmost Boundary,* 53:42
and that He caused laughter and caused weeping, 53:43
and that He caused to die and gave life 53:44
and it is He, He created the pairs, the male and the female 53:45
from seminal fluid when it is emitted, 53:46
and that with Him is another growth 53:47
and it is He, He Who Enriched and made rich 53:48
and that He, He is the Lord of Sirius 53:49
and that He caused to perish the previous Ad 53:50
and Thamud. He caused none to remain 53:51
and the folk of Noah before. Truly, they had been they who do greater wrong and ones who are defiant. 53:52 ***

He caused to tumble that which are cities overthrown, 53:53
then, enwrapped them with what enwrapped. 53:54
Then, which of the benefits of **your** *Lord will* **you** *quarrel with?* 53:55
This is a warner among the previous warnings. 53:56

I bear witness that *Muhammad* (Q48:29), peace and the mercy of God be upon him, is *His servant* (Q17:1) and *Prophet.* (Q7:158) He sent him for enforcement of His commands, for exhausting His pleas and for presenting warnings against eternal punishment. Sermon 82

The Impending Day is impending. 53:57

When the earthquake occurs, the Day of Resurrection approaches with all its severities, the people of every worshipping place cling to it, all the devotees cling to the object of their devotion and all the followers cling to their leader. Then on that day even the opening of an eye in the air and the sound of a footstep on the ground will be assigned its due through His Justice and His Equity. On that day many an argument will prove void and a contention for excuses will stand rejected. Sermon 222

There is not other than God, One Who Uncovers it. 53:58
Then, at this discourse you marvel? 53:59
Will you laugh and not weep 53:60

while you are ones who pass life in enjoyment? **53:61**

I bear witness that *there is no god but God,* (Q47:19), the One. I bear witness that *there is no god but God,* (Q47:19), the One. He has no like. My bearing witness has been tested. Its essence is our belief. We shall cling to it for as long as we live and shall store it facing the tribulations that overtake us because it is the foundation stone of faith and the first step towards good actions and divine pleasure. It is the means to keep Satan away. Sermon 2

So, prostrate yourselves to God and worship Him. **53:62**

He was asked whether he had seen God, when he replied: Do I worship one whom I have not seen? Then he enquired: How have you seen Him? Then he replied: Eyes cannot see Him face to face, but hearts perceive Him through the realities of belief. He is near to things, but not physically contiguous. He is far from them, but not physically separate. He is a speaker, but not with reflection. He intends, but not with preparation. He molds, but not with the assistance of limbs. He is subtle, but cannot be attributed with being concealed. He is great, but cannot be attributed with haughtiness. He sees, but cannot be attributed with the sense of sight. He is Merciful, but cannot be attributed with weakness of heart. Faces feel low before His greatness and hearts tremble out of fear of Him. Sermon 179

Chapter 54: The Moon (al-Qamar)

The Hour neared and the moon was split. **54:1**
If they see a sign, they turn aside and say: Incessant sorcery! **54:2**

I bear witness that *there is no god but God,* (Q47:19), by virtue of belief, certainty, sincerity and conviction. I also bear witness that *Muhammad* (Q48:29), peace and the mercy of God be upon him, is *His servant* (Q17:1) and *Prophet* (Q7:158) whom He deputed when the signs of guidance were obliterated and the ways of religion were desolate. So he threw open the truth, gave advice to the people, guided them towards righteousness and ordered them to be moderate. May God bless him ... Sermon 194

They denied and followed their own desires. Every affair is that which is settled. **54:3**
Certainly, the tidings drew near them wherein was that which is to deter **54:4**
—namely that which is far reaching wisdom— yet warnings avail not. **54:5**
So, turn **you** *away from them on a Day when One Who Calls will call to a horrible thing.* **54:6**

Then there remain a few people in whose case the remembrance of their return to God on the Day of Judgment keeps their eyes bent and the fear of Resurrection moves their tears. Some of them are scared away from the world and dispersed. Some are frightened and subdued. Some are quiet as if muzzled. Some are praying sincerely. Some are grief-stricken and pain-ridden whom fear has confined to namelessness and disgrace has shrouded them, so they are in the sea of bitter water, their mouths are closed and their hearts are bruised. They preached until they were tired. They were oppressed until they were disgraced. They were killed until their numbers dwindled. Sermon 32

Their sight will be that which is humbled and they will go forth from the tombs as if they had been dispersed locusts, **54:7**
ones who run forward with their eyes fixed in horror towards The One Who Calls. The ones who are ungrateful will say: This is a difficult Day! **54:8**

If you wish you can reflect on the locust as well. God gave it two red eyes, lighted for them two moon-like pupils, made for it small ears, opened for it a suitable mouth and gave it keen sense, gave it two teeth to cut with and two sickle-like feet to grip with. The farmers are afraid of it in the matter of their crops since they cannot drive it away even though they may join together. The locust attacks the fields and satisfies its desires of hunger from them although its body is not equal to a thin finger. Sermon 185

The folk of Noah denied before them. They denied Our servant and said: One who is possessed! He was deterred. **54:9**
So, he called to his Lord saying: I am one who is vanquished, so ***You*** *help me.* **54:10**
So, We opened the doors of heaven with torrential water. **54:11**
We caused the earth to gush forth with springs so the waters were to meet one another from a command that was measured. **54:12**
We carried him on a vessel of planks and caulked, **54:13**
running under Our eyes, a recompense for Noah who had been disbelieved. **54:14**
Certainly, We left this as a sign. Then, is there one who recalls? **54:15**
So, how had been My punishment and My warning? **54:16** ***
Certainly, We made the Quran easy as a Remembrance. Then, is there one who recalls? **54:17**
Ad denied. So, how had been My punishment and My warning? **54:18**
Truly, We sent a raging wind against them on a day of continuous misfortune, **54:19**
tearing out humanity as if they had been uprooted palm trees, uprooted. **54:20**
So, how had been My punishment and My warning? **54:21**
Certainly, We made the Quran easy as a Remembrance. Then, is there one who recalls? **54:22**
Thamud denied the warning **54:23**
for they said: Follow we a lone mortal from among us? Truly, we would be going astray and insane. **54:24**
Is it that the Remembrance was cast down to Salih from among us? Nay! He is a rash liar! **54:25**
They will know tomorrow who the rash liar is! **54:26**
Truly, We are ones who sent the she-camel as a test for them. So, ***you*** *be on the watch for them and maintain patience.* **54:27**
Tell them that the division of the water is between them. Every drink was that which is divided in turn. **54:28**
But they cried out to their companion, and he took her in hand and crippled her. **54:29**
So, how had been My punishment and My warning? **54:30**
Truly, We sent against them one Cry and they had been like straw for the one who is a builder of animal enclosures. **54:31**
Certainly, We made the Quran easy as a Remembrance. Then, is there one who recalls? **54:32**
The folk of Lot denied the warning. **54:33**
Truly, We sent against them a sand storm, but the family of Lot. We delivered them at the breaking of day **54:34**
as a divine blessing from Us. Thus, We gave recompense to him who gave thanks. **54:35**
Certainly, he warned them of Our attack but they quarreled over the warning. **54:36**
Certainly, they solicited his guests, so We obliterated their eyes. Then, experience My punishment and My warning. **54:37**
Certainly, it came in the morning, early morning at dawn, a settled punishment. **54:38**
Then, experience My punishment and My warning. **54:39**

Certainly, We made the Quran easy as a Remembrance. Then, is there one who recalls? **54:40**
Certainly, drew near the warning to the people of Pharaoh. **54:41**
They denied Our signs, all of them. So, We took them with a taking, One Who is Almighty, Omnipotent. **54:42**
Are ones who are ungrateful better than those? Or have you an immunity in the ancient scrolls? **54:43**
Or say they: We are aided altogether. **54:44**
Their multitude will be put to flight and they will turn their backs. **54:45**
Nay! The Hour is what is promised them and the Hour will be more calamitous and more distasteful. **54:46** ***

Truly, ones who sin are going astray and insane. **54:47**

I advise you, O people, to fear God and to praise Him profusely for His favors to you and His reward for you and His obligations on you. See how He chose you for favors and dealt with you with mercy. You sinned openly. He kept you covered. You behaved in a way to incur His punishment, but He gave you more time. Sermon 188

On a Day they will be dragged into the fire on their faces: Experience the touch of Saqar! **54:48**

Pledge yourself with prayer and remain steady with it. Offer prayer as much as possible and seek nearness to God through it, because it is imposed upon the believers as a timed ordinance: *Truly, the formal prayer had been—for the ones who believe—a timed prescription.* (Q4:103) Have you not heard the reply of the people of Hell when they were asked: *What thrust you into Saqar? They would answer: We were not of the ones who formally pray.* (Q74:42-43) Sermon 198

Truly, We created all things in measure **54:49**
and Our command is not but one as the twinkling of the eye. **54:50**

Praise belongs to God (Q1:2) Who is High above all else, and is Near the creation through His bounty. He is the Giver of all reward and distinction, and Dispeller of all calamities and hardships. I praise Him for His continuous mercy and His copious bounties. Sermon 82

Certainly, We caused to perish their partisans. Is there, then, one who recalls? **54:51**

I bear witness that *there is no god but God* (Q47:19), the One, there is no partner with Him, nor is there with Him any god other than Himself, and that *Muhammad* (Q48:29), peace and the mercy of God be upon him, is *His servant* (Q17:1) and *Prophet.* (Q7:158) Sermon 35

Everything they accomplished is in the ancient scrolls. **54:52**

Certainly, there are examples before you of God's wrath, punishment, days of tribulations and happenings. Therefore, do not disregard His promises. Do not ignore His punishment or make light His wrath and not expect His violence, because God, the Almighty, did not curse the past ages unless they had left off asking others to do good acts and refraining them from bad acts. In fact, God cursed the foolish for committing sins and the wise because they gave up refraining others from evil. Be aware! You have broken the bonds of Islam, transgressed its limits, and destroyed its commands. Sermon 192

Every small and great thing is that which is written. 54:53
Truly, the ones who are God-conscious will be in Gardens and rivers, 54:54
in positions of sincerity near an Omnipotent King. 54:55

The Book of God is that through which you see, you speak and you hear. Sermon 133

CHAPTER 55: THE MERCIFUL (al-Raḥmān)

The Merciful. 55:1
He taught the Quran. 55:2

The Book of God ... does not create differences about God, nor does it mislead its own follower from the path of God. Sermon 133

He created the human being. 55:3
He taught him the clear explanation. 55:4
The sun and the moon are to keep count. 55:5
The stars and the trees both prostrate. 55:6
The heaven He exalted. He set in place the Balance 55:7
that you be not defiant in the Balance. 55:8
Set up the weighing with justice and skimp not in the Balance. 55:9
He set the earth in place for the human race. 55:10
On and in it are many kinds of sweet fruit and date palm trees with sheathed fruit trees 55:11
and grain possessor of husks and fragrant herbs. 55:12
So, which of the benefits of the Lord of you both will you both deny? 55:13

This world and the hereafter have submitted to Him their reins. The skies and earths have flung their keys towards Him. The thriving trees bow to Him in the morning and evening, producing for Him flaming fire from their branches and, at His command, turn their own feed into ripe fruits. Sermon 133

He created the human being from earth mud like potter's clay. 55:14
He created the ones who are spirits from a smokeless flame of fire. 55:15
So, which of the benefits of the Lord of you both will you both deny? 55:16
The Lord of the Two Easts, and the Lord of the Two Wests! 55:17
So, which of the benefits of the Lord of you both will you both deny? 55:18
He let forth the two seas to meet one another. 55:19
Between them is a barrier which they wrong not. 55:20
So, which of the benefits of the Lord of you both will you both deny? 55:21

How great is **Your** creation that we see, but how small is this greatness by the side of **Your** Might! How awe-striking is **Your** realm that we notice, but how humble is this against what is hidden from us out of **Your** authority! How extensive are **Your** bounties in this world, but how small are they against the bounties of the next world! Sermon 108

From both of them go forth pearls and coral. 55:22
So, which of the benefits of the Lord of you both will you both deny? 55:23

How awe-striking is **Your** realm that we notice, but how humble is this against what is hidden from us out of **Your** authority! How extensive are **Your** bounties in this world, but how small are they against the bounties of the next world! Sermon 108

His are ones that run with that which is displayed in the sea like landmarks. **55:24**
So, which of the benefits of the Lord of you both will you both deny? **55:25**

You did not create the creation on account of loneliness, nor did **You** make them work for gain. He whom **You** catch cannot go farther than **You**, and he whom **You** hold cannot escape **You**. Sermon 108

All who are in or on it are ones who are being annihilated, **55:26**
yet the Countenance of ***your*** *Lord will remain forever, Possessor of The Majesty and The Splendor.* **55:27**
So, which of the benefits of the Lord of you both will you both deny? **55:28**

Do I worship one whom I have not seen? Then he enquired: How have you seen Him? Then he replied: Eyes cannot see Him face to face, but hearts perceive Him through the realities of belief. He is near to things, but not physically contiguous. He is far from them, but not physically separate. He is a speaker, but not with reflection. He intends, but not with preparation. He molds, but not with the assistance of limbs. He is subtle, but cannot be attributed with being concealed. He is great, but cannot be attributed with haughtiness. He sees, but cannot be attributed with the sense of sight. He is Merciful, but cannot be attributed with weakness of heart. Faces fall low before His greatness and hearts tremble out of fear of Him. Sermon 179

Of Him asks whoever is in the heavens and in and on the earth. Every day He is on some matter. **55:29**
So, which of the benefits of the Lord of you both will you both deny? **55:30**
We will attend to you at leisure, O you two dependents. **55:31**
So, which of the benefits of the Lord of you both will you both deny? **55:32**

Everything submits to Him. Everything exists by Him. He is the satisfaction of every poor, dignity of the low, energy for the weak and shelter for the oppressed. Sermon 108

O you both, assembly of jinn and humankind! If you were able to pass through the areas of the heavens and the earth, then, pass through them! But you will not pass through, but with an authority. **55:33**
So, which of the benefits of the Lord of you both will you both deny? **55:34**

He who disobeys **You** does not decrease **Your** authority. He who obeys **You** does not add to **Your** Might. Sermon 108

There will be sent against you both a flame of fire and heated brass. Will you not, then, help yourselves? **55:35**
So, which of the benefits of the Lord of you both will you both deny? **55:36**

You are the highest aim. There is no escape from **You**. **You** are the promised point of return from which there is no deliverance except towards **You**. In **Your** hand is the forelock of every creature. To **You** is the return of every living being. Sermon 108

Then, when the heaven was split then, it had been crimson like red leather, **55:37**
so which of the benefits of the Lord of you both will you both deny? **55:38**

He who turns away from **Your** command cannot do without **You**. Sermon 108

On that Day no one will be asked about his impiety neither humankind nor ones who are spirits. **55:39**
So, which of the benefits of the Lord of you both will you both deny? **55:40**

The human being should ... fear the Day of Judgment before it arrives. He should appreciate the shortness of his life and the shortness of his sojourn in the place of stay which has only to last for his change over to the next place. He should, therefore, do something for his change over and for the known stages of his departure. Blessed be he who possesses a virtuous heart, obeys one who guides him, keeps away from one who takes him to ruin, catches the path of safety with the help of him who provides him light of guidance and, by obeying the leader who commands him, hastens towards guidance before its doors are closed, opens the door of repentance and removes the stain of sins. He has certainly been put on the right path and guided towards the straight path. Sermon 214

Ones who sin will be recognized by their mark and they will be taken by their forelocks and their feet. **55:41**
So, which of the benefits of the Lord of you both will you both deny? **55:42**

Ones who sin will be recognized by their mark. (Q55:41) What vision does not reach **You** and what sight does not grasp **You**? **You** see the eyes and count the ages. **You** hold people as servants ... *and they will be taken by their forelocks and their feet* ... (Q55:41). We see **Your** creation and wonder over it because of **Your** might, and describe it as a result of **Your** great authority whereas what is hidden from us, of which our sight has fallen short, which our intelligence has not attained, and between which and ourselves curtains of the unknown have been cast, is far greater. He who frees his heart from all other engagements and exerts his thinking in order to know how **You** established **Your** throne, how **You** created **Your** creatures, how **You** suspended the air in **Your** skies and how **You** spread **Your** earth on the waves of water, his eyes would return tired, his intelligence defeated, his ears eager and his thinking wander. Sermon 160

This is hell which the ones who sin deny! **55:43**
They will go around between it and between scalding boiling water! **55:44**
So, which of the benefits of the Lord of you both will you both deny? **55:45**

Be aware the world is wrapping itself up. It has announced its departure. Its known things have become strangers and it is speedily moving backward. It is advancing its inhabitants towards destruction and driving its neighbors towards death. Its sweet enjoyments have become sour. Its clear things have become polluted. Consequently, what has remained of it is just like the remaining water in a vessel or a mouthful of water in a measuring cup. If a thirsty person drinks it, his thirst is not quenched. Sermon 52

For him who feared the station before his Lord are two Gardens. **55:46**
So, which of the benefits of the Lord of you both will you both deny? **55:47**

God, the Almighty, has sent down a guiding Book wherein He has explained virtue and vice. You should adopt the course of virtue whereby you will have guidance, and keep aloof from the direction of vice so that you remain on the right way. Mind the obligations! Mind the obligations! Fulfill them for God and they will take you to the Garden. Surely,

God has made unlawful the things which are not unknown and made lawful the things which are without defect. Sermon 167

Possessor of wide shade. **55:48**
So, which of the benefits of the Lord of you both will you both deny? **55:49**
Two springs will be running. **55:50**
So, which of the benefits of the Lord of you both will you both deny? **55:51**
In them both every kind of sweet fruit of diverse pairs. **55:52**
So, which of the benefits of the Lord of you both will you both deny? **55:53**
Ones who are reclining on places of restfulness the inner linings of which are of brocade. The fruit plucked from trees while fresh, that which draws near from the two Gardens. **55:54**
So, which of the benefits of the Lord of you both will you both deny? **55:55**
In them both are ones who are restraining their (f) glance. No humankind touched them (f) sexually before nor ones who are spirits. **55:56**
So, which of the benefits of the Lord of you both will you both deny? **55:57**

The perfection of believing in His Oneness is to regard Him Pure. The perfection of His purity is to deny Him attributes, because every attribute is a proof that it is different from that to which it is attributed and everything to which something is attributed is different from the attribute. Thus, whoever attaches attributes to God recognizes His like. Whoever recognizes His like regards Him as two. Whoever regards Him as two recognizes parts for Him. Whoever recognizes parts for Him mistakes Him. Whoever mistakes Him points at Him. Whoever points at Him admits limitations for Him. Whoever admits limitations for Him numbers Him. Sermon 1

They are as if they were like rubies and coral. **55:58**
So, which of the benefits of the Lord of you both will you both deny? **55:59**
Is the recompense for kindness other than kindness? **55:60**
So, which of the benefits of the Lord of you both will you both deny? **55:61**
Besides these are two other Gardens. **55:62**
So, which of the benefits of the Lord of you both will you both deny? **55:63**

God seeks you to thank Him and assigns to you His affairs. He has allowed time in the limited field of life so that you may vie with each other in seeking the reward of the Garden. Therefore, tighten up your girdles and wrap up the skirts. High courage and dinners do not go together. Sleep causes weakness in the big affairs of the day and its darkness obliterates the memories of courage. Sermon 24

Dark green. **55:64**
So, which of the benefits of the Lord of you both will you both deny? **55:65**
In them both are two springs gushing. **55:66**
So, which of the benefits of the Lord of you both will you both deny? **55:67**

God sent Muhammad, peace and the mercy of God be upon him, with the Truth so that he may take out His people from the worship of idols towards His worship and from obeying Satan towards obeying Him. God sent him with the Quran which He explained and made strong in order that the people may know their Sustainer (God), since they were ignorant of Him, may acknowledge Him, since they were denying Him and accept Him, since they were refusing to believe in Him. Sermon 147

In them both are sweet fruits and date palm trees and pomegranates. **55:68**
So, which of the benefits of the Lord of you both will you both deny? **55:69**
In them both are the good deeds, fairer. **55:70**
So, which of the benefits of the Lord of you both will you both deny? **55:71**
Most beautiful eyed ones who will be restrained in edifices. **55:72**
So, which of the benefits of the Lord of you both will you both deny? **55:73**
No humankind touched them (f) sexually before nor ones who are spirits. **55:74**
So, which of the benefits of the Lord of you both will you both deny? **55:75**
Ones who are reclining on green pillows and fairer carpets. **55:76**
So, which of the benefits of the Lord of you both will you both deny? **55:77**
Blessed be the Name of ***your*** *Lord, Possessor of The Majesty and The Splendor.* **55:78**

Praise belongs to God (Q1:2) Who is proof of His existence through His creation, of His being eternal through the newness of His creation, and through their mutual similarities of the fact that nothing is similar to Him. Sermon 152

Chapter 56: The Inevitable (al-Wāqi^{c}ah)

When The Inevitable came to pass, **56:1**
its descent is not like that which lies. **56:2**
It will be one that abases, one that exalts. **56:3**
When the earth will rock with a rocking **56:4**
and the mountains be crumbled to dust, crumbling, **56:5**
then, they had been dust scattered about. **56:6**
You had been of three diverse pairs. **56:7**
Then, the Companions of the Right—who are the Companions of the Right? **56:8**
The Companions of the Left—who are Companions of the Left? **56:9**
Ones who take the lead are the ones who take the lead. **56:10**
Those are the ones who are brought near **56:11**
in the Gardens of Bliss. **56:12**
A throng of the ancient ones **56:13**
and a few of the later ones **56:14**
are on lined couches, **56:15**
ones who are reclining on them, ones who are facing one another. **56:16**
Immortal children go around them **56:17**
with cups and ewers and goblets from a spring of water. **56:18**
Neither will they suffer headaches nor will they be intoxicated, **56:19**
and sweet fruit of what they specify **56:20**
and the flesh of birds for which they lust **56:21**
and most beautiful eyed ones, **56:22**
like the parable of the well-guarded pearls, **56:23**
a recompense for what they had been doing. **56:24**
They will not hear any idle talk in it nor accusation of sinfulness, **56:25**
but the saying of Peace! Peace! **56:26**
The Companions of the Right—who are the Companions of the Right? **56:27**
They will be among thornless lote-trees **56:28**
and acacias, one on another, **56:29**

and spread out shade **56:30**
and outpoured water **56:31**
and many sweet fruit. **56:32**
There will be neither that which is severed nor that which is inaccessible. **56:33**
It is an exalted place of restfulness. **56:34**
Truly, We caused them (f) to grow, a good forming, **56:35**
and made them (f) virgins, **56:36**
full of love, of the same age, **56:37**
for the Companions of the Right. **56:38**
A throng of the ancient ones **56:39**
and a throng from the later ones, **56:40**
and the Companions of the Left—who are the Companions of the Left? **56:41**
Those who are in burning wind and scalding water **56:42**
and shade of black smoke **56:43**
neither that which is cool nor generous. **56:44**
Truly, they had been before that ones who are given ease **56:45**
and they had been persisting in tremendous wickedness. **56:46**
They had been saying: When we died and had been earth dust and bones, will we, then, be ones who are raised up? **56:47**
Our ancient fathers? **56:48**
Say: Truly, the ancient ones and the later ones **56:49**
will be ones who will be gathered to a time appointed on a known Day. **56:50**
Again, you, O ones who go astray, are the ones who deny. **56:51**
Certainly, you will be ones who eat from the Zaqqum tree. **56:52**
Then, you will be ones who fill your bellies from it, **56:53**
then, ones who drink scalding water after it. **56:54**
So, you will be ones who drink like the drinking of thirsty camels. **56:55**
This will be their hospitality on the Day of Judgment! **56:56**
We, We created you. Why establish it not as true? **56:57**
Considered you what you spill of human seed? **56:58**
Is it you who create it? Or are We the ones who are the creators? **56:59**
We ordained death among you and We will not be ones who will be outrun **56:60**
in that We will substitute your likeness and We caused you to grow in a way you know not. **56:61**
Certainly, you knew the first growth. Will you not, then, recollect? **56:62**
Considered you the soil that you till? **56:63**
Is it you who sows it? Or are We the ones who sow? **56:64**
If We will, We would make it into chaff and you would continue to joke saying: **56:65**
We are ones who are debt-loaded! **56:66**
Nay! We are ones who are deprived. **56:67**
Considered you the water that you drink? **56:68**
Is it you who caused it to descend from the cloud vapors? Or are We the ones who caused it to descend? **56:69**
If We will, We would make it bitter. Why, then, give you not thanks? **56:70**
Considered you the fire which you strike? **56:71**
Is it you who caused the tree to grow? Or are We the ones who cause it to grow? **56:72**
We made it an admonition and sustenance for ones who are desert people. **56:73**

Then, glorify with the name of ***your*** *Lord, The Sublime.* **56:74**
But no! I swear by the orbit of the stars **56:75**
and, truly, that is an oath to be sworn if you know, sublime. **56:76**
Truly, it is a generous Recitation **56:77**
in a well-guarded Book. **56:78**
None touches it but the ones who are purified, **56:79**
a sending down successively from the Lord of the worlds. **56:80**
Then, is it this discourse that you are ones who scorn? **56:81**
You make it your provision that you, you deny the Recitation. **56:82**
Then, why not intervene when it reached the wind-pipe **56:83**
and you are looking on at the time? **56:84**
We are nearer to him than you, yet you perceive not. **56:85**
Then, why had you not been—if you are not ones to be judged— **56:86**
returning the soul to the body, if you had been ones who are sincere? **56:87**
If he had been among the ones who are brought near, **56:88**
there is solace and fragrant herbs and a Garden of Bliss. **56:89**
If he had been of the Companions of the Right, **56:90**
then: Peace for ***you*** *from the Companions of the Right.* **56:91**
Yet if he had been of the ones who go astray, ones who deny, **56:92**
then, a hospitality of scalding water **56:93**
and broiling in hellfire. **56:94**
Truly, this is The Truth of certainty. **56:95**

Blessed is the man who always kept the life after death in his view, who remembered the Day of Judgment through all his deeds, who led a contented life and who was happy with the lot that God had destined for him. Saying 44

So, glorify the Name of ***your*** *Lord, The Almighty.* **56:96**

Almighty are **You**, the Creator, the Worshipped. On account of **Your** good trials of **Your** creatures, **You** created a house (Paradise) and provided in it for feasting, drinks, foods, spouses, servants, places, streams, plantations and fruits. Then **You** sent a Messenger to invite towards it ... Sermon 108

Chapter 57: Iron (al-Ḥadīd)

Whatever is in the heavens glorified God and whatever is in and on the earth. He is The Almighty, The Wise. **57:1**
To Him belongs the dominion of the heavens and the earth. He gives life and causes to die. He is Powerful over everything. **57:2**
He is The First and The Last, The One Who is Outward and The One Who is Inward. He is Knowing of everything. **57:3**

Praise belongs to God (Q1:2) Who is present in the hidden inwardness of things and Whose being is indicated by the signs of manifest things. The eye of the onlooker cannot behold Him so the eye of one who does not see Him cannot deny His reality, nor can the heart of one who affirms His reality see Him. He is utmost in elevation, so no thing is more elevated than He, but He is also close in His nearness, so no thing is closer than He ... God has not made the intellects capable of defining His qualities, but He has also not veiled the intellects from essential knowledge of Him. Sermon 49*

It is He Who created the heavens and the earth in six days. Again, He turned His attention to the Throne. He knows what penetrates into the earth and what goes forth from it, and what comes down from the heaven and what goes up to it. He is with you wherever you had been. God is Seeing of what you do. **57:4**
To Him belongs the dominion of the heavens and the earth. All commands are returned to God. **57:5**

The face of right has become clear for the wanderer. The approaching moment has raised the veil from its face and signs have appeared for those who search for them. Sermon 108

He causes the nighttime to be interposed into the daytime and causes the daytime to be interposed into the nighttime. He is Knowing of whatever is in the breasts. **57:6**

He hung in its vastness its sky and put therein its decoration consisting of small bright pearls and lamp-like stars. He shot at the over-hearers arrows of bright meteors. He put them in motion on their appointed routine and made them into fixed stars, moving stars, descending stars, ascending stars, ominous stars and lucky stars. Sermon 91

Believe in God and His Messenger and spend out of what He made you ones who are successors in it. Those among you who believed and spent, for them is a great compensation. **57:7**

God never allowed His creation to remain without a Prophet, one deputized by Him, or a Book sent down from Him, or a binding argument, or a standing plea. These Messengers were such that they did not fear that they were few in comparison to the large numbers of their falsifiers. Among them was either a predecessor who would name the one to follow or the follower who had been introduced by the predecessor. Sermon 1

What is the matter with you that you believe not in God while the Messenger calls to you to believe in your Lord and He took your solemn promise, if you had been ones who believe? **57:8**

God sent His Messengers and series of His prophets towards people to get them to fulfill the pledges of His creation, to recall to them His bounties, to exhort them by preaching, to unveil before them the hidden virtues of wisdom and show them the signs of His Omnipotence, namely the sky which is raised over them, the earth that is placed beneath them, means of living that sustain them, deaths that make them die, ailments that turn them old and incidents that successively betake them. Sermon 1

It is He Who sends down to His servant clear portents, signs, that He brings you out from the shadows into the light. Truly, God is to you Gentle, Compassionate. **57:9**

I bear witness that *there is no god but God* (Q47:19), by virtue of belief, certainty, sincerity and conviction. I also bear witness that *Muhammad* (Q48:29), peace and the mercy of God be upon him, is *His servant* (Q17:1) and *Prophet* (Q7:158) whom He deputed when the signs of guidance were obliterated and the ways of religion were desolate. So he threw open the truth, gave advice to the people, guided them towards righteousness and ordered them to be moderate. May God bless him ... Sermon 194

What is the matter with you that you spend not in the way of God while to God belongs the heritage of the heavens and the earth? Not on the same level among you are whoever spent before the victory and fought. Those are more sublime in degree than those who spent afterwards and fought. God promised the fairer to all. God is Aware of what you do. **57:10**

I have seen your flight and your dispersal from the lines. You were surrounded by rude and low people and Bedouins of Syria, although you are the chiefs of Arabs and summit of distinction and possess the dignity of the high nose and big hump of the camel. The sigh of my bosom can subside only when I eventually see you surrounding them as they surrounded you and see you dislodging them from their position as they dislodged you, killing them with arrows and striking them with spears so that their forward rows might fall on the rear ones just like the thirsty camels who have been turned away from their place of drink and removed from their water-points. Sermon 107

Who is he who will lend to God a fairer loan that He multiply it for him and he will have a generous compensation? **57:11**

He, the Sublime. has said: *Who is he who will lend to God a fairer loan that He multiply it for him and he will have a generous compensation?* (Q57:11) He does not seek your support because of any weakness, nor does He demand a loan from you because of shortage. He seeks your help, although He possesses all the armies of the skies and the earth and He is strong and wise. He seeks a loan from you, although He owns the treasures of the skies and the earth and He is rich and praiseworthy. Rather He intends to try you as to which of you performs good acts. You should, therefore, be quick in performance of good acts so that your way be with His neighbors in His abode. He made His Prophet's companions of these neighbors and made the angels to visit them. He has honored their ears so that the sound of Hell fire may never reach them. Sermon 182

On a Day **you** *will see the males, ones who believe and the females, ones who believe, their light coming eagerly in advance of them and on their right: Good tidings for you this Day, Gardens beneath which rivers run, ones who will dwell in them forever. That, it is the winning the sublime triumph!* **57:12**

Mind the obligations! Mind the obligations! Fulfill them for God and they will take you to the Garden. Surely, God has made unlawful the things which are not unknown and made lawful the things which are without defect. Sermon 167

On a Day will say the males, ones who are hypocrites and females, the ones who are hypocrites to those who believed: Wait for us that we will borrow from your light. It will be said: Return behind and search out for a light. There would be a fence set up between them for which there is a door. That which is inward is mercy and that which is outward is towards the punishment. **57:13**

People did not take light from the lights of his wisdom, nor did they produce flame from the flint of sparkling knowledge. So in this matter, they are like grazing cattle and hard stones. Nevertheless, hidden things have appeared for those who perceive. The face of right has become clear for the wanderer. The approaching moment has raised the veil from its face. Signs have appeared for those who search for them. Sermon 108

The hypocrites will cry out to the believers: Have we not been with you? They will say: Yea! You let yourselves be tempted and you awaited and you were in doubt and you were deluded by following your fantasies until the command of God drew near and the deluder deluded you in regard to God. **57:14**

The opponents have entered the oceans of disturbance and have taken to innovations instead of the *sunna*, while the believers have sunk down. The misguided and the liars are speaking. We are the near ones, companions, treasure holders and doors to the *sunna*. Houses are not entered save through their doors. Whoever enters them from other than the door is called a thief. Sermon 153

So, this Day ransom will not be taken from you nor from those who were ungrateful. Your place of shelter will be the fire. It is your defender. Miserable will be the Homecoming! **57:15**

They are wrong who liken **You** to their idols, and dress **You** with apparel of the creatures by their imagination, attribute to **You** parts of body by their own thinking and consider **You** after the creatures of various types, through the working of their intelligence. I bear witness that whoever equated **You** with anything out of **Your** creation took a partner for **You**. Whoever takes a partner for **You** is ungrateful according to what is stated in **Your** unambiguous verses and indicated by the evidence of **Your** clear arguments. I also bear witness that **You** are that God Who cannot be confined in the fetters of intelligence so as to admit change of condition by entering its imagination, nor in the shackles of the mind so as to become limited and an object of alterations. Sermon 91

Is it not time for those who believed that their hearts be humbled by the Remembrance of God and to The Truth that came down to them and that they not be like those who were given the Book before? Then, the space of time was long for them so their hearts became hard. Many of them were ones who disobey. **57:16**

Has not the moment come for the believers, that their hearts be humbled to the remembrance of God and to what has been revealed of the truth and that they not become as those who were given the book before: *Then, the space of time was long for them so their hearts became hard.* Many of them are evil-doers. Sermon 90*

Know you that God gives life to the earth after its death. Surely, We made manifest the signs to you so that perhaps you will be reasonable. **57:17**

I bear witness that *there is no god but God* (Q47:19), by virtue of belief, certainty, sincerity and conviction. I also bear witness that *Muhammad* (Q48:29), peace and the mercy of God be upon him, is *His servant* (Q17:1) and *Prophet* (Q7:158) whom He deputed when the signs of guidance were obliterated and the ways of religion were desolate. So he threw open the truth, gave advice to the people, guided them towards righteousness and ordered them to be moderate. May God bless him ... Sermon 194

Truly, the males, ones who are charitable and the females, ones who are charitable and who lent a fairer loan to God, it will be multiplied for them and for them there is a generous compensation. **57:18**

Those who believed in God and His Messengers, those, they are the just persons. The witnesses to their Lord. For them is their compensation and their light. Those who were ungrateful and denied Our signs, those are the Companions of Hellfire. **57:19**

Where are the hearts dedicated to God and devoted to the obedience of God? Sermon 144

Know that this present life is only a pastime, a diversion and an adornment and a mutual boasting among you and a rivalry in respect to wealth and children as the likeness of plenteous rain water. The plants impressed ones who are ungrateful. Again, it withers; then, **you** *see it yellowing. Again, it becomes chaff while in the world to come there is severe punishment and forgiveness from God and contentment. This present life is nothing but a delusion of enjoyment.* **57:20**

O my God! Have mercy on their bewilderment and their passages and their groaning in their yards. Sermon 115

Move quickly towards forgiveness from your Lord and the Garden whose depth is as the breadth of the heavens and earth. It was prepared for those who believed in God and His Messengers. That is the grace of God. He gives it to whom He wills. God is The Possessor of the Sublime Grace. **57:21**

You should therefore be quick in performance of good acts so that you may be with His neighbors in His abode; He made His Prophet's companions of these neighbors and made the angels to visit them. He has honored their ears so that the sound of hellfire may never reach them, and He has afforded protection to their bodies from weariness and fatigue: *That is the grace of God. He gives it to whom He wills. God is The Possessor of the Sublime Grace.* (Q57:21) I say what you are hearing. I seek God's help for myself and yourselves: *God is enough for us and how excellent is He, the Trustee.* (Q3:173) Sermon 182

No affliction lit on the earth nor on yourselves but it is in a Book that We fashion before. Truly, that is easy for God, **57:22**
so that you not grieve over what slipped away from you nor be glad because of what was given to you. God loves not any proud, boaster, **57:23**
those who are misers and who command humanity to miserliness, and whoever turns away then, God, He is The Sufficient, The Worthy of Praise. **57:24**

Praise belongs to God (Q1:2), Creator of the human being. He has spread the earth. He makes streams to flow and vegetation to grow on high lands. His primordiality has no beginning, nor has His eternity any end. He is the First and forever. He is the everlasting without limit. Foreheads bow before Him and lips declare His Oneness. He determined the limits of things at the time of His creating them, keeping Himself away from any likeness. Sermon 163

Certainly, We sent Our Messengers with the clear portents and We caused the Book to descend with them and the Balance so that humanity may uphold equity. We caused iron to descend in which is vigorous might and profits for humanity that perhaps God would know whoever helps Him and His Messengers in the unseen. Truly, God is Strong, Almighty. **57:25**

The Book of God is among you. It speaks. Its tongue does not falter. It is a house whose pillars do not fall down. It is a power whose supporters are never defeated. Sermon 132

Certainly, We sent Noah and Abraham and We assigned to their offspring prophethood and the Book. Of them are ones who are truly guided while many of them are ones who disobey. **57:26**
Again, We sent Our Messengers following their footsteps. We sent following them Jesus son of Mary. We gave him the Gospel. We assigned in the hearts of those who followed him, tenderness and mercy. But as for monasticism, they made it up themselves. We prescribed it not for them but they were so looking for the contentment of God. Then, they gave it not the attention giving its right attention so We gave those who believed among them their compensation. Many of them are ones who disobey. **57:27**

O those who believed! Be God-conscious and believe in His Messenger. He will give you a double like part of His mercy. He assigns you a light to walk by. He will forgive you. God is Forgiving, Compassionate. **57:28**

The beginning of the action of one who sees with his heart and acts with eyes is to assess whether the action will go against him or for him. If it is for him, he indulges in it, but if it is against him, he keeps away from it. For he who acts without knowledge is like one who treads without a path. His deviation from the path keeps him at a distance from his aim. He who acts according to knowledge is like He who treads the clear path. Therefore, he who can see, should see whether he should proceed or return. Sermon 153

Certainly, the People of the Book know that they have no power over anything of the grace of God and that the grace of God is in the hand of God. He gives it to whomever He wills. God is Possessor of the Sublime Grace. **57:29**

God is The Possessor of the Sublime Grace. (Q57:21) Sermon 182

CHAPTER 58: SHE WHO DISPUTES (al-Mujādilah)

Surely, God heard the saying of she who disputes with **you** *about her spouse and she complains to God and God hears conversing between you both. Truly, God is Hearing, Seeing.* **58:1**
Those who say to their wives: Be as my mother's back, they (f) are not their mothers. Their mothers are only those (f) who gave them birth. Truly, they say that which is unlawful among their sayings and an untruth. Truly, God is Pardoning, Forgiving. **58:2**
Those who say: Be as my mother's back, to their wives and again, retract what they said, then, the letting go of a bondsperson before they both touch one another. That is of what you are admonished. God is Aware of what you do. **58:3**
He who finds not such means then, formal fasting for two successive months before they both touch one another. For him who is unable to fast, the feeding of sixty needy persons. That is so that you believe in God and His Messenger. Those are the ordinances of God. For the ones who are ungrateful, a painful punishment. **58:4**
Truly, those who oppose God and His Messenger, they were suppressed as those who before them were suppressed. Surely, We caused clear portents, signs to descend. For the ones who are ungrateful is a despised punishment **58:5**
on a Day when God will raise them up altogether and tell them of what they did. God counted it while they forgot it. God is a Witness over everything. **58:6**

God never allowed His creation to remain without a Prophet, one deputized by Him, or a Book sent down from Him or a binding argument or a standing plea. These Messengers were such that they did not fear that they were few in comparison to the large numbers of their falsifiers. Among them was either a predecessor who would name the one to follow or the follower who had been introduced by the predecessor. Sermon 1

Have **you** *not considered that God knows whatever is in the heavens and whatever is in and on the earth. There will be no conspiring secretly of three, but He is their fourth nor of five, but He is the sixth, nor of fewer than that nor of more, but He is with them wherever they had been. Again, He will tell them of what they did on the Day of Resurrection. Truly, God is Knowing of everything.* **58:7**

Have **you** *not considered those who were prohibited from conspiring secretly? Again, they revert to what they were prohibited from and hold secret counsel in sin and deep-seated dislike and in opposition to the Messenger? When they drew near* **you** *they gave* **you** *greetings with that with which God gives not as a greeting to* **you** *and they say to themselves: Why punishes us not God for what we say? Hell will be enough for them. They will roast in it. Then, miserable will be the Homecoming!* **58:8**

Desires will be cut. Hearts will sink quietly. Voices will be lowered. Sweat will choke the throat. Fear will increase. Ears will resound with the thundering voice of the announcer calling towards the final judgment, award of recompense, striking of punishment and paying of reward. Sermon 82

O those who believed! When you hold secret counsel, hold not secret counsel in sin and deep-seated dislike and in opposition to the Messenger. But hold secret counsel for virtuous conduct and God-consciousness and be God-conscious before Whom you will be assembled. **58:9**

Conspiring secretly is only from Satan that he dishearten those who believed. But he is not one who injures them at all, but with the permission of God. In God let the ones who believe put their trust. **58:10**

I bear witness that *there is no god but God* (Q47:19), the One.... It is the means to keep Satan away. Sermon 2

O those who believed! When it was said to you: Make ample space in the assemblies, then, make room. God will make room for you. When it was said: Move up, then, move up. God will exalt those among you who believed and those who were given the knowledge in degrees. God is Aware of what you do. **58:11**

O those who believed! When you consulted with the Messenger, put charity forward in advance of your conversing privately. That is better for you and purer. But if you find not the means, then, truly, God is Forgiving, Compassionate. **58:12**

I bear witness that *there is no god but God* (Q47:19), by virtue of belief, certainty, sincerity and conviction. I also bear witness that *Muhammad* (Q48:29), peace and the mercy of God be upon him, is *His servant* (Q17:1) and *Prophet* (Q7:158) whom He deputed when the signs of guidance were obliterated and the ways of religion were desolate. So he threw open the truth, gave advice to the people, guided them towards righteousness and ordered them to be moderate. May God bless him ... Sermon 194

Are you apprehensive to put forward charity in advance of your conversing privately? If, then, you accomplish it not, God turned in forgiveness to you. Perform the formal prayer and give the purifying alms and obey God and His Messenger. God is Aware of what you do. **58:13**

Certainly, only doubtful innovations cause ruin except those from which God may protect. In God's authority lies the safety of your affairs. Therefore, render Him such obedience as is neither blameworthy nor insincere. Sermon 169

Have **you** *considered those who turned in friendship to a folk against whom God was angry? They are not of you, nor are you of them and they swear to a lie while they know.* **58:14**

God prepared a severe punishment for them. Truly, they, how evil is what they had been doing! **58:15**

They took their oaths to themselves as a pretext and they barred from the way of God. So, for them

is a despised punishment. **58:16**
Avails them not their wealth and their children against God at all. Those will be the Companions of the Fire. They are ones who will dwell in it forever. **58:17**
On a Day when God will raise them up altogether, then, they will swear to Him as they swear to you, assuming that they are something. They, they are ones who lie. **58:18**

Be aware! You have been ordered insistently to march. You have been guided as to how to provide for the journey. Truly, the most frightening thing which I am afraid of about you is that you will follow desires and widen your hopes. Provide for yourself from this world what would save you tomorrow on the Day of Judgment. Sermon 28

Satan gained mastery over them, so he caused them to forget the Remembrance of God. Those are of the Party of Satan. Regard the Party of Satan, they will be the ones who are losers. **58:19**

They eulogize each other and expect reward from each other. When they ask something they insist on it. If they reprove any one, they disgrace him. If they pass verdict, they commit excess. They have adopted for every truth a wrong way, for every erect thing a bender, for every living being a killer, for every closed door a key and for every night a lamp. They covet, but with despair, in order to maintain with it their markets and to popularize their handsome merchandise. When they speak, they create doubts. When they describe, they exaggerate. First they offer easy paths, but afterwards they make them narrow. In short, they are the party of Satan and the stings of fire. *Regard the Party of Satan. They will be the ones who are losers.* (Q58:19) Sermon 193

Truly, those who oppose God and His Messenger, those are among the humiliated in spirit. **58:20**

Every one of you has to bear his own burden. It has been kept light for the ignorant. God is Merciful. Faith is straight. *The Prophet* (Q7:158), peace and the mercy of God be upon him, is the holder of knowledge. Yesterday I was with you; today I have become the object of a lesson for you, and tomorrow I shall leave you. May God forgive me and you! Sermon 149

God prescribed: I will prevail, truly, I and My Messengers. Truly, God is Strong, Almighty. **58:21**
You *will not find any folk who believe in God and the Last Day who make friends with whoever opposed God and His Messenger even if they had been their fathers or their sons or their brothers or their kinspeople. Those, He prescribed belief in their hearts, and confirmed them with a Spirit from Himself. He will cause them to enter Gardens beneath which rivers run as ones who will dwell in them forever. God was well-pleased with them and they were well-pleased with Him. Those are the Party of God. Lo! the Party of God. They are the ones who prosper.* **58:22**

God, the Sublime, also says: *Truly, of humanity closest to Abraham are those who followed him and this Prophet and those who believed. God is Protector of the ones who believe.* (Q3:68) Letter 28

CHAPTER 59: THE BANISHMENT (al-Hashr)

Whatever is in the heavens glorified God and whatever is in and on the earth. He is The Almighty, The Wise. **59:1**
It is He Who drove out those who were ungrateful—among the People of the Book—from their

abodes at the first assembling. You thought that they would not go forth. They thought that they are ones who are secure in their fortresses from God. But God approached them from where they anticipate not. He hurled alarm into their hearts. They devastate their own houses with their own hands and the hands of the ones who believe. Then, take warning, O those imbued with insight! **59:2**

Everything submits to Him. Everything exists by Him. He is the satisfaction of every poor, dignity of the low, energy for the weak and shelter for the oppressed. Whoever speaks, He hears his speaking, and whoever keeps quiet, He knows his secret. On Him is the livelihood of everyone who lives, and to Him returns whoever dies. Sermon 108

If God prescribed not banishment for them, He would have punished them in the present. For them in the world to come would be the punishment of the fire. **59:3**

Be God-conscious, be God-conscious, O God's human being, because the world is behaving with you in the usual way and you and the Day of Judgment are in the same rope close to each other. Sermon 190

That is because they make a breach with God and His Messenger. Whoever made a breach with God, then, truly, God is Severe in repayment. **59:4**

God never allowed His creation to remain without a Prophet, one deputized by Him, or a Book sent down from Him or a binding argument or a standing plea. These Messengers were such that they did not fear that they were few in comparison to the large numbers of their falsifiers. Among them was either a predecessor who would name the one to follow or the follower who had been introduced by the predecessor. Sermon 1

Whatever palm trees you severed or left them as ones that arise from their roots, it was with the permission of God and so that He might cover with shame the ones who disobey. **59:5**

Where are those who protect honor, and those self-respecting persons who defend respectable persons in the time of hardship? Shame is behind you while the Garden is in front of you. Sermon 171

What God gave as spoils of war to His Messenger from them, you spurred not an animal for an expedition, neither any horse nor riding camel, but God gives authority to His Messengers over whomever He wills. God is Powerful over everything. **59:6**

What God gave to His Messenger as spoils of war from the people of the towns is for God and His Messenger and the possessors of kinship and the orphans and the needy and the traveler of the way so that it be changing not hands between the rich among you. Whatever the Messenger gave you, take it. Refrain yourselves from what he prohibited you. Be God-conscious. Truly, God is Severe in repayment. **59:7**

God deputized *the Prophet* (Q7:158), peace and the mercy of God be upon him, after a gap from the previous Prophets when there was much talk among the people. With him God exhausted the series of Prophets and ended the revelation. He then fought for Him those who were turning away from Him and were equating others with Him. Sermon 133

For the poor who were of the ones who emigrate, those who were driven out from their abodes and their property, looking for grace from God and His contentment and they help God and His Messenger, there is also a share. Those, they are the ones who are sincere. **59:8**

Do you command me that I should seek support by oppressing those over whom I have been placed? By God, I will not do so as long as the world goes on and as long as one star leads another in the sky. Even if it were my property, I would have distributed it equally among them. Then why not when the property is that of God? Sermon 126

Those who took their abodes as dwellings and had belief before them, love them who emigrated to them and they find not in their breasts any need for what the emigrants were given and hold them in greater favor over themselves even though they themselves had been in destitution. Whoever is protected from his own stinginess, then, those, they are the ones who prosper. **59:9**

I want to caution you about the poor. Be God-conscious about their conditions and your attitude towards them. They have no support, no resources and no opportunities. They are poor. They are destitute and many of them are cripples and unfit for work. Some of them come out begging and some who maintain self-respect who do not beg, but their conditions speak of their distress, poverty, destitution and wants. For the sake of God, Malik, protect them and their rights. He has laid the responsibility of this upon your shoulders. You must fix a share for them from the Government Treasury. Besides this reservation in cash, you must also reserve a share in kinds of crops etc. from government granaries in cities where food-grains are stored as are cultivated on State-owned land because in this storage the share of those living far away from any particular city is equal to the share of those living nearby. Let me remind you once again that you are made responsible for guarding the rights of the poor people and for looking after their welfare. Take care that the conceit of your position and vanity of wealth may not deceive you to lose sight of such a grave and important responsibility. Yours is such an important post that you cannot claim immunity from the responsibility of even minor errors of commission or omission with an excuse that you were engrossed in the major problems of the State which you have solved diligently. Letter 53

Those who drew near after them, they say: Our Lord! Forgive us and our brothers/sisters who preceded us in belief and make not in our hearts any grudge against those who believed. Our Lord! Truly, ***You*** *are Gentle, Compassionate.* **59:10**

O the Most Merciful of all! O my God! Surely, **You** are powerful over whatever **You** will. Sermon 143

Have ***you*** *not considered those who are ones who are hypocrites? They say to their brothers—those who were ungrateful— among the People of the Book: If you were driven out, we, certainly, will go forth with you and we will never obey anyone against you ever. If you were fought against, we will, certainly, help you. God bears witness that they, truly, are ones who lie.* **59:11**

Certainly, if they were driven out, they would not go forth with them. If they were fought against they would not help them. If they had helped them, they would turn their backs. Again, they would not be helped by them. **59:12**

Truly, you are a more severe fright in their breasts than God. That is because they are a folk who understand not. **59:13**

They fight not against you altogether, but in fortified towns or from behind walls. Their might among themselves is very severe. You would assume them united, but their hearts are diverse. That is because they are a folk who are not reasonable. **59:14**

As the likeness of those who were before them, they experienced the immediate mischief of their affair and for them is a painful punishment. **59:15**

Certainly, if they were driven out, they would not go forth with them. If they were fought against, they would not help them. If they had helped them, they would turn their backs. Again, *they would not be helped by them.* (Q59:12) Sermon 91

As the likeness of Satan when he said to the human being: Be Ungrateful! Then, when he was ungrateful, Satan said: I am free of ***you****. I fear God, the Lord of the worlds.* **59:16**
The Ultimate End of both of them will be that they be in the fire, ones who will dwell in it forever. That is the recompense of the ones who are unjust. **59:17**

Be God-conscious and do not let Satan drive you wherever he wants. Letter 55

O those who believed! Be God-conscious and let every soul look on what is put forward for tomorrow. Be God-conscious. Truly, God is Aware of what you do. **59:18**
Be not like those who forgot God and He caused them to forget themselves. Those, they are the ones who disobey. **59:19**

One of the firm decisions of God in the Wise Reminder (Quran), upon which He bestows reward or gives punishment and through which He likes or dislikes, is that it will not benefit a person, even though he exerts himself and acts sincerely, if he leaves this world to meet God with one of these acts without repenting, namely that he believed in a partner with God during his obligatory worship or appeased his own anger by killing an individual or spoke about acts committed by others or sought fulfillment of his needs from people by introducing an innovation in his religion or met people with a double face or moved among them with a double tongue. Understand this because an illustration is a guide for its like. Sermon 153

The Companions of the Fire are not equal to the Companions of the Garden. The Companions of the Garden, they are the ones who are victorious. **59:20**
If We had caused this, the Quran, to descend on a mountain, ***you*** *would have seen it as that which is humbled, one that is split open from dreading God. There are the parables that We propound for humanity so that perhaps they will reflect.* **59:21**

You should also know that no one will need anything after guidance from the Quran and no one will be free from want before guidance from the Quran. Seek cure from it for your ailments and seek its assistance in your distress. It contains a cure for the worst diseases, namely unbelief, hypocrisy, revolt and misguidance. Pray to God through it and turn to God with its love.... There is nothing comparable to it by which the people should turn to God, the Sublime. Sermon 176

He is God; there is no god but He, One Who Knows of the unseen and the visible. He is The Merciful, The Compassionate. **59:22**
He is God besides whom there is no god but He, The King, The Holy, The Peaceable, One Who is The Bestower, Preserver, The Almighty, The Compeller, The One Who is The Supreme. Glory be to God above partners they ascribe. **59:23**

I bear witness that *there is no god but God* (Q47:19), and I bear witness that *Muhammad* (Q48:29), peace and the mercy of God be upon him, is *His servant* (Q17:1) and *Prophet* (Q7:158) and His chosen and His selected one. Sermon 150

He is God, the One Who is Creator, The One Who Fashions, The One Who is The Giver of Form.

To Him belongs the Fairer Names. Whatever is in the heavens glorifies Him and whatever is in and on the earth and He is The Almighty, The Wise. **59:24**

How great is **Your** creation that we see, but how small is this greatness by the side of **Your** Might! How awe-striking is **Your** realm that we notice, but how humble is this against what is hidden from us out of **Your** authority! How extensive are **Your** bounties in this world, but how small are they against the bounties of the next world! Sermon 108

Chapter 60: She Who is Put to a Test (al-Mumtaḥinah)

O those who believed! Take not My enemies to yourselves and your enemies as protectors, giving a proposal of affection towards them while they were ungrateful for what drew near you of The Truth. They drive out the Messenger and you because you believe in God, your Lord. If you had been going forth struggling in My way and looking for My goodwill, you keep secret affection for them. Yet I am greater in knowledge of what you concealed and what you spoke openly. Whoever accomplishes that among you, surely, he went astray from the right path. **60:1**

One should not be afraid of the scarcity of those who tread on the right path, a counsel to tread the clear path of guidance. O people! Do not be desolate at the small number of those who follow the right path, because people throng only round the table of this world where the duration of satiety is short and its hunger is prolonged. Sermon 201

If they come upon you, they will be enemies against you. They extend their hands against you and their tongues with evil. They wished that you be ungrateful. **60:2**

If you refuse to stop claiming that I have gone wrong and been misled, why do you consider that the common men among the followers of *the Prophet* (Q7:158), peace and the mercy of God be upon him, have gone astray like me, and accuse them with my wrong, and hold them ungrateful on account of my sins? You are holding your swords on your shoulders and using them right and wrong. You are confusing those who have committed sins with those who have not. Sermon 127

Your blood relations will never profit you nor your children. On the Day of Resurrection, He will distinguish among you. God is Seeing of what you do. **60:3**

Surely, there had been a fairer, good example for you in Abraham and those with him when they said to their folk:Truly, we are released from obligation to you and whatever you worship other than God. We disbelieved in you. Shown itself between us and between you was enmity and hatred eternally until you believe in One God, but for Abraham saying to his father:Truly, I will ask for forgiveness for you and I possess not anything for you before God. Our Lord! In You we put our trust and to You we were penitent and to You is the Homecoming! **60:4**

Our Lord! Make us not be a cause of their pleasure for those who were ungrateful and forgive us. Our Lord; truly, ***You, You*** *alone are The Almighty, The Wise.* **60:5**

Certainly, there had been a fairer, good example in them for you for whoever had been hoping for God and the Last Day. Whoever turns away, then, truly, God, He is Sufficient, Worthy of Praise. **60:6**

He produces affection among inimical things. He fuses together diverse things, brings near remote things and separates things that are joined together. He is not confined by limits, nor counted by numbers. Material parts can surround things of their own kind, and organs can point out things similar to themselves. Sermon 186

Perhaps God will assign between you and between those to whom you were at enmity with them, affection. God is Powerful. God is Forgiving, Compassionate. **60:7**

O the Most Merciful of all! O my God! We have come out to **You** to complain when the severe troubles have forced us, drought-stricken famines have driven us, distressing wants have made us helpless and troublesome mischief has incessantly befallen us. O my God! We beseech **You** not to send us back disappointed, nor to return us with down-cast eyes, nor to address us harshly for our sins, nor deal with us according to our deeds. Sermon 143

God prohibits you not from those who fight not against you because of your way of life nor drive you out of your abodes so be good and act justly towards them. Truly, God loves the ones who act justly. **60:8**

God prohibits you only from those who fought against you in your way of life and drove you out of your abodes and were behind expelling you, that you turn to them in friendship. Whoever turns to them in friendship, then, those, they are the ones who are unjust. **60:9**

O my God! We seek **Your** protection from turning away from **Your** command, or revolting against **Your** religion, or being led away by our desires instead of by guidance that comes from **You.** Sermon 215

O those who believed! When the females, ones who believe, drew near to you, ones who emigrate (f), put them (f) to a test. God is greater in knowledge as to their (f) belief. Then, if you knew them (f) as ones who believe (f), return them (f) not to the ones who are ungrateful. They (f) are not allowed to them (m) nor are they (m) lawful for them (f). Give them (m) what they (m) have spent. There is no blame on you that you (m) marry them (f) when you have given them (f) their compensation. Hold back conjugal ties with the ones who are ungrateful and ask for what you (m) spent and let them ask for what they (m) spent. That is the determination of God. He gives judgment among you. God is Knowing, Wise. **60:10**

If any slipped away from you of your spouses to the ones who are ungrateful, then, you retaliated and give the like to whose spouses went of what they (m) spent. Be God-conscious in Whom you are ones who believe. **60:11**

O Prophet! When drew near ***you*** *the females, ones who are believers, to take the pledge of allegiance to* ***you*** *that they will ascribe nothing as partners with God nor will they steal nor will they commit adultery nor will they kill their children, nor will they approach making false charges to harm another's reputation that they devise between their (f) hands and their (f) feet, and that they rebel not against* ***you*** *in anything that is honorable. Then, take their (f) pledge of allegiance and ask forgiveness from God for them (f). Truly, God is Forgiving, Compassionate.* **60:12**

During the days of *the Prophet* (Q7:158), peace and the mercy of God be upon him, we had strict orders not to touch, molest or insult women though they were unbelievers. Even in pre-Islamic days it was the custom that if a man struck a woman, even with a stick or a stone, the revenge had to be taken by his sons and descendants. Letter 14

O those who believed! Turn not in friendship to a folk against whom God was angry. Surely, they gave up hope for the world to come, just as gave up hope the ones who are ungrateful of the occupants of the graves. **60:13**

Their magnificent places and spread-out carpets were changed to stones, laid-in-blocks and cave-like dug out graves whose very foundation is based on ruins and whose construction has been made with soil. Their positions are contiguous, but those settled in them are like far flung strangers. They are among the people of their area, but feel lonely, and they are free from work, but still engaged in activity. They feel no attachment with homelands, nor do they keep contact among themselves like neighbors despite nearness of neighborhood and priority of abodes. How can they meet each other when decay has ground them with its chest, and stones and earth have eaten them. Sermon 225

Chapter 61: The Ranks (al-Ṣaff)

Whatever is in the heavens glorified God and whatever is in and on the earth. He is The Almighty, The Wise. **61:1**
O those who believed! Why say you what you accomplish not? **61:2**
It was most troublesome, repugnant to God that you say what you accomplish not. **61:3**

The practice of boasting over the favors done undoes the good done, the habit of exaggerating and thinking very highly of our good actions will make us lose the guidance of God, and the habit of breaking one's promises is disliked both by God and by people: *it was most troublesome, repugnant to God that you say what you accomplish not.*(Q 61:3) Letter 53

Truly, God loves those who fight in His way, ranged in rows as if they were a well-compacted structure. **61:4**

Fight, whenever required, to defend the cause of God. Letter 31

When Moses said to his folk: O my folk! Why malign me while, surely, you know that I am the Messenger of God to you? So, when they swerved, God caused their hearts to swerve. God guides not the folk, the ones who disobey. **61:5**
When Jesus son of Mary said: O Children of Jacob! I am the Messenger of God to you, one who establishes as true what was in advance of me in the Torah and one who gives good tidings of a Messenger to approach after me. His name will be Ahmad. But when he brought about the clear portents to them, they said: This is clear sorcery! **61:6** ***

Who does greater wrong than he who devised the lie against God while he is being called to submission to God? God guides not the folk, ones who are unjust. **61:7**
They want to extinguish the light of God with their mouths but God is One Who Fulfills His light even though the ones who are ungrateful disliked it. **61:8**
He it is Who sent His Messenger with guidance and the way of life of The Truth to uplift it over all other ways of life even though the ones who are polytheists disliked it. **61:9**

O my God! I seek **Your** protection from becoming destitute despite **Your** riches, from being misguided despite **Your** guidance, from being molested in **Your** realm and from being humiliated while authority rests with **You.** O my God! Let my spirit be the first of those good objects that **You** take from me and the first trust out of **Your** favors held in trust with me. Sermon 215

O those who believed! Shall I point you to a transaction that will rescue you from a painful punishment? **61:10**
You believe in God and His Messenger and struggle in the way of God with your wealth and your lives. That is better for you if you had been knowing. **61:11**

Only the middle way is the right path which is the Everlasting Book and the traditions of *the Prophet* (Q7:158), peace and the mercy of God be upon him. From it the *sunna* has spread and towards it is the eventual return. He who claims otherwise is ruined. He who concocts falsehood is disappointed. He who opposes right is destroyed. It is enough ignorance for a person not to know himself. He who is strong rooted in God-consciousness is not destroyed. The plantation of a people based on God-consciousness never remains without water. Reform yourselves. Repent. One should praise only God and condemn only one's self. Sermon 16

He will forgive you your impieties and cause you to enter into Gardens beneath which rivers run, and into good dwellings in the Gardens of Eden, the winning the sublime triumph. **61:12**
He gives another thing you love, help is from God and victory in the near future, so give good tidings to the ones who believe. **61:13**

God, the Almighty, has sent down a guiding Book wherein He has explained virtue and vice. You should adopt the course of virtue whereby you will have guidance, and keep aloof from the direction of vice so that you remain on the right way. Sermon 167

O those who believed! Be helpers of God as Jesus son of Mary said to the disciples: Who are my helpers for God? The disciples said: We are the helpers for God. Then, a section believed of the Children of Jacob and a section were ungrateful. So, We confirmed those who believed against their enemies. They became ones who are prominent. **61:14**

Those are the fortunate people, who adopt piety as the principle of their lives and are fully attentive to their welfare for the hereafter. They accept bare earth as the most comfortable bed and water as the most pleasant drink. They adopt the Quran and prayers as their guide and protector. Like Prophet Jesus Christ, they forsake the world and its vicious pleasure. Saying 104

Chapter 62: The Congregation (al-Jumu^c^ah)

Whatever is in the heavens glorifies God and whatever is in and on the earth, The King, The Holy, The Almighty, The Wise. **62:1**
He it is Who raised up among the unlettered a Messenger from among them who recounts His signs to them and makes them pure and teaches them the Book and wisdom even though they had been before certainly, clearly going astray **62:2**
and to others among them who join them not. He is The Almighty, The Wise. **62:3**
That is the grace of God. He gives it to whom He wills. God is Possessor of the Sublime Grace. **62:4**

Certainly, these people are in agreement in disliking my authority. I will carry on until I perceive disunity among you, because if they succeed in spite of the unsoundness of their view, the whole organization of Muslims will be shattered. They are hankering after this world out of jealousy against him on whom God has bestowed it. So they intend to revert the matters to the pre-Islamic period. On us it is obligatory, for your sake, to abide by the Book of God (Quran), the Sublime, and the conduct of *the Prophet* (Q7:158), peace and the mercy of God be upon him, to stand by His rights and to revive his *sunna*. Sermon 169

The parable of those who were entrusted with the Torah, and, again, carries it not is as the parable

of a donkey who carries writings. Miserable was the parable of a folk who denied the signs of God! God guides not the folk, the ones who are unjust. **62:5**
Say: O those who became Jews! If you claimed that you are the protectors of God to the exclusion of humanity, then, covet death if you had been ones who are sincere. **62:6**
But they will not covet it ever because of what their hands put forward. God is Knowing of the ones who are unjust. **62:7**
Say: Truly, the death that you run away from, then, it will be, truly, that which you encounter. Again, you will be returned to the One Who Knows of the unseen and the visible and He will tell you what you had been doing. **62:8**
O those who believed! When the formal prayer was proclaimed on the day of congregation, then, hasten about to the Remembrance of God and forsake trading. That is better for you if you had been knowing. **62:9**
Then, when the formal prayer had ended, disperse through the earth looking for the grace of God. Remember God frequently so that perhaps you will prosper. **62:10**
When they considered a transaction or a diversion, they broke away toward it, and left ***you*** *as one who is standing up. Say: What is with God is better than any diversion or than any transaction. God is Best of the ones who provide.* **62:11**

People did not take light from the lights of his wisdom, nor did they produce flame from the flint of sparkling knowledge. So in this matter, they are like grazing cattle and hard stones. Nevertheless, hidden things have appeared for those who perceive. The face of right has become clear for the wanderer. The approaching moment has raised the veil from its face. Signs have appeared for those who search for them. Sermon 108

Chapter 63: The Hypocrites (al-Munāfiqūn)

When the ones who are hypocrites drew near ***you****. They said: We bear witness that* ***you*** *art, truly, the Messenger of God. God knows that* ***you*** *art, truly, His Messenger and God bears witness that the ones who are hypocrites are ones who lie.* **63:1**
They took their oaths to themselves as a pretext. Then, they barred from the way of God. Truly, they, how evil is what they had been doing! **63:2**
so a seal was set on their hearts so they understand not **63:3**
When ***you*** *see them, their physiques impress* ***you****. When they speak,* ***you*** *have heard their saying. It is as if they had been propped up timber. They assume that every Cry is against them. They are the enemy so beware of them. God took the offensive. How they are misled!* **63:4**
When it was said to them: Approach now. The Messenger of God asks forgiveness for you. They twist their heads and ***you*** *had seen them dissuading while they are ones who grow arrogant.* **63:5**
It is the same to them whether ***you*** *had asked for forgiveness for them or* ***you*** *had not asked for forgiveness for them. God will never forgive them. Truly, God guides not the folk, the ones who disobey.* **63:6**
They are those who say: Spend not on such ones who are with the Messenger of God until they break away. To God belongs the treasures of the heavens and the earth but the ones who are hypocrites understand not. **63:7**
They say: If we returned to the city, certainly, would drive out the more mighty, the ones humble spirited from it. Yet to God belongs the great glory and to His Messenger and to the ones who believe. But the ones who are hypocrites know not. **63:8**

O God's human being! I advise you to fear God and I warn you of the hypocrites, because they are themselves misguided and misguide others, and they have slipped and make others slip too. They change into many colors and adopt various ways. They support you with all sorts of supports and lie in waiting for you at every lookout. Their hearts are diseased while their faces are clean. They walk stealthily and tread like the approach of sickness over the body. Their words speak of cure, but their acts are like incurable diseases. They are jealous of ease, intensify distress and destroy hopes. Their victims are found lying down on every path, while they have means to approach every heart and they have false tears for every grief. Sermon 193

O those who believed! Let not your wealth divert you nor your children from the Remembrance of God. Whoever accomplishes that, then, those, they are the ones who are losers. **63:9**
Spend of what We provided you before approaches death to any of you. Then, he will say: My Lord! If only **You** *would postpone it for a little term then, I would be charitable and be among the ones in accord with morality.* **63:10**
But God never postpones it for a soul when its term drew near. God is Aware of what you do. **63:11**

Those before you passed away because of the lengthening of their desires and the forgetting of their death, until that promised event befell them about which excuses are turned down, repentance is denied and punishment and retribution is inflicted. Sermon 146

Chapter 64: The Mutual Loss and Gain (al-Taqābun)

Whatever is in the heavens glorifies God and whatever is in and on the earth. His is the dominion and to Him belongs all the praise. He is Powerful over everything. **64 1**

Praise belongs to God (Q1:2) Who is proof of His existence through His creation, of His being external through the newness of His creation, and through their mutual similarities of the fact that nothing is similar to Him. Senses cannot touch Him and curtains cannot veil Him, because of the difference between the Maker and the made, the Limiter and the limited and the Sustainer and the sustained. He is One, but not by the first in counting, is Creator, but not through activity or labor, is Hearer, but not by means of any physical organ, is Looker, but not by a stretching of eyelids, is Witness, but not by nearness, is Distinct, but not by measurement of distance, is Manifest, but not by seeing and is Hidden, but not by subtlety of body. He is Distinct from things because He overpowers them and exercises might over them, while things are distinct from Him because of their subjugation to Him and their turning towards Him. He who describes Him limits Him. He who limits Him numbers Him. He who numbers Him rejects His eternity. He who said "how" sought a description for Him. He who said "where" bounded him. He is the Knower even though there be nothing to be known. He is the Sustainer even though there be nothing to be sustained. He is the Powerful even though there be nothing to be overpowered. Sermon 151

He it is Who created you: So, some of you are ones who disbelieve and some of you are ones who believe. God is Seeing of what you do. **64:2**

He originated the creation without any example which He could follow and without any specimen prepared by any creator who would have been before Him. He showed us the realm of His Might, and such wonders which speak of His Wisdom. The confession of the created things that their existence owes itself to Him made us realize that argument has been furnished about knowing Him so that there is no excuse against it. The signs of His creative power and standard of His wisdom are fixed in the wonderful things He has created. Whatever He has created is an argument in His favor and a guide towards Him. Even a silent thing is a guide towards Him as though it speaks, and its guidance towards the Creator is clear. Sermon 91

He created the heavens and the earth with The Truth and He formed you and formed your forms well. To Him is the Homecoming! **64:3**

I bear witness that *there is no god but God* (Q47:19), by virtue of belief, certainty, sincerity and conviction. I also bear witness that *Muhammad* (Q48:29), peace and the mercy of God be upon him, is *His servant* (Q17:1), and *Prophet* (Q7:158) whom He deputed when the signs of guidance were obliterated and the ways of religion were desolate. So he threw open the truth, gave advice to the people, guided them towards righteousness and ordered them to be moderate. May God bless him ... Sermon 194

He knows what is in the heavens and the earth and He knows what you keep secret and what you speak openly. God is Knowing of what is in the breasts. **64:4**

Whoever speaks, He hears his speaking. Whoever keeps quiet, He knows his secret. On Him is the livelihood of everyone who lives. To Him returns whoever dies. Sermon 108

Approaches you not the tiding of those who were ungrateful before? They experienced the mischief of their affair and there is a painful punishment for them. **64:5**
So, they were ungrateful and turned away. God is Self-Sufficient. God is Rich, Worthy of Praise. **64:6**

Praise belongs to God (Q1:2) Who made me such that I have not died, nor am I sick, nor have my veins been infected with disease, nor have I been hauled up for my evil acts, nor am I without progeny, nor have I forsaken my religion, nor do I disbelieve in my Lord, nor do I feel strangeness with my faith, nor is my intelligence affected, nor have I been punished with the punishment of peoples before me. I am a servant in **Your** possession. I have been guilty of excesses over myself. **You** have exhausted **Your** pleas over me and I have no plea before **You**. I have no power to take except what **You** give me. I cannot evade except what **You** save me from. Sermon 215

Those who were ungrateful claimed that they will never be raised up. Say: Yea! By my Lord, you will, certainly, be raised up. Again, you will be told of what you did. That is easy for God. **64:7**
So, believe in God and His Messenger, and in the Light which We caused to descend. God is Aware of what you do. **64:8**
On a Day when He will amass you for the Day of Gathering, that will be the day of the mutual loss and gain, and whoever believes in God and does as one in accord with morality, He will absolve him of his evil deeds and He will cause him to enter Gardens beneath which rivers run as ones who will dwell in them forever, eternally. That will be winning the sublime triumph. **64:9**
But for those who were ungrateful and denied Our signs, those are the Companions of the Fire, ones who will dwell in it forever. Miserable will be the Homecoming! **64:10**

The truthful Prophet has said: God may love a person, but hate his action, and may love the action, but hate the person. You should also know that every action is like vegetation, and vegetation cannot do without water while waters are different. So where the water is good the plant is good and its fruits are sweet, whereas where the water is bad the plant will also be bad and its fruits will be bitter. Sermon 154

No affliction lit but with the permission of God. Whoever believes in God, He guides his heart. God is Knowing of everything. **64:11**

Believers do not entertain pride so as to make much of their acts. Their humility before the glory of God does not allow them to esteem their own virtues. Languor does not affect them despite their long affliction. Their longings for Him do not lessen so that they might turn away from hope in God, their Sustainer. The tips of their tongues do not get dry by constant prayers to God. Engagements in other matters do not betake them so as to turn their loud voices for Him into faint ones. Their shoulders do not get displaced in the postures of worship. They do not move their necks this and that way for comfort in disobedience to His command. Follies of negligence do not act against their determination to strive, and the deceptions of desires do not overcome their courage. Sermon 90

Obey God and obey the Messenger. Then, if you turned away, then, it is only for Our Messenger the delivering the clear message. **64:12**
God, there is no god but He. In God let the ones who believe put their trust. **64:13**

I bear witness that *there is no god but God* (Q47:19), the One, there is no partner with Him, nor is there with Him any god other than Himself, and that *Muhammad* (Q48:29), peace and the mercy of God be upon him, is *His servant* (Q17:1) and *Prophet.* (Q7:158) Sermon 35

O those who believed! Truly, there are among your spouses and your children enemies for you, so beware of them. If you would pardon, overlook and forgive, then, truly, God is Forgiving, Compassionate. **64:14**
Your wealth and your children are only a test. God, with Him is a sublime compensation. **64:15**
So, be God-conscious as much as you were able and hear and obey and spend. That is good for your souls, and whoever is protected from his own self's stinginess, then, those, they are the ones who prosper. **64:16**
If you lend to God a fairer loan, He will multiply it for you and will forgive you. God is Ready to Appreciate, Forbearing, **64:17**

O God's human being! I advise you to be God-conscious. It is He Who has furnished illustrations and Who has timed for you your lives. He has given you covering of dress. He has scattered a livelihood for you. He has surrounded you with His knowledge. He has ordained rewards. He has bestowed upon you vast bounties and extensive gifts. He has warned you through far reaching arguments. He has counted you by numbers. He has fixed for you an age to live in this place of testing and house of instruction. You are on a test in this world and have to render an account regarding it. Sermon 82

One Who Knows the unseen and the visible, The Almighty, The Wise. **64:18**

If God, the Almighty, had placed His sacred House and His great signs among plantations, streams, soft and level plains, plenty of trees, an abundance of fruits, a thick population, close habitats, golden wheat, lush gardens, green land, watered plains, thriving orchards and crowded streets, the amount of recompense would have decreased because of the lightness of the trial. If the foundation on which the House is borne and the stones with which it has been raised had been of green emerald and red rubies, and there had been brightness and effulgence, then this would have lessened the action of doubts in the breasts, would have dismissed the effect of Satan's activity from the hearts and would have stopped the surging of misgivings in people, but God tries His creatures by means of different troubles, wants them to render worship through hardships and involves them in distresses, all in order to extract out vanity from their hearts, to settle down humbleness in their spirits and to make all this an open door for His favors and an easy means for His forgiveness for their sins. Sermon 192

Chapter 65: Divorce (Ṭalāq)

O Prophet! When you divorced your wives, then, divorce them (f) after their (f) waiting periods and count their (f) waiting periods. Be God-conscious, your Lord. Drive them (f) not out from their (f) houses nor let them (f) go forth unless they approach a manifest indecency. These are the ordinances of God. Whoever violates the ordinances of God, then, truly, he did wrong to himself. ***You*** *are not informed so that perhaps God will cause to evoke something after that affair.* **65:1**
Then, when they (f) reached their (f) term, either hold them (f) back as one who is honorable or part from them (f) as one who is honorable and call to witnesses from two possessors of justice from among you and perform testimony for God. That is admonished for whomever had been believing in God and the Last Day. He who is God-conscious, He will make a way out for him. **65:2**

By God, even if I had found that by such money women have been married or servant-maids have been purchased, I would have returned it to its owners because there is wide scope in dispensation of justice. He who finds it hard to act justly will find it harder to deal with injustice. Sermon 15

He will provide him with where he not anticipate. Whoever puts his trust in God, then, He will be enough for him. God is One Who Reaches Through His command. Surely, God assigned a measure to everything. **65:3**

Praise belongs to God (Q1:2) Who is recognized without being seen and Who creates without trouble. He created the creation with His Might and receives the devotion of rulers by virtue of His dignity. He exercises superiority over great men through His generosity. It is He who made His creation to populate the world and sent towards the jinn and human beings His Messengers to unveil it for them, to warn them of its harm, to present to them its examples, to show them its defects and to place before them a whole collection of matters containing lessons about the changings of health and sickness in this world, its lawful things and unlawful things and all that God has ordained for the obedient and the disobedient, namely Paradise and Hell and honor and disgrace. I extend my praise to His Being as He desires His creation to praise Him. He has fixed: *Surely God has assigned a measure to everything* (Q65:3) *for every measure a time limit,* and ... *for every term there is a Book.* (Q13:38) Sermon 183

As for those who gave up hope of menstruation among your women, if you were in doubt, their (f) waiting period is three months and for those who have not yet menstruated. As for those (f) who are imbued with pregnancy, their (f) term is that they (f) bring forth their (f) burden. Whoever is God-conscious, He will make his affair with ease for him. **65:4**

Among the God-conscious are the people of distinction. Their speech is to the point. Their dress is moderate. Their gait is humble. They keep their eyes closed to what God has made unlawful for them. They put their ears to that knowledge which is beneficial to them. They remain in the time of trials as though they remain in comfort. If there had not been fixed periods of life ordained for each, their spirits would not have remained in their bodies even for the twinkling of an eye because of their eagerness for the reward and fear of chastisement. The greatness of the Creator is seated in their heart, and so everything else appears small in their eyes. Thus to them Paradise is as though they see it and are enjoying its favors. To them, Hell is also as if they see it and are suffering punishment in it. Sermon 193

That is the command of God which He caused to descend to you. Whoever is God-conscious, He will absolve him of his evil deeds and will enhance for him a compensation. **65:5**

Whoever entertains God-consciousness, troubles remain away from him after having been near. Affairs become sweet after their bitterness. Waves of troubles recede from him after having crowded over him. Difficulties become easy for him after occurring. Generosity rains fast over him after there had been famine. Mercy bends over him after it had been loath. The favors of God spring forth on him after they had been dried. Blessings descend over him in showers after being scanty. So be God-conscious Who benefits you with His good advice, preaches to you through *His Messenger* (Q3:101) and obliges you with His favors. Devote yourselves to His worship. Sermon 198

Cause them (f) to dwell where you inhabited according to what you are able to afford and be not pressing them (f), putting them (f) in straits. If they (f) had been imbued with pregnancy, then, spend on them (f) until they bring forth their (f) burden. Then, if they (f) breast feed for you, give them (f) their compensation. Each of you take counsel between you as one who is honorable. But if you make difficulties for one another, then, another would breast feed on behalf of the father. **65:6**
The possessor of plenty spends from his plenty. He whose provisions were measured, he will spend out of what God gave him. God places not a burden on any person beyond what He gave him. God will make ease after hardship. **65:7**

The hardships of this world are easier to bear than the hardships of the next world. Sermon 54

How many a town defied the command of its Lord and His Messengers, so we made a reckoning, a severe reckoning and We punished it with a horrible punishment. **65:8**
So, it experienced the mischief of its affair and the Ultimate End of its affair had been loss. **65:9**
God prepared for them a severe punishment. So, be God-conscious, O those imbued with intuition, those who believed! Surely, God caused to descend to you a Remembrance, **65:10**
a Messenger who recounts to you the signs of God, ones that are made manifest, that he brings out those who believed and did as the ones in accord with morality from the shadows to the light. Whoever believes in God and does as one in accord with morality, He will cause him to enter into Gardens beneath which rivers run, ones who will dwell in them forever, eternally. Surely, God did good with provision for him. **65:11**
It is God Who created the seven heavens and of the earth, a similar number like them. The command comes forth between them so that perhaps you would know that God is Powerful over everything

and that God, truly, enclosed everything in His Knowledge. **65:12**

(The Prophet) has enjoined upon himself to follow justice. The first step of his justice is the rejection of desires from his heart. He describes right and acts according to it. There is no good which he has not aimed at or any likely place of virtue to which he has not proceeded. He has placed his reins in the hands of the Quran. Therefore, the Quran is his guide and leader. He gets down when the Quran puts down its weight and he settles where the Quran settles down. Sermon 87

Chapter 66: The Forbidding (al-Taḥrīm)

O Prophet! Why have ***you*** *forbidden what God permitted to* ***you****. Looking for the goodwill of* ***your*** *spouses? God is Forgiving, Compassionate.* **66:1**
God imposed on you the dissolution of such of your oaths. God is your Defender. He is The Knowing, The Wise. **66:2**
Mention when the Prophet confided to one of his spouses a discourse, she, then, told it to another. God disclosed to him of it. He acquainted her with some of it and turned aside some of it. When he told her about it, she said: Who communicated this to ***you****? He said: The Knowing, The Aware told me.* **66:3**
If you two repent to God, the hearts of you both will be bent towards it. If you helped one another against him, then, truly, God, He is his Defender and Gabriel and ones in accord with morality, the ones who believe. The angels after that are his sustainers. **66:4**
Perhaps if he divorced you (f), his Lord will cause in exchange for him spouses better than you (f), ones who submit (f) to One God, ones who believe (f), ones who are morally obligated (f), ones who repent, ones who worship (f), ones who are inclined to fasting (f), women previously married and virgins. **66:5**

God has protected His creatures who are believers by means of prayers, alms-giving and suffering the hardship of fasting in the days in which it has been made obligatory, in order to give their limbs peacefulness, to cast fear in their eyes, to make their spirits humble, to give their hearts humility and to remove haughtiness from them. All this is achieved through the covering of their delicate cheeks with dust in humility, prostrating their main limbs on the ground in humbleness and retracting of their bellies so as to reach to their backs due to fasting by way of lowliness before God, besides giving all sorts of products of the earth to the needy and the destitute by way of alms. Sermon 191

O those who believed! Protect yourselves and your people from a fire whose fuel is humanity and rocks over which are angels, harsh, severe who rebel not against whatever God commanded them and they accomplish what they are commanded. **66:6**

Perform good acts while you are still in the vastness of life. The books are open for recording of actions. Repentance is allowed. The runner away from God is being called and the sinner is being given hope of forgiveness before the light of action is put off, time expires, life ends, the door for repentance is closed and angels ascend to the sky. Therefore, a person should derive benefit from himself for himself, from the living for the dead, from the mortal for the lasting and from the departer for the stayer. A person should be God-conscious while he is given age to live up to his death and is allowed time to act. A person should control his self by the rein and hold it with its bridle. By the rein, he should prevent it from disobedience towards God. By the bridle, he should lead it towards obedience to God. Sermon 236

O those who were ungrateful! Make not excuses this Day. You are only given recompense for what you had been doing. **66:7**

For every action there is a reaction. Letter 31

O those who believed! Turn to God for forgiveness remorsefully, faithfully. Perhaps your Lord will absolve you of your evil deeds and cause you to enter into Gardens beneath which rivers run. On the Day God will not cover the Prophet with shame and those who believed with him. Their light will hasten about between them and on their right. They will say: Our Lord! Fulfill for us our light and forgive us. Truly, ***You*** *are Powerful over everything.* **66:8**

O my God! Preserve the grace of my face with easiness of life and do not disgrace my countenance with destitution, lest I may have to beg a livelihood from those who beg from **You,** try to seek the favor of **Your** evil creatures, engage myself in praising those who give to me and be tempted in abusing those who do not give to me, although behind all these **You** are the master of giving and denying. *Truly,* ***You*** *over all things, are the Powerful over everything.* (Q66:8) Sermon 223

O Prophet! Struggle against the ones who are ungrateful and the ones who are hypocrites and be ***you*** *harsh against them. Their place of shelter will be hell. Miserable will be the Homecoming!* **66:9**

Truly, God sent Muhammad, peace and the mercy of God be upon him, as a warner against vice for all the worlds and a trustee of His revelation, while you people of Arabia were following the worst religion and you resided among rough stones and venomous serpents. You drank dirty water and ate filthy food. You shed each other's blood and cared not for your relationships. Idols were worshipped among you and your sins were clinging to you. Sermon 26

God propounded an example for those, ones who are ungrateful like the woman of Noah and the woman of Lot. They both had been beneath two servants of Our servants, ones who are in accord with morality. But they both (f) betrayed them so they avail them not against God at all. It was said: Enter the fire along with ones who enter. **66:10**
God propounded an example for those who believed: Behold the woman of Pharaoh; she said: My Lord, build for me near ***You*** *a house in the Garden and deliver* ***You*** *me from Pharaoh and his actions and deliver me from the folk, the ones who are unjust.* **66:11**
Mary, the daughter of Imran, who guarded her private parts, so We blew into it of Our Spirit and she established as true the Words of her Lord and His Books and she had been among the ones who are morally obligated. **66:12**

Chapter 67: The Dominion (al-Mulk)

Blessed be He in whose hands is the dominion and He is Powerful over everything! **67:1**
He Who created death and this life that He try you as to which of you is fairer in action. He is The Almighty, The Forgiving, **67:2**

The hidden thing, namely death, which is being driven towards you by two ever new phenomena—the day and the night—is certainly quick to approach. The traveler that is approaching with success or failure deserves the best of provision. So acquire such provision from this world while you are here with which you may shield yourself tomorrow on the Day of Judgment. Sermon 64

Who created the seven heavens one on another? **You** *have not seen any imperfection in the creation of The Merciful. Then, return* **your** *sight! Have* **you** *seen any flaw?* **67:3**

Everything submits to Him. Everything exists by Him. He is the satisfaction of every poor, dignity of the low, energy for the weak and shelter for the oppressed. Whoever speaks, He hears his speaking. Whoever keeps quiet, He knows his secret. On Him is the livelihood of everyone who lives. To Him returns whoever dies. Sermon 108

Again, return **your** *sight twice again and* **your** *sight will turn about to* **you**, *one that is dazzled while it is weary.* **67:4**

People did not take light from the lights of his wisdom, nor did they produce flame from the flint of sparkling knowledge. So in this matter, they are like grazing cattle and hard stones. Nevertheless, hidden things have appeared for those who perceive. The face of right has become clear for the wanderer. The approaching moment has raised the veil from its face. Signs have appeared for those who search for them. Sermon 108

Certainly, We made to appear pleasing the lower heaven with lamps and We assigned them things to stone satans. We made ready for them the punishment of the blaze. **67:5**

I am among you like a lamp in the darkness. Whoever enters by it will be lit from it. So listen, O people, preserve it and remain attentive with the ears of your hearts so that you may understand. Sermon 187

For those who were ungrateful to their Lord is the punishment of hell. Miserable will be the Homecoming! **67:6**
When they were cast down into it, they would hear it sighing while it is boiling **67:7**
and about to burst with rage. As often as a unit of them were cast down into it, the ones who are keepers there asked them: Approaches not a warner to you? **67:8**
They will say: Yea! A warner drew near us, but we denied him. We said: God sent not down anything. You are not but in a great going astray. **67:9**
They would say: If we had been hearing or are reasonable, we would not have been Companions of the Blaze. **67:10**
They would acknowledge their impiety. Then, hell for the Companions of the Blaze! **67:11**

Everyone of them is ... alone although they are a group, and they are strangers, even though friends. They are unaware of morning after a night and of evening after a day. The night or the day when they departed has become ever existent for them. They found the dangers of their place of stay more serious than they had apprehended. They witnessed that its signs were greater than they had guessed. The two objectives, namely Paradise and Hell, have been stretched for them up to a point beyond the reach of fear or hope. Had they been able to speak they would have become dumb to describe what they witnessed or saw. Sermon 220

Truly, those who dread their Lord in the unseen, for them is forgiveness and a great compensation. **67:12**

Keep your saying secret or publish it, truly, He is Knowing of what is in your breasts. **67:13**

Now, if you portray them in your mind, or if the curtains concealing them are removed from them for you, in this state when their ears have lost their power and turned deaf, their eyes have been filled with dust and sunk down, their tongues which were very active have been cut into pieces, their hearts which were ever wakeful have become motionless in their chests, in every limb of theirs a peculiar decay has occurred which has deformed it, and has paved the way for calamity towards it, all these lie powerless, with no hand to help them and no heart to grieve over them, then you would certainly notice the grief of their hearts and the dirt of their eyes. Sermon 220

Would He who created not know? He is The Subtle, The Aware. **67:14**

I praise Him for His continuous mercy and His copious bounties. Sermon 82

It is He who made the earth submissive to you, so walk in its tracts and eat of His provision. To Him is the rising. **67:15**

The whole creation is dependent upon Him for sustenance. He has guaranteed their livelihood and ordained their sustenance. He has prepared the way for those who turn to Him and those who seek what is with Him. He is as generous about what He is asked as He is about that for which He is not asked. He is the First for whom there was no"“before” so that there could be anything before Him. Sermon 91

Were you safe from He Who is in the heaven that He will not cause the earth to swallow you up when it spins? **67:16**

Were you safe from He Who is in the heavens that He will not send against you a sand storm? You will know how My warner has been right! **67:17**

God sent Muhammad, peace and the mercy of God be upon him, as a warner for all the worlds and a trustee of His revelation. Sermon 26

Certainly, those who were before them denied. Then, how horrible had been My reproach! **67:18**

Everyone should be God-conscious, should admonish himself, should send forward his repentance and should overpower his desire because his death is hidden from him. His desires deceive him. Satan keeps posted about him. He beautifies his sin for him so that he may commit it. He prompts him to delay repentance until his desires cause him to be the most negligent. Pity is for the negligent person whose life itself would be a proof against him and his own days, passed in sin, will lead him to punishment. Sermon 64

Consider they not the birds above them ones standing in ranks and closing their wings? Nothing holds them back but The Merciful. Truly, He is Seeing of everything. **67:19**

They have different kinds of wings, and various characteristics. They are controlled by the rein of God's authority. They flutter with their wings in the expanse of the vast firmament and the open atmosphere. He brought them into existence from non-existence in strange external shapes and composed them with joints and bones covered with flesh. He prevented some of them from flying easily in the sky because of their heavy bodies and allowed them to use their wings only close to the ground. He has set them in different colors by His delicate might and exquisite creative power. Among them are those which are tinted with one hue and there is no other hue except the one in which they have been dyed. There are others which are tinted with one color, and they have a neck ring of a different color than that with which they are tinted. Sermon 165

Who is this who would be an army for you to help you other than The Merciful? Truly, ones who are ungrateful are not but in delusion. **67:20**

We hold a promise from God. He will fulfill His promise and support His army. Sermon 146

Or who is this who will provide for you if He held back His provision? Nay! They were resolute, turning in disdain and aversion. **67:21**

Then is whoever walks as one who is prone on his face better guided, or he who walks without fault on a straight path? **67:22**

Say: It is He who caused you to grow and assigned you the ability to hear, sight, and minds. But you give little thanks! **67:23**

Do not forget gratitude when receiving blessings for God has exhausted the excuses before you through clear, shining arguments and open, bright books. Sermon 81

Say: It is He who made you numerous on the earth and to Him you will be assembled. **67:24**

They say: When is this promise if you had been ones who are sincere? **67:25**

Praise belongs to God. (Q1:2) He is such that senses cannot perceive Him, place cannot contain Him, eyes cannot see Him and veils cannot cover Him. He proves His eternity by the coming into existence of His creation, and also by originating His creation He proves His existence, and by their mutual similarity He proves that there is nothing similar to Him. He is true in His promise. He is too high to be unjust to His creatures. He stands by equity among His creation and practices justice over them in His commands. He provides evidence through the creation of things of His being from ever, through their marks of incapability of His power, and through their powerlessness against death of His eternity. Sermon 185

Say: The knowledge of this is only with God and I am only a clear warner. **67:26**

God sent the *Prophet* (Q33:6), peace and the mercy of God be upon him, for enforcement of His commands, for exhausting His pleas and for presenting warnings against eternal punishment. Sermon 82

But when they saw the punishment nigh, the faces were troubled of those who were ungrateful. It will be said to them: This is what you had been calling for. **67:27**

Say: Considered you if God would cause me to perish and whoever is with me or had mercy on us, who will grant protection to the ones who are ungrateful from a painful punishment? **67:28**

If you refuse to stop claiming that I have gone wrong and been misled, why do you consider that the common men among the followers of *the Prophet* (Q7:158), peace and the mercy of God be upon him, have gone astray like me, and accuse them with my wrong, and hold them ungrateful on account of my sins? You are holding your swords on your shoulders and using them right and wrong. You are confusing those who have committed sins with those who have not. Sermon 127

Say: He is The Merciful. We believed in Him and in Him we put our trust. Then, you will know who he is, one who is clearly gone astray. **67:29**

God sent *the Prophet* (Q7:158), peace and the mercy of God be upon him, at a time when the people were going astray in perplexity and were moving here and there in mischief. Desires had deflected them and self-conceit had swerved them. Extreme ignorance had made them foolish. They were confounded by the unsteadiness of matters and the evils of ignorance. Then *the Prophet* (Q7:158), peace and the mercy of God be upon him, did his best in giving them sincere advice, himself trod on the right path and called them towards wisdom and good counsel. Sermon 94

Say: Considered you? If it came to be in the morning that your water be sinking into the ground, who approaches you with assistance from water springs ? **67:30**

When the excitement of water subsided under the earth's sides and under the weight of the high and lofty mountains placed on its shoulders, God flowed springs of water from its high tops and distributed them through plains and low places and moderated their movement by fixed rocks and high mountain tops. Then its trembling came to a standstill because of the penetration of mountains in various parts of its surface and their being fixed in its deep areas, and their standing on its plains. Sermon 91

CHAPTER 68: THE PEN (al-Qalam)

Nun! By the pen and what they inscribe: **68:1**
***You** are not, by the divine blessing of **your** Lord, one who is possessed.* **68:2**
*Truly, there is for **you** certainly, compensation, that which is unfailing.* **68:3**
*Truly, **you** are of sublime morals.* **68:4**
***You** will perceive and they will perceive* **68:5**
which of you is the one who is demented. **68:6**
*Truly, **your** Lord, He is greater in knowledge of whoever went astray from His Way and He is greater in knowledge of ones who are truly guided.* **68:7**
Then, obey not ones who deny. **68:8**

I bear witness that *there is no god but God* (Q47:19), alone Who has no partner—a testimony whose sincerity has been tested and whose essence has been assimilated with conviction. Sermon 194

*They wished that **you** would compromise with them and they would compromise with **you**.* **68:9**
*But obey **you** not every worthless swearer, defamer,* **68:10**
one who goes about with slander, slandering, **68:11**
who delays good, a sinful, exceeder of limits, **68:12**
cruel and after that, ignoble, **68:13**
because he had been possessor of wealth and children. **68:14**
When Our signs are recounted to him, he said: Fables of the ancient ones! **68:15**
We will mark him on the snout! **68:16**
Truly, We tried them as We tried the Companions of the Garden when they swore an oath that they would pluck fruit, in that which is happening in the morning. **68:17**
They make no exception by saying if God wills. **68:18**
*Then, a visitation from **your** Lord visited it while they were ones who sleep,* **68:19**
in that which is happening in the morning, it was like a plucked garden! **68:20**

They called to one another in that which is morning: **68:21**
Set forth in the early morning dawn to your cultivation if you had been ones who pluck fruit. **68:22**
So, they set out and they whisper, saying: **68:23**
There will, truly, not enter it today on you any needy person. **68:24**
They set forth in the early morning, designing, assuming they were ones who have the power. **68:25**
But when they saw it, they said: We are, certainly, ones who go astray! **68:26**
Nay! We are ones who are deprived. **68:27**
The most moderate of them said: Say I not to you: Why glorify you not God? **68:28**
They said: Glory be to God, our Lord! Truly, we had been ones who are unjust. **68:29**
Then, they came forward, some with some others blaming one another. **68:30**
They said: O woe be to us! Truly, we had been ones who are defiant. **68:31**
Perhaps our Lord will cause to exchange for us better than it. Truly, we are ones who quest our Lord. **68:32**
Thus, this is the punishment of this present life, but the punishment of the world to come is greater, if they had been knowing! **68:33**

Mind the obligations! Mind the obligations! Fulfill them for God and they will take you to the Garden. Surely, God has made unlawful the things which are not unknown and made lawful the things which are without defect. Sermon 167

Truly, for ones who are God-conscious are Gardens of Bliss with their Lord. **68:34**

Believers are humble. Believers are admonishers. Believers are God-conscious. Sermon 153

Will We make ones who submit to God as ones who sin? **68:35**
What is the matter with you? How you give judgment! **68:36**
Or have you a Book by which you study **68:37**
that you will have in it whatever you specify? **68:38**
Or are there oaths from Us, ones that reach through to the Day of Resurrection providing that you will have what you yourselves give as judgment? **68:39**

On that day God will collect on it the front and the back, to stand in obedience for the exaction of accounts and for the award of recompense for deeds. Sweat would flow up to their mouths like reins while the earth would be trembling under them. In the best condition among them would be he who has found a resting place for both his feet and an open place for his breath. Sermon 102

Ask them, then, which of them will be a guarantor for that. **68:40**
Or have they ones they ascribe as associate with God? Then, let them approach with their ascribed associates if they had been ones who are sincere. **68:41**

I bear witness that *there is no god but God* (Q47:19), the One, there is no partner with Him, nor is there with Him any god other than Himself, and that *Muhammad* (Q48:29), peace and the mercy of God be upon him, is *His servant* (Q17:1) and *Prophet.* (Q7:158) Sermon 35

On a Day the great calamity will be uncovered and they will be called to prostration, then, they will not be able to do so. **68:42**

Your ultimate goal of reward or punishment is before you. Behind your back is the hour of Resurrection which is driving you on. Keep yourself light and overtake the forward ones. The first ones who have preceded await your last ones. Sermon 21

Their sight will be that which is humbled. Abasement will come over them and they had before this been called to prostration while they were ones who are healthy. **68:43**
So, forsake Me. Whoever denies this discourse, We will draw them on gradually from where they know not **68:44**
and I will grant indulgence to them. Truly, My cunning is sure. **68:45**
Or have **you** *asked them for a compensation, so that they would be weighed down from something owed?* **68:46**
Or have they knowledge of the unseen with them so that they write it down? **68:47**

People did not take light from the lights of his wisdom, nor did they produce flame from the flint of sparkling knowledge. So in this matter, they are like grazing cattle and hard stones. Nevertheless, hidden things have appeared for those who perceive. The face of right has become clear for the wanderer. The approaching moment has raised the veil from its face. Signs have appeared for those who search for them. Sermon 108

So, be **you** *patient until the determination of* **your** *Lord and be not like the Companion of the Great Fish when he cried out, one who is suppressed by grief.* **68:48**
If a divine blessing not followed him one after another from His Lord he would be cast forth on the naked shore while he was one who is condemned. **68:49**
But his Lord elected him and made him among the ones in accord with morality. **68:50** ***

It was almost as if those who were ungrateful looked at **you** *sternly with their sight when they heard the Remembrance, and they say: He is one who is possessed!* **68:51**
It is, certainly, not but a Remembrance to the worlds. **68:52**

Know that this Quran is an adviser who never deceives, a leader who never misleads and a narrator who never speaks a lie. No one will sit beside this Quran, but when he rises, he will achieve one addition or one diminution—addition in his guidance or elimination in his spiritual blindness. You should also know that no one will need anything after guidance from the Quran and no one will be free from want before guidance from the Quran. Seek cure from the Quran for your ailments and seek its assistance in your distress. It contains a cure for the worst diseases, namely unbelief, hypocrisy, revolt and misguidance. Pray to God through it and turn to God with its love ... There is nothing like it through which the people should turn to God, the Sublime. Sermon 176

CHAPTER 69: THE REALITY (al-Hāqqah)

The Reality! **69:1**
What is The Reality? **69:2**
What would cause **you** *to recognize what The Reality is?* **69:3**

I praise Him for His continuous mercy and His copious bounties. Sermon 82

Thamud and Ad denied the Day of Disaster. **69:4**
Then, as for Thamud, they were caused to perish by a storm of thunder and lightning. **69:5**

As for Ad, they were caused to perish by a fierce and roaring, raging wind. **69:6**
It compelled against them for seven uninterrupted nights and eight days so will **you** *see the folk in it laid prostrate as if they had been uprooted fallen down date palm trees?* **69:7**
Then, will **you** *see of them any ones who endure?* **69:8**
Pharaoh and whoever draw near before him and the ones that are cities overthrown were ones of inequity **69:9**
and they rebelled against the Messenger of their Lord, so He took them with a swelling, taking. **69:10**
When the waters became turbulent, we carried you in that which runs on water, **69:11**
that We make it an admonition for you, and attentive ears would hold onto it. **69:12**

I praise God for whatever matter He ordained and whatever action He destines ... Sermon 180

When the trumpet will be blown with one gust, **69:13**
and the earth and the mountains will be mounted, then, will be ground to powder in one grinding, **69:14**
so on that Day will have come to pass The Reality **69:15**
and the heaven will be split. For on that day they will be as ones who are frail, **69:16**
and the angels will be at its borders. The Throne of **your** *Lord above them will be carried by eight on that Day.* **69:17**
That Day you will be presented. Your private matters will not be hidden. **69:18**

Be aware! ... You have been guided as to how to provide for the journey. Sermon 28

For him who will be given his book in his right hand he will say: Lo and behold! Recite my book! **69:19**

In God's authority lies the safety of your affairs. Therefore, render Him such obedience as is neither blameworthy nor insincere. By God, you must do so otherwise God will take away from you the power of Islam and will never thereafter return it to you until it reverts to others. Sermon 169

Truly, I thought that I would be one who encounters my reckoning. **69:20**

Your ultimate goal of reward or punishment is before you. Behind your back is the hour of Resurrection which is driving you on. Keep yourself light and overtake the forward ones. The first ones who have preceded await your last ones. Sermon 21

He will have a well-pleasing, pleasant life **69:21**
in a magnificent Garden. **69:22**
Its clusters, that which draws near. **69:23**
Eat and drink wholesomely for what you did in the past, in the days, that which have gone by. **69:24**

The human being should ... fear the Day of Judgment before it arrives. He should appreciate the shortness of his life and the shortness of his sojourn in the place of stay which has only to last for his change over to the next place. He should, therefore, do something for his change over and for the known stages of his departure. Blessed be he who possesses a virtuous heart, obeys one who guides him, keeps away from one who takes him to ruin, catches the path of safety with the help of him who provides him light of guidance and, by obeying the leader who commands him, hastens towards guidance before its doors are closed, opens the door of repentance and removes the stain of sins. He has certainly been put on the right path and guided towards the straight path. Sermon 214

But as for him who is given his book to his left he will say: O would that I was not given my book, **69:25**
and that I was not informed of my reckoning! **69:26**
O would that my death had been my expiry! **69:27**

In this state when he was getting ready to depart from the world and leave his beloved ones, such a serious choking overtook him that his senses became bewildered and the dampness of his tongue dried up. Now, there was many an important question whose reply he knew about he could not utter it, and many a voice that was painful for his heart that he heard, but remained unmoved as though he was deaf to the voice of either an elder whom he used to respect or of a younger whom he used to caress. The pangs of death are too hideous to be covered by description or to be appreciated by the hearts of the people in this world. Sermon 220

My wealth availed me not. **69:28**
Perished from me is my authority. **69:29**
It will be said: Take him and restrict him. **69:30**
Again, broil him in hellfire **69:31**
and after that in a chain of the length of seventy cubits. So, insert him in it. **69:32**
Truly, he had not been believing in God, The Sublime, **69:33**
nor did he urge food for the needy. **69:34**
This day he is not to have any loyal friend here **69:35**
and no food, but foul pus **69:36**
which none eat but ones of inequity. **69:37**

Everyone of them is ... alone although they are a group, and they are strangers, even though friends. They are unaware of morning after a night and of evening after a day. The night or the day when they departed has become ever existent for them. They found the dangers of their place of stay more serious than they had apprehended, and they witnessed that its signs were greater than they had guessed. The two objectives, namely Paradise and Hell, have been stretched for them up to a point beyond the reach of fear or hope. Had they been able to speak they would have become dumb to describe what they witnessed or saw. Sermon 220

So, I swear an oath by what you perceive **69:38**
and what you perceive not. **69:39**

Praise belongs to God. (Q1:2) He is such that senses cannot perceive Him, place cannot contain Him, eyes cannot see Him and veils cannot cover Him. He proves His eternity by the coming into existence of His creation, and also by originating His creation He proves His existence, and by their mutual similarity He proves that there is nothing similar to Him. He is true in His promise. He is too high to be unjust to His creatures. He stands by equity among His creation and practices justice over them in His commands. He provides evidence through the creation of things of His being from ever, through their marks of incapability of His power, and through their powerlessness against death of His eternity. Sermon 185

Truly, it is the saying of a generous Messenger, **69:40**
and not the saying of a poet. Little do you believe! **69:41**
Nor is it the saying of a soothsayer. Little do you recollect! **69:42**
It is a sending down from the Lord of the worlds. **69:43**
If he fabricated against Us some sayings, **69:44**
truly, We would have taken him by the right hand **69:45**
and, again, We would have severed his life-vein. **69:46**

God deputized *the Prophet* (Q7:158), peace and the mercy of God be upon him, after a gap from the previous Prophets when there was much talk among the people. With him God exhausted the series of Prophets and ended the revelation. He then fought for Him those who were turning away from Him and were equating others with Him. Sermon 133

There is none of you who would be ones who hinder Us from him. **69:47**

Know that this Quran is an adviser who never deceives, a leader who never misleads and a narrator who never speaks a lie. No one will sit beside this Quran, but when he rises, he will achieve one addition or one diminution—addition in his guidance or elimination in his spiritual blindness. You should also know that no one will need anything after guidance from the Quran and no one will be free from want before guidance from the Quran. Sermon 176

Truly, it is an admonition to ones who are God-conscious. **69:48**

O God's human being! Be God-conscious. Keep in view the reason why He created you. Be afraid of Him to the extent He has advised you to do. Make yourself deserve what He has promised you by having confidence in the truth of His promise and entertaining fear of the Day of Judgment. Sermon 82

We well know that there are among you, ones who deny. **69:49**
Truly, it will be a regret for ones who are ungrateful. **69:50**

He will direct desires towards the path of guidance, while people will have turned guidance towards desires. He will turn their views to the direction of the Quran, while the people will have turned the Quran to their views. Before this Enjoiner of Good, matters will deteriorate until war will rage among you with full force, showing forth its teeth, with udders full of sweet milk, but with a sour tip. Be aware! It will be tomorrow and the morrow will come soon with things which you do not know. The person in power, not from this crowd, will take to task all those were formerly appointed for their ill deeds and the earth will pour forth its eternal treasures and fling before him easily the keys. He will show you the just way of behavior and revive the Quran and *sunna* which have become lifeless among people.... You should know that Satan makes his ways easy so that you may follow him on his heels. Sermon 137

Truly, it is The Truth of certainty. **69:51**
So, glorify the Name of ***your*** *Lord, The Sublime.* **69:52**

Praise belongs to God (Q1:2) Who is above all similarity to creatures, is above the words of describers Who displays the wonders of His management for the on-lookers, is hidden from the imagination of thinkers by virtue of the greatness of His glory, has knowledge without acquiring it by adding to it or drawing it from someone, and Who is the ordainer of all matters without reflecting or thinking. He is such that gloom does not concern Him, nor does He seek light from brightness. Night does not overtake Him, nor does the day pass over Him so as to affect Him in any manner. His comprehension of things is not through eyes. His knowledge is not dependent on being informed. Sermon 213

Chapter 70: The Stairways of Ascent (al-Maᶜārij)

One who supplicates asked for a punishment that will fall **70:1**
on the ones who are ungrateful for which there will be no one to avert **70:2**
from God, the Possessor of the Stairways of Ascent. **70:3**
The angels and the Spirit go up to Him on a Day whose measure had been fifty thousand years. **70:4**

They the angels do not entertain pride so as to make much of their acts. Their humility before the glory of God does not allow them to esteem their own virtues. Languor does not affect them despite their long affliction. Their longings for Him do not lessen so that they might turn away from hope in God, their Sustainer. The tips of their tongues do not get dry by constant prayers to God. Engagements in other matters do not betake them so as to turn their loud voices for Him into faint ones. Their shoulders do not get displaced in the postures of worship. They do not move their necks this and that way for comfort in disobedience of His command. Follies of negligence do not act against their determination to strive, and the deceptions of desires do not overcome their courage. Sermon 91

So, have ***you*** *patience with a graceful patience.* **70:5**

Praise belongs to God (Q1:2) Who made me such that I have not died, nor am I sick, nor have my veins been infected with disease, nor have I been hauled up for my evil acts, nor am I without progeny, nor have I forsaken my religion, nor do I disbelieve in my Lord, nor do I feel strangeness with my faith, nor is my intelligence affected, nor have I been punished with the punishment of peoples before me. I am a servant in **Your** possession. I have been guilty of excesses over myself. **You** have exhausted **Your** pleas over me and I have no plea before **You**. I have no power to take except what **You** give me. I cannot evade except what **You** save me from. Sermon 215

Truly, they see it as distant, **70:6**
but We see it as near at hand. **70:7**
On a Day the heaven will become as molten copper **70:8**
and the mountains be as wool clusters **70:9**
and no loyal friend will ask a loyal friend, **70:10**
although they are given sight of them. One who sins would wish that he offer for ransom—from the punishment of that day—his children **70:11**
or his companion wife, or his brother **70:12**
or his relatives who gave him refuge, **70:13**
or whoever is on the earth altogether, again, if that would rescue him. **70:14**
No indeed. Truly, it is the furnace of hell **70:15**
removing their scalps, **70:16**

calling whoever drew back and turned away **70:17**
and gathered wealth and amassed. **70:18**
Truly, the human being was created fretful. **70:19**
When the worst afflicted him, he is impatient. **70:20**
When the good afflicted him, begrudging. **70:21**
But the ones who formally pray, **70:22**
those, they are ones who continue with their formal prayers **70:23**
and those who in their wealth there is a known obligation towards **70:24**
the one who begs and the one who is deprived **70:25**
and those who sincerely validate the Day of Judgment. **70:26**

This is the thing against which God has protected His creatures who are believers by means of prayers, alms-giving and suffering the hardship of fasting in the days in which it has been made obligatory in order to give their limbs peacefulness, to cast fear in their eyes, to make their spirits humble, to give their hearts humility and to remove haughtiness from them. All this is achieved through the covering of their delicate cheeks with dust in humility, prostrating their main limbs on the ground in humbleness and retracting of their bellies so as to reach to their backs due to fasting by way of lowliness before God, in addition to giving all sorts of products of the earth to the needy and the destitute by way of alms. Look what there is in these acts by way of curbing the appearance of pride and suppressing the traces of vanity. Sermon 192

Those, they are ones who are apprehensive of the punishment of their Lord. **70:27**
Truly, as to the punishment of their Lord, there is no one who is safe from it. **70:28**

O God's human being! Where are those who were allowed long ages to live? They enjoyed bounty. They were taught. They learned. They were given time. They passed it in vain. They were kept healthy. They forgot their duty. They were allowed a long period of life, were handsomely provided for, were warned of grievous punishment and were promised great rewards. You should avoid sins that lead to destruction and vices that attract the wrath of God. Sermon 82

Those, they are ones who guard their private parts, **70:29**
but not from their spouses or what their right hands possessed. Truly, they are not ones who will be reproached. **70:30**
But whoever was looking beyond that, those, they are ones who turn away. **70:31**
Those, they who in their trusts and to their compacts are ones who shepherd. **70:32**
Those, they who, giving their testimony, are ones who uphold. **70:33**
Those, they who over their formal prayers are watchful. **70:34**
Those will be in Gardens, ones who are honored. **70:35**
What is with those who were ungrateful—ones who run forward towards ***you****, eyes fixed in horror,* **70:36**
to the right and the left, tied in knots. **70:37**
Is not every man of them desirous of being caused to enter into a Garden of Bliss? **70:38**
No indeed. Truly, We created them out of what they know. **70:39**
So, I swear an oath by the Lord of the rising places and the setting places, that We certainly are ones who have power **70:40**
to substitute better for them. We are not ones who are outrun. **70:41**

So, let them engage in idle talk and play until they encounter the Day of theirs that they are promised, **70:42**
the Day when they will go forth swiftly from their tombs as though they had been hurrying to a goal **70:43**
with their sight, that which is humbled. Abasement will come over them. That is the Day which they had been promised. **70:44**

O God's human being! Be God-conscious. Keep in view the reason why He created you. Be afraid of Him to the extent He has advised you to do. Make yourself deserve what He has promised you by having confidence in the truth of His promise and entertaining fear of the Day of Judgment. Sermon 82

CHAPTER 71: NOAH (Nūḥ)

Truly, We sent Noah to his folk saying: Warn **your** *folk before a painful punishment approaches them.* **71:1**
He said: O my folk! Truly, I am a clear warner to you: **71:2**
Worship God and be God-conscious of Him and obey me. **71:3**
He forgives you some of your impieties and postpones for you a term, that which is determined. Truly, when the term of God drew near, it will not be postponed if you had been but knowing. **71:4**
He said: My Lord! Truly, I called to my folk nighttime and daytime, **71:5**
but my supplication increases not but their running away. **71:6**
Truly, as often as I called to them that **You** *would forgive them, they laid their fingertips over their ears and covered themselves with their garments. They maintained growing arrogant as they grew arrogant.* **71:7**
Again, truly, I called to them with openness. **71:8**
Again, I spoke openly to them and confided in them, keeping secret our converse. **71:9**
I said: Ask for forgiveness of your Lord. Truly, He had been a Forgiver. **71:10**
He sends from heaven abundant rain for you. **71:11**
He will furnish you relief with wealth and children. He will assign for you Gardens and will assign for you rivers. **71:12**

Certainly, God tries His creatures in respect of their evil deeds by decreasing fruits, holding back blessings and closing the treasures of good, so that he who wishes to repent may repent. He who wishes to turn away from evils may turn away. He who wishes to recall forgotten good may recall. He who wishes to abstain from evil may abstain. God, the Almighty, has made the seeking of His forgiveness a means for the pouring down of livelihood and mercy on the people. *Ask for forgiveness of your Lord. Truly, He had been a Forgiver. He sends from heaven abundant rain for you. He will furnish you relief with wealth and children. He will assign for you Gardens and will assign for you rivers.* (Q71:10-12) Sermon 142

What is it with you that you hope not for dignity from God? **71:13**
Surely, He created you in stages? **71:14**
Consider you not how God created the seven heavens, one on another? **71:15**
How He made the moon in them as a light and how He made the sun as a light-giving lamp? **71:16**

How God caused you to develop, bringing you forth from the earth. **71:17**
Again, He will cause you to return into it and bring you out in an expelling. **71:18**
How God made for you the earth as a carpet **71:19**
that you may tread in it ways through ravines. **71:20**
Noah said: My Lord! Truly, they rebelled against me. They followed such a one whose wealth and children increase him not, but in loss. **71:21**
They planned a magnificent plan. **71:22**
They said: You will by no means forsake your gods, nor will you forsake Wadd nor Suwa nor Yaghuth nor Yauq nor Nasr. **71:23**
Truly, they are going much astray. Increase ***You*** *not ones who are unjust but in causing them to go astray.* **71:24**
Because of their transgressions, they were drowned and were caused to enter into a fire. They find not for themselves any helpers other than God. **71:25**
Noah said: My Lord! Allow not even one on the earth from among the ones who are ungrateful! **71:26**
Truly, ***You****, if* ***You*** *were to allow them, they would cause* ***Your*** *servants to go astray and they will but procreate immoral ingrates.* **71:27**
My Lord! Forgive me and ones who are my parents and whoever entered my house as one who believes—the males, ones who believe and the females, ones who believe and increase not the ones who are unjust, but in ruin. **71:28**

The best deed of a great man is to forgive and forget. Saying 203

Chapter 72: The Jinn (al-Jinn)

Say: It was revealed to me that a group of jinn listened to me. They said: Truly, we heard a wondrous Recitation. **72:1**

Go ahead with the remembrance of God, for it is the best remembrance. Long for that which He has promised to the pious, for His promise is the most true promise. Tread the course of *the Prophet* (Q7:158), peace and the mercy of God be upon him, for it is the most distinguished course. Follow his *sunna*, for it is the most right of all behaviors. Learn the Quran, for it is the fairest of discourses. Understand it thoroughly, for it is the best blossoming of hearts. Seek cure with its light, for it is the cure for hearts. Recite it beautifully, for it is the most beautiful narration. Certainly, a scholar who acts not according to his knowledge is like the off-headed ignorant who does not find relief from his ignorance, but the plea of God is greater on the learned and grief more incumbent. He is more blameworthy before God. Sermon 110

It guides to the right judgment, so we believed in it. We will never ascribe partners with our Lord anyone. **72:2**

I bear witness that *there is no god but God* (Q47:19), the One, there is no partner with Him, nor is there with Him any god other than Himself, and that *Muhammad* (Q48:29), peace and the mercy of God be upon him, is *His servant* (Q17:1) and *Prophet.* (Q7:158) Sermon 35

Truly, He, exalted be the grandeur of our Lord. He took no companion (f) to Himself, nor a son, **72:3**

and yet a foolish one among us had been saying an outrageous lie about God! **72:4**
But we, truly, thought that the humankind, nor the jinn would ever say a lie about God **72:5**
and that there had been men of humankind who would take refuge with the masculine of the jinn, but they increased them in vileness. **72:6**

Praise belongs to God (Q1:2) Who is recognized without being seen and Who creates without trouble. He created the creation with His Might and receives the devotion of rulers by virtue of His dignity. He exercises superiority over great men through His generosity. It is He who made His creation to populate the world and sent towards the jinn and human beings His Messengers to unveil it for them, to warn them of its harm, to present to them its examples, to show them its defects and to place before them a whole collection of matters containing lessons about the changings of health and sickness in this world, its lawful things and unlawful things and all that God has ordained for the obedient and the disobedient, namely Paradise and Hell and honor and disgrace. I extend my praise to His Being as He desires His creation to praise Him. He has fixed: *Surely God has assigned a measure to everything* ... (Q65:3) for every measure a time limit, and ... *for every term there is a Book.* (Q13:38) Sermon 183

They thought as you thought, that God will never raise up anyone. **72:7**
We stretched towards the heaven. Then, we found it was filled with stern guards and burning flames. **72:8**
We had been sitting in positions having the ability to hear. But whoever listens now will find a burning flame and watchers for him. **72:9**

O my God! Whoever listens to our words which are just and which seek the prosperity of religion and the worldly life and do not seek mischief, they reject after listening. He certainly turns away from **Your** support and desists from strengthening **Your** religion. We make **You** a Witness over him. **You** are the greatest of all witnesses. We make all those who inhabit **Your** earth and **Your** skies witness over him. Thereafter, **You** alone can make us needless of his support and question him for his sin. Sermon 212

We were not informed whether the worst was intended for those who are on earth or whether their Lord intended for them right mindedness. **72:10**
There are among us, the ones in accord with morality. There are among us other than that. We had been of ways differing from one another. **72:11**

Among the proofs of His creation is the creation of the skies which are fastened without pillars and stand without support. He called them. They responded obediently and humbly without being lazy or loathsome. If they had not acknowledged His Godhead and obeyed Him, He would not have made them the place for His throne, the abode of His angels and the destination: *To Him Words of what is good rise and He exalts an action in accord with morality* ... (Q35:10) of the creatures. Sermon 182

We, truly, thought that we will never be able to weaken God on the earth and we will never weaken Him by flight. **72:12**
So, truly, when we heard the guidance, we believed in it. Whoever believes in his Lord, he will fear neither meagerness nor vileness. **72:13**

O my God! I seek **Your** protection from becoming destitute despite **Your** riches, from being misguided despite **Your** guidance, from being molested in **Your** realm and from

being humiliated while authority rests with **You**. O my God! Let my spirit be the first of those good objects that **You** take from me and the first trust out of **Your** favors held in trust with me. Sermon 215

Truly, we are the ones who submit to God. Among us there are the ones who swerve from justice. Whoever submitted to God, then, those sought right mindedness. **72:14**

In case you cannot avoid vanity, your vanity should be for good qualities, praiseworthy acts and admirable matters with which the dignified and noble chiefs of the Arab families distinguished themselves such as attractive manners, high thinking, respectable position and good performances. You, too, should show vanity in praiseworthy habits like the protection of the neighbor, the fulfillment of agreements, obedience to the virtuous, opposition to the haughty, extending generosity to others, abstention from rebellion, keeping aloof from bloodshed, doing justice to people, suppressing anger and avoiding trouble on the earth. You should also fear what calamities befell peoples before you on account of their evil deeds and detestable actions. Remember, during good or bad circumstances, what happened to them. Be cautious that you do not become like them. Sermon 192

As for the ones who swerve from justice, they had been as firewood for hell. **72:15**
If they went straight on the way, We would have satiated them with copious water **72:16**
so that We try them in it. But whoever turns aside from the Remembrance of his Lord, He will dispatch him to a rigorous punishment. **72:17**

When the excitement of water subsided under the earth's sides and under the weight of the high and lofty mountains placed on its shoulders, God flowed springs of water from its high tops and distributed them through plains and low places and moderated their movement by fixed rocks and high mountain tops. Then its trembling came to a standstill because of the penetration of mountains in various parts of its surface and their being fixed in its deep areas and their standing on its plains. Sermon 91

Truly, the places of prostration belong to God so call not to anyone with God. **72:18**
Truly, when the servant of God stood up, calling to Him, they be about to swarm upon him. **72:19**

He is the Giver of all reward and distinction, and Dispeller of all calamities and hardships. Sermon 82

Say: Truly, I call only to my Lord, and I ascribe not as partners with Him anyone. **72:20**

I bear witness that *there is no god but God* (Q47:19), the One, there is no partner with Him, nor is there with Him any god other than Himself, and that *Muhammad* (Q48:29), peace and the mercy of God be upon him, is *His servant* (Q17:1) and *Prophet.* (Q7:158) Sermon 35

Say: Truly, I possess not the power to hurt nor to bring right mindedness for you. **72:21**

The beginning of the action of one who sees with his heart and acts with eyes is to assess whether the action will go against him or for him. If it is for him, he indulges in it, but if it is against him, he keeps away from it. For he who acts without knowledge is like one who treads without a path. His deviation from the path keeps him at a distance from his aim. He who acts according to knowledge is like He who treads the clear path. Sermon 153

Say: Truly, none would grant me protection from God—not anyone! I will never find other than Him that which is a haven **72:22**
unless I be delivering messages from God, His messages. Whoever disobeys God and His Messenger, then, for him is the fire of hell, ones who will dwell in it forever, eternally. **72:23**

Certainly, only doubtful innovations cause ruin except those from which God may protect. In God's authority lies the safety of your affairs. Therefore, render Him such obedience as is neither blameworthy nor insincere. Sermon 169

Until when they saw what they are promised, then, they will know who is weaker of ones who help and fewer in number. **72:24**
Say: I am not informed if what you are promised is near, or if my Lord will assign for it a space of time. **72:25**

Praise belongs to God. (Q1:2) He is such that senses cannot perceive Him, place cannot contain Him, eyes cannot see Him and veils cannot cover Him. He proves His eternity by the coming into existence of His creation, and also by originating His creation He proves His existence, and by their mutual similarity He proves that there is nothing similar to Him. He is true in His promise. He is too high to be unjust to His creatures. He stands by equity among His creation and practices justice over them in His commands. He provides evidence through the creation of things of His being from ever, through their marks of incapability of His power, and through their powerlessness against death of His eternity. Sermon 185

He is The One Who Knows of the unseen! He discloses not the unseen to anyone, **72:26**
but a Messenger with whom He was content. Then, truly, He dispatches in advance of him and from behind him, watchers **72:27**
that He know that they expressed the messages of their Lord. He enclosed whatever is with them and He counted everything with numbers. **72:28**

God, the Sublime, says: *Truly, of humanity closest to Abraham are those who followed him and this Prophet and those who believed. God is Protector of the ones who believe.* (Q3:68) Letter 28

Chapter 73: The One Who is Wrapped (al-Muzzammil)

O ***you*** *, the one who is wrapped,* **73:1**
stand up during the night, but for a little part, **73:2**
for half of it or reduce it a little. **73:3**
Or increase it and chant the Quran, a good chanting, **73:4**
for We will cast on ***you*** *a weighty saying.* **73:5**
Truly, one who begins in the night, is when impression is strongest and speech more upright. **73:6**
Truly, for ***you*** *in the daytime is a lengthy occupation.* **73:7**
Remember ***you*** *the Name of* ***your*** *Lord. Devote* ***your****self to Him with total devotion.* **73:8**
The Lord of the East and of the West, there is no god but He. So, take Him to ***your****self as* ***your*** *Trustee.* **73:9**
Have ***you*** *patience with regard to what they say and abandon them with a graceful abandoning.* **73:10**
Forsake to Me the ones who deny, those imbued with prosperity and respite them for a little. **73:11**
Truly, with Us are shackles and hellfire **73:12**

and food which sticks in the throat and chokes and a painful punishment. **73:13**
On a Day when the earth will quake and the mountains, and the mountains will become a poured forth heap of sand. **73:14**

The human being should ... fear the Day of Judgment before it arrives. He should appreciate the shortness of his life and the shortness of his sojourn in the place of stay which has only to last for his change over to the next place. He should, therefore, do something for his change over and for the known stages of his departure. Blessed be he who possesses a virtuous heart, obeys one who guides him, keeps away from one who takes him to ruin, catches the path of safety with the help of him who provides him light of guidance and, by obeying the leader who commands him, hastens towards guidance before its doors are closed, opens the door of repentance and removes the stain of sins. He has certainly been put on the right path and guided towards the straight path. Sermon 214

Truly, We sent you a Messenger, one who bears witness to you, as We sent to Pharaoh a Messenger. **73:15**

I cling to (my bearing witness) always, for as long as we endure, storing it up as protection against the terrors that will befall us. For truly, it renders faith resolute, pens up spiritual virtue, pleases The Compassionate, repels Satan. Sermon 2*

But Pharaoh rebelled against the Messenger so We took him a taking remorselessly. **73:16**
How will you fend off a day if you were ungrateful, that will make the children gray haired? **73:17**
The heaven will be that which is split apart from it. His promise had been one that is accomplished. **73:18** ***

Truly, this is an admonition; so let whoever willed take himself a way to his Lord. **73:19**
Truly, ***your*** *Lord knows that* ***you*** *be standing up for nearly two thirds of the nighttime, or a half of it or a third of it along with a section of those who are with* ***you****. God ordains the nighttime and the daytime. He knew that you would not be able to keep count of it, so He turned towards you in forgiveness, then recite of the Quran as much as was easy. He knew that some of you are sick and others travel on the earth looking for the grace of God and others fight in the way of God. So, recite of it as much as was easy. Perform the formal prayer and give the purifying alms and lend to God a fairer loan. For whatever of good you put forward for your souls, you will find the same with God. It is good and a sublime compensation. Ask God for forgiveness. Truly, God is Forgiving, Compassionate.* **73:20**

O my God! Forgive me what **You** know about me more than I do. If I return to sins, **You** return to forgiveness. My God! Forgive me what I had promised to myself, but **You** did not find its fulfillment with me. My God! Forgive me that with what I sought nearness to **You** with my tongue, but my heart opposed and did not perform it. My God, forgive me the winkings of the eye, vile utterances, desires of the heart and errors of speech. Sermon 77

Chapter 74: The One Who is Wrapped in a Cloak (al-Muddaththir)

O ***you****, the one who wrapped himself in a cloak!* **74:1**
Stand up and warn! **74:2**

Magnify **your** *Lord* **74:3**
and purify **your** *garments* **74:4**
and abandon contamination! **74:5**
Reproach not others to acquire more for yourself. **74:6**
For **your** *Lord, then, have* **you** *patience.* **74:7**
Then, when the horn is sounded, **74:8**
truly, that Day will be a difficult day, **74:9**
and not easy for the ones who are ungrateful. **74:10**
Forsake to Me whom I alone created. **74:11**
I assigned to him the spreading out of wealth **74:12**
and children as ones who bear witness. **74:13**
I have made affairs smooth for him, a making smooth **74:14**
Again, he is desirous that I increase it. **74:15**
No indeed; he had been stubborn about Our signs. **74:16**
I will constrain him with a hard ascent. **74:17**
Truly, he deliberated and calculated. **74:18**
Then, perdition to him! How he calculated! **74:19**
Again, perdition to him! How he calculated! **74:20**
Again, he looked on **74:21**
and, again, he frowned and scowled. **74:22**
Again, he drew back and grew arrogant. **74:23**
He said: This is nothing but fabricated old sorcery. **74:24**
This is nothing but the saying of a mortal. **74:25**
I will scorch him in Saqar. **74:26**
How will **you** *recognize what Saqar is?* **74:27**
It forsakes not nor causes anything to remain, **74:28**
scorching the mortal. **74:29**
Over it there are nineteen. **74:30**
We assigned none but angels to be wardens of the Fire and We made the amount of them not but as a test for those who were ungrateful. So, those who were given the Book are reassured and those who believed, add to their belief. Will not doubt those who were given the Book and the ones who believe. Say to those who in their hearts is a sickness and the ones who are ungrateful: What had God wanted by this example? Thus, God causes to go astray whom He wills, and He guides whom He wills. None knows the armies of **your** *Lord but He. It is not other than a reminder for the mortals.* **74:31**

God, the Almighty, has sent down a guiding Book wherein He has explained virtue and vice. You should adopt the course of virtue, whereby you will have guidance. Detach yourself from the direction of vice, so that you remain on the right way. Mind the obligations! Mind the obligations! Fulfill them for God and they will take you to the Garden. Surely, God has made unlawful the things which are not unknown and made lawful the things which are without defect. Sermon 167

No indeed! By the moon **74:32**
and the night when it drew back **74:33**
and polished is the morning. **74:34**
Truly, it is one of the greatest of all things **74:35**
as a warner to the mortals, **74:36**

to whomever willed among you that he go forward or remain behind. **74:37**

He originated the creation without any example which He could follow and without any specimen prepared by any creator who would have been before Him. He showed us the realm of His Might, and such wonders which speak of His Wisdom. The confession of the created things that their existence owes itself to Him made us realize that argument has been furnished about knowing Him so that there is no excuse against it. The signs of His creative power and standard of His wisdom are fixed in the wonderful things He has created. Whatever He has created is an argument in His favor and a guide towards Him. Even a silent thing is a guide towards Him as though it speaks, and its guidance towards the Creator is clear. Sermon 91

Every soul is a pledge for what it earned **74:38**
but the Companions of the Right **74:39**
will be in Gardens and will demand of one another **74:40**
about the ones who sin: **74:41**
What thrust you into Saqar? **74:42**

Have you not heard the reply of the people of Hell when they were asked: *What thrust you into Saqar (Hell)? They would say: We be not among the ones who formally pray.* (Q74:42-43) Certainly, prayer drops out sins like the dropping of leaves of trees, and removes them as ropes are removed from the necks of cattle. *The Messenger of God* (Q48:29), peace and the mercy of God be upon him, likened it to a hot bath situated at the door of a person who bathes in it five times a day. Will then any dirt remain on him? Sermon 198

They would say: We be not among the ones who formally pray **74:43**
and we were not those who feed the needy. **74:44**
We had been ones who engage in idle talk along with the ones who engage in idle talk. **74:45**

Pledge yourself with prayer and remain steady on it; offer prayer as much as possible and seek nearness of God through it, because it is imposed upon the believers as a timed ordinance: *Truly the formal prayer has been—for the ones who believe—a timed prescription.* (Q4:103). Sermon 198

We had been denying the Day of Judgment **74:46**
until the certainty of the Hour approached us. **74:47**

On that day God will collect on it the front and the back, to stand in obedience for the exaction of accounts and for the award of recompense for deeds. Sweat would flow up to their mouths like reins while the earth would be trembling under them. In the best condition among them would be he who has found a resting place for both his feet and an open place for his breath. Sermon 102

Then, intercession will not profit them from the ones who are intercessors. **74:48**

Know that the Quran is an interceder and its intercession will be accepted. It is a speaker who bears witness. For whoever the Quran intercedes on the Day of Judgment, its intercession for him would be accepted. He about whom the Quran speaks ill on the Day of Judgment shall testify to it. On the Day of Judgment, an announcer will announce: Be aware! Every sower of a crop is in distress except the sowers of the Quran. Therefore, you should be among the sowers of the Quran and its followers. Make it your guide towards

God. Seek its advice for yourselves, do not trust your views against it and regard your desires in the matter of the Quran as deceitful. Sermon 176

Then, what is the matter with them that they are ones who turn aside from the admonition, **74:49**
as though they had been frightened donkeys **74:50**
that ran away from a lion? **74:51**
Nay! Every man among them wants to be given unrolled scrolls. **74:52**
No indeed! Nay! They fear not the world to come. **74:53**
No indeed! Truly, it is an admonition. **74:54**
So, let whoever willed, remember it. **74:55**
But they will not remember unless God wills. He is Worthy of God-consciousness and He is Worthy of granting The Forgiveness. **74:56**

The Prophet (Q7:158), peace and the mercy of God be upon him, said: The belief of a person cannot be firm unless his heart is firm, and his heart cannot be firm unless his tongue is firm. So whoever of you can manage to meet God, the Sublime, in such a position that his hands are unsmeared with the blood of Muslims and their property and his tongue is safe from exposing them, he should do so. Sermon 176

Chapter 75: The Resurrection (al-Qiyāmah)

I swear an oath by the Day of Resurrection. **75:1**
I swear an oath by the reproachful soul. **75:2**
Assumes the human being that We will never gather his bones? **75:3**
Yea! We are ones who have power to shape his fingers again. **75:4**
Nay! The human being wants to act immorally in front of him. **75:5**
He asks: When is this Day of Resurrection? **75:6**
But when their sight will be astonished **75:7**
and the moon will cause the earth to be swallowed **75:8**
and the sun and the moon will be gathered, **75:9**
the human being will say on that Day: Where is a place to run away to? **75:10**
No indeed! There is no refuge. **75:11**
*With **your** Lord on this Day will be **your** recourse.* **75:12**
The human being will be told on that Day what he put forward and what he postponed. **75:13**
Nay! The human being is clear evidence against himself. **75:14**
Although he would cast his excuses, **75:15**
*impel not **your** tongue to hasten it.* **75:16**
Truly, on Us is his amassing and its Recitation. **75:17**
*But when We recited it, follow **you** its Recitation.* **75:18**

Go ahead with the remembrance of God, for it is the best remembrance. Long for that which He has promised to the pious, for His promise is the most true promise. Tread the course of *the Prophet* (Q7:158), peace and the mercy of God be upon him, for it is the most distinguished course. Follow his *sunna*, for it is the most right of all behaviors. Learn the Quran, for it is the fairest of discourses. Understand it thoroughly, for it is the best blossoming of hearts. Seek cure with its light, for it is the cure for hearts. Recite it beautifully, for it is the most beautiful narration. Certainly, a scholar who acts not according to his knowledge is like the off-headed ignorant who does not find relief from his ignorance, but the plea of God is greater on the learned and grief more incumbent. He is more blameworthy before God. Sermon 110

From Us after that is its clear explanation. 75:19
No indeed! Nay! You love that which hastens away 75:20
and forsake the world to come. 75:21
Faces on that Day will be ones that beam, 75:22
ones that look towards their Lord. 75:23
Faces on that day will be ones that scowl. 75:24
***You** will think that against them is wreaked a crushing calamity.* 75:25
No indeed! When it reached the collar bones at death 75:26
and it was said: Where is one who is a wizard to save me? 75:27
He thought it to be his parting 75:28
and one leg was intertwined with the other leg, 75:29
that Day he will be driving toward ***your*** *Lord* 75:30
for he established not the true nor invoked blessings 75:31
and he denied and turned away. 75:32
He went to his people again, going arrogantly. 75:33
Closer to ***you**! Closer to* ***you**!* 75:34
Again closer to ***you**! Closer to* ***you**!* 75:35
Assumes the human being that he will be left aimless? 75:36
Was he not a sperm-drop to be emitted in seminal fluid? 75:37
Again, he had been a clot and He created him and shaped him. 75:38
Then, He made of him two pairs, the male and the female. 75:39
Is not that One Who Has Power over that able to give life to the dead? 75:40

Do you not see that your predecessors did not come back and the surviving followers did not remain? Do you not observe that the people of the world pass mornings and evenings in different conditions? Thus, somewhere the dead is wept for, someone is being condoled, someone is prostrate in distress, someone is enquiring about the sick, someone is passing his last breath, someone is hankering after the world while death is looking for him, someone is forgetful, but he is not forgotten by death, and the survivors walk in the footsteps of the predecessors. Sermon 99

CHAPTER 76: THE HUMAN BEING (al-Insān)

Approached the human being a long course of time when he will be nothing remembered? 76:1
Truly, We made the human being of a mingling of seminal fluid that We may test him. So, We made him hearing, seeing. 76:2
Truly, We guided him on the way, whether he be one who is thankful or ungrateful. 76:3
Truly, We made ready for ones who are ungrateful chains and yokes and a blaze. 76:4
Truly, the pious will drink from a cup that had been a mixture of camphor, 76:5
a spring where the servants of God will drink, causing it to gush forth, a great gushing. 76:6
They live up to their vows and they fear a Day when the worst will be that which flies far and wide. 76:7

In spite of their love for it, they feed with food one who is needy and the orphan and the prisoner of war saying: **76:8**
We feed you only for the Countenance of God. We want no recompense from you nor any thankfulness. **76:9**
Truly, we fear our Lord on a frowning, inauspicious Day. **76:10**
So, God would protect them from worse on that day, and would make them find radiancy and joyfulness. **76:11**
He will give them recompense for their enduring patiently with a Garden and silk, **76:12**
and ones who are reclining in it on raised benches. In it they will see neither sun nor excessive cold of the moon. **76:13**
That which draws near them is its shade and clusters of grapes will be subdued, a subduing. **76:14**
Are passed around among them receptacles of silver and goblets that had been of crystal, **76:15**
crystal like silver, and that they calculated a calculating. **76:16**
They are given to drink in it a cup that had been with a mixture of ginger. **76:17**
There is a spring in it named Salsabil. **76:18**
*Ones who are immortal youths will go around them whom, when **you** had seen them, **you** would assume them to be scattered pearls.* **76:19**
*When **you** had seen them, again, **you** will have seen bliss and a great dominion.* **76:20**
Upon them are garments of fine green silk and brocade. They will be adorned with bracelets of silver. Their Lord will give to drink undefiled drink. **76:21**
Truly, this had been your recompense. What had been that which is your endeavoring. **76:22**
*Truly, We sent down to **you** the Quran, a sending down successively.* **76:23**

God, the Almighty, has sent down a guiding Book wherein He has explained virtue and vice. You should adopt the course of virtue, whereby you will have guidance. Detach yourself from the direction of vice, so that you remain on the right way. Sermon 167

*So, have **you** patience for the determination of **your** Lord and obey not any one of them, not the ones who are perverted nor the ungrateful.* **76:24**
*Remember **you** the Name of **your** Lord at early morning dawn and eventide.* **76:25**
*During the night, prostrate **your**self to Him and glorify Him a lengthy part of the night.* **76:26**
Truly, these are they who love that which hastens away and they forsake a weighty day behind them. **76:27**

O God's human being! Weigh yourselves before you are weighed and assess yourselves before you are assessed. Breathe before suffocation of the throat. Be submissive before you are harshly driven. Know that if one does not help himself in acting as his own adviser and warner, then no one else can effectively be his adviser or warner. Sermon 90

We created them and We strengthened their frame. When We willed, We will substitute their likes with a substitution. **76:28**
Truly, this is an admonition. Whoever willed, he took himself on a way to his Lord. **76:29**

The best means by which seekers of nearness to God, the Almighty, the Exalted, seek nearness, is the belief in Him and His Prophet, fighting in His cause for it is the high pinnacle of Islam, and to believe in the expression of divine purification for it is just nature and the establishment of prayer for it is the basis of community, payment of the purifying tax (*zakat*) for it is a compulsory obligation, fasting for the month of Ramadan for it is the shield against chastisement, the performance of the pilgrimage to the House of God (Kabah) and its visitation (*umra*) (other than annual visit) for these two acts banish poverty and wash away sins, regard for kinship for it increases wealth and length of life, giving alms secretly for it covers shortcomings, giving alms openly for it protects against a bad death and extending benefits to people for it saves from positions of disgrace. Sermon 109

But you will it not unless God wills it. For God had been Knowing, Wise. **76:30**
He causes to enter whom He wills into His mercy. The ones who are unjust, He prepared for them a painful punishment. **76:31**

Praise belongs to God (Q1:2) Who is above all similarity to creatures, is above the words of describers Who displays the wonders of His management for the on-lookers, is hidden from the imagination of thinkers by virtue of the greatness of His glory, has knowledge without acquiring it by adding to it or drawing it from someone, and Who is the ordainer of all matters without reflecting or thinking. He is such that gloom does not concern Him, nor does He seek light from brightness. Night does not overtake Him, nor does the day pass over Him so as to affect Him in any manner. His comprehension of things is not through eyes. His knowledge is not dependent on being informed. God deputized *the Prophet* (Q7:158), peace and the mercy of God be upon him, with light and accorded him the highest precedence in selection. Through him God united those who were divided, overpowered the powerful, overcame difficulties and leveled rugged ground and, thus, removed misguidance from right and left. Sermon 213

Chapter 77: The Ones Who are Sent (al-Mursalāt)

By ones who are sent successively, **77:1**
by the storm and raging tempest, **77:2**
by that which causes vegetation to revive, unfolding **77:3**
by the ones who separate a separating **77:4**
by ones who cast a remembrance **77:5**
as excusing or warning, **77:6**
truly, what you are promised will be that which falls. **77:7**
Then, when the stars will be obliterated **77:8**
and when the heaven will be cleaved asunder **77:9**
and when the mountains will be scattered **77:10**
and when the time will be set for the Messengers, **77:11**
for which Day were these appointed? **77:12**
For the Day of Decision. **77:13**
What would cause ***you*** *to recognize what the Day of Decision is?* **77:14**
Woe on that Day to the ones who deny! **77:15**
Caused We not the ancient ones to perish? **77:16**
Again, We will pursue the later ones. **77:17**
Thus, We accomplish this with the ones who sin. **77:18**
Woe on that Day to the ones who deny! **77:19**
Create We you not of despicable water? **77:20**

You, O God, made angels reside in **Your** skies and placed them high above from **Your** earth. They have the most knowledge about **You** and **Your** whole creation, the most consciousness of **You**, and are the nearest to **You**. They never stayed in loins nor were retained in wombs. They were not created from *despicable water.* (Q77:20)

Then, We made it in a secure stopping place **77:21**
for a known measuring? **77:22**

... and placed in a still place for a known length: *Then We made it in a secure stopping place for a known measuring* (Q77:21-22) and an ordained time. You used to move in the womb of your mother as an embryo, neither responding to a call nor hearing any voice. Sermon 163

We measured. How bountiful are the ones who measure! **77:23**
Woe on that day to the ones who deny! **77:24**

He is One, but not by the first in counting, is Creator, but not through activity or labor, is Hearer, but not by means of any physical organ, is Looker, but not by a stretching of eyelids, is Witness, but not by nearness, is Distinct, but not by measurement of distance, is Manifest, but not by seeing and is Hidden, but not by subtlety of body. He is Distinct from things because He overpowers them and exercises might over them, while things are distinct from Him because of their subjugation to Him and their turning towards Him. Sermon 152

Make We not the earth a place of drawing together **77:25**
the living and the lifeless? **77:26**
We made on it soaring, firm mountains. We satiated you with water of the sweetest kind. **77:27**
Woe on that Day to the ones who deny! **77:28**
Set out toward what you had been in it denying. **77:29**
Set out to the shade. It is possessor of three columns, **77:30**
having no shade nor availing you against the flaming! **77:31**
Truly, it will throw up sparks of fire like the palace, **77:32**
as though it was a string of saffron-colored male camels. **77:33**
Woe on that Day to the ones who deny! **77:34**
This Day they will not speak for themselves **77:35**
nor will they be given permission so that they make excuses. **77:36**
Woe on that Day to the ones who deny! **77:37**
This is the Day of Decision; We gathered you and the ancient ones. **77:38**
So, if you had been cunning, then, try to outwit Me. **77:39**
Woe on that Day to the ones who deny! **77:40**
Truly, the ones who are God-conscious will be amidst shade and springs **77:41**
and sweet fruit for which they lust: **77:42**

Make obedience to God your way of life and not only your outside covering. Make it your inner habit instead of only outer routine, subtle enough to enter through your ribs up to the heart, the guide for all your affairs, the watering place for your getting down on the Day of Judgment, the interceder for the achievement of your aims, asylum for the day of your fear, the lamp of the interior of your graves, company for your long loneliness and deliverance from the troubles of your abodes. Certainly, obedience to God is a protection against encircling calamities, expected dangers and the flames of burning fires. Sermon 198

Eat and drink wholesomely for what you had been doing. 77:43
Truly, We, thus, give recompense to the ones who are doers of good. 77:44
Woe on that Day to the ones who deny! 77:45
Eat, take joy for a little. You are ones who sin. 77:46
Woe on that Day to the ones who deny! 77:47
When it will be said: Bow down, they bow not down. 77:48
Woe on that Day to the ones who deny! 77:49
Then, in which discourse after this will they believe? 77:50

God, the Almighty, has sent down a guiding Book wherein He has explained virtue and vice. You should adopt the course of virtue whereby you will have guidance, and keep aloof from the direction of vice so that you remain on the right way. Mind the obligations! Mind the obligations! Fulfill them for God and they will take you to the Garden. Surely, God has made unlawful the things which are not unknown and made lawful the things which are without defect. Sermon 167

Chapter 78: The Tiding (al-Nabāᵓ)

About what demand you of one another? 78:1
Of the sublime tiding 78:2
about which they are ones who are at variance in it? 78:3
No indeed! Soon they will know. 78:4
Again, no indeed! Soon they will know. 78:5
Make We not the earth for a cradling 78:6
and the mountains as stakes? 78:7
We created not you in pairs 78:8
and We made your sleep as a rest. 78:9
We made the nighttime as a garment. 78:10
We made the daytime for you to earn a living. 78:11
We built over you seven superior ones. 78:12
We made a bright, light-giving lamp. 78:13
We caused to descend that which are clouds bringing rain, water cascading, 78:14
with which We bring about grain and plants 78:15
and luxuriant Gardens. 78:16
Truly, the Day of Decision would be a time appointed, 78:17
a Day the trumpet is blown. Then, you approach in units 78:18
and the heaven will be let loose and will be all doors. 78:19
The mountains will be set in motion and will be as vapor. 78:20
Truly, hell will be on the watch, 78:21
a destination for the ones who are defiant, 78:22
one who lingers in expectation in it for many years. 78:23
They experience in it not any coolness nor any drink, 78:24
but scalding water and filth, 78:25
a suitable recompense! 78:26
Truly, they had been not hoping not for a reckoning 78:27
and they denied Our signs with a denial. 78:28

But We counted everything in a Book. **78:29**
Experience it! We will never increase you but in punishment. **78:30**
Truly, for the ones who are God-conscious, there is a place of security, **78:31**
fertile gardens and grapevines, **78:32**
and full breasted maidens of the same age **78:33**
and a cup overflowing. **78:34**
No idle talk will they hear in it nor any denial, **78:35**
a recompense from **your** *Lord, a gift, a reckoning.* **78:36**
from the Lord of the heavens and the earth and of whatever is between them, The Merciful. against Whom they possess no argument. **78:37**
On a Day when the Spirit and the angels will stand up ranged in rows. They will not assert themselves but he to whom the Merciful gave permission and who said what is correct. **78:38**

If God had wanted to create Adam from a light whose glare would have dazzled the eyes, whose handsomeness would have amazed the wits and whose fragrance would have caught the breath, He could have done so. If He had done so people would have bowed to him in humility and the trial of the angels through him would have become easier, but God, the Almighty, tries His creatures by means of those things whose real nature they do not know in order to distinguish good and bad for them through the trial, and to remove vanity from them and keep them away from pride and self-admiration. Sermon 192

That is the Day of The Truth; so whoever willed took his Lord to himself as the destination. **78:39**

You are supporters of Truth and brethren in faith. You are the shield on the day of tribulation and my trustees among the rest of the people. With your support I strike the runner away and hope for the obedience of him who advances forward. Therefore, extend to me support which is free from deceit and pure from doubt because, by God, I am the most preferable of all for the people. Sermon 118

We warned you of a near punishment on a Day when a man will look on what his hands put forward and the ones who are ungrateful will say: O would that I had been earth dust! **78:40**

They are wrong who liken **You** to their idols, dress **You** with apparel of the creatures by their imagination, attribute to **You** parts of body by their own thinking and consider **You** after the creatures of various types through the working of their intelligence. I bear witness that whoever equated **You** with anything out of **Your** creation took a partner for **You**. Whoever takes a partner for **You** is ungrateful according to what is stated in **Your** unambiguous verses and indicated by the evidence of **Your** clear arguments. I also bear witness that **You** are that God Who cannot be confined in the fetters of intelligence so as to admit change of condition by entering its imagination, nor in the shackles of the mind so as to become limited and an object of alterations. Sermon 91

Chapter 79: The Ones Who Tear Out (al-Nāziᶜāt)

By the ones who tear out vehemently, **79:1**
by the ones who draw out a drawing out, **79:2**
by the ones who are swimmers, swimming, **79:3**
the ones who take the lead, taking the lead, **79:4**
by the ones who manage a command, **79:5**

on a Day when the quake quakes, **79:6**
succeeds the one that comes close behind it, **79:7**
hearts beating painfully on that Day, **79:8**
their sight, that which is humble. **79:9**
They say: Will we be restored to our original state **79:10**
when we had been crumbled bones? **79:11**
They said: That is a return again of one who is a loser. **79:12**
Truly, there will be but one scare. **79:13**
That is when they would be the ones awakening. **79:14**
Approached **you** *the discourse of Moses* **79:15**
when his Lord cried out to him in the sanctified valley of Tuwa: **79:16**
Be **you** *gone to Pharaoh. Truly, he was defiant.* **79:17**
Say: Would **you** *purify* **your***self?* **79:18**
I will guide **you** *to* **your** *Lord, then,* **you** *will dread Him.* **79:19**
He caused him to see the greater sign. **79:20**
But Pharaoh denied and rebelled. **79:21**
Again, Pharaoh drew back, hastening about. **79:22**
Then, Pharaoh assembled them; then, proclaimed. **79:23**
Then, Pharaoh said: I am your lofty lord. **79:24**
So, God took him with an exemplary punishment for the last and for the first. **79:25**
Truly, in that is a lesson for whoever dreads God. **79:26**

Glorified is He who ... solidified (the earth) after the watery state of its sides. In this way He made it a cradle for His creatures and spread it for them in the form of a floor over the deep ocean which is stationary, does not move, is fixed and does not flow. Severe winds move it here and there and clouds draw up water from it: *Truly, in that is a lesson for whoever dreads God.* (Q79:26) Sermon 210

Is your constitution harder to create or the heaven which He built? **79:27**
He exalted its vault and shaped it **79:28**
and He made its night dark and brought out its forenoon. **79:29**
After that, He spread out the earth. **79:30**
He brought out from it its water and its pasture. **79:31**
The mountains He set firm, **79:32**
an enjoyment for you and for your flocks. **79:33**
When the Greater Catastrophe would draw near, **79:34**
on that Day the human being will recollect for what he endeavored. **79:35**

Your ultimate goal of reward or punishment is before you. Behind your back is the hour of Resurrection which is driving you on. Keep yourself light and overtake the forward ones. The first ones who have preceded await your last ones. Sermon 21

Hellfire will be advanced for whoever sees. **79:36**
As for whoever was defiant **79:37**
and held this present life in greater favor, **79:38**
then, truly, hellfire will be the place of shelter! **79:39**
As for him who feared the Station of his Lord and prohibited desire from his soul, **79:40**
truly, the Garden will be the place of shelter! **79:41**

They ask **you** *about the Hour. When will it berth?* **79:42**
Then, what are **you** *about that* **you** *remind of it?* **79:43**
To **your** *Lord is the Utmost Boundary of it.* **79:44**
You *are only one who warns to such a one whoever dreads it.* **79:45**
It will be as though a Day they see it, they linger not in expectation but an evening or a forenoon. **79:46**

Their hearts are grieved. Others are protected from their evil. Their bodies are thin. Their needs are scanty. Their souls are chaste. They endured hardship for a short while. As a consequence, they secured comfort for a long time. It is a beneficial transaction that God made easy for them. The world aimed at them, but they did not aim at it. It captured them, but they freed themselves from it by a ransom. During the night, they are standing on their feet, reading portions of the Quran and reciting it in a well-measured way, creating through it grief and seeking by it the cure for their ailments. If they come across a verse creating eagerness for Paradise, they pursue it avidly. Their spirits turn towards it eagerly. They feel as if it is in front of them. When they come across a verse which contains fear of Hell, they bend the ears of their hearts towards it and feel as though the sound of Hell and its cries are reaching their ears. They bend themselves from their backs, prostrate themselves on their foreheads, their palms, their knees and their toes, and beseech God, the Sublime, for their deliverance. Sermon 193

Chapter 80: He Frowned (al-ᶜAbasa)

He frowned and turned away **80:1**
So, let whoever willed, remember it **80:1**
that the blind man drew near him. **80:2**
What will cause **you** *to recognize so that perhaps he will purify himself* **80:3**
or yet recollect and a reminder profit him? **80:4**
But as for he who was self-complacent, **80:5**
then, **you** *have attended to him* **80:6**
and not upon **you** *is any blame if he purifies not himself.* **80:7**
Yet as for him who drew near to **you***, coming eagerly for knowledge* **80:8**
and he dreads God, **80:9**
then, **you** *have paid no heed to him?* **80:10**
No indeed! Truly, this is an admonition. **80:11**
So, whoever has willed will remember it **80:12**
in scrolls to be held in esteem, **80:13**
ones that are exalted and ones that are purified **80:14**
by the hands of generous writers **80:15**
and ones who are kindly, generous. **80:16**
Perdition to the human being! How ungrateful he is! **80:17**
From which thing did He create him? **80:18**
He created him from seminal fluid then, ordained that he be. **80:19**
He made the way easy for him again. **80:20**
Again, He caused him to die and be buried. **80:21**
Again, when He willed, He will revive him. **80:22**

No indeed! The human being finishes not what He commanded him. **80:23**
Then, let the human being look on his food— **80:24**
how We, truly, unloosed rain water with a pouring out. **80:25**
Again, We split the earth, a splitting. **80:26**
We put forth in it grain **80:27**
and grapevines and reeds **80:28**
and olives and date palm trees **80:29**
and dense fertile gardens **80:30**
and sweet fruits and whatever grows on the earth, **80:31**
an enjoyment for you and your flocks. **80:32**
Then, when the blare drew near, **80:33**
that Day a man will run away from his brother **80:34**
and his mother and his father **80:35**
and his companion wife and his children. **80:36**
For every man of them on that Day will be a matter that will preoccupy him. **80:37**
Faces that Day will be ones that are polished, **80:38**
ones who are laugh and ones who rejoice at good tidings. **80:39**

Then there remain a few people in whose case the remembrance of their return to God on the Day of Judgment keeps their eyes bent and the fear of Resurrection moves their tears. Some of them are scared away from the world and dispersed. Some are frightened and subdued. Some are quiet as if muzzled. Some are praying sincerely. Some are grief-stricken and pain-ridden whom fear has confined to namelessness and disgrace has shrouded them, so they are in the sea of bitter water, their mouths are closed and their hearts are bruised. They preached until they were tired. They were oppressed until they were disgraced. They were killed until their numbers dwindled. Sermon 32

Faces on that Day will be dust-stained. **80:40**
Gloom will come over them. **80:41**
Those, they are the ones who are ungrateful, ones who act immorally. **80:42**

They are wrong who liken **You** to their idols, dress **You** with apparel of the creatures by their imagination, attribute to **You** parts of body by their own thinking and consider **You** after the creatures of various types through the working of their intelligence. I bear witness that whoever equated **You** with anything out of **Your** creation took a partner for **You**. Whoever takes a partner for **You** is ungrateful according to what is stated in **Your** unambiguous verses and indicated by the evidence of **Your** clear arguments. I also bear witness that **You** are that God Who cannot be confined in the fetters of intelligence so as to admit change of condition by entering its imagination, nor in the shackles of the mind so as to become limited and an object of alterations. Sermon 91

Chapter 81: The Darkening (al-Takwīr)

When the sun will be darkened **81:1**
and when the stars plunge down **81:2**
and when the mountains will be set in motion **81:3**
and when the pregnant camels are ignored **81:4**

and when the savage beasts will be assembled together **81:5**
and when the seas are caused to overflow **81:6**
and when the souls will be mated **81:7**
and when the buried infant girl will be asked **81:8**
for which impiety she was slain **81:9**
and when the scrolls will be unfolded **81:10**
and when the heaven is stripped off **81:11**
and when hellfire will be caused to burn fiercely **81:12**
and when the Garden will be brought close, **81:13**
every soul will know to what it was prone. **81:14**
So, no! I swear an oath by the stars that recede, **81:15**
by the ones that run, the setting stars **81:16**
and by the night when it swarmed **81:17**
and by the morning, when it sighed, **81:18**
truly, the Quran is a saying from a generous Messenger, **81:19**
possessed of strength, with the Possessor of the Throne, secure, **81:20**
one who is obeyed and, again, trustworthy. **81:21**
Your companion is not one who is possessed. **81:22**

God never allowed His creation to remain without a Prophet, one deputized by Him, or a Book sent down from Him, or a binding argument, or a standing plea. These Messengers were such that they did not fear that they were few in comparison to the large numbers of their falsifiers. Among them was either a predecessor who would name the one to follow or the follower who had been introduced by the predecessor. Sermon 1

Certainly, he saw him on the clear horizon. **81:23**
He is not avaricious for the unseen, **81:24**
nor is it the saying of the accursed Satan. **81:25**
So, where are you going? **81:26**

So, where are you going? (Q81:26) and *How then are you misled?* Signs of guidance are standing, indications of virtue are clear, and the minarets of light have been fixed. Where are you being taken astray and how are you groping? Sermon 91

Truly, it is not but a Remembrance to the worlds **81:27**
to whoever among you willed to go straight. **81:28**
But you will not, unless God wills, the Lord of the worlds. **81:29**

Every one of you has to bear his own burden. It has been kept light for the ignorant. God is Merciful. Faith is straight. *The Prophet* (Q7:158), peace and the mercy of God be upon him, is the holder of knowledge. Yesterday I was with you; today I have become the object of a lesson for you, and tomorrow I shall leave you. May God forgive me and you! Sermon 149

Chapter 82: The Splitting Apart (al-Infiṭār)

When the heaven will be split apart **82:1**
and when the stars will be scattered **82:2**
and when the seas will be caused to gush forth **82:3**

and when the graves will be scattered about **82:4**
every soul would know what it put forward and what it postponed. **82:5**
O human being! What deluded **you** *as to* **your** *generous Lord,* **82:6**

O human being! What deluded **you** *as to* **your** *generous Lord ...* (Q82:6) The addressee in this verse is devoid of argument. His excuse is most deceptive. He is detaining himself in ignorance. Sermon 221

He Who created **you**, *then, shaped* **you** *in proportion.* **82:7**
He composed **you** *in whichever form He willed.* **82:8**
No indeed! Nay! You deny this way of life! **82:9**
Truly, there are ones who guard over you, **82:10**
ones who are generous scribes. **82:11**
They know whatever you accomplish. **82:12**
Truly, the pious will be in bliss. **82:13**
Truly, the ones who act immorally will be in hellfire. **82:14**
They will roast on the Day of Judgment. **82:15**
They will not be of ones who are absent. **82:16**
What will cause **you** *to recognize what the Day of Judgment is?* **82:17**
Again, what will cause **you** *to recognize what the Day of Judgment is?* **82:18**
It is a Day whereon a soul will not possess anything to avail another soul and the command on that Day will belong to God. **82:19**

Know that you have to pass over the pathway (sirat) where steps waver, feet slip away and there are fearful dangers at every step. O God's human being! Be God-conscious, like the fearing of a wise man whom the thought of the next world has turned away from other matters. God-consciousness has afflicted his body with trouble and pain. His engagement in the night prayer has turned even his short sleep into awakening. Hope of eternal recompense keeps him thirsty in the day. Abstention has curbed his desires. Remembrance of God is ever moving his tongue. He entertains awareness before dangers. He avoids uneven ways in favor of clear ones. He follows the shortest route to secure his purpose. Wishfulness does not twist his thinking. Ambiguities do not blind his eyes. He enjoys deep sleep and passes his day happily because of the happiness of good tidings and the pleasure of eternal bounties. He passes the pathway of this world in a praiseworthy manner. He reaches the next world with virtues. He hastens towards virtue out of awareness for vice. He moves briskly during the short time of life in this world. He devotes himself in seeking eternal good. He runs away from evil. Today he is mindful of tomorrow. He keeps the future in his view. Certainly, Paradise is the best reward and achievement while Hell is appropriate punishment and suffering. God is the best Avenger and Helper and the Quran is the best argument and confronter. Sermon 82

Chapter 83: The Ones Who Give Short Measure (al-Muṭaffifīn)

Woe be to the ones who give short measure, **83:1**
those who when they measure against humanity obtained full measure. **83:2**
Yet when they wanted to measure for them, or weigh for them, they skimp. **83:3**

Think those not that they will be ones who are raised up **83:4**
on the sublime Day, **83:5**
a Day when humanity will stand up for the Lord of the worlds? **83:6**
No indeed! Truly, the Book of the ones who act immorally is in Sijjin. **83:7**
What will cause ***you*** *to recognize what Sijjin is?* **83:8**
It is a written book. **83:9**
Woe on that Day to the ones who deny— **83:10**
those who deny the Day of Judgment! **83:11**
None denies it but every sinful, exceeder of limits, **83:12**
who, when Our signs are recounted to him, he said: Fables of the ancient ones! **83:13**
No indeed! Nay! Their hearts will be overcome with rust from what they had been earning. **83:14**
No indeed! They will be from their Lord on that Day ones who are alienated. **83:15**
Truly, again, they will be ones who roast in hellfire. **83:16**
Again, it will be said to them after that: This is what you had been denying. **83:17**
No indeed! Truly, the book of the pious is in Illiyyun. **83:18**
What will cause ***you*** *to recognize what Illiyyun is?* **83:19**
It is a written book. **83:20**
Bearing witness to it are the ones who are brought near to God. **83:21**

We bear witness.... Sermon 114

Truly, the pious will be in bliss, **83:22**
on raised benches, looking on. **83:23**
You *will recognize on their faces the radiancy of bliss.* **83:24**
They will be given to drink sealed over exquisite wine. **83:25**
Its seal will have the lingering smell of musk. So, for that, then, the ones who strive, strive. **83:26**
The mixture will be of Tasnim, **83:27**
a spring from which will drink the ones who are brought near to it. **83:28**
Truly, those who sinned—at those who believed—had been laughing. **83:29**
When they passed by them, they would wink at one another, **83:30**
and when they would turn about to their people, they would turn about acting as ones who are unconcerned. **83:31**
When they saw them, they would say: Truly, these are ones who go astray. **83:32**
They were sent as ones who guard over them. **83:33**
Then, on this Day, those who believed laugh at the ones who are ungrateful, **83:34**
seated on raised benches, they look on. **83:35**
Were the ones who are ungrateful not rewarded for what they had been accomplishing? **83:36**

The Prophet (Q7:158) lit flames for the seeker and put bright signs for the impeded. So he is **Your** trustworthy trustee, **Your** witness on the Day of Judgment. Sermon 105

Chapter 84: The Splitting Open (al-Inshiqāq)

When the heaven was split open **84:1**
and gave ear to its Lord as it will be justly disposed to do **84:2**
and when the earth stretches out **84:3**
and cast what is in it and voided itself **84:4**

and gave ear to its Lord as it will be justly disposed to do, **84:5**
O human being! Truly, **you** *are one who is laboring towards* **your** *Lord laboriously and* **you** *will be one who encounters Him.* **84:6**
As for him who will be given his book in his right hand, **84:7**
then, he will be made a reckoning, an easy reckoning, **84:8**
and will turn about to his people as one who is joyous. **84:9**
But for whoever will be given his book behind his back, **84:10**
he will call for damnation **84:11**
and roast in a blaze. **84:12**
He had been one who is joyous with his people. **84:13**
Truly, he thought he would never retreat. **84:14**
Yea! Truly, his Lord had been seeing him. **84:15**
So, no! I swear an oath by the twilight **84:16**
and by the night and whatever it enveloped **84:17**
and by the moon when it was full **84:18**
that you will, truly, ride plane after plane. **84:19**
Then, what is for them who believe not **84:20**
when the Quran was recited to them, they prostrate not themselves?‡ **84:21**
Nay! Those who were ungrateful deny, **84:22**
but God is greater in knowledge of what they amass. **84:23**
So, give them good tidings of a painful punishment. **84:24**
But those who believed and did as the ones in accord with morality, for them is compensation, that which is unfailing. **84:25**

God, the Almighty, has sent down a guiding Book wherein He has explained virtue and vice. You should adopt the course of virtue, whereby you will have guidance. Detach yourself from the direction of vice, so that you remain on the right way. Mind the obligations! Mind the obligations! Fulfill them for God and they will take you to the Garden. Surely, God has made unlawful the things which are not unknown and made lawful the things which are without defect. Sermon 167

CHAPTER 85: THE CONSTELLATIONS (al-Burūj)

By the heaven possessing the constellations, **85:1**
by the promised Day, **85:2**
by ones who bear witness and ones who are witnessed, **85:3**
the Companions of the Ditch were slain, **85:4**
possessors of the fuel of the fire **85:5**
above which they were ones who sit, **85:6**
as they were, in what they accomplish against the ones who believe, ones who bore witness. **85:7**
They sought revenge on them only because they believe in God, The Almighty, The Worthy of Praise, **85 8**
Him to whom belongs the dominion of the heavens and the earth. God is Witness over everything. **85:9**
Truly, those who persecuted the males, ones who believe and the females, ones who believe and again repent not after that, for them is the punishment of hell and for them is the punishment of

the burning. **85:10**
Truly, those who believed and did as the ones in accord with morality, for them will be Gardens beneath which rivers run. That will be the Great Triumph. **85:11**
Truly, the seizing by force by **your** *Lord is severe.* **85:12**
Truly, He causes to begin and He causes to return. **85:13**
He is The Forgiving, The Loving, **85:14**
the Possessor of the Glorious Throne **85:15**
Achiever of what He wants. **85:16**
Approached **you** *the discourse of the armies* **85:17**
of Pharaoh and of Thamud? **85:18**
Nay! Those who were ungrateful are belying **85:19**
and God is One Who Encloses them from behind. **85:20**
Nay! It is a glorious Recitation **85:21**
inscribed on the Guarded Tablet. **85:22**

Go ahead with the remembrance of God, for it is the best remembrance. Long for that which He has promised to the pious, for His promise is the most true promise. Tread the course of *the Prophet* (Q7:158), peace and the mercy of God be upon him, for it is the most distinguished course. Follow his *sunna*, for it is the most right of all behaviors. Learn the Quran, for it is the fairest of discourses. Understand it thoroughly, for it is the best blossoming of hearts. Seek cure with its light, for it is the cure for hearts. Recite it beautifully, for it is the most beautiful narration. Certainly, a scholar who acts not according to his knowledge is like the off-headed ignorant who does not find relief from his ignorance, but the plea of God is greater on the learned and grief more incumbent. He is more blameworthy before God. Sermon 110

CHAPTER 86: THE NIGHT VISITOR (al-Ṭāriq)

By the heaven and the night visitor, **86:1**
what will cause **you** *to recognize what the night visitor is?* **86:2**
It is the piercing star. **86:3**
Truly, every soul has one who guards it. **86:4**
So, let the human being look on of what he was created. **86:5**
He was created of water, that which gushes forth, **86:6**
going forth from between the loins and the breast bone. **86:7**
Truly, He, in returning him, certainly is One Who Has Power. **86:8**
On a Day all secret thoughts will be tried, **86:9**
then, there will not be for him any strength nor one who helps. **86:10**
By the heaven possessing the returning **86:11**
and by the earth splitting with verdure, **86:12**
truly, the Quran is a decisive saying **86:13**
and it is not for mirth. **86:14**
Truly, they are strategizing a strategy. **86:15**
I am strategizing a strategy. **86:16**
So, respite the ones who are ungrateful! Grant **you** *them a delay for a while.* **86:17**

God, the Almighty, has not counseled anyone on other than the lines of this Quran, for it is the strong rope of God and His trustworthy means. It contains the blossoming of the heart and springs of knowledge. For the heart there is no other gloss than the Quran, although those who remembered it have passed away, while those who forgot or pretended to have forgotten it have remained. If you see any good, give your support to it, but if you see evil, evade it, because *the Messenger of God* (Q48:29), peace and the mercy of God be upon him, used to say: O son of Adam, do good and evade evil. By doing so you will be treading correctly. Sermon 176

CHAPTER 87: THE LOFTY (al-A^{c}lā)

Glorify the Name of ***your*** *Lord, The Lofty* **87:1**
Who created and shaped **87:2**
and who ordained and, then, guided **87:3**
and who brought out the pasture **87:4**
then, made it dark colored refuse. **87:5**
We will make ***you*** *recite and* ***you*** *will not forget* **87:6**
but what God willed. Truly, He knows the openly published and whatever is hidden. **87:7**
We will make easy for ***you*** *an easing.* **87:8**
So, remind if a reminder profited them. **87:9**
Whoever dreads God will recollect, **87:10**
but the disappointed will scorn it— **87:11**
even he who will roast in the great fire, **87:12**
again, neither dying in it nor living. **87:13**
He, surely, prospered, he who purified himself, **87:14**
and remembered the Name of his Lord and invoked blessings. **87:15**
Nay! You hold this present life in greater favor, **87:16**
yet the world to come is better, and one that endures. **87:17**
Truly, this is in the previous scrolls, **87:18**
the scrolls of Abraham and Moses. **87:19**

Praise belongs to God (Q1:2) Who is above all similarity to the creatures, is above the words of describers, Who displays the wonders of His management for the on-lookers, is hidden from the imagination of thinkers by virtue of the greatness of His glory, has knowledge without acquiring it, adding to it or drawing it from someone, and Who is the ordainer of all matters without reflecting or thinking. He is such that gloom does not concern Him, nor does He seek light from brightness, night does not overtake Him, nor does the day pass over Him so as to affect Him in any manner. His comprehension of things is not through eyes and His knowledge is not dependent on being informed. God deputized *the Prophet* (Q7:158), peace and the mercy of God be upon him, with light, and accorded him the highest precedence in selection. Through him God united those who were divided, overpowered the powerful, overcame difficulties and leveled rugged ground, and thus removed misguidance from right and left. Sermon 213

CHAPTER 88: THE OVERWHELMING EVENT (al-Ghāshiyah)

Approached ***you*** *the discourse of the Overwhelming Event?* **88:1**

Faces on that Day will be ones that are humbled, 88:2
ones that work and ones that are fatigued, 88:3
roasting in a hot fire. 88:4
They will be given to drink from boiling receptacles. 88:5
Is it not that there is no food for them but a thorny fruit. 88:6
It will not fatten nor will it avail hunger. 88:7
Faces on that Day will be ones that are pleasant, 88:8
ones who are well-pleased by their endeavoring 88:9
in a magnificent Garden. 88:10
They will hear no babble in it. 88:11
In it is a running spring. 88:12
In it are exalted couches 88:13
and goblets that are set down 88:14
and cushions arrayed 88:15
and rugs, ones that are dispersed. 88:16
Will they not, then, look on the camel, how it was created? 88:17
Of the heaven, how it was lifted up? 88:18
The mountains, how they were hoisted up? 88:19
The earth, how it was stretched out? 88:20
Then, remind for ***you*** *are only one who reminds.* 88:21
You *are not over them one who is a register of their deeds.* 88:22
But whoever turned away and is one who is ungrateful, 88:23
God will punish him with the greater punishment. 88:24
Truly, to Us is their reversion. 88:25
Again, truly, on Us is their reckoning. 88:26

God, the Almighty, has sent down a guiding Book wherein He has explained virtue and vice. You should adopt the course of virtue, whereby you will have guidance. Detach yourself from the direction of vice, so that you remain on the right way. Mind the obligations! Mind the obligations! Fulfill them for God and they will take you to the Garden. Surely, God has made unlawful the things which are not unknown and made lawful the things which are without defect. Sermon 167

Chapter 89: The Dawn (al-Fajr)

By the dawn 89:1
and the ten nights, 89:2
by the even number and the odd number 89:3
and at night when it sets out. 89:4
Is there not in that an oath to be sworn for a possessor of intelligence? 89:5
Have ***you*** *not considered how* ***your*** *Lord accomplished with Ad,* 89:6
with Iram of the pillars 89:7
of which are not created the likes in the land? 89:8
With Thamud, those who hollowed out the rocks in the valley? 89:9
With Pharaoh, the possessor of the stakes, 89:10
those who were defiant in the land 89:11

and made much corruption in it? **89:12**
So, **your** *Lord unloosed on them a scourge of punishment.* **89:13**
Truly, **your** *Lord is, surely, on the watch.* **89:14**
Then, as for the human being, when his Lord tested him and honored him and lauded him, he says: My Lord honored me. **89:15**
But whenever He tested him and constricted his provision for him, he says: My Lord despised me. **89:16**
No indeed! Nay! You honor not the orphan **89:17**
and you encouraged not one another about food for the needy **89:18**
and you consume the inheritance, a greedy consuming, **89:19**
and you love wealth with an ardent cherishing. **89:20**
No indeed! When the earth will be ground to powder, ground to powder, ground to powder, **89:21**
and **your** *Lord will draw near, and the angels, ranged in rows,* **89:22**
on the Day hell is brought about. On that Day the human being will recollect. How will the reminder be for him? **89:23**
He will say: O would that I had put forward from this life for the world to come! **89:24**
Then, on that Day, He will punish no one the like of His punishment. **89:25**
No one will bind as His restraints. **89:26**
O soul, one that is at peace! **89:27**
Return to **your** *Lord, one that is well-pleasing, well-pleased:* **89:28**
Enter **you** *among My servants* **89:29**
and **you** *enter My Garden!* **89:30**

Their hearts are grieved. Others are protected from their evil. Their bodies are thin. Their needs are scanty. Their souls are chaste. They endured hardship for a short while. As a consequence, they secured comfort for a long time. It is a beneficial transaction that God made easy for them. The world aimed at them, but they did not aim at it. It captured them, but they freed themselves from it by a ransom. Sermon 193

Chapter 90: The Land (al-Balad)

I swear an oath by this land **90:1**
you *are allowed in this land* **90:2**
and by ones who are your parents and what is procreated, **90:3**
truly, We created the human being in trouble. **90:4**
Assumes he that none has power over him? **90:5**
He says: I have caused abundant wealth to perish. **90:6**
Assumes he that none sees him? **90:7**
Make we not two eyes for him **90:8**
and a tongue and two lips **90:9**
and guided him to the two open highways? **90:10**
Yet he rushed not onto the steep ascent. **90:11**
What will cause **you** *to recognize what the steep ascent is?* **90:12**
It is the liberating of a bondsperson **90:13**
or feeding on a day possessing famine **90:14**
an orphan, possessor of kinship, **90:15**

or a needy, possessor of misery. **90:16**
Again, it had been among those who believed and counseled one another to having patience and counseled one another to clemency. **90:17**
Those will be the Companions of the Right. **90:18**
But they who were ungrateful for Our signs they will be the Companions of the Left **90:19**
and over them will be fire, that which is closing in. **90:20**

Your benign rule and humane treatment will so affect them that they will come to your help at the time of your difficulties and you will be able to rely on their support. Your kindness, your clemency and your justice will be a kind of moral training to them, and the contented, happy and prosperous life, for which they will be grateful to you, will be the best support, strongest protection and the greatest treasury for you. Letter 53

Chapter 91: The Sun (al-Shams)

By the sun and its forenoon **91:1**
and by the moon when it related to it **91:2**
and by the daytime when it displayed it **91:3**
and by the nighttime when it overcomes it **91:4**
and by the heaven and what built it **91:5**
and by the earth and what widened it **91:6**
and by the soul and what shaped it **91:7**
and, then, inspired it to its acting immorally and God-consciousness, **91:8**
he who made it pure prospered. **91:9**
Surely, is frustrated whoever seduced it. **91:10**

The gazing of people's eyes is not hidden from Him, nor the repetition of words, nor the glimpse of hillocks, nor the tread of a footstep in the dark night or in the deep gloom, where the shining moon casts its light and the effulgent sun comes in its wake, through its setting and appearing again and again with the rotation of time and periods, by the approach of the advancing night or the passing away of the running day. Sermon 162

Thamud denied because of their overboldness. **91:11**
When the disappointed among them were aroused, **91:12**
and the Messenger of God said to them: Allow watering to the she-camel of God. **91:13**
Then, they denied him; then, they crippled her. So, their Lord doomed them for their impiety. **91:14**
Then, He leveled them. He fears not its Ultimate End. **91:15** ***

Chapter 92: The Night (al-Layl)

By the nighttime when it overcomes, **92:1**
by the daytime when it self-disclosed, **92:2**
by Him Who created the male and the female, **92:3**
truly, your endeavoring is diverse. **92:4**
As for him who gave and was God-conscious **92:5**
and established the fairer as true, **92:6**
We will make easy for him the easing. **92:7**

As for him who was a miser and was self-sufficient **92:8**
and denied the fairer, **92:9**
We will make falling into difficulty easy for him. **92:10**
His wealth will not avail him when he succumbed. **92:11**
Truly, guidance is from Us **92:12**
and, truly, to Us belongs the last and the first. **92:13**
I warned you of a fire that blazes fiercely. **92:14**
It roasts none but the vile **92:15**
who denied and turned away. **92:16**
But the devout will be caused to turn aside from it. **92:17**
He who gives of his wealth to purify himself, **92:18**
and with him there is none for which recompense is expected to be given for divine blessing, **92:19**
but only looks for the Countenance of his Lord, The Lofty. **92:20**
He will be well-pleased. **92:21**

I praise God for whatever matter He ordained and whatever action He destines and for my trial with you, O group of people who do not obey when I order and do not respond when I call you. If you are at ease you engage in conceited conversation, but if you are faced with battle you show weakness. Sermon 180

Chapter 93: The Forenoon (al-Duḥā)

By the forenoon **93:1**
and by the night when it brooded, **93:2**
***your** Lord deserted **you** not, nor is He in hatred of **you**.* **93:3**
*Truly, the last will be better for **you** than the first.* **93:4**
***Your** Lord will give to **you**. Then, **you** will be well-pleased.* **93:5**
*Found He **you** not an orphan and He gave **you** refuge?* **93:6**
*Found He **you** one who goes astray, then, He guided **you**?* **93:7**
*Found He **you** one who wants, then, He enriched **you**?* **93:8**
So, as for the orphan, oppress him not. **93:9**
As for one who begs, scold him not. **93:10**
*As for the divine blessing of **your** Lord, divulge it!* **93:11**

Certainly, God Almighty sent Muhammad, peace and the mercy of God be upon him, as Prophet while no one among the Arabs read the Book, nor claimed prophethood or revelation. He had to fight those who disobeyed him in company with those who followed him, leading them towards their salvation and hastening with them lest death overtook them. When any weary person sighed or a distressed one stopped, he stood with him until he got him his aim, except the worst in whom there was no virtue at all. Eventually he showed them their goal and carried them to their places of deliverance. Consequently, their affairs moved on and their hand-mill began to rotate, their position gained strength, their spears were straightened. By God, I was among their rear-guard until they turned back on their sides and were flocked in their rope. I never showed weakness or lack of courage, nor did I betray or become languid. By God, I shall split the wrong until I extract right from its flanks. Sermon 104

CHAPTER 94: THE EXPANSION (al-Inshirāh)

Expand We not ***your*** *breast* **94:1**
and lifted from ***you*** *the heavy loaded burden,* **94:2**
that weighed heavily on ***your*** *back?* **94:3**
Exalted We not ***your*** *remembrance?* **94:4**
So, truly, with hardship, ease. **94:5**
Truly, with hardship, ease. **94:6**
When ***you*** *had finished* ***your*** *duties, then, work on supplication,* **94:7**
and quest ***your*** *Lord.* **94:8**

Hearts achieved guidance through (the Prophet) after being ridden with troubles. He introduced clearly guiding signs and shining injunctions. He is **Your** trusted trustee, the treasurer of **Your** treasured knowledge, **Your** witness on the Day of Judgment, **Your** envoy of truth and **Your** Messenger towards the people. May God prepare a large place for him under **Your** shade and award him multiplying good by **Your** bounty. Sermon 71

CHAPTER 95: THE FIG (al-Tīn)

By the fig and the olive **95:1**
and by Mount Sinai **95:2**
and by this trustworthy land, **95:3**
We have created the human being of the fairer symmetry. **95:4**
Again, We returned him to the lowest of the low. **95:5**
But those who believed and did as the ones in accord with morality, for them is compensation, that which is unfailing. **95:6**
What will cause ***you*** *to deny the Judgment after that?* **95:7**
Is not God The Most Just of ones who judge? **95:8**

Praise belongs to God (Q1:2) for Whom one condition does not proceed another so that He may be the First before being the Last or He may be Outward or Manifest before being Inward or Hidden. Anyone called one except Him is by virtue of being small in number. Anyone enjoying honor other than Him is humble. Any powerful person other than Him is weak. Any master other than Him is a servant. Sermon 65

CHAPTER 96: THE BLOOD CLOT (al-ᶜAlaq)

Recite in the Name of ***your*** *Lord Who created.* **96:1**
He created the human being from a clot. **96:2**
Recite: ***Your*** *Lord is the Most Generous,* **96:3**
He Who taught by the pen. **96:4**
He taught the human being what he knows not. **96:5**
No indeed! The human being is, truly, defiant. **96:6**
He considered himself self-sufficient. **96:7**
Truly, to ***your*** *Lord is the returning.* **96:8**
Have ***you yourself*** *considered he who prohibits* **96:9**

a servant when he invoked blessings? **96:10**
*Have **you** considered if he had been on guidance* **96:11**
or commanded God-consciousness? **96:12**
*Have **you** considered if he denied and turned away?* **96:13**
Knows he not that God sees? **96:14**
No indeed! Truly, if he refrains himself not, We will, surely, lay hold of him by the forelock, **96:15**
a lying, inequitable forelock. **96:16**
Let him call to his conclave. **96:17**
We will call to the guards of hell. **96:18**
*No indeed! Truly, obey **you** him not but prostrate **your**self to God and be near to Him.* **96:19**

Pledge yourself with prayer and remain steady on it; offer prayer as much as possible and seek nearness of God through it, because it is imposed upon the believers as a timed ordinance: *Truly the formal prayer has been—for the ones who believe—a timed prescription.* (Q4:103) Sermon 198

CHAPTER 97: THE NIGHT OF POWER (al-Qadr)

Truly, We caused it to descend on the night of power. **97:1**
*What will cause **you** to recognize what is the night of power?* **97:2**
The night of power is better than a thousand months. **97:3**
The angels come forth and the Spirit during it with their Lord's permission, with every command. **97:4**
Peace it is until the time of the rising dawn. **97:5**

God the Almighty, has not counseled anyone on the lines of this Quran, for it is the strong rope of God and His trustworthy means. It contains the blossoming of the heart and springs of knowledge. For the heart there is no other gloss than the Quran although those who remembered it have passed away while those who forgot or pretended to have forgotten it have remained. If you see any good give your support to it, but if you see evil evade it, because *the Messenger of God* (Q48:29), peace and the mercy of God be upon him, used to say: O son of Adam, do good and evade evil; by doing so you will be treading correctly. Sermon 176

CHAPTER 98: THE CLEAR PORTENT (al-Bayyinah)

Not would those who were ungrateful from among the People of the Book, nor the ones who are polytheists to be ones who set aside their beliefs until the clear portent approaches them: **98:1**
A Messenger from God, who recounts to them purified scrolls **98:2**
wherein are truth-loving Books. **98:3**
Split up not among themselves those to whom the Book was given until after the clear portent drew near them. **98:4**
They were commanded but to worship God as ones who are sincere and devoted in the way of life to Him, as monotheists and they perform the formal prayer and they give the purifying alms. That is the truth-loving way of life. **98:5**
Truly, those who were ungrateful among the People of the Book and the ones who are polytheists will be in the fire of hell, ones who will dwell in it forever. Those are the worst of creatures. **98:6**

But those who believed and did as the ones in accord with morality, those are the best of creatures. **98:7**
Their recompense is with their Lord—Gardens of Eden, beneath which rivers run, ones who will dwell in them forever, eternally. God was well-pleased with them and they were well-pleased with Him. That is for him who dreaded his Lord. **98:8**

Their recompense is with their Lord—Gardens of Eden, beneath which rivers run, ones who will dwell in them forever, eternally. *God was well-pleased with them and they were well-pleased with Him. That is for him who dreaded his Lord.* (Q98:8) Sermon 167

CHAPTER 99: THE CONVULSION (al-Zalzalah)

When the earth will be convulsed with a convulsion, **99:1**
and the earth brought out its ladings **99:2**
and the human being said: What is with it (the earth)*?* **99:3**
On that Day it will divulge its news **99:4**
for your Lord revealed it. **99:5**
On that Day humanity will issue, separately, that they may be caused to see their actions. **99:6**
Whoever does the weight of an atom of good will see it. **99:7**
Whoever does the weight of an atom of the worst will see it. **99:8**

Your party had decided to select two persons. So we took their pledge that they would act according to the Quran and would not commit excess, that their tongues should be with it and that their hearts should follow it, but they deviated from it, abandoned what was right although they had it before their eyes. Wrong-doing was their desire, and going astray was their behavior. Although we had settled with them to decide with justice, to act according to the light and without the interference of their evil views and wrong judgment. Now that they have abandoned the course of right and have come out with just the opposite of what was settled, we have strong ground to reject their verdict. Sermon 177

CHAPTER 100: THE CHARGERS (al-ᶜĀdiyāt)

By the chargers, panting, **100:1**
by ones who strike a fire, striking fire, **100:2**
by the ones who are raiders in the morning, **100:3**
then, they plowed it to a trail of dust, **100:4**
and they penetrated the center with it, a multitude. **100:5**
Truly, the human being is unthankful to his Lord. **100:6**
Truly, he is a witness to that. **100:7**
He is more severe in the cherishing of good. **100:8**
Knows he not that when all that is in the graves will be scattered about **100:9**
and will be shown forth what is in the breasts? **100:10**
Truly, their Lord on that Day is Aware of them. **100:11**

Praise belongs to God (Q1:2) for Whom one condition does not proceed another so that He may be the First before being the Last or He may be Outward or Manifest before being Inward or Hidden. Anyone called one except Him is by virtue of being small in number. Anyone enjoying honor other than Him is humble. Any powerful person other than Him is weak. Any master other than Him is a servant. Sermon 65

Chapter 101: The Disaster (al-Qāriᶜah)

The Disaster! **101:1**
What is the Disaster? **101:2**
What will cause ***you*** *to recognize what the Disaster is?* **101:3**
On a Day humanity will be like dispersed moths **101:4**
and the mountains will be like plucked wool clusters. **101:5**
Then, for him whose balance was heavy will be **101:6**
one whose life is pleasant, well-pleasing. **101:7**
But he whose balance was made light, **101:8**
his abode of rest will be the pit. **101:9**
What will cause ***you*** *to recognize what it is?* **101:10**
It is a hot fire. **101:11**

Then there remain a few people in whose case the remembrance of their return to God on the Day of Judgment keeps their eyes bent and the fear of Resurrection moves their tears. Some of them are scared away from the world and dispersed. Some are frightened and subdued. Some are quiet as if muzzled. Some are praying sincerely. Some are grief-stricken and pain-ridden whom fear has confined to namelessness and disgrace has shrouded them, so they are in the sea of bitter water, their mouths are closed and their hearts are bruised. They preached until they were tired. They were oppressed until they were disgraced. They were killed until their numbers dwindled. Sermon 32

Chapter 102: The Rivalry (al-Takāthur)

Rivalry diverted you **102:1**
until you stopped by the cemetery. **102:2**

He recited the verse: *Rivalry diverted you until you have stopped by the cemetery.* (Q102:1-2) Then he said: How distant from achievement is their aim, how neglectful are these visitors and how difficult is the affair. They have not taken lessons from things which are full of lessons, but they took them from far off places. Do they boast on the dead bodies of their fore-fathers, or do they regard the number of dead persons as a ground for feeling boastful of their number? They want to revive the bodies that have become spiritless and the movements that have ceased. They are more entitled to be a source of lesson than a source of pride. They are more suitable for being a source of humility than of honor. Sermon 220

No indeed! You will know! **102:3**
Again, no indeed! You will know! **102:4**
No indeed! If you will know with the knowledge of certainty, **102:5**
you will, certainly, see hellfire. **102:6**
Again, you will see it with the eye of certainty. **102:7**
Again, you will, certainly, be asked on that day about the bliss. **102:8**

I bear witness that *there is no god but God* (Q47:19), the One. I bear witness that *there is no god but God* (Q47:19), the One. He has no like. My bearing witness has been tested. Its essence is our belief. We shall cling to it for as long as we live and shall store it facing the tribulations that overtake us because it is the foundation stone of faith and the first step towards good actions and divine pleasure. It is the means to keep Satan away. Sermon 2

Chapter 103: By Time (al-ᶜAṣr)

By time through the ages, **103:1**
truly, the human being is, surely, in a loss **103:2**
but those who believed and did as the ones in accord with morality, and counseled one another to The Truth, and counseled one another to having patience. **103:3**

Praise belongs to God (Q1:2) Who is High above all else, and is Near the creation through His bounty. He is the Giver of all reward and distinction, and Dispeller of all calamities and hardships. I praise Him for His continuous mercy and His copious bounties. Sermon 82

Chapter 104: The Slanderer (al-Humazah)

Woe to every slandering backbiter **104:1**
who gathered wealth and counted it over and over! **104:2**
He assumes that his wealth made him immortal. **104:3**
No indeed! He will be cast forth into the Crusher. **104:4**
What will cause **you** *to recognize what the Crusher is?* **104:5**
It is the fire of God, that which is kindled eternally, **104:6**
that peruses the minds, **104:7**
that which will be closing in on them **104:8**
with its pillars, ones that are outstretched. **104:9**

The devastation of the land only comes about through the destitution of its inhabitants. The destitution of its inhabitants only comes about when the desire to amass wealth rules the souls of the governors, when they have doubts about what endures, and when they profit little from exemplary teachings. *Woe to every slandering backbiter who gathered wealth and counted it over and over! He assumes that his wealth made him immortal. No indeed! He will be cast forth into the Crusher.* Letter 53*

Chapter 105: The Elephant (al-Fīl)

Have **you** *not considered what* **your** *Lord accomplished with the Companions of the Elephant?* **105:1**
Makes He not their cunning leading to nothing? **105:2**
He sent upon them flocks of birds, **105:3**
throwing at them rocks of baked clay. **105:4**
Then, made He them like ones who are consumed by stalks of husked grain. **105:5**

Praise belongs to God (Q1:2) Who is above all similarity to creatures, is above the words of describers Who displays the wonders of His management for the on-lookers, is hidden from the imagination of thinkers by virtue of the greatness of His glory, has knowledge without acquiring it by adding to it or drawing it from someone and Who is the ordainer of all matters without reflecting or thinking. He is such that gloom does not concern Him, nor does He seek light from brightness. Night does not overtake Him, nor does the day pass over Him so as to affect Him in any manner. His comprehension of things is not through eyes. His knowledge is not dependent on being informed. God deputized *the Prophet* (Q7:158), peace and the mercy of God be upon him, with light and accorded him the highest precedence in selection. Through him God united those who were divided, overpowered the powerful, overcame difficulties and leveled rugged ground and, thus, removed misguidance from right and left. Sermon 213

CHAPTER 106: THE QURAYSH (al-Quraysh)

For the solidarity of the Quraysh, **106:1**
their solidarity is the winter and the summer travel. **106:2**
Let them worship the Lord of this House **106:3**
Who fed them against hunger and secured them against fear. **106:4**

Praise belongs to God (Q1:2) Who is High above all else, and is Near the creation through His bounty. He is the Giver of all reward and distinction, and Dispeller of all calamities and hardships. I praise Him for His continuous mercy and His copious bounties. Sermon 82

CHAPTER 107: ASSISTANCE (al-Mā^cūn)

Had ***you*** *considered one who denies this way of life?* **107:1**
That is he who drives away with force the orphan **107:2**
and urges not to give food to the needy. **107:3**
So, woe to ones who formally pray, **107:4**
ones who are inattentive to their formal prayers, **107:5**
those who make display, **107:6**
yet they repulse giving the assistance. **107:7**

Know that the slightest pretention is polytheism. Sermon 85

CHAPTER 108: THE ABUNDANCE (al-Kawthar)

Truly, We gave ***you*** *the abundance.* **108:1**
So, invoke blessings for ***your*** *Lord and make sacrifice.* **108:2**
Truly, the one who detests ***you****, he is the one who is cut off.* **108:3**

Indeed, there is a group who worship God out of desire for something not yet attained: this is the worship of the merchants. There is a group who worship God out of fear. This is the worship of the servants. There is a group who worship God out of gratitude. This is the worship of the free. Saying 238*

Chapter 109: The Ungrateful (al-Kāfirūn)

Say: O ones who are ungrateful! **109:1**
I worship not what you worship; **109:2**
and you are not ones who worship what I worship. **109:3**
I am not one who worships what you worshipped. **109:4**
You are not ones who worship what I worship. **109:5**
For you is your way of life, and for me is my way of life. **109:6**

O my God! We seek **Your** protection from turning away from **Your** command or revolting against **Your** religion, or being led away by our desires instead of by guidance that comes from **You**. Sermon 215

Chapter 110: The Help (al-Naṣr)

When the help of God drew near and the victory **110:1**
and ***you*** *had seen humanity entering into the way of life of God in units,* **110:2**
then, glorify the praise of ***your*** *Lord and ask for His forgiveness. Truly, He had been ever The Accepter of Repentance.* **110:3**

I praise God for whatever matter He ordained and whatever action He destines and for my trial with you, O group of people, who do not obey when I order and do not respond when I call you. If you are at ease, you engage in conceited conversation, but if you are faced with battle you show weakness. Sermon 180

Chapter 111: Rope of Palm Fibers (al-Masad)

Ruined were the hands of Abu Lahab and he was ruined. **111:1**
His wealth availed him not nor whatever he earned. **111:2**
He will roast in a fire, possessing flames **111:3**
and his woman, the carrier of firewood, **111:4**
around her long neck is a rope of palm fibers. **111:5**

Chapter 112: The Sincere Expression (al-Ikhlās)

Say: He is God, One **112:1**
God, the Everlasting Refuge. **112:2**
He procreated not nor was He procreated **112:3**
and there be not anything comparable with Him. **112:4**

I bear witness that *there is no god but God* (Q47:19), the One. I bear witness that *there is no god but God* (Q47:19), the One. He has no like. My bearing witness has been tested. Its essence is our belief. We shall cling to it for as long as we live and shall store it facing the tribulations that overtake us because it is the foundation stone of faith and the first step towards good actions and divine pleasure. It is the means to keep Satan away. Sermon 2

Chapter 113: The Daybreak (al-Falaq)

Say: I take refuge with the Lord of Daybreak **113:1**
from the worst of things that He created **113:2**
and from the worst of the darkness of the night when the dark intensified, **113:3**
and from the worst of the women who practice magic, blowing on the knots **113:4**
and from the worst of one who is jealous when jealous. **113:5**

I bear witness that *Muhammad* (Q48:29), peace and the mercy of God be upon him, is *His servant* (Q17:1) and *Prophet* (Q7:158) whom He deputed when the signs of guidance were obliterated and the ways of religion were desolate. So he threw open the truth, gave advice to the people, guided them towards righteousness and ordered them to be moderate. May God bless him. Sermon 194

Chapter 114: Humanity (al-Nās)

Say: I take refuge with the Lord of humanity, **114:1**
King of humanity, **114:2**
God of humanity, **114:3**
from the worst of the sneaking whisperer of evil **114:4**
who whispers evil in the breasts of humanity, **114:5**
from among the genie and humanity. **114:6**

God never allowed His creation to remain without a Prophet, one deputized by Him, or a Book sent down from Him or a binding argument or a standing plea. These Messengers were such that they did not fear that they were few in comparison to the large numbers of their falsifiers. Among them was either a predecessor who would name the one to follow or the follower who had been introduced by the predecessor. Sermon 1